Social Psychology

FIFTH EDITION

Social Psychology

David G. Myers

Hope College
Holland, Michigan

The McGraw-Hill Companies, Inc.

New York   St. Louis   San Francisco   Auckland   Bogotá   Caracas
Lisbon   London   Madrid   Mexico City   Milan   Montreal
New Delhi   San Juan   Singapore   Sydney   Tokyo   Toronto

McGraw-Hill

*A Division of The **McGraw·Hill** Companies*

Social Psychology

Acknowledgments appear on pages 683–686 and on this page by reference.

This book is printed on acid-free paper.

1 2 3 4 5 6 7 8 9 0   DOW   DOW   9 0 9 8 7 6 5

ISBN 0-07-044377-7

This book was set in Palatino by York Graphics Services, Inc.
The editors were Jane Vaicunas, Jeannine Ciliotta, and James R. Belser;
the designer was Wanda Siedlecka;
the production supervisor was Paula Keller.
The photo editor was Elyse Rieder.
Cover photo and part-opener photos by Roman Kossak.
New drawings were done by Vantage Art.
R. R. Donnelley & Sons Company was printer and binder.

Library of Congress Cataloging-in-Publication Data

Myers, David G.
    Social psychology / David G. Myers.—5th ed.
       p.   cm.
    Includes bibliographical references and index.
    ISBN 0-07-044377-7
    1. Social psychology. I. Title.
HM251.M897 1996
302—dc20   95-39693

INTERNATIONAL EDITION

Copyright 1996. Exclusive rights by The McGraw-Hill Companies, Inc., for manufacture and export. This book cannot be re-exported from the country to which it is consigned by McGraw-Hill. The International Edition is not available in North America.

When ordering this title, use ISBN 0-07-114508-7.

ABOUT THE AUTHOR

David G. Myers is the John Dirk Werkman Professor of Psychology at Michigan's Hope College, where he has taught for 28 years and been voted "Outstanding Professor" by students. Myers' love of teaching psychology is evident in his writing for the lay public. He has written for many magazines, including *Scientific American* and *Today's Education*, and has authored or co-authored ten books, most recently, *The Pursuit of Happiness: Who Is Happy—and Why* (Avon Books, 1993) and *Exploring Social Psychology* (McGraw-Hill, 1994).

Also an award-winning researcher, Dr. Myers received the Gordon Allport Prize from Division 9 of the American Psychological Association for his work on group polarization. His scientific articles have appeared in more than two dozen journals, including *Science, American Scientist, Psychological Bulletin*, and *Psychological Science*. He has served his discipline as consulting editor to the *Journal of Experimental Social Psychology* and the *Journal of Personality and Social Psychology*.

In his spare time he has chaired his city's Human Relations Commission, helped found a Community Action center that assists poverty-level families, and spoken to numerous collegiate and religious groups. David and Carol Myers are parents of two grown sons and a daughter in college.

CONTENTS IN BRIEF

CONTENTS

PART III ■ SOCIAL RELATIONS   387

P R E F A C E

In all of recorded history, human social behavior has been scientifically studied for just one century—our century. Considering that we have barely begun, the results are gratifying. We have amassed significant insights into belief and illusion, love and hate, conformity and independence. Much about human behavior remains a mystery, yet social psychology can now offer partial answers to many intriguing questions: Will people act differently if we can first persuade them to adopt new attitudes? If so, how can we best persuade them? What leads people sometimes to hurt and sometimes to help one another? What kindles social conflict, and how can we transform closed fists into helping hands? Answering such questions expands our self-understanding and sensitizes us to the social forces at work upon us.

When first invited to write this book I envisioned a text that would be at once solidly scientific and warmly human, factually rigorous and intellectually provocative. It would reveal social psychology as an investigative reporter might, by providing an up-to-date summary of important social phenomena, and of how scientists uncover and explain such phenomena. It would be reasonably comprehensive, yet would also stimulate students' *thinking*—their readiness to inquire, to analyze, to relate principles to everyday happenings.

How does one select material for inclusion in a "reasonably comprehensive" introduction to the discipline? I have sought to present theories and findings that are neither too esoteric for the typical undergraduate nor better suited to other courses, such as developmental and personality psychology. I have chosen instead to emphasize material that casts social psychology in the intellectual tradition of the liberal arts. By the teaching of great literature, philosophy, and science, liberal education seeks to expand our thinking and awareness and to liberate us from the confines of the present. Social psychology can contribute to these goals. Many undergraduate social psychology students are not psychology majors; virtually all will enter other professions. By focusing on humanly significant issues, one can present the fundamental content that preprofessional psychology students need in ways that are stimulating and useful to all students.

The book opens with a single chapter that introduces our methods of inquiry. The chapter also warns students how findings can seem obvious—once you know them—and how social psychologists' own values permeate the discipline. The intent is to give students just enough to prepare them for what follows.

The book then unfolds around its definition of social psychology: the scientific study of how people *think about* (Part One), *influence* (Part Two), and *relate* (Part Three) to one another.

Part One on *social thinking* examines how we view ourselves and others. It assesses the accuracy of our impressions, intuitions, and explanations.

Part Two explores *social influence*. By appreciating the cultural sources of our attitudes, and by learning the nature of conformity, persuasion, and group influence, we can better recognize subtle social forces at work upon us.

Part Three considers the attitudinal and behavioral manifestations of both negative and positive *social relations*. It flows from prejudice to aggression, and from attraction to altruism, and concludes by exploring the dynamics of conflict and peacemaking.

Applications of social psychology are both interwoven throughout every chapter and highlighted with the applied chapter that concludes each section. One such chapter, "Social Cognition and Human Well-Being," includes material on social psychology's contribution to the study of health.

This edition, like its predecessors, has a multicultural emphasis that can be seen in the thoroughly revised treatment of cultural influences in Chapter 6 and throughout the book in the inclusion of research from various cultural settings. The book's focus remains the fundamental principles of social thinking, social influence, and social relations as revealed by careful empirical research. But these principles are more and more illustrated transnationally, thereby broadening our awareness of the whole human family.

The book is again thoroughly updated, with 600 new citations. This fifth edition offers expanded coverage of

■ the self—in the new Chapter 2 on "The Self in a Social World,"

■ evolutionary psychology—in a heavily revised Chapter 6, now titled, "Gender, Genes, and Culture," and

■ close relationships—in the retitled Chapter 13, "Attraction and Intimacy."

There are also fresh "Behind the Scenes" personal reflections by selected investigators, and a fresh pedagogical strategy that breaks chapters into digestible modules: typically three or four major sections begin with previews and end with section summaries that highlight the organization and key concepts.

Believing with Thoreau that "Anything living is easily and naturally expressed in popular language," I have sought, paragraph by paragraph, to craft the most engaging and effective book possible. A bright four-color design complements the text revisions and enhances the impact of the photos and figures. As before, definitions of key terms appear both in the margins and in the end-of-book Glossary.

Social Psychology, fifth edition, is accompanied by a comprehensive teaching-learning package. Martin Bolt's acclaimed *Teacher's Resource Manual* contains a wealth of classroom ideas, including dozens of ready-to-use demonstrations. For many students, the most helpful supplement to this text will be Bolt's *Study Guide,* which provides chapter objectives, chapter reviews, practice tests, and ideas and resources for papers. For this edition, Bolt has also prepared an extensive new test-item file of basic knowledge and application items.

In collaboration with Martin Bolt, McGraw-Hill also now offers a videodisc of classic social psychology experiments. These 4- to 8-minute clips (also available on videotape) are drawn from social psychology archives and arranged to complement the text. A second videodisc (or videotape), edited and produced by Philip Zimbardo and Allen Funt, offers 3- to 5-minute clips from the original Candid Camera shows. These too follow the text organization and can enrich and stimulate class discussion. Information on how to obtain the supplements is available from local McGraw-Hill representatives.

■ IN APPRECIATION

Although only one person's name appears on this book's cover, the truth is that a whole community of scholars has invested itself in it. Although none of these people should be held responsible for what I have written—nor do any of them fully agree with everything said—their suggestions made this a better book than it could otherwise have been.

This new edition still retains many of the improvements contributed by consultants and reviewers on the first four editions. To the following esteemed colleagues I therefore remain indebted:

Robert Arkin, Ohio State University
Susan Beers, Sweet Briar College
George Bishop, National University of Singapore
Martin Bolt, Calvin College
Dorothea Braginsky, Fairfield University
Russell Clark, Florida State University
Jack Croxton, State University of New York at Fredonia
Anthony Doob, University of Toronto
Philip Finney, Southeast Missouri State University
William Froming, Pacific Graduate School of Psychology
Stephen Fugita, Santa Clara University
David A. Gershaw, Arizona Western College
Mary Alice Gordon, Southern Methodist University
Ranald Hansen, Oakland University
Elaine Hatfield, University of Hawaii
James L. Hilton, University of Michigan
Bert Hodges, Gordon College
William Ickes, University of Texas at Arlington
Marita Inglehart, University of Michigan
Chester Insko, University of North Carolina
Edward Jones, Princeton University
Judi Jones, Georgia Southern College
Martin Kaplan, Northern Illinois University

Janice Kelly, Purdue University
Douglas Kenrick, Arizona State University
Norbert Kerr, Michigan State University
Charles Kiesler, University of Missouri
David McMillen, Mississippi State University
Robert Millard, Vassar College
Arthur Miller, Miami University
Teru Morton, Vanderbilt University
Darren Newtson, University of Virginia
Chris O'Sullivan, Bucknell University
Paul Paulus, University of Texas at Arlington
Scott Plous, Wesleyan University
Nicholas Reuterman, Southern Illinois University of Edwardsville
Linda Silka, University of Lowell
Royce Singleton, Jr., College of the Holy Cross
Stephen Slane, Cleveland State University
Mark Snyder, University of Minnesota
Garold Stasser, Miami University
Homer Stavely, Keene State College
Elizabeth Tanke, University of Santa Clara
William Titus, Braircliff College
Tom Tyler, University of California, Berkeley
Rhoda Unger, Montclair State College
Billy Van Jones, Abilene Christian College
Mary Stewart Van Leeuwen, Calvin College
Ann L. Weber, University of North Carolina at Asheville
Gary Wells, Iowa State University
Bernard Whitley, Ball State University
Kipling Williams, University of Toledo
Midge Wilson, DePaul University

This fifth edition additionally benefited from cover-to-cover reviews offering countless constructive suggestions, by Galen V. Bodenhausen, Michigan State University; David Buss, University of Michigan; Cynthia Crown, Xavier University; Mary Alice Gordon, Southern Methodist University; Allen Hart, University of Iowa; Marjorie Krebs, Gannon University; Robert D. Ridge, Brigham Young University; Richard A. Smith, University of Kentucky; Sheldon Solomon, Skidmore College; Ann L. Weber, University of North Carolina, Asheville; and Daniel M. Wegner, University of Virginia. I am indebted to each of these colleagues.

Hope College, Michigan, and the University of St. Andrews, Scotland, have been wonderfully supportive of these successive editions. Both the people and the environment provided by these two institutions have helped make the gestation of *Social Psychology* a pleasure. At Hope College, poet-essayist Jack Ridl helped shape the voice you will hear in these pages, and Kathy Adamski has again contributed here good cheer along with her secretarial excellence. Phyllis and Rick Vandervelde assisted the extensive recrafting of this new edition by preparing each of the successive drafts with their usual skill and efficiency. Ntsiki Sisulu and MaryLee Pikey assisted with essential library research and proofreading. MaryLee Pikey also painstakingly created the name index and page-referenced bibliography.

Were it not for the inspiration of Nelson Black of McGraw-Hill, it never would have occurred to me to write a textbook. Alison Meersschaert guided and encouraged the formative first edition. Editor Jeannine Ciliotta gently nurtured this new edition, suggesting numerous revisions and offering countless ideas and editorial touches along the way. And James Belser has patiently guided the process of converting each of the editions from manuscript into finished book.

To all in this supporting cast, I am indebted. Working with all these people has made the creation of this book a stimulating, gratifying experience.

DAVID G. MYERS
Hope College
Holland, MI 49422-9000
e-mail: myers @hope.edu

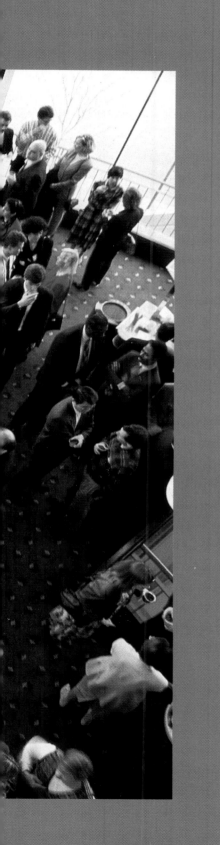

C H A P T E R 1

INTRODUCING SOCIAL PSYCHOLOGY

1

"Our lives are connected by a thousand invisible threads," said the novelist Herman Melville. Social psychology—the science that studies our human connections—aims to illuminate those threads. It does so by asking questions that have intrigued us all:

How Much of Social Reality Is in Our Heads? Social behavior varies not just with the objective situation but with how people construe it. Happily married people will attribute their spouse's acid "Can't you ever put that where it goes?" to something external ("He must have had a frustrating day"). Unhappily married people will attribute the same remark to a mean disposition ("Geesh, is he ever hostile!"), and may therefore respond with a counterattack. Moreover, *expecting hostility* from their spouse, they may behave resentfully, thereby eliciting the hostility they expect.

As we will see in later chapters, people who expect a doctor's child to be bright, an attractive person to be warm, or a person from another group to be uncooperative also often get what they expect. Distrusting each other, the Soviet Union and the United States squandered vast resources on a nuclear arms race. "My suspicion," acknowledged Senator J. William Fulbright, is that the USSR's behavior "is as much influenced by suspicion of our intentions as ours is by suspicion of theirs. This would mean that we have great influence on their behavior—that, by treating them as hostile, we assure their hostility."

Are our own social beliefs similarly self-fulfilling? And do others ever prejudge us in ways that influence our reactions? Might someone, construing your shyness as unfriendliness, snub you—leading you to bad-mouth the person, thereby confirming her suspicion of your "antagonism"?

What group influences might have led President Kennedy and his advisors to blunder into a fiasco during the Bay of Pigs invasion?

Are Ten Heads Dumber Than One?   In the early 1960s, President John F. Kennedy worked on major decisions with a bright and loyal group of advisers. One of their first major decisions was to approve a Central Intelligence Agency plan to invade Cuba, where communist Fidel Castro had taken control. The group's high morale fostered a sense that the plan couldn't fail. Because no one sharply disagreed with the idea, it appeared to have everyone's support. The result, however, was a fiasco: The small band of U.S.-trained and -supplied invaders was easily captured and soon linked to the American government, causing Kennedy to wonder aloud, "How could we have been so stupid?" In his book *A Thousand Days*, Arthur Schlesinger, a member of Kennedy's inner circle, later reproached himself "for having kept so silent in the cabinet room. I can only explain my failure to do more than raise a few timid questions by reporting that one's impulse to blow the whistle on this nonsense was simply undone by the circumstances of the discussion" (1965, p. 255).

Again, we wonder: Are you and I similarly affected by our participation in groups? To what extent and in what ways do other people influence our attitudes and actions? How can we as individuals resist social pressure or even sway a group?

Throughout this book, sources for information are cited parenthetically, then fully provided in the reference section that begins on page 609.

To Help or to Help Oneself?   As bags of cash tumbled from an armored truck on a fall day in 1987, $2 million was scattered along a Columbus, Ohio, street. Some motorists who stopped to help returned $100,000. Judging from what disappeared, many more stopped to help themselves. When similar incidents occurred several months later in San Francisco and Toronto, the results were the same: Passersby grabbed most of the money (Bowen, 1988).

What situations trigger people to be helpful or greedy? For that matter, what stimulates us to like or dislike and to be friendly or antagonistic toward others?

A common thread runs through these questions: They all deal with how people view and affect one another. And that is what social psychology is all about. Social psychologists explore such questions using the scientific method. They study attitudes and beliefs, conformity and independence, love and hate. To put it formally, we might say that **social psychology** is *the scientific study of how people think about, influence, and relate to one another.*

Social psychology is still a young science. We keep reminding people of this, partly as an excuse for our incomplete answers to some of its questions. But it's true. The first social psychology experiments were not reported until the late 1800s. No book on social psychology was published before this century. Not until the 1930s did social psychology assume its current form. And it was not until World War II, when psychologists contributed imaginative studies of persuasion and soldier morale, that it began to emerge as the vibrant field it is today. In just the last quarter-century the number of social psychology periodicals has more than doubled.

Social psychology: The scientific study of how people think about, influence, and relate to one another.

Today the expanding field of social psychology emphasizes:

■ *The power of the situation.* We are creatures of our cultures and contexts. Thus, evil situations sometimes overwhelm good intentions, inducing people to follow falsehoods or comply with cruelty. In the early 1990s, in a bitter conflict with Bosnian Muslims, scores of Serbian young men whom we would have welcomed as neighbors became vicious rapists.

■ *The power of the person.* We also are the creators of our social worlds. If a group is evil, its members contribute to (or resist) its being so. Facing the same situation, different people may react differently. Emerging from years of political imprisonment, one person exudes bitterness. Another, such as South Africa's Nelson Mandela, lays bitterness aside and works for peace and reconciliation.

■ *The importance of cognition.* People react differently partly because they think differently. How we intuitively reason matters. How we react to a friend's insult depends on how we explain it—as reflecting hostility, or as just a bad day. Social reality is something we subjectively construct. Our beliefs about ourselves also matter. Do we have an optimistic outlook? Do we sense that we are in control? Do we see ourselves as superior or inferior? Such thoughts (cognitions) influence our attitudes and our behaviors.

■ *The applicability of social psychological principles.* As we will see, social psychologists are more and more applying their concepts and methods to current social concerns, such as emotional well-being, health, courtroom decision making, and the quest for peace.

But what are social psychology's concepts and methods? How does the field differ from sociology and from other areas of psychology? Are social psychologists influenced by their own personal and cultural values? What are social psychology's research tactics, and how might we apply these in everyday life? In this chapter, these are our questions.

■ SOCIAL PSYCHOLOGY AND RELATED DISCIPLINES

S ocial psychologists are keenly interested in how people think about, influence, and relate to one another. But so are sociologists and personality psychologists. How does social psychology differ?

SOCIAL PSYCHOLOGY AND SOCIOLOGY

People often confuse social psychology with sociology. Sociologists and social psychologists do share an interest in studying how people behave in groups. But most sociologists study groups, from small to very large (societies), while most social psychologists study individuals—how one person thinks about others, is influenced by them, relates to them. This includes studies of how groups affect individual people and how an individual affects a group.

Some examples: In studying close relationships, a sociologist might study trends in marriage, divorce, and cohabitation rates, while a psychologist might examine how certain individuals become attracted to one another. Or a sociologist might investigate how the racial attitudes of middle-class people as a group differ from those of lower-income people. A social psychologist might study how racial attitudes develop within the individual.

Although sociologists and social psychologists use some of the same research methods, social psychologists rely much more heavily upon experiments in which they *manipulate* a factor, such as the presence or absence of peer pressure, to see what effect it has. The factors that sociologists study, such as economic class, are typically difficult or unethical to manipulate.

SOCIAL PSYCHOLOGY AND PERSONALITY PSYCHOLOGY

Social psychology and personality psychology are allies in their focus on the individual. Thus, the American Psychological Association includes the two subfields in the same journals (the *Journal of Personality and Social Psychology* and the *Personality and Social Psychology Bulletin*). Their difference lies in social psychology's *social* character. Personality psychologists focus on private internal functioning and on *differences* between individuals—for example, why some individuals are more aggressive than others. Social psychologists focus on our common humanity—on how people, in general, view and affect one another. They ask how social situations can lead *most* people to act kind or cruel, to conform or be independent, to feel liking or prejudice.

There are other differences: Social psychology has a shorter history. Many of personality psychology's heroes—people like Sigmund Freud, Carl Jung, Karen Horney, Abraham Maslow, and Carl Rogers—lived and worked during the first two-thirds of this century. Most of social psychology's leading contributors are still active. And social psychology has fewer famous heroes (people who have invented grand theories) and many more unsung ones—creative researchers who contribute smaller-scale concepts. We will meet some of these people in the autobiographical "Behind the Scenes" boxes sprinkled throughout this book.

"You can never foretell what any man will do, but you can say with precision what an average number will be up to. Individuals may vary, but percentages remain constant."
Sherlock Holmes, in Sir Arthur Conan Doyle's
A Study in Scarlet, 1887

LEVELS OF EXPLANATION

We study human beings from the different perspectives that we know as academic disciplines. These perspectives range from basic sciences, such as physics and chemistry, to integrative disciplines, such as philosophy and theology. Which perspective is relevant depends on what you want to talk about. Take love, for example. A physiologist might describe love as a state of arousal. A social psychologist might examine how various characteristics and conditions—good looks, the partners' similarity, sheer repeated exposure—enhance the feeling we call love. A poet would extol the sublime experience love can sometimes be. A theologian might describe love as the God-given goal of human relationships.

We needn't assume that any one of these levels is the *real* explanation. The physiological and emotional perspectives on love, for example, are simply two ways of looking at the same event. One type of explanation need not compete with others. Scientific explanations needn't discredit or replace the perspectives of literature and philosophy. An evolutionary explanation of universal incest taboos (in terms of the genetic penalty offspring pay for inbreeding) does not replace a sociological explanation (which might see incest taboos as a way of preserving the family unit) or a theological one (which might focus on moral truth). The various explanations can complement one another (Figure 1–1).

If all truth is part of one fabric, then different levels of explanation should fit together to form a whole picture, just as we can assemble different two-dimensional perspectives of an object into a three-dimensional whole image. Recognizing the complementary relationship of various explanatory levels liberates us from useless argument over whether we should view human nature scientifically or subjectively. It's not an either/or matter; both scientific and subjective perspectives are valuable. Although this book pays particular attention to the results of scientific research, we ought not ignore the rich insights of other approaches. Sociologist Andrew Greeley (1976) explains: "Try as it might, psychology cannot explain the purpose of human existence, the meaning of human life, the ultimate destiny of the human person." Social psychologists ask some very important questions, but these are not among them. Social psychology is *one* important perspective from which we can view and understand ourselves, but it is not the only one.

"Knowledge is one. Its division into subjects is a concession to human weakness."
Sir Halford John MacKinder, 1887

SUMMING UP

Social psychology is the scientific study of how people think about, influence, and relate to one another. Sociology and psychology are social psychology's parent disciplines. Social psychology tends to be more individualistic in its content and more experimental in its method than other areas of sociology. Compared to personality psychology, social psychology focuses less on differences among individuals and more on how people, in general, view and affect one another.

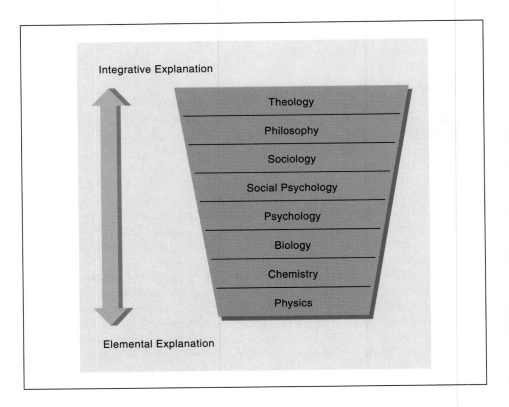

■ FIGURE 1–1
Partial hierarchy of disciplines *The disciplines range from basic sciences that study nature's building blocks up to integrative disciplines that study complex systems. A successful explanation of human functioning at one level need not contradict explanations at other levels.*

Different sciences offer different perspectives.

Social psychology is an environmental science; it reveals how social circumstances influence behavior. There are many additional perspectives on human nature, each of which asks its own set of questions and provides its own set of answers. These different perspectives are complementary, not contradictory.

■ SOCIAL PSYCHOLOGY AND HUMAN VALUES

Social psychologists' values penetrate their work in ways both obvious and subtle. What are such ways?

Social psychology, I have just suggested, views human behavior from a scientific rather than a subjective perspective. Social psychology is less a collection of findings than a set of scientific strategies for answering questions. In science, as in courts of law, personal opinions are inadmissible. When ideas are put on trial, evidence determines the verdict. But are social psychologists really this objective? As human beings, don't our values—our personal convictions about what is desirable and how people ought to behave—seep into our work? And if they do, can social psychology really be scientific?

OBVIOUS WAYS IN WHICH VALUES ENTER

Values enter the picture with our choice of research topics. It was no accident that the study of prejudice flourished during the 1940s as fascism raged in Europe; that the 1950s, a time of look-alike fashions and McCarthyist intolerance of differing views, gave us studies of conformity; that the 1960s saw increased interest in aggression as riots and rising crime rates plagued America; that the 1970s provided a wave of research on gender and sexism; that the 1980s offered a resurgence of attention to psychological aspects of the arms race; and that the 1990s are marked by heightened interest in how people respond to multicultural diversity. These trends reflect the social concerns of their time. Social psychology reflects social history.

Values also influence the type of people attracted to various disciplines (Campbell, 1975; Moynihan, 1979). At your school, too, do the students attracted to the humanities, the natural sciences, and the social sciences noticeably differ? Do psychology and sociology attract people who are eager to challenge tradition, people who would rather shape the future than preserve the past?

Finally, values obviously enter the picture as the *object* of social-psychological analysis. Social psychologists investigate how values form, why they change, and how they influence attitudes and actions. None of this, however, tells us which values are "right."

NOT-SO-OBVIOUS WAYS IN WHICH VALUES ENTER

We less often recognize the subtler ways in which value commitments masquerade as objective truth. Consider three not-so-obvious ways in which values enter social psychology and related areas.

Science Has Subjective Aspects

"Science does not simply describe and explain nature; it is part of the interplay between nature and ourselves; it describes nature as exposed to our method of questioning."
Werner Heisenberg, *Physics and Philosophy*, 1958

There has been a growing awareness among both scientists and philosophers that science is not so purely objective as we thought. Scientists do not merely read what's out there in the book of nature. Rather, they interpret nature, using their own mental categories. In our daily lives, too, we view the world through the lens of our preconceptions. Pause a moment: What do you see in Figure 1–2?

Can you see a Dalmatian sniffing the ground at the center of the picture? Without this expectation, most people are blind to what those who have the preconception can see. But once your mind has the preconception, it controls your interpretation of the picture—so much so that it becomes difficult *not* to see the dog. This is the way our minds work. While reading these words you have been unaware, until this moment, that you are also looking at your nose. Your mind blocks from awareness something that is there, if only you were predisposed to perceive it. This tendency to prejudge reality based on our expectations is a basic fact about the human mind.

A 1951 Princeton-Dartmouth football game provided a classic demonstration of how opinions control interpretations (Hastorf & Cantril, 1954; see also Loy & Andrews, 1981). The game lived up to its billing as a grudge match; it turned out to be one of the roughest and dirtiest games in the history of either school. A Princeton All-American was gang-tackled, piled on, and finally forced out of the game with a broken nose. Fistfights erupted, and there were further injuries on both sides.

■ FIGURE 1–2
What do you see?

Not long afterward, two psychologists, one from each school, showed films of the game to students on each campus as part of a social psychology experiment. When the students played the role of scientist, noting each infraction as they watched and who was responsible for it, they could not set aside their loyalties. The Princeton students were much more likely than the Dartmouth students to see Princeton players as victims of illegal aggression. The Princeton students, for example, saw twice as many Dartmouth violations as the Dartmouth students saw. There *is* an objective reality out there. But, in science as in everyday life, we always view it through the lens of our beliefs and values.

Because the community of scholars at work in any given area often share a common viewpoint or come from the same culture, their assumptions may go unchallenged. What we take for granted—the shared beliefs that European social psychologists call our **social representations** (Augoustinos & Innes, 1990; Moscovici, 1988)—are our most important but also most unexamined convictions. Sometimes, however, someone from outside the camp will call attention to these assumptions. During the 1980s, feminists and Marxists exposed some of social psychology's unexamined assumptions. Feminist critics called attention to subtle biases—for example, to the political conservatism of many scientists who favor a biological interpretation of gender differences in social behavior (Unger, 1985). Marxist critics called attention to competitive,

Social representations:
Socially shared beliefs. Widely held ideas and values, including our assumptions and cultural ideologies. Our social representations help us make sense of our world.

individualist biases—for example, the assumption that conformity is bad and that individual rewards are good. Marxists and feminists, of course, make their own assumptions. In Chapter 2 we will see more ways in which our preconceptions guide our interpretations. What's crucial for our behavior is less the situation-as-it-is than the situation-as-we-construe-it.

Psychological Concepts Contain Hidden Values

Values also influence concepts. Consider psychologists' attempts to specify the good life. We refer to people as mature or immature, as well-adjusted or poorly adjusted, as mentally healthy or mentally ill. We talk as if these were statements of fact, when really they are value judgments. The personality psychologist Abraham Maslow, for example, was known for his sensitive descriptions of "self-actualized" people—people who, with their needs for survival, safety, "belongingness," and self-esteem satisfied, go on to fulfill their human potential. Few readers notice that Maslow himself, guided by his own values, selected the sample of self-actualized people he described. The resulting description of self-actualized personalities—as spontaneous, autonomous, mystical, and so forth—reflected Maslow's personal values. Had he begun with someone else's heroes—maybe Napoleon, Alexander the Great, and John D. Rockefeller, Sr.—the resulting description of self-actualization would have been quite different (Smith, 1978).

Psychological advice also reflects the advice giver's personal values. When mental health professionals advise us how to live our lives, when child-rearing experts tell us how to handle our children, and when some psychologists encourage us to live free of concern for others' expectations, they are expressing their personal values. Many people, unaware of this, defer to the "professional." Because value decisions concern us all, we should not feel intimidated by scientists and professionals. Science can help us discern how better to achieve our goals, once we have settled on them. But science does not and cannot answer questions of ultimate moral obligation, of purpose and direction, and of life's meaning.

Hidden values even seep into psychology's research-based concepts. Pretend you have taken a personality test and the psychologist, after scoring your answers, announces: "You scored high in self-esteem. You are low in anxiety. And you have exceptional ego-strength." "Ah," you think, "I suspected as much, but it feels good to know that." Now another psychologist gives you a similar test. For some peculiar reason this test asks some of the same questions. Afterward the psychologist informs you that you seem defensive, for you scored high in "repressiveness." "How could this be," you wonder, "the other psychologist said such nice things about me." It could be because all these labels describe the same set of responses (a tendency to say nice things about oneself and not to acknowledge problems). Shall we call it high self-esteem or defensiveness? The label reflects the researcher's value judgment about the trait.

That value judgments are often hidden within our social-psychological language is no reason to fault social psychology. This is true of all human language, which offers us "purr-words" and "snarl-words" for describing the same thing. Whether we label someone engaged in guerrilla warfare a "terrorist" or a "freedom fighter" depends on our view of the cause. Whether we call public assistance "welfare" or "aid to the needy" reflects our political views. When

Hidden (and not-so-hidden) values seep into psychological advice. They permeate popular psychology books that offer guidance on living and loving.

"they" exalt their country and people, it's nationalism; when "we" do it, it's patriotism. Whether someone involved in an extramarital affair is practicing "open marriage" or "adultery" depends on one's personal values. Brainwashing is social influence we do not approve of. Perversions are sex acts we do not practice. Remarks about "ambitious" men and "aggressive" women, or about "cautious" boys and "timid" girls, convey a hidden message.

To repeat, values lie hidden within our definitions of mental health and self-esteem, our psychological advice for living, and our psychological labels. Throughout this book I will call your attention to additional examples of hidden values. The point will never be that the implicit values are necessarily bad. The point is that scientific interpretation, even at the level of labeling phenomena, is a very human activity. It is therefore quite natural and quite inevitable that prior beliefs and values will influence what social psychologists think and write.

There Is No Bridge From "Is" to "Ought"

A seductive error for those who work in the social sciences is sliding from a description of *what is* into a prescription of *what ought to be*. Philosophers call this the **naturalistic fallacy**. The gulf between "is" and "ought," between scientific description and ethical prescription, remains as wide today as when philosopher David Hume pointed it out 200 years ago. No survey of human behavior—say, of sexual practices—logically dictates what is "right" behavior. If most people don't do something, that does not make it wrong. If most people do it, that does not make it right. We inject our values whenever we move from objective statements of fact to prescriptive statements of what ought to be.

Naturalistic fallacy:
The error of defining what is good in terms of what is observable. For example: What's typical is normal; what's normal is good.

In such ways, both obvious and subtle, social psychologists' personal values influence their work. We do well to remember this and also to remember that what is true of them is true of each of us. Our values and assumptions color our view of the world. To discover how much our assumed values and social representations shape what we take for granted, we need to encounter a different cultural world—as from time to time we will throughout this book.

So what do we conclude: That because science has its subjective side, we should dismiss it? Quite the contrary: The realization that human thinking always involves interpretation is precisely why we need scientific analysis. By constantly checking our beliefs against the facts, as best we know them, we check and restrain our biases. Observation and experimentation help us clean the lens through which we see reality.

FOCUS

SOCIAL PSYCHOLOGY IN THREE WORLDS

Psychology's roots are international as well as interdisciplinary. The pioneering experimenter Ivan Pavlov was a Russian physiologist. Child watcher Jean Piaget was a Swiss biologist. Sigmund Freud was an Austrian physician. But it was in the United States that these and other transplanted roots flourished, thanks to abundant laboratories, sophisticated equipment, and a wealth of trained personnel. Surveying the world scene, social psychologist Fathali Moghaddam (1987, 1990) describes the United States as the psychological first world—the superpower of academic psychology, especially of social psychology. Social psychology's "professional center of gravity" is in the United States, observes Michael Bond (1988) from the Chinese University of Hong Kong. Because U.S. and Canadian social psychology are intermeshed—"indistinguishable" says Moghaddam—we could as well speak of "North American" social psychology.

The other industrialized nations form social psychology's second world. Great Britain, for example, shares with North America a strong tradition of scientific psychology. But because of its much smaller university system, Britain has only one-twenty-fifth as many academic psychologists as does the United States. Likewise, the Soviet Union has a similar population to the United States but one-tenth as many psychologists (Kolominsky, 1991).

Some social psychologists in Britain, Germany, France, and the other European countries are contributing new approaches. Their methodology supplements laboratory experiments with natural observation of behavior and social discourse.

European and North American social psychologists share interests in the personal and interpersonal levels of explaining social behavior, but European scholars tend to give more attention to the intergroup and societal levels as well (Doise, 1986; Hewstone, 1988). Thus European views may question U.S. individualism; conflict, they say, arises not so much from the misperceptions of individuals as from a power struggle between groups. The European political agenda stimulates their interests in social issues, such as unemployment, political ideology, and relations between different linguistic and ethnic groups.

The developing nations, such as Bangladesh, Cuba, and Nigeria, form social psychology's third world. Hampered by their limited resources, such countries have had to import their psychology from the first- and second-world nations. Yet their problems are distinctive: pressing issues related to poverty, conflict, and traditional agricultural lifestyles demand attention. In third-world societies, social psychologists seldom have the luxury of exploring the basics of human nature, nor can illiterate people answer questionnaires.

A complete social psychology would draw upon the insights of psychologists in all three worlds in describing processes of social thinking, social influence, and social relations common to all humans. As the global village continues to shrink and as we share knowledge and viewpoints, a world-based social psychology may indeed become possible.

BEHIND THE SCENES

After being born in Iran and educated in England, I joined hundreds of thousands of Iranians returning home after the revolution of 1978. I soon found that my new Ph.D. ill-equipped me for work in a culture that was suspicious of western psychology and demanding that my teaching and research reflect Iranian concerns and values. Through my experiences there, and subsequently with the United Nations Development Programme, I became aware of the urgent need for a psychology that is appropriate to the poor and illiterate masses of third world people. Believing that internationalizing psychology will benefit psychologists in all three worlds, I am now working to bridge the gap between social psychology in North America and other parts of the world and to educate psychologists for work in the third world.

FATHALI M. MOGHADDAM, *Georgetown University*

SUMMING UP

Social psychologists' values penetrate their work in obvious ways, such as their choice of research topics, and in subtler ways, such as their hidden assumptions when forming concepts, choosing labels, and giving advice. There is a growing awareness of the subjectivity of scientific interpretation, of values hidden in social psychology's concepts and labels, and of the gulf between scientific description of what is and ethical prescription of what ought to be. This penetration of values into science is not unique to social psychology, nor is it anything to be embarrassed about. That human thinking is seldom dispassionate is precisely (1) why we need systematic observation and experimentation if we are to check our cherished ideas against reality and (2) why social psychologists in different cultures are eager to exchange ideas and findings.

■ I KNEW IT ALL ALONG: IS SOCIAL PSYCHOLOGY SIMPLY COMMON SENSE?

But do social psychology's theories provide new insight into the human condition? Or do they only describe the obvious?

Many of the conclusions presented in this book will probably have already occurred to you, for social psychology is all around you. Every day we observe people thinking about, influencing, and relating to one another. For centuries, philosophers, novelists, and poets have observed and commented upon social behavior, often with keen insight.

Might it therefore be said that social psychology is only common sense in different words? Social psychology faces two contradictory criticisms: One is that it is trivial because it documents the obvious; the second is that it is dangerous because its findings could be used to manipulate people. Is the first objection valid—does social psychology simply formalize what any amateur social psychologist already knows intuitively?

Cullen Murphy (1990) thinks so: "Day after day social scientists go out into the world. Day after day they discover that people's behavior is pretty much what you'd expect." Nearly a half-century earlier, historian Arthur Schlesinger, Jr., (1949) reacted similarly to social scientists' studies of American World War II soldiers as reported in the two volumes of *The American Soldier*—"ponderous demonstrations" of common sense knowledge, he said.

What were the findings? Another reviewer, Paul Lazarsfeld (1949), offered a sample with interpretive comments, a few of which I paraphrase:

1. Better-educated soldiers suffered more adjustment problems than less-educated soldiers. (Intellectuals were less prepared for battle stresses than street-smart people.)
2. Southern soldiers coped better with the hot South Sea Island climate than Northern soldiers. (Southerners are more accustomed to hot weather.)
3. White privates were more eager to be promoted to noncommissioned officers than Black privates. (Years of oppression take a toll on achievement motivation.)
4. Southern Blacks preferred Southern to Northern White officers (because Southern officers were more experienced and skilled in interacting with Blacks).
5. As long as the fighting continued, soldiers were more eager to return home than after the war ended. (During the fighting, soldiers knew they were in mortal danger.)

"A first-rate theory predicts; a second-rate theory forbids; and a third-rate theory explains after the event."
Aleksander Isaakovich Kitaigorodskii

One problem with common sense, however, is that we invoke it *after* we know the facts. Events are far more "obvious" and predictable in hindsight than beforehand. Experiments reveal that when people learn the outcome of an experiment, that outcome suddenly seems unsurprising—certainly less surprising than it is to people who are simply told about the experimental procedure and the possible outcomes (Slovic & Fischhoff, 1977).

Daphna Baratz (1983) gave college students supposed social findings. Some were true (for example, "In prosperous times people spend a larger proportion of their income than during a recession" or "People who go to church regularly tend to have more children than people who go to church infrequently"). Some were the opposite of the truth. Whether given the truth or its opposite, most students rated a supposed finding as something "I would have predicted."

You perhaps experienced this phenomenon when reading Lazarsfeld's summary of findings from *The American Soldier*. For actually, Lazarsfeld went on to say, "*every one of these statements is the direct opposite of what was actually found.*" In reality, the book reported that poorly educated soldiers adapted more poorly. Southerners were *not* more likely than Northerners to adjust to a tropical climate. Blacks were *more* eager than Whites for promotion, and so forth. "If we had mentioned the actual results of the investigation first [as Schlesinger experienced], the reader would have labelled these 'obvious' also. Obviously something is wrong with the entire argument of obviousness. . . . Since every kind of human reaction is conceivable, it is of great importance to know which reactions actually occur most frequently and under what conditions."

In hindsight, events seem obvious and predictable.

Likewise, in everyday life we often do not expect something to happen until it does. We *then* suddenly see clearly the forces that brought it to be and feel unsurprised. After Ronald Reagan's presidential victory over Jimmy Carter in 1980, commentators—forgetting that the election had been "too close to call" until the campaign's final few days—found the Reagan landslide unsurprising and easily understandable. When, the day before the election, Mark Leary (1982) asked people what percentage of votes they thought each candidate would receive, the average person, too, foresaw but a slim Reagan victory. The day after the election Leary asked other people what result they *would have predicted* the day before the election; most indicated a Reagan vote that was closer to the final result. As the Danish philosopher-theologian Sören Kierkegaard put it, "Life is lived forwards, but understood backwards."

If this **hindsight bias** (also called the I-knew-it-all-along phenomenon) is pervasive, you may now be feeling that you already knew about it. Indeed, almost any conceivable result of a psychological experiment can seem like common sense—*after* you know the result. You can demonstrate the phenomenon. Ask half a group to predict the outcome of some current event, such as an upcoming election. Ask the other half, a week after the outcome is known, what they would have predicted. For example, when Martin Bolt and John Brink (1991) invited Calvin College students to predict the U.S. Senate vote on controversial Supreme Court nominee Clarence Thomas, 58 percent predicted his approval. A week after his confirmation, Bolt asked other students to recall what they would have predicted. "I thought he would be approved," said 78 percent.

Or give half a group one psychological finding and the other half the opposite result. For example, tell half:

Hindsight bias:
The tendency to exaggerate, *after* learning an outcome, one's ability to have foreseen how something turned out. Also known as the *I-knew-it-all-along phenomenon.*

Social psychologists have found that, whether choosing friends or falling in love, we are most attracted to people whose traits are different from our own. There seems to be wisdom in the old saying, "Opposites attract."

Tell the other half:

Social psychologists have found that, whether choosing friends or falling in love, we are most attracted to people whose traits are similar to our own. There seems to be wisdom in the old saying, "Birds of a feather flock together."

Ask the people first to explain the result. Then ask them to say whether it is "surprising" or "not surprising." Virtually all will find whichever result they were given "not surprising."

As these examples show, we can draw upon the stockpile of ancient proverbs to make almost any result seem to make sense. Because nearly every possible outcome is conceivable, there are proverbs for various occasions. Shall we say with John Donne, "No man is an island," or with Thomas Wolfe, "Every man is an island"? If a social psychologist reports that separation intensifies romantic attraction, Joe Public responds, "You get paid for this? Everybody knows that 'absence makes the heart grow fonder.'" Should it turn out that separation weakens attraction, Judy Public may say, "My grandmother could have told you, 'Out of sight, out of mind.'" No matter what happens, there will be someone who knew it would.

Karl Teigen (1986) must have had a few chuckles when asking University of Leicester (England) students to evaluate actual proverbs and their opposites. When given the actual proverb "Fear is stronger than love," most rated it as true. But so did students who were given its reversed form, "Love is stronger than fear." Likewise, the genuine proverb "He that is fallen cannot help him who is down," was rated highly; but so, too, was "He that is fallen can help him who is down." My favorites, however, were the two highly rated proverbs:

Perhaps best remembered for his banal discourses and frequent use of clichés was the early Greek philosopher, Mediocrates.

COMPETING PROVERBS

Cullen Murphy (1990), managing editor of *The Atlantic*, faults "sociology, psychology, and other social sciences far too often merely discerning the obvious or confirming the commonplace." His own casual survey of social science findings "turned up no ideas or conclusions that can't be found in *Bartlett's* or any other encyclopedia of quotations." So true, because for many a conceivable finding there is a quotation (Evens & Berent, 1993). As the philosopher Alfred North Whitehead (1861–1947) once remarked, "Everything important has been said before." Nevertheless, to sift the truth of competing quotations we need research. Consider . . .

Is it more true that . . .	Or that . . .
Too many cooks spoil the broth.	Two heads are better than one.
The pen is mightier than the sword.	Actions speak louder than words.
You can't teach an old dog new tricks.	You're never too old to learn.
Blood is thicker than water.	Many kinfolk, new friends.
He who hesitates is lost.	You should look before you leap.
Forewarned is forearmed.	You shouldn't cross the bridge until you come to it.

"Wise men make proverbs and fools repeat them" (authentic) and its made-up counterpart, "Fools make proverbs and wise men repeat them."

The hindsight bias creates a problem for many psychology students. When you read the results of experiments in your textbooks, the material often seems easy, even obvious. When you later take a multiple-choice test on which you must choose among several plausible conclusions, the task may become surprisingly difficult. "I don't know what happened," the befuddled student later moans. "I thought I knew the material." (A word to the wise: Beware of this phenomenon when studying for exams, lest you fool yourself into thinking that you know the material better than you do.)

The I-knew-it-all-along phenomenon not only can make social science findings seem like common sense, it also can have pernicious consequences. It is conducive to arrogance—an overestimation of our own intellectual powers. After the invention and acceptance of the typewriter, in hindsight, people said it was a machine that demanded invention and that, once invented, had to be a success. But to Christopher Latham Sholes, creator of the Remington, its success was not so obvious beforehand. In an 1872 letter he confided: "My apprehension is [that] it will have its brief day and be thrown aside."

Moreover, because outcomes seem as if they should have been foreseeable, we are more likely to blame decision makers for what are in retrospect "obvious" bad choices than to praise them for good choices, which also seem "obvious." *After* the 1991 Persian Gulf War, it seemed obvious that the overwhelming air superiority of the United States and its allies would rout the Iraqi military, though that was hardly clear to most politicians and pundits beforehand. *After* Japan's 1941 attack on Pearl Harbor, hints of the impending attack seemed similarly obvious to Monday morning historians, who chastised the politicians and the U.S. military leadership for not having anticipated what happened.

Likewise, we sometimes blame ourselves for "stupid mistakes"—perhaps for not having handled a situation or a person better. Looking back, we see how we should have handled it. (Recall Arthur Schlesinger's regret "for having kept so silent" during discussions of the CIA plan to invade Cuba's Bay of Pigs.) But sometimes we are too hard on ourselves. We forget that what is obvious to us *now* was not nearly so obvious at the time. Physicians told both a patient's symptoms and the cause of death (as determined by autopsy) sometimes wonder how an incorrect diagnosis could have been made. Other physicians, given only the symptoms, don't find the diagnosis nearly so obvious (Dawson & others, 1988). (Would juries be slower to assume malpractice if they were forced to take a foresight rather than a hindsight perspective?)

"It is easy to be wise after the event."
Sherlock Holmes, in Arthur Conan Doyle's "The Problem of Thor Bridge"

So what shall we conclude—that common sense is usually wrong? Sometimes it is. Until science dethroned the commonsense view, centuries of daily experience assured people that the sun revolved around the earth. Medical experience assured doctors that bleeding was an effective treatment for typhoid fever, until someone in the middle of the last century bothered to experiment—to divide patients into two groups, one bled, the other given mere bed rest.

Other times, conventional wisdom is right—or it falls on both sides of an issue: Does happiness come from knowing the truth, or preserving illusions? From being with others, or living in peaceful solitude? From living a virtuous life, or getting away with evil? Opinions are a dime a dozen; no matter what we find, there will be someone who foresaw it. But which of the many competing ideas best fit reality? So the point is not that common sense is predictably wrong. Rather, common sense usually is right *after the fact*. We therefore easily deceive ourselves into thinking that we know and knew more than we do and did. And this is precisely why we need psychological science—to help us sift reality from illusion, and genuine predictions from easy hindsight.

SUMMING UP

Social psychology's findings sometimes seem obvious. However, experiments reveal that outcomes are more "obvious" after the facts are known. This hindsight bias often makes people overconfident about the validity of their judgments and predictions.

■ HOW WE DO SOCIAL PSYCHOLOGY

Social psychologists predict behavior using correlational studies, often conducted in natural settings. And they seek to explain behavior by conducting experiments that manipulate one or more factors under controlled conditions. Their findings enable them to evaluate theories that organize their observations and imply testable or practical hypotheses.

Unlike other scientific disciplines, social psychology has nearly 6 billion amateur practitioners. People-watching is a universal hobby—in parks, at the beach, at school. As we observe people, we form ideas about how human beings think about, influence, and relate to one another. Professional social psychologists do the same, only more painstakingly, often with experiments that create miniature social dramas that pin down cause and effect.

■ FIGURE 1–3
Status and Longevity Tall grave pillars commemorated people who also tended to live longer. (Adapted from Carroll & others, 1994.)

Most of what you will learn about social-psychological research methods you will absorb as you read later chapters. But let us go backstage now and take a brief look at how social psychology is done. This glimpse behind the scenes will be just enough, I trust, for you to appreciate findings discussed later and to think critically about everyday social events.

Social-psychological research varies by location. It can take place in the *laboratory* (a controlled situation) or in the **field** (everyday situations). And it varies by method—being either **correlational** (asking whether two factors are naturally associated) or **experimental** (manipulating some factor to see its effect on another). If you want to be a critical reader of psychological research reported in newspapers and magazines, it will pay you to understand the difference between correlational and experimental research.

Field research:
Research done in natural, real-life settings outside the laboratory.

CORRELATIONAL RESEARCH: DETECTING NATURAL ASSOCIATIONS

Using some real examples, let's first consider the advantages of **correlational research** (often involving important variables in natural settings) and the disadvantage (ambiguous interpretation of cause and effect). As we will see in Chapter 5, psychologists are relating personal and social factors to human health. Among the researchers are Douglas Carroll at Glasgow Caledonian University and his colleagues George Davey Smith and Paul Bennett (1994). In search of possible links between socioeconomic status and health, the researchers ventured into Glasgow's old graveyards. As a measure of health, they noted from grave markers the life spans of 843 individuals. As an indication of status, they measured the height of pillars over the grave, reasoning that height reflected cost and therefore affluence. As Figure 1–3 shows, higher markers were related to longer lives, for both men and women.

Correlational research:
The study of the naturally occurring relationships among variables.

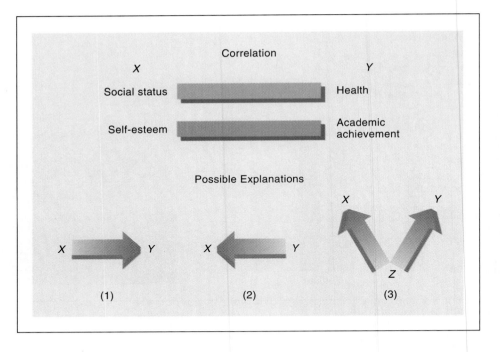

■ FIGURE 1–4
When two variables correlate, any combination of three explanations is possible.

Carroll and his colleagues explain how other researchers, using contemporary data, have confirmed the status-longevity correlation. Scottish postal-code regions having the least overcrowding and unemployment also have the greatest longevity. In the United States, income correlates with longevity (poor and lower status people are more at risk for premature death). In Britain, occupational status correlates with longevity. Across times and places, the status-health correlation seems reliable.

Correlation versus Causation

The status-longevity question illustrates the most irresistible thinking error made by both amateur and professional social psychologists. When two factors like status and health go together, it is terribly tempting to conclude that one is causing the other. Status, we might presume, somehow protects a person from health risks. Or might it be the other way around? Maybe health promotes vigor and success. Perhaps people who live longer accumulate more wealth (enabling more expensive grave pillars). Correlational research allows us to *predict*, but it cannot tell us whether changing one variable (such as social status) will *cause* changes in another (such as health).

The correlation-causation confusion is behind much muddled thinking in popular psychology. Consider another very real correlation—between self-esteem and academic achievement. Children with high self-esteem tend also to have high academic achievement. (As with any correlation, we can also state this the other way around: High achievers tend to have high self-esteem.) Why do you suppose this is (Figure 1–4)?

Some people believe a "healthy self-concept" contributes to achievement. Thus, boosting a child's self-image may also boost the child's school achievement. Others argue that high achievement produces a favorable self-image. A study of 635 Norwegian schoolchildren suggests that a string of gold stars by one's name on the spelling chart and constant praise from an admiring teacher can boost a child's self-esteem (Skaalvik & Hagtvet, 1990). It's also possible that self-esteem and achievement correlate because both are linked to underlying intelligence and family social status. That possibility was raised in two studies—one a nationwide sample of 1600 young American men, another of 715 Minnesota youngsters (Bachman & O'Malley, 1977; Maruyama & others, 1981). When the researchers statistically removed the effect of intelligence and family status, the correlation between self-esteem and achievement evaporated. Similarly, John McCarthy and Dean Hoge (1984) dispute the idea that the correlation between low self-esteem and delinquency means that low self-esteem causes delinquency; rather, their study of 1658 teenagers suggests, delinquent acts lower self-esteem. Breaking rules leads to condemnation, which leads to lowered self-esteem.

Advanced correlational techniques can *suggest* cause-effect relations. *Time-lagged* correlations reveal the *sequence* of events (for example, by indicating whether changed achievement more often precedes or follows changed self-esteem). Researchers can also use statistical techniques that extract the influence of "confounded" variables. Thus, the researchers just mentioned saw the self-esteem—achievement correlation evaporate after extracting differences in intelligence and family status. (Among people of similar intelligence and family status, the self-esteem–achievement relationship was minimal.) Similarly, the Scottish research team wondered whether the status-longevity relationship would survive their removing the effect of cigarette smoking, which is now much less common among those higher in status. It did, which suggested that some other factors, such as increased stress and decreased feelings of control, must also account for the greater mortality of the poor.

So, the great strength of correlational research is that it tends to occur in real-world settings where we can examine factors like race, sex, and social status that we cannot manipulate in the laboratory. Its great disadvantage lies in the ambiguity of the results. Knowing that two variables change together enables us to predict one when we know the other. But this does not give us cause and effect.

Researchers have found a modest but positive correlation between adolescents' preference for heavy metal music and their having attitudes favorable to premarital sex, pornography, satanism, and drug and alcohol use (Landers, 1988). What are the possible explanations for this correlation?

Survey Research

How, then, do we measure such variables as status and health? One way is by surveying representative samples of people. Survey researchers obtain a representative group by taking a **random sample**—one in which every person in the total group has an equal chance of participating. With this procedure any subgroup of people—red-haired people, for example—will tend to be represented in the survey to the extent that they are represented in the total population.

It is an amazing fact that whether we survey people in a city or in a whole country, 1200 randomly selected participants will enable us to be 95 percent confident of describing the entire population with an error margin of 3 percent or less. Imagine a huge jar filled with beans, 50 percent red and 50 percent white. Randomly sample 1200 of these, and you will be 95 percent certain to draw out between 47 percent and 53 percent red beans—regardless of whether

Random sample:
Survey procedure in which every person in the population being studied has an equal chance of inclusion.

A state-of-the-art survey research center. The University of Michigan's Institute for Social Research has 60 interviewing carrels with monitoring stations. Staff and visitors must sign a pledge to honor the strict confidentiality of all interviews.

the jar contains 10,000 beans or 100 million beans. If we think of the red beans as supporters of one presidential candidate and white beans as supporters of the other candidate, we can understand why, since 1950, the Gallup polls taken just before U.S. national elections have diverged from election results by an average of only 1.4 percent. As a tube of blood can speak for the whole body, so can a random sample speak for a population.

Bear in mind that polls do not actually *predict* voting; they only *describe* public opinion as of the moment they are taken. Public opinion can shift. To evaluate surveys, we must also bear in mind four potentially biasing influences: unrepresentative samples, the order of questions, the response options, and the wording of the questions.

Unrepresentative Samples

Not only does sample size matter in a survey but also how closely the sample represents the population under study. In 1984, columnist Ann Landers accepted a letter writer's challenge to poll her readers on the question of whether women find affection more important than sex. Her question: "Would you be content to be held close and treated tenderly and forget about 'the act'?" Of the more than 100,000 women who replied, 72 percent said yes. An avalanche of worldwide publicity followed. In response to critics, Landers (1985, p. 45) granted that "the sampling may not be representative of all American women. But it does provide honest—valuable—insights from a cross section of the public. This is because my column is read by people from every walk of life, approximately 70 million of them." Still, one wonders, are the 70 million readers representative of the entire population? And are the 1 in 700 readers who participated representative of the 699 in 700 who did not?

The importance of representativeness was effectively demonstrated in 1936, when a weekly news magazine, *Literary Digest*, mailed a postcard presidential election poll to 10 million Americans. Among the more than 2 million returns, Alf Landon won by a landslide over Franklin D. Roosevelt. When the actual votes were counted a few days later, Landon carried only two states. The magazine sent the poll only to people whose names it had obtained from telephone books and automobile registrations—thus omitting all those who could afford neither (Cleghorn, 1980).

Sampling bias can plague even the best survey. Simultaneous political opinion polls, each supposedly having a 3 percent error margin, commonly vary from one another by more than 3 percent. Philip Converse and Michael Traugott (1986) attribute such discrepancies partly to the fact that some 30 percent of those sampled refuse to cooperate or are unavailable, which makes the sample obtained not a perfect random sample. For instance, when voters were surveyed by phone during the 1984 presidential race, those answering when their home was first called favored President Reagan by a slim 3 percent margin. After the interviewers persisted in callbacks until they reached everyone, President Reagan's margin increased by 13 percentage points. (Republican voters apparently were less often home.)

Order of Questions

Given a representative sample, we must also contend with other sources of bias, such as the order in which we ask questions. Asked whether "the Japanese government should be allowed to set limits on how much American industry can sell in Japan," most Americans answered no (Schuman & Ludwig, 1983). Simultaneously, two-thirds of an equivalent sample were answering yes to the same question because they were first asked whether "the American government should be allowed to set limits on how much Japanese industry can sell in the United States." Most of these people said the United States has the right to limit imports. To appear consistent, they then said that Japan should have the same right.

Consider this example: Do you favor or oppose increased spending for welfare programs? If you are like the people in one survey (Tourangeau & others, 1989), you would be likely to *favor* increased spending—if shortly before you had been asked whether "in America, any person who is willing to work hard has a good chance of succeeding." But you would be more likely to *oppose* increased spending if previously you were asked whether "some people in America really need help from the government." (Both prior questions elicited overwhelming agreement.)

Response Options

Consider, too, the dramatic effects of the response options. When Joop van der Plight and his co-workers (1987) asked English voters what percentage of Britain's nuclear energy they wished came from nuclear power, the average

Survey researchers must be sensitive to subtle—and not so subtle—biases.

preference was 41 percent. They asked others what percentage they wished came from (1) nuclear, (2) coal, and (3) other sources. Their average preference for nuclear power was 21 percent.

A similar effect occurred when Howard Schuman and Jacqueline Scott (1987) asked Americans, "What do you think is the most important problem facing this country today—the energy shortage, the quality of public schools, legalized abortion, or pollution—or if you prefer, you may name a different problem as most important." Given these choices, 32 percent felt that the quality of public schools was the biggest problem. Among others they simply asked, "What do you think is the most important problem facing this country today?" only 1 percent named the schools. So remember: The form of the question may guide the answer.

Wording

The precise wording of questions may also influence answers. One poll found that only 23 percent of Americans thought their government was spending too much "on assistance to the poor." Yet 53 percent thought the government was spending too much "on welfare" (Time, 1994). Even subtle changes in the tone of a question can have large effects (Schuman & Kalton, 1985). "Forbidding" something may be the same as "not allowing" it. But in 1940 when two comparable samples of Americans were asked, "Do you think the U.S. should forbid public speeches against democracy?" or "Do you think the U.S. should allow public speeches against democracy?" 54 percent said the United States should "forbid" such speeches and 75 percent said the United States should "not allow" them. Survey questioning is a very delicate matter. Even when people say they feel strongly about an issue, a question's form and wording may affect their answer (Krosnick & Schuman, 1988).

Response, order, and wording effects enable political manipulators to use surveys to show public support for their views—for or against nuclear power, welfare, or unrestrained speech. Consultants, advertisers, and physicians can have similar disconcerting influences upon our decisions by how they "frame" them. No wonder the meat lobby in 1994 objected to a new U.S. food labeling law that requires declaring ground beef, for example, as "30% fat," rather than "70% lean, 30% fat."

The moral: The way choices are worded can make a big difference. A young monk was once rebuffed when asking if he could smoke while he prayed. Ask a different question, advised a friend: Ask if you can pray while you smoke (Crossen, 1993).

EXPERIMENTAL RESEARCH: SEARCHING FOR CAUSE AND EFFECT

The near impossibility of discerning cause and effect among naturally correlated events prompts most social psychologists to create laboratory simulations of everyday processes whenever this is feasible and ethical. These simulations are similar to how aeronautical engineers work. They don't begin by observing how flying objects perform in a wide variety of natural environments. The variations in both atmospheric conditions and flying objects are so complex that they would surely find it difficult to organize and use such data to design better aircraft. Instead, they construct a simulated reality that is under their control—a wind tunnel. Now they can manipulate wind conditions and ascertain the precise effect of particular wind conditions on particular wing structures.

Control: Manipulating Variables

Like aeronautical engineers, social psychologists experiment by constructing social situations that simulate important features of our daily lives. By varying just one or two factors at a time—called **independent variables**—the experimenter pinpoints how changes in these one or two things affect us. As the wind tunnel helps the aeronautical engineer discover principles of aerodynamics, so the experiment enables the social psychologist to discover principles of social thinking, social influence, and social relations. The ultimate aim of wind tunnel simulations is to understand and predict the flying characteristics of complex aircraft; social psychologists experiment to understand and predict human behavior.

Independent variable:
The experimental factor that a researcher manipulates.

Social psychologists have used the experimental method in about three-fourths of their research studies (Higbee & others, 1982), and in two out of three studies the setting has been a research laboratory (Adair & others, 1985). To illustrate the laboratory experiment, consider two experiments that typify research from upcoming chapters on prejudice and aggression. Each suggests possible cause-effect explanations of correlational findings.

The first concerns prejudice against people who are obese. People often perceive the obese as slow, lazy, and sloppy (Ryckman & others, 1989). Do such attitudes spawn discrimination? In hopes of finding out, Steven Gortmaker and his colleagues (1993) studied 370 obese 16- to 24-year-olds. When they restudied them seven years later, two-thirds of the women were still obese, and these were less likely to be married and earning high salaries than a comparison group of some 5000 other women. Even after correcting for any differences in aptitude test scores, race, and parental income, the obese women's incomes were $7000 a year below average.

A billboard for the Stop the Violence, Save the Child program in New York City. Does viewing violence on TV or in other media lead to imitation, especially among children? Experiments suggest that it does.

Although correcting for certain other factors makes it look like discrimination might explain the correlation between obesity and lower status, we can't be sure. (Can you think of other possibilities?) Enter social psychologists Mark Snyder and Julie Haugen (1994). They asked 76 University of Minnesota men students to have a getting acquainted phone conversation with one of 76 women students. Each man was shown a photo *said* to picture his conversational partner. Half were shown an obese woman (not the actual partner), the other half a normal weight woman. In one part of the experiment, the men were asked to form an impression of the women's traits. Later analysis of just the women's side of the conversation revealed that when women were being evaluated they spoke less warmly and happily if they were presumed obese. Clearly, the men's beliefs induced them to behave in a way that led their supposedly obese partners to confirm the idea that such women are undesirable. Prejudice and discrimination were having an effect.

As a second example of how an experiment can clarify causation, consider the correlation between television viewing and children's behavior. Children who watch many violent television programs tend to be more aggressive than those who watch few. This suggests that children might be learning from what they see on the screen. But, as I hope you now recognize, this is a correlational finding. Figure 1–4 reminds us that there are two other cause-effect interpretation that do not implicate television as the cause of the children's aggression. (What are they?)

Social psychologists have therefore brought television viewing into the laboratory, where they control the amount of violence the children see. By exposing children to violent and nonviolent programs, researchers can observe how the amount of violence affects behavior. Robert Liebert and Robert Baron (1972) showed young Ohio boys and girls a violent excerpt from a gangster television show or an excerpt from an exciting track race. The children who viewed the violence were subsequently most likely to press vigorously a special red button that supposedly would heat a rod, causing a burning pain to another child. This measure of behavior we call the **dependent variable**. (Actually, there was no other child, so no one was really harmed.) Such experiments indicate that television *can* be one cause of children's aggressive behavior.

So far we have seen that the logic of experimentation is simple: By creating and controlling a miniature reality, we can vary one factor and then another and discover how these factors, separately or in combination, affect people. Now let's go a little deeper and see how an experiment is done.

Every social-psychological experiment has two essential ingredients. One we have just considered—*control*. We manipulate one or two independent variables while trying to hold everything else constant. The other ingredient is *random assignment*.

Random Assignment: The Great Equalizer

Recall that we were reluctant, on the basis of a correlation, to assume that obesity *caused* lower status (via discrimination) or that violence viewing *caused* aggressiveness. A survey researcher might measure and statistically extract other possibly pertinent factors and see if the correlations survive. But one can never control for all the factors that might distinguish obese from nonobese, and violence-viewers from nonviewers. Maybe violence-viewers differ in education, culture, intelligence—or in dozens of ways the researcher hasn't considered.

In one fell swoop, **random assignment** eliminates all such extraneous factors. With random assignment, each person has an equal chance of viewing the violence or the nonviolence. Thus, the people in both groups would, in every conceivable way—family status, intelligence, education, initial aggressiveness—average about the same. Highly intelligent people, for example, are equally likely to appear in both groups. Because random assignment creates equivalent groups, any later aggression difference between the two groups must have something to do with the only way they differ—whether or not they viewed violence (Figure 1–5). And thanks to random assignment of the Min-

Dependent variable:
The variable being measured, so-called because it may *depend* on manipulations of the independent variable.

Experimental research:
Studies that seek clues to cause-effect relationships by manipulating one or more factors (independent variables) while controlling others (holding them constant).

Random assignment:
The process of assigning participants to the conditions of an experiment such that all persons have the same chance of being in a given condition. (Note the distinction between random *assignment* in experiments and random *sampling* in surveys. Random assignment helps us infer cause and effect. Random sampling helps us generalize to a population.)

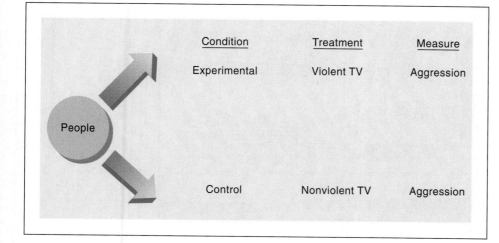

	Condition	Treatment	Measure
People	Experimental	Violent TV	Aggression
	Control	Nonviolent TV	Aggression

■ **FIGURE 1–5**
Randomly assigning people either to a condition that receives the experimental treatment or to a control condition that does not gives the researcher confidence that any later difference is somehow caused by the treatment.

nesota students to the photo conditions, the women's behavior *must* have been influenced by the men's beliefs about their obesity.

The Ethics of Experimentation

Our television example illustrates why some experiments are ethically sensitive. Social psychologists would not, over long time periods, expose one group of children to brutal violence. Rather, they briefly alter people's social experience and note the effects. Sometimes the experimental treatment is a harmless, perhaps even enjoyable experience to which people give their knowing consent. Sometimes, however, researchers find themselves operating in that gray area between the harmless and the risky.

Social psychologists often venture into that ethical gray area when they design experiments that really engage people's thoughts and emotions. Experiments need not have what Elliot Aronson, Marilynn Brewer, and Merrill Carlsmith (1985) call **mundane realism**. That is, laboratory behavior (for example, delivering electric shocks as part of an experiment on aggression) need not be literally the same as everyday behavior. For many researchers, that sort of realism is indeed mundane—not important. But the experiment *should* have **experimental realism**—it should absorb and involve the participants. Experimenters do not want their people consciously play-acting or ho-humming it; they want to engage real psychological processes. Forcing people to choose whether to give intense or mild electric shock to someone else can, for exam-

Mundane realism:
Degree to which an experiment is superficially similar to everyday situations.
Experimental realism:
Degree to which an experiment absorbs and involves its participants.

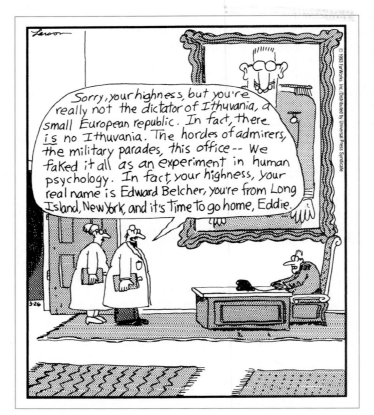

The Far Side

ple, be a realistic measure of aggression. It functionally simulates real aggression.

Achieving experimental realism often requires deceiving people. If the person in the next room is actually not receiving the shocks, the experimenter does not want the participants to know this. That would destroy the experimental realism. Thus, about one-third of social-psychological studies (though a decreasing number) have required deception (Korn & Nicks, 1993; Vitelli, 1988).

Experimenters also seek to hide their predictions lest the participants, in their eagerness to be "good subjects," merely do what's expected—or, in an ornery mood, do the opposite. In subtle ways, the experimenter's words, tone of voice, and gestures may call forth desired responses. To minimize such **demand characteristics**—cues that seem to "demand" certain behavior—experimenters typically standardize their instructions or even write or tape-record them.

Researchers often walk a tightrope in designing experiments that will be involving yet ethical. To believe that you are hurting someone, or to be subjected to strong social pressure to see if it will change your opinion or behavior, may be temporarily uncomfortable. Such experiments raise the age-old question of whether ends justify means. Do the insights gained justify deceiving and sometimes distressing people?

University ethics committees now review social-psychological research to ensure that it will treat people humanely. Ethical principles developed by the American Psychological Association (1981, 1992) and the British Psychological Society (1991) urge investigators to:

- Tell potential participants enough about the experiment to enable their **informed consent**.
- Be truthful. Use deception only if justified by a significant purpose and if there is no alternative.
- Protect people from harm and significant discomfort.
- Treat information about the individual participants confidentially.
- Fully explain the experiment afterward, including any deception. The only exception to this rule is when the feedback would be distressing, say by making people realize they have been stupid or cruel.

The experimenter should be sufficiently informative *and* considerate that people leave feeling at least as good about themselves as when they came in. Better yet, the participants should be repaid by having learned something about the nature of psychological inquiry. When treated in a courteous, nonmanipulative way, few participants mind being deceived (Christensen, 1988; Sharpe & others, 1992). Indeed, say social psychology's defenders, we provoke far greater anxiety and distress by giving and returning course exams than we now do in our experiments.

EXPLAINING AND PREDICTING: USING THEORIES

Although basic research often produces practical benefits, there are other reasons for doing social psychology. Many of us are in the profession because we have a hard time thinking of anything more fascinating than human existence.

Demand characteristics: Cues in an experiment that tell the participant what behavior is expected.

Informed consent: An ethical principle requiring that research participants be told enough to enable them to choose whether they wish to participate.

"Nothing has such power to broaden the mind as the ability to investigate systematically and truly all that comes under thy observation in life."
Marcus Aurelius, *Meditations*

Theory:
An integrated set of principles that explain and predict observed events.

If, as Socrates counseled, "The unexamined life is not worth living," then simply "knowing thyself" seems a worthy enough goal.

As we wrestle with human nature to pin down its secrets, we organize our ideas and findings into theories. A **theory** is an integrated set of principles that explain and predict phenomena. Some people wonder why social psychologists are so preoccupied with theories: Why don't they just gather facts? Our aeronautical engineering analogy is again useful. The engineers would soon be overwhelmed if, without any guiding principles, they tried by trial and error to create an exhaustive catalog of how different wind conditions affect different wing structures. So, they formulate broad concepts or theories about how air movements interact with wing structures and use the wind tunnel to test predictions derived from these concepts. Theories are a scientific shorthand.

In everyday conversation, "theory" often means "less than fact"—a middle rung on a confidence ladder going down from fact to theory to guess. But to any kind of scientist, facts and theories are different things, not different points on a continuum. Facts are agreed-upon statements about what we observe. Theories are *ideas* that summarize and explain facts. "Science is built up with facts, as a house is with stones," said Jules Henri Poincaré, "but a collection of facts is no more a science than a heap of stones is a house."

Hypothesis:
A testable proposition that describes a relationship that may exist between events.

Theories not only summarize, they also imply testable predictions, which we call **hypotheses**. Hypotheses serve several purposes. First, they allow us to *test* the theories on which they are based. By making specific predictions, a theory puts its money where its mouth is. Second, predictions give *direction* to research. Any scientific field will mature more rapidly if its researchers have a sense of direction. Theoretical predictions suggest new areas for research; they send investigators looking for things they might never have thought of. Third, the predictive feature of good theories can also make them *practical*. What, for example, would be of greater practical value today than a theory of aggression that would predict when to expect it and how to control it? As Kurt Lewin, one of modern social psychology's founders, declared, "There is nothing so practical as a good theory."

Consider how this works. Say we observe that people sometimes explode violently when in crowds. We might therefore theorize that the presence of other people makes individuals feel anonymous and lowers their inhibitions. Let's let our minds play with this idea for a moment. Perhaps we could test it by constructing a laboratory experiment similar to execution by electric chair. What if we asked individuals in groups to administer punishing shocks to a hapless victim without knowing which one of the group was actually shocking the victim? Would these individuals administer stronger shock than individuals acting alone, as our theory predicts?

We might also manipulate anonymity: Would people hiding behind masks deliver stronger shocks because they could not be identified? If the results confirm our hypothesis, they might suggest some practical applications. Perhaps police brutality could be reduced by having officers wear large name tags and drive cars identified with large numbers or by videotaping their arrests.

But how do we conclude that one theory is better than another? A good theory does all these jobs well: (1) It effectively summarizes a wide range of observations. (2) And it makes clear predictions that we can use to (a) confirm or modify the theory, (b) generate new exploration, and (c) suggest practical ap-

British fans at a game in Dusseldorf, Germany. What influences occasionally trigger postgame violence among European soccer fans? Social psychologists have proposed hypotheses which have been tested with groups behaving under controlled conditions.

plication. When we discard theories, usually it's not because they have been proved false. Rather, like an old car, they get replaced by newer, better models.

GENERALIZING FROM LABORATORY TO LIFE

As the TV experiment illustrates, social psychology mixes everyday experience and laboratory analysis. Throughout this book we will do the same by drawing our data mostly from the laboratory and our illustrations mostly from life. Social psychology displays a healthy interplay between laboratory research and everyday life. Hunches gained from everyday experience often inspire laboratory research, which deepens our understanding of our experience. This interplay appears in the research on children's television. What people saw in everyday life suggested experiments. Although constrained by economics and politics, network and government policymakers are now aware of the results.

However, we must generalize from laboratory to life cautiously. Although the laboratory uncovers basic secrets of human existence, it is still a simplified, controlled reality. It tells us what effect to expect of variable x, all other things being equal—which in real life they never are. Moreover, as you will see, the participants in many social-psychological experiments are college students. While this may help you identify with them, college students are hardly a random sample of all humanity. Would we get similar results with people of different ages, educational levels, and cultures? This is always an open question.

Nevertheless, we can distinguish between the *content* of people's thinking and acting (their attitudes, for example) and the *process* by which they think and act (for example, how attitudes affect actions and vice versa). The content varies more from culture to culture than does the process. People of different cultures may hold different opinions, yet form them in similar ways. Consider:

> College students in Puerto Rico report greater loneliness than do collegians on the U.S. mainland. Yet in both cultures the ingredients of loneliness are much the same— shyness, uncertain purpose in life, low self-esteem (Jones & others, 1985).
>
> Ethnic groups differ in school achievement and delinquency, but the differences are "no more than skin deep," report David Rowe and his colleagues (1994). To the extent that family structure, peer influences, and parental education predict achievement or delinquency for one ethnic group, they do so for other groups. Our behaviors may differ, yet be influenced by the same social forces.

SUMMING UP

Most social psychological research is either correlational or experimental. Correlational studies, sometimes conducted with systematic survey methods, discern the relationship between variables, such as between amount of education and amount of income. Knowing two things are naturally related is valuable information, but it seldom indicates what is causing what. When possible, social psychologists prefer to conduct experiments that explore cause and effect.

By constructing a miniature reality that is under their control, experimenters can vary one thing and then another and discover how these things, separately or in combination, affect behavior. We randomly assign participants to an experimental condition, which receives the experimental treatment, or to a control condition, which does not. We can then attribute any resulting difference between the two conditions to the independent variable.

In creating experiments, social psychologists sometimes stage situations that engage people's emotions. In doing so, they are obliged to follow professional ethical guidelines, such as obtaining people's informed consent, protecting them from harm, and fully disclosing afterward any temporary deceptions.

Social psychologists organize their ideas and findings into theories. A good theory will distill an array of facts into a much shorter list of predictive principles. We can use these predictions to confirm or modify the theory, to generate new exploration, and to suggest practical application. Laboratory experiments enable social psychologists to test ideas gleaned from life experience and then to apply the principles and findings back in the real world.

■ FOR FURTHER READING

To see social psychology firsthand in its primary sources, skim, for North American social psychology, the *Journal of Personality and Social Psychology* or *Personality and Social Psychology Bulletin*, both published by the American Psychological Association.

To sample European social psychology, see the *European Journal of Social Psychology* (published by the European Association of Experimental Social Psychology) or the *British Journal of Social Psychology* (published by the British Psychological Society).

For a carefully selected sample of influential articles from the literature of social psychology, see Steve Ellyson and Amy Halberstadt's *Exploring Social Psychology: The Readings* (McGraw-Hill, 1995).

SOCIAL THINKING

*Change the way people think and
things will never be the same.*

Stephen Biko
SOUTH AFRICAN CIVIL RIGHTS MARTYR

This book unfolds around its definition of social psychology: the scientific study of how we *think about* (Part I), *influence* (Part II), and *relate to* (Part III) one another.

These chapters on social thinking examine how we view ourselves and others. In varying ways, each chapter confronts an overriding question: How reasonable are our social attitudes, explanations, and beliefs? Are our impressions of ourselves and others generally accurate? How is our social thinking prone to bias and error, and how might we bring it closer to reality?

Chapter 2 explores the interplay between our sense of self and our social worlds. How do our social surroundings shape our self-identity? How does self-interest color our social judgments and motivate our social behavior?

Chapter 3 looks at the amazing and sometimes rather amusing ways in which we form beliefs about our social worlds and reveals a half-dozen ways in which we are prone to err.

Chapter 4 explores the links between attitudes and behaviors: Do our attitudes determine our behaviors? Do our behaviors determine our attitudes? Or does it work both ways?

Chapter 5 examines the implications of this research on attitudes, explanations, and beliefs for the mental health professions. For example, how do people explain their emotional and health problems? And how might psychologists and physicians diagnose people more accurately and treat them more effectively?

THE SELF IN A SOCIAL WORLD

Our behavior arises from the interplay between what's going on inside our heads and what's happening outside, between our sense of self and our social surroundings. A few examples:

■ *Social Surroundings Affect Self-Awareness*: As individuals in a group of a different culture, race, or sex, we become self-conscious of how we differ and sensitive to how others are reacting to our difference. On the day I wrote these words, a European-American friend just back from Nepal explained how self-consciously White he felt while living in a rural village; an hour later an African-American friend told me how self-consciously *American* she felt while in Africa.

■ *Self-Interest Colors Social Judgments*: We are not objective, dispassionate judges of events. When problems arise in a close relationship such as marriage, we usually attribute more responsibility to our partners than to ourselves. Few divorced people blame themselves. When things go *well* at home or work or play, we see ourselves as more responsible. In competing for prizes, scientists seldom underrate their own contributions. After Frederick Banting and John Macleod received a 1923 Nobel Prize for discovering insulin, Banting claimed that Macleod, who headed the laboratory, had been more a hindrance than a help. Macleod omitted Banting's name in speeches about the discovery (Ross, 1981).

■ *Self-Concern Motivates Social Behavior*: Our actions are often strategic. In hopes of making a positive impression, we spend billions on cosmetics and diet programs. Like politicians, we also monitor others' behavior and expectations and adjust our behavior accordingly. Concern for self-image drives much of our behavior.

As these examples suggest, the traffic between self and society runs both ways. Your ideas and feelings about yourself affect how you interpret events, how you recall them, and how you respond to others. Others, in turn, help shape your sense of self. For such reasons, no topic in psychology is today more researched than the self. In 1993 the word "self" appeared in nearly 5400 book and article summaries in *Psychological Abstracts*—quadruple the number in 1970. Our sense of self organizes our thoughts, feelings, and actions. We therefore begin our tour of social psychology with a look at how well we know ourselves, how we feel about ourselves, and how our sense of self drives our attitudes and actions.

■ SELF-CONCEPT

How do our beliefs about ourselves influence our thoughts and actions? How accurately do we know ourselves? How does our culture shape our sense of self?

Who are you? As a unique and complex creature you have many ways to complete the sentence "I am_____." (What five answers might you give?) Taken together, your answers define your *self-concept*. The elements of your self-concept, the specific beliefs by which you define who you are, are your

self-schemas (Markus & Wurf, 1987). *Schemas* are mental templates by which we organize our worlds. Our *self*-schemas—our perceiving ourselves as athletic, overweight, smart, or whatever—powerfully affect how we process social information. They influence how we perceive, remember, and evaluate both other people and ourselves. If athletics is a central part of our self-concept (if being an athlete is one of our self-schemas), then we will tend to notice others' bodies and skills. We will quickly recall sports-related experiences. And we will welcome information that is consistent with our self-schema (Kihlstrom & Cantor, 1984). Thus the self-schemas that make up our self-concept serve as a sort of mental Dewey Decimal System for cataloguing and retrieving information.

Consider how the self influences memory, a phenomenon known as the **self-reference effect**: When information is relevant to our self-concepts, we process it quickly and remember it well (Higgins & Bargh, 1987; Kuiper & Rogers, 1979; Reeder & others, 1987). If asked whether specific words, such as "outgoing" describe *us*, we later remember those words better than if asked whether they describe someone else. If asked to compare ourselves with a character in a short story, we remember that character better. Two days after a conversation with someone, our recall is best for what the person said about us (Kahan & Johnson, 1992). Thus, memories form around our primary interest: ourselves. When we think about something in relation to ourselves, we remember it better.

The self-reference effect illustrates a basic fact of life: Our sense of self is at the center of our worlds. Because we tend to see ourselves as center stage, we overestimate the extent to which others' behavior is aimed at us. And we often see ourselves as responsible for events in which we played only a small part (Fenigstein, 1984).

Our self-concepts include not only our beliefs about who we currently are but also who we might become—our **possible selves**. Hazel Markus and her colleagues (Inglehart & others, 1989; Markus & Nurius, 1986) note that our possible selves include our visions of the self we dream of becoming—the rich self, the thin self, the passionately loved and loving self. They also include the self we fear becoming—the unemployed self, the sick self, the academically failed self. Such possible selves motivate us with specific goals—a vision of the life we long for.

Is **self-esteem**—our overall self-evaluation—the summation of all our self-schemas and possible selves? If we see ourselves as attractive, athletic, smart, and destined to be rich and loved, will we have high self-esteem? That's what psychologists assume when they suggest that to help people feel better about themselves, one must first make them feel more attractive, athletic, smarter, and so forth. But Jonathon Brown and Keith Dutton (1994) argue that this "bottom-up" view of self-esteem is backwards. The causal arrow, they believe, goes the other way. People who value themselves in a general way—those with high self-esteem—are more likely to accept their looks, abilities, and so forth. They are like new parents who, loving their infant, delight in its fingers, toes, and hair. (The parents do not first evaluate their infant's fingers or toes and then decide how much to value the whole baby.)

To test their idea that global self-esteem affects specific self-perceptions ("top down"), they introduced University of Washington students to a supposed trait, "integrative ability." (They gave the students sets of three words—for example: "car," "swimming," "cue"—and challenged them to think of a word that linked the three words. Hint: the word begins with *p*.) High self-esteem people were more likely to report having this ability if told it was very important

Self-schema:
Beliefs about self that organize and guide the processing of self-relevant information.

Self-reference effect:
The tendency to process efficiently and remember well information related to oneself.

Possible selves:
Images of what we dream of or dread becoming in the future.

Self-esteem:
A person's overall self-evaluation or sense of self worth.

Oprah Winfrey's imagined possible selves, including the dreaded overweight self and the rich self, motivated her to work to achieve the life she wanted.

than if told there was no known use for the ability. Feeling good about oneself in a general way, it seems, casts a rosy glow over one's specific self-schemas and possible selves.

Consistent with this top-down view of self-esteem, Stephen Smith and Richard Petty (1995) have shown how high self-esteem people maintain positive emotions. Put low self-esteem people in a negative mood and they will retrieve mostly negative memories from their past and from newspaper headlines. Put high self-esteem people in a negative mood, and they will often restore their mood by retrieving *positive* memories. Likewise, if put in a negative mood, low self-esteem people will usually imagine a mood-consistent negative story in response to an ambiguous picture. If put in the same negative mood, high self-esteem people will usually spin a mood-enhancing positive story.

So, global self-esteem colors our feelings about our traits and abilities, and colors our memories and thoughts. But what determines our self-esteem? There are, as we will see, multiple influences: secure early attachments to parents, others' appraisal of us, comparisons we make with others, culturally influenced identities, and even the bottom-up influence of achieving specific competencies. As we conquer challenges and learn skills that set us apart from others, our successes breed a more hopeful, confident approach to the world. Although self-esteem influences our thinking, top down, it also is fed through the roots of daily experience.

SELF-KNOWLEDGE

"Know thyself," admonished the Greek philosopher Socrates. We certainly try. We readily form beliefs about ourselves, and we don't hesitate to explain why we feel and do as we do. But how well do we actually know ourselves?

"There is one thing, and only one in the whole universe which we know more about than we could learn from external observation," noted C. S. Lewis (1960, pp. 18–19). "That one thing is [ourselves]. We have, so to speak, inside information; we are in the know." Indeed. Yet sometimes we *think* we know, but our inside information is wrong. This is the unavoidable conclusion of some fascinating recent research.

Explaining Our Behavior

Why did you choose your college? Why did you lash out at your roommate? Why did you fall in love with that special person? Sometimes we know. Sometimes we don't know. Asked why we have felt or acted as we have, we produce plausible answers. Yet, when causes and determinants are not obvious, our self-explanations often err. Factors that have big effects we sometimes report as innocuous. Factors that have little effect we sometimes perceive as influential.

Richard Nisbett and Stanley Schachter (1966) demonstrated this by asking Columbia University students to take a series of electric shocks of steadily increasing intensity. Beforehand, some took a fake pill that, they were told, would produce heart palpitations, breathing irregularities, and butterflies in the stomach—the very symptoms that usually accompany being shocked. Nisbett and Schachter anticipated that people would attribute the symptoms of shock to the pill rather than to the shock, thus they should tolerate more shock than people not given the pill. Indeed, the effect was enormous—people given the fake pill took four times as much shock.

When informed they had taken more shock than average, and asked why, their answers did not mention the pill. When pressed (even after the experimenter explained the hypotheses in detail), they denied the pill's influence. They would usually say the pill probably did affect some people, but not them. A typical reply was, "I didn't even think about the pill."

> "You don't know your own mind."
> Jonathan Swift, Polite Conversation, 1738

Sometimes people think they *have* been affected by something that has had no effect. Nisbett and Timothy Wilson (1977) had University of Michigan students rate a documentary film. While some of them watched, a power saw roared just outside the room. Most people felt that this distracting noise affected their ratings. But it didn't; their ratings were similar to those of control subjects who viewed the film without distraction.

Even more thought-provoking are studies in which people recorded their moods every day for two or three months (Stone & others, 1985; Weiss & Brown, 1976; Wilson & others, 1982). They also recorded factors that might affect their moods—the day of the week, the weather, the amount they slept, and so forth. At the end of each study, the people judged how much each factor had affected their moods. Remarkably (given that their attention was being drawn to their daily moods), there was little relationship between their perceptions of how important a factor was and how well the factor actually predicted their mood. These findings raise a disconcerting question: How much insight do we really have into what makes us happy or unhappy?

> "There are three things extremely hard, Steel, a Diamond, and to know one's self."
> Benjamin Franklin

Predicting Our Behavior

People also err when predicting their behavior. Asked whether they would obey demands to deliver severe electric shocks or would hesitate to help a victim if several other people were present, people overwhelmingly deny their

Predicting behavior, even one's own, is no easy matter—which may be why this visitor to Burma has turned to an astrologer for help.

vulnerability to such influences. But as we will see, experiments have shown that many of us are vulnerable. Moreover, consider what Sidney Shrauger (1983) discovered when he had college students predict the likelihood of their experiencing dozens of different events during the ensuing two months (becoming romantically involved, being sick, and so forth): Their self-predictions were hardly more accurate than predictions based on the average person's experience. The surest thing we can say about your individual future is that it is sometimes hard for even you to predict. When predicting yourself, the best advice is to consider your past behavior in similar situations (Osberg & Shrauger, 1986, 1990).

The Wisdom and Delusions of Self-Analysis

So, to a striking extent, our intuitions are often dead wrong about what has influenced us and what we will feel and do. But let's not overstate the case. When the causes of our behavior are conspicuous and the correct explanation fits our intuition, our self-perceptions will be accurate (Gavanski & Hoffman, 1987). Peter Wright and Peter Rip (1981) found that California high school juniors *could* discern how such features of a college as its size, tuition, and distance from home influenced their reactions to it. But when the causes of behavior are not obvious to an observer, they are not obvious to the person, either.

As Chapter 3 will explain, we are unaware of much that goes on in our minds. Studies of perception and memory show that our awareness is mostly of the *results* of our thinking and not of the *process*. Gazing across our mental sea, we behold little below its conscious surface. We experience the *results* of our mind's unconscious workings when we set a mental clock to record the passage of time and to awaken us at an appointed hour, or when we somehow achieve a spontaneous creative insight after a problem has unconsciously "incubated." Creative scientists and artists, for example, often cannot report the thought process that produced their insights.

Social psychologist Timothy Wilson (1985) offers a bold idea: the mental processes that *control* our social behavior are distinct from the mental processes through which we *explain* our behavior. Our rational explanations may therefore omit the gut-level attitudes that actually guide our behavior. In nine experiments, Wilson and his co-workers (1989) found that people's expressed attitudes—toward things or toward others—usually predicted their later behavior reasonably well. However, if they first asked the people to *analyze* their feelings, their attitude reports became useless. For example, dating couples' happiness with their relationship was a reasonably good predictor of whether they were still dating several months later. But if before rating their happiness they first listed all the reasons they could think of why their relationship was good or bad, then their attitude reports were useless in predicting the future of the relationship! Apparently the process of dissecting the relationship drew people's attention to easily verbalized factors that actually were less important than other aspects of the relationship that were harder to verbalize.

In a later study, Wilson and his co-workers (1993) had people choose one of two art posters to take home. Those asked first to identify *reasons* for their choice preferred a humorous poster (whose positive features they could more easily verbalize). But a few weeks later, they were less satisfied with their choice than were those who just went by their gut feelings, and generally chose the other poster.

Murray Millar and Abraham Tesser (1992) believe that Wilson overstates our ignorance of self. Their research suggests that, yes, drawing people's attention to *reasons* diminishes the usefulness of attitude reports in predicting behaviors that are driven by *feelings*. If instead of having people analyze their romantic relationships Wilson had first asked them to get more in touch with their

"Self-contemplation is a curse That makes an old confusion worse."
Theodore Roethke, The Collected Poems of Theodore Roethke, 1975

An inventor with his monocycle. Like everyone else, creative people are more aware of the results of their thinking than of the underlying cognitive processes.

feelings ("How do you feel when you are with and apart from your partner?"), their attitude reports might have been *more* insightful. Other behavior domains—say, choosing which school to attend based on considerations of cost, career advancement, and so forth—seem more cognitively driven. For these, an analysis of reasons rather than feelings may be most useful. While the heart has its reasons, sometimes the mind's own reasons are decisive.

This research on the limits of our self-knowledge has two practical implications. The first is for psychological inquiry. Although people's intuitions may provide useful clues to their psychological processes, *self-reports are often untrustworthy.* Errors in self-understanding limit the scientific usefulness of subjective personal reports.

The second implication is for our everyday lives. The sincerity with which people report and interpret their experiences is no guarantee of the validity of these reports. Personal testimonies are powerfully persuasive, but they may also convey error. Keeping this potential for error in mind can help us feel less intimidated by others and be less gullible.

SELF AND CULTURE

How did you complete the "I am_____" statement? With information about your individual traits, such as "I am honest," "I am tall," or "I am outgoing"? Or also with information about your social connections and group identity, such as "I am Roman Catholic," "I am a MacDonald," or "I am Canadian"?

For some people, especially those in industrialized western cultures, identity is pretty much self-contained. Adolescence is a time of separating from parents and defining one's personal, *independent self.* Uprooted and placed in a foreign land, one's identity—as a unique individual with particular abilities, traits, values, and dreams—would remain intact. The psychology of western cultures assumes that your life will be enriched by defining your possible selves and believing in your power of personal control. Don't conform to others' expectations. Rather, be true to yourself. Seek your own bliss. Do your own thing. To love others, first love yourself.

Western literature, from the *Iliad* to *The Adventures of Huckleberry Finn*, celebrates the self-reliant individual. Movie plots feature rugged heroes who buck the establishment. Songs proclaim that "I Did it My Way" and "I Gotta Be Me" and revere "The Greatest Love of All"—loving oneself (Schoeneman, 1994).

As we will see in Chapter 6, "Gender, Genes, and Culture," such individualism is bred by certain social conditions and entails certain consequences. For now, it is enough to note that many nonwestern cultures nurture what Shinobu Kitayama and Hazel Markus (in press) call the *interdependent self.* In cultures native to Asia, Africa, and Central and South America, identity is defined more in relation to others. Malaysians, for example, are much more likely than Australians and Britishers, and Japanese more likely than Americans, to complete the "I am" statement with their group identities (Bochner, 1994; Markus & Kitayama, 1991).

With an interdependent self one has a greater sense of belonging. Uprooted and cut off from family, colleagues, and loyal friends, one would lose the social connections that define who one is. One has not one self but many selves: self-with-parents, self-at-work, self-with-friends (Cross & others, 1992). As Figure 2–1 and Table 2–1 suggest, the interdependent self is embedded in, and

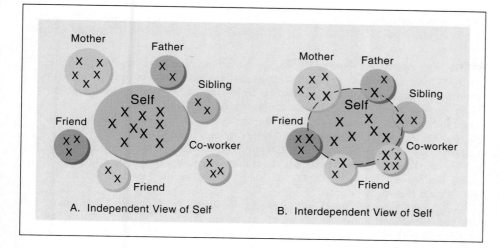

■ FIGURE 2–1
Self-construal as Independent or Interdependent. The independent self acknowledges relationships with others. But the interdependent self is more deeply embedded in others. (From Markus & Kitayama, 1991.)

TABLE 2–1 *Self-Concept: Independent or Interdependent*

	INDEPENDENT	INTERDEPENDENT
Identity is	Personal, defined by individual traits and goals	Social, defined by connections with others
What matters	Me—personal achievement and fulfillment; my rights and liberties	We—group goals and solidarity; our social responsibilities and relationships
Disapproves of	Conformity	Egotism
Illustrative motto	"To thine own self be true"	"No one is an island"
Cultures that support	Individualistic western	Collectivistic Asian and third world

partly defined by, social memberships. Thus the goal of social life is not so much to enhance one's individual self as to harmonize with and support one's communities. Self-esteem correlates closely with "what others think of me and my group." For those in individualistic cultures, and especially for minorities who have learned to discount others' prejudices, others' appraisal of oneself and one's group matter somewhat less (Crocker, 1994; Crocker & others, 1994).

So, when East meets West—as happens, for example, thanks to western influences in urban Japan and to Japanese exchange students visiting western countries—does the self-concept become more individualized? Does being bombarded with examples of promotions based on individual achievement rather than seniority, admonitions to "believe in one's own possibilities," and movies in which the heroic individual police officer catches the crook *despite* others' interference, have an influence? It may, indeed, report Steven Heine and Darrin Lehman (1995). Self-esteem increased among Japanese exchange students after spending seven months at the University of British Columbia. Self-esteem is also higher among long-term Asian immigrants to Canada than among more recent immigrants and among those living in Asia.

In 1991, after nearly ten years of research and teaching at the Universities of Michigan and Oregon, I visited my Japanese alma mater, Kyoto University, and met with Japanese graduate students to plan some cross-cultural research on self-concept. When I explained the western idea of the independent self to these very bright students, they were astounded. "This oversimplified statement about self does no justice to the full complexity of social life," they insisted. I persisted in explaining this western notion of self-concept—one that my American students understood intuitively—and finally began to persuade them that, indeed, many Americans do have such a disconnected notion of self. Still, one of them, sighing deeply, said at the end, "Could this *really* be true?"

As a person who has lived and learned in both the West and the East, I have been fascinated by the surprising variability of the self in our differing cultures. As we come to understand this variability better, perhaps social psychology's horizon can expand. And, more significantly, perhaps we will better appreciate the relative strengths of our world's many cultures.

SHINOBU KITAYAMA, *Kyoto University*

SUMMING UP

Our sense of self helps organize our thoughts and actions. When we process information with reference to ourselves, we remember it well (a phenomenon called the *self-reference* effect). The elements of our self-concept are the specific *self-schemas* that guide our processing of self-relevant information and the *possible selves* that we dream of or dread. Our *self-esteem* is an overall sense of self-worth that influences how we appraise our traits and abilities.

Our self-knowledge is, however, flawed. We often do not know why we behave the way we do. When powerful influences upon our behavior are not so conspicuous that any observer could spot them, we, too, can miss them.

People differ in their self-conceptions. Some people, especially in individualistic western cultures, assume an *independent self*. Others, often in Asian and third world cultures, assume an *interdependent self*. These contrasting ideas contribute to cultural differences in social behavior (as Chapter 6 will further explain).

■ SELF-EFFICACY

It helps not only to know ourselves without glaring self-delusions but also to believe in ourselves. In experiments, people who imagine themselves being hardworking and successful outperform on challenging tasks those who imagine themselves failing (Ruvolo & Markus, 1992). Envision your positive possibilities and you become more likely to plan and enact a successful strategy.

High self-esteem also pays dividends. Compared to those with low self-esteem, people with a sense of self-worth are happier, less neurotic, less troubled by ulcers and insomnia, less prone to drug and alcohol addictions (Brockner & Hulton, 1978; Brown, 1992). Additional research on *locus of control* and *learned helplessness* confirms the benefits of seeing oneself as competent and effective. Albert Bandura (1986) merges much of this research into a concept called **self-efficacy**, a scholarly version of the wisdom behind the power of positive thinking. An optimistic belief in our own possibilities pays dividends. People with strong feelings of self-efficacy are more persistent, less anxious and depressed, and more academically successful (Gecas, 1989; Maddux, 1991; Scheier & Carver, 1992). Your self-efficacy is how competent you feel to do something. What then? If you can do it, will it make a difference? Do you have *control* over your outcomes?

Self-efficacy:
A sense that one is competent and effective. Distinguished from self-esteem, a sense of one's self-worth. A bombardier might feel high self-efficacy and low self-esteem.

LOCUS OF CONTROL

"I have no social life," complained a 40-something single man to student therapist Jerry Phares. At Phares' urging, the patient went to a dance, where several women danced with him. "I was just lucky," he later reported, "it would never happen again." When Phares reported this to his mentor, Julian Rotter, it crystallized an idea he had been forming. In Rotter's experiments and in his clinical practice, some people seemed to persistently "feel that what happens to them is governed by external forces of one kind or another, while others feel that what happens to them is governed largely by their own efforts and skills" (quoted by Hunt, 1993, p. 334).

Rotter called this attitude **locus of control**. With Phares, he developed 29 paired statements to measure a person's locus of control. What do you think? Are people more often captains of their destinies or victims of their circumstances? The playwrights, directors, and actors of their own lives or prisoners of invisible situations? Specifically, which do you more strongly believe?

Locus of control:
The extent to which people perceive their lives as internally controllable by their own efforts and actions or as externally controlled by chance or outside forces.

In the long run people get the respect they deserve in this world.	*or* Unfortunately, people's worth often passes unrecognized no matter how hard they try.
What happens to me is my own doing.	*or* Sometimes I feel that I don't have enough control over the direction my life is taking.
The average person can have an influence in government decisions.	*or* This world is run by the few people in power, and there is not much the little guy can do about it.

Do your answers to such questions (from Rotter, 1973) indicate that you believe you control your own destiny (*internal* locus of control)? Or that chance or outside forces determine your fate (*external* locus of control)? Those who see themselves as internally controlled are more likely to do well in school, successfully stop smoking, wear seat belts, practice birth control, deal with marital problems directly, make lots of money, and delay instant gratification in order to achieve long-term goals (Findley & Cooper, 1983; Lefcourt, 1982; Miller & others, 1986).

How competent and effective we feel depends on how we explain setbacks. Perhaps you have known students who view themselves as victims—who, say, blame poor grades on things beyond their control—their feelings of stupidity or their "poor" teachers, texts, or tests. If such students are coached to adopt a more hopeful attitude—to believe that effort, good study habits, and self-discipline can make a difference—their grades tend to go up (Noel & others, 1987; Peterson & Barrett, 1987).

Successful people are more likely to see setbacks as a fluke or to think "I need a new approach." New life insurance sales representatives who view failures as controllable ("It's difficult, but with persistence I'll get better") sell more policies. They are half as likely as their more pessimistic colleagues to quit during their first year (Seligman & Schulman, 1986). Among college swimming team members, those with an optimistic explanatory style are more likely than pessimists to perform beyond expectations (Seligman & others, 1990). As the Roman poet Virgil said in the *Aeneid*, "They can because they think they can."

LEARNED HELPLESSNESS VERSUS SELF-DETERMINATION

The benefits of self-efficacy also appear in animal research. Dogs that learn a sense of helplessness (by being taught they cannot escape shocks) will later fail to take the initiative in another situation when they *could* escape the punishment. Dogs that learn personal control (by escaping their first shocks successfully) adapt easily to a new situation. Researcher Martin Seligman (1975, 1991) notes similarities to this **learned helplessness** in human situations. Depressed or oppressed people, for example, become passive because they believe their efforts have no effect. Helpless dogs and depressed people both suffer paralysis of the will, passive resignation, even motionless apathy (Figure 2–2).

Here is a clue to how institutions—whether malevolent, like concentration camps, or benevolent, like hospitals—can dehumanize people. In hospitals, "good patients" don't ring bells, don't ask questions, don't try to control what's happening (Taylor, 1979). Such passivity may be good for hospital efficiency, but it is bad for people. Feelings of efficacy, of an ability to control one's life, enhance health and survival. Losing control over what you do and what others do to you can make unpleasant events profoundly stressful (Pomerleau & Rodin, 1986). Several diseases are associated with feelings of helplessness and diminished choice. So is the rapidity of decline and death in concentration camps and nursing homes. Hospital patients who are trained to believe in their ability to control stress require fewer pain relievers and sedatives and nurses see them as exhibiting less anxiety (Langer & others, 1975).

Ellen Langer and Judith Rodin (1976) showed the importance of personal control by treating elderly patients in a high-rated Connecticut nursing home

Learned helplessness:
The hopelessness and resignation learned when a human or animal perceives no control over repeated bad events.

■ FIGURE 2–2
Learned Helplessness *When animals and people experience uncontrollable bad events, they learn to feel helpless and resigned.*

Personal control: Inmates of Spain's modern Valencia prison can, with appropriate behavior, gain access to classes, sports facilities, and cultural opportunities. Salary earned for work is credited to an account, which they can charge for extra snacks.

in one of two ways. With one group the benevolent caregivers stressed "our responsibility to make this a home you can be proud of and happy in." They treated the patients as passive recipients of the normal well-intentioned, sympathetic care. Three weeks later, most were rated by themselves, by interviewers, and by nurses as further debilitated. Langer and Rodin's other treatment promoted personal control. It stressed opportunities for choice, the possibilities for influencing nursing-home policy, and the person's responsibility "to make of your life whatever you want." These patients were given small decisions to make and responsibilities to fulfill. Over the ensuing three weeks, 93 percent of this group showed improved alertness, activity, and happiness.

The experience of the first group must have been similar to that of James MacKay (1980), an 87-year-old psychologist:

> I became a nonperson last summer. My wife had an arthritic knee which put her in a walker, and I chose that moment to break my leg. We went to a nursing home. It was all nursing and no home. The doctor and the head nurse made all decisions; we were merely animate objects. Thank heavens it was only two weeks. . . . The top man of the nursing home was very well trained and very compassionate; I considered it the best home in town. But we were nonpersons from the time we entered until we left.

Studies confirm that systems of governing or managing people that promote self-efficacy will indeed promote health and happiness (Deci & Ryan, 1987).

■ Prisoners given some control over their environments—by being able to move chairs, control TV sets, and switch the lights—experience less stress, exhibit fewer health problems, and commit less vandalism (Ruback & others, 1986; Wener & others, 1987).

■ Workers given leeway in carrying out tasks and making decisions experience improved morale (Miller & Monge, 1986).

■ Institutionalized residents allowed choice in such matters as what to eat for breakfast, when to go to a movie, whether to sleep late or get up early, may live longer and certainly are happier (Timko & Moos, 1989).

■ Homeless shelter residents who perceive little choice in when to eat and sleep, and little control over their privacy, are more likely to have a passive, helpless attitude regarding finding housing and work (Burn, 1992).

COLLECTIVE EFFICACY

"If my mind can conceive it and my heart can believe it, I know I can achieve it. Down with dope! Up with hope! I am somebody!"
Jesse Jackson, civil rights march on Washington, 1983

Although it is commonly thought that hopelessness breeds militant social action, the truth is that it more often breeds apathy. Compared to apathetic people, protesting members of aggrieved groups generally have more self-pride and a stronger belief in their ability to influence events (Caplan, 1970; Forward & Williams, 1970; McKenzie-Mohr & Dyal, 1991). In many countries, university students (not the most severely disadvantaged members of the society) spearhead political activism. "People who have a sense of collective efficacy," notes Bandura (1982),

> will mobilize their efforts and resources to cope with external obstacles to the changes they seek. But those convinced of their inefficacy will cease trying even though changes are attainable through concerted effort . . . As a society, we enjoy the benefits left by those before us who collectively resisted inhumanities and worked for social reforms that permit a better life. Our own collective efficacy will, in turn, shape how future generations will live their lives.

Self-efficacy: Hope and control rather than helplessness marks the lives of these new American citizens.

"This gives my confidence a real boost."

Confidence and feelings of self-efficacy grow from successes.

Although this psychological research and comment on self-efficacy is new, the emphasis on taking charge of one's life and realizing one's potential is not. The you-can-do-it theme of Horatio Alger's rags-to-riches books is an enduring American idea. We find it in Norman Vincent Peale's 1950s best-seller, *The Power of Positive Thinking* ("If you think in positive terms you will get positive results. That is the simple fact."). We find it in self-help books and videos that urge people to succeed through positive mental attitudes.

Research on self-efficacy gives us greater confidence in traditional virtues such as perseverance and hope. Yet Bandura believes that self-efficacy grows not primarily by self-persuasion ("I think I can, I think I can") or by puffing people up like hot-air balloons ("You're terrific! You are somebody! You are beautiful!"). Its chief source is undertaking challenging yet realistic tasks and succeeding. After mastering the physical skills needed to repel a sexual assault, women feel less vulnerable, less anxious, and more in control (Ozer & Bandura, 1990). After experiencing academic success, students develop higher appraisals of their academic ability, which in turn often stimulate them to work harder and achieve more (Felson, 1984). To do one's best and achieve is to feel more confident and empowered.

"Argue for your limitations, and sure enough they're yours." Richard Bach, Illusions: Adventures of a Reluctant Messiah, 1977

Several lines of research show the benefits of the *self-efficacy* that comes from succeeding at challenging tasks. People who believe in their own competence and effectiveness, and who have an internal locus of control cope better and achieve more than do those who have learned a helpless, pessimistic outlook. Groups that feel collective efficacy often are activist.

SUMMING UP

■ SELF-SERVING BIAS

A s *we process self-relevant information, a potent bias intrudes. We readily excuse our failures, accept credit for our successes, and in many ways see ourselves as better than average. Such self-enhancing perceptions enable most people to enjoy the benefits of high self-esteem, while occasionally suffering the perils of pride.*

It is widely believed that most of us suffer low self-esteem. A generation ago, humanistic psychologist Carl Rogers (1958) concluded that most people he knew "despise themselves, regard themselves as worthless and unlovable." Many popularizers of humanistic psychology concur. "All of us have inferiority complexes," contends John Powell (1989). "Those who seem not to have such a complex are only pretending." As Groucho Marx (1960) lampooned, "I don't want to belong to any club that would accept me as a member."

Self-serving bias:
The tendency to perceive oneself favorably.

Actually, most of us have a good reputation with ourselves. In studies of self-esteem, even low-scoring people respond in the midrange of possible scores. (A low self-esteem person responds to such statements as "I have good ideas" with a qualifying adjective, such as "somewhat" or "sometimes.") Moreover, one of social psychology's most provocative yet firmly established conclusions concerns the potency of **self-serving bias**.

FOCUS

DEVELOPMENT OF THE SOCIAL SELF

The self has become a major topic in psychology because it helps organize our social thinking and energize our social behavior. But what influences our sense of self? This chapter discusses two ingredients of self:

- *Culture.* Individualist western cultures nurture an independent, detached sense of self. Collectivist Asian and third world cultures nurture a more interdependent, socially connected sense of self.
- *Personal experience.* Self-efficacy arises from mastery experiences. To succeed at a challenging task builds one's sense of competence.

Future chapters will explore other ingredients of self:

- *Other people's judgments.* We see ourselves, in part, as reflected in others' impressions and judgments. Children whom others label as gifted, hard working, or helpful tend to incorporate such ideas into their self-concepts and behavior (see Chapter 3).

- *The roles we play.* As we enact a new role—as college student, parent, salesperson, and so forth—we may initially feel self-conscious. Gradually, however, what begins as play-acting in the theatre of life gets absorbed into our sense of self. Pretense becomes reality (see Chapter 4).
- *Self-justification and self-perception.* We sometimes feel discomfort after speaking or acting insincerely. Or we may speak in support of something we haven't really thought much about. In such cases, we can justify our actions by identifying ourselves with them. Moreover, observing ourselves can be self-revealing; we may now perceive ourselves as holding the views we expressed (see Chapter 4).
- *Social comparison.* At any moment, we tend to be most self-aware of ways we differ from those around us. As a solo female in a group of men, or as a solo Canadian in a group of Europeans, we are self-conscious of our uniqueness (see Chapter 7). Comparisons with others also shape our self-identity as rich or poor, smart or dumb, tall or short (Chapter 12).

EXPLANATIONS FOR POSITIVE AND NEGATIVE EVENTS

Time and again, experimenters have found that people readily accept credit when told they have succeeded (attributing the success to their ability and effort), yet attribute failure to such external factors as bad luck or the problem's inherent "impossibility" (Whitley & Frieze, 1985). Similarly, in explaining their victories, athletes commonly credit themselves, but attribute losses to something else: bad breaks, bad referee calls, or the other team's super effort or dirty play (Grove & others, 1991; Lalonde, 1992; Mullen & Riordan, 1988). And how much responsibility do you suppose car drivers tend to accept for their accidents? On insurance forms, drivers have described their accidents in words such as these: "An invisible car came out of nowhere, struck my car and vanished," "As I reached an intersection, a hedge sprang up, obscuring my vision and I did not see the other car," "A pedestrian hit me and went under my car" (*Toronto News*, 1977). Situations that combine skill and chance (games, exams, job applications) are especially prone to the phenomenon: Winners can easily attribute their successes to their skill, while losers can attribute their losses to chance. When I win at Scrabble, it's because of my verbal dexterity; when I lose, it's because, "Who could get anywhere with a *Q* but no *U*?"

Michael Ross and Fiore Sicoly (1979) observed a marital version of self-serving bias. They found that young married Canadians usually felt they took more responsibility for such activities as cleaning the house and caring for the children than their spouses credited them for. In a survey of Americans, 91 percent of wives but only 76 percent of husbands credited the wife with doing most of the food shopping (Burros, 1988). In another study, husbands estimated

Adam's excuse:
"The woman whom you gave to be with me, she gave me fruit from the tree, and I ate."

"I'm drawing up a list of all my good points and all my flaws, and so far my good points are running way, way ahead of my flaws."

The self-serving bias.

they did slightly more of the housework than their wives did; the wives, however, estimated their efforts were more than double their husbands' (Fiebert, 1990). Every night, my wife and I pitch our laundry at the foot of our bedroom clothes hamper. In the morning, one of us puts it in. When she suggested that I take more responsibility for this, I thought, "Huh? I already do it 75 percent of the time." So I asked her how often she thought she picked up the clothes. "Oh," she replied, "about 75 percent of the time." Small wonder that divorced people usually blame their partner for the breakup (Gray & Silver, 1990), or that managers usually blame poor performance on workers' lack of ability or effort (Imai, 1994; Rice, 1985). (Workers are more likely to blame something external—inadequate supplies, excessive workload, difficult co-workers, ambiguous assignments.)

Students also exhibit self-serving bias. After receiving an exam grade, those who do well tend to accept personal credit. They judge the exam to be a valid measure of their competence (Arkin & Maruyama, 1979; Davis & Stephan, 1980; Gilmor & Reid, 1979; Griffin & others, 1983). Those who do poorly are much more likely to criticize the exam.

Reading this research, I couldn't resist a satisfied "knew-it-all-along" feeling. But consider teachers' ways of explaining students' good and bad performances. When there is no need to feign modesty, those assigned the role of teacher tend to take credit for positive outcomes and blame failure on the student (Arkin & others, 1980; Davis, 1979). Teachers, it seems, are likely to think, "With my help, Maria graduated with honors. Despite all my help, Melinda flunked out."

CAN WE ALL BE BETTER THAN AVERAGE?

Self-serving bias also appears when people compare themselves to others. If the sixth-century B.C. Chinese philosopher Lao-tzu was right that "at no time in the world will a man who is sane over-reach himself, over-spend himself, over-rate himself," then most of us are a little insane. For on nearly any dimension that is both *subjective* and *socially desirable*, most people see themselves as better than average. This is especially so when comparing oneself to people in general rather than to known individuals (Alicke & others. 1995). Consider:

- Most businesspeople see themselves as more ethical than the average businessperson (Baumhart, 1968; Brenner & Molander, 1977). Ninety percent of business managers rate their performance as superior to their average peer (French, 1968).
- In Australia, 86 percent of people rate their job performance as above average, 1 percent as below average (Headey & Wearing, 1987).
- In The Netherlands, most high school students rate themselves as more honest, persistent, original, friendly, and reliable than the average high school student (Hoorens, 1993, in press).
- Most drivers—even most drivers who have been hospitalized for accidents—believe themselves to be safer and more skilled than the average driver (Guerin, 1994; Svenson, 1981).
- Most people perceive themselves as more intelligent than their average peer (Wylie, 1979), as better looking (*Public Opinion*, 1984), and as less prejudiced than others in their communities (Fields & Schuman, 1976; Lenihan, 1965; Messick & others, 1985; O'Gorman & Garry, 1976).

"I dread to think of all the inaccuracies there would be if you wrote my biography after I'm gone."

Most people perceive themselves as better than average.

- Most adults believe they support their aging parents more than do their siblings (Lerner & others, 1991).
- Los Angeles residents view themselves as healthier than most of their neighbors, and most college students believe they will outlive their actuarially predicted age of death by about 10 years (Larwood, 1978; C. R. Snyder, 1978).

Every community, it seems, is like Garrison Keillor's fictional Lake Wobegon, where "all the women are strong, all the men are good-looking, and all the children are above average." Perhaps one reason for this optimism is that although 12 percent of people feel old for their age, many more—66 percent—think they are young for their age (*Public Opinion*, 1984). All of which calls to mind Freud's joke about the man who told his wife, "If one of us should die, I think I would go live in Paris."

Subjective dimensions (such as "disciplined") trigger greater self-serving bias than objective behavioral dimensions (such as "punctual"). Students are more likely to rate themselves superior in "moral goodness" than in "intelligence" (Allison & others, 1989; Van Lange, 1991). And community residents overwhelmingly see themselves as *caring* more than most others about the environment, about hunger, and about other social issues, though they don't see themselves as *doing* more, such as contributing time or money to those issues (White & Plous, 1994). This is partly because subjective qualities give us so much leeway in constructing our own definitions of success (Dunning & others, 1989, 1991). Rating my "athletic ability," I ponder my basketball play, not the agonizing weeks I spent as a Little League baseball player hiding in right field. Assessing my "leadership ability," I conjure up an image of a great leader whose style is similar to mine. By defining ambiguous criteria in our own terms, each of us can see ourselves as relatively successful. In one College Entrance Examination Board survey of 829,000 high school seniors, 0 percent rated themselves below average in "ability to get along with others" (a subjective, desirable trait), 60 percent rated themselves in the top 10 percent, and 25 percent saw themselves among the top 1 percent!

We also support our self-image by assigning importance to the things we're good at. Over a semester, those who ace an introductory computer science course come to place a higher value on their identity as a computer-literate person in today's world. Those who do poorly are more likely to scorn computer geeks and to exclude computer skills as pertinent to their self-image (Hill & others, 1989).

UNREALISTIC OPTIMISM

Optimism predisposes a positive approach to life. "The optimist," notes H. Jackson Brown (1990, p. 79), "goes to the window every morning and says, 'Good morning, God.' The pessimist goes to the window and says, 'good god, morning.'" However, many of us have what researcher Neil Weinstein (1980, 1982) terms "an unrealistic optimism about future life events." At Rutgers University, for example, students perceive themselves as far more likely than their classmates to get a good job, draw a good salary, and own a home, and as far less likely to experience negative events, such as developing a drinking problem, having a heart attack before age 40, or being fired. In Scotland, most late adolescents think they are much less likely than their peers to become infected by the AIDS virus (Abrams, 1991). After experiencing the 1989 earthquake, San Francisco Bay–area students did lose their optimism about being less vulnerable than their classmates to injury in a natural disaster, but within three months their illusory optimism had rebounded (Burger & Palmer, 1991).

Linda Perloff (1987) notes how illusory optimism increases our vulnerability. Believing ourselves immune to misfortune, we do not take sensible pre-

"Views of the future are so rosy that they would make Pollyanna blush."
Shelley E. Taylor, Positive Illusions, 1989

FOCUS

THE ILLUSION OF INVULNERABILITY

In a 1943 Harvard Chapel meditation, psychologist Gordon W. Allport (1978, pp. 19–20) described the perils of unrealistic optimism:

Recently I examined two hundred life histories written by refugees from Nazi Germany. With scarcely an exception these people had found themselves blinded by their own hopes.

Not one of them would at first believe that Hitlerism could bring such a catastrophe on them.

In 1932 they hoped and therefore believed that Hitler would never come to power.

In 1933 they hoped and therefore believed that he could not put his threats into execution.

In 1934 they hoped and therefore believed that the nightmare would soon pass.

In 1938 the Austrians were certain that Hitler could never come to Austria, because they hoped that Austrians were different from Germans.

Another example comes from a study of college undergraduates who were asked to estimate their income in five years' and in ten years' time after leaving college. The results, I regret to report, are quite fantastic. Most of them picture themselves as well-to-do, quite overlooking probabilities.

If they were headed for medicine, they estimated their income within a range which only about 5 percent of the medical profession achieves. If they were to become airplane pilots, they figured a salary above that obtained by any pilot.

Hope based on ignorance may spring eternal, but it certainly spells a fall. It is more of a vice than a virtue.

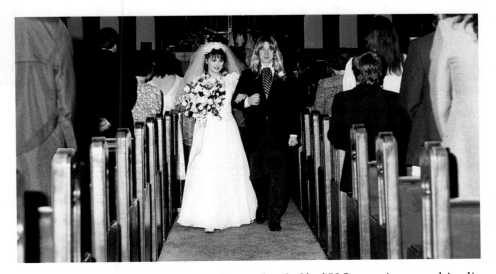

Illusory optimism: Most couples marry feeling confident of long-term love. Actually, in individualistic cultures, new marriages often fail.

cautions. Most young Americans know that half of U.S. marriages end in divorce but persist in believing that *theirs* will not (Lehman & Nisbett, 1985). Sexually active undergraduate women who don't consistently use contraceptives perceive themselves, compared to other women at their university, as much *less* vulnerable to unwanted pregnancy (Burger & Burns, 1988). Those who cheerfully shun seat belts, deny the effects of smoking, and stumble into ill-fated relationships remind us that blind optimism, like pride, may, as the ancient proverb warns, go before a fall.

Although optimism beats pessimism in promoting self-efficacy, a dash of pessimism can save us from the perils of unrealistic optimism. Self-doubt can energize students, most of whom—especially those destined for low grades—exhibit excess optimism about upcoming exams (Prohaska, 1994; Sparrell & Shrauger, 1984). Students who are overconfident tend to underprepare. Their equally able but more anxious peers, fearing that they are going to bomb on the upcoming exam, study furiously and get higher grades (Goodhart, 1986; Norem & Cantor, 1986; Showers & Ruben, 1987). The moral: Success in school and beyond requires enough optimism to sustain hope and enough pessimism to motivate concern.

"O God, give us grace to accept with serenity the things that cannot be changed, courage to change the things which should be changed, and the wisdom to distinguish the one from the other."
Reinhold Niebuhr, "The Serenity Prayer," 1943

FALSE CONSENSUS AND UNIQUENESS

We have a curious tendency to further enhance our self-image by overestimating or underestimating the extent to which others think and act as we do—a phenomenon called the **false consensus effect**. On matters of *opinion*, we find support for our positions by overestimating the extent to which others agree (Krueger & Clement, 1994; Marks & Miller, 1987; Mullen & Goethals, 1990). If we favor a Canadian referendum or support New Zealand's National Party, we wishfully overestimate the extent to which others agree (Babad & others, 1992; Koestner, 1993). When we behave badly or fail in a task, we reassure ourselves by thinking that such lapses are common. We guess that others think and act as we do: "I do it, but so does everyone else." If we cheat on our income taxes or smoke, we are likely to overestimate the number of other people who do likewise.

False consensus effect: The tendency to overestimate the commonality of one's opinions and one's undesirable or unsuccessful behaviors.

"I admit it does look very impressive. But you see nowadays everyone graduates in the top ten per cent of his class."

Can we all be better than average?
(William W. Haefeli/Saturday Review, 1/20/79.)

Penthouse publisher Bob Guccione, responding to a national survey revealing that 83 percent of adults reported zero or one sexual partner in the past year: "Positively, outrageously stupid

TABLE 2–2   *False Uniqueness: Who Follows the Ten Commandments?*

TEN COMMANDMENTS	I FOLLOW	MOST OTHERS FOLLOW
Do Not Take the Lord's Name in Vain		

- Judging from photos, we not only guess that attractive people have desirable personalities, we also guess that they have personalities more like our own than do unattractive people (Marks & others, 1981).

- We like to associate ourselves with the glory of others' success. If we find ourselves linked with (say, born on the same day as) some reprehensible person, we boost ourselves by softening our view of the rascal (Finch & Cialdini, 1989).

So, is pop psychology right that most people suffer from low self-esteem and insufficient self-love? Many streams of evidence suggest otherwise. To paraphrase Elizabeth Barrett Browning, "How do I love me? Let me count the ways!"

SELF-ESTEEM MOTIVATION

Why do people perceive themselves in self-enhancing ways? One explanation sees the self-serving bias as a by-product of how we process and remember information about ourselves. Recall the study in which married people credited themselves for more housework than did their spouses. Might this not be due, as Michael Ross and Fiore Sicoly (1979) believe, to our greater recall for what we've actively done and our lesser recall for what we've not done or merely observed others doing? I can easily picture myself picking up the laundry, but I have difficulty picturing myself absentmindedly overlooking it.

But are the biased perceptions simply a perceptual error, an unemotional bent in how we process information? Or are self-serving *motives* also involved? It's now clear from research that we have multiple motives. Questing for self-knowledge, we're eager to *assess* our competence (Brown, 1990). Questing for self-confirmation, we're eager to *verify* our self-conceptions (Sanitioso & others, 1990; Swann, 1990). Questing for self-affirmation, we're *especially* motivated to *enhance* our self-image (Sedikides, 1993).

Experiments confirm that a motivational engine powers our cognitive machinery (Kunda, 1990). Facing failure, high self-esteem people sustain their self-worth by perceiving other people as failing, too, and by exaggerating their superiority over others (Agostinelli & others, 1992; Brown & Gallagher, 1992). The more physiologically aroused people are after a failure, the more likely they are to excuse the failure with self-protective attributions (Brown & Rogers, 1991). We are not just cool information-processing machines.

Abraham Tesser (1988) at the University of Georgia reports that a "self-esteem maintenance" motive predicts a variety of interesting findings, even friction among brothers and sisters. Do you have a sibling of the same sex who is close to you in age? If so, people probably compared the two of you as you grew up. Tesser presumes that people's perceiving one of you as more capable than the other will motivate the less able one to act in ways that maintain his or her self-esteem. (Tesser thinks the threat to self-esteem is greatest for an older child with a highly capable younger sibling.) Men with a brother of differing ability typically recall not getting along well with him; men with a brother of similar ability are more likely to recall very little friction. Self-esteem threats occur among friends and married partners, too. Although shared interests are healthy, *identical* career goals may produce tension or jealousy (Clark & Bennett, 1992).

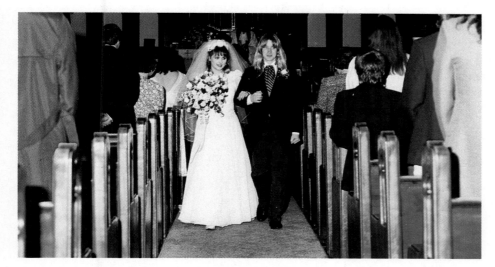

Illusory optimism: Most couples marry feeling confident of long-term love. Actually, in individualistic cultures, new marriages often fail.

cautions. Most young Americans know that half of U.S. marriages end in divorce but persist in believing that *theirs* will not (Lehman & Nisbett, 1985). Sexually active undergraduate women who don't consistently use contraceptives perceive themselves, compared to other women at their university, as much *less* vulnerable to unwanted pregnancy (Burger & Burns, 1988). Those who cheerfully shun seat belts, deny the effects of smoking, and stumble into ill-fated relationships remind us that blind optimism, like pride, may, as the ancient proverb warns, go before a fall.

Although optimism beats pessimism in promoting self-efficacy, a dash of pessimism can save us from the perils of unrealistic optimism. Self-doubt can energize students, most of whom—especially those destined for low grades—exhibit excess optimism about upcoming exams (Prohaska, 1994; Sparrell & Shrauger, 1984). Students who are overconfident tend to underprepare. Their equally able but more anxious peers, fearing that they are going to bomb on the upcoming exam, study furiously and get higher grades (Goodhart, 1986; Norem & Cantor, 1986; Showers & Ruben, 1987). The moral: Success in school and beyond requires enough optimism to sustain hope and enough pessimism to motivate concern.

"O God, give us grace to accept with serenity the things that cannot be changed, courage to change the things which should be changed, and the wisdom to distinguish the one from the other."
Reinhold Niebuhr, "The Serenity Prayer," 1943

FALSE CONSENSUS AND UNIQUENESS

We have a curious tendency to further enhance our self-image by overestimating or underestimating the extent to which others think and act as we do—a phenomenon called the **false consensus effect**. On matters of *opinion*, we find support for our positions by overestimating the extent to which others agree (Krueger & Clement, 1994; Marks & Miller, 1987; Mullen & Goethals, 1990). If we favor a Canadian referendum or support New Zealand's National Party, we wishfully overestimate the extent to which others agree (Babad & others, 1992; Koestner, 1993). When we behave badly or fail in a task, we reassure ourselves by thinking that such lapses are common. We guess that others think and act as we do: "I do it, but so does everyone else." If we cheat on our income taxes or smoke, we are likely to overestimate the number of other people who do likewise.

False consensus effect: The tendency to overestimate the commonality of one's opinions and one's undesirable or unsuccessful behaviors.

Penthouse publisher Bob Guccione, responding to a national survey revealing that 83 percent of adults reported zero or one sexual partner in the past year: "Positively, outrageously stupid and unbelievable. I would say five partners a year is the average for men"
(Elmer-DeWitt, 1994).

TABLE 2–2 *False Uniqueness: Who Follows the Ten Commandments?*

TEN COMMANDMENTS	I FOLLOW	MOST OTHERS FOLLOW
Do Not Take the Lord's Name in Vain	64%	15%
Worship None Before God	64%	22%
Honor Your Mother and Father	95%	49%
Do Not Kill	91%	71%
Attend Services on Holy Days	86%	45%
Do Not Commit Adultery	90%	54%
Do Not Steal	88%	33%
Do Not Bear False Witness	76%	23%
Do Not Covet Your Neighbor's Spouse	84%	42%
Do Not Envy Your Neighbor's Possessions	81%	49%

Source: National Survey of Americans reported by Rosenblatt (1993).

One might argue that false consensus occurs because we generalize from a limited sample, which prominently includes ourselves (Dawes, 1990). Lacking other information, why not use our own responses as a clue to others' likely responses? But on matters of *ability* or when we behave well or successfully, a **false uniqueness effect** more often occurs (Goethals & others, 1991). We serve our self-image by seeing our talents and moral behaviors as relatively unusual (Table 2–2). Thus those who drink heavily but use seat belts will *over*estimate (false consensus) the number of other heavy drinkers and *under*estimate (false uniqueness) the commonality of seat belt use (Suls & others, 1988). Simply put, people see their failings as normal, their virtues as rare.

False uniqueness effect:
The tendency to underestimate the commonality of one's abilities and one's desirable or successful behaviors.

Other Self-serving Tendencies

These tendencies toward self-serving attributions, self-congratulatory comparisons, and illusory optimism are not the only signs of favorably biased self-perceptions. Earlier we noted that most of us overestimate how desirably we would act in a given situation. Chapter 3 explains that we also display a "cognitive conceit" by overestimating the accuracy of our beliefs and judgments, and by misremembering our own past in self-enhancing ways.

Additional streams of evidence converge to form a river:

"How little we should enjoy life if we never flattered ourselves!"
La Rochefoucauld, Maxims, 1665

■ If an undesirable act cannot be misremembered or undone, then, as we will see in Chapter 4, we may justify it.

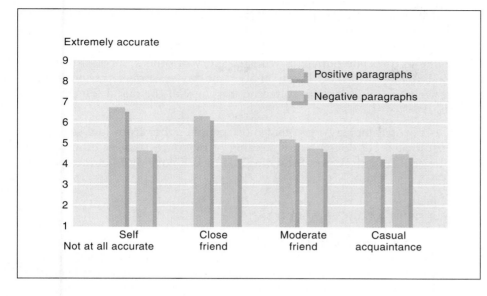

Extremely accurate

Not at all accurate

Categories: Self, Close friend, Moderate friend, Casual acquaintance

Positive paragraphs
Negative paragraphs

■ FIGURE 2–3

"If it's positive, it sounds like me" (and my best friend). Joel Johnson and his colleagues (1985) found that subjects judged favorable descriptions (such as, "finds it easy to be open and demonstrative") to be (a) not especially accurate descriptions of their casual acquaintances, (b) better descriptions of their friends, and (c) even better descriptions of themselves.

- The more favorably we perceive ourselves on some dimension (intelligence, persistence, sense of humor), the more we use that dimension as a basis for judging others (Lewicki, 1983).
- The more favorably we view ourselves, the more we think others perceive us in flattering ways (Kenny & DePaulo, 1993).
- If a test or some other source of information—even a horoscope—flatters us, then we believe it, and we evaluate positively both the test and any evidence suggesting that the test is valid (Ditto, 1994; Glick & others, 1989; Pyszczynski & others, 1985). (See Figure 2–3.)
- Most university students, however, think the Scholastic Assessment Test underestimates their ability (Shepperd, 1993). (In fact, however, the higher scores they *think* they deserved would *less* accurately predict their obtained grades.)

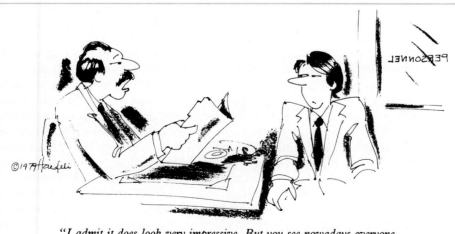

"I admit it does look very impressive. But you see nowadays everyone graduates in the top ten per cent of his class."

Can we all be better than average?
(William W. Haefeli/Saturday Review, 1/20/79.)

- Judging from photos, we not only guess that attractive people have desirable personalities, we also guess that they have personalities more like our own than do unattractive people (Marks & others, 1981).

- We like to associate ourselves with the glory of others' success. If we find ourselves linked with (say, born on the same day as) some reprehensible person, we boost ourselves by softening our view of the rascal (Finch & Cialdini, 1989).

So, is pop psychology right that most people suffer from low self-esteem and insufficient self-love? Many streams of evidence suggest otherwise. To paraphrase Elizabeth Barrett Browning, "How do I love me? Let me count the ways!"

SELF-ESTEEM MOTIVATION

Why do people perceive themselves in self-enhancing ways? One explanation sees the self-serving bias as a by-product of how we process and remember information about ourselves. Recall the study in which married people credited themselves for more housework than did their spouses. Might this not be due, as Michael Ross and Fiore Sicoly (1979) believe, to our greater recall for what we've actively done and our lesser recall for what we've not done or merely observed others doing? I can easily picture myself picking up the laundry, but I have difficulty picturing myself absentmindedly overlooking it.

But are the biased perceptions simply a perceptual error, an unemotional bent in how we process information? Or are self-serving *motives* also involved? It's now clear from research that we have multiple motives. Questing for self-knowledge, we're eager to *assess* our competence (Brown, 1990). Questing for self-confirmation, we're eager to *verify* our self-conceptions (Sanitioso & others, 1990; Swann, 1990). Questing for self-affirmation, we're *especially* motivated to *enhance* our self-image (Sedikides, 1993).

Experiments confirm that a motivational engine powers our cognitive machinery (Kunda, 1990). Facing failure, high self-esteem people sustain their self-worth by perceiving other people as failing, too, and by exaggerating their superiority over others (Agostinelli & others, 1992; Brown & Gallagher, 1992). The more physiologically aroused people are after a failure, the more likely they are to excuse the failure with self-protective attributions (Brown & Rogers, 1991). We are not just cool information-processing machines.

Abraham Tesser (1988) at the University of Georgia reports that a "self-esteem maintenance" motive predicts a variety of interesting findings, even friction among brothers and sisters. Do you have a sibling of the same sex who is close to you in age? If so, people probably compared the two of you as you grew up. Tesser presumes that people's perceiving one of you as more capable than the other will motivate the less able one to act in ways that maintain his or her self-esteem. (Tesser thinks the threat to self-esteem is greatest for an older child with a highly capable younger sibling.) Men with a brother of differing ability typically recall not getting along well with him; men with a brother of similar ability are more likely to recall very little friction. Self-esteem threats occur among friends and married partners, too. Although shared interests are healthy, *identical* career goals may produce tension or jealousy (Clark & Bennett, 1992).

Among sibling relationships, the threat to self-esteem is greatest for an older child with a highly capable younger brother or sister.

What underlies our motive to maintain self-esteem? Mark Leary and his colleagues (1995; Leary & Downs, 1995) believe that our self-esteem feelings are like a fuel gauge. As social creatures, good relationships are conducive to our surviving and thriving. Thus, the self-esteem gauge alerts us to threatened social rejection, motivating us to act with greater sensitivity to others' expectations. Studies confirm that social rejection lowers our self-esteem, strengthening our eagerness for approval. Spurned or jilted, we feel unattractive or inadequate. This pain can motivate self-improvement and a search for acceptance elsewhere.

REFLECTIONS ON SELF-EFFICACY AND SELF-SERVING BIAS

No doubt many readers are finding all this either depressing or contrary to their own occasional feelings of inadequacy. To be sure, most of us who exhibit the self-serving bias may still feel inferior to specific individuals, especially those who are a step or two higher on the ladder of success, attractiveness, or skill. And not everyone operates with a self-serving bias. Some people *do* suffer from low self-esteem. Do such people hunger for esteem and therefore often exhibit self-serving bias? Is self-serving bias just a cover-up? This is what some theorists, such as Erich Fromm, have proposed (Shrauger, 1975).

And it's true: When feeling good about ourselves, we are less defensive (Epstein & Feist, 1988). We are also less thin-skinned and judgmental—less likely to inflate those who like us and berate those who don't (Baumgardner & others, 1989). In experiments, people whose self-esteem is temporarily bruised—

"Narcissism, like selfishness, is an overcompensation for the basic lack of self-love."
Erich Fromm, Escape from Freedom, 1941

say, by being told they did miserably on an intelligence test—are more likely to disparage others. More generally, people who are down on themselves tend also to be down on others (Wills, 1981). And those whose ego has recently been wounded are more prone to self-serving explanations of success or failure than are those whose ego has recently received a boost (McCarrey & others, 1982). So, threats to self-esteem may provoke self-protective defensiveness. When feeling unaffirmed, people may offer self-affirming boasts, excuses, and put-downs of others. Mockery says as much about the mocker as the one mocked.

Nevertheless, high self-esteem goes hand in hand with self-serving perceptions. Those who score highest on self-esteem tests (who say nice things about themselves) also say nice things about themselves when explaining their successes and failures (Ickes & Layden, 1978; Levine & Uleman, 1979; Rosenfeld, 1979; Schlenker & others, 1990), when evaluating their group (Brown & others, 1988), and when comparing themselves to others (Brown, 1986).

The Self-Serving Bias as Adaptive

Without the self-serving bias, and its accompanying excuses, people with low self-esteem are more vulnerable to anxiety and depression (Snyder & Higgins, 1988). As we will see in Chapter 5, although most people excuse their failures on laboratory tasks or perceive themselves as being more in control than they are, depressed people's self-appraisals are more accurate: sadder but wiser.

And consider: Thanks to people's reluctance to criticize, it's easy to overestimate how others are really perceiving us (DePaulo & others, 1987; Kenny & Albright, 1987). Mildly depressed people are less prone to illusions; they generally see themselves *as* other people see them—which may, at times, be understandably depressing (Lewinsohn & others, 1980). This prompts the unsettling thought that Pascal may have been right: "I lay it down as a fact that, if all men knew what others say of them, there would not be four friends in the world."

As this new research on depression suggests, there may be some practical wisdom in self-serving perceptions. Cheaters give a more convincing display of honesty if they believe in their honesty. Belief in our superiority can also motivate us to achieve—creating a self-fulfilling prophecy—and can sustain a sense of hope in difficult times.

Self-Serving Bias as Maladaptive

Although self-serving pride may help protect us from depression, it can at times be maladaptive. People who blame others for their social difficulties are often unhappier than people who can acknowledge their mistakes (C. A. Anderson & others, 1983; Newman & Langer, 1981; Peterson & others, 1981). Moreover, the most self-enhancing people often come across to others as egotistical, condescending, and deceitful (Colvin & others, 1995). In human history, expansive egos have marked genocidal dictators, White supremacists, and drunken spouse-abusers (Baumeister and others, 1996). When someone's inflated self-esteem is challenged by others' criticisms or taunts, the result is sometimes an abusive or murderous rage.

Research by Barry Schlenker (1976; Schlenker & Miller, 1977a, 1977b) has also shown how self-serving perceptions can poison a group. In nine experiments at the University of Florida, Schlenker had people work together on some task. He then falsely informed them that their group had done either well or

"No one speaks of us in our presence as in our absence."
Pascal, Pensées, 1670

"Victory finds a hundred fathers but defeat is an orphan."
Count Galeazzo Ciano, The Ciano Diaries, 1938

poorly. In every one of these studies the members of successful groups claimed more responsibility for their group's performance than did members of groups that supposedly failed at the task. Most presented themselves as contributing more than the others in their group when the group did well; few said they contributed less.

Such self-deception can lead individual group members to expect greater than average rewards when their organization does well and less than average blame when it does not. If most individuals in a group believe they are underpaid and underappreciated relative to their contributions, disharmony and envy are likely. College presidents and academic deans will readily recognize the phenomenon. Ninety percent or more of college faculty members rate themselves as superior to their average colleague (Blackburn & others, 1980; Cross, 1977). It is therefore inevitable that when merit salary raises are announced and half receive an average raise or less, many will feel themselves victims of injustice.

Biased self-assessments also distort managerial judgment. When groups are comparable, most people consider their own group superior (Codol, 1976; Taylor & Doria, 1981; Zander, 1969). Thus, most corporation presidents predict more growth for their own firms than for their competition (Larwood & Whittaker, 1977). And most production managers overpredict their production (Kidd & Morgan, 1969). Such overoptimism can produce disastrous consequences. If those who deal in the stock market or in real estate perceive their business intuition to be superior to that of their competitors, they may be in for severe disappointment. Even the seventeenth-century economist Adam Smith, a defender of human economic rationality, foresaw that people would overestimate their chances of gain. This "absurd presumption in their own good fortune," he said, arises from "the overweening conceit which the greater part of men have of their own abilities" (Spiegel, 1971, p. 243).

BEHIND THE SCENES

In my high school and college days I was, for fun and profit, a guitarist in a rock group. Two observations from that period influenced my later research.

First, the performance was as important as the music. I came to see that the same is true in everyday social interactions: What matters is not just what people are like on the inside, but how they present themselves to others. I became curious about how people manage information to create desired impressions, and this curiosity led to a research program that has kept me busy for 20 years.

Second, most musicians I met seemed convinced that their group was special because of its exceptional instrumental artistry, singing talent, song-writing skill, stage presence, or managerial direction. Also, rock band members typically overestimated their contributions to a group's success and underestimated their contributions to failure. I admit to similar feelings about my own group and my contributions to it. I saw many good bands disintegrate from the problems caused by these self-glorifying tendencies. My later research revealed that self-serving bias is common in groups and identified the conditions that foster it.

BARRY SCHLENKER, *University of Florida*

"Hubris is back in town."
W. C. Fields

That people see themselves with a favorable bias is hardly new—the tragic flaw portrayed in ancient Greek drama was *hubris*, or pride. Like the subjects of our experiments, the Greek tragic figures were not self-consciously evil; they merely thought too highly of themselves. In literature, the pitfalls of pride are portrayed again and again. In religion, pride has long been first among the "seven deadly sins."

If pride is akin to the self-serving bias, then what is humility? Is it self-contempt? Or can we be self-affirming and self-accepting without a self-serving bias? To paraphrase the English scholar-writer C. S. Lewis, humility is not handsome people trying to believe they are ugly and clever people trying to believe they are fools. False modesty can actually be a cover for pride in one's better-than-average humility. (Perhaps you, like most readers of this book before you, congratulate yourself on being relatively free of self-serving bias—Friedrich, in press.) True humility is more like self-forgetfulness than false modesty. It leaves people free to rejoice in their special talents and, with the same honesty, to recognize others.

"Half the truth is often a great lie."
Benjamin Franklin, Poor Richard's Almanac, 1758

Studies of self-efficacy, self-esteem, and self-serving bias expose some deep truths about human nature. They also remind us of what Pascal taught 300 years ago: No single truth is ever sufficient, because the world is complex. Any truth, separated from its complementary truth, is a half-truth.

The truth concerning self-efficacy encourages us to not resign ourselves to bad situations, to persist despite initial failures, to exert effort without being overly distracted by self-doubts. High self-esteem—a sense of self-worth—is adaptive. When we believe in our positive possibilities, we are less vulnerable to depression and we increase our chances for success.

The truth concerning illusory optimism and other forms of self-serving bias reminds us that self-efficacy is not the whole story of the self in a social world.

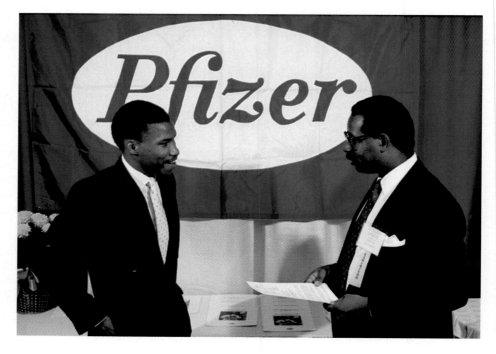

After just one brief conversation with a prospective employee, interviewers are prone to overconfidence in their intuitive judgments.

"Then we're in agreement. There's nothing rotten here in Denmark. Something is rotten everywhere else."

Self-serving pride in group settings can become especially dangerous.

If positive thinking can accomplish *anything*, then if we are unhappily married, poor, or depressed we have only ourselves to blame. For shame! If only we had tried harder, been more disciplined, less stupid. Failing to appreciate that difficulties sometimes reflect the oppressive power of social situations can tempt us to blame people for their problems and failures, or even to blame ourselves too harshly for our own. Life's greatest achievements, but also its greatest disappointments, are born of the highest expectations.

SUMMING UP

Contrary to the presumption that most people suffer from low self-esteem or feelings of inferiority, researchers consistently find that most people exhibit a *self-serving bias*. In experiments and everyday life, we often blame failures on the situation while taking credit for successes. We typically rate ourselves as better than average on subjective, desirable traits and abilities. Believing in ourselves, we exhibit unrealistic optimism about our futures. And we overestimate the commonality of our opinions and foibles (*false consensus*) while underestimating the commonality of our abilities and virtues (*false uniqueness*). Such perceptions arise partly from a motive to maintain and enhance self-esteem, a motive that protects people from depression but contributes to misjudgment and group conflict.

■ SELF-PRESENTATION

We humans seem motivated not only to perceive ourselves in self-enhancing ways but also to present ourselves to others in desired ways. How might our tactics of "impression management" lead to false modesty or to self-defeating behavior?

So far we have seen that the self is at the center of our social worlds, that self-esteem and self-efficacy pay dividends, and that self-serving pride biases self-evaluations. But are self-enhancing expressions always sincere? Do people privately feel as they publicly talk? Or will they put on a positive face even while living with self-doubt?

FALSE MODESTY

There is indeed evidence that people sometimes present a different self than they feel. The clearest example, however, is not false pride but false modesty. Perhaps you have by now recalled times when someone was not self-praising but self-disparaging. Such put-downs can be subtly self-serving, for often they elicit reassuring "strokes." "I felt like a fool" may trigger a friend to reassure that "you did fine!" Even a remark such as "I wish I weren't so ugly," may elicit at least a, "Come now. I know a couple of people who are uglier than you."

There is another reason people disparage themselves and praise others. Think of the coach who, before the big game, extols the opponent's strength. Is the coach utterly sincere? When coaches publicly exalt their opponents, they convey an image of modesty and good sportsmanship, and set the stage for a favorable evaluation no matter what the outcome. A win becomes a praiseworthy achievement, a loss attributable to the opponent's "great defense." Modesty, said the seventeenth-century philosopher Francis Bacon, is but one of the "arts of ostentation." Thus, Robert Gould, Paul Brounstein, and Harold Sigall (1977) found that, in a laboratory contest, their University of Maryland students similarly aggrandized their anticipated opponent, but only when the assessment was made publicly. Anonymously, they credited their future opponent with much less ability.

False modesty also appears in people's autobiographical accounts of their achievements. At awards ceremonies, honorees graciously thank others for their support. Upon receiving an Academy Award, Maureen Stapleton thanked "my family, my children, my friends, and everyone I have ever met in my entire life." Does such generous sharing of credit contradict the common finding that people readily attribute success to their own effort and competence?

To find out, Roy Baumeister and Stacey Ilko (1995) invited students to write a description of "an important success experience." Those whom they asked to sign their names and who anticipated reading their story to others often acknowledged the help or emotional support they had received. Those who wrote anonymously rarely made such mentions; rather, they portrayed themselves achieving their successes on their own. To Baumeister and Ilko, these results

"Humility is often but a trick whereby pride abases itself only to exalt itself later."
La Rochefoucauld, Maxims, 1665

suggest "shallow gratitude"—superficial gratitude offered to *appear* humble, while "in the privacy of their own minds" the subjects credited themselves for their successes.

SELF-HANDICAPPING

Sometimes people sabotage their chances for success by presenting themselves as shy, ill, or handicapped by past traumas. Far from being deliberately self-destructive, such behaviors typically have a self-protective aim (Arkin & others, 1986; Baumeister & Scher, 1988; Rhodewalt, 1987): "I'm not a failure—I'm okay except for this problem that handicaps me."

Why would people handicap themselves with self-defeating behavior? Recall that we eagerly protect our self-images by attributing failures to external factors. Can you see why, *fearing failure*, people might handicap themselves by partying half the night before a job interview or playing video games instead of studying before a big exam? When self-image is tied up with performance, it can be more self-deflating to try hard and fail than to have a ready excuse. If we fail while working under a handicap, we can cling to a sense of competence; if we succeed under such conditions, it can only boost our self-image. Handicaps protect our self-esteem and public image by allowing us to attribute failures to something temporary or external ("I was feeling sick"; "I was out too late the night before") rather than to lack of talent or ability.

This analysis of **self-handicapping**, proposed by Steven Berglas and Edward Jones (1978), has been confirmed. One experiment was said to concern "drugs and intellectual performance." Imagine yourself in the position of their Duke University subjects. You guess answers to some difficult aptitude questions and then are told, "Yours was one of the best scores seen to date!" Feeling incredibly lucky, you are then offered a choice between two drugs before answering more of these items. One drug will aid intellectual performance and the other will inhibit it. Which drug do you want? Most students wanted the drug that would supposedly disrupt their thinking and thus provide a handy excuse for anticipated poorer performance.

Researchers have documented other ways in which people self-handicap. Fearing failure, people will:

- Reduce their preparation for important individual athletic events (Rhodewalt & others, 1984)
- Not try as hard as they could during a tough ego-involving task (Hormuth, 1986; Pyszczynski & Greenberg, 1983; Riggs, 1992; Turner & Pratkanis, 1993)
- Give their opponent an advantage (Shepperd & Arkin, 1991)
- Report feeling depressed (Baumgardner, 1991)
- Perform poorly at the beginning of a task in order not to create unreachable expectations (Baumgardner & Brownlee, 1987)

After losing to some younger rivals, tennis great Martina Navratilova confessed that she was "afraid to play my best. . . . I was scared to find out if they could beat me when I'm playing my best because if they can, then I am finished" (Frankel & Snyder, 1987).

Self-handicapping:
Protecting one's self-image by creating a handy excuse for failure.

"With no attempt there can be no failure; with no failure no humiliation."
William James, Principles of Psychology, 1890

IMPRESSION MANAGEMENT

Self-serving bias, false modesty, and self-handicapping reveal the depth of our concern for self-image. To varying degrees, we are continually managing the impressions we create. Whether we wish to impress, to intimidate, or to seem helpless, we are social animals, playing to an audience.

Self-presentation refers to our wanting to present a desired image both to an external audience (other people) and to an internal audience (ourselves). We work at managing the impressions we create. We express our identities (we "self-identify") by showing ourselves to be a particular type of person (Schlenker & others, in press). Intentionally or not, we excuse, justify, or apologize as necessary to shore up our self-esteem and verify our self-image (Schlenker & Weigold, 1992). In familiar situations, this happens without conscious effort. In unfamiliar situations, perhaps at a party with people we would like to impress or in conversation with someone of the other sex, we are acutely self-conscious of the impression we are creating (Leary & others, 1994). Preparing to present ourselves in a photograph, we may even try out different faces in a mirror.

No wonder, say self-presentation researchers, that people will self-handicap when failure might make them look bad (Arkin & Baumgardner, 1985). No wonder that people take health risks—tanning their skin with wrinkle- and cancer-causing radiation; becoming anorexic; failing to obtain and discuss condoms; yielding to peer pressures to smoke, get drunk, and do drugs (Leary & others, 1994). No wonder people express more modesty when their self-flattery is vulnerable to being debunked or when experts will be scrutinizing their self-evaluations (Arkin & others, 1980; Riess & others, 1981; Weary & others, 1982). Professor Smith will express less confidence in the significance of her work when presenting it to professional colleagues than when presenting to students.

For some people, conscious self-presentation is a way of life. By continually monitoring their own behavior and noting how others react, they adjust their social performance when it's not having the desired effect. Those who score high on a scale of **self-monitoring** tendency (who, for example, agree that "I tend to be what people expect me to be") act like social chameleons—they adjust their behavior in response to external situations (Snyder, 1987). Having attuned their behavior to the situation, they are more likely to espouse an attitude they don't really hold (Zanna & Olson, 1982). Being conscious of others, they are less likely to act on their own attitudes. For high self-monitors, attitudes, therefore, serve a social adjustment function; they help these people adapt to new jobs, roles, and relationships (Snyder & DeBono, 1989; Snyder & Copeland, 1989).

Those who score low in self-monitoring care less about what others think. They are more internally guided and thus more likely to talk and act as they feel and believe (McCann & Hancock, 1983). Most of us fall somewhere between the high self-monitoring extreme of the con artist and the low self-monitoring extreme of stubborn insensitivity to others.

Presenting oneself in ways that create a desired impression is a very delicate matter. People want to be seen as able, but also as modest and honest (Carlston & Shovar, 1983). Modesty creates a good impression, and unsolicited boasting creates a bad impression (Forsyth & others, 1981; Holtgraves & Srull, 1989;

Self-presentation:
The act of expressing oneself and behaving in ways designed to create a favorable impression or an impression that corresponds to one's ideals.

Self-monitoring:
Being attuned to the way one presents oneself in social situations and adjusting one's performance to create the desired impression.

"Public opinion is always more tyrannical towards those who obviously fear it than towards those who feel indifferent to it."
Bertrand Russell, The Conquest of Happiness, 1930

Dance class in a Tokyo kindergarten. In Asian countries, self-presentation is restrained. Children learn to identify themselves with their groups.

Schlenker & Leary, 1982). Thus, the false modesty phenomenon: We often display *less* self-esteem than we privately feel (Miller & Schlenker, 1985). But when we have obviously done extremely well, false disclaimers ("I did well, but it's no big deal") may come across as feigned humility. To make good impressions—as modest yet competent—requires social skill.

The tendency to self-present modesty and restrained optimism is especially great in cultures that value self-restraint, such as those of China and Japan (Heine & Lehman, 1995; Markus & Kitayama, 1991; Wu & Tseng, 1985). In Japan, children learn to share credit for success and accept responsibility for failures. In western countries, children learn to feel pride in success while attributing failure to the situation. The result, reports Philip Zimbardo (1993), is greater modesty and shyness among the Japanese.

Despite such self-presentational concerns, people worldwide privately are self-enhancing. Self-serving bias has been noted among Dutch high school and university students, Belgian basketball players, Indian Hindus, Japanese drivers, Australian students and workers, Chinese students, and French people of all ages (Codol, 1976; de Vries & van Knippenberg, 1987; Feather, 1983; Hagiwara, 1983; Jain, 1990; Liebrand & others, 1986; Lefebvre, 1979; Murphy-Berman & Sharma, 1986; and Ruzzene & Noller, 1986, respectively).

"It is not, therefore, necessary for a prince to have all the desirability qualities . . . but it is very necessary to seem to have them."
Niccolo Machiavelli, 1469–1527

A s social animals, we adjust our words and actions to suit our audiences. To varying degrees, we *self-monitor*, we note our performance and adjust it to create a desired impression. Such *impression management* tactics explain examples of false modesty, in which people put themselves down, extol future competitors, or publicly credit others when privately they credit themselves. Sometimes people will even *self-handicap* with self-defeating behaviors that protect self-esteem by providing excuses for failure.

SUMMING UP

■ FOR FURTHER READING

Leary, M. R. (1995). *Self-presentation: Impression management and interpersonal behavior*. Madison, WI: Brown & Benchmark. A state-of-the-art analysis of the motives and tactics underlying our self-presenations, and of the effects they have on others—and ourselves.

Seligman, M. (1991). *Learned optimism*. New York: Knopf. Describes research on learned helplessness and optimism, showing why optimism is important and how to gain it.

Taylor, S. E. (1989). *Positive illusions*. New York: Basic Books. The ancient wisdom to "know thyself" notwithstanding, mental health may instead reflect the art of being well deceived. Or so social psychologist Taylor suggests in this captivating summary of research on the benefits of positive, if self-serving, thinking.

SOCIAL BELIEFS AND JUDGMENTS

In September 1983, off their Pacific coast, the Soviet Union shot down Korean Airlines Flight 007, killing all 269 people on board. The United States' reaction was swift and harsh: The Soviets were condemned for slaying innocent people on an obviously off-course civilian flight.

In July 1988, the destroyer USS *Vincennes*, in battle with Iranian gunboats in the Persian Gulf, shot down Iran Airbus Flight 655, killing all 290 people on board. Now the Soviets condemned the Americans for slaying innocent people on an on-course civilian flight.

Was each country right to attribute the other's action to evil intent and to doubt the other's claim to have misidentified the aircraft as a military one? Or was each act an understandable response in the situation? Were Soviet perceptions clouded by incidents of border invasion and aircraft spying? Were U.S. perceptions clouded by recent air-launched missile damage to another U.S. destroyer?

As these cases illustrate, our judgments of what nations and people do depend on how we explain their behavior. Depending on our explanation, we may judge killing someone as murder, manslaughter, self-defense, or patriotism. Depending on our explanation, we may view a woman's lower pay as discriminatory or justified. Depending on our explanation, we may attribute friendliness toward us as reflecting affection or as an attempt at ingratiation. Because our explanations matter, social psychologists study how we explain and judge what people do.

■ EXPLAINING OTHERS

*P*eople make it their business to explain other people, and social psychologists make it their business to explain people's explanations. So, how—and how accurately—do people explain others' behavior? Attribution theory suggests some answers.

The airplane tragedies illustrate a question we face daily. In trying to understand people, we wonder *why* they act that way. The human mind wants to make sense of its world. If worker productivity declines, do we assume the workers are getting lazier? Or has their equipment become less efficient? Does a young boy who hits his classmates have a hostile personality? Or is he responding to relentless teasing? When a salesperson says, "That outfit really looks nice on you," does this reflect genuine feeling? Or is it a sales ploy?

ATTRIBUTING CAUSALITY: TO THE PERSON OR THE SITUATION?

We endlessly analyze and discuss why things happen as they do, especially when something negative or unexpected occurs (Bohner & others, 1988; Weiner, 1985). Amy Holtzworth-Munroe and Neil Jacobson (1985, 1988) report that married people often analyze their partners' behaviors, especially their negative behaviors. Cold hostility is more likely than a warm hug to leave the part-

Anita Hill testifying at the Senate hearings. In 1991, Americans debated their explanations for why Anita Hill might accuse Supreme Court candidate Clarence Thomas of sexual harassment, and why he might deny it. Research suggests that men's attributing friendliness to sexual interest can lead to behavior that women regard as sexual harassment.

ner wondering "why?" Spouses' answers correlate with their marriage satisfaction. Those who interpret their partner's negative acts as selfish and characteristic ("She's a cold, crabby person") are usually unhappily married. Those who externalize their partner's negative acts ("She's frustrated because of how I acted"; "He's had a bad day") find it easier to accept and love the partner (Fincham & Bradbury, 1993; Fletcher & others, 1990).

Our conclusions about why people act as they do are profoundly important: They determine our reactions to others and our decisions regarding them. Antonia Abbey (1987, 1991) and her colleagues have repeatedly found that men are more likely than women to attribute a woman's friendliness to mild sexual interest. This misreading of warmth as a sexual come-on (called "misattribution") can lead to behavior the woman regards as sexual harassment (Johnson & others, 1991; Saal & others, 1989). It also helps explain the greater sexual assertiveness exhibited by men across the world (Kenrick & Trost, 1987).

Sexually aggressive men are especially likely to misread women's communications (Malamuth & Brown, 1994). Such misattributions contribute both to date rape and to the greater tendency of men than women in various cultures, from Boston to Bombay, to justify rape by blaming the victim's behavior (Kanekar & Nazareth, 1988; Muehlenhard, 1988; Shotland, 1989). Misattributions also help explain why the 23 percent of American women who say they have been forced into unwanted sexual behavior is eight times the 3 percent of American men who say they have ever forced a woman into a sexual act (Laumann & others, 1994).

To what should we attribute this student's sleepiness? To lack of sleep? to boredom? Whether we make internal or external attributions depends on whether we notice him consistently sleeping in this and other classes, and to whether other students react as he does to this particular class.

Attribution theory:
The theory of how people explain others' behavior—for example, by attributing it either to internal *dispositions* (enduring traits, motives, and attitudes) or to external *situations*.

Attribution theory analyzes how we explain people's behavior. The variations of attribution theory share some common assumptions. As Daniel Gilbert and Patrick Malone (1995) explain, each "construes the human skin as a special boundary that separates one set of 'causal forces' from another. On the sunny side of the epidermis are the external or situational forces that press inward upon the person, and on the meaty side are the internal or personal forces that exert pressure outward. Sometimes these forces press in conjunction, sometimes in opposition, and their dynamic interplay manifests itself as observable behavior."

Fritz Heider (1958), widely regarded as attribution theory's originator, analyzed the "commonsense psychology" by which people explain everyday events. Heider concluded that people tend to attribute someone's behavior to *internal* causes (for example, the person's disposition) or *external* causes (for example, something about the person's situation). A teacher may wonder whether a child's underachievement is due to lack of motivation and ability (a "dispositional attribution") or to physical and social circumstances (a "situational attribution").

This distinction between internal (dispositional) and external (situational) causes often blurs, because external situations produce internal changes (White, 1991). To say a schoolchild "is fearful" may be a short semantic leap from saying "School frightens the child." Moreover, situations act upon dispositions. A bowling ball rolls toward the pins because it is round and disposed to roll, *and* because it is pushed. Nevertheless, social psychologists have discovered that we often attribute the behavior of *others* either to their dispositions *or* to the situation. Thus when Constantine Sedikides and Craig Anderson (1991) asked American students why Americans have defected to the Soviet Union, 8 in 10 attributed the behavior to a "confused," "ungrateful," or "traitorous" personality. But 9 in 10 attributed mirror-image Soviet defections to the oppressiveness of the Soviet situation.

Inferring Traits

Edward Jones and Keith Davis (1965) noted that we often infer that other people's intentions and dispositions *correspond* to their actions. If I observe Rick making a sarcastic comment to Linda, I am likely to infer that Rick is a hostile person. Jones and Davis's "theory of correspondent inferences" specifies the conditions under which such attributions are most likely. For example, normal or expected behavior tells us less about the person than does unusual behavior. If Rick is sarcastic in a job interview, where a person would normally be pleasant, this tells us more about Rick than if he is sarcastic about his new car just being dented in a parking lot.

The ease with which we infer traits is remarkable. In experiments at New York University, James Uleman (1989) gave students statements to remember, like "The librarian carries the old woman's groceries across the street." The students would instantly, unintentionally, and unconsciously infer a trait. When later they were helped to recall the sentence, the most valuable clue word was not "books" (to cue librarian) or "bags" (to cue groceries) but "helpful"— the inferred trait that I suspect you, too, spontaneously attributed to the librarian.

"So! If it's good, it's Mister Coffee. If it's bad, it's me."

We tend to attribute someone's behavior or the outcome of an event either to internal (dispositional) or external (situational) causes.

© 1976, The New Yorker Magazine, Inc.

Commonsense Attributions

As these examples suggest, attributions often are rational. In testimony to the reasonable ways in which we explain behavior, attribution theorist Harold Kelley (1973) described how we use information about "consistency," "distinctiveness," and "consensus" (Figure 3–1). When explaining why Edgar is having trouble with his XYZ5000 computer, most people appropriately use information concerning *consistency* (Does Edgar usually have trouble with his computer?), *distinctiveness* (Does Edgar have trouble with other computers, or only the XYZ?), and *consensus* (Do other people have similar problems with the XYZ?). If we learn that Edgar and Edgar alone consistently has trouble with this and other computers, we likely will attribute the troubles to Edgar, not to defects in the XYZ.

So our commonsense psychology often explains behavior logically. But Kelley also found that in everyday explanations, people often discount a contributing cause of behavior if other plausible causes are already known. If I can specify one or two reasons a student might have done poorly on an exam, I may ignore or discount other possibilities.

Information Integration

Further evidence of the reasonableness of our social judgments comes from research on information integration. Norman Anderson (1968, 1974) and his collaborators discerned some rules by which we combine different pieces of information about a person into an overall impression. Suppose that you have an upcoming blind date with someone described as intelligent, daring, lazy, and sincere. Research on how people combine such information suggests that you would likely weight each item of information according to its importance. If you consider sincerity especially important, you will give it more weight. If you are like the participants in experiments by Solomon Asch (1946), Bert Hodges (1974), and Roos Vonk (1993), you may also give extra weight to information that comes first, and you may be more sensitive to negative information.

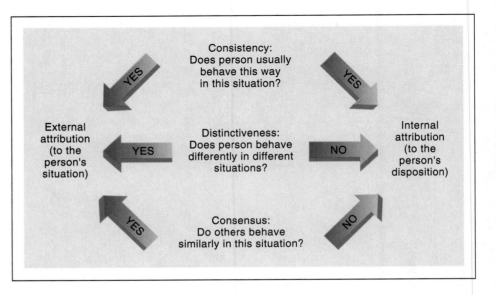

■ FIGURE 3–1

Harold Kelley's theory of attributions. Three factors—consistency, distinctiveness, and consensus—influence whether we attribute someone's behavior to internal or external causes.

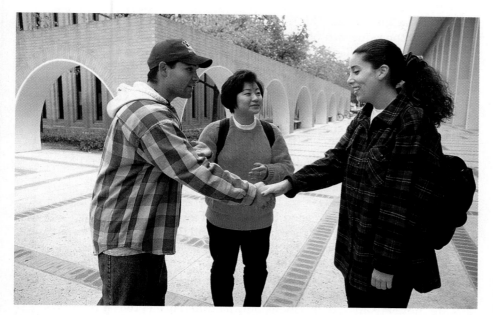

First impressions matter, for they can color later information and judgments.

First impressions can color your interpretation of later information. Having been told that someone is "intelligent," you may then interpret the person's being "daring" as meaning courageous rather than reckless. Negative information, such as "she is dishonest," also has extra potency, perhaps because it is more unusual. Once you have interpreted and weighed each piece of information, you then use your mental algebra to integrate the different items. The result is your overall impression of your "blind" date.

WHY WE STUDY ATTRIBUTION ERRORS

So far, so good. We form impressions and explain behavior in some reasonable ways. More fascinating, though, are the intriguing errors we make. This chapter, like the one before, explains some foibles and fallacies in our social thinking. Reading these may make it seem, as one student put it, that "social psychologists get their kicks out of playing tricks on people." Actually, the experiments are not designed to demonstrate "what fools these mortals be" (although some of the experiments *are* amusing); their purpose is to reveal how we think about ourselves and others. As we noted in Chapter 2, other psychologists study visual illusions for the same reason—for what they reveal about how the human cognitive system processes information.

If our capacity for illusion and self-deception is shocking, remember that our modes of thought are generally adaptive. Illusory thinking is often a by-product of our mind's strategies for simplifying complex information. It parallels our perceptual mechanisms, which generally give us a useful image of the world, but sometimes lead us astray.

A second reason for focusing on the biases that penetrate our thinking is that we are mostly unaware of them. My hunch is that you will find more surprises, more challenges, and more benefit in an analysis of errors and biases than you would in a string of testimonies to our human capacity for logic and intellectual achievement. This is also why epics of world literature so often portray the consequences of pride and other human failings. Liberal education exposes us to fallacies in our thinking in the hope that we will become more rational, more in touch with reality. The hope is not in vain: Psychology students explain behavior less simplistically than equally able natural science students (Fletcher & others, 1986). So, remembering this overriding aim—*developing our capacity for critical thinking*—let us continue looking at how the new research on social thinking can enhance our social reasoning.

THE FUNDAMENTAL ATTRIBUTION ERROR

As later chapters will reveal, social psychology's most important lesson concerns how much we are affected by our social environment. At any moment, our internal state, and therefore what we say and do, depends on the situation, as well as on what we bring to the situation. In experiments, a slight difference between two situations sometimes greatly affects how people respond. I see this when I teach classes at both 8:30 A.M. and 7:00 P.M. Silent stares greet me at 8:30; at 7:00 I have to break up a party. In each situation some individuals are more talkative than others, but the difference between the two situations exceeds the individual differences.

Attribution researchers have found that we often fail to appreciate this important lesson. When explaining someone's behavior, we underestimate the impact of the situation and overestimate the extent to which it reflects the individual's traits and attitudes. Thus, even knowing the effect of the time of day on classroom conversation, I find it terribly tempting to assume that the people in the 7:00 P.M. class are more extraverted than the "silent types" who come at 8:30 A.M.

Fundamental attribution error:

The tendency for observers to underestimate situational influences and overestimate dispositional influences upon others' behavior. (Also called *correspondence bias*, because we so often see behavior as corresponding to a disposition.)

This discounting of the part played by the situation, dubbed by Lee Ross (1977) the **fundamental attribution error,** appears in many experiments. In the first such study, Edward Jones and Victor Harris (1967) had Duke University students read debaters' speeches supporting or attacking Cuba's leader, Fidel Castro. When the position taken was said to have been chosen by the debater, the students logically enough assumed it reflected the person's own attitude. But what happened when the students were told that the debate coach had assigned the position? People write stronger statements than you'd expect from those feigning a position they don't hold (Allison & others, 1993; Miller & others, 1990). Thus, even knowing that the debater had been told to take a pro-Castro position did not prevent students' inferring that the debater in fact had some pro-Castro leanings (Figure 3–2). People seemed to think, "Yeah, I know he was assigned that position, but to some extent I think he really believes it." What do you suppose happens when people also read another essay supposedly written a week or more later in which the debater followed instructions to endorse the other position?

The attribution error is so irresistible that even when people know they are causing someone else's behavior, they still underestimate external influences. If subjects dictate an opinion that someone else must then express, they still tend to see the person as actually holding that opinion (Gilbert & Jones, 1986). If subjects are asked to be either self-enhancing or self-deprecating during an interview, they are very aware of why they are acting so. But they are *un*aware of their effect on another person. If Juan acts modest, his naive partner Bob is

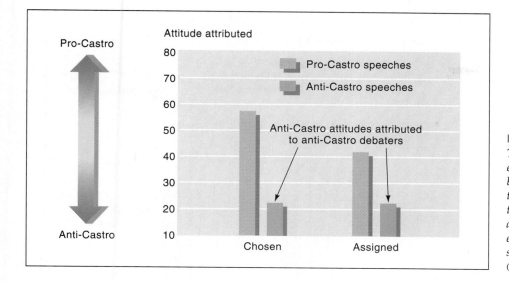

■ **FIGURE 3–2**
The fundamental attribution error. When people read a debate speech supporting or attacking Fidel Castro, they attributed corresponding attitudes to the speech writer, even when the debate coach assigned the writer's position.
(Data from Jones & Harris, 1967.)

likely to exhibit modesty as well. Juan will easily understand his own apparent modesty, but he will think that poor Bob suffers low self-esteem (Baumeister & others, 1988). In short, we tend to presume that others *are* the way they act.

We commit the fundamental attribution error when explaining *other people's* behavior. We often explain our own behavior in terms of the situation while holding others responsible for their behavior. John might attribute his behavior to the situation ("I was angry because everything was going wrong"), but Alice might think, "John was hostile because he is an angry person." When referring to ourselves, we typically use verbs that describe our actions and reactions ("I get annoyed when . . ."). Referring to someone else, we more often describe what that person *is* ("He is nasty") (Fiedler & others, 1991; McGuire & McGuire, 1986; White & Younger, 1988).

The Fundamental Attribution Error in Everyday Life

If we know the checkout cashier is programmed to say, "Thank you and have a nice day," do we nevertheless automatically conclude that the cashier is a friendly, grateful person? We certainly know how to discount behavior that we attribute to ulterior motives (Fein & others, 1990). Yet consider what happened when Williams College students talked with a supposed clinical psychology graduate student who acted either warm and friendly or aloof and critical. Researchers David Napolitan and George Goethals (1979) told half the students beforehand that her behavior would be spontaneous. They told the other half that for purposes of the experiment she had been instructed to feign friendly (or unfriendly) behavior. The effect of the information? None. If she acted friendly, they assumed she was really a friendly person; if she acted unfriendly, they assumed she was an unfriendly person. As when viewing a dummy on the ventriloquist's lap or a movie actor playing a "good-guy" or "bad-guy" role, we find it difficult to escape the illusion that the programmed behavior reflects an inner disposition. Perhaps this is why Leonard Nimoy, who played Mr. Spock on the original *Star Trek*, entitled his book *I Am Not Spock*.

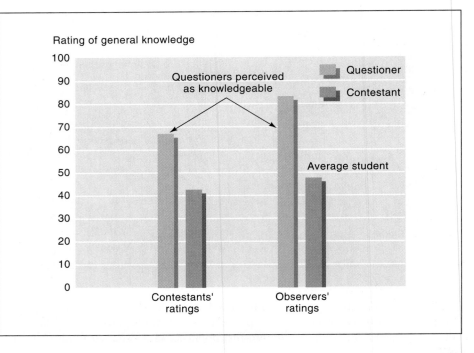

■ FIGURE 3–3
Both contestants and observers of a simulated quiz game assumed that a person who had been randomly assigned the role of questioner was actually far more knowledgeable than the contestant. Actually the assigned roles of questioner and contestant simply made the questioner seem more knowledgeable. The failure to appreciate this illustrates the fundamental attribution error.

(Data from Ross, Amabile, & Steinmetz, 1977.)

The discounting of social constraints was further revealed in a thought-provoking experiment by Lee Ross and his collaborators (Ross & others, 1977). The experiment re-created Ross's firsthand experience of moving from graduate student to professor. His doctoral oral exam had proved a humbling experience as his apparently brilliant professors quizzed him on topics they specialized in. Six months later, *Dr.* Ross was himself an examiner, now able to ask penetrating questions on *his* favorite topics. Ross's hapless student later confessed to feeling exactly as Ross had a half year before—dissatisfied with his ignorance and impressed with the apparent brilliance of the examiners.

In the experiment, with Teresa Amabile and Julia Steinmetz, Ross set up a simulated quiz game. He randomly assigned some Stanford University students to play the role of questioner, some to play the role of contestant, and others to observe. The researchers invited the questioners to make up difficult questions that would demonstrate their wealth of knowledge. It's fun to imagine the questions: "Where is Bainbridge Island?" "What is the seventh book in the Old Testament?" "Which has the longer coastline, Europe or Africa?" If even these few questions have you feeling a little uninformed, then you will appreciate the results of this experiment.*

Everyone had to know that the questioner would have the advantage. Yet both contestants and observers (but not the questioners) came to the erroneous conclusion that the questioners *really were* more knowledgeable than the contestants (Figure 3–3). Follow-up research shows that these misimpressions are

---

* Bainbridge Island is across Puget Sound from Seattle. The seventh Old Testament book is Judges. Although the African continent is more than double the area of Europe, Europe's coastline is longer. (It is more convoluted, with lots of harbors and inlets, a geographical fact that contributed to its role in the history of maritime trade.)

hardly a reflection of low social intelligence. If anything, intelligent and socially competent people are *more* likely to make the attribution error (Block & Funder, 1986).

In real life, those with social power usually initiate and control conversation, which often leads underlings to overestimate their knowledge and intelligence. Medical doctors, for example, are often presumed to be experts on all sorts of questions unrelated to medicine. Similarly, students often overestimate the brilliance of their teachers. (As in the experiment, teachers are questioners on subjects of their special expertise.) When some of these students later become teachers, they are usually amazed to discover that teachers are not so brilliant after all.

To illustrate the fundamental attribution error, most of us need look no further than our own experience. Determined to make some new friends, Bev plasters a smile on her face and anxiously plunges into a party. Everyone else seems quite relaxed and happy as they laugh and talk with one another. Bev wonders to herself, "Why is everyone always so at ease in groups like this while I'm feeling shy and tense?" Actually, everyone else is feeling nervous, too, and making the same attributional error in assuming that Bev and the others *are* as they *appear*—confidently convivial.

Attributions of responsibility are at the heart of many judicial decisions (Fincham & Jaspars, 1980). In 1988, after Colonel Oliver North was indicted on charges of theft, fraud, and conspiracy, a controversy ensued: Was North accountable for illegal activity and should he therefore be jailed? Or was North acting under orders in the line of duty? (In a 1991 book, he maintained that even President Reagan knew of the orders he was following.) The case exemplifies many judicial controversies: The prosecution argues, "You are to blame, for you could have done otherwise"; the defendant replies, "It wasn't my fault; I was a victim of the situation" or "Under the circumstance I did no wrong."

Why Do We Make the Attribution Error?

So far we have seen a bias in the way we explain other people's behavior: We often ignore powerful situational determinants. Why do we tend to underestimate the situational determinants of others' behavior but not our own?

Perspective and Situational Awareness

Attribution theorists point out that we have a different perspective when observing others than when acting (Jones & Nisbett, 1971; Jones, 1976). When we act, the environment commands our attention. When we watch another person act, that *person* occupies the center of our attention and the situation becomes relatively invisible. To use the perceptual analogy of figure and ground, the person is the figure that stands out from the surrounding environmental ground. So the person seems to cause whatever happens. If this is true, what might we expect if the perspectives were reversed? What if we could see ourselves as others see us and if we saw the world through their eyes? Shouldn't this eliminate or reverse the typical attribution error?

See if you can predict the result of a clever experiment conducted by Michael Storms (1973). Picture yourself as a subject in Storms' experiment. You are seated facing another student with whom you are to talk for a few minutes. Beside you is a TV camera that shares your view of the other student. Facing you from alongside the other student are an observer and another TV camera.

Afterward, both you and the observer judge whether your behavior was caused more by your personal characteristics or by the situation.

Question: Which of you—subject or observer—will attribute the least importance to the situation? Storms found it was the observer (another demonstration of the fundamental attribution tendency). What if we reverse points of view by having you and the observer each watch the videotape recorded from the other's perspective? (You now view yourself, while the observer views what you saw.) This reverses the attributions: The observer now attributes your behavior mostly to the situation you faced, while you now attribute it to your person. *Remembering* an experience from an observer's perspective—by "seeing" oneself from the outside—has the same effect (Frank & Gilovich, 1989).

In another experiment, people viewed a videotape of a suspect confessing during a police interview. If they viewed the confession through a camera focused on the suspect, they perceived the confession as genuine. If they viewed it through a camera focused on the detective, they perceived it as more coerced (Lassiter & Irvine, 1986). In courtrooms, most confession videotapes focus on the confessor. As we might expect, note Daniel Lassiter and Kimberly Dudley (1991), such tapes yield a nearly 100 percent conviction rate when played by prosecutors. Perhaps a more impartial videotape would show both interrogator and suspect.

Time can also change observers' perspectives. As the once-visible person recedes in their memory, observers often give more and more credit to the situation. Immediately after hearing someone argue an assigned position, people assume that's how the person really felt. A week later they are much more likely to credit the situational constraints (Burger, 1991). The day after the 1988 presidential election, Jerry Burger and Julie Pavelich (1994) asked Santa Clara, California, voters why the election turned out as it did. Most attributed the outcome to the candidates' personal traits and positions (Bush was likeable; challenger Dukakis ran a poor campaign). When they asked other voters the same question a year later, only a third attributed the verdict to the candidates. More people now credited circumstances, such as the country's good mood and the robust economy.

Editorial reflections on the six U.S. presidential elections between 1964 and 1988 show the same growth in situational explanations with time (Burger & Pavelich, 1994). Just after the 1978 election, editorial pundits focused on Ford's and Carter's campaigns and personalities. Two years later the situation loomed larger: "The shadows of Watergate . . . cleared the way for [Carter's] climb to the Presidency," noted one editorial in the *New York Times*.

Circumstances can also shift our perspective on ourselves. Seeing ourselves on television redirects our attention to ourselves. Seeing ourselves in a mirror, hearing our tape-recorded voices, having our pictures taken, filling out biographical questionnaires similarly focus our attention inward, making us *self-conscious* instead of *situation*-conscious.

Robert Wicklund, Shelley Duval, and their collaborators have explored the effects of becoming **self-aware** (Duval & Wicklund, 1972; Wicklund, 1979, 1982). When our attention focuses upon ourselves, we attribute more responsibility to ourselves. Allan Fenigstein and Charles Carver (1978) demonstrated this by having students imagine themselves in hypothetical situations. Those who were made self-conscious by thinking they were hearing their own heartbeats while pondering the situation saw themselves as more responsible for the imag-

Self-awareness:
A self-conscious state in which attention focuses on oneself. It makes people more sensitive to their own attitudes and dispositions.

inary outcome than did those who thought they were just hearing extraneous noises.

Some people are typically quite self-conscious. In experiments, people who report themselves as privately self-conscious (who agree with statements such as "I'm generally attentive to my inner feelings") behave similarly to people whose attention has been self-focused with a mirror (Carver & Scheier, 1978). Thus, people whose attention focuses on themselves—either briefly during an experiment or because they are self-conscious persons—view themselves more as observers typically do; they attribute their behavior more to internal factors and less to the situation.

Here then is one good reason for the attribution error: *We find causes where we look for them.* To see this in your own experience, consider: Would you say your social psychology instructor is a quiet or a talkative person?

My guess is you inferred that he or she is fairly outgoing. But consider further: Your attention focuses on your instructor while he or she behaves in a public context that demands speaking. The instructor also observes his or her own behavior in many different situations—in the classroom, in meetings, at home. "Me talkative?" your instructor might say. "Well, it all depends on the situation. When I'm in class or with good friends, I'm rather outgoing. But at conventions and in unfamiliar situations I feel and act rather shy."

If we are acutely aware of how our behavior varies with the situation, we should also see ourselves as more variable than other people. And that is precisely what studies in the United States, Canada, and Germany have found (Baxter & Goldberg, 1987; Kammer, 1982; Sande & others, 1988). Moreover, the less opportunity we have to observe people's behavior in context, the more we attribute to their personalities. Thomas Gilovich (1987) explored this by showing people a videotape of someone and then having them describe the person's actions to other people. The secondhand impressions were more extreme. Similarly, people's impressions of someone they have often heard about from a friend are typically more extreme than their friend's firsthand impressions. The better you know someone, the less prone you are to overgeneralized impressions (Prager & Cutler, 1990).

Culture Differences

Cultures also influence the attribution error (Ickes, 1980; Watson, 1982). Our western worldview predisposes us to assume that people, not situations, cause events. Jerald Jellison and Jane Green (1981) reported that among University of Southern California students, internal explanations are more socially approved. "You can do it!" we are assured by the pop psychology of positive-thinking western culture.

The assumption here is that, with the right disposition and attitude, anyone can surmount almost any problem: You get what you deserve and deserve what you get. Thus we often explain bad behavior by labeling the person as "sick," "lazy," or "sadistic." As children grow up in western culture, they increasingly explain behavior in terms of the other's personal characteristics (Rholes & others, 1990; Ross, 1981). As a first-grader, one of my sons brought home an example. He unscrambled the words "gate the sleeve caught Tom on his" into "The gate caught Tom on his sleeve." His teacher, applying the western cultural assumptions of the curriculum materials, marked this wrong. The "right" answer located the cause within Tom: "Tom caught his sleeve on the gate."

Some languages promote external attributions. Instead of "I was late," Spanish idiom allows one to say, "The clock caused me to be late." In less individualist cultures, people less often perceive others in terms of personal dispositions (Zebrowitz-McArthur, 1988). They are less likely to spontaneously interpret a behavior as reflecting an inner trait (Newman, 1993). When told of someone's actions, Hindus in India are less likely than Americans to offer dispositional explanations ("She is kind") and more likely to offer situational explanations ("Her friends were with her") (Miller, 1984).

HOW FUNDAMENTAL IS THE FUNDAMENTAL ATTRIBUTION ERROR?

Like most provocative ideas, the presumption that we're all prone to a fundamental attribution error has its critics. Granted, say some, there is an attribution *bias*. But in any given instance, this may or may not produce an "error," just as parents who are biased to believe their child does not use drugs may or may not be correct (Harvey & others, 1981). We can be biased to believe what is true. Moreover, some everyday circumstances, such as being in church or on a job interview, are like the experiments we have been considering: As actors realize better than observers, the circumstances involve clear constraints. Hence the attribution error. But in other settings—in one's room, at a park—people exhibit their individuality. In such settings, people may see their own behavior as *less* constrained than do observers (Monson & Snyder, 1977; Quattrone, 1982). So it's an overstatement to say that at all times and in all settings observers underestimate situational influences. For this reason, many social psychologists follow Edward Jones in referring to the fundamental attribution error—seeing behavior as corresponding to an inner disposition—as the *correspondence bias*.

Nevertheless, experiments reveal that the bias occurs even when we are aware of the situational forces—when we know that an assigned debate posi-

BEHIND THE SCENES

Once upon a time there was a boy who loved nothing more than hearing and telling stories about people. So it seemed quite natural that the boy should grow up to become a writer. By the time he was 20, he had dropped out of school and published many stories. One day he decided to take a psychology course at a local college—just to see what all the fuss was about—and within a few months he knew he would rather spend his life understanding people than inventing them.

In making the switch from writing science fiction to researching science fact, I've been puzzled about one thing. We all know that we can be cajoled and bribed and threatened and embarrassed into being polite to those we dislike, or unkind to those we adore. Our actions needn't mirror our private attitudes. Yet we seem quite willing to take *other people's* actions at face value. How can we realize something about ourselves and ignore it when understanding others? Aided by our experiments, we are seeking to explain when and why people believe that others are as they act.

DANIEL T. GILBERT, *University of Texas*

The fundamental attribution error: People are biased to assume that people's behavior corresponds to their inner dispositions. Such assumptions are sometimes, but not always, correct. Some weekend bikers are weekday professionals.

tion is not a good basis for inferring someone's real attitudes (Croxton & Morrow, 1984; Croxton & Miller, 1987; Reeder & others, 1989) or that the questioners' role in the quiz game gives them an advantage (Johnson & others, 1984). It is sobering to think that you and I can know about a social process that distorts our thinking and still be susceptible to it. Perhaps that's because it takes more mental effort to assess social effects on someone's behavior than merely to attribute it to a disposition (Gilbert & others, 1988, 1992; Webster, 1993). It's as if the busy person thinks, "This isn't a very good basis for making a judgment, but it's easy and all I've got time to look at." Less analytical people are especially prone to snap trait judgments that discount the situation (D'Agostino & Fincher-Keifer, 1992).

In many ways, this is adaptive (psychologists generally assume that even our biases serve a purpose, or else nature would have rejected rather than selected those who exhibit them). Attributing behavior to dispositions rather than to situations is not only efficient, it often does little harm. For one thing, our dispositions often lead us to choose our situations. If bankers dress conservatively, note Daniel Gilbert and Patrick Malone (1995), that may reflect not only their profession's demands but also the conservative person's choice of a profession. Assume that the banker really is more conservative than the artist and you are likely right. Some situations really are of our own making. Moreover, when we experience people only in a single role—as a banker, teacher, or grandmother—we can predict their behavior equally well whether attributing it to their role or to their disposition. It's only when we experience a person in a new situation that our disposition-based predictions may go astray. And remember: Even when it is logically incorrect, assuming an internal locus of control may gain us the psychological dividends of self-efficacy noted in Chapter 2.

The attribution error is, however, *fundamental* because it colors our explanations in basic and important ways. Researchers in Britain, India, Australia, and the United States have found, for example, that people's attributions predict their attitudes toward the poor and unemployed (Feather, 1983; Furnham, 1982; Pandey & others, 1982; Wagstaff, 1983; Zucker & Weiner, 1993). Those who attribute poverty and unemployment to personal dispositions ("They're just lazy and undeserving") tend to adopt political positions unsympathetic to such people. Their views differ from those who make external attributions ("If you or I were to live with the same overcrowding, poor education, and discrimination, would we be any better off?"). French investigators Jean-Leon Beauvois and Nicole Dubois (1988) report that "relatively privileged" middle-class people are more likely than less advantaged people to assume that people's behaviors have internal explanations. (Those who have made it tend to assume that you get what you deserve.)

"Most poor people are not lazy. . . . They catch the early bus. . . . They raise other people's children. . . . They clean the streets. No, no, they're not lazy."
The Reverend Jesse Jackson, address to the Democratic National Convention, July 1988.

How might we benefit from being aware of the bias? Perhaps being sensitive to it can help. Recently, I assisted with some interviews for a faculty position. One candidate was interviewed by six of us at once; each of us had the opportunity to ask two or three questions. I came away thinking, "What a stiff, awkward person he is." The second candidate I met privately over coffee, and we immediately discovered we had a close, mutual friend. As we talked, I became increasingly impressed by what a "warm, engaging, stimulating person she is." Only later did I remember the fundamental attribution error and reassess my analysis. I had attributed his stiffness and her warmth to their dispositions; in fact, I later realized, such behavior resulted partly from the difference in their interview situations. Had I viewed these interactions through their eyes instead of my own, I might have come to different conclusions.

SUMMING UP

Attribution researchers study how we explain people's behavior. When will we attribute someone's behavior to a person's disposition and when to the situation? By and large we make reasonable attributions. However, when explaining other people's behavior, we often commit the *fundamental attribution error* (also called *correspondence bias*). We attribute their behavior so much to their inner traits and attitudes that we discount situational constraints, even when these are obvious. If a balloon moves because it is pushed by an invisible wind, we don't assume it is internally propelled. But people are not inanimate objects; thus, when a *person* acts we more often discount the situational winds and assume internal propulsion.

We make this attribution error partly because when we watch someone act, that *person* is the focus of our attention and the situation is relatively invisible. When *we* act, our attention is usually on what we are reacting to—the situation is more visible. Thus we are more sensitive to the situational influences upon ourselves. With time, however, our perspectives, and our explanations, often change.

■ JUDGING OTHERS

As we have already noted, our cognitive mechanisms are efficient and adaptive, yet error-prone. Usually they serve us well, but sometimes clinicians misjudge patients, employers misjudge employees, people of one race misjudge another, and spouses misjudge their mates. The results are misdiagnoses, labor strife, prejudices, and divorces. So, how—and how well—do we make intuitive social judgments?

When historians describe social psychology's first century, they will surely record the last 25 years as the era of social cognition. By drawing upon advances in cognitive psychology—in how people perceive, represent, and remember events—social psychologists have shed welcome light on how we form judgments. Let's look at what this research reveals of the marvels and mistakes of our social intuition.

INTUITION: OUR POTENTIAL FOR INNER KNOWING

What are our powers of intuition—of immediately knowing something without reasoning or analysis? Advocates of "intuitive management" believe we should tune into our hunches. When judging others, we should plug into the nonlogical smarts of our "right brain." When hiring, firing, and investing, we should listen to our premonitions. In making judgments, we should follow the example of *Star Wars'* Luke Skywalker by switching off our computer guidance systems and trusting the force within.

Are the intuitionists correct that important information is immediately available apart from our conscious analysis? Or are the skeptics right in saying that intuition is "our knowing we are right, whether we are or not"?

The Powers of Intuition

"The heart has its reasons which reason does not know," observed seventeenth-century philosopher-mathematician Blaise Pascal. Three centuries later, scientists have proved Pascal correct. We know more than we know we know. Studies of our unconscious information processing confirm our limited access to what's going on in our minds (Bargh, 1994; Greenwald & Banaji, 1995). Our thinking is partly controlled (deliberate and conscious) and—more than most of us once supposed—partly *automatic* (effortless and without our awareness). Automatic thinking occurs not "on screen" but off screen, out of sight, where reason does not know. Consider:

■ *Schemas*—mental templates—automatically, intuitively, guide our perceptions and interpretations of our experience. Whether we hear someone speaking of religious *sects* or *sex* depends not only on the word spoken but on how we automatically interpret the sound.

■ Some *emotional reactions* are nearly instantaneous, before there is time for deliberate thinking. Simple likes, dislikes, and fears typically involve little analysis. Although our intuitive reactions sometimes defy logic, they may still be adaptive. Our ancestors who intuitively feared a sound in the bushes were usually fearing nothing, but they were more likely to survive to pass their genes down to us than their more deliberative cousins.

■ Given sufficient *expertise,* people may intuitively know the answer to a problem. The situation cues information stored in their memory. Without knowing quite how we do it, we recognize a friend's voice after the first spoken word of a phone conversation. Master chess players intuitively recognize meaningful patterns that novices miss.

■ Some things—facts, names, and past experiences—we remember explicitly (consciously). But other things—skills and conditioned dispositions—we remember *implicitly,* without consciously knowing and declaring that we know. It's true of us all, but most strikingly evident in brain-damaged persons who cannot form new explicit memories. Having learned how to solve a block-stacking puzzle or play golf, they will deny ever having experienced the task. Yet (surprisingly to themselves) they perform like practiced experts.

■ Equally dramatic are the cases of *blindsight*. Having lost a portion of the visual cortex to surgery or stroke, people may be functionally blind in part of their field of vision. Shown a series of sticks in the blind field, they report seeing nothing. After correctly guessing whether the sticks are vertical or horizontal, the patients are astounded when told, "You got them all right." Again, these people know more than they know they know. There are, it seems, little minds—parallel processing units—operating unseen.

■ *Prosopagnosia* patients suffer damage to a brain area involved in face recognition. They can see familiar people but are unable to recognize them as their spouses or children. Yet, shown pictures of such people, their heart knows them; its rate increases as their body shows signs of unconscious recognition.

■ For that matter, consider your own taken-for-granted capacity to intuitively recognize a face. As you look at a photo, your brain breaks the visual information into subdimensions such as color, depth, movement, and form and works on each aspect simultaneously before reassembling the components. Finally, somehow, your brain compares the perceived image with previously stored images. Voilà! Instantly and effortlessly, you recognize your grandmother. If intuition is immediately knowing something without reasoned analysis, perceiving is intuition par excellence.

■ Although below our threshold for conscious awareness, *subliminal* stimuli may nevertheless have intriguing effects. Shown certain geometric figures for less than 0.01 second each, people will deny having seen anything more than a flash of light. Yet they will later express a preference for the forms they saw. Sometimes we intuitively feel what we cannot explain. Likewise, invisible flashed words can *prime* or predispose our responses to later questions. If the word "bread" is flashed too briefly to recognize, we may then detect a flashed, related word such as "butter" more easily than an unrelated word such as "bottle."

To repeat, many routine cognitive functions occur automatically, unintentionally, without awareness. Our minds function rather like big corporations. Our CEO—our controlled consciousness—attends to the most important or novel issues and assigns routine affairs to subordinates. This delegation of attentional resources enables us to react to many situations quickly, efficiently, *intuitively*, without taking limited time to reason and analyze.

The Limits of Intuition

Although researchers affirm that unconscious information processing can produce flashes of intuition, they have their doubts about its brilliance. Elizabeth Loftus and Mark Klinger (1992) speak for today's cognitive scientists in reporting "a general consensus that the unconscious may not be as smart as previously believed." For example, although subliminal stimuli can trigger a weak, fleeting response—enough to evoke a feeling if not conscious awareness—there is no evidence that commercial subliminal tapes can "reprogram your unconscious mind" for success. [Indeed, a mass of new evidence indicates that they can't (Greenwald & others, 1991).]

Moreover, our intuitive judgments err often enough to understand why poet T. S. Eliot would describe "The hollow man . . . Headpiece filled with straw." Social psychologists have explored our error-prone hindsight judgments (our intuitive sense, after the fact, that we knew-it-all-along). Other domains of psychology have explored our capacity for illusion—perceptual misinterpretations, fantasies, and constructed beliefs. Michael Gazzaniga (1992) reports that patients whose brain hemispheres have been surgically separated will instantly fabricate—and believe—explanations of puzzling behaviors. If the patient gets up and takes a few steps after the experimenter flashes the instruction "walk" to the patient's nonverbal right hemisphere, the verbal left hemisphere will instantly invent a plausible explanation ("I felt like getting a drink").

Illusory thinking also appears in the vast new literature on how we take in, store, and retrieve social information. As perception researchers study visual illusions for what they reveal about our normal perceptual mechanisms, social psychologists study illusory thinking for what it reveals about normal information processing. These researchers want to give us a map of everyday social thinking, with the hazards clearly marked. As we examine some of these efficient thinking patterns, remember this: Demonstrations of how people create counterfeit beliefs do not prove that all beliefs are counterfeit. Still, to recognize counterfeiting, it helps to know how it's done. So let's explore how efficient information processing can go awry, beginning with our self-knowledge.

"People are good enough to get through life, poor enough to make predictable and consequential mistakes."
Baruch Fischhoff, 1981

CONSTRUCTING INTERPRETATIONS AND MEMORIES

Chapter 1 noted a significant fact about the human mind—that our preconceptions guide how we perceive and interpret information. People will grant that preconceptions influence social judgments, yet fail to realize how great the effect is. Let's look at some recent experiments. Some examine how *pre*judgments affect the way people perceive and interpret information. Others plant a judgment in people's minds *after* they have been given information to study how after-the-fact ideas bias recall. The overarching point: We respond not to reality as it is but to reality as we construe it.

Perceiving and Interpreting Events

The effects of prejudgments and expectations are standard fare for psychology's introductory course. Recall the Dalmatian photo in Chapter 1. Or consider this phrase:

A
BIRD
IN THE
THE HAND

Did you notice anything wrong with it? There is more to perception than meets the eye. This was tragically demonstrated when the USS *Vincennes* crew misperceived the Iranian airliner and shot it down. As social psychologist Richard Nisbett (1988) noted in a congressional hearing on the incident, "The effects of expectations on generating and sustaining mistaken hypotheses can be dramatic."

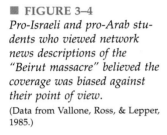

■ FIGURE 3–4

Pro-Israeli and pro-Arab students who viewed network news descriptions of the "Beirut massacre" believed the coverage was biased against their point of view.

(Data from Vallone, Ross, & Lepper, 1985.)

The same is true of social perception. Because social perceptions are very much in the eye of the beholder, even a simple stimulus may strike two people quite differently. Saying Canada's Jean Chrétien is "an okay prime minister" may sound like a put-down to one of his ardent admirers and as positively biased to someone who regards him with contempt. When social information is subject to multiple interpretations, preconceptions matter (Hilton & von Hippel, 1990).

An experiment by Robert Vallone, Lee Ross, and Mark Lepper (1985) reveals just how powerful preconceptions can be. They showed pro-Israeli and pro-Arab students six network news segments describing the 1982 killing of civilian refugees at two camps in Lebanon. As Figure 3–4 illustrates, each group perceived the networks as hostile to its side. The phenomenon is commonplace: Presidential candidates and their supporters nearly always view the news media as unsympathetic to their cause. A 1994 Gallup poll found African Americans twice as likely as other Americans to perceive media coverage of O. J. Simpson's arrest as too harsh. Sports fans perceive referees as partial to the other side. People in conflict (married couples, labor and management, opposing racial groups) see impartial mediators as biased against them.

Our shared assumptions about the world can even make contradictory evidence seem supportive. For example, Ross and Lepper assisted Charles Lord (1979) in asking students to evaluate the results of two supposedly new research studies. Half the students favored capital punishment and half opposed it. One study confirmed and the other disconfirmed the students' beliefs about the deterrence effect of the death penalty. The results: both proponents and opponents of capital punishment readily accepted evidence that confirmed their belief but were sharply critical of disconfirming evidence. Showing the two sides an *identical* body of mixed evidence had therefore not lessened their

"As I am, so I see."
Ralph Waldo Emerson, *Essays*

disagreement but *increased* it. Each side perceived the evidence as supporting its belief and now believed even more strongly. In general, people are less critical of information when it supports their preferred conclusions (Ditto & Lopez, 1992).

Is this why, in politics, religion, and science, ambiguous information often fuels conflict? Presidential TV debates in the United States have mostly reinforced predebate opinions. By nearly a 10 to 1 margin, those who already favored one candidate or the other in the 1960, 1976, and 1980 debates perceived their candidate as having won (Kinder & Sears, 1985).

Preconceptions sway scientists, too. In Chapter 1 we noted that beliefs and values penetrate science. Philosophers of science remind us that our observations are "theory-laden." There is an objective reality out there, but we view it through the spectacles of our beliefs, attitudes, and values. This is one reason our beliefs are so important; they shape our interpretation of everything else. Often, this is justifiable. Your preconceptions of the editorial standards of certain tabloid newspapers probably justify your disregarding headlines proclaiming, "Computers talk with the dead." So preconceptions can be useful: The occasional biases they create are the price we pay for their helping us filter and organize vast amounts of information efficiently.

Experiments have manipulated preconceptions with astonishing effects upon how people interpret and recall what they observe. Myron Rothbart and Pamela Birrell (1977) had University of Oregon students assess the facial ex-

"Once you have a belief, it influences how you perceive all other relevant information. Once you see a country as hostile, you are likely to interpret ambiguous actions on their part as signifying their hostility."
Political scientist Robert Jervis (1985)

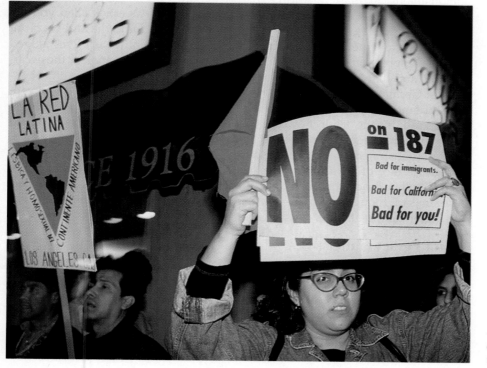

Supporters of a particular candidate or cause tend to see the media as favoring the other side.

■ **FIGURE 3–5**
The photo of "Kurt Walden" as shown by Myron Rothbart and Pamela Birrell. Judge for yourself: Is this man cruel or kind?

"The error of our eye directs our mind: What error leads must err."
Shakespeare, *Troilus and Cressida*, 1601–1602

"We hear and apprehend only what we already half know."
Henry David Thoreau, 1817–1862

pression of the man shown in Figure 3–5. Those told he was a Gestapo leader responsible for barbaric medical experiments on concentration camp inmates during World War II intuitively judged his expression as cruel. (Can you see that barely suppressed sneer?) Those told he was a leader in the anti-Nazi underground movement whose courage saved thousands of Jewish lives judged his facial expression as warm and kind. (On second thought, look at those caring eyes and that almost smiling mouth.)

West German researcher Harald Wallbott (1988) controlled people's perceptions of emotion by manipulating the setting in which they see a face. Filmmakers call this the "Kulechov effect," after a Russian film director who would skillfully guide viewers' inferences by manipulating their assumptions. Kulechov demonstrated the phenomenon by creating three short films that presented the face of an actor with a neutral expression after viewers had first been shown a dead woman, a dish of soup, or a girl playing—making the actor seem sad, thoughtful, or happy. The moral: There is a reality out there, but our understanding of it is construed in our minds.

Belief Perseverance

If a false idea biases information processing, will later discrediting erase its effects? Imagine a baby-sitter who decides, during an evening with a crying infant, that bottle feeding produces colicky babies: "Come to think of it, cow's milk obviously better suits calves than babies." If the infant turns out to be suffering a high fever, will the sitter nevertheless persist in believing that bottle feeding causes colic (Ross & Anderson, 1982)? To find out, Lee Ross, Craig Anderson, and their colleagues planted a falsehood in people's minds and then tried to discredit it.

Their experiments reveal that it is surprisingly difficult to demolish a false-hood, once the person conjures up a rationale for it. Each experiment first implanted a belief, either by proclaiming it was true or by inducing people to come to that conclusion after inspecting two sample cases. Then the people were asked to explain *why* it is true. Finally, the researchers totally discredited the initial information by telling the person the truth: The information was manufactured for the experiment, and half the people in the experiment had received opposite information. Nevertheless, the new belief survived about 75 percent intact, presumably because the people still retained their invented explanations for the belief. This phenomenon, named **belief perseverance,** shows that beliefs can take on a life of their own, and survive discrediting of the evidence that gave them birth.

For instance, Anderson, Lepper, and Ross (1980) asked people, after giving them two concrete cases to inspect, to decide whether people who take risks make good or bad firefighters. One group considered a risk-prone person who was a successful firefighter and a cautious person who was an unsuccessful one. The other group considered cases suggesting the opposite conclusion. After forming their theory that risk-prone people make better or worse firefighters, the individuals wrote explanations for it—for example, that risk-prone people are brave or that cautious people are careful. Once formed, each explanation could exist independently of the information that initially created the belief. When that information was discredited, the people still held their self-generated explanations and therefore continued to believe that risk-prone people really *do* make better or worse firefighters.

These experiments also show that the more we examine our theories and explain how they *might* be true, the more closed we become to information that challenges our belief. To a lesser extent, false beliefs about other individuals or even oneself may also survive discrediting (DiFonzo, 1994). Once we con-

Belief perseverance:
Persistence of one's initial conceptions, as when the basis for one's belief is discredited but an explanation of why the belief might be true survives.

"No one denies that new evidence can change people's beliefs. Children do eventually renounce their belief in Santa Claus. Our contention is simply that such changes generally occur slowly, and that more compelling evidence is often required to alter a belief than to create it."
Lee Ross & Mark Lepper (1980)

Do people who take risks make the best firefighters? Or the worst?

sider why an accused person might be guilty, why someone of whom we have a negative first impression acts that way, or why a favored stock might rise in value, our explanations may survive challenging evidence to the contrary (Jelalian & Miller, 1984). Once we attribute our failure at the hands of an incompetent teacher to our own incompetence, our low self-image may persevere (Lepper & others, 1986).

"Two-thirds of what we see is behind our eyes."
Chinese proverb

The evidence is compelling: Our beliefs and expectations powerfully affect how we mentally construct events. Usually we benefit from our preconceptions, just as scientists benefit from creating theories that guide them in noticing and interpreting events. But the benefits sometimes entail a cost; we become prisoners of our own thought patterns. Thus the "canals" that were so often seen on Mars turned out to be the product of intelligent life—an intelligence on earth's side of the telescope.

Is there any way we can restrain belief perseverance? There is a simple remedy: *Explain the opposite.* Charles Lord, Mark Lepper, and Elizabeth Preston (1984) repeated the capital punishment study described earlier and added two variations. First, they asked some of their subjects when evaluating the evidence to be "*as objective* and *unbiased* as possible.*"* It was to no avail; whether for or against capital punishment, those who received this plea made evaluations as biased as those who did not.

The researchers asked a third group of subjects to consider the opposite—to ask themselves "whether you would have made the same high or low evaluations had exactly the same study produced results on the *other* side of the issue." After imagining an opposite finding, these people were much less biased in their evaluations of the evidence for and against their views. In his experiments, Craig Anderson (1982; Anderson & Sechler, 1986) consistently found that explaining why an opposite theory might be true—why a cautious rather than a risk-taking person might be a better firefighter—reduces or eliminates belief perseverance. So, to counteract belief perseverance, force yourself to explain why the opposite belief might be true.

Constructing Memories

Do you agree or disagree with this statement?

> Memory can be likened to a storage chest in the brain into which we deposit material and from which we can withdraw it later if needed. Occasionally, something is lost from the "chest," and then we say we have forgotten.

About 85 percent of college students agree (Lamal, 1979). As a 1988 ad in *Psychology Today* put it, "Science has proven the accumulated experience of a lifetime is preserved perfectly in your mind."

Actually, psychological research has proved the opposite. Many memories are not copies of experiences that remain on deposit in a memory bank. Rather, we construct memories at the time of withdrawal, for memory involves backward reasoning. It infers what must have been, given what we now believe or know. Like a paleontologist inferring the appearance of a dinosaur from bone fragments, we reconstruct our distant past by combining fragments of information using our current feelings and expectations (Hirt, 1990; Ross & Buehler, 1994). Thus we can easily (though unconsciously) revise our memories to suit our current knowledge. When one of my sons complained, "The June issue of *Cricket* never came," and was then shown where it was, he delightedly responded, "Oh good, I knew I'd gotten it."

"Memory isn't like reading a book: it's more like writing a book from fragmentary notes."
John F. Kihlstrom (1994)

Unlike photos, memories get reconstructed when withdrawn from the memory bank.

Reconstructing Past Attitudes

Five years ago, how did you feel about nuclear power? About Bill Clinton or Jean Chrétien? About your parents? If your attitudes have changed, do you know the extent of the change?

Experimenters have tried to answer such questions, and the results have been unnerving. People whose attitudes have changed often insist that they have always felt much as they now feel. Daryl Bem and Keith McConnell (1970) took a survey among Carnegie-Mellon University students. Buried in it was a question concerning student control over the university curriculum. A week later the students agreed to write an essay opposing student control. After doing so, their attitudes shifted toward greater opposition to student control. When asked to recall how they had answered the question before writing the essay, they "remembered" holding the opinion that they *now* held and denied that the experiment had affected them. After observing Clark University students similarly denying their former attitudes, researchers D. R. Wixon and James Laird (1976) commented: "The speed, magnitude, and certainty" with which the students revised their own histories "was striking."

In 1973, University of Michigan researchers interviewed a national sample of high school seniors and then reinterviewed them in 1982 (Markus, 1986). When recalling their 1973 attitudes on issues such as aid to minorities, the legalization of marijuana, and equality for women, people's reports were much closer to their 1982 attitudes than to those they actually expressed in 1973. As George Vaillant (1977, p. 197) noted after following some adults for a period of time: "It is all too common for caterpillars to become butterflies and then to maintain that in their youth they had been little butterflies. Maturation makes liars of us all."

"A man should never be ashamed to own that he has been in the wrong, which is but saying, in other words, that he is wiser today than he was yesterday."
Jonathan Swift,
Thoughts on Various Subjects, 1711

The construction of positive memories does brighten our recollections. Terence Mitchell and Leigh Thompson (1994) report that people often exhibit *rosy retrospection*—they *recall* mildly pleasant events more favorably than they experienced them. College students on a three-week bike trip, older adults on a guided tour of Austria, and undergraduates on vacation all report enjoying their experiences as they have them. But they later recall such experiences even more fondly, minimizing the unpleasant or boring aspects and remembering the high points. Thus, the pleasant times during which I have sojourned in Scotland I now (back in my office facing deadlines and interruptions) romanticize as pure bliss. With any positive experience, some of the pleasure resides in the anticipation, some in the actual experience, and some in the rosy retrospection.

Cathy McFarland and Michael Ross (1985) found that we also revise our recollections of other people as our relationships with them change. They had university students rate their steady dating partners. Two months later, they rated them again. Students who were more in love than ever had a tendency to recall love at first sight. Those who had broken up were more likely to recall having recognized the partner as somewhat selfish and bad-tempered.

Diane Holmberg and John Holmes (1994) discovered the same phenomenon among 373 newlywed couples, most of whom reported being very happy. When resurveyed two years later, those whose marriages had soured recalled that things had always been bad. The results are "frightening," say Holmberg and Holmes: "Such biases can lead to a dangerous downward spiral. The worse your current view of your partner is, the worse your memories are, which only further confirms your negative attitudes."

It's not that we are totally unaware of how we used to feel, just that when memories are hazy, current feelings guide our recall. Parents of every generation bemoan the values of the next generation, partly because they misrecall their youthful values as being closer to their current values.

Reconstructing Past Behavior

Memory construction enables us to revise our own histories. Michael Ross, Cathy McFarland, and Garth Fletcher (1981) exposed some University of Waterloo students to a message convincing them of the desirability of toothbrushing. Later, in a supposedly different experiment, these students recalled brushing their teeth more often during the preceding two weeks than did students who had not heard the message. Likewise

- When representative samples of Americans are asked about their cigarette smoking and their reports are projected to the nation as a whole, at least a third of the 600 billion cigarettes sold annually are unaccounted for (Hall, 1985).

- In a recent Census Bureau (1993) survey, 61 percent of adult Americans reported voting in the last presidential election, in which 55 percent of adults voted.

- Most people think their lifestyle is healthier than that of their average peer. If challenged by information about the actual frequency with which their peers drink to excess, eat greasy foods and so forth, people revise their recollections and report engaging in such behaviors even less often (Klein & Kunda, 1993).

"Travel is glamorous only in retrospect."
Paul Theroux,
in *The Observer*

"Vanity plays lurid tricks with our memory."
Novelist Joseph Conrad,
1857–1924

Noting the similarity of such findings to happenings in George Orwell's *Nineteen Eighty-Four*—where it was "necessary to remember that events happened in the desired manner"—social psychologist Anthony Greenwald (1980) surmised that we all have "totalitarian egos" that revise the past to suit our present views.

Sometimes our present view is that we've improved—in which case we may misrecall our past as more *un*like the present than it actually was. This tendency resolves a puzzling pair of consistent findings: Those who participate in self-improvement programs (weight-control programs, antismoking programs, exercise programs, psychotherapy) show only modest improvement on average. Yet they often claim considerable benefit (Myers, 1995). Michael Conway and Michael Ross (1985) explain why: Having expended so much time, effort, and money on self-improvement, people may think, "I may not be perfect now, but I was worse before; this did me a lot of good." For example, the participants in a study-skills course emerged from the experience thinking their skills had improved, especially in comparison to their now biased memories about how terrible they were before the course. But despite their belittling of their past, and their optimism about their academic future, the sad truth is that their grades did not change (Conway & Ross, 1984).

Reconstructing Our Experiences

In experiments involving more than 20,000 people, Elizabeth Loftus has revealed our tendency to construct memories we recall with great confidence but sometimes little accuracy. In the typical experiment, people witness an event, receive misleading information about it (or not), and then take a memory test. The repeated finding is the **misinformation effect**. People incorporate the misinformation into their memories: They recall a yield sign as a stop sign, hammers as screwdrivers, *Vogue* magazine as *Mademoiselle*, Dr. Henderson as "Dr. Davidson," breakfast cereal as eggs, and a clean-shaven man as a fellow with a mustache (Loftus & others, 1989). Suggested misinformation may even produce false memories of supposed child sexual abuse, argues Loftus (1993).

In one famous experiment with John Palmer, Loftus showed University of Washington students a film of a traffic accident and then asked them questions about what they had witnessed (Loftus & Palmer, 1974). People asked "How fast were the cars going when they smashed into each other?" gave higher estimates than those asked "How fast were the cars going when they hit each other?" A week later they were also asked whether they recalled seeing any broken glass. There was no broken glass. Yet people who had been asked the "smashed into" question were more than twice as likely as those asked the "hit" question to report seeing broken glass.

What is more, it's difficult for untrained observers to distinguish between unreal memories (those constructed from suggestion, as with the broken glass) and memories of actual experience (Schooler & others, 1986). As such experiments show, in constructing a memory, we unconsciously use our general knowledge and beliefs to fill in the holes, thus organizing fragments from our actual past into a convincing story.

This process affects our recall of social as well as physical events. Jack Croxton and his colleagues (1984) had students spend 15 minutes talking with someone. Those later informed that this person reported liking them recalled the person's behavior as relaxed, comfortable, and happy. Those informed that the

Misinformation effect: Incorporating "misinformation" into one's memory of the event, after witnessing an event and receiving misleading information about it.

Pause to recall a scene from a favorite past experience. . . . Do you see yourself in the scene? If so, your memory must be a reconstruction, for in reality you did not see yourself.

person disliked them recalled the person as nervous, uncomfortable, and not so happy.

To understand why, it helps to have an idea of how our memories work. We can think of memories as stored in a web of associations. To retrieve a memory, we need to activate one of the strands that leads to it, a process called **priming** (Bower, 1986). Priming is what the philosopher-psychologist William James described as the "wakening of associations."

Priming:
Activating particular associations in memory.

Events may awaken or prime our associations without our realizing it. Watching a scary movie while alone at home can prime our thinking—by activating frightening memories that cause us to interpret furnace noises as an intruder. For many psychology students, reading about psychological disorders primes how they interpret their own anxieties and gloomy moods. In experiments, ideas implanted in people's minds act like preconceptions: They automatically—unintentionally, effortlessly, and without awareness—influence how people interpret and recall events (Bargh, 1989, 1994). Having recently seen words such as "adventurous" and "self-confident," people will later, in a different context, form positive impressions of an imagined mountain climber or Atlantic sailor. If, instead, their thinking is primed with such negative words as "reckless," their impressions are more negative (Higgins & others, 1977).

In Chapter 5 we will see that psychiatrists and clinical psychologists are not immune to these human tendencies. We all selectively notice, interpret, and recall events in ways that sustain our ideas. Our social judgments are a mix of observation and expectation, reason and passion.

JUDGMENTAL OVERCONFIDENCE

So far we have seen that our cognitive system processes a vast amount of information efficiently and automatically, resulting in those impressive intuitive judgments. But our adaptive efficiency has a trade-off; as we interpret our experiences and construct memories, our intuitive judgments are sometimes wrong. Usually, we are unaware of our flaws. The "intellectual conceit" evident in judgments of past knowledge ("I knew it all along") extends to estimates of current knowledge.

Overconfidence phenomenon:
The tendency to be more confident than correct—to overestimate the accuracy of one's beliefs.

To explore this **overconfidence phenomenon**, Daniel Kahneman and Amos Tversky (1979) gave people factual questions and asked them to fill in the blanks, as in: "I feel 98 percent certain that the air distance between New Delhi and Beijing is more than _____ miles but less than _____ miles." Most subjects were overconfident: About 30 percent of the time, the correct answers lay outside the range they felt 98 percent confident about.

To find out whether overconfidence extends to social judgments, David Dunning and his associates (1990) created a little game show. They asked Stanford University students to guess a stranger's answers to a series of questions, such as, "Would you prepare for a difficult exam alone or with others?" and "Would you rate your lecture notes as neat or messy?" Knowing the type but not the actual questions, the subjects first interviewed their target person about background, hobbies, academic interests, aspirations, astrological sign—anything they thought might be helpful. Then, while the targets answered 20 of the two-choice questions, the interviewers predicted their target's answers and rated their own confidence in the predictions.

The interviewers guessed right 63 percent of the time, beating chance by 13 percent. But, on average, they *felt* 75 percent sure of their predictions. When guessing their own roommates' responses, they were 68 percent correct and 78 percent confident. Moreover, the most confident people were most likely to be *over*confident.

Are people better at predicting their own behavior? To find out, Robert Vallone and his colleagues (1990) had college students predict in September whether they would drop a course, declare a major, elect to live off campus next year, and so forth. Although the students felt, on average, 84 percent sure of these self-predictions, they were wrong nearly twice as often as they expected to be. Even when feeling 100 percent sure of their predictions, they erred 15 percent of the time.

In estimating their chances for success on a task, such as a major exam, people's confidence runs highest when removed in time from "the moment of truth." By exam day, the possibility of failure looms larger and confidence typically drops (Gilovich & others, 1993). Roger Buehler and his colleagues (1994) report that most students also confidently underestimate how long it will take them to complete papers and other major assignments. They are not alone:

- Planners routinely underestimate the time and expense of projects. In 1969, Montreal Mayor Jean Drapeau proudly announced that a $120 million stadium with a retractable roof would be built for the 1976 Olympics. The roof was completed in 1989 and cost $120 million by itself.

- Investment experts market their services with the confident presumption that they can beat the stock market average, forgetting that for every stockbroker or buyer saying "Sell!" at a given price there is another saying "Buy!" A stock's price is the balance point between these mutually confident judgments. Thus, incredible as it may seem, economist Burton Malkiel (1985) reports that mutual fund portfolios selected by investment analysts have not outperformed randomly selected stocks.

  The air distance between New Delhi and Beijing is 2500 miles.

- Editors' assessments of manuscripts also reveal surprising error. Writer Chuck Ross (1979), using a pseudonym, mailed a typewritten copy of Jerzy Kosinski's novel *Steps* to 28 major publishers and literary agencies. All rejected it, including Random House, which had published the book in 1968 and watched it win the National Book Award and sell more than 400,000 copies. The novel came closest to being accepted by Houghton Mifflin, publisher of three other Kosinski novels: "Several of us read your untitled novel here with admiration for writing and style. Jerzy Kosinski comes to mind as a point of comparison. . . . The drawback to the manuscript, as it stands, is that it doesn't add up to a satisfactory whole."

  "The wise know too well their weakness to assume infallibility; and he who knows most, knows best how little he knows."
  Thomas Jefferson, *Writings*

- Overconfident decision makers can wreak havoc. It was a confident Adolf Hitler who from 1939 to 1945 waged war against the rest of Europe. It was a confident Lyndon Johnson who in the 1960s invested U.S. weapons and soldiers in the effort to salvage democracy in South Vietnam. It was a confident Saddam Hussein who in 1990 marched his army into Kuwait.

  Regarding the atomic bomb: *"That is the biggest fool thing we have ever done. The bomb will never go off, and I speak as an expert in explosives."*
  Admiral William Leahy to President Truman, 1945

What produces overconfidence? Why does experience not lead us to a more realistic self-appraisal? There are several reasons (Klayman & Ha, 1987; Sanbomatsu & others, 1993; Skov & Sherman, 1986). For one thing, people tend not to seek information that might disprove what they believe. P. C. Wason

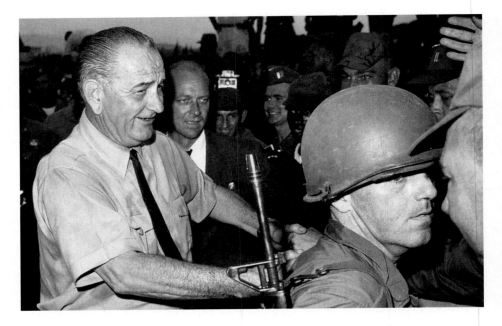

President Lyndon Johnson on a Vietnam visit, 1966. Overconfidence, such as he exhibited in committing troops to a failed war, underlies many blunders, both large and small.

"When you know a thing, to hold that you know it; and when you do not know a thing, to allow that you do not know it; this is knowledge."
Confucius, *Analects*

Confirmation bias:
A tendency to search for information that confirms one's preconceptions.

(1960) demonstrated this, as you can, by giving people a sequence of three numbers—2, 4, 6—which conformed to a rule he had in mind (the rule was simply *any three ascending numbers*). To enable the people to discover the rule, Wason invited each person to generate sets of three numbers. Each time Wason told the person whether or not the set conformed to his rule. When they were sure they had discovered the rule, the people were to stop and announce it.

The result? Seldom right but never in doubt: 23 of the 29 people convinced themselves of a wrong rule. They typically formed some erroneous belief about the rule (for example, counting by two's) and then searched for *confirming* evidence (for example, by testing 8, 10, 12) rather than attempting to *disconfirm* their hunches. We are eager to verify our beliefs but less inclined to seek evidence that might disprove them. We call this phenomenon the **confirmation bias**.

Our preference for confirming information helps explain why our self-images are so remarkably stable. In experiments at the University of Texas at Austin, William Swann and Stephen Read (1981a, b; Swann & others, 1992, 1994) discovered that students seek, elicit, and recall feedback that confirms their beliefs about themselves. People seek as friends and spouses those who bolster their own self views—even if they think poorly of themselves (Swann & others, 1991, 1992, in press). Swann and Read liken this *self-verification* to how someone with a domineering self-image might behave at a party. Upon arriving, the person *seeks* those guests whom she knows acknowledge her dominance. In conversation she then presents her views in ways that *elicit* the respect she expects. After the party, she has trouble recalling conversations in which her influence was minimal and more easily *recalls* her persuasiveness in the conversations that she dominated. Thus her experience at the party confirms her self-image.

Remedies for Overconfidence

What lessons can we draw from research on overconfidence? One lesson is to be careful about other people's dogmatic statements. Even when people seem sure that they are right, they may be wrong. Confidence and competence need not coincide.

Two techniques have successfully reduced the overconfidence bias. One is prompt feedback (Lichtenstein & Fischhoff, 1980). In everyday life, weather forecasters and those who set the odds in horse racing both receive clear, daily feedback. Experts in both groups, therefore, do quite well at estimating their probable accuracy (Fischhoff, 1982).

When people think about why an idea *might* be true it begins to seem true (Koehler, 1991). Thus, another way to reduce overconfidence is to get people to think of one good reason *why their judgments might be wrong:* force them to consider disconfirming information (Koriat & others, 1980). Managers might foster more realistic judgments by insisting that all proposals and recommendations include reasons why they might not work.

Still, we should be careful not to undermine people's self-confidence to a point where they spend too much time in self-analysis or where self-doubts begin to cripple decisiveness. In times when their wisdom is needed, those lacking self-confidence may shrink from speaking up or making tough decisions. *Over*confidence can cost us, but realistic self-confidence is adaptive.

HEURISTICS

With such precious little time to process so much information, our cognitive system specializes in mental shortcuts. With remarkable ease, we form impressions, make judgments, and invent explanations. In many situations, our snap generalizations—"That's dangerous!"—are adaptive. Their speed promotes our survival. Thinking's biological purpose is less to make us right than to keep us alive. In some situations, however, haste makes error.

Representativeness Heuristic

> Twice divorced, Frank spends most of his free time hanging around the country club. His clubhouse bar conversations often center around his regrets at having tried to follow his esteemed father's footsteps. The long hours he had spent at academic drudgery would have been better invested in learning how to be less quarrelsome in his relations with other people.

> *Question:* What is the probability that Frank is a lawyer rather than an engineer?

Asked to guess Frank's occupation, more than 80 percent of University of Oregon students surmised he was one of the lawyers (Fischhoff & Bar-Hillel, 1984). Fair enough. But how do you suppose their estimates changed when the sample description was changed to say that 70 percent were engineers? Not in the slightest. The students took no account of the base rate of engineers and lawyers; in their minds Frank was more *representative* of lawyers, and that was all that seemed to matter.

To judge something by intuitively comparing it to our mental representation of a category is to use the **representativeness heuristic**. *Heuristics* are simple,

Representativeness heuristic:
The strategy of judging the likelihood of things by how well they represent, or match, particular prototypes; may lead one to ignore other relevant information.

efficient thinking strategies—implicit rules of thumb. Like most heuristics, representativeness usually is a reasonable guide to reality. But not always. Consider Linda, who is 31, single, outspoken, and very bright. She majored in philosophy in college. As a student she was deeply concerned with discrimination and other social issues, and she participated in antinuclear demonstrations. Based on this description, would you say it is more likely that:

a. Linda is a bank teller.
b. Linda is a bank teller and active in the feminist movement.

Most people think *b* is more likely, partly because Linda better *represents* their image of feminists. Consider: Is there a better chance that Linda is *both* a bank teller *and* a feminist than that she's a bank teller (whether feminist or not)? As Amos Tversky and Daniel Kahneman (1983) remind us, the conjunction of two events can't be more likely than either event alone.

Ignoring Base-Rate Information

As these experiments show, anecdotal information is persuasive. A research team led by Richard Nisbett (1976) explored the tendency to overuse such information. They showed University of Michigan students videotaped interviews of people who supposedly had participated in an experiment in which most subjects failed to assist a seizure victim. Learning how *most* subjects acted had little effect upon people's predictions of how the individual they observed acted. The apparent niceness of this individual was more vivid and compelling than the general truth about how most subjects really acted: "Ted seems so

Vivid, memorable—and therefore cognitively available—events influence our perceptions of the social world.

pleasant that I can't imagine him being unresponsive to another's plight." This experiment illustrates the **base-rate fallacy:** Focusing upon the specific individual can push into the background useful information about the population the person came from and distort our perception of what is generally true. Our impressions of a group, for example, tend to be overly influenced by its extreme members. When an American murdered a Norwegian some years ago, there was talk in Norway of expelling all Americans (Triandis, 1994). As psychologist Gordon Allport put it, "Given a thimbleful of facts we rush to make generalizations as large as a tub."

People *will* use base-rate data when their relevance is obvious (Ginossar & Trope, 1987; Krosnick & others, 1990). If told that students taking a particular exam had a high failure rate, we infer the exam was difficult. This lowers our estimated likelihood of a particular student passing the exam. Moreover, argues Norbet Schwarz (1994), subjects in experiments overuse anecdotal information because they presume—following the normal rules of conversation—that "if the experimenter provides it, I should use it."

Nevertheless, the research reveals a basic principle of social thinking: People are slow to deduce particular instances from a general truth but are remarkably quick to infer general truth from a vivid instance. No wonder that after hearing and reading countless instances of rapes, robberies, and beatings, 9 out of 10 Canadians overestimate—usually by a considerable margin—the percentage of crimes that involve violence (Doob & Roberts, 1988).

Sometimes the vivid example is a personal experience. Before buying a new Honda, I consulted the *Consumer Reports* survey of car owners and found the repair record of the Dodge Colt, which for a time I considered, to be quite good. A short while later, I mentioned my interest in the Colt to a student. "Oh no," he moaned, "don't buy a Colt. I worked in a garage last summer and serviced two Dodge Colts that kept falling apart and being brought in for one thing after another." How did I use this information—and the glowing testimonies from two friends who were Honda owners? Did I simply add to the *Consumer Reports* surveys of Colt and Honda owners two more people each? Although I knew that, logically, that is what I should have done, it was nearly impossible to ignore my awareness of those vivid accounts. I bought the Honda.

The Availability Heuristic

Consider: Does the letter *k* appear more often as the first letter of a word or as the third letter? Do more people live in Cambodia or Tanzania?

You probably answered in terms of how readily instances of them come to mind. If examples are readily *available* in our memory—as letters beginning with *k* and as Cambodians tend to be—then we presume that the event is commonplace. Usually it is, so we are often well served by this cognitive rule of thumb, called the **availability heuristic.** But sometimes the rule deludes us. Vivid, easy-to-imagine events, such as diseases with easy-to-picture symptoms, may seem more likely than harder-to-picture events (MacLeod & Campbell, 1992; Sherman & others, 1985). Even fictional happenings in novels, television, and movies leave images that later penetrate our judgments (Gerrig & Prentice, 1991).

The availability heuristic explains why powerful anecdotes are often more compelling than base-rate statistical information, and why perceived risk is

Base-rate fallacy:
The tendency to ignore or underuse base-rate information (information that describes most people) and instead to be influenced by distinctive features of the case being judged.

"Most people reason dramatically, not quantitatively."
Jurist Oliver Wendell Holmes, Jr., 1809–1894

"Testimonials may be more compelling than mountains of facts and figures (as mountains of facts and figures in social psychology so compellingly demonstrate)."
Mark Snyder (1988)

Availability heuristic:
An efficient but fallible rule-of-thumb that judges the likelihood of things in terms of their availability in memory. If instances of something come readily to mind, we presume it to be commonplace.

■ **FIGURE 3–6**
Menstruation, actual mood, and perceived mood. Ontario women's daily mood reports did not vary across their menstrual cycle. Yet they perceived that their moods were generally worse just before and during menstruation and better at other times of the cycle.
(Data from C. McFarland & others, 1989.)

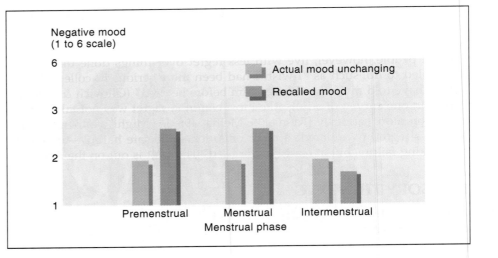

"I see men ordinarily more eager to discover a reason for things than to find out whether the things are so."
French essayist Montaigne, 1533–1592

Illusion of control: Perception of uncontrollable events as subject to one's control or as more controllable than they are.

irritability? Because, say Kato and Ruble, their implicit theories of menstruation lead them to notice and remember the joint appearances of negative moods and the onset of menstruation, but not to notice and remember bad moods two weeks later.

This intense human desire to find order, even in random events, leads us to seek reasons for unusual happenings or mystifying mood fluctuations. By attributing events to a cause, we order our worlds and make things seem more predictable and controllable. Again, this tendency is usually adaptive but occasionally leads us astray.

Illusion of Control

Our tendency to perceive random events as related feeds an **illusion of control**—the idea that chance events are subject to our influence. This is what keeps gamblers going, and what makes the rest of us do all sorts of unlikely things. During the 1988 summer drought, for example, retired farmer Elmer Carlson arranged a rain dance by 16 Hopis in Audubon, Iowa. The next day it rained 1 inch. "The miracles are still here, we just have to ask for them," explained Carlson (Associated Press, 1988).

Gambling

Ellen Langer (1977) demonstrated the illusion of control with experiments on gambling. Compared to those given an assigned lottery number, people who chose their own number demanded four times as much money when asked about selling their ticket. When playing a game of chance against an awkward and nervous person, they bet significantly more than when playing against a dapper, confident opponent. In these and other ways, Langer and others consistently find people acting as if they can control chance events.

Observations of real-life gamblers confirm these experimental findings. Dice players may throw softly for low numbers and hard for high numbers (Henslin, 1967). The gambling industry thrives on gamblers' illusions. Gamblers attribute wins to their skill and foresight. Losses become "near misses" or "flukes"—perhaps (for the sports gambler) a bad call by the referee or a freakish bounce of the ball (Gilovich & Douglas, 1986). When their sense of control is undermined by stress, people prefer to *predict* their roll of a die (giving them an illusion of control) rather than to guess the outcome *after* the roll (Friedland & others, 1992).

Regression Toward the Average

Tversky and Kahneman (1974) noted another way by which an illusion of control may arise: We fail to recognize the statistical phenomenon of **regression toward the average**. Because exam scores fluctuate partly by chance, most students who get extremely high scores on an exam will get lower scores on the next exam. Because their first score is at the ceiling, their second score is more likely to fall back ("regress") toward their own average than to push the ceiling even higher. (This is why a student who does consistently good work, even

Regression toward the average:
The statistical tendency for extreme scores or extreme behavior to return toward one's average.

"The next dance you will see is for partly cloudy conditions with moderating temperatures."

Peter Steiner

The illusion of control takes many forms.

Regression to the average: When we are at an extremely low point, anything we try, like meditation or yoga, will usually seem effective as we return to our more usual state.

if never the best, will sometimes end a course at the top of the class.) Conversely, the lowest-scoring students on the first exam are likely to improve. If those who scored lowest go for tutoring after the first exam, the tutors are likely to feel effective when the student improves, even if the tutoring had no effect.

Indeed, when things reach a low point, we will try anything, and whatever we try—going to a psychotherapist, starting a new diet-exercise plan, reading a self-help book—is more likely to be followed by improvement than by further deterioration. Sometimes we recognize that events are not likely to continue at an unusually good or bad extreme. Experience has taught us that when everything is going great, something will go wrong, and that when life is dealing us terrible blows, we can usually look forward to things getting better. Often, though, we fail to recognize this regression effect. We puzzle at why baseball's rookie-of-the-year often has a more ordinary second year—did he become overconfident? self-conscious? We forget that exceptional performance tends to regress toward normality.

To simulate the consequences of using praise and punishment, Paul Schaffner (1985) invited Bowdoin College students to train an imaginary fourth-grade boy, "Harold," to come to school by 8:30 each morning. For each school day of a three-week period, a computer displayed Harold's arrival time, which was always between 8:20 and 8:40. The subjects would then select a response to Harold, ranging from strong praise to strong reprimand. As you might expect, they usually praised Harold when he arrived before 8:30 and reprimanded him when he arrived after 8:30. Because Schaffner had programmed the computer to display a random sequence of arrival times, Harold's arrival time tended to improve (to regress toward 8:30) after being reprimanded. For example, if Harold arrived at 8:39, he was almost sure to be reprimanded, and his randomly selected next-day arrival time was likely to be earlier than 8:39. Thus, *even though their reprimands were having no effect,* most subjects ended the experiment believing that their reprimands had been effective.

This experiment demonstrates Tversky and Kahneman's provocative conclusion: Nature operates in such a way that we often feel punished for rewarding others and rewarded for punishing them. In actuality, as every student of psychology knows, positive reinforcement for doing things right is usually more effective and has fewer negative side effects.

MOOD AND JUDGMENT

Social judgment involves efficient, though fallible, information processing. It also involves our feelings: Our moods infuse our judgments. We are not cool computing machines, we are emotional creatures. The extent to which feeling infuses cognition appears in new studies comparing happy and sad individuals (Myers, 1993). Unhappy people—especially those bereaved or depressed—tend to be lethargic, socially withdrawn, even hostile. They also are more self-focused and brooding. Unless it overwhelms people with hopelessness, a depressed mood motivates intense thinking—a search for information that makes one's environment more understandable and controllable (Weary & Edwards, 1994).

Happy people, by contrast, are strikingly energetic, decisive, creative, and sociable. Compared to unhappy people, they are more trusting, more loving, more responsive. If made temporarily happy by receiving a small gift while mall-shopping, they will report, a few moments later on an unrelated survey, that their cars and TV sets are working beautifully—better, if you took their word for it, than those belonging to folks who didn't receive a gift.

Happy people tolerate more frustration. Whether temporarily or enduringly happy, they are more loving and forgiving and less likely to exaggerate or over-interpret slight criticism. They choose long-term rewards over immediate small pleasures. Given a chance to look at happy pictures (people laughing, playing) and sad pictures (funerals, disasters), they literally spend more time looking at the brighter side. Sad people look more at the gloomy side of life, and prefer less upbeat people, stories, movies, and music.

The dramatic effect of moods pervades our thinking. To West Germans enjoying their team's World Cup soccer victory (Schwarz & others, 1987) and to Australians emerging from a heartwarming movie (Forgas & Moylan, 1987), people seem good-hearted, life seems wonderful. After (but not before) a 1990 football game between rivals Alabama and Auburn, victorious Alabama fans deemed war less likely and potentially devastating than did the gloomier Auburn fans (Schweitzer & others, 1992). In a happy mood, the world seems friendlier, decisions are easier, good news more readily comes to mind (Johnson & Tversky, 1983; Isen & Means, 1983; Stone & Glass, 1986). When we *feel* happy, we *think* happy and optimistic thoughts. *Currently* depressed people recall their parents as having been rejecting and punitive. But *formerly* depressed people recall their parents in the same positive terms as do never-depressed people (Lewinsohn & Rosenbaum, 1987).

Let our mood turn gloomy, and our thoughts switch onto a different track. Off come the rose-colored glasses; on come the dark glasses. Now the bad mood primes our recollections of negative events (Bower, 1987; Johnson & Magaro, 1987). Our relationships seem to sour. Our self-image takes a dive. Our hopes for the future dim. Other people's behavior seems more sinister (Brown & Taylor, 1986; Mayer & Salovey, 1987).

Imagine yourself in an experiment by Joseph Forgas and his colleagues (1984). Using hypnosis, they put you in a good or bad mood and then have you watch a videotape (made the day before) of yourself talking with someone. If made to feel happy, you feel pleased with what you see, and you are able to detect many instances of your poise, interest, and social skill. If put in a bad mood, viewing the same tape seems to reveal a quite different you—one who is frequently stiff, nervous, and inarticulate (Figure 3–7). Given how your mood colors your judgments, you feel relieved at how things brighten when the experimenter switches you to a happy mood before leaving the experiment. Curiously, note Michael Ross and Garth Fletcher (1985), we don't attribute our changing perceptions to our mood shifts. Rather, the world really seems different.

Our moods color how we see our worlds partly by bringing to mind past experiences associated with the mood. In a bad mood we have more depressing thoughts. Mood-related thoughts may distract us from complex thinking about something else. Thus, when emotionally aroused—when angry or even in a very good mood—we become more likely to make snap judgments and evaluate others based on stereotypes (Bodenhausen & others, 1994; Paulhus & Lim, 1994). (Besides, why risk a postgame great mood by thinking deeply about some novel issue, such as the likelihood of a war?)

Curiously, our moods have less effect on simple, "automatic" thinking than on complex, "effortful" thinking (Hartlage & others, 1993). Thus, notes Forgas (1994, 1995), moods are most likely to invade thinking when we evaluate unusual rather than typical people, explain complex rather than simple human conflicts, and make sense of odd rather than well-matched couples. Thus, the more we think, the more our moods may infuse our thinking.

SUMMING UP

Research psychologists have for a long time explored the mind's impressive capacity for processing information. We have an enormous capacity for automatic, efficient, intuitive thinking. Our cognitive efficiency, though generally adaptive, comes at the price of occasional error. Since we are generally unaware of these errors entering our thinking, it can pay us to identify ways in which we form and sustain false beliefs—"reasons for unreason."

■ FIGURE 3–7

A temporary good or bad mood strongly influenced people's ratings of their videotaped behavior. Those in a bad mood detected far fewer positive behaviors.

(Forgas & others, 1984.)

BEHIND THE SCENES

We all know moody people, and I have often been struck by how their feelings seem to invade their thinking. It almost appears that their memories and judgments change with the color of their mood. For some years now, I have been trying to understand how and why this mood infusion occurs.

One day while sitting in a restaurant, I noticed an odd couple at the next table—a beautiful young woman with an unattractive elderly man. As I found myself repeatedly wondering about this relationship, it occurred to me that the more I thought about them, the more opportunity there might be for my mood to infuse my thoughts. Testing this idea in the laboratory, we found that, indeed, mood had a greater effect on complex judgments of odd couples than on snap judgments of well-matched couples. Such findings have helped us to develop a theory that predicts when moodiness will infuse judgments.

JOSEPH FORGAS, *University of New South Wales*, Sydney, Australia

First, our preconceptions strongly influence how we interpret and remember events. In experiments, people's prejudgments have striking effects upon how they perceive and interpret information. Other experiments have planted judgments or false ideas in people's minds *after* they have been given information. These experiments reveal that as before-the-fact judgments bias our perceptions and interpretations, so after-the-fact judgments bias our recall.

Second, we often overestimate our judgments. This "overconfidence phenomenon" stems partly from the much greater ease with which we can imagine why we might be right than why we might be wrong. Moreover, people are much more likely to search for information that can confirm their beliefs than information that can disconfirm them.

Third, when given compelling anecdotes or even useless information, we often ignore useful base-rate information. This is partly due to the later ease of recall ("availability") of vivid information.

Fourth, we are often swayed by illusions of correlation and personal control. It is tempting to perceive correlations where none exist ("illusory correlation") and to think we can control events which are really beyond our control (the "illusion of control").

Finally, moods infuse judgments. Good and bad moods trigger memories of experiences associated with those moods. Moods color our interpretation of current experiences. And by distracting us, moods can also influence how deeply or superficially we think when making judgments.

■ SELF-FULFILLING BELIEFS

*H*aving considered how we explain and judge others—efficiently, adaptively, but sometimes wrongly—we conclude by pondering the effects of our social judgments. Do our beliefs about social reality change reality?

formance. Teachers were judged most capable when assigned a student who nonverbally conveyed positive expectations.

To see whether such effects might also occur in actual classrooms, a research team led by David Jamieson (1987) experimented with four Ontario high school classes taught by a newly transferred teacher. During individual interviews they told students in two of the classes that both other students and the research team rated the teacher very highly. Compared to the control classes, whose expectations they did not raise, the students given positive expectations paid better attention during class. At the end of the teaching unit, they also got better grades and rated the teacher as clearer in her teaching. The attitudes that a class has toward its teacher are as important, it seems, as the teacher's attitude toward the students.

GETTING FROM OTHERS WHAT WE EXPECT

So, the expectations of experimenters and teachers, though usually reasonably accurate assessments, occasionally act as self-fulfilling prophecies. How general is this effect? Do we get from others what we expect of them? There are times when negative expectations of someone lead us to be extra nice to that person, which induces them to be nice in return—thus *dis*confirming our expectations. But a more common finding in studies of social interaction is that, yes, we do to some extent get what we expect (Olson & others, 1996).

In laboratory games, hostility nearly always begets hostility: People who *perceive* their opponents as noncooperative will readily induce them to *be* noncooperative (Kelley & Stahelski, 1970). Self-confirming beliefs abound when there is conflict. Each party's perception of the other as aggressive, resentful, and vindictive induces the other to display these behaviors in self-defense, thus creating a vicious self-perpetuating circle. Whether I expect my wife to be in a bad mood or in a warm, loving mood may affect how I relate to her, thereby inducing her to confirm my belief.

Several experiments conducted by Mark Snyder (1984) at the University of Minnesota show how, once formed, erroneous beliefs about the social world can induce others to confirm those beliefs, a phenomenon called **behavioral confirmation**. In a now-classic study, Snyder, Elizabeth Tanke, and Ellen Berscheid (1977) had men students talk on the telephone with women they thought (from having been shown a picture) were either attractive or unattractive. Analysis of just the women's comments during the conversations revealed that the supposedly attractive women spoke more warmly than the supposedly unattractive women. The men's erroneous beliefs had become a self-fulfilling prophecy by leading them to act in a way that influenced the women to fulfill their stereotype that beautiful people are desirable people.

Expectations influence children's behavior, too. After observing the amount of litter in three classrooms, Richard Miller and his colleagues (1975) had the teacher and others repeatedly tell one class that they should be neat and tidy. This persuasion increased the amount of litter placed in wastebaskets from 15 to 45 percent, but only temporarily. Another class, which also had been placing only 15 percent of its litter in wastebaskets, was repeatedly congratulated for being so neat and tidy. After eight days of hearing this, and still two weeks later, these children were fulfilling the expectation by putting more than 80 percent of their litter in wastebaskets. Repeatedly tell children they are hard-work-

Behavioral confirmation:
A type of self-fulfilling prophecy whereby people's social expectations lead them to act in ways that cause others to confirm their expectations.

ing and kind (rather than lazy and mean), and they may live up to their label.

These experiments help us understand how social beliefs, such as stereotypes about people with disabilities or about people of a particular race or sex, may be self-confirming. We help construct our own social realities. How others treat us reflects how we and others have treated them.

As with every social phenomenon, the tendency to confirm others' expectations has its limits. Expectations often predict behavior simply because they are accurate (Jussim, 1993). Also, people who are forewarned about another's expectation may work to overcome it (Hilton & Darley, 1985; Swann, 1987). If Chuck knows Jane thinks he's an airhead, he may strive to disprove her impression. If Jane knows that Chuck expects her to be aloof, she may actively refute his expectation.

William Swann and Robin Ely (1984) report another condition under which we are unlikely to confirm others' expectations: when our expectations clash with a clear self-concept. For example, Swann and Ely found that when a strongly outgoing person was interviewed by someone who expected her to be introverted, the interviewer's perceptions changed, not the interviewee's behavior. In contrast, interviewees who were unsure of themselves more often lived up to the interviewer's expectations.

Our beliefs about ourselves can also be self-fulfilling. In several experiments, Steven Sherman (1980) found that people often fulfill predictions they make of their own behavior. When Bloomington, Indiana, residents were called and asked to volunteer three hours to an American Cancer Society drive, only 4 percent agreed to do so. When a comparable group of other residents were

---

FOCUS

THE SELF-FULFILLING PSYCHOLOGY OF THE STOCK MARKET

On the evening of January 6, 1981, Joseph Granville, a popular Florida investment adviser, wired his clients: "Stock prices will nose-dive; sell tomorrow." Word of Granville's advice soon spread, and January 7 became the heaviest day of trading in the previous history of the New York Stock Exchange. All told, stock values lost $40 billion.

Nearly a half-century ago, John Maynard Keynes likened such stock market psychology to the popular beauty contests then conducted by London newspapers. To win, one had to pick the six faces out of a hundred that were, in turn, chosen most frequently by the other newspaper contestants. Thus, as Keynes wrote, "Each competitor has to pick not those faces which he himself finds prettiest, but those which he thinks likeliest to catch the fancy of the other competitors."

Investors likewise try to pick not the stocks that touch their fancy but the stocks that other investors will favor. The name of the game is predicting others' behavior. As one Wall Street fund manager explained, "You may or may not agree with Granville's view—but that's usually beside the point." If you think his advice will cause others to sell, then you want to sell quickly, before prices drop more. If you expect others to buy, you buy now to beat the rush.

The self-fulfilling psychology of the stock market worked to an extreme on Monday, October 19, 1987, when the Dow Jones Industrial average crashed 508 points, causing people to lose—on paper—about 20 percent of the value of their stock investments. Part of what happens during such slides is that the media and rumor mill focus on whatever bad news is available to explain them. Once reported, the explanatory news stories further diminish people's expectations, causing declining prices to fall still lower—and vice versa with a focus on good news when stock prices are rising.

called and asked to *predict* how they would react if they were to receive such a request, almost half predicted they would agree to help—and most of these did indeed agree to do so when they were contacted by the Cancer Society. Formulating a plan for how we would want to act in a given situation makes it more likely that we will really do it.

S U M M I N G   U P

Our beliefs sometimes take on a life of their own. Usually, our beliefs about others have a basis in reality. But studies of experimenter bias and teacher expectations show that an erroneous belief that certain people are unusually capable (or incapable) can lead teachers and researchers to give those people special treatment. This may elicit superior (or inferior) performance and, therefore, seem to confirm an assumption that is actually false. Similarly, in everyday life we often get "behavioral confirmation" of what we expect.

■ CONCLUSIONS

Social cognition studies reveal that our information-processing powers are impressive for their efficiency and adaptiveness ("in apprehension how like a god!" exclaimed Shakespeare's Hamlet), yet vulnerable to predictable errors and misjudgments ("headpiece filled with straw," said T. S. Eliot). What practical lessons, and what insights into human nature, can we take home from this research?

We could extend our list of reasons for unreason, but surely this has been a sufficient glimpse at how people come to believe what may be untrue. We cannot easily dismiss these experiments: Most of their participants were intelligent people, mostly students at leading universities. Moreover, these predictable distortions and biases occurred even when payment for right answers motivated people to think optimally. As one researcher concluded, the illusions "have a persistent quality not unlike that of perceptual illusions" (Slovic, 1972).

Research in cognitive social psychology thus mirrors the mixed review given humanity in literature, philosophy, and religion. Many research psychologists have spent lifetimes exploring the awesome capacities of the human mind (Manis, 1977). We are smart enough to have cracked our own genetic code, to have invented talking computers, to have sent people to the moon. Three cheers for human reason.

Well, two cheers—because the mind's premium on efficient judgment makes our intuition more vulnerable to *mis*judgment than we suspect. With remarkable ease, we form and sustain false beliefs. Led by our preconceptions, overconfident, persuaded by vivid anecdotes, perceiving correlations and control even where none may exist, we construct our social beliefs and then influence others to confirm them. "The naked intellect," observed novelist Madeline L'Engle, "is an extraordinarily inaccurate instrument."

"In creating these problems, we didn't set out to fool people. All our problems fooled us, too."
Amos Tversky (1985)

But have these experiments just been intellectual tricks played on hapless participants, thus making them look worse than they are? Richard Nisbett and Lee Ross (1980) contend that, if anything, laboratory procedures *over*estimate our intuitive powers. The experiments usually present people with clear evidence and warn them that their reasoning ability is being tested. Seldom does life say to us: "Here is some evidence. Now put on your intellectual Sunday best and answer these questions."

Often our everyday failings are inconsequential, but not always so. False impressions, interpretations, and beliefs can produce serious consequences. Even small biases can have profound social effects when we are making important social judgments: Why are so many people homeless? unhappy? homicidal? Does my friend love me or my money? Cognitive biases even creep into sophisticated scientific thinking. Apparently human nature has not changed in the 3000 years since the Psalmist noted that "no one can see his own errors."

Lest we succumb to the cynical conclusion that *all* beliefs are absurd, I hasten to balance the picture. The elegant analyses of the imperfections of our thinking are themselves a tribute to human wisdom. (Were one to argue that *all* human thought is illusory, the assertion would be self-refuting, for it, too, would be but an illusion. It would be logically equivalent to contending "all generalizations are false, including this one.")

As medical science assumes that any given body organ serves a function, so behavioral scientists find it useful to assume that *our modes of thought and behavior are generally adaptive* (Funder, 1987; Kruglanski & Ajzen, 1983; Swann, 1984). The rules of thought that produce false beliefs and striking deficiencies in our statistical intuition usually serve us well. Frequently, the errors are a by-product of our mental shortcuts that simplify the complex information we receive.

Nobel laureate psychologist Herbert Simon (1957) was among the modern researchers who first described the bounds of human reason. Simon contends that to cope with reality, we simplify it. Consider the complexity of a chess game: The number of possible games is greater than the number of particles in the universe. How do we cope? We adopt some simplifying rules of thumb—heuristics. These heuristics sometimes lead us to defeat. But they do enable us to make efficient snap judgments.

Illusory thinking can likewise spring from useful heuristics that aid our survival. The belief in our power to control events helps maintain hope and effort. If things are sometimes subject to control and sometimes not, we maximize our outcomes by positive thinking. Optimism pays dividends. We might even say that our beliefs are like scientific theories—sometimes in error yet useful as generalizations. As Susan Fiske (1992) says, "thinking is for doing."

As we constantly seek to improve our theories, might we not also work to reduce error in our social thinking? In school, math teachers teach, teach, teach until the mind is finally trained to process numerical information accurately and automatically. We assume that such ability does not come naturally; otherwise, why bother with the years of training? Research psychologist Robyn Dawes (1980)—who is dismayed that "study after study has shown [that] people have very limited abilities to process information on a conscious level, particularly social information"—suggests that we should also teach, teach, teach how to process social information.

Richard Nisbett and Lee Ross (1980) believe that education could indeed reduce our vulnerability to certain types of error. They propose that:

■ We train people to recognize likely sources of error in their own social intuition.

"The purposes in the human mind are like deep water, but the intelligent will draw them out."
Proverbs 20:5

"The spirit of liberty is the spirit which is not too sure that it is right; the spirit of liberty is the spirit which seeks to understand the minds of other men and women; the spirit of liberty is the spirit which weighs their interests alongside its own without bias."
Learned Hand, *The Spirit of Liberty*, 1952

FOCUS

HOW JOURNALISTS THINK: COGNITIVE BIAS IN NEWSMAKING

"That's the way it is," concluded CBS anchorperson Walter Cronkite at the end of each newscast. And that's the journalistic ideal—to present reality the way it is. The *Wall Street Journal* reporters' manual states the ideal plainly: "A reporter must never hold inflexibly to his preconceptions, straining again and again to find proof of them where little exists, ignoring contrary evidence. . . . Events, not preconceptions, should shape all stories to the end" (Blundell, 1986, p. 25).

We might wish that it were so. But journalists are human, conclude Indiana University journalism professor Holly Stocking and New York psychologist-lawyer Paget Gross in their 1989 book, *How Do Journalists Think?* Like laypeople and scientists, journalists "construct reality." The cognitive biases considered in this chapter therefore color newsmaking, in at least six ways.

1. *Preconceptions may control interpretations.* Typically, reporters "go after an idea," which may then affect how they interpret information. Beginning with the idea that homelessness reflects a failure of mental health programs, a reporter may interpret ambiguous information accordingly while discounting other complicating factors.
2. *Confirmation bias may guide them toward sources and questions that will confirm their preconceptions.* Hoping to report the newsworthy story that a radiation leak is causing birth defects, a reporter might interview someone who accepts the idea and then someone else recommended by the first person. Believing that devastating disabilities can be overcome, a reporter might ask disabled people, "How did you overcome the obstacles you faced?" Assuming that a coach is disliked, a reporter may interview the coach's detractors and ask *how* the coach offends people.
3. *Belief perseverance may sustain preconceptions in the face of discrediting.* While "greedy" Ivan Boesky

awaited sentencing on a 1987 Wall Street insider-trading scandal, he looked for volunteer work, something "a lot of white-collar crooks do to impress sentencing judges," noted a contemptuous reporter. On the other hand, a politician caught lying can, if respected, be reported as "confused" or "forgetful."

4. *Compelling anecdotes may seem more informative than base-rate information.* Like their readers, journalists may be more persuaded by vivid stories of ESP and other psychic happenings than by dispassionate research. They may be more taken by someone's apparent "cure" by a new therapy than by statistics on the therapy's success rate. After an air crash, they may describe "the frightening dangers of modern air travel," without noting its actual safety record.
5. *Events may seem correlated when they are not.* A striking co-occurrence—say three minority athletes' problems with drugs—may lead reporters to infer a relationship between race and drug use in the absence of representative evidence.
6. *Hindsight makes for easy after-the-fact analysis.* President Carter's ill-fated attempt to rescue American hostages in Iran was "doomed from the start"; so said journalists *after* they knew it had failed. George Bush's choice of Dan Quayle as his running mate was scorned by journalists *after* the negative public reaction and Quayle's gaffes and humbling television debate with his vice-presidential opponent. Decisions that turn out poorly have a way of seeming *obviously* dumb, after the fact.

Indeed, surmise Stocking and Gross, given all the information that reporters and editors must process quickly, how could they be immune to the illusory thinking tendencies that penetrate human thinking? But on the positive side, exposing these points of bias may alert journalists to ways of reducing them—by considering opposite conclusions, by seeking sources and asking questions that might counter their ideas, by seeking statistical information first and then seeking representative anecdotes, by remembering that well-meaning people make decisions without advance knowledge of their consequences.

■ We set up statistics courses geared to everyday problems of logic and social judgment. Given such training, people do in fact reason better about everyday events (Lehman & others, 1988; Nisbett & others, 1987).

■ We make such teaching more effective by richly illustrating it with concrete, vivid anecdotes and examples from everyday life.

■ We teach memorable and useful slogans, such as: "It's an empirical question." Or, "Which hat did you draw that sample out of?" Or, "You can lie with statistics, but a well-chosen example does the job better."

Is research on pride and error *too* humbling? Surely we can acknowledge the hard truth of our human limits and still sympathize with the deeper message that people are more than machines. Our subjective experiences are the stuff of our humanity—our art and our music, our enjoyment of friendship and love, our mystical and religious experiences.

The cognitive and social psychologists who explore illusory thinking are not out to remake us into logical machines. They know that intuition and feeling not only enrich human experience but also are an important source of creative ideas. They add, however, the humbling reminder that our susceptibility to error also makes clear the need for disciplined training of the mind. Norman Cousins (1978) called this "the biggest truth of all about learning: that its purpose is to unlock the human mind and to develop it into an organ capable of thought—conceptual thought, analytical thought, sequential thought."

"Rob the average man of his life-illusion, and you rob him also of his happiness."
Henrik Ibsen, *The Wild Duck*, 1884

R esearch on social beliefs and judgments reveals how we form and sustain beliefs that usually serve us well, but sometimes lead us astray. Even our misjudgments are by-products of thinking strategies (heuristics) that usually serve us well, just as visual illusions are a by-product of perceptual mechanisms that help us organize sensory information. But they are still errors, errors that can warp our perceptions of reality and prejudice our judgments of others.

SUMMING UP

■ FOR FURTHER READING

Fiske, S. T., & Taylor, S. E. (1991). *Social cognition*, 2d ed. New York: McGraw-Hill. A comprehensive, state-of-the-art introduction to how we form impressions and social beliefs and how we explain people's behavior.

Gilovich, T. (1991). *How we know what isn't so: The fallibility of human reason in everyday life*. New York: Free Press. A witty yet scientific book that offers fascinating examples of disastrous reasoning in everyday life.

Maital, S. (1982). *Minds, markets, and money: Psychological foundations of economic behavior*. New York: Basic Books. Insightfully applies social-psychological principles to people's beliefs and behavior regarding inflation, consumption, and the stock market.

BEHAVIOR AND ATTITUDES

Each year throughout the industrialized world, the tobacco industry kills some 2 million of its best customers (Peto & others, 1992). Given present trends, estimates a 1994 World Health Organization report, *half a billion* people alive today will be killed by tobacco. In the United States, for example, smoking kills 420,000 people a year—surpassing the combined fatalities from homicide, suicide, AIDS, car accidents, and alcohol and drug abuse. Although quick assisted suicide may be illegal, slow-motion suicide assisted by the tobacco industry is not.

People wonder: With the tobacco industry responsible for fatalities equal to 14 loaded and crashed jumbo jets a day (not including those in the expanding but hard to count third world market), how do tobacco company executives live with themselves? At Philip Morris, one of the world's two largest tobacco advertisers, upper-level executives—mostly intelligent, family-oriented, community-minded people—resent being called "mass murderers." They defend smokers' right to choose. "Is it an addiction issue?" asks one vice-president. "I don't believe it. People do all sorts of things to express their individuality and to protest against society. And smoking is one of them, and not the worst" (Rosenblatt, 1994).

Social psychologists wonder: Do such statements reflect privately held attitudes—or social pressure to say things one doesn't believe? Does this executive really think smoking is a comparatively healthy expression of individuality? If so, how are such attitudes internalized?

When people question someone's attitude, they refer to beliefs and feelings related to a person or event and their resulting behavior. Taken together, favorable or unfavorable *evaluative reactions*—whether exhibited in beliefs, feel-

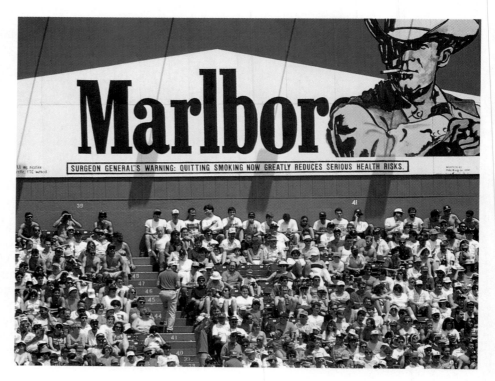

SURGEON GENERAL'S WARNING: QUITTING SMOKING NOW GREATLY REDUCES SERIOUS HEALTH RISKS.

Attitudes and actions: Many sports events, which glorify health and physical prowess, are sponsored by manufacturers of products like cigarettes, which are dangers to health. And the ads themselves are incongruous: Here's the stalwart cowboy, the Marlboro Man—accompanied by the Surgeon General's warning.

ings, or inclinations to act—define a person's **attitude** toward something (Olson & Zanna, 1993). Attitudes are an efficient way to size up the world. When we have to respond quickly to something, how we *feel* about it can guide how we react (Breckler & Wiggins, 1989; Sanbonmatsu & Fazio, 1990). For example, a person who *believes* a particular ethnic group is lazy and aggressive may *feel* dislike for such people and therefore *intend to act* in a discriminatory manner. When assessing attitudes, we tap one of these three dimensions. You can remember them as the ABCs of attitudes: *a*ffect (feelings), *b*ehavior (intention), and *c*ognition (thoughts).

The study of attitudes is close to social psychology's heart, and historically was one of its first concerns. So we continue our look at social thinking by asking, how do our attitudes affect our actions?

Attitude:
A favorable or unfavorable evaluative reaction toward something or someone, exhibited in one's beliefs, feelings, or intended behavior.

■ DO ATTITUDES DETERMINE BEHAVIOR?

To what extent, and under what conditions, do the attitudes of the heart drive our actions? Why were social psychologists at first surprised by a seeming lack of connection between attitudes and actions?

Asking whether attitudes determine behavior asks a basic question about human nature: What is the relationship between what we *are* (on the inside) and what we *do* (on the outside)? Philosophers, theologians, and educators have long speculated about the connection between thought and action, character and conduct, private word and public deed. The prevailing assumption, which underlies most teaching, counseling, and child rearing, has been that our private beliefs and feelings determine our public behavior. So, if we want to alter the way people act, we need to change their hearts and minds.

"The ancestor of every action is a thought."
Ralph Waldo Emerson,
Essays, First Series, 1841

ARE WE ALL HYPOCRITES?

In the beginning, social psychologists agreed: To know people's attitudes is to predict their actions. But in 1964, Leon Festinger—judged by some to have been social psychology's most important contributor (Gerard, 1994)—concluded the evidence did *not* show that changing attitudes changes behavior. Festinger believed the attitude-behavior relation works the other way around, with our behavior as the horse and our attitudes as the cart. As Robert Abelson (1972) put it, we are "very well trained and very good at finding reasons for what we do, but not very good at doing what we find reasons for."

A further blow to the supposed power of attitudes came in 1969, when social psychologist Allan Wicker reviewed several dozen research studies covering a wide variety of people, attitudes, and behaviors, and offered a shocking conclusion: People's expressed attitudes hardly predicted their varying behaviors. Student attitudes toward cheating bore little relation to the likelihood of their actually cheating. Attitudes toward the church were but modestly linked with church attendance on any given Sunday. Self-described racial attitudes provided little clue to behaviors in actual situations.

*"Between the idea
And the reality
Between the motion
And the Act
Falls the Shadow."*
T. S. Eliot, *The Hollow Men,*
1925

This was dramatically apparent during the early 1930s, when many Americans were expressing intense prejudice against Asians. To discern the extent of such prejudice, Richard LaPiere (1934) wrote 251 restaurants and hotels, asking, "Will you accept members of the Chinese race as guests in your establishment?" Among the 128 who replied, 92 percent said no, and only one said yes. But LaPiere and a "personable and charming" young Chinese couple had traveled the country six months previously and actually received courteous treatment at all but one of these establishments. Faced with specific people who defied the stereotypes, the proprietors laid aside their negative attitudes and behaved warmly.

If people don't play the same game that they talk, it's little wonder that attempts to change behavior by changing attitudes often fail. Warnings about the dangers of smoking only minimally affect those who already smoke. Increasing public awareness of the desensitizing and brutalizing effects of a prolonged diet of television violence has stimulated many people to voice a desire for less violent programming—yet they still watch media murder as much as ever. Appeals for safe driving have had far less effect on accident rates than have lower speed limits, divided highways, and drunk driving penalties (Etzioni, 1972).

While Wicker and others were describing the weakness of attitudes, some personality psychologists were saying that personality traits also fail to predict behavior (Mischel, 1968). If we want to know how helpful people are going to be, we usually won't learn much by giving them tests of self-esteem, anxiety, or defensiveness. If the situation makes clear-cut demands, we are better off knowing how they react. Likewise, many psychotherapists began to argue that talking therapies, such as psychoanalysis, seldom "cure" problems. Instead of analyzing personality defects, they began to try to change the problem behavior.

All in all, the developing picture of what controls behavior emphasized external social influences and played down internal factors, such as attitudes and personality. The emerging image was of little billiard balls that have different stripes and colors, to be sure, but are all buffeted by outside forces. In short, the original thesis that attitudes determine actions was countered during the 1960s by the antithesis that attitudes determine virtually nothing. Thesis. Antithesis. Is there a synthesis? The surprising finding that what people say often differs from what they do sent social psychologists scurrying to find out why. Surely, we reasoned, convictions and feelings *must* sometimes make a difference.

Indeed. In fact, what I am about to explain now seems so obvious that I wonder why most social psychologists (myself included) were not thinking this way before the early 1970s. I must remind myself that truth never seems obvious until it is known.

WHEN DO ATTITUDES PREDICT BEHAVIOR?

We sometimes violate our expressed attitudes because, as Figure 4–1 suggests, our behavior and our expressed attitudes are both subject to other influences. One social psychologist counted 40 separate factors that complicate their relationship (Triandis, 1982; see also Kraus, 1995). If we could just neutralize the other influences—make all other things equal—might attitudes accurately predict behaviors? Let's see.

"It may be desirable to abandon the attitude concept."
Alan Wicker (1971)

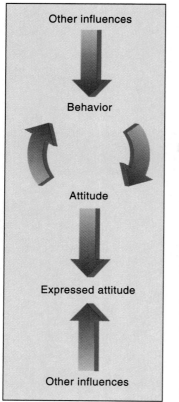

■ FIGURE 4–1
Our expressed attitudes imperfectly predict our behavior because both are subject to other influences.

Minimizing Social Influences on Expressed Attitudes

Unlike a physician measuring heart rate, social psychologists never get a direct reading on attitudes. Rather, we measure *expressed* attitudes. Like other behaviors, expressions are subject to outside influences. This was vividly demonstrated when the U.S. House of Representatives once overwhelmingly passed a salary increase for itself in an off-the-record vote, then moments later overwhelmingly defeated the same bill on a roll-call vote. Fear of criticism had distorted the true sentiment on the roll-call vote. We sometimes say what we think others want to hear.

Knowing that people don't wear their hearts on their sleeves, social psychologists have longed for a "pipeline to the heart." Edward Jones and Harold Sigall (1971) therefore devised a **bogus pipeline** method for measuring attitudes. In one experiment, conducted with Richard Page, Sigall (1971) had University of Rochester students hold a locked wheel that, if unlocked, could turn a pointer to the left, indicating disagreement, or to the right, indicating agreement. When electrodes were attached to their arms, the fake machine supposedly measured tiny muscular responses said to gauge their tendency to turn the wheel left (disagree) or right (agree). To demonstrate this amazing new machine, the researcher asked the students some questions. After a few moments of impressive flashing lights and whirring sounds, a meter on the machine announced the student's attitude—which was nothing more than an attitude the student had earlier expressed as part of a now-forgotten survey. The procedure convinced everyone.

Once the students were convinced, the attitude meter was hidden and they were asked questions concerning their attitudes toward African Americans and requested to guess what the meter revealed. How do you suppose these White collegians responded? Compared to other students who responded through a typical questionnaire, those responding by the bogus pipeline admitted more negative belief. Unlike those responding to the paper-and-pencil scale—who rated African Americans as being more sensitive than other Americans—those responding through the bogus pipeline reversed these judgments. It was as if they were thinking, "I'd better tell the truth or the experimenter will think I'm out of touch with myself."

Such findings suggest a reason why subjects who are first persuaded that lie detectors work may then admit the truth. They also suggest one reason for a weak attitude-behavior link: Under everyday conditions, such as those faced by tobacco executives and politicians, people sometimes express attitudes they don't privately hold.

Minimizing Other Influences on Behavior

Social influences color other behaviors as well. As Chapters 6 to 9 will illustrate again and again, social influences can be enormous—enormous enough to induce people to violate their deepest convictions. Before Jesus' crucifixion, his disciple Peter denied ever knowing him. Presidential aides may go along with actions they know are wrong. Prisoners of war may lie to placate their captors.

On any occasion it's not only our inner attitudes that guide us but also the situation we face. Would *averaging* many occasions enable us to detect more clearly the impact of our attitudes? Predicting people's behavior is like predicting a baseball player's hitting. The outcome of any particular time at bat is

Bogus pipeline:
A false procedure that fools people into disclosing their attitudes. Participants are first convinced that a new machine can use their psychological responses to measure their private attitudes. Then they are asked to predict the machine's reading, thus revealing their attitudes.

"Do I contradict myself? Very well then I contradict myself. (I am large, I contain multitudes.)"
Walt Whitman, *Song of Myself,* 1855

nearly impossible to predict, because it is affected not only by the batter but also by what the pitcher throws and by chance factors. When we aggregate many times at bat, we neutralize these complicating factors. Knowing the players, we can predict their approximate batting *averages*.

To use a comparable example from research, people's general attitude toward religion poorly predicts whether they will go to church next Sunday (because the weather, the preacher, how one is feeling, and so forth also influence church attendance). But religious attitudes predict quite well the total quantity of religious behaviors over time (Fishbein & Ajzen, 1974; Kahle & Berman, 1979). The findings define a *principle of aggregation*: The effects of an attitude on behavior become more apparent when we look at a person's aggregate or average behavior rather than at isolated acts.

Examining Attitudes Specific to the Behavior

Other conditions further improve the predictive accuracy of attitudes. As Icek Ajzen and Martin Fishbein (1977; Ajzen, 1982) point out, when the measured attitude is general—say, an attitude toward Asians—and the behavior is very specific—say, a decision whether to help the particular Asian couple in LaPiere's study—we should not expect a close correspondence between words and actions. Indeed, report Fishbein and Ajzen, in 26 out of 27 such research studies, attitudes did not predict behavior. But attitudes *did* predict behavior in all 26 studies they could find in which the measured attitude was directly pertinent to the situation. Thus, attitudes toward the general concept of "health fitness" poorly predict specific exercise and dietary practices. Whether people jog is more likely to depend on their opinions about the costs and benefits of *jogging*.

Further studies confirmed that specific, relevant attitudes *do* predict behavior (Kim & Hunter, 1993). For example, attitudes toward contraception strongly

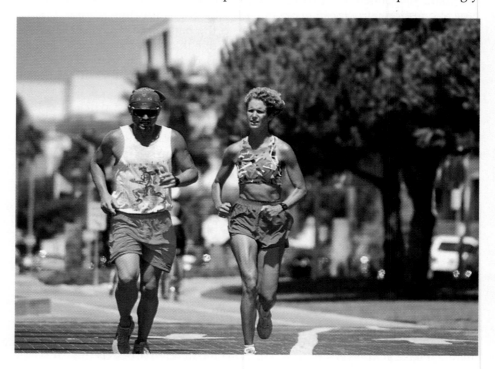

Compared to their general attitudes toward a healthy lifestyle, people's specific attitudes regarding jogging predict their jogging behavior much better.

predict contraceptive use (Morrison, 1989). And attitudes toward recycling (but not general attitudes toward environmental issues) predict participation in recycling (Oskamp, 1991). To change health habits through persuasion, we should alter people's attitudes toward *specific* practices (Olson & Zanna, 1981; Ajzen & Timko, 1986).

So far we have seen two conditions under which attitudes will predict behavior: (1) when we minimize other influences upon our attitude statements and our behavior and (2) when the attitude is specifically relevant to the observed behavior. There is a third condition: An attitude predicts behavior better when it is potent.

Maximizing Attitude Potency

Our attitudes often lie dormant when we act automatically, without pausing to consider them. We act out familiar scripts, without reflecting on what we're doing. We respond to people we meet in the hall with an automatic "Hi." We answer the restaurant cashier's question, "How was your meal?" by saying, "Fine," even if we found it terrible. Such mindless reaction is adaptive. It frees our minds to work on other things. As the philosopher Alfred North Whitehead argued, "Civilization advances by extending the number of operations which we can perform without thinking about them."

Bringing Attitudes to Mind

In novel situations our behavior is less automatic; lacking a script, we think before we act. If they are prompted to think about their attitudes before acting, will people be truer to themselves? Mark Snyder and William Swann (1976) wanted to find out. So two weeks after 120 of their University of Minnesota students indicated their attitudes toward affirmative-action employment policies, Snyder and Swann invited them to act as jurors in a sex-discrimination court case. Only if they first induced the students to remember their attitudes—by giving them "a few minutes to organize your thoughts and views on the affirmative-action issue"—did attitudes predict verdicts. Similarly, people who take a few moments to review their past behavior express attitudes that better predict their future behavior (Zanna & others, 1981). Our attitudes guide our behavior *if* they come to mind.

Self-conscious people usually are in tune with their own attitudes (Miller & Grush, 1986). This suggests another way experimenters can induce people to focus on their inner convictions: *Make* people self-conscious, perhaps by having them act in front of a mirror (Carver & Scheier, 1981). Maybe you can recall suddenly being acutely aware of yourself upon entering a room with a large mirror. Making people self-aware in this way promotes consistency between words and deeds (Gibbons, 1978; Froming & others, 1982).

Edward Diener and Mark Wallbom (1976) noted that nearly all college students *say* that cheating is morally wrong. But will they follow the advice of Shakespeare's Polonius, "To thine own self be true"? Diener and Wallbom set University of Washington students to work on an anagram-solving task (said to predict IQ) and told them to stop when a bell in the room sounded. Left alone, 71 percent cheated by working past the bell. Among students made self-aware—by working in front of a mirror while hearing their tape-recorded voices—only 7 percent cheated. It makes one wonder: Would eye-level mirrors in stores make people more conscious of their attitudes about stealing?

"Thinking is easy, acting difficult, and to put one's thoughts into action, the most difficult thing in the world."
German poet Goethe, 1749–1832

"Without doubt it is a delightful harmony when doing and saying go together."
Montaigne, *Essays*, 1588

Attitudes, we noted earlier, involve evaluations. An attitude is our association between an object and our evaluation of it. When this association is strong, the attitude becomes accessible: Encountering the object (perhaps a person of a different sexual orientation) calls up the associated evaluation. To strengthen the associations between object and evaluation, researchers have gotten people to rehearse their attitudes (by repeatedly stating their like or dislike of something or someone, for example). The more the rehearsal, the stronger the association between object and evaluation. And the stronger the association, the more accessible and potent the attitude of like or dislike (Fazio, 1995).

Situations may then automatically activate certain attitudes. Without conscious intention, our evaluative response to a liked or disliked group may influence how we *perceive* and *interpret* events, and therefore, how we react (Fazio, Presson, C.C., Chassin, L., Bensenberg, M., Corty, E., & Olshavsky, R., 1990). A basketball game activates fans' evaluations of the two teams. These spontaneously activated attitudes influence perceptions of who is fouling whom, and thus their reactions to referees' calls.

The Potency of Attitudes Forged through Experience

Finally, we acquire attitudes in a manner that makes them sometimes potent, sometimes not. An extensive series of experiments by Russell Fazio and Mark Zanna (1981) shows that when attitudes arise from experience, they are far more likely to endure and to guide actions. They conducted one of their studies with the unwitting help of Cornell University. A housing shortage forced the university to assign some first-year students to several weeks on cots in dormitory lounges, while others basked in the relative luxury of permanent rooms.

When questioned by Dennis Regan and Fazio (1977), students in both groups had equally negative attitudes about the housing situation and how the administration was dealing with it. Given opportunities to act upon their attitudes—to sign a petition and solicit other signatures, to join a committee to investigate the situation, to write a letter—only those whose attitudes grew from direct experience with the temporary housing acted. Moreover, compared to attitudes formed passively, those forged in the fire of experience are more thoughtful, more certain, more stable, more resistant to attack, and more accessible (Sherman & others, 1983; Watts, 1967; Wu & Shaffer, 1988).

Some Conclusions

To summarize, our attitudes predict our actions if

■ Other influences are minimized
■ The attitude is specific to the action
■ The attitude is potent—because something reminds us of it, because the situation activates an unconscious attitude that subtly guides how we perceive and react to events, or because we gained it in a manner that makes it strong

Do these conditions seem obvious? It may be tempting to think we "knew them all along." But remember: They were not obvious to researchers in 1970. Nor were they obvious to the German university students who were unable to guess the outcomes of published studies on attitude-behavior consistency (Six & Krahe, 1984).

So it is now plain that, depending on the circumstances, the relationship between attitude statements and behavior can range from no relationship to a

"It is easier to preach virtue than to practice it."
La Rochefoucauld, *Maxims,* 1665

strong one (Kraus, 1995). Yet we can breathe a sigh of relief that our attitudes are, after all, *one* determinant of our actions. To return to our philosophical question, there *is* a connection between what we are and what we do, even if that connection is looser than most of us would have guessed.

Ηow do our inner attitudes relate to our external actions? Social psychologists agree that attitudes and actions feed each other. Popular wisdom stresses the impact of attitudes on action. Surprisingly, our attitudes—usually assessed as our feelings toward some object or person—are often poor predictors of our actions. Moreover, changing people's attitudes typically fails to produce much change in their behavior. These findings sent social psychologists scurrying to find out why we so often fail to play the game we talk. The answer: Our expressions of attitudes and our behaviors are each subject to many influences.

Our attitudes *will* predict our behavior (1) if these "other influences" are minimized, (2) if the attitude corresponds very closely to the predicted behavior (as in voting studies), and (3) if the attitude is potent (because something reminds us of it, because the situation subtly activates it, or because we acquired it in a manner that makes it strong). Thus there *is* a connection between what we think and feel and what we do, but in many situations that connection is looser than we'd like to believe.

SUMMING UP

■ DOES BEHAVIOR DETERMINE ATTITUDES?

If social psychology has taught us anything during the last 25 years, it is that we are likely not only to think ourselves into a way of acting but also to act ourselves into a way of thinking. What lines of evidence support this assertion?

Now we turn to the more startling idea that behavior determines attitudes. It's true that we sometimes stand up for what we believe, but it's also true that we come to believe in what we stand up for (Figure 4–2). Social-psychological

"Thought is the child of Action."
Benjamin Disraeli, *Vivian Grey*, 1826

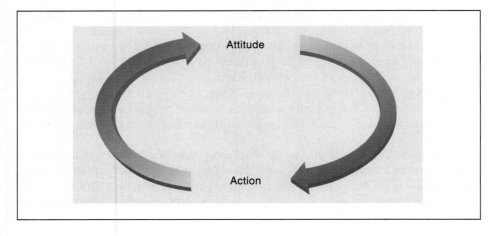

■ FIGURE 4–2
Attitudes and actions generate one another, like chickens and eggs.

theories inspired much of the research that underlies this conclusion. Instead of beginning with these theories, I think it more interesting to first present the wide-ranging evidence that behavior affects attitudes. Now you can play theorist as you read. Speculate *why* actions affect attitudes, and then compare your ideas with the explanations proposed by social psychologists.

Consider the following incidents, each based on actual happenings:

■ Sarah is hypnotized and told to take off her shoes when a book drops on the floor. Fifteen minutes later a book drops, and Sarah quietly slips out of her loafers. "Sarah," asks the hypnotist, "why did you take off your shoes?" "Well . . . my feet are hot and tired," Sarah replies. "It has been a long day." The act produces the idea.

■ George has electrodes temporarily implanted in the brain region that controls his head movements. When neurosurgeon José Delgado (1973) stimulates the electrode by remote control, George always turns his head. Unaware of the remote stimulation, he offers a reasonable explanation for it: "I'm looking for my slipper." "I heard a noise." "I'm restless." "I was looking under the bed."

■ Carol's severe seizures were relieved by surgically separating her two brain hemispheres. Now, in an experiment, psychologist Michael Gazzaniga (1985) flashes a picture of a nude woman to the left half of Carol's field of vision and thus to her nonverbal right brain hemisphere. A sheepish smile spreads over her face, and she begins chuckling. Asked why, she invents—and apparently believes—a plausible explanation: "Oh—that funny machine." Frank, another split-brain patient, has the word "smile" flashed to his nonverbal right hemisphere. He obliges and forces a smile. Asked why, he explains, "This experiment is very funny."

The mental aftereffects of our behavior indeed appear in a rich variety of social situations. The following examples will illustrate the power of self-persuasion—of attitudes following behavior.

ROLE PLAYING

Role:
A set of norms that define how people in a given social position ought to behave.

The word **role** is borrowed from the theater and, as in the theater, refers to prescribed actions—actions expected of those who occupy a particular social position. When stepping into a new social role, we must perform its actions, even if we feel phony. But our sense of phoniness seldom lasts.

Think of a time when you stepped into some new role—perhaps your first days on a job, or at college, or in a sorority or fraternity. That first week on campus, for example, you may have been supersensitive to your new social situation and tried valiantly to act appropriately and root out your high school behavior. At such times we feel self-conscious. We observe our new speech and actions because they aren't natural to us. Then one day an amazing thing happens: We notice that our sorority enthusiasm or our pseudo-intellectual talk no longer feels forced. The role has begun to fit as comfortably as our old jeans and T-shirt.

"No man, for any considerable period, can wear one face to himself and another to the multitude without finally getting bewildered as to which may be true."
Nathaniel Hawthorne, 1850

In one study, college men volunteered to spend time in a simulated prison constructed in Stanford's psychology department by Philip Zimbardo (1971). Zimbardo, like so many others, wondered whether prison brutality is a product of evil prisoners and malicious guards, or whether the institutional roles of

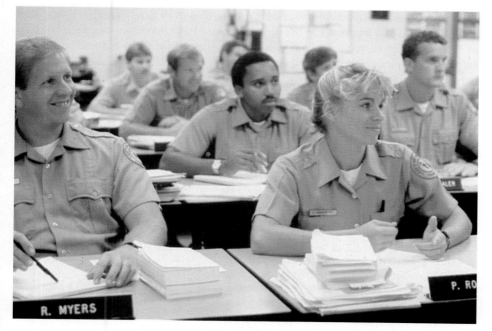

Before long, these Austin, Texas, police cadets will be internalizing attitudes appropriate to their new role.

guard and prisoner would embitter and harden even compassionate people? Do the people make the place violent? Or does the place make the people violent?

By a flip of a coin, he designated some students as guards. He gave them uniforms, billy clubs, and whistles and instructed them to enforce the rules. The other half, the prisoners, were locked in cells and made to wear humiliating outfits. After a jovial first day of "playing" their roles, the guards and prisoners, and even the experimenters, got caught up in the situation. The guards began to disparage the prisoners, some also devising cruel and degrading routines. The prisoners broke down, rebelled, or became apathetic. There developed, reported Zimbardo (1972b), a "growing confusion between reality and illusion, between role-playing and self-identity. . . . This prison which we had created . . . was absorbing us as creatures of its own reality." Observing the emerging social pathology, Zimbardo was forced to call off the planned two-week simulation after only six days.

The effect of behavior on attitude appears even in the theater. Self-conscious acting may diminish as the actor becomes absorbed in the role and experiences genuine emotion. In William Golding's novel *Lord of the Flies*, a group of shipwrecked English boys become wild and exhibit brutal, uncivilized behavior. When a movie version of the book was made, the youngsters who acted in it became the creatures defined by their roles. The director, Peter Brook (1969), reported that "Many of their off-screen relationships completely paralleled the story, and one of our main problems was to encourage them to be uninhibited within the shots but disciplined in between them" (p. 163). Jonathan Winters has remarked that a hazard for stand-up comics like himself is that "You get to believing your own stuff." After several years of constructing fantastic characters, Winters underwent therapy to treat a confused personal identity (Elliott, 1986).

"My whole personality changed during the time I was doing the part."
Ian Charleson on his role as serene and devout Olympic hero Eric Liddell in *Chariots of Fire*

The deeper lesson of role-playing studies concerns how what is unreal (an artificial role) can evolve into what is real. In a new career, as teacher, soldier, or businessperson, we act a role that shapes our attitudes. Imagine playing the role of slave—not just for six days but for decades. If a few days altered the behavior of those in Zimbardo's "prison," then imagine the corrosive effects of decades of subservient behavior. The master may be even more profoundly affected, because the master's role is chosen. Frederick Douglass, a former slave, recalls his slave mistress's transformation as she absorbed her role:

> My new mistress proved to be all she appeared when I first met her at the door—a woman of the kindest heart and finest feelings. She had never had a slave under her control previously to myself, and prior to her marriage she had been dependent upon her own industry for a living. She was by trade a weaver; and by constant application to her business, she had been in a good degree preserved from the blighting and dehumanizing effects of slavery. I was utterly astonished at her goodness. I scarcely knew how to behave towards her. She was entirely unlike any other white woman I had ever seen. I could not approach her as I was accustomed to approach other white ladies. My early instruction was all out of place. The crouching servility, usually so acceptable a quality in a slave, did not answer when manifested toward her. Her favor was not gained by it; she seemed to be disturbed by it. She did not deem it impudent or unmannerly for a slave to look her in the face. The meanest slave was put fully at ease in her presence, and none left without feeling better for having seen her. Her face was made of heavenly smiles, and her voice of tranquil music.
>
> But, alas! this kind heart had but a short time to remain such. The fatal poison of irresponsible power was already in her hands, and soon commenced its infernal work. That cheerful eye, under the influence of slavery, soon became red with rage; that voice, made all of sweet accord, changed to one of harsh and horrid discord; and that angelic face gave place to that of a demon. (Douglass, 1845, pp. 57–58)

SAYING BECOMES BELIEVING

Closely related to role playing's effect is the *saying-becomes-believing* effect. Consider, first, the human tendency to adapt what we say to please our listeners:

■ We are quicker to tell people good news than bad, and we adjust our message toward our listener's position (Manis & others, 1974; Tesser & others, 1972; Tetlock, 1983).

■ Faculty members writing supposedly candid letters of recommendation to graduate schools are more glowing in their comments when the students reserve their right to inspect the letters (Ceci & Peters, 1984).

■ Social psychologist Philip Tetlock (1981b, 1995) has found that the policy statements of American presidents tend to be simplistic during the political campaign ("To bring down the deficit we need major spending cuts"). After the election their statements become more complex—until the next campaign.

■ The urge to shade one's views to suit one's audience seems strongest in Asian cultures. One study asked people to consider a father's best response to his daughter's introducing her fiance from another race. Although the father privately thought he "would never allow them to marry," 2 percent of Americans and 44 percent of Japanese felt he should tell them he "was in favor of their marriage" (Iwao, 1988).

In 1785, Thomas Jefferson hypothesized that shaded messages can affect the messenger: "He who permits himself to tell a lie once finds it much easier to

"*Good God! He's giving the white-collar voters' speech to the blue collars.*"

Impression management: In expressing our thoughts to others, we sometimes tailor our words to what we think the others will want to hear.

do it a second and third time, till at length it becomes habitual; he tells lies without attending to it, and truths without the world's believing him. This falsehood of the tongue leads to that of the heart, and in time depraves all its good dispositions." Experiments have proved Jefferson right. People induced to give spoken or written witness to something about which they have real doubts will often feel bad about their deceit. Nevertheless, they begin to believe what they are saying—*provided* they weren't bribed or coerced into doing so. When there is no compelling external explanation for one's words, saying becomes believing (Klaas, 1978).

Tory Higgins and his colleagues (Higgins & Rholes, 1978; Higgins & McCann, 1984) illustrated how saying becomes believing. They had university students read a personality description of someone and then summarize it for someone else who was believed either to like or dislike this person. The students wrote a more positive description when the recipient liked the person, and, having said positive things, then liked the person more themselves. Asked to recall what they had read, they remembered the description as being more positive than it was. In short, it seems that we are prone to adjust our messages to our listeners, and having done so, to believe the altered message.

"I had thought I was humoring [my captors] by parroting their clichés and buzz words without personally believing in them. . . . In trying to convince them I convinced myself."
Kidnap victim Patricia Campbell Hearst,
Every Secret Thing, 1982

ACTING ONESELF INTO BELIEF—SAYING IS BELIEVING

University of Oregon psychologist Ray Hyman (1981) described how acting the role of a palm reader convinced him that palmistry worked.

> I started reading palms when I was in my teens as a way to supplement my income from doing magic and mental shows. When I started I did not believe in palmistry. But I knew that to "sell" it I had to act as if I did. After a few years I became a firm believer in palmistry. One day the late Stanley Jaks, who was a professional mentalist and a man I respected, tactfully suggested that it would make an interesting experiment if I deliberately gave readings opposite to what the lines indicated. I tried this out with a few clients. To my surprise and horror my readings were just as successful as ever. Ever since then I have been interested in the powerful forces that convince us, [palm] reader and client alike, that something is so when it really isn't. (p. 86)

THE FOOT-IN-THE-DOOR PHENOMENON

Most of us can recall times when, after agreeing to help out with a project or an organization, we ended up more involved than we ever intended, vowing that in the future we would say no to such requests. How does this happen? Experiments suggest that if you want people to do a big favor for you, one technique is to get them to do a small favor first. In the best-known demonstration of this **foot-in-the-door** principle, researchers posing as safety-drive volunteers asked Californians to permit the installation of a huge, poorly lettered "Drive Carefully" sign in their front yards. Only 17 percent consented. Others were first approached with a small request: Would they display a 3-inch "Be a safe driver" window sign? Nearly all readily agreed. When approached two weeks later to allow the large, ugly sign in their front yards, 76 percent consented (Freedman & Fraser, 1966). One project helper who went from house to house later recalled that, not knowing who had been previously visited, "I was simply stunned at how easy it was to convince some people and how impossible to convince others" (Ornstein, 1991).

Foot-in-the-door phenomenon:
The tendency for people who have first agreed to a small request to comply later with a larger request.

BLONDIE ® by Dean Young and Stan Drake

A foot in the door. To get people to donate blood or money, it often helps to first elicit a smaller commitment to the same cause.

Other researchers have confirmed the foot-in-the-door phenomenon with altruistic behaviors.

- Patricia Pliner and her collaborators (1974) found 46 percent of Toronto suburbanites willing to give to the Cancer Society when approached directly. Others, asked a day ahead to wear a lapel pin publicizing the drive (which all agreed to do), were nearly twice as likely to donate.

- Among the residents of one middle-class Israeli city, 53 percent gave to a collection for the mentally impaired when approached by canvassers working for Joseph Schwarzwald and his colleagues (1983). Two weeks earlier, other residents had been approached to sign a petition supporting a recreation center for the impaired; among these, 92 percent now gave.

- Anthony Greenwald and his co-researchers (1987) approached a sample of registered voters the day before the 1984 U.S. presidential election and asked them a small question: "Do you expect that you will vote or not?" All said yes. Compared to other voters not asked their intentions, they were 41 percent more likely to vote.

- Angela Lipsitz and others (1989) report that ending blood-drive reminder calls with, "We'll count on seeing you then, OK? [pause for response]" increased the show-up rate from 62 to 81 percent.

"You will easily find folk to do favors if you cultivate those who have done them."
Publilius Syrus, 42 B.C.

Note that in these experiments the initial compliance—signing a petition, wearing a lapel pin, stating one's intention—was voluntary. We will see again and again that when people commit themselves to public behaviors *and* perceive these acts to be their own doing, they come to believe more strongly in what they have done.

Robert Cialdini and his collaborators (1978) demonstrated a variation of the foot-in-the-door phenomenon by experimenting with the **low-ball technique**, a tactic reportedly used by some car dealers. After the customer agrees to buy a new car because of its great price and begins completing the sales forms, the salesperson removes the price advantage by charging for options the customer

Low-ball technique:
A tactic for getting people to agree to something. People who agree to an initial request will often still comply when the requester ups the ante. People who receive only the costly request are less likely to comply with it.

thought were included or by checking with a boss who disallows the deal because, "We'd be losing money." Folklore has it that more customers now stick with the higher-priced purchase than would have agreed to it at the outset. Airlines and hotels have also used the tactic by attracting inquiries with great deals available on only a few seats or rooms, then hoping the customer will agree to a higher priced option. Cialdini and his collaborators found that this technique indeed works. When they invited introductory psychology students to participate in an experiment at 7:00 A.M., only 24 percent showed up. But if the students first agreed to participate without knowing the time and only then were asked to participate at 7:00 A.M., 53 percent came.

Marketing researchers and salespeople have found that the principle works even when we are aware of a profit motive (Cialdini, 1988). A harmless initial commitment—returning a card for more information and a gift, agreeing to listen to an investment possibility—often moves us toward a larger commitment. The day after I wrote this sentence, a life insurance salesperson came to my office and offered a thorough analysis of my family's financial situation. He did not ask whether I wished to buy his life insurance, or even whether I wished to try his free service. His question was instead a small foot-in-the-door, one carefully calculated to elicit agreement: Did I think people should have such information about their financial situation? I could only answer yes, and before I realized what was happening, I had agreed to the analysis. But I'm learning. Just the other evening a paid fund-raiser came to my door, first soliciting a petition signature supporting environmental cleanup, then welcoming my contribution to what I had signed my support of. (I sign, but resisting manipulation, don't give.)

Salespeople may exploit the power of small commitments when trying to bind people to purchase agreements. Many states now have laws that allow customers of door-to-door salespeople a few days to think over their purchases and cancel. To combat the effect of these laws, many companies use what the sales-training program of one encyclopedia company calls "a very important psychological aid in preventing customers from backing out of their contracts" (Cialdini, 1988, p. 78). They simply have the customer, rather than the salesperson, fill out the agreement. Having written it themselves, people usually live up to their commitment.

This process of step-by-step commitment, of spiraling action and attitude, contributed to the escalation of the U.S. involvement in the Vietnam war. After making and defending difficult decisions, political and military leaders seemed blind to information incompatible with their acts. They noticed and remembered comments that harmonized with their actions but ignored or dismissed information that undermined their assumptions. As Ralph White (1971) put it, "There was a tendency, when actions were out of line with ideas, for decision-makers to align their ideas with their actions."

The foot-in-the-door phenomenon is well worth learning about. Someone trying to seduce us, financially, politically, or sexually, usually will try to create a momentum of compliance. Before agreeing to a small request, think about what may follow.

EVIL ACTS AND ATTITUDES

The attitudes-follow-behavior principle works with more immoral acts as well. Evil sometimes results from gradually escalating commitments. A trifling evil act can make a less trifling evil act easier. Evil acts gnaw at the moral sensitivity of the actor. To paraphrase La Rochefoucauld's *Maxims* (1665), it is not as difficult to find a person who has never succumbed to a given temptation as to find a person who has succumbed only once.

For example, cruel acts corrode the consciences of those who perform them. Harming an innocent victim—by uttering hurtful comments or delivering electric shocks—typically leads aggressors to disparage their victims, thus helping them justify their behavior (Berscheid & others, 1968; Davis & Jones, 1960; Glass, 1964). We tend not only to hurt those we dislike but to dislike those we hurt. In studies establishing this, people would justify an action especially when coaxed, not coerced, into it. When we voluntarily agree to do a deed, we take more responsibility for it.

The phenomenon almost always appears in wartime, as soldiers denigrate their victims: American World War II soldiers called their enemy "the Japs." In the 1960s American soldiers dehumanized the Vietnamese people as "gooks."

Cruel acts, such as the massacre of these Rwandan Tutsis, breed even crueler and more hate-filled attitudes.

This is another instance of spiraling action and attitude: The more one commits atrocities, the easier it becomes. Conscience mutates. The same holds for prejudice. If one group holds another in slavery, it is likely to perceive the slaves as having traits that justify their oppression. Actions and attitudes feed one another, sometimes to the point of moral numbness.

"Our self-definitions are not constructed in our heads; they are forged by our deeds."
Robert McAfee Brown, *Creative Dislocation—The Movement of Grace*, 1980

If evil acts shape the self, so, thankfully, do moral acts. Character, it is said, is reflected in what we do when we think no one is looking. Researchers have tested character by giving children temptations when it seems no one is watching. Consider what happens when children resist the temptation. They internalize the conscientious act *if* the deterrent is strong enough to elicit the desired *behavior* yet mild enough to leave them with a sense of *choice*. In a dramatic experiment, Jonathan Freedman (1965) introduced elementary school children to an enticing battery-controlled robot, instructing them not to play with it while he was out of the room. Freedman used a severe threat with half the children and a mild threat with the others. Both were sufficient to deter the children.

Several weeks later a different researcher, with no apparent relation to the earlier events, left each child to play in the same room with the same toys. Of the 18 children who had been given the severe threat, 14 now freely played with the robot; but two-thirds of those who had been given the mild deterrent still resisted playing with it. Having made the conscious choice *not* to play with the toy, the mildly deterred children apparently internalized their decision. This new attitude controlled their subsequent action. Thus, moral action, especially when chosen rather than coerced, affects moral thinking.

INTERRACIAL BEHAVIOR AND RACIAL ATTITUDES

If moral action feeds moral attitudes, will positive interracial behavior reduce racial prejudice? This was part of social scientists' testimony before the U.S. Supreme Court's 1954 decision to desegregate schools. Their argument ran like this: If we wait for the heart to change—through preaching and teaching—we will wait a long time for racial justice. But if we legislate moral action, we can, under the right conditions, indirectly affect heartfelt attitudes.

This idea runs counter to the presumption that "you can't legislate morality." Yet attitude change has, in fact, followed desegregation. Consider the results of this mammoth social experiment:

■ Since the Supreme Court decision, the percentage of White Americans favoring integrated schools has more than doubled, and now includes nearly everyone.

■ In the 10 years after the Civil Rights Act of 1964, the percentage of White Americans who described their neighborhoods, friends, co-workers, or other students as all-White declined by about 20 percent for each of these measures. Interracial behavior was increasing. During the same period, the percentage of White Americans who said that Blacks should be allowed to live in any neighborhood increased from 65 percent to 87 percent (ISR Newsletter, 1975). Attitudes were changing, too.

■ More uniform national standards against discrimination were followed by decreasing differences in racial attitudes among people of differing religions, classes, and geographic regions. As Americans came to act more alike, they came to think more alike (Greeley & Sheatsley, 1971; Taylor & others, 1978).

Experiments confirm that positive behavior toward someone fosters liking for that person. Doing a favor for an experimenter or another subject, or tutoring a student, usually increases liking of the person helped (Blanchard & Cook, 1976). It is a lesson worth remembering: If you wish to love someone more, act as if you do.

In 1793, Benjamin Franklin tested the idea that doing a favor engenders liking. As clerk of the Pennsylvania General Assembly, he was disturbed by opposition from another important legislator. So Franklin set out to win him over:

> I did not . . . aim at gaining his favour by paying any servile respect to him but, after some time, took this other method. Having heard that he had in his library a certain very scarce and curious book I wrote a note to him expressing my desire of perusing that book and requesting he would do me the favour of lending it to me for a few days. He sent it immediately and I return'd it in about a week, expressing strongly my sense of the favour. When we next met in the House he spoke to me (which he had never done before), and with great civility; and he ever after manifested a readiness to serve me on all occasions, so that we became great friends and our friendship continued to his death. (Rozenzweig, 1972, p. 769)

SOCIAL MOVEMENTS

The effect of a society's behavior on its racial attitudes suggests the possibility, and the danger, of employing the same idea for political socialization on a mass scale. For many people in Nazi Germany, participation in mass meetings, wearing uniforms, demonstrating, and especially the public greeting "Heil Hitler" established a profound inconsistency between behavior and belief. Historian Richard Grunberger (1971) reports that for those who had their doubts about Hitler, "The 'German greeting' was a powerful conditioning device. Having once decided to intone it as an outward token of conformity, many experienced schizophrenic discomfort at the contradiction between their words and their feelings. Prevented from saying what they believed, they tried to establish their psychic equilibrium by consciously making themselves believe what they said" (p. 27).

The practice is not limited to totalitarian regimes. Political rituals—the daily flag salute by schoolchildren, singing the national anthem—use public conformity to build a private belief in patriotism. I recall participating in air-raid drills in an elementary school not far from the Boeing Company in Seattle. After we repeatedly acted as if we were the objects of Soviet attack, many of us came to fear the Soviets. Observers noted how the civil rights marches of the 1960s strengthened the demonstrators' commitments. Their actions expressed an idea whose time had come and drove that idea more deeply into their hearts. The 1980s move toward inclusive language (by referring, say, to "human nature" rather than "man's nature") has similarly strengthened inclusive attitudes.

Many people assume that the most social indoctrination comes through *brainwashing*, a term coined to describe what happened to American prisoners of war (POWs) during the 1950s Korean war. Actually, the Chinese "thought-control" program, developed to re-educate the Chinese populace into communism, was not nearly as irresistible as this term suggests. But it was disconcerting that hundreds of prisoners cooperated with their captors, that 21 chose to remain after being granted permission to return to America, and that many of those who did return came home believing "although communism won't work in America, I think it's a good thing for Asia" (Segal, 1954).

"We do not love people so much for the good they have done us, as for the good we have done them."
Leo Tolstoy, *War and Peace*, 1867–1869

"One does what one is; one becomes what one does."
Robert Musil, *Kleine Prosa*, 1930

Celebrating Canada Day: Patriotic actions strengthen patriotic attitudes.

"You can use small commitments to manipulate a person's self-image; you can use them to turn citizens into 'public servants,' prospects into 'customers,' prisoners into 'collaborators.'"
Robert Cialdini, *Influence*, 1988

Edgar Schein (1956) interviewed many of the POWs during their journey home and reported that the captors' methods included a gradual escalation of demands. The Chinese always started with trivial requests and gradually worked up to more significant ones. "Thus after a prisoner had once been 'trained' to speak or write out trivia, statements on more important issues were demanded." Moreover, they always expected active participation, be it just copying something or participating in group discussions, writing self-criticism, or uttering public confessions. Once a prisoner had spoken or written a statement, he felt an inner need to make his beliefs consistent with his acts. This often drove prisoners to persuade themselves of what they had done. The "start-small-and-build" tactic was an effective application of the foot-in-the-door technique, as it continues to be today in the socialization of terrorists and torturers (Chapter 7).

REFLECTIONS ON THE EVIDENCE

From these observations—of the effects of role playing, the foot-in-the-door experience, moral and immoral acts, interracial behavior, social movements, and brainwashing—there is a powerful practical lesson: If we want to change ourselves in some important way, it's best not to wait for insight or inspiration. Sometimes we need to act—to begin writing that paper, to make those phone calls, to see that person—even if we don't feel like acting. Jacques Barzun (1975) recognized the energizing power of action when he advised aspiring writers to engage in the act of writing even if contemplation had left them feeling uncertain about their ideas:

"If we wish to conquer undesirable emotional tendencies in ourselves we must . . . coldbloodedly go through the outward motions of those contrary dispositions we prefer to cultivate."
William James, *"What Is an Emotion?"* 1884

> If you are too modest about yourself or too plain indifferent about the possible reader and yet are required to write, then you have to pretend. Make believe that you want

to bring somebody around to your opinion; in other words, adopt a thesis and start expounding it. . . . With a slight effort of the kind at the start—a challenge to utterance—you will find your pretense disappearing and a real concern creeping in. The subject will have taken hold of you as it does in the work of all habitual writers. (pp. 173–174)

This attitudes-follow-behavior phenomenon is not irrational or magical, for that which prompts us to act may also prompt us to think. Writing an essay, or role-playing an opposing view, forces us to consider arguments we otherwise might have ignored. What is more, we remember information best when we have actively explained it in our own terms. In one experiment, Gordon Bower and Mark Masling (1979) gave Stanford students a list of bizarre correlations like this one: "As the number of fire hydrants in an area decreases the crime rate increases." Students who simply studied or were given explanations for these correlations recalled only about 40 percent of them when tested later. But students who invented their own explanations recalled 73 percent of the correlations.

The memorability of self-produced information is one reason we are most affected by information we have reformulated in our own terms (Greenwald, 1968; Petty & others, 1981). As one student wrote me, "It wasn't until I tried to verbalize my beliefs that I really understood them." As a teacher and a writer, I must therefore remind myself not always to lay out finished results. It is better to stimulate students to think through the implications of a theory, to make them active listeners and readers. Even taking notes deepens the impression. The philosopher-psychologist William James (1899) made the same point a century ago: "No reception without *reaction*, no impression without correlative expression—this is the great maxim which the teacher ought never to forget."

So let me ask you, before reading further, to play theorist. Ask yourself: Why in these studies and real-life examples did attitudes follow behavior?

The attitude-action relation also works in the reverse direction: We are likely not only to think ourselves into action but also to act ourselves into a way of thinking. When we act, we amplify the idea underlying what we have done, especially when we feel responsible for it. Many streams of evidence converge on this principle. The actions prescribed by social roles mold the attitudes of the role players. Research on the foot-in-the door phenomenon reveals that committing a small act (for example, agreeing to do a small favor) later makes people more willing to do a larger one. Actions also affect our moral attitudes: That which we have done we tend to justify as right. Similarly, our racial and political behaviors help shape our social consciousness: We not only stand up for what we believe, we also believe in what we have stood up for.

∎ WHY DO ACTIONS AFFECT ATTITUDES?

What theories help explain the attitudes-follow-behavior phenomenon? How does the contest between these competing ideas illustrate the process of scientific explanation?

We have seen that several streams of evidence merge to form a river: the effect of actions on attitudes. Do these observations contain any clues to *why* action affects attitude? Social psychology's detectives suspect three possible sources. **Self-presentation theory** assumes that for strategic reasons we express attitudes that make us *appear* consistent. **Cognitive dissonance theory** assumes that to reduce discomfort, we *justify* our actions to ourselves. **Self-perception theory** assumes that our actions are *self-revealing* (when uncertain about our feelings or beliefs, we look to our behavior, much as anyone else would). Let's examine each.

SELF-PRESENTATION: IMPRESSION MANAGEMENT

The first explanation began as a simple idea: Who among us does not care what people think? We spend countless dollars on clothes, diets, cosmetics, even plastic surgery—all because we worry about what others think of us. To make a good impression is often to gain social and material rewards, to feel better about ourselves, even to become more secure in our social identities (Leary, 1994).

Indeed, no one wants to look foolishly inconsistent. To avoid seeming so, we express attitudes that match our actions. To *appear* consistent, we may even feign attitudes we don't really believe in. Even if it means displaying a little insincerity or hypocrisy, it can pay to manage the impression one is making. Or so *self-presentation theory* suggests.

Self-presentation theory assumes that our behavior aims to create desired impressions.

© 1987, The New Yorker Magazine, Inc.

"My not wearing a hairpiece indicates to others that I'm comfortable with myself."

We have seen that people do engage in "impression management." They will adjust what they say to please rather than offend. Sometimes it may take a bogus pipeline to cut through the pretense. Moreover, people take longer to deliver news of failure (for example, signaling wrong answers on an IQ-type test) than news of success; but this effect occurs only if the bearers of the news are identifiable and therefore concerned about making a bad impression (Bond & Anderson, 1987).

For some people, making a good impression is a way of life. By continually monitoring their own behavior and noting how others react, they adjust their social performance when it's not having the desired effect. Those who score high on a scale of **self-monitoring** tendency (who, for example, agree that "I tend to be what people expect me to be") act like social chameleons—they adjust their behavior in response to external situations (Snyder, 1987). Having attuned their behavior to the situation, they are more likely to espouse an attitude they don't really hold (Zanna & Olson, 1982). Being conscious of others, they are less likely to act on their own attitudes. By self-monitoring, such people readily adapt to new jobs, roles, and relationships (Snyder & DeBono, 1989; Snyder & Copeland, 1989).

Those who score low in self-monitoring care less about what others think. They are more internally guided and thus more likely to talk and act as they feel and believe (McCann & Hancock, 1983). Most of us fall somewhere between the high self-monitoring extreme of the con artist and the low self-monitoring extreme of stubborn insensitivity to others.

Does our eagerness to *appear* consistent explain why expressed attitudes shift toward consistency with behavior? To some extent, yes—people exhibit a much smaller attitude change when a bogus pipeline inhibits trying to make a good impression (Paulhus, 1982; Tedeschi & others, 1987). Moreover, self-presentation involves not just impressing others but expressing our ideals and identity (Baumeister, 1982, 1985; Schlenker, 1986, 1987).

But there is more to the attitude changes we have reviewed than self-presentation, for people express their changed attitudes even to someone who doesn't know how they have behaved. (There is no need to present a consistent attitude when talking to someone who is unaware of their behavior.) Two other theories explain why people sometimes internalize their self-presentations as genuine attitude changes.

Self-monitoring:
Being attuned to the way one presents oneself in social situations and adjusting one's performance to create the desired impression.

SELF-JUSTIFICATION: COGNITIVE DISSONANCE

One theory is that our attitudes change because we are motivated to maintain consistency among our cognitions. This is the implication of Leon Festinger's (1957) **cognitive dissonance theory**. The theory is simple, but its range of application is enormous. It assumes we feel tension ("dissonance") when two thoughts or beliefs ("cognitions") are psychologically inconsistent—as when we decide to say or do something we have mixed feelings about. Festinger argued that to reduce this unpleasant arousal, we often adjust our thinking.

Dissonance theory pertains mostly to discrepancies between behavior and attitudes. We are aware of both. Thus if we sense an inconsistency, we feel pressure for change. That helps explain why smokers justify smoking—and why, in a British survey, half of cigarette smokers therefore disagreed with the near-

Cognitive dissonance:
Tension that arises when one is simultaneously aware of two inconsistent cognitions. For example, dissonance may occur when we realize that we have, with little justification, acted contrary to our attitudes or made a decision favoring one alternative despite reasons favoring another.

When the essay argues something they don't believe in—say, a tuition increase—the underpaid essay writers begin to feel somewhat greater sympathy with the policy. Advocating a policy favorable to another race may improve your attitudes not only toward the policy but toward the race. This is especially so if something makes you face the inconsistency or if you think important people will actually read an essay with your name on it (Leippe & Eisenstadt, 1994; Leippe & Elkin, 1987). Feeling responsible for statements you have made, you will now believe them more strongly. Pretense has become reality.

Earlier we noted how the insufficient justification principle works with punishments. Children were more likely to internalize a request not to play with an attractive toy if given a mild threat that insufficiently justified their compliance. When a parent says, "Clean up your room, Johnny, or I'll knock your block off," Johnny won't need to internally justify cleaning his room. The severe threat is a sufficient justification.

Note that cognitive dissonance theory focuses on what *induces* a desired action, rather than the relative effectiveness of rewards and punishments administered *after* the act. It aims to have Johnny say, "I am cleaning up my room because I want a clean room," rather than, "I am cleaning up my room because my parents will kill me if I don't." The principle: We accept responsibility for our behavior if we have chosen it without obvious pressure and incentives.

These implications of dissonance theory have led some to view it as an integration of humanistic and scientific perspectives. Authoritarian management will be effective, the theory predicts, only when the authority is present, be-

Dissonance theory suggests that parents should aim to elicit desired behavior noncoercively, thus motivating children to internalize the appropriate attitudes.

cause people are unlikely to internalize forced behavior. Bree, a formerly enslaved talking horse in C. S. Lewis's *The Horse and His Boy* (1974), observes that "One of the worst results of being a slave and being forced to do things is that when there is no one to force you any more you find you have almost lost the power of forcing yourself" (p. 193). Dissonance theory insists that encouragement and inducement should be enough to elicit the desired action. But it suggests that managers, teachers, and parents should use only enough incentive to elicit the desired behavior.

Dissonance after Decisions

The emphasis on perceived choice and responsibility implies that *decisions* produce dissonance. When faced with an important decision—what college to attend, whom to date, which job to accept—we are sometimes torn between two equally attractive alternatives. Perhaps you can recall a time when, having committed yourself, you become painfully aware of dissonant cognitions—the desirable features of what you had rejected and the undesirable features of what you had chosen. If you decided to live on campus, you may have realized you were forgoing the spaciousness and freedom of an apartment in favor of cramped, noisy dorm quarters. If you elected to live off campus, you may have realized that your decision meant physical separation from campus and friends and having to cook for yourself.

After making important decisions, we usually reduce dissonance by upgrading the chosen alternative and downgrading the option we passed over. In the first published dissonance experiment (1956), Jack Brehm had University of Minnesota women rate eight products, such as a toaster, a radio, and a hair dryer. Brehm then showed the women two objects they had rated closely and told them they could have whichever they chose. Later, when rerating the eight objects, the women increased their evaluations of the item they had chosen and decreased their evaluations of the rejected item. It seems that when we have made our choice, the grass does *not* then grow greener on the other side of the fence.

With simple decisions, this deciding-becomes-believing effect can occur very quickly. Robert Knox and James Inkster (1968) found that racetrack bettors who had just put down their money on a horse felt more optimistic about their bet than did those who were about to bet. In the few moments that intervened between standing in line and walking away from the betting window, nothing had changed—except the decision and the person's feelings about it. Contestants in carnival games of chance feel more confident of winning right after agreeing to play than right before. And voters indicate more esteem and confidence in a candidate just after voting than just before (Younger & others, 1977). There may sometimes be but a slight difference between the two options, as I can recall in helping make faculty tenure decisions. The competence of one faculty member who barely makes it and that of another who barely loses seem not very different—until after you make and announce the decision.

These experiments and examples suggest that, once made, decisions grow their own legs of support—self-justifying reasons why the commitment was wise. Often, these new legs are strong enough that when one leg is pulled away—perhaps the original one—the decision does not collapse. Alison de-

"Every time you make a choice you are turning the central part of you, the part of you that chooses, into something a little different from what it was before."
C. S. Lewis, *Mere Christianity*, 1943

Big decisions can produce big dissonance when one later ponders the negative aspects of what is chosen and the positive aspects of what is not chosen.

cides to take a trip home if it can be done for an airfare under $400. It can, so she makes her reservation and begins to think of additional reasons why she is glad she is going. When she goes to buy the tickets, however, she learns there has been a fare increase to $475. No matter, she is now determined to go. As when being low-balled by a car dealer, it never occurs to people, reports Robert Cialdini (1984, p. 103), "that those additional reasons might never have existed had the choice not been made in the first place."

SELF-PERCEPTION

Although dissonance theory has inspired much research, an even simpler theory explains its phenomena. Consider how we make inferences about other people's attitudes. We see how a person acts in a particular situation, and then we attribute the behavior either to the person's traits and attitudes or to environmental forces. If we see parents coercing their little Susie into saying, "I'm sorry," we attribute Susie's reluctant behavior to the situation, not to her personal regret. If we see Susie apologizing with no apparent inducement, we attribute the apology to Susie herself.

Self-perception theory (proposed by Daryl Bem, 1972) assumes that we make similar inferences when we observe our own behavior. When our attitudes are weak or ambiguous, we are in the position of someone observing us from the outside. As we discern people's attitudes by looking closely at their actions when they are free to act as they please, so we discern our own attitudes. Hearing myself talk informs me of my attitudes; seeing my actions provides clues to how strong my beliefs are. This is especially so when I can't eas-

Self-perception theory: The theory that when unsure of our attitudes, we infer them much as would someone observing us—by looking at our behavior and the circumstances under which it occurs.

ily attribute my behavior to external constraints. The acts we freely commit are self-revealing.

William James proposed a similar explanation for emotion a century ago. We infer our emotions, he suggested, by observing our bodies and our behaviors. A stimulus such as a growling bear confronts a woman in the forest. She tenses, her heartbeat increases, adrenaline flows, and she runs away. Observing all this, she then experiences fear. At a college where I am to lecture, I awake before dawn and am unable to get back to sleep. Noting my wakefulness, I conclude that I must be anxious.

You may be skeptical of the self-perception effect. I was when I first heard it. However, experiments on the effects of facial expressions suggest a way for you to experience it. When James Laird (1974, 1984; Duclos & others, 1989) induced college students to frown while attaching electrodes to their faces—"contract these muscles," "pull your brows together"—they reported feeling angry. It's more fun to try out Laird's other finding: Those induced to make a smiling face felt happier and found cartoons more humorous.

"Self-knowledge is best learned, not by contemplation, but action."
Goethe, 1749–1832

"I can watch myself and my actions, just like an outsider."
Anne Frank, *The Diary of a Young Girl,* 1947

According to German psychologist Fritz Strack and colleagues (1988), people find cartoons funnier while holding a pen with their teeth (using a smiling muscle) than while holding it with their lips (using muscles incompatible with smiling).

*"I don't sing because I am happy. I am
happy because I sing."*

We have all experienced this phenomenon. We're feeling crabby, but then the phone rings or someone comes to the door and elicits from us warm, polite behavior. "How's everything?" "Just fine, thanks. How are things with you?" "Oh, not bad. . . ." If our feelings are not intense, this warm behavior may change our whole attitude. It's tough to smile and feel grouchy. When Miss America parades her smile, she may, after all, be helping herself feel happy. As Rodgers and Hammerstein reminded us, when afraid it may help to "whistle a happy tune." Going through the motions can trigger the emotions.

The effect sometimes endures into later behavior. After people are induced to *act* in an outgoing, talkative manner (during an interview), their self-presentation may carry over into greater self-perceived outgoingness and more outgoing social behavior (Schlenker & others, 1994; Tice, 1992). Act *as if* you are energetically outgoing, and you may become more so.

Even your gait can affect how you feel. When you get up from reading this chapter, walk for a minute taking short, shuffling steps, with eyes downcast. It's a great way to feel depressed. "Sit all day in a moping posture, sigh, and reply to everything with a dismal voice, and your melancholy lingers," noted William James (1890, p. 463). Want to feel better? Walk for a minute taking long strides with your arms swinging and your eyes straight ahead. Can you, like the participants in an experiment by Sara Snodgrass (1986), feel the difference?

If our expressions influence our feelings, then would imitating others' expressions help us know what they are feeling? An experiment by Katherine Burns Vaughan and John Lanzetta (1981) suggests it would. They asked Dartmouth College students to observe someone receiving electric shock. They told some of the observers to make a pained expression whenever the shock came on. If, as Freud and others supposed, expressing an emotion allows us to discharge it, then the pained expression should be inwardly calming (Cacioppo & others, 1991). Actually, compared to other students who did not act out the expressions, these grimacing students perspired *more* and had a faster heart rate whenever they saw the person shocked. Acting out the person's emotion apparently enabled the observers to feel more empathy. The implication: To sense how other people are feeling, let your own face mirror their expressions.

Actually, you hardly need try. Observing others' faces, postures, and voices, we naturally and unconsciously mimic their moment-to-moment reactions (Hatfield & others, 1992). We synchronize our movements, postures, and tones of voice with theirs. Doing so helps us tune in to what they're feeling. It also makes for "emotional contagion," helping explain why it's fun to be around happy people and depressing to be around depressed people (Chapter 5).

Our facial expressions also influence our attitudes. In a clever experiment, Gary Wells and Richard Petty (1980) had University of Alberta students "test headphone sets" by making either vertical or horizontal head movements while listening to a radio editorial. Who most agreed with the editorial? Those who had been nodding their heads up and down. Why? Wells and Petty surmised that positive thoughts are compatible with vertical nodding and incompatible with horizontal motion. Try it yourself when listening to someone: Do you feel more agreeable when nodding rather than shaking your head?

In an even zanier experiment, John Cocioppo and his colleagues (1993) had people rate Chinese characters when pressing their arms upward (as when lifting food) or downward (as when pushing something or someone away). Which flex condition do you suppose triggered the most positive ratings? It was the upward flex. (Try it out: Do you get a more positive feeling while lifting a table edge with upturned hands rather than pressing down? Might this motion-affects-emotion phenomenon predispose people to feel better at parties while holding food or drink?)

Overjustification and Intrinsic Motivations

Recall the insufficient justification effect—the *smallest* incentive that will get people to do something is usually the most effective in getting them to like the activity and keep on doing it. Cognitive dissonance theory offers one explanation for this: When external inducements are insufficient to justify our behavior, we reduce dissonance by justifying it internally.

Self-perception theory offers another explanation: People explain their behavior by noting the conditions under which it occurs. Imagine hearing someone proclaim the wisdom of a tuition increase after being paid $20 to do so. Surely the statement would seem less sincere than if you thought the person

"The free expression by outward signs of emotion intensifies it. On the other hand, the repression as far as possible, of all outward signs softens our emotions."
Charles Darwin, *The Expression of the Emotions in Man and Animals,* 1897

was expressing those opinions for no pay. Perhaps we make similar inferences when observing ourselves.

Self-perception theory goes even a step further. Contrary to the notion that rewards always increase motivation, it suggests that unnecessary rewards sometimes have a hidden cost. Rewarding people for doing what they already enjoy may lead them to attribute their doing it to the reward, thus undermining their self-perception that they do it because they like it. Experiments by Edward Deci and Richard Ryan (1991) at the University of Rochester, by Mark

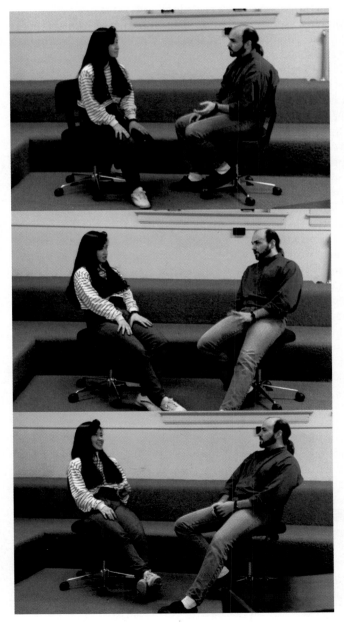

Natural mimicry and emotional contagion. People in sync, like these volunteers videotaped during an Oregon State University study by Frank Bernieri and colleagues, feel more rapport with each other.

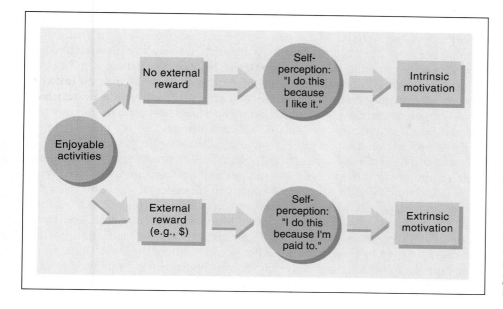

■ FIGURE 4–4
When people do something they enjoy, without reward or coercion, they attribute their behavior to their love of the activity. External rewards undermine intrinsic motivation by leading people to attribute their behavior to the incentive.

Lepper and David Greene (1979) at Stanford, and by Ann Boggiano and her colleagues (1985, 1987) at the University of Colorado confirm this **overjustification effect.** Pay people for playing with puzzles, and they will later play with the puzzles less than those who play without being paid; promise children a reward for doing what they intrinsically enjoy (for example, playing with magic markers) and you will turn their play into work (Figure 4–4).

A folktale illustrates the overjustification effect. An old man lived alone on a street where boys played noisily every afternoon. The din annoyed him, so one day he called the boys to his door. He told them he loved the cheerful sound of children's voices and promised them each 50 cents if they would return the next day. Next afternoon the youngsters raced back and played more lustily than ever. The old man paid them and promised another reward the next day. Again they returned, whooping it up, and the man again paid them; this time 25 cents. The following day they got only 15 cents, and the man explained that his meager resources were being exhausted. "Please, though, would you come to play for 10 cents tomorrow?" The disappointed boys told the man they would not be back. It wasn't worth the effort, they said, to play all afternoon at his house for only 10 cents.

As self-perception theory implies, an *unanticipated* reward does *not* diminish intrinsic interest, because people can still attribute their action to their own motivation (Bradley & Mannell, 1984; Tang & Hall, 1994). (It's like the heroine who, having fallen in love with the woodcutter, now learns that he's really a prince.) And if compliments for a good job make us feel more competent and successful, this can actually *increase* our intrinsic motivation. The overjustification effect occurs when someone offers an unnecessary reward beforehand in an obvious effort to control behavior. What matters is what a reward implies: Rewards and praise that *inform* people of their achievements (that make them feel, "I'm very good at this") *boost* intrinsic motivation. Rewards that seek to *control* people and lead them to believe it was the reward that caused their effort ("I did it for the money") *diminish* the intrinsic appeal of an enjoyable task (Rosenfeld & others, 1980; Sansone, 1986).

Overjustification effect: The result of bribing people to do what they already like doing; they may then see their action as externally controlled rather than intrinsically appealing.

How then can we cultivate people's enjoyment of tasks that are not intrinsically appealing? Young Maria may find her first piano lessons frustrating. Tommy may not have an intrinsic love of fifth-grade science. Sandra may not look forward to making those first sales calls. In such cases, the parent, teacher, or manager should probably use some incentives to coax the desired behavior (Boggiano & Ruble, 1985; Workman & Williams, 1980). After the person complies, suggest an intrinsic reason for doing so: "I knew you'd share your toys because you're a generous person" (Cialdini & others, 1992).

If we provide students with *just enough* justification to perform a learning task and use rewards and labels to help them feel competent, we may enhance their enjoyment and their eagerness to pursue the subject on their own. When there is too much justification—as happens in classrooms where teachers dictate behavior and use rewards to control the children—child-driven learning may diminish (Deci & Ryan, 1985, 1991). My younger son eagerly consumed six or eight library books a week—until our library started a reading club which promised a party to those who read ten books in three months. Three weeks later he began checking out only one or two books during our weekly visit. Why? "Because you only need to read ten books, you know."

COMPARING THE THEORIES

We have seen one explanation of why our actions *seem* to affect our attitudes (self-presentation theory). And we have seen two explanations of why our actions *genuinely* affect our attitudes: (1) the dissonance-theory assumption that we justify our behavior to reduce our internal discomfort and (2) the self-perception-theory assumption that we observe our behavior and make reasonable inferences about our attitudes, as we do when observing other people.

Olympic athletes at Barcelona in 1992. When people are not overly rewarded or coerced into an activity they already enjoy, it feels more internally controlled and intrinsically appealing.

The last two explanations seem to contradict one another. Which is right? It's difficult to find a definitive test. In most instances they make the same predictions, and we can bend each theory to accommodate most of the findings we have considered (Greenwald, 1975). Daryl Bem (1972), the self-perception theorist, even suggested it boils down to a matter of loyalties and esthetics. This illustrates the subjectivity of scientific theorizing (see Chapter 1). Neither dissonance theory nor self-perception theory has been handed to us by nature. Both are products of human imagination—creative attempts to simplify and explain what we've observed.

It is not unusual in science to find that a principle, such as "attitudes follow behavior," is predictable from more than one theory. Physicist Richard Feynman (1967) marveled that "one of the amazing characteristics of nature" is the "wide range of beautiful ways" in which we can describe it: "I do not understand the reason why it is that the correct laws of physics seem to be expressible in such a tremendous variety of ways" (pp. 53–55). Like different roads leading to the same place, different sets of assumptions can lead to the same principle. If anything, this *strengthens* our confidence in the principle. It becomes credible not only because of the data supporting it but also because it rests on more than one theoretical pillar.

Dissonance as Arousal

Can we say that one of our theories is better? On one key point, strong support has emerged for dissonance theory. Recall that dissonance is, by definition, an aroused state of uncomfortable tension. To reduce this tension, we supposedly change our attitudes. Self-perception theory says nothing about tension being aroused when our actions and attitudes are not in harmony. It assumes merely that when our attitudes are weak to begin with, we will use our behavior and its circumstances as a clue to those attitudes (like the person who said, "How do I know how I feel until I hear what I say?").

Are conditions that supposedly produce dissonance (for example, making decisions or acting contrary to one's attitudes) actually *uncomfortably arousing*? Clearly yes, providing that the behavior has unwanted consequences for which the person feels responsible (Cooper & Fazio, 1984; Elliot & Devine, 1994; Scher & Cooper, 1989). If in the privacy of your closet you say something you don't believe, dissonance will be minimal. But it will be much greater if there are unpleasant results—if someone hears and believes you, if the negative effects are irrevocable, and if the person harmed is someone you like. If, moreover, you feel responsible for these consequences—if you can't easily excuse your act because you freely agreed to it and if you could foresee its consequences—then uncomfortable dissonance will be aroused (Figure 4–5). Moreover, the arousal will be detectable as increased perspiration and heart rate (Cacioppo & Petty, 1986; Croyle & Cooper, 1983; Losch & Cacioppo, 1990).

There is a reason why "volunteering" to say or do undesirable things is arousing, suggests Claude Steele (1988). Such acts are embarrassing. They make us feel foolish. They threaten our sense of personal competence and goodness. Justifying our actions and decisions is therefore self-protective; it affirms our sense of integrity and self-worth.

So what do you suppose happens if, after committing a self-contradictory act, we offer people some other way to reaffirm their sense of self-worth, such as by doing a good deed? In several experiments Steele found that, with their self-concepts secure, people (especially those who came to the experiments with strong self-concepts) felt much less need to justify their acts (Steele & others, 1993). Therefore, says Steele, people are aroused by undesirable dissonant behaviors because such acts threaten their positive self-concepts. Had the Chinese in Korea used torture to gain compliance, the POWs would have had less

People rarely internalize coerced behavior.

"No, Hoskins, you're not going to do it just because I'm telling you to do it. You're going to do it because you believe in it."

© 1988, The New Yorker Magazine, Inc.

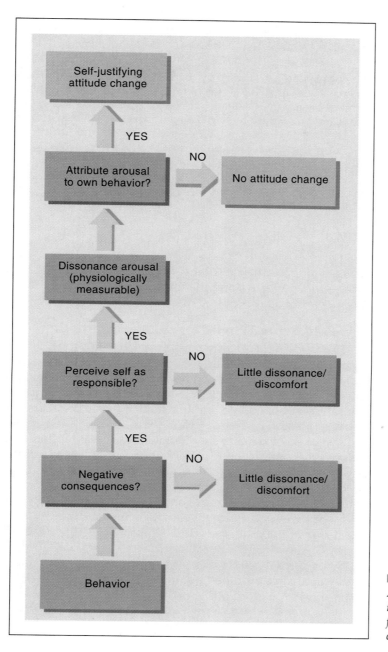

■ **FIGURE 4–5**
A revised version of dissonance theory: the sequence that leads from behavior to attitude change.

need to justify their acts to themselves. You don't need to feel guilty about, or to justify, forced acts.

So dissonance conditions do indeed arouse tension, especially when they threaten self-worth. But is this arousal necessary for the attitudes-follow-behavior effect? Steele and his colleagues (1981) believe the answer is yes. When drinking alcohol reduces dissonance-produced arousal, the attitudes-follow-behavior effect disappears. In one of their experiments, they induced University of Washington students to write an essay favoring a big tuition increase. The students reduced their resulting dissonance by softening their antituition attitudes—*unless* after writing the unpleasant essay, they drank alcohol, supposedly as part of a beer- or vodka-tasting experiment.

Self-Perceiving When Not Self-Contradicting

So dissonance procedures are uncomfortably arousing, which leads to self-persuasion after acting contrary to one's attitudes. But dissonance theory cannot explain all the findings. When people argue a position that is in line with their opinion, although a step or two beyond it, procedures that usually eliminate arousal do not eliminate attitude change (Fazio & others, 1977, 1979). Dissonance theory also does not explain the overjustification effect, since being paid to do what you like to do should not arouse great tension. And what about situations where the action really does not contradict any attitude—when, for example, people are induced to smile or grimace. Here, too, there should be no dissonance. For these cases, self-perception theory has a ready explanation.

In short, it appears that dissonance theory successfully explains what happens when we act contrary to clearly defined attitudes: We feel tension, so we adjust our attitudes to reduce it. Dissonance theory, then, explains attitude *change*. In situations where our attitudes are not well formed, self-perception theory explains attitude *formation*. As we act and reflect, we develop a more readily accessible attitude to guide our future behavior (Fazio, 1987; Roese & Olson, 1994).

SUMMING UP

Three competing theories explain *why* our actions affect our attitude reports. *Self-presentation theory* assumes that people, especially those who self-monitor their behavior hoping to create a good impression, will adapt their attitude reports to *appear* consistent with their actions. The available evidence confirms that people do adjust their attitude statements out of concern for what other people will think. But it also shows that some genuine attitude change occurs.

Two theories propose that our actions trigger genuine attitude change. *Dissonance theory* explains this attitude change by assuming that we feel tension after acting contrary to our attitudes or making a difficult decision. To reduce this arousal, we internally justify our behavior. Dissonance theory further proposes that the less external justification we have for an undesirable action, the more we feel responsible for it, and thus the more dissonance arises and the more attitudes change.

Self-perception theory assumes that when our attitudes are weak, we simply observe our behavior and its circumstances and infer our attitudes. One interesting implication of self-perception theory is the "overjustification effect": Rewarding people to do what they like doing anyway can turn their pleasure into drudgery (if the reward leads them to attribute their behavior to the reward). Evidence supports predictions from both theories, suggesting that each describes what happens under certain conditions.

■ FOR FURTHER READING

Cialdini, R. B. (1993). *Influence: Science and practice* (3rd ed.). New York: HarperCollins. An engrossing summary of six "weapons of influence" revealed by social-psychological research and exploited in everyday situations. See, especially, Chapter 3, "Commitment and Consistency: Hobgoblins of the Mind."

Petty, R. E., & Krosnick, J. A. (1995). *Attitude strength: Antecedents and consequences.* Hillsdale, NJ: Erlbaum. What are the roots and fruits of strong (persistent, influential) attitudes? This scholarly book offers experts' answers.

Zimbardo, P. G., & Leippe, M. R. (1991). *The psychology of attitude change and social influence.* New York: McGraw-Hill. A basic introduction to attitudes, including how they influence, and are influenced by, our actions.

SOCIAL COGNITION AND HUMAN WELL-BEING

If you are a typical college student, you may occasionally feel mildly depressed, dissatisfied with your life, discouraged about the future, sad, lacking appetite and energy, unable to concentrate, perhaps even wondering if life is worth it. Maybe you think disappointing grades have jeopardized your career goals. Perhaps the breakup of a relationship has left you in despair. At such times your self-focused brooding only worsens your feelings. For some 10 percent of men and nearly twice that many women, life's down times are not just temporary blue moods but one or more major depressive episodes that last for weeks without any obvious cause.

Among the many thriving areas of applied social psychology is one that relates research on social cognition (described in Chapters 2 to 4) to such problems as depression. This bridge-building research between social psychology and **clinical psychology** seeks answers to three important questions: (1) As laypeople or as professional psychologists, how can we improve our judgments and predictions about others? (2) How can the ways in which we think about self and others feed such problems as depression, loneliness, anxiety, and even physical illness? (3) How might these maladaptive thought patterns be reversed? In this chapter we explore some answers by examining social psychology's contribution to improving the process of clinical *judgment and prediction* to the *understanding of disorders* such as depression, and to their *treatment*.

Clinical psychology:
The study, assessment, and treatment of people with psychological difficulties.

■ MAKING CLINICAL JUDGMENTS

Do the influences on our social judgment discussed in earlier chapters also affect clinicians' judgments of clients? If so, what biases should clinicians (and their clients) be wary of?

Clinical psychologists struggle to make accurate judgments, recommendations, and predictions in any number of real situations: Is Susan suicidal? Should John be committed to a mental hospital? If released, will Tom be a homicide risk?

Such clinical judgments are also *social* judgments, and thus vulnerable to illusory correlations, overconfidence bred by hindsight, and self-confirming diagnoses (Leary & Maddux, 1987). Let's see how—and why—alerting mental health workers, interviewers, and others to how people form both impressions and *mis*impressions might help avert misjudgments and perhaps fatal mistakes.

"To free a man of error is to give, not to take away. Knowledge that a thing is false is a truth."
Arthur Schopenhauer, 1788–1860

ILLUSORY CORRELATIONS

Consider the following court transcript in which a seemingly confident psychologist (PSY) is being questioned by an attorney (ATT):

> **ATT**: You asked the defendant to draw a human figure?
> **PSY**: Yes.
> **ATT**: And this is the figure he drew for you? What does it indicate to you about his personality?

PSY: You will note this is a rear view of a male. This is very rare, statistically. It indicates hiding guilt feelings, or turning away from reality.

ATT: And this drawing of a female figure, does it indicate anything to you; and, if so, what?

PSY: It indicates hostility toward women on the part of the subject. The pose, the hands on the hips, the hard-looking face, the stern expression.

ATT: Anything else?

PSY: The size of the ears indicates a paranoid outlook, or hallucinations. Also, the absence of feet indicates feelings of insecurity. (Jeffery, 1964)

The assumption here, as in so many clinical judgments, is that test results reveal something important. Do they? There is a simple way to find out. Have one clinician administer and interpret the test. Have another clinician assess the same person's symptoms. Repeat this process with many people. The proof is in the pudding: Are test outcomes in fact correlated with reported symptoms? Some tests are indeed predictive. Others, such as the Draw-a-Person test above, have correlations far weaker than their users suppose. Why, then, do clinicians continue to express confidence in uninformative or ambiguous tests?

Pioneering experiments by Loren Chapman and Jean Chapman (1969, 1971) help us see why. They invited both college students and professional clinicians to study some test performances and diagnoses. If the students or clinicians *expected* a particular association they generally *perceived* it, regardless of whether the data were supportive. For example, clinicians who believed that suspicious people draw peculiar eyes on the Draw-a-Person test perceived such a relationship—even when shown cases in which suspicious people drew peculiar eyes *less* often than nonsuspicious people. Believing that a relationship existed between two things, they were more likely to notice confirming instances. To believe is to see.

In fairness to clinicians, illusory thinking also occurs among political analysts, historians, sportscasters, personnel directors, stockbrokers, and many other professionals, including the research psychologists who point them out. As a researcher I have often been blind to the shortcomings of my theoretical analyses. I so eagerly presume that my idea of truth is *the* truth that, no matter how hard I try, I cannot see my own error. This is evident in the editorial review process that precedes any research publication. During the last 25 years I have read dozens of reviews of my own manuscripts and have been a reviewer for dozens of others. My experience is that it is far easier to spot someone else's sloppy thinking than to perceive one's own.

"No one can see his own errors."
Psalms 19:12

HINDSIGHT AND OVERCONFIDENCE

If someone we know commits suicide, how do we react? One common reaction is to think that we, or those close to the person, should have been able to predict and therefore to prevent the suicide. In hindsight, we can see the suicidal signs and the pleas for help: "We should have known." One experiment gave people a description of a depressed person who later committed suicide. Compared to those not informed of the suicide, those told the person committed suicide were more likely to say they "would have expected " it (Goggin & Range, 1985). Moreover, if they were told of the suicide, their reactions to the victim's family were more negative. After a tragedy, an I-should-have-

Kurt Cobain, member of the Nirvana rock group, whose songs often expressed depressed, suicidal thinking. Should others have used such signs to predict or prevent his suicide?

"Undergraduate psychology can, and I believe should, seek to liberate the student from ignorance, but also from the arrogance of believing we know more about ourselves and others than we really do."
David L. Cole (1982)

known-it-all-along phenomenon can leave family, friends, and therapists feeling guilty. When a client becomes violent, a therapist may, in retrospect, seem negligent for not having foreseen the danger and taken appropriate measures.

David Rosenhan (1973) and seven associates provided a striking example of potential error in after-the-fact explanations. To test mental health workers' clinical insights, they each made an appointment with a different mental hospital admissions office and complained of "hearing voices." Apart from giving false names and vocations, they reported their life histories and emotional states honestly and exhibited no further symptoms. Most got diagnosed as schizophrenic and remained hospitalized for two to three weeks. The clinicians then searched for early incidents in the pseudo-patients' life histories and hospital behavior that "confirmed" and "explained" the diagnosis. Rosenhan tells of one pseudo-patient who truthfully explained to the interviewer that he

> had a close relationship with his mother but was rather remote from his father during his early childhood. During adolescence and beyond, however, his father became a close friend, while his relationship with his mother cooled. His present relationship with his wife was characteristically close and warm. Apart from occasional angry exchanges, friction was minimal. The children had rarely been spanked.

The interviewer, "knowing" the person suffered from schizophrenia, explained the problem this way:

> This white 39-year-old male . . . manifests a long history of considerable ambivalence in close relationships, which begins in early childhood. A warm relationship with his mother cools during his adolescence. A distant relationship to his father is described as becoming very intense. Affective stability is absent. His attempts to control emotionality with his wife and children are punctuated by angry outbursts and, in the case of the children, spankings. And while he says that he has several good friends, one senses considerable ambivalence embedded in those relationships also.

Rosenhan later told some staff members (who had heard about his controversial experiment but doubted such mistakes could occur in their hospital) that during the next three months one or more pseudo-patients would seek admission to their hospital. After the three months, he asked the staff to guess which of the 193 patients admitted during that time were really pseudo-patients. Of the 193 new patients, 41 were accused by at least one staff member of being normal. Actually, there were none.

SELF-CONFIRMING DIAGNOSES

So far we've seen that mental health workers sometimes perceive illusory correlations and that hindsight explanations are often questionable. A third problem with clinical judgment is that people may also supply information that fulfills clinicians' expectations. In a clever series of experiments at the University of Minnesota, Mark Snyder (1984, 1992), in collaboration with William Swann and others, gave interviewers some hypotheses to test concerning individuals' traits. To get a feel for their experiments, imagine yourself on a blind date with someone who has been told that you are an uninhibited, outgoing person. To see whether this is true, your date slips questions into the conversation, such as, "Have you ever done anything crazy in front of other people?" As you answer such questions, will your date meet a different "you" than if you were probed for instances when you were shy and retiring?

Snyder and Swann found that people often test for a trait by looking for information that confirms it. If they are trying to find out if someone is an extravert, they often solicit instances of extraversion ("What would you do if you wanted to liven things up at a party?"). Testing for introversion, they are more likely to ask, "What factors make it hard for you to really open up to people?" Such questioning leads those being tested for extraversion to behave more sociably and those being tested for introversion to appear more shy and reserved. By *our* behavior, it seems, we create the kind of people we expect to see.

At Indiana University, Russell Fazio and his colleagues (1981) reproduced this finding and also discovered that those asked the "extraverted questions" later perceived themselves as actually more outgoing than those asked the introverted questions. Moreover, they really became noticeably more outgoing. An accomplice of the experimenter later met each subject in a waiting room and 70 percent of the time correctly guessed from the subject's behavior which condition the subject had come from.

When given the structured list of questions to choose from, even experienced psychotherapists prefer the extraverted questions when testing for extraversion and thus unwittingly trigger extraverted behavior among their interviewees (Dallas & Baron, 1985; Copeland & Snyder, in press; Snyder & Thomsen, 1988). Even when making up their own questions, interviewers' expectations may influence their questioning *if* they have definite preexisting ideas (Devine & others, 1990; Hodgins & Zuckerman, 1993; Swann & Giuliano, 1987). Strong beliefs may generate their own confirmation.

Confirmation bias also appears when people evaluate themselves. Consider for a moment: Are you happy with your social life? Zva Kunda and colleagues (1993) put this question to students at the University of Waterloo and elsewhere. The students searched their memories for confirming instances and thus ended up feeling happier than students asked, "Are you unhappy with your social life?" Search and you shall see.

In other experiments, Snyder and his colleagues (1982) tried to get people to search for behaviors that would *disconfirm* the trait they were testing. In one experiment, they told the interviewers "it is relevant and informative to find out ways in which the person . . . may not be like the stereotype." In another experiment Snyder (1981a) offered "$25 to the person who develops the set of questions that tell the most about . . . the interviewee." Still, confirmation bias persisted: People resisted choosing "introverted" questions when testing for extraversion.

Based on Snyder's experiments, can you see why the behaviors of people undergoing psychotherapy come to fit the theories of their therapists (Whitman & others, 1963)? When a psychologist and a psychiatrist, Harold Renaud and Floyd Estess (1961), conducted life-history interviews of 100 healthy, successful adult men, they were startled to discover that their subjects' childhood experiences were loaded with "traumatic events," tense relations with certain people, and bad decisions by their parents—the very factors usually used to explain psychiatric problems. When Freudian therapists go fishing for traumas in early childhood experiences, they often find their hunches confirmed. Thus, surmises Snyder (1981):

> The psychiatrist who believes (erroneously) that adult gay males had bad childhood relationships with their mothers may meticulously probe for recalled (or fabricated) signs of tension between their gay clients and their mothers, but neglect to so carefully interrogate their heterosexual clients about their maternal relationships. No doubt, any individual could recall some friction with his or her mother, however minor or isolated the incidents.

Skeptics argue that therapists' search for hunch-confirming information explains many "recovered memories." Books such as Ellen Bass and Laura Davis's (1988) *The Courage to Heal* suggest that survivors of child sex abuse are likely to experience feelings of depression, shame, unworthiness, perfectionism, and powerlessness. When patients present such symptoms (which may actually result from many causes), some therapists will actively search for evidence that confirms their suspicions of sex abuse (Harris, 1994; Loftus & Ketcham, 1994; Poole & others, 1995). The therapist may explain that "people who've been abused often have your symptoms, so you probably were abused." If the patient cannot remember any abuse, the therapist may use hypnosis, guided imagery, or dream interpretation in hopes of recovering confirming information. In some cases, such confirmation-seeking tactics have led clients to create memories for events that never happened.

CLINICAL VERSUS STATISTICAL PREDICTION

Given these hindsight- and diagnosis-confirming tendencies, it will come as no surprise that most clinicians and interviewers express more confidence in their intuitive assessments than in statistical data. Yet when researchers pit statistical prediction (as when predicting graduate school success using a formula that includes grades and aptitude scores) against intuitive prediction, the statistics usually win. Statistical predictions are indeed unreliable, but human intuition—even expert intuition—is even more unreliable (Dawes & others, 1989; Faust & Ziskin, 1988; Meehl, 1954).

Three decades after demonstrating the superiority of statistical over intuitive prediction, Paul Meehl (1986) found the evidence stronger than ever:

> There is no controversy in social science which shows [so many] studies coming out so uniformly in the same direction as this one. . . . When you are pushing 90 investigations, predicting everything from the outcome of football games to the diagnosis of liver disease and when you can hardly come up with a half dozen studies showing even a weak tendency in favor of the clinician, it is time to draw a practical conclusion. . . .

In *House of Cards: Psychology and Psychotherapy Built on Myth*, Robyn Dawes (1994) explodes the pretensions of clinical intuition. For example, during the 1970s the University of Texas Medical School at Houston admitted 150 students annually based on interviewers' ratings of their 800 most qualified candidates. When the legislature suddenly required them to admit 50 more students, they admitted the only ones still available—those to whom the interviewers had given low ratings. So what was the difference in performance between the two groups? Nil. The top-rated 150 and bottom 50 each had 82 percent of their group receive the M.D. and similar proportions receive honors. Even after the first year of residency, both groups were doing equally well. The unavoidable conclusion: Some people interview better than others. Nevertheless, the medical school interviews—by medical professionals who *thought* they could judge future competence—were a waste of time.

Ah, but what if we combined statistical prediction with clinical intuition? What if we gave professional clinicians the statistical prediction of someone's future academic performance or risk of parole violation or suicide, and asked them to refine or improve on the prediction? Alas, in the few studies where this has been done, prediction was better if the "improvements" were ignored (Dawes, 1994).

So, why do so many clinicians continue to interpret Rorschach inkblot tests and offer intuitive predictions about parolees, suicide risks, and likelihood of

When the Texas Pardon and Parole Board meets to decide prisoner releases, its members would do best to consider statistical predictors of risk rather than their own impressions.

"The effect of Meehl's work on clinical practice in the mental health area can be summed up in a single word: Zilch. He was honored, elected to the presidency of [the American Psychological Association] at a very young age in 1962, recently elected to the National Academy of Sciences, and ignored."
Robyn M. Dawes (1989)

child abuse? Partly out of sheer ignorance, says Meehl, but also partly out of "mistaken conceptions of ethics":

> If I try to forecast something important about a college student, or a criminal, or a depressed patient by inefficient rather than efficient means, meanwhile charging this person or the taxpayer 10 times as much money as I would need to achieve greater predictive accuracy that is not a sound ethical practice. That it feels better, warmer, and cuddlier to me as predictor is a shabby excuse indeed.

Such words are shocking. Do Meehl and the other researchers underestimate our intuition? To see why their findings are apparently true, consider the assessment of human potential by graduate admissions interviewers. Dawes (1976) explained why statistical prediction is so often superior to an interviewer's intuition when predicting certain outcomes such as graduate school success:

> What makes us think that we can do a better job of selection by interviewing (students) for a half hour, than we can by adding together relevant (standardized) variables, such as undergraduate GPA, GRE score, and perhaps ratings of letters of recommendation. The most reasonable explanation to me lies in our overevaluation of our cognitive capacity. And it is really cognitive conceit. Consider, for example, what goes into a GPA. Because for most graduate applicants it is based on at least $3^{1}/_{2}$ years of undergraduate study, it is a composite measure arising from a minimum of 28 courses and possibly, with the popularity of the quarter system, as many as 50. . . . Yet you and I, looking at a folder or interviewing someone for a half hour, are supposed to be able to form a better impression than one based on $3^{1}/_{2}$ years of the cumulative evaluations of 20–40 different professors. . . . Finally, if we do wish to ignore GPA, it appears that the only reason for doing so is believing that the candidate is particularly brilliant even though his or her record may not show it. What better evidence for such brilliance can we have than a score on a carefully devised aptitude test? Do we really think we are better equipped to assess such aptitude than is the Educational Testing Service, whatever its faults?

IMPLICATIONS

"'I beseech ye in the bowels of Christ, think that ye may be mistaken.' I shall like to have that written over the portals of every church, every school, and every courthouse, and, may I say, of every legislative body in the United States."
Judge Learned Hand, 1951, echoing Oliver Cromwell's 1650 plea to the Church of Scotland

Although psychotherapy often helps troubled individuals (Smith & others, 1980; Elkin, 1986), we have seen possible problems with clinical judgments. Professional clinicians:

- Can easily convince clients of worthless diagnoses
- Are frequently the victims of illusory correlation
- Are too readily convinced of their own after-the-fact analyses
- Often fail to appreciate that erroneous diagnoses can be self-confirming

The implications for mental health workers are more easily stated than practiced: Be mindful that clients' verbal agreement with what you say does not prove its validity. Beware of the tendency to see relationships that you expect to see or that are supported by striking examples readily available in your memory. Rely on your notes more than your memory. Recognize that hindsight is seductive: It can lead you to feel overconfident and sometimes to judge yourself too harshly for not having foreseen outcomes. Guard against the tendency to ask questions that assume your preconceptions are correct; consider opposing ideas and test them, too (Garb, 1994).

When analyzing clients, mental health workers, like all of us, are vulnerable to cognitive illusions.

Research on illusory thinking has implications not only for mental health workers but for all psychologists. What Lewis Thomas (1978) said of biology may as justly be said of psychology:

> The solidest piece of scientific truth I know of, the one thing about which I feel totally confident, is that we are profoundly ignorant about nature. Indeed, I regard this as the major discovery of the past 100 years of biology. . . . It is this sudden confrontation with the depth and scope of ignorance that represents the most significant contribution of 20th century science to the human intellect. We are, at last, facing up to it. In earlier times, we either pretended to understand how things worked or ignored the problem, or simply made up stories to fill the gaps.

Psychology has crept only a little way across the edge of insight into our human condition. Ignorant of their ignorance, some psychologists invent theories to fill gaps in their understanding. Intuitive observation seems to support these theories, even if they are mutually contradictory. Research on illusory thinking therefore leads us to a new humility concerning the truth of our unchecked speculation. It reminds research psychologists why they must test their preconceptions before presenting them as truth. To seek the hard facts, even if they threaten cherished illusions, is the goal of every science.

I am *not* arguing that the scientific method can answer all human questions. There are questions that it cannot address and ways of knowing that it cannot capture. But science *is* one means for examining claims about nature, human nature included. Propositions that imply observable results are best evaluated by systematic observation and experiment—which is the whole point of social psychology. We also need inventive genius, lest we test only trivialities. But whatever unique and enduring insights psychology can offer will be hammered out by research psychologists sorting through competing claims. Science always involves an interplay between intuition and rigorous test, between creative hunch and skepticism.

"One thing I have learned in a long life: that all our science, measured against reality, is primitive and childlike—and yet it is the most precious thing we have."
Albert Einstein, in B. Hoffman & H. Dukes, *Albert Einstein: Creator and Rebel*, 1973

"Science is the great antidote to the poison of enthusiasm and superstition."
Adam Smith, *Wealth of Nations*, 1776

VIEWPOINT

A PHYSICIAN LOOKS AT SOCIAL PSYCHOLOGY

Reading this book helps me understand the human behaviors I observe in my work as a cancer specialist and as medical director of a large staff of physicians. A few examples:

Reviews of medical records illustrate the "I-knew-it-all-along phenomenon." Physician reviewers who assess the medical records of their colleagues often believe, in hindsight, that problems such as cancer or appendicitis should clearly have been recognized and treated much more quickly. Once you know the correct diagnosis, it's easy to look back and interpret the early symptoms accordingly.

For many physicians I have known, the intrinsic motives behind their entering the profession—to help people, to be scientifically stimulated—soon become "overjustified" by the high pay. Before long, the joy is lost. The extrinsic rewards become the reason to practice, and the physician, having lost the altruistic motives, works to increase "success," measured in income.

"Self-serving bias" is ever present. We physicians gladly accept personal credit when things go well. When they don't—when the patient is misdiagnosed or doesn't get well or dies—we attribute the failure elsewhere. We were given inadequate information or the case was ill-fated from the beginning.

I also observe many examples of "belief perseverance." Even when presented with the documented facts about, say, how AIDS is transmitted, people will strangely persist in wrongly believing that it is just a "gay" disease or that they should fear catching it from mosquito bites. It makes me wonder: How can I more effectively persuade people of what they need to know and act upon?

Indeed, as I observe medical attitudes and decision making I feel myself submerged in a giant practical laboratory of social psychology. To understand the goings-on around me, I find social psychological insights invaluable and would strongly advise premed students to study the field. (Burton F. VanderLaan, Chicago, Illinois)

SUMMING UP

To review and apply principles of social cognition discussed in previous chapters, this chapter considers some of social psychology's contributions to clinical understanding, treatment, and judgment. As psychiatrists and clinical psychologists diagnose and treat their clients, they may perceive illusory correlations. Hindsight explanations of people's difficulties are sometimes too easy. Indeed, after-the-fact explaining can breed overconfidence in clinical judgment. When interacting with clients, erroneous diagnoses are sometimes self-confirming, because interviewers tend to seek and recall information that verifies what they are looking for.

Research on the errors that so easily creep into intuitive judgments illustrates the need for rigorous testing of intuitive conclusions. The scientific method cannot answer all questions and is itself vulnerable to bias. Thankfully, however, it can help us sift truth from falsehood.

■ SOCIAL COGNITION IN PROBLEM BEHAVIORS

One of psychology's most intriguing research frontiers concerns the cognitive processes that accompany psychological disorders. What are the memories, attributions, and expectations of depressed, lonely, shy, or illness-prone people?

SOCIAL COGNITION AND DEPRESSION

As we all know from experience, depressed people are negative thinkers. They view life through dark-colored glasses. With seriously depressed people—those who are feeling worthless, lethargic, disinterested in friends and family, and unable to sleep or eat normally—the negative thinking becomes self-defeating. Their intensely pessimistic outlook leads them to magnify bad experiences and minimize good ones. A depressed young woman illustrates: "The real me is worthless and inadequate. I can't move forward with my work because I become frozen with doubt" (Burns, 1980, p. 29).

Distortion or Realism?

Are all depressed people unrealistically negative? To find out, Lauren Alloy and Lyn Abramson (1979) studied college students who were either mildly depressed or not depressed. They had the students observe whether their pressing a button was linked with a light coming on. Surprisingly, the depressed students were quite accurate in estimating their degree of control. It was the nondepressives whose judgments were distorted, who exaggerated the extent of their control.

This surprising phenomenon of **depressive realism**, nicknamed the "sadder-but-wiser effect," shows up in various judgments of one's control or skill (Ackermann & DeRubeis, 1991; Alloy & others, 1990). Shelley Taylor (1989, p. 214) explains:

> Normal people exaggerate how competent and well liked they are. Depressed people do not. Normal people remember their past behavior with a rosy glow. Depressed people [unless severely depressed] are more evenhanded in recalling their successes and failures. Normal people describe themselves primarily positively. Depressed people describe both their positive and negative qualities. Normal people take credit for successful outcomes and tend to deny responsibility for failure. Depressed people accept responsibility for both success and failure. Normal people exaggerate the control they have over what goes on around them. Depressed people are less vulnerable to the illusion of control. Normal people believe to an unrealistic degree that the future holds a bounty of good things and few bad things. Depressed people are more

Depressive realism:
The tendency of mildly depressed people to make accurate rather than self-serving judgments, attributions, and predictions.

Stresses challenge some people and defeat others. Researchers have sought to understand the "explanatory style" that makes some people more vulnerable to depression than others.

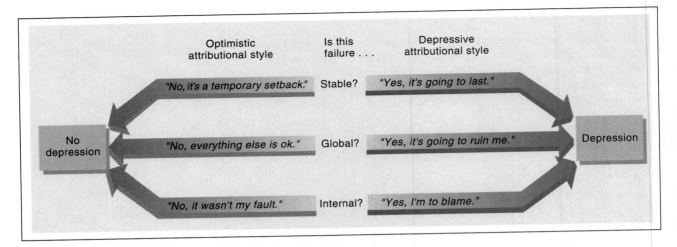

Is this failure . . .

Optimistic attributional style		Depressive attributional style
"No, it's a temporary setback."	Stable?	"Yes, it's going to last."
"No, everything else is ok."	Global?	"Yes, it's going to ruin me."
"No, it wasn't my fault."	Internal?	"Yes, I'm to blame."

No depression ← ... → Depression

■ **FIGURE 5–1**

Depressive explanatory style. Depression is linked with a negative, pessimistic way of explaining and interpreting failures.

Explanatory style:
One's habitual way of explaining life events. A negative pessimistic, depressive explanatory style attributes failures to stable, global, and internal causes.

"Life is the art of being well deceived."
William Hazlitt, 1778–1830

realistic in their perceptions of the future. In fact, on virtually every point on which normal people show enhanced self-regard, illusions of control, and unrealistic visions of the future, depressed people fail to show the same biases. "Sadder but wiser" does indeed appear to apply to depression.

Underlying the thinking of depressed people are their attributions of responsibility. Consider: If you fail an exam and blame yourself, you may conclude that you are stupid or lazy, and feel depressed. If you attribute the failure to an unfair exam or to other circumstances beyond your control, you are more likely to feel angry. In over 100 studies involving 15,000 subjects (Sweeney & others, 1986), depressed people have been more likely than nondepressed people to exhibit a negative **explanatory style** (Figure 5–1). They are more likely to attribute failure and setbacks to causes that are *stable* ("It's going to last forever"), *global* ("It's going to affect everything I do"), and *internal* ("It's all my fault"). The result of this pessimistic, overgeneralized, self-blaming thinking, say Abramson and her colleagues (1989), is a depressing sense of hopelessness.

Compared to this depressive explanatory style, self-serving illusions are adaptive. Although positive illusions can breed false optimism and self-righteousness, such illusions make us happier, more productive, and less self-preoccupied. Mental health, conclude researchers Shelley Taylor and Jonathan Brown (1988), derives from "overly positive self-evaluations, exaggerated perceptions of control or mastery, and unrealistic optimism."

Is Negative Thinking a Cause or a Result of Depression?

The cognitive accompaniments of depression raise a chicken-and-egg question: Do depressed moods cause negative thinking, or does negative thinking cause depression?

Depressed Moods Cause Negative Thinking

As we saw in Chapter 3, our moods definitely color our thinking. When we *feel* happy, we see and recall a good world. But let our mood turn gloomy, and our thoughts switch on to a different track. Off come the rose-colored glasses; on come the dark glasses. Now the bad mood primes our recollections of negative events (Bower, 1987; Johnson & Magaro, 1987). Our relationships seem to sour, our self-image takes a dive, our hopes for the future dim, people's behavior seems more sinister (Brown & Taylor, 1986; Mayer & Salovey, 1987). Thus, as depression increases, memories and expectations plummet; when depression lifts, thinking brightens (Barnett & Gotlib, 1988; Kuiper & Higgins, 1985).

As Edward Hirt and his colleagues (1992) demonstrated in a study of some rabid Indiana University basketball fans, a bad mood induced by rejection or defeat can darken our thinking. After the fans were either depressed by watching their team lose or elated by a victory, the researchers asked them to predict the team's future performance, and their own. After a loss, people offered bleaker assessments not only of the team's future but also of their own likely performance at throwing darts, solving anagrams, and getting a date. When things aren't going our way, it may seem as though they never will.

A depressed mood also affects behavior. The person who is withdrawn, glum, and complaining does not elicit joy and warmth in others. Stephen Strack and James Coyne (1983) found that depressed people were realistic in thinking that others didn't appreciate their behavior. Their pessimistic outlooks and, especially, their bad moods trigger social rejection (Carver & others, 1994). Depressed behavior can also trigger reciprocal depression in others. College students who have depressed roommates tend to become a little depressed themselves (Burchill & Stiles, 1988; Joiner, 1994; Sanislow & others, 1989). Depressed people are therefore at risk for being divorced, fired, or shunned, thus magnifying their depression (Coyne & others, 1991; Gotlib & Lee, 1989; Sacco & Dunn, 1990). They may also seek out those whose unfavorable views of them verify, and further magnify, their low self-image (Swann & others, 1991).

So being depressed has cognitive and behavioral effects. Does it also have cognitive origins?

Negative Thinking Causes Depressed Moods

Many people feel depressed when experiencing severe stress—losing a job, getting divorced or rejected, suffering physical trauma—anything that disrupts their sense of who they are and why they are a worthy human being (Hamil-

BEHIND THE SCENES

As graduate students we were shocked to discover that the popular and clinical lore that depressed people distort reality had never been tested. We were further surprised when our own studies revealed that nondepressed people often distort reality—in an optimistic direction. This phenomenon of depressive realism—what we call the "sadder but wiser effect"—makes us wonder: Does realism about oneself and one's world make people more vulnerable to depression? Or is realism a consequence of depression?

LAUREN ALLOY, *Temple University*
LYN ABRAMSON, *University of Wisconsin*

ton & others, 1993; Kendler & others, 1993). Such brooding can be adaptive; insights gained during times of depressed inactivity may later result in better strategies for interacting with the world. But depression-prone people respond to bad events in an especially self-focused, self-blaming way (Pyszczynski & others, 1991; Wood & others, 1990a,b). Their self-esteem fluctuates more rapidly up with boosts and down with threats (Butler & others, 1994).

Why are some people so readily depressed by *minor* stresses? New evidence suggests that a negative explanatory style contributes to depressive reactions. Colin Sacks and Daphne Bugental (1987) asked some young women to get acquainted with a stranger who sometimes acted cold and unfriendly, creating an awkward social situation. Unlike optimistic women, those with a pessimistic explanatory style—who characteristically offer stable, global, and internal attributions for bad events—reacted to the social failure by feeling depressed. Moreover, they then behaved more antagonistically toward the next person they met. Their negative thinking had led to a negative mood response, which then led to negative behavior.

Outside the laboratory, studies of children, teenagers, and adults confirm that those with the pessimistic explanatory style are more likely to become depressed when bad things happen (Alloy & Clements, 1992; Brown & Siegel, 1988; Nolen-Hoeksema & others, 1986). "A recipe for severe depression is pre-existing pessimism encountering failure," notes Martin Seligman (1991, p. 78). Moreover, patients who end therapy no longer feeling depressed but still with a negative explanatory style tend to relapse as bad events occur (Seligman, 1992). If those with a more optimistic explanatory style relapse, they often recover quickly (Metalsky & others, 1993; Needles & Abramson, 1990). Do you view negative events such as money problems, bad grades, or social rejections as within your power to control? If so, you are probably less vulnerable to depression.

Researcher Peter Lewinsohn and his colleagues (1985) have assembled these findings into a coherent psychological understanding of depression. In their view, the negative self-image, attributions, and expectations of a depressed person are an essential link in a vicious cycle that is triggered by negative experience—perhaps academic or vocational failure, or family conflict, or social rejection (Figure 5–2). In those vulnerable to depression, such stresses trigger

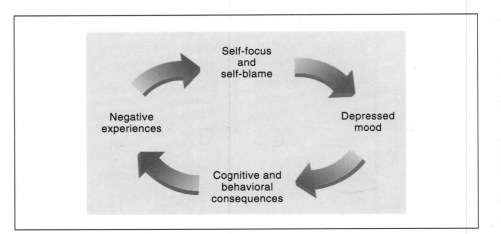

■ **FIGURE 5–2**
The vicious cycle of depression.

brooding, self-focused, self-blaming thoughts (Pyszczynski & others, 1991; Wood & others, 1990a,b). Such ruminations create a depressed mood that drastically alters the way a person thinks and acts, which then fuels further negative experiences, self-blame, and depressed mood. Depression is therefore *both* a cause and a consequence of negative cognitions.

Martin Seligman (1991) believes that self-focus and self-blame help explain the near-epidemic levels of depression in the western world today. In North America, for example, young adults today are three times as likely as their grandparents to have suffered depression—despite their grandparents' greater years at risk (Cross-National Collaborative Group, 1992). Seligman believes that the decline of religion and family, plus the growth of the individualist "you can do it" attitude, breeds hopelessness and self-blame when things don't go well. Failed courses, careers, and marriages produce despair when we stand alone, with nothing and no one to fall back on. If, as a macho *Fortune* ad declared, you can "make it on your own," on "your own drive, your own guts, your own energy, your own ambition," then whose fault is it if you *don't* make it on your own? In nonwestern cultures, where close-knit relationships and cooperation are the norm, major depression is less common and less tied to guilt and self-blame over perceived failure. In Japan, for example, depressed people instead tend to report feeling shame over letting down their family or co-workers (Draguns, 1990).

These insights into the thinking style linked with depression have prompted social psychologists to study thinking patterns associated with other problems. How do those who are plagued with excessive loneliness, shyness, or substance abuse view themselves? How well do they recall their successes and their failures? To what do they attribute their ups and downs? Is their attention focused on themselves or on others?

SOCIAL COGNITION AND LONELINESS

If depression is the common cold of psychological disorders, then loneliness is the headache. Loneliness, whether chronic or temporary, is a painful awareness that our social relationships are less numerous or meaningful than we desire. Jenny de Jong-Gierveld (1987) observed in her study of Dutch adults that unmarried and unattached people are more likely to feel lonely. This prompted her to speculate that the modern emphasis on individual fulfillment and the depreciation of marriage and family life may be "loneliness-provoking" (as well as depression-provoking).

But loneliness need not coincide with aloneness. One can feel lonely in the middle of a party. And one can be utterly alone—as I am while writing these words in the solitude of an isolated turret office at a British university 5000 miles from home—without feeling lonely. To feel lonely is to feel excluded from a group, unloved by those around you, unable to share your private concerns, or different and alienated from those in your surroundings (Beck & Young, 1978; Davis & Franzoi, 1986). Adolescents experience such feelings more commonly than do adults. When beeped by an electronic pager at various times during a week and asked to record what they were doing and how they felt, adolescents more often than adults reported feeling lonely when alone (Larson & others, 1982). Males and females feel lonely under somewhat different cir-

Close relationships and a positive explanatory style help protect people from feelings of loneliness.

cumstances—males when isolated from group interaction, females when deprived of close one-to-one relationships (Berg & McQuinn, 1988; Stokes & Levin, 1986).

Like depressed people, chronically lonely people seem caught in a vicious cycle of self-defeating social cognitions and social behaviors. They have some of the negative explanatory style of the depressed; they blame themselves for their poor social relationships and see most things as beyond their control (Anderson & others, 1994; Snodgrass, 1987). Moreover, they perceive others in negative ways. When paired with a stranger of the same sex or with a first-year college roommate, lonely students are more likely to perceive the other person negatively (Jones & others, 1981; Wittenberg & Reis, 1986).

These negative views may both reflect and color the lonely person's experience. Believing in their social unworthiness and feeling pessimistic about others inhibits lonely people from acting to reduce their loneliness. Lonely people often do find it hard to introduce themselves, make phone calls, and participate in groups (Rook, 1984; Spitzberg & Hurt, 1987). They tend to be self-conscious and low in self-esteem (Cheek & Melchior, 1990; Vaux, 1988). When talking with a stranger, they spend more time talking about themselves and take less interest in their conversational partners than do nonlonely people (Jones & others, 1982). After such conversations, the new acquaintances often come away with more negative impressions of the lonely people (Jones & others, 1983).

SOCIAL COGNITION AND SOCIAL ANXIETY

Being interviewed for a much-wanted job, dating someone for the first time, stepping into a roomful of strangers, performing before an important audience, or—that most common of phobias—giving a speech can make almost anyone feel anxious. Some people, especially those who are shy or easily embarrassed, feel anxious in almost any situation in which they might be evaluated. For these people, anxiety is more a trait than a temporary state.

What causes us to feel anxious in social situations? Why are some people shackled in the prison of their own shyness? Barry Schlenker and Mark Leary (1982b, 1985; Leary, 1984, 1986; Maddux & others, 1988) answer these questions by applying self-presentation theory. As you may recall from Chapters 2 and 4, self-presentation theory assumes that we are eager to present ourselves in ways that make a good impression. The implications for social anxiety are straightforward: *We feel anxious when we are motivated to impress others but doubt our ability to do so.* This simple principle helps explain a variety of research findings, each of which may ring true in your own experience. We feel most anxious when:

- Dealing with powerful, high-status people—people whose impressions of us matter
- In an evaluative context, as when making a first impression on the parents of one's fiancé
- The interaction focuses on something central to our self-image, as when a college professor presents ideas before peers at a professional convention
- We are in novel or unstructured situations, such as a first school dance or first formal dinner, where we are unsure of the social rules
- We are self-conscious (as shy people often are) and our attention is focused on ourselves and how we are coming across

The natural tendency in all such situations is to be cautiously self-protective: to talk less; to avoid topics that reveal one's ignorance; to be guarded about oneself; to be unassertive, agreeable, and smiling. Ironically, such anxious concern with making a good impression often makes a not-good impression (Broome & Wegner, 1994; Meleshko & Alden, 1993).

Shyness is a form of social anxiety characterized by self-consciousness and worry about what others think (Anderson & Harvey, 1988; Asendorpf, 1987;

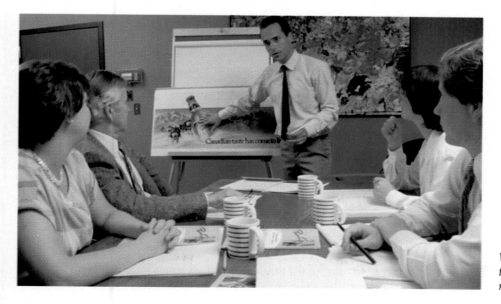

When eager to impress important people, social anxiety is natural.

Carver & Scheier, 1986). Self-conscious people (whose numbers include many adolescents) see incidental events as somehow relevant to themselves (Fenigstein, 1984; Fenigstein & Vanable, 1992). They overpersonalize situations, a tendency that breeds anxious concern and, in extreme cases, paranoia. Shown someone they think is interviewing them live (actually a videotaped interviewer), they perceive the interviewer as less accepting and interested in them (Pozo & others, 1991). They also overestimate the extent to which other people are watching and evaluating them. If their hair won't comb right or they have a facial blemish, they assume everyone else notices and judges them accordingly.

To reduce social anxiety, some people turn to alcohol. Alcohol lowers anxiety as it reduces self-consciousness (Hull & Young, 1983). Thus, chronically self-conscious people are especially likely to drink following a failure. If they become alcoholics, they are more likely than those low in self-consciousness to relapse from treatment when they again experience stress or failure.

Symptoms as diverse as anxiety and alcohol abuse can also serve a self-handicapping function. Labeling oneself as anxious, shy, depressed, or under the influence of alcohol can provide an excuse for failure (Snyder & Smith, 1986). Behind a barricade of symptoms, the person's ego stands secure. "Why don't I date? Because I'm shy, so people don't easily get to know the real me." The symptom is an unconscious strategic ploy to explain away negative outcomes.

What if we were to remove the need for such a ploy by providing people with a handy alternative explanation for their anxiety and therefore for possible failure? Would a shy person no longer need to be shy? That is precisely what Susan Brodt and Philip Zimbardo (1981) found when they brought shy and not-shy college women to the laboratory and had them converse with a handsome male who posed as another subject. Before the conversation, the women were cooped up in a small chamber and blasted with loud noise. Some of the shy women (but not others) were told that the noise would leave them with a pounding heart, a common symptom of social anxiety. Thus when these women later talked with the man, they could attribute their pounding heart and any conversational difficulties to the noise, not to their shyness or social inadequacy. Compared to the shy women who were not given this handy explanation for their pounding hearts, these women were no longer so shy. They talked fluently once the conversation got going and asked questions of the man. In fact, unlike the other shy women (whom the man could easily spot as shy), these women were to him indistinguishable from the not-shy women.

SOCIAL COGNITION AND PHYSICAL ILLNESS

Behavioral medicine:
An interdisciplinary field that integrates and applies behavioral and medical knowledge about health and disease.

In the industrialized world, at least half of all deaths are linked with behavior—with consuming cigarettes, alcohol, drugs, and harmful foods; with reactions to stress; with lack of exercise and not following a doctor's orders. Efforts to study and change these behavioral contributions to illness helped create a new interdisciplinary field called **behavioral medicine.**

Health Psychology

Health psychology:
A subfield of psychology that provides psychology's contribution to behavioral medicine.

Psychology's contribution to this interdisciplinary science is its new subfield **health psychology**. Its numbers include many of the estimated 3500 psychologists now working in Canadian and U.S. medical schools (Michaelson, 1993).

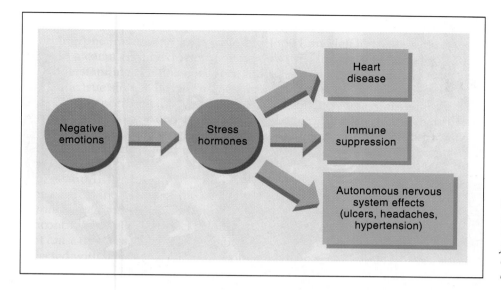

■ FIGURE 5–3
Stress-caused negative emo-tions may have various ef-fects on health. This is espe-cially so for depressed or anger-prone people.

Among health psychology's questions (and some tentative answers), are the following:

1. Do characteristic emotions, and ways of responding to stressful events, pre-dict susceptibility to heart disease, stroke, cancer, and other ailments (Fig-ure 5–3)?

   ■ Heart disease has been linked with a competitive, an impatient, and—the aspect that matters—an *anger-prone* personality (Matthews, 1988; Williams, 1993). Under stress, reactive, anger-prone "Type A" people se-crete more of the stress hormones believed to accelerate the buildup of plaque on the walls of the heart's arteries.

   ■ Sustained stress suppresses the disease-fighting immune system, leav-ing us more vulnerable to infections and malignancy (Cohen & others, 1991, 1993; Institute of Medicine, 1989). Experiments reveal that the im-mune system's activity can also be influenced by conditioning.

2. How can we control or even reduce stress?

   ■ Health psychologists are exploring the benefits of aerobic exercise (an ef-fective antidote to mild depression and anxiety), relaxation training (to help control such tension-related ailments as headaches and high blood pressure), and supportive close relationships (which can help buffer the impact of stress).

3. How do people decide whether they are ill, and what can be done to en-sure that they seek medical help and follow a treatment regimen?

   ■ We decide we are sick when symptoms fit one of our existing "schemas" for disease (Bishop, 1991). Does the small cyst match our idea of a ma-lignant lump? Is the stomachache bad enough to be appendicitis? Is the pain in the chest area merely—as many heart attack victims suppose—a muscle spasm?

   ■ Patients are more willing to follow treatment instructions when they have a warm relationship with their doctor, when they help plan their treat-

The Delaney sisters, both over 100, attribute their longevity to a positive outlook on life.

Peterson, Seligman, and George Valliant (1988) offer other findings: Harvard graduates who expressed the most optimism when interviewed in 1946 were healthiest when restudied in 1980. Virginia Tech introductory psychology students who offered optimistic explanations for bad events suffered fewer colds, sore throats, and flus a year later. Michael Scheier and Charles Carver (1992) similarly report that optimists (who agree, for example, that "I usually expect the best") are less often bothered by various illnesses and recover faster from coronary bypass surgery.

Even cancer patients appear more likely to survive if their attitude is hopeful and determined rather than pessimistic and stoical (Levy & others, 1988; Pettingale & others, 1985). One study of 86 women undergoing breast cancer therapy reported a finding that stunned the researchers: Those who participated in morale-boosting weekly support group sessions survived an average of 37 months, double the 19-month average survival time among the nonparticipants (Spiegel & others, 1989). (At least a half-dozen research teams are now attempting to replicate this finding.) Blood tests suggest a possible reason, by linking the pessimistic explanatory style with weaker immune defenses (Kamen & others, 1988). Compared to UCLA cancer patients in a control group, those who participated in support groups became more upbeat, with an associated increase in immune cells (Cousins, 1989). Beliefs, it seems, can boost biology.

From their own studies, researchers Howard Tennen and Glenn Affleck (1987) agree that a positive, hopeful explanatory style is generally good medicine. But they also remind us that every silver lining has a cloud. Optimists may see themselves as invulnerable and thus fail to take sensible precautions. (Those who smoke hazardous high-tar cigarettes optimistically underestimate the risks involved—Segerstrom & others, 1993.) And when things go wrong in a big way—when the optimist encounters a devastating illness—adversity can be shattering. Optimism *is* good for health. But remember: Even optimists have a mortality rate of 100 percent.

S ocial psychologists are actively exploring the attributions and expecta- tions of depressed, lonely, socially anxious, and physically ill people. De- pressed people have a negative explanatory style. Compared to nonde- pressed people, they engage in more self-blame, they interpret and recall events in a more negative light, and they are less hopeful about the future. Despite their more negative judgments, mildly depressed people in labora- tory tests tend to be surprisingly realistic.

Depressed thinking has consequences for the depressed person's behav- ior, which in turn helps maintain a self-defeating cycle. Much the same can be said of those who suffer chronic loneliness and states of social anxiety, such as extreme shyness. The mushrooming new field of health psychology is exploring the links among illness, stress, and a pessimistic explanatory style.

"You are dust, and to dust you shall return."
Genesis 3:19

S U M M I N G   U P

■ SOCIAL-PSYCHOLOGICAL APPROACHES TO TREATMENT

W e have considered patterns of social thinking that are linked with problems in living, ranging from serious depression to everyday shyness to physical illness. Do these maladaptive thought patterns suggest any treatments?

There is no single social-psychological therapy. But therapy is a social en- counter, and social psychologists are now suggesting how their principles might be integrated into existing treatment techniques (Leary & Maddux, 1987; Strong & others, 1992). Building on what we have learned, let's consider three examples (with a fourth to come in Chapter 7, "Persuasion").

INDUCING INTERNAL CHANGE THROUGH EXTERNAL BEHAVIOR

In Chapter 4, we reviewed a broad range of evidence for a simple but power- ful principle: Our actions affect our attitudes. The roles we play, the things we say and do, and the decisions we make influence who we are. Our uncoerced behaviors are self-persuasive.

Consistent with the attitudes-follow-behavior principle, several psychother- apy techniques prescribe action. Behavior therapists try to shape behavior and, if they care about inner dispositions, assume that these will tag along after the behavior changes. Assertiveness training employs the foot-in-the-door proce- dure. The individual first role-plays assertiveness in a supportive context, then gradually becomes assertive in everyday life. Rational-emotive therapy as- sumes that we generate our own emotions; clients receive "homework" as- signments to act in new ways that will generate new emotions. Self-help groups subtly induce participants to behave in new ways in front of the group—to express anger, cry, act with high self-esteem, express positive feelings. All these techniques share a common assumption: If we cannot directly control our feelings by sheer will power, we can influence them indirectly through our behavior.

Experiments confirm that what we say about ourselves can affect how we feel. In one experiment, students were induced to write self-laudatory essays (Mirels & McPeek, 1977). These students, more than others who wrote essays about a current social issue, later expressed higher self-esteem when privately rating themselves for a different experimenter. In several more experiments, Edward Jones and his associates (1981; Rhodewalt & Agustsdottir, 1986) influenced students to present themselves to an interviewer in either self-enhancing or self-deprecating ways. Again, the public displays—whether upbeat or downbeat—carried over to later private responses on a test of actual self-esteem. Saying is believing, even when we talk about ourselves. This was especially true when the students were made to feel responsible for how they presented themselves.

The importance of perceived choice was also apparent in an experiment by Pamela Mendonca and Sharon Brehm (1983). They invited one group of overweight children who were about to begin a weight-loss program to choose the treatment they preferred. Then they periodically reminded them that they had chosen their treatment. Compared to no-choice children who simultaneously experienced the same eight-week program, those who felt responsible for their treatment had lost more weight when reweighed at the end of the eight weeks and three months later.

When a sense of choice and personal responsibility is yoked with a high level of effort, the impact is even greater, report Danny Axom and Joel Cooper (1985; Axom, 1989). They put women who wanted to lose weight through some supposedly (but not actually) therapeutic tasks, such as making perceptual judgments. Those who committed the most effort to the tasks lost the most weight. This result is especially evident when the commitment is freely chosen. The most therapeutic commitments are both uncoerced and effortful.

BREAKING VICIOUS CYCLES

If depression, loneliness, and social anxiety maintain themselves through a vicious cycle of negative experiences, negative thinking, and self-defeating behavior, it should be possible to break the cycle at any of several points—by changing the environment, by training the person to behave more constructively, by reversing negative thinking. And it is. Several different therapy methods help free people from depression's vicious cycle.

Social Skills Training

Depression, loneliness, and shyness are not just problems in someone's mind. To be around a depressed person for any length of time can be irritating and depressing. As lonely and shy people suspect, they may indeed come across poorly in social situations. In these cases, social skills training may help. By observing and then practicing new behaviors in safe situations, the person may develop the confidence to behave more effectively in other situations.

Social skills training: When shy, anxious people observe, then rehearse, then try out more assertive behaviors in real situations, their social skills often improve.

As the person begins to enjoy the rewards of behaving more skillfully, a more positive self-perception develops. Frances Haemmerlie and Robert Montgomery (1982, 1984, 1986) demonstrated this in several heartwarming studies with shy, anxious college students. Those who are inexperienced and nervous around those of the other sex may say to themselves: "I don't date much, so I must be socially inadequate, so I shouldn't try reaching out to anyone." To reverse this negative sequence, Haemmerlie and Montgomery enticed such students into pleasant interactions with people of the other sex.

In one experiment, college men completed social anxiety questionnaires and then came to the laboratory on two different days. Each day they enjoyed 12-minute conversations with each of six young women. The men thought the women were also subjects. Actually, the women had been asked to carry on a natural, positive, friendly conversation with each of the men.

The effect of these two and a half hours of conversation was remarkable. As one subject wrote afterward, "I had never met so many girls that I could have a good conversation with. After a few girls, my confidence grew to the point where I didn't notice being nervous like I once did." Such comments were supported by a variety of measures. Unlike men in a control condition, those who experienced the conversations reported considerably less female-related anxiety when retested one week and six months later. Placed alone in a room with an attractive female stranger, they also became much more likely to start a conversation. Outside the laboratory they actually began occasional dating.

Haemmerlie and Montgomery note that not only did all this occur without any counseling but it may very well have occurred *because* there was no counseling. Having behaved successfully on their own, the subjects could now perceive themselves as socially competent. Although seven months later the researchers did debrief the subjects, by that time the men had presumably enjoyed enough social success to maintain their internal attributions for success. "Nothing succeeds like success," concluded Haemmerlie (1987)—"as long as there are no external factors present that the client can use as an excuse for that success!"

Explanatory Style Therapy

The vicious cycles that maintain depression, loneliness, and shyness can be broken by social skills training, by positive experiences that alter self-perceptions, *and* by changing negative thought patterns. Some people have social skills, but their experiences with hypercritical friends and family have convinced them they do not. For such people it may be enough to help them reverse their negative beliefs about themselves and their futures. Among the cognitive therapies with this aim is an *explanatory style therapy* proposed by social psychologists (Abramson, 1988; Försterling, 1986; Greenberg & others, 1992).

One such program taught depressed college students to change their typical attributions. Mary Anne Layden (1982) first explained the advantages of making attributions more like those of the typical nondepressed person (by accepting credit for successes and seeing how circumstances can make things go wrong). After assigning a variety of tasks, she helped the students see how they typically interpreted success and failure. Then came the treatment phase: Layden instructed each person to keep a diary of daily successes and failures, noting how they contributed to their own successes and noting external reasons for their failures. When retested after a month of this attributional retraining and compared with an untreated control group, their self-esteem had risen and their attributional style had become more positive. And the more their explanatory style improved, the more their depression lifted. By changing their attributions, they had changed their emotions.

MAINTAINING CHANGE THROUGH INTERNAL ATTRIBUTIONS FOR SUCCESS

Two of the principles considered so far—that internal change may follow behavior change and that changed self-perceptions and self-attributions can help break a vicious cycle—converge on a corollary principle: Once achieved, improvements endure best if people attribute them to factors under their own control rather than to a treatment program.

As a rule, coercive techniques trigger the most drastic and immediate behavior changes (Brehm & Smith, 1986). By making the unwanted behavior extremely costly or embarrassing and the healthier behavior extremely rewarding, a therapist may achieve quick and dramatic results. The problem, as 30 years of social-psychological research reminds us, is that coerced behavior changes soon wane.

To appreciate why, consider the experience of Martha, who is concerned with her mild obesity and frustrated with her inability to do anything about it. Martha is considering several different commercial weight-control programs. Each claims it achieves the best results. She chooses one and is ordered onto a strict 1200-calorie-a-day diet. Moreover, she is required to record and report her calorie intake each day and to come in once a week and be weighed so she and her instructor can know precisely how she is doing. Confident of the program's value and not wanting to embarrass herself, Martha adheres to the program and is delighted to find the unwanted pounds gradually disappearing. "This unique program really does work!" Martha tells herself as she reaches her target weight.

Sadly, however, after graduating from the program, Martha's experience repeats that of most weight-control graduates (Wing & Jeffrey, 1979): She regains the lost weight. On the street, she sees her instructor approaching. Embarrassed, she moves to the other side of the sidewalk and looks away. Alas, she is recognized by the instructor, who warmly invites her back into "the program." Admitting that the program achieved good results for her the first time, Martha grants her need of it and agrees to return, beginning a second round of yo-yo dieting.

Martha's experience typifies that of the participants in several weight-control experiments, including one by Janet Sonne and Dean Janoff (1979). Half the participants were led, like Martha, to attribute their changed eating behavior to the program. The others were led to credit their own efforts. Both groups lost weight during the program. But when reweighed 11 weeks later, those in the self-control condition had maintained the weight loss best. These people, like those in the shy-man-meets-women study described earlier, illustrate the benefits of self-efficacy. Having learned to cope successfully and believing that *they did it,* they now felt more confident and were more effective.

Having emphasized what changed behavior and thought patterns can accomplish, we do well to remind ourselves of their limits. Social skills training and positive thinking cannot transform us into consistent winners who are loved and admired by everyone. Furthermore, temporary depression, loneliness, and shyness are perfectly appropriate responses to profoundly sad events. It is when such feelings exist chronically and without any discernible cause that there is reason for concern and a need to change the self-defeating thoughts and behaviors.

SUMMING UP

Among the social-psychological principles that may be usefully applied in treatment are these three: (1) Changes in external behavior can trigger internal change. (2) A self-defeating cycle of negative attitudes and behaviors can be broken by training more skillful behavior, by positive experiences that alter self-perceptions, and by changing negative thought patterns. (3) Improved states are best maintained after treatment if people attribute their improvement to internal factors under their continued control rather than to the treatment program itself.

■ FOR FURTHER READING

Dawes, R. M. (1994). *House of cards: Psychology and psychotherapy built on myth.* New York: Free Press. A critical analysis of therapists' beliefs and powers. Provocative and controversial, but informed by research and logic.

Friedman, H. S. (1991). *The self-healing personality: Why some people achieve health and others succumb to illness.* New York: Holt. Health psychologist Friedman offers a lucid, state-of-the-art analysis of how our genes, habits, and emotions make us disease-prone or health-prone.

Peterson, C., & Bossio, L. M. (1991). *Health and optimism.* New York: Free Press. A leading researcher shows how social cognition—especially, an optimistic versus pessimistic explanatory style—influences physical well-being.

Snyder, C. R., & Forsyth, D. F. (Eds.) (1991). *Handbook of social and clinical psychology: The health perspective.* New York: Pergamon Press. Experts offer state-of-the-art summaries of social psychology's contributions to the diagnosis, understanding, and treatment of mental and physical disorders.

PART II

SOCIAL INFLUENCE

Social psychology studies not only how we think about one another—our topic in the preceding chapters—but also how we influence and relate to one another. In Chapters 6 through 10 we therefore probe social psychology's central concern: the powers of social influence.

What are these unseen social forces that push and pull us? How powerful are they? Research on social influence helps illuminate the invisible strings by which our social worlds move us about. This unit reveals these subtle powers, especially the cultural sources of attitudes and behavior (Chapter 6), the forces of social conformity (Chapter 7), the principles of persuasion (Chapter 8), the consequences of participation in groups (Chapter 9), and how all these influences operate together in everyday situations. In Chapter 10, we take a close look at the social influences at work in a specific setting—the courtroom.

Seeing these influences, we may better understand why people feel and act as they do. And we may ourselves become less vulnerable to unwanted manipulation and more adept at pulling our own strings.

GENDER, GENES, AND CULTURE

Approaching earth from light-years away, alien scientists assigned to study the species *Homo sapiens* can hardly contain their excitement. Their plan: to observe, then abduct two randomly sampled humans for a week of study. Their first subject, Peter, is a verbally combative Los Angeles trial lawyer who grew up in Nashville but moved west seeking the "California lifestyle." After a series of brief affairs and a divorce, Peter is enjoying a second marriage, and wishes he had more time to spend with his two children. Friends describe him as self-confident, competitive, an independent thinker, and somewhat domineering in relationships.

Their second subject, Pomoko, lives with her husband and daughter in a rural Japanese village, a walk from the homes of both their parents. Pomoko prides herself on being a good daughter, loyal wife, and protective mother. Friends describe Pomoko as kind, gentle, respectful, sensitive, and supportive of her extended family.

From their small sample of two people of differing gender and culture, what might our alien scientists conclude about human nature? Would they wonder whether both are actually of the same species? Or would they be struck by deeper similarities beneath the surface differences?

The questions faced by our alien scientists are those faced by today's earth-bound scientists: How do we humans differ? How are we alike? These questions are central to a world where social diversity has become, as historian Arthur Schlesinger (1991) said, "the explosive problem of our times." In a world ripped apart by ethnic, cultural, and gender differences, how can we learn to accept our diversity, value our cultural identity, *and* recognize the extent of our human kinship?

In many important ways, Peter and Pomoko are more alike than different. As members of one great family with common ancestors, they share not only a common biology but common behavior tendencies. Each perceives the world, feels thirst, and develops grammar through identical mechanisms. Peter and Pomoko both prefer sweet tastes to sour and divide the visual spectrum into similar colors. They and their kin across the globe all similarly interpret frowns and smiles. They join groups, conform, and recognize distinctions of social status. As children, they feared strangers beginning about 8 months of age, and as adults favor members of their own groups. Confronted by those with dissimilar attitudes or attributes, they react warily or negatively. Peter and Pomoko are both intensely social creatures who feast and sing, laugh and cry, and prefer living with others to living alone. Such commonalities define their shared human nature. In truth, Peter and Pomoko are more alike than different.

Among their similarities, the most important is their capacity to learn and adapt. Their shared biology enables their social diversity. It enables those in one **culture** to value promptness, welcome frankness, and accept premarital sex, while those in another culture do not. Whether we equate beauty with slimness or shapeliness depends on when and where we live. Whether we define social justice as equality (all receive the same) or as equity (those who produce more receive more) depends on whether Marxism or capitalism shapes our ideology. Whether we tend to be expressive or reserved, casual or formal, hinges partly on whether we have spent our lives in an African, a European, or an Asian culture.

In viewing human similarities and differences, two perspectives dominate current thinking: an *evolutionary* perspective, emphasizing human kinship, and

Culture:
The enduring behaviors, ideas, attitudes, and traditions shared by a large group of people and transmitted from one generation to the next.

a *cultural* perspective, emphasizing human diversity. Nearly everyone agrees that we need both: Our genes design an adaptive human brain—a hard drive that receives the culture's software.

Evolutionary psychologists, however, highlight the universal human nature that has evolved through natural selection. Nature has selected behavior tendencies that, when triggered by the environment, contribute to the preservation and spread of one's genes. (Those not inclined to gene-promoting behaviors were less likely to have had their genes preserved in today's population.) Thanks to our evolved human nature, all human societies engage in communal sharing. All rank people by authority and status. And all have ideas about economic justice (Fiske, 1992). Cultures provide the specific rules for working out these elements of social life.

Evolutionary psychology incorporates environmental influences. Environments interact with evolved mechanisms to produce behavior much as environmental friction interacts with evolved skin mechanisms to produce callouses. Nevertheless the cultural perspective, while acknowledging that all behavior requires our evolved genes, highlights human adaptability. The diversity of our languages, customs, and expressive behaviors suggests that much of our behavior is socially programmed, not hardwired. The genetic leash is long. As sociologist Ian Robertson (1987) notes:

> Americans eat oysters but not snails. The French eat snails but not locusts. The Zulus eat locusts but not fish. The Jews eat fish but not pork. The Hindus eat pork but not beef. The Russians eat beef but not snakes. The Chinese eat snakes but not people. The Jalé of New Guinea find people delicious. (p. 67)

The range of dress habits is equally great. If you were a traditional Muslim woman, you would cover your entire body, even your face, and be thought deviant if you didn't. If you were a North American woman, you would expose your face, arms, and legs, but you would cover your breasts and pelvic region, and be thought deviant if you didn't. If you were a Tasaday tribe woman in the Philippines, you would go about your daily activities naked, and be thought deviant if you didn't.

To see the evolutionary and cultural perspectives at work, let's consider an important issue that illustrates them: How are women and men alike? How do they differ—and how do the evolutionary and cultural perspectives explain their differences?

Evolutionary psychology: The study of the evolution of behavior using the principles of natural selection; assumes that natural selection favors information processing and behaviors that, in particular environments, contribute to the preservation and spread of one's genes.

■ GENDER SIMILARITIES AND DIFFERENCES

*B*oth evolutionary psychologists and psychologists working from a cultural perspective have sought to explain gender variations. Before considering their views, let's see what there is to explain: As males and females, how are we alike? How do we differ?

There are many obvious dimensions of human diversity—height, weight, hair color, to name just a few. But for people's self-concepts and social relationships, the two dimensions that matter most, and that people first attune

Gender:
In psychology, the characteristics, whether biologically or socially influenced, by which people define male and female. Because "sex" is a biological category, social psychologists often refer to biologically based gender differences as "sex differences."

to, are race and, especially, sex (Stangor & others, 1992). In Chapter 11, we will look closely at how race and sex affect the way others regard and treat us. For now, let's consider **gender**—the characteristics people associate with male and female. What behaviors *are* universally characteristic and expected of males? of females?

The sexes are similar in many physical traits, such as age of sitting, teething, and walking. They also are alike in many psychological traits, such as overall vocabulary, intelligence, happiness, and self-esteem. But the occasional differences are what capture attention and make news. Men enter puberty two years later, grow 15 percent bigger, and die five years sooner. Women are twice as vulnerable to anxiety disorders and depression, though one-third as vulnerable to suicide and one-fifth as vulnerable to alcoholism. Women have a slightly better sense of smell. They more easily become rearoused immediately after orgasm. And they are much less likely to suffer hyperactivity or speech disorders as children and to display antisocial personalities as adults.

During the 1970s, many scholars worried that studies of such gender differences might reinforce stereotypes and that gender differences might be construed as women's deficits. Focusing attention on gender differences will provide "battle weapons against women" warned sociologist Jesse Bernard (1976, p. 13). And it's true that explanations for differences usually focus on the group that's seen as different (Miller & others, 1991). In discussing the "gender gap" in American presidential voting, for example, commentators more often wonder why women so often vote Democratic than why men so often vote Republican. People more often wonder what causes homosexuality than what causes heterosexuality (or what determines sexual orientation). People ask why Asian Americans so often excel in math and science, not why other groups less often excel. In each case, people define the standard by one group and wonder why the other is "different." From "different" it is but a short leap to "deviant" or "substandard."

Since the 1980s, scholars have felt freer to explore gender diversity (Ashmore, 1990). Initially, gender difference research "furthered the cause of gender equality" by reducing overblown stereotypes (Eagly, 1986). Then, during the 1980s and 1990s, reports Alice Eagly (1995), many studies revealed gender differences—differences as large as "important" behavior differences in other areas of psychology. Some findings confirm gender stereotypes by suggesting that women are less aggressive, more nurturant, and more sensitive (Swim, 1994). Such gender differences may explain why most people rate their feelings regarding "women" as more favorable than their feelings regarding "men" (Eagly, 1994; Haddock & Zanna, 1994).

Let's compare men's and women's social connections, dominance, aggressiveness, and sexuality. Having described these differences, we can then consider how the evolutionary and cultural perspectives might explain them. Do gender differences reflect tendencies predisposed by natural selection? Or are they culturally constructed?

INDEPENDENCE VERSUS CONNECTEDNESS

Individual men display outlooks and behavior varying from fierce competitiveness to caring nurturance. So do individual women. Without denying that, psychologists Nancy Chodorow (1978, 1989), Jean Baker Miller (1986), and

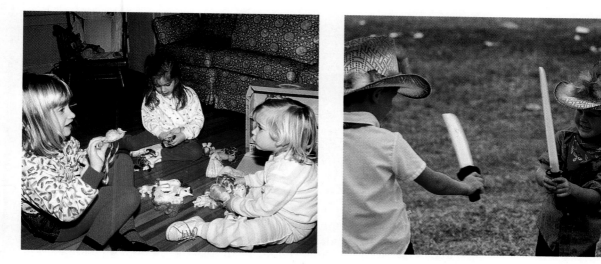

Carol Gilligan and her colleagues (1982, 1990) contend that women more than men give priority to relationships.

The difference surfaces in childhood. Boys strive for independence; they define their identity in separation from the caregiver, usually their mother. Girls welcome *inter*dependence; they define their identity through their social connections. Boys' play often involves group activity. Girls' play occurs in smaller groups, with less aggression, more sharing, more imitation of relationships, and more intimate discussion (Lever, 1978).

Adult relationships extend this gender difference. In conversation, men more often focus on tasks, women on relationships (Tannen, 1990). In groups, men talk more to give information; women talk more to share lives, give help, or show support (Dindia & Allen, 1992; Eagly, 1987). In most of the U.S. caregiving professions, such as social worker, teacher, and nurse, women outnumber men. Among first-year college students, 5 in 10 males and 7 in 10 females say it is *very* important to "help others who are in difficulty" (Astin & others, 1993). Women seem more charitable: Among individuals leaving estates more than $5 million, 48 percent of women and 35 percent of men make a charitable bequest, and women's colleges have unusually supportive alumni (National Council for Research on Women, 1994). Women's greater "ethic of care" helps explain why, in survey after survey, American women are more likely than men to support the Democratic Party's social agenda and to oppose military initiatives (*American Enterprise*, 1991).

Women's connections as mothers, daughters, sisters, and grandmothers bind families (Rossi & Rossi, 1990). Women spend more time caring for both preschoolers and aging parents (Eagly & Crowley, 1986). They buy most birthday gifts and greeting cards (DeStefano & Colasanto, 1990; Hallmark, 1990). Asked to provide photos that portray whom they are, women include more photos of parents and of themselves with others (Clancy & Dollinger, 1993). For women, especially, a sense of mutual support is crucial to marital satisfaction (Acitelli & Antonucci, 1994).

When surveyed, women are far more likely to describe themselves as having **empathy**, as being able to feel what another feels—to rejoice with those

Girls' play is often in small groups and imitates relationships. Boys' play is more often competitive or aggressive.

"In the different voice of women lies the truth of an ethic of care."
Carol Gilligan (1982, p. 173)

Empathy:
The vicarious experience of another's feelings; putting oneself in another's shoes.

Sally Forth by Greg Howard, with permission of North American Syndicate.

who rejoice and weep with those who weep. Although to a lesser extent, the empathy difference extends to laboratory studies. Shown slides or told stories, girls react with more empathy (Hunt, 1990). Women are more likely to cry or report feeling distressed at another's distress (Eisenberg & Lennon, 1983). And this helps explain why, compared to friendships with men, both men and women report friendships with women to be more intimate, enjoyable, and nurturing (Rubin, 1985; Sapadin, 1988). When they want empathy and understanding, someone to whom they can disclose their joys and hurts, both men and women usually turn to women.

Women's greater connectedness also gets expressed in their smiling (Hecht & others, 1993). When Marianne LaFrance (1985) analyzed 9000 college yearbook photos and when Amy Halberstadt and Martha Saitta (1987) studied 1100 magazine and newspaper photos and 1300 people in shopping malls, parks, and streets, they consistently found that females were more likely to smile.

One explanation for this male-female empathy difference is that women tend to be better at reading others' emotions. In her analysis of 125 studies of men's and women's sensitivity to nonverbal cues, Judith Hall (1984) discerned that women are generally superior at decoding others' emotional messages. For example, shown a two-second silent film clip of the face of an upset woman, women guess more accurately whether she is criticizing someone or discussing her divorce. Women's sensitivity to nonverbal cues helps explain their greater emotional responsiveness in both depressing and joyful situations (Grossman & Wood, 1993; Sprecher & Sedikides, 1993; Stoppard & Gruchy, 1993). Women also are more skilled at *expressing* emotions nonverbally, reports Hall.

Whether considered feminine or human, traits such as gentleness, sensitivity, and warmth are a boon to close relationships. In a study of married couples in Sydney, Australia, John Antill (1983) found that when either the husband or wife had these traditionally feminine qualities—or better, when *both* did—marital satisfaction was higher. People find marriage rewarding when their spouse is nurturant and emotionally supportive.

What do you think: Should western women become more self-reliant and more attuned to their culture's individualism? Or might women's relational approach to life help transform power-oriented western societies (marked by high levels of child neglect, loneliness, and depression) into more caring communities?

SOCIAL DOMINANCE

Imagine two people: One is "adventurous, autocratic, coarse, dominant, forceful, independent, and strong." The other is "affectionate, dependent, dreamy, emotional, submissive, and weak." If the first person sounds more to you like a man and the second like a woman, you are not alone, report John Williams and Deborah Best (1990a, p. 15). The world around, from Asia to Africa and Europe to Australia, people rate men as more dominant, driven, and aggressive.

These perceptions and expectations correlate with reality. In essentially every society, men *are* socially dominant. At the end of 1990 they were 96 percent of the heads of nations and 97 percent of the world's cabinet ministers (United Nations, 1991). From the founding of the U.S. Congress through the end of 1994, 98.6 percent of its 11,377 members have been men (Feinsilber, 1994). Men are half of all jurors but 90 percent of elected jury leaders and most of the leaders of ad hoc laboratory groups (Davis & Gilbert, 1989; Kerr & others, 1982). As is typical of those in higher-status positions, men initiate most of the inviting for dates.

Men's style of communicating undergirds their social power. As leaders in situations where roles aren't rigidly scripted, men tend to be directive, women to be democratic (Eagly & Johnson, 1990). Men tend to excel as directive, task-focused leaders, women as social leaders who build team spirit (Eagly & Karau, 1991; Eagly & others, 1995; Wood & Rhodes, 1991). Men more than women place priority on winning, getting ahead, and dominating others (Sidanius & others, 1994). When leading democratically, women leaders get evaluated as favorably as men. When leading autocratically, women get evaluated less favorably (Eagly & others, 1992). People will accept a man's "strong, assertive" leadership more readily than a woman's "pushy, aggressive" leadership.

Men's conversational style reflects their concern for independence, women's for connectedness. Men are more likely to act as powerful people often do—talking assertively, interrupting, touching with the hand, staring more, smiling less (Carli, 1991; Ellyson & others, 1991; Major & others, 1990). Stating the results from a female perspective, women's influence style (especially in mixed-sex groups) tends to be more indirect—less interruptive, more sensitive, more polite, less cocky.

Aware of such findings, Nancy Henley (1977) has argued that women should stop feigning smiles, averting their eyes, and tolerating interruptions and

When women achieve equal status with men, will they, should they, feel as free as men to initiate formal dates?

"A little further, dear."

Drawing by W. Steig; © 1989 The New Yorker Magazine, Inc.

should instead look people in the eye and speak assertively. Judith Hall (1984), however, values women's less autocratic communication style and therefore objects to the idea

> that women should change their nonverbal style so as to appear more affectively distant and insensitive. . . . What would be sacrificed is the deeper value to self and society of a behavioral style that is adaptive, socially wise, and likely to facilitate positive interaction, understanding, and trust. . . . Whenever it is assumed that women's nonverbal behavior is undesirable, yet another myth is perpetuated: that male behavior is "normal" and that it is women's behavior that is deviant and in need of explanation. (pp. 152–153)

AGGRESSION

Aggression:
Physical or verbal behavior intended to hurt someone. In laboratory experiments, this might mean delivering electric shocks or saying something likely to hurt another's feelings. By this social psychological definition, one can be socially assertive without being aggressive.

By **aggression**, psychologists mean behavior intended to hurt. Throughout the world, hunting, fighting, and warring are primarily men's activities. In surveys, men admit to more aggression than do women. In laboratory experiments, men indeed exhibit more physical aggression, for example, by administering what they believe are hurtful electric shocks (Eagly & Steffen, 1986; Hyde, 1986). In Canada, the male-to-female arrest rate is 11 to 1 for murder and 8 to 1 for assault (Colombo, 1994). In the United States, it is 10 to 1 for murder and 5 to 1 for assault (FBI, 1994). Across the world, murder rates vary. Yet in all regions, men are roughly 20 times more likely to murder men than women are to murder women (Daly & Wilson, 1989). In less assaultive forms of aggression—say, slapping a family member or verbally attacking someone—women are no less aggressive than men (Björkqvist, 1994; White & Kowalski, 1994).

SEXUALITY

There is also a gender gap in sexual attitudes and assertiveness. It's true that in their physiological and subjective responses to sexual stimuli, women and men are "more similar than different" (Griffitt, 1987). Yet consider:

- Susan Hendrick and her colleagues (1985) report that many studies, including their own, reveal that women are "moderately conservative" about casual sex and men are "moderately permissive."
- The American Council on Education's recent survey of a quarter million first-year college students is illustrative. "If two people really like each other, it's all right for them to have sex even if they've known each other for only a very short time," agreed 56 percent of men but only 32 percent of women (Astin & others, 1994).
- In a survey of 3400 randomly selected Americans, half as many men (25 percent) as women (48 percent) cited affection for the partner as a reason for first intercourse (Laumann & others, 1994).
- Data gleaned from 177 studies of 130,000 people confirm that men are much more accepting of casual sex (Oliver & Hyde, 1993).

The gender difference in sexual attitudes carries over to behavior. "With few exceptions anywhere in the world," report cross-cultural psychologist Marshall Segall and his colleagues (1990, p. 244), "males are more likely than females to initiate sexual activity." Moreover, among people of both sexual orientations (though especially among those with a homosexual orientation) "men without women have sex more often, with more different partners, than women without men" (Baumeister, 1991, p. 151; Bailey & others, 1994). Casual hit-and-run sex is most common among males with traditional masculine attitudes (Pleck & others, 1993). Not only in sexual relations but also in courtship and touching, males tend to take more initiative (Hendrick, 1988; Kenrick 1987). Like their human counterparts, the males of most animal species, too, are more sexually assertive and less selective about their partners (Hinde, 1984).

Sexual fantasies express the gender difference (Ellis & Symons, 1990). In male-oriented erotica, women are unattached and lust driven. In romance novels, a tender male is emotionally consumed by his devoted passion for the heroine. Social scientists aren't the only ones to have noticed. "Women can be fascinated by a four-hour movie with subtitles wherein the entire plot consists of a man and a woman yearning to have, but never actually having a relationship," observes humorist Dave Barry (1995). "Men HATE that. Men can take maybe 45 seconds of yearning, and they want everybody to get naked. Followed by a car chase. A movie called 'Naked People in Car Chases' would do really well among men."

As detectives are more intrigued by crime than virtue, so psychological detectives are more intrigued by differences than similarities. Let us therefore remind ourselves: *Individual* differences in independence, dominance, and most other social behaviors far exceed gender differences. Females and males are hardly opposite (altogether different) sexes. Rather, they differ like two folded hands—similar but not the same, fitting together yet differing as they grasp each other. In explaining those differences, inquiry has focused on two culprits: evolution and culture.

Which would you prefer: finding a great bargain on clothes or having great sex?

	Women	Men
Bargain	46%	14%
Sex	41%	76%

Source: Yankelovich poll in *Time* (1994).

S U M M I N G   U P

B oys and girls, and men and women, are in many ways alike. Yet their differences attract more attention. Although individual differences among women and among men exceed their gender differences, social psychologists have explored gender differences in independence versus connectedness. Women typically do more caring, express more empathy and emotion, and define themselves more in terms of relationships. Men and women also tend to exhibit differing social dominance, aggression, and sexuality.

■ EVOLUTION AND BEHAVIOR

A lthough evolutionary psychologists remind us of human adaptability to varying environments (and therefore of our cultural variability), they emphasize universal principles of behavior. Our human kinship is manifest in certain universal social behaviors and norms—and, say the evolutionists, in some universal gender differences in mating preferences.

Since Darwin, most biologists have assumed that for millions of years organisms have competed to survive and leave descendants. Genes that increased the odds of leaving descendants became more abundant. In the snowy Arctic environment, for example, polar bear genes programming a thick coat of camouflaging white fur have won the genetic competition and now predominate. Evolutionary psychology studies how this process may predispose not just adaptive physical traits, such as polar bear coats, but also psychological traits and social behaviors.

Humans, too, are the way we are, say evolutionary psychologists, because natural selection predisposed behaviors that enabled our ancestors' survival and reproduction. We are the descendants of ancestors who preferred nutritious, energy-providing foods rich in protein, sugar, and fat and who disliked bitter, sour, often toxic tastes. (Those who lacked such preferences were less likely to survive to become our ancestors.) Because these food preferences supported survival, we today carry such preferences. We long for whatever helped our ancestors to survive, reproduce, and nurture offspring.

Although survival in regions from the Arctic to equatorial jungles required adaptability, some social tasks, such as finding mates and negotiating relationships, are common to people everywhere. Thus, we all have inherited certain emotional reactions and behaviors that help us solve recurring problems. This explains why even cross-cultural psychologists see beneath the veneer of cultural differences "an essential universality" (Lonner, 1980). As members of one species, we are more alike than different.

Before considering the possible evolution of universal gender differences, let's see an example of a universal behavior tendency.

> "I am confident that [if] modern psychology had developed in, let us say, India, the psychologists there would have discovered most of the principles discovered by the Westerners."
> Cross-cultural psychologist John E. Williams (1993)

UNIVERSAL NORMS

All cultures have their accepted ideas about appropriate behavior. People often view these social expectations, or **norms,** as a negative force that imprisons us all in a blind effort to perpetuate tradition. Norms restrain and control us so successfully and so subtly that we hardly sense their existence. Like fish in the ocean, we are so immersed in our culture that we must leap out of it to understand it. There is no better way to learn the norms of our culture than to visit another culture and see that its members do things *that* way, while we do them *this* way. I tell my children that yes, Europeans eat meat with the fork facing down in the left hand, but we Americans consider it good manners to cut the meat and then transfer the fork to the right hand: "I admit it's inefficient. But it's the way *we* do it."

Norms may seem arbitrary and confining. However, just as a play moves smoothly when the actors know their lines, so social behavior occurs smoothly when people know what to expect. Norms grease the social machinery. In unfamiliar situations, when the norms may be unclear, we monitor others' behavior and adjust our own accordingly. In familiar situations, our words and acts come effortlessly.

Although norms vary by culture, humans do hold some norms in common. Best known is the taboo against incest: Parents are not to have sexual relations with their children, nor siblings with one another. Although the taboo apparently is violated more often than psychologists once believed, the norm is still universal. Every society disapproves of incest. Given the biological penalties for inbreeding, evolutionary psychologists can easily understand why people everywhere are predisposed against incest.

Norms:
Rules for accepted and expected behavior. Norms *prescribe* "proper" behavior. (In a different sense of the word, norms also *describe* what most others do—what is *normal*.)

Norms—rules for accepted and expected behavior—vary by culture.

People everywhere also have some common norms for friendship. From studies conducted in Britain, Italy, Hong Kong, and Japan, Michael Argyle and Monika Henderson (1985) noted several cultural variations in the norms that define the role of friend (in Japan it's especially important not to embarrass a friend with public criticism). But there are also some apparently universal norms: Respect the friend's privacy, make eye contact while talking, don't divulge things said in confidence. These are among the rules of the friendship game. Break them and the game is over.

Roger Brown (1965, 1987; Kroger & Wood, 1992) noticed another universal norm. Everywhere—in 27 languages studied to date—people not only form status hierarchies, they also talk to higher-status people in the respectful way they often talk to strangers. And they talk to lower-status people in the more familiar, first name way they speak to friends. Patients call their physician "Dr. So and So"; the physician often replies using their first name. Students and professors typically address one another in a similar nonmutual way.

Most languages have two forms of the English pronoun "you": a respectful form and a familiar form (for example, *Sie* and *du* in German, *vous* and *tu* in French, *usted* and *tu* in Spanish). People typically use the familiar form with intimates and subordinates (not only with close friends and family members but also in speaking to children and dogs). A German child receives a boost when strangers begin addressing the child as "Sie" instead of "du." Nouns, too, can express assumed social inequalities. Among faculty studied by Rebecca Rubin (1981), young female professors were far more likely than young male professors to have students call them by their first name. Women tennis players will empathize: Sportscasters 53 percent of the time have referred to them,

In The Female Eunuch, *Germaine Greer notes how the language of affection reduces women to foods and baby animals—honey, lamb, sugar, sweetie-pie, kitten, chick.*

Despite the enormous cultural variation in norms, we humans do hold some norms in common.

"*Look, everyone here loves vanilla, right? So let's start there.*"

though only 8 percent of the time to men players, using only their first name (*Harper's Index,* 1991).

This first aspect of Brown's universal norm—that *forms of address communicate not only social distance but also social status*—correlates with a second aspect: *Advances in intimacy are usually suggested by the higher-status person.* In Europe, where most twosomes begin a relationship with the polite, formal "you" and may eventually progress to the more intimate "you," someone obviously has to initiate the increased intimacy. Who do you suppose does so? On some congenial occasion, the elder, or richer, or more distinguished of the two may say, "Why don't we say *du* to one another?"

This norm extends beyond language to every type of advance in intimacy. It is more acceptable to borrow a pen from or put a hand on the shoulder of one's intimates and subordinates than to behave in such a casual way with strangers or superiors. Similarly, the president of my college invites faculty to his home before they invite him to theirs. In general, then, the higher-status person is the pacesetter in the progression toward intimacy.

THE EVOLUTION OF THE SEXES: DOING WHAT COMES NATURALLY

"What do you think is the main reason men and women have different personalities, interests, and abilities?" asked the Gallup Organization (1990) in a national survey. "Is it mainly because of the way men and women are raised, or are the differences part of their biological makeup?" Among the 99 percent who answered the question (apparently without questioning its assumptions), nearly equal numbers answered "upbringing" and "biology."

There are, of course, salient biological sex differences. Men have penises; women have vaginas. Men produce sperm; women, eggs. Men have the muscle mass to hunt with a spear; women can breast-feed. Are biological sex differences limited to these obvious distinctions in reproduction and physique? Or do men's and women's genes, hormones, and brains differ in ways that also contribute to behavior differences?

Gender and Mating Preferences

Noting the worldwide persistence of gender differences in aggressiveness, dominance, and sexuality, evolutionary psychologist Douglas Kenrick (1987) suggests that "we cannot change the evolutionary history of our species, and some of the differences between us are undoubtedly a function of that history." Evolutionary psychology predicts no sex differences in all those domains in which the sexes faced similar adaptive challenges (Buss, 1995b). Both sexes regulate heat with sweat, have similar taste preferences to nourish their bodies, and grow callouses where the skin meets friction. But evolutionary psychology does predict sex differences in behaviors relevant to mating and reproduction.

Consider, for example, the male's greater sexual initiative. The average male produces many trillions of sperm in his lifetime, making sperm cheap compared to eggs. Moreover, while a female brings one fetus to term and then nurses it, a male can spread his genes by fertilizing many females. Thus females invest their reproductive opportunities carefully, by looking for signs of health and resources. Meanwhile, males compete with other males for chances to send their genes into the future. Thus, say the evolutionists, men seek to reproduce widely, women wisely. Moreover, evolutionary psychology suggests, physically dominant males gained more access to females, which over generations enhanced male aggression and dominance.

Mind you, little of this is conscious. No one stops to calculate, "How can I maximize the number of genes I leave to posterity?" Rather, say evolutionary

Secretariat, the greatest racehorse of modern times, sired 400 foals.

"I hunt and she gathers—otherwise, we couldn't make ends meet."

"A hen is only an egg's way of making another egg."
Samuel Butler, 1835–1901

psychologists, our natural yearnings are our genes' way of making more genes. Emotions execute evolution's dispositions. "Humans are living fossils—collections of mechanisms produced by prior selection pressures," says David Buss (1995a). And that, evolutionary psychologists believe, helps explain not only male aggression but also the differing sexual attitudes and behaviors of females and males. Although men's interpreting a woman's smile as sexual interest usually proves wrong, the reproductive payoff for occasionally being right may underlie this common misattribution.

Evolutionary psychology also predicts that men will strive to offer what women will desire—external resources and physical protection—and that women will strive to offer men the youthful, healthy appearance (connoting fertility) that men will desire. And sure enough, note Buss (1994a) and Alan Feingold (1992), women's and men's mate preferences confirm these predictions. We today carry the preferences of our successful ancestors. Consider:

■ Studies in 37 cultures, from Australia to Zambia, reveal that men everywhere feel attracted to women whose physical features, such as youthful face and form, suggest fertility. Women everywhere feel attracted to men whose wealth, power, and ambition promise resources for protecting and nurturing offspring (Figure 6–1). Men's greater interest in physical form also makes them the consumers of most of the world's visual pornography. But there are gender similarities, too: Whether residing on an Indonesian island or in urban São Paulo, both women and men desire kindness, love, and mutual attraction.

■ Men feel most jealous over their mate's having sex with someone else. Women tend to feel greater jealously over their mate's becoming emotionally attached to someone else. Evolutionary psychologists say this gender difference reflects men's natural concern with their offspring's paternity and women's natural concern with their mate's provision of resources (Buss, 1994a).

■ FIGURE 6–1
Human mating preferences.
David Buss and 50 collaborators surveyed more than 10,000 people from all races, religions, and political systems on six continents and five islands. Everywhere, men preferred attractive physical features suggesting youth and health—and reproductive fitness. Everywhere, women preferred men with resources and status.
(From Buss, 1994b.)

In life's mating game, men often desire women with beauty and youth and women desire men with wealth and power. For evolutionary psychologists, Donald Trump and Marla Maples illustrate men's desire for features that connote fertility and women's desire for features that connote protection and support for their offspring.

■ Men everywhere tend to marry younger women. Moreover, the older the man the greater the age difference he prefers when selecting a mate. In their twenties, men prefer, and marry, women only slightly younger. In their sixties, men prefer, and marry, women averaging about 10 years younger (Kenrick & Keefe, 1992). Women of all ages prefer men just slightly older than themselves. Once again, say the evolutionary psychologists, we see that natural selection predisposes men to feel attracted to female features associated with fertility.

Even the masculine concern for independence and competitive achievement may reflect naturally selected gender differences, suggest some evolutionary psychologists. "Male achievement is ultimately a courtship display," says Glenn Wilson (1994), "parallel in a sense to the peacock's tail." Men, he suggests, are motivated to attain and display the sort of status and resources that women will find attractive, as illustrated in the lives of super-rich men who have relationships with a succession of beautiful women.

Gender and Hormones

If genes predispose gender-related traits, they must do so by their effects on our bodies. As the results of architectural blueprints appear in physical structures, so the effects of our genetic blueprints appear in the sex hormones that differentiate males and females. In male embryos, the genes direct the formation of testes which begin to secrete *testosterone*, the principal male sex hormone. Expose female rat, monkey, or human embryos to high levels of male sex hormones and, voila!, they, too, will exhibit masculine appearance and behavior (Berenbaum & Hines, 1992; Hines & Green, 1991). So, do biological hormone differences predispose psychological gender differences?

BEHIND THE SCENES

When I began work in the field in 1982, no one knew whether some mating desires were universal, or whether culture exerts so powerful an influence that it overrides any evolved preferences. So, I departed from traditional mainstream psychology to explore the mating behaviors predicted from evolutionary principles.

I found, somewhat to my astonishment, that men and women across the world differ in their mate preferences in precisely the ways predicted by the evolutionists. Just as our fears of snakes, heights, and spiders provide a window for viewing the survival hazards of our evolutionary ancestors, our mating desires provide a window for viewing the resources our ancestors needed for reproduction. We all carry with us today the desires of our successful forebears.

DAVID M. BUSS, *University of Michigan*

The gender gap in aggression does seem influenced by testosterone. In various animals, administering testosterone heightens aggressiveness. In humans, violent male criminals have higher than normal testosterone levels, as do National Football League players and rambunctious fraternity members (Dabbs & others, 1990, 1993). Moreover, for both humans and monkeys the gender difference in aggression appears early in life (before culture has much effect) and wanes as testosterone levels decline during adulthood. No one of these lines of evidence is conclusive. Taken together, they convince most scholars that sex hormones matter. But so, as we will see, does culture.

As people mature to middle age and beyond, a curious thing happens. Women become more assertive and self-confident, men more empathic and less domineering (Lowenthal & others, 1975; Pratt & others, 1990). Hormone changes are one possible explanation for the shrinking gender differences. Role demands are another. Some speculate that during courtship and early parenthood, social expectations lead both sexes to emphasize traits that enhance their roles. While courting, providing, and protecting, men play up their macho sides and forgo their needs for interdependence and nurturance (Gutmann, 1977). While courting and rearing young children, young women restrain their impulses to assert and be independent. As men and women graduate from these early adult roles, they supposedly express more of their restrained tendencies. Each becomes more *androgynous*—capable of both assertiveness and nurturance.

"The finest people marry the two sexes in their own person."
Ralph Waldo Emerson,
Journals, 1843

Reflections on Evolutionary Psychology

Without disputing the principle of natural selection—that nature tends to select physical and behavioral traits that enhance gene survival—critics see two problems with evolutionary explanations. First, such an explanation sometimes starts with an effect (such as the male-female difference in sexual initiative) and then works backward to conjecture an explanation for it. This approach is reminiscent of functionalism, a dominant theory in psychology during the 1920s. "Why does that behavior occur? Because it serves such and such a function." The theorist can hardly lose at this game.

The way to prevent the hindsight bias is to imagine things turning out otherwise. Let's try it. If human males were never known to have extramarital affairs, might we not see the evolutionary wisdom behind their fidelity? After all, argues Dorothy Einon (1994), women will mate throughout the menstrual cycle and while pregnant or lactating—which means that a man who mates at random is no more likely than a faithful married man to fertilize a woman. Moreover, because there is more to bringing offspring to maturity than merely depositing sperm, men and women both gain by jointly investing in their children. Males who are loyal to their mates and offspring are more apt to ensure that their young will survive to perpetuate their genes. (This is, in fact, an evolutionary explanation for why humans, and certain other species whose young require a heavy parental investment, tend to pair off and be monogamous. Love between man and woman is universal because of its genetic payoffs: The offspring of devoted males were less vulnerable to predators.) Or imagine that women were the stronger, more physically aggressive sex. "But of course!" someone might say, "all the better for protecting their young."

Evolutionary psychologists reply that such criticisms are "flat-out wrong." Hindsight plays no less a role in cultural explanations: Why do women and men differ? Because their culture *socializes* their behavior! When, as we will see, people's roles vary across time and place, "culture" describes more than it explains that fact. And far from being mere hindsight conjecture, their field is an empirical science that tests evolutionary predictions with data from animal behavior, cross-cultural observations, and hormonal and genetic studies. As in many scientific fields, observations inspire a theory that generates new, testable predictions (Figure 6–2). The predictions alert us to unnoticed phenomena and allow us to confirm, refute, or revise the theory.

Also, the evolutionary psychologist reminds us, evolutionary wisdom is *past* wisdom. It tells us what behaviors worked in the past. Whether such tenden-

"Sex differences in behavior may have been relevant to our ancestors gathering roots and hunting squirrels on the plains of Northern Africa, but their manifestations in modern society are less clearly 'adaptive.' Modern society is information oriented—big biceps and gushing testosterone have less direct relevance to the president of a computer firm."
Douglas Kenrick (1987)

Marriage patterns vary. Worldwide, monogamy is most common. But polygamy, illustrated by this Cameroon man with many wives, occurs in some cultures.

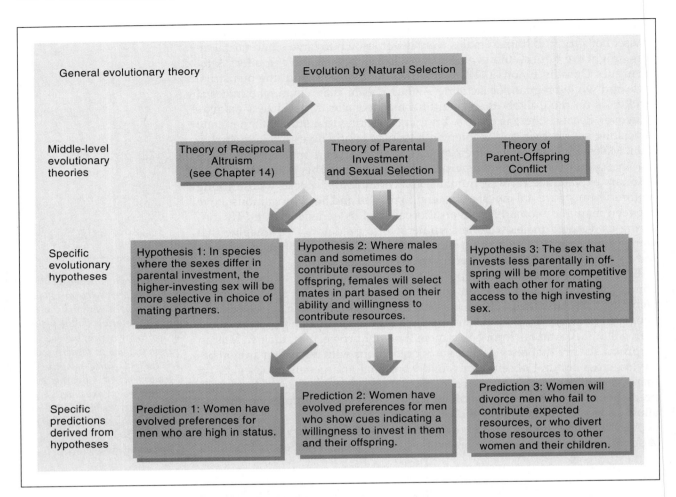

■ FIGURE 6–2

Sample predictions derived from evolutionary psychology by David Buss (1995a).

cies are still adaptive is a different question. For example, although people tend to be attracted to potential mates whose appearance and behavior fit typical masculine or feminine images, people actually report more satisfying relationships with those who are androgynous (Ickes, 1993).

Critics acknowledge that evolution helps explain both our commonalities and our differences (a certain amount of diversity aids survival, and genetic predispositions may be triggered only in certain environmental contexts). But they say our common evolutionary heritage does not, by itself, predict the enormous cultural variation in human marriage patterns (from one spouse to a succession of spouses to multiple wives to multiple husbands to spouse swapping). Nor does it explain cultural changes in behavior patterns over mere decades of time. The most significant trait that nature has endowed us with, it seems, is the capacity to adapt—to learn and to change. Therein lies what all agree is culture's shaping power.

SUMMING UP

Evolutionary psychologists emphasize the kinship of all humans that results from our shared human nature. Our kinship extends to our social behaviors. Despite their differences, cultures share some norms in common. One apparently universal norm concerns how people of unequal status relate to one another. The more formal way we communicate with strangers is the same way we communicate with superiors. Moreover, increased intimacy (for example, a social invitation) is usually initiated by the person with higher status.

Evolutionary psychologists theorize how evolution might have predisposed gender differences in behaviors such as aggression and sexual initiative. Nature's mating game, they suggest, favors male sexual initiative toward females—especially those with physical features suggesting fertility—and aggressive dominance in competing with other males. Females, who have a greater stake in not squandering their fewer reproductive chances, place a greater priority on selecting mates with the ability to commit resources to protecting and nurturing their young.

■ CULTURE AND BEHAVIOR

The biological legacy of our ancestral past matters. But so, thanks to our endowed adaptability, do social influences, including the cultural waters in which we swim. Consider some differing cultural norms. For example, in what ways does our culture shape the individualism of our values and our definitions of gender roles?

To appreciate the impact of culture, we need only confront another culture. American males may feel uncomfortable when Middle Eastern heads of state greet the U.S. president with a kiss on the cheek. A German student, accustomed to speaking rarely to "Herr Professor," considers it strange that at my institution most faculty office doors are open and students stop by freely. An Iranian student on her first visit to an American McDonald's restaurant fumbles around in her paper bag looking for the eating utensils until she sees the other customers eating their french fries with, of all things, their hands. In many areas of the globe your and my best manners are a serious breach of etiquette. Foreigners visiting Japan often struggle to master the rules of the social game—when to take their shoes off, how to pour the tea, when to give and open gifts, how to act toward someone higher or lower in the social hierarchy.

Cultures also vary in their norms for expressiveness and personal space. To someone from a relatively formal northern European culture, a person whose roots are in an expressive Mediterranean culture may seem "warm, charming, inefficient, and time-wasting." To the Mediterranean person, the northern European may seem "efficient, cold, and overconcerned with time" (Triandis, 1981). Latin American business executives who arrive late for a dinner engagement may be mystified by how obsessed their American counterparts are with punctuality.

Personal space is a sort of portable bubble or buffer zone that we like to maintain between ourselves and others. As the situation changes, the bubble varies in size. With strangers we maintain a fairly large personal space, keeping a distance of 4 feet or more between us. On uncrowded buses, or in restrooms or libraries, we protect our space and respect others' space. We let friends come closer, often within 2 or 3 feet.

Individuals differ: Some people prefer more personal space than others (Smith, 1981; Sommer, 1969; Stockdale, 1978). Groups differ, too: Adults main-

Personal space:
The buffer zone we like to maintain around our bodies. Its size depends on our familiarity with whomever is near us.

"Women kiss women good night. Men kiss women good night. But men do not kiss men good night—especially in Armonk."

Although some norms are universal, every culture has its own norms—rules for accepted and expected social behavior.

"Some 30 inches from my nose, the frontier of my person goes."
W. H. Auden, 1907–1973

tain more distance than children. Men keep more distance from one another than do women. For reasons unknown, cultures near the equator prefer less space and more touching and hugging. Thus the British and Scandinavians prefer more distance than the French and Arabs; Americans prefer more space than Latin Americans.

To see the effect of encroaching on another's personal space, play space invader. Stand or sit but a foot or so from a friend and strike up a conversation. Does the person fidget, look away, back off, show other signs of discomfort? These are some signs of arousal noted by space-invading researchers (Altman & Vinsel, 1978).

INDIVIDUALISM VERSUS COLLECTIVISM

One pervasive culture difference arises from social values that stress either individual control and achievement or the bonds of social solidarity. To reflect on your own orientation, consider these questions from the Individualism-Collectivism Scale, developed by C. Harry Hui (1988):
Would you agree that

I would help if a colleague at work told me that he/she needed money to pay utility bills.

Young people should take into consideration their parents' advice when making education/career plans.

I am often influenced by the moods of my neighbors.

Do your answers suggest that you place a greater value on your individual goals and identity or on your social bonds?

Industrialized western cultures typically value **individualism**. They give more priority to self-reliance and personal well-being than to social identity. Western books and movies often celebrate rugged individuals who seek their own fulfillment rather than fulfilling others' expectations. Individualism flourishes under conditions of affluence, mobility, urbanism, and exposure to mass media (Triandis & others, 1993).

Asian and third-world cultures place a greater value on **collectivism**. They give more priority to the goals and welfare of their groups—family, clan, work group. Books and movies often celebrate those who, despite temptations to self-indulgence, remember who they are and do their social duty. When Kobe, Japan, was struck by the devastating 1995 earthquake, western reporters were struck by the absence of looting and the orderly way in which people lined up for relief supplies—"as if they were waiting for a bus." Collectivism flourishes where people face shared threats such as famine, where families are large, and where life requires cooperation, as when building canals or harvesting and stor-

Individualism:
The concept of giving priority to one's own goals over group goals and defining one's identity in terms of personal attributes rather than group identifications.

Collectivism:
The concept of giving priority to the goals of one's groups (often one's extended family or work group) and defining one's identity accordingly.

"*You're not one of those guys who are afraid of intimacy, are you?*"

Drawing by Mankoff; © 1988 The New Yorker Magazine, Inc.

Depending partly on their culture, some people prefer more personal space than others.

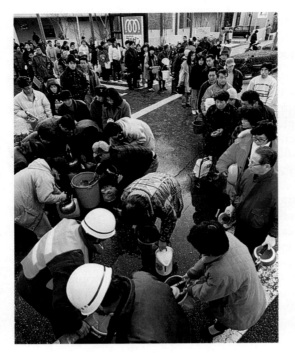

Collectivism in action: People resisted the temptation to loot and acted with civility following the 1995 earthquake in Kobe, a major Japanese city. Here they line up for water.

ing food. In Australia, for example, Aboriginal people tend to value collectivism, while non-Aboriginal people value individualism (Fogarty & White, 1994).

Without discounting individual differences within cultures, cross-cultural psychologists such as Harry Triandis, Richard Brislin, and C. Harry Hui (1988; Triandis, 1994) have shown how a culture's individualism or collectivism affects self-concept, social relations, and child rearing.

Self-Concept

Recall the Chapter 2 discussion of "Self and Culture."

Shorn of their social connections—separated from family, friends, and work group—individualists retain their identity, their sense of "me." Thus individualists feel free to leave jobs, homes, churches, and extended families in search of better opportunities for themselves. As adolescents they struggle to separate from parents and define their own personal sense of self. "Get in touch with yourself, accept yourself, be true to yourself," they hear from their culture's individualistic advice givers. Don't be "codependent" (by supporting, loving, and staying tied to a troubled partner). Therapist Fritz Perls (1973, p. 70) epitomized the individualism of western popular psychology: "I do my thing, and you do your thing. I am not in this world to live up to your expectations. And, you are not in this world to live up to mine." Superstar Frank Sinatra sings the idea: "I did it my way," for "I gotta be me."

In collectivist cultures, where communal solidarity is prized, such words would seldom be spoken. For collectivists, social networks provide one's bearings and help define who one is. Extended families are close-knit. One's family name may even be written first to emphasize one's social identity (Hui Harry). Self-reliance means not "doing one's own thing" but "being responsible" (Triandis & others, 1993). Compared to U.S. magazine ads, for example, Korean magazine ads are less likely to appeal to individual interests ("She's got a style all her own") and more likely to appeal to collective interests ("We have a way of bringing people closer together") (Han & Shavitt, 1994).

Child Rearing

In individualist cultures, parents and schools teach children to be independent and to think for themselves. Immediately after birth, parents begin fostering independence. Babies sleep, bathe, and spend their days separated from their mothers. Children and adolescents typically decide their own restaurant orders, open their own mail, choose their own boyfriends and girlfriends, and chart their own goals en route to leaving the family nest. Schools teach children to clarify their own values and think for themselves. As young adults, individualists dream their own dreams and separate from their parents, who already live separated from the grandparents.

If you live in a western culture, you probably take all this for granted. If you live in Asia, you may wince at such individualism, preferring instead to teach children the values of communal sensitivity and cooperation, to guide or decide children's choices, and to maintain the extended family by providing care for aging parents (Hui, 1990). If you live in Africa, you may also enjoy your community's support in caring for children.

"It takes a whole village to raise a child."
African proverb

Social Relations

Collectivists may have fewer relationships, but they are deeper and longer lasting. Compared to North American students, university students in Hong Kong talk during a day with fewer people for longer periods (Wheeler & others, 1989). In the United States, feeling good is linked with disengaged positive feelings (for example, feeling proud—an emotion that westerners often feel) (Kitayama & others, in press). In Japan, feeling good more often links with feeling interpersonally engaged (for example, having friendly feelings). In collectivist cultures, employer-employee relations are marked by mutual loyalty. Valuing social solidarity, people seek to maintain harmony by showing respect and allowing others to save face. They avoid confrontation, blunt honesty, and boasting. Instead, they stay away from touchy topics, defer to others, and display a self-effacing humility (Kitayama & Markus, 1995). People do favors for one another and remember who has done favors for them. For collectivists, no one is an island. The self is not independent but *inter*dependent. What matters is less "me" than "we."

"The squeaky wheel gets the grease."
American saying

"The nail that stands out gets pounded down."
Japanese saying

Because social identity is so important, collectivists are, however, somewhat quicker to prejudge people by their groups. In their culture, they explain, it *helps* to know people's group identities—"tell me a person's family, schooling, and employment and you tell me a lot about the person." In Japan, people exchange cards when first meeting—cards that tell their social identity (name, occupation, address). Individualists warn against stereotyping and prefer not to judge people by their backgrounds and affiliations: "Everyone's an individual, so you shouldn't make assumptions just from knowing a person's sex, race, or background." Individualists do prejudge people but often by obvious personal attributes, such as physical attractiveness (Dion & others, 1990). And they more often attribute someone's behavior to their disposition, as when attributing a violent act to a "very bad temper" rather than a personal conflict or rivalry (Morris & Peng, 1994).

BEHIND THE SCENES

As a Hong Kong native who has studied in North America, I am sometimes asked whether I am an individualist or a collectivist. My North American and British friends consider me a collectivist. In their eyes, I seldom contradict people and I'm rarely assertive. My decisions seem to give consideration to my family members and relatives. But my extended Chinese family sees me as an individualist. On a vacation with 10 relatives, I insisted on us each going our own ways—to shop, to eat, to tour buildings as we wished. I didn't want my preference for tranquillity to cut short someone's shopping trip. They, however, found less enjoyment in where they went than in experiencing things TOGETHER. Who am I? Am I both individualist and collectivist? Or neither?

C. HARRY HUI, *University of Hong Kong*

When people from different cultures interact, sensitivity to their differing social relations helps minimize misunderstandings and awkward moments. When visiting collectivist cultures, Triandis, Brislin, and Hui (1988) advise individualists to

■ Avoid confrontation
■ Cultivate long-term relationships without expecting instant intimacy
■ Present oneself modestly
■ Attend to people's positions in their group hierarchies
■ Let them know one's own social position

When visiting individualist cultures, collectivists should feel freer than usual to

■ Criticize
■ Get right to business
■ Disclose one's skills and accomplishments
■ Pay more attention to personal attitudes than to group memberships and positions

Each cultural tradition offers benefits, for a price. In competitive, individualist cultures, people enjoy more personal freedom, take greater pride in their own achievements, and are less restricted by others' prejudgments. They also enjoy more privacy, behave more spontaneously, and feel freer to move about and choose their own lifestyles. Innovation and creativity are celebrated.

But the price is more frequent loneliness, more divorce, more homicide, and more stress-related disease (Popenoe, 1993; Triandis & others, 1988). Individualists expect more passion and personal fulfillment in a marriage, which puts the relationship under greater pressure (Dion & Dion, 1993). "Keeping romance alive" was rated as important to a good marriage by 78 percent of American women surveyed and 29 percent of Japanese women (*American Enterprise*, 1992). "Rampant individualism," suggests clinical researcher Martin Seligman (1988), helps explain a huge increase in rates of depression in western countries, resulting partly from the "meaninglessness" that occurs when there is no "attachment to something larger than you are."

Communitarianism

Cross-cultural research on collectivist values converges with gender research on the valuing of social connections. Both research strands remind us of alternatives to power-oriented, self-reliant individualism. In view of such findings, social psychologists Hazel Markus and Shinobu Kitayama (1991) propose a new understanding of dependence: "Being dependent does not invariably mean being helpless, powerless, or without control. It often means being *interdependent.*" It means valuing close relationships, being sensitive and responsive to others, giving and receiving support. It means defining oneself not just as a unique self but also as loyally attached to important others.

Hoping to blend the best of individualist and collectivist values, some social scientists are now exploring a **communitarian** synthesis that aims to balance individual rights with the collective right to communal well-being. Communitarians welcome incentives for individual initiative and appreciate why Marxist economies have crumbled. "If I were, let's say, in Albania at this moment," said communitarian sociologist Amitai Etzioni (1991), "I probably would argue that there's too much community and not enough individual rights." But they also question the other extreme—the rugged individualism and self-indulgence of the 1960s ("Do your own thing"), the 1970s (the "Me decade"), and the 1980s ("Greed is good"). Unrestrained personal freedom, they say, destroys a culture's social fabric; unrestrained commercial freedom, they add, plunders our shared environment. Echoing the French Revolutionists, their motto might well be "liberty, equality, *and* fraternity."

During the last half-century, western individualism has intensified. Parents have become more likely to prize independence and self-reliance in their children, and less concerned with obedience (Alwin, 1990; Remley, 1988). Clothing and grooming styles have become more diverse, personal freedoms have increased, and common values have waned (Schlesinger, 1991). Accompanying this growing individualism has been not only increased depression but other indicators of social recession. In the United States since 1960:

- The divorce rate has doubled.
- The teen suicide rate has tripled.
- The known rape rate has quadrupled.
- Reports of child abuse and neglect have quintupled.
- The proportion of children born to single parents has increased sixfold, as has the juvenile violent crime rate.

Some words of caution: Such trends have multiple causes. Thus, the mere correlation over time between increased individualism and decreased social well-being does not prove cause and effect. Also, communitarians are not advocating a nostalgia trip—a return, for example, to the more restrictive and unequal gender roles of the 1950s. Rather, they propose a middle ground between the individualism of the West and the collectivism of the East, between the macho independence traditionally associated with males and the caregiving connectedness traditionally associated with females, between concerns for indi-

Communitarianism:
An effort to synthesize aspects of both individualism (respecting basic individual rights) and collectivism (caring for the well-being of families and communities).

"This is the age of the individual."
President Ronald Reagan, Address on Wall Street, 1982

"There is no society. There are only individuals and their families."
Prime Minister Margaret Thatcher, after her third election

vidual rights and for communal well-being, between liberty and fraternity, between me-thinking and we-thinking.

A communitarian blend of individualist and collectivist values can already be seen in some western cultures, as in Britain's attempt to strengthen the individual incentives of a free-market economy while restricting individual rights of gun ownership; in Canada's openness to cultural diversity while restraining violent pornography; and in America's effort to foster a "new covenant" of mutual responsibility between the government and the governed, between what society gives individuals (as in funding public education) and what individuals give back in voluntary service. In each case, there is an effort to affirm some individual liberties while constraining others that, unhindered, might harm collective well-being.

As with luggage searches at airports, smoking bans on planes, and sobriety checkpoints and speeding limits on highways, societies are accepting some adjustments to individual rights in order to protect the public good. Environmental restraints on individual freedoms (to pollute, to whale, to deforest) similarly exchange certain short-term liberties for long-term communal gain. Some individualists warn that such constraints on individual liberties may plunge us down a slippery slope leading to the loss of more important liberties. If today we let them search our luggage, tomorrow they'll be knocking down the doors of our houses. If today we censor cigarette ads on television, tomorrow they'll be removing books from our libraries. If today we ban handguns, tomorrow they'll take our hunting rifles. In protecting the interests of the majority do we risk suppressing the basic rights of minorities? Communitarians reply that if we don't balance concern for individual rights with concern for our collective well-being, we risk worse civic disorder, which in turn *will* fuel cries for an autocratic crackdown. As the political debate between individual and collective rights heats up, the new cross-cultural and gender scholarship illuminates alternative cultural values and makes visible our own assumed values.

So, culture's impact is plainly evident as differing norms and social values. The force of culture also appears in the roles that people play. Chapter 4 illustrated a powerful phenomenon: Playing a role often leads people to internalize their behavior. Acting becomes believing. Let's now see how roles vary, within and across cultures, and how assigning individuals to gender roles helps create gender differences.

SOCIAL ROLES

All the world's a stage,
And all the men and women merely players:
They have their exits and their entrances;
And one man in his time plays many parts.
William Shakespeare

Role theorists assume, as did William Shakespeare, that social life is like acting on a theatrical stage, with all its scenes, masks, and scripts. Like the role of Jaques, who speaks these lines in *As You Like It,* social roles, such as parent, student, and friend, outlast those who play them. And, as Jaques says, these roles allow some freedom of interpretation to those who act them out; great

Heiress Patricia Hearst as "Tanya" the revolutionary and as a suburban socialite.

performances are defined by the way the role is played. However, some aspects of any role *must* be performed. A student must at least show up for exams, turn in papers, and maintain some minimum grade point average.

When only a few norms are associated with a social category (for example, sidewalk pedestrians should keep to the right and not jaywalk), we do not regard the position as a social role. It takes a whole cluster of norms to define a **role**. I could readily generate a long list of norms prescribing my activities as a professor or as a father. Although I may acquire my particular image by violating the least important norms (valuing efficiency, I rarely arrive early for anything), violating my role's most important norms (failing to meet my classes, abusing my children) could lead to my being fired or divorced.

Roles have powerful effects. In Chapter 4, we noted that we tend to absorb our roles. On a first date or on a new job, we may act the role self-consciously. As we internalize the role, self-consciousness subsides. What felt awkward now feels genuine.

"Nowhere is social psychology further apart from public consciousness," noted Philip Brickman (1978), "than in its understanding of how things become real for people." Take the case of kidnapped newspaper heiress Patricia Hearst. In 1974, while held by some young revolutionaries who called themselves the Symbionese Liberation Army (SLA), she renounced her former life, her wealthy parents, and her fiancé. Announcing that she had joined her captors, she asked that people "try to understand the changes I've gone through." Twelve days later a bank camera recorded her participation in an SLA armed holdup.

Eventually, Hearst was apprehended and, after "deprogramming," resumed her role as an heiress. Then she became a suburban Connecticut housewife and mother who devoted much of her time to charitable causes (Johnson, 1988). If Patricia Hearst had really been a dedicated revolutionary all along, or had she only pretended to cooperate with her captors, people could have understood her actions. What they could not understand (and what therefore helped make this one of the biggest news stories of the 1970s) was, as Brickman wrote, "that she could really be an heiress, really a revolutionary, and then perhaps really

Role:
A set of norms that define how people in a given social position ought to behave.

an heiress again." It's mind-blowing. Surely, this could not happen to you or me—or could it?

Yes and no. As we'll see in the last section of this chapter, our actions depend not only on the social situation but also on our dispositions. Not everyone responds in the same way to pressure. In Patricia Hearst's predicament, you and I might respond differently. Nevertheless, some social situations can move most "normal" people to behave in "abnormal" ways. This is clear from experiments that put well-intentioned people in a bad situation to see whether good or evil prevails. To a dismaying extent, evil wins. Nice guys often don't finish nice.

High- and Low-Status Roles

In George Orwell's *Animal Farm*, the livestock overthrow their human masters and form an egalitarian society in which "All animals are equal." As the story unfolds, the pigs—who assume the managerial role—soon evade chores and accept comforts they consider appropriate to their status. "All animals are equal," they affirm, "but some animals are more equal than others."

Lawrence Messé, Norbert Kerr, and David Sattler (1992) note that the effects of status on self-perceptions aren't limited to pigs. In many everyday and laboratory situations, people assigned a superior status come to see themselves as meriting favorable treatment or as capable of superior performance. Ronald Humphrey (1985) showed this when he set up a simulated business office. By lottery, some people became managers, others clerks. As in real offices, the managers gave orders to the clerks and did higher-level work. Afterward, both clerks and managers perceived the equally able (randomly assigned) managers as *more* intelligent, assertive, and supportive—as really being more leaderlike.

Likewise, playing a *subservient* role can have demeaning effects. Ellen Langer and Ann Benevento (1978) discovered this when they had pairs of New York City women solve arithmetic problems. After solving the problems individually, the women solved more problems together, with one of the women designated "boss" and the other "assistant." When they then went back to working individually, the "bosses" now solved more problems than they had in the first round, and the "assistants" solved fewer. Similar effects of assigned status on performance have been found in experiments with elementary school children (Jemmott & Gonzalez, 1989; Musser & Graziano, 1991): Demeaning roles undermine self-efficacy.

Role Reversal

Role playing can also be a positive force. By intentionally playing a new role, people sometimes change themselves or empathize with people whose roles differ from their own. Psychodrama, a form of psychotherapy, uses role playing for just this purpose. In George Bernard Shaw's *Pygmalion*, Eliza Doolittle, the cockney flower vendor, discovers that if she plays the role of a lady, and is viewed by others as a lady, then she in fact is a lady. What wasn't real now is.

Roles often come in pairs defined by relationships—parent and child, husband and wife, teacher and student, doctor and patient, employer and employee, police and citizen. To help each understand the other, role reversals can help. The problem with much human conversation and argument, observed La Rochefoucauld, is that people pay more attention to their own utterances than to giving exact answers to questions. "Even the most charming and clever do

"It is the peculiar triumph of society—and its loss—that it is able to convince those people to whom it has given inferior status of the reality of this decree."
James Baldwin,
Notes of a Native Son, 1955

"Great Spirit, grant that I may not criticize my neighbor until I have walked for a moon in his moccasins."
Native American prayer

little more than appear attentive, while in their eyes one may see a look of bewilderment as one talks, so anxious are they to return to their own ideas" (1665, No. 139). A negotiator or group leader can therefore create better communication by having the two sides reverse roles, with each arguing the other's position. Or each side can be asked to restate the other party's point (to the other's satisfaction) before replying. The next time you get into a difficult argument with a friend or parent, try to stop it in the middle and have each of you restate the other's perceptions and feelings before going on with your own. Likely, your mutual understanding will increase.

So far in this chapter we have affirmed our biological kinship as members of one human family, we have acknowledged our cultural diversity, and we have noted how norms and roles vary with culture and over time. Remember that our primary quest in social psychology is not to catalog differences but to identify universal principles of behavior. Our aim is what cross-cultural psychologist Walter Lonner (1989) calls "a universalistic psychology—a psychology that is as valid and meaningful in Omaha and Osaka as it is in Rome and Botswana." Attitudes and behaviors will always vary with culture, but the processes by which attitudes influence behavior vary much less. People in Nigeria and Japan define gender roles differently than do those in Europe and North America, but in all cultures role expectations guide social relations. G. K. Chesterton had the idea nearly a century ago: When someone "has discovered why men in Bond Street wear black hats he will at the same moment have discovered why men in Timbuctoo wear red feathers."

GENDER ROLES

The shaping power of cultural expectations is conspicuous in our ideas about how men and women should behave. Even in contemporary, dual-career, North American marriages, men do most of the household repairs and women arrange

In western cultures, gender roles are changing, but not this much.

Doonesbury copyright 1981 G.B. Trudeau.

the child care (Biernat & Wortman, 1991). In the United States women have been 3 percent of top executives at the 1000 largest corporations, 4 percent of the Marine Corps, 97 percent of nurses, and 99 percent of secretaries (Castro, 1990; Saltzman, 1991; Williams, 1989). In countries everywhere, girls spend more time helping with housework and child care, while boys spend more time in unsupervised play (Edwards, 1991).

Gender socialization, it has been said, gives girls "roots" and boys "wings." In Caldecott Award children's books over the last half-century, girls have four times more often than boys been shown using household objects (such as broom, sewing needle, or pots and pans), and boys have five times more often than girls been shown using production objects (such as pitchfork, plow, or gun) (Crabb & Bielawski, 1994). The adult result: "Everywhere," reports the United Nations (1991), women do most household work. And "everywhere, cooking and dishwashing are the least shared household chores." Such behavior expectations for males and females define **gender roles.**

Gender role:
A set of behavior expectations (norms) for males or females.

In an experiment with Princeton University undergraduate women, Mark Zanna and Susan Pack (1975) showed the impact of gender role expectations. The women answered a questionnaire on which they described themselves to a tall, unattached, senior man they expected to meet. Those led to believe his ideal woman was home-oriented and deferential to her husband presented themselves as more traditionally feminine than did women expecting to meet a man who liked strong, ambitious women. Moreover, given a problem-solving test, those expecting to meet the nonsexist man behaved more intelligently: They solved 18 percent more problems than those expecting to meet the man with the traditional views. This adapting of themselves to fit the man's image was much less pronounced if the man was less desirable—a short, already attached freshman. In a companion experiment by Dean Morier and Cara Seroy (1994), men similarly adapted their self-presentations to meet desirable women's gender role expectations.

Do you ever present one self to members of your own sex and a different self to members of the other sex?

BEHIND THE SCENES

When I began my career at Princeton in 1970, the first group of female undergraduates had just enrolled at this formerly all-male bastion. These pioneers were incredibly bright and very ambitious. Indeed, the majority intended to become doctors, lawyers, or professors! It was Susan Pack's intuition that, despite the great capabilities and high achievement motivation of her female peers, they still "acted dumb" when confronted with the typical attractive, though chauvinistic, Princeton male.

Susan's undergraduate honors thesis, designed to test this notion, demonstrated that Princeton females "acted dumb" or "acted smart" depending, in part, on whether they believed an attractive Princeton male held chauvinistic or liberated attitudes about women. I wonder: Would these results hold today at Princeton? At other colleges? Would males, too, act to fulfill the gender stereotypes of attractive females?

MARK ZANNA, *University of Waterloo*

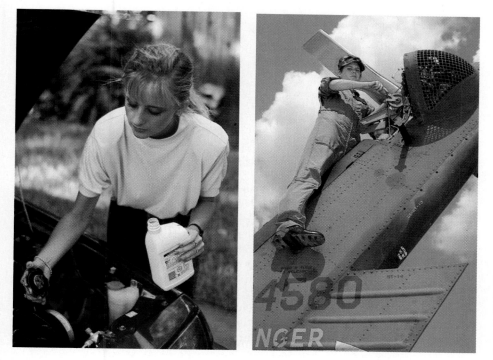

In western countries, gender roles are becoming more flexible. No longer is housework necessarily women's work, and mechanical work necessarily men's work.

But does culture construct gender roles? Or do gender roles merely reflect behavior naturally appropriate for men and women? The variety of gender roles across cultures and over time shows that culture indeed constructs our gender roles.

Gender Roles Vary with Culture

Should women do the housework? Should they be more concerned with promoting their husband's career than with their own? John Williams, Debra Best, and their collaborators (1990b) asked such questions of university students in 14 cultures. In nearly every one, women students had slightly more egalitarian views than their male peers. But the differences among the countries were far greater. Nigerian and Pakistani students, for example, had much more traditional ideas about distinct roles for men and women than did Dutch and German students. Iftikhar Hassan (1980) of Pakistan's National Institute of Psychology explains the traditional status of Pakistani women:

> She knows that parents are not happy at the birth of a girl and she should not complain about parents not sending her to school as she is not expected to take up a job. She is taught to be patient, sacrificing, obedient. . . . If something goes wrong with her marriage she is the one who is to be blamed. If any one of her children do not succeed in life, she is the main cause of their failure. And in the rare circumstance that she seeks a divorce or receives a divorce her chances of second marriage are very slim because Pakistani culture is very harsh on divorced women.

In nomadic, food-gathering societies, boys and girls receive much the same education and men and women do much the same work. In agricultural societies, gender roles are more distinct: Women work the fields and stay with the

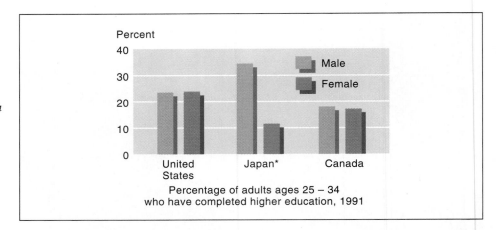

■ **FIGURE 6–3**

Gender and education. In North America, young adult men and women are equally likely to have completed college. In Japan, men are three times as likely as women to have done so.

(Data from American Council on Education, 1994.)

children, while men roam more freely (Segall & others, 1990; Van Leeuwen, 1978). In industrialized societies, roles vary enormously (Figure 6–3). Women fill 2 percent of managerial positions in South Korea, 17 percent in the United States, 28 percent in Austria, and 48 percent in Switzerland (Triandis, 1994). In North America, most doctors and dentists are men; in Russia most doctors are women, as are most dentists in Denmark.

Gender Roles Vary over Time

In the last half-century—a thin slice of our long history—gender roles have changed dramatically. In 1938, 1 in 5 Americans approved "of a married woman holding a job in business or industry if her husband is able to support her." By 1993, 86 percent approved (Newport, 1993)—although nearly 2 in 3 still think that for children the "ideal family situation" is "father has a job and mother stays home and cares for the children" (Gallup, 1990). In 1967, 57 percent of first-year American collegians agreed that "the activities of married women are best confined to the home and family." In 1994, 25 percent agreed (Astin & others, 1987, 1994).

American husbands do 72 percent of the outdoor work and 91 percent of the auto maintenance, but only 19 percent of the meal preparation, 16 percent of the housecleaning, and 12 percent of the laundry
(Blair & Lichter, 1991).

Behavior changes have accompanied this attitude shift. Between 1960 and 1995, the proportion of American women in the workforce increased from 1 in 3 to nearly 3 in 5. Since 1970, increasing numbers of women have been training to become lawyers, doctors, and dentists (Figure 6–4).

Between 1965 and 1985, American women were spending progressively less time in household tasks and men more time, raising the proportion of housework done by men from 15 to 33 percent (Robinson, 1988). But the culture effect still looms large. In Japan, the average husband devotes some 4 hours a week to domestic chores, while Swedish husbands clock some 18 hours per week (Juster & Stafford, 1991).

SUMMING UP

The remarkably wide diversity of attitudes and behaviors from one culture to another indicates the extent to which we are the products of cultural norms.

For example, cultures vary in their norms regarding eating and personal space. Another important difference arises from the valuing of individual self-reliance (as in western cultures) versus collective solidarity and group

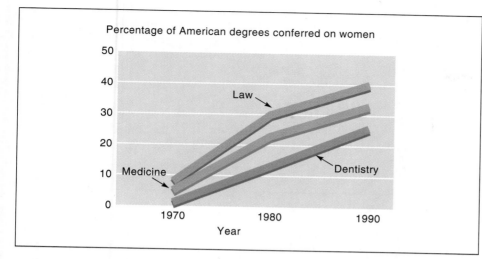

Percentage of American degrees conferred on women

■ **FIGURE 6–4**
Changing gender roles in the workplace. The number of law, medical, and dental degrees conferred on women is steadily rising.
(Data from Bianchi, in press.)

identity (as in many Asian and third-world cultures). The priority that cultures place on individualism or collectivism influences self-concepts, social relations, and child rearing.

A role is a set of norms associated with a given social position. The most heavily researched of roles, gender roles, illustrate culture's impact. Gender roles vary sharply from culture to culture and from time to time.

■ CONCLUSIONS

B iology and culture do not exist in isolation, because culture works upon what is biologically given. How, then, do biology and culture interact? And how do our individual personalities interact with our situations?

BIOLOGY *AND* CULTURE

We needn't think of biology and culture as competitors. Cultural norms subtly but powerfully affect our attitudes and behavior. But they don't do so independent of biology. Everything social and psychological is ultimately biological. If others' expectations influence us, that is part of our biological programming. Moreover, what our biological heritage initiates, culture may accentuate. If genes and hormones predispose males to be more physically aggressive than females, culture may amplify this difference through norms that expect males to be tough and females to be the kinder, gentler sex.

Biology and culture may also **interact**. In humans, biological traits influence how the environment reacts. People respond differently to a Sylvester Stallone than to a Woody Allen. Men, being 8 percent taller and averaging almost double the proportion of muscle mass, may likewise have different experiences than women. Or consider this: A very strong cultural norm dictates that males

Interaction:
The effect of one factor (such as biology) depends on another factor (such as environment).

■ **FIGURE 6–5**

A social-role theory of gender differences in social behavior. Various influences, including childhood experiences and biological factors, bend males and females toward differing roles. It is the expectations and the skills and beliefs associated with these differing roles that affect men's and women's behavior.

(Adapted from Eagly, 1987, and Eagly & Wood, 1991.)

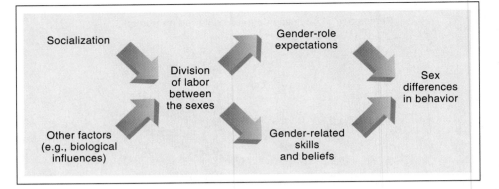

should be taller than their female mates. In one study, only 1 in 720 married couples violated this norm (Gillis & Avis, 1980). With hindsight, we can speculate a psychological explanation: Perhaps being taller (and older) helps men perpetuate their social power over women. But we can also speculate evolutionary wisdom that might underlie the cultural norm: If people preferred partners of the same height, tall men and short women would often be without partners. As it is, evolution dictates that men tend to be taller than women, and culture dictates the same for couples. So the height norm might well be a result of biology *and* culture.

In her book *Sex Differences in Social Behavior,* Alice Eagly (1987) theorizes a process by which biology and culture interact (Figure 6–5). She believes that a variety of factors, including biological influences and childhood socialization, predispose a sexual division of labor. In adult life the immediate causes of gender differences in social behavior are the *roles* that reflect this sexual division of labor. Men tend to be found in roles demanding social and physical power, and women in more nurturant roles. Each sex tends to exhibit the behaviors expected of those who fill such roles and to have their skills and beliefs shaped accordingly. The effects of biology and socialization may be important insofar as they influence the social roles that people play, for the roles we play influence who we become. If men are more assertive and women more nurturing, this may be an *effect* of their playing powerful versus caregiving roles. (Regardless of their sex, people in subordinate roles tend to be sensitive to powerful people's feelings—Snodgrass, 1992.)

THE GREAT LESSON OF SOCIAL PSYCHOLOGY

Food for thought: If Bohr's statement is a great truth, what is its opposite?

"There are trivial truths and great truths," declared the physicist Niels Bohr. "The opposite of a trivial truth is plainly false. The opposite of a great truth is also true." Each chapter in this unit on social influence teaches a great truth: the power of the social situation. This great truth about the power of external pressures would sufficiently explain our behavior if we were passive, like tumbleweed. But unlike tumbleweed, we are not just blown here and there by the environment. We act; we react. We respond, and we get responses. We can resist the social situation and sometimes even change it. Thus each of these "social influence" chapters concludes by calling attention to the opposite of the great truth: the power of the person.

Perhaps stressing the power of culture leaves you somewhat uncomfortable. Most of us resent any suggestion that external forces determine our behavior; we see ourselves as free beings, as the originators of our actions (well, at least of our good actions). We sense that believing in social determinism can lead to what philosopher Jean-Paul Sartre called "bad faith"—evading responsibility by blaming something or someone for one's fate.

Actually, social control (the power of the situation) and personal control (the power of the person) no more compete with one another than do biological and cultural explanations. Social and personal explanations of our social behavior are both valid, for at any moment we are both the creatures and the creators of our social worlds. We may well be the products of our genes and environment. But it is also true that the future is coming, and it is our job to decide where it is going. Our choices today determine our environment tomorrow.

Social situations do profoundly influence individuals. But individuals also influence the social situation. The two *interact.* Asking whether external situations or inner dispositions (or culture or evolution) determine behavior is like asking whether length or width determines the area of a field.

The interaction occurs in at least three ways (Snyder & Ickes, 1985). First, a given social situation often affects different people somewhat differently. Because our minds do not see reality identically, we each respond to a situation as we construe it. And some people are more sensitive and responsive to social situations than others (M. Snyder, 1983). The Japanese, for example, are more responsive to social expectations than the British (Argyle & others, 1978).

"The words of truth are always paradoxical."
Lao-tzu, *The Simple Way*

Only very occasionally do couples violate the male-taller norm.

Second, interaction between persons and situations also occurs because people can choose to be part of a particular situation (Ickes & others, 1990). Given a choice, sociable people elect situations that evoke social interaction. When you chose your college, you were also choosing to expose yourself to a specific set of social influences. Ardent political liberals are unlikely to settle in Orange County, California, and join the Chamber of Commerce. They are more likely to live in Toronto and join Greenpeace—in other words, to choose a social world that reinforces their inclinations.

Third, people often create their situations. Recall again that our preconceptions can be self-fulfilling: If we expect someone to be extraverted, hostile, feminine, or sexy, our actions toward the person may induce the very behavior we expect. What, after all, composes a social situation but the people in it? A liberal environment is created by liberals. What takes place in the sorority is created by the members. The social environment is not like the weather—something that just happens to us. It is more like our homes—something we make for ourselves.

This reciprocal causation between situations and persons allows us to see people as either *reacting to* or *acting upon* their environment. Each perspective is correct, for we are both the products and the architects of our social worlds. However, is one perspective wiser? In one sense, it is wise to see ourselves as the creatures of our environments (lest we become too proud of our achievements and blame ourselves too much for our problems) and to see others as free actors (lest we become paternalistic and manipulative).

However, perhaps we would do well more often to assume the reverse—to view ourselves as free agents and to view others as influenced by their environments. We would then assume self-efficacy as we view ourselves and seek understanding and social reform as we relate to others. (If we view others as influenced by their situations, we are more likely to understand and empathize than smugly to judge unpleasant behavior as freely chosen by "immoral," "sadistic," or "lazy" persons.) Most religions encourage us to take responsibility for ourselves but to refrain from judging others. Does religion teach this because our natural inclination is to excuse our own failures while blaming others for theirs?

"If we explain poverty, or emotional disorders, or crime and delinquency, or alcoholism, or even unemployment, as resulting from personal, internal, individual defects . . . then there simply is not much we can do about prevention."
George Albee (1979)

S U M M I N G   U P

Biological and cultural explanations need not be contradictory. Indeed, they interact. Biological factors operate within a cultural context, and culture builds upon a biological foundation.

The great truth about the power of social influence is but half the truth if separated from its complementary truth: the power of the person. Persons and situations interact in at least three ways. First, individuals vary in how they interpret and react to a given situation. Second, people choose many of the situations that influence them. Third, people help create their social situations. Thus power resides both in persons and in situations. We create and are created by our social worlds.

■ FOR FURTHER READING

Buss, D. M. (1994). *The evolution of desire: Strategies of human mating.* New York: Basic Books. Psychologist David Buss suggests how motives forged by our common evolutionary past influence the attractions and sexual choices of women and of men worldwide.

Eagly, A. H. (1987). *Sex differences in social behavior: A social-role explanation.* Hillsdale, NJ: Erlbaum. How and why are men and women alike and different in aggressiveness, altruism, influenceability, and nonverbal behavior? Eagly digests all the available research studies and cogently explains the outcomes.

Lonner, W. J., & Malpass, R. (Eds.) (1994). *Psychology and culture.* Needham Heights, MA: Allyn & Bacon. In 43 crisp essays, leading cross-cultural psychologists offer their most important findings.

Triandis, H. (1994). *Culture and social behavior.* New York: McGraw-Hill. How are we humans alike? How do we differ? Drawing on his research and experience in many cultures, a senior cross-cultural researcher provides answers.

Triandis, H. C., (1995). *Individualism and collectivism.* Boulder, CO: Westview Press. Cross-cultural psychologist Triandis shows how the cultural patterns represented by individualism and collectivism influence people's social perceptions and relations.

Unger, R., & Crawford, M. (1992). *Women and gender.* New York: McGraw-Hill. A state-of-the-art look at how we become gendered, with special attention to women's experiences, achievements, and stresses.

CONFORMITY

It was a long-awaited May afternoon. Three thousand family members and friends had gathered for the celebration. On cue, 400 Hope College seniors rose to hear the college president declare, "I hereby confer upon each of you the degree of Bachelor of Arts, with all the rights and privileges appertaining thereto." The declaration finished, the 25 new alumni in the first row began filing forward to receive their diplomas. As they did so, the other 375 eyed one another nervously, each thinking: "Weren't we instructed to sit down now and await our turn?" But no one sat. The seconds ticked by. Half the first row now had diplomas in hand. Outwardly, the standing herd kept its cool. But inside each head thoughts were buzzing: "We could be standing here for a half hour before it is our row's turn. . . . We're blocking the view of spectators seated behind us. . . . Why doesn't someone sit down?" Still, no one sat. Now two minutes had elapsed. The graduation marshal, whose instructions at the graduation rehearsal they were ignoring, strode up to the first standing row and subtly signaled it to sit down. No one sat. So he moved to the next row and audibly ordered it to "Sit down!" Within two seconds, 375 much-relieved people were happily relaxing in their chairs.

"The race of men, while sheep in credulity, are wolves for conformity."
Carl Van Doren,
Why I Am an Unbeliever

This scene raised three sets of questions for me. First, why, given the diversity of individuals among that large group, was their behavior so uniform? Is social pressure sometimes powerful enough to obliterate individual differences? Where were the rugged individualists?

Second, 25 percent of those graduates had been my students in social psychology. Although it was the furthest thing from their minds at the moment, they knew about conformity. When studying the topic, many of them had privately assured themselves that they would never be so docile as subjects in the famous conformity experiments. But here they were, participating in one of life's parallels. In everyday life, is courage always more easily fantasized than performed? Are we more susceptible to social influence than we realize? Does learning about social influence not liberate us from it?

Third, is conformity as bad as my description of this docile "herd" implies? Should I have been pleased at their "group solidarity" and "social sensitivity" rather than dismayed at their "mindless conformity"?

Let us take the last question first. Is conformity good or bad? This is another question that has no scientific answer. But assuming the values most of us share, we can say two things. First, conformity is at times bad (when it leads someone to drink and drive), at times good (when it inhibits people from cutting in front of us in a theater line), and at times inconsequential (when it disposes us to wear white when playing tennis).

"Whatever crushes individuality is despotism, by whatever name it may be called."
John Stuart Mill,
On Liberty, 1859

Second, the word "conformity" does carry a negative value judgment. How would you feel if you overheard someone describing you as a "real conformist"? I suspect you would feel hurt, because western cultures don't prize the trait of submitting to peer pressure. Hence American and European social psychologists more often give it negative labels (conformity, submission, compliance) than positive ones (communal sensitivity, responsiveness, cooperative team play).

"The social pressures community brings to bear are a mainstay of our moral values."
Amitai Etzioni,
The Spirit of Community, 1993

In Japan, going along with others is not a sign of weakness, but of tolerance, self-control, and maturity (Markus & Kitayama, 1994). "Everywhere in Japan," observed Lance Morrow (1983) "one senses an intricate serenity that comes to a people who know exactly what to expect from each other."

The moral: We choose labels to suit our values and judgments. In retrospect, I view the U.S. senators who cast unpopular votes against the Vietnam war as "independent" and "inner-directed" and those who cast unpopular votes against civil rights legislation as "eccentric" and "self-centered." Labels both describe and evaluate—and they are inescapable. We cannot discuss the topics of this chapter without labels. So let us be clear on the meanings of the following labels: "conformity," "compliance," "acceptance."

When, as part of a crowd, you rise to cheer a game-winning touchdown, are you conforming? When, along with millions of others, you drink milk or coffee, are you conforming? When you and everyone else agree that men look better with combable hair than with crewcuts, are you conforming? Maybe, maybe not. The key is whether your behavior and beliefs would be the same apart from the group. Would you rise to cheer the touchdown if you were the only fan in the stands? Conformity is not just acting as other people act, it is being affected by how they act. It is acting differently from the way you would act alone. Thus **conformity** is "a change in behavior or belief . . . as a result of real or imagined group pressure" (Kiesler & Kiesler, 1969, p. 2).

There are two varieties of conformity. Sometimes we conform without really believing in what we are doing. We put on the necktie or dress, though we dislike doing so. This insincere, outward conformity is **compliance**. We comply primarily to reap a reward or avoid a punishment. If our compliance is to an explicit command, we call it obedience.

Sometimes we genuinely believe in what the group has convinced us to do. We may join millions of others in drinking milk because we are convinced that milk is nutritious. This sincere, inward conformity is called **acceptance**. Acceptance sometimes follows compliance. As Chapter 4 emphasized, attitudes follow behavior. Thus, unless we feel no responsibility for our behavior, we usually become sympathetic to what we have stood up for.

Conformity:
A change in behavior or belief as a result of real or imagined group pressure.

Compliance:
Conformity that involves publicly acting in accord with social pressure while privately disagreeing.

Acceptance:
Conformity that involves both acting and believing in accord with social pressure.

The American People Finally Speak Up

Sometimes it is difficult to avoid complying.

Sherif and others have used this technique to answer questions about people's suggestibility. When people were retested alone a year later, would their estimates again diverge or would they continue to follow the group norm? Remarkably, they continued to support the group norm (Rohrer & others, 1954). (Does this suggest compliance or acceptance?)

Struck by culture's seeming power to perpetuate false beliefs, Robert Jacobs and Donald Campbell (1961) studied the transmission of false beliefs in their Northwestern University laboratory. Using the autokinetic phenomenon, they had a **confederate** give an inflated estimate of how far the light moved. The confederate then left the experiment and was replaced by another real subject who was in turn replaced by a still newer member. The inflated illusion persisted for five generations. These people had become "unwitting conspirators in perpetuating a cultural fraud." The lesson of these experiments: Our views of reality are not ours alone.

In everyday life the results of suggestibility are sometimes amusing. In late March 1954, Seattle newspapers reported damage to car windshields in a city 80 miles to the north. On the morning of April 14, similar windshield damage was reported 65 miles away and later that day only 45 miles away. By nightfall, the windshield-pitting agent had reached Seattle. Before the end of April 15, the Seattle police department had received complaints of damage to more than 3000 windshields (Medalia & Larsen, 1958). That evening the mayor of Seattle called on President Eisenhower for help.

I was an 11-year-old in Seattle at the time. I recall searching our windshield, frightened by the explanation that a Pacific H-bomb test was raining fallout on Seattle. However, on April 16 the newspapers hinted that the real culprit might be mass suggestibility. After April 17 there were no more complaints. Later analysis of the pitted windshields concluded that the cause was ordinary road damage. Why did we notice this only after April 14? Given the suggestion, we had looked carefully *at* our windshields instead of *through* them.

In real life suggestibility is not always so amusing. Hijackings, UFO sightings, and even suicides tend to come in waves. Sociologist David Phillips and his colleagues (1985, 1989) report that known suicides, and fatal auto accidents and private airplane crashes (which sometimes disguise suicides), increase after well-publicized suicides. For example, following Marilyn Monroe's August 6, 1962, suicide, there were 200 more August suicides in the United States than normal. Moreover, the increase happens only in areas where the suicide story is publicized. The more publicity, the greater the increase in later fatalities.

A copycat suicide phenomenon has also occurred in Germany (Jonas, 1992). Moreover, in both Germany and the United States, suicide rates rise slightly following fictional suicides on soap operas, and, ironically, even after serious dramas that focus on the suicide problem (Gould & Shaffer, 1986; Hafner & Schmidtke, 1989; Phillips, 1982). Phillips reports that teenagers are most susceptible, which would help explain the clusters of teen suicides that occasionally occur in some communities.

ASCH'S STUDIES OF GROUP PRESSURE

Participants in the autokinetic experiments faced an ambiguous reality. Consider a less ambiguous perceptual problem, such as faced by a young boy named Solomon Asch. While attending the traditional Jewish seder at Passover, recalls Asch,

Confederate:
An accomplice of the experimenter.

"Why doth one man's yawning make another yawn?"
Robert Burton,
Anatomy of Melancholy, 1621

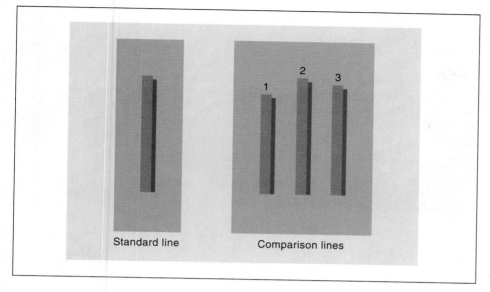

■ **FIGURE 7–2**
Sample comparison from Solomon Asch's conformity procedure. The participants judged which of three comparison lines matched the standard.

I asked my uncle, who was sitting next to me, why the door was being opened. He replied, "The prophet Elijah visits this evening every Jewish home and takes a sip of wine from the cup reserved for him."

I was amazed at this news and repeated, "Does he really come? Does he really take a sip?"

My uncle said, "If you watch very closely, when the door is opened you will see—you watch the cup—you will see that the wine will go down a little."

And that's what happened. My eyes were riveted upon the cup of wine. I was determined to see whether there would be a change. And to me it seemed—it was tantalizing, and of course, it was hard to be absolutely sure—that indeed something was happening at the rim of the cup, and the wine did go down a little. (Quoted by Aron & Aron, 1989, p. 27)

Years later, social psychologist Asch re-created his boyhood experience in his laboratory. Imagine yourself as one of Asch's volunteer subjects. You are seated sixth in a row of seven people. After explaining that you will be taking part in a study of perceptual judgments, the experimenter asks you to say which of the three lines in Figure 7–2 matches the standard line. You can easily see that it's line 2. So it's no surprise when the five people responding before you all say "line 2."

The next comparison proves as easy, and you settle in to endure a boring experiment. But the third trial startles you. Although the correct answer seems just as clear-cut, the first person gives a seemingly wrong answer. When the second person gives the same answer, you sit up in your chair and stare at the cards. The third person agrees with the first two. Your jaw drops; you start to perspire. "What is this?" you ask yourself. "Are they blind? Or am I?" The fourth and fifth people agree with the others. Then the experimenter looks at you. Now you are experiencing an "epistemological nightmare": "How am I to know what is true? Is it what my peers tell me or what my eyes tell me?"

Dozens of college students experienced this conflict during Asch's experiments. Those in a control condition who answered alone were correct more than 99 percent of the time. Asch wondered: If several others ("confederates"

In one of Asch's conformity experiments (top), subject number 6 experienced uneasiness and conflict after hearing five people before him give a wrong answer.

"He who sees the truth, let him proclaim it, without asking who is for it or who is against it."
Henry George,
The Irish Land Question, 1881

Ethical Note: Professional ethics usually dictate explaining the experiment afterward (see Chapter 1). Pretend you were an experimenter who had just finished a session with a conforming participant. Could you explain the deception without making the person feel gullible and dumb?

coached by the experimenter) gave identical wrong answers, would people declare what they would otherwise have denied? Although some people never conformed, three quarters did so at least once. All told, 37 percent of the responses were conforming (or should we say "trusting of others"?). Of course, that means 63 percent of the time people did not conform. Despite the independence shown by many of his subjects, Asch's (1955) feelings about the conformity were as clear as the correct answers to his questions: "That reasonably intelligent and well-meaning young people are willing to call white black is a matter of concern. It raises questions about our ways of education and about the values that guide our conduct."

Asch's procedure became the standard for hundreds of later experiments. These experiments lack what Chapter 1 called the "mundane realism" of everyday conformity, but they do have "experimental realism." People get emotionally involved in the experience. However, the procedure is expensive and difficult to control because it requires a troupe of confederates who must act with near-perfect consistency from subject to subject. Richard Crutchfield (1955) remedied this by automating Asch's experiment. Five participants—each a real subject—sat in adjacent booths and viewed questions projected on the wall across the room. Each booth had a panel of lights and switches that allowed the subjects to declare their judgments and to see how others responded. After a few warm-up trials, all subjects found themselves responding last after seeing the purported responses of the other four.

The technique lets the researcher present a variety of questions. Crutchfield tested military officers by presenting a circle and a star side by side (Figure 7–3). The area of the circle was one-third greater. But when each officer thought the others had judged the star to be larger, 46 percent of them denied the evidence of their senses and voted with the group. Tested privately, each of the officers rejected the statement, "I doubt whether I would make a good leader." Of course—these *are* leaders. Yet, when they believed all the other officers had accepted the statement, almost 40 percent agreed with it.

Even ideologically objectionable positions got approval when the group approved. Not long before the 1960s free-speech movement surfaced at the University of California, Berkeley, Crutchfield and his colleagues found 58 percent of the students willing to go along with the group and agree that "free speech being a privilege rather than a right, it is proper for a society to suspend free speech when it feels itself threatened" (Krech & others, 1962).

The Sherif, Asch, and Crutchfield results are startling because in none of them is there any open, obvious pressure to conform—there are no rewards for "team play," no punishments for individuality. If people are this compliant in response to such minimal pressure, how much more compliant will they be if they are directly coerced? Could someone force the average North American to perform cruel acts? I would have guessed not: North Americans' humane, democratic, individualistic values would make them resist such pressure. Besides, the easy verbal pronouncements of these experiments are a giant step away from actually harming someone; you and I would never yield to coercion to hurt another. Or would we? Social psychologist Stanley Milgram wondered.

"It is too easy to go over to the majority."
Seneca, *Epistulae ad Lucilium*

Which is bigger?

(a)   (b)

■ FIGURE 7–3
Richard Crutchfield's conformity-testing procedure. People sit in adjacent booths and answer questions presented on the wall in front of them after witnessing others' purported answers.

MILGRAM'S OBEDIENCE EXPERIMENTS

Milgram's (1965, 1974) experiments on what happens when the demands of authority clash with the demands of conscience have become the most famous and controversial experiments in social psychology. "Perhaps more than any other empirical contributions in the history of social science," notes Lee Ross (1988), "they have become part of our society's shared intellectual legacy—that small body of historical incidents, biblical parables, and classic literature that serious thinkers feel free to draw on when they debate about human nature or contemplate human history."

Here is the scene staged by Milgram, a creative artist who wrote stories and stage plays: Two men come to Yale University's psychology laboratory to participate in a study of learning and memory. A stern experimenter in a gray technician's coat explains that this is a pioneering study of the effect of punishment on learning. The experiment requires one of them to teach a list of word pairs to the other and to punish errors by delivering shocks of increasing intensity. To assign the roles, they draw slips out of a hat. One of the men, a mild-mannered, 47-year-old accountant who is the experimenter's confederate, pretends that his slip says "learner" and is ushered into an adjacent room. The "teacher" (who has come in response to a newspaper ad) takes a mild sample shock and then looks on as the experimenter straps the learner into a chair and attaches an electrode to his wrist.

Teacher and experimenter then return to the main room where the teacher takes his place before a "shock generator" with switches ranging from 15 to 450 volts in 15-volt increments. The switches are labeled "Slight Shock," "Very Strong Shock," "Danger: Severe Shock," and so forth. Under the 435- and 450-volt switches appears "XXX." The experimenter tells the teacher to "move one level higher on the shock generator" each time the learner gives a wrong answer. With each flick of a switch, lights flash, relay switches click, and an electric buzz sounds.

An obedient subject in Milgram's "touch" condition forces the victim's hand onto the shock plate. Usually, however, "teachers" were more merciful to victims who were this close to them.

THE LEARNER'S SCHEDULE OF PROTESTS IN MILGRAM'S "HEART DISTURBANCE" EXPERIMENTS

75 volts   Ugh!

90 volts   Ugh!

105 volts   Ugh! (*Louder*)

120 volts   Ugh! Hey, this really hurts.

135 volts   Ugh!!

150 volts   Ugh!!! Experimenter! That's all. Get me out of here. I told you I had heart trouble. My heart's starting to bother me now. Get me out of here, please. My heart's starting to bother me. I refuse to go on. Let me out.

165 volts   Ugh! Let me out! (*Shouting*)

180 volts   Ugh! I can't stand the pain. Let me out of here! (*Shouting*)

195 volts   Ugh! Let me out of here. Let me out of here. My heart's bothering me. Let me out of here! You have no right to keep me here! Let me out! Let me out of here! Let me out! Let me out of here! My heart's bothering me. Let me out! Let me out!

210 volts   Ugh! Experimenter! Get me out of here. I've had enough. I won't be in the experiment any more.

225 volts   Ugh!

240 volts   Ugh!

255 volts   Ugh! Get me out of here.

270 volts   (*Agonized scream*) Let me out of here. Let me out of here. Let me out of here. Let me out. Do you hear? Let me out of here.

285 volts   (*Agonized scream*)

300 volts   (*Agonized scream*) I absolutely refuse to answer any more. Get me out of here. You can't hold me here. Get me out. Get me out of here.

315 volts   (*Intensely agonized scream*) I told you I refuse to answer. I'm no longer part of this experiment.

330 volts   (*Intense and prolonged agonized scream*) Let me out of here. Let me out of here. My heart's bothering me. Let me out. I tell you. (*Hysterically*) Let me out of here. Let me out of here. You have no right to hold me here. Let me out! Let me out! Let me out! Let me out of here! Let me out! Let me out!

From *Obedience to Authority* by Stanley Milgram. New York: Harper & Row, 1974, pp. 56–57.

If the subject complies with the experimenter's requests, he hears the learner grunt at 75, 90, and 105 volts. At 120 volts the learner shouts that the shocks are painful. And at 150 volts he cries out, "Experimenter, get me out of here! I won't be in the experiment anymore! I refuse to go on!" By 270 volts his protests have become screams of agony, and he continues to insist to be let out. At 300 and 315 volts he screams his refusal to answer. After 330 volts he falls silent. In answer to the teacher's inquiries and pleas to end the experiment, the experimenter states that the nonresponses should be treated as wrong answers. To keep the subject going, he uses four verbal prods:

Prod 1: Please continue (*or* Please go on).

Prod 2: The experiment requires that you continue.

Prod 3: It is absolutely essential that you continue.

Prod 4: You have no other choice; you *must* go on.

How far would you go? Milgram described the experiment to 110 psychiatrists, college students, and middle-class adults. People in all three groups guessed that they would disobey by about 135 volts; none expected to go beyond 300 volts. Recognizing that self-estimates may reflect self-serving bias, Milgram asked them how far they thought *other* people would go. Virtually no one expected anyone to proceed to XXX on the shock panel. (The psychiatrists guessed about one in a thousand.)

But when Milgram conducted the experiment with 40 men—a vocational mix of 20- to 50-year-olds—25 of them (63 percent) went clear to 450 volts. In fact, all who reached 450 volts complied with a command to *continue* the procedure until, after two further trials, the experimenter called a halt.

Given this disturbing result, Milgram next made the learner's protests even more compelling. As the learner was strapped into the chair, the teacher heard him mention his "slight heart condition" and heard the experimenter's reassurance that "although the shocks may be painful, they cause no permanent tissue damage." The learner's anguished protests (see "Focus: The Learner's Schedule") were to little avail; of 40 new men in this experiment, 26 (65 percent) fully complied with the experimenter's demands (Figure 7–4).

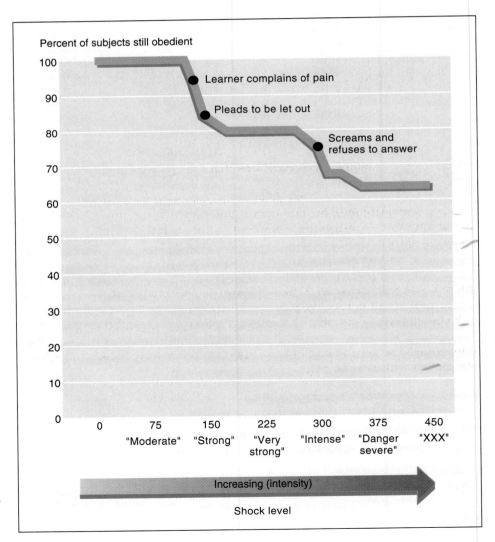

■ **FIGURE 7–4**

The Milgram obedience experiment. Percentage of subjects complying despite the learner's cries of protest and failure to respond.

(From Milgram, 1965.)

The obedience of his subjects disturbed Milgram. The procedures he used disturbed many social psychologists (Miller, 1986). The "learner" in these experiments actually received no shock (he disengaged himself from the electric chair and turned on a tape recorder that delivered the protests). Nevertheless, some critics said that Milgram did to his subjects what they did to their victims: He stressed them against their will. Indeed, many of the "teachers" did experience agony. They sweated, trembled, stuttered, bit their lips, groaned, or even broke into uncontrollable nervous laughter. A *New York Times* reviewer complained that the cruelty inflicted by the experiments "upon their unwitting subjects is surpassed only by the cruelty that they elicit from them" (Marcus, 1974). Critics also argued that the participants' self-concepts may have been altered. One participant's wife told him, "You can call yourself Eichmann" (referring to Nazi death camp administrator Adolf Eichmann). CBS television depicted the results and controversy in a two-hour dramatization, *The Tenth Level*, starring William Shatner of *Star Trek* fame as Milgram.

In his own defense, Milgram pointed to the lessons taught by his nearly two dozen experiments with a diverse sample of more than 1000 subjects. He also reminded critics of the support he received from the participants after the deception was revealed and the experiment explained. When surveyed afterward, 84 percent said they were glad to have participated; only 1 percent regretted volunteering. A year later, a psychiatrist interviewed 40 of those who had suffered most and concluded that, despite the temporary stress, none was harmed.

> *"If a system of death camps were set up in the United States of the sort we had in Nazi Germany, one would be able to find sufficient personnel for those camps in any medium-sized American town."*
> Stanley Milgram, on CBS "Sixty Minutes," 1979

> *"History, despite its wrenching pain, Cannot be unlived, and if faced With courage, need not be lived again."*
> Maya Angelou, Presidential Inaugural Poem, January 20, 1993

WHAT BREEDS OBEDIENCE?

Milgram did more than reveal the extent to which people will obey an authority; he also examined the conditions that breed obedience. In further experiments, he varied the social conditions and got compliance ranging from 0 to 93 percent fully obedient. The determining factors were these four: the victim's emotional distance, the authority's closeness and legitimacy, whether or not the authority is institutionalized, and the liberating effects of a disobedient fellow subject.

Emotional Distance of the Victim

Milgram's subjects acted with least compassion when the "learners" could not be seen (and could not see them). When the victim was remote and the teachers heard no complaints, nearly all obeyed calmly to the end. When the learner was in the same room, "only" 40 percent obeyed to 450 volts. Full compliance dropped to 30 percent when teachers were required to force the learner's hand into contact with a shock plate.

In everyday life, too, it is easiest to abuse someone who is distant or depersonalized. People will be unresponsive even to great tragedies. Executioners depersonalize those being executed by placing hoods over their heads. The ethics of war allow one to bomb a helpless village from 40,000 feet but not to shoot an equally helpless villager. In combat with an enemy they can see, many soldiers either do not fire or do not aim. Such disobedience is rare among those given orders to kill with the more distant artillery or aircraft weapons (Padgett, 1989).

On the positive side, people act most compassionately toward those who are personalized. This is why appeals for the unborn or the hungry are nearly al-

FOCUS

PERSONALIZING THE VICTIMS

Innocent victims trigger more compassion if personalized. In a week when a soon-forgotten earthquake in Iran kills 3000 people, a lone boy dies, trapped in a well shaft in Italy, and the whole world grieves. The projected death statistics of a nuclear war are impersonal to the point of being incomprehensible. So international law professor Roger Fisher proposed a way to personalize the victims:

> It so happens that a young man, usually a navy officer, accompanies the President wherever he goes. This young man has a black attaché case which contains the codes that are needed to fire nuclear weapons.
>
> I can see the President at a staff meeting considering nuclear war as an abstract question. He might conclude, "On SIOP Plan One, the decision is affirmative. Commu-

nicate the Alpha line XYZ." Such jargon keeps what is involved at a distance.

> My suggestion, then, is quite simple. Put that needed code number in a little capsule and implant that capsule right next to the heart of a volunteer. The volunteer will carry with him a big, heavy butcher knife as he accompanies the President. If ever the President wants to fire nuclear weapons, the only way he can do so is by first, with his own hands, killing one human being.
>
> "George," the President would say, "I'm sorry, but tens of millions must die." The President then would have to look at someone and realize what death is—what an *innocent* death is. Blood on the White House carpet: it's reality brought home.
>
> When I suggested this to friends in the Pentagon, they said, "My God, that's terrible. Having to kill someone would distort the President's judgment. He might never push the button."

Adapted from "Preventing Nuclear War" by Roger Fisher, *Bulletin of the Atomic Scientists*, March 1981, pp. 11–17.

Imagine you had the power to prevent either a tidal wave that would kill 25,000 people in Pakistan, a crash that would kill 250 people at your local airport, or a car accident that would kill an acquaintance. Which would you prevent?

ways personalized with a compelling photograph or description. Perhaps even more compelling is an ultrasound picture of one's own developing fetus. When queried by John Lydon and Christine Dunkel-Schetter (1994), expectant women expressed more commitment to their pregnancy if they had earlier seen an ultrasound picture of their fetus that clearly displayed body parts. In his 1790 *Theory of Moral Sentiments*, Scottish economist Adam Smith imagined that "the great empire of China, with all its myriads of inhabitants, was suddenly swallowed up by an earthquake." Your average European, he guessed, would on hearing the news "express very strongly his sorrow for the misfortune of that unhappy people, would make many melancholy reflections upon the precariousness of human life . . . and when all this fine philosophy was over [would resume] his business or his pleasure . . . as if no such accident had happened."

Closeness and Legitimacy of the Authority

The physical presence of the experimenter also affected obedience. When Milgram gave the commands by telephone, full obedience dropped to 21 percent (although many lied and said they were obeying). Other studies confirm that when the one making the request is physically close, compliance increases. Given a light touch on the arm, people are more likely to lend a dime, sign a petition, or sample a new pizza (Kleinke, 1977; Smith & others, 1982; Willis & Hamm, 1980).

However, the authority must be perceived as legitimate. In another twist on the basic experiment, the experimenter received a rigged telephone call that required him to leave the laboratory. He said that since the equipment recorded data automatically, the teacher should just go ahead. After the experimenter left, another subject who had been assigned a clerical role (actually a second confederate) assumed command. The clerk "decided" that the shock should be increased one level for each wrong answer and instructed the teacher accordingly. Now 80 percent of the teachers refused to comply fully. The confederate, feigning disgust at this defiance, then came and sat down in front of the shock generator and tried to take over the teacher's role. At this point most of the defiant participants protested. Some tried to unplug the generator. One large man lifted the zealous shocker from his chair and threw him across the room. This rebellion against an illegitimate authority contrasted sharply with the deferential politeness usually shown the experimenter.

It also contrasts with the behavior of hospital nurses who in one study were called by an unknown physician and ordered to administer an obvious overdose of a drug (Hofling & others, 1966). The researchers told one group of nurses and nursing students about the experiment and asked how they would react. Nearly all said they would not have given the medication as ordered. One explained that she would have replied, "I'm sorry, sir, but I am not authorized to give any medication without a written order, especially one so large over the usual dose and one that I'm unfamiliar with. If it were possible, I would be glad to do it, but this is against hospital policy and my own ethical standards." Nevertheless, when 22 other nurses were actually given the phoned-in overdose order, all but one obeyed without delay (until being intercepted on their way to the patient). Although not all nurses are so compliant (Rank & Jacobson, 1977), these nurses were following a familiar script: Doctor (a legitimate authority) orders; nurse obeys.

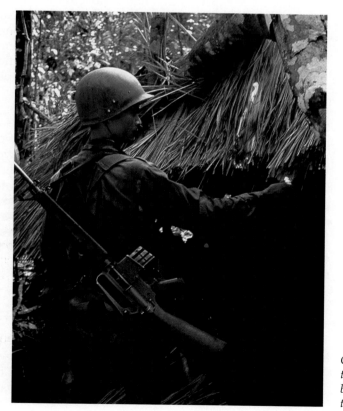

Given orders, most soldiers will torch people's homes or kill— behaviors that in other contexts they would consider immoral.

Compliance with legitimate authority was also apparent in the strange case of the "rectal ear ache" (Cohen & Davis, 1981, cited by Cialdini, 1988). A doctor ordered ear drops given to a patient suffering infection in the right ear. On the prescription, the doctor abbreviated "place in right ear" as "place in R ear." Reading the order, the compliant nurse put the required drops in the compliant patient's rectum.

Institutional Authority

If the prestige of the authority is this important, then perhaps the institutional prestige of Yale University legitimized the Milgram experiment commands. In postexperimental interviews, many participants volunteered that had it not been for Yale's reputation, they would not have obeyed. To see whether this was true, Milgram moved the experiment to Bridgeport, Connecticut. He set himself up in a modest commercial building as the "Research Associates of Bridgeport." When the usual "heart disturbance" experiment was run with the same personnel, what percentage of the men do you suppose fully obeyed? Though reduced, the rate remained remarkably high—48 percent.

In everyday life, too, authorities backed by institutions wield social power. Robert Ornstein (1991) tells of a psychiatrist-friend who was called to the edge of a cliff above San Mateo, California, where one of his patients, Alfred, was threatening to jump. When the psychiatrist's reasoned reassurance failed to dislodge Alfred, the psychiatrist could only hope that a police crisis expert would soon arrive.

Although no expert came, another police officer, unaware of the drama, happened on to the scene, took out his power bullhorn, and yelled at the assembled cliffside group: "Who's the ass who left that Pontiac station wagon double-parked out there in the middle of the road? I almost hit it. Move it *now*, whoever you are." Hearing the message, Alfred obediently got down at once, moved the car, and then without a word got into the policeman's car for a trip to the nearby hospital.

The Liberating Effects of Group Influence

These classic experiments give us a negative view of conformity. Can conformity be constructive? Perhaps you can recall a time you felt justifiably angry at an unfair teacher, or with someone's offensive behavior, but you hesitated to object. Then one or two others objected, and you followed their example. Milgram captured this liberating effect of conformity by placing the teacher with two confederates who were to help conduct the procedure. During the experiment, both defied the experimenter, who then ordered the real subject to continue alone. Did he? No. Ninety percent liberated themselves by conforming to the defiant confederates.

REFLECTIONS ON THE CLASSIC STUDIES

The common response to Milgram's results is to note their counterparts in recent history: the "I was only following orders" defenses of Adolf Eichmann in Nazi Germany; of Lieutenant William Calley, who in 1968 directed the unprovoked slaughter of hundreds of Vietnamese in the village of My Lai; and of the

"If the commander-in-chief tells this lieutenant colonel to go stand in the corner and sit on his head, I will do so."
Oliver North, 1987

"ethnic cleansing" occurring more recently in Iraq, Rwanda, and Bosnia. A Bosnian victim explains:

> I was raped and tortured too, because they knew that I am a wife of a leader of the Muslim party. My neighbor tortured me the most, the one my husband respected as his own brother. By the end of June, Chetniks brought another neighbor of ours and with a gun pointed at him they forced him to rape a 14-year-old girl. He stood trembling and stuttering with fear. Then he turned to a Chetnik he believed was a leader and said: "Don't make me do it. I have known her since she was born. . . ." They beat him in front of us until he died. It was an example to the other Serbs that there is no pity, that one must do what leaders order them to do. (Drakuli, 1992)

Soldiers are trained to obey superiors. In the United States, the military acknowledges that even Marines should disobey *inappropriate* orders, but the military does not train soldiers to recognize an illegal or immoral order (Staub, 1989). Thus one participant in the My Lai massacre recalled:

> [Lieutenant Calley] told me to start shooting. So I started shooting, I poured about four clips into the group. . . . They were begging and saying, "No, no." And the mothers were hugging their children and. . . . Well, we kept right on firing. They was waving their arms and begging. (Wallace, 1969)

The "safe" scientific contexts of the obedience experiments differ from the wartime contexts. The obedience experiments also differ from the other conformity experiments in the strength of the social pressure: Compliance is explicitly commanded. Without the coercion, people did not act cruelly. Yet both the Asch and Milgram experiments share certain commonalities. They show how compliance can take precedence over moral sense. They succeeded in pressuring people to go against their own conscience. They did more than teach us an academic lesson; they sensitized us to moral conflicts in our own lives. And they illustrate and affirm some familiar social psychological principles: the link between behavior and attitudes, the power of the situation, and the strength of the fundamental attribution error.

Behavior and Attitudes

In Chapter 4 we noted that attitudes fail to determine behavior when external influences override inner convictions. These experiments vividly illustrate this principle. When responding alone, Asch's subjects nearly always gave the correct answer. It was another matter when they stood alone against a group. In the obedience experiments, a powerful social pressure (the experimenter's commands) overcame a weaker one (the remote victim's pleas). Torn between the pleas of the victim and the orders of the experimenter, between the desire to avoid doing harm and the desire to be a good subject, a surprising number chose to obey. As Milgram explained,

> Some subjects were totally convinced of the wrongness of what they were doing [yet] felt that—within themselves, at least—they had been on the side of the angels. What they failed to realize is that subjective feelings are largely irrelevant to the moral issue at hand so long as they are not transformed into action. Political control is effected through action. . . . Tyrannies are perpetuated by difficult men who do not possess the courage to act out their beliefs. Time and again in the experiment people disvalued what they were doing but could not muster the inner resources to translate their values into action. (Milgram, 1974, p. 10)

BEHIND THE SCENES

While working for Solomon E. Asch, I wondered whether his conformity experiments could be made more humanly significant. First, I imagined an experiment similar to Asch's except that the group induced the person to deliver shocks to a protesting victim. But a control was needed to see how much shock a person would give in the absence of group pressure. Someone, presumably the experimenter, would have to instruct the subject to give the shocks. But now a new question arose: Just how far would a person go when ordered to administer such shocks? In my mind, the issue had shifted to the willingness of people to comply with destructive orders. It was an exciting moment for me. I realized that this simple question was both humanly important and capable of being precisely answered.

The laboratory procedure gave scientific expression to a more general concern about authority, a concern forced upon members of my generation, in particular upon Jews such as myself, by the atrocities of World War II. The impact of the Holocaust on my own psyche energized my interest in obedience and shaped the particular form in which it was examined.

STANLEY MILGRAM (1933–1984), *City University of New York*

Abridged from the original for this book and from Milgram, 1977, with permission of Alexandra Milgram.

Why were the participants unable to disengage themselves? How had they become trapped? Imagine yourself as the teacher in yet another version of Milgram's experiment, one he never conducted. Assume that when the learner gives the first wrong answer, the experimenter asks you to zap him with 330 volts. After flicking the switch, you hear the learner scream, complain of a heart disturbance, and plead for mercy. Do you continue?

I think not. Recall the step-by-step entrapment of the foot-in-the-door phenomenon (Chapter 4) as we compare this hypothetical experiment to what Milgram's subjects experienced. Their first commitment was mild—15 volts—and it elicited no protest. You, too, would agree to do that much. By the time they delivered 75 volts and heard the learner's first groan, they already had complied five times. On the next trial the experimenter asked them to commit an act only slightly more extreme than what they had already repeatedly committed. By the time they delivered 330 volts, after 22 acts of compliance, the subjects had reduced some of their dissonance. They were therefore in a different psychological state from that of someone beginning the experiment at that point. As we saw in Chapter 4, external behavior and internal disposition can feed one another, sometimes in an escalating spiral. Thus, reported Milgram (1974, p. 10):

> Many subjects harshly devalue the victim *as a consequence* of acting against him. Such comments as "He was so stupid and stubborn he deserved to get shocked," were common. Once having acted against the victim, these subjects found it necessary to view him as an unworthy individual, whose punishment was made inevitable by his own deficiencies of intellect and character.

During the early 1970s, the military junta then in power in Greece used this "blame-the-victim" process to train torturers (Haritos-Fatouros, 1988; Staub, 1989). In Greece, as in the training of SS officers in Nazi Germany, the military selected candidates based on their respect for and submission to authority. But such tendencies alone do not a torturer make. Thus they would first assign the trainee to guard prisoners, then to participate in arrest squads, then to hit prisoners, then to observe torture, and only then to practice it. Step by step, an obedient but otherwise decent person evolved into an agent of cruelty. Compliance bred acceptance.

From his study of human genocide across the world, Ervin Staub (1989) shows where this process can lead. Too often, criticism produces contempt, which licenses cruelty, which, when justified, leads to brutality, then killing, then systematic killing. Evolving attitudes both follow and justify actions. Staub's disturbing conclusion: "Human beings have the capacity to come to experience killing other people as nothing extraordinary"(p. 13).

But then humans also have a capacity for heroism. During the Holocaust, French Jews destined for deportation to Germany were sheltered by the villagers of Le Chambon. These people were mostly Protestants, descendants of a persecuted group, and people whose own authorities, their pastors, had taught them to "resist whenever our adversaries will demand of us obedience contrary to the orders of the Gospel" (Rochat, 1993). Ordered to divulge the sheltered Jews, the head pastor modeled disobedience: "I don't know of Jews, I only know of human beings." Without knowing how terrible the war would be or how much they would suffer, the resisters made an initial commitment and then—supported by their beliefs, by their own authorities, and by one another—remained defiant to the war's end. Here and elsewhere, the ultimate response to Nazi occupation usually came early. The first acts of compliance or resistance bred attitudes that influenced behavior, which strengthened attitudes. Initial helping heightened commitment, leading to more helping.

The Power of the Situation

The most important lesson of Chapter 6—that culture is a powerful shaper of lives—and this chapter's most important lesson—that immediate situational forces are just as powerful—reveal the strength of the social context. To feel this for yourself, imagine violating some minor norms: standing up in the middle of a class; singing out loud in a restaurant; greeting some distinguished senior professors by their first names; wearing shorts to church; playing golf in a suit; munching Cracker Jacks at a piano recital. In trying to break with social constraints, we suddenly realize how strong they are.

Some of Milgram's own students learned this lesson when he and John Sabini (1983) asked their help in studying the effects of violating a simple social norm: asking riders on the New York City subway system for their seats. To their surprise, 56 percent gave up their seats, even when no justification was given. The students' own reactions to making the request were as interesting: Most found it extremely difficult. Often, the words got stuck in their throat, and they had to withdraw. Once having made a request and gotten a seat, they sometimes justified their norm violation by pretending to be sick. Such is the power of the unspoken rules governing our public behavior.

There is also a lesson here about evil. Evil sometimes results from a few bad apples. That's the image of evil symbolized by depraved killers in suspense

"Men's actions are too strong for them. Show me a man who has acted and who has not been the victim and slave of his action."
Ralph Waldo Emerson,
Representative Men: Goethe, 1850

"Eichmann did not hate Jews, and that made it worse, to have no feelings. To make Eichmann appear a monster renders him less dangerous than he was. If you kill a monster you can go to bed and sleep, for there aren't many of them. But if Eichmann was normality, then this is a far more dangerous situation."
Hannah Arendt, *Eichmann in Jerusalem*, 1963

(Arendt, 1963). Or consider the German police battalion responsible for shooting nearly 40,000 Jews in Poland, many of them women, children, and elderly people who were shot in the back of the head, gruesomely spraying their brains. Christopher Browning (1992) portrays the "normality" of these men. They were not Nazis, SS members, or racial fanatics. They were laborers, salesmen, clerks, and artisans—family men who were too old for military service, but who, when directly ordered to kill, were unable to refuse.

Milgram's conclusion also makes it hard to attribute the Holocaust to unique character traits in the German people: "The most fundamental lesson of our study," he noted, is that "ordinary people, simply doing their jobs, and without any particular hostility on their part, can become agents in a terrible destructive process" (Milgram, 1974, p. 6). As Mister Rogers often reminds his preschool television audience, "Good people sometimes do bad things." Perhaps then, we should be more wary of political leaders whose charming dispositions lull us into supposing they would never do evil. Under the sway of evil forces, even nice people are sometimes corrupted.

The classic conformity experiments answered some questions but raised others: (1) Sometimes people conform; sometimes they do not. When do they? (2) Why do people conform? Why don't they ignore the group and "to their own selves be true?" (3) Is there a type of person who is likely to conform? Let's take these questions one at a time.

SUMMING UP

Conformity—changing one's behavior or belief as a result of group pressure—comes in two forms. *Compliance* is outwardly going along with the group while inwardly disagreeing. *Acceptance* is believing as well as acting in accord with social pressure.

Three classic sets of experiments illustrate how researchers have studied conformity and how conforming people can be. Muzafer Sherif observed that others' judgments influenced people's estimates of the illusory movement of a point of light. Norms for "proper" answers emerged and survived both over long periods of time and through succeeding generations of subjects. This laboratory suggestibility parallels suggestibility in real life.

Solomon Asch used a task that was as clear-cut as Sherif's was ambiguous. Asch had people listen to others' judgments of which of three comparison lines was equal to a standard line and then make the same judgment themselves. When the others unanimously gave a wrong answer, the subjects conformed 37 percent of the time.

Sherif's procedure elicited acceptance; Stanley Milgram's obedience experiments, on the other hand, elicited an extreme form of compliance. Under optimum conditions—a legitimate, close-at-hand commander, a remote victim, and no one else to exemplify disobedience—65 percent of his adult male subjects fully obeyed instructions to deliver what were supposedly traumatizing electric shocks to a screaming innocent victim in an adjacent room.

These classic experiments expose the potency of social forces and the ease with which compliance breeds acceptance. Evil is not just the product of bad people in a nice world but also of powerful situations that induce people to conform to falsehoods or capitulate to cruelty.

■ WHEN DO PEOPLE CONFORM?

*S*ome situations trigger much conformity, others little conformity. If you want to produce maximum conformity, what conditions would you choose?

Social psychologists wondered: If even Asch's noncoercive, unambiguous situation could elicit a conformity rate of 37 percent, would other settings produce even more? Researchers soon discovered that conformity did grow if the judgments were difficult or if the subjects felt incompetent. The more insecure we are about our judgments, the more influenced we are by others.

Researchers have also found that the nature of the group has an important influence. Conformity is highest when the group has three or more people and is cohesive, unanimous, and high in status. Conformity is also highest when the response is public and made without prior commitment.

GROUP SIZE

In laboratory experiments a group need not be large to have a large effect. Asch and other researchers found that three to five people will elicit much more conformity than just one or two. Increasing the number of people beyond five yields diminishing returns (Gerard & others, 1968; Rosenberg, 1961). In a field experiment, Milgram and his colleagues (1969) had 1, 2, 3, 5, 10, or 15 people pause on a busy New York City sidewalk and look up. As Figure 7–5 shows, the percentage of passersby who also looked up increased as the number looking up increased from one to five persons.

Bibb Latané (1981) accounts for the diminishing returns of increases in group size with his "social impact theory," which assumes that social influence in-

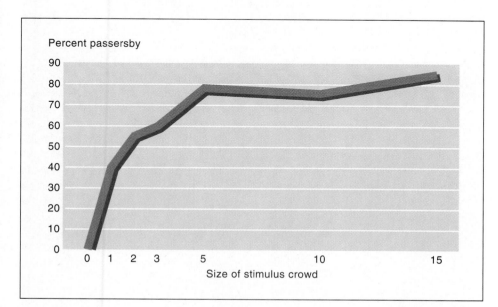

■ **FIGURE 7–5**
Group size and conformity. The percentage of passersby who imitated a group looking upward increased as group size increased to five persons.
(Data from Milgram, Bickman, & Berkowitz, 1969.)

creases with the immediacy and size of the group. But there are diminishing increments with increasing numbers: The second person has less social impact than the first, and person n has less effect than person $n - 1$.

The way the group is "packaged" also makes a difference. Researcher David Wilder (1977) gave University of Wisconsin students a jury case. Before giving their own judgments, the students watched videotapes of four confederates giving their judgments. When presented as two independent groups of two people, the participants conformed more than when the four confederates presented their judgments as a single group. Similarly, two groups of three people elicited more conformity than one group of six, and three groups of two people elicited even more. Evidently, the agreement of several small groups makes a position more credible.

UNANIMITY

Imagine yourself in a conformity experiment where all but one of the people responding before you give the same wrong answer. Would the example of this one nonconforming confederate be as liberating as it was for the subjects in Milgram's obedience experiment? Several experiments reveal that someone who punctures a group's unanimity deflates its social power (Allen & Levine, 1969; Asch, 1955; Morris & Miller, 1975). As Figure 7–6 illustrates, subjects will nearly always voice their convictions if just one other person has also done so. The subjects in such experiments often later say they felt warm toward and close to their nonconforming ally, but deny that the ally influenced them: "I would have answered just the same if he weren't there."

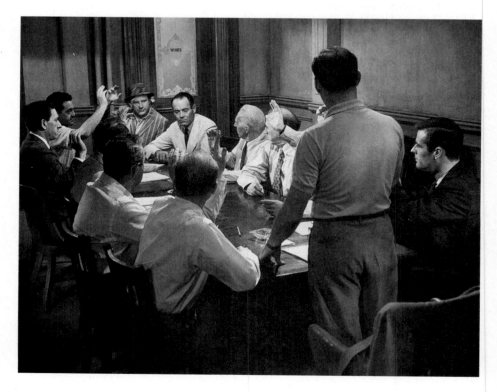

It is difficult to stand alone as a minority of one. But doing so sometimes makes a hero, as was the lone dissenting jury member played by Henry Fonda in the classic movie, 12 Angry Men.

Percent conformity

■ FIGURE 7–6
The effect of unanimity on conformity. When someone giving correct answers punctures the group's unanimity, subjects conform only one-fourth as often.
(From Asch, 1955.)

It's difficult to be a minority of one; few juries are hung because of one dissenting juror. These experiments teach the practical lesson that it is easier to stand up for something if you can find someone else to stand up with you. Many religious groups recognize this. Following the example of Jesus, who sent his disciples out in pairs, the Mormons send two missionaries into a neighborhood together. The support of the one comrade greatly increases a person's social courage.

Observing someone else's dissent—even when it is wrong—can increase our own independence. Charlan Nemeth and Cynthia Chiles (1988) discovered this after having people observe a lone individual in a group of four misjudge blue stimuli as green. Although the dissenter was wrong, observing him enabled the observers to exhibit their own form of independence. In a follow-up experiment, 76 percent of the time they correctly labeled red slides "red" even when everyone else was calling them "orange." Lacking this model of courage, 70 percent of the time observers went along with the group in calling red "orange."

"My opinion, my conviction, gains infinitely in strength and success, the moment a second mind has adopted it."
Novalis, Fragment

COHESION

A minority opinion from someone outside the groups we identify with—from someone at another college or of a different religion—sways us less than the same minority opinion from someone within our group (Clark & Maass, 1988, 1989). A heterosexual arguing for gay rights would more effectively sway heterosexuals than would a homosexual. The more **cohesive** a group is, the more power it gains over its members. In college sororities, for example, friends tend to share binge-eating tendencies, especially as they grow closer (Crandall, 1988).

In experiments, too, group members who feel attracted to the group are more responsive to its influence (Berkowitz, 1954; Lott & Lott, 1961; Sakurai, 1975). They do not like disagreeing with other group members. Fearing rejection by people they like, they allow them a certain power. In his *Essay Concerning Human Understanding*, the seventeenth-century philosopher John Locke recognized

Cohesiveness:
A "we feeling"—the extent to which members of a group are bound together, such as by attraction for one another.

the cohesiveness factor: "Nor is there one in ten thousand who is stiff and insensible enough to bear up under the constant dislike and condemnation of his own club."

STATUS

As you might suspect, higher-status people tend to have more impact (Driskell & Mullen, 1990). Studies of jaywalking behavior, conducted with the unwitting aid of nearly 24,000 pedestrians, reveal that the baseline jaywalking rate of 25 percent decreases to 17 percent in the presence of a nonjaywalking confederate and increases to 44 percent in the presence of another jaywalker (Mullen & others, 1990). The nonjaywalker does best in discouraging jaywalking when he or she is well dressed (although, strangely, jaywalking confederates do not trigger more jaywalking when well dressed). Clothes seem to "make the person" in Australia, too. Michael Walker, Susan Harriman, and Stuart Costello (1980) found that Sydney pedestrians were more compliant when approached by a well-dressed survey taker than one who was poorly dressed.

Milgram (1974) reports that in his obedience experiments people of lower status accepted the experimenter's commands more readily than people of higher status. After delivering 450 volts, one subject, a 37-year-old welder, turned to the experimenter and deferentially asked, "Where do we go from here, Professor?" (p. 46). Another subject, a divinity school professor who disobeyed at 150 volts, said: "I don't understand why the experiment is placed above this person's life," and plied the experimenter with questions about "the ethics of this thing"(p. 48).

PUBLIC RESPONSE

One of the first questions researchers sought to answer was this: Would people conform more in their public responses than in their private opinions? Or would they wobble more in their private opinions but be unwilling to conform publicly, lest they appear wishy-washy? The answer is now clear: In experiments, people conform more when they must respond publicly before others than when they write their answer privately. Asch's subjects, after hearing others respond, were less influenced by group pressure if they could write an answer that only the experimenter would see. It is much easier to stand up for what we believe in the privacy of the voting booth than before a group.

"If you worry about missing the boat—remember the Titanic."
Anonymous

NO PRIOR COMMITMENT

In 1980, Genuine Risk became the second filly to win the Kentucky Derby. In her next race, the Preakness, she came off the last turn gaining on the leader, Codex, a colt. As they came out of the turn neck and neck, Codex moved sideways toward Genuine Risk, causing her to hesitate and giving him a narrow victory. Had Codex brushed Genuine Risk? Had his jockey even whipped Genuine Risk in the face? The race referees huddled. After a brief deliberation they judged that no foul had occurred and confirmed Codex as the winner. The decision caused an uproar. On the televised instant replays, it appeared that Codex had indeed brushed Genuine Risk, the sentimental favorite. A protest was filed. The officials reconsidered their decision, but they did not change it.

Did Codex brush against Genuine Risk? Once race referees publicly announced their decision, no amount of evidence could budge them.

Did their judgment immediately after the race affect officials' openness toward reaching a different decision later? We will never know. However, we can put people through a laboratory version of this event—with and without the immediate commitment—and observe whether the commitment makes a difference. Again, imagine yourself in an Asch-type experiment. The experimenter displays the lines and asks you to respond first. After you have given your judgment and then heard everyone else disagree, the experimenter offers you an opportunity to reconsider. In the face of group pressure, do you now back down?

People almost never do (Deutsch & Gerard, 1955); once having made a public commitment, they stick to it. At most, they will change their judgments in later situations (Saltzstein & Sandberg, 1979). So we may expect that judges of diving contests, for example, will seldom change their ratings of a dive after seeing the other judges' ratings, although they might adjust their ratings of later dives.

Prior commitments restrain persuasion, too. When simulated juries make decisions, hung verdicts are more likely in cases when jurors are polled by a show of hands rather than by secret ballot (Kerr & MacCoun, 1985). Making a public commitment makes people hesitant to back down. Smart persuaders know this. Salespeople ask questions that prompt us to make statements for, rather than against, what they are marketing. Environmentalists ask people to commit themselves to recycling, energy conservation, or bus riding—and find that behavior changes more than when environmental appeals are heard without inviting a commitment (Katzev & Wang, 1994). Religious evangelists invite people "to get up out of your seat," knowing that people are more likely to hold to their new faith if they make a public commitment to it.

Public commitment may reduce conformity not only because people are more accepting after making a commitment but also because they hate to appear indecisive. Compared to people whose attitudes are stable, those whose attitudes change seem less reliable (Allgeier and others, 1979). People who "wander, waver, waffle, and wiggle," as President Ford said contemptuously of candidate Jimmy Carter in 1976, lose respect.

"Those who never retract their opinions love themselves more than they love truth."
Joubert, *Pensées*

Drawing by Mankoff; © 1980 The New Yorker Magazine, Inc.

"All right! Have it your own way. It was a ball."

Prior commitment: Once they commit themselves to a position, people seldom yield to social pressure. Real umpires and referees rarely reverse their initial judgments.

SUMMING UP

Using conformity testing procedures, experimenters have explored the circumstances that produce conformity. Certain situations appear to be especially powerful. For example, conformity is affected by the characteristics of the group: People conform most when faced with the unanimous reports of three or more attractive, high-status people. People also conform most when their responses are public (in the presence of the group) and made without prior commitment.

■ WHY CONFORM?

Do you see yonder cloud that's almost in the shape of a camel?" asks Shakespeare's Hamlet of Polonius. *"Tis like a camel indeed,"* replies Polonius. *"Methinks it is a weasel,"* says Hamlet a moment later. *"It is backed like a weasel,"* acknowledges Polonius. *"Or like a whale?"* wonders Hamlet. *"Very like a whale,"* agrees Polonius. Question: Why does Polonius so readily agree with the Prince of Denmark?

Here I was, an American attending my first lecture during an extended visit at a German university. As the lecturer finished, I lifted my hands to join in the clapping. But rather than clap, the other people began rapping the tables with their knuckles. What did this mean? Did they disapprove of the speech? Surely, not everyone would be so openly rude to a visiting dignitary. Nor did their faces express displeasure. No, I decided, this must be a German ovation. Whereupon, I added my knuckles to the chorus.

What prompted this conformity? Why had I not clapped even while the others rapped? There are two possibilities: A person may bow to the group to be accepted and avoid rejection or to obtain important information. Morton Deutsch and Harold Gerard (1955) named these two possibilities **normative influence** and **informational influence**.

Normative conformity is "going along with the crowd" to avoid rejection, to stay in people's good graces, or to gain their approval. Perhaps Polonius sought Hamlet's favor. In the laboratory and in everyday life, groups often reject those who consistently deviate (Miller & Anderson, 1979; Schachter, 1951). Can you recall such an experience? As most of us know, social rejection is painful; when we deviate from group norms, we often pay an emotional price.

Sometimes the high price of deviation compels people to support what they do not believe in. Fearing they would be court-martialed for disobedience, some of the soldiers at My Lai participated in the massacre. Normative influence commonly leads to compliance. This is especially true for people seeking to climb a group's status ladder (Hollander, 1958). As John F. Kennedy (1956) recalled, "'The way to get along,' I was told when I entered Congress, 'is to go along'"(p. 4).

Informational influence, on the other hand, leads people to acceptance. When reality is ambiguous, as it was for subjects in the autokinetic situation, other people can be a valuable source of information. The subject may reason, "I can't tell how far the light is moving. But this guy seems to know." Others' responses may also affect how we interpret ambiguous stimuli. Viewing a changing, am-

Normative influence: Conformity based on a person's desire to fulfill others' expectations, often to gain acceptance.

Informational influence: Conformity that results from accepting evidence about reality provided by other people.

"Do as most do and men will speak well of thee."
Thomas Fuller, *Gnomologia*

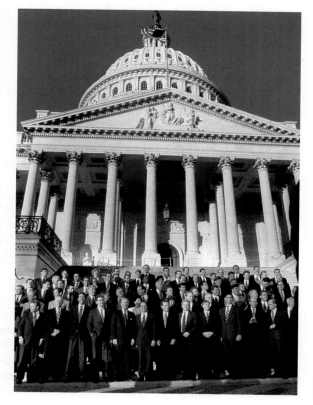

Normative influence: Newly elected politicians often dream of changing the system. Then, seeking to climb within the system, normative influences compel them to comply with its social rules.

biguous cloud, Polonius may actually see what Hamlet helps him see. People who witness others agreeing that "free speech should be limited" may infer a different meaning in the statement than those who witness others disagreeing (Allen & Wilder, 1980). *After* concurring with a group, people are especially likely to construe a meaning that justifies their decision (Buehler & Griffin, 1994).

So, concern for social image produces normative influence. The desire to be correct produces informational influence. In day-to-day life, normative and informational influence often occur together. I was not about to be the only person in the room clapping (normative influence), yet the others' behavior also showed me how to express my appreciation (informational influence).

Some of the experiments on "when people conform" have isolated either normative or informational influence. Conformity is greater when people respond before a group; this surely reflects normative influence (because subjects receive the same information whether they respond publicly or privately). What is more, the larger the group, the greater the difference between public and private responding (Insko & others, 1985). On the other hand, conformity is greater when participants feel incompetent, when the task is difficult, or when the subjects care about being right. Why do we conform? For two main reasons: Because we want to be liked and approved or because we want to be right.

SUMMING UP

Experiments reveal two reasons people conform. *Normative influence* results from a person's desire for acceptance. *Informational influence* results from others' providing evidence about reality. The tendency to conform more when responding publicly reflects normative influence, and the tendency to conform more on difficult decision-making tasks reflects informational influence.

■ WHO CONFORMS?

Conformity varies not only with situations but also with persons. How much so? And in what social contexts do personality traits best shine through?

Are some people generally more susceptible (or, should I say, more *open*) to social influence? Among your friends, can you identify some who are "conformists" and others who are "independent"? I suspect that most of us can. Researchers are exploring several areas in their search for the conformer. Let us look briefly at three: gender, personality, and culture.

GENDER

Among Americans tested in group-pressure situations during the last 30 years, there has been a slight tendency for women to conform more than men. Alice Eagly and Linda Carli (1981; also Becker, 1986) discerned this by statistically combining results from the dozens of available studies. However, newer conformity experiments and those conducted by women seldom find females more conforming. Most other gender differences in social behavior also appear uninfluenced by the sex of the investigator, reports Eagly (1987).

BEHIND THE SCENES

I began my work on gender and social influence in the early 1970s. Like many feminist activists of the day, I initially assumed that, despite negative cultural stereotypes about women, the behavior of women and men is substantially equivalent. Over the years, my views have evolved considerably. I have found that women and men do behave somewhat differently, especially in relatively unstructured situations in which gender roles become important. Although most of these differences are gender-stereotypic, feminists should not assume that these differences necessarily reflect unfavorably on women. Women's tendencies to be more attuned to other people's concerns and to treat others more democratically are assets in many situations. In fact, my recent research (Eagly & others, 1991) on gender stereotypes shows that, if we take both negative and positive qualities into account, the stereotype of women is currently more favorable than the stereotype of men.

ALICE EAGLY, *Northwestern University*

Is labeling this small gender effect a "conformity difference" a negative judgment on the women "conformers"? Remember, our label for the phenomenon is something we choose. Perhaps we should instead call the difference a greater "people orientation." (Recall from Chapter 6 that women are somewhat more empathic and socially sensitive.) Perhaps we should say that women are slightly more flexible, more open and responsive to their social environment, more concerned with interpersonal relations. Such language carries quite different connotations from saying that women are more conforming.

To say that women are slightly more influenceable because they are more concerned with interpersonal relations attributes the difference to personality. Eagly and Wendy Wood (1985) believe that gender differences in conformity may instead be a product of men's and women's typical social roles. Male-female differences are not just a gender difference but also (or instead) status differences. In everyday life, men tend to occupy positions of greater status and power, so we often see men exerting and women accepting influence. This explains why people *perceive* a much greater gender difference in everyday conformity than has been found in experiments that assign men and women identical roles.

Although Milgram's 1000 subjects (1974) were nearly all males, 40 female subjects did experience the "heart-disturbance" obedience procedure. Milgram assumed that women were generally more compliant yet also more empathic and less aggressive. What he found was no difference: 65 percent were fully compliant.

PERSONALITY

The history of social-psychological thinking about the relationship between personality traits and social behavior parallels the history of thinking about attitudes and behavior. During the 1950s and early 1960s psychologists studied how inner motives and dispositions influenced people's actions. For example, those who described themselves as needing social approval were more conforming (Snyder & Ickes, 1985). During the late 1960s and 1970s, efforts to link personal characteristics with social behaviors, such as conformity, found only weak connections (Mischel, 1968). In contrast to the demonstrable power of situational factors, personality scores were poor predictors of individuals' behavior. If you wanted to know how conforming or aggressive or helpful someone was going to be, it seemed you were better off knowing the details of the situation than the person's scores on a battery of psychological tests. As Milgram (1974) concluded: "I am certain that there is a complex personality basis to obedience and disobedience. But I know we have not found it"(p. 205).

Reflecting on his prison simulation and other experiments, Philip Zimbardo argued that the ultimate message

> is to say what it is we have to do to break through your egocentricism, to say you're not different, anything any human being has ever done cannot be alien to you, you can't divorce it! We must break through this "we-they" idea that our dispositional orientation promotes and understand that the situational forces operating on a person at any given moment could be so powerful as to override everything prior—values, history, biology, family, church. (Bruck, 1976)

During the 1980s, the idea that personal dispositions make little difference prompted personality researchers to pinpoint the circumstances under which traits *do* predict behavior. Their research affirms a principle that we met in Chapter 4: While internal factors (attitudes, traits) seldom precisely predict a specific action, they better predict a person's average behavior across many situations (Epstein, 1980; Rushton & others, 1983). An analogy may help: Just as your response to a single test item is hard to predict, so is your behavior in a single situation. And just as your total score across the many items of a test is more predictable, so is your total conformity (or outgoingness or aggressiveness) across many situations.

Personality also predicts behavior better when the trait is specific to a situation (such as "speech anxiety" rather than anxiety in general) and when social influences are weak. Like many other laboratory studies, Milgram's obe-

"Wait! Wait! Listen to me! . . . We don't HAVE to be just sheep!"

A group's unanimity versus nonunanimity affects conformity more than does individual personality.

Personality effects loom larger when we note people's differing reactions to the same situation, as when one person reacts with terror and another with delight to a roller coaster ride.

dience experiments created "strong" situations; their clear-cut demands made it difficult for personality differences to operate. Still, Milgram's subjects differed widely in how obedient they were, and there is good reason to suspect that sometimes his subjects' hostility, respect for authority, and concern for meeting expectations affected their obedience (Blass, 1990, 1991). In the Nazi extermination camps, too, some guards displayed kindness, while others used live infants as shooting targets or hurled them into the fire. Personality matters.

In "weaker" situations—as when two strangers sit in a waiting room with no cues to guide their behavior—individual personalities are even freer to shine (Ickes & others, 1982; Monson & others, 1982). If we compare two similar personalities in very different situations, the situational effect will overwhelm the personality difference. If we compare a group of Saddam Hussein types with a group of Mother Teresa types in a smattering of everyday situations, the personality effect will look much stronger.

Behavioral styles persist across situations. David Funder and Randall Colvin (1991) of the University of California, Riverside, videotaped pairs of students while they got acquainted in casual conversation, then videotaped them again a few weeks later while casually chatting with a new acquaintance and while participating in a debate. Those who spoke loudly or were energetic, outgoing, or relaxed in one situation usually behaved much the same way in the other situations.

It is interesting to note how the pendulum of professional opinion swings. Without discounting the undeniable power of social forces, the pendulum is now swinging back toward an appreciation of individual personality. Like the attitude researchers we considered earlier, personality researchers are clarifying and reaffirming the connection between who we are and what we do. Thanks to their efforts, virtually every social psychologist today would agree with theorist Kurt Lewin's (1936) dictum: "Every psychological event depends upon the state of the person and at the same time on the environment, although their relative importance is different in different cases" (p. 12).

CULTURE

Does cultural background help predict how conforming people will be? Indeed it does. James Whittaker and Robert Meade (1967) repeated Asch's conformity experiment in several countries and found similar conformity rates in most— 31 percent in Lebanon, 32 percent in Hong Kong, 34 percent in Brazil—but 51 percent among the Bantu of Zimbabwe, a tribe with strong sanctions for nonconformity. When Milgram (1961) used a different conformity procedure to compare Norwegian and French students, he consistently found the Norwegian students to be the more conforming. However, cultures may change. Replications of Asch's experiment with university students in Britain, Canada, and the United States sometimes trigger less conformity than Asch observed two or three decades earlier (Lalancette & Standing, 1990; Larsen, 1974, 1990; Nicholson & others, 1985; Perrin & Spencer, 1981).

When researchers in Germany, Italy, South Africa, Australia, Austria, Spain, and Jordan repeated the obedience experiments, how do you think the results compared to those with American subjects? The obedience rates were similar, or even higher—85 percent in Munich (Mantell, 1971; Meeus & Raaijmakers, 1986; Milgram, 1974).

In a study of "administrative obedience" in the Netherlands, Wim Meeus and Quinten Raaijmakers (1986) ordered Dutch adults who had volunteered for an experiment to disrupt a job applicant who was taking an employment test, causing the applicant to fail the test and supposedly remain unemployed. In the guise of an experiment on the effects of stress, the subjects had to trigger 15 derogatory computer messages that caused the applicant to become progressively more upset. As the applicant's tension turned to irritation and finally to despair, the subjects found the procedure unfair and their task disagreeable. Yet by shifting responsibility to the experimenter, 90 percent fully complied.

So, conformity and obedience are universal phenomena, yet they vary by culture (Bond, 1988; Triandis & others, 1988). Euro-American cultures teach individualism: You are responsible for yourself. Follow your own conscience. Be true to yourself. Define your unique gifts. Meet your own needs. Respect one another's privacy. Asian and nonwestern cultures are more likely to teach collectivism: Your family or clan is responsible for its individual members, whose actions therefore reflect shame or honor upon it. So bring honor to your group. Be true to your traditions. Show respect for elders and superiors. Cultivate harmony, and do not criticize another publicly. Be loyal to family, company, nation. Live communally, without assuming that you have a private self separate from your social context. An analysis by Rod Bond and Peter Smith (in press) of 133 studies in 17 countries confirms that these cultural values have an impact on conformity. Compared to people in individualistic countries, those in collectivist countries are more responsive to others' influence.

"I don't want to get adjusted to this world."
Woody Guthrie

S U M M I N G   U P

The question "Who conforms?" has produced fewer definitive answers. In experiments, females have, on the average, been slightly more conforming than males. (If this sounds negative it's because labels such as "conformity" evaluate as well as describe behavior. Call the trait "openness" or "communal sensitivity," and it takes on a more positive connotation.) Global personality scores are poor predictors of specific acts of conformity but better predict average tendencies to conformity (and other social behaviors). Trait effects are strongest in "weak" situations where social forces do not overwhelm individual differences. Although conformity and obedience are universal, culture socializes people to be more or less socially responsive.

■ RESISTING SOCIAL PRESSURE

*W*ill people ever actively resist social pressure? When compelled to do A will they instead do Z? What would motivate such anticonformity?

This chapter, like Chapter 6, emphasizes the power of social forces. It is therefore fitting that we conclude by again reminding ourselves of the power of the person. We are not just billiard balls; we act in response to the forces that push upon us. Knowing that someone is trying to coerce us may even prompt us to react in the *opposite* direction.

"To do just the opposite is also a form of imitation."
Lichtenberg, *Aphorismen,* 1764–1799

REACTANCE

Individuals value their sense of freedom and self-efficacy (Baer & others, 1980). So when social pressure becomes so blatant that it threatens their sense of freedom, they often rebel. Think of Romeo and Juliet, whose love was intensified by their families' opposition. Or think of children asserting their freedom and independence by doing the opposite of what their parents ask. Savvy parents therefore offer their children choices instead of commands: "It's time to clean up: Do you want a bath or a shower?"

The theory of psychological **reactance**—that people do indeed act to protect their sense of freedom—is supported by experiments showing that attempts to restrict a person's freedom often produce a "boomerang effect" (Brehm & Brehm, 1981; Nail & Van Leeuwen, 1993). Suppose someone stops you on the street and asks you to sign a petition that advocates something you mildly support. While considering the petition, you are told that someone else believes "people absolutely should not be allowed to distribute or sign such petitions." Reactance theory predicts that such blatant attempts to limit freedom will ac-

Reactance:
A motive to protect or restore one's sense of freedom. Reactance arises when someone threatens our freedom of action.

Reactance at work? Underage students have been found to be less often abstinent and more often drinking to excess than students over the legal drinking age.

tually increase the likelihood of your signing. When Madeline Heilman (1976) staged this experiment on the streets of New York City, that is precisely what she found. Clinical psychologists sometimes use the reactance principle by ordering resistant clients to enact the to-be-eliminated behavior (Brehm & Smith, 1986; Seltzer, 1983). By resisting the therapist, the clients get better.

Reactance may also contribute to underage drinking. In the United States, where alcohol sales are illegal to persons under age 21, a survey of 3375 students on a cross section of 56 campuses revealed a 25 percent rate of abstinence among students of legal drinking age but only a 19 percent abstinence rate among students under 21. The researchers, Ruth Engs and David Hanson (1989), also found that 15 percent of the legal-age students and 24 percent of the underage students were heavy drinkers. They suspect this reflects a reactance against the restriction. It probably also reflects peer influence. With alcohol use, as with drugs, peers influence attitudes, provide the substance, and offer a context for its use. This helps explain why college students, living in a peer culture that often supports alcohol use, drink more alcohol than their non-college peers (Atwell, 1986).

Reactance can escalate into social rebellion. Like obedience, rebellion can be produced and observed in experiments. That's what William Gamson, Bruce Fireman, and Steven Rytina (1982) learned when they posed as members of a commercial research firm. They recruited people from towns near the University of Michigan to come to a hotel conference room for "a group discussion of community standards." Once there, the people learned that the discussions were to be videotaped on behalf of a large oil company seeking to win a legal case against a local station manager who had spoken out against high gas prices.

In the first discussion, virtually everyone sided with the station manager. Hoping to convince the court that people in the local community were on its side, the "company representative" then began to tell more and more group members to defend the company. In the end, he told everyone to attack the station manager and asked them to sign an affidavit giving the company permission to edit the tapes and use them in court. By leaving the room from time to time, the experimenter gave the group members repeated opportunities to interpret and react to the injustice.

Most rebelled, objecting to and resisting the demand that they misrepresent their opinions to help the oil company. Some groups even mobilized themselves to stop the whole effort. They made plans to go to a newspaper, the Better Business Bureau, a lawyer, or the court.

By brewing small social rebellions, the researchers saw how a revolt is born. They found that successful resistance often begins very quickly. The more a group complies with unjust demands, the harder it later is to break free. And someone must be willing to seed the process by expressing the reservations the others are feeling.

These demonstrations of reactance reassure us that people are not puppets. Sociologist Peter Berger (1963) expressed the point vividly:

> We see the puppets dancing in their miniature stage, moving up and down as the strings pull them around, following the prescribed course of their various little parts. We learn to understand the logic of this theater and we find ourselves in its motions. We locate ourselves in society and thus recognize our own position as we hang from its subtle strings. For a moment we see ourselves as puppets indeed. But then we grasp a decisive difference between the puppet theater and our own drama. Unlike the puppets, we have the possibility of stopping in our movements, looking up and perceiving the machinery by which we have been moved. In this act lies the first step towards freedom. (p. 176)

ASSERTING UNIQUENESS

Imagine a world of complete conformity where there were no differences among people. Would such a world be a happy place? If nonconformity can create discomfort, can sameness create comfort?

People feel uncomfortable when they appear too different from others. But, at least in western cultures, they also feel uncomfortable when they appear exactly like everyone else. As experiments by C. R. Snyder and Howard Fromkin (1980) have shown, people feel better when they see themselves as unique. Moreover, they act in ways that will assert their individuality. In one experiment, Snyder (1980) led Purdue University students to believe that their "10 most important attitudes" were either distinct from or nearly identical to the attitudes of 10,000 other students. When they then participated in a conformity experiment, those deprived of their feeling of uniqueness were most likely to assert their individuality by nonconformity. In another experiment, people who heard others express attitudes identical to their own altered their positions to maintain their sense of uniqueness.

Seeing oneself as unique also appears in people's "spontaneous self-concepts" William McGuire and his Yale University colleagues (McGuire & Padawer-Singer, 1978; McGuire & others, 1979) report that when children are invited to "tell us about yourself," they are most likely to mention their distinctive attributes. Foreign-born children are more likely than others to mention their birthplace. Redheads are more likely than black- and brown-haired children to volunteer their hair color. Light and heavy children are the most likely to refer to their body weight. Minority children are the most likely to mention their race. Likewise we become more keenly aware of our gender when we are with people of the other sex (Cota & Dion, 1986).

"When I'm in America, I have no doubt I'm a Jew, but I have strong doubts about whether I'm really an American. And when I get to Israel, I know I'm an American, but I have strong doubts about whether I'm a Jew."
Leslie Fiedler,
Fiedler on the Roof, 1991

Asserting our uniqueness. While not wishing to be greatly deviant, most of us express our distinctiveness through our personal styles and dress.

"*Self-consciousness, the recognition of a creature by itself as a 'self,' [cannot] exist except in contrast with an 'other,' a something which is not the self.*"
C. S. Lewis,
The Problem of Pain, 1940

The principle, says McGuire, is that "one is conscious of oneself insofar as, and in the ways that, one is different." Thus, "If I am a Black woman in a group of White women, I tend to think of myself as a Black; if I move to a group of Black men, my blackness loses salience and I become more conscious of being a woman" (McGuire & others, 1978). This insight helps us understand why any minority group tends to be conscious of its distinctiveness and how the surrounding culture relates to it. The majority group, being less conscious of race, may see the minority group as "hypersensitive." Living for a year in Scotland, where my American accent marks me as a foreigner, I am conscious of my national identity and sensitive to how others react to it.

When the people of two cultures are nearly identical, they still will notice their differences, however small. Even trivial distinctions may provoke scorn and conflict. Jonathan Swift satirized the phenomenon in *Gulliver's Travels*— the Little-Endians war against the Big-Endians. Their difference: The Little-Endians preferred to break their eggs on the small end, the Big-Endians on the large end. On a world scale, the differences may not seem great between Scots and English, Hutus and Tutus, Serbs and Croatians, or Catholic and Protestant Northern Irelanders. But small differences can mean big conflict (Rothbart & Taylor, 1992). Rivalry is often most intense when the other group most closely resembles you.

So it seems that while we do not like being greatly deviant, we are, ironically, all alike in wanting to feel distinctive and noticing how we are distinctive. But as research on self-serving bias (Chapter 3) makes clear, it is not just any kind of distinctiveness we seek but distinctiveness in the right direction. Our quest is not merely to be different from the average, but *better* than average.

Finally, a comment on the experimental method used in conformity research: Conformity situations in the laboratory differ from those in everyday life. How

"*There are no exceptions to the rule that everybody likes to be an exception to the rule.*"
Malcolm Forbes,
Forbes Magazine

often are we asked to judge line lengths or administer shock? As combustion is similar for a burning match and a forest fire, so we assume that psychological processes in the laboratory and in everyday life are similar (Milgram, 1974). We must be careful in generalizing from the simplicity of a burning match to the complexity of a forest fire. Yet, controlled experiments on burning matches can give us insights into combustion that we cannot gain by observing forest fires. So, too, the social-psychological experiment offers insights into behavior not readily revealed in everyday life. The experimental situation is unique, but so is every social situation. By testing with a variety of unique tasks, and by repeating experiments in different times and places, researchers probe for the common principles that lie beneath the surface diversity.

S ocial psychology's emphasis on the power of social pressure must be joined by a complementary emphasis on the power of the person. We are not puppets. When social coercion becomes blatant, people often experience *reactance*—a motivation to defy the coercion in order to maintain their sense of freedom. When group members experience reactance simultaneously, the result may be rebellion.

SUMMING UP

We are not comfortable being too different from a group, but neither do we want to appear the same as everyone else. Thus, we act in ways that preserve our sense of uniqueness and individuality. In a group, we are most conscious of how we differ from the others.

■ FOR FURTHER READING

Kelman, H. C., & Hamilton, V. L. (1989). *Crimes of obedience: Toward a social psychology of authority and responsibility*. New Haven, CT: Yale University Press. Social psychologist Kelman and sociologist Hamilton analyze crimes ordered by authority (Nazi war crimes, the My Lai massacre, Watergate, the Iran-Contra affair). They show "how responsibility may be 'lost' where it is most essential to retain it: in the military and bureaucratic hierarchies of the modern world."

Milgram, S. (1974). *Obedience to authority*. New York: Harper & Row. The complete but simply written account of the experiments that, in the words of Milgram's biographer, now belong "to the self-understanding of literate people in our age."

Miller, A. G. (1986). *The obedience experiments: A case study of controversy in social science*. New York: Praeger. A skillful review of the nearly two dozen obedience experiments conducted by Stanley Milgram and of the ensuing replications, critiques, and controversies. As one reviewer notes, this is a book that "any serious student of social psychology would profit from reading."

Staub, E. (1989). *The roots of evil: The origins of genocide and other group violence*. New York: Cambridge University Press. Why do human beings kill and brutalize other human beings? This book powerfully analyzes the social psychological roots of human torture and slaughter as practiced in Turkey, Nazi Germany, Argentina, Cambodia, Russia, and Greece.

PERSUASION

SEX CAN BE A REAL SCREAM.

Teenagers who go all the way don't often go very far.
THE CHILDREN'S DEFENSE FUND.

Teenage pregnancy has social consequences for both parent and child. How persuasive is this message in addressing the problem?

"Remember that to change thy mind and to follow him that sets thee right, is to be none the less a free agent."
Marcus Aurelius Antoninus,
Meditations

"A fanatic is one who can't change his mind and won't change the subject."
Winston Churchill, 1954

Our social behavior is influenced not only by our cultural experience and our current situation but also by our attitudes. Those who wish to influence behavior therefore seek to change attitudes.

Consider Joseph Goebbels, Nazi Germany's minister of "popular enlightenment" and propaganda from 1933 to 1945. Given control of publications, radio programs, motion pictures, and the arts, he undertook to persuade Germans to accept Nazi ideology. Julius Streicher, another member of the Nazi group, published *Der Stürmer*, a weekly anti-Semitic (anti-Jewish) newspaper with a circulation of 500,000 and the only paper read cover to cover by his intimate friend, Adolf Hitler. Streicher also published anti-Semitic children's books and spoke with Goebbels at the mass rallies that became a part of the Nazi propaganda machine.

How effective were Goebbels, Streicher, and other Nazi propagandists? Did they, as the Allies alleged at Streicher's Nuremberg trial, "inject poison into the minds of millions and millions" (Bytwerk, 1976)? Most Germans were not persuaded to feel raging hatred for the Jews. But some were. Others became sympathetic to anti-Semitic measures. And most of the rest became either sufficiently uncertain or sufficiently intimidated to allow the Holocaust to happen.

Powerful persuasive forces are also at work in today's world. In the wake of publicized research on the physical and social consequences of marijuana use, adolescent attitudes have changed rapidly. Among the 16,000 U.S. high school seniors surveyed annually by the University of Michigan, the proportion who believe there is "great risk" to regular marijuana use has doubled—from 35 percent in 1978 to 73 percent in 1993 (Johnston & others, 1994). Simultaneously, support for the legalization of marijuana dropped among the quarter of a million new college students surveyed annually by the American Council on Education—from 50 percent to 32 percent (Astin & others, 1987, 1994). Behavior changed too. Marijuana use within the month preceding the survey dropped from 37 percent of high school seniors to 16 percent. Canadian teens underwent similar attitude and marijuana-use changes (Smart & others, 1991). Thanks to health promotion campaigns, the Center for Disease Control and Prevention reports that the American cigarette smoking rate has plunged to 26 percent, barely more than half the rate of 30 years ago.

But some persuasive efforts flop. One massive governmental experiment to persuade people to use seat belts had no discernible effect (seven carefully designed cable TV messages were broadcast 943 times during prime time to 6400 households). Psychologist Paul Slovic (1985) thought he and his colleagues might do better. Their hunch was that only 10 percent of people use seat belts because most people perceive themselves to be invulnerable. Although it's true that only 1 trip in 100,000 produces an injury, 50,000 trips taken in an average lifetime mean that for many people the feeling of safety eventually turns out to be an "illusion of invulnerability."

With the support of the National Traffic Safety Administration, Slovic and his colleagues produced 12 TV messages designed to persuade people of the risks of driving without seat belts. After pretesting with hundreds of people, several thousand people at a "screening house" evaluated six messages. The three best messages were repeatedly presented to yet another group of people. Alas, the messages had no effect on their seat-belt use. Because each safe trip reinforces nonuse of seat belts, concluded Slovic, "There seems to be no form

Persuasion is everywhere. When we approve it, we may call it "education."

of educational campaign or message that will persuade more than a small percentage of American motorists to voluntarily wear seat belts."

As these examples show, efforts to persuade are sometimes diabolical, sometimes salutary; sometimes effective, sometimes futile. Persuasion is neither inherently good nor bad. It is usually the content of the message that elicits judgments of good or bad. The bad we call "propaganda." The good we call "education." True, education is more factually based and less coercive than mere propaganda. Yet generally we call it "education" when we believe it, "propaganda" when we don't (Lumsden & others, 1980).

Our opinions have to come from somewhere. Persuasion—whether it be education or propaganda—is therefore inevitable. Indeed, persuasion is everywhere—at the heart of politics, marketing, courtship, parenting, negotiation, evangelism, and courtroom decision making. Social psychologists therefore seek to understand what makes a message effective: What factors influence us to change? And how, as persuaders, can we most effectively "educate" others?

Imagine that you are a marketing or advertising executive, one of those responsible for the nearly $300 billion spent annually worldwide on advertising (Brown & others, 1993). Or imagine that you are a preacher, trying to increase love and charity among your parishioners. Or imagine that you want to promote energy conservation, to encourage breast feeding, or to campaign for a political candidate. What could you do to make yourself, and your message, persuasive? Or, if you are wary of being manipulated by such appeals, what tactics should you be alert to?

To answer such questions, social psychologists usually study persuasion the way some geologists study erosion—by observing the effects of various factors

"To swallow and follow, whether old doctrine or new propaganda, is a weakness still dominating the human mind." Charlotte Perkins Gilman, *Human Work*, 1904

If you live in North America, advertisers spend about $500 annually trying to influence you (Brown & others, 1993).

in brief controlled experiments. The effects are small and are most potent on weak attitudes that don't touch our values (Johnson & Eagly, 1989; Petty & Krosnick, 1995). Yet they enable us to better understand how, given enough time, such factors could produce big effects.

■ TWO ROUTES TO PERSUASION

What two paths lead to influence? What type of cognitive processing does each involve—and with what effects?

In choosing tactics, you must first decide: Should you focus mostly on building strong *central arguments*? Or should you make your message appealing by associating it with favorable *peripheral cues*? Persuasion researchers Richard Petty and John Cacioppo (1986; Petty, 1994) and Alice Eagly and Shelly Chaiken (1992) report that people who are able and motivated to think through an issue are best persuaded through a **central route** to persuasion—one that marshals systematic arguments to stimulate favorable thinking. Computer ads, for

Central route persuasion: Persuasion that occurs when interested people focus on the arguments and respond with favorable thoughts.

Computer ads take the central route to persuasion, by offering cogent information that aims to stimulate favorable cognitive responses.

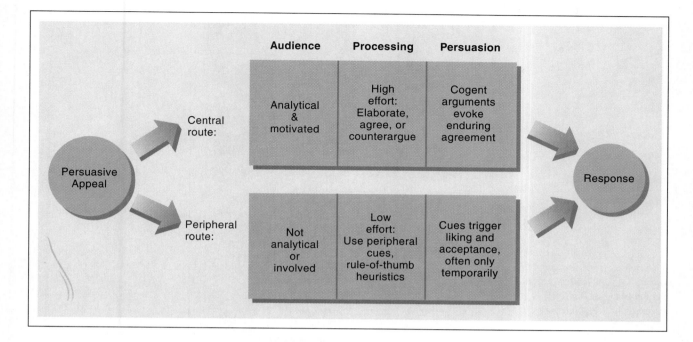

Audience	Processing	Persuasion
Central route: Analytical & motivated	High effort: Elaborate, agree, or counterargue	Cogent arguments evoke enduring agreement
Peripheral route: Not analytical or involved	Low effort: Use peripheral cues, rule-of-thumb heuristics	Cues trigger liking and acceptance, often only temporarily

Persuasive Appeal → Response

example, seldom feature Hollywood stars or great athletes; instead they offer their analytical customers competitive features and prices.

Some people are analytical, note Petty and Cacioppo. They like to think about issues and mentally elaborate them. Such people rely not just on the cogency of persuasive appeals but on their own cognitive responses to them as well. It's not so much the arguments that are persuasive as what they get people thinking. And when people think deeply rather than superficially, any changed attitude will more likely persist, resist attack and influence behavior (Petty & others, 1995; Verplanken, 1991).

On issues that don't and won't engage people's thinking, a **peripheral route**—one that provides cues that trigger acceptance without much thinking—works better. Instead of providing product information, cigarette ads merely associate the product with images of beauty and pleasure. So do soft drink ads that promote "the real thing" or "the Pepsi generation" with images of youth, vitality, and joy.

Even analytical people sometimes form tentative opinions using peripheral heuristics, such as "trust experts" or "long messages are credible" (Chaiken & Maheswaran, 1994). Residents of my community recently voted on a complicated issue involving the legal ownership of our local hospital. I didn't have the time or interest to study this question myself (I had this book to write). But I noted that referendum supporters were all people I either liked or regarded as experts. So I used a simple heuristic—friends and experts can be trusted—and voted accordingly. We all make snap judgments using other rule-of-thumb heuristics: If a speaker is articulate and appealing, has apparently good motives, and has several arguments (or better, if the different arguments come from different sources), we take the easy peripheral route and accept the message without much thought (Figure 8–1).

■ **FIGURE 8–1**
The central and peripheral routes to persuasion. Computer ads typically take the central route, by assuming their audience wants to systematically compare features and prices. Soft-drink ads usually take the peripheral route, by merely associating their product with glamour, pleasure, and good moods.

Peripheral route persuasion: Persuasion that occurs when people are influenced by incidental cues, such as a speaker's attractiveness.

Through its written arguments, this ad uses the central route to persuasion. But it also takes a peripheral route. Note how it suggests that mother and infant can derive happiness from simulating the natural mother-infant relationship.

SUMMING UP

Sometimes persuasion occurs as people focus on arguments and respond with favorable thoughts. Such systematic, or "central route," persuasion occurs when people are naturally analytical or involved in the issue. When issues don't engage people's systematic thinking, persuasion may occur through a faster "peripheral route" as people use heuristics or incidental cues to make snap judgments. Central route persuasion, being more thoughtful and less superficial, is more durable and more likely to influence behavior.

■ THE ELEMENTS OF PERSUASION

Among the central and peripheral ingredients of persuasion explored by social psychologists are these four: (1) the communicator, (2) the message, (3) how the message is communicated, and (4) the audience. In other words, who says what by what means to whom?

WHO SAYS? THE EFFECT OF THE COMMUNICATOR

Imagine the following scene: I. M. Wright, a middle-aged American, is watching the evening news. In the first segment, a small group of radicals is shown burning an American flag. As they do, one shouts through a bullhorn that whenever any government becomes oppressive, "it is the Right of the People to alter or to abolish it. . . . It is their right, it is their duty, to throw off such government!" Angered, Mr. Wright mutters to his wife, "It's sickening to hear them spouting that Communist line." In the next segment, a presidential candidate speaking before an antitax rally declares, "Thrift should be the guiding principle in our government expenditure. It should be made clear to all government workers that corruption and waste are very great crimes." An obviously pleased Mr. Wright relaxes and smiles: "Now that's the kind of good sense we need. That's my kinda guy."

Now switch the scene. Imagine Mr. Wright hearing the same revolutionary line at a July 4 oration of the Declaration of Independence (from which the line comes) and hearing a Communist speaker read the thrift quote from *Quotations from Chairman Mao Zedong* (from which they come). Would he now react differently?

Social psychologists have found that who is saying something makes a big difference. In one experiment, when the Socialist and Liberal leaders in the Dutch parliament argued identical positions using the same words, each was most effective with members of his own party (Wiegman, 1985). Obviously, it's not just the central message that matters, but a peripheral *cue*—who says it. But what makes one communicator more persuasive than another?

Credibility

Any of us would find a statement about the benefits of exercise more believable if it came from the National Academy of Sciences rather than a tabloid newspaper. But the effects of source **credibility** (perceived expertise and trustworthiness) diminish after a month or so. If a credible person's message is persuasive its impact may fade as its source is forgotten or dissociated from the message. The impact of a noncredible person may correspondingly *increase* over time (if people remember the message better than the reason for discounting it) (Cook & Flay, 1978; Gruder & others, 1978; Pratkanis & others, 1988). This delayed persuasion, after people forget the source or its connection with the message, is called the **sleeper effect**.

Credibility:
Believability. A credible communicator is perceived as both expert and trustworthy.

Sleeper effect:
A delayed impact of a message; occurs when we remember the message but forget a reason for discounting it.

"If I seem excited, Mr. Bolling, it's only because I know that I can make you a very rich man."

Effective persuaders know how to convey a message effectively.

"Believe an expert."
Virgil, *Aeneid*

Perceived Expertise

How does one become "expert"? One way is to begin by saying things the audience agrees with, which makes you seem smart. Another is to be introduced as someone who is *knowledgeable* on the topic. A message about toothbrushing from "Dr. James Rundle of the Canadian Dental Association" is much more convincing than the same message from "Jim Rundle, a local high school student who did a project with some of his classmates on dental hygiene" (Olson & Cal, 1984). After more than a decade studying high school marijuana use, the University of Michigan researchers (Bachman & others, 1988) concluded that scare messages from unreliable sources did not affect marijuana use during the 1960s and 1970s. But from a credible source, scientific reports of the biological and psychological results of long-term marijuana use "can play an important role in reducing . . . drug use."

Another way to appear credible is to *speak confidently*. Bonnie Erickson and her collaborators (1978) had University of North Carolina students evaluate courtroom testimony given in the straightforward manner said to be characteristic of "men's speech" or in the more hesitant manner of "women's speech." For example:

> **QUESTION:** Approximately how long did you stay there before the ambulance arrived?
>
> **ANSWER:** [*Straightforward*] Twenty minutes. Long enough to help get Mrs. David straightened out.
>
> [*Hesitating*] Oh, it seems like it was about uh, twenty minutes. Just long enough to help my friend Mrs. David, you know, get straightened out.

The students found the straightforward witnesses much more competent and credible.

Perceived Trustworthiness

Speech style also affects a speaker's apparent trustworthiness. Gordon Hemsley and Anthony Doob (1978) found that if, while testifying, videotaped witnesses looked their questioner straight in the eye instead of gazing downward, they impressed people as more believable.

Trustworthiness is also higher if the audience believes the communicator is not trying to persuade them. In an experimental version of what later became the "hidden-camera" method of television advertising, Elaine Hatfield and Leon Festinger (Walster & Festinger, 1962) had some Stanford University undergraduates eavesdrop on graduate students' conversations. (What they actually heard was a tape recording.) When the conversational topic was relevant to the eavesdroppers (having to do with campus regulations), supposedly unsuspecting speakers were more influential than speakers said to be aware that someone was listening. After all, if people don't know someone's listening, why would they be less than fully honest?

People also perceive as sincere those who argue against their own self-interest. Alice Eagly, Wendy Wood, and Shelly Chaiken (1978) presented University of Massachusetts students with a speech attacking a company's pollution of a river. When they said the speech was given by a political candidate with a business background or to an audience of company supporters, it seemed unbiased and was persuasive. When the same antibusiness speech was supposedly given to environmentalists by a pro-environment politician, listeners could attribute the politician's arguments to personal bias or to the audience. Being willing to suffer for one's beliefs—which many great leaders have done—can help convince people of one's sincerity (Knight & Weiss, 1980).

These experiments all point to the importance of attribution: To what do we attribute a speaker's position—to the speaker's bias and selfish motives or to the evidence? Wood and Eagly (1981) report that when a speaker argues an *unexpected* position, we are more likely to attribute the message to compelling evidence and find it persuasive. Arguments for generous compensation in a personal-injury case are most persuasive when they come from a stingy, Scrooge-type person. Arguments for stingy compensation are most persuasive when they come from a normally warm, generous person (Wachtler & Counselman, 1981). We could therefore expect that a Northern Ireland peace treaty would be most trusted by followers of both sides if negotiated by hard-line leaders.

Norman Miller and his colleagues (1976) at the University of Southern California found that both trustworthiness and credibility increase when people talk fast. People in the Los Angeles area who listened to tape-recorded messages on topics such as "the dangers of coffee drinking" rated fast speakers (about 190 words per minute) as more objective, intelligent, and knowledgeable than slow speakers (about 110 words per minute). They also found the more rapid speakers more persuasive.

But is it speed alone that makes rapid speakers more persuasive? Or is it something that accompanies rapid speech, like higher intensity or pitch? To find out, marketing researcher James MacLachlan (1979; MacLachlan & Siegel, 1980) electronically compressed radio and television commercials without altering the speaker's pitch, inflection, and intensity. (He deleted small segments, about a fiftieth of a second in length, from all parts of the speech.) Speed itself was a factor. When the commercials were speeded up 25 percent, the listeners comprehended as well, rated the speakers as more knowledgeable, intelligent, and sincere, and found the messages more interesting. In fact, the normal 140- to 150-word-per-minute speech rate can be almost doubled before comprehension begins to drop abruptly (Foulke & Sticht, 1969). John F. Kennedy, an exceptionally effective public speaker, sometimes spoke in bursts approaching 300 words per minute. To Americans (though not to Koreans) fast speech conveys power and competence (Peng & others, 1993). Although fast speech doesn't leave listeners time to elaborate favorable thoughts, it also cuts short any unfavorable thoughts (Smith & Shaffer, 1991). If an advertiser is persuading you at 70 miles per hour it's tough to counterargue at the same speed.

Some television ads are obviously constructed to make the communicator appear both expert and trustworthy. Drug companies peddle pain relievers using a white-coated speaker, who declares confidently that most doctors recommend their ingredient (the ingredient, of course, is aspirin). Given such peripheral cues, people who don't care enough to analyze the evidence may reflexively infer the product's value. Other ads seem not to use the credibility principle. Was Bill Cosby really a trustworthy expert on Jell-O desserts? And are you and I more likely to drink Pepsi because Shaquille O'Neal recommends it?

Attractiveness

Most people deny that endorsements by star athletes and entertainers affect them. Everyone knows that stars are seldom knowledgeable about the products. Besides, we know the intent is to persuade us; we don't just accidentally eavesdrop on Cosby lapping Jell-O. Such ads are based on another characteristic of an effective communicator: attractiveness. We may think we are not influenced by attractiveness or likeability, but researchers have found otherwise. Our liking may open us up to their arguments (central route persuasion) or may trigger positive associations when we later see the product (peripheral route persuasion).

Attractiveness:
Having qualities that appeal to an audience. An appealing communicator (often someone similar to the audience) is most persuasive on matters of subjective preference.

Attractiveness varies in several ways. *Physical appeal* is one. Arguments, especially emotional ones, are often more influential when they come from beautiful people (Chaiken, 1979; Dion & Stein, 1978; Pallak & others, 1983). *Similarity* is another. As Chapter 13 will emphasize, we tend to like people who are like us. We also are influenced by them. For example, Theodore Dembroski, Thomas Lasater, and Albert Ramirez (1978) gave African-American junior high students a taped appeal for proper dental care. When a dentist assessed the cleanliness of their teeth the next day, those who heard the appeal from an African-American dentist had cleaner teeth. As a general rule, people respond better to a message that comes from someone in their group (Van Knippenberg & Wilke, 1992; Wilder, 1990).

Is similarity more important than credibility? Sometimes yes, sometimes no. Timothy Brock (1965) found paint store customers more influenced by the testimony of an ordinary person who had recently bought the same amount of paint they planned to buy than by an expert who had recently purchased 20 times as much. But recall that a leading dentist (a dissimilar but expert source) was more persuasive than a student (a similar but inexpert source) when discussing dental hygiene.

Such seemingly contradictory findings as this bring out the detective in the scientist. They suggest that an undiscovered factor is at work—that similarity is more important given factor X and credibility is more important given not-X. But what is factor X? As George Goethals and Erick Nelson (1973) discovered, it is whether the topic is one of *subjective preference* or *objective reality*. When the choice concerns matters of personal value, taste, or way of life, similar communicators have the most influence. But on judgments of fact—Does Sydney have less rainfall than London?—confirmation of belief by a *dissimilar* person does more to boost confidence. A dissimilar person provides a more independent judgment.

WHAT IS SAID? THE CONTENT OF THE MESSAGE

It matters not only who says a thing (a peripheral cue), but *what* that person says. If you were to help organize an appeal to get people to vote for school taxes, or to stop smoking, or to give money to world hunger relief, you might wonder how to concoct a recipe for central route persuasion. Common sense can be made to argue on either side of these questions:

■ Is a carefully reasoned message most persuasive—or one that arouses emotion?

- Will you get more opinion change by advocating a position only slightly discrepant from the listeners' existing opinions? Or by advocating an extreme point of view?
- Should the message express your side only, or should it acknowledge and attempt to refute opposing views?
- If people are to present both sides—say, in successive talks at a community meeting—is there an advantage to going first or last?

Let's take these questions one at a time.

Reason versus Emotion

Suppose you were campaigning in support of world hunger relief. Would it be best to itemize your arguments and cite an array of impressive statistics? Or would you be more effective presenting an emotional approach—say, the compelling story of one starving child? Of course, an argument can be both reasonable and emotional. Still, which is more influential—reason or emotion? Was Shakespeare's Lysander right: "The will of man is by his reason sway'd"? Or was Lord Chesterfield's advice wiser: "Address yourself generally to the senses, to the heart, and to the weaknesses of mankind, but rarely to their reason"?

The answer: It depends on the audience. Well-educated or analytical people are more responsive to rational appeals than are less educated or less analytical people (Cacioppo & others, 1983; Hovland & others, 1949). Thoughtful, involved audiences travel the central route; they are most responsive to reasoned arguments. Disinterested audiences travel the peripheral route; they are more affected by how much they like the communicator (Chaiken, 1980; Petty & others, 1981). To judge from interviews before major elections, many voters are uninvolved. Americans' voting preferences are more predictable from emotional reactions to the candidates (for example, whether Ronald Reagan ever made them feel happy) than from their beliefs about the candidates' traits and likely behaviors (Abelson & others, 1982).

The Effect of Good Feelings

Messages also become more persuasive through association with good feelings. Irving Janis and his colleagues (1965; Dabbs & Janis, 1965) found that Yale students were more convinced by persuasive messages if they were allowed to enjoy peanuts and Pepsi while reading them (Figure 8–2). Similarly, Mark Galizio and Clyde Hendrick (1972) found Kent State University students more persuaded by folk-song lyrics accompanied by pleasant guitar music than by unaccompanied lyrics. Those who like conducting business over sumptuous lunches with soft background music can celebrate these results.

Good feelings enhance persuasion—partly by enhancing positive thinking (when people are motivated to think) and partly by linking good feelings with the message (Petty & others, 1993). As noted in Chapter 3, in a good mood, people view the world through rose-colored glasses. They also make faster, more impulsive decisions; they rely more on peripheral cues (Bodenhausen, 1993; Schwarz & others, 1991). Unhappy people ruminate more before reacting, so they are less easily swayed by weak arguments. Thus, if you can't make a strong case, it's a smart idea to put your audience in a good mood and hope they'll feel good about your message without thinking too much about it.

"The truth is always the strongest argument."
Sophocles, *Phaedra*

"Opinion is ultimately determined by the feelings and not by the intellect."
Herbert Spencer, *Social Statics*, 1851

Advertising research, as in one study of the persuasiveness of 168 television commercials (Agres, 1987), reveals that the most effective ads invoke both reasons ("You'll get whiter whites with Detergent X") and emotions ("Choosy mothers choose Jif").

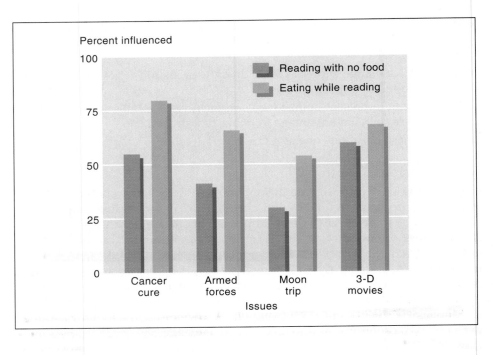

People who snacked as they read were more persuaded than those who read without snacking.
(Data from Janis, Kaye, & Kirschner, 1965.)

The Effect of Arousing Fear

Messages also can be effective by evoking negative emotions. In trying to convince people to cut down on smoking, brush their teeth more often, get a tetanus shot, or drive carefully, a fear-arousing message can be potent (Muller & Johnson, 1990). Showing cigarette smokers the horrible things that sometimes happen to people who smoke too much adds to persuasiveness. But how much fear should you arouse? Should you evoke just a little fear, lest people become so frightened that they tune out your painful message? Or should you try to scare the daylights out of them? Experiments by Howard Leventhal (1970) and his collaborators at the University of Wisconsin and by Ronald Rogers and his collaborators at the University of Alabama (Robberson & Rogers, 1988) show that, often, the more frightened people are, the more they respond.

The effectiveness of fear-arousing communications is being applied in ads discouraging smoking, drinking and driving, and risky sexual behaviors. Dawn Wilson and her colleagues (1987, 1988) had doctors send a letter to their patients who smoked. Of those who received a positively framed message (explaining that by quitting they would live longer), 8 percent tried to quit smoking. Of those who received a fear-framed message (explaining that by continuing to smoke they would likely die sooner), 30 percent tried to quit. Similarly, when Claude Levy-Leboyer (1988) found that attitudes toward alcohol and drinking habits among French youth were effectively changed by fear-arousing pictures, the French government incorporated this kind of information in its TV spots.

But playing on fear won't always make a message more potent. If you don't tell people how to avoid the danger, frightening messages can be overwhelming (Leventhal, 1970; Rogers & Mewborn, 1976). Fear messages are more effective if you lead people not only to fear the severity and likelihood of a threatened event (say, a lung cancer death due to cigarette smoking) but also to perceive an effective protective strategy (Maddux & Rogers, 1983). Many ads aimed at reducing sexual risks aim both to arouse fear—"AIDS kills"—and to offer a protective strategy: abstain or wear a condom or save sex for a committed relationship. During the 1980s, fear of AIDS indeed persuaded many men to alter their behavior. One study of 5000 gay men found that as the AIDS crisis mushroomed between 1984 and 1986 the number saying they were celibate or monogamous rose from 14 to 39 percent (Fineberg, 1988).

Vividly imagined diseases seem a more likely threat than hard-to-picture diseases (Sherman & others, 1985). That little fact helps explain why health warnings like those on cigarette ads are so ineffective—"a yawnful concentration of legal jargon," say Timothy Brock and Laura Brannon (1991)—and hardly make a dent in the ad's visual impact. Making the warnings as vivid as the ad—with color photos of lung cancer surgery—makes them more effective in changing attitudes and intentions. This is especially so when the ad draws attention to a persuasive image rather than, as sexual images sometimes do, distracting the audience (Frey & Eagly, 1993). When it comes to persuasion, a pertinent, dramatic picture can indeed be worth a thousand words.

Vivid propaganda often exploits fears. Streicher's *Der Stürmer* aroused fear with hundreds upon hundreds of unsubstantiated anecdotes about Jews who were said to have ground rats to make hash, seduced non-Jewish women, and cheated families out of their life savings. Streicher's appeals, like most Nazi propaganda, were emotional, not logical. The appeals also gave clear, specific

"If those who have studied the art of writing are in accord on any one point, it is on this: the surest way to arouse and hold the attention of the reader is by being specific, definite, and concrete."
William Strunk and E. B. White, *The Elements of Style*, 1979

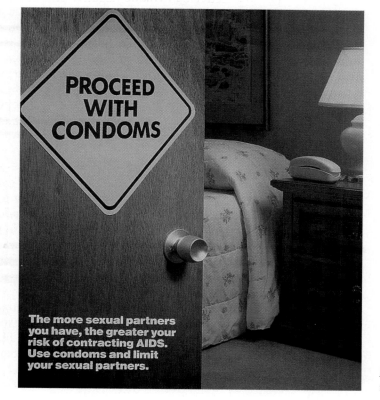

Health warnings are most effective when made vivid.

instructions on how to combat "the danger": They listed Jewish businesses so readers would avoid them, encouraged readers to submit for publication the names of Germans who patronized Jewish shops and professionals, and directed readers to compile lists of Jews in their area (Bytwerk & Brooks, 1980). This was vivid hard-to-forget propaganda.

Discrepancy

Picture the following scene: Wanda arrives home on spring vacation and hopes to convert her portly, middle-aged father to her new "health-fitness lifestyle." She runs 5 miles a day. Her father says his idea of exercise is "channel surfing." Wanda thinks: "Would I be more likely to get Dad off his duff by urging him to try a modest exercise program, say a daily walk, or by trying to get him involved in something strenuous, say a program of calisthenics and running? Maybe if I asked him to take up a rigorous exercise program he would compromise and at least take up something worthwhile. But then again maybe he'd think I'm crazy and do nothing."

Like Wanda, social psychologists can reason either way. Disagreement produces discomfort, and discomfort prompts people to change their opinions (recall from Chapter 4 the effects of dissonance). So perhaps greater disagreement will produce more change. But then again, a communicator who proclaims an uncomfortable message may get discredited. One study found that people who disagree with conclusions drawn by a newscaster rate the newscaster as more biased, inaccurate, and untrustworthy. People are more open to conclusions within their range of acceptability (Liberman & Chaiken, 1992; Zanna, 1993). So perhaps greater disagreement will produce *less* change.

Given these considerations, Elliot Aronson, Judith Turner, and Merrill Carlsmith (1963) reasoned that only a *credible source*—one hard to discount—would elicit considerable opinion change when advocating a position *greatly discrepant* from the recipient's. Sure enough, when T. S. Eliot was said to have highly praised a disliked poem, people changed their opinion more than when he gave it faint praise. But when "Agnes Stearns, a student at Mississippi State Teachers College," evaluated a disliked poem, faint praise was as persuasive as high praise. Thus, as Figure 8–3 shows, discrepancy and credibility *interact*: The effect of a large versus small discrepancy depends on whether or not the communicator is credible.

So the answer to Wanda's question—"Should I argue an extreme position?"—is, "It depends." Is Wanda in her adoring father's eyes a highly prestigious, authoritative source? If so, Wanda should push for a complete fitness program. If not, Wanda would be wise to make a more modest appeal.

The answer also depends on how involved her father is in the issue. Deeply involved people tend to accept only a narrow range of views. To them, a moderately discrepant message may seem foolishly radical, especially if the message argues an opposing view rather than being a more extreme version of a view they already agree with (Pallak & others, 1972; Petty & Cacioppo, 1979; Rhine & Severance, 1970). If Wanda's father has not yet thought or cared much about exercise, she can probably take a more extreme position than if he is strongly committed to not exercising. So, if you are a credible authority and your audience isn't much concerned with your issue, you should feel free to advocate a discrepant view.

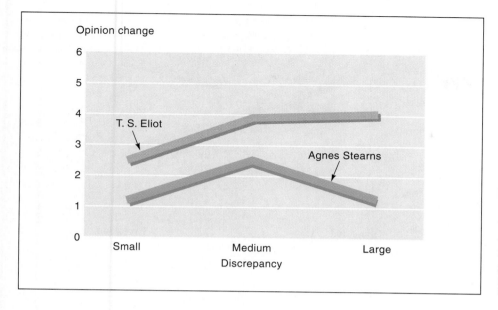

Opinion change

T. S. Eliot

Agnes Stearns

Small   Medium   Large

Discrepancy

■ FIGURE 8–3
Discrepancy interacts with communicator credibility. Only a highly credible communicator maintains effectiveness when arguing an extreme position.
(Data from Aronson, Turner, & Carlsmith, 1963.)

One-Sided versus Two-Sided Appeals

Persuaders face another practical issue: how to deal with opposing arguments. Once again, common sense offers no clear answer. Acknowledging the opposing arguments might confuse the audience and weaken the case. On the other hand, a message might seem fairer, more disarming, if it recognizes the opposition's arguments.

After Germany's defeat in World War II, the U.S. Army did not want soldiers to relax and think that the still ongoing war with Japan now would be easy. So social psychologist Carl Hovland and his colleagues (1949) in the Army's Information and Education Division designed two radio broadcasts arguing that the war in the Pacific would last at least two more years. One broadcast was one-sided; it did not acknowledge the existence of contradictory arguments, such as the advantage of fighting only one enemy instead of two. The other broadcast was two-sided; it mentioned and responded to the opposing arguments. As Figure 8–4 illustrates, the effectiveness of the message depended on the listener. A one-sided appeal was most effective with those who already agreed. An appeal that acknowledged opposing arguments worked better with those who disagreed.

Later experiments revealed that if people are (or will be) aware of opposing arguments, a two-sided presentation is more persuasive and enduring (Jones & Brehm, 1970; Lumsdaine & Janis, 1953). In simulated trials, a defense case becomes more credible when the defense brings up damaging evidence before the prosecution does (Williams & others, 1993). Apparently, a one-sided message stimulates an informed audience to think of counterarguments and to view the communicator as biased. Thus, a political candidate speaking to a politically informed group would indeed be wise to respond to the opposition. So, if your audience includes or will be exposed to opposing views, offer a two-sided appeal.

"Opponents fancy they refute us when they repeat their own opinion and pay no attention to ours."
Goethe, *Maxims and Reflections,* early nineteenth century

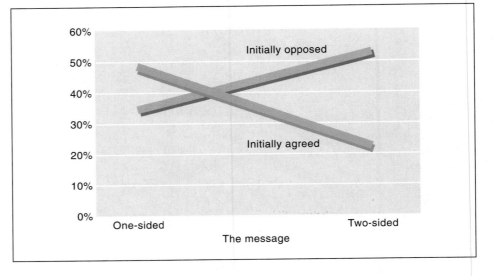

■ **FIGURE 8–4**
The interaction of initial opinion with one- versus two-sidedness. After Germany's defeat in World War II, American soldiers skeptical of a message suggesting Japan's strength were more persuaded by a two-sided communication. Soldiers initially agreeing with the message were strengthened more by a one-sided message.
(Data from Hovland, Lumsdaine, & Sheffield, 1949.)

Primacy versus Recency

Imagine yourself a consultant to a prominent politician who must soon debate another prominent politician regarding a proposed arms limitation treaty. Three weeks before the vote, each politician is to appear on the nightly news and present a prepared statement. By the flip of a coin, your side receives the choice of whether to speak first or last. Knowing that you are a former social psychology student, everyone looks to you for advice.

You mentally scan your old books and lecture notes. Would first be best? People's preconceptions control their interpretations. Moreover, a belief, once formed, is difficult to discredit. So going first could give people ideas that would favorably bias how they would perceive and interpret the second speech. Besides, people may pay most attention to what comes first. But then again, people remember recent things best. Might it really be more effective to speak last?

Primacy effect:
Other things being equal, information presented first usually has the most influence.

Your first line of reasoning predicts what is most common, a **primacy effect:** Information presented early is most persuasive. First impressions *are* important. For example, can you sense a difference between these two descriptions?

■ John is intelligent, industrious, impulsive, critical, stubborn, and envious.
■ John is envious, stubborn, critical, impulsive, industrious, and intelligent.

When Solomon Asch (1946) gave these sentences to college students in New York City, those who read the adjectives in the intelligent-to-envious order rated the person more positively than did those given the envious-to-intelligent order. The earlier information seemed to color their interpretation of the later information, producing the primacy effect. A similar effect occurs in experiments where people succeed on a guessing task 50 percent of the time. Those whose successes come early seem more able than those whose successes come mostly after early failures (Jones & others, 1968; Langer & Roth, 1975; McAndrew, 1981).

Is primacy the rule in persuasion as well as judgment? Norman Miller and Donald Campbell (1959) gave Northwestern University students a condensed transcript from an actual civil trial. They placed the plaintiff's testimony and arguments in one block, those for the defense in another. The students read both blocks. When they returned a week later to declare their opinions, most sided with the information they had read first. Using the transcript of an actual criminal case, Gary Wells and his colleagues (1985) found a similar primacy effect when they varied the timing of a defense attorney's opening statement. The statement was more effective if presented *before* the prosecution's presentation of the evidence.

What about the opposite possibility? We have all experienced what the book of Proverbs observed: "The one who first states a case seems right, until the other comes and cross-examines." So, will our better memory for recent information ever create a **recency effect**? We know from our experience (as well as from memory experiments) that today's events can temporarily outweigh significant past events. To test this, Miller and Campbell gave another group of students one block of testimony to read. A week later the researchers had them read the second block and then immediately state their opinions. Now the results were just the reverse—a recency effect. Apparently the first block of arguments, being a week old, had largely faded from memory. Forgetting creates the recency effect (1) when enough time separates the two messages *and* (2) when the audience commits itself soon after the second message. When the two messages are back to back, followed by a time gap, a primacy effect usually occurs (Figure 8–5). This is especially so when the first message stimulates thinking (Haugtvedt & Wegener, 1994). So, what advice would you give to the political debater?

HOW IS IT SAID? THE CHANNEL OF COMMUNICATION

Active Experience or Passive Reception?

In Chapter 4 we noted that our actions shape who we are. When we act, we amplify the idea behind what we've done, especially when we feel responsible. We also noted that attitudes rooted in our own experience—rather than

Recency effect:
Information presented last sometimes has the most influence. Recency effects are less common than primacy effects.

■ **FIGURE 8–5**
Primacy effect versus recency effect. When two persuasive messages are back to back and the audience then responds at some later time, the first message has the advantage (primacy effect). When the two messages are separated in time and the audience responds soon after the second message, the second message has the advantage (recency effect).

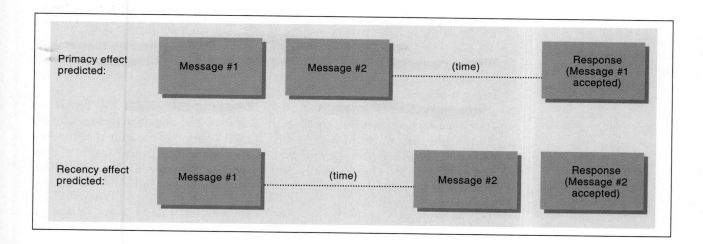

Channel of communication: The way the message is delivered—whether face to face, in writing, on film, or in some other way.

learned secondhand—are more likely to endure and to affect our behavior. Compared to attitudes formed passively, experience-based attitudes are more confident, more stable, and less vulnerable to attack.

Commonsense psychology nevertheless places faith in the power of written words. How do we try to get people out to a campus event? We post notices. How do we get drivers to slow down and keep their eyes on the road? We put "Drive Carefully" messages on billboards. How do we discourage students from dropping trash on campus? We litter campus bulletin boards and mailboxes with antilitter messages.

Are people so easily persuaded? Consider two well-intentioned efforts. At Scripps College in California, a week-long antilitter campaign urged students to "Keep Scripps' campus beautiful," "Let's clean up our trash," and so forth. Such slogans were placed in students' mailboxes each morning and displayed on prominent posters across the campus. The day before the campaign began, social psychologist Raymond Paloutzian (1979) placed litter near a trash can along a well-traveled sidewalk. Then he stepped back to record the behavior of 180 passers-by. No one picked up anything. On the last day of the campaign he repeated the test with 180 more passers-by. Did the pedestrians now race one another in their zeal to comply with the appeals? Hardly. Only 2 of the 180 picked up the trash.

Are spoken appeals more persuasive? Not necessarily. Those of us who do public speaking, as teachers or persuaders, become so easily enamored of our spoken words that we are tempted to overestimate their power. Ask college students what aspect of their college experience has been most valuable or what they remember from their first year, and few, I am sad to say, recall the brilliant lectures that we faculty remember giving. Thomas Crawford (1974) and his associates tested the impact of the spoken word by going to the homes of people from 12 churches shortly before and after they heard sermons opposing racial bigotry and injustice. When asked during the second interview whether they had heard or read anything about racial prejudice or discrimination since the previous interview, only 10 percent spontaneously recalled the sermons. When the remaining 90 percent were asked directly whether their priest had "talked about prejudice or discrimination in the last couple of weeks," more than 30 percent denied hearing such a sermon. It is therefore hardly surprising that the sermons left racial attitudes unaffected.

When you stop to think about it, the preacher has so many hurdles to surmount, it's a wonder that preaching affects as many people as it does. As Figure 8–6 shows, persuasive speakers must deliver a message that not only gets attention but also is understandable, convincing, memorable, and compelling. A carefully thought-out appeal must consider each of these steps in the persuasion process.

Passively received appeals, however, are not always futile. My drugstore sells two brands of aspirin, one heavily advertised and one unadvertised. Apart from slight differences in how fast each tablet crumbles in your mouth, any pharmacist will tell you the two brands are identical. Aspirin is aspirin. Our bodies cannot tell the difference. But our pocketbooks can. The advertised brand sells for three times the price of the unadvertised brand. And sell it does, to millions of people.

With such power, can the media help a wealthy political candidate buy an election? Joseph Grush (1980) analyzed candidate expenditures in all the 1976

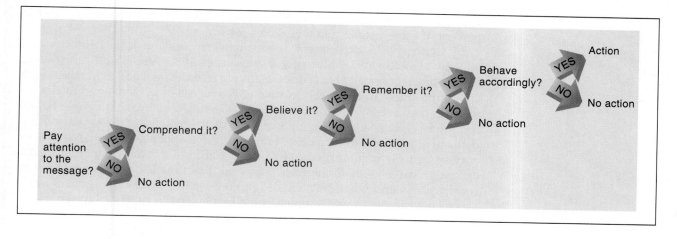

■ FIGURE 8–6
To elicit action, a persuasive message must clear several hurdles. What is crucial is not so much remembering the message itself as remembering one's own thoughts in response.
(Adapted from McGuire, 1978.)

Democratic presidential primaries and found that those who spent the most in any election usually got the most votes. As Grush noted, the effect of this exposure was often to make an unfamiliar candidate into a familiar one. (This parallels laboratory experiments in which mere exposure to unfamiliar stimuli breeds liking—see Chapter 13.) Their message, too, may gain with repetition. People rated trivial statements, like "Mercury has a higher boiling point than copper," as more truthful if they had read and rated them a week before. Mere repetition can make things believable. Researcher Hal Arkes (1990) views such findings as "scary." As political manipulators know, demagoguery can triumph over reason. Believable lies can displace hard truths. Echoed clichés can cover complex realities.

Would the media be as effective with familiar candidates and important issues? Probably not. Researchers have time and again found little effect of political advertising on voters' attitudes in the general presidential election (although, of course, even a small effect could swing a close election) (Kinder & Sears, 1985; McGuire, 1986).

Because passively received appeals are sometimes effective and sometimes not, can we specify in advance the topics on which a persuasive appeal will be successful? There is a simple rule: Persuasion *decreases* as the significance and familiarity of the issue *increase*. On minor issues, such as which brand of aspirin to buy, it's easy to demonstrate the media's power. On more familiar and important issues, such as racial attitudes in racially tense cities, persuading people is like trying to push a piano uphill. It is not impossible, but one shove won't do it.

Personal versus Media Influence

Persuasion studies demonstrate that the major influence upon us is not the media but our contact with people. Two field experiments illustrate the strength of personal influence. Some years ago, Samuel Eldersveld and Richard Dodge (1954) studied political persuasion in Ann Arbor, Michigan. They divided citizens intending not to vote for a revision of the city charter into three groups. Of those exposed only to what they saw and heard in the mass media, 19 percent voted for the revision on election day. Of a second group, who received four mailings in support of the revision, 45 percent voted for it. People in a third group were visited personally and given the appeal face to face, and 75 percent of these people cast their votes for it.

In another field experiment, a research team led by John Farquhar and Nathan Maccoby (1977; Maccoby & Alexander, 1980; Maccoby, 1980) tried to reduce the frequency of heart disease among middle-aged adults in three small California cities. To check the relative effectiveness of personal and media influence, they interviewed and medically examined some 1200 people before the project began and at the end of each of the following three years. Residents of Tracy, California, received no persuasive appeals other than those occurring in their regular media. In Gilroy, California, a two-year multimedia campaign used TV, radio, newspapers, and direct mail to teach people about coronary risk and what they could do to reduce it. In Watsonville, California, this media campaign was supplemented by personal contacts with two-thirds of those whose blood pressure, weight, and age put them in a high-risk group. Using behavior-modification principles, the researchers helped people set specific goals and reinforced their successes.

As Figure 8–7 shows, after one, two, and three years the high-risk people in Tracy (the control town) were about as much at risk as before. High-risk people in Gilroy, which was deluged with media appeals, improved their health habits and were now somewhat less at risk. Those in Watsonville, who also received the personal contacts, changed most.

I suspect college students will have little trouble recognizing the potency of personal influence from their own experience. In retrospect, most say they learned more from their friends and other students than from contact with books or professors. Educational researchers have confirmed the students' intuition: Out-of-class personal relationships powerfully influence how students mature during college (Astin, 1972; Wilson & others, 1975).

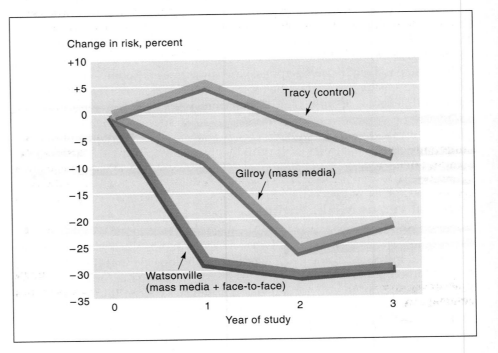

■ FIGURE 8–7

Percentage change from baseline (0) in coronary risk after one, two, or three years of health education.

(Data from Maccoby, 1980.)

Opinion change

Difficult message

Easy message

Written   Audio tape   Video tape

■ **FIGURE 8–8**
Easy-to-understand messages are most persuasive when video-taped. Difficult messages are most persuasive when written. Thus the difficulty of the message interacts with the medium to determine persuasiveness.
(Data from Chaiken & Eagly, 1978.)

Although face-to-face influence is usually greater than media influence, we should not underestimate the media's power. Those who personally influence our opinions must get their ideas somewhere, and often their sources are the media. Elihu Katz (1957) observed that much of the media's effects operate in a **two-step flow of communication**—from media to opinion leaders to the rank and file. If I want to evaluate computer equipment, I defer to the opinions of my son, who gets many of his ideas from the printed page.

The two-step flow model oversimplifies. The media also communicate directly with mass audiences. But the model does remind us that media influences penetrate the culture in subtle ways. Even if the media had little direct effect upon people's attitudes, they could still have a big indirect effect. Those rare children who grow up without watching television do not grow up beyond television's influence. Unless they live as hermits, they will join in TV-imitative play on the school ground. They will ask their parents for the TV-related toys their friends have. They will beg or demand to watch their friend's favorite programs. Parents can just say no, but they cannot switch off television's influence.

Lumping together all media, from mass mailings to television, also oversimplifies. Studies comparing different media find that the more lifelike the medium, the more persuasive its message. Thus the order of persuasiveness seems to be: live, videotaped, audiotaped, and written. But to add to the complexity, messages are best *comprehended* and *recalled* when written. Comprehension is one of the first steps in the persuasion process (recall Figure 8–6). Shelly Chaiken and Alice Eagly (1978) reasoned that if a message is difficult to comprehend, persuasion, too, could be greatest when the message is written. They gave University of Massachusetts students easy or difficult messages in writing, on audiotape, or videotape. Figure 8–8 displays their results: Difficult messages were indeed most persuasive when written, easy messages when videotaped. By drawing attention to the communicator and away from the message itself, the TV medium also draws attention to the communicator's characteristics (Chaiken & Eagly, 1983).

Two-step flow of communication:
The process by which media influence often occurs through opinion leaders, who in turn influence others.

BEHIND THE SCENES

My interest in studying persuasion was spurred when my graduate advisor, Alice Eagly, pointed me to William McGuire's analysis of media effects. McGuire reasoned that different factors might affect someone's *comprehending* a persuasive argument and their *yielding* to it. This took me back to my preteen experience watching John F. Kennedy demolish (or so I thought) Richard Nixon during their presidential debates. Yet, I later learned, the perception that Kennedy "won" may have run stronger among people who *viewed* the debates than among people who only *heard* them or *read* them. Had my verdict been influenced more than I'd imagined by my hero's attractive appearance and bearing?

My master's thesis research (Figure 8–8) confirmed that the medium of communication indeed matters. Moreover, this led to the idea that people sometimes process messages *heuristically*, basing judgments on extrinsic factors such as the communicator's likability or attractiveness. I like to take credit for this idea, but it's high time I thanked Alice Eagly, Bill McGuire, and President Kennedy for their input.

SHELLY CHAIKEN, *New York University*

TO WHOM IS IT SAID? THE AUDIENCE

As we saw in Chapter 7, people's traits often don't predict their response to social influence. A particular trait may enhance one step in the persuasion process (Figure 8–6) but work against another. Take self-esteem. People with low self-esteem are often slow to comprehend a message and therefore hard to persuade. Those with high self-esteem may comprehend yet remain confident of their own opinions; thus self-esteem alone won't directly predict persuadability. The conclusion: People with moderate self-esteem are the easiest to influence (Rhodes & Wood, 1992).

Let's also consider two other characteristics of those who receive a message: their age and their thoughtfulness.

How Old Are They?

People today tend to have different social and political attitudes depending on their age. There are two explanations for the difference. One is a *life-cycle explanation*: Attitudes change (for example, become more conservative) as people grow older. The other is a *generational explanation*: The attitudes older people adopted when they were young persist largely unchanged; because these attitudes are different from those now being adopted by young people today, a generation gap develops.

The evidence mostly supports the generational explanation. In surveying and resurveying groups of younger and older people over several years, the attitudes of older people usually change less than do those of young people. As David Sears (1979, 1986) puts it, researchers have "almost invariably found generational rather than life cycle effects."

The point is not that older adults are inflexible; most people in their fifties and sixties have more liberal sexual and racial attitudes than they had in their thirties and forties (Glenn, 1980, 1981). The point is that the teens and early twenties are important formative years (Krosnick & Alwin, 1989), and the attitudes formed then tend to be stable thereafter. Such people might therefore be advised to choose intentionally their social influences—the groups they join, the media they imbibe, the roles they adopt.

A striking example: During the late 1930s and early 1940s, students at Vermont's Bennington College—women from privileged, conservative families—encountered a free-spirited environment led by a left-leaning young faculty. One of those faculty, social psychologist Theodore Newcomb, later denied the faculty was trying to make "good little liberals" out of its students. Nevertheless, they succeeded. The students became much more liberal than was typical of those from their social backgrounds. Moreover, attitudes formed at Bennington endured. A half-century later, the Bennington women, now seventyish, voted Democratic by a 3 to 1 margin in the 1984 presidential election, while other seventyish college-educated women were voting Republican by a 3 to 1 margin (Alwin & others, 1991). The views embraced in the impressionable years of transition to adulthood had survived a lifetime of wider experience.

Experiences during adolescence and early adulthood are formative partly because they make deep and lasting impressions. When Howard Schuman and Jacqueline Scott (1989) asked people to name the one or two most important national or world events over the last half century, most recalled events from their teens or early twenties. For those who experienced the Great Depression or World War II as 16- to 24-year-olds, those events overshadowed the civil rights movement and the Kennedy assassination of the early sixties, the Vietnam war and moon landing of the late sixties, and the women's movement of the seventies, each of which imprinted themselves on the minds of those who experienced them as 16- to 24-year-olds. We may expect that memories of the fall of the Berlin Wall and the democratization of Eastern Europe will be indelible turning points in world history for today's young adults.

What Are They Thinking

In central route persuasion, what's crucial is not the message itself but what responses it evokes in a person's mind. Our minds are not sponges that soak up whatever pours over them. If the message summons favorable thoughts, it persuades us. If it provokes us to think of contrary arguments, we remain unpersuaded.

Forewarned Is Forearmed—If You Care Enough to Counterargue

What circumstances breed counterarguing? One is a *forewarning* that someone is going to try to persuade you. If you had to tell your family that you wanted to drop out of school, you would likely anticipate their trying to persuade you to stay. So, you might develop a list of arguments to counter every conceivable argument they might make. Jonathan Freedman and David Sears (1965) demonstrated the difficulty of trying to persuade someone under such circumstances. They forewarned one group of California high schoolers that they were going to hear a talk: "Why Teenagers Should Not Be Allowed to Drive." Those forewarned, did not budge. Others, not forewarned, did.

"To be forewarned and therefore forearmed . . . is eminently rational if our belief is true; but if our belief is a delusion, this same forewarning and forearming would obviously be the method whereby the delusion rendered itself incurable."
C. S. Lewis,
Screwtape Proposes a Toast, 1965

suader's point of view? If the answer is yes, quality arguments will be persuasive. During the closing days of a closely contested 1980 presidential cam-

Sneak attacks on attitudes are especially useful with involved people. Given

BEHIND THE SCENES

We spent many hours during graduate school trying to convince each other of our personal views. After these marathon debates, it seemed that the vulnerability of our attitudes depended on the merits of our arguments. We therefore were surprised what happened when, for a class project, we gained admittance to an introductory "cult" meeting. The cult leaders achieved success less by relying on arguments than by using peripheral cues such as source attractiveness, social approval, and the trappings of credibility. We left the meeting convinced that there were multiple routes by which attitudes change. Some people, in some situations, respond more to a central (argument-based) route; others, in other situations, respond more to peripheral cues. That basic idea is the core of our theory of persuasion, and the individual differences we observed gave birth to our research on need for cognition.

RICHARD PETTY and JOHN CACIOPPO, *Ohio State University*

paign, Ronald Reagan effectively used rhetorical questions to stimulate desired thoughts in voters' minds. His summary statement in the presidential debate began with two potent rhetorical questions that he repeated often during the campaign's remaining week: "Are you better off than you were four years ago? Is it easier for you to go and buy things in the stores than it was four years ago?" Most people answered no, and Reagan, thanks partly to this bit of central-route persuasion, won by a bigger-than-expected margin.

SUMMING UP

What makes persuasion effective? Researchers have explored four factors: the communicator, the message, the channel, and the audience.

Credible communicators are perceived as trustworthy experts. People who speak unhesitatingly, who talk fast, and who look listeners straight in the eye seem more credible. So are people who argue against their own self-interest. An attractive communicator also is effective on matters of taste and personal values.

Associating a message with the good feelings one has while eating, drinking, or listening to music makes it more convincing. People often make snappier, less reflective judgments while in good moods. Some messages that arouse fear can also be effective, perhaps because they are vivid and memorable.

How discrepant a message should be from an audience's existing opinions depends on the communicator's credibility. And whether a message is most persuasive when it presents only one position or when it introduces the opposing side as well depends on the listeners. When the audience already agrees with the message, is unaware of opposing arguments, and is unlikely later to consider the opposition, a one-sided appeal is most effective. With more sophisticated audiences or with those not already in agreement, two-sided messages are most successful.

When two sides of an issue are included, do the arguments presented first or second have the advantage? The common finding is a primacy effect: Information presented early is most potent. However, if a time gap separates the presentations, the effect of the early information diminishes; if a decision is made right after hearing the second side, which is therefore still fresh in the mind, the result will likely be a recency effect.

Another important consideration is *how* the message is communicated. Although not as potent as face-to-face personal influence, the mass media can be effective when the issue is minor (such as which brand of aspirin to buy) or unfamiliar (such as deciding between two otherwise unknown political candidates).

Finally, it matters *who* receives the message. What does the audience think while receiving a message? Do they think agreeing thoughts? Do they counterargue? Forewarning that a disagreeable message is coming reduces persuasion by stimulating counterarguments; distracting people while they hear a disagreeable message can increase persuasion by interfering with their counterarguing. The age of the audience also makes a difference. Researchers who have resurveyed people over time find that young people's attitudes are less stable.

■ CASE STUDIES IN PERSUASION

What persuasion and group influence principles are applied by religious cults? by mental health professionals?

The persuasion principles described in this chapter get applied, consciously or not, in ways that reveal their power. Consider the social influences that have caused hundreds of thousands of people to join religious cults and that have benefited many who undergo counseling and psychotherapy.

CULT INDOCTRINATION

Hare Krishna chanters, Moonies, and cult suicide victims—what persuades them to adopt radically new beliefs? Do their experiences illustrate the dynamics of human persuasion? Bear two things in mind: First, this is hindsight analysis. It uses persuasion principles as categories for explaining, after the fact, a fascinating social phenomenon.

Second, explaining *why* people believe something says nothing about the *truth* of their beliefs. That is a logically separate issue. A psychology of religion might tell us *why* a theist believes in God and an atheist disbelieves, but it cannot tell us who is right. Explaining either belief does not explain it away. So if someone tries to discount your beliefs by saying, "You just believe that because . . . ," you might recall the reply of Archbishop William Temple. After giving an address at Oxford, a questioner opened the discussion with a challenge: "Well, of course, Archbishop, the point is that you believe what you believe because of the way you were brought up." To which the Archbishop

What persuasive powers lead people to follow cult leaders even to death, as these members of a Canadian-Swiss cult did in May 1994 at a chalet in Switzerland? Forty-three bodies were found in the "Temple of the Sun."

Cult:

A group typically characterized by (1) the distinctive ritual of its devotion to a god or a person, (2) isolation from the surrounding "evil" culture, and (3) a charismatic leader. (A *sect*, by contrast, is a spinoff from a major religion.)

replied: "That is as it may be. But the fact remains that you believe I believe what I believe because of the way I was brought up, because of the way you were brought up."

In recent decades, several **cults** have gained much publicity: Sun Myung Moon's Unification Church and Jim Jones's People's Temple. The Reverend Moon's mixture of Christianity, anticommunism, and glorification of Moon himself as a new messiah attracted a worldwide following. In response to Moon's declaration, "What I wish must be your wish," many committed themselves and their incomes to the Unification Church. How were they persuaded to do so?

In 1978 in Guyana, 914 followers of the Reverend Jones, who had followed him there from San Francisco, shocked the world when they died by following his order to down a strawberry drink laced with tranquilizers, painkillers, and a lethal dose of cyanide.

In 1993, high-school dropout David Koresh used his talent for memorizing Scripture and mesmerizing people to seize control of a faction of a sect called the Branch Davidians. Over time, members were gradually relieved of their bank accounts and possessions. Koresh also persuaded the men to live celibately while he slept with their wives and daughters, and he convinced his 19 "wives" that they should bear his children. Under seige after a shootout that killed six members and four federal agents, Koresh told his followers they would soon die and go with him straight to heaven. When the federal agents rammed the compound with tanks, hoping to inject tear gas, cult members set it afire, consuming 86 people in the flames.

How could such things happen? What persuaded these people to give such total allegiance? In hindsight, it looks as if the attitude-change principles have been at work.

Attitudes Follow Behavior

Compliance Breeds Acceptance

As Chapter 4 showed over and again, people usually internalize commitments made voluntarily, publicly, and repeatedly. Cult leaders seem to know this. New converts soon learn that membership is no trivial matter. They are quickly made active members of the team. Rituals within the cult community, and public canvassing and fund-raising, strengthen the initiates' identities as members. As those in social-psychological experiments come to believe in what they bear witness to (Aronson & Mills, 1959; Gerard & Mathewson, 1966), so cult initiates become committed advocates. The greater the personal commitment, the more the need to justify it.

The Foot-in-the-Door Phenomenon

How are we induced to make commitments? Seldom by an abrupt, conscious decision. One does not just decide, "I'm through with mainstream religion. I'm gonna find a cult." Nor do cult recruiters approach people on the street with, "Hi. I'm a Moonie. Care to join us?" Rather, the recruitment strategy exploits the foot-in-the-door principle. Unification Church recruiters would invite people to a dinner and then to a weekend of warm fellowship and discussions of philosophies of life. At the weekend retreat, they encouraged the attenders to join them in songs, activities, and discussion. Potential converts were then urged to sign up for longer training retreats. Eventually the activities became more arduous—soliciting contributions and attempting to convert others.

Jim Jones also used this foot-in-the-door technique. Psychologist Robert Ornstein (1991) recalls Jones explaining his recruitment successes to the San Francisco mayor and himself. Unlike other street solicitors on behalf of the poor,

"You go on home without me, Irene. I'm going to join this man's cult."

© 1982, The New Yorker Magazine, Inc.

Hundreds of thousands of people in recent years have been recruited by members of some 2500 religious cults, but seldom through an abrupt decision.

Group Effects

Cults illustrate the next chapter's theme: the power of a group to shape members' views and behavior. The cult typically separates members from their previous social support systems and isolates them with other cultists. There may then occur what Rodney Stark and William Bainbridge (1980) call a "social implosion": External ties weaken until the group socially collapses inward, each person engaging only with other group members. Cut off from families and former friends, they lose access to counterarguments. The group now defines reality. Because the cult frowns on or punishes disagreements, the apparent consensus helps eliminate any lingering doubts.

Contrary to the idea that cults turn hapless people into mindless robots, these techniques—increasing behavioral commitments, persuasion, and group isolation—do not have unlimited power. The Unification Church successfully recruits fewer than 1 in 10 people who attend its workshops (Ennis & Verrilli, 1989). David Koresh ruled with a mix of persuasion, intimidation, and violence. As Jim Jones made his demands more extreme, he, too, increasingly had to control people with intimidation. He used threats of harm to those who fled the community, beatings for noncompliance, and drugs to neutralize disagreeable members. By the end, he was as much an arm twister as a mind bender.

Moreover, cult influence techniques are in some ways similar to techniques used by groups more familiar to us. Fraternity and sorority members, for example, have reported that the initial "love bombing" of potential cult recruits is not unlike their own "rush" period. Members lavish prospective pledges with attention and make them feel special. During the pledge period, new members are somewhat isolated, cut off from old friends who did not pledge. They spend time studying the history and rules of their new group. They suffer and commit time on its behalf. They are expected to comply with all its demands. Not surprisingly, the result is usually a committed new member.

Military training in El Salvador: Terrorist and commando organizations create cohesion and commitment through some of the same tactics used by cult leaders.

Much the same is true of some therapeutic communities for recovering drug and alcohol abusers. Like religious cults, zealous self-help groups form a cohesive "social cocoon," have intense beliefs, and exert a profound influence on members' behavior (Galanter, 1989, 1990). Terrorist organizations exploit similar principles in recruiting and indoctrinating members (McCauley & Segal, 1987).

I chose the examples of fraternities, sororities, and self-help groups not to disparage them but to illustrate two concluding observations. First, if we attribute cult indoctrination to the leader's mystical force or to the followers' peculiar weaknesses, we may delude ourselves into thinking we are immune to social control techniques. In truth, our own groups—and countless salespeople, political leaders, and other persuaders—successfully use many of these tactics on us. Between education and indoctrination, enlightenment and propaganda, conversion and coercion, there is but a blurry line.

Second, that Jim Jones abused the power of persuasion does not mean persuasion is intrinsically bad. Nuclear power enables us to light up homes or wipe out cities. Sexual power enables us to express and celebrate committed love or exploit people for selfish gratification. Persuasive power enables us to enlighten or deceive. That these powers can be harnessed for evil purposes should alert us to guard against their immoral use. But the powers themselves are neither inherently evil nor inherently good; how we use them determines whether their effect is destructive or constructive. Condemning persuasion because of deceit is like condemning eating because of gluttony.

PERSUASION IN COUNSELING AND PSYCHOTHERAPY

One constructive use of persuasion is in counseling and psychotherapy, which social-counseling psychologist Stanley Strong views "as a branch of applied social psychology" (1978, p.101). Like Strong, psychiatrist Jerome Frank (1974, 1982) recognized years ago that it takes persuasion to change self-defeating attitudes and behaviors. Frank noted that the psychotherapy setting, like cults and zealous self-help groups, provides (1) a supportive, confiding social relationship, (2) an offer of expertise and hope, (3) a special rationale or myth that explains one's difficulties and offers a new perspective, and (4) a set of rituals and learning experiences that promises a new sense of peace and happiness.

By the 1990s, psychologists more and more accepted the idea that social influence—one person affecting another—is at the heart of therapy. Having noted in Chapter 5 the therapeutic value of changing maladaptive behaviors and attributions, let's look now at verbal persuasion. Strong (1991) offers a prototypical example: A thirtyish woman comes to a therapist complaining of depression. The therapist gently probes her feelings and her situation. She explains her helplessness and her husband's demands. Although admiring her devotion, the therapist helps her see how she takes responsibility for his problems. She protests. But the therapist persists. In time, she grants that her husband may not be as fragile as she presumed. She begins to see how she can respect both her husband and herself. With the therapist, she plans strategies for each new week. At the end of a long stream of reciprocal influences between therapist and client, she emerges no longer depressed and with new ways of behaving.

Early analyses of psychotherapeutic influence focused on how therapists establish credible expertise and trustworthiness and how their credibility enhances their influence (Strong, 1968). More recent analyses have focused less on the therapist than on how the interaction affects the client's thinking (Cacioppo & others, 1991; McNeill & Stoltenberg, 1991; Neimeyer & others, 1991). Peripheral cues, such as therapist credibility, may open the door for ideas that the therapist can now get the client to think about. But the central route to persuasion provides the most enduring attitude and behavior change. Therapists should therefore aim not to elicit a client's superficial agreement with their expert judgment but to change the client's own thinking.

Fortunately, most clients entering therapy are motivated to take the central route, thinking deeply about their problems under the therapist's guidance. The therapist's task is to offer arguments and raise questions calculated to elicit favorable thoughts. The therapist's insights matter less than the thoughts they evoke in the client. The therapist needs to put things in ways that a client can hear and understand, that will prompt agreement rather than counterargument, and that allow time and space for the client to reflect. Questions, such as, "How do you respond to what I just said?" can stimulate the client's thinking.

Martin Heesacker (1989) illustrates with the case of Dave, a 35-year-old male graduate student. Having seen what Dave denied—an underlying substance abuse problem—the counselor drew on his knowledge of Dave, an intellectual person who liked hard evidence, in persuading him to accept the diagnosis and join a treatment-support group. The counselor said, "OK, if my diagnosis is wrong, I'll be glad to change it. But let's go through a list of the characteristics of a substance abuser to check out my accuracy." The counselor then went through each criterion slowly, giving Dave time to think about each point. As he finished, Dave sat back and exclaimed, "I don't believe it: I'm a damned alcoholic."

In an experiment, John Ernst and Heesacker (1993) showed the effectiveness of escorting participants in an assertion training workshop through the central route to persuasion. Some participants experienced the typical assertiveness workshop by learning and rehearsing concepts of assertiveness. Others learned the same concepts but also volunteered a time when they hurt themselves by being unassertive. Then they heard arguments that Ernst and Heesacker knew were likely to trigger favorable thoughts (for example, "By failing to assert yourself, you train others to mistreat you"). At the workshop's end, Ernst and Heesacker asked the people to stop and reflect on how they now felt about all they had learned. Compared to those in the first group, those who went through the thought-evoking workshop left the experience with more favorable attitudes and intentions regarding assertiveness. Moreover, their roommates noticed greater assertiveness during the ensuing two weeks.

In his 1620 *Pensées*, the philosopher Pascal foresaw this principle: "People are usually more convinced by reasons they discover themselves than by those found by others." It's a principle worth remembering in our own lives.

SUMMING UP

The successes of religious cults provide an opportunity to see powerful persuasion processes at work. It appears that their success has resulted partly by their eliciting behavior commitments (as described in Chapter 4), by applying principles of effective persuasion (this chapter), and by isolating members in like-minded groups (to be discussed in Chapter 9).

Mental health workers also are recognizing that changing clients' attitudes and behaviors requires persuasion. Therapists, aided by their image as expert, trustworthy communicators, aim to stimulate healthier thinking by offering cogent arguments and raising questions.

■ RESISTING PERSUASION: ATTITUDE INOCULATION

Having perused the "weapons of influence," we consider, finally, some tactics for resisting influence.

This consideration of persuasive influences has perhaps made you wonder if it is possible to *resist* unwanted persuasion. Daniel Gilbert and his colleagues (1990, 1993) report that 'tis easier to accept persuasive messages than to doubt them. To *understand* an assertion (say, that lead pencils are a health hazard) is to *believe* it—at least temporarily, until one actively undoes the initial, automatic acceptance. If a distracting event prevents the undoing, the acceptance lingers.

Still, blessed with logic, information, and motivation, we do resist falsehoods. If, because of an aura of credibility, the repairperson's uniform and doctor's title have intimidated us into unquestioning agreement, we can rethink our habitual responses to authority. We can seek more information before committing time or money. We can question what we don't understand.

STRENGTHENING PERSONAL COMMITMENT

Chapter 7 presented another way to resist: Before encountering others' judgments, make a public commitment to your position. Having stood up for your convictions, you will become less susceptible (or should we say less "open"?) to what others have to say. In mock civil trials, straw polls of jurors can foster a hardening of expressed positions, leading to more deadlocks (Davis & others, 1993).

Challenging Beliefs

How might we stimulate people to commit themselves? From his experiments, Charles Kiesler (1971) offers one possible way: Mildly attack their position. Kiesler found that when committed people were attacked strongly enough to cause them to react, but not so strongly as to overwhelm them, they became even more committed. Kiesler explains:

> When you attack a committed person and your attack is of inadequate strength, you drive him to even more extreme behaviors in defense of his previous commitment. His commitment escalates, in a sense, because the number of acts consistent with his belief increases. (p. 88)

Perhaps you can recall a time when this happened in an argument, as those involved escalated their rhetoric, committing themselves to increasingly extreme positions.

Developing Counterarguments

There is a second reason a mild attack might build resistance. Like inoculations against disease, weak arguments prompt counterarguments, which are then available for a stronger attack. William McGuire (1964) documented this in a series of experiments. McGuire wondered: Could we inoculate people against persuasion much as we inoculate them against a virus? Is there such a thing as **attitude inoculation**? Could we take people raised in a "germ-free ideological environment"—people who hold some unquestioned belief—and stimulate their mental defenses? And would subjecting them to a small dose of belief-threatening material inoculate them against later persuasion?

That is what McGuire did. First, he found some cultural truisms, such as, "It's a good idea to brush your teeth after every meal if at all possible." He then showed that people were vulnerable to a massive, credible assault upon these truisms (for example, prestigious authorities were said to have discovered that too much toothbrushing can damage one's gums). If, however, before having their belief attacked, they were "immunized" by first receiving a small challenge to their belief, *and* if they read or wrote an essay in refutation of this mild attack, then they were better able to resist the powerful attack.

CASE STUDIES: LARGE-SCALE INOCULATION PROGRAMS

Inoculating Children against Peer Pressure to Smoke

In a clear demonstration of how laboratory research findings can lead to practical application, a research team led by Alfred McAlister (1980) had high school students "inoculate" seventh graders against peer pressures to smoke. The seventh graders were taught to respond to advertisements implying that liberated women smoke by saying, "She's not really liberated if she is hooked on tobacco." They also acted in role plays in which, after being called "chicken" for not taking a cigarette, they answered with statements like, "I'd be a real chicken if I smoked just to impress you." After several such sessions during the seventh and eighth grades, the inoculated students were half as likely to begin smoking as uninoculated students at another junior high school that had an identical parental smoking rate (Figure 8–11).

Other research teams have confirmed that such inoculation procedures can indeed greatly reduce the teenage smoking rate (Evans & others, 1984; Flay & others, 1985). Most newer efforts emphasize strategies for resisting social pressure. One study exposed sixth to eighth graders to antismoking films or to information about smoking, together with role plays of student-generated ways of refusing a cigarette (Hirschman & Leventhal, 1989). A year and a half later 31 percent of those who watched the antismoking films had taken up smoking. Among those who role-played refusing, only 19 percent had done so. Another study involved the entire seventh-grade class in a diverse sample of 30 junior high schools. It warned students about pressures to smoke and use drugs and offered them strategies for resisting (Ellickson & Bell, 1990). Among nonusers of marijuana, the training curbed initiation by a third; among users, it reduced usage by half.

Antismoking and drug education programs apply other persuasion principles, too. They use attractive peers to communicate information. They trigger

---

Attitude inoculation: Exposing people to weak attacks upon their attitudes so that when stronger attacks come, they will have refutations available.

"The SLA . . . read me news items they clipped from the newspapers almost every day. Some of their stories were indisputable, sometimes I did not know what to believe. It was all very confusing. I realized that my life prior to my kidnapping had indeed been very sheltered; I had taken little or no interest in foreign affairs, politics, or economics."
Patricia Campbell Hearst, *Every Secret Thing*, 1982

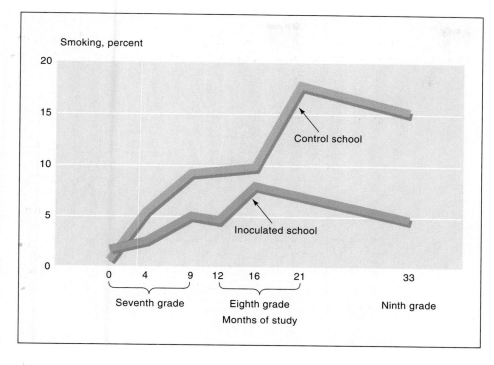

Smoking, percent

Seventh grade
Eighth grade
Ninth grade
Months of study

Control school

Inoculated school

■ FIGURE 8–11
The percentage of cigarette smokers at an "inoculated" junior high school was much less than at a matched control school using a more typical smoking education program.
(Data from McAlister & others, 1980; Telch & others, 1981.)

the students' own cognitive processing ("Here's something you might want to think about"). They get the students to make a public commitment (by making a rational decision about smoking and then announcing it, along with their reasoning, to their classmates). Some of these smoking-prevention programs require only two to six 1-hour class sessions, using prepared printed materials or videotapes. Today any school district or teacher wishing to use the social-psychological approach to smoking prevention can do so easily, inexpensively, and with the hope of significant reductions in future smoking rates and associated health costs.

Inoculating Children against the Influence of Advertising

Researchers have also studied how to immunize young children so they can more effectively analyze and evaluate television commercials. This research was prompted partly by studies showing that children, especially those under 8 years, (1) have trouble distinguishing commercials from programs and fail to grasp their persuasive intent, (2) trust television advertising rather indiscriminately, and (3) desire and badger their parents for advertised products (Adler & others, 1980; Feshbach, 1980; Palmer & Dorr, 1980). Children, it seems, are an advertiser's dream: gullible, vulnerable, an easy sell. Moreover, half the 20,000 ads the typical child sees in a year are for low-nutrition, often sugary foods.

Armed with such data, citizen's groups have given the advertisers of such products a chewing out (Moody, 1980): "When a sophisticated advertiser spends millions to sell unsophisticated, trusting children an unhealthy product, this can only be called exploitation. No wonder the consumption of dairy products has declined since the start of television, while soft-drink consump-

A debated question: What is the cumulative effect on children's materialism of watching some 350,000 commercials during their growing-up years?

Children are the advertiser's dream. Researchers have therefore studied ways to inoculate children against the 20,000 or so ads they see each year, many as they are glued to a TV set.

tion has almost doubled." On the other side are the commercial interests, who claim that such ads allow parents to teach their children consumer skills and, more important, finance children's television programs. In the United States, the Federal Trade Commission has been in the middle, pushed by research findings and political pressures while trying to decide whether to place new constraints on TV ads aimed at young children.

Meanwhile, researchers have wondered whether children can be taught to resist deceptive ads. In one such effort, a team of investigators led by Norma Feshbach (1980; Cohen, 1980) gave small groups of Los Angeles–area elementary school children three half-hour lessons in analyzing commercials. The children were inoculated by viewing ads and discussing them. For example, after viewing a toy ad, they were immediately given the toy and challenged to make it do what they had just seen in the commercial. Such experiences helped breed a more realistic understanding of commercials.

IMPLICATIONS

Inoculation research also has some provocative implications. The best way to build resistance to brainwashing may not be, as some U.S. senators thought after the Korean war, to have more courses on patriotism. William McGuire advised that teachers use inoculation techniques: Challenge the concepts and principles of democracy and explain alternatives such as communism and constitutional monarchy, and so help students to develop defenses.

For the same reason, religious educators should be wary of creating a "germ-free ideological environment" in their churches and schools. An attack, if refuted, is more likely to solidify one's position than to undermine it, particularly if the threatening material can be examined with like-minded others. Cults apply this principle by forewarning members of how families and friends will attack the cult's beliefs. When the expected challenge comes, the member is armed with counterarguments.

Another implication is that, for the persuader, an ineffective appeal can be worse than none. Can you see why? Those who reject an appeal are inoculated against further appeals. Consider an experiment in which Susan Darley and Joel Cooper (1972) invited students to write essays advocating a strict dress code. Because this was against the students' own positions and the essays were to be published, all chose *not* to write the essay—even those offered money to do so. After turning down the money, they became even more extreme and confident in their anti-dress-code opinions. Having made an overt decision against the dress code, they became even more resistant to it. Those who have rejected initial appeals to quit smoking may likewise become immune to further appeals. Thus, ineffective persuasion, by stimulating the listener's defenses, may be counterproductive. Rebuffed appeals "harden the heart" against later appeals.

Inoculation research has a personal implication, too. Do you want to build your resistance to persuasion without becoming closed to valid messages? Be an active listener and a critical thinker. Force yourself to counterargue. After hearing a political speech, discuss it with others. In other words, don't just listen; react. If the message cannot withstand careful analysis, so much the worse for it. If it can, its effect on you will be the more enduring.

H ow do people resist persuasion? A prior public commitment to one's own position, stimulated perhaps by a mild attack on the position, breeds resistance to later persuasion. A mild attack can also serve as an inoculation, stimulating one to develop counterarguments that will then be available if and when a strong attack comes. This implies, paradoxically, that one way to strengthen existing attitudes is to challenge them, though the challenge must not be so strong as to overwhelm them.

SUMMING UP

BEHIND THE SCENES

I confess to having felt like Mr. Clean when doing this immunization work because I was studying how to help people resist being manipulated. Then, after our research was published, an advertising executive called and said, "Very interesting, Professor: I was delighted to read about it." Somewhat righteously, I replied, "Very nice of you to say that, Mr. Executive, but I'm really on the other side. You're trying to persuade people, and I'm trying to make them more resistant." "Oh, don't underrate yourself, Professor," he said. "We can use what you're doing to diminish the effect of our competitors' ads." And sure enough, it has become almost standard for advertisers to mention other brands and deflate their claims.

WILLIAM MCGUIRE, *Yale University*

■ FOR FURTHER READING

Cialdini, R. B. (1993). *Influence: Science and practice* (3d. ed.). Glenview, IL: Scott, Foresman. An entertaining and informative description of how and why people agree to things. Cialdini explains how skillful car salespeople, Tupperware dealers, realtors, and cult recruiters exploit the "weapons of influence."

Eagly, A. H., & Chaiken, S. (1992). *The psychology of attitudes.* San Diego: Harcourt Brace Jovanovich. A comprehensive summary of what we've learned from a half-century of research and theorizing on attitudes and how they change.

Perloff, R. M. (1993). *The dynamics of persuasion.* Hillsdale, NJ: Erlbaum. An easy-to-read manual of the roots and fruits of persuasion. Offers many practical examples of the application of persuasion principles in contexts ranging from cult indoctrination to public information campaigns.

Pratkanis, A. R., & Aronson, E. (1992). *Age of propaganda: The everyday use and abuse of persuasion.* New York: Freeman. Two social psychologists explain how persuasion principles can be used (for example, to promote environmentally conscious behaviors) and abused (to exploit gullible people).

Zimbardo, P. G., & Leippe, M. R. (1991). *The psychology of attitude change and social influence.* New York: McGraw-Hill. A basic and skillful introduction to the study of persuasion and behavior change.

GROUP INFLUENCE

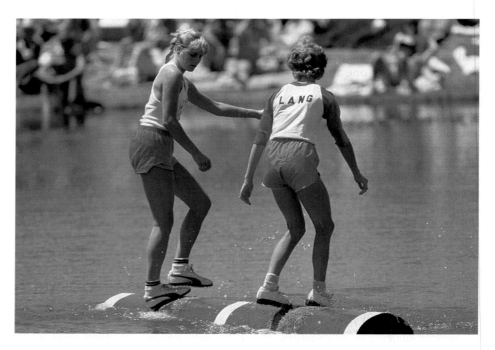

Social facilitation: Two contestants in the world championship timber carnival for loggers. The motivating presence of a co-actor or audience strengthens well-learned responses.

Saying that the presence of others sometimes facilitates performance and sometimes hinders it is about as satisfying as a weather forecast predicting that it might be sunny but then again it might rain. By 1940, research activity in this area had ground to a halt. It lay dormant for 25 years until awakened by the touch of a new idea.

Social psychologist Robert Zajonc (pronounced *Zy-ence*, rhymes with *science*) wondered whether these seemingly contradictory findings could be reconciled. As often happens at creative moments in science, Zajonc (1965) used one field of research to illuminate another. In this case the illumination came from a well-established principle in experimental psychology: Arousal enhances whatever response tendency is dominant. Increased arousal enhances performance on easy tasks for which the most likely—"dominant"—response is the correct one. People solve easy anagrams, such as *akec*, fastest when they are anxious. On complex tasks, for which the correct answer is not dominant, increased arousal promotes *incorrect* responding. On harder anagrams people do worse when anxious.

Could this principle solve the mystery of social facilitation? It seemed reasonable to assume that others' presence will arouse or energize people. (Most of us can recall feeling more tense or excited before an audience.) If social arousal facilitates dominant responses, it should boost performance on easy tasks and hurt performance on difficult tasks. Now the confusing results made sense. Winding fishing reels, doing simple multiplication problems, and eating were all easy tasks for which the responses were well learned or naturally dominant. And sure enough, having others around boosted performance. On the other hand, learning new material, doing a maze, and solving complex math problems were more difficult tasks for which the correct responses were initially less probable. And sure enough, the presence of others increased the number of *incorrect* responses on these tasks. The same general rule—*arousal*

"Mere social contact begets . . . a stimulation of the animal spirits that heightens the efficiency of each individual workman."
Karl Marx, *Das Kapital*, 1867

facilitates dominant responses—worked in both cases. Suddenly, what had looked like contradictory results no longer seemed contradictory.

Zajonc's solution, so simple and elegant, left other social psychologists thinking what Thomas H. Huxley thought after first reading Darwin's *Origin of the Species:* "How extremely stupid not to have thought of that!" It seemed obvious—once Zajonc had pointed it out. Perhaps, however, the pieces appeared to merge so neatly only because we viewed them through the spectacles of hindsight. Would the solution survive direct experimental tests?

After almost 300 studies conducted with the help of more than 25,000 volunteer subjects, it has survived (Bond & Titus, 1983; Guerin, 1993). Several experiments in which Zajonc and his associates manufactured an arbitrary dominant response confirmed that an audience enhanced this response. In one, Zajonc and Stephen Sales (1966) asked people to pronounce various nonsense words between 1 and 16 times. Then they told the people that the same words would appear on a screen, one at a time. Each time, they were to guess which had appeared. When the people were actually shown only random black lines for a hundredth of a second, they "saw" mostly the words they had pronounced most frequently. These words had become the dominant responses. People who took the same test in the presence of two others were even more likely to guess the dominant words (Figure 9–1).

In various ways, later experiments confirmed that social arousal facilitates dominant responses, whether right or wrong. Peter Hunt and Joseph Hillery (1973) found that in the presence of others, University of Akron students took less time to learn a simple maze and more time to learn a complex one (just as the cockroaches do). And James Michaels and his collaborators (1982) found that good pool players in the Virginia Polytechnic Institute student union (who had made 71 percent of their shots while being unobtrusively observed) did even better (80 percent) when four observers came up to watch them play. Poor

"Discovery consists of seeing what everybody has seen and thinking what nobody has thought."
Albert Axent-Gyorgyi,
The Scientist Speculates

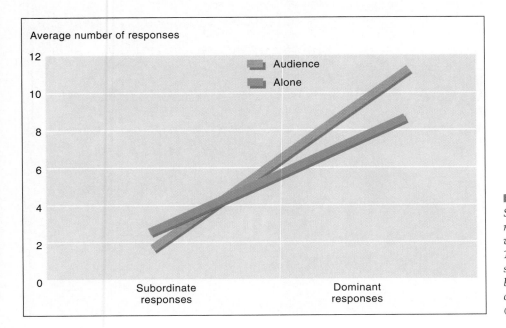

■ **FIGURE 9–1**
Social facilitation of dominant responses. People responded with dominant words (practiced 16 times) more frequently, and subordinate words (practiced but once) less frequently, when observers were present.
(Data from Zajonc & Sales, 1966.)

TABLE 9–1 *Home Advantage in Major Team Sports*

SPORT	GAMES STUDIED	HOME TEAM WINNING PERCENTAGE
Baseball	135,665	54.3%
Football	2,592	57.3
Ice hockey	4,322	61.1
Basketball	13,596	64.4
Soccer	37,202	69.0

Data from Courneya & Carron (1992), except for major league baseball, 1900 to 1992, from Schlenker & others, 1995.

shooters (who had previously averaged 36 percent) did even worse (25 percent) when closely observed.

Athletes perform well-practiced skills, which helps explain why they often perform best when energized by the responses of a supportive crowd. Studies of more than 80,000 college and professional athletic events in Canada, the United States, and England reveal that home teams win about 6 in 10 games (somewhat fewer for baseball and football, somewhat more for basketball and soccer—see Table 9–1). The home advantage may, however, also stem from the players' familiarity with their home environment, less travel fatigue, feelings of dominance derived from territorial control, or increased team identity when cheered by fans (Zillmann & Paulus, 1993).

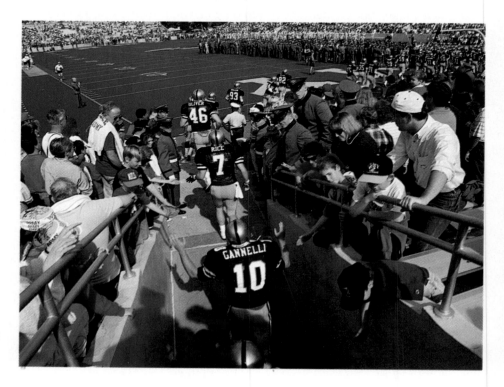

The Army football team entering the stadium at West Point. A supportive home crowd helps create a home advantage in every sport studied.

CROWDING: THE PRESENCE OF MANY OTHERS

So, people do respond to the presence of others. But does the presence of observers really arouse people? In times of stress, a comrade can be comforting. Nevertheless, researchers have found that with others present, people perspire more, breathe faster, tense their muscles more, and have higher blood pressure and a faster heart rate (Geen & Gange, 1983; Moore & Baron, 1983).

The effect of other people increases with their number (Jackson & Latane, 1981; Knowles, 1983). Sometimes the arousal and self-conscious attention created by a large audience interferes even with well-learned, automatic behaviors, such as speaking. Given extreme pressure, we're vulnerable to choking. Stutterers tend to stutter more in front of larger audiences than when speaking to just one or two people (Mullen, 1986). College basketball players become slightly *less* accurate in their free-throw shooting when highly aroused by a packed fieldhouse (Sokoll & Mynatt, 1984).

Being *in* a crowd also intensifies positive or negative reactions. When they sit close together, friendly people are liked even more, and *un*friendly people are *dis*liked even more (Schiffenbauer & Schiavo, 1976; Storms & Thomas, 1977). In experiments with Columbia University students and with Ontario Science Center visitors, Jonathan Freedman and his co-workers (1979, 1980) had an accomplice listen to a humorous tape or watch a movie with other subjects. When all sat close together, the accomplice could more readily induce them to laugh and clap. As theater directors and sports fans know, and as researchers have confirmed (Aiello & others, 1983; Worchel & Brown, 1984), a "good house" is a full house.

Perhaps you've noticed that a class of 35 students feels more warm and lively in a room that seats just 35 than when spread around a room that seats 100. This occurs partly because when others are close by, we are more likely to notice and join in their laughter or clapping. But crowding also enhances arousal, as Gary Evans (1979) found. He tested 10-person groups of University of Massachusetts students, either in a room 20 by 30 feet or in one 8 by 12 feet. Compared to those in the large room, those densely packed had higher pulse rates and blood pressure (indicating arousal). Though their performance on simple tasks did not suffer, on difficult tasks they made more errors. In a study of university students in India, Dinesh Nagar and Janak Pandey (1987) similarly found that crowding hampered performance only on complex tasks, such as solving difficult anagrams. So, crowding enhances arousal, which facilitates dominant responses.

WHY ARE WE AROUSED IN THE PRESENCE OF OTHERS?

To this point we have seen that what you do well, you will be energized to do best in front of others (unless you become hyperaroused and self-conscious). What you find difficult may seem impossible in the same circumstances. What is it about other people that causes arousal? Is it their mere presence? There is evidence to support three possible factors.

Evaluation Apprehension

Nickolas Cottrell surmised that observers make us apprehensive because we wonder how they are evaluating us. To test whether **evaluation apprehension**

Evaluation apprehension: Concern for how others are evaluating us.

exists, Cottrell and his associates (1968) repeated Zajonc and Sales' nonsense-syllable study at Kent State University and added a third condition. In this "mere presence" condition they blindfolded observers, supposedly in preparation for a perception experiment. In contrast to the effect of the watching audience, the mere presence of these blindfolded people did *not* boost well-practiced responses. Other experiments confirmed Cottrell's conclusion: The enhancement of dominant responses is strongest when people think they are being evaluated. In one experiment, joggers on a University of California at Santa Barbara jogging path sped up as they came upon a woman seated on the grass—*if* she was facing them rather than sitting with her back turned (Worringham & Messick, 1983).

Evaluation apprehension also helps explain:

■ Why people perform best when their coactor is slightly superior (Seta, 1982)
■ Why arousal lessens when a high-status group is diluted by adding people whose opinions don't matter to us (Seta & Seta, 1992)
■ Why people who worry most about others' evaluations are the ones most affected by their presence (Gastorf & others, 1980; Geen & Gange, 1983)
■ Why social-facilitation effects are greatest when the others are unfamiliar and hard to keep an eye on (Guerin & Innes, 1982)

The self-consciousness we feel when being evaluated can also interfere with behaviors that we perform best automatically (Mullen & Baumeister, 1987). If self-conscious basketball players analyze their body movements while shooting critical free throws, they are more likely to miss.

Driven by Distraction

Glenn Sanders, Robert Baron, and Danny Moore (1978; Baron, 1986) carried evaluation apprehension a step further. They theorized that when people wonder how coactors are doing or how an audience is reacting, they get distracted. This *conflict* between paying attention to others and paying attention to the task overloads the cognitive system, causing arousal. Evidence that people are indeed "driven by distraction" comes from experiments that produce social facilitation not just by the presence of another person but even by a nonhuman distraction, such as bursts of light (Sanders, 1981a, 1981b).

Mere Presence

Zajonc, however, believes that the mere presence of others produces some arousal even without evaluation apprehension or distraction. For example, people's color preferences are stronger when they make judgments with others present (Goldman, 1967). On such a task, there is no "good" or "right" answer for others to evaluate and thus no reason to be concerned with their reactions.

That response facilitation effects also occur with animals, which probably are not consciously worrying about how other animals are evaluating them, hints at an innate social arousal mechanism common to much of the zoological world. At the human level, most joggers feel energized when jogging with someone else, even one who neither competes nor evaluates.

This is a good time to remind ourselves of the purpose of a theory. As we noted in Chapter 1, a good theory is a scientific shorthand: It simplifies and

■ FIGURE 9–2
In the "open-office plan" people work in the presence of others. How might this affect worker efficiency?
(Photo courtesy of Herman Miller Inc.)

summarizes a variety of observations. Social-facilitation theory does this well. It is a simple summary of many research findings. A good theory also offers clear predictions that (1) help confirm or modify the theory, (2) guide new exploration, and (3) suggest practical application. Social-facilitation theory has definitely generated the first two types of prediction: (1) The basics of the theory (that the presence of others is arousing and that this social arousal enhances dominant responses) have been confirmed, and (2) the theory has brought new life to a long dormant field of research. Does it also suggest (3) some practical applications?

Application is properly the last research phase. In their study of social facilitation, researchers have yet to work much on this. That gives us the opportunity to speculate on what some applications might be. As Figure 9–2 shows, many new office buildings are replacing private offices with large, open areas divided by low partitions. Might the resulting awareness of others' presence help energize the performance of well-learned tasks but disrupt creative thinking on complex tasks? Can you think of other possible applications?

S ocial psychology's most elementary issue concerns the mere presence of others. Some early experiments on this question found that performance improved with observers or coactors present. Others found that the presence of others can hurt one's performance. Robert Zajonc reconciled these findings by applying a well-known principle from experimental psychology: Arousal facilitates dominant responses. Because the presence of others is arousing, the presence of observers or coactors boosts performance on easy tasks (for which the correct response is dominant) and hinders performance on difficult tasks (for which incorrect responses are dominant).

But why are we aroused by others' presence? Experiments suggest that the arousal stems partly from "evaluation apprehension" and partly from a conflict between paying attention to others and concentrating on the task.

SUMMING UP

Other experiments, including some with animals, suggest that the presence of others can be somewhat arousing even when we are not evaluated or distracted.

■ SOCIAL LOAFING

In a team tug-of-war, will eight people on a side exert as much force as the sum of their best efforts in individual tugs of war? If not, why not? And what level of individual effort can we expect from members of work groups?

Social facilitation usually occurs when people work toward individual goals and when their efforts, whether winding fishing reels or solving math problems, can be individually evaluated. These situations parallel some everyday work situations, but not those where people cooperatively pool their efforts toward a *common* goal and where individuals are *not* accountable for their efforts. A team tug-of-war provides one such example. Organizational fund-raising—pooling candy sale proceeds to pay for the class trip—provides another. So does a class group project where all get the same grade. On such "additive tasks"—tasks where the group's achievement depends on the sum of the individual efforts—will team spirit boost productivity? Will bricklayers lay bricks faster when working as a team than when working alone? One way to attack such questions is with laboratory simulations.

MANY HANDS MAKE LIGHT WORK

Nearly a century ago, French engineer Max Ringelmann (reported by Kravitz & Martin, 1986) found that the collective effort of such teams was but half the sum of the individual efforts. Contrary to the common notion that "in unity there is strength," this suggests that group members may actually be *less* motivated when performing additive tasks. Maybe, though, poor performance stemmed from poor coordination—people pulling in slightly different directions at slightly different times. A group of Massachusetts researchers led by Alan Ingham (1974) cleverly eliminated this problem by making individuals think others were pulling with them, when in fact they were pulling alone. Blindfolded participants assigned the first position in the apparatus shown in Figure 9–3 and told to "pull as hard as you can" pulled 18 percent harder when they knew they were pulling alone than when they believed that behind them two to five people were also pulling.

At Ohio State University, researchers Bibb Latané, Kipling Williams, and Stephen Harkins (1979; Harkins & others, 1980) kept their ears open for other ways to investigate this phenomenon, which they labeled **social loafing**. They observed that the noise produced by six people shouting or clapping "as loud as you can" was less than three times that produced by one person alone. However, like the tug-of-war task, noisemaking is vulnerable to group inefficiency. So Latané and his associates followed Ingham's example by leading participants to believe others were shouting or clapping with them, when in fact they were doing so alone.

Social loafing:
The tendency for people to exert less effort when they pool their efforts toward a common goal than when they are individually accountable.

■ FIGURE 9–3
The rope-pulling apparatus. People in the first position pulled less hard when they thought people behind them were also pulling.
(Data from Ingham, Levinger, Graves, & Peckham, 1974. Photo by Alan G. Ingham.)

Their method was to blindfold six people, seat them in a semicircle, and have them put on headphones, over which they were blasted with the sound of people shouting or clapping. People could not hear their own shouting or clapping, much less that of others. On various trials they were instructed to shout or clap either alone or along with the group. People who were told about this experiment guessed the subjects would shout louder when with others, because they would be less embarrassed (Harkins, 1981). The actual result? Social loafing: When the participants believed five others were also either shouting or clapping, they produced one-third less noise than when they thought themselves alone. Social loafing occurred even when the subjects were high school cheerleaders who believed themselves to be cheering together or alone (Hardy & Latané, 1986).

Curiously, those who clapped both alone and in groups did not view themselves as loafing; they perceived themselves clapping equally in both situations. This parallels what happens when students work on group projects yielding a shared grade. Williams reports that all agree that loafing occurs—but no one admits to doing the loafing.

John Sweeney (1973), a political scientist interested in the policy implications of social loafing, obtained similar results in an experiment at the University of Texas. He found that students pumped exercise bicycles more energetically (as measured by electrical output) when they knew they were being individually monitored than when they thought their output was being pooled with that of other riders. In the group condition, people were tempted to **free-ride** on the group effort.

Free riders:
People who benefit from the group but give little in return.

In this and some 160 other studies (Karau & Williams, 1993, and Figure 9–4), we see a twist on one of the psychological forces that makes for social facilitation: evaluation apprehension. In the social loafing experiments, individuals believe they are evaluated only when they act alone. The group situation (rope pulling, shouting, and so forth) *decreases* evaluation apprehension.

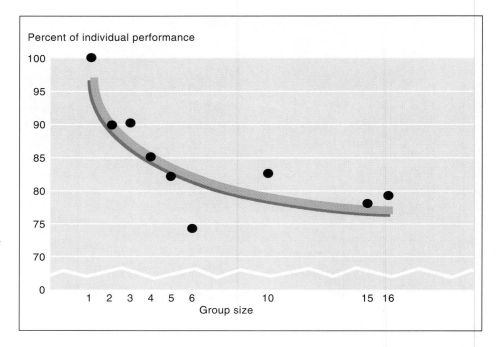

■ FIGURE 9–4

A statistical digest of 49 studies, involving more than 4000 participants, revealed that effort decreases (loafing increases) as the size of the group increases. Each dot represents the aggregate data from one of these studies.

(From Williams & others, 1992.)

When people are not accountable and cannot evaluate their own efforts, responsibility is diffused across all group members (Harkins & Jackson, 1985; Kerr & Bruun, 1981). By contrast, the social-facilitation experiments *increased* people's exposure to evaluation. When made the center of attention, people self-consciously monitor their behavior (Mullen & Baumeister, 1987). So the principle is the same: When being observed *increases* evaluation concerns, social facilitation occurs; when being lost in a crowd *decreases* evaluation concerns, social loafing occurs.

To motivate group members, one strategy is to make performance individually identifiable. Some football coaches do this by individually filming and evaluating each player. The Ohio State researchers had group members wear individual microphones while engaged in group shouting (Williams & others, 1981). Whether in a group or not, people exert more effort when their outputs are individually identifiable: University swim team members swim faster in intrasquad relay races when someone monitors and announces their individual times (Williams & others, 1989).

SOCIAL LOAFING IN EVERYDAY LIFE

How widespread is social loafing? In the laboratory, the phenomenon occurs not only among people who are pulling ropes, cycling, shouting, and clapping but also among those who are pumping water or air, evaluating poems or editorials, producing ideas, typing, and detecting signals. Do these results generalize to everyday worker productivity?

On their collective farms under communism, Russian peasants worked one field one day, another field the next, with little direct responsibility for any given plot. For their own use, they were given small private plots. In one analysis, the private plots occupied 1 percent of the agricultural land, yet produced 27 percent of the Soviet farm output (H. Smith, 1976). In Hungary, private plots accounted for only 13 percent of the farmland but produced one-third of the output (Spivak, 1979). In China, where farmers are now allowed to sell food grown in excess of that owed to the state, food production increased 8 percent each year after 1978—2 $1/2$ times the rate in the preceding 26 years (Church, 1986).

In North America, workers who do not pay dues or volunteer time to their union or professional association nevertheless are usually happy to accept its benefits. So, too, are public television viewers who don't respond to their station's fund drives. This hints at another possible explanation of social loafing. When rewards are divided equally, regardless of how much one contributes to the group, any individual gets more reward per unit of effort by free-riding on the group. So people may be motivated to slack off when their efforts are not individually monitored and rewarded.

In a pickle factory, for example, the key job is picking the right-size dill-pickle halves off the conveyor belt and stuffing them in jars. Unfortunately, workers are tempted to stuff any size pickle in, because their output is not identifiable (the jars go into a common hopper before reaching the quality-control section). Williams, Harkins, and Latané (1981) note that research on social loafing suggests "making individual production identifiable, and raises the question: 'How many pickles could a pickle packer pack if pickle packers were only paid for properly packed pickles?'"

But surely collective effort does not always lead to slacking off. Sometimes the goal is so compelling and maximum output from everyone is so essential that team spirit maintains or intensifies effort. In an Olympic crew race, will the individual rowers in an eight-person crew pull their oars with less effort than those in a one- or two-person crew?

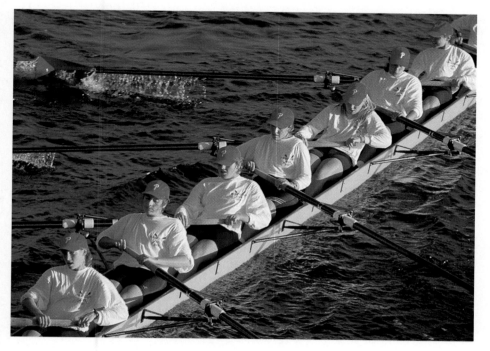

Teamwork at the Charles River regatta in Boston. Social loafing occurs when people work in groups but without individual accountability—except if the task is challenging, appealing, or involving and the group members are friends.

The evidence assures us they will not. People in groups loaf less when the task is *challenging, appealing,* or *involving* (Karau & Williams, 1993). On challenging tasks, people may perceive their efforts as indispensable (Harkins & Petty, 1982; Kerr, 1983; Kerr & Bruun, 1983). When people see others in their group as unreliable or as unable to contribute much, they work harder (Vancouver & others, 1991; Williams & Karau, 1991). Adding incentives or challenging a group to strive for certain standards also promotes collective effort (Harkins & Szymanski, 1989; Shepperd & Wright, 1989). So does intergroup competition (Erev & others, 1993).

Groups also loaf less when their members are *friends* rather than strangers (Davis & Greenlees, 1992). Latané notes that Israel's communal kibbutz farms have actually outproduced Israel's noncollective farms (Leon, 1969). Cohesiveness intensifies effort. So, will social loafing not occur in group-centered cultures? To find out, Latané and his co-researchers (Gabrenya & others, 1985) headed for Asia where they repeated their sound production experiments in Japan, Thailand, Taiwan, India, and Malaysia. Their findings? Social loafing was evident in all these countries, too. Sixteen later studies in Asia reveal that people in collectivist cultures exhibit less social loafing than do people in individualist cultures (Karau & Williams, 1993). As we noted in Chapter 6, loyalty to family and work groups runs strong in collectivist cultures. Likewise, women exhibit less social loafing than men (who, as Chapter 6 also explained, tend to be more individualistic).

Some of these findings parallel those from studies of everyday work groups. When groups are given challenging objectives, when they are rewarded for group success, and when there is a spirit of commitment to the "team," group members work hard (Hackman, 1986). So, while social loafing is a common occurrence when group members work collectively and without individual accountability, many hands need not always make light work.

SUMMING UP

Social-facilitation researchers study people's performance on tasks where they can be individually evaluated. However, in many work situations people pool their efforts and work toward a common goal without individual accountability. Studies show that group members often work less hard when performing such "additive tasks." This finding parallels everyday situations with diffused responsibility that tempts individual group members to free-ride on the group's effort.

■ DEINDIVIDUATION

In 1991 an eyewitness videotaped four Los Angeles police officers hitting unarmed Rodney King more than 50 times—fracturing his skull in nine places with their nightsticks and leaving him brain damaged and missing teeth—while 23 other officers watched passively. Replays of the tape shocked the nation into a prolonged discussion of police brutality and group violence. People wondered: Where was the officers' humanity? What had happened to standards of professional conduct? What evil force could provoke such behavior?

Rodney King's beating by Los Angeles police officers made people wonder: How do group situations release people from normal restraints?

DOING TOGETHER WHAT WE WOULD NOT DO ALONE

Social facilitation experiments show that groups can arouse people. Social loafing experiments show that groups can diffuse responsibility. When arousal and diffused responsibility combine, normal inhibitions may diminish. The result may be acts ranging from a mild lessening of restraint (throwing food in the dining hall, snarling at a referee, screaming during a rock concert) to impulsive self-gratification (group vandalism, orgies, thefts) to destructive social explosions (police brutality, riots, lynchings). In a 1967 incident, 200 University of Oklahoma students gathered to watch a disturbed fellow student threatening to jump from a tower. They began to chant "Jump. Jump. . . ." The student jumped to his death (UPI, 1967).

These unrestrained behaviors have something in common: They are somehow provoked by the power of a group. Groups can provoke a sense of excitement, of being caught up in something bigger than self. It is harder to imagine a single rock fan screaming deliriously at a private rock concert, a single Oklahoma student trying to coax someone to suicide, or even a single police officer beating a defenseless motorist. In certain kinds of group situations people are more likely to abandon normal restraints, to lose their sense of individual responsibility, to become what Leon Festinger, Albert Pepitone, and Theodore Newcomb (1952) labeled **deindividuated**. What circumstances elicit this psychological state?

Deindividuation:
Loss of self-awareness and evaluation apprehension; occurs in group situations that foster anonymity and draw attention away from the individual.

Group Size

A group has the power not only to arouse its members but also to render them unidentifiable. The snarling crowd hides the snarling basketball fan. A lynch mob enables its members to believe they will not be prosecuted; they perceive the action as the *group's*. Rioters, made faceless by the mob, are freed to loot. In an analysis of 21 instances in which crowds were present as someone threatened to jump from a building or bridge, Leon Mann (1981) found that when

"A mob is a society of bodies
voluntarily bereaving them-
selves of reason."
Ralph Waldo Emerson,
"Compensation," Essays,
First Series, 1841

the crowd was small and exposed by daylight, people usually did not try to bait the person. But when a large crowd or the cover of night gave people anonymity, the crowd usually baited and jeered. Brian Mullen (1986) reports a similar effect of lynch mobs: The bigger the mob, the more its members lose self-awareness and become willing to commit atrocities, such as burning, lacerating, or dismembering the victim. In each of these examples, from sports crowds to lynch mobs, evaluation apprehension plummets. And because "everyone is doing it," all can attribute their behavior to the situation rather than to their own choices.

Philip Zimbardo (1970) speculated that the mere immensity of crowded cities produces anonymity and thus norms that permit vandalism. He purchased two 10-year-old cars and left them with the hoods up and license plates removed, one on a street near the old Bronx campus of New York University and one near the Stanford University campus in Palo Alto, a much smaller city. In New York the first auto strippers arrived within 10 minutes, taking the battery and radiator. After three days and 23 incidents of theft and vandalism (by neatly dressed White people) the car was reduced to a battered, useless hulk of metal. By contrast, the only person observed to touch the Palo Alto car in over a week was a passer-by who lowered the hood when it began to rain.

Physical Anonymity

How can we be sure that the crucial difference between the Bronx and Palo Alto is greater anonymity in the Bronx? We can't. But we can experiment with anonymity to see if it actually lessens inhibitions. In one creative experiment, Zimbardo (1970) dressed New York University women in identical white coats and hoods, rather like Ku Klux Klan members (Figure 9–5). Asked to deliver electric shocks to a woman, they pressed the shock button twice as long as did women who were visible and wearing large name tags.

A research team led by Ed Diener (1976) cleverly demonstrated the effect both of being in a group *and* of being physically anonymous. At Halloween, they observed 1352 Seattle children trick-or-treating. As the children, either alone or in groups, approached 1 of 27 homes scattered throughout the city, an experimenter greeted them warmly, invited them to "take *one* of the candies,"

■ FIGURE 9–5
*Anonymous women delivered
more shock to helpless victims
than did identifiable women.*

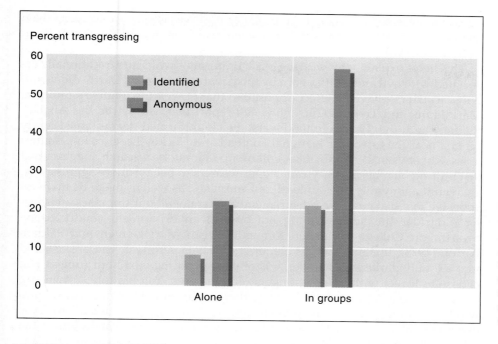

Percent transgressing

■ FIGURE 9–6
Children were more likely to transgress by taking extra Halloween candy when in a group, when anonymous, and, especially, when deindividuated by the combination of group immersion and anonymity.
(Data from Diener & others, 1976.)

and then left the room. Hidden observers noted that, compared to solo children, those in groups were more than twice as likely to take extra candy. Also, compared to children who had been asked their names and where they lived, those left anonymous were also more than twice as likely to transgress. The transgression rate thus varied dramatically with the situation. As Figure 9–6 shows, when group immersion was combined with anonymity, the deindividuated children usually stole extra candy.

These experiments make me wonder about the effect of wearing uniforms. Preparing for battle, warriors in some tribal cultures depersonalize themselves with body and face paints or special masks. After the battle, some cultures kill, torture, or mutilate any remaining enemies; other cultures take prisoners alive. Robert Watson (1973) scrutinized anthropological files and discovered that the cultures with depersonalized warriors were also the cultures that brutalized the enemy. The uniformed Los Angeles police officers who beat Rodney King were angered and aroused by his defiant refusal to stop his car, enjoying one another's camaraderie, and unaware that outsiders would view their actions. Thus, forgetting their normal standards, they were swept away by the situation.

Does becoming physically anonymous *always* unleash our worst impulses? Fortunately, no. For one thing, the situations in which some of these experiments took place had clear antisocial cues. Robert Johnson and Leslie Downing (1979) point out that the Klan-like outfits worn by Zimbardo's subjects may have encouraged hostility. In an experiment at the University of Georgia, they had women put on nurses' uniforms before deciding how much shock someone should receive. When those wearing the nurses' uniforms were made anonymous, they became *less* aggressive in administering shocks than when their names and personal identities were stressed. Evidently, being anonymous makes one less self-conscious and more responsive to cues present in the situaation, whether negative (Klan uniforms) or positive (nurses' uniforms). Given altruistic cues, deindividuated people even give more money (Spivey & Prentice-Dunn, 1990).

This helps explain why wearing black uniforms—which are traditionally associated with evil and death, worn by medieval executioners, Darth Vader, and Ninja warriors—have an effect opposite to that of wearing a nurse's uniform. Mark Frank and Thomas Gilovich (1988) report that, led by the Los Angeles Raiders and the Philadelphia Flyers, black-uniformed teams consistently ranked near the top of the National Football and Hockey Leagues in penalties assessed between 1970 and 1986. Follow-up laboratory research suggests that just putting on a black jersey can trigger wearers to behave more aggressively.

Even if anonymity does unleash our impulses, as well as make us more responsive to social cues, we must remember that not all our impulses are sinister. Consider the heartwarming outcome of an experiment conducted by Swarthmore College researchers Kenneth Gergen, Mary Gergen, and William Barton (1973). Imagine that, as a subject in this experiment, you are ushered into a totally darkened chamber, where you spend the next hour (unless you choose to leave) with seven strangers of both sexes. You are told, "There are no rules as to what you should do together. At the end of the time period you will be escorted from the room alone, and will subsequently depart from the experimental site alone. There will be no opportunity to [formally] meet the other participants."

Control participants, who spent the hour in a lighted room with more conventional expectations, chose simply to sit and talk. By contrast, the experience of being anonymous in the dark room with unclear expectations "unleashed" intimacy and affection. People in the dark talked less, but they talked more about "important" things. Ninety percent purposefully touched someone; 50 percent hugged another. Few disliked the anonymity; most deeply enjoyed it and volunteered to return without pay. Anonymity had "freed up" intimacy and playfulness.

Arousing and Distracting Activities

Aggressive outbursts by large groups are often preceded by minor actions that arouse and divert people's attention. Group shouting, chanting, clapping, or dancing serve both to hype people up and to reduce self-consciousness. One Moonie observer recalls how the "choo-choo" chant helped deindividuate:

> All the brothers and sisters joined hands and chanted with increasing intensity, choo-choo-choo, Choo-choo-choo, CHOO-CHOO-CHOO! YEA! YEA! POWW!!! The act made us a group, as though in some strange way we had all experienced something important together. The power of the choo-choo frightened me, but it made me feel more comfortable and there was something very relaxing about building up the energy and releasing it. (Zimbardo & others, 1977, p. 186)

Ed Diener's experiments (1976, 1979) have shown that such activities as throwing rocks and group singing can set the stage for more disinhibited behavior. There is a self-reinforcing pleasure in doing an impulsive act while observing others doing it also. When we see others act as we are acting, we think they feel as we do, and so feel reinforced in our own feelings (Orive, 1984). Moreover, impulsive group action absorbs our attention. When we yell at the referee, we are not thinking about our values; we are reacting to the immediate situation. Later, when we stop to think about what we have done or said,

"The use of self-control is like the use of brakes on a train. It is useful when you find yourself going in the wrong direction, but merely harmful when the direction is right."
Bertrand Russell, *Marriage and Morals*

we sometimes feel chagrined. Sometimes. At other times we seek deindividuating group experiences—dances, worship experiences, group encounters—where we can enjoy intense positive feelings and feel close to others.

DIMINISHED SELF-AWARENESS

Group experiences that diminish self-consciousness tend to disconnect behavior from attitudes. Experiments by Ed Diener (1980) and Steven Prentice-Dunn and Ronald Rogers (1980, 1989) reveal that unself-conscious, deindividuated people are less restrained, less self-regulated, more likely to act without thinking about their own values, more responsive to the situation. These findings complement and reinforce the experiments on *self-awareness* considered in Chapter 3.

Self-awareness is the other side of the coin from deindividuation. Those made self-aware, say by acting in front of a mirror or TV camera, exhibit *increased* self-control, and their actions more clearly reflect their attitudes. People made self-aware are less likely to cheat (Beaman & others, 1979; Diener & Wallbom, 1976). So are those who generally have a strong sense of themselves as distinct and independent (Nadler & others, 1982). People who are self-conscious, or who are temporarily made so, exhibit greater consistency between their words outside a situation and their deeds in it. They also become more thoughtful and therefore less vulnerable to appeals that run counter to their values (Hutton & Baumeister, 1992).

Circumstances that decrease self-awareness, as alcohol consumption does, therefore increase deindividuation (Hull & others, 1983). And deindividuation decreases in circumstances that increase self-awareness: mirrors and cameras, small towns, bright lights, large name tags, undistracted quiet, individual clothes and houses (Ickes & others, 1978). When a teenager leaves for a party, a parent's parting advice could well be: "Have fun, and remember who you are." In other words, enjoy being with the group, but be self-aware; don't become deindividuated.

> *"Attending a service in the Gothic cathedral, we have the sensation of being enclosed and steeped in an integral universe, and of losing a prickly sense of self in the community of worshippers."*
> Yi-Fu Tuan, 1982

When high levels of social arousal combine with diffused responsibility, people may abandon their normal restraints and lose their sense of individuality. Such "deindividuation" is especially likely when, after being aroused and distracted, people feel anonymity while in a large group or wearing concealing clothing or costumes. The result is diminished self-awareness and self-restraint and increased responsiveness to the immediate situation, be it negative or positive.

SUMMING UP

■ GROUP POLARIZATION

Many conflicts grow as people on both sides respond to a crisis by talk, mostly with like-minded others. Does such interaction amplify preexisting attitudes? If so, why?

Which effects—good or bad—does group interaction more often have? Police brutality and mob violence demonstrate its destructive potential. Yet support-group leaders, management consultants, and educational theorists proclaim its benefits. And social and religious movements and collectivist cultures urge their members to strengthen their identities by fellowship with like-minded others.

Research helps clarify our understanding of such effects. From studies of people in small groups, a principle emerges that helps explain both destructive and constructive outcomes: Group discussion often strengthens members' initial inclinations, good or bad. The unfolding of this research on "group polarization" illustrates the process of inquiry—how an interesting discovery often leads researchers to hasty and erroneous conclusions, which ultimately get replaced with more accurate conclusions. This is one scientific mystery I can discuss firsthand, having been one of the detectives.

THE CASE OF THE "RISKY SHIFT"

A research literature of more than 300 studies began with a surprising finding by James Stoner (1961), then an MIT graduate student. For his master's thesis in industrial management, Stoner compared risk taking by individuals and groups. To test the commonly held belief that groups are more cautious than individuals, Stoner posed decision dilemmas faced by fictional characters. The participant's task was to advise the character how much risk to take. Put yourself in the participant's shoes: What advice would you give the character in this situation?

> Helen is a writer who is said to have considerable creative talent but who so far has been earning a comfortable living by writing cheap westerns. Recently she has come up with an idea for a potentially significant novel. If it could be written and accepted, it might have considerable literary impact and be a big boost to her career. On the other hand, if she cannot work out her idea or if the novel is a flop, she will have expended considerable time and energy without remuneration.
>
> Imagine that you are advising Helen. Please check the *lowest* probability that you would consider acceptable for Helen to attempt to write the novel.
>
> Helen should attempt to write the novel if the chances that the novel will be a success are at least:
>
> ____ 1 in 10
>
> ____ 2 in 10
>
> ____ 3 in 10
>
> ____ 4 in 10
>
> ____ 5 in 10
>
> ____ 6 in 10
>
> ____ 7 in 10
>
> ____ 8 in 10
>
> ____ 9 in 10
>
> ____ 10 in 10 (Place a check here if you think Helen should attempt the novel only if it is certain that the novel will be a success.)

After making your decision, guess what this book's average reader would advise.

Having marked their advice on a dozen such items, five or so individuals would then discuss and reach agreement on each item. How do you think the group decisions compared to the average decision before the discussions? Would the groups be likely to take greater risks? be more cautious? stay the same?

To everyone's amazement, the group decisions were usually riskier. Dubbed the risky shift phenomenon, this finding set off a wave of investigation into group risk taking. The studies revealed that this effect occurs not only when a group decides by consensus; after a brief discussion, individuals, too, will alter their decisions. What is more, researchers successfully repeated Stoner's finding with people of varying ages and occupations in a dozen different nations.

During discussion opinions converged. Curiously, however, the point toward which they converged was usually a lower (riskier) number than their initial average. Here was a delightful puzzle. The small risky shift effect was reliable, unexpected, and without any immediately obvious explanation. What group influences produce such an effect? And how widespread is the effect? Do discussions in juries, business committees, and military organizations also promote risk taking?

After several years of study and speculation about group risk taking, we became aware that the risky shift was not universal. We could write decision dilemmas on which people became more *cautious* after discussion. One of these featured "Roger," a young married man with two school-age children and a secure but low-paying job. Roger can afford life's necessities but few of its luxuries. He hears that the stock of a relatively unknown company may soon triple in value if its new product is favorably received or decline considerably if it does not sell. Roger has no savings. To invest in the company, he is considering selling his life insurance policy.

Can you see a general principle that predicts both the tendency to give riskier advice after discussing Helen's situation and more cautious advice after discussing Roger's?

If you are like most people, you would advise Helen to take greater risk than Roger, even before talking with others. It turns out there is a strong tendency for discussion to accentuate these initial leanings.

We therefore began to realize that this group phenomenon was not, as originally assumed, a consistent shift to risk, but rather a tendency for group discussion to *enhance* the individuals' initial leanings. This idea led investigators to propose what Serge Moscovici and Marisa Zavalloni (1969) called a **group polarization** phenomenon: Discussion typically strengthens the average inclination of group members.

Group polarization: Group-produced enhancement of members' preexisting tendencies; a strengthening of the members' *average* tendency, not a split within the group.

DO GROUPS INTENSIFY OPINIONS?

Experiments on Group Polarization

This new view of the changes induced by group discussion prompted experimenters to have people discuss statements that most of them favored or most of them opposed. Would talking in groups enhance their initial inclinations as it did with the decision dilemmas? That's what the group polarization hypothesis predicts (Figure 9–7).

Dozens of studies confirm group polarization. Moscovici and Zavalloni (1969) observed that discussion enhanced French students' initially positive attitude toward their premier and negative attitude toward Americans. Mititoshi

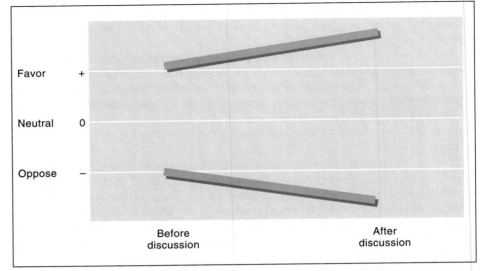

■ FIGURE 9–7

The group-polarization hypothesis predicts that discussion will strengthen an attitude shared by group members. If people initially tend to favor something (say, risk on a life dilemma question), they tend to favor it even more after discussion. If they tend to oppose something, they tend to oppose it even more after discussion.

Isozaki (1984) found that Japanese university students gave more pronounced judgments of "guilty" after discussing a traffic case. And Glen Whyte (1993) reports that groups exacerbate the "too much invested to quit" phenomenon that has cost many businesses huge sums of money. Canadian business students imagined themselves having to decide whether to invest more money in the hope of preventing losses in various failing projects (for example, whether to make a high-risk loan to protect an earlier investment). They exhibited the typical effect: 72 percent reinvested money they would seldom have invested if they were considering it as a new investment on its own merits. When making the same decision in groups, 94 percent opted for reinvestment.

Another research strategy has been to pick issues on which opinions are divided and then isolate people who hold the same view. Does discussion with like-minded people strengthen shared views? Does it magnify the attitude gap that separates the two sides?

George Bishop and I wondered. So we set up groups of relatively prejudiced and unprejudiced high school students and asked them to respond—before and after discussion—to issues involving racial attitudes, such as property rights versus open housing (Myers & Bishop, 1970). We found that the discussions among like-minded students did indeed increase the initial gap between the two groups (Figure 9–8). Such polarization helps explain another repeated finding: that groups compete more against one another, and cooperate less, than do individuals interacting with individuals (Schopler & others, 1991).

Naturally Occurring Group Polarization

In everyday life people associate mostly with others whose attitudes are similar to their own (Chapter 13). (Look at your own circle of friends.) So, does everyday group interaction with like-minded friends intensify shared attitudes? In natural situations it's hard to disentangle cause and effect. But the laboratory phenomenon does have real-life parallels.

One such parallel is what education researchers have called the "accentua-

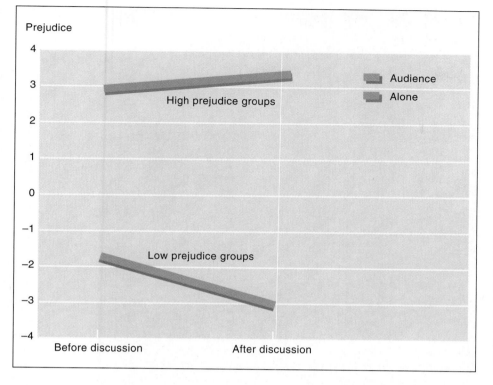

■ FIGURE 9–8
Discussion increased polarization between homogeneous groups of high- and low-prejudice high school students. Talking over racial issues increased prejudice in a high-prejudice group and decreased it in a low-prejudice group.
(Data from Myers & Bishop, 1970.)

tion phenomenon": Over time, initial differences among college-student groups become accentuated. If the students at college X are initially more intellectual than the students at college Y, that gap is likely to grow during college. Likewise, compared to fraternity and sorority members, independents tend to have more liberal political attitudes, a difference that grows with time in college (Pascarella & Terenzini, 1991). Researchers believe this results partly from group members reinforcing shared inclinations (Chickering & McCormick, 1973; Feldman & Newcomb, 1969; Wilson & others, 1975).

Polarization also occurs in communities. During community conflicts, like-minded people increasingly associate with one another. This amplifies their shared tendencies. Gang delinquency emerges from a process of mutual reinforcement within neighborhood gangs, whose members have a common socioeconomic and ethnic background (Cartwright, 1975). From their analysis of terrorist organizations around the world, Clark McCauley and Mary Segal (1987) note that terrorism does not erupt suddenly. Rather, it arises among people whose shared grievances bring them together. As they interact in isolation from moderating influences, they become progressively more extreme. The social amplifier brings the signal in stronger. The result is violent acts that the individuals, apart from the group, might never have contemplated.

In two trials, South African courts reduced sentences after learning how social-psychological phenomena, including deindividuation and group polarization, led crowd members to commit murderous acts (Colman, 1991). Would you agree that courts should consider social-psychological phenomena as possible extenuating circumstances when determining guilt and pronouncing sentence?

EXPLAINING POLARIZATION

Why do groups adopt stances that are more exaggerated than the average opinions of their individual members? Researchers hoped that solving the mystery

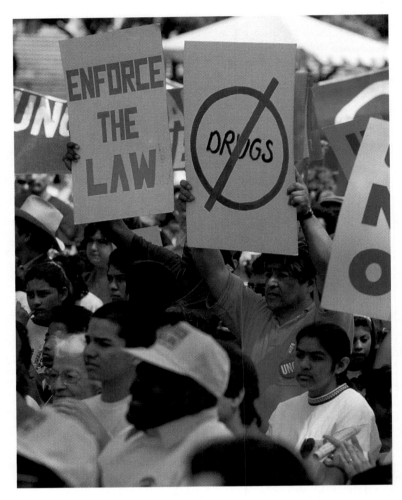

Group polarization: An anti-crime rally. Group interaction among like-minded people tends to strengthen their shared attitudes.

of group polarization might provide some insights. Solving small puzzles sometimes provides clues for solving larger ones.

Among several proposed theories of group polarization, two survived scientific scrutiny. One deals with the arguments presented during a discussion, the other with how members of a group view themselves vis-à-vis the other members. The first idea is an example of informational influence (influence that results from accepting evidence about reality). The second is an example of normative influence (influence based on a person's desire to be accepted or admired by others).

Informational Influence

According to the best-supported explanation, group discussion elicits a pooling of ideas, most of which favor the dominant viewpoint. Ideas that were common knowledge to group members will often be brought up in discussion or, even if unmentioned, will jointly influence their discussion (Gigone & Hastie, 1993; Larson & others, 1994; Stasser, 1991). Other ideas may include persuasive arguments that some group members had not previously consid-

FOCUS

GROUP POLARIZATION

Shakespeare portrayed the polarizing power of the like-minded group in this dialogue of Julius Caesar's followers:

ANTONY: Kind souls, what weep you when you but behold/Our Caesar's vesture wounded? Look you here./ Here is himself, marr'd, as you see, with traitors.

FIRST CITIZEN: O piteous spectacle!

SECOND CITIZEN: O noble Caesar!

THIRD CITIZEN: O woeful day!

FOURTH CITIZEN: O traitors, villains!

FIRST CITIZEN: O most bloody sight!

SECOND CITIZEN: We will be revenged!

ALL: Revenge! About! Seek! Burn! Fire! Kill! Slay! Let not a traitor live!

From *Julius Caesar* by William Shakespeare, Act III, Scene ii, lines 199–209.

---

ered. When discussing Helen the writer, someone may say, "Helen should go for it, because she has little to lose—if her novel flops, she can always go back to writing cheap westerns." Such statements often entangle information about the person's *arguments* with cues concerning the person's *position* on the issue. But when people hear relevant arguments without learning the specific stands other people assume, they still shift their positions (Burnstein & Vinokur, 1977; Hinsz & Davis, 1984). *Arguments*, in and of themselves, matter.

But there's more to attitude change than merely hearing someone else's arguments. *Active participation* in discussion produces more attitude change than passive listening. Participants and observers hear the same ideas, but when participants put them into their own words, the verbal commitment magnifies the impact. The more group members repeat one another's ideas, the more they rehearse and validate them (Brauer & others, 1995).

This illustrates a point made in Chapter 8: People's minds are not just blank tablets for persuaders to write on. In central route persuasion, what people *think* in response to a message is crucial. Indeed, just thinking about an issue for a couple of minutes can strengthen opinions (Tesser & others, 1995). (Perhaps you can recall your feelings becoming polarized as you merely thought about someone you disliked, or liked.) Even just *expecting* to discuss an issue with an equally expert person holding an opposing view can motivate people to marshal their arguments and thus to adopt a more extreme position (Fitzpatrick & Eagly, 1981).

Normative Influence

A second explanation of polarization involves comparison with others. As Leon Festinger (1954) argued in his influential theory of **social comparison**, it is human nature to want to evaluate our opinions and abilities, something we can do by comparing our views with others'. We are most persuaded by people in groups we identify with (Abrams & others, 1990; Hogg & others, 1990). Moreover, wanting people to like us, we may express stronger opinions after discovering that others share our views.

Perhaps you can recall a time when you and others were guarded and reserved in a group, until someone broke the ice and said, "Well, to be perfectly

Social comparison: Evaluating one's opinions and abilities by comparing oneself to others.

honest, I think . . ." Soon you were all surprised to discover strong support for your shared views. Sometimes when a professor asks if anyone has any questions, no one will respond, leading each student to infer that he or she is the only one confused. All believe that fear of embarrassment explains their own silence but that everyone else's silence means they understand the material.

Dale Miller and Cathy McFarland (1987) bottled this familiar phenomenon in a laboratory experiment. They asked people to read an incomprehensible article and to seek help if they ran into "any really serious problems in understanding the paper." Although none of the subjects sought help, they presumed *other* subjects would not be similarly restrained by fear of embarrassment. They wrongly inferred that people who didn't seek help didn't need any. To overcome such **pluralistic ignorance**, someone must break the ice and enable others to reveal and reinforce their shared reactions.

When we ask people (as I asked you earlier) to predict how others would respond to items such as the "Helen" dilemma, they typically exhibit pluralistic ignorance: They don't realize how much others support the socially preferred tendency (in this case, writing the novel). A typical person will advise writing the novel even if its chance of success is only 4 in 10, but estimate that most other people would require 5 or 6 in 10. When the discussion begins, most people discover they are not outshining the others as they had supposed. In fact, some others are ahead of them, having taken an even stronger position for writing the novel. No longer restrained by a misperceived group norm, they are liberated to voice their preferences more strongly.

This social comparison theory prompted experiments that exposed people to others' positions but not to their arguments. This is roughly the experience we have when reading the results of an opinion poll. When people learn others' positions—without discussion—will they adjust their responses to main-

Pluralistic ignorance:
A false impression of how other people are thinking, feeling, or responding.

This finding is reminiscent of the self-serving bias (Chapter 2): People tend to view themselves as better-than-average embodiments of socially desirable traits and attitudes.

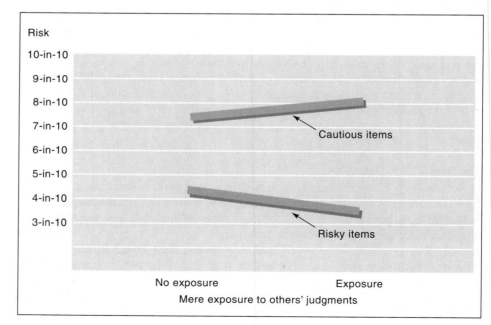

■ FIGURE 9–9
On "risky" dilemma items (such as the case of Helen), mere exposure to others' judgments enhanced individuals' risk-prone tendencies. On "cautious" dilemma items (such as the case of Roger), exposure to others' judgments enhanced their cautiousness.
(Data from Myers, 1978.)

tain a socially favorable position? When people have made no prior commitment to a particular response, seeing others' responses *does* stimulate a small polarization (Goethals & Zanna, 1979; Sanders & Baron, 1977). (See Figure 9–9 for an example.) This polarization from mere social comparison is usually less than that produced by a lively discussion. Still, it's surprising that, instead of simply conforming to the group average, people often go it one better. Are people "one-upping" the observed norm to differentiate themselves from the group? Is this another example of our need to feel unique (Chapter 7)?

Group polarization research illustrates the complexity of social-psychological inquiry. As much as we like our explanations to be simple, one explanation of a phenomenon seldom accounts for all the data. Because people are complex, more than one factor frequently influences a phenomenon. In group discussions, persuasive arguments predominate on issues that have a factual element ("Is she guilty of the crime?"). Social comparison sways responses on value-laden judgments ("How long a sentence should she serve?") (Kaplan, 1989). On the many issues that have both factual and value-laden aspects, the two factors work together. Discovering that others share one's feelings (social comparison) unleashes arguments (informational influence) supporting what everyone secretly favors.

Potentially positive and negative results arise from group discussion. While trying to understand the curious finding that group discussion enhanced risk taking, investigators discovered that discussion actually tends to strengthen whatever is the initially dominant point of view, whether risky or cautious. In everyday situations, too, group interaction tends to intensify opinions.

The group polarization phenomenon provided a window through which researchers could observe group influence. Experiments confirmed two group influences: informational and normative. The information gleaned from a discussion mostly favors the initially preferred alternative, thus reinforcing support for it. Moreover, people may go further out on the limb when, after comparing positions, they discover surprising support for their initial inclinations.

■ GROUPTHINK

When do group influences hinder smart decisions? When do groups promote good decisions, and how can we lead groups to make optimal decisions?

Do the social-psychological phenomena we have been considering in these first nine chapters occur in sophisticated groups like corporate boards or the president's cabinet? Is there likely to be self-justification? Self-serving bias? A cohesive "we feeling" provoking conformity and rejection of dissent? Public commitment producing resistance to change? Group polarization? Social psychologist Irvin Janis (1971, 1982a) wondered whether such phenomena might help explain good and bad group decisions made by recent American presidents and their advisers. To find out, he analyzed the decision-making procedures that led to several major fiascos:

Pearl Harbor   In the weeks preceding the December 1941 Pearl Harbor attack that put the United States into World War II, military commanders in Hawaii received a steady stream of information about Japan's preparations for an attack on the United States somewhere in the Pacific. Then military intelligence lost radio contact with Japanese aircraft carriers, which had begun moving straight for Hawaii. Air reconnaissance could have spotted the carriers or at least provided a few minutes' warning. But complacent commanders decided against such precautions. The result: No alert was sounded until the attack on a virtually defenseless base was under way, claiming 18 ships, 170 planes, and 3,700 lives.

The Bay of Pigs Invasion   In 1961 President John Kennedy and his advisers tried to overthrow Fidel Castro by invading Cuba with 1400 CIA-trained Cuban exiles. Nearly all the invaders were soon killed or captured, the United States was humiliated, and Cuba allied itself even closer to the U.S.S.R. After learning the outcome, Kennedy wondered aloud, "How could we have been so stupid?"

The Vietnam War   From 1964 to 1967 President Lyndon Johnson and his "Tuesday lunch group" of policy advisers escalated the war in Vietnam on the assumption that U.S. aerial bombardment, defoliation, and search-and-destroy missions would bring North Vietnam to the peace table with the appreciative support of the South Vietnamese populace. They continued the escalation despite warnings from government intelligence experts and nearly all U.S. allies. The resulting disaster cost 46,500 American and more than 1 million Vietnamese lives, drove the president from office, and created huge budget deficits that helped fuel inflation in the 1970s.

Janis believed these blunders were bred by the tendency of decision-making groups to suppress dissent in the interests of group harmony, a phenomenon he called **groupthink**. In work groups, camaraderie boosts productivity (Mullen & Copper, 1994). But when making decisions, close-knit groups may pay a price. Janis believed that the soil from which groupthink sprouts includes an amiable, *cohesive* group; relative *isolation* of the group from dissenting viewpoints; and a *directive leader* who signals what decision he or she favors. When planning the ill-fated Bay of Pigs invasion, the newly elected President Kennedy and his advisers enjoyed a strong esprit de corps. Arguments critical of the plan were suppressed or excluded, and the president himself soon endorsed the invasion.

Groupthink:
"The mode of thinking that persons engage in when concurrence-seeking becomes so dominant in a cohesive in-group that it tends to override realistic appraisal of alternative courses of action."
Irving Janis (1971)

SYMPTOMS OF GROUPTHINK

From historical records and the memoirs of participants and observers, Janis identified eight groupthink symptoms. These symptoms are a collective form of dissonance reduction that surface as group members try to maintain their positive group feeling when facing a threat (Turner & others, 1992, 1994). An ironic example was a threatened President Nixon and his advisers plotting the cover-up of the Watergate burglary of Democratic Party offices, even as Janis was plotting the completion of his theory of groupthink.

The first two groupthink symptoms lead group members to *overestimate their group's might and right*.

■ **An illusion of invulnerability:** The groups Janis studied all developed an excessive optimism that blinded them to warnings of danger. Told that his forces had lost radio contact with the Japanese carriers, Admiral Kimmel, the chief naval officer at Pearl Harbor, joked that maybe they were about to round Honolulu's Diamond Head. Their planes were, but Kimmel's laughing at the idea dismissed the very possibility of its being true.

■ **Unquestioned belief in the group's morality:** Group members assume the inherent morality of their group and ignore ethical and moral issues. The Kennedy group knew that adviser Arthur Schlesinger, Jr., and Senator J. William Fulbright had moral reservations about invading a small, neighboring country. But the group never entertained or discussed these moral qualms.

Group members also become *closed-minded:*

■ **Rationalization:** The groups discount challenges by collectively justifying their decisions. President Johnson's Tuesday lunch group spent far more time rationalizing (explaining and justifying) than reflecting upon and rethinking prior decisions to escalate. Each initiative became an action to defend and justify.

■ **Stereotyped view of opponent:** Participants in these groupthink tanks consider their enemies too evil to negotiate with or too weak and unintelligent to defend themselves against the planned initiative. The Kennedy group convinced itself that Castro's military was so weak and his popular support so shallow that a single brigade could easily overturn his regime.

Finally, the group suffers from *pressures toward uniformity:*

■ **Conformity pressure:** Group members rebuffed those who raised doubts about the group's assumption and plans, at times not by argument but by personal sarcasm. Once, when President Johnson's assistant Bill Moyers arrived at a meeting, the president derided him with, "Well, here comes Mr. Stop-the-Bombing." Most people fall into line when faced with such ridicule.

■ **Self-censorship:** Since disagreements were often uncomfortable and the groups seemed in consensus, members withheld or discounted their misgivings. In the months following the Bay of Pigs invasion, Arthur Schlesinger (1965, p. 255) reproached himself "for having kept so silent during those crucial discussions in the Cabinet Room, though my feelings of guilt were tempered by the knowledge that a course of objection would have accomplished little save to gain me a name as a nuisance."

■ **Illusion of unanimity:** Self-censorship and pressure not to puncture the consensus create an illusion of unanimity. What is more, the apparent consensus confirms the group's decision. This appearance of consensus was evident in these three fiascos and in other fiascos before and since. Albert Speer (1971), an adviser to Adolf Hitler, describes the atmosphere around Hitler as one where pressure to conform suppressed all deviation. The absence of dissent created an illusion of unanimity:

People "are never so likely to settle a question rightly as when they discuss it freely."
John Stuart Mill,
On Liberty, 1859

CONSISTENCY

More influential than a minority that wavers is a minority that sticks to its position. Moscovici and his associates (1969, 1985) have found that if a minority consistently judges blue slides as green, members of the majority will occasionally agree. But if the minority wavers, saying "blue" to one-third of the blue slides and "green" to the rest, virtually no one in the majority will ever agree with "green."

Still debated is the nature of this influence (Clark & Maass, 1990; Levine & Russo, 1987). Moscovici believes that a minority's following the majority usually reflects just public compliance, but a majority's following a minority usually reflects genuine acceptance—really recalling the blue slide as greenish. In public, people may wish not to align themselves with a deviant minority view (Wood & others, 1994). A majority can also give us a rule of thumb for deciding truth ("All those smart cookies can't be wrong"), while a minority influences us by making us think more deeply (Burnstein & Kitayama, 1989; Mackie, 1987). Minority influence is therefore more likely to take the thought-filled central route to persuasion (see Chapter 8).

Experiments show—and experience confirms—that nonconformity, especially persistent nonconformity, is often painful (Levine, 1989). If you set out to be Emerson's minority of one, prepare yourself for ridicule—especially when you argue an issue that's personally relevant to the majority and when the group is wanting to settle an issue by reaching consensus (Kameda & Sugimori, 1993; Kruglanski & Webster, 1991; Trost & others, 1992). People may attribute your dissent to psychological peculiarities, such as your presumed dogmatism (Papastamou & Mugny, 1990). When Charlan Nemeth (1979) planted a minority of two within a simulated jury and had them oppose the majority's opinions, the duo was inevitably disliked. Nevertheless, the majority acknowledged that the persistence of the two did more than anything else to make them rethink their positions.

In so doing, a minority may stimulate creative thinking (Mucchi-Faina & others, 1991; Peterson & Nemeth, in press). With dissent from within one's own group, people take in more information, think about it in new ways, and often make better decisions. Believing that one need not win friends to influence people, Nemeth quotes Oscar Wilde: "We dislike arguments of any kind; they are always vulgar, and often convincing."

A persistent minority is influential, even if not popular, partly because it soon becomes the focus of debate (Schachter, 1951). Being the center of conversation allows one to contribute a disproportionate number of arguments. And Nemeth reports that in experiments on minority influence, as in the studies dealing with group polarization, the position supported by the most arguments usually wins. Talkative group members are usually influential (Mullen & others, 1989).

SELF-CONFIDENCE

Consistency and persistence convey self-confidence. Furthermore, Nemeth and Joel Wachtler (1974) reported that any behavior by a minority that conveys self-confidence—for example, taking the head seat at the table—tends to raise self-doubts among the majority. By being firm and forceful, the minority's apparent self-assurance may prompt the majority to reconsider its position.

DEFECTIONS FROM THE MAJORITY

A persistent minority punctures any illusion of unanimity. When a minority consistently doubts the majority wisdom, members of the majority who might otherwise have self-censored their own doubts feel freer to express them and may even switch to the minority position. In research with University of Pittsburgh students, John Levine (1989) found that a minority person who had defected from the majority was more persuasive than a consistent minority voice. In her jury-simulation experiments, Nemeth found that once defections begin, others often soon follow, initiating a snowball effect.

Are these factors that strengthen minority influence unique to minorities? Sharon Wolf and Bibb Latané (1985; Wolf, 1987) and Russell Clark (1995) believe not. They argue that the same social forces work for both majorities and minorities. Informational and normative influence fuels both group polarization and minority influence. And if consistency, self-confidence, and defections from the other side strengthen the minority, such variables strengthen a majority also. The social impact of any position—whether held by a majority or a minority—depends on the strength, immediacy, and number of those who support it. Minorities have less influence than majorities simply because they are smaller.

However, Anne Maass and Russell Clark (1984, 1986) agree with Moscovici that minorities are more likely to convert people to *accepting* their views. Nemeth (1986) also believes that the stress of being in the minority differs from the majority's more relaxed reflection. And from their analyses of how groups evolve over time, John Levine and Richard Moreland (1985) conclude that new recruits to a group exert a different type of minority influence than do long-time members. Newcomers exert influence through the attention they receive and the group awareness they trigger in the old-timers. Established members feel freer to dissent and to exert leadership.

There is a delightful irony in this new emphasis on how individuals can influence the group. Until recently, the idea that the minority could sway the majority was itself a minority view in social psychology. Nevertheless, by arguing consistently and forcefully, Moscovici, Nemeth, and others have convinced the majority of group influence researchers that minority influence is a phenomenon worthy of study.

IS LEADERSHIP MINORITY INFLUENCE?

One example of the power of individuals is **leadership,** the process by which certain individuals mobilize and guide groups. Leadership matters, note Robert Hogan and associates (1994). In 1910, the Norwegians and English engaged in an epic race to the South Pole. The Norwegians, effectively led by Roald Amundsen, made it. The English, ineptly led by Robert Falcon Scott, did not; Scott and three team members died. Abraham Lincoln's Civil War army was going nowhere until Lincoln appointed Ulysses S. Grant as its leader. Some coaches move from team to team, transforming losers into winners each time.

Some leaders are formally appointed or elected; others emerge informally as the group interacts. What makes for good leadership often depends on the situation—the best person to lead the engineering team may not make the best leader of the sales force. Some people excel at *task leadership*—at organizing

Leadership:
The process by which certain group members motivate and guide the group.

BEHIND THE SCENES

My heroes always stood up and told the truth as they saw it. Often they were vilified, though history would come to treat them more kindly. In 1968 at the University of Chicago, I saw colleagues tell the truth as they saw it and end up bloodied. In the midst of this conflict over ideas and values, I experienced one of the most intellectually and morally invigorating periods of my life. The next year, while a visiting professor in England and France, I had the good fortune of working with Henri Tajfel and Serge Moscovici. The three of us were "outsiders"—I an American Roman Catholic female in Europe, they having survived World War II as Eastern European Jews. Sensitivity to the value and the struggles of the minority perspective came to dominate our work. While studying jury deliberations, I discovered that, even when wrong, minority views can stimulate productive thinking. This helped me see why Senator William Fulbright was wise to say that we should "welcome and not fear the voices of dissent."

CHARLAN JEANNE NEMETH, *University of California, Berkeley*

work, setting standards, and focusing on goal attainment. Others excel at *social leadership*—at building teamwork, mediating conflicts, and being supportive.

Task leaders often have a directive style—one that can work well if the leader is bright enough to give good orders (Fiedler, 1987). Being goal oriented, such leaders also keep the group's attention and effort focused on its mission. Experiments show that the combination of specific, challenging goals and periodic progress reports helps motivate high achievement (Locke & Latham, 1990).

Women more often than men have a democratic leadership style.
(Eagly & Johnson, 1990)

Social leaders often have a democratic style—one that delegates authority and welcomes input from team members. Many experiments reveal that such leadership is good for morale. Group members usually feel more satisfied when they participate in making decisions (Spector, 1986; Vanderslice & others, 1987). Given control over their tasks, workers also become more motivated to achieve (Burger, 1987). People who value good group feeling and take pride in achievement therefore thrive under democratic leadership.

Democratic leadership can be seen in the move by many businesses toward "participative management," a management style common in Sweden and Japan (Naylor, 1990; Sundstrom & others, 1990). Ironically, a major influence on this "Japanese-style" management was M.I.T. social psychologist Kurt Lewin. In laboratory and factory experiments, Lewin and his students demonstrated the benefits of inviting workers to participate in decision making. Shortly before World War II, Lewin visited Japan and explained his findings to industrial and academic leaders (Nisbett & Ross, 1991). Japan's collectivist culture provided a receptive audience for Lewin's group-centered ideas about teamwork. Eventually, his influence circled back to North America.

The once-popular "great person" theory of leadership—that all great leaders share certain traits—has fallen into disrepute. Effective leadership styles, we now know, vary with the situations. Recently, however, social psychologists have again wondered if there might be qualities that mark a good leader in many situations (Hogan & others, 1994). British social psychologists Peter Smith and Monir Tayeb (1989) report that studies done in India, Taiwan, and Iran have found that the most effective supervisors in coal mines, banks, and government offices score high on tests of *both* task and social leadership. They are actively concerned with how work is progressing *and* sensitive to the needs of their subordinates.

Studies also reveal that many effective leaders of laboratory groups, work teams, and large corporations exhibit behaviors that promote minority influence. They engender trust by consistently sticking to their goals. And they often exude a self-confident charisma that kindles the allegiance of their followers (Bennis, 1984; House & Singh, 1987). Charismatic leaders typically have a compelling *vision* of some desired state of affairs, an ability to *communicate* this to others in clear and simple language, and enough optimism and faith in their group to *inspire* others to follow. Not surprisingly, then, personality tests reveal that effective leaders tend to be outgoing, energetic, conscientious, agreeable, emotionally stable, and self-confident (Hogan & others, 1994).

To be sure, groups also influence their leaders. Sometimes those at the front of the herd have simply sensed where it is already heading. Political candidates know how to read the opinion polls. A leader who deviates too radically from the group's standards may be rejected. Smart leaders usually remain with the majority and spend their influence prudently. Nevertheless, effective individual leaders can sometimes exhibit a type of minority influence by mobilizing and guiding their group's energy.

In rare circumstances, the right traits matched with the right situation yield history-making greatness, notes Dean Keith Simonton (1994). To have a Winston Churchill or a Margaret Thatcher, a Thomas Jefferson or a Karl Marx, a Napoleon or an Adolph Hitler, an Abraham Lincoln or a Martin Luther King, takes the right person in the right place at the right time. When an apt com-

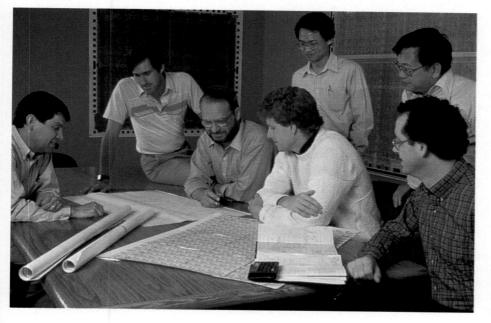

Participative management, illustrated in this "Quality Circle," requires democratic rather than autocratic leaders.

bination of intelligence, skill, determination, self-confidence, and social charisma meets a rare opportunity, the result is sometimes a championship, a Nobel Prize, or a social revolution. Just ask Rosa Parks.

SUMMING UP

If minority viewpoints never prevailed, history would be static and nothing would ever change. In experiments, a minority is most influential when consistent and persistent in its views, when its actions convey self-confidence, and when it begins to elicit some defections from the majority. Even if such factors do not persuade the majority to adopt the minority's views, they will increase the majority's self-doubts and prompt it to consider other alternatives, often leading to better, more creative decisions.

Through their task and social leadership, formal and informal group leaders exert disproportionate influence. Those who consistently press toward their goals and exude a self-confident charisma often engender trust and inspire others to follow.

■ FOR FURTHER READING

Janis, I. L. (1982). *Groupthink: Psychological studies of policy decisions and fiascos*. Boston: Houghton Mifflin. An informative and captivating analysis of the group decision processes that led to several historical fiascoes, from the failure to anticipate the Pearl Harbor attack to the Watergate cover-up.

Janis, I. L. (1989). *Crucial decisions: Leadership in policy making and crisis management*. New York: Free Press. Janis draws upon social-psychological research and his close study of policymakers' mistakes in formulating guidelines for better executive and managerial decisions. Includes a profile of 20 effective leadership practices.

Paulus, P. B. (Ed.) (1989). *The psychology of group influence* (2d ed.). Hillsdale, NJ: Erlbaum. Experts provide state-of-the-art reviews of recent research on group influence. Includes further information on many of the topics discussed in this chapter.

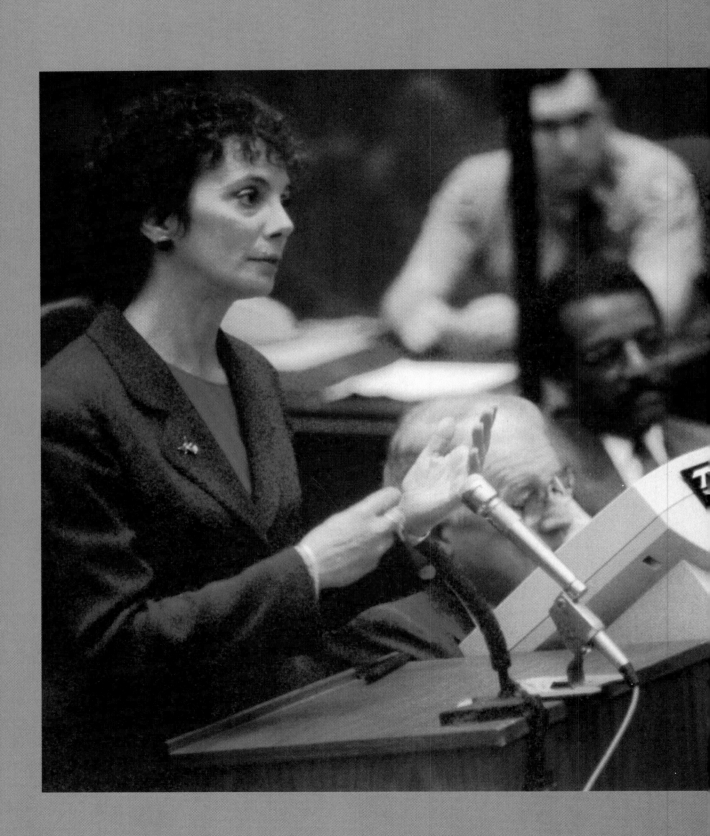

SOCIAL PSYCHOLOGY IN COURT

It was the most publicized criminal case in human history: football hero, actor, and broadcaster O. J. Simpson accused of brutally murdering his estranged wife and a male acquaintance. The evidence was compelling, the prosecution argued. Simpson's behavior fit a longstanding pattern of spouse abuse and threats of violence. Blood tests confirmed that his blood was at the crime scene and his victims' blood was on his glove, his car, even on a sock in his bedroom. His travels the night of the murders and his later fleeing when arrest was imminent fit the crime.

Simpson's defense attorneys argued that racial prejudice may have motivated the officer who allegedly found the bloody glove at Simpson's estate. Moreover, they said, Simpson could not receive a fair trial. Would the jurors—two-thirds of whom were women—be kindly disposed to a man alleged to have abused and murdered a woman? And how likely was it that jurors could heed the judge's instructions to ignore prejudicial pretrial publicity?

The case dripped with other questions pertinent to social psychology:

■ There were no eyewitnesses to this crime. How influential is eyewitness testimony? How trustworthy are eyewitness recollections?

■ Simpson was handsome, beloved, rich, and famous. Can jurors ignore, as they should, a defendant's attractiveness and social status?

■ How well do jurors comprehend important information, such as statistical probabilities involved in DNA blood tests?

■ The jury was composed mostly of women and Blacks, but also included men, Hispanics, and nonHispanic Whites. Do jurors' characteristics bias their verdicts? If so, can lawyers use the jury selection process to stack a jury in their favor?

■ In cases such as this, a 12-member jury deliberates extensively before delivering a verdict. During deliberations, how do jurors influence one another? Can a minority win over the majority? Do 12-member juries reach the same decisions as 6-member juries?

Such questions fascinate lawyers, judges, and defendants. And they are questions to which social psychology can suggest answers, as some 100 American law schools have recognized by hiring one or more professors of "law and social science" (Melton & others, 1987).

We can think of a courtroom as a miniature social world, one that magnifies everyday social processes with major consequences for those involved. Here, as elsewhere, people think about and influence one another. There is, then, a long list of topics pertinent to both social psychology and law. For example:

■ How do a culture's norms and traditions influence its legal decisions? How, say, do cultural ideas about women's and men's roles in child rearing influence whether judges in divorce cases award child custody to the mother or father?

■ What legal procedures strike people as fair? How important are perceptions of the judge's or mediator's neutrality and honesty? (Quite important, reports Tom Tyler, 1988, 1989.) Most English-speaking countries have an adversarial justice system in which attorneys "zealously" represent their side. Most other countries have a nonadversarial system in which the court takes

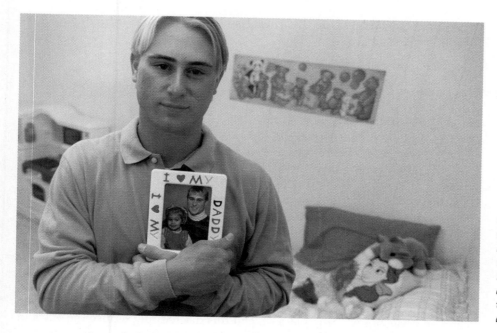

Cultural norms governing men's and women's roles were debated in a recent child custody case in which Steven Smith obtained custody of his daughter because the mother worked and left the daughter in day care.

a more active role. Which procedure do people in English-speaking and non-English-speaking countries regard as fairer? (In both North America and Europe, most people regard the adversarial system as fairer, report Allan Lind & others, 1976, 1978).

■ In cases of civil liability, why do clients and their attorneys spend such enormous sums on legal fees before reaching settlements? Is it partly because cognitive bias leads defendants to overestimate their own case and therefore to reject reasonable settlement offers? (Jeffrey Rachlinski's 1990 analysis of civil cases reveals the answer is yes.)

In criminal cases, psychological factors may influence decisions involving arrest, interrogation, prosecution, plea bargaining, sentencing, and parole. Of criminal cases disposed of in U.S. district courts, 4 in 5 never come to trial (U.S. Department of Justice, 1980). Much of the trial lawyer's work therefore "is not persuasion in the courtroom but bargaining in the conference room" (Saks & Hastie, 1978, pp. 119–120). Even in the conference room, decisions are made based on speculation about what a jury or judge might do.

So, whether a case reaches a jury verdict or not, the social dynamics of the courtroom matter. Let's therefore consider two sets of factors that have been heavily researched: (1) features of the courtroom drama that can influence jurors' judgments of a defendant and (2) characteristics of both the jurors and their deliberations.

■ WHAT INFLUENCES JUDGMENTS?

As the courtroom drama unfolds, jurors hear testimony, form impressions of the defendant, listen to instructions from the judge, and render a verdict. Let's take these steps one at a time. When do biases erode fair judgments? And what reforms could reduce bias?

EYEWITNESS TESTIMONY

How Persuasive Is Eyewitness Testimony?

In Chapter 3 we noted that anecdotes and personal testimonies, being vivid and concrete, can be powerfully persuasive, often more so than information that is logically compelling but abstract. There's no better way to end an argument than to say, "I saw it with my own eyes!" Seeing is believing.

At the University of Washington, Elizabeth Loftus (1974, 1979) found that those who had "seen" were indeed believed, even when their testimony was shown to be useless. When students were presented with a hypothetical robbery-murder case with circumstantial evidence but no eyewitness testimony, only 18 percent voted for conviction. Other students received the same information but with the addition of a single eyewitness. Now, knowing that someone had declared, "That's the one!" 72 percent voted for conviction. For a third group, the defense attorney discredited this testimony (the witness had 20/400 vision and was not wearing glasses). Did this discrediting reduce the effect of the testimony? Hardly—68 percent still voted for conviction.

Follow-up experiments revealed that, although discrediting reduces the number of guilty votes, a discredited eyewitness is more convincing than no eyewitness at all (Whitley, 1987). Unless contradicted by another eyewitness (Leippe, 1985), a vivid eyewitness account is difficult to erase from jurors' minds. That helps explain why, compared to criminal cases lacking eyewitness testimony, those that have eyewitness testimony are more likely to produce convictions (Visher, 1987).

Ah, but can't jurors spot erroneous testimony? To find out, Gary Wells, R. C. L. Lindsay, and their colleagues staged hundreds of eyewitnessed thefts of a University of Alberta calculator. Afterward, they asked each eyewitness to identify the culprit from a photo lineup. Other people, acting as jurors, observed the eyewitnesses being questioned and then evaluated their testimony. Are incorrect eyewitnesses believed less often than those who are accurate? As it happened, both correct and incorrect eyewitnesses were believed 80 percent of the time (Wells & others, 1979). This led the researchers to speculate "that human observers have absolutely no ability to discern eyewitnesses who have mistakenly identified an innocent person" (Wells & others, 1980).

In a follow-up experiment, Lindsay, Wells, and Carolyn Rumpel (1981) staged the theft under conditions that sometimes allowed witnesses a good, long look at the thief and sometimes didn't. The jurors believed the witnesses more when conditions were good. But even when conditions were so poor that two-thirds of the witnesses had actually misidentified an innocent person, 62 percent of the jurors still usually believed the witnesses.

Wells and Michael Leippe (1981) also have found that jurors are more skeptical of eyewitnesses whose memory for trivial details is poor—though these tend to be the most *accurate* witnesses. Jurors think a witness who can remember that there were three pictures hanging in the room must have "really been paying attention" (Bell & Loftus, 1988, 1989). Actually, those who pay attention to details are *less* likely to pay attention to the culprit's face.

Eyewitness recall of detail is sometimes impressive. When John Yuille and Judith Cutshall (1986) studied accounts of a midafternoon murder on a busy Burnaby, British Columbia, street, they found that eyewitnesses' recall for detail was 80 percent accurate.

"As it turned out, my battery of lawyers was no match for their battery of eyewitnesses."

How Accurate Are Eyewitnesses?

Is eyewitness testimony, in fact, often inaccurate? Stories abound of innocent people who have wasted years in prison because of the testimony of eyewitnesses who were sincerely wrong (Brandon & Davies, 1973). In the United States alone, eyewitnesses accuse some 75,000 people a year of crimes (Goldstein & others, 1989). So even dozens of such cases would not prove that eyewitness accounts are unreliable. To assess the accuracy of eyewitness recollections, we

BEHIND THE SCENES

The legal system has always struck me as relying heavily on doctrine and precedent in making assumptions. What attracted me to social psychology was the possibility of scientifically testing many of these assumptions. Consider the assumption that eyewitnesses to crimes can report reliably on events they have observed. Using staged crimes, I have shown that eyewitnesses can be highly inaccurate and yet sincerely confident. This research reveals that people's confidence in the accuracy of their memories reflects social and personality factors rather than the quality of their memories. One exciting development from this research is that I have been able to devise ways to improve eyewitness accuracy. This shows that social psychologists can do more than identify problems, we can also develop solutions.

GARY L. WELLS, *Iowa State University*

need to learn their overall rates of "hits" and "misses." One way to gather such information is to stage crimes comparable to those in everyday life and then solicit eyewitness reports.

This has now been done many times, sometimes with disconcerting results. For example, at the California State University, Hayward, 141 students witnessed an "assault" on a professor. Seven weeks later, when Robert Buckhout (1974) asked them to identify the assailant from a group of six photographs, 60 percent chose an innocent person. It's not surprising that eyewitnesses to actual crimes sometimes disagree about what they saw.

Of course, some witnesses are more confident than others. And Wells and his colleagues report that it's the confident witnesses jurors find most believable. So it is disconcerting that unless conditions are very favorable, as when the culprit is very distinctive-looking, the certainty of witnesses bears little relation to their accuracy (Bothwell & others, 1987; Brigham, 1990; Luus & Wells, 1994). Although intuitive confidence does correlate somewhat with accuracy, some people—whether right or wrong—chronically express themselves more assertively. And that, says Michael Leippe (1994), explains why mistaken eyewitnesses are so often confident-seeming and persuasive.

This finding would surely come as a surprise to members of the 1972 U.S. Supreme Court. In a judgment that established the position of the U.S. judiciary system regarding eyewitness identifications, the Court declared that among the factors to be considered in determining accuracy is "the level of certainty demonstrated by the witness" (Wells & Murray, 1983).

Sources of Error: How Memories Are Constructed

Errors sneak into our perceptions and our memories because our minds are not videotape machines. Rather, we construct our memories, based partly on what we perceived at the time and partly on our expectations, beliefs, and current knowledge (Figures 10–1 and 10–2).

■ **FIGURE 10–1**
Sometimes believing is seeing. Cultural expectations affect perceiving, remembering, and reporting. In a 1947 experiment on rumor transmission, Gordon Allport and Leo Postman showed people this picture of a White man holding a razor blade and then had them tell a second person about it, who then told a third person, and so on. After six tellings, the razor blade in the White man's hand usually shifted to the Black man's.

(From "Eyewitness Testimony" by Robert Buckhout. Copyright © 1974 by Scientific American, Inc. All rights reserved.)

MISTAKEN IDENTITY

Fifty years ago, Yale law professor Edwin Borchard (1932) documented 65 convictions of people whose innocence was ultimately established beyond a doubt. Most resulted from mistaken identifications of the culprit by eyewitnesses. Borchard observed that in several of the cases the convicted prisoner, later proved innocent, was saved from hanging or electrocution by a hairbreadth. Only by rare good fortune were some of the sentences of hanging and electrocution commuted to life imprisonment, so the error could still be corrected. How many wrongfully convicted persons have actually been executed it is impossible to say. Eyewitness misidentification put Randall Ayers, shown here with his sisters on his first day of freedom in eight years, behind bars for a rape he didn't commit. The actual culprit—who strikingly resembles Ayers—confessed to the rape when arrested for the murders of two women. Jurors later admitted being bothered by the absence of supporting evidence and by Ayers' being an inch shorter than the victim, although the attacker was supposedly an inch or two taller. Nevertheless, the eyewitnesses' repeated and confident identification of Ayers was persuasive.

The Misinformation Effect

Elizabeth Loftus and her associates (1978) provided a dramatic demonstration of memory construction. They showed University of Washington students 30 slides depicting successive stages of an automobile-pedestrian accident. One

■ **FIGURE 10–2**
Expectations affect perception. Is the drawing on the far right a face or figure?
(From Fisher, 1968, adapted by Loftus, 1979. Drawing by Anne Canevari Green.)

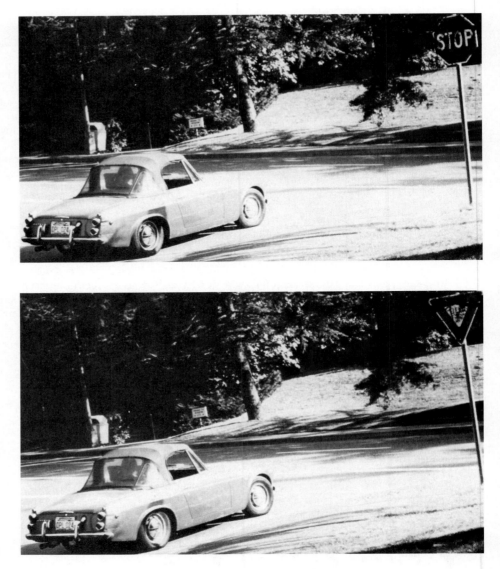

■ FIGURE 10–3
When shown one of these two pictures and then asked a question suggesting the sign from the other photo, most people later "remembered" seeing the sign they had never actually seen.
(From Loftus, Miller, & Burns, 1978. Photos courtesy of Elizabeth Loftus.)

Misinformation effect:
Witnessing an event, receiving misleading information about it, and then incorporating the "misinformation" into one's memory of the event.

critical slide showed a red Datsun stopped at a stop sign or a yield sign. Afterward they asked half the students, among other questions, "Did another car pass the red Datsun while it was stopped at the stop sign?" They asked the other half the same question but with the words "stop sign" replaced by "yield sign." Later, when shown both slides in Figure 10–3 and asked which one they had previously seen, those earlier asked the question consistent with what they had seen were 75 percent correct. Those previously asked the misleading question were only 41 percent correct; more often than not, they denied seeing what they had actually seen and instead "remembered" the picture they had never seen!

In other studies of this **misinformation effect** (remembering wrong information) Loftus (1979) found that after suggestive questions witnesses may believe that a red light was actually green or that a robber had a mustache when

"Well, first you say you *saw* the defendant at the scene and now you say you *think* you saw him! ... Let's cut to the chase, Ms. Sunbeam — is it possible your entire testimony is nothing more than a mere fairy tale?"

he didn't. When questioning eyewitnesses, police and attorneys commonly ask questions framed by their own understanding of what happened. So it is troubling to discover how easily witnesses incorporate misleading information into their memories, especially when they believe the questioner is well informed (Smith & Ellsworth, 1987).

It also is troubling to realize that false memories feel and look like real memories. Thus, they can be as persuasive as real memories—convincingly sincere, yet sincerely wrong. This is true of young children (who are especially susceptible to misinformation) as well as adults. Stephen Ceci and Maggie Bruck (1993a,b) demonstrated children's suggestibility by asking children, once a week for 10 weeks, to "Think real hard, and tell me if this ever happened to you." For example, "Can you remember going to the hospital with the mousetrap on your finger." Remarkably, when then interviewed by a new adult who asked the same question, 58 percent of preschoolers produced false and often detailed stories about the fictitious event. One boy explained that his brother had pushed him into a basement woodpile, where his finger got stuck in the trap. "And then we went to the hospital, and my mommy, daddy, and Colin drove me there, to the hospital in our van, because it was far away. And the doctor put a bandage on this finger."

Given such vivid stories, professional psychologists were often fooled. They could not reliably separate real from false memories. Nor could the children. Told the incident never actually happened, some protested. "But it really did happen. I remember it!," explained one. For Ceci (1993), such findings raise the possibility of false accusations, such as in alleged child sex abuse cases where children's memories may have been contaminated by repeated suggestive questioning and where there is no corroborating evidence.

Retelling

Retelling events commits people to their recollections, accurate or not. An accurate retelling helps them later resist misleading suggestions (Bregman & McAllister, 1982). At other times, the more we retell a story, the more we convince ourselves of a falsehood. Wells, Ferguson, and Lindsay (1981) demonstrated this by having eyewitnesses to a staged theft rehearse their answers to questions before taking the witness stand. Doing so increased the confidence of those who were wrong, and thus made jurors who heard their false testimony more likely to convict the innocent person.

In Chapter 4 we noted that we often adjust what we say to please our listeners and, having done so, come to believe the altered message. Imagine witnessing an argument that erupts into a fight in which one person injures the other. Afterward, the injured party sues, and before the trial a smooth lawyer for one of the two parties interviews you. Might you slightly adjust your testimony, giving a version of the fight that supports this lawyer's client? If you did so, might your later recollections in court be similarly slanted?

Blair Sheppard and Neil Vidmar (1980) report that the answer to both questions is yes. At the University of Western Ontario, they had some students serve as witnesses to a fight and others as lawyers and judges. When interviewed by lawyers for the defendant, the witnesses later gave the judge testimony that was more favorable to the defendant. In a follow-up experiment, Vidmar and Nancy Lair (1983) noted that witnesses did not omit important facts from their testimony; they just changed their tone of voice and choice of words depending on whether they thought they were a witness for the defendant or for the plaintiff. Even this was enough to bias the impressions of those who heard the testimony. So it's not only suggestive questions that can distort eyewitness recollections but also their own retellings, which may be subtly adjusted to suit their audience.

Reducing Error

Given these error-prone tendencies, what constructive steps can be taken to increase the accuracy of eyewitnesses and jurors? Experts have several ideas.

Train Police Interviewers

When Ronald Fisher and his co-workers (1987) examined tape-recorded interviews of eyewitnesses conducted by experienced Florida police detectives, they found a typical pattern. Following an open-ended beginning ("Tell me what you recall"), the detectives would occasionally interrupt with follow-up questions, including questions eliciting terse answers ("How tall was he?"). Fisher and Edward Geiselman say interviews should begin by allowing eyewitnesses to offer their own unprompted recollections.

The recollections will be most complete if the interviewer jogs the memory by first guiding people to reconstruct the setting. Have them visualize the scene and what they were thinking and feeling at the time. Even showing pictures of the setting—of, say, the store checkout lane with a clerk standing where she was robbed—can promote accurate recall (Cutler & Penrod, 1988). After giving witnesses ample, uninterrupted time to report everything that comes to mind, the interviewer jogs their memory with evocative questions ("Was there anything unusual about the voice? Was there anything unusual about the person's appearance or clothing?"). When Fisher and his colleagues (1989, 1994) trained detectives to question in this way, the information they elicited from eyewitnesses increased 50 percent. In response to such results, this "cognitive interview" procedure is being adopted by police forces in North America and Britain (Memon & Bull, 1991).

However, interviewers must be careful to keep their questions free of hidden assumptions. Loftus and Guido Zanni (1975) found that questions such as, "Did you see the broken headlight?" triggered twice as many "memories" of nonexistent events as did questions without the hidden assumption: "Did you see a broken headlight?" Likewise, flooding eyewitnesses with an array of mugshots reduces accuracy in later identifying the culprit (Brigham & Cairns, 1988). Witnesses who analytically compare photos to narrow the choices err more often than witnesses for whom one face just pops out as that of the culprit (Dunning & Stern, 1994).

Minimize False Lineup Identifications

The case of Ron Shatford illustrates how the composition of a police lineup can promote misidentification (Doob & Kirshenbaum, 1973). After a suburban Toronto department store robbery, the cashier involved could only recall that the culprit was not wearing a tie and was "very neatly dressed and rather good looking." When police put the good-looking Shatford in a lineup with 11 unattractive men, all of whom wore ties, the cashier readily identified him as the culprit. Only after he had served 15 months of a long sentence did another person confess, allowing Shatford to be retried and found not guilty. Many eyewitnesses will identify the lineup member who *most resembles* the culprit.

> *"While the rules of evidence and other safeguards provide protection in the courtroom, they are absent in the backroom of the precinct station."*
> Ernest Hilgard & Elizabeth Loftus (1979)

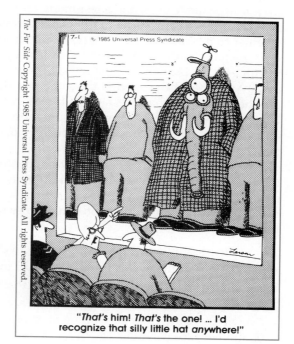

"*That's* him! *That's* the one! ... I'd recognize that silly little hat *anywhere!*"

Lineup fairness? From the suspect's perspective a lineup is fair, note John Brigham, David Ready and Stacy Spier (1990), when "the other lineup members are reasonably similar in general appearance to the suspect."

Gary Wells (1984, 1993) reports that one way to reduce such misidentifications is to give eyewitnesses a "blank" lineup that contains no suspects and screen out those who make false identifications. Those who do not make such errors turn out to be more accurate when they later face the actual lineup. Mistakes can also be reduced by having witnesses simply make individual yes or no judgments in response to a *sequence* of people (Cutler & Penrod, 1988; Lindsay & Wells, 1985). Witnesses viewing just one suspect (in a "show-up") are more likely to say "not there" than those viewing a lineup (Gonzalez & others, 1993). If witnesses view a group of photos or people simultaneously, they are more likely to choose whoever most resembles the culprit.

Police can also minimize false identifications by including instructions acknowledging that the offender may not be in the lineup (Malpass & Devine, 1984). Compared to lineups of several suspects, a lineup composed of one suspect and several people known to be innocent further reduces misidentifications (Wells, 1993). Lineups containing innocent people enable police to disregard eyewitnesses who make errors; with all-suspect lineups, there is no opportunity to weed out those who are guessing.

Such procedures make police lineups more like good experiments. They contain a control group (a no-suspect lineup or a lineup in which mock witnesses try to guess the suspect based merely on a general description). They have an experimenter who is blind to the hypotheses (an officer who doesn't know which person is the suspect). And questions are worded so they don't subtly demand a particular response (the procedure doesn't imply the culprit *is* in the lineup). Using these social-psychological insights, Canada's Law Reform Commission has recommended new eyewitness identification procedures to reduce the likelihood of future Ron Shatfords (Wells & Luus, 1990).

Educate Jurors

Do jurors evaluate eyewitness testimony critically? Do they intuitively understand how the circumstances of a lineup determine its reliability? Do they know whether to take an eyewitness's self-confidence into account? Do they realize how memory can be influenced by earlier misleading questions, by stress at the time of the incident, by the interval between the event and the questioning, by whether the suspect is the same or a different race, by whether recall of other details is sharp or hazy? Studies in Canada, Great Britain, and the United States reveal that jurors discount most of these factors, all of which are known to influence eyewitness testimony (Cutler & others, 1988; Noon & Hollin, 1987; Wells & Turtle, 1987).

To educate jurors, experts are now frequently asked (usually by defense attorneys) to testify about eyewitness testimony. Their aim is to offer jurors the sort of information you have been reading, which should help them evaluate the testimony of both prosecution and defense witnesses. These experts explain that:

■ Eyewitnesses often perceive events selectively.

■ Discussions of the events can alter or add to their memories.

■ Research using staged crimes has shown that witnesses often choose a wrong person from a lineup.

■ Eyewitnesses are especially prone to error when trying to identify someone of another race (Chapter 11).

TABLE 10–1 *Influences upon Eyewitness Testimony*

PHENOMENON	RELIABLE ENOUGH?*
1. *Question wording.* An eyewitness's testimony about an event can be affected by how the questions put to that eyewitness are worded.	97
2. *Lineup instructions.* Police instructions can affect an eyewitness's willingness to make an identification and/or the likelihood that he or she will identify a particular person.	95
3. *Postevent information.* Eyewitness testimony about an event often reflects not only what they actually saw but information they obtained later on.	87
4. *Accuracy versus confidence.* An eyewitness's confidence is not a good predictor of his or her identification accuracy.	87
5. *Attitudes and expectations.* An eyewitness's perception and memory for an event may be affected by his or her attitudes and expectations.	85

*Percentage of eyewitness experts agreeing, "This phenomenon is reliable enough for psychologists to present it in courtroom testimony."

From S. M. Kassin, P. C. Ellsworth, & V. L. Smith (1989).

■ Jurors should disregard the confidence with which an eyewitness offers testimony.

Table 10–1, drawn from a survey of 63 experts on eyewitness testimony, lists the most agreed-upon phenomena.

Experiments show that such information can prompt jurors to analyze eyewitness reports more skeptically and discuss them more fully (Loftus, 1980; Maass & others, 1985; Wells & others, 1980). Taught the conditions under which eyewitness accounts *are* trustworthy, jurors become more likely to trust such testimony (Cutler & others, 1989; Wells, 1986).

THE DEFENDANT'S CHARACTERISTICS

According to the famed trial lawyer Clarence Darrow (1933), jurors seldom convict a person they like or acquit one they dislike. He argued that the main job of the trial lawyer is to make a jury like the defendant. Was he right? And is it true, as Darrow also said, that "facts regarding the crime are relatively unimportant"?

Darrow overstated the case. One study of more than 3500 criminal cases and some 4000 civil cases found that 4 times in 5 the judge agreed with the jury's decision (Kalven & Zeisel, 1966). Although both may have been wrong, the evidence usually is clear enough that jurors can set aside their biases, focus on the facts, and agree on a verdict (Saks & Hastie, 1978; Visher, 1987). Darrow was too cynical; facts do matter.

Nevertheless, when jurors are asked to make social judgments—would *this* defendant commit *this* offense? intentionally?—facts are not all that matter. As we noted in Chapter 8, communicators are more persuasive if they seem credible and attractive. Jurors cannot help forming impressions of the defendant. Can they put these impressions aside and decide the case based on the facts alone? To judge from the more lenient treatment often received by high-status defendants (McGillis, 1979), it seems that some cultural bias lingers. But actual cases vary in so many ways—in the type of crime, in the status, age, sex, and race of the defendant—that it's hard to isolate the factors that influence jurors. So experimenters have controlled such factors by giving mock jurors the same basic facts of a case while varying, say, the defendant's attractiveness or similarity to the jurors.

Physical Attractiveness

As we will see in Chapter 13, there is a physical attractiveness stereotype: Beautiful people seem like good people. Michael Efran (1974) wondered whether this stereotype would bias students' judgments of someone accused of cheating. He asked some of his University of Toronto students whether attractiveness should affect presumption of guilt. Their answer: "No, it shouldn't." But did it? Yes. When Efran gave other students a description of the case with a photograph of either an attractive or an unattractive defendant, they judged the most attractive as least guilty and recommended that person for the least punishment.

Other experimenters have confirmed that when the evidence is meager or ambiguous, justice is not blind to a defendant's looks (Mazzela & Feingold, 1994). Diane Berry and Leslie Zebrowitz-McArthur (1988) discovered this when they asked people to judge the guilt of baby-faced and mature-faced defen-

Other things being equal, people often judge physically appealing defendants more leniently.

And so I ask the jury . . . is that the face of a mass murderer?

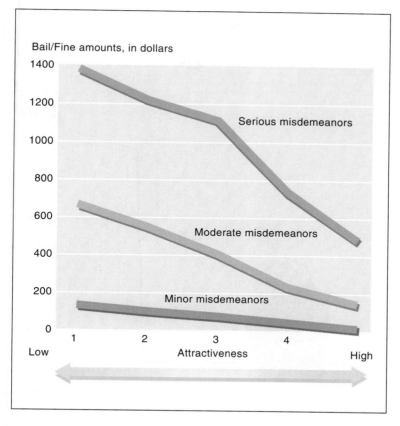

Bail/Fine amounts, in dollars

Serious misdemeanors

Moderate misdemeanors

Minor misdemeanors

Low   Attractiveness   High

■ **FIGURE 10–4**
Attractiveness and legal judg-
ments. Texas Gulf Coast judges
set higher bails and fines for
less attractive defendants.
(Data from Downs & Lyons, 1991.)

dants. Baby-faced adults (people with large, round eyes and small chins) seemed more naive and were found guilty more often of crimes of negligence and less often of intentional criminal acts. If convicted, unattractive people also strike people as more dangerous, especially if they are sexual offenders (Esses & Webster, 1988). O. J.'s being, as one prospective juror put it, "a hunk of a fellow" probably hasn't hurt his cause.

To see if these findings extend to the real world, Chris Downs and Phillip Lyons (1991) asked police escorts to rate the physical attractiveness of 1742 defendants appearing before 40 Texas judges in misdemeanor cases. Whether the misdemeanor was serious (such as forgery), moderate (such as harassment), or minor (such as public intoxication), the judges set greater bails and fines for less attractive defendants (Figure 10–4). What explains this dramatic effect? Are unattractive people also lower in status? Are they indeed more likely to flee or to commit crime, as the judges perhaps suppose? Or are judges simply ignoring the Roman statesman Cicero's advice: "The final good and the supreme duty of the wise man is to resist appearance."

Similarity to the Jurors

If Clarence Darrow was even partly right in his declaration that liking or disliking a defendant colors judgments, then other factors that influence liking should also matter. Among such influences is the principle, noted in Chapter

"Surely not guilty. Next case."

8, that likeness (similarity) leads to liking. When people pretend they are jurors, they are indeed more sympathetic to a defendant who shares their attitudes, religion, race, or (in cases of sexual assault) gender (Selby & others, 1977; Towson & Zanna, 1983; Ugwuegbu, 1979).

Some examples:

■ When Paul Amato (1979) had Australian students read evidence concerning a left- or right-wing person accused of a politically motivated burglary, they judged the defendant less guilty if his or her political views were similar to their own.

■ When Cookie Stephan and Walter Stephan (1986) had English-speaking people judge someone accused of assault, they were more likely to think the person not guilty if the defendant's testimony was in English, rather than translated from Spanish or Thai.

■ For "White crimes," such as embezzlement and fraud, (mostly White) mock jurors punish White defendants more severely (Mazzella & Feingold, 1994). For violent crimes, mock jurors punish Black defendants more severely (Sweeney & Haney, 1992). And in actual capital cases, data from "all over the country," reports Craig Haney (1991), "show that Blacks are overpunished as defendants or undervalued as victims, or both." Thus, Blacks who kill Whites are more often sentenced to death than are Whites who kill Blacks.

It seems we are more sympathetic toward a defendant with whom we can identify. If we think *we* wouldn't have committed that criminal act, we may assume that someone like us is also unlikely to have done it. That helps explain why a national survey before the O. J. Simpson trial got under way found that 77 percent of Whites, but only 45 percent of Blacks, saw the case against him as at least "fairly strong" (Smolowe, 1994). And it helps explain the riotous outrage that followed the initial acquittal (by a jury with no Blacks) of the White officers who clubbed Rodney King. People debated: If an unarmed White man had been arrested after a car chase by four Black officers, who were videotaped beating him mercilessly, would the same jury have acquitted them?

Ideally, jurors would leave their biases outside the courtroom and begin a trial with open minds. So implies the Sixth Amendment to the U.S. Constitution: "The accused shall enjoy the right to a speedy and public trial by impartial jury." In its concern for objectivity, the judicial system is similar to science: Both scientists and jurors are supposed to sift and weigh the evidence. Both the courts and science have rules about what evidence is relevant. Both keep careful records and assume that others given the same evidence would decide similarly.

When the evidence is clear and jurors focus on it (as when they reread and debate the meaning of testimony), their biases are indeed minimal (Kaplan & Schersching, 1980). The quality of the evidence matters more than the prejudices of the jurors.

THE JUDGE'S INSTRUCTIONS

In the courtroom, judges instruct jurors to ignore biasing information. All of us can recall courtroom dramas in which an attorney exclaimed, "Your honor, I object!" whereupon the judge sustained the objection and ordered the jury to ignore the other attorney's suggestive question or the witness's remark. Nearly all states in the United States now have "rape shield" statutes that prohibit or limit testimony concerning the victim's prior sexual activity. Such testimony, though irrelevant to the case at hand, tends to make jurors more sympathetic to the accused rapist's claim that the woman consented to sexual relations (Borgida, 1981; Cann & others, 1979).

If such reliable, illegal, or prejudicial testimony is nevertheless slipped in by the defense or blurted out by a witness, will jurors follow a judge's instruction to ignore it? And is it enough for the judge to remind jurors that "the issue is not whether you like or dislike the defendant but whether the defendant committed the offense"?

Very possibly not. Several experimenters report that it is hard for jurors to ignore inadmissible evidence, such as the defendant's previous convictions. In one study, Stanley Sue, Ronald Smith, and Cathy Caldwell (1973) gave University of Washington students a description of a grocery store robbery-murder and a summary of the prosecution's case and the defense's case. When the prosecution's case was weak, no one judged the defendant guilty. When a tape recording of an incriminating phone call made by the defendant was added to the weak case, about one-third judged the person guilty. The judge's instructing jurors that the tape was not legal evidence and they should ignore it did nothing to erase the effect of the damaging testimony.

Indeed, Sharon Wolf and David Montgomery (1977) found that a judge's order to ignore testimony—"It must play no role in your consideration of the case. You have no choice but to disregard it"—can even boomerang, adding to the testimony's impact. Perhaps such statements create **reactance** in the jurors. Or perhaps they sensitize jurors to the inadmissible testimony, as what happens when I warn you *not* to look at your nose as you finish this sentence. Judges can more easily strike inadmissible testimony from the court records than from the jurors' minds. As trial lawyers sometimes say, "You can't unring a bell."

Reactance:
The desire to assert one's sense of freedom (see p. 265).

Pretrial publicity is also hard for jurors to ignore, as Geoffrey Kramer and his colleagues (1990) confirmed. In a massive experiment, they exposed nearly 800 mock jurors (most from actual jury rolls) to incriminating news reports about the past convictions of a man accused of robbing a supermarket. After the jurors viewed a videotaped reenactment of the trial, they either did or did not hear the judge's instructions to disregard the pretrial publicity. The effect of the judicial admonition was nil. Moreover, people whose opinions are biased by such publicity typically deny its effect on them, and this denial makes it hard to eliminate biased jurors (Moran & Cutler, 1991). In experiments, even getting mock jurors to pledge their impartiality and their willingness to disregard prior information has not eliminated the pretrial publicity effect (Dexter & others, 1992). O. J. Simpson's attorneys, it seems, had reason to worry about the massive pretrial publicity. And Judge Ito had reason to order jurors not to view pertinent media publicity, and to isolate them during the trial.

Nevertheless, judges do influence jurors. Judges come to trials with their own opinions, which they subtly communicate to jurors. Jurors sometimes de-

A newsstand display just after O. J. Simpson's arrest for the murder of his ex-wife and her friend. Will jurors clear their minds of pretrial publicity that might bias their evaluation of evidence? Although jurors will deny being biased, experiments have shown otherwise.

"The jury will disregard the witness's last remarks."

It is not easy for jurors to erase inadmissible testimony from memory.

tect and reflect judges' opinions (Hart, 1995). One analysis of municipal court judges' behavior during videotaped trials revealed that their pretrial opinions of the case influenced their nonverbal behaviors—the tone of their instructions, their head nods, their smiles, their frowns—which in turn related to the jury's later verdict (Blanck & others, 1985).

To minimize the effects of inadmissible testimony, judges can *forewarn* jurors that certain types of evidence, such as a rape victim's sexual history, are irrelevant. Once jurors form impressions based on such evidence, a judge's admonitions have much less effect (Borgida & White, 1980; Kassin & Wrightsman, 1979). Thus, reports Vicki Smith (1991), a pretrial training session pays dividends. Teaching jurors legal procedures and standards of proof improves their understanding of the trial procedure and their willingness to withhold judgment until after they have heard all the trial information.

Better yet, judges could cut inadmissible testimony before the jurors hear it—by videotaping testimonies and removing the inadmissible parts. Live and videotaped testimony have much the same impact as do live and videotaped lineups (Cutler & others, 1989; Miller & Fontes, 1979). Perhaps, then, courtrooms of the future will have life-size television monitors. Critics object that the procedure prevents jurors from observing how the defendant and others react to the witness. Proponents argue that videotaping not only enables the judge to edit out inadmissible testimony but also speeds up the trial and allows witnesses to talk about crucial events before memories fade.

OTHER ISSUES

We have considered three courtroom factors—eyewitness testimony, the defendant's characteristics, and the judge's instructions. Researchers are also

BEHIND THE SCENES

While I was a new University of Illinois graduate student, my advisor, James Davis, began studying how a group's size affects its decisions. Coincidentally, the Supreme Court had just guessed that jury size wouldn't much matter. So Jim, with my help, decided to experiment with jury size. As I eavesdropped on the mock juries I became fascinated by the jurors' insightful arguments, their mix of amazing recollections and memory fabrications, their prejudices, their attempts to persuade or coerce, and their occasional courage in standing alone. Here brought to life before me were so many of the psychological processes I had been studying! Although our student jurors understood they were only simulating a real trial, they really cared about reaching a fair verdict. Ever since listening in on those first jury deliberations, I've been hooked on studying juror behavior.

NORBERT KERR, *Michigan State University*

studying the influence of many other factors. For example, at Michigan State University, Norbert Kerr and his colleagues (1978, 1981, 1982) have studied these issues: Does a severe potential punishment (for example, a death penalty) make jurors less willing to convict—and was it therefore strategic for the Los Angeles prosecutors not to seek the death penalty for O. J. Simpson? Do experienced jurors' judgments differ from those of novice jurors? Are defendants judged more harshly when the *victim* is attractive or has suffered greatly? Kerr's research suggests that the answer to all three questions is yes.

Experiments by Mark Alicke and Teresa Davis (1989) and Michael Enzle and Wendy Hawkins (1992) show that the victim's characteristics can affect jurors' judgments of blame and punishment even when the defendant was unaware of them. Consider the 1984 case of the "subway vigilante" Bernard Goetz. When four teens asked Goetz for $5 on a New York subway, the frightened Goetz pulled out a loaded gun and shot each of them, leaving one partly paralyzed. When Goetz was charged with attempted homicide, there was an outcry of public support for him based partly on the disclosure that the youths had extensive criminal records and that three of them were carrying concealed, sharpened screwdrivers. Although Goetz didn't know any of this, he was acquitted of the attempted homicide charge and convicted only of illegal firearm possession.

SUMMING UP

In hundreds of recent experiments, courtroom procedures have been on trial. Social psychologists have conducted these experiments believing that the courtroom offers a natural context for studying how people form judgments and that social psychology's principles and methods can shed new light on important judicial issues.

During a trial, jurors hear testimony, form impressions of the defendant, and listen to the judge's instructions. At each of these stages, subtle factors may influence their judgments.

Experiments reveal that both witnesses and jurors readily succumb to an illusion that a given witness's mental-recording equipment functions free of significant error. But as witnesses construct and rehearse memories of what they have observed, errors creep in. Research suggests ways to lessen such error, both in eyewitness reports and in jurors' use of such reports.

The facts of a case are usually compelling enough that jurors can lay aside their biases and render a fair judgment. When the evidence is ambiguous, jurors are more likely to interpret it with their preconceived biases and to feel sympathetic to a defendant who is attractive or similar to themselves.

When jurors are exposed to damaging pretrial publicity or to inadmissible evidence, will they follow a judge's instruction to ignore it? In simulated trials, the judge's orders were sometimes followed, but often, especially when the judge's admonition came *after* an impression was made, they were not.

■ THE JURORS AS INDIVIDUALS

Verdicts depend on what happens in the courtroom—the eyewitness testimonies, the defendant's characteristics, the judge's instructions. But verdicts also depend on how the jurors, individually and then as a group, process information.

Courtroom influences on "the average juror" are worth pondering. But no juror is the average juror; each carries into the courthouse individual attitudes and personalities. And when deliberating, jurors influence one another. A key question is: How are their verdicts influenced by their individual dispositions and by their working together as a group?

JUROR COMPREHENSION

To gain insight into juror comprehension, Nancy Pennington and Reid Hastie (1993) have studied the thought processes of mock jurors, sampled from courthouse jury pools, while viewing reenactments of actual trials. In making their decisions, jurors first construct a story that makes sense of all the evidence. After observing one murder trial, some jurors concluded that a quarrel made the defendant angry, triggering him to get a knife, search for the decedent, and stab him to death. Others surmised that the frightened defendant picked up a knife that he used to defend himself when he later encountered the decedent. When the jurors begin deliberating, they are often surprised to discover that others have constructed stories different from their own. This implies—and research confirms—that jurors are persuaded when attorneys present evidence like a narrative story. In felony cases—where the national conviction rate is 80 percent—the prosecution case follows a story structure more often than the defense case.

Next the jurors must grasp the judge's instructions concerning the available verdict categories. For these instructions to be effective, jurors must first understand them. Study after study has found that many people do not understand the standard legalese of judicial instructions. Depending on the type of case, a jury may be told that the standard of proof is a "preponderance of the evidence," "clear and convincing evidence," or "beyond a reasonable doubt."

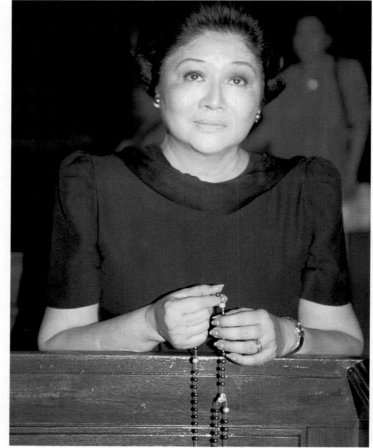

Faced with an incomprehensibly complex accounting of Imelda Marcos's alleged thefts of public money, jurors fell back on their intuitive assessments of the seemingly devout and sincere woman.

Such statements may have one meaning for the legal community and different meanings in the minds of jurors (Kagehiro, 1990). In one study of Nevada criminal instructions, viewers of videotaped instructions could answer only 15 percent of 89 questions posed to them about what they had heard (Elwork & others, 1982).

After observing actual cases and later interviewing the jurors, Stephen Adler (1994) found "lots of sincere, serious people who—for a variety of reasons—were missing key points, focusing on irrelevant issues, succumbing to barely recognized prejudices, failing to see through the cheapest appeals to sympathy or hate, and generally botching the job." In the trial of Imelda Marcos, charged with transferring hundreds of millions of dollars of Philippine money into American banks for her own use, lawyers eliminated anyone who was aware of her role in her husband's dictatorship. Ill-equipped to follow the complex money transactions, the uninformed people who made it onto the jury fell back on sympathy for Imelda, whom they would see dressed in black, clutching her rosaries, and wiping away tears (Adler, 1994).

Jurors may be further confused if the criteria change as proceedings move from the trial phase that determines guilt or innocence into the penalty phase

(Luginbuhl, 1992). In North Carolina, for example, jurors are to convict only if there is "proof beyond a reasonable doubt." But a "preponderance of the evidence" is sufficient when judging whether mitigating circumstances, such as an abusive childhood, should preclude a death sentence.

Finally, jurors must compare their explanation with the verdict categories. When using the judge's definition of, say, justifiable self-defense, jurors must decide whether "pinned against a wall" matches their understanding of the required circumstance "unable to escape." Often a judge's abstract, jargon-filled definition of verdict categories loses in the competition with the jurors' own images ("mental prototypes") of these crimes. Vicki Smith (1991) reports that, regardless of the judge's definition, if a defendant's actions match jurors' images of "vandalism," "assault," or "robbery," they likely will find the person guilty.

Tests on blood found at the scene where O. J. Simpson's wife and her fellow victim were murdered revealed bloodstains that match Simpson's mix of blood proteins, but not the victims'. Learning that only 1 in 200 people share this blood type, some people assumed the chances were 99.5 percent that Simpson was the culprit. But 1 in 200 means the culprit could be any one of at least 40,000 people in the Los Angeles area, noted the defense. Faced with such arguments, 3 in 5 people will discount the relevance of the blood-type evidence, report William Thompson and Edward Schumann (1987). Actually, both attorneys are wrong. The evidence *is* relevant because few of the other 40,000 people can reasonably be considered suspects. But the 99.5 percent argument ignores the fact that the defendant was charged partly because his blood type matched.

When a more precise DNA match with Simpson's blood was found, prosecutors contended that the odds were 1 in 170 million of such a match, while the defense showed that experts disagreed about the reliability of DNA testing. But Gary Wells (1992) reports that even when people (including experienced trial judges) understand naked statistical probabilities, they may be unpersuaded. The numbers, it seems, must be supported by a convincing story. Thus, reports Wells, one Toronto mother lost a paternity suit seeking child support from her child's alleged father despite a blood test showing a 99.8 percent probability that the man was her child's father. She lost after the man took the stand and persuasively denied the allegation.

Understanding how jurors misconstrue judicial instructions and statistical information is a first step toward better decisions. A next step might be giving jurors access to transcripts rather than forcing them to rely on their memories in processing complex information (Bourgeois & others, 1993). A further step is devising and testing clearer, more effective ways to present information—a task on which several social psychologists are currently at work. For example, when a judge quantifies the required standard of proof (as, say, 51, 71, or 91 percent certainty) jurors understand and respond appropriately (Kagehiro, 1990). And surely there must be a simpler way to tell jurors, as required by the Illinois Death Penalty Act, not to impose the death sentence in murder cases when there are justifying circumstances: "If you do not unanimously find from your consideration of all the evidence that there are no mitigating factors sufficient to preclude imposition of a death sentence, then you should sign the verdict requiring the court to impose a sentence other than death" (Diamond, 1993).

a real jury would. In a series of such studies at the University of Illinois, James Davis, Robert Holt, Norbert Kerr, and Garold Stasser tested various mathematical schemes for predicting group decisions, including decisions by mock juries (Davis & others, 1975, 1977, 1989; Kerr & others, 1976). Will some mathematical combination of people's initial decisions predict their final group decision? Davis and his colleagues found that the scheme that predicts best varies according to the nature of the case. But in several experiments, a "two-thirds-majority" scheme fared best: The group verdict was usually the alternative favored by at least two-thirds of the jurors at the outset. Without such a majority, a hung jury was likely.

Likewise, in Kalven and Zeisel's survey of juries, 9 in 10 reached the verdict favored by the majority on the first ballot. Although you or I might fantasize about someday being the courageous lone juror who sways the majority, the fact is it seldom happens.

MINORITY INFLUENCE

Minority influence:
See pages 347–352.

Seldom, yet sometimes, what was initially a minority prevails. In the Mitchell-Stans trial the four jurors who favored acquittal persisted and eventually prevailed. From the research on minority influence we know that jurors in the minority will be most persuasive when they are consistent, persistent, and self-confident, especially if they can begin to trigger some defections from the majority.

Ironically, the most influential minority juror in the Mitchell-Stans trial, Andrew Choa, was a well-educated *New York Times* reader—someone who did not fit the survey profile of a juror sympathetic to the defense. But Choa was also a dedicated supporter of Richard Nixon and a bank vice-president who ingratiated himself with the other jurors through various favors, such as taking them to movies in his bank's private auditorium (Zeisel & Diamond, 1976). Choa also illustrates a common finding from jury experiments: High-status male jurors tend to be most influential (Gerbasi & others, 1977).

GROUP POLARIZATION

Group polarization:
See pages 331–339.

Jury deliberation shifts people's opinions in other intriguing ways as well. In experiments, deliberation often magnifies initial sentiments. For example, Robert Bray and Audrey Noble (1978) had University of Kentucky students listen to a 30-minute tape of a murder trial. Then, assuming the defendant was found guilty, they recommended a prison sentence. Groups of high authoritarians initially recommended strong punishments (56 years) and after deliberation were even more punitive (68 years). The low-authoritarian groups were initially more lenient (38 years) and after deliberation became more so (29 years).

Confirmation that group polarization can occur in juries comes from an ambitious study in which Reid Hastie, Steven Penrod, and Nancy Pennington (1983) put together 69 twelve-person juries from Massachusetts citizens on jury duty. Each jury was shown a reenactment of an actual murder case, with roles played by an experienced judge and actual attorneys. Then they were given unlimited time to deliberate the case in a jury room. As Figure 10–5 shows, the

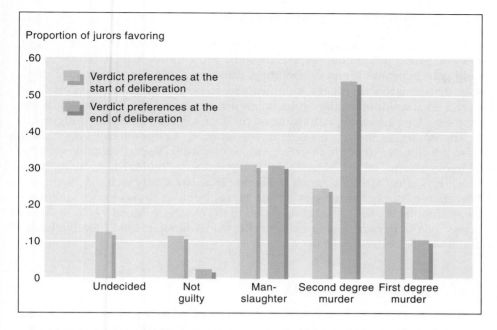

■ FIGURE 10–5
Group polarization in juries. In highly realistic simulations of a murder trial, 828 Massachusetts jurors stated their initial verdict preferences, then deliberated the case for periods ranging from three hours to five days. Deliberation strengthened initial tendencies, which favored the prosecution.
(From Hastie & others, 1983.)

evidence was incriminating: Four out of five jurors voted guilty before deliberation, but felt unsure enough that a weak verdict of manslaughter was their most popular preference. After deliberation, nearly all agreed the accused was guilty, and most now preferred a stronger verdict—second-degree murder. Through deliberation, their initial leanings had grown stronger.

LENIENCY

In many experiments, one other curious effect of deliberation has surfaced: Especially when the evidence is not highly incriminating, as it was in the experiment just described, deliberating jurors often become more lenient (MacCoun & Kerr, 1988). This qualifies the "two-thirds-majority-rules" finding, for if even a bare majority initially favors *acquittal,* it usually will prevail (Stasser & others, 1981). Moreover, a minority that favors acquittal stands a better chance of prevailing than one that favors conviction (Tindale & others, 1990).

Once again, a survey of actual juries confirms the laboratory results. Kalven and Zeisel (1966) report that in those cases where the majority does not prevail, it usually shifts to acquittal (as in the Mitchell-Stans trial). When a judge disagrees with the jury's decision, it is usually because the jury acquits someone the judge would have convicted.

Might "informational influence" (stemming from others' persuasive arguments) account for the increased leniency? The "innocent-unless-proved-guilty" and "proof-beyond-a-reasonable-doubt" rules put the burden of proof on those who favor conviction. Perhaps this makes evidence of the defendant's innocence more persuasive. Or perhaps "normative influence" creates the leniency effect, as jurors who view themselves as fair-minded confront other jurors who are even more concerned with protecting a possibly innocent defendant.

"It is better that ten guilty persons escape than one innocent suffer."
William Blackstone, 1769

ARE 12 HEADS BETTER THAN 1?

In Chapter 9 we saw that on thought problems where there is an objective right answer, group judgments surpass those by most individuals. Does the same hold true in juries? When deliberating, jurors not only exert normative pressure by trying to shift others' judgments by the sheer weight of their own but they also share information, thus enlarging one another's knowledge of the case. So, does informational influence produce superior collective judgment?

The evidence, though meager, is encouraging. Groups recall information from a trial better than do their individual members (Vollrath & others, 1989). Moreover, some of the biases that contaminate individual judgments have much less effect after the jurors deliberate (Kaplan & Schersching, 1980). Deliberation not only cancels out certain biases but also draws jurors' attention away from their own prejudgments and to the evidence. Moreover, it restrains jurors' use of inadmissible evidence (Kerwin & Shaffer, 1994). Twelve heads are, it seems, better than one.

ARE 6 HEADS AS GOOD AS 12?

In keeping with their British heritage, juries in the United States and Canada have traditionally been composed of 12 people whose task is to reach consensus—a unanimous verdict. However, in several cases appealed during the early 1970s, the U.S. Supreme Court declared that in civil cases and state criminal cases not potentially involving a death penalty, courts could use six-person juries. Moreover, the Court affirmed a state's right to allow less than unanimous verdicts, even upholding one Louisiana conviction based on a 9 to 3 vote (Tanke & Tanke, 1979). There is no reason to suppose, argued the Court, that smaller juries, or juries not required to reach consensus, will deliberate or decide differently from the traditional jury.

The Court's assumptions triggered an avalanche of criticism from both legal scholars and social psychologists (Saks, 1974). Some criticisms were matters of simple statistics. For example, if 10 percent of a community's total jury pool is Black, then 72 percent of 12–member juries but only 47 percent of 6–member juries may be expected to have at least one Black person. So smaller juries are less likely to reflect a community's diversity. And if, in a given case, one-sixth of the jurors initially favor acquittal, that would be a single individual in a 6-member jury and 2 people in a 12-member jury. The Court assumed that, psychologically, the two situations would be identical. But as you may recall from our discussion of conformity, resisting group pressure is far more difficult for a minority of one than for a minority of two. Psychologically speaking, a jury split 10 to 2 is not equivalent to a jury split 5 to 1. Not surprisingly, then, 12-person juries are more likely than 6-person juries to have hung verdicts (Kerr & MacCoun, 1985).

Other criticisms were based on experiments by Michael Saks (1977), Charlan Nemeth (1977), and James Davis and others (1975). In these mock jury experiments, the overall distribution of verdicts from small or nonunanimous juries did not differ much from the verdicts pronounced by unanimous 12-member juries (although verdicts from the smaller juries were slightly more unpredictable). There are, however, greater effects on deliberation. A smaller jury has the advantage of greater and more evenly balanced participation per juror but the disadvantage of eliciting less total deliberation. Moreover, once they realize that the necessary majority has been achieved, juries not required to reach consensus seem to discuss minority views rather superficially (Davis & others, 1975; Foss, 1981; Hastie & others, 1983; Kerr & others, 1976).

In 1978, after some of these studies were reported, the Supreme Court rejected Georgia's 5-member juries (although it still retains the 6-member jury). Announcing the Court's decision, Justice Harry Blackmun drew upon both the logical and the experimental data to argue that 5-person juries would be less representative, less reliable, less accurate (Grofman, 1980). Ironically, many of these data actually involved comparisons of 6- versus 12-member juries, and thus also argued against the 6-member jury. But having made and defended a public commitment to the 6-member jury, the Court was not convinced that the same arguments applied (Tanke & Tanke, 1979).

"We have considered [the social science studies] carefully because they provide the only basis, besides judicial hunch, for a decision about whether smaller and smaller juries will be able to fulfill the purposes and functions of the Sixth Amendment."
Justice Harry Blackmun, *Ballew v. Georgia,* 1978

■ FROM LAB TO LIFE: SIMULATED AND REAL JURIES

Perhaps while reading this chapter, you have wondered what some critics (Tapp, 1980; Vidmar, 1979) have wondered: Isn't there an enormous gulf between college students discussing a hypothetical case and real jurors deliberating a real person's fate? Indeed there is. It is one thing to ponder a pretend decision given minimal information and quite another to agonize over the complexities and profound consequences of an actual case. So Reid Hastie, Martin Kaplan, James Davis, Eugene Borgida, and others have asked their participants, who sometimes are drawn from actual juror pools, to view enactments of actual trials. The enactments are so realistic that sometimes participants forget the trial they are watching on television is staged (Thompson & others, 1981).

The U.S. Supreme Court (1986) debated the usefulness of jury research in its decision regarding the use of "death-qualified" jurors in capital punishment cases. The dissenting judges argued that a defendant's constitutional "right to a fair trial and an impartial jury whose composition is not biased toward the prosecution" is violated when jurors include only those who accept the death penalty. Their argument, they said, was based chiefly on "the essential unanimity of the results obtained by researchers using diverse subjects and varied methodologies." The majority of the judges, however, declared their "serious doubts about the value of these studies in predicting the behavior of actual jurors." The dissenting judges replied that it is the courts themselves that have not allowed experiments with actual juries; thus "defendants claiming prejudice from death qualification should not be denied recourse to the only available means of proving their case."

Researchers also defend the laboratory simulations, by noting that the laboratory offers a practical, inexpensive method for studying important issues under controlled conditions (Bray & Kerr, 1982; Dillehay & Nietzel, 1980). What is more, as researchers have begun testing them in more realistic situations, findings from the laboratory studies have often held up quite well. No one contends that the simplified world of the jury experiment mirrors the complex world of the real courtroom. Rather, the experiments help us formulate theories with which we interpret the complex world.

Attorneys are using new technology to present crime stories in ways jurors can easily grasp, as in this computer simulation of a homicide generated on the basis of forensic evidence.

Come to think of it, are these jury simulations any different from social psychology's other experiments, all of which create simplified versions of complex realities? By varying just one or two factors at a time in this simulated reality, the experimenter pinpoints how changes in one or two aspects can affect us. And that is the essence of social psychology's experimental method.

SUMMING UP

What matters is what happens not only in the courtroom but also within and among the jurors themselves.

In forming their judgments, individual jurors (1) construct a story that explains the evidence, (2) consider the judge's instructions, and (3) compare their understandings with the possible verdicts. In a close case, the jurors' own characteristics can influence their verdicts. Jurors who favor capital punishment or who are highly authoritarian appear more likely to convict certain types of defendants. Thus lawyers seek to identify and eliminate potential jurors likely to be unsympathetic to their side. Nevertheless, what matters most is not the jurors' personalities and general attitudes but rather the situation they must react to.

Juries are groups, and are swayed by the same influences that bear upon other types of groups—patterns of majority and minority influence, group polarization, information exchange. Researchers have also examined and questioned the assumptions underlying several recent U.S. Supreme Court decisions permitting smaller juries and nonunanimous juries.

Simulated juries are not real juries, so we must be cautious in generalizing research findings to actual courtrooms. Yet, like all experiments in social psychology, laboratory jury experiments help us formulate theories and principles that we can use to interpret the more complex world of everyday life.

■ FOR FURTHER READING

Hans, V. P., & Vidmar, N. (1986). *Judging the jury*. New York: Plenum. A graceful review of the history of the jury, of two decades of jury research, of important court decisions, and of highly publicized trials. Examines issues involved in insanity, rape, and death penalty cases.

Kassin, S. M., & Wrightsman, L. S. (1988). *The American jury on trial: Psychological perspectives*. New York: Hemisphere. An easy-to-read and authoritative review of the entire process of trial by jury, from jury selection to verdict.

Loftus, E., & Ketcham, K. (1991). *Witness for the defense: The accused, the eyewitness, and the expert who puts memory on trial*. New York: St. Martin's. Memory researcher and frequent expert witness Elizabeth Loftus shows how memory construction can produce persuasive but flawed eyewitness reports by adults and children.

Ross, D. F., Read, J. D., & Toglia, M. P. (Eds.) (1994). *Adult eyewitness testimony: Current trends and developments*. Cambridge, England: Cambridge University Press. Experts summarize what research reveals about eyewitness recall and lineup construction.

PART III

SOCIAL RELATIONS

Having explored how we think about (Part I) and influence (Part II) one another, we come finally to social psychology's third facet—how we relate to one another. Our feelings and actions toward people are sometimes negative, sometimes positive. Chapter 11, "Prejudice," and 12, "Aggression," examine the unpleasant aspects of human relations: Why do we dislike, even despise, one another? Why and when do we hurt one another? Then in Chapters 13, "Attraction and Intimacy," and 14, "Altruism," we explore the more pleasant aspects: Why do we like or love particular people? When will we offer help to friends or strangers? Lastly in Chapter 15, "Conflict and Peacemaking," we consider how social conflicts develop and how they can often be justly and amicably resolved.

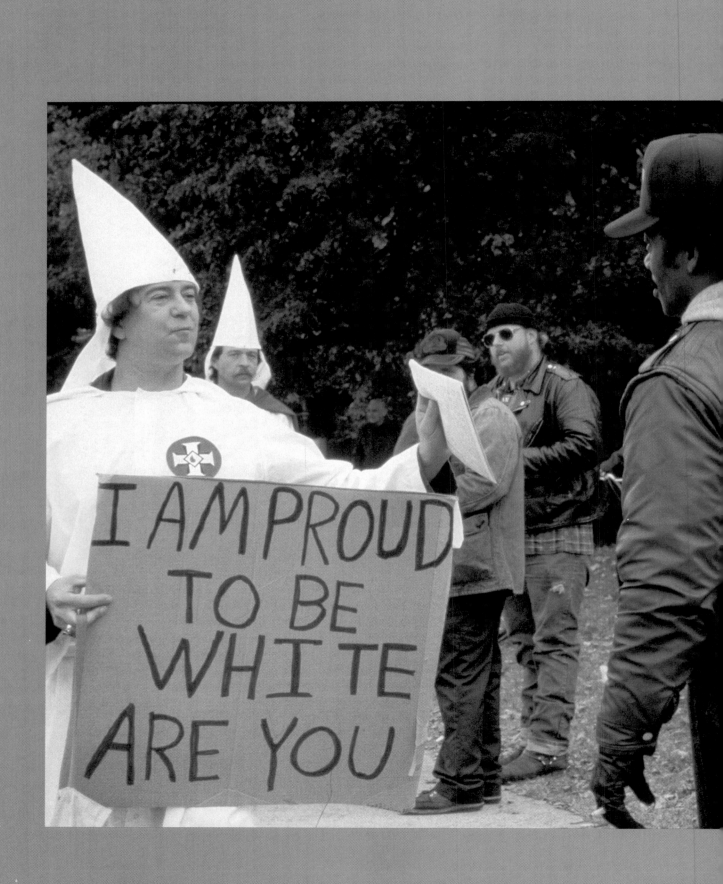

PREJUDICE: DISLIKING OTHERS

Prejudices come in many forms—against "northeastern liberals" or "southern rednecks," against Arab "terrorists" or Christian "fundamentalists," against people who are short, or fat, or homely. Consider a few actual occurrences:

In 1961, African-American Charlayne Hunter, now PBS newscaster Charlayne Hunter-Gault, needed a federal judge to compel the University of Georgia to admit her. A week after she enrolled, state officials asked the court whether they also were compelled to allow her to eat on campus (Menand, 1991).

Prejudice against girls and women is sometimes subtle, sometimes devastating. Nowhere in the modern world are female infants left on a hillside to die of exposure, as was the occasional practice in ancient Greece. Yet in many developing countries, death rates for girls exceed those for boys. During the 1976–1977 Bangladesh famine, preschool girls were more malnourished than boys (Bairagi, 1987).

When men seek roles traditionally associated with women, discrimination can run the other direction. Elizabeth Turner and Anthony Pratkanis (1994) sent identical job-inquiry letters from a community college student in a child-care program to 56 child-care centers and preschools in seven cities. When the letter was signed "Mary E. Johnson" nearly half the centers returned a stamped postcard, checking "we would be interested in discussing a position." When the letter was signed "David E. Johnson" only 1 in 10 replied with similar encouragement.

A group of homosexual students at the University of Illinois announced that the motto for one spring day would be: "If you are gay, wear blue jeans today." When the day dawned, many students who usually wore jeans woke up with an urge to dress up in a skirt or slacks. The gay group had made its point—that attitudes toward homosexuals are such that many would rather give up their usual clothes lest anyone suspect (*RCAgenda*, 1979).

■ THE NATURE AND POWER OF PREJUDICE

How is "prejudice" distinct from "stereotyping," "discrimination," "racism," and "sexism"? Are stereotypes necessarily false or malicious? Over time, how much have racial and gender attitudes changed? What forms does prejudice assume today?

WHAT IS PREJUDICE?

Prejudice, stereotyping, discrimination, racism, sexism: The terms often overlap. Before seeking to understand prejudice, let's clarify the terms. Each of the situations just described involved a negative evaluation of some group. And that is the essence of **prejudice**: an unjustifiable negative attitude toward a group and its individual members. Prejudice is *prejudgment*; it biases us against a person based solely on our identifying the person with a particular group.

Prejudice is an attitude. As we saw in Chapter 4, an attitude is a distinct combination of feelings, inclinations to act, and beliefs. This combination is the ABC of attitudes: *a*ffect (feelings), *b*ehavior tendency (inclination to act),

Prejudice:
An unjustifiable negative attitude toward a group and its individual members.

and *c*ognition (beliefs). A prejudiced person might *dislike* those different from self and *behave* in a discriminatory manner, *believing* them ignorant and dangerous.

The negative evaluations that mark prejudice can stem from emotional associations, from the need to justify behavior, or from negative beliefs, called **stereotypes**. To stereotype is to generalize. To simplify the world, we generalize all the time: The British are reserved; Americans are outgoing. Professors are absentminded, Serbs are cruel. Here are some widely shared stereotypes uncovered in recent research:

- Women who assume the title of "Ms." are more assertive and ambitious than those who call themselves "Miss" or "Mrs." (Dion, 1987; Dion & Cota, 1991; Dion & Schuller, 1991).

- In 19 nations, older adults are seen as likeable but less strong and active than younger adults (Williams, 1993).

- Europeans view southern Europeans such as Italians as more emotional and less efficient than northern Europeans, such as Germans and Scandinavians (Linssen & Hagendoorn, 1994). The stereotype of the southerner as more expressive even holds within countries: James Pennebaker and his colleagues (in press) report that across 20 Northern Hemisphere countries (but not in six Southern Hemisphere countries), southerners within a country are perceived as more expressive than northerners.

Such generalizations can have a germ of truth. Old people are less active. Southern countries in the Northern Hemisphere do have higher rates of violence. People living in the south in these countries do report being more expressive than those in the northern regions of their country. "Stereotypes," note Lee Jussim, Clark McCauley, and Yueh-Ting Lee (1995), "may be positive or negative, accurate or inaccurate." An accurate stereotype may even be desirable. We call it "sensitivity to diversity" or "cultural awareness in a multicultural world." To stereotype the British as more concerned than Mexicans about showing up on time is to understand what to expect and how to act with minimal friction in each culture.

A problem with stereotypes arises when they are *overgeneralized* or just plain wrong. Someone who stereotypes African Americans as more likely than European Americans to bear babies outside of marriage or to be on welfare would be correct. But to presume that most nonmarital births or most welfare clients are African American is to overgeneralize because it just isn't so.

Another problem arises when people attribute negatively evaluated differences to racial biology, ignoring toxic social forces. People may see that race correlates with family disintegration, but not see an underlying corroding factor: poverty. Take out the "confounding" poverty factor (for example, by comparing middle-class Blacks and Whites) and the race difference often disappears (Coontz, 1992; Schaller & O'Brien, 1992).

Prejudice is a negative *attitude*; **discrimination** is negative *behavior*. Discriminatory behavior often, but not always, has its source in prejudicial attitudes (Dovidio & others, in press). How distant we want to be from certain people stems more directly from our feelings than our beliefs about them, note Charles Stangor and his colleagues (1991).

As Chapter 4 emphasized, however, attitudes and behavior are often loosely linked, partly because our behavior reflects more than our inner convictions.

Stereotype:
A belief about the personal attributes of a group of people. Stereotypes can be overgeneralized, inaccurate, and resistant to new information.

Discrimination:
Unjustifiable negative behavior toward a group or its members.

Racism:
(1) An individual's prejudicial attitudes and discriminatory behavior toward people of a given race, or (2) institutional practices (even if not motivated by prejudice) that subordinate people of a given race.

Sexism:
(1) An individual's prejudicial attitudes and discriminatory behavior toward people of a given sex, or (2) institutional practices (even if not motivated by prejudice) that subordinate people of a given sex.

Prejudiced attitudes need not breed hostile acts, nor does all oppression spring from prejudice. **Racism** and **sexism** are institutional practices that discriminate, even when there is no prejudicial intent.

Imagine a police force that set a height requirement of 5 feet, 10 inches, for all its officers. If this requirement were irrelevant to on-the-job effectiveness and tended to exclude Hispanics, Asians, and women, someone might label the requirement racist and sexist. Note that we could make this allegation even if no one intended discrimination. Similarly, if word-of-mouth hiring practices in an all-White business have the effect of excluding non-White employees, the practice could be called racist—even if an employer intended no discrimination. This chapter explores the roots and fruits of prejudiced attitudes. Mindful that racist and sexist policies need not involve prejudiced attitudes, I leave it to sociologists and political scientists to explore racism and sexism in their institutional forms.

HOW PERVASIVE IS PREJUDICE?

Is prejudice inevitable? Can we eradicate it? Let's look at the most heavily studied examples of prejudice—racial and gender prejudice.

Racial Prejudice

In the context of the world, every race is a minority. Non-Hispanic Whites, for example, are but one-fifth of the world's people and will be but one-eighth within another half-century. Thanks to mobility and migration during the past two centuries, the world's races now intermingle, in relations that are sometimes hostile, sometimes amiable.

Is Racial Prejudice Disappearing?

Psychologists capitalize Black and White to emphasize that these are race labels, not literal color labels for persons of African and European ancestry.

To judge from what Americans tell survey takers, racial prejudice toward African Americans has plummeted since the early 1940s. In 1942, most Americans agreed: "There should be separate sections for Negroes on streetcars and buses" (Hyman & Sheatsley, 1956). Today, the question would seem bizarre. In 1942, fewer than a third of all Whites (only 1 in 50 in the south) supported school integration; by 1980, support for it was 90 percent. Considering what a thin slice of history is covered by the years since 1942, or even since slavery was practiced, the changes are dramatic.

African Americans' attitudes also have changed since the 1940s, when Kenneth Clark and Mamie Clark (1947) demonstrated that many held anti-Black prejudices. In making its historic 1954 decision declaring segregated schools unconstitutional, the Supreme Court found it noteworthy that when the Clarks gave African-American children a choice between Black dolls and White dolls, most chose the White. In studies from the 1950s through the 1970s, Black children were increasingly likely to prefer Black dolls. And adult Blacks came to view Blacks and Whites as similar in traits such as intelligence, laziness, and dependability (Jackman & Senter, 1981; Smedley & Bayton, 1978).

So, shall we conclude that racial prejudice is extinct in the United States? No. Although no longer fashionable, racial prejudice still exists. It usually surfaces when a person thinks it is safe to express it.

Prejudice appears among White Americans who, as Figure 11–1 shows, openly dislike African Americans. Most Americans believe that "the increas-

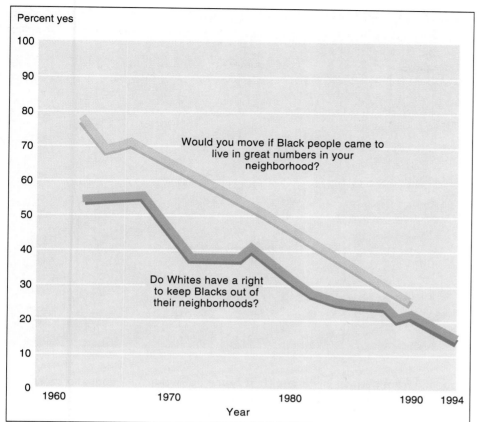

■ **FIGURE 11–1**
Expressed racial attitudes of White Americans from 1963 to 1993.
(Data from Gallup & Hugick, 1990; Niemi & others, 1989; Smith, 1994.)

ing diversity that immigrants bring to this country . . . mostly *threatens* American culture" (Moore, 1993). This is especially so for immigrants whose ethnic identities differ from their own. During the late 1980s and into the 1990s, "hate crimes"—slurs, vandalism, physical violence—victimized a growing number of African Americans and gay men and lesbians (Goleman, 1990; Herek, 1990; Levine, 1990). In other cultures, open ethnic hostilities are common, as Serbs and Muslims in the former Yugoslavia, and Tutsis and Hutus in Rwanda know well.

Questions concerning intimate interracial contacts still detect prejudice. "I would probably feel uncomfortable dancing with a Black person in a public place," detects more racial feeling than, "I would probably feel uncomfortable riding a bus with a Black person." This helps explain why, in a survey of students at 390 colleges and universities, 53 percent of African-American students felt excluded from social activities (Hurtado & others, 1994). (Similar feelings were reported by 24 percent of Asian Americans, 16 percent of Mexican Americans, and 6 percent of European Americans.) In another survey, only 3 percent of Whites said they wouldn't want their child to attend an integrated school, but 57 percent acknowledged they would be unhappy if their child *married* a Black person (*Life*, 1988).

This phenomenon of *greatest prejudice in the most intimate social realms* seems universal. In India, people who accept the caste system will typically allow

In 1992 there were 246,000 Black-White married couples in the United States, quadruple the 65,000 in 1970.

Racial attitude changes appear in the growing market for ethnic dolls.

someone from a lower caste into their home but would not consider marrying such a person (Sharma, 1981). In a national survey of Americans, 75 percent said they would "shop at a store owned by a homosexual" but only 39 percent would "see a homosexual doctor" (Henry, 1994).

Subtle Forms of Prejudice

Recall from Chapter 4 that when White students indicate racial attitudes while hooked up to a supposed lie detector, they admit to prejudice. Other researchers have invited people to evaluate someone's behavior, that someone being either White or Black. Birt Duncan (1976) had White students at the University of California, Irvine, observe a videotape of one man lightly shoving another during a brief argument. When a White shoved a Black man, only 13 percent of the observers rated the act as "violent behavior." They interpreted the shove as "playing around" or "dramatizing." Not so when a Black shoved a White man: Then, 73 percent said the act was "violent."

Many experiments have assessed people's *behavior* toward Blacks and Whites. As we will see in Chapter 15, Whites are equally helpful to any person in need—except when the needy person is remote (say, a wrong-number caller with a Black accent who needs a message relayed). Likewise, when asked to use electric shocks to "teach" a task, White people give no more (if anything less) shock to a Black than to a White person—except when they are angered or when the recipient can't retaliate or know who did it (Crosby & others, 1980; Rogers & Prentice-Dunn, 1981) (Figure 11–2). Thus, discriminatory behavior surfaces not when a behavior would *look* like prejudice but when it can hide behind the screen of some other motive. In France, Britain, Germany, and the Netherlands, too, subtle prejudice (exaggerating ethnic differences, feeling less admiration and affection for minorities, rejecting minorities for supposedly nonracial reasons) is replacing blatant prejudice (Pettigrew & Meertens, 1995). Some researchers therefore call such subtle prejudice "modern racism."

My community's school board recently took the unprecedented step of overruling their search committee's recommendation of a new high school principal. The recommended candidate happened to be African American. The school board's appointee happened to share the community's Dutch heritage. During the ensuing controversy, the local newspapers asked various school board members whether race had been a factor in their votes. "Definitely not!" was the typical reply. Perhaps they were right. But this much seems clear: Modern prejudice is seldom consciously intended. (Virtually no one will answer such a question with "Yes, I'd have voted for him if he'd been White like me.") Rather, prejudice appears more subtly, such as through our preferences for what is familiar, similar, and comfortable (Dovidio & others, 1992; Esses & others, 1993a).

Prejudice may also linger where we least expect it. Mary Inman and Robert Baron (1996) report that people readily perceive prejudice and discrimination where they expect it: White against Black, male against female, young against old. In such cases, our suspicions are readily aroused. Sometimes they produce "false alarms"—perceptions of prejudicial motives where none exist. People are slower to detect prejudice when the identical bias occurs in the reverse direction, or within a group (say, a female discriminating against a female). Thus, prejudice among blacks, Hispanics, and Koreans may go unnoticed until it erupts into violence.

As blatant prejudice subsides, automatic emotional reactions linger. Patricia Devine and her colleagues (1989, 1995) report that those low and high in prejudice are aware of the same stereotypes and often have similar automatic reactions. They differ because the low-prejudice person consciously tries to suppress prejudicial thoughts and feelings. It's like consciously breaking a bad habit, says Devine. Try as we might to suppress unwanted thoughts—thoughts about food, thoughts about romance with a friend's partner, judgmental

Race sensitivity leads to exaggerated reactions to isolated minority persons—both overpraising their accomplishments and overcriticizing their mistakes (Fiske, 1989; Hass & others, 1991).

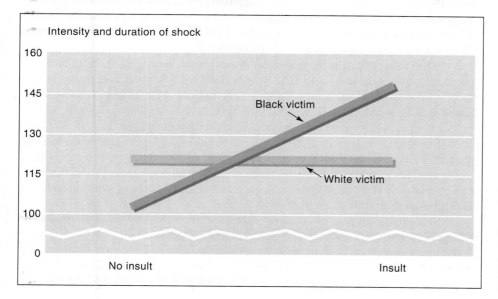

■ FIGURE 11–2

Does anger trigger latent prejudice? When White students administered electric shock, supposedly as part of a "behavior-modification experiment," they behaved less aggressively toward an agreeable Black victim than toward a White victim. But when the victim insulted the subjects, they responded with more aggression if the victim was Black.

(Data from Rogers & Prentice-Dunn, 1981.)

BEHIND THE SCENES

"Are you Catholic?" Although initially puzzled by the question, it so reliably followed the disclosure that I have seven siblings that it became clear to me that many people relate number of children to religious affiliation. Similarly, while moving around a lot as a child, I observed that knowing others' ethnic group, cued by their last names, triggered unwarranted stereotypes about their personalities, interests, and behaviors. Such inferences were so quickly and easily supplied that they seemed automatic—even for those who believed that stereotypes and prejudice are wrong.

Why would such negative thoughts persist, even when people embrace nonprejudiced values? Could such unintentional stereotyping be overcome? In working through such issues I came to see that overcoming prejudice is like breaking a habit. As in breaking any habit, it's not easy. It requires a great deal of effort, practice, and relearning.

PATRICIA DEVINE, *University of Wisconsin*

"There is a real anti-black sentiment in American life, but it is no longer as powerful as we remember it. Our memory makes us like the man who wears a heavy winter coat in springtime because he was frostbitten in winter."
Shelby Steele,
The Content of Our Character: A New Vision of Race in America,
1990

thoughts about another group—they sometimes refuse to go away (Macrae & others, 1994; Wegner & Erber, 1992). Unwanted thoughts and feelings often persist.

Thomas Pettigrew (1987, p. 20) illustrates: "Many [people] have confessed to me . . . that even though in their minds they no longer feel prejudice toward Blacks, they still feel squeamish when they shake hands with a Black. These feelings are left over from what they learned in their families as children." Likewise, those with accepting and those with disapproving attitudes toward homosexuals may both feel uncomfortable sitting with a gay male on a bus seat (Monteith, 1993). Thus prejudice operates partly as an unconscious, unintended response (Greenwald & Banaji, 1995). As in the experiments with the shoves, shocks, and wrong phone numbers, unconscious prejudice appears mostly when people react to someone for the first time, with their conscious attention focused on something other than the person's race.

Even the very social scientists who study prejudice seem vulnerable to it, note Anthony Greenwald and Eric Schuh (1994). They analyzed biases in authors' citations of social science articles by people with selected non-Jewish names (Erickson, McBride, and so forth) and Jewish names (Goldstein, Siegel, and so forth). After analyzing nearly 30,000 citations, including 17,000 citations of prejudice research, they had a remarkable finding: Compared to Jewish authors, non-Jewish authors had 40 percent higher odds of citing non-Jewish names. (Greenwald and Schuh could not determine whether Jewish authors were overciting their Jewish colleagues, non-Jewish authors were overciting their non-Jewish colleagues, or both.)

To summarize, there is good news: During the past four decades, open prejudice against African Americans has nearly vanished. White racial attitudes are far more egalitarian than a generation ago. The bad news pertains to all people of color, including Native Americans and Hispanics (Trimble, 1988; Ramirez, 1988): Though now camouflaged by a more pleasant exterior, resentments and bias still lurk beneath the surface. And what is true in the United States is true everywhere: In a world still torn by ethnic tensions, old hatreds die slowly.

Gender Prejudice

How pervasive is prejudice against women? In Chapter 6, we examined gender-role norms—people's ideas about how women and men *ought* to behave. Here we first consider gender *stereotypes*—people's beliefs about how women and men *do* behave.

Gender Stereotypes

From research on stereotypes, two conclusions are indisputable: Strong gender stereotypes exist, and, as often happens, members of the stereotyped group accept the stereotypes. Men and women agree that you *can* judge the book by its sexual cover. Analyzing responses from a University of Michigan survey, Mary Jackman and Mary Senter (1981) found that gender stereotypes were much stronger than racial stereotypes. For example, only 22 percent of men thought the two sexes equally "emotional." Of the remaining 78 percent, those who believed females were more emotional outnumbered those who thought males were by 15 to 1. And what did the women believe? To within 1 percentage point, their responses were identical.

Consider, too, a study by Natalie Porter, Florence Geis, and Joyce Jennings Walstedt (1983). They showed students pictures of "a group of graduate students working as a team on a research project" (Figure 11–3). Then they gave them a test of "first impressions," asking them to guess who contributed most to the group. When the group was either all male or all female, the students overwhelmingly chose the person at the head of the table. When the group

"All the pursuits of men are the pursuits of women also, and in all of them a woman is only a lesser man."
Plato, *Republic*

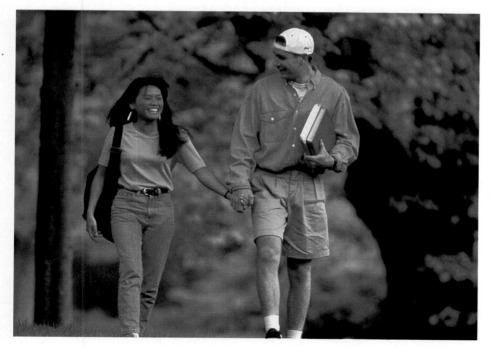

Although prejudice dies last in socially intimate contacts, interracial romance and marriage is much more common today than in 1970.

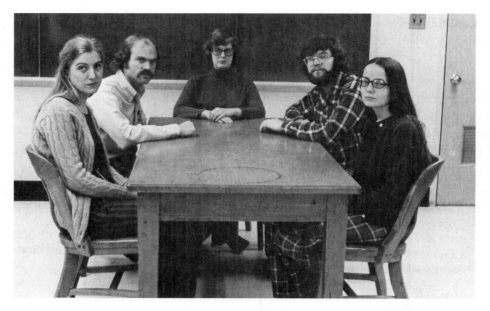

■ **FIGURE 11–3**
Which one of these people would you guess is the group's strongest contributor? Shown this picture, college students usually guessed one of the two men, although those shown photos of same-sex groups most commonly guessed the person at the head of the table.

was mixed sex, a man occupying that position was again overwhelmingly chosen. But a woman occupying that position was usually ignored. Each of the men in Figure 11–3 received more of the leadership choices than all three women combined! This stereotype of men as leaders was true not only of women as well as men but also of feminists as well as nonfeminists. How pervasive are gender stereotypes? Quite pervasive.

Remember that stereotypes are generalizations about a group of people and may be true, false, or overgeneralized from a kernel of truth. In Chapter 6 we noted that the average man and woman do differ somewhat in social connectedness, empathy, social power, aggressiveness, and sexual initiative. Do we then conclude that gender stereotypes are accurate? Often they are, observed Janet Swim (1994). She found that Pennsylvania State University students' stereotypes of men's and women's restlessness, nonverbal sensitivity, aggressiveness, and so forth were reasonable approximations of actual gender differences.

Carol Lynn Martin (1987) surmised as much after querying visitors to the University of British Columbia. She asked them to check which of several traits described them and to estimate what percentage of North American males and females had each trait. Males were *slightly* more likely than females to describe themselves as assertive and dominant and were *slightly* less likely to describe themselves as tender and compassionate. But stereotypes of these differences were greatly exaggerated: The people perceived North American males as almost twice as likely as females to be assertive and dominant and roughly half as likely to be tender and compassionate. The conclusion: Although actual differences between the sexes are small, stereotypes are sometimes strong.

Stereotypes (beliefs) are not prejudices (attitudes). Stereotypes may support prejudice. But then again one might believe, without prejudice, that men and women are "different yet equal." Let us therefore see how researchers probe for gender prejudice.

Gender Attitudes

Judging from what people tell survey researchers, attitudes toward women have changed as rapidly as racial attitudes. In 1937, one-third of Americans said they would vote for a qualified woman whom their party nominated for president; in 1988, 9 in 10 said they would (Figure 11–4). In 1967, 56 percent of first-year American college students agreed that, "The activities of married women are best confined to the home and family"; by 1993, only 24 percent agreed (Astin & others, 1987, 1993). In 1970, Americans were split 50-50 on whether they favored or opposed "efforts to strengthen women's status." By the end of the decade, this tenet of the women's movement was favored by better than 2 to 1. And should there be "equal pay for women and men when they are doing the same job?" (NBC, 1977). Yes, say both men and women— by a 16 to 1 margin, as close to absolute consensus as Americans ever get.

Alice Eagly and her associates (1991) and Geoffrey Haddock and Mark Zanna (1994) also report that people don't respond to women with gut-level negative emotions as they do to certain other groups. Most people like "women" more than "men." They perceive women as more understanding, kind, and helpful. Thus, a *favorable* stereotype—which Eagly (1994) dubs the *women-are-wonderful effect*—results in a favorable attitude. Affection, however, needn't entail admiration. One can like grandmothers and day-care workers (or women in general) without admiring them. And some people admire the achievements of Jews, Germans, or Japanese, note Susan Fiske and Janet Ruscher (1993), without liking them.

But there is still more good news for those who are upset by sex bias. One heavily publicized finding of prejudice against women came from a 1968 study in which Philip Goldberg gave women students at Connecticut College several short articles, and asked them to judge the value of each. Sometimes a given article was attributed to a male author (for example, John T. McKay) and sometimes to a female author (for example, Joan T. McKay). In general, the articles received lower ratings when attributed to a female. The historic mark of oppression—self-deprecation—surfaced clearly: Women were prejudiced against women.

> "Women are wonderful primarily because they are [perceived] so nice. [Men are] perceived as superior to women in agentic [competitive, dominant] attributes that are viewed as equipping people for success in paid work, especially in male-dominated occupations."
> Alice Eagly (1994)

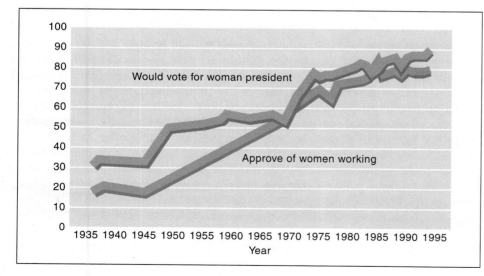

■ **FIGURE 11–4**
Prejudice against women: an idea whose time has passed? The percentage of Americans who say that they approve of a married woman's working for money if she has a capable husband and that they would vote for a qualified woman candidate for President has steadily increased since the mid-1930s. (Data from Niemi & others, 1989; Tom Smith, personal correspondence.)

Eager to demonstrate the subtle reality of gender prejudice, I obtained Goldberg's materials and repeated the experiment for my own students' benefit. They showed no such tendency to deprecate women's work. So, Janet Swim, Eugene Borgida, Geoffrey Maruyama, and I (1989) searched the literature and corresponded with investigators to learn all we could about studies of gender bias in the evaluation of men's and women's work. To our surprise, the biases that occasionally surfaced were as often against men as women. But the most common result across 104 studies involving almost 20,000 people was *no difference*. On most comparisons, judgments of someone's work were unaffected by whether the work was attributed to a female or a male. Summarizing other studies of people's evaluations of women and men as leaders, professors, and so forth, Alice Eagly (1994) says that "experiments have *not* demonstrated any *overall* tendency to devalue women's work."

The attention given highly publicized studies of prejudice against women's work illustrates a familiar point: Social scientists' values often seep into their conclusions. The researchers who conducted the publicized studies did as they should in reporting their findings. However, my colleagues and I more readily accepted and reported findings supporting our preconceived biases than those opposing them.

So, is gender bias fast becoming extinct in western countries? Has the women's movement nearly completed its work? As with race prejudice, blatant gender prejudice is dying, but subtle bias lives. The bogus-pipeline method, for example, exposes bias. As we noted in Chapter 4, men who believe an experimenter can read their true attitudes with a sensitive lie detector express less sympathy toward women's rights. Even on paper-and-pencil questionnaires, Janet Swim and her co-researchers (1995) found a subtle ("modern") sexism that parallels subtle ("modern") racism. Both appear in denials of discrimination and in antagonism toward efforts to promote equality.

We can also detect bias in behavior. That's what a research team led by Ian Ayres (1991) did while visiting 90 Chicago-area car dealers and using a uniform strategy to negotiate the lowest price on a new car that cost the dealer about $11,000. White males were given a final price that averaged $11,362; White females were given an average price of $11,504; Black males were given an average price of $11,783; and Black females were given an average price of $12,237.

Most women know that gender bias exists. They believe that sex discrimination affects most working women, as shown by the lower salaries for women and for jobs, such as child care, that are filled mostly by women. Garbage haulers (mostly men) make more than preschool teachers (mostly women). Curiously, however, Faye Crosby and her colleagues (1989) have repeatedly found that most women deny feeling personally discriminated against. Discrimination, they believe, is something *other* women face. Their employer is not villainous. They are doing better than the average woman. Hearing no complaints, managers—even in discriminatory organizations—can persuade themselves that justice prevails. Similar denials of *personal* disadvantage, while perceiving discrimination against one's *group*, occur among unemployed people, out-of-the-closet lesbians, African Americans, and Canadian minorities (Taylor & others, 1990).

In the world beyond democratic western countries, gender discrimination looms even larger.

Question: *"Misogyny" is the hatred of women. What is the corresponding word for the hatred of men?*
Answer: *In most dictionaries, no such word exists.*

"And just why do we always call <u>my</u> income the second income?"

Gender prejudice gets expressed subtly.

■ Two-thirds of the world's unschooled children are girls. The world's 600 million illiterate women exceed its 350 million illiterate men by 70 percent (United Nations, 1991).

■ In Saudi Arabia, women are forbidden to drive. In the Sudan, they may not leave the country without the permission of husband, father, or brother (Beyer, 1990).

■ In South Korea, male births exceed female births by 14 percent, in China by 18 percent. Sex-selective abortions and infanticide have led to 76,000,000— let's say that slowly, seventy-six *million*—"missing women" (Kristof, 1993; Klasen, 1994).

To conclude, overt prejudice against people of color and against women is far less common today than it was four decades ago. Nevertheless, techniques that are sensitive to subtle prejudice still detect widespread bias. And in parts of the world, gender prejudice is literally deadly. We therefore need to look carefully and closely at the problem of prejudice and its causes. Let's examine its social, cognitive, and emotional sources.

*S*tereotypes are *beliefs* about another group, beliefs that may be accurate, inaccurate, or overgeneralized but based on a kernel of truth. *Prejudice* is an unjustifiable negative *attitude*. Discrimination is unjustifiable negative *behavior*. *Racism* and *sexism* may refer to individuals' prejudicial attitudes or discriminatory behavior, or to oppressive institutional practices (even if not intentionally prejudicial).

Stereotypical beliefs, prejudicial attitudes, and discriminatory behavior have long poisoned human existence. Judging by what Americans have told survey researchers during the last four decades, their prejudice against Blacks and women has plunged. Nevertheless, subtle survey questions, and

SUMMING UP

indirect methods for assessing people's attitudes and behavior, still reveal strong gender stereotypes and a fair amount of disguised racial and gender bias. Though less obvious, prejudice yet lurks.

■ SOCIAL SOURCES OF PREJUDICE

What social conditions breed prejudice? How does society maintain prejudice?

Prejudice springs from several sources because it serves several functions (Herek, 1986, 1987). Prejudice may express our sense of who we are and gain us social acceptance. It may defend our sense of self against anxiety that arises from insecurity or inner conflict. And it may promote our self-interest by supporting what brings us pleasure and opposing what doesn't. Consider first how prejudice can function to defend self-esteem and social position.

SOCIAL INEQUALITIES

Unequal Status and Prejudice

A principle to remember: *Unequal status breeds prejudice*. Masters view slaves as lazy, irresponsible, lacking ambition—as having just those traits that justify the slavery. Historians debate the forces that create unequal status. But once these inequalities exist, prejudice helps justify the economic and social superiority of those who have wealth and power. You tell me the economic relationship between two groups and I'll predict the intergroup attitudes. Prejudice and discrimination support each other: Discrimination breeds prejudice, and prejudice legitimizes discrimination.

Examples abound of prejudice rationalizing unequal status. Until recently, prejudice was greatest in regions where slavery was practiced. Nineteenth-century European politicians and writers justified imperial expansion by describing exploited, colonized people as "inferior," "requiring protection," and a "burden" to be borne (G. W. Allport, 1958, pp. 204–205). Four decades ago,

"Prejudice is never easy unless it can pass itself off for reason."
William Hazlitt (1778–1830), "On Prejudice"

Racial prejudice often begins during times of conflict, as during World War II when Japanese-Americans were sent to internment camps.

sociologist Helen Mayer Hacker (1951) noted how stereotypes of Blacks and women helped rationalize the inferior status of each: Many people thought both groups were mentally slow, emotional and primitive, and "contented" with their subordinate role. Blacks were "inferior"; women were "weak." Blacks were all right in their place; women's place was in the home.

In times of conflict, attitudes easily adjust to behavior. People often view enemies as subhuman and depersonalize them with a label. During World War II, the Japanese people became "the Japs." After the war was over, they became "the intelligent, hardworking Japanese." Attitudes are amazingly adaptable. Cruel acts breed cruel attitudes.

Gender stereotypes, too, help rationalize gender roles. After studying these stereotypes worldwide, John Williams and Deborah Best (1990) noted that if women provide most of the care to young children, it is reassuring to think women are naturally nurturant. And if males run the businesses, hunt, and fight wars, it is comforting to suppose that men are aggressive, independent, and adventurous. In experiments, people perceive members of unknown groups as having traits that suit their roles (Hoffman & Hurst, 1990).

"It is human nature to hate those whom we have injured."
Tacitus, *Agricola*

Religion and Prejudice

Those who benefit from social inequalities yet avow that "all are created equal" need to justify keeping things the way they are. And what more powerful justification than to believe God has ordained the existing social order? For all sorts of cruel deeds, noted William James, "Piety is the mask" (1902, p. 264)—a mask that sometimes portrays lovely expressions while hiding ugly motives.

In almost every country, leaders invoke religion to sanctify the present order. In a remarkable turnabout, Father George Zabelka (1980), chaplain to the aircrews that bombed Hiroshima, Nagasaki, and other civilian targets in Japan, years later came to regret that he had provided religion's blessing for these missions of devastation: "The whole structure of the secular, religious, and military society told me clearly that it was all right to 'let the Japs have it.' God was on the side of my country."

The use of religion to support injustice helps explain a consistent pair of findings concerning Christianity, North America's dominant religion: (1) Church members express more racial prejudice than nonmembers and (2) those professing traditional or fundamentalist Christian beliefs express more prejudice than those professing less traditional beliefs (Altemeyer & Hunsberger, 1992; Batson & others, 1993; Gorsuch, 1988).

Knowing the correlation between two variables—religion and prejudice—tells us nothing about their causal connection. There might be no connection at all. Perhaps people with less education are both more fundamentalist and more prejudiced. Perhaps prejudice causes religion, by leading people to create religious ideas to support their prejudices. Or perhaps religion causes prejudice, by leading people to believe that because all individuals possess free will, impoverished minorities have no one but themselves to blame for any perceived lack of virtue or achievement.

If indeed religion causes prejudice, then more religious church members should also be more prejudiced. But three other findings consistently indicate that this plainly is not so.

■ Among church members, faithful church attenders were, in 24 out of 26 comparisons, *less* prejudiced than occasional attenders (Batson & Ventis, 1982).

Second, Gordon Allport and Michael Ross (1967) found that those for whom religion is an end in itself (those who agree, for example, with the statement, "My religious beliefs are what really lie behind my whole approach to life") express *less* prejudice than those for whom religion is more a means to other ends (who agree, "A primary reason for my interest in religion is that my church is a congenial social activity"). Those for whom religion is an open-ended quest (not an attachment to pat answers) exhibit little prejudice (Batson & others, 1986). And those who score highest on Gallup's "spiritual commitment" index are more welcoming of a person of another race moving in next door (Gallup & Jones, 1992).

■ Protestant ministers and Roman Catholic priests gave more support to the civil rights movement than did lay people (Fichter, 1968; Hadden, 1969). And in Germany, 45 percent of clergy in 1934 had aligned themselves with the Confessing Church, organized to oppose the Nazi regime (Reed, 1989).

What, then, is the relationship between religion and prejudice? The answer we get depends on *how* we ask the question. If we define religiousness as church membership or willingness to agree at least superficially with traditional beliefs, then the more religious are the more racially prejudiced—the Ku Klux Klan rationalizes bigotry with religion. However, if we assess depth of religious commitment in any of several other ways, then the very devout are less prejudiced—hence the religious roots of the modern civil rights movement, among whose leaders were many ministers and priests. As Gordon Allport concluded, "The role of religion is paradoxical. It makes prejudice and it unmakes prejudice" (1958, p. 413).

Discrimination's Impact: The Self-Fulfilling Prophecy

Attitudes may agree with the social order not only as a rationalization for it but also because discrimination affects its victims. "One's reputation," wrote Gordon Allport, "cannot be hammered, hammered, hammered into one's head without doing something to one's character" (1958, p. 139). If we could snap our fingers and end all discrimination, it would be naive then to say: "The tough times are all over, folks! You can now put on suits or dresses and be attache-carrying executives and professionals." When the oppression ends, its effects linger, like a societal hangover.

In his classic book, *The Nature of Prejudice*, Allport catalogued 15 possible effects of victimization. Allport believed these reactions were reducible to two basic types—those that involve blaming oneself (withdrawal, self-hate, aggression against one's own group) and those that involve blaming external causes (fighting back, suspiciousness, increased group pride). If the net results are negative—say, higher rates of crime—people can use them to justify the discrimination that helps maintain them: "If we let those people in our nice neighborhood, property values will plummet."

Does discrimination affect its victims in this way? We must be careful not to overstate the point. The soul and style of Black culture is for many a proud heritage, not just a response to victimization (Jones, 1983). Cultural differences need not imply social deficits.

Nevertheless, social beliefs *can* be self-confirming, as demonstrated in a clever pair of experiments by Carl Word, Mark Zanna, and Joel Cooper (1974). In the first experiment, Princeton University White men interviewed White and

"We have just enough religion to make us hate, but not enough to make us love one another."
Jonathan Swift,
Thoughts on Various Subjects

"It is understandable that the suppressed people should develop an intense hostility towards a culture whose existence they make possible by their work, but in whose wealth they have too small a share."
Sigmund Freud,
The Future of an Illusion, 1927

Black job applicants. When the applicant was Black, the interviewers sat farther away, ended the interview 25 percent sooner, and made 50 percent more speech errors than when the applicant was White. Imagine being interviewed by someone who sat at a distance, stammered, and ended the interview rather quickly. Would it affect your performance or your feelings about the interviewer?

To find out, the researchers conducted a second experiment in which trained interviewers treated students as the interviewers in the first experiment had treated either the White or Black applicants. When videotapes of the interviews were later rated, those who were treated like the Blacks in the first experiment seemed more nervous and less effective. Moreover, the interviewees could themselves sense a difference; those treated as were the Blacks judged their interviewers as less adequate and less friendly. The experimenters concluded "that the 'problem' of Black performance resides not entirely within the Blacks, but rather within the interaction setting itself."

Recall, too (from Chapter 3), that social beliefs can be self-fulfilling. Placed in a situation where others expect you to perform poorly, your anxiety may cause you to confirm the belief. Claude Steele and his colleagues call this phenomenon **stereotype vulnerability**—a self-confirming apprehension that one's behavior will verify a negative stereotype. In several experiments, Steven Spencer and Steele (1995) gave a very difficult math test to men and women students who had similar math abilities and course experience. Told that men and women usually perform equally on the test, the women's performance consistently equaled the men's. Told that women usually underperform men on the test, the women dramatically confirmed the stereotype (Figure 11–5). Frustrated by the extremely difficult items, they apparently felt added apprehension, which undermined their performance.

"If we foresee evil in our fellow man, we tend to provoke it; if good, we elicit it."
Gordon Allport,
The Nature of Prejudice, 1958

Stereotype vulnerability:
A disruptive apprehension that one will verify a negative stereotype.

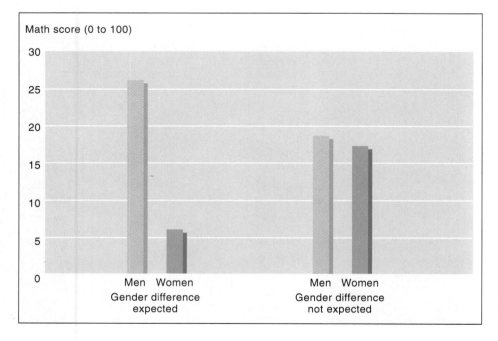

■ **FIGURE 11–5**
Stereotype vulnerability and women's math performance. Steven Spencer and Claude Steele (1995) gave equally capable men and women a difficult math test. When subjects were led to expect inferior performance by women, women fulfilled the stereotype by scoring lower.

Might racial stereotypes be similarly self-fulfilling? Steele and Joshua Aronson (in press) confirmed this when giving difficult verbal abilities tests to Whites and Blacks. Taking the tests under conditions designed to make Blacks "stereotype vulnerable" depressed their scores relative to Whites.

INGROUP AND OUTGROUP

Ingroup:
"Us"—a group of people who share a sense of belonging, a feeling of common identity.

Outgroup:
"Them"—a group that people perceive as distinctively different from or apart from their ingroup.

Ingroup bias:
The tendency to favor one's own group.

The social definition of who you are—your race, religion, sex, academic major—implies a definition of who you are not. The circle that includes "us" (the **ingroup**) excludes "them" (the **outgroup**). Thus, the mere experience of being formed into groups may promote **ingroup bias**. Ask children, "Which are better, the children in your school or the children at [another school nearby]?" Virtually all will say their own school has the better children.

In a series of experiments, British social psychologists Henri Tajfel (pronounced TOSH-fel) and Michael Billig (1974; Tajfel, 1970, 1981, 1982) discovered how little it takes to provoke favoritism toward *us* and unfairness toward *them*. Even when the us-them distinction was trivial, people still favored their own group. In one study Tajfel and Billig had British teenagers evaluate modern abstract paintings and then told them that they and some others had favored the art of Paul Klee over that of Wassily Kandinsky. Finally, without ever meeting the other members of their group, the teens divided some money among members of both groups. In experiment after experiment, defining groups even in this trivial way produced favoritism. David Wilder (1981) summarizes the typical result: "When given the opportunity to divide 15 points [worth money], subjects generally award 9 or 10 points to their own group and 5 or 6 points to the other group." This bias occurs with both sexes and with people of all ages and nationalities, though especially with people from individualist cultures (Gudykunst, 1989). (People in communal cultures identify more with all their peers and so treat everyone more the same.)

In Rwanda, ingroup bias lay behind the murder of half the minority Tutsi population and to a huge refugee exodus when the majority Hutus were defeated.

We also are more prone to ingroup bias when our group is small relative to the outgroup (Mullen & others, 1992). When we're part of a small group surrounded by a larger group, we are also more conscious of our group membership; when our ingroup is the majority, we think less about it. To be a foreign student, or to be a Black student on a mostly White campus or a White student on a mostly Black campus, is to feel one's social identity more keenly and to react accordingly. In Britain, where the English outnumber the Scots 10 to 1, Scottish identity defines itself partly by differences with the English. "To be Scottish is, to some degree, to dislike or resent the English" (Meech & Kilborn, 1992). The English, as the majority, are less conscious of being not-Scottish.

Even forming conspicuous groups on *no* logical basis—say, merely by composing groups X and Y with the flip of a coin—will produce some ingroup bias (Billig & Tajfel, 1973; Brewer & Silver, 1978; Locksley & others, 1980). In Kurt Vonnegut's novel *Slapstick*, computers gave everyone a new middle name; all "Daffodil-11's" then felt unity with one another and distance from "Raspberry-13's." The self-serving bias (Chapter 2) rides again, enabling people to achieve a more positive social identity: "We" are better than "they," even when "we" and "they" are alike.

Because we evaluate ourselves partly by our group memberships, seeing our own groups as superior helps us feel good about ourselves. What is more, our whole self-concept—our sense of who we are—contains not just our personal identity (our sense of our personal attributes and attitudes) but our **social identity** (Abrams, 1994; Hogg & Abrams, 1988). Having a sense of "we-ness" strengthens our self concept. It *feels* good. So much so, report Charles Perdue and his associates (1990), that just pairing a nonsense syllable such as *yof* with words like "we" and "us" makes the syllable seem more pleasant than if it is associated with "they" or "them."

Because of our social identifications, we conform to our group norms. We sacrifice ourselves for team, family, nation. We dislike outgroups. The more important our social identity and the more strongly attached we feel to a group, the more we react prejudicially to threats from another group (Crocker & Luhtanen, 1990; Hinkle & others, 1992). Names such as Serbian, Tamil, Kurd, and Estonian represent ingroup identities for which people are prepared to die. Israeli historian and former Jerusalem deputy mayor Meron Benvenisti (1988) reports that among Jerusalem's Jews and Arabs, social identity is so central to self-concept that it constantly reminds them of who they are not. Thus, on the integrated street where he lives, his own children—to his dismay—"have not acquired a single Arab friend."

When our group has actually been successful, we can also make ourselves feel better by identifying more strongly with it. When queried after their football team's victory, college students frequently report *"we* won." When questioned after their team's defeat, students are more likely to say *"they* lost." Basking in the reflected glory of a successful ingroup is strongest among those who have just experienced an ego blow, such as learning they did poorly on a "creativity test" (Cialdini & others, 1976). We can also bask in the reflected glory of a friend's achievement—except when the friend outperforms us on something pertinent to our identity (Tesser & others, 1988). If you think of yourself as an outstanding psychology student, you will likely take more pleasure in a friend's excelling in mathematics.

"There is a tendency to define one's own group positively in order to evaluate oneself positively."
John C. Turner (1984)

Social identity:
The "we" aspect of our self-concept. The part of our answer to "Who am I?" that comes from our group memberships. Examples: "I am Australian." "I am Catholic."

Drawing by Ed Fisher; © 1987 The New Yorker Magazine, Inc.

"Uh-oh! They seem to have loved it!"

Something favored by an "out-group" may be cast in a negative light.

Father, Mother, and Me,
* sister and Auntie say*
All the people like us are We,
* and every one else is They.*
And They live over the sea,
* While We live over the way.*
But—would you believe it?—
they
* look upon We*
* As only a sort of They!*
Rudyard Kipling, 1926 (quoted
by Mullen, 1991)

Ingroup bias is the favoring of one's group. Such favoritism could reflect (1) liking for the ingroup, (2) dislike for the outgroup, or both. If both, loyalty to one's group should produce a devaluing of other groups. Is that true? Does ethnic pride cause prejudice? Does a strong feminist identity lead women to dislike men? Does loyalty to a particular fraternity or sorority lead its members to deprecate independents and members of other fraternities and sororities?

Experiments support both explanations. Outgroup stereotypes prosper when people feel keenly their ingroup identity, as when with other ingroup members (Wilder & Shapiro, 1991). At a club meeting, we sense most strongly our differences from those in another club. When anticipating bias against our group, we more strongly disparage the outgroup (Vivian & Berkowitz, 1993).

Yet ingroup bias results primarily from perceiving that one's own group is good (Brewer, 1979) and to a lesser extent from a sense that other groups are bad (Rosenbaum & Holtz, 1985). So it seems that positive feelings for our own groups need not be mirrored by equally strong negative feelings for outgroups. Granted, devotion to one's own race, religion, and social group can predispose a person to devalue other races, religions, and social groups. But the sequence is not automatic.

CONFORMITY

Once established, prejudice is maintained largely by inertia. If prejudice is socially accepted, many people will follow the path of least resistance and conform to the fashion. They will act not so much out of a need to hate as out of a need to be liked and accepted.

Studies by Thomas Pettigrew (1958) of Whites in South Africa and the American south revealed that during the 1950s those who conformed most to other social norms were also most prejudiced; those who were less conforming mirrored less of the surrounding prejudice. The price of nonconformity was painfully clear to the ministers of Little Rock, Arkansas, where the Supreme Court's 1954 school desegregation decision was implemented. Most ministers favored integration but usually only privately; they feared that advocating it openly would lose them members and contributions (Campbell & Pettigrew, 1959). Or consider the Indiana steelworkers and West Virginia coal miners of the same era. In the mills and the mines, the workers accepted integration. In the neighborhood, the norm was rigid segregation (Reitzes, 1953; Minard, 1952). Prejudice was clearly *not* a manifestation of "sick" personalities but simply of the norms that operated in a given situation. Nearly a half-century later, the racial attitudes of parents and peers are still major predictors of prejudice (Agnew & others, 1994).

Conformity also maintains gender prejudice. "If we have come to think that the nursery and the kitchen are the natural sphere of a woman," wrote George Bernard Shaw in an 1891 essay, "we have done so exactly as English children come to think that a cage is the natural sphere of a parrot—because they have never seen one anywhere else." Children who *have* seen women elsewhere—children of employed women—have less stereotyped views of men and women (Hoffman, 1977).

In all this, there is a message of hope. If prejudice is not deeply ingrained in personality, then as fashions change and new norms evolve, prejudice can diminish. And so it has.

BEHIND THE SCENES

One's best ideas in social psychology often evolve from direct experience. As a White southerner, I realized when reading *The Authoritarian Personality* as an undergraduate that the book did not explain most of what I thought I knew about anti-Black prejudice in the south. I knew many people who were racially prejudiced but did not appear to be authoritarian personalities. To explain the discrepancy, I needed only to recall the times I had been expelled from the public schools of Richmond, Virginia, for opposing the traditional racial norms. These ideas led directly to my research on how societal pressures to conform shape individual attitudes and behavior.

THOMAS PETTIGREW, *University of California, Santa Cruz*

INSTITUTIONAL SUPPORTS

Segregation is one way that social institutions (schools, government, the media) bolster widespread prejudice. Politics is another. Political leaders may both reflect and reinforce prevailing attitudes. When Arkansas Governor Orville Faubus barred the doors of Central High School in Little Rock, he was doing more than representing his constituents; he was legitimating their views.

Schools, too, reinforce dominant cultural attitudes. One analysis of stories in 134 children's readers written before 1970 found that male characters outnumbered female characters 3 to 1 (Women on Words and Images, 1972). Who was portrayed as showing initiative, bravery, and competence? Note the answer in this excerpt from the classic "Dick and Jane" children's reader: Jane, sprawled out on the sidewalk, her roller skates beside her, listens as Mark explains to his mother;

> "She cannot skate," said Mark.
> "I can help her.
> I want to help her.
> Look at her, mother.
> Just look at her.
> She's just like a girl.
> She gives up."

Not until the 1970s, when changing ideas about males and females brought new perceptions of such portrayals, was this blatant stereotyping widely noticed and changes made in the textbooks. Institutional supports for prejudice often go unnoticed. Usually, they are not deliberate, hateful attempts to oppress a group; more often, they simply reflect a culture's assumptions, as when the one "flesh"-colored crayon in the Crayola box was pinkish white.

What contemporary examples of institutionalized biases still go unnoticed? Here is one most of us have never noticed, although it is frequently right be-

An exception to face-ism: a rare instance in which an ad focuses on a male's entire body.

fore our eyes: By examining 1750 photographs of people in magazines and newspapers, Dane Archer and his associates (1983) discovered that about two-thirds of the average male photo, but less than half of the average female photo, is devoted to the face. As Archer widened his search, he discovered that such "face-ism" is common. He found it in the periodicals of 11 other countries, in 920 portraits gathered from the artwork of six centuries, and in the amateur drawings of students at the University of California, Santa Cruz. Georgia Nigro and her colleagues (1988) confirmed the face-ism phenomenon in more magazines, including *Ms*.

The researchers suspect that the visual prominence given men's faces and women's bodies both reflects and perpetuates sex bias. In research in Germany, Norbert Schwarz and Eva Kurz (1989) confirmed that people whose faces are prominent in photos seem more intelligent and ambitious. But better a whole-body depiction than none at all. When Ruth Thibodeau (1989) examined the previous 42 years of *New Yorker* cartoons, she could find only a single instance in which an African American appeared in a cartoon unrelated to race. (It is therefore much easier to integrate this book's photos than its cartoons.)

Films and television programs also embody and reinforce prevailing cultural attitudes. The muddle-headed wide-eyed Black butlers and maids in 1930s movies helped perpetuate the stereotypes they reflected. Today most of us would find such images offensive, yet we might fail to notice stereotyped portrayals of "savage" Native Americans (Trimble, 1988), fanatical Arabs (Shaheen, 1990), or bird-brained women. Women continue to be stereotyped and underrepresented: Men have outnumbered women 2 to 1 in MTV videos, 3 to 1 in prime-time television, and 9 to 1 as authoritative narrators of commercials (Bretl & Cantor, 1988; Gerbner & others, 1986; Lovdal, 1989; Sommers-Flanagan & others, 1993).

Attitudes toward Japanese Americans during World War II illustrate the impact of the media and other social institutions. In California, many people said good-riddance when Japanese Americans were taken from their communities and banished to internment camps. Few people came to help them pack their belongings or say good-bye. Anyone who sold insurance to protect Japanese property while they were gone risked being derided as a "White Jap" and boycotted. Newspaper magnate William Randolph Hearst supported these attitudes with influential editorials warning of the "yellow peril" (Sperling, 1994). When the war was over, the returnees were sometimes greeted with armed resistance, arson, or "No Japs here" signs.

On Bainbridge Island, Washington, from which the first Japanese Americans were removed to internment camps, the reaction could hardly have differed more. Islanders knew these people as community leaders, school classmates, and friends. "We are fighting the war against different Japanese," they said. Insurance agents (among them, my father) insured their property, sometimes overcoming strong objections from insurance companies. The *Bainbridge Review* wrote many supportive editorials, noting that "These Japanese Americans of ours haven't bombed anybody. In the past, they have shown every indication of loyalty to this nation." When forced to leave, other islanders helped them pack and store their possessions, and came to say a final good-bye. During the ordeal, the newspaper published letters from camps, keeping islanders in touch with their friends. When the war was over, the returnees were welcomed home.

SUMMING UP

The social situation breeds and maintains prejudice in several ways. A group that enjoys social and economic superiority will often justify its standing with prejudicial beliefs. Moreover, prejudice can lead people to treat others in ways that trigger expected behavior, thus seeming to confirm the prejudiced view. Experiments also reveal that an ingroup bias often arises from the mere fact that people are divided into groups. Once established, prejudice continues partly through the inertia of conformity and partly through institutional supports, such as the mass media.

■ EMOTIONAL SOURCES OF PREJUDICE

Although prejudice is bred by social situations, emotional factors often add fuel to the fire: Frustration and aggression can feed prejudice, as can personality factors like status needs and authoritarian tendencies. Let's see how.

FRUSTRATION AND AGGRESSION: THE SCAPEGOAT THEORY

As we will see in Chapter 12, pain and frustration (the blocking of a goal) often evoke hostility. When the cause of our frustration is intimidating or vague, we often redirect our hostility. This phenomenon of "displaced aggression" may have contributed to the lynchings of African Americans in the south after the Civil War. Between 1882 and 1930, there were more lynchings in years when cotton prices were low and economic frustration was therefore presumably high (Hepworth & West, 1988; Hovland & Sears, 1940). Ethnic peace is easier to maintain during prosperous times.

"*And now at this point in the meeting I'd like to shift the blame away from me and onto someone else.*"

Drawing by Maslin; © 1985 The New Yorker Magazine, Inc.

Scapegoats provide an outlet for frustrations and hostilities.

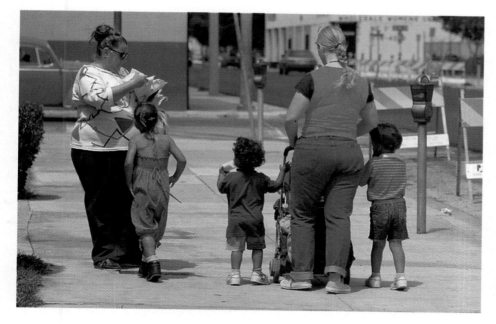

Scapegoating: In difficult times, when budgets are slashed and taxes are high, homeless women with small children are often targets of hostility because they are perceived as responsible for their situation and as a drain on scarce social resources.

Targets for this displaced aggression vary. Following their defeat in World War I and their country's subsequent economic chaos, many Germans saw Jews as villains. Long before Hitler came to power, one German leader explained: "The Jew is just convenient. . . . If there were no Jews, the anti-Semites would have to invent them" (quoted by G. W. Allport, 1958, p. 325). In earlier centuries people vented their fear and hostility on witches, whom they sometimes burned or drowned in public. Today's economic frustrations are often attributed to "lazy welfare bums" or "greedy corporations."

A famous experiment by Neal Miller and Richard Bugelski (1948) confirmed the scapegoat theory. They asked college-age men working at a summer camp to state their attitudes toward Japanese and Mexicans. Some did so before, and then after, being forced to stay in camp to take tests rather than attend a long-awaited free evening at a local theater. Compared to a control group that did not undergo this frustration, the deprived group afterward displayed increased prejudice. Passions provoked prejudice.

One source of frustration is competition. When two groups compete for jobs, housing, or social prestige, one group's goal fulfillment can become the other group's frustration. Thus the **realistic group conflict theory** suggests that prejudice arises when groups compete for scarce resources. A corresponding ecological principle, Gause's law, states that maximum competition will exist between species with identical needs. In western Europe, for example, some people agree that "over the last five years people like yourself have been economically worse off than most [name of country's minority group]." These frustrated people express relatively high levels of blatant prejudice (Pettigrew & Meertens, 1995). Researchers have consistently detected the strongest anti-Black prejudice among Whites who are closest to Blacks on the socioeconomic ladder (Greeley & Sheatsley, 1971; Pettigrew, 1978; Tumin, 1958). When interests clash, prejudice pays, for some people.

"Whoever is dissatisfied with himself is continually ready for revenge."
Nietzsche, *The Gay Science*, 1882–1887

Realistic group conflict theory:
The theory that prejudice arises from competition between groups for scarce resources.

PERSONALITY DYNAMICS

Any two people, with equal reason to feel frustrated or threatened, will often not be equally prejudiced. This suggests that prejudice serves other functions besides advancing competitive self-interest. Sometimes, suggested Sigmund Freud, people hold to beliefs and attitudes that satisfy unconscious needs.

Need for Status and Belonging

Status is relative: To perceive ourselves as having status, we need people below us. Thus one psychological benefit of prejudice, or of any status system, is a feeling of superiority. Most of us can recall a time when we took secret satisfaction in another's failure—perhaps seeing a brother or sister punished, or a classmate's failing a test. Prejudice is often greater among those low or slipping on the socioeconomic ladder and among those whose positive self-image is being threatened (Lemyre & Smith, 1985; Thompson & Crocker, 1985). In one study at Northwestern University, members of lower-status sororities were more disparaging of other sororities than were members of higher-status sororities (Crocker & others, 1987). Perhaps people whose status is secure have less need to feel superior.

But other factors associated with low status could also account for prejudice. Imagine yourself as one of the Arizona State University students who took part in an experiment by Robert Cialdini and Kenneth Richardson (1980). You are walking alone across campus. Someone approaches you and asks your help with a five-minute survey. You agree. After the researcher gives you a brief "creativity test," he deflates you with the news that "you have scored relatively low on the test." The researcher then completes the survey by asking you some evaluative questions about either your school or its traditional rival, the University of Arizona. Would your feelings of failure affect your ratings of either school? Compared with those in a control group whose self-esteem was not threatened, the students who experienced failure gave higher ratings to their own school and lower ratings to their rival. Apparently, boasting about one's own group and denigrating outgroups can boost one's ego.

James Meindl and Melvin Lerner (1984) found that a humiliating experience—accidentally knocking over a stack of someone's important computer cards—provoked English-speaking Canadian students to express increased hostility toward French-speaking Canadians. And Teresa Amabile and Ann Glazebrook (1982) found that Dartmouth College men who were made to feel insecure judged others' work more harshly. Thinking about your own mortality—by writing a short essay on dying and the emotions aroused by thinking about death—also provokes enough insecurity to intensify ingroup favoritism and outgroup prejudice (Greenberg & others, 1990, 1994).

All this suggests that a man who doubts his own strength and independence might, by proclaiming women to be pitifully weak and dependent, boost his masculine image. Indeed, when Joel Grube, Randy Kleinhesselink, and Kathleen Kearney (1982) had Washington State University men view young women's videotaped job interviews, men with low self-acceptance disliked strong, nontraditional women. Men with high self-acceptance preferred them.

A despised outgroup serves yet another need: the need to belong to an ingroup. As we will see in Chapter 15, the perception of a common enemy unites a group. School spirit is seldom so strong as when the game is with the arch-

"By exciting emulation and comparisons of superiority, you lay the foundation of lasting mischief; you make brothers and sisters hate each other."
Samuel Johnson, quoted in James Boswell's *Life of Samuel Johnson*

rival. The sense of comradeship among workers is often highest when they all feel a common antagonism toward management. To solidify the Nazi hold over Germany, Hitler used the "Jewish menace." Despised outgroups can strengthen the ingroup.

The Authoritarian Personality

The emotional needs that contribute to prejudice are said to predominate in the "authoritarian personality." In the 1940s, University of California, Berkeley, researchers—two of whom had fled Nazi Germany—set out on an urgent research mission. They wanted to uncover the psychological roots of an anti-Semitism so poisonous that it caused the slaughter of millions of Jews and turned many millions of Europeans into indifferent spectators. In studies of American adults, Adorno and his colleagues (1950) discovered that hostility toward Jews often coexisted with hostility toward other minorities. Prejudice appeared to be less an attitude specific to one group than a way of thinking about those who are different. Moreover, these judgmental, **ethnocentric** people shared authoritarian tendencies—an intolerance for weakness, a punitive attitude, and a submissive respect for their ingroup's authorities, as reflected in their agreement with such statements as, "Obedience and respect for authority are the most important virtues children should learn."

As children, authoritarian people often were harshly disciplined. This supposedly led them to repress their hostilities and impulses and to "project" them onto outgroups. The insecurity of authoritarian children seemed to predispose them toward an excessive concern with power and status and an inflexible right-wrong way of thinking that made ambiguity difficult to tolerate. Such people therefore tended to be submissive to those with power over them and aggressive or punitive toward those beneath them.

Scholars criticized the research for a focus on right-wing authoritarianism that overlooked dogmatic authoritarianism of the left. Still, its main conclusion has survived: Authoritarian tendencies, sometimes reflected in ethnic tensions, surge during threatening times of economic recession and social upheaval

Ethnocentrism:
A belief in the superiority of one's own ethnic and cultural group, and a corresponding disdain for all other groups.

Authoritarian tendencies feed on social upheaval.

(Doty & others, 1991; Sales, 1973). In contemporary Russia, individuals scoring high in authoritarianism have tended to support a return to Marxist-Leninist ideology and to oppose democratic reform (McFarland & others, 1992).

Moreover, contemporary studies of right-wing authoritarians by University of Manitoba psychologist Bob Altemeyer (1988, 1992) confirm that there *are* individuals whose fears and self-righteous hostilities surface as prejudice. Feelings of moral superiority may go hand in hand with brutality toward perceived inferiors. Some contemporary examples:

■ Although the prejudices that maintained *apartheid* in South Africa arose from social inequalities, socialization, and conformity (Louw-Potgieter, 1988), those who most strongly favored separation usually had authoritarian attitudes (Van Staden, 1987).

■ In repressive regimes across the world, people who become torturers typically have an authoritarian liking for hierarchical chains of command and a contempt for those who are weak or resistant (Staub, 1989).

■ Different forms of prejudice—toward Blacks, gays and lesbians, women, old people, fat people, AIDS victims, the homeless—*do* tend to coexist in the same individuals (Bierly, 1985; Crandall, 1994; Peterson & others, 1993; Snyder & Ickes, 1985). As Altemeyer concludes, right-wing authoritarians tend to be "equal opportunity bigots." The same is true of those with a "social dominance orientation"—who view people in terms of hierarchies of merit or goodness. By contrast, those with a more communal orientation—who presume "universal human rights" enjoyed by "all God's children"—are more accepting of those who differ from themselves (Pratto & others, 1994).

SUMMING UP

Prejudice has emotional roots, too. Frustration breeds hostility, which people sometimes vent on scapegoats and sometimes express more directly against competing groups perceived as responsible for one's frustration. By providing a feeling of social superiority, prejudice may also help cover feelings of inferiority. Different types of prejudice are often found together in those who have an "authoritarian" attitude.

■ COGNITIVE SOURCES OF PREJUDICE

To understand stereotyping and prejudice, it also helps to remember how our minds work. How do the ways in which we think about the world, and simplify it, influence our stereotypes? And how do our stereotypes affect our judgments?

Much of the explanation of prejudice so far could have been written in the 1960s—but not what follows. This new look at prejudice, fueled by 1500 research articles on stereotyping in the last 10 years (Dovidio & others, in press), applies the new research on social thinking. The basic point is this: Stereotyped beliefs and prejudiced attitudes exist not only because of social conditioning, or because they enable people to displace and project hostilities, but also as by-products of normal thinking processes. Many stereotypes spring less from malice than from how we simplify our complex worlds. They are like perceptual illusions, a by-product of our knack for interpreting the world.

CATEGORIZATION

One way we simplify our environment is to "categorize"—to organize the world by clustering objects into groups. A biologist, for example, classifies plants and animals. Once we organize people into categories, we can think about them more easily. If persons in a group are similar, it helps to know their group. Customs inspectors and airplane antihijack personnel are therefore given "profiles" of suspicious individuals (Kraut & Poe, 1980). In these cases, categorization helps—it provides useful information with a minimum amount of effort (Macrae & others, 1994). It's especially easy and efficient to rely on stereotypes when

- Pressed for time (Kaplan & others, 1993)
- Preoccupied (Gilbert & Hixon, 1991)
- Tired (Bodenhausen, 1990)
- Emotionally aroused (Esses & others, 1993b; Stroessner & Mackie, 1993)
- Too young to appreciate diversity (Biernat, 1991)

Ethnicity and sex are, in our current world, powerful ways of categorizing people. Imagine Tom, a 40-year-old, African-American real estate agent in New Orleans. I suspect that your image of "Black male" predominates over the categories "middle-aged," "businessperson," and "southerner." Experiments expose our spontaneous categorization of people by race. When subjects view different people making statements, they often forget who said what, yet remember the race of the person who made each statement (Hewstone & others, 1991; Stroessner & others, 1990; Taylor & others, 1978). By itself, such categorization is not prejudice, but it does provide a foundation for prejudice.

Perceived Similarities and Differences

Picture the following objects: apples, chairs, pencils.

There is a strong tendency to see objects within a group as being more uniform than they really are. Were your apples all red? your chairs all straight-backed? your pencils all yellow? Once we classify two days in the same month, they seem more alike, temperature-wise, than the same interval across months. People guess the eight-day average temperature difference between, say, November 15th and 23rd to be less than the eight-day difference between November 30th and December 8th.

It's the same with people. Once we assign people to groups—athletes, drama majors, math professors—we are likely to exaggerate the similarities within groups and the differences between them (S. E. Taylor, 1981; Wilder, 1978). Mere division into groups can create an **outgroup homogeneity effect**—a sense that *they* are "all alike" and different from "us" and "our" group (Ostrom & Sedikides, 1992). Because we generally like people we think are similar to us and dislike those we perceive as different, the natural result is ingroup bias (Byrne & Wong, 1962; Rokeach & Mezei, 1966; Stein & others, 1965).

Bad or good moods can amplify the outgroup stereotyping. Feeling bad, we perceive people and events in a more negative light. But even positive emotions can interfere with complex thinking, leading us to perceive folks in another group as more alike than they are. Happy people, feeling contented, seem to commit less effort to wrestling with differences. Moreover, suggest Galen Bodenhausen and his colleagues (1994), feeling really good may prime feelings of relative superiority.

The mere fact of a group decision can also lead outsiders to overestimate a group's unanimity. If a conservative wins a national election by a slim majority, observers infer "the people have turned conservative." If a liberal won by a similarly slim margin, voter attitudes would hardly have differed, but observers would now attribute a "liberal mood" to the country. (Seven months after Bill Clinton's 1992 victory with 43 percent of the votes, University of Richmond students recalled his getting 56 percent of the votes.) Whether the decision is made by majority rule or by a designated group executive, people usually presume that it reflects the entire group's attitudes (Allison & others, 1985, 1987, 1990, 1995). So it happened in the 1994 U.S. elections when Republicans captured the Congress with 53 percent of the votes (in an election in which most adults did not vote)—producing what commentators interpreted as a "revolutionary," "landslide," "sea change" in American politics.

When the group is our own, we are more likely to see diversity (which includes our unique identity):

- Many non-Europeans see the Swiss as a fairly homogeneous people. But to the people of Switzerland, the Swiss are diverse, encompassing French-, German-, and Italian-speaking people.
- Many Anglo-Americans lump "Latinos" together. Mexican Americans, Cuban Americans, and Puerto Ricans see important differences, especially between their own subgroup and the others (Huddy & Virtanen, 1995).
- White Americans readily identify "Black leaders" who supposedly can speak for Black Americans, and White reporters sometimes find it newsworthy that the "Black community is divided" on an issue such as immigration policy. Whites apparently presume their own racial group is more diverse: They do not assume there are "White leaders" who can speak for White America, nor is it newsworthy that not all Whites agree on an issue. (No newspaper would headline, "White leaders divided over immigration policy.")

Outgroup homogeneity effect:
Perception of outgroup members as more similar to one another than are ingroup members. Thus "they are alike; we are diverse."

"Women are more like each other than men [are]."
Lord (not Lady) Chesterfield

Likewise, sorority sisters perceive the members of any other sorority as less diverse than the mix in their own (Park & Rothbart, 1982). And business majors and engineering majors overestimate the uniformity of the other group's traits and attitudes (Judd & others, 1991). In general, the greater our familiarity with a social group, the more we see its diversity (Brown & Wootton-Millward, 1993; Linville & others, 1989). The less our familiarity, the more we stereotype. Also, the smaller and less powerful the group, the more we stereotype (Fiske, 1993; Mullen & Hu, 1989). To those in power, we pay attention.

Perhaps you have noticed: *They*—the members of any racial group other than your own—even *look* alike. Many of us can recall embarrassing ourselves by confusing two people of another racial group, prompting the person we've misnamed to say, "You think we all look alike." Experiments by John Brigham, June Chance, Alvin Goldstein, and Roy Malpass in the United States and by Hayden Ellis in Scotland reveal that people of other races do in fact *seem* to look more alike than do people of one's own race (Brigham & Williamson, 1979; Chance & Goldstein, 1981; Ellis, 1981). When White students are shown faces of a few White and a few Black individuals and then asked to pick these individuals out of a photographic lineup, they more accurately recognize the White faces than the Black.

I am White. When I first read this research I thought, of course: White people *are* more physically diverse than Blacks. But my reaction was apparently just an illustration of the phenomenon. For if my reaction were correct, Black people, too, would better recognize a White face among a lineup of Whites than a Black face in a lineup of Blacks. But in fact, as Figure 11–6 illustrates, Blacks more easily recognize another Black than they do a White (Bothwell & others,

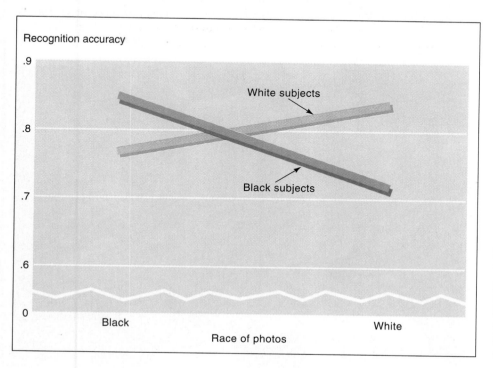

■ FIGURE 11–6

The own-race bias. White subjects more accurately recognize the faces of Whites than of Blacks; Black subjects more accurately recognize the faces of Blacks than of Whites.

(From Devine & Malpass, 1985.)

The term "own-race bias" is a misnomer in the case of Anglo and Hispanic identifications. Most Hispanic people are classified as Caucasians.

1989). And Hispanics more readily recognize another Hispanic whom they saw a couple of hours earlier than they do an Anglo (Platz & Hosch, 1988).

This intriguing "own-race bias" appears to be an automatic cognitive phenomenon, for it is usually unrelated to the perceiver's racial attitudes (Brigham & Malpass, 1985). But experience may play a role. June Chance (1985) reports that White students have difficulty recognizing individual Japanese faces (although Japanese facial features are actually as varied as those of White faces). But White students become markedly better at recognizing Japanese faces if over several training sessions, they view pairs of Japanese faces, which they must learn to differentiate. Chance's hunch is that experience enables people to become attuned to the types of faces they frequently encounter. Her hunch is questioned by research showing that Asian and Caucasian students have trouble with cross-race identification, regardless of experience (Ng & Lindsay, 1994). But it helps explain why Black people in White cultures are slightly better than Whites at recognizing faces from another race (Anthony & others, 1992). And it also explains why to me all Cabbage Patch dolls looked alike, though they hardly looked alike to my nine-year-old daughter and her friends.

DISTINCTIVE STIMULI

Distinctive People

Other ways we perceive our worlds also breed stereotypes. Distinctive people and vivid or extreme occurrences often capture attention and distort judgments.

Have you ever found yourself in a situation where you were the only person present of your sex, race, or nationality? If so, your difference from the others probably made you more noticeable and the object of more attention. A

Distinctive people—like this tourist visiting a Saturday market in Menghum, China—draw attention. Their salience may cause exaggerated perceptions of their good and bad qualities.

Black in an otherwise White group, a man in an otherwise female group, or a woman in an otherwise male group seems more prominent and influential and to have exaggerated good and bad qualities (Crocker & McGraw, 1984; S. E. Taylor & others, 1979). This occurs because when someone in a group is made salient (conspicuous), we tend to see that person as causing whatever happens (Taylor & Fiske, 1978). If we are positioned to look at Joe, an average group member, Joe will seem to have a greater than average influence upon the group. People who capture our attention seem more responsible for what happens.

Ellen Langer and Lois Imber (1980) asked Harvard students to watch a video of a man reading. The students paid closer attention when they were led to think he was out of the ordinary—a cancer patient, a homosexual, or a millionaire. They detected characteristics that other viewers ignored, and their evaluation of him was more extreme. Those who thought the man a cancer patient noticed distinctive facial characteristics and bodily movements and thus perceived him as much more "different from most people" than did the other viewers. The extra attention we pay to distinctive people creates an illusion that they differ more from others than they really do. If people thought you had the IQ of a genius, they would probably notice things about you that otherwise would pass unnoticed.

However, sometimes we perceive others as reacting to our distinctiveness when actually they aren't. At Dartmouth College, researchers Robert Kleck and Angelo Strenta (1980) discovered this when they led college women to feel disfigured. The women thought the purpose of the experiment was to assess how someone would react to a facial scar created with theatrical makeup; the scar was on the right cheek, running from the ear to the mouth. Actually, the purpose was to see how the women themselves, when made to feel deviant, would perceive others' behavior toward them. After applying the makeup, the experimenter gave each subject a small hand mirror so she could see the authentic-looking scar. When she put the mirror down, he then applied some "moisturizer" to "keep the makeup from cracking." What the "moisturizer" really did was remove the scar.

The scene that followed was poignant. A young woman, feeling terribly self-conscious about her supposedly disfigured face, talked with another woman who sees no such disfigurement and knows nothing of what has gone on before. If you have ever felt similarly self-conscious—perhaps about a physical handicap, acne, even just a bad hair day—then perhaps you can sympathize with the self-conscious woman. Compared to women led to believe their conversational partner merely thought they had an allergy, the "disfigured" women became acutely sensitive to how their partners were looking at them. They rated their partners as more tense, distant, and patronizing. But in fact, observers who later analyzed videotapes of how the partners treated "disfigured" persons could find no such differences in treatment. Self-conscious about being different, the "disfigured" women misinterpreted mannerisms and comments they would otherwise not notice.

Self-consciousness interactions between a majority and minority person can therefore feel tense even when both are well-intentioned (Devine & others, in press). Tom, who is known to be gay, meets Bill, who is straight. Tolerant Bill wants to respond without prejudice. But feeling unsure of himself, he holds back a bit. Tom, expecting negative attitudes from most people, misreads Bill's hesitancy as hostility and responds with a seeming chip on his shoulder.

The self-consciousness created by being a token minority—say, a man in a group of women or a woman in a group of men—can also disrupt one's normal thinking and memory processes, thereby making the token person seem inept (Lord & Saenz, 1985).

Vivid Cases

Our minds also use distinctive cases as a shortcut to judging groups. Are Blacks good athletes? "Well, there's Barry Sanders and Venus Williams and Shaquille O'Neal. Yeah, I'd say so." Note the thought processes at work here: We recall instances of a particular category and, based on those recalled, generalize. The problem is that vivid instances, though more available in memory, are seldom representative of the larger group. Exceptional athletes, though distinctive and memorable, are not the best basis for judging the distribution of athletic talent among an entire group.

Those in a numerical minority, being more conspicuous, also may be numerically overestimated by the majority. What proportion of your country's population would you say is Muslim? People in non-Muslim countries often overestimate this proportion—which repeated U.S. surveys, by Gallup (1994) and others, show is less than 1 percent. Or consider a 1990 Gallup poll report that the average American estimated 32 percent of the U.S. population was Black and 21 percent Hispanic. The real figures were 12 and 9 percent (Gates, 1993).

Myron Rothbart and his colleagues (1978) showed how distinctive cases also fuel stereotypes. They had University of Oregon students view 50 slides, each of which stated the man's height. For one group of students, 10 of the men were slightly over 6 feet (up to 6 feet, 4 inches). For other students, these 10 men were well over 6 feet (up to 6 feet, 11 inches). When asked later how many of the men were over 6 feet, those given the moderately tall examples recalled 5 percent too many. In a follow-up experiment, students read descriptions of the actions of 50 men, 10 of whom had committed either nonviolent crimes, such as forgery, or violent crimes, such as rape. Of those shown the list with the violent crimes, most overestimated the number of criminal acts.

Because they are distinctive, we most easily remember extreme cases—and because they alone are newsworthy, they dominate our images of various groups. The attention-getting power of distinctive, extreme cases helps explain why middle-class people so greatly exaggerate the dissimilarities between themselves and the underclass. Contrary to stereotypes of "welfare queens" driving Cadillacs, people living in poverty generally share the aspirations of the middle class and would rather provide for themselves than accept public assistance (Cook & Curtin, 1987). Moreover, the less we know about a group, the more we are influenced by a few vivid cases (Quattrone & Jones, 1980). To see is to believe.

Distinctive Events

Stereotypes assume a correlation between group membership and individuals' characteristics ("Italians are emotional," "Jews are shrewd," "Accountants are perfectionists"). Even under the best of conditions, our attentiveness to unusual occurrences can create **illusory correlations**. Because we are sensitive to distinctive events, the co-occurrence of two such events is especially noticeable—more noticeable than each of the times the unusual events do not occur together. Thus Rupert Brown and Amanda Smith (1989) found that British faculty members overestimated the number of (relatively rare, though noticeable) female senior faculty at their university.

David Hamilton and Robert Gifford (1976) demonstrated illusory correlation in a clever experiment. They showed students slides on which various

Illusory correlation:
A false impression that two variables correlate. See Chapter 2.

people, members of "Group A" or "Group B," were said to have done something desirable or undesirable. For example, "John, a member of Group A, visited a sick friend in the hospital." Twice as many statements described members of Group A as Group B, but both groups did nine desirable acts for every four undesirable behaviors. Since both Group B and the undesirable acts were less frequent, their co-occurrence—for example, "Allen, a member of Group B, dented the fender of a parked car and didn't leave his name"—was an unusual combination that caught people's attention. The students therefore overestimated the frequency with which the "minority" group (B) acted undesirably and judged Group B more harshly.

Remember, Group B members actually committed undesirable acts in the same proportion as Group A members. Moreover, the students had no preexisting biases for or against Group B, and they received the information more systematically than daily experience ever offers it. Although researchers debate why it happens, they agree that illusory correlation occurs and provides yet another source for the formation of racial stereotypes (Hamilton & Sherman, 1994).

The mass media reflect and feed this phenomenon. When a self-described homosexual murders someone, homosexuality often gets mentioned. When a heterosexual murders someone, this is a less distinctive event and the person's sexual orientation is seldom mentioned. Likewise, when ex-mental patients like Mark Chapman and John Hinckley, Jr., shoot John Lennon and President Reagan, respectively, the person's mental history commands attention. Assassins and mental hospitalization are both relatively infrequent, making the combination especially newsworthy. Such reporting adds to the illusion of a large correlation between (1) violent tendencies and (2) homosexuality or mental hospitalization.

Unlike those who judged groups A and B, we often have preexisting biases. Further research by Hamilton with Terrence Rose (1980) reveals that our preexisting stereotypes can lead us to "see" correlations that aren't there. They had University of California, Santa Barbara, students read sentences in which various adjectives described the members of different occupational groups ("Doug, an accountant, is timid and thoughtful"). In actuality, each occupation was described equally often by each adjective; accountants, doctors, and salespeople were equally often timid, wealthy, and talkative. However, the students *thought* they had more often read descriptions of timid accountants, wealthy doctors, and talkative salespeople. Their stereotyping led them to perceive correlations that weren't there, thus helping to perpetuate the stereotypes. To believe is to see.

ATTRIBUTION: IS IT A JUST WORLD?

In explaining others' actions, we frequently commit the fundamental attribution error. We attribute their behavior so much to their inner dispositions that we discount important situational forces. The error occurs partly because our attention focuses on the persons, not on the situation. A person's race or sex is vivid and attention-getting; to an observer, the situational forces working upon that person are usually less visible. Slavery was often overlooked as an explanation for slave behavior; the behavior was instead attributed to the slaves' own nature. Until recently, the same was true of how we explained the

Fundamental attribution error:
See Chapter 2.

perceived differences between women and men. Because gender-role constraints were hard to see, we attributed men's and women's behavior solely to their innate dispositions.

Group-Serving Bias

Thomas Pettigrew (1979, 1980) argues that attribution errors bias people's explanations of group members' behaviors. They grant members of their own group the benefit of the doubt: "She donated because she has a good heart; he refused because he had to under the circumstances." When explaining acts by members of other groups, people more often assume the worst: "He donated to gain favor; she refused because she's selfish." Hence, as we noted earlier in this chapter, the shove that Whites perceive as mere "horsing around" when done by another White becomes a "violent gesture" when done by a Black.

Positive behavior by outgroup members is more often dismissed. It may be seen as a "special case" ("He is certainly bright and hardworking—not at all like other Hispanics"), as owing to luck or some special advantage ("She probably got admitted just because her med school had to fill its quota for women applicants"), as demanded by the situation ("Under the circumstances, what could the cheap Scot do but pay the whole check?"), or as attributable to extra effort ("Jewish students get better grades because they're so compulsive"). Disadvantaged groups and groups that stress modesty (such as the Chinese) exhibit less of this **group-serving bias** (Fletcher & Ward, 1989; Hewstone & Ward, 1985; Jackson & others, 1993).

The group-serving bias can subtly color our language. A team of Italian researchers led by Anne Maass (1995) has found that positive behaviors by a fellow ingroup member often get described as general dispositions (for example, "Lucy is helpful"). When performed by an outgroup member, the same behavior often gets described as a specific, isolated act ("Lucy held the door open for somebody").

Earlier we noted that blaming the victim can justify the blamer's own superior status. Blaming occurs as people attribute an outgroup's failures to its

Group-serving bias: Explaining away outgroup members' positive behaviors; also attributing negative behaviors to their dispositions (while excusing such behavior by one's own group).

BEHIND THE SCENES

I still remember that day in 1979 when, as an Oxford graduate student, I was told by one of my advisors after a trip to the United States that "attribution theory was finished." Having hoped to integrate North American attribution theory with European theory about intergroup relations and prejudice, I was dismayed. Fortunately, my second advisor supported my exploring how people attribute motives to those in other groups. This research illustrates how the international field of social psychology benefits from both the North American and European perspectives. It also reminds me that, when rebuffed, students should seek a second opinion. If you glimpse an important phenomenon that begs to be studied, don't be easily deterred by current research fads and fashions.

MICHAEL HEWSTONE, *University of Wales*

members' flawed dispositions, notes Miles Hewstone (1990): "They fail because they're stupid; we fail because we didn't try." If women, Blacks, or Jews have been abused, they must somehow have brought it on themselves. When the British marched a group of German civilians around the Bergen-Belsen concentration camp at the close of World War II, one German responded: "What terrible criminals these prisoners must have been to receive such treatment."

The Just-World Phenomenon

In a series of experiments conducted at the Universities of Waterloo and Kentucky, Melvin Lerner and his colleagues (Lerner & Miller, 1978; Lerner, 1980) discovered that merely *observing* another person being innocently victimized is enough to make the victim seem less worthy. Imagine that you along with some others are participating in one of their studies—supposedly on the perception of emotional cues (Lerner & Simmons, 1966). One of the participants, a confederate, is selected by lottery to perform a memory task. This person receives painful shocks whenever she gives a wrong answer. You and the others note her emotional responses.

After watching the victim receive these apparently painful shocks, the experimenter asks you to evaluate her. How would you respond? With compassionate sympathy? We might expect so. As Ralph Waldo Emerson wrote, "The martyr cannot be dishonored." On the contrary, the experiments revealed that martyrs *can* be dishonored. When observers were powerless to alter the victim's fate, they often rejected and devalued the victim. Juvenal, the Roman satirist, anticipated these results: "The Roman mob follows after Fortune . . . and hates those who have been condemned."

Linda Carli and her colleagues (1989, 1990) report that this **just-world phenomenon** colors our impressions of rape victims. Carli had people read detailed descriptions of interactions between a man and a woman. Some read a scenario that has a happy ending: "Then he led me to the couch. He held my hand and asked me to marry him." In hindsight, people find the ending unsurprising and admire the man's and woman's character traits. Others read the same scenario with a different ending: "But then he became very rough and pushed me onto the couch. He held me down on the couch and raped me." Given this ending, people see it as more inevitable and blame the woman for prior behavior that seems faultless when it has a happier outcome.

Lerner (1980) believes such disparaging of hapless victims results from our need to believe that "I am a just person living in a just world, a world where people get what they deserve." From early childhood, he argues, we are taught that good is rewarded and evil punished. Hard work and virtue pay dividends; laziness and immorality do not. From this it is but a short leap to assuming that those who flourish must be good and those who suffer must deserve their fate. The classic illustration is the Old Testament story of Job, a good person who suffers terrible misfortune. Job's friends surmise that, this being a just world, Job must have done something wicked to elicit such terrible suffering.

This suggests that people are indifferent to social injustice not because they have no concern for justice but because they *see* no injustice. They believe that rape victims must have behaved seductively (Borgida & Brekke, 1985), that battered spouses must have provoked their beatings (Summers & Feldman, 1984), that poor people don't deserve better (Furnham & Gunter, 1984), and that sick

Just-world phenomenon: The tendency of people to believe the world is just and that people therefore get what they deserve and deserve what they get.

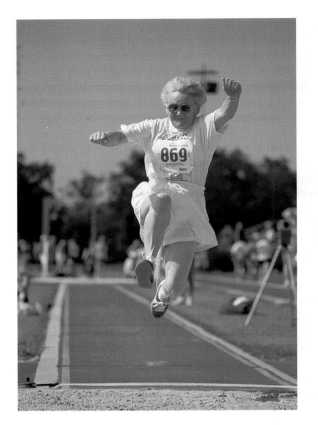

When people violate our stereotypes, we salvage the stereotype by splitting off a new subgroup stereotype, such as "senior Olympians."

rival of a first Black neighbor, they found initial opposition melting. Fears that the new neighbors would not take care of their property or that property values would decline had apparently proved groundless.

Still, negative ideas about a person or a group are often hard to dislodge (Rothbart & John, 1985). For one thing, a positive image—that one is gentle, sincere, or dependable—is easily reversed by just a few contrary behaviors. An unfavorable image—that one is deceitful, hostile, or unethical—is not so easily changed (Rothbart & Park, 1986). If suspicious, we can easily misinterpret someone's genuine friendliness as superficial smoothness.

The resistance of negative stereotypes to disconfirming facts is sometimes alarming. In congressional testimony, California governor Earl Warren warned of subversion by Japanese Americans during World War II: "I take the view that this [lack of subversive activity] is the most ominous sign in our whole situation. It convinces me more than perhaps any other factor that the sabotage we are to get [is] timed just like Pearl Harbor was timed" (Daniels, 1975).

We do notice information that is strikingly inconsistent with a stereotype. Still, when the "exceptions" seem concentrated in a few atypical people, we can salvage the stereotype by splitting off a new category (Brewer, 1988; Hewstone, 1994). Homeowners who have desirable Black neighbors can form a new stereotype of "professional, middle-class" Blacks. This subgroup stereotype helps maintain the larger stereotype that *most* Blacks make irresponsible neighbors. The positive image British schoolchildren form of their friendly school police officers—whom they perceive as in a special category—doesn't improve their image of police officers in general (Hewstone & others, 1992). One who believes that women are basically passive and dependent can split off a new category of "aggressive feminist" to handle women who don't fit the basic stereotype (S. E. Taylor, 1981). Similarly, people split their stereotypes of the elderly into the "grandmotherly" type, the "elder-statesman" type, and the inactive "senior-citizen" type (Brewer & Lui, 1984).

Do Stereotypes Bias Judgments of Individuals?

There is an upbeat note on which we can conclude this chapter: *People often evaluate individuals more positively than the groups they compose* (Miller & Felicio, 1990). Anne Locksley, Eugene Borgida, and Nancy Brekke have found that once someone knows a person, "stereotypes may have minimal, if any, impact on judgments about that person" (Borgida & others, 1981; Locksley & others, 1980, 1982). They discovered this by giving University of Minnesota students anecdotal information about recent incidents in the life of "Nancy." In a supposed transcript of a telephone conversation, Nancy told a friend how she responded to three different situations (for example, being harassed by a seedy character while shopping). Some of the students read transcripts portraying Nancy responding assertively (telling the seedy character to leave); others read a report of passive responses (simply ignoring the character until he finally drifts away). Still other students received the same information, except that the person was named "Paul" instead of Nancy. A day later the students predicted how Nancy (or Paul) would respond to other situations.

Did knowing the person's sex have any effect on these predictions? None at all. Expectations of the person's assertiveness were influenced solely by what they had learned about that individual the day before. Even their judgments of masculinity and femininity were unaffected by knowing the person's sex. Gender stereotypes had been left on the shelf; the students evaluated Nancy and Paul as individuals.

The explanation for this finding is implied by an important principle discussed in Chapter 3. Given (1) general (base-rate) information about a group and (2) trivial but vivid information about a particular group member, the vivid information usually overwhelms the effect of the general information. This is especially so when the person doesn't fit our image of the typical group member (Fein & Hilton, 1992; Lord & others, 1991). For example, imagine yourself being told how most people in an experiment actually behaved and then viewing a brief interview with one of the supposed subjects. Would you react like the typical viewer—by guessing the person's behavior from the interview, ignoring the base-rate information on how most people actually behaved?

Stereotypes are general beliefs about the distribution of traits in groups of people. For example, "assertiveness is found mostly in men, passiveness in women." People often believe such stereotypes, yet ignore them when given vivid, anecdotal information. Thus, many people believe "politicians are crooks" but "our Senator Jones has integrity." (No wonder people have such a low opinion of politicians yet usually reelect their own representatives.) Similarly, the bigot who holds extreme stereotypes may claim, "But one of my best friends is. . . ." Borgida, Locksley, and Brekke explain: "People may sustain general prejudices while simultaneously treating individuals with whom they frequently interact in a nonprejudicial manner."

"There are no good women climbers. Women climbers either aren't good climbers or they aren't real women."
Anonymous climber (cited by Rothbart & Lewis, 1988)

These findings resolve a puzzling set of findings considered early in this chapter. We know that gender stereotypes (1) are strong yet (2) have little effect on people's judgments of work attributed to a man or a woman. Now we see why. People may have strong gender stereotypes yet ignore them when judging a particular individual.

Strong stereotypes do, however, color our judgments of individuals. When Thomas Nelson, Monica Biernat, and Melvin Manis (1990) had students estimate the heights of individually pictured men and women, they judged the individual men as taller—even when their heights were equal, even when they were told that in this sample sex didn't predict height, and even when they were offered cash rewards for accuracy.

In a follow-up study, Nelson, Michele Acker, and Manis (1994) showed University of Michigan students photos of other students from the university's engineering and nursing schools, along with descriptions of each student's interests. Even when informed that the sample contained an equal number of males and females from each school, the same description was judged more likely to come from a nursing student when attached to a female face. Thus, even when a strong gender stereotype is known to be irrelevant, it has an irresistible force.

Also, sometimes we make judgments, or begin interacting with someone, with little to go on but our stereotype. In such cases stereotypes can strongly bias our interpretations and memories of people. For example, Charles Bond and his colleagues (1988) found that, after getting to know their patients, White psychiatric nurses equally often put Black and White patients in physical restraints. But they restrained *incoming* Black patients more often than their White counterparts. With little else to go on, stereotypes mattered.

Such bias can also operate more subtly. In an experiment by John Darley and Paget Gross (1983), Princeton University students viewed a videotape of a fourth-grade girl, Hannah. The tape depicted her either in a depressed urban neighborhood, supposedly the child of lower-class parents, or in an affluent suburban setting, the child of professional parents. Asked to guess Hannah's ability level in various subjects, both groups of viewers refused to use Hannah's class background to prejudge her ability level; each group rated her ability level at her grade level. Other students also viewed a second videotape, showing Hannah taking an oral achievement test in which she got some questions right and some wrong.

Those who had previously been introduced to upper-class Hannah judged her answers as showing high ability and later recalled her getting most questions right; those who had met lower-class Hannah judged her ability as below grade level and recalled her missing almost half the questions. But remember: The second videotape was *identical* for both groups. So we see that when stereotypes are strong and the information about someone is ambiguous (unlike the cases of Nancy and Paul), stereotypes can *subtly* bias our judgments of individuals.

Finally, stereotypes sometimes bias our judgments of individuals by producing a contrast effect. A woman who rebukes someone cutting in front of her in a movie line ("Shouldn't you go to the end of the line?") may seem more assertive than a man who reacts similarly (Manis & others, 1988). Aided by the testimony of social psychologist Susan Fiske and her colleagues (1991), the U.S. Supreme Court saw such stereotyping at work when Price Waterhouse,

Martina Navratilova, world-famous tennis champion who is open about her homosexuality. People sometimes maintain general prejudices (such as against gays and lesbians) without applying their prejudice to particular individuals whom they know and respect.

one of the nation's top accounting firms, denied Ann Hopkins' promotion to partner. Among the 88 candidates for promotion, Hopkins, the only woman, was number one in the amount of business she brought in to the company and, by all accounts, was hardworking and exacting. By other accounts, she needed a "course at charm school," where she could learn to "walk more femininely, talk more femininely, dress more femininely. . . ." After reflecting on this, the Supreme Court in 1989 decided that encouraging men to be aggressive, but not women, is to act "on the basis of gender":

> We sit not to determine whether Ms. Hopkins is nice, but to decide whether the partners reacted negatively to her personality because she is a woman. . . . An employer who objects to aggressiveness in women but whose positions require this trait places women in an intolerable Catch 22: out of a job if they behave aggressively and out of a job if they don't.

Stereotypes more often bias our judgments of groups. Sometimes we judge groups as a whole. On such occasions, whether we personally know any members of the group is irrelevant. What matters—what shapes public policy—is our impression of the group as a whole. Once we come to know a particular person, we are often able to set aside stereotypes and prejudices. Yet both remain potent social forces.

BEHIND THE SCENES

We risked a lot by testifying on Ann Hopkins' behalf, no doubt about it. As far as we knew, no one had ever introduced the social psychology of stereotyping in a gender case before. Race discrimination cases have used social science evidence ever since the landmark 1954 *Brown v. Board of Education* decision ending school segregation. But gender cases had used only common sense or statistics, not social psychology, as evidence of discriminatory intent. I was a fresh assistant professor, sitting alone in my office, when attorney Sally Burns (now of New York University Law School) called me and proposed such testimony. Other people told me I was wasting my time, but I couldn't resist, as it seemed so exciting a chance. If we succeeded, we would get the latest stereotyping research out of the dusty journals and into the muddy trenches of legal debate, where it might be useful. If we failed, we might hurt the client, slander social psychology, and damage my reputation as a scientist. At the time I had no idea that the testimony would eventually make it successfully through the Supreme Court.

SUSAN T. FISKE, *University of Massachusetts, Amherst*

Can We Reduce Prejudice?

Social psychologists have been more successful in explaining prejudice than in alleviating it. Because prejudice results from many interrelated factors, there is no simple remedy. Nevertheless, we can now anticipate techniques for reducing prejudice (discussed further in chapters to come): If unequal status breeds prejudice, then we can seek to create cooperative, equal-status relationships. If prejudice often rationalizes discriminatory behavior, then we can mandate nondiscrimination. If social institutions support prejudice, then we can pull out those supports (for example, have the media model interracial harmony). If outgroups seem more unlike one's own group than they really are, then we can make efforts to personalize their members. These are some of the antidotes for the poison of prejudice.

Since the end of World War II in 1945, a number of these antidotes have been applied, and racial and gender prejudices have indeed diminished. It now remains to be seen whether, during the remaining years of this century, progress will continue or whether, as could easily happen in a time of increasing population and diminishing resources, antagonisms will again erupt into open hostility.

SUMMING UP

A fresh look at prejudice in recent research shows how the stereotyping that underlies prejudice is a by-product of our thinking—our ways of simplifying the world. First, clustering people into categories exaggerates the uniformity within a group and the differences between groups. Second, a distinctive individual, such as a lone minority person, has a compelling quality. Such persons make us aware of differences that would otherwise go unnoticed. The occurrence of two distinctive events—say a minority person committing an unusual crime—helps create an illusory correlation between people and behavior. Third, attributing others' behavior to their dispositions can lead to the group-serving bias: assigning outgroup members' negative behavior to their natural character while explaining away their positive behaviors. Blaming the victim also results from the common presumption that because this is a just world, people get what they deserve.

Stereotypes have cognitive consequences and cognitive sources. By directing interpretations and memory, they lead us to "find" supportive evidence, even when none exists. Stereotypes are therefore resistant to change. Stereotypes are more potent when strong, when judging unknown individuals, and when deciding policies regarding whole groups. Stereotypes can also subtly color our assessments of individuals' behavior, though we tend to discard group stereotypes in interpreting the behavior of people we know.

■ FOR FURTHER READING

Altemeyer, B. (1988). *Enemies of freedom: Understanding right-wing authoritarianism*. San Francisco: Jossey-Bass. The complete report of a prize-winning analysis of why some people—notably those with self-righteous, authoritarian tendencies—belittle and brutalize socially disparaged outgroups.

Jones, J. M. (1996). *The psychology of racism and prejudice*. New York: McGraw-Hill. A new, authoritative summary of the causes and effects of stereotyping and prejudice.

Taylor, D. M., & Moghaddam, F. M. (1987). *Theories of intergroup relations: International social psychological perspectives*. New York: Praeger. A skillful summary and evaluation of major theories of prejudice and group attitudes.

CHAPTER 12

AGGRESSION: HURTING OTHERS

Our behavior toward one another seems increasingly destructive. Although Woody Allen's prediction that "by 1990 kidnapping will be the dominant mode of social interaction" has not been fulfilled, images of 1990s violence have horrified people across the world.

■ The British, shocked by the beating death of 2-year-old James Bulger at the hands of two 10-year-old boys, debated reasons for rising brutality in their once-genteel culture.

■ Germans, appalled by neo-Nazis murdering and harassing Turkish immigrants, decried the decline of humane values.

■ In Rwanda, some 500,000 people—including half the Tutsi population—were slaughtered in the genocidal summer of 1994.

■ In a Canadian government survey of 12,300 women, 29 percent reported being physically or sexually assaulted by their partner (Rodgers, 1994).

■ In the United States, reported assaults now exceed 1 million annually, and the arrest rate for juvenile violence has increased sixfold since 1960. Stunned by random carjackings, assassinations of tourists on Florida highways, and children gunning down children, Americans are, in President Clinton's words, "finally coming to grips with the accumulated wave of crime and violence and the breakdown of family and community." The result: a 1994 anti-crime bill with billions for building more prisons and hiring more police.

■ Worldwide, spending for arms and armies approaches $3 billion per *day*— $3 billion that could daily feed, educate, and protect the environment of the world's impoverished millions.

Why this propensity to hurt others? Is it because we, like the mythical Minotaur, are half human, half beast? What circumstances prompt hostile outbursts? Can we control aggression? In this chapter, these are our questions. However, we first need to clarify this term, "aggression."

"Every gun that is made, every warship launched, every rocket fired signifies, in the final sense, a theft from those who hunger and are not fed, those who are cold and are not clothed."
President Dwight Eisenhower, Speech to the American Society of Newspaper Editors, 1953

■ WHAT IS AGGRESSION?

"Aggression" has varied meanings. Clearly, the original Thugs, members of a criminal fraternity in northern India, were aggressing when between 1550 and 1850 they strangled more than 2 million people, claiming to do so in the service of a goddess. But when "aggressive" describes a dynamic salesperson, it takes on a different meaning. What is the difference?

Social psychologists debate how to define aggression, but they agree on this much: We should sharpen our vocabulary by distinguishing self-assured, energetic, go-getting behavior from behavior that hurts, harms, or destroys. The former is assertiveness, the latter aggression.

In Chapter 6 we defined **aggression** as physical or verbal behavior intended to hurt someone. This excludes auto accidents, dental treatments, and sidewalk collisions. It includes slaps, direct insults, even gossipy "digs." Researchers typically measure aggression by having people decide how much to hurt someone, such as how much electric shock to impose.

Aggression:
Physical or verbal behavior intended to hurt someone.

Our definition covers two distinct types of aggression. Animals exhibit *social* aggression, characterized by displays of rage, and *silent* aggression, as when a predator stalks its prey. Peter Marler (1974) reports that social and silent aggression involve separate brain regions. In humans, psychologists label the two types "hostile aggression" and "instrumental aggression." **Hostile aggression** springs from anger. Its goal is to injure. **Instrumental aggression** aims to hurt only as a means to some other end. In 1990, political leaders justified the Persian Gulf war not as a hostile effort to kill 100,000 Iraqis but as a means toward liberating Kuwait. Hostile aggression is "hot"; instrumental aggression is "cool."

Distinguishing between hostile and instrumental aggression is sometimes difficult. What begins as a cool, calculating act can ignite hostility. Still, social psychologists find the distinction useful. Most murders, for example, are hostile. They are impulsive, emotional outbursts—which explains why data from 110 nations show that enforcing the death penalty has not resulted in fewer homicides (Wilkes, 1987). But some murders are instrumental. Most of Chicago's 1000+ mob murders since 1919 were cool and calculated.

Hostile aggression:
Aggression driven by anger and performed as an end in itself.

Instrumental aggression:
Aggression that is a means to some other end.

■ THEORIES OF AGGRESSION

In analyzing causes of hostile and instrumental aggression, social psychologists have focused on three big ideas: (1) There is an inborn aggressive drive. (2) Aggression is a natural response to frustration. (3) Aggressive behavior is learned.

IS AGGRESSION INBORN?

Philosophers have long debated whether our human nature is fundamentally that of a benign, contented "noble savage" or that of a potentially explosive brute. The first view, popularly associated with the eighteenth-century philosopher Jean-Jacques Rousseau, blames society, not human nature, for social evils. The second, associated with the philosopher Thomas Hobbes (1588–1679), sees society's restrictions as necessary to restrain and control the human brute. In this century, the "brutish" view—that aggressive drive is inborn and thus inevitable—was argued by Sigmund Freud in Vienna and Konrad Lorenz in Germany.

Our behavior toward each other is the strangest, most unpredictable, and most unaccountable of all the phenomena with which we are obliged to live. In all of nature, there is nothing so threatening to humanity as humanity itself."
Lewis Thomas (1981)

Instinct Theory

Freud, the pioneering psychoanalyst, speculated that human aggression springs from our redirecting toward others the energy of a primitive death urge (which, loosely speaking, he called the "death instinct"). Lorenz, who studied animal behavior, saw aggression as adaptive rather than self-destructive. But both agreed that aggressive energy is instinctual. If not discharged, it supposedly builds up until it explodes or until an appropriate stimulus "releases" it, like a mouse releasing a mousetrap. Although Lorenz (1976) also argued that we have innate mechanisms for inhibiting aggression (such as making ourselves defenseless), he feared the implications of arming our "fighting instinct" with-

Instinctive behavior:
An innate, unlearned behavior pattern exhibited by all members of a species.

A 19th century engraving of Spanish warriors conquering Montezuma's Indian empire.

out arming our inhibitions. The imbalanced equipping of aggressive tendencies helps explain why more people have been killed in war during this century than in all of prior human history (Sivard, 1991).

The idea that aggression is an instinct collapsed as the list of supposed human instincts grew to include nearly every conceivable human behavior. Nearly 6000 supposed instincts were enumerated in one 1924 survey of social science books (Barash, 1979). What the social scientists had tried to do was *explain* social behavior by *naming* it. It's tempting to play this explaining-by-naming game: "Why do sheep stay together?" "Because of their herd instinct."

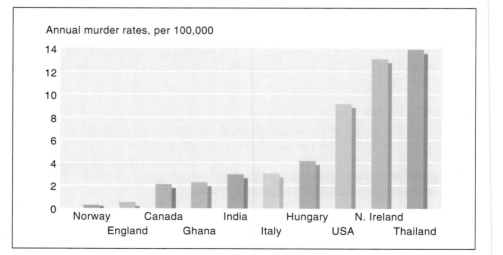

■ FIGURE 12–1

Aggression varies by culture. Homicide rates during the early 1970s varied widely from country to country.

(Data from Archer & Gartner, 1984.)

"How do you know they have a herd instinct?" "Just look at them: They're always together!" Such circular explanation is, of course, no explanation at all.

Instinct theory also fails to account for the variation in aggressiveness, from person to person and culture to culture. How would a shared human instinct for aggression explain the difference between the peaceful Iroquois before White invaders came and the hostile Iroquois after the invasion (Hornstein, 1976)? In today's world, cultures range from nonviolent Norway, where murder is rare, to the South American Yanomamo, nearly half of whose surviving adult males have been involved in a killing (Chagnon, 1988; see also Figure 12–1).

Biological Influences

Although the human propensity to aggress may not qualify as an instinct, aggression *is* biologically influenced.

Neural Influences

Because aggression is a complex behavior, no one spot in the brain controls it. But in both animals and humans, researchers have found neural systems that facilitate aggression. When they activate these areas in the brain, hostility increases; when they deactivate them, hostility decreases. Docile animals can thus be provoked into rage, and raging animals into submission.

"Of course, we'll never actually <u>use</u> it against a potential enemy, but it will allow us to negotiate from a position of strength."

John Ruge

Humanity has armed its capacity for destruction without comparably arming its capacity for the inhibition of aggression.

In one experiment, researchers placed an electrode in an aggression-inhibiting area of a domineering monkey's brain. Given a button that activated the electrode, one small monkey learned to push it every time the tyrant monkey became intimidating. Brain activation works with human patients, too. After receiving painless electrical stimulation in her amygdala (a part of the brain core), one woman became enraged and smashed her guitar against the wall, barely missing her psychiatrist's head (Moyer, 1976).

Genetic Influences

Heredity influences the neural system's sensitivity to aggressive cues. It has long been known that animals of many species can be bred for aggressiveness. Sometimes this is done for practical purposes (the breeding of fighting cocks). Sometimes, breeding is done for research. Kirsti Lagerspetz (1979), a Finnish psychologist, took normal albino mice and bred the most aggressive ones together and the least aggressive ones. After repeating the procedure for 26 generations, she had one set of fierce mice and one set of placid mice.

Aggressiveness similarly varies among primates and humans (Asher, 1987; Olweus, 1979). Our temperament—how intense and reactive we are—is partly something we bring with us into the world, influenced by our sympathetic nervous system's reactivity (Kagan, 1989). Identical twins, when asked separately, are more likely than fraternal twins to agree on whether they have "a violent temper" (Rushton & others, 1986). A person's temperament, observed in infancy, usually endures (Larsen & Diener, 1987; Wilson & Matheny, 1986). A fearless, impulsive, temper-prone child is at risk for violent behavior in adolescence (American Psychological Association, 1993).

Genes predispose the pit bull's aggressiveness.

Biochemical Influences

Blood chemistry is another influence on neural sensitivity to aggressive stimulation. Both laboratory experiments and police data indicate that when people are provoked, alcohol unleashes aggression (Bushman & Cooper, 1990; Bushman, 1993; Taylor & Chermack, 1993; Taylor & Leonard, 1983). Violent people are more likely (1) to drink, and (2) to become aggressive when intoxicated (White & others, 1993). In experiments, intoxicated people administer stronger shocks or higher pain buttons. In the real world, people who have been drinking commit about half of rapes and other violent crimes (Abbey & others, 1993; Reiss & Roth, 1993). In 65 percent of homicides, the murderer and/or the victim had been drinking (American Psychological Association, 1993). Alcohol enhances aggressiveness by reducing people's self-awareness, and by reducing their ability to consider consequences (Hull & Bond, 1986; Steele & Southwick, 1985). Alcohol deindividuates and disinhibits.

Aggressiveness is also influenced by the male sex hormone, testosterone. Although hormonal influences appear much stronger in lower animals than in humans, drugs that diminish testosterone levels in violent human males will subdue their aggressive tendencies. After people reach age 25, their testosterone and rates of violent crime decrease together. Among prisoners convicted of unprovoked violent crimes, testosterone levels tend to be higher than among those imprisoned for nonviolent crimes (Dabbs, 1992; Dabbs & others, 1995). And among the normal range of teen boys and adult men, those with high testosterone levels are more prone to delinquency, hard drug use, and aggressive responses to provocation (Archer, 1991; Dabbs & Morris, 1990; Olweus & others, 1988).

So, there exist important neural, genetic, and biochemical influences on aggression. But is aggression so much a part of human nature that it makes peace unattainable? The Council of Representatives of the American Psychological Association and the directors of the International Council of Psychologists have joined other organizations in unanimously endorsing a statement on violence developed by scientists from a dozen nations (Adams, 1991): "It is scientifically incorrect [to say that] war or any other violent behavior is genetically programmed into our human nature [or that] war is caused by 'instinct' or any single motivation." Thus there are, as we will see, ways to reduce human aggression.

Question: Some violent sex offenders, wishing to free themselves of persistent, damaging impulses and to reduce their prison terms, have requested castration, an operation that is less invasive than a hysterectomy. Should their requests be granted? If so, and if they are deemed no longer at risk of sexual violence, should their prison terms be reduced or eliminated?

IS AGGRESSION A RESPONSE TO FRUSTRATION?

It is a warm evening. Tired and thirsty after two hours of studying, you borrow some change from a friend and head for the nearest soft-drink machine. As the machine devours the change, you can almost taste the cold, refreshing cola. But when you push the button, nothing happens. You push it again. Then you flip the coin return button. Still nothing. Again, you hit the buttons. You slam them. And finally you shake and whack the machine. You stomp back to your studies, empty-handed and short-changed. Should your roommate beware? Are you now more likely to say or do something hurtful?

One of the first psychological theories of aggression, the popular frustration-aggression theory, answers yes. "Frustration always leads to some form of ag-

Frustrating situations, like that experienced by Haitians fleeing to the United States at the Guantanamo naval base in Cuba, help fuel aggressive reactions.

Frustration:
The blocking of goal-directed behavior.

Displacement:
The redirection of aggression to a target other than the source of the frustration. Generally, the new target is a safer or more socially acceptable target.

gression," said John Dollard and his colleagues (1939, p. 1). **Frustration** is anything (such as the malfunctioning vending machine) that blocks our attaining a goal. Frustration grows when our motivation to achieve a goal is very strong, when we expected gratification, and when the blocking is complete.

As Figure 12–2 suggests, the aggressive energy need not explode directly against its source. We learn to inhibit direct retaliation, especially when others might disapprove or punish; instead we *displace* our hostilities to safer targets. **Displacement** occurs in the old anecdote about a man who, humiliated by his boss, berates his wife, who yells at their son, who kicks the dog, which bites the mail carrier.

■ **FIGURE 12–2**
The classic frustration-aggression theory. Frustration creates a motive to aggress. Fear of punishment or disapproval for aggressing against the source of frustration may cause the aggressive drive to be displaced against some other target or even redirected against oneself.
(Based on Dollard & others, 1939, and Miller, 1941.)

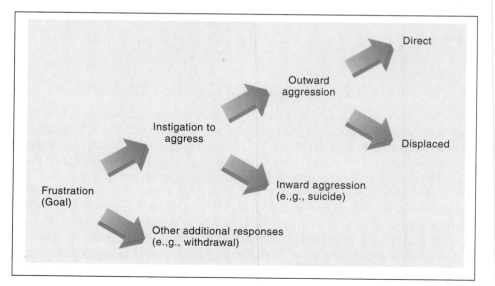

Frustration-Aggression Theory Revised

Laboratory tests of the frustration-aggression theory produced mixed results: Sometimes frustration increased aggressiveness, sometimes not. For example, if the frustration was understandable—if, as in one experiment by Eugene Burnstein and Philip Worchel (1962), a confederate disrupted a group's problem solving because his hearing aid malfunctioned (rather than just because he paid no attention)—then frustration led to irritation, not aggression.

Note that frustration-aggression theory is designed to explain hostile aggression, not instrumental aggression.

Knowing that the original theory overstated the frustration-aggression connection, Leonard Berkowitz (1978, 1989) revised it. Berkowitz theorized that frustration produces anger, an emotional readiness to aggress. Anger arises when someone who frustrates us could have chosen to act otherwise (Averill, 1983; Weiner, 1981). A frustrated person is especially likely to lash out when aggressive cues pull the cork, releasing bottled-up anger. Sometimes the cork will blow without such cues. But cues associated with aggression amplify aggression (Carlson & others, 1990).

Berkowitz (1968, 1981, 1995) and others have found that the sight of a weapon is such a cue. In one experiment, children who had just played with toy guns became more willing to knock down another child's blocks. In another, angered University of Wisconsin men gave more electric shocks to their tormenter when a rifle and a revolver were nearby (supposedly left over from a previous experiment) than when badminton racquets had been left behind (Berkowitz & LePage, 1967). Thus, Berkowitz is not surprised that half of all U.S. murders are committed with handguns and that handguns in homes are far more likely to kill household members than intruders. "Guns not only permit violence," he reported, "they can stimulate it as well. The finger pulls the trigger, but the trigger may also be pulling the finger."

Nor would Berkowitz be surprised that countries that ban handguns have lower murder rates. Compared to the United States, Britain has one-fourth as many people and one-sixteenth as many murders. The United States has 10,000 handgun homicides a year; Britain has about 10. Vancouver, British Columbia, and Seattle, Washington, have similar populations, climates, economies, and rates of criminal activity and assault—except that Vancouver, which carefully restricts handgun ownership, has one-fifth as many handgun murders as Seattle and thus a 40 percent lower overall murder rate (Sloan & others, 1988). When Washington, D.C. adopted a law restricting handgun possession, the numbers of gun-related murders and suicides each abruptly dropped about 25 percent. No changes occurred in other methods of murder and suicide, nor did adjacent areas outside the reach of this law experience any such declines (Loftin & others, 1991).

Guns not only serve as aggression cues, they also put psychological distance between aggressor and victim. As Milgram's obedience studies taught us, remoteness from the victim facilitates cruelty. A knife attack can kill someone but is more difficult and less likely than pulling a trigger from a distance (Figure 12–3).

Is Frustration the Same as Deprivation?

Picture someone feeling extremely frustrated—economically, sexually, or politically. My hunch is that most of you will imagine someone economically, sexually, or politically *deprived*. But frustration may be unrelated to deprivation. The most sexually frustrated people are probably not celibate. The most

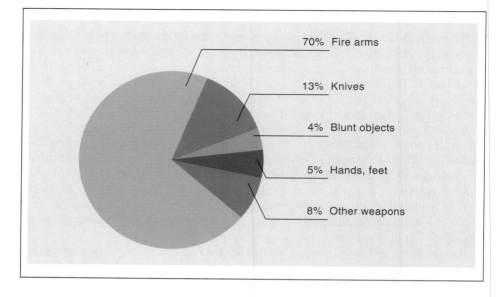

70% Fire arms

13% Knives

4% Blunt objects

5% Hands, feet

8% Other weapons

■ **FIGURE 12–3**

Weapons used to commit murder in the United States in 1993.

(Source: *FBI Uniform Crime Reports,* 1994.)

"I would say a person is deprived if he lacks a goal object people generally regard as attractive or desirable, but is frustrated only when he had been anticipating the pleasure to be gotten from this object and then cannot fulfill this expectation."
Leonard Berkowitz (1972)

"Evils which are patiently endured when they seem inevitable become intolerable when once the idea of escape from them is suggested."
Alexis de Tocqueville, 1856

economically frustrated people are probably not the impoverished residents of Jamaican shantytowns. As the 1969 National Commission on the Causes and Prevention of Violence concluded, economic advancement may even increase frustration and escalate violence. Let's pause to examine this paradoxical conclusion.

Just before Detroit's 1967 riot, in which 43 people were killed and 683 structures burned, Michigan's Governor George Romney appeared on television's *Meet the Press.* He boasted about his state's leadership in civil rights legislation and about the $367 million in federal aid pumped into Detroit during the five preceding years. No sooner were his words broadcast than a large Black neighborhood in Detroit exploded into this century's worst U.S. civil disorder.

People were stunned. Why Detroit? Although things were still bad there relative to the affluence of the White populace, there were greater injustices elsewhere. The National Advisory Commission on Civil Disorders, established to answer the question, concluded that one immediate psychological cause was the frustration of expectations fueled by the legislative and judicial civil rights victories of the 1960s. When there occurs a "revolution of rising expectations," as happened in Detroit and elsewhere, frustrations may escalate, even while conditions improve.

The principle works everywhere. The political scientist-social psychologist team of Ivo and Rosaline Feierabend (1968, 1972) applied the frustration-aggression theory in a study of political instability within 84 nations. When people in rapidly modernizing nations become urbanized and literacy improves, they become more aware of material improvements. However, since affluence usually diffuses slowly, the increasing gap between aspirations and achievements intensifies frustration. Even as deprivation diminishes, frustration and political aggression may therefore escalate. Expectation outstrips reality.

The point is not that actual deprivation and social injustice are irrelevant to social unrest; injustice can be a root cause, even if not the immediate psychological cause. The point is this: Frustration arises from the *gap* between expectations and attainments.

Does Money Alleviate Frustration?

The principle "frustration equals expectations minus attainments" helps us understand why economic satisfaction and frustration fluctuate. Consider the following rather bewildering set of facts:

■ *Fact 1*: Although people deny that "money buys happiness," they will usually grant that a little more money would make them a *little* happier (Myers, 1993). Among entering collegians in 1993, "being very well off financially" was therefore the top-rated objective, outranking "raising a family" and "helping others in difficulty" (Astin & others 1993).

■ *Fact 2*: During the recent decades of economic growth, people in the western world have gained a little more money—many times over. The average American, for example, enjoys *double* the real income of the mid-1950s and has half as many children to spend it on. Doubled incomes have meant doubled purchases, including twice as many cars per person, not to mention the color TVs, VCRs, microwave ovens, home computers, and other trappings of greater wealth.

■ *Fact 3*: Although they have gotten more of the much desired money and possessions, people today are no happier. For example, Americans in recent years have been no more likely than those of the 1950s to report feeling happy and satisfied with their lives. In 1957, 35 percent reported themselves "very happy." In 1994, 29 percent said the same (Figure 12–4). By some measures, such as the rapidly rising rates of depression and teen suicide, modern affluence has been accompanied by greater despair. The same trends—increasing wealth without increasing well-being—mark other nations from Europe to Australia (Easterlin, in press; Cross-National Collaborative Group, 1992). William Cowper's 1782 observation has proved correct: "Happiness depends, as nature shows, less on exterior things than most suppose."

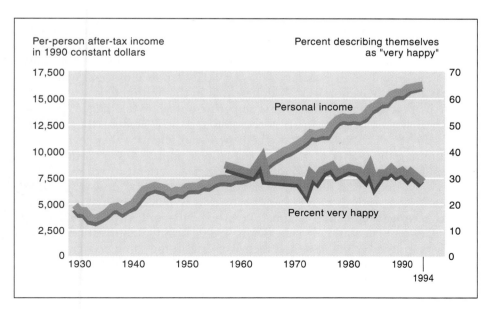

■ FIGURE 12–4
Does money buy happiness? Although buying power has doubled since the 1950s, self-reported happiness has not increased.

(Income data from *Historical Statistics of the U.S.* and *Economic Indicators.* Happiness data cited by Niemi & others, 1989, and Tom Smith, personal communications.)

Why are we not happier given our improving affluence? And how have yesterday's luxuries—color television, air conditioning, CD sound systems—become today's necessities?

The Adaptation-Level Phenomenon

Adaptation-level phenomenon:
The tendency to adapt to a given level of stimulation and thus to notice and react to changes from that level.

Two principles developed by research psychologists help explain rising expectations and therefore continuing frustrations. The **adaptation-level phenomenon** implies that feelings of success and failure, satisfaction and dissatisfaction, are relative to prior achievements. If our current achievements fall below what we previously accomplished, we feel dissatisfied, frustrated; if they rise above that level, we feel successful, satisfied.

If we continue to achieve, however, we soon adapt to success. What formerly felt good registers as neutral, and what formerly felt neutral now feels like deprivation. This helps explain why, despite the rapid increase in real income during the past several decades, the average American is no happier.

Parkinson's second law: Expenditures rise to meet income.

Most of us have experienced the adaptation-level phenomenon. More consumer goods, academic achievement, or social prestige provide an initial surge of pleasure. Yet, all too soon the feeling wanes. Now, we need an even higher level to give us another surge of pleasure. "Even as we contemplate our satisfaction with a given accomplishment, the satisfaction fades," noted Philip Brickman and Donald Campbell (1971), "to be replaced finally by a new indifference and a new level of striving."

"People are never happy for a thousand days."
Chinese proverb

A study of state lottery winners illustrates. Brickman and his colleagues, Dan Coates and Ronnie Janoff-Bulman (1978), found that at first the winners typically felt elated: "Winning the lottery was one of the best things that ever happened to me." Yet their self-reported overall happiness did not increase. In fact, ordinary activities they had previously enjoyed, such as reading or eating a good breakfast, became less pleasurable. Winning the lottery was apparently such an emotional high that, by comparison, their ordinary pleasures paled.

Relative Deprivation

"A house may be large or small; as long as the surrounding houses are equally small, it satisfies all social demands for a dwelling. But let a palace arise beside the little house, and it shrinks from a little house into a hut."
Karl Marx

The dissatisfaction that comes with adapting to new highs is often compounded when we compare ourselves to others. Workers' feelings of well-being depend on whether their compensation is equitable compared to others in their line of work (Yuchtman, 1976). A salary raise for a city's police officers, while temporarily lifting their morale, may deflate that of the fire fighters.

Much of our misery springs from comparing ourselves to others. When people experience an increase in affluence, status, or achievement, they raise the standards by which they evaluate their own attainments. When feeling good and climbing the ladder of success, people look up, not down (Gruder, 1977; Suls & Tesch, 1978; Wheeler & others, 1982). They attend to where they are going, often neglecting where they have come from. This "upward comparison" can cause feelings of **relative deprivation** (Williams, 1975; Wood, 1989).

Relative deprivation:
The perception that one is less well off than others to whom one compares oneself.

Such feelings predict the reactions to perceived inequities by minority groups in the United States and Canada (Dion, 1985). Relative deprivation explains why women who make less than men working in the same occupations feel underpaid only if they compare themselves with male rather than female colleagues (Bylsma & Major, 1994; Zanna & others, 1987). And it explains why the East Germans revolted against their communist regime: they had a higher

PEANUTS reprinted by permission of USF, Inc.

standard of living than some western European countries, but a frustratingly lower one than their West German neighbors (Baron & others, 1992).

The term *relative deprivation* was coined by researchers studying the satisfaction felt by American soldiers in World War II (Merton & Kitt, 1950; Stouffer & others, 1949). Ironically, those in the Air Corps, felt *more* frustrated about their own rate of promotion than those in the Military Police, for whom promotions were slower and more unpredictable. The Air Corps' promotion rate was rapid, and most Air Corps personnel probably perceived themselves as better than the average Air Corps member (the self-serving bias). Thus, their aspirations soared higher than their achievements. The result? Frustration. And where there is frustration, aggression often follows.

One possible source of such frustration today is the affluence depicted in television programs and commercials. In cultures where television is a universal appliance, it helps turn absolute deprivation (lacking what others have) into relative deprivation (feeling deprived). Karen Hennigan and her co-workers (1982) analyzed crime rates in American cities around the time television was introduced. In 34 cities where television ownership became widespread in 1951, the 1951 larceny theft rate (for crimes such as shoplifting and bicycle stealing) took an observable jump. In 34 other cities, where a government freeze had delayed the introduction of television until 1955, a similar jump in the theft rate occurred—in 1955. Why? Hennigan and her colleagues believe

> television caused younger and poorer persons (the major perpetrators of theft) to compare their life-styles and possessions with (a) those of wealthy television characters and (b) those portrayed in advertisements. Many of these viewers may have felt resentment and frustration over lacking the goods they could not afford, and some may have turned to crime as a way of obtaining the coveted goods and reducing any "relative deprivation."

Some Conclusions

The principles of adaptation-level and relative deprivation have a thought-provoking implication: Seeking satisfaction through material achievement requires continually expanding affluence merely to maintain satisfaction. "Poverty," said Plato, "consists not in the decrease of one's possessions, but in the increase of one's greed."

Fortunately, adaptation also can enable us to adjust downward, should we choose or be forced to simplify our lives. If our buying power shrinks, we initially feel some pain. But eventually we adapt to the new reality. In the aftermath of the 1970s gas price hikes, North Americans managed to substantially reduce their "need" for large, gas-slurping cars. Even paraplegics, the

Could Lucy ever experience enough "ups"? Not according to the adaptation-level phenomenon.

"Women's discontent increases in exact proportion to her development."
Elizabeth Cady Stanton, 1815–1902, American suffragette

"All our wants, beyond those which a very moderate income will supply, are purely imaginary."
Henry St. John, *Letter to Swift*, 1719

blind, and other people with severe handicaps usually show remarkable re-silience. They adapt to their disability and achieve a normal or near-normal level of life satisfaction (Brickman & others, 1978; Chwalisz & others, 1988; Schulz & Decker, 1985). Victims of traumatic incidents surely must envy those who are not paralyzed, as many of us envy those who have won a state lottery. Yet, after a period of adjustment, the astonishing fact is that none of these three groups differs appreciably from the others in moment-to-moment happiness. Human beings have an enormous capacity to adapt.

Finally, experiences that lower our comparison standards can renew our contentment. A research team led by Marshall Dermer (1979) put University of Wisconsin-Milwaukee women through some imaginative exercises in deprivation. After viewing depictions of how grim life was in Milwaukee in 1900, or after imagining and then writing about being burned and disfigured, the women expressed greater satisfaction with their own lives. In another experiment, Jennifer Crocker and Lisa Gallo (1985) found that those who five times completed the sentence "I'm glad I'm not a . . ." afterward felt less depressed and more satisfied with life than did those who had completed sentences beginning "I wish I were a. . . ." For this reason, people facing personal threat often search for a silver lining and boost their self-esteem by comparing downward (Gibbons & Gerrard, 1989; Reis & others, 1993; Taylor, 1989). Realizing that others have it worse helps people feel better about themselves.

"However great the discrepancies between men's lots, there is always a certain balance of joy and sorrow which equalizes all."
La Rochefoucauld, *Maxims*, 1665

IS AGGRESSION LEARNED SOCIAL BEHAVIOR?

Theories of aggression based on instinct and frustration assume that hostile urges erupt from inner emotions, which naturally "push" aggression from within. Social psychologists contend that learning also "pulls" aggression out of us.

The Rewards of Aggression

By experience and by observing others, we learn that aggression often pays. Experiments have transformed animals from docile creatures into ferocious fighters. Severe defeats, on the other hand, create submissiveness (Ginsburg & Allee, 1942; Kahn, 1951; Scott & Marston, 1953).

People, too, can learn the rewards of aggression. A child whose aggressive acts successfully intimidate other children will likely become increasingly aggressive (Patterson & others, 1967). Aggressive hockey players—the ones sent most often to the penalty box for rough play—score more goals than nonaggressive players (McCarthy & Kelly, 1978a, 1978b). Canadian teenage hockey players whose fathers applaud physically aggressive play show the most aggressive attitudes and style of play (Ennis & Zanna, 1991). In these cases, aggression is instrumental in achieving certain rewards.

Collective violence can also pay. After the 1980 riot in Miami's Liberty City neighborhood, President Carter came to the neighborhood to assure residents personally of his concern and of forthcoming federal aid. After the 1967 Detroit riot, the Ford Motor Company accelerated its efforts to hire minority workers, prompting comedian Dick Gregory to joke, "Last summer the fire got too close to the Ford plant. Don't scorch the Mustangs, baby." After the 1985 riots in South Africa became severe, the government repealed laws forbidding mixed marriages, offered to restore Black "citizenship rights" (not including

Aggression can be instrumental, as it is for this Palestinian terrorist, shown on videotape with Israeli soldier Nachson Waxman, who was later killed.

the right to vote), and eliminated the hated pass laws controlling the movement of Blacks. The point is not that people consciously plan riots for their instrumental value but that aggression sometimes has payoffs. If nothing more, it gets attention.

The same is true of terrorist acts, which enable powerless people to garner widespread attention. "Kill one, frighten ten thousand," asserts an ancient Chinese proverb. In this age of global communications, killing only a few can frighten tens of millions—as happened when the terrorist-caused deaths of 25 Americans in several incidents during 1985 struck more fear into the hearts of travelers than the car-accident deaths of 46,000, or when the 1995 Oklahoma City bombing of a federal building captured a nation's attention. Deprived of what Margaret Thatcher called "the oxygen of publicity," terrorism would surely diminish, concludes Jeffrey Rubin (1986). It's like the 1970s incidents of naked spectators "streaking" onto football fields for a few seconds of television exposure. Once the networks decided to ignore the incidents, the phenomenon ended.

Observational Learning

Albert Bandura, the leading proponent of the **social learning theory** of aggression, believes that we learn aggression not only by experiencing its payoffs but also by observing others. As with most social behaviors, we acquire aggression by watching others act and noting the consequences.

Picture this scene from one of Bandura's experiments (Bandura & others, 1961). A Stanford nursery school child is put to work on an interesting art activity. An adult is in another part of the room, where there are Tinker Toys, a mallet, and a big inflated doll. After a minute of working with the Tinker Toys,

Social learning theory:
The theory that we learn social behavior by observing and imitating and by being rewarded and punished.

the adult gets up and for almost 10 minutes attacks the inflated doll. She pounds it with the mallet, kicks it, and throws it, all the while yelling, "Sock him in the nose. . . . Knock him down. . . . Kick him."

After observing this outburst, the child goes to a different room with many very attractive toys. But after two minutes the experimenter interrupts, saying these are her best toys and she must "save them for the other children." The frustrated child now goes into another room with various toys for aggressive and nonaggressive play, two of which are a Bobo doll and a mallet.

Seldom did children not exposed to the aggressive adult model display any aggressive play or talk. Although frustrated, they nevertheless played calmly. Those who had observed the aggressive adult were many times more likely to pick up the mallet and lash out at the doll. Watching the adult's aggressive behavior lowered their inhibitions. Moreover, the children often reproduced the model's acts and said her words. Observing aggressive behavior had both lowered their inhibitions and taught them ways to aggress.

Bandura (1979) believes that everyday life exposes us to aggressive models in the family, the subculture, and the mass media.

The Family

Children of physically punitive parents tend to use similar aggression when relating to others. Their parents often disciplined them by screaming, slapping, and beating—thus modeling aggression as a method of dealing with problems (Patterson & others, 1982). These parents often themselves had parents who were physically punitive (Bandura & Walters, 1959; Straus & Gelles, 1980). Although most abused children do not become criminals or abusive parents, 30 percent do later abuse their own children—four times the national rate (Kaufman & Zigler, 1987; Widom, 1989). Within families, violence often leads to violence.

Family influence also appears in higher violence rates in cultures and families where the father plays a minimal role (Triandis, 1994). The U.S. Bureau of Justice Statistics reports that 70 percent of juveniles in detention did not grow up with two parents (Beck & others, 1988). Two-parent families differ not only in increased care and positive discipline by fathers but also in less poverty and greater educational achievement. The correlation between parental absence (usually father absence) and violence holds across races, income levels, education, and locations (Staub, 1996; Zill, 1988).

The correlation also appears over time. In the United States of 1960, barely over 1 in 10 children did not live with two parents and only 16,000 juveniles were arrested for violent crime. In 1992, nearly 3 in 10 children did not live with two parents, and a similar-sized juvenile population produced 96,000 arrests for violent crime. The point is not that children from father-absent homes are likely to become delinquent or violent (nurtured by a caring mother and extended family, most such children do not act out). But the risk is increased. The situation, it seems, matters.

The Subculture and the Mass Media

The social environment outside the home also provides models. In communities where "macho" images are admired, aggression is readily transmitted to new generations (Cartwright, 1975; Short, 1969). The violent subculture of teenage gangs, for instance, provides its junior members with aggressive mod-

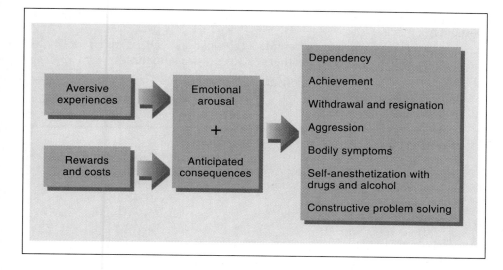

■ **FIGURE 12–5**
The social learning view of aggression. The emotional arousal stemming from an aversive experience motivates aggression. Whether aggression or some other response actually occurs depends on what consequences we have learned to expect.
(Based on Bandura, 1979.)

els. At sporting events such as soccer games, player violence precedes most incidents of fan violence (Goldstein, 1982).

Richard Nisbett (1993) explored the subculture effect by studying violence rates in southern American towns settled by Scotts-Irish herders whose tradition emphasized "manly honor" and the aggressive protection of one's flock. Their cultural descendants today have triple the homicide rates of Whites in New England towns settled by gentler Puritan, Quaker, and Dutch farmer-artisans. They also express more support for spanking children, initiating war, and owning guns.

Although family or subculture may model aggression, television offers a much wider range of violent models. As we will see, viewing televised violence tends to (1) increase aggressiveness, (2) desensitize viewers to violence, and (3) shape their assumptions about social reality.

So, people learn aggressive responses both by experience and by observing aggressive models. But when will aggressive responses actually occur? Bandura (1979) contends that aggressive acts are motivated by a variety of aversive experiences—frustration, pain, insults (Figure 12–5). Such experiences arouse us emotionally. But whether we act aggressively depends upon the consequences we anticipate. Aggression is most likely when we are aroused *and* it seems safe and rewarding to aggress.

A ggression manifests itself in two forms: *hostile aggression*, which springs from emotions such as anger and intends to injure, and *instrumental aggression*, which is a means to some other end.

There are three broad theories of aggression. The *instinct* view is most commonly associated with Sigmund Freud and Konrad Lorenz. It contends that aggressive energy will accumulate from within, like water accumulating behind a dam. Although the available evidence offers little support for the instinct view, aggression *is* biologically influenced by heredity, blood chemistry, and the brain.

According to the second view, *frustration* causes anger and hostility. Given aggressive cues, this anger may provoke aggression. Frustration stems not

SUMMING UP

from deprivation itself but from the gap between expectations and achievements.

The *social learning* view presents aggression as learned behavior. By experience and by observing others' success, we sometimes learn that aggression sometimes pays.

■ INFLUENCES ON AGGRESSION

*U*nder what conditions do we aggress? The factors tugging at our trigger include: aversive incidents, arousal, the media, and the group context.

AVERSIVE INCIDENTS

Pain

Researcher Nathan Azrin wanted to know if switching off foot shocks would reinforce two rats' positive interactions with each other. Azrin planned to turn on the shock and then, once the rats approached each other, cut off the pain. To his great surprise, the experiment proved impossible. As soon as the rats felt pain, they attacked each other, before the experimenter could switch off the shock. The greater the shock (and pain) the more violent the attack.

Is this true of rats alone? The researchers found that with a wide variety of species, the cruelty the animals imposed upon each other matched zap for zap the cruelty imposed upon them. As Azrin (1967) explained, the pain-attack response occurred

> in many different strains of rats. Then we found that shock produced attack when pairs of the following species were caged together: some kinds of mice, hamsters, opossums, raccoons, marmosets, foxes, nutria, cats, snapping turtles, squirrel monkeys, ferrets, red squirrels, bantam roosters, alligators, crayfish, amphiuma (an amphibian), and several species of snakes including the boa constrictor, rattlesnake, brown rat-snake, cottonmouth, copperhead, and black snake. The shock-attack reaction was clearly present in many very different kinds of creatures. In all the species in which shock produced attack it was fast and consistent, in the same "push-button" manner as with the rats.

Today's ethical guidelines restrict researchers' use of painful stimuli.

The animals were not choosy about their targets. They would attack animals of their own species and also those of a different species, or stuffed dolls, or even tennis balls.

The researchers also varied the source of pain. They found that not just shocks induce attack; intense heat and "psychological pain"—for example, suddenly not rewarding hungry pigeons that have been trained to expect a grain reward after pecking at a disk—brought the same reaction as shocks. "Psychological pain" is, of course, what we call frustration.

Pain heightens aggressiveness in humans, also. Many of us can recall such a reaction after stubbing a toe or suffering a headache. Leonard Berkowitz and his associates demonstrated this by having University of Wisconsin students hold one hand in lukewarm water or painfully cold water. Those whose hands were submerged in the cold water reported feeling more irritable and more annoyed, and they were more willing to blast another person with unpleasant

The pain-attack reaction: Upon receiving a shock or other painful effect, many animals will automatically attack whatever animal is within reach.

noise. In view of such results, Berkowitz (1983, 1989) now believes that aversive stimulation rather than frustration is the basic trigger of hostile aggression. Frustration is certainly one important type of unpleasantness. But any aversive event, whether a dashed expectation, a personal insult, or physical pain, can incite an emotional outburst. Even the torment of a depressed state increases the likelihood of hostile aggressive behavior.

Heat

People have theorized for centuries about the effect of climate on human action. Hippocrates (ca. 460–377 B.C.), comparing the civilized Greece of his day to the savagery in what we now know as Germany and Switzerland, believed the cause to be northern Europe's harsh climate. Later, the English attributed their "superior" culture to *England's* ideal climate. French thinkers proclaimed the same for France. Because climate remains steady while cultural traits change, the climate theory of culture obviously has limited validity.

However, temporary climate variations can affect behavior. Offensive odors, cigarette smoke, and air pollution have all been linked with aggressive behavior (Rotton & Frey, 1985). But the most-studied environmental irritant is heat.

William Griffitt (1970; Griffitt & Veitch, 1971) found that compared to students who answered questionnaires in a room with a normal temperature, those who did so in an uncomfortably hot room (over 90°F.) reported feeling more tired and aggressive and expressed more hostility toward a stranger. Follow-up experiments revealed that heat also triggers retaliative actions (Bell, 1980; Rule & others, 1987).

Does uncomfortable heat increase aggression in the real world as well as in the laboratory? Consider:

■ The riots occurring in 79 U.S. cities between 1967 and 1971 were more likely on hot than on cool days (Figure 12–6).

■ When the weather is hot in Houston, Texas, violent crimes are more likely. The same is true in Des Moines, Iowa (Cotton, 1981); Dayton, Ohio (Rotton & Frey, 1985); Indianapolis, Indiana (Cotton, 1986); and Dallas, Texas (Harries & Stadler, 1988).

■ Not only do hotter days have more violent crimes, so do hotter seasons of the year and hotter summers (Anderson, 1989).

■ In heat-stricken Phoenix, Arizona, drivers without air conditioning are more likely to honk at a stalled car (Kenrick & MacFarlane, 1986).

■ During the 1986 to 1988 major league baseball seasons, the number of batters hit by a pitch was two-thirds greater for games played in the 90s than for games played below 80° (Reifman & others, 1991). Pitchers weren't wilder on hot days—they had no more walks and wild pitches. They just clobbered more batters.

Do these real-world findings show that heat discomfort directly fuels aggressiveness? Although the conclusion appears plausible, these *correlations* between temperature and aggression don't prove it. People certainly could be more irritable in hot, sticky weather. However, there may be other contribut-

"I pray thee, good Mercutio, let's retire;
The day is hot, the Capulets abroad,
And, if we meet, we shall not 'scape a brawl,
For now, these hot days, is the mad blood stirring."
Shakespeare, *Romeo and Juliet*

■ **FIGURE 12–6**
Between 1967 and 1971 the likelihood of a riot increased with temperature. (This does not mean that most riots occurred at temperatures above 90°F. Rather, on any given day above 90°F a riot was more likely than on any other given day of lower temperature.)
(Data from Carlsmith & Anderson, 1979.)

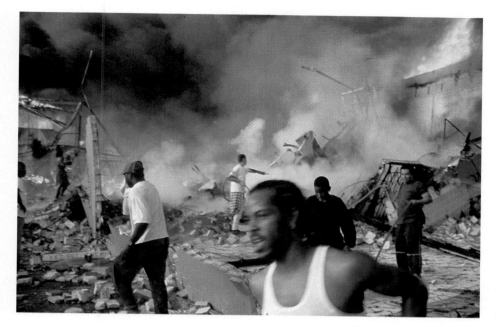

Los Angeles, May 1993. Riots are more likely during hot summer weather.

ing factors. Maybe hot summer evenings drive people into the streets. There, other group influence factors may well take over. Judging from experiments on aversive stimulation and group aggression (see pages 452 and 470), my hunch is that such behavior is stimulated by *both* the heat and the group.

Attacks

Being attacked or insulted by another is especially conducive to aggression. Experiments at Kent State University by Stuart Taylor (Taylor & Pisano, 1971), at Washington State University by Harold Dengerink (Dengerink & Myers, 1977), and at Osaka University by Kennichi Ohbuchi and Toshihiro Kambara (1985) confirm that intentional attacks breed retaliatory attacks. In most of these experiments one person competes with another in a reaction-time contest. After each test trial, the winner chooses how much shock to give the loser. Actually, each subject is playing a programmed opponent, who steadily escalates the amount of shock. Do the real subjects respond charitably? Hardly. Extracting "an eye for an eye" is the more likely response.

Crowding

Crowding—the subjective feeling of not having enough space—is stressful. Crammed in the back of a bus, trapped in slow-moving freeway traffic, or living three to a small room in a college dorm diminishes one's sense of control (Baron & others, 1976; McNeel, 1980). Might such experiences also heighten aggression?

The stress experienced by animals allowed to overpopulate a confined environment does heighten aggressiveness (Calhoun, 1962; Christian & others, 1960). But it is a rather large leap from rats in an enclosure or deer on an island to humans in a city. Nevertheless, it's true that dense urban areas do experience higher rates of crime and emotional distress (Fleming & others, 1987;

Crowding:
A subjective feeling of not enough space per person.

Kirmeyer, 1978). Even when they don't suffer higher crime rates, residents of crowded cities may *feel* more fearful. Toronto's crime rate is four times higher than Hong Kong's. Yet people from Hong Kong, which is four times more densely populated than Toronto, report feeling more fearful on their city's streets than do people from Toronto (Gifford & Peacock, 1979).

AROUSAL

So far we have seen that various aversive stimulations can arouse anger. Do other types of arousal, such as those that accompany exercise or sexual excitement, have a similar effect? Imagine that Tawna, having just finished a stimulating short run, comes home to discover that her date for the evening has called and left word that he has made other plans. Will Tawna more likely explode in fury after her run than if she discovered the same message after awakening from a nap? Or, having just exercised, will her aggressive tendencies be exorcised? To discover an answer, let's examine some intriguing research on how we interpret and label our bodily states.

In a now famous experiment, Stanley Schachter and Jerome Singer (1962) found we can experience an aroused bodily state in different ways. They aroused University of Minnesota men by injecting adrenaline. The drug produced body flushing, heart palpitation, and more rapid breathing. When forewarned that the drug would produce these effects, the men felt little emotion, even when waiting with either a hostile or a euphoric person. Of course, they could readily attribute their bodily sensations to the drug. Schachter and Singer led another group of men to believe the drug produced no such side effects. Then they, too, were placed in the company of a hostile or euphoric person. How did they feel and act? Angered when with the hostile person; amused when with the person who was euphoric. The seeming principle: *A given state of bodily arousal feeds one emotion or another, depending on how the person interprets and labels the arousal.*

Other experiments indicate that arousal is not as emotionally undifferentiated as Schachter believed. Yet being physically stirred up does intensify just

■ FIGURE 12–7

Elements of hostile aggression. An aversive situation can trigger aggression by provoking hostile cognitions, hostile feelings, and arousal. These reactions make us more likely to perceive harmful intent and to react aggressively.

(Adapted from Anderson, Deuser, and DeNeve, 1995.)

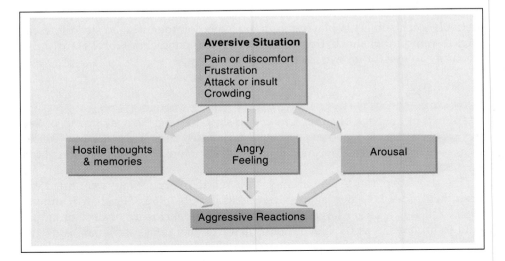

about any emotion (Reisenzein, 1983). For example, Paul Biner (1991) reports that people find radio static unpleasant, *especially* when they are aroused by bright lighting. And Dolf Zillmann (1988), Jennings Bryant, and their collaborators found that people who have just pumped an exercise bike or watched a film of a Beatles rock concert find it easy to misattribute their arousal to a provocation. They then retaliate with heightened aggression. While common sense might lead us to assume that Tawna's run would have drained her aggressive tensions, enabling her to accept bad news calmly, these studies show that arousal feeds emotions.

Sexual arousal and other forms of arousal, such as anger, can therefore amplify one another (Zillmann, 1989). Love is never so passionate as after a fight or a fright. In the laboratory, erotic stimuli are more arousing to people who have just been frightened. The arousal of a roller-coaster ride may similarly spill over into romantic feeling for one's partner.

A frustrating, hot, crowded, or insulting situation heightens arousal. When it does, the arousal, combined with hostile thoughts and feelings, may form a recipe for aggressive behavior (Figure 12–7). Angered and aroused by a defiant Rodney King's refusal to stop his car, Los Angeles police officers confronted him in an aggressive frame of mind, and then beat him.

THE MEDIA

The increase in reported violent crime, especially among juveniles, prompts us to wonder: Why the change? What social forces have caused the mushrooming violence?

Alcohol contributes to aggression, but alcohol use has not appreciably changed since 1960 (McAneny, 1994). Might the surging violence instead be fueled by the growth in individualism and materialism? by the growing gap

Is violent crime rising? Americans' perceptions of dramatically increased crime have triggered a wave of gun purchases and new laws allowing the carrying of concealed weapons (which are more likely to be used against a household member than as intended—against an intruder or attacker). Most other Western countries tolerate many fewer guns, and have a much lower murder rate.

between the powerful rich and the powerless poor? by the media's increasing modeling of violence and unrestrained sexuality? The latter question arises because increased rates of violence and sexual coercion have coincided with increases in media mayhem and sexual suggestion. Is the historical correlation a coincidence? What are the social consequences of pornography (which *Webster's* defines as erotic depictions intended to excite sexual arousal)? And what are the effects of modeling violence in movies and on television?

PORNOGRAPHY AND SEXUAL VIOLENCE

Repeated exposure to erotic films featuring quick, uncommitted sex has several effects. It can

- Decrease attraction for a less exciting partner (see page 492)
- Increase acceptance of extramarital sex and of women's sexual submission to men (Zillmann, 1989)
- Increase men's perceiving women in sexual terms (Frable & others, 1994; Hansen & Hansen, 1989; 1990)

Social-psychological research on pornography has, however, focused mostly on depictions of sexual violence. A typical sexually violent episode finds a man forcing himself upon a woman. She at first resists and tries to fight off her attacker. Gradually she becomes sexually aroused, and her resistance melts. By the end she is in ecstasy, pleading for more. We have all viewed or read nonpornographic versions of this sequence: She resists, he persists. Dashing man grabs and forcibly kisses protesting woman. Within moments, the arms that were pushing him away are clutching him tight, her resistance overwhelmed by her unleashed passion. In *Gone with the Wind*, Scarlett O'Hara is carried to bed protesting and kicking, and wakes up singing.

Social psychologists report that viewing such fictional scenes of a man overpowering and arousing a woman can (1) distort one's perceptions of how women actually respond to sexual coercion and (2) increase men's aggression against women, at least in laboratory settings.

Distorted Perceptions of Sexual Reality

Does viewing sexual violence reinforce the myth that some women would welcome sexual assault—that "'no' doesn't really mean no"? To find out, Neil Malamuth and James Check (1981) showed University of Manitoba men either two nonsexual movies or two movies depicting a man sexually overcoming a woman. A week later, when surveyed by a different experimenter, those who saw the films with mild sexual violence were more accepting of violence against women. Note that the sexual message (that many women enjoy being "taken") was subtle and unlikely to elicit counterarguing. (Recall from Chapter 8 that more persuasion occurs when a disagreeable message slips in without provoking people to counterargue.)

Viewing slasher movies has much the same effect. Men shown films such as the *Texas Chainsaw Massacre* become desensitized to brutality and more likely to view rape victims unsympathetically (Linz & others, 1988, 1989). In fact, said researchers Edward Donnerstein, Daniel Linz, and Steven Penrod (1987), what better way for an evil character to get people to react calmly to

"Pornography that portrays sexual aggression as pleasurable for the victim increases the acceptance of the use of coercion in sexual relations."
Social science consensus at Surgeon General's Workshop on Pornography and Public Health (Koop, 1987)

the torture and mutilation of women than to show a gradually escalating series of such films?

Aggression against Women

Evidence also accumulates that pornography may contribute to men's actual aggression toward women. Correlational studies suggest that possibility. John Court (1984) notes that across the world, as pornography became more widely available during the 1960s and 1970s, the rate of reported rapes sharply increased—except in countries and areas where pornography was controlled. (The examples that counter this trend—such as Japan, where violent pornography is available but the rape rate is low—remind us that other factors are also important.) In Hawaii, the number of reported rapes rose ninefold between 1960 and 1974, dropped when restraints on pornography were temporarily imposed, and rose again when the restraints were lifted.

In another correlational study, Larry Baron and Murray Straus (1984) discovered that the sales of sexually explicit magazines (such as *Hustler* and *Playboy*) in the 50 states correlates with state rape rates. After controlling for other factors, such as the percentage of young males in each state, a positive relationship remained. Alaska ranked first in sex magazine sales and first in rape. Nevada was second on both measures.

When interviewed, Canadian and American sexual offenders commonly acknowledge pornography use. For example, William Marshall (1989) reports that Ontario rapists and child molesters use pornography much more than men

"Pornography is the theory and rape the practice."
Robin Morgan (1980, p. 139)

Was the use of pornography by Milwaukee mass murderer Jeffery Dahmer (in whose apartment police found pornographic tapes) merely a symptom of his derangement, or also a contributing cause? Did Ted Bundy's (1989) comments on the eve of his execution for a series of rape-murders acknowledge pornography's toll, or make it a handy excuse?: "The most damaging kinds of pornography [involve] sexual violence. Like an addiction, you keep craving something that is harder, harder, something which, which gives you a greater sense of excitement. Until you reach a point where the pornography only goes so far, you reach that jumping off point where you begin to wonder if maybe actually doing it would give you that which is beyond just reading it or looking at it."

who are not sexual offenders. An FBI study also reports considerable exposure to pornography among serial killers, as does the Los Angeles Police Department among most child sex abusers (Bennett, 1991; Ressler & others, 1988). Of course, this *correlation* cannot prove that pornography is a contributing *cause* of rape. Maybe the offenders' use of pornography is merely a symptom and not a cause of their basic deviance.

Although limited to the sorts of short-term behaviors that can be studied in the laboratory, controlled experiments reveal cause and effect. A consensus statement by 21 leading social scientists sums up the results: "Exposure to violent pornography increases punitive behavior toward women" (Koop, 1987). One of these social scientists, Edward Donnerstein (1980), had shown 120 University of Wisconsin men a neutral, an erotic, or an aggressive-erotic (rape) film. Then, the men, supposedly as part of another experiment, "taught" a male or female confederate some nonsense syllables by choosing how much shock to administer for incorrect answers. Especially when angered, the men who had watched the rape film administered markedly stronger shocks—but only to female victims (Figure 12–8).

If the ethics of conducting such experiments trouble you, rest assured that these researchers appreciate the controversial and powerful experience they are giving participants. Only after giving their knowing consent do people participate. Moreover, after the experiment researchers debunk any myths the film communicated. One hopes that such debriefing sufficiently offsets the vivid image of a supposedly euphoric rape victim. Judging from studies with University of Manitoba and Winnipeg students by James Check and Neil Malamuth (1984; Malamuth & Check, 1984), it does. Those who read erotic rape stories and were then fully debriefed became *less* accepting of the "women-enjoy-rape" myth than students who had not seen the film. Similarly, Donnerstein and Berkowitz (1981) found that Wisconsin students who viewed pornography *and* were then thoroughly debriefed were later *less* likely than other students to agree that "being roughed up is sexually stimulating to many women."

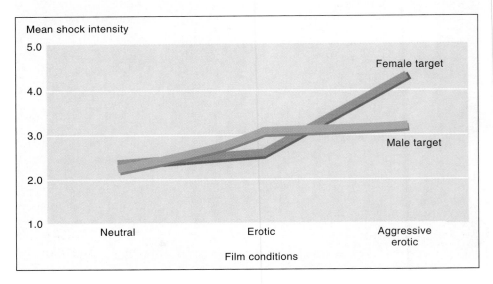

■ FIGURE 12–8
After viewing an aggressive-erotic film, college men delivered stronger shocks than before, especially to a woman.
(Data from Donnerstein, 1980.)

TABLE 12–1 *Reported Rape Experiences in Five Countries*

COUNTRY	SAMPLE OF WOMEN	COMPLETED & ATTEMPTED RAPE
Canada	National sample at 95 colleges and universities	23% rape or sexual assault
New Zealand	Convenience sample of psychology students	25%
United Kingdom	Convenience sample at 22 universities	19%
United States	Representative sample at 32 colleges and universities	28%
Seoul, Korea	Adult women	22%

Source: Studies reported by Koss, Heise, and Russo (1994)

Justification for this experimentation is not only scientific but also humanitarian. In a careful national survey, 22 percent of women reported having been forced by a man to do something sexually (Laudmann & others, 1994). In surveys of 6200 college students nationwide and 2200 Ohio working women, Mary Koss and her colleagues (1988, 1990, 1993) found that 28 percent of the women reported an experience that met the legal definition of rape or attempted rape. Surveys in other industrialized countries produce similar results (Table 12–1). Three in four stranger rapes and nearly all acquaintance rapes went unreported to police. Thus the known rape rate *greatly* underestimates the actual rape rate. Moreover, many more women—half in one recent survey of college women (Sandberg & others, 1985)—report having suffered some form of sexual assault while on a date, and even more have experienced verbal sexual coercion or harassment (Craig, 1990; Pryor, 1987).

Eight different surveys have asked college males whether there was any chance they would rape a woman "if you could be assured that no one would know and that you could in no way be punished" (Stille & others, 1987). A disturbing proportion—about one-third—admit to at least a slim possibility of doing so. Compared to men who indicate no possibility of raping, these men are more like convicted rapists in their belief in rape myths, their being sexually aroused by rape depictions, and their behaving aggressively toward women—in both laboratory and dating situations. Aggression is greatest among those who have formed the sort of rape-supportive attitudes that pornography cultivates. Men who behave in sexually coercive, aggressive ways typically desire dominance, exhibit hostility toward women, and are sexually experienced (Malamuth, 1986, 1989).

Most, having been overcome on a date or by an acquaintance, didn't label it as such. Women's "scripts" for rape usually involve violence by a stranger. (Kahn & others, 1994).

FOCUS

IS RAPE ON THE INCREASE?

Across the world, people are alarmed and angry about increasing violent crime. The American experience illustrates. By a 6 to 1 margin, Americans report being "dissatisfied" rather than "satisfied" with how safe they feel (Hugick & McAneny, 1992). There is therefore now a booming business in home security systems, bedside guns, and bodyguards.

By one measure—the counting of violent crimes by local police and sheriffs, as reported in the FBI's annual *Uniform Crime Report*—America's violent crime rate has indeed increased, dramatically so. Since 1960, reported violent crime (homicides, rapes, assaults, and robberies per 100,000 people) has *quintupled*.

By another measure—the Census Bureau's National Crime Victimization Survey (NCVS) for the Bureau of Justice Statistics, conducted annually since 1973—the violent crime rate has not increased by one iota. Despite frightening TV images of violence, despite pockets of drug-related violence, this survey of random households reassures us: Things aren't so bad. In fact, women's vulnerability to rape has, the survey suggests, been decreasing since 1973 (see Figure 12–9).

So which do we believe? The government's crime report from law enforcement agencies? Or the government's crime report from citizens? Perhaps the contradiction in rape statistics is easily explained: Does the surge in reported rapes merely reflect women's increasing willingness to report? We could wish it were so, but the NCVS reveals no increase over time in the percentage of women who report a rape. Might the surge instead reflect more recording (and therefore reporting) of rape complaints by officers and dispatchers—more of whom now are women? Sociologists Gary Jensen and Maryaltani Karpos (1993) find that a much more likely explanation, because increased female participation in police forces parallels the increased recording and reporting of rape.

But consider this: The crime survey question and interview format primarily detects violent stranger rapes, and only some of those. Rapes known to police (a fraction of all rapes, everyone agrees) are nearly double the number of rapes that the NCVS estimates were reported to police. Noting these problems, psychologist Mary Koss (1992) is skeptical about the NCVS conclusions. And consider this: If the actual rape rate is steady, older women should be more likely to report ever having been raped (because of their greater years at risk). But if the rate has recently increased, today's young women should be more likely than older women to report ever having been raped (because older women would have experienced their most vulnerable teen years and twenties long ago, when rape would have been less common). It is indeed the case that *younger* women are more likely to report having been raped (Sorenson & others, 1987). Assuming that women of any age would be unlikely to for-

Malamuth, Donnerstein, and Zillmann are among those alarmed by women's increasing risk of being sexually harassed or raped. They caution against oversimplifying the complex causes of rape—which is no more attributable to any one cause than is cancer. Yet they conclude that viewing violence, especially sexual violence, can have antisocial effects. Just as most Germans quietly tolerated the degrading anti-Semitic images that fed the Holocaust, so most people today tolerate media images of women that feed what some call the growing "female holocaust" of sexual harassment, abuse, and rape.

Media Awareness

In the contest of individual versus collective rights, people in most western nations side with individual rights. So, as an alternative to censorship, many psychologists favor "media awareness training." Recall that pornography researchers have successfully resensitized and educated participants to women's actual responses to sexual violence. Could educators similarly promote criti-

■ **FIGURE 12–9**
Disparity in Rape
Statistics. *Is rape
increasing, as the FBI's
Uniform Crime Report
indicates? Or decreasing,
as the Census Bureau's
National Crime
Victimization Survey
indicates?*
(Data from Jensen & Karpos,
1993.)

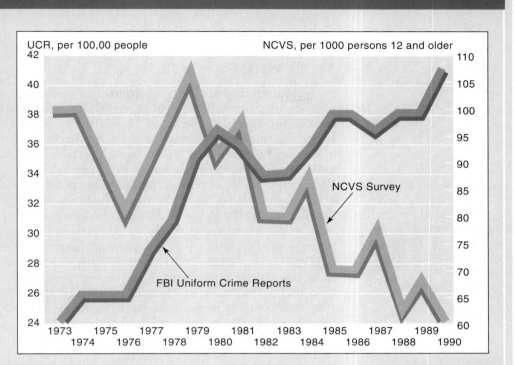

get a rape experience, this survey result suggests that sexual violence *has* increased (though probably at less than the rate of increase reported by the FBI).

The moral: Truth is elusive. As so often happens, simple questions—Is rape increasing?—are not simply answered. Different methods sometimes give us differing answers. From different perspectives, we glimpse different aspects of reality. By attacking a question in different ways, we restrain error and form a clearer, if still hazy, image of truth.

cal viewing skills? By sensitizing people to the view of women that predominates in pornography and to issues of sexual harassment and violence, it should be possible to counter the myth that women enjoy being coerced. "Our utopian and perhaps naive hope," say Edward Donnerstein, Daniel Linz, and Steven Penrod (1987, p. 196), "is that in the end the truth revealed through good science will prevail and the public will be convinced that these images not only demean those portrayed but also those who view them."

Is such a hope naive? Consider: Without banning cigarettes, the number of smokers has dropped from 43 percent in 1972 to 27 percent in 1994 (Gallup, 1994). Without censoring racism, once-common media images of African Americans as childlike, superstitious buffoons have nearly disappeared. As public consciousness changed, script writers, producers, and media executives decided that exploitative images of minorities were not good. More recently they have decided that drugs are not glamorous, as many films and songs from the 1960s and 1970s implied, but dangerous—and high school seniors' marijuana

"What we're trying to do is raise the level of awareness of violence against women and pornography to at least the level of awareness of racist and Ku Klux Klan literature."
Gloria Steinem (1988)

use during the previous month has dropped from 37 percent in 1979 to 16 percent in 1993 (Johnston & others, 1994). Will we one day look back with embarrassment on the time when movies entertained people with scenes of exploitation, mutilation, and sexual coercion?

TELEVISION

We have seen that watching an aggressive model can unleash children's aggressive urges and teach them new ways to aggress. And we have seen that after viewing sexual violence, many angry men will act more violently toward women. Does television have any similar effects?

Consider these few facts about watching television. In 1945, the Gallup poll asked Americans, "Do you know what television is?" (Gallup, 1972, p. 551). Today, in America, as in much of the industrialized world, 98 percent of households have a TV set, more than have bathtubs or telephones. With MTV and CNN spanning the globe, and *Baywatch* having a billion viewers in 142 countries, television is creating a global pop culture (McDougal, 1994).

In the average home, the set is on seven hours a day, with individual household members averaging four hours. Women watch more than men, non-Whites more than Whites, preschoolers and retired people more than those in school or working, and the less educated more than the highly educated (Nielsen, 1990). For the most part, these facts about Americans' viewing habits also characterize Europeans, Australians, and Japanese (Murray & Kippax, 1979).

During all those hours, what social behaviors are modeled? Since 1967, George Gerbner and other TV watchers (1993) at the University of Pennsylvania have been sampling U.S. network prime-time and Saturday morning entertainment programs. Their findings? Two of three programs contain violence ("physically compelling action that threatens to hurt or kill, or actual hurting or killing"). What does it add up to? By the end of elementary school, the average child views some 8000 TV murders and 100,000 other violent acts (Huston & others, 1992). Reflecting on his 22 years of cruelty counting, Gerbner (1994) lamented: "Humankind has had more bloodthirsty eras but none as filled with *images* of violence as the present. We are awash in a tide of violent representations the world has never seen . . . drenching every home with graphic scenes of expertly choreographed brutality."

Does it matter? Does prime-time crime stimulate the behavior it depicts? Or, as viewers vicariously participate in aggressive acts, do the shows drain off aggressive energy?

The latter idea, a variation on the **catharsis** hypothesis, maintains that watching violent drama enables people to release their pent-up hostilities. Defenders of the media cite this theory frequently and remind us that violence predates television. In an imaginary debate with one of television's critics, the medium's defender might argue, "Television played no role in the genocides of Jews and Native Americans. Television just reflects and caters to our tastes." "Agreed," responds the critic, "but it's also true that during America's TV age reported violent crime has increased several times faster than the population rate. Surely you don't mean the popular arts are mere passive reflections, without any power to influence public consciousness." The defender replies: "The violence epidemic results from many factors. TV may even reduce aggression by keeping people off the streets and by offering them a harmless opportunity to vent their aggression."

The problem with television is that people must sit and keep their eyes glued on a screen: the average American family hasn't time for it. Therefore, the showmen are convinced that . . . television will never be a serious competitor of [radio] broadcasting."
New York Times, March 19, 1939

Catharsis:
Emotional release. The catharsis view of aggression is that aggressive drive is reduced when one "releases" aggressive energy, either by acting aggressively or by fantasizing aggression.

The debate goes on. Studies of television viewing and aggression aim to identify effects more subtle and pervasive than the occasional "copy-cat" murders that capture public attention. They ask: How does television affect viewers' *behavior?* viewers' *thinking?*

Television's Effects on Behavior

Do viewers imitate violent models? Examples abound of people reenacting television crimes. In one survey of 208 prison convicts, 9 of 10 admitted that they learned new criminal tricks by watching crime programs. And 4 out of 10 said they had attempted specific crimes seen on television (*TV Guide*, 1977).

Correlation of TV Viewing and Behavior

Crime stories are not scientific evidence. Researchers therefore use correlational and experimental studies to examine the effects of viewing violence. One technique, commonly used with schoolchildren, asks whether their TV watching predicts their aggressiveness. To some extent it does. The more violent the content of the child's TV viewing, the more aggressive the child (Eron, 1987; Turner & others, 1986). The relationship is modest but consistently found in the United States, Europe, and Australia.

So can we conclude that a diet of violent TV fuels aggression? Perhaps you are already thinking that because this is a correlational study, the cause-effect relation could also work in the opposite direction. Maybe aggressive children prefer aggressive programs. Or maybe some underlying third factor, such as lower intelligence, predisposes some children both to prefer aggressive programs and to act aggressively.

Researchers have developed two ways to test these alternative explanations. They test the "hidden third factor" explanation by statistically pulling out the influence of some of these possible factors. For example, British researcher William Belson (1978; Muson, 1978) studied 1565 London boys. Compared to those who watched little violence, those who watched a great deal (especially realistic rather than cartoon violence) admitted to 50 percent more violent acts

" I TOLD YOU THE KIDS WERE WATCHING TOO MUCH TELEVISION."

during the preceding six months (for example, "I busted the telephone in a telephone box"). Belson also examined 22 likely third factors, such as family size. The heavy and light viewers still differed after equating them with respect to potential third factors. So Belson surmised that the heavy viewers were indeed more violent *because* of their TV exposure.

Similarly, Leonard Eron and Rowell Huesmann (1980, 1985) found that violence viewing among 875 eight-year-olds correlated with aggressiveness even after statistically pulling out several obvious possible third factors. Moreover, when they restudied these individuals as 19-year-olds, they discovered that viewing violence at age 8 modestly predicted aggressiveness at age 19, but that aggressiveness at age 8 did *not* predict viewing violence at age 19. Aggression followed viewing, not the reverse. They confirmed these findings in follow-up studies of 758 Chicago-area and 220 Finnish youngsters (Huesmann & others, 1984). What is more, when Eron and Huesmann (1984) examined the later criminal conviction records of their initial sample of 8-year-olds, they found that at age 30, those men who as children had watched a great deal of violent television were more likely to have been convicted of a serious crime (Figure 12–10).

Even murder rates increase when and where television comes. In Canada and the United States, the homicide rate doubled between 1957 and 1974 as violent television spread. In census regions where television came later, the homicide rate jumped later, too. In White South Africa, where television was not introduced until 1975, a similar near doubling of the homicide rate did not begin until after 1975 (Centerwall, 1989). And in a closely studied rural Canadian town where television came late, playground aggression doubled soon after (Williams, 1986).

Notice that these studies illustrate how researchers are now using correlational findings to *suggest* cause and effect. Yet, an infinite number of possible third factors could be creating a merely coincidental relation between viewing violence and aggression. Fortunately, however, the experimental method can control these extraneous factors. If we randomly assign some children to watch a violent film and others a nonviolent film, any later aggression difference be-

"I rarely turn down an invitation to speak to a PTA meeting or other civic groups in order to warn parents and other caretakers that they must control their children's viewing habits."
Leonard Eron (1985)

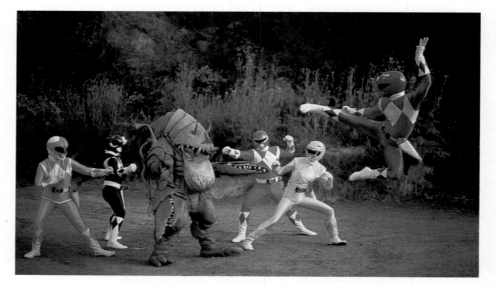

After viewing TV's Power Rangers, children have imitated many of the aggressive behaviors that are characteristic of the program.

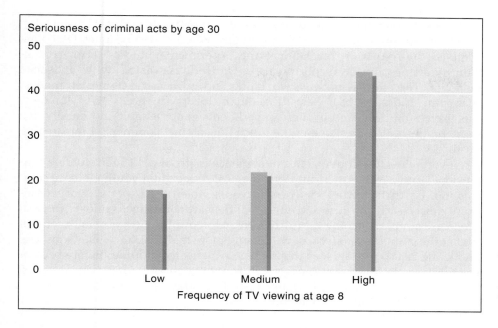

Seriousness of criminal acts by age 30

■ **FIGURE 12–10**
Children's television viewing and later criminal activity. Violence viewing at age 8 was a predictor of a serious criminal offense by age 30.
(Data from Eron & Huesmann, 1984.)

tween the two groups will be due to the only factor that distinguishes them: what they watched.

TV Viewing Experiments

The pioneering experiments by Albert Bandura and Richard Walters (1963) sometimes had young children view the adult pounding the inflated doll on film instead of observing it live—with much the same effect. Then Leonard Berkowitz and Russell Geen (1966) found that angered college students who viewed a violent film acted more aggressively than did similarly angered students who viewed nonaggressive films. These laboratory experiments, coupled with growing public concern, were sufficient to prompt the U.S. Surgeon General to commission 50 new research studies during the early 1970s. By and large, these studies confirmed that viewing violence amplifies aggression.

In a later series of experiments, research teams led by Ross Parke (1977) in the United States and Jacques Leyens (1975) in Belgium showed institutionalized American and Belgian delinquent boys a series of either aggressive or nonaggressive commercial films. Their consistent finding: "Exposure to movie violence . . . led to an increase in viewer aggression." Compared to the week preceding the film series, physical attacks increased sharply in cottages where boys were viewing violent films.

Chris Boyatzis and his colleagues (in press) observed a similar effect when they showed some elementary school children, but not others, an episode of television's most popular—and violent—children's program, "Power Rangers." Immediately after viewing the episode, the viewers committed seven times as many aggressive acts per 2-minute interval as the nonviewers. As in Bandura's pioneering Bobo doll studies, the boy viewers often precisely imitated the characters' acts, such as their flying karate kicks. In Norway in 1994 a 5-year-old girl was stoned, kicked, and left to freeze in the snow by playmates reportedly imitating acts seen on the show—triggering the show's banning by three Scandinavian countries (Blucher, 1994).

"Then shall we simply allow our children to listen to any story anyone happens to make up, and so receive into their minds ideas often the very opposite of those we shall think they ought to have when they are grown up?"
Plato, *The Republic*

Television research has involved a variety of methods and participants. Researchers Susan Hearold (1986) and Wendy Wood and colleagues (1991) assembled the results of correlational and experimental studies. Their conclusion: Viewing antisocial portrayals is indeed associated with antisocial behavior. The effect is not overwhelming and is, in fact, at times so modest that some critics doubt it exists (Freedman, 1988; McGuire, 1986). Moreover, the aggression provoked in these experiments is not assault and battery; it's more on the scale of a shove in the lunch line, a cruel comment, a threatening gesture.

"There is absolutely no doubt that higher levels of viewing violence on television are correlated with increased acceptance of aggressive attitudes and increased aggressive behavior."
American Psychological Association Commission on Violence and Youth, 1993

Nevertheless, the convergence of evidence is striking. "The irrefutable conclusion," said a 1993 American Psychological Association youth violence commission, is "that viewing violence increases violence." Experimental studies point most clearly to cause and effect, but they are sometimes remote from real life (for example, pushing a hurt button). Moreover, the experiments can but hint at the cumulative effects of witnessing more than 100,000 violent episodes and some 20,000 murders, as the average American child does before becoming the average American teenager (Murray & Lonnborg, 1989). Uncontrolled influences complicate the correlational studies, but such studies do tap the cumulative effects of real-life viewing.

Why Does TV Viewing Affect Behavior?

The conclusion drawn by the Surgeon General and by these researchers is *not* that television and pornography are primary causes of social violence, any more than cyclamates are a primary cause of cancer. Rather they say television is *a* cause. Even if it is just one ingredient in a complex recipe for violence, it is one that, like cyclamates, is potentially controllable. Given the convergence of correlational and experimental evidence, researchers have explored *why* viewing violence has this effect.

Consider three possibilities (Geen & Thomas, 1986). One is that it's not the violent content itself that causes social violence but the *arousal* it produces (Mueller & others, 1983; Zillmann, 1989). As we noted earlier, arousal tends to spill over: One type of arousal energizes other behaviors.

Question: *Might there be a similar effect of repeated playing of violent video games such as Mortal Kombat (in which women are attacked and dismembered)? Might such play teach youth "scripts"—mental tapes for how to act when facing conflict?*

Other research shows that viewing violence *disinhibits*. In Bandura's experiment, the adult's punching the Bobo doll seemed to legitimate such outbursts and to lower the children's own inhibitions. Viewing violence primes the viewer for aggressive behavior by activating violence-related thoughts (Berkowitz, 1984; Bushman & Geen, 1990; Josephson, 1987).

Media portrayals also evoke *imitation*. The children in Bandura's experiments reenacted the specific behaviors they had witnessed. The commercial television industry is hard-pressed to dispute that television leads viewers to imitate what they have seen: Its advertisers model consumption. Television's critics agree—and are troubled that on TV programs acts of assault outnumber affectionate acts 4 to 1 and that, in other ways as well, television models an unreal world (Table 12–2). TV cops fire their guns in almost every episode; actual Chicago police officers fire their guns an average of once every 27 years (Radecki, 1989).

Prosocial behavior:
Positive, constructive, helpful social behavior; the opposite of antisocial behavior.

If the ways of relating and problem solving modeled on television do trigger imitation, especially among young viewers, then modeling **prosocial behavior** should be socially beneficial. Chapter 14 contains good news: Television's subtle influence can indeed teach children positive lessons in behavior.

TABLE 12–2 *America's Television World versus the Real World*
How closely does prime-time network television drama mirror the world around us? Compare the percentages of people and behaviors on TV dramas with those in the real world. Television may reflect culture's mythology, but it distorts the reality.

ITEM VIEWED	SEEN ON TELEVISION (%)	IN THE REAL WORLD (%)
Female	33	51
Married	10	61
Blue collar	25	67
Having a religious affiliation	6	88
Implied intercourse: partners unmarried	85	Unknown
Beverages consumed: percentage alcoholic	45	16

From an analysis of nearly 35,000 television characters since 1969 by George Gerbner (1993; Gerbner & others, 1986). TV sex data from Fernandez-Collado & others (1978). TV religion data from Skill & others (1994); actual religion data from Saad & McAneny (1994)—percent for whom religion is fairly or very important. Alcohol data from NCTV (1988). Percentage of sex acts that occur among unmarried partners is surely a fraction of that depicted on TV, given that most adults are married, that frequency of intercourse is higher among the married than among singles, and that extramarital sex is rarer than commonly believed (Greeley, 1991; Laudmann & others, 1994).

Television's Effects on Thinking

We have focused on television's effect on behavior. Researchers have also examined the cognitive effects of viewing violence: Does prolonged viewing desensitize us to cruelty? Does it distort perceptions of reality?

Take some emotion-arousing stimulus, like an obscene word, and repeat it over and over. What happens? From introductory psychology you may recall that the emotional response will "extinguish." After witnessing thousands of acts of cruelty, there is good reason to expect a similar emotional numbing. The most common response might well become, "Doesn't bother me at all." Such a response is precisely what Victor Cline and his colleagues (1973) observed when they measured the physiological arousal of 121 Utah boys who watched a brutal boxing match. Compared to boys who watched little television, the responses of those who watched habitually were more a shrug than a concern.

Of course, these boys might differ in ways other than television viewing. But in experiments on the effects of viewing sexual violence, similar desensitization—a sort of psychic numbness—occurs among young men who view slasher films. Moreover, experiments by Ronald Drabman and Margaret Thomas (1974, 1975, 1976) confirmed that such viewing breeds a more blasé reaction when later viewing the film of a brawl or when actually observing two children fighting.

Does television's fictional world also mold our conceptions of the real world? George Gerbner and his University of Pennsylvania associates (1979, 1994) suspect this is television's most potent effect. Their surveys of both adolescents

"All television is educational. The question is, what is it teaching?"
Nicholas Johnson, Former Commissioner, Federal Communications Commission, 1978

"Those of us who have been active over more than 15 years in studying [television] cannot fail to be impressed with the significance of this medium for the emerging consciousness of the developing child."
Jerome Singer and Dorothy G. Singer (1988)

and adults show that heavy viewers (four hours a day or more) are more likely than light viewers (two hours or less) to exaggerate the frequency of violence in the world around them and to fear being personally assaulted. Similarly, a national survey of American 7- to 11-year-old children found that heavy viewers were more likely than light viewers to admit fears "that somebody bad might get into your house" or that "when you go outside, somebody might hurt you" (Peterson & Zill, 1981). Adults better distinguish television crime from the events in their own neighborhoods. Those who watch crime dramas (more than those who don't) see New York as a dangerous place. They even believe that their own city could be dangerous. But they are not more afraid of their own neighborhood (Heath & Petraitis, 1987; Tyler & Cook, 1984).

Perhaps, though, television's biggest effect occurs indirectly, as it each year replaces in people's lives a thousand or more hours of other activities. If, like most others, you have spent a thousand-plus hours per year watching TV, think how you might have used that time if there were no television. What difference would that have made in who you are today?

GROUP INFLUENCES

We have considered what provokes *individuals* to aggress. If frustrations, insults, and aggressive models heighten the aggressive tendencies of isolated people, then such factors are likely to prompt the same reaction in groups. As a riot begins, aggressive acts often spread rapidly after the "trigger" of one antagonistic person. Seeing looters freely helping themselves to TV sets, normally law-abiding bystanders may drop their moral inhibitions and imitate.

Groups can amplify aggressive reactions partly by diffusing responsibility. Decisions to attack in war typically are made by strategists remote from the

"The worst barbarity of war is that it forces men collectively to commit acts against which individually they would revolt with their whole being."
Ellen Key, *War, Peace, and the Future*, 1916

People who watch many hours of television see the world as a dangerous place.

front lines. The strategists have a buffer between themselves and the actual violence: They give orders, but others carry them out. Does such distancing make it easier to recommend aggression?

Jacquelin Gaebelein and Anthony Mander (1978) simulated this situation in the laboratory. They asked their University of North Carolina at Greensboro students to *shock* someone or to *advise* someone how much shock to administer. When the recipient provoked the front-line subjects, they and the advisers independently favored approximately the same amount of shock. But when the recipient was innocent of any provocation, as are most victims of mass aggression, the front-line subjects gave less shock than recommended by the advisers, who felt less directly responsible for any hurt.

Diffusion of responsibility increases not only with distance but also with numbers. (Recall from Chapter 9 the phenomenon of deindividuation.) When Brian Mullen (1986) analyzed information from 60 lynchings that occurred between 1899 and 1946, he made an interesting discovery: The greater the number of people in a lynch mob, the more vicious the murder and mutilation.

Such situations also involve group interaction. Through social "contagion," groups magnify aggressive tendencies, much as they polarize other tendencies. As group identity develops, conformity pressures and deindividuation increase (Staub, 1996). Self-identity diminishes as members give themselves over to the group, often feeling a satisfying oneness with the others. Examples are youth gangs, soccer fans, rapacious soldiers, urban rioters, and what Scandinavians call "mobbing"—schoolchildren repeatedly harassing or attacking an insecure, weak schoolmate. Mobbing occurs as a group activity. One bully alone is less likely to taunt or attack a victim (Lagerspetz & others, 1982).

Experiments by Israeli social psychologists Yoram Jaffe and Yoel Yinon (1983) confirm that groups can polarize aggressive tendencies. In one, university men angered by a supposed fellow subject retaliated with decisions to give much stronger shocks when in groups than when alone. In another experiment (Jaffe & others, 1981), people decided, either alone or in groups, how much punishing shock to give someone for incorrect answers on an ESP task. As Figure 12–11 shows, individuals gave progressively more of the assumed shock as the experiment proceeded, and group decision making magnified this individual tendency. So, when circumstances provoke an individual's aggressive reaction, the addition of group interaction will often amplify it.

A versive experiences include not only frustrations but also discomfort, pain, and personal attacks, both physical and verbal. Arousal from almost any source, even physical exercise or sexual stimulation, can be steered by the environment into anger.

SUMMING UP

Television portrays considerable violence. Correlational and experimental studies converge on the conclusion that viewing violence (1) breeds a modest increase in aggressive behavior and (2) desensitizes viewers to aggression and alters their perceptions of reality. These two findings parallel the results of research on the effects of viewing violent pornography, which can increase men's aggression against women and distort their perceptions of women's responses to sexual coercion.

Much aggression is committed by groups. Circumstances that provoke individuals may also provoke groups. By diffusing responsibility and polarizing actions, group situations amplify aggressive reactions.

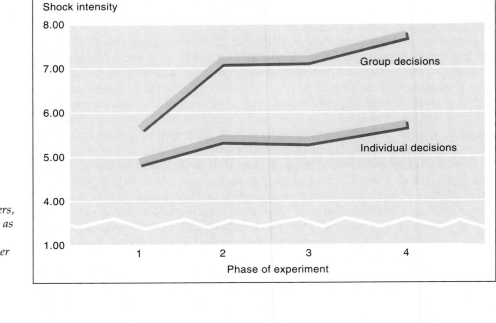

■ **FIGURE 12–11**
When individuals chose how much shock to administer as punishment for wrong answers, they escalated the shock level as the experiment proceeded. Group decision making further polarized this tendency.
(Data from Jaffe & others, 1981.)

■ REDUCING AGGRESSION

*W*e have examined instinct, frustration-aggression, and social learning theories of aggression, and we have scrutinized influences on aggression. How, then, can we reduce aggression? Do theory and research suggest ways to control aggression?

CATHARSIS

"Youngsters should be taught to vent their anger." So advised Ann Landers (1969). If a person "bottles up his rage, we have to find an outlet. We have to give him an opportunity of letting off steam." So asserted the prominent psychiatrist Fritz Perls (1973). Both statements assume the "hydraulic model"—accumulated aggressive energy that, like dammed-up water, needs a release.

The concept of catharsis is usually credited to Aristotle. Although Aristotle actually said nothing about aggression, he did argue that we can purge emotions by experiencing them and that viewing the classic tragedies therefore enabled a catharsis ("purgation") of pity and fear. To have an emotion excited, he believed, is to have that emotion released (Butcher, 1951). The catharsis hypothesis has been extended to include the emotional release supposedly obtained not only by observing drama but also through recalling and reliving past events, through expressing emotions, and through various actions. In such ways, we supposedly "blow off a little steam."

Assuming that aggressive action or fantasy drains pent-up aggression, some therapists and group leaders encourage people to ventilate suppressed aggression by acting it out—by whopping one another with foam bats or beating a bed with a tennis racket while screaming. Some psychologists advise parents to encourage children's release of emotional tension through aggressive play. Many Americans have bought the idea, as reflected in their nearly 2 to 1 agreement with the statement, "Sexual materials provide an outlet for bottled-up impulses" (Niemi & others, 1989). But then other national surveys reveal that most Americans also agree, "Sexual materials lead people to commit rape." So, is the catharsis approach valid or not?

If viewing erotica provides an outlet for sexual impulses, then people should afterward experience diminished sexual desire and men should be less likely to view and treat women as sexual objects. But experiments show the opposite is true (Kelley & others, 1989; McKenzie-Mohr & Zanna, 1990). The near consensus among social psychologists is that catharsis does not occur as Freud, Lorenz, and their followers supposed (Geen & Quanty, 1977). For example, Robert Arms and his associates report that Canadian and American spectators of football, wrestling, and hockey games exhibit *more* hostility after viewing the event than before (Arms & others, 1979; Goldstein & Arms, 1971; Russell, 1983). Not even war seems to purge aggressive feelings. After a war, a nation's murder rate tends to jump (Archer & Gartner, 1976).

In laboratory tests of the catharsis hypothesis, Jack Hokanson and his colleagues (1961, 1962a,b, 1966) found that when Florida State University students were allowed to counterattack someone who had provoked them, their arousal (as measured by their blood pressures) did more quickly return to normal. But this calming effect of retaliation occurs only in specific circumstances—when the target is the actual tormentor, not a substitute. Moreover, the retaliation must be justifiable and the target nonintimidating, so the person does not afterward feel guilty or anxious.

Does such aggressing reduce later aggression? In some experiments, aggressing has led to heightened aggression. Ebbe Ebbesen and his co-researchers (1975) interviewed 100 engineers and technicians shortly after they were angered by layoff notices. Some were asked questions that gave them an opportunity to express hostility against their employer or supervisor—for example, "What instances can you think of where the company has not been fair with you?" Afterward, they answered a questionnaire assessing attitudes toward the company and the supervisor. Did the previous opportunity to "vent" or "drain off" their hostility reduce it? To the contrary, their hostility increased. Expressing hostility bred more hostility.

Sound familiar? Recall from Chapter 4 that cruel acts beget cruel attitudes. Furthermore, as we noted in analyzing Stanley Milgram's obedience experiments, little aggressive acts can breed their own justification. People derogate their victims, rationalizing further aggression. Even if retaliation sometimes (in the short run) reduces tension, in the long run it reduces inhibitions.

Should we therefore bottle up anger and aggressive urges? Silent sulking is hardly more effective, because it allows us to continue reciting our grievances as we conduct conversations in our head. Fortunately, there are nonaggressive ways to express our feelings and to inform others how their behavior affects us. Across cultures, those who reframe accusatory "you" messages as "I" messages—"I'm angry," or "When you talk like that I feel irritated"—communicate their feelings in a way that better enables the other person to make a positive response (Kubany & others, 1995). We can be assertive without being aggressive.

"He who gives way to violent gestures will increase his rage."
Charles Darwin, *The Expression of Emotion in Man and Animals*, 1872

A SOCIAL LEARNING APPROACH

If aggressive behavior is learned, then there is hope for its control. Let us briefly review factors that influence aggression and speculate how to counteract them.

Aversive experiences such as frustrated expectations and personal attacks predispose hostile aggression. So it is wise to refrain from planting false, unreachable expectations in people's minds. Anticipated rewards and costs influence instrumental aggression. This suggests that we should reward cooperative, nonaggressive behavior. In experiments, children become less aggressive when their aggressive behavior is ignored and when their nonaggressive behavior is reinforced (Hamblin & others, 1969). Punishing the aggressor is less consistently effective. Threatened punishment deters aggression only under ideal conditions—when the punishment is strong, prompt, and sure; when it is combined with reward for the desired behavior; and when the recipient is not angry (R. A. Baron, 1977). Lacking such deterence, aggression may erupt. This was evident in 1969 when the Montreal police force went on a 16-hour strike, and in 1992 when helicopter TV coverage of the Los Angeles riot showed areas abandoned by police. In both cases, looting and destruction erupted—until the police returned.

But there are limits to punishment's effectiveness. Most mortal aggression is impulsive, hot aggression—the result of an argument, an insult, or an attack. Thus, we must *prevent* aggression before it happens. We must teach nonaggressive conflict-resolution strategies. If only mortal aggression were cool and instrumental we could hope that waiting till it happens and severely punishing the criminal afterward would deter such acts. In that world, states that impose the death penalty might have a lower murder rate than states without the death penalty. But in our world of hot homicide, that is not so.

Physical punishment can also have negative side effects. Punishment is aversive stimulation; it models the behavior it seeks to prevent. And it is coercive (recall that we seldom internalize actions coerced with strong external justifications). These are reasons violent teenagers and child-abusing parents so often come from homes where discipline took the form of harsh physical punishment.

To foster a gentler world we could model and reward sensitivity and cooperation from an early age, perhaps by training parents how to discipline without violence. Often, modeling violence—screaming, slapping, spanking—is precisely what exasperated parents do. Training programs encourage parents to reinforce desirable behaviors and to frame statements positively ("When you finish cleaning your room you can go play," rather than "If you don't clean your room, you're grounded.") One "aggression-replacement program" has reduced re-arrest rates of juvenile offenders and gang members by teaching the youths and their parents communication skills, training them to control anger, and raising their level of moral reasoning (Goldstein & Glick, 1994).

If observing aggressive models lowers inhibitions and elicits imitation, then we might also reduce brutal, dehumanizing portrayals in films and on television—steps comparable to those already taken to reduce racist and sexist portrayals. We can also inoculate children against the effects of media violence. Despairing that the TV networks would ever "face the facts and change their programming," Eron and Huesmann (1984) taught 170 Oak Park, Illinois, children that television portrays the world unrealistically, that aggression is less

"It was in the middle of rising expectations and the increased, though inadequate, social spending of the great society that the U.S. riots of 1967 and 1968 took place."
Jesse Jackson (1981)

common and effective than TV suggests, and that aggressive behavior is undesirable. (Drawing upon attitude research, Eron and Huesmann encouraged children to draw these inferences themselves and to attribute their expressed criticisms of television to their own convictions.) When restudied two years later, these children were less influenced by TV violence than were untrained children.

Aggression is also triggered by aggressive stimuli. This suggests reducing the availability of weapons such as handguns. Jamaica in 1974 implemented a sweeping anticrime program that included strict gun control and censorship of gun scenes from television and movies (Diener & Crandall, 1979). In the following year, robberies dropped 25 percent, nonfatal shootings 37 percent. In Sweden, the toy industry has discontinued the sale of war toys. The Swedish Information Service (1980) states the national attitude: "Playing at war means learning to settle disputes by violent means."

Suggestions such as these can help us minimize aggression. But given the complexity of aggression's causes and the difficulty of controlling them, who can feel the optimism expressed by Andrew Carnegie's forecast that in the twentieth century, "To kill a man will be considered as disgusting as we in this day consider it disgusting to eat one." Since Carnegie uttered those words in 1900, some 200 million human beings have been killed. It is a sad irony that although today we understand human aggression better than ever before, humanity's inhumanity is hardly diminished.

S U M M I N G   U P

How can we minimize aggression? Contrary to the catharsis hypothesis, expressing aggression more often breeds than reduces aggression. The social learning approach suggests controlling aggression by counteracting the factors that provoke it—by reducing aversive stimulation, by rewarding and modeling nonaggression, and by eliciting reactions incompatible with aggression.

■ FOR FURTHER READING

Baron, R. A., & Richardson, D. R. (1994). *Human aggression*, 2d ed. New York: Plenum. A 400-page review of the development, determinants, and consequences of aggression and its control.

Berkowitz, L. (1993). *Aggression: Its causes, consequences, and control*. New York: McGraw-Hill. A leading expert offers a state-of-the-art summary of what we have learned about the roots of aggressive behavior.

Groebel, J., & Hinde, R. (Eds.) (1988). *Aggression and war: Their biological and social bases*. New York: Cambridge University Press. Prominent aggression researchers summarize current understandings of the biological, psychological, and cultural sources of aggression.

Huston, A. C., & others (1992). *Big world, small screen: The role of television in American society*. Lincoln, NB: University of Nebraska. Nine psychologists, members of an American Psychological Association Task Force on Television and Society, collaborate in assessing television's influence.

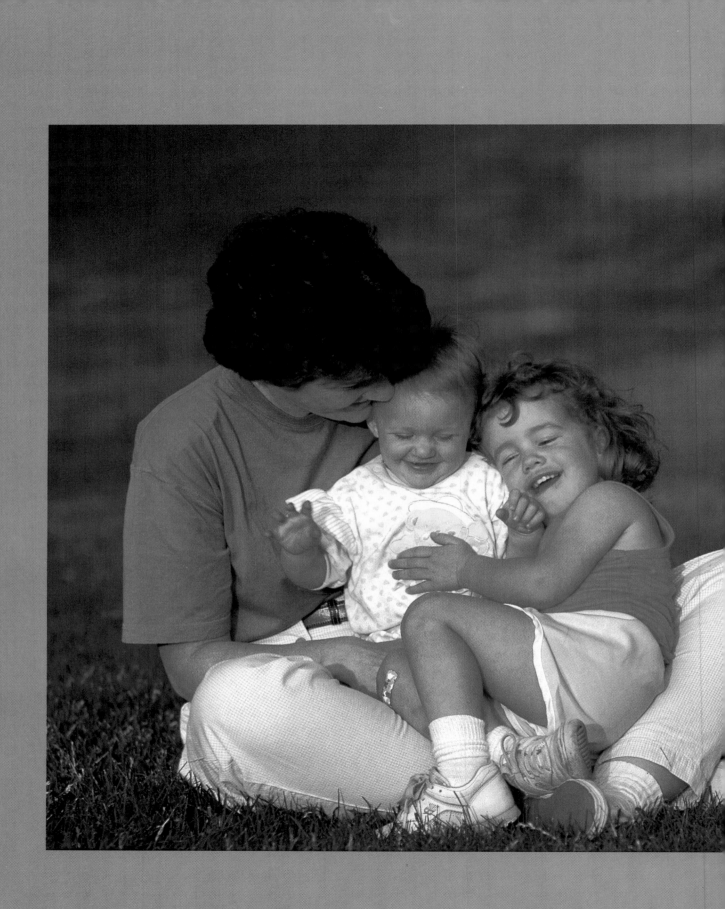

ATTRACTION AND INTIMACY

Need to belong:
A motivation to bond with others in relationships that provide ongoing, positive interactions.

In the beginning there was attraction—the attraction between a particular man and a particular woman to which we each owe our existence. Our lifelong dependence on one another puts relationships at the core of our existence. As what Aristotle called "the social animal," we have an intense **need to belong**—to connect with others in enduring, close relationships.

Social psychologists Roy Baumeister and Mark Leary (1995) illustrate the power of social attractions bred by our need to belong.

- For our ancestors, mutual attachments enabled group survival. When hunting game or erecting shelter, 10 hands were better than 2.
- For a woman and a man, the bonds of love lead to children, whose survival chances are boosted by the nurturing of two bonded parents.
- For children and their caregivers, social attachments enhance survival. Unexplainably separated from one another, parent and toddler may each panic, until reunited in tight embrace.
- For people everywhere, actual and hoped-for close relationships preoccupy thinking and color emotions. Finding a supportive soul mate in whom we can confide, we feel accepted and prized as we are. Falling in love, we feel irrepressible joy. Longing for acceptance and love, we spend billions on cosmetics, clothes, and diets.
- For the jilted, the widowed, and the sojourner in a strange place, the loss of social bonds triggers pain, anger, or withdrawal. Reared under extreme neglect or in institutions without belonging to anybody, children become pathetic, anxious creatures. Losing a soul-mate relationship, adults feel jealous, lonely, distraught, or bereaved. Exiled, imprisoned, or in solitary confinement, people ache for their own people and places. We are, indeed, social animals. We need to belong.

The architecture of friendship. People who live in close proximity, as do these college students, are more likely to become good friends.

■ BELONGING AND WELL-BEING

Supportive close relationships—feeling liked, affirmed, and encouraged by intimate friends and family—are linked with both health and happiness.

Our relationships are fraught with stress. "Hell is others," wrote Jean-Paul Sartre. When Peter Warr and Roy Payne (1982) asked a representative sample of British adults what, if anything, had emotionally strained them the day before, "family" was their most frequent answer. And stress, as we all by now know, aggravates health problems such as coronary heart disease, hypertension, and suppression of our disease-fighting immune system.

Still, on balance, close relationships contribute less to illness than to health and happiness. Asked what prompted yesterday's times of pleasure, the same British sample, by an even larger margin, again answered "family." Close relationships provide our greatest heartaches, but also our greatest joys.

LINKS WITH HEALTH

Six massive investigations, each interviewing thousands of people across several years, have reached a common conclusion: Close relationships promote health (Cohen, 1988; House & others, 1988). Compared to those with few social ties, those who have close relationships with friends, kin, or other members of close-knit religious or community organizations are less likely to die prematurely. And losing such ties heightens the risk of disease. A Finnish study of 96,000 widowed people found their risk of death doubled in the week following their partner's death (Kaprio & others, 1987). A National Academy of Sciences study reveals that those recently widowed become more vulnerable to disease and death (Dohrenwend & others, 1982).

So, there is a link between social support and health, but why? Perhaps those who enjoy close relationships eat better, exercise more, and smoke and drink less. Perhaps a supportive network helps us evaluate and overcome stressful events. Perhaps friends and family help bolster our self-esteem. When wounded by someone's dislike or the loss of a job, a friend's advice, help, and reassurance may indeed be good medicine (Cutrona, 1986; Rook, 1987). Even when the problem isn't mentioned, friends provide us with distraction and a sense that, come what may, we're accepted, liked, and respected. "Friendship is a sovereign antidote against all calamities," said Seneca.

With someone we consider a close friend, we may confide painful feelings. In one study, James Pennebaker and Robin O'Heeron (1984) contacted the surviving spouses of suicide or car accident victims. Those who bore their grief alone had more health problems than those who expressed it openly. When Pennebaker (1990) surveyed more than 700 college women, he found 1 in 12 reported a traumatic sexual experience in childhood. Compared with women who had experienced nonsexual traumas, such as parental death or divorce, the sexually abused women reported more headaches, stomach ailments, and other health problems, *especially if they had kept their secret to themselves.*

To isolate the confiding, confessional side of close relationships, Pennebaker asked the bereaved spouses to share what upsetting events had been preying on their minds. Those they first asked to describe a trivial event were physically tense. They stayed tense until they confided their troubles. They then relaxed. Writing about personal traumas in a diary also seems to help. When volunteers in another experiment did so, they had fewer health problems during the next six months. One participant explained, "Although I have not talked with anyone about what I wrote, I was finally able to deal with it, work through the pain instead of trying to block it out. Now it doesn't hurt to think about it." Even if it's only "talking to my diary," it helps to be able to confide.

LINKS WITH HAPPINESS

Dealing creatively with stress bolsters our shaken self-esteem, and confiding painful feelings is good not only for the body but for the soul as well. That's the conclusion of studies showing that people are happier when supported by a network of friends and family.

"Woe to him who is alone when he falls and has not another to lift him up."
Ecclesiastes 4:10b

Some studies, summarized in Chapter 6, compare people in a competitive, individualistic culture, such as that of the United States, Canada, and Australia, with those in collectivist cultures, such as those of Japan and many third world countries. Individualistic cultures offer independence, privacy, and pride in personal achievements. The tighter social bonds of collectivist cultures offer protection from loneliness, alienation, divorce, and stress-related diseases.

Other studies compare individuals with few or many close relationships. Being attached to friends with whom we can share intimate thoughts has two effects, observed the seventeenth-century philosopher Francis Bacon. "It redoubleth joys, and cutteth griefs in half." So it seems from answers to a question asked of Americans by the National Opinion Research Center (Burt, 1986): "Looking over the last six months, who are the people with whom you discussed matters important to you?" Compared to those who could name no such intimate, those who named five or more such friends were 60 percent more likely to feel "very happy."

Other findings confirm the importance of social networks.

- The happiest university students are those who feel satisfied with their love life (Emmons & others, 1983).
- Those who enjoy close relationships cope better with various stresses, including bereavement, rape, job loss, and illness (Abbey & Andrews, 1985; Perlman & Rook, 1987).
- Compared to Army soldiers in large units with changing memberships, those on stable, cohesive, 12-person A-teams experience greater social support, better physical and mental health, and more career satisfaction (Manning & Fullerton, 1988).
- People report greater well-being if their friends and families support their goals, by frequently expressing interest and offering help and encouragement (Israel & Antonucci, 1987; Ruehlman & Wolchik, 1988).
- Among 800 alumni of Hobart and William Smith Colleges surveyed by Wesley Perkins, those with "Yuppie values"—those who preferred a high income and occupational success and prestige to having very close friends and a close marriage—were twice as likely as their former classmates to describe themselves as "fairly" or "very" unhappy (Perkins, 1991).
- Asked, "What is necessary for your happiness?" or "What is it that makes your life meaningful?" most people mention—before anything else—satisfying

"Better is a dinner of vegetables where love is than a fatted ox and hatred with it."
Proverbs 15:17

close relationships with family, friends, or romantic partners (Berscheid, 1985; Berscheid & Peplau, 1983). As C. S. Lewis (1949) said, "the sun looks down on nothing half so good as a household laughing together over a meal." Happiness hits close to home.

Writer Lois Wyse (1991) realized as much after riding on a hotel elevator when the press was expecting Elizabeth Taylor. When the doors opened at the lobby level she put her head down as she was greeted by a burst of flashbulbs. "There she is," someone yelled. When she lifted her head, another reporter said, "Oh, it's nobody." Well, yes and no, she thought. "Who we are, what we do, and the way we do it matter to only a small group of people. But it does matter deeply to them." To those who love us, if we are fortunate to have a small circle of such people, we are somebody.

W̶e humans have an intense *need to belong*. Bonding with others in close, enduring relationships facilitates survival of individuals and groups. Seeking relationships, we spend time and money to make ourselves attractive. Gaining an intimate relationship, we feel joy. Losing a soul-mate relationship, we feel pain. Studies link close relationships with both physical health and emotional well-being.

S U M M I N G   U P

■ FRIENDSHIPS

W̶*hat factors nurture liking and loving? Let's start with those that help initiate attraction: proximity, physical attractiveness, similarity, and feeling liked.*

What predisposes one person to like, or to love, another? Few questions about human nature arouse greater interest. The ways affections flourish and fade form the stuff and fluff of soap operas, popular music, novels, and much of our everyday conversation. Long before I knew there was such a field as social psychology, I had memorized Dale Carnegie's recipe for *How to Win Friends and Influence People.*

So much has been written about liking and loving that almost every conceivable explanation—and its opposite—has been already proposed. Does absence make the heart grow fonder? Or is someone who is out of sight also out of mind? Is it likes that attract? Or opposites? How much do good looks matter? What has fostered your close relationships?

With so many possibilities, let's narrow our focus to specific influences on attraction. For most people—for you—what factors nurture liking and loving? Let's start with those that help a friendship begin and then consider those that sustain and deepen a relationship.

"I cannot tell how my ankles bend, nor whence the cause of my faintest wish, Nor the cause of the friendship I emit, nor the cause of the friendship I take again."
Walt Whitman, *Song of Myself,* 1855

PROXIMITY

One of the most powerful predictors of whether any two people are friends is sheer **proximity**. Proximity can also breed hostility; most assaults and murders involve people living close together. (Guns purchased for self-defense are much more likely to be turned on family members than against intruders.) But far

Proximity:
Geographical nearness. Proximity (more precisely, "functional distance") powerfully predicts liking.

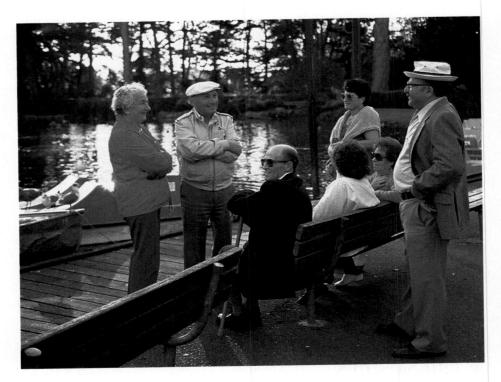

Close relationships with friends and family contribute to health and happiness.

more often, proximity kindles liking. Though it may seem trivial to those pondering the mysterious origins of romantic love, sociologists have found that most people marry someone who lives in the same neighborhood, or works at the same company or job, or sits in the same class (Bossard, 1932; Burr, 1973; Clarke, 1952; Katz & Hill, 1958). Look around. If you choose to marry, it will likely be to someone who has lived or worked or studied within walking distance.

Interaction

Actually, it is not geographical distance that is critical but "functional distance"—how often people's paths cross. We frequently become friends with those who use the same entrances, parking lots, and recreation areas. Randomly assigned college roommates, who of course can hardly avoid frequent interaction, are far more likely to become good friends than enemies (Newcomb, 1961). Such interaction enables people to explore their similarities, to sense one another's liking, and to perceive themselves as a social unit (Arkin & Burger, 1980).

At the college where I teach, the men and women students once lived on opposite sides of the campus. They understandably bemoaned the lack of cross-sex friendships. Now that they occupy different areas of the same dormitories and share common sidewalks, lounges, and laundry facilities, cross-sex friendships are far more frequent. So, if you're new in town and want to make friends, try to get an apartment near the mailboxes, an office desk near the coffee pot, a parking spot near the main buildings. Such is the architecture of friendship.

The chance nature of such contacts helps explain a surprising finding. Consider: If you had an identical twin who became engaged to someone, wouldn't you (being in so many ways similar to your twin) expect to share your twin's attraction to this person? But no, report researchers David Lykken and Auke Tellegen (1993); only half of identical twins recall really liking their twin's selection, and only 5 percent said "I could have fallen for my twin's fiancée." Romantic love is often rather like ducklings' imprinting, surmised Lykken and Tellegen. With repeated exposure to someone, our infatuation may fix upon almost anyone who has roughly similar characteristics and who reciprocates our affection.

But why does proximity breed liking? One factor is availability; obviously there are fewer opportunities to get to know someone who attends a different school or lives in another town. But there is more to it than that. Most people like their roommates, or those one door away, better than those two doors away. Those just a few doors away, or even a floor below, hardly live at an inconvenient distance. Moreover, those close by are potential enemies as well as friends. So why does proximity encourage affection more often than animosity?

> "When I'm not near the one I love, I love the one I'm near."
> E. Y. Harburg, *Finian's Rainbow*, London: Chappell Music, 1947

Anticipation of Interaction

Already we have noted one answer: Proximity enables people to discover commonalities and exchange rewards. What is more, merely *anticipating* interaction boosts liking. John Darley and Ellen Berscheid (1967) discovered this when they gave University of Minnesota women ambiguous information about two other women, one of whom they expected to talk with intimately. Asked how much they liked each one, the women preferred the person they expected to meet. Expecting to date someone similarly boosts liking (Berscheid & others, 1976). A positive expectation—anticipating the person will be pleasant and compatible—increases the chance of a rewarding relationship (Knight & Vallacher, 1981; Klein & Kunda, 1992; Miller & Marks, 1982).

The phenomenon is adaptive. Our lives are filled with relationships with people whom we may not have chosen but with whom we need to have continuing interactions—roommates, grandparents, teachers, classmates, co-workers. Liking such people is surely conducive to better relationships with them, which in turn makes for happier, more productive living.

Mere Exposure

Proximity leads to liking for yet another reason: More than 200 experiments reveal that, contrary to the old proverb, familiarity does not breed contempt. Rather it breeds fondness (Bornstein, 1989). **Mere exposure** to all sorts of novel stimuli—nonsense syllables, Chinese characters, musical selections, faces—boosts people's ratings of them. Do the supposed Turkish words *nansoma*, *saricik*, and *afworbu* mean something better or something worse than the words *iktitaf*, *biwojni*, and *kadirga*? University of Michigan students tested by Robert Zajonc (1968, 1970) preferred whichever of these words they had seen most frequently. The more times they had seen a meaningless word or a Chinese ideograph, the more likely they were to say it meant something good (Figure 13–1).

Or consider: What are your favorite letters of the alphabet? People of differing nationalities, languages, and ages prefer the letters appearing in their own name and those that frequently appear in their own language (Hoorens & others, 1990, 1993; Nuttin, 1987). French students rate capital *W*, the least frequent letter in French, as their least favorite letter.

Mere-exposure effect: The tendency for novel stimuli to be liked more or rated more positively after the rater has been repeatedly exposed to them.

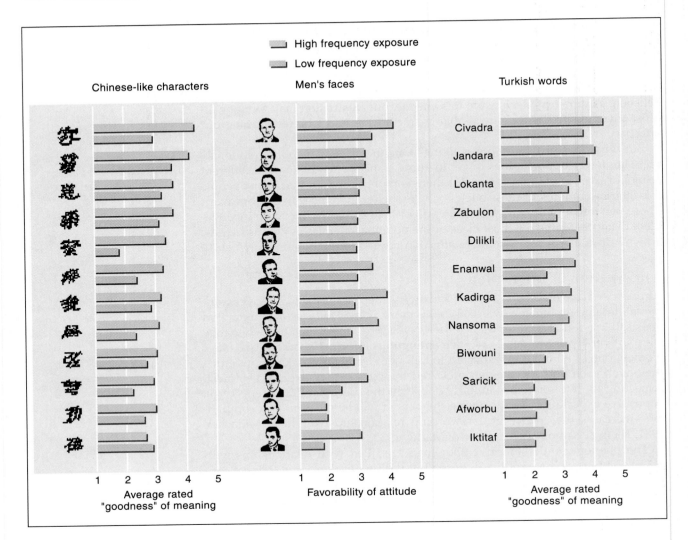

■ **FIGURE 13–1**

The mere-exposure effect. Students rated stimuli more positively after being shown them repeatedly.

(From Zajonc, 1968.)

The mere-exposure effect violates the commonsense prediction of *decreased* interest in repeatedly heard music or tasted foods (Kahneman & Snell, 1992). But unless the repetitions are incessant ("Even the best song becomes tiresome if heard too often," says a Korean proverb), liking usually increases. When completed in 1889, the Eiffel Tower in Paris was mocked as grotesque (Harrison, 1977). Today it is the beloved symbol of Paris. Such changes make one wonder about initial reactions to new things. Do visitors to the Louvre in Paris really adore the *Mona Lisa*, or are they simply delighted to find a familiar face? It might be both: To know her is to like her.

Zajonc and his co-workers, William Kunst-Wilson and Richard Moreland, reported that exposure leads to liking even when people don't know that they have been exposed (Kunst-Wilson & Zajonc, 1980; Moreland & Zajonc, 1977; Wilson, 1979). In fact, mere exposure has an even stronger effect when people perceive stimuli without awareness (Bornstein & D'Agostino, 1992). In one experiment, women students listened through headphones in one ear to a prose passage. They also repeated the words out loud and compared them to a written version to check for errors. Meanwhile, brief, novel melodies played in their other ear. This procedure focused the women's attention upon the verbal material and away from the tunes. Later, when they heard the tunes interspersed among similar ones not previously played, they did not recognize them. Nevertheless, they *liked best* the tunes they had previously heard. In another experiment, people were shown a series of geometric figures, one at a time, each for a millisecond—long enough to perceive only a flash of light. Although later they were unable to recognize the figures they had been shown, they nevertheless *liked* them best.

Note that in both experiments conscious judgments about the stimuli were a far less reliable clue to what people had heard or seen than were instant feelings. You can probably recall immediately liking or disliking something or someone without consciously knowing why. Zajonc (1980) argues that emotions are often more instantaneous, more primitive than thought. Fearful or prejudicial feelings are not always expressions of stereotyped beliefs; sometimes the beliefs arise later as justifications for intuitive feelings.

The mere-exposure effect colors our evaluations of others: Familiar people we like more (Swap, 1977). We even like ourselves better when we are the way we're used to seeing ourselves. In a delightful experiment, Theodore Mita, Marshall Dermer, and Jeffrey Knight (1977) photographed women students at the University of Wisconsin-Milwaukee and later showed each one her actual picture along with a mirror image of it. Asked which picture they liked better, most preferred the mirror image—the image they were used to seeing. (No wonder our photographs never look quite right.) When close friends of the subjects were shown the same two pictures, they preferred the true picture—the image *they* were used to seeing.

Advertisers and politicians exploit this phenomenon. When people have no strong feelings about a product or a candidate, repetition alone can increase sales or votes (McCullough & Ostrom, 1974; Winter, 1973). After endless repetition of a commercial, shoppers often have an unthinking, automatic, favorable response to the product. If candidates are relatively unknown, those with the most media exposure usually win (Patterson, 1980; Schaffner & others, 1981). Political strategists who understand the mere-exposure effect have replaced reasoned argument with brief ads that hammer home a candidate's name and sound-bite message.

The respected Washington state Supreme Court Chief Justice Keith Callow learned this lesson when in 1990 he lost to a nominal opponent, Charles Johnson. Johnson, an unknown attorney who handled minor criminal cases and divorces, filed for the seat on the principle that judges "need to be challenged." Neither man campaigned, and the media ignored the race. On election day the two candidates' names appeared without any identification—just one name next to the other. The result: a 53 percent to 47 percent Johnson victory. "There are a lot more Johnsons out there than Callows," offered the ousted judge afterward to a stunned legal community. Indeed, a Seattle newspaper counted 27 Charlie Johnsons in Seattle alone. There was Charles Johnson, the King County judge. And down in Tacoma there was television anchorman Charles Johnson, whose broadcasts were seen on statewide cable TV. Forced to choose between two unknown names, many voters apparently preferred the comfortable, familiar name of Charlie Johnson.

"'Tis strange—but true; for truth is always strange—Stranger than fiction."
Lord Byron, *Don Juan*

PHYSICAL ATTRACTIVENESS

What do (or did) you look for in a potential date? Sincerity? Good looks? Character? Conversational ability? Sophisticated, intelligent people are unconcerned with such superficial qualities as good looks; they know "beauty is only skin deep" and "you can't judge a book by its cover." At least they know that's how they *ought* to feel. As Cicero counseled, "The final good and the supreme duty of the wise man is to resist appearance."

The belief that looks matter little may be another instance of our denying real influences upon us, for there is now a file drawer full of research studies showing that appearance *does* matter. The consistency and pervasiveness of this effect is disconcerting. Good looks are a great asset.

Attractiveness and Dating

Like it or not, a young woman's physical attractiveness is a moderately good predictor of how frequently she dates. A young man's attractiveness is slightly less a predictor of how frequently he dates (Berscheid & others, 1971; Krebs & Adinolfi, 1975; Reis & others, 1980, 1982; Walster & others, 1966). Does this imply, as many have surmised, that women are better at following Cicero's advice? Or does it merely reflect the fact that men more often do the inviting? If women were to indicate their preferences among various men, would looks be as important to them as to men? Philosopher Bertrand Russell (1930, p. 139) thought not: "On the whole women tend to love men for their character while men tend to love women for their appearance."

To see whether indeed men are more influenced by looks, researchers provide men and women students with various pieces of information about someone of the other sex, including a picture of the person. Or they briefly introduce a man and a woman and later ask each about their interest in dating the other. In such experiments, men do put somewhat more value on opposite-sex physical attractiveness than do women (Feingold, 1990, 1991; Sprecher & oth-

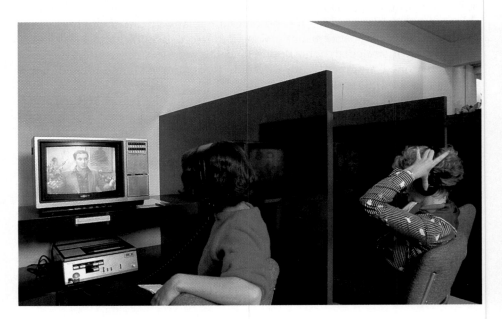

Attractiveness and dating. For video dating customers, looks are part of what is offered and sought.

ers, 1994). Perhaps sensing this, women more than men worry about their appearance and constitute 90 percent of cosmetic surgery patients (Dion & others, 1990). But women, too, respond to a man's looks.

In one ambitious study, Elaine Hatfield and her co-workers (1966) matched 752 University of Minnesota first-year students for a "Welcome Week" computer dance. The researchers gave each student personality and aptitude tests but then matched the couples randomly. On the night of the dance, the couples danced and talked for two and one-half hours and then took a brief intermission to evaluate their dates. How well did the personality and aptitude tests predict attraction? Did people like someone better who was high in self-esteem, or low in anxiety, or different from themselves in outgoingness? The researchers examined a long list of possibilities. But so far as they could determine, only one thing mattered: how physically attractive the person was. The more attractive a woman was, the more he liked her and wanted to date her again. And the more attractive the man was, the more she liked him and wanted to date him again. Pretty pleases.

The Matching Phenomenon

Not everyone can end up paired with someone stunningly attractive. So how do people pair off? Judging from research by Bernard Murstein (1986) and others, they pair off with people who are about as attractive as they are. Several studies have found a strong correspondence between the attractiveness of husbands and wives, of dating partners, and even of those within particular fraternities (Feingold, 1988). People tend to select as friends and especially to marry those who are a "good match" not only to their level of intelligence but also to their level of attractiveness.

Experiments confirm this **matching phenomenon**. When choosing whom to approach, knowing the other is free to say yes or no, people usually approach someone whose attractiveness roughly matches their own (Berscheid & others, 1971; Huston, 1973; Stroebe & others, 1971). Good physical matches may also be conducive to good relationships, as Gregory White (1980) found in a study of UCLA dating couples. Those who were most similar in physical attractiveness were most likely, nine months later, to have fallen more deeply in love.

So, who might we expect to be most closely matched for attractiveness—married couples or couples casually dating? White found, as have other researchers, that married couples are better matched.

Perhaps this research prompts you to think of happy couples who are not similarly attractive. In such cases, the less attractive person often has compensating qualities. Each partner brings assets to the social marketplace, and the value of the respective assets creates an equitable match. Personal advertisements exhibit this exchange of assets (Koestner & Wheeler, 1988; Rajecki & others, 1991). Men typically offer status and seek attractiveness; women more often do the reverse: "Attractive, bright woman, 38, slender, seeks warm, professional male." The asset-matching process helps explain why beautiful young women often marry older men of higher social status (Elder, 1969).

The Physical-Attractiveness Stereotype

Does the attractiveness effect spring entirely from sexual attractiveness? Clearly not, as Vicky Houston and Ray Bull (1994) discovered when they used a make-up artist to give an accomplice an apparently scarred, bruised, or birth-marked

Matching phenomenon: The tendency for men and women to choose as partners those who are a "good match" in attractiveness and other traits.

"Love is often nothing but a favorable exchange between two people who get the most of what they can expect, considering their value on the personality market."
Erich Fromm, *The Sane Society*, 1955

face. When riding on a Glasgow commuter rail line, people of both sexes avoided sitting next to the accomplice when she appeared facially disfigured. Moreover, much as adults are biased toward attractive adults, young children are biased toward attractive children (Dion, 1973; Dion & Berscheid, 1974; Langlois & Stephan, 1981). To judge from how long they gaze at someone, even babies prefer attractive faces (Langlois & others, 1987).

Adults show a similar bias when judging children. Margaret Clifford and Elaine Hatfield (Clifford & Walster, 1973) gave Missouri fifth-grade teachers identical information about a boy or girl but with the photograph of an attractive or unattractive child attached. The teachers perceived the attractive child as more intelligent and successful in school. Think of yourself as a playground supervisor having to discipline an unruly child. Might you, like the women studied by Karen Dion (1972), show less warmth and tact to an unattractive child? The sad truth is that most of us assume what we might call a "Bart Simpson effect"—that homely children are less able and socially competent than their beautiful peers.

What is more, we assume that beautiful people possess certain desirable traits. Other things being equal, we guess beautiful people are happier, sexually warmer, and more sociable, intelligent, and successful, though not more honest or concerned for others (Eagly & others, 1991; Feingold, 1992b; Jackson & others, 1995). Added together, the findings define a **physical-attractiveness stereotype**: What is beautiful is good. Children learn the stereotype quite early. Snow White and Cinderella are beautiful—and kind. The witch and the stepsisters are ugly—and wicked. As one kindergarten girl put it when asked what it means to be pretty, "It's like to be a princess. Everybody loves you" (Dion, 1979).

If physical attractiveness is this important, then permanently changing people's attractiveness should change the way others react to them. But is it ethical to alter someone's looks? Such manipulations are performed millions of times a year by plastic surgeons and orthodontists. With teeth and nose straightened, hair replaced and dyed, face lifted, and (for more than 1 million American women) breasts enlarged, can a self-dissatisfied person now find happiness?

To examine the effect of such alterations, Michael Kalick (1977) had Harvard students rate their impressions of eight women based on profile photographs taken before or after cosmetic surgery. Not only did they judge the women as more physically attractive after the surgery but also as kinder, more sensitive, more sexually warm and responsive, more likable, and so on. Ellen Berscheid (1981) notes that although such cosmetic improvements can boost self-image, they can also be temporarily disturbing:

> Most of us—at least those of us who have *not* experienced swift alterations of our physical appearance—can continue to believe that our physical attractiveness level plays a minor role in how we are treated by others. It is harder, however, for those who have actually experienced swift changes in appearance to continue to deny and to minimize the influence of physical attractiveness in their own lives—and the fact of it may be disturbing, even when the changes are for the better.

To say that attractiveness is important, other things being equal, is not to say that physical appearance always outranks other qualities. Attractiveness probably most affects first impressions. But first impressions are important—

Physical-attractiveness stereotype:
The presumption that physically attractive people possess other socially desirable traits as well: What is beautiful is good.

"Even virtue is fairer in a fair body."
Virgil, *Aeneid*

and are becoming more so as societies become increasingly mobile and urbanized and as contacts with people become more fleeting (Berscheid, 1981).

Though interviewers may deny it, attractiveness and grooming affect first impressions in job interviews (Cash & Janda, 1984; Mack & Rainey, 1990; Marvelle & Green, 1980). This helps explain why attractive people have more prestigious jobs, make more money, and describe themselves as happier (Umberson & Hughes, 1987). Patricia Roszell and her colleagues (1990) looked at the attractiveness of a national sample of Canadians whom interviewers had rated on a 1 (homely) to 5 (strikingly attractive) scale. They found that for each additional scale unit of rated attractiveness, people earned, on average, an additional $1988 annually. Irene Hanson Frieze and her associates (1991) did the same analysis with 737 MBA graduates after rating them on a similar 1 to 5 scale using student picture book photos. For each additional scale unit of rated attractiveness, men earned an added $2600 and women earned an added $2150.

Do beautiful people indeed have desirable traits? Or was Leo Tolstoy correct when he wrote that it's "a strange illusion . . . to suppose that beauty is goodness"? There is a trace of truth to the stereotype. Attractive children and young adults are neither more nor less academically capable (contrary to the negative stereotype that "beauty times brains equals a constant") (Sparacino & Hansell, 1979). However, they are somewhat more relaxed and socially polished (Feingold, 1992b). William Goldman and Philip Lewis (1977) demonstrated this by having 60 University of Georgia men call and talk for five minutes with each of three women students. Afterward the men and women rated their unseen telephone partners who happened to be most attractive as somewhat more socially skillful and likeable.

These small average differences between attractive and unattractive people probably result from self-fulfilling prophecies. Attractive people are valued and favored, and so many develop more social self-confidence. (Recall from Chapter 2 an experiment in which men evoked a warm response from unseen women they *thought* were attractive.) By this analysis, what's crucial to your social skill is not how you look but how people treat you and how you feel about yourself—whether you accept yourself, like yourself, feel comfortable with yourself.

Despite all the advantages of being beautiful, attraction researchers Elaine Hatfield and Susan Sprecher (1986) report there is also an ugly truth about beauty. Exceptionally attractive people may suffer unwelcome sexual advances, and resentment from those of their own sex. They may be unsure whether others are responding to their inner qualities or just to their looks, which in time will fade. Moreover, if they can coast on their looks, they may be less motivated to develop themselves in other ways. Ellen Berscheid wonders whether we might still be lighting our houses with candles if Charles Steinmetz, the homely and exceptionally short genius of electricity, had instead been subjected to the social enticements experienced by a Mel Gibson.

Who Is Attractive?

I have described attractiveness as if it were an objective quality like height, which some people have more of, some less. Strictly speaking, attractiveness is whatever the people of any given place and time find attractive. This, of course, varies. The beauty standards by which Miss Universe is judged hardly apply to the whole planet. Even in a given place and time, people (fortunately) disagree about who's attractive (Morse & Gruzen, 1976).

Generally, however, "attractive" facial and bodily features do not deviate too drastically from average (Beck & others, 1976; Graziano & others, 1978; Symons, 1981). People perceive noses, legs, or statures that are not unusually large or small as relatively attractive. Judith Langlois and Lori Roggman (1990, 1994) showed this by digitizing the faces of up to 32 college students and using a computer to average them. Students judged the composite faces as more appealing than 96 percent of the individual faces. So in some respects, perfectly average is strikingly attractive.

What makes for an attractive face depends somewhat on the person's sex. Consistent with men's historically having greater social power, people judge women more attractive if they have "baby-faced" features, such as large eyes, that suggest nondominance (Cunningham, 1986; Keating, 1985). Men seem more attractive when their faces—and their behaviors—suggest maturity and dominance (Sadalla & others, 1987). Curiously, among homosexuals these preferences tend to reverse: Many gay males prefer baby-faced males, and many lesbians seem not to prefer baby-faced females. With this exception, report Michael Cunningham and colleagues (1995), people across the world show remarkable agreement about the features of an ideal male face and female face when judging any ethnic group.

Psychologists working from the evolutionary perspective explain these gender differences in terms of reproductive strategy (Chapter 6). They assume that evolution predisposes men to favor female features that imply youth and health—and therefore good reproductive potential. And they assume evolution predisposes women to favor male traits that signify an ability to provide and protect resources. That, David Buss (1989) believes, explains why the males he studied in 37 cultures—from Australia to Zambia—did indeed prefer female characteristics that signify reproductive capacity. And it explains why physically attractive females tend to marry high-status males and why men compete with such determination to achieve fame and fortune.

From yesterday's Stone Age figurines to today's centerfolds and beauty pageant winners, men feel most attracted to women whose waists are roughly a third narrower than their hips—a shape associated with sexual fertility.
(Singh, 1993).

"I'LL TELL YOU WHY WE'RE BECOMING EXTINCT. BECAUSE WE'RE SOLITARY CREATURES, EVEN DURING THE <u>MATING</u> SEASON — THAT'S WHY WE'RE BECOMING EXTINCT."

© 1991 by Sidney Harris; American Scientist Magazine.

"Love is only a dirty trick played on us to achieve a continuation of the species."
Novelist W. Somerset Maugham, 1874–1965

What's attractive to you also depends on your comparison standards. Douglas Kenrick and Sara Gutierres (1980) had male confederates interrupt Montana State University men in their dormitory rooms and explain, "We have a friend coming to town this week and we want to fix him up with a date, but we can't decide whether to fix him up with her or not, so we decided to conduct a survey. . . . We want you to give us your vote on how attractive you think she is . . . on a scale of 1 to 7." Shown a picture of an average young woman, those who had just been watching three beautiful women on television's *Charlie's Angels* rated her less attractive than those who hadn't.

Standards of beauty differ from culture to culture. Yet some people, especially those with youthful features that suggest health and fertility, are considered attractive throughout most of the world.

Laboratory experiments confirm this "contrast effect." To men who have recently been gazing at centerfolds, average women—or even their own wives—seem less attractive (Kenrick & others, 1989). Viewing pornographic films simulating passionate sex similarly decreases satisfaction with one's own partner (Zillmann, 1989). Being sexually aroused may *temporarily* make a person of the other sex seem more attractive. But the lingering effect of exposure to perfect "10s," or of unrealistic sexual depictions, is to make one's own partner seem less appealing—more like a "6" than an "8." It works the same way with our self-perceptions. After viewing a superattractive person of the same sex, people *feel* less attractive than after viewing a homely person (Brown & others, 1992; Thornton-Moore, 1993).

Let's conclude our discussion of attractiveness on an upbeat note. Not only do we perceive attractive people as likeable, we also perceive likeable people as attractive. Perhaps you can recall individuals who, as you grew to like them, became more attractive. Their physical imperfections were no longer so noticeable. Alan Gross and Christine Crofton (1977) had University of Missouri–St. Louis students view someone's photograph after reading a favorable or unfavorable description of the person's personality. When portrayed as warm, helpful, and considerate, people *looked* more attractive. Discovering someone's similarities to us also makes the person seem more attractive (Beaman & Klentz, 1983; Klentz & others, 1987). Moreover, love sees loveliness: The more in love a woman is with a man, the more physically attractive she finds him (Price & others, 1974). And the more in love people are, the *less* attractive they find all others of the opposite sex (Johnson & Rusbult, 1989; Simpson & others, 1990). "The grass may be greener on the other side," note Rowland Miller and Jeffry Simpson (1990), "but happy gardeners are less likely to notice." To paraphrase Benjamin Franklin, when Jill's in love, she finds Jack more handsome than his friends.

SIMILARITY VERSUS COMPLEMENTARITY

From our discussion so far, one might surmise Leo Tolstoy was entirely correct: "Love depends . . . on frequent meetings, and on the style in which the hair is done up, and on the color and cut of the dress." However, as people get to know one another, other factors influence whether acquaintanceship develops into friendship.

Do Birds of a Feather Flock Together?

Of this much we may be sure: Birds that flock together are of a feather. Friends, engaged couples, and spouses are far more likely than people randomly paired to share common attitudes, beliefs, and values. Furthermore, the greater the similarity between husband and wife, the happier they are and the less likely they are to divorce (Byrne, 1971; Caspi & Herbener, 1990). Such correlational findings are intriguing. But cause and effect remain an enigma. Does similarity lead to liking? Or does liking lead to similarity?

Likeness Begets Liking

To discern cause and effect, we experiment. Imagine that at a campus party Laura gets involved in a long discussion of politics, religion, and personal likes

"Do I love you because you are beautiful, or are you beautiful because I love you?"
Prince Charming, in Rogers & Hammerstein's *Cinderella*

"Love to faults is always blind, Always is to joy inclined."
Poet William Blake, 1791

"Can two walk together except they be agreed?"
Amos 3:3

"Pardon me, but I can't help noticing that we share similar tastes in tropical-fruit-flavored chewing gum."

and dislikes with Les and Larry. She and Les discover they agree on almost everything, she and Larry on few things. Afterward, she reflects: "Les is really intelligent. And he's so likeable. I hope we meet again." In experiments, Donn Byrne (1971) and his colleagues captured the essence of Laura's experience. Over and over again they found that the more similar someone's attitudes are to your own, the more likeable you will find the person. This "likeness-leads-to-liking" relationship holds true not only for college students but also for children and the elderly, for people of various occupations, and for those in various nations.

This agreement effect has been tested in real-life situations by noting who comes to like whom.

■ At the University of Michigan, Theodore Newcomb (1961) studied two groups of 17 unacquainted male transfer students. After 13 weeks of living together in a boardinghouse, those whose agreement was initially highest were most likely to have formed close friendships. One group of friends was composed of five liberal arts students, each a political liberal with strong intellectual interests. Another was made up of three conservative veterans who were all enrolled in the engineering college.

■ William Griffitt and Russell Veitch (1974) compressed the getting-to-know-you process by confining 13 unacquainted men in a fallout shelter. (The men were paid volunteers.) Knowing the men's opinions on various issues, the researchers could predict with better-than-chance accuracy those each man would most like and most dislike.

■ When Susan Sprecher and Steve Duck (1994) put 83 student couples together on blind get-acquainted dates, the 16 percent who saw each other again were especially likely to see themselves as similar.

So, similarity breeds content. Birds of a feather *do* flock together. Surely you have noticed this upon discovering a special someone who shares your ideas, values, and desires, a soul mate who likes the same music, the same activities, even the same foods you do.

Do birds of a feather flock together?

Or do opposites attract?

"And they are friends who have come to regard the same things as good and the same things as evil, they who are friends of the same people, and they who are the enemies of the same people. . . . We like those who resemble us, and are engaged in the same pursuits."
Aristotle, *Rhetoric*

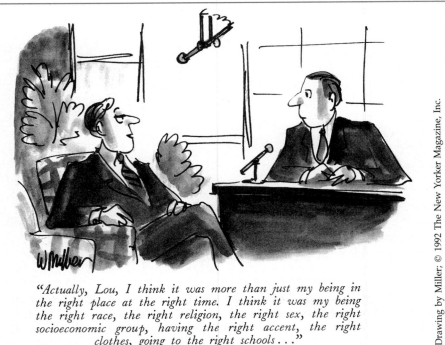

"*Actually, Lou, I think it was more than just my being in the right place at the right time. I think it was my being the right race, the right religion, the right sex, the right socioeconomic group, having the right accent, the right clothes, going to the right schools...*"

Drawing by Miller; © 1992 The New Yorker Magazine, Inc.

Without doubt, the most appealing people are those who are like us.

Dissimilarity Breeds Dislike

We have a bias—the false consensus bias—toward assuming that others share our attitudes. When we discover that someone does not, we may dislike the person. Iowa Democrats surveyed in one study were not so much fond of other Democrats as they were disdainful of Republicans (Rosenbaum, 1986; Hoyle, 1993). The extent to which people perceive those of another race as similar or dissimilar therefore helps determine racial attitudes. When people perceived Jews or Native Americans as a lower species of life, genocide was not far behind. Wherever one group of people regards another as "other"—as creatures who speak differently, live differently, think differently—the potential for oppression is high.

In fact, except for intimate relationships such as dating, the perception of like minds seems more important for attraction than like skins. Most Whites express more liking for, and willingness to work with, a like-minded Black than a dissimilarly minded White (Insko & others, 1983; Rokeach, 1968). "Cultural racism" persists, argues James Jones (1988), because cultural differences are a fact of life. Black culture tends to be present-oriented, expressive, spiritual, and emotionally driven. White culture tends to be more future-oriented, individualistic, materialistic, and achievement-driven. Rather than trying to eliminate such differences, says Jones, we might better appreciate what they "contribute to the cultural fabric of a multicultural society." There are situations in which expressiveness is advantageous and situations in which future orientation is advantageous. Each culture has much to learn from the other. In countries such as Canada, Britain, and the United States, where migration and different birthrates make for growing diversity, educating people to respect and enjoy those who differ is a major challenge.

Do Opposites Attract?

But are we not also attracted to people who are in some ways *different* from ourselves, different in ways that complement our own characteristics? Researchers have explored this question by comparing not only the attitudes and beliefs of friends and spouses but also their age, religion, race, smoking behavior, economic level, education, height, intelligence, and appearance. In all these ways and more, similarity still prevails (Buss, 1985; Kandel, 1978). Smart birds flock together. So do rich birds, Protestant birds, tall birds, pretty birds.

Still we resist: Are we not attracted to people whose needs and personalities complement our own? Would a gratifying relationship develop from the meeting of a sadist and a masochist? Even the *Reader's Digest* tells us that "opposites attract. . . . Socializers pair with loners, novelty-lovers with those who dislike change, free spenders with scrimpers, risk-takers with the very cautious" (Jacoby, 1986). Sociologist Robert Winch (1958) reasoned that the needs of someone who is outgoing and domineering would naturally complement those of someone who is shy and submissive. The logic seems compelling, and most of us can think of couples who view their differences as complementary: "My husband and I are perfect for each other. I'm Aquarius—a decisive person. He's Libra—can't make decisions. But he's always happy to go along with arrangements I make."

Given the idea's persuasiveness, the inability of researchers to confirm it is astonishing. For example, most people feel attracted to expressive, outgoing people (Friedman & others, 1988). Would this be especially so when one is down in the dumps? Do depressed people seek those whose gaiety will cheer them up? To the contrary, it is *non*depressed people who most prefer the com-

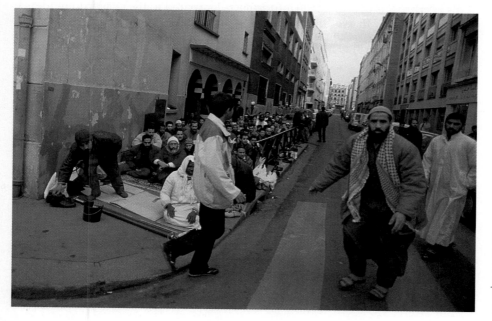

Dissimilarity breeds dislike: Muslims living in France have encountered hostility and suffered attacks because their culture is so visibly different from that of the majority.

BEHIND THE SCENES

As a Yale graduate student I was invited to write a book on prejudice. Wanting to take readers past the individual blame aspect of prejudice, I entitled the volume *Prejudice and Racism*, and explained how race problems are embedded in society. Prejudice is ultimately not a race problem but a culture problem. European- and African-heritage cultures differ, and their differences are the soil from which springs cultural racism—the intolerance of those whose culture differs. In today's world of ethnic mixing, we must learn to accept our cultural diversity even as we seek unifying ideals.

JAMES JONES, *University of Delaware*

pany of happy people (Locke & Horowitz, 1990; Rosenblatt & Greenberg, 1988, 1991; Wenzlaff & Prohaska, 1989). When you're feeling blue, another's bubbly personality can be aggravating. The contrast effect that makes average people feel homely in the company of beautiful people also makes sad people more conscious of their misery in the company of cheerful people.

Some **complementarity** may evolve as a relationship progresses (even a relationship between two identical twins). Yet people seem slightly more prone to marry those whose needs and personalities are *similar* (Berscheid & Walster, 1978; Buss, 1984; Fishbein & Thelen, 1981a, 1981b; Nias, 1979). Perhaps we shall yet discover some ways (other than heterosexuality) in which differences commonly breed liking. But researcher David Buss (1985) doubts it: "The tendency of opposites to marry, or mate . . . has never been reliably demonstrated, with the single exception of sex." So it seems that the "opposites-attract" rule, if it's ever true, is of minuscule importance compared to the powerful tendency of likes to attract likes.

Complementarity:
The supposed tendency, in a relationship between two people, for each to complete what is missing in the other. The questionable complementarity hypothesis proposes that people attract those whose needs are different, in ways that complement their own.

Opposites who didn't stay attracted. Prince Charles loved opera, art museums, and Scotland vacations. Diana, 13 years younger, loved rock concerts, nightclubs, and London. When lovers don't love the same things, their love usually wanes.

"Well—and I'm not just saying this because you're my husband—it stinks."

LIKING THOSE WHO LIKE US

Proximity and attractiveness influence our initial attraction to someone, and similarity influences longer-term attraction as well. If we have a deep need to belong and to feel liked and accepted, would we not take a liking to those who like us? Are the best friendships mutual admiration societies? Indeed, one person's liking for another predicts the other's liking in return (Kenny & Nasby, 1980). Liking is usually mutual.

But does one person's liking another *cause* the other to return the appreciation? People's reports of how they fell in love suggest yes (Aron & others, 1989). Discovering that an appealing someone really likes you seems to awaken romantic feelings. Experiments confirm it: Those told that certain others like or admire them usually feel a reciprocal affection (Berscheid & Walster, 1978).

Ellen Berscheid and her colleagues (1969) even found that people like better another student who says eight positive things about them than one who says seven positive things and one negative thing. We are sensitive to the slightest hint of criticism. Writer Larry L. King speaks for many in noting, "I have discovered over the years that good reviews strangely fail to make the author feel as good as bad reviews make him feel bad." Whether we are judging ourselves or others, negative information carries more weight because, being less usual, it grabs more attention (Yzerbyt & Leyens, 1991). People's votes are more influenced by their impressions of presidential candidates' weaknesses than by their impressions of strengths (Klein, 1991), a phenomenon that has not been lost on those who design negative campaigns.

This principle—that we like and treat warmly those we perceive as liking us—was recognized long before social psychologists confirmed it. Observers from the ancient philosopher Hecato ("If you wish to be loved, love") to Ralph Waldo Emerson ("The only way to have a friend is to be one") to Dale Carnegie ("Dole out praise lavishly") anticipated the findings. What they did not anticipate was the precise conditions under which the principle works.

"The average man is more interested in a woman who is interested in him than he is in a woman with beautiful legs."
Marlene Dietrich (1901–1992), Legendary actress

compensating qualities). Positive attributions about attractive people define a physical-attractiveness stereotype—an assumption that what is beautiful is good.

Two other factors further help determine whether acquaintance becomes friendship. Liking for another is greatly aided by *similarity* of attitudes, beliefs, and values. Likeness leads to liking, opposites rarely attract. We are also likely to develop friendships with people who *like us*.

■ LOVE

What is this thing called "love"? Can love in its passionate form endure? If not, what can replace it?

Loving is more complex than liking and thus more difficult to measure, more perplexing to study. People yearn for it, live for it, die for it. Yet only in the last few years has loving become a serious topic in social psychology.

Most researchers have studied what is most easily studied—responses during brief encounters between strangers. The influences on our initial liking of another—proximity, attractiveness, similarity, being liked—also influence our long-term, close relationships. The impressions that dating couples quickly form of each other therefore provide a clue to their long-term future (Berg, 1984; Berg & McQuinn, 1986). Indeed, if romances in the United States flourished *randomly*, without regard to proximity and similarity, then most Catholics (being a minority) would marry Protestants, most Blacks would marry Whites, and college graduates would be as apt to marry high school dropouts as fellow graduates.

So first impressions are important. Nevertheless, long-term loving is not merely an intensification of initial liking. Social psychologists have therefore shifted their attention from the mild attraction experienced during first encounters to the study of enduring, close relationships.

PASSIONATE LOVE

The first step in scientifically studying romantic love, as in studying any variable, is to decide how to define and measure it. We have ways to measure aggression, altruism, prejudice, and liking—but how do we measure love?

Elizabeth Barrett Browning asked a similar question: "How do I love thee? Let me count the ways." Social scientists have counted various ways. Psychologist Robert Sternberg (1988) views love as a triangle, whose three sides (of varying lengths) are passion, intimacy, and commitment (Figure 13–2). Drawing from ancient philosophy and literature, sociologist John Alan Lee (1988) and psychologists Clyde Hendrick and Susan Hendrick (1993) identify three primary love styles—*eros* (passion), *ludus* (game playing), and *storge* (friendship)—which, like the primary colors, combine to form secondary love styles. Pioneering love researcher Zick Rubin (1970, 1973) discerned somewhat different factors. To tap each, he wrote questionnaire items:

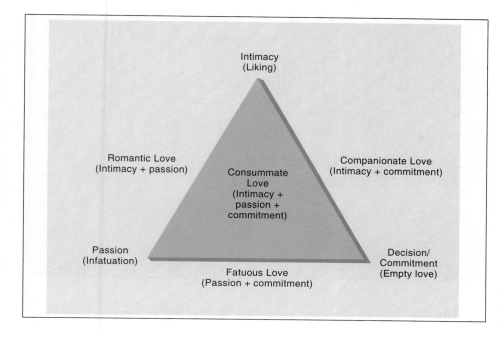

■ **FIGURE 13–2**
Robert Sternberg's (1988) conception of kinds of loving as combinations of three basic components of love.

1. *Attachment* (for example, "If I were lonely, my first thought would be to seek_____out.")
2. *Caring* (for example, "If_____were feeling bad, my first duty would be to cheer him [her] up.")
3. *Intimacy* (for example, "I feel that I can confide in_____about virtually everything.")

Some elements are common to all loving relationships: mutual understanding, giving and receiving support, enjoying the loved one's company. Some elements are distinctive. If we experience passionate love, we express it physically, we expect the relationship to be exclusive, and we are intensely fascinated with our partner. You can see it in our eyes. Rubin confirmed this. He administered his Love Scale to hundreds of University of Michigan dating couples. Later, from behind a one-way mirror in a laboratory waiting room, he clocked eye-contact among "weak-love" and "strong-love" couples. His result will not surprise you: The strong-love couples gave themselves away by gazing long into one another's eyes.

Passionate love is emotional, exciting, intense. Hatfield (1988) defines it as *"a state of intense longing for union with another"* (p. 193). If reciprocated, one feels fulfilled and joyous; if not, one feels empty or despairing. Like other forms of emotional excitement, passionate love involves a mix of elation and gloom, tingling exhilaration and dejected misery.

A Theory of Passionate Love

To explain passionate love, Hatfield notes that a given state of arousal can be steered into any of several emotions, depending on how we attribute the arousal. An emotion involves both body and mind—both arousal and how we interpret

Passionate love:
A state of intense longing for union with another. Passionate lovers are absorbed in one another, feel ecstatic at attaining their partner's love, and are disconsolate on losing it.

and label the arousal. Imagine yourself with pounding heart and trembling hands: Are you experiencing fear, anxiety, joy? Physiologically, one emotion is quite similar to another. You may therefore experience the arousal as joy if you are in a euphoric situation, anger if your environment is hostile, and passionate love if the situation is romantic. In this view, passionate love is the psychological experience of being biologically aroused by someone we find attractive.

If indeed passion is a revved-up state that's labeled "love," then whatever revs one up should intensify feelings of love. In several experiments, college men aroused sexually by reading or viewing erotic materials had a heightened response to a woman (for example, by scoring much higher on Rubin's Love Scale when describing their girlfriend) (Carducci & others, 1978; Dermer & Pyszczynski, 1978; Stephan & others, 1971). Proponents of the **two-factor theory of emotion** argue that when the revved-up men responded to a woman, they easily misattributed some of their arousal to her.

Two-factor theory of emotion:
Arousal × label = emotion.

According to this theory, being aroused by *any* source should intensify passionate feelings—providing the mind is free to attribute some of the arousal to a romantic stimulus. Donald Dutton and Arthur Aron (1974, 1989) invited University of British Columbia men to participate in a learning experiment. After meeting their attractive female partner, some were frightened with the news that they would be suffering some "quite painful" electric shocks. Before the experiment was to begin, the researcher gave a brief questionnaire "to get some information on your present feelings and reactions, since these often influence performance on the learning task." Asked how much they would like to date and kiss their female partner, the aroused (frightened) men expressed more intense attraction toward the woman.

Does this phenomenon occur outside the laboratory? Dutton and Aron (1974) had an attractive young woman approach individual young men as they crossed a narrow, wobbly 450-foot-long suspension walkway hanging 230 feet above British Columbia's rocky Capilano River. The woman asked each man to help her fill out a class questionnaire. When he had finished, she scribbled her name and phone number and invited him to call if he wanted to hear more

"When in doubt, Sis, you've got to listen to your heart. If it's going thump, thump, thump, slow and steady, you've got the wrong guy."

about the project. Most accepted the phone number, and half who did so called. By contrast, men approached by the woman on a low, solid bridge, and men approached on the high bridge by a *male* interviewer, rarely called. Once again, physical arousal accentuated romantic responses. Scary movies, roller-coaster rides, and physical exercise have the same effect (Cohen & others, 1989; White & Kight, 1984). Adrenaline makes the heart grow fonder.

"The 'adrenaline' associated with a wide variety of highs can spill over and make passion more passionate. (Sort of a 'Better loving through chemistry' phenomenon.)"
Elaine Hatfield and Richard Rapson (1987)

Variations in Love

There is always a temptation to assume that most others share our feelings and ideas. We assume, for example, that love is a precondition for marriage. But this assumption is not shared in cultures that practice arranged marriages. Moreover, until recently in North America, marital choices, especially those by women, were strongly influenced by considerations of economic security, family background, and professional status. But by the mid-1980s, almost 9 in 10 young adults surveyed indicated that love was essential for marriage (Simpson & others, 1986).

Our liking and disliking of people is influenced by the events with which they are associated.

BEHIND THE SCENES

When I was an undergraduate, I studied learning and motivation in rats. By the time I entered Stanford, I had become less interested in rats and more interested in the very human phenomena of passionate love and emotions. Learning theory didn't do a very good job of explaining these powerful experiences. My fellow graduate students, who were mostly hard scientists interested in constructing mathematical models of rat learning, warned me to avoid such topics. They dismissed love and emotions as taboo, impossibly difficult to study, and trivial, though common sense argued for their significance. Luckily, I've always followed my own passions and have been able to spend my time studying those subjects I had always wondered about: passionate love, emotions, and the place of physical attractiveness in personal encounters.

ELAINE HATFIELD, *University of Hawaii*

Cultures vary in the importance they place upon romantic love. Most cultures—89 percent in one analysis of 166 cultures—have a concept of romantic love, as reflected in flirtation or couples running off together (Jankowiak & Fischer, 1992). But not all cultures build marriage on romance. In western cultures today, love generally precedes marriage; in others, it more often follows.

Self-Monitoring

Within any given place and time, individuals also vary in their approach to heterosexual relationships. Some seek a succession of short involvements; others value the intimacy of an exclusive and enduring relationship. In a series of studies, Mark Snyder and his colleagues (1985, 1988; Snyder & Simpson, 1985) identified a personality difference linked with these two approaches to romance. In Chapter 4 we noted that some people—those high in *self-monitoring*—skillfully monitor their own behavior to create the desired effect in any given situation. Others—those low in self-monitoring—are more internally guided, more likely to report that they act the same way regardless of the situation.

Which type of person—someone high or low in self-monitoring—would you guess to be more affected by a prospect's physical appearance? to be more willing to end a relationship in favor of a new partner and therefore to date more people for shorter periods of time? to be more sexually promiscuous?

Snyder and Simpson report that in each case the answer is the person high in self-monitoring. Such people are skilled in managing first impressions but tend to be less committed to deep and enduring relationships. Low self-monitors, being less externally focused, are more committed and display more concern for people's inner qualities. When reading folders with information on potential dates or employees, they place a higher premium on personal attributes than on appearance. Given a choice between someone who shares their attitudes or their preferred activities, low self-monitors (unlike high self-monitors) feel drawn to those with kindred attitudes (Jamieson & others, 1987).

Gender

Do males and females differ in how they experience passionate love? Studies of men and women falling in and out of love reveal some surprises. Most people, including the writer of the following letter to a newspaper advice columnist, suppose that women fall in love more readily:

> Dear Dr. Brothers:
>
> Do you think it's effeminate for a 19-year-old guy to fall in love so hard it's like the whole world's turned around? I think I'm really crazy because this has happened several times now and love just seems to hit me on the head from nowhere. . . . My father says this is the way girls fall in love and that it doesn't happen this way with guys—at least it's not supposed to. I can't change how I am in this way but it kind of worries me.—P.T. (quoted by Dion & Dion, 1985)

P.T. would be reassured by the repeated finding that it is actually *men* who tend to fall more readily in love (Dion & Dion, 1985; Peplau & Gordon, 1985). Men also seem to fall out of love more slowly and are less likely than women to break up a premarital romance. However, women in love are typically as emotionally involved as their partners, or more so. They are more likely to report feeling euphoric and "giddy and carefree," as if they were "floating on a cloud." Women are also somewhat more likely than men to focus on the intimacy of the friendship and on their concern for their partner. Men are more likely than women to think about the playful and physical aspects of the relationship.

COMPANIONATE LOVE

Although passionate love burns hot, it inevitably simmers down. The longer a relationship endures, the fewer its emotional ups and downs (Berscheid & others, 1989). The high of romance may be sustained for a few months, even a couple of years. But as we noted in Chapter 12, no high lasts forever. The intense absorption in the other, the thrill of the romance, the giddy "floating on a cloud" feeling, fades. After two years of marriage, spouses express affection about half as often as when they were newlyweds (Huston & Chorost, 1994). About four years after marriage the divorce rate peaks in cultures worldwide (Fisher, 1994). If a close relationship is to endure, it will settle to a steadier but still warm afterglow that Hatfield calls **companionate love**.

Unlike the wild emotions of passionate love, companionate love is lower key; it's a deep, affectionate attachment. And it is just as real. Nisa, a !Kung San woman of the African Kalahari Desert, explains: "When two people are first together, their hearts are on fire and their passion is very great. After a while, the fire cools and that's how it stays. They continue to love each other, but it's in a different way—warm and dependable" (Shostak, 1981).

It won't surprise those who know the rock song, "Addicted to Love," to find out that the flow and ebb of romantic love follows the pattern of addictions to coffee, alcohol, and other drugs. At first, a drug gives a big kick, perhaps a high. With repetition, opponent emotions gain strength and tolerance develops. An amount that once was highly stimulating no longer gives a thrill. However, stopping the substance does not return you to where you started. Rather, it triggers withdrawal symptoms—malaise, depression, the blahs. The same of-

"When two people are under the influence of the most violent, most insane, most delusive, and most transient of passions, they are required to swear that they will remain in that excited, abnormal, and exhausting condition continuously until death do them part."
George Bernard Shaw

Companionate love:
The affection we feel for those with whom our lives are deeply intertwined.

FOCUS

LOVE—EAST AND WEST

After four years' studying in America, a college graduate returns home to Indonesia—and writes back to one of her professors:
I am very happy to be at home again. I stay with my parents again and I will try to get a job. I know that in the western part of the world living with parents is the last thing young people would choose. But despite my education, I am still very much an eastern woman and so are my parents. We consider that it is the best for me to stay home with my family or my relatives.

I do not know whether I am going to get married soon. It just happened that in my last year at United States I met a person I really like. A brother of my best friend. I would like very much to marry him but in our society marriage is not only about love.

If my family (especially my mother) does not like the idea of me getting married to this guy, I have nothing to say but to obey. That is only if I want to be a good Muslim woman. If this happens, I do not know what I will do next. But whatever happens, I know I would never date like many people do. My family whom can be my cousins, uncles, and aunts would introduce me to the son of someone they know. I would only see him and talk to him once or twice or maybe more but not very often and if I like the guy I would only need to say *yes*. If I do not like the guy or I do not feel comfortable with him, I still can say *no*. I do believe if a person has a good heart, love will grow easily and beautifully around him or her.

ten happens in love. The passionate high is fated to become lukewarm. The no-longer-romantic relationship becomes taken for granted—until it ends. Then the jilted lover, the widower, the divorcee, are surprised at how empty life now seems without the person they long ago stopped feeling passionately attached to. Having focused on what was not working, they stopped noticing what was (Carlson & Hatfield, 1992).

The cooling of passionate love over time and the growing importance of other factors, such as shared values, can be seen in the feelings of those who enter arranged versus love-based marriages in India. Usha Gupta and Pushpa

Unlike passionate love, companionate love can last a lifetime.

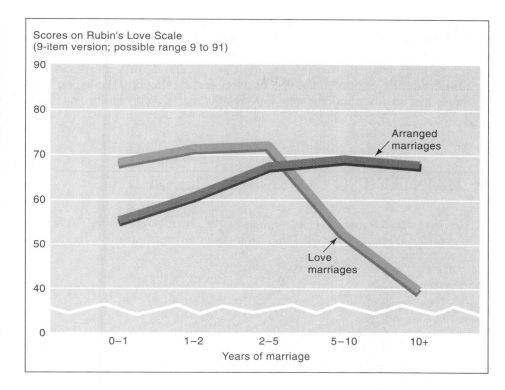

Scores on Rubin's Love Scale
(9-item version; possible range 9 to 91)

Arranged
marriages

Love
marriages

Years of marriage

■ **FIGURE 13–3**
*Romantic love between partners
in arranged or love marriages in
Jaipur, India.*
(Data from Gupta & Singh, 1982.)

Singh (1982) asked 50 couples in Jaipur, India, to complete Zick Rubin's Love Scale. They found that those who married for love reported diminishing feelings of love if they had been married more than five years. By contrast, those in arranged marriages reported *more* love if they were not newlyweds (Figure 13–3).

The cooling of intense romantic love often triggers a period of disillusion, especially among those who regard such love as essential both for a marriage (recall Figure 13–2) and for its continuation. Jeffry Simpson, Bruce Campbell, and Ellen Berscheid (1986) suspect "the sharp rise in the divorce rate in the past two decades is linked, at least in part, to the growing importance of intense positive emotional experiences (e.g., romantic love) in people's lives, experiences that may be particularly difficult to sustain over time." Compared to North Americans, Asians tend to focus less on personal feelings and more on the practical aspects of social attachments (Dion & Dion, 1988; Sprecher & others, 1994). Thus, they are less vulnerable to disillusion. Asians are also less prone to the self-focused individualism that in the long run can undermine a relationship and lead to divorce (Dion & Dion, 1991; Triandis & others, 1988).

The decline in intense mutual fascination may be natural and adaptive for species survival. The result of passionate love frequently is children, whose survival is aided by the parents' waning obsession with one another (Kenrick & Trost, 1987). Nevertheless, for those married more than 20 years, some of the lost romantic feeling is often renewed as the family nest empties and the parents are once again free to focus their attention on each other (Hatfield & Sprecher, 1986). "No man or woman really knows what love is until they have been married a quarter of a century," said Mark Twain. If the relationship has been intimate and mutually rewarding, companionate love deepens.

*"To marry a woman you love
and who loves you is to lay a
wager with her as to who will
stop loving the other first."*
Alfred Capus,
Notes et Pensées, 1926

Occasionally, an acquaintance develops not just into friendship but into *passionate love*. Such love is often a bewildering confusion of ecstasy and anxiety, elation and pain. The two-factor theory of emotion suggests that in a romantic context arousal from any source, even painful experiences, can be steered into passion. In the best of relationships, the initial romantic high settles to a steadier, more affectionate relationship called *companionate love*.

■ MAINTAINING CLOSE RELATIONSHIPS

What factors influence the ups and downs of our close relationships? We consider several: attachment styles, relationship rewards, intimacy, equity, and commitment.

ATTACHMENT

We are, in our roots, social creatures, destined to bond with others. Cooperation promoted our species' survival. In solo combat, our ancestors were not the toughest predators. But as hunter-gatherers, and in fending off predators, they gained strength from numbers. Because group dwellers survived and reproduced, we today carry genes that predispose such bonds.

Our infant dependency strengthens our human bonds. Soon after birth we exhibit various social responses—love, fear, anger. But the first and greatest of

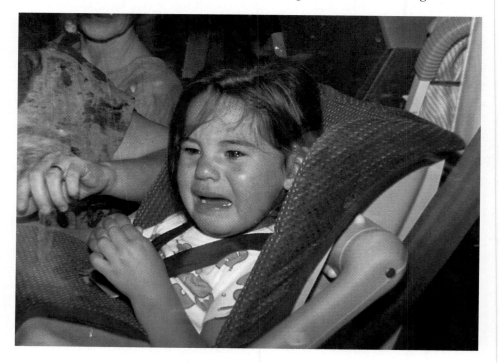

Attachment, especially to caretakers, is a powerful survival impulse. In August 1993, after an emotional custody battle, a distraught 2 1/2-year-old Jessica DeBoer is wrenched from the only family she has known, to be returned to her biological parents.

these is love. As babies, we almost immediately prefer familiar faces and voices. We coo and smile when our parents give us attention. By eight months, we crawl after mother or father and typically let out a wail when separated from them. Reunited, we cling. By keeping infants close to their caregivers, social attachment serves as a powerful survival impulse.

Deprived of familiar attachments, sometimes under conditions of extreme neglect, children may become withdrawn, frightened, silent. After studying the mental health of homeless children for the World Health Organization, psychiatrist John Bowlby (1980, p. 442) reflected that "Intimate attachments to other human beings are the hub around which a person's life revolves, not only when he is an infant or a toddler or a schoolchild but throughout his adolescence and his years of maturity as well, and on into old age. From these intimate attachments a person draws his strength and enjoyment of life. . . ."

Researchers have compared the nature of attachment and love in various close relationships—between parents and children, same-sex friends, and spouses or lovers (Davis, 1985; Maxwell, 1985; Sternberg & Grajek, 1984). Some elements are common to all loving attachments: mutual understanding, giving and receiving support, valuing and enjoying being with the loved one. Passionate love is, however, spiced with some added features: physical affection, an expectation of exclusiveness, and an intense fascination with the loved one.

Passionate love is not just for lovers. Phillip Shaver and his co-workers (1988) note that year-old infants display a passionate attachment to their parents. Much like young adult lovers, they welcome physical affection, feel distress when separated, express intense affection when reunited, and take great pleasure in the significant other's attention and approval. But knowing that infants vary in their styles of relating to caregivers, Shaver and Cindy Hazan (1993, 1994) wondered whether infant attachment styles might carry over to adult relationships.

Attachment Styles

Some babies, when placed in a strange situation (usually a laboratory playroom), show *secure attachment*. They play comfortably in their mother's presence, happily exploring this strange environment. If she leaves, they get distressed; when she returns, they run to her, hold her, then relax and return to exploring and playing. Other infants show the anxiousness and ambivalence of *insecure attachment*. In the strange situation, they are more likely to cling anxiously to their mother. If she leaves, they cry; when she returns they may be indifferent or even hostile. Still others show *avoidant attachment*. Although internally aroused, they reveal little distress during separation or attachment upon reunion (Ainsworth, 1973, 1989).

Some researchers attribute these varying attachment styles to parental responsiveness. Sensitive, responsive mothers—mothers who engender a sense of basic trust in the world's reliability—typically have securely attached infants, observed Mary Ainsworth (1979) and Erik Erikson (1963). Other researchers believe attachment styles may reflect inherited temperament. Regardless, early attachment styles do seem to lay a foundation for future relationships.

Shaver, Hazan and others (Feeney & Noller, 1990; Simpson & others, 1992) have explored adult versions of the infant attachment styles. *Secure* individuals find it easy to get close to others and don't fret about getting too dependent or being abandoned. As lovers, they enjoy sexuality within the context of a continuing relationship. *Anxious-ambivalent* individuals are less trusting, and therefore more possessive and jealous. They may break up repeatedly with the same person. *Avoidant* individuals fear closeness, and therefore become less invested in relationships and more likely to leave them. They also are more likely to engage in one-night stands of sex without love.

Marital Attachment and Happiness

Earlier we noted links between close relationships and health and happiness. For more than 9 in 10 people worldwide, one eventual example of a close relationship is marriage. So, does marriage correlate positively with happiness? Or is there more happiness in the pleasure-seeking single life than in the "bondage," "chains," and "yoke" of marriage?

A mountain of data reveal that most people are happier attached than unattached. Survey after survey of many tens of thousands of Europeans and Americans has produced a consistent result: Compared to those single or widowed, and especially compared to those divorced or separated, married people report being happier and more satisfied with life (Inglehart, 1990; Gove & others, 1990). During the 1970s and 1980s in the United States, for example, 24 percent of never-married adults, but 39 percent of married adults, reported being "very happy" (Figure 13–4).

Is marriage, as is so often supposed, more strongly associated with men's happiness than women's? Given women's greater contribution to household work and to supportive nurturing, we might expect so. However, the married vs. never-married happiness gap is only slightly greater among men than women. Moreover, in European surveys, and in a statistical digest of 93 other

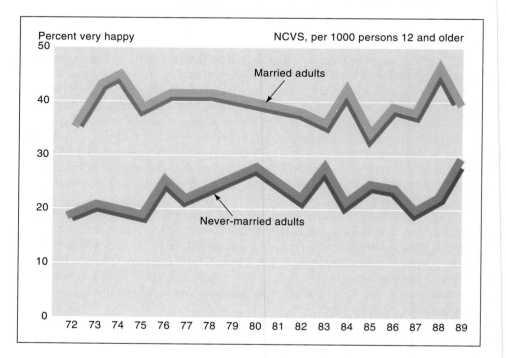

■ **FIGURE 13–4**

Marriage and happiness.

(Data from National Opinion Research Center surveys summarized by Lee & others, 1991.)

studies, this happiness gap is virtually identical for men and women (Ingle-hart, 1990; Wood & others, 1989). Although a bad marriage is often more depressing to a woman than a man, the myth that single women are happier than married women can be laid to rest. Throughout the western world, married people of both sexes report more happiness than those never married, divorced, or separated.

However, more important than being married is the marriage's quality. People who say their marriage is satisfying—who find themselves still in love with their partner—rarely report being unhappy, discontented with life, or depressed. Fortunately, most married people *do* declare their marriages happy ones. In the United States, almost two-thirds say their marriage is "very happy." Three out of four say their spouse is their best friend. Four out of five people say they would marry the same person again. The consequence? Most such people feel quite happy with life as a whole.

But why are married people generally happier? Does marriage promote happiness? Or does happiness promote marriage? Are happy people more appealing as marriage partners? Do grouchy or depressed people more often stay single or suffer divorce? Certainly, happy people are more fun to be with. They are, as we have seen, more outgoing, trusting, compassionate, and focused on others. Unhappy people, as we noted in Chapter 5, are more often socially rejected. For these reasons, positive, happy people more readily form happy relationships.

But marriage also enhances happiness, for at least two reasons. First, married people are more likely to enjoy an enduring, supportive, intimate relationship, and are less likely to suffer loneliness. No wonder male medical students in a study by UCLA's Robert Coombs survived medical school with less stress and anxiety if married (Coombs, 1991). A good marriage gives each partner a dependable companion, a lover, a friend.

There is a second, more prosaic, reason why marriage promotes happiness, or at least buffers us from misery. Marriage offers the roles of spouse and parent, which can provide additional sources of self-esteem (Crosby, 1987). True, multiple roles can multiply stress. Our circuits can and do overload. Yet each also provides rewards, status, avenues to enrichment, escape from stress faced in other parts of one's life. When our personal identity stands on several legs, it more easily holds up under the loss of any one. If I mess up at work, well, I can tell myself I'm still a good husband and father, and in the final analysis, these parts of me are what matter most.

RELATIONSHIP REWARDS

Asked why they are friends with someone or why they were attracted to their partner, most people can readily answer. "I like Carol because she's warm, witty, and well-read." What such explanations leave out—and what social psychologists believe is most important—is ourselves. Attraction involves the one who is attracted as well as the attractor. Thus a more psychologically accurate answer might be, "I like Carol because of how I feel when I'm with her." We are attracted to those *we* find it satisfying and gratifying to be with. Attraction is in the eye (and brain) of the beholder.

The point can be expressed as a simple **reward theory of attraction:** Those who reward us, or whom we associate with rewards, we like. If a relationship

Reward theory of attraction: The theory that we like those whose behavior is rewarding to us or whom we associate with rewarding events.

gives us more rewards than costs, we will like it and will wish it to continue. This will be especially true if the relationship is more profitable than alternative relationships (Burgess & Huston, 1979; Kelley, 1979; Rusbult, 1980). In his 1665 book of *Maxims*, La Rochefoucauld conjectured similarly: "Friendship is a scheme for the mutual exchange of personal advantages and favors whereby self-esteem may profit."

We not only like people who are rewarding to be with; we also, according to the second version of the reward principle, like those we *associate* with good feelings. According to theorists Donn Byrne and Gerald Clore (1970), and to Albert Lott and Bernice Lott (1974), social conditioning creates positive feelings toward those linked to rewarding events. When, after a strenuous week, we relax in front of a fire, enjoying good food, drink, and music, we will likely feel a special warmth toward those around us. We are less likely to take a liking to someone we meet while suffering a splitting headache.

Pawel Lewicki (1985) tested this liking-by-association principle. In one experiment, University of Warsaw students were virtually 50-50 in choosing which of two pictured women (A or B in Figure 13–5) looked friendlier. Other students, having interacted with a warm, friendly experimenter who resembled woman A, chose woman A, by a 6 to 1 margin. In a follow-up study, the experimenter acted *un*friendly toward half the subjects. When these subjects later had to turn in their data to one of two women, they nearly always *avoided* the one who resembled the experimenter. (Perhaps you can recall a time when you reacted positively or negatively to someone who reminded you of someone else.)

Other experiments confirm this phenomenon of liking—and disliking— by association. In one, college students who evaluated strangers in a pleasant room liked them better than those who evaluated them in an uncomfortably hot room (Griffitt, 1970). In another, people evaluated photographs of other people while

■ **FIGURE 13–5**
Liking by association. After interacting with a friendly experimenter, people preferred someone who looked like her (A) to one who didn't (B). After interacting with an un*friendly experimenter, people avoided the woman who resembled her (Lewicki, 1985).*

Experimenter   Person A   Person B

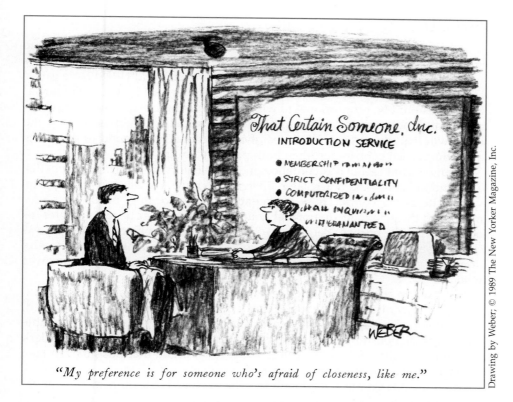

That Certain Someone, Inc.
INTRODUCTION SERVICE

● MEMBERSHIP
● STRICT CONFIDENTIALITY
● COMPUTERIZED

"My preference is for someone who's afraid of closeness, like me."

Drawing by Weber; © 1989 The New Yorker Magazine, Inc.

in either an elegant, sumptuously furnished, softly lit room or in a shabby, dirty, stark room (Maslow & Mintz, 1956). Again, the warm feelings evoked by the elegant surroundings transferred to the people being rated. Elaine Hatfield and William Walster (1978) found a practical tip in these research studies: "Romantic dinners, trips to the theatre, evenings at home together, and vacations never stop being important. . . . If your relationship is to survive, it's important that you *both* continue to associate your relationship with good things."

This simple theory of attraction—we like those who reward us and those we associate with rewards—helps us understand some of the influences on attraction:

■ *Proximity* is rewarding. It costs less time and effort to receive friendship's benefits with someone who lives or works close by.

■ We like *attractive* people because we perceive that they offer other desirable traits and because we benefit by associating with them.

■ If others have *similar* opinions, we feel rewarded because we presume that they like us in return. Moreover, those who share our views help validate them. We especially like people if we have successfully converted them to our way of thinking (Lombardo & others, 1972; Riordan, 1980; Sigall, 1970).

■ We like to be liked and love to be loved. Thus, liking is usually mutual. We like those who like us.

EQUITY

If both partners in a relationship pursue their personal desires willy-nilly, the friendship will die. Therefore, our society teaches us to exchange rewards by what Elaine Hatfield, William Walster, and Ellen Berscheid (1978) have called an **equity** principle of attraction: What you and your partner get out of a relationship should be proportional to what you each put into it. If two people receive equal outcomes, they should contribute equally; otherwise one or the other will feel it is unfair. If both feel their outcomes correspond to the assets and efforts each contributes, then both perceive equity.

Strangers and casual acquaintances maintain equity by exchanging benefits: You lend me your class notes; later, I'll lend you mine. I invite you to my party; you invite me to yours. Those in an enduring relationship, including roommates and those in love, do not feel bound to trade similar benefits—notes for notes, parties for parties (Berg, 1984). They feel freer to maintain equity by exchanging a variety of benefits ("When you drop by to lend me your notes, why don't you stay for dinner?") and eventually to stop keeping track of who owes whom.

Is it crass to suppose that friendship and love are rooted in an equitable exchange of rewards? Don't we sometimes give in response to a loved one's need, without expecting any sort of return? Indeed, those involved in an equitable long-term relationship are unconcerned with short-term equity. Margaret Clark and Judson Mills (1979, 1993; Clark, 1984, 1986) argue that people even take pains to *avoid* calculating any exchange benefits. When we help a good friend, we do not want instant repayment. If someone has us for dinner, we wait before reciprocating, lest the person attribute the motive for our return invitation to be merely paying off a social debt. True friends tune into one another's needs even when reciprocation is impossible (Clark & others, 1986, 1989). One clue that an acquaintance is becoming such a friend is the person's sharing when sharing is unexpected (Miller & others, 1989). Happily married people tend *not* to keep score of how much they are giving and getting (Buunk & Van Yperen, 1991).

In experiments with University of Maryland students, Clark and Mills confirmed that *not* being calculating is a mark of friendship. Tit-for-tat exchanges boosted people's liking when the relationship was relatively formal but *diminished* liking when the two sought friendship. Clark and Mills surmise that marriage contracts in which each partner specifies what is expected from the other are more likely to undermine than enhance love. Only when the other's positive behavior is voluntary can we attribute it to love.

Still, the long-term equity principle explains why people usually bring equal assets to romantic relationships. Recall that often they are matched for attractiveness, status, and so forth. If they are mismatched in one area, such as attractiveness, they tend to be mismatched in some other area, such as status. But in total assets, they are an equitable match. No one says, and few even think, "I'll trade you my good looks for your big income." But especially in relationships that last, equity is the rule.

Those in an equitable relationship are more content (Fletcher & others, 1987; Hatfield & others, 1985; Van Yperen & Buunk, 1990). Those who perceive their relationship as *in*equitable feel discomfort: The one who has the better deal

Equity:
A condition in which the outcomes people receive from a relationship are proportional to what they contribute to it. Note: Equitable outcomes needn't always be equal outcomes.

"Love is the most subtle kind of self-interest."
Holbrook Johnson

Perceived inequity—thinking one contributes more to a relationship and receives less than one's spouse—predicts marital distress and dissatisfaction.

may feel guilty and the one who senses a raw deal may feel strong irritation. (Given the self-serving bias, the person who is "overbenefited" is less sensitive to the inequity.)

Robert Schafer and Patricia Keith (1980) surveyed several hundred married couples of all ages, noting those who felt their marriage was somewhat unfair because one spouse contributed too little to the cooking, housekeeping, parenting, or providing. Inequity took its toll: Those who perceived inequity also felt more distressed and depressed. During the child-rearing years, when wives often feel underbenefitted and husbands overbenefitted, marital satisfaction tends to dip. During the honeymoon and empty-nest stages, spouses are more likely to perceive equity and to feel satisfaction with their marriage (Feeney & others, 1994). When both partners freely give and receive, and make decisions together, the odds of sustained, satisfying love are good.

SELF-DISCLOSURE

Deep, companionate relationships are intimate. They enable us to be known as we truly are and feel accepted. We discover this delicious experience in a good marriage or a close friendship—a relationship where trust displaces anxiety and where we are therefore free to open ourselves without fear of losing the other's affection (Holmes & Rempel, 1989). Such relationships are characterized by what the late Sidney Jourard called **self-disclosure** (Derlega & others, 1993). As a relationship grows, self-disclosing partners reveal more and more of themselves to one another; their knowledge of one another penetrates to deeper and deeper levels until it reaches an appropriate depth. Lacking such opportunities for intimacy, we experience the pain of loneliness (Berg & Peplau, 1982; Solano & others, 1982).

Self-disclosure:
Revealing intimate aspects of oneself to others.

Experiments have probed both the *causes* and the *effects* of self-disclosure. When are people most willing to disclose intimate information concerning "what you like and don't like about yourself" or "what you're most ashamed and most proud of"? And what effects do such revelations have upon those who reveal and receive them?

We disclose more when distressed—when angry or anxious (Stiles & others, 1992). But the most reliable finding is the **disclosure reciprocity** effect: Disclosure begets disclosure (Berg, 1987; Miller, 1990; Reis & Shaver, 1988). We reveal more to those who have been open with us. But intimacy is seldom instant; far more often, it progresses like a dance: I reveal a little, you reveal a little—but not too much. You then reveal more, and I reciprocate.

Some people are especially skilled "openers"—they easily elicit intimate disclosures from others, even from those who normally don't reveal very much of themselves (Miller & others, 1983; Pegalis & others, 1994). Such people tend to be good listeners. During conversation they maintain attentive facial expressions and appear to be comfortably enjoying themselves (Purvis & others, 1984). They may also express interest by uttering supportive phrases while their conversational partner is speaking. They are what psychologist Carl Rogers (1980) called "growth-promoting" listeners—people who are *genuine* in revealing their own feelings, who are *accepting* of others' feelings, and who are *empathic*, sensitive, reflective listeners.

What are the effects of such self-disclosure? Jourard (1964) argued that dropping our masks, letting ourselves be known as we are, nurtures love. He presumed that it is gratifying to open up to another and then to receive the trust another implies by being open with us. For example, having an intimate friend with whom we can discuss threats to our self-image seems to help us survive such stresses (Swann & Predmore, 1985). A true friendship is a special relationship that helps us cope with our other relationships. "When I am with my friend," reflected the Roman playwright Seneca, "methinks I am alone, and as much at liberty to speak anything as to think it." At its best, marriage is such a friendship, sealed by commitment.

Although intimacy is rewarding, the results of many experiments caution us not to presume that self-disclosure will automatically kindle love. It's just not that simple. It's definitely true that we like best those to whom we've disclosed ourselves, and usually we also like those who open up with us (Collins & Miller, 1994). But we are not always fond of those who most intimately reveal themselves to us. Someone who early in an acquaintanceship rushes to tell us intimate details may seem indiscreet, immature, even unstable (Dion & Dion, 1978; Miell & others, 1979). Usually, though, people prefer an open, self-disclosing person to one who holds back. This is especially so when the disclosure is appropriate to the conversation. We feel pleased when a normally reserved person says that something about us "made me feel like opening up" and share confidential information (Archer & Cook, 1986; D. Taylor & others, 1981). It's gratifying to be singled out for another's disclosure.

Intimate self-disclosure is one of companionate love's delights. Dating and married couples who most reveal themselves to one another express most satisfaction with their relationship and are more likely to endure in it (Berg & McQuinn, 1986; Hendrick & others, 1988; Sprecher, 1987). In a recent Gallup national marriage survey, 75 percent of those who prayed with their spouse (and

Disclosure reciprocity:
The tendency for one person's intimacy of self-disclosure to match that of a conversational partner.

"What is a Friend? I will tell you. It is a person with whom you dare to be yourself."
Frank Crane, *A Definition of Friendship*

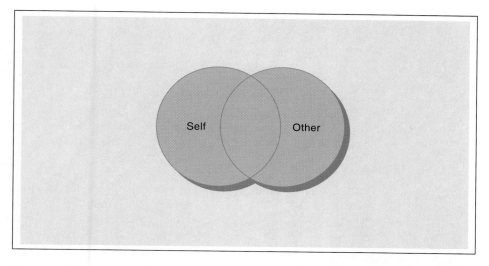

■ **FIGURE 13–6**
Love: An overlapping of selves—you become part of me, I part of you.
(From Aron & Aron, 1994.)

57 percent of those who didn't) reported their marriage as very happy (Greeley, 1991). Among believers, shared prayer from the heart is a humbling, intimate, soulful exposure. Those who pray together also more often say they discuss their marriage together, respect their spouse, and rate their spouse as a skilled lover.

Researchers have also found that women are often more willing to disclose their fears and weaknesses than are men (Cunningham, 1981). As Kate Millett (1975) put it, "Women express, men repress." Nevertheless, men today, particularly men with egalitarian gender-role attitudes, seem increasingly willing to reveal intimate feelings and to enjoy the satisfactions that accompany a relationship of mutual trust and self-disclosure. And that, say Arthur Aron and Elaine Aron (1994), is the essence of love—two selves connecting, disclosing, and identifying with one another; two selves, each retaining their individuality, yet sharing activities, delighting in similarities, and mutually supporting (Figure 13–6).

■ ENDING RELATIONSHIPS

In 1971, a man wrote a love note to his bride, slipped it into a bottle, and dropped it into the Pacific Ocean between Seattle and Hawaii. A decade later, a jogger found it on a Guam beach:

> *If, by the time this letter reaches you, I am old and gray, I know that our love will be as fresh as it is today.*
>
> *It may take a week or it may take years for this note to find you. . . . If this should never reach you, it will still be written in my heart that I will go to extreme means to prove my love for you. Your husband, Bob.*

The woman to whom the love note was addressed was reached by phone. The note was read to her. She burst out laughing. And, the more she heard the harder she laughed. "We're divorced," she finally said, and slammed down the phone.

So it often goes. Comparing their unsatisfying relationship with the support and affection they imagine is available elsewhere, people are divorcing more often—at double the 1960 rate. Slightly more than half of American marriages and roughly 40 percent of Canadian marriages now end in divorce. "We are living longer, but loving more briefly," quips Os Guiness (1993, p. 309).

Sociologist Norval Glenn (1991) analyzed national opinion data gathered on thousands of Americans from 1972 to 1988. He followed the course of marriages that began in the early 1970s. By the late 1980s, only a third of the starry-eyed newlyweds were still married *and* proclaiming their marriages "very happy." Allowing for some overreporting of marital happiness—it's easier to tell an interviewer you've succeeded than failed in your marriage—Glenn concludes that "the real proportion of those marriages that were successful . . . may well have been under a fourth." From a 1988 national survey, the Gallup Organization offers a similarly dismal conclusion: Two out of three 35- to 54-year-olds had divorced, separated, or been close to separation (Colasanto & Shriver, 1989). If this pattern continues, "our nation will soon reach the point where the dominant experience of adults will have been marital instability."

The House of Windsor knows well the hazards of modern marriage. The fairy tale marriages of Princess Margaret, Princess Anne, and Prince Charles have all crumbled, smiles replaced with glowers. Shortly after her 1986 marriage to Britain's Prince Andrew, Sarah Ferguson gushed, "I love his wit, his charm, his looks. I worship him." Andrew reciprocated her euphoria: "She is the best thing in my life." Six years later, Andrew, having decided her friends were "philistines," and Sarah, having derided Andrew's boorish behavior as "terribly gauche," called it quits (*Time*, 1992).

WHO DIVORCES?

Divorce rates vary widely by country, ranging from .01 percent of the population annually in Bolivia, the Philippines, and Spain to 4.7 percent in the world's most divorce-prone country, the United States. To predict a culture's divorce rates it helps to know its values (Triandis, 1994). Individualistic cultures (where love is a feeling and people ask, "What does my heart say?") have more divorce than do communal cultures (where love entails obligation and people ask, "What will other people say?").

Risk of divorce also depends on who marries whom (Fergusson & others, 1984; Myers, 1995b; Tzeng, 1992). People usually stay married if they

- Married after age 20
- Both grew up in stable, two-parent homes
- Dated for a long while before marriage
- Are well and similarly educated
- Enjoy a stable income from a good job
- Live in a small town or on a farm
- Did not cohabit or become pregnant before marriage
- Are religiously committed
- Are of similar age, faith, and education

None of these predictors, by itself, is essential to a stable marriage. But if none of these things is true for someone, marital breakdown is an almost sure bet. If all are true, they are *very* likely to stay together until death. The English perhaps had it right, several centuries ago, when presuming that the temporary intoxication of passionate love was a foolish basis for permanent marital decisions. Better, they felt, to choose a mate based on stable friendship and compatible backgrounds, interests, habits, and values (Stone, 1977).

"Passionate love is in many ways an altered state of consciousness. . . . In many states today, there are laws that a person must not be in an intoxicated condition when marrying. . . . But passionate love is a kind of intoxication."
Roy Baumeister, *Meanings of Life*, 1991

THE DETACHMENT PROCESS

Severing bonds produces a predictable sequence of agitated preoccupation with the lost partner, followed by deep sadness and, eventually, the beginnings of emotional detachment and a return to normal living (Hazan & Shaver, 1994). Even newly separated couples who have long ago ceased feeling affection are often surprised at their desire to be near the former partner. Deep and long-standing attachments seldom break quickly; detaching is a process, not an event.

Among dating couples, the closer and longer the relationship and the fewer the available alternatives, the more painful the breakup (Simpson, 1987). Surprisingly, Roy Baumeister and Sara Wotman (1992) report that months or years later people recall more pain over spurning someone's love than over having been spurned. Their distress arises from guilt over hurting someone, from upset over the heartbroken lover's persistence, or from uncertainty over how to respond. Among married couples, breakup has additional costs: shocked parents and friends, restricted parental rights, guilt over broken vows. Still, each year millions of couples are willing to pay such costs to extricate themselves from what they perceive as the greater costs of continuing a painful, unrewarding relationship. Such costs include, in one study of 328 married couples, a tenfold increase in depression symptoms when a marriage is marked by discord rather than satisfaction (O'Leary & others, 1994).

When relationships suffer, there are alternatives to divorce. Caryl Rusbult and her colleagues (1986, 1987) have explored three other ways of coping with a failing relationship. Some people exhibit *loyalty*—by passively but optimistically waiting for conditions to improve. The problems are too painful to speak of and the risks of separation are too great, so the loyal partner perseveres, hoping the good old days will return. Others (especially men) passively allow the relationship to deteriorate. When painful dissatisfactions are ignored, an insidious emotional uncoupling ensues as the partners talk less and begin redefining their lives without each other. Still others will *voice* their concerns and take active steps to improve the relationship, by discussing problems, seeking advice, and attempting to change.

Study after study reveals that unhappy couples disagree, command, criticize, and put down. Happy couples more often agree, approve, assent, and laugh (Noller & Fitzpatrick, 1990). After observing 2000 couples, John Gottman (1994) noted that healthy marriages were not necessarily devoid of conflict. Rather, they were marked by an ability to reconcile differences and to overbalance criticism with affection. In successful marriages, positive interactions (smiling, touching, complimenting, laughing) outnumbered negative interactions (sarcasm, disapproval, insults) by at least a 5 to 1 ratio.

Successful couples have learned, sometimes aided by communication training, to restrain the cancerous putdowns and gut-level fire-with-fire reactions, to fight fair (by stating feelings without insulting), and to depersonalize conflict with comments like "I know it's not your fault" (Markman & others, 1988; Notarius & Markman, 1993; Yovetich & Rusbult, 1994). Would unhappy relationships get better if the partners agreed to *act* more as happy couples do— by complaining and criticizing less? by affirming and agreeing more? by setting times aside to voice their concerns? by praying or playing together daily? As attitudes trail behaviors, do affections trail actions?

Joan Kellerman, James Lewis, and James Laird (1989) wondered whether actions produce affection. They knew that among couples passionately in love, eye gazing is typically prolonged and mutual (Rubin, 1973). Would intimate eye gazing similarly stir feelings between those not in love? To find out, they asked unacquainted male-female pairs to gaze intently for two minutes either at one another's hands or in one another's eyes. When they separated, the eye gazers reported a tingle of attraction and affection toward each other. Simulating love had begun to stir it.

By enacting and expressing love, researcher Robert Sternberg (1988) believes the passion of initial romance can evolve into enduring love:

> "Living happily ever after" need not be a myth, but if it is to be a reality, the happiness must be based upon different configurations of mutual feelings at various

times in a relationship. Couples who expect their passion to last forever, or their intimacy to remain unchallenged, are in for disappointment. . . . We must constantly work at understanding, building, and rebuilding our loving relationships. Relationships are constructions, and they decay over time if they are not maintained and improved. We cannot expect a relationship simply to take care of itself, any more than we can expect that of a building. Rather, we must take responsibility for making our relationships the best they can be.

Given the psychological ingredients of marital happiness—kindred minds, social and sexual intimacy, equitable giving and receiving of emotional and material resources—it becomes possible to contest the French saying, "Love makes the time pass and time makes love pass." But it takes effort to stem love's decay. It takes effort to carve out time each day to talk over the day's happenings. It takes effort to forgo nagging and bickering and instead to disclose and hear one another's hurts, concerns, and dreams. It takes time to make a relationship into "a classless utopia of social equality" (Sarnoff & Sarnoff, 1989), in which both partners freely give and receive, share decision making, and enjoy life together.

For those who commit themselves to creating an equitable, intimate, mutually supportive relationship there may come the security, and the joy, of enduring, companionate love. When someone "loves you for a long, long time," explained the wise, old Skin Horse to the Velveteen Rabbit,

"not just to play with, but REALLY loves you, then you become Real."
"Does it hurt?" asked the Rabbit.
"Sometimes," said the Skin Horse, for he was always truthful. "When you are Real you don't mind being hurt."
"Does it happen all at once, like being wound up," he asked, "or bit by bit?"
"It doesn't happen all at once," said the Skin Horse. "You become. It takes a long time. That's why it doesn't often happen to people who break easily, or have sharp edges, or who have to be carefully kept. Generally, by the time you are Real, most of your hair has been loved off, and your eyes drop out and you get loose in the joints and very shabby. But these things don't matter at all, because once you are Real you can't be ugly, except to people who don't understand."

From infancy to old age, attachments are central to human life. Secure attachments, as in an enduring marriage, mark happy lives. They do so thanks partly to the rewards offered by a supportive relationship: We like people whose behavior we find rewarding or whom we have associated with rewarding events.

One reward of companionate love is the opportunity for intimate self-disclosure, a state achieved gradually as each partner reciprocates the other's increasing openness. Companionate love is most likely to endure when both partners feel it to be equitable, with both perceiving themselves receiving from the relationship in proportion to what they contribute to it.

Often, however, love does not endure. As divorce rates rose, researchers discerned predictors of marital dissolution and the process through which couples either detach or rebuild their relationship.

■ FOR FURTHER READING

Harvey, J. (1995). *Odyssey of the heart: The search for closeness, intimacy, and love.* New York: Freeman. An overview of what social psychologists know about love. Illustrates significant findings with real cases.

Hendrick, C., & Hendrick, S. S. (1993). *Romantic Love.* Newbury Park, CA: Sage. A literate summary of the roots, the history, and the meaning of different types of love.

Hendrick, S. S., & Hendrick, C. (1992). *Liking, loving and relating.* Pacific Grove, CA: Brooks/Cole. A brief, authoritative overview of what psychologists have learned about the types and stages of close personal relationships.

Pennebaker, J. (1990). *Opening up: The healing power of confiding in others.* New York: Wiliam Morrow. Researcher James Pennebaker explains why disclosing oneself to others is good for both body and soul.

Weber, A. L., & Harvey, J. H. (Eds.) (1994). *Perspectives on close relationships.* Boston: Allyn & Bacon. Experts give state-of-the-art summaries of research on attraction, attachment, communication, support, sexuality, and other dimensions of close relationships.

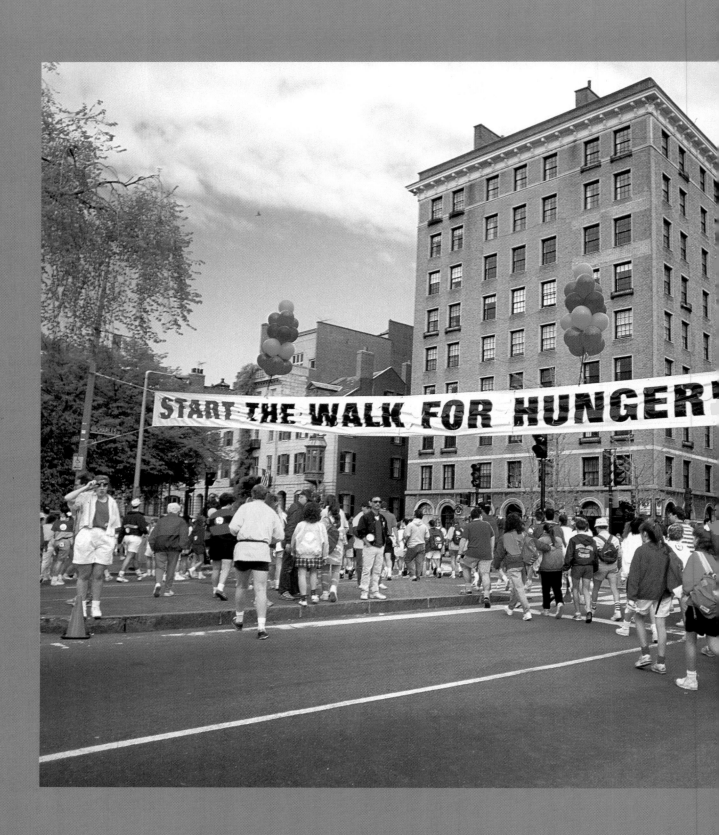

CHAPTER 14

ALTRUISM: HELPING OTHERS

On March 13, 1964, bar manager Kitty Genovese is set upon by a knife-wield-ing rapist as she returns to her Queens, New York, apartment house at 3:00 A.M. Her screams of terror and pleas for help—"Oh my God, he stabbed me! Please help me! Please help me!"—arouse 38 of her neighbors. Many come to their windows and watch while for 35 minutes she struggles to escape her at-tacker. Not until her attacker departs does anyone so much as call the police. Soon after, she dies.

Why had Genovese's neighbors not come to her aid? Were they callous? in-different? apathetic? If so, there are many such people. Consider:

- Andrew Mormille is knifed in the stomach as he rides the subway home. Af-ter his attackers leave the car, 11 other riders watch the young man bleed to death.

- An 18-year-old switchboard operator, working alone, is sexually assaulted. She momentarily escapes and runs naked and bleeding to the street and screams for help. Forty pedestrians watch as the rapist tries to drag her back inside. Fortunately, two police officers happen by and arrest the assailant.

- Eleanor Bradley trips and breaks her leg while shopping. Dazed and in pain, she pleads for help. For 40 minutes the stream of shoppers simply parts and flows around her. Finally, a cab driver helps her to a doctor (Darley & La-tané, 1968).

What is shocking is not that in these cases some people failed to help but that in each of these groups (of 38, 11, 40, and 100s) almost 100 percent of those involved failed to respond. Why? In the same or similar situations, would you or I react as they did? Or would we be heroes, like these people:

- Hearing the rumble of an approaching New York subway train, Everett Sanderson leapt down onto the tracks and raced toward the approaching headlights to rescue Michelle De Jesus, a four-year-old who had fallen from the platform. Three seconds before the train would have run her over, Sander-son flung Michelle into the crowd above. As the train roared in, he himself failed in his first effort to jump back to the platform. At the last instant, by-standers pulled him to safety (Young, 1977).

- It was 2:00 on a mid-summer's afternoon in 1983 when Joe Delaney, a Kansas City Chiefs football player, saw people standing around a huge water-filled hole. Three boys had waded in, unaware that a short way out the bottom dropped off. Suddenly they were in over their heads and thrashing and screaming for help. As Joe alone dashed for the pond, a little boy asked, "Can you swim?" "I can't swim good," Joe answered, "but I've got to save those kids. If I don't come up, get somebody." One boy struggled back to safety. Later the other two—and Joe Delaney—were hauled out by rescuers, dead (Deford, 1983).

- Skydiving instructor Gregory Robertson and six other jumpers had just re-leased from their exhilarating hand-to-hand airborne circle when calamity struck. After the split, Debbie Williams collided headfirst with another jumper, leaving her unconscious and spinning like Raggedy Ann, earthbound at 160 miles per hour. From above, Robertson, seeing the collision's effect, threw caution to the wind. Streamlining his body, Superman-like, he rock-eted toward her—and the ground—at 200 miles per hour. As he approached he spread his limbs to slow down, grabbed her harness with one hand, and pulled her parachute release cord with the other, sparing her life. Finally, just 2000 feet from impact he opened his own chute, sparing his life as well (*Time-Life*, 1994).

■ On a hillside in Jerusalem, 800 trees form a simple line, the Avenue of the Righteous. Beneath each tree is a plaque with the name of a European Christian who gave refuge to one or more Jews during the Nazi Holocaust. These "righteous Gentiles" knew that if the refugees were discovered, Nazi policy dictated that both host and refugee would suffer a common fate. Many did (Hellman, 1980; Wiesel, 1985).

Less dramatic acts of comforting, caring, and helping abound: Without asking anything in return, people offer directions, donate money, give blood, volunteer time. Why, and when, will people perform altruistic acts? And what can be done to lessen indifference and increase altruism? These are this chapter's primary questions.

Altruism is selfishness in reverse. An altruistic person is concerned and helpful even when no benefits are offered or expected in return. Jesus' parable of the Good Samaritan provides the classic illustration:

> A man was going down from Jerusalem to Jericho, and fell into the hands of robbers, who stripped him, beat him, and went away, leaving him half dead. Now by chance a priest was going down that road; and when he saw him, he passed by on the other side. So likewise a Levite, when he came to the place and saw him, passed by on the other side. But a Samaritan while traveling came near him; and when he saw him, he was moved with pity. He went to him and bandaged his wounds, having poured oil and wine on them. Then he put him on his own animal, brought him to an inn, and took care of him. The next day he took out two denarii, gave them to the innkeeper, and said, "Take care of him; and when I come back, I will repay you whatever more you spend." (Luke 10:30–35)

The Samaritan illustrates pure altruism. Filled with compassion, he gives a total stranger time, energy, and money while expecting neither repayment nor appreciation.

Altruism:
A motive to increase another's welfare without conscious regard for one's self-interests.

■ WHY DO WE HELP?

To study altruistic acts, social psychologists examine the conditions under which people perform such deeds. Before looking at what the experiments reveal, let's consider what motivates altruism. Three complementary theories offer some answers.

SOCIAL EXCHANGE

One explanation for altruism comes from **social-exchange theory**: Human interactions are guided by a "social economics." We exchange not only material goods and money but also *social* goods—love, services, information, status (Foa & Foa, 1975). In doing so, we use a "minimax" strategy—minimize costs, maximize rewards. Social-exchange theory does not contend that we consciously monitor costs and rewards, only that such considerations predict our behavior.

Social-exchange theory:
The theory that human interactions are transactions that aim to maximize one's rewards and minimize one's costs.

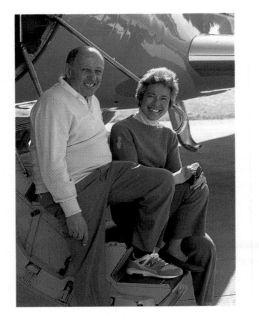

What motivates volunteers in the Corporate Angel Network? Recovered cancer patients Jay Weinberg and Pat Blum match flight schedules of hundreds of corporate planes with cancer patients' destinations and desired flight days. By putting patients in empty executive seats and expediting their travel, "we offer them a bit of dignity," says Blum.

"Men do not value a good deed unless it brings a reward."
Ovid, *Epistulae ex Ponto*

Suppose your campus is having a blood drive and someone asks you to participate. Might you not weigh the *costs* of donating (needle prick, time, fatigue) versus those of not donating (guilt, disapproval)? Might you not also weigh the *benefits* of donating (feeling good about helping someone, free refreshments) versus those of not donating (saving the time, discomfort, and anxiety)? According to social-exchange theory—and to studies of Wisconsin blood donors by Jane Allyn Piliavin, Dorcas Evans, and Peter Callero (1982)—such subtle calculations precede decisions to help or not.

Helping as Disguised Self-Interest

Rewards that motivate helping may be external or internal. When businesses donate money to improve their corporate images or when someone offers another a ride hoping to receive appreciation or friendship, the reward is external. We give to get. Thus we are most eager to help someone attractive to us, someone whose approval we desire (Krebs, 1970; Unger, 1979).

The benefits of helping also include internal self-rewards. Near someone in distress, we typically respond with empathy. A woman's scream outside your window arouses and distresses you. If you cannot reduce your arousal by interpreting the scream as a playful shriek, then you may investigate or give aid, thereby reducing your distress (Piliavin & Piliavin, 1973). Indeed, Dennis Krebs (1975) found that Harvard University men whose physiological responses and self-reports revealed the most distress in response to another's distress also gave the most help to the person. As Everett Sanderson remarked after saving the child who fell from the subway platform, "If I hadn't tried to save that little girl, if I had just stood there like the others, I would have died inside. I would have been no good to myself from then on." Altruistic acts also increase our sense of self-worth. Nearly all blood donors in Jane Piliavin's research agreed that giving blood "makes you feel good about yourself" and "gives you a feeling of self-satisfaction."

From their analyses of why people volunteer, as when befriending AIDS patients, Mark Snyder, Allen Omoto, and Gil Clary (Clary & Snyder, 1993) have discerned six motivations:

- **Knowledge:** to better understand people or learn skills
- **Career:** to enhance job prospects with experience and contacts
- **Social adjustment:** to be part of a group and gain approval
- **Ego defense:** to reduce guilt or escape personal problems
- **Esteem enhancement:** to boost self-worth and confidence
- **Value expression:** to act on humanitarian values and concern for others

Because only the value-expression function allows for selfless altruism, this cost-benefit analysis can seem demeaning. In defense of the theory, however, is it not a credit to humanity that we can derive pleasure from helping others? that much of our behavior is not antisocial but "prosocial"? that we can find fulfillment in the giving of love? How much worse if we gained pleasure only by serving ourselves.

"True," some readers may reply. "Still, doesn't social-exchange theory imply that a helpful act is never truly altruistic—that we merely *call* it 'altruistic' when its rewards are inconspicuous? If we help the screaming woman so we can gain social approval, relieve our distress, or boost our self image, is it really altruistic?" This is reminiscent of B. F. Skinner's (1971) analysis of altruism. We credit people for their good deeds, said Skinner, only when we can't explain them. We attribute their behavior to their inner dispositions only when we lack external explanations. When the external causes are obvious, we credit the causes, not the person.

There is, however, a weakness in social-exchange theory: It easily degenerates into explaining-by-naming. If someone volunteers for the Big Sister tutor program, it is tempting to "explain" her compassionate action by the satisfaction it brings her. But such after-the-fact naming of rewards creates a circular explanation: "Why did she volunteer?" "Because of the inner rewards." "How do you know there are inner rewards?" "Why else would she have volunteered?" Because of this flaw, **egoism**—the idea that self-interest motivates all behavior—has fallen into disrepute.

To escape the circularity, we must define the rewards and costs independently of the altruistic behavior. If social approval motivates helping, then in experiments we should find that when approval follows helping, helping increases. And it does (Staub, 1978). Moreover, the cost-benefit analysis says something else. It suggests that the passive bystanders who observed the switchboard operator being dragged by the rapist may not have been apathetic. They may actually have been greatly distressed, yet paralyzed by their awareness of the potential costs of intervening.

Egoism:
A motive (supposedly underlying all behavior) to increase one's own welfare. The opposite of *altruism*, which aims to increase another's welfare.

Empathy as a Source of Genuine Altruism

Are life-saving heroes, everyday blood donors, and Peace Corps volunteers *ever* motivated by an ultimate goal of selfless concern for another? Or is their ultimate goal always some form of self-benefit, such as relief from distress or avoidance of guilt?

Abraham Lincoln illustrated the philosophical issue in a conversation with another passenger in a horse-drawn coach. After Lincoln argued that selfish-

"Are you all right, Mister? Is there anything I can do?"

"Young man, you're the only one who bothered to stop! I'm a millionaire and I'm going to give you five thousand dollars!"

We never know what benefits may come from helping someone in distress.

ness prompts all good deeds, he noticed a sow making a terrible noise. Her piglets had gotten into a pond and were in danger of drowning. Lincoln called the coach to a halt, jumped out, ran back, and lifted the little pigs to safety. Upon his return, his companion remarked, "Now, Abe, where does selfishness come in on this little episode?" "Why, bless your soul, Ed, that was the very essence of selfishness. I should have had no peace of mind all day had I gone and left that suffering old sow worrying over those pigs. I did it to get peace of mind, don't you see?" (F. C. Sharp, cited by Batson & others, 1986). Until recently, psychologists would have sided with Lincoln. They would have sided with skeptics who, noting ex-President Jimmy Carter's devoting his retirement to building houses for the poor, renewing Atlanta slums, and being a peacemaker between nations, wonder what motivates all this good—a lust, perhaps, for a Nobel Peace Prize?

Psychologist Daniel Batson (1991, 1995), however, theorizes that our willingness to help is influenced by both self-serving *and* selfless considerations (Figure 14–1). Distress over someone's suffering motivates us to relieve our upset, either by escaping the distressing situation (like the priest and Levite) or by helping (like the Samaritan). But especially when we feel attached to someone, report Batson and his colleagues, we also feel *empathy*. Loving parents suffer when their children suffer and rejoice over their children's joys—an empathy lacking in child abusers and other perpetrators of cruelty (Miller & Eisenberg, 1988).

When feeling empathy we focus not so much on our own distress as on the sufferer. Genuine sympathy and compassion motivate us to help the person for his or her own sake. Such empathy comes naturally. Even day-old infants cry more when they hear another infant cry (Hoffman, 1981). In hospital nurseries, one baby's crying sometimes evokes a chorus of crying. We come, it seems, hard-wired for empathy.

Often distress and empathy together motivate responses to a crisis. In 1983, people watched on television as an Australian bushfire wiped out hundreds of homes near Melbourne. Afterward, Paul Amato (1986) studied donations of money and goods. He found that those who felt angry or indifferent gave less than those who felt either distressed (shocked and sickened) or empathic (sympathetic and worried for the victims). Children's generosity, too, varies with their capacity for distress and empathy. George Knight and his Arizona State University co-researchers (1994) found that some six- to nine-year-olds more than others reported feeling sorry when others were sad or being picked on. After watching a video of a burned girl, these sympathetic children were also the most generous when given a chance to give some of their research earnings to a children's burn unit.

To separate egoistic distress reduction from altruistic empathy, Batson's research group conducted studies that aroused feelings of empathy. Then the researchers noted whether the aroused people would reduce their own distress by escaping the situation or whether they would go out of their way to aid the person. The results were consistent: Their empathy aroused, they usually helped.

In one of these experiments, Batson and his associates (1981) had University of Kansas women observe a young woman suffering while she supposedly received electric shocks. During a pause in the experiment, the obviously upset victim explained to the experimenter that a childhood fall against an electric fence left her acutely sensitive to shocks. In sympathy, the experimenter suggested that perhaps the observer (the actual subject in this experiment) might trade places and take the remaining shocks for her. Previously, half of these actual subjects had been led to believe the suffering person was a kindred spirit on matters of values and interests (thus arousing their empathy). Some also were led to believe that their part in the experiment was completed, so that in

"Elaine" experiments

■ **FIGURE 14–1**

Egoistic and altruistic routes to helping. Viewing another's distress can evoke a mixture of self-focused distress and other-focused empathy. Researchers agree that distress triggers egoistic motives. But they debate whether empathy can trigger a pure altruistic motive.
(Adapted from Batson, Fultz, & Schoenrade, 1987.)

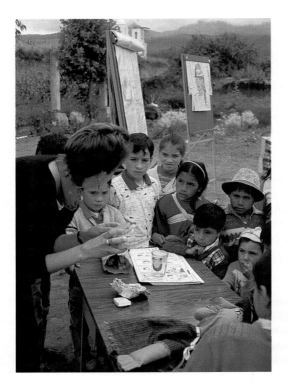

Might genuine empathy motivate a Peace Corps worker's explaining dental hygiene to Ecuadorian children? Daniel Batson believes yes.

any case they were done observing the woman's suffering. Nevertheless, their empathy aroused, virtually all these student observers willingly offered to substitute for the victim.

Is this pure altruism? Mark Schaller and Robert Cialdini (1988) doubt it. Feeling empathy for a sufferer makes one sad, they note. In one of their experiments they led people to believe that their sadness was going to be relieved by a different sort of mood-boosting experience—listening to a comedy tape. Under such conditions, people who felt empathy were not especially helpful. Schaller and Cialdini concluded that if we feel empathy but know that something else will make us feel better, we aren't so likely to help.

Other findings suggest that genuine altruism may exist:

■ Empathy produces helping only when people believe the other will receive the needed help (Dovidio & others, 1990).

■ People whose empathy is aroused will help even when they believe no one will know about their helping. Their concern continues until someone *has* helped (Fultz & others, 1986).

■ People will sometimes persist in wanting to help a suffering person even when they believe their distressed mood has been temporarily frozen by a "mood-fixing" drug (Schroeder & others, 1988).

■ Sensing that empathy triggers altruism, people will sometimes avoid situations that arouse their empathy, so they can avoid possible over-involvement (Shaw & others, 1994).

"How selfish soever man may be supposed, there are evidently some principles in his nature, which interest him in the fortune of others, and render their happiness necessary to him, though he derives nothing from it except the pleasure of seeing it."
Adam Smith, *The Theory of Moral Sentiments*, 1759

To summarize, everyone agrees that some helpful acts are either obviously egoistic (done to gain rewards or avoid punishment) or subtly egoistic (done to relieve inner distress). Is there a third type of helpfulness—an altruism that aims simply to increase another's welfare (producing happiness for oneself merely as a by-product)? Is empathy-based helping a source of such altruism? Cialdini (1991) and his colleagues Mark Schaller and Jim Fultz still doubt it. They note that no experiment rules out all possible egoistic explanations for helpfulness. But after some 25 experiments testing egoism versus empathy, Batson (1991, 1995) and others (Dovidio, 1991; Staub, 1991; Wallach & Wallach, 1983) believe that sometimes people *do* focus on others' welfare, not on their own.

During the Vietnam war 63 soldiers received Medals of Honor for using their bodies to shield their buddies from exploding devices (Hunt, 1990). Most were in close-knit combat groups. Most threw themselves on live hand grenades. In doing so, 59 made the ultimate sacrifice. Unlike other altruists, such as the 50,000 Gentiles now believed to have rescued 200,000 Jews from the Nazis, these soldiers had no time to reflect upon the shame of cowardice or the eternal rewards of self-sacrifice. Yet something drove them to act. With energy and creativity, today's social psychologists explore and debate what that something is.

SOCIAL NORMS

Often we help others not because we have consciously calculated that such behavior is in our self-interest but simply because something tells us we *ought* to. We ought to help a new neighbor move in. We ought to turn off a parked car's

BEHIND THE SCENES

At age 14, I was traumatized when my family moved from Vancouver, B. C. to California. I fell from President of my junior high school to an object of social ridicule because of my clothes, accent, and behavior. The skills I had acquired boxing soon generated a quite different reputation from the one I enjoyed in Canada. I sank lower and lower until, after several bouts with the law and several visits to juvenile detention homes, I was arrested for driving under the influence of drugs. I escaped from jail, hitchhiked to a logging camp in Oregon, and eventually made my way back to British Columbia. I was admitted to university on probation, graduated at the top of my class, won a Woodrow Wilson Fellowship, and was accepted at Harvard.

Concerned about my record in California, I turned myself in and suffered through the ensuing publicity. I was pardoned, in large part because of the tremendous support I received from many people. I attended Harvard, where, after three years, I was hired as an Assistant Professor. Eventually, I returned to British Columbia to chair the Psychology Department at Simon Fraser University. Though it makes me somewhat uncomfortable, I disclose this history as a way of encouraging people with two strikes against them to remain in the game. A great deal of the energy I have invested in understanding morality has stemmed from a need to understand why I went wrong, and my interest in altruism has been fueled by the generosity of those who helped me overcome my past. I'm now working on a theory of self-deception.

DENNIS KREBS, *Simon Fraser University*

BEHIND THE SCENES

Attempting to answer the question of altruism versus egoism—of whether we humans are capable of genuine caring for each other or only of caring for ourselves—has been like coming home for me. It's the kind of question about human nature that I often asked, first in college studying philosophy and later in seminary studying theology. When Jay Coke and I began studying people's emotional reactions to witnessing others in need, I realized that we were approaching a long-standing philosophical and theological puzzle. I was excited to think that if we could ascertain whether people's concerned reactions were genuine, and not simply a subtle form of selfishness, then we could shed new light on a basic issue regarding human nature.

C. DANIEL BATSON, *University of Kansas*

lights. We ought to return the wallet we found. We ought to protect our combat buddies from harm. Norms (as you may recall from Chapter 6) are social expectations. They *prescribe* proper behavior, the *oughts* of our lives. Researchers studying helping behavior have identified two social norms that motivate altruism.

The Reciprocity Norm

Reciprocity norm:
An expectation that people will help, not hurt, those who have helped them.

Sociologist Alvin Gouldner (1960) contended that one universal moral code is a **norm of reciprocity**: To those who help us, we should return help, not harm. Gouldner believed this norm is as universal as the incest taboo. We "invest" in others and expect dividends. Mail surveys and solicitations sometimes include a little gift of money or individualized address labels, on the assumption that many people will reciprocate the favor. Politicians know that the one who gives a favor can later expect a favor in return. The reciprocity norm even applies with marriage. Sometimes one may give more than one receives. But in the long run, one expects the exchange to balance out. In all such interactions, to receive without giving in return violates the reciprocity norm.

"There is no duty more indispensable than that of returning a kindness."
Cicero

The norm applies most strongly to interactions with equals. Those who do not see themselves as inferior or as dependent especially feel the need to reciprocate. If they cannot reciprocate, they may feel threatened and demeaned by accepting aid. Thus, compared to low self-esteem people, they are more reluctant to seek help (Nadler & Fisher, 1986). With people who clearly are dependent and unable to reciprocate—children, the severely impoverished and disabled, and others perceived as unable to return as much as they receive—another social norm motivates our helping.

The Social-Responsibility Norm

The reciprocity norm reminds us to balance giving and receiving in social relations. However, if the only norm was reciprocity, the Samaritan would not have been the Good Samaritan. In the parable, Jesus obviously had something more humanitarian in mind, something explicit in another of his teachings: "If you love those who love you [the reciprocity norm], what right have you to claim any credit? . . . I say to you, Love your enemies" (Matthew 5:46, 44).

The belief that people should help those who need help, without regard to future exchanges, is the **norm of social responsibility** (Berkowitz, 1972b; Schwartz, 1975). The norm motivates people to retrieve a dropped book for a person on crutches. In India, a relatively collectivist culture, people support the social-responsibility norm more strongly than in the individualist west (Miller & others, 1990). They voice an obligation to help even when the need is not life-threatening or the needy person is outside their family circle.

Experiments show that even when helpers remain anonymous and have no expectation of any reward, they often help needy people (Shotland & Stebbins, 1983). However, they usually apply the social-responsibility norm selectively to those whose need appears not to be due to their own negligence. Especially among political conservatives (Skitka & Tetlock, 1993), the norm seems to be: Give people what they deserve. If they are victims of circumstance, like natural disaster, then by all means be generous. If they seem to have created their own problems, by laziness, immorality, or lack of foresight, then they should get what they deserve. Responses are thus closely tied to *attributions*. If we attribute the need to an uncontrollable predicament, we help. If we attribute the need to the person's choices, fairness does not require us to help; we say it's the person's own fault (Weiner, 1980).

Imagine yourself as one of the University of Wisconsin students in a study by Richard Barnes, William Ickes, and Robert Kidd (1979). You receive a call from a "Tony Freeman" who explains that he is in your introductory psychology class. He says that he needs help for the upcoming exam and that he has gotten your name from the class roster. "I don't know. I just don't seem to take good notes in there," Tony explains. "I know I can, but sometimes I just don't feel like it, so most of the notes I have aren't very good to study with." How

Social-responsibility norm: An expectation that people will help those dependent upon them.

When 18-month-old Jessica McClure fell 22 feet into an abandoned well, it took 2 1/2 days for workers in Midland, Texas to free her. Driven by a sense of social responsibility, "Baby Jessica's" rescuers worked round the clock.

sympathetic would you feel toward Tony? How much of a sacrifice would you make to lend him your notes? If you are like the students in this experiment, you would probably be much less inclined to help than if Tony had just explained that his troubles were beyond his control. So, when people need our help, we are moved by the social-responsibility norm—unless we blame them for their problem.

EVOLUTIONARY PSYCHOLOGY

The third explanation of altruism comes from evolutionary theory. As you may recall from Chapters 6 and 13, evolutionary psychology contends that the essence of life is gene survival. Our genes drive us in ways that have maximized their chance of survival. When our ancestors died, their genes lived on.

As suggested by the title of Richard Dawkins' (1976) popular book *The Selfish Gene*, evolutionary psychology offers a humbling human image—one that psychologist Donald Campbell (1975a,b) has called a biological reaffirmation of a deep, self-serving "original sin." Genes that predispose individuals to selflessly promote strangers' welfare would not survive in the evolutionary competition. Genetic selfishness should, however, predispose us toward two specific types of selfless or even self-sacrificial altruism: kin protection and reciprocity.

Kin Protection

Our genes dispose us to care for relatives in whom they reside. Thus one form of self-sacrifice that *would* increase gene survival is devotion to one's children. Parents who put their children's welfare ahead of their own are more likely to pass their genes on than parents who neglect their children. As David Barash (1979, p. 153) has said, "Genes help themselves by being nice to themselves, even if they are enclosed in different bodies." Although evolution favors altruism toward one's children, children have less at stake in the survival of their parents' genes. Thus, parents are generally more devoted to their children than their children are to them.

Other relatives share genes in proportion to their biological closeness. You share one-half your genes with your brothers and sisters, one-eighth with your cousins. That led the evolutionary biologist J. B. S. Haldane to jest that while he would not give up his life for his brother, he would sacrifice himself for *three* brothers—or for nine cousins. Haldane would not have been surprised that, compared to fraternal twins, genetically identical twins are noticeably more mutually supportive (Segal, 1984).

The point is not that we calculate genetic relatedness before helping but that nature programs us to care about close relatives. The Carnegie medal for heroism is never awarded for saving a relative. That we expect. What we do not expect (and therefore honor) is the altruism of those who, like our subway hero Everett Sanderson, risk themselves to save a stranger.

We also share common genes with many others. Blue-eyed people share particular genes with other blue-eyed people. But how do we detect the people in which copies of our genes occur most abundantly? As the blue-eyes example suggests, one clue lies in physical similarities (Rushton & others, 1984). Also, in evolutionary history genes were shared more with neighbors than with foreigners. Are we therefore biologically biased to act more altruistically toward

"Fallen heroes do not have children. If self-sacrifice results in fewer descendants, the genes that allow heroes to be created can be expected to disappear gradually from the population."
E. O. Wilson (1978, pp. 152–153)

those similar to us and those who live near us? In the aftermath of natural disasters and other life-and-death situations, the order of who gets helped would not surprise an evolutionary psychologist: the young before the old, family members before friends, neighbors before strangers (Burnstein & others, 1994; Form & Nosow, 1958).

Some evolutionary psychologists say we can also expect ethnic ingroup favoritism—the root of countless historical and contemporary conflicts (Rushton, 1991). E. O. Wilson (1978) noted that **kin selection**—favoritism toward those who share our genes—is "the enemy of civilization. If human beings are to a large extent guided . . . to favor their own relatives and tribe, only a limited amount of global harmony is possible" (p. 167).

> **Kin selection:**
> The idea that evolution has selected altruism toward one's close relatives to enhance the survival of mutually shared genes.

Reciprocity

Genetic self-interest also predicts reciprocity. An organism helps another, biologist Robert Trivers argues, because it expects help in return (Binham, 1980). The giver expects later to be the getter, while failure to reciprocate gets punished: The cheat, the turncoat, and the traitor are universally despised.

Reciprocity works best in small, isolated groups, groups in which one will often see the people for whom one does favors. If a vampire bat has gone a day or two without food—it can't go much more than 60 hours without starving to death—it asks a well-fed nestmate to regurgitate food for a meal (Wilkinson, 1990). The donor bat does so willingly, losing fewer hours till starvation than the recipient gains. But such favors occur only among familiar nestmates who share in the give and take. Those who always take and never give, and those who have no relationship with the donor bat, go hungry.

For similar reasons, reciprocity is stronger in the remote Cook Islands of the South Pacific than in New York City (Barash, 1979, p. 160). Small schools, towns, churches, work teams, and dorms are all conducive to a community spirit in which people care for each other. Compared to people in small-town or rural environments, those in big cities are less willing to relay a phone message, less likely to mail "lost" letters, less cooperative with survey interviewers, less helpful to a lost child, and less willing to do small favors (Hedge & Yousif, 1992; Steblay, 1987).

If individual self-interest inevitably wins in genetic competition, then why does nonreciprocal altruism toward strangers occur? What causes a Mother Teresa to act as she does? What causes soldiers to throw themselves on grenades?

Donald Campbell's (1975) answer is that human societies evolved ethical and religious rules that serve as brakes on the biological bias toward self-interest. Commandments, such as "Love your neighbor," admonish us to balance self-concern with concern for the group, and so contribute to the survival of the group. Richard Dawkins (1976) offered a similar conclusion: "Let us try to *teach* generosity and altruism, because we are born selfish. Let us understand what our selfish genes are up to, because we may then at least have the chance to upset their designs, something no other species has ever aspired to" (p. 3).

Some evolutionary psychologists contend that selflessness might also arise from *group* selection (Wilson & Sober, 1994). Groups offer protection from predators and from other groups, and they enable cooperative hunting and farming. Thus, groups with individuals disposed to reciprocal altruism may have been more likely to survive.

COMPARING AND EVALUATING THEORIES OF ALTRUISM

By now you have perhaps noticed similarities among the social-exchange, social norm, and evolutionary views of altruism. The parallels are indeed striking. As Table 14–1 shows, each proposes two types of prosocial behavior: a tit-for-tat reciprocal exchange and a more unconditional helpfulness. They do so at three complementary levels of explanation. If the evolutionary view is correct, then our genetic predispositions *should* manifest themselves in psychological and sociological phenomena.

Each theory appeals to logic. Yet each is vulnerable to charges of being speculative and after the fact. When we start with a known effect (the give and take of everyday life) and explain it by conjecturing a social-exchange process, a "reciprocity norm," or an evolutionary origin, we might be merely explaining-by-naming. The argument that a behavior occurs because of its survival function is hard to disprove. With hindsight, it's easy to think it had to be that way. If we can explain *any* conceivable behavior after the fact as the result of a social exchange, a norm, or natural selection, then we cannot disprove the theories. Each theory's task is therefore to generate predictions that enable us to test it.

An effective theory also provides a coherent scheme for summarizing a variety of observations. On this criterion, the three altruism theories get higher marks. Each offers us a broad perspective from which we can understand both enduring commitments of time or resources and spontaneous help, such as that studied in the experiments described in the following sections.

SUMMING UP

Three theories explain altruistic behavior. The *social-exchange theory* assumes that helping, like other social behaviors, is motivated by a desire to minimize costs and maximize rewards. Other psychologists believe that a genuine altruistic concern for another's welfare also motivates people.

Social norms also mandate helping. The *reciprocity norm* stimulates us to return help, not harm, to those who have helped us. The *social-responsibility norm* beckons us to help needy people, even if they cannot reciprocate, so long as they are deserving.

Evolutionary psychology assumes two types of altruism: devotion to kin and reciprocity. However, most evolutionary psychologists believe that the genes of selfish individuals are more likely to survive than the genes of self-sacrificing individuals and that society must therefore teach altruism.

TABLE 14–1 *Comparing Theories of Altruism*

THEORY	LEVEL OF EXPLANATION	HOW IS ALTRUISM EXPLAINED?	
		MUTUAL "ALTRUISM"	INTRINSIC ALTRUISM
Social norms	Sociological	Reciprocity norm	Social responsibility norm
Social exchange	Psychological	External rewards for helping	Distress→inner rewards for helping
Evolutionary	Biological	Reciprocity	Kin selection

These three theories are complementary. Each uses psychological, sociological, or biological concepts to account for two types of altruism: (1) an "altruism" of reciprocal exchange and (2) an unconditional altruism.

■ WHEN WILL WE HELP?

*W*hat are the circumstances that prompt people to help, or not to help? How *and why is helping influenced by the number and behavior of other bystanders? by mood states? by traits and values?*

Social psychologists were curious and concerned about bystanders' lack of involvement during such events as the Kitty Genovese rape-murder. So they undertook experiments to identify when people will help in an emergency.

More recently, researchers have broadened the question to ask: Who is likely to help in nonemergencies—by such deeds as giving money, donating blood, or contributing time? Let's examine these experiments by looking first at the *circumstances* that enhance helpfulness and then at the characteristics of the *people* who help.

SITUATIONAL INFLUENCES: NUMBER OF BYSTANDERS

Bystander passivity during emergencies prompted social commentators to lament people's "alienation," "apathy," "indifference," and "unconscious sadistic impulses." By attributing the nonintervention to the bystanders' dispositions, we can reassure ourselves that as caring people, we *would* have helped. But were the bystanders such dehumanized characters?

Social psychologists Bibb Latané and John Darley (1970) were unconvinced. So they staged ingenious emergencies and found that a single situational factor—the presence of other bystanders—greatly decreased intervention. By 1980 some four dozen experiments had compared help given by bystanders who

BEHIND THE SCENES

Shocked by the Kitty Genovese murder, Bibb Latané and I met over dinner and began to analyze the bystanders' reactions. Being social psychologists, we thought not about the personality flaws of the "apathetic" individuals, but rather about how anyone in that situation might react as did these people. By the time we finished our dinner, we had formulated several factors that together could lead to the surprising result: no one helping. Then we set about conducting experiments that isolated each factor and demonstrated its importance in an emergency situation.

JOHN M. DARLEY, *Princeton University*

■ **FIGURE 14–2**
Latané and Darley's decision tree. Only one path up the tree leads to helping. At each fork of the path, the presence of other bystanders may divert a person down a branch toward not helping.
(Adapted from Darley & Latané, 1968.)

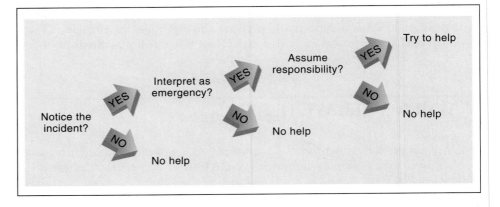

perceived themselves to be either alone or with others. In about 90 percent of these comparisons, involving nearly 6000 people, lone bystanders were more likely to help (Latané & Nida, 1981).

Sometimes, the victim was actually less likely to get help when many people were around. When Latané, James Dabbs (1975), and 145 collaborators "accidentally" dropped coins or pencils during 1497 elevator rides, they were helped 40 percent of the time when one other person was on the elevator and less than 20 percent of the time when there were six passengers. Why? Latané and Darley surmised that as the number of bystanders increases, any given bystander is less likely to *notice* the incident, less likely to *interpret* the incident as a problem or emergency, and less likely to *assume responsibility* for taking action (Figure 14–2).

Noticing

Twenty minutes after Eleanor Bradley has fallen and broken her leg on a crowded city sidewalk, you come along. Your eyes are on the backs of the pedestrians in front of you (it is bad manners to stare at those you pass) and your private thoughts are on the day's events. Would you therefore be less likely to notice the injured woman than if the sidewalk were virtually deserted?

To find out Latané and Darley (1968) had Columbia University men fill out a questionnaire in a room, either by themselves or with two strangers. While they were working (and being observed through a one-way mirror), there was a staged emergency: Smoke poured into the room through a wall vent. Solitary students, who often glanced idly about the room while working, noticed the smoke almost immediately—usually in less than five seconds. Those in groups kept their eyes on their work. It typically took them about 20 seconds to *notice* the smoke.

Interpreting

Once we notice an ambiguous event, we must interpret it. Put yourself in the room filling with smoke. Though worried, you don't want to embarrass yourself by getting flustered. You glance at the others. They look calm, indifferent. Assuming everything must be okay, you shrug it off and go back to work. Then one of the others notices the smoke and, noting your apparent unconcern, reacts similarly. This is yet another example of informational influence (Chapter 7). Each person uses others' behavior as clues to reality.

So it happened in the actual experiment. When those working alone noticed the smoke, they usually hesitated a moment, then got up, walked over to the vent, felt, sniffed, and waved at the smoke, hesitated again, and then went to report it. In dramatic contrast, those in groups of three did not move. Among the 24 men in 8 groups, only one person reported the smoke within the first four minutes (Figure 14–3). By the end of the six-minute experiment, the smoke was so thick it was obscuring the men's vision and they were rubbing their eyes and coughing. Still, in only three of the eight groups did even a single person leave to report the problem.

Equally interesting, the group's passivity affected its members' interpretations. What caused the smoke? "A leak in the air conditioning," "Chemistry labs in the building," "Steam pipes," "Truth gas." They offered many explanations. Not one said, "Fire." The group members, in serving as nonresponsive models, influenced each other's interpretation.

This experimental dilemma parallels dilemmas each of us face. Are the shrieks outside merely playful antics or the desperate screams of someone being assaulted? Is the boys' scuffling a friendly tussle or a vicious fight? Is the person slumped in the doorway sleeping, or seriously ill, perhaps in a diabetic coma? That surely was the question confronting those who passed by Sidney Brookins (Goleman, 1993). Brookins, who had suffered a concussion when beaten, died after lying near the door to a Minneapolis apartment house for two days.

Unlike the smoke-filled-room experiment, however, each of these everyday situations involves danger to another person. To see if the same **bystander effect** occurs in such situations, Latané and Judith Rodin (1969) staged an experiment around a woman in distress. A female researcher set Columbia University men to work on a questionnaire and then left through a curtained doorway to work in an adjacent office. Four minutes later she could be heard (from a high-fidelity tape recorder) climbing on a chair to reach some papers. This was followed by a scream and a loud crash as the chair collapsed and she fell to the floor. "Oh, my God, my foot . . . I . . . I . . . can't move it," she sobbed.

Bystander effect:
The finding that a person is less likely to provide help when there are other bystanders.

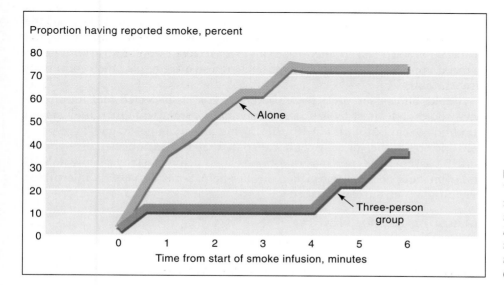

■ **FIGURE 14–3**
The smoke-filled room experiment. Smoke pouring into the testing room was much more likely to be reported by individuals working alone than by three-person groups.
(Data from Latané & Darley, 1968.)

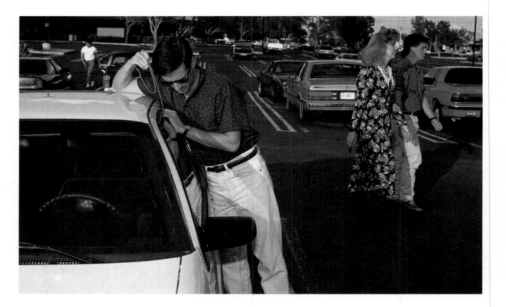

Interpretations matter. Is this man locked out of his car or a burglar? Our answer affects how we respond.

"Oh . . . my ankle . . . I . . . can't get this . . . thing . . . off me." Only after two minutes of moaning did she manage to make it out her office door.

Seventy percent of those alone when they overheard the "accident" came into the room or called out to offer help. Among pairs of strangers confronting the emergency, only 40 percent of the time did either person offer help. Those who did nothing apparently interpreted the situation as a nonemergency. "A mild sprain," said some. "I didn't want to embarrass her," explained others. This again demonstrates the bystander effect: As the number of people known to be aware of an emergency increases, any given person becomes less likely to help. For the victim, there is therefore no safety in numbers.

People's interpretations also affect their reactions to street crimes. In staging physical fights between a man and a woman, Lance Shotland and Margaret Straw (1976) found that bystanders intervened 65 percent of the time when the woman shouted, "Get away from me; I don't know you," but only 19 percent of the time when she shouted, "Get away from me; I don't know why I ever married you." Spouse abuse, it seems, just doesn't trigger as much concern as stranger abuse.

Harold Takooshian and Herzel Bodinger (1982) suspected that interpretations could also affect bystanders' reactions to burglaries. When they staged hundreds of car burglaries in 18 cities (using a coat hanger to gain access to a valuable object, such as a TV set or fur coat), they were astonished. Fewer than 1 in 10 passers-by so much as questioned their activity. Many people noticed and even stopped to stare, snicker, or offer help. Some apparently interpreted the "burglar" as the car's owner.

Assuming Responsibility

Misinterpretation is not the bystander effect's only cause. Even when a shabby 14-year-old was the "burglar," when someone simultaneously broke into two adjacent cars, or when onlookers saw a different person breaking into the car than had just gotten out of it, Takooshian and Bodinger report there still was virtually no intervention by New Yorkers. And what about those times when an emergency is obvious? Those who saw and heard Kitty Genovese's pleas for help correctly interpreted what was happening. But the lights and silhouetted figures in neighboring windows told them that others were also watching. This diffused the responsibility for action.

Few of us have observed a murder. But all of us have at times been slower to react to a need when others were present. Passing a stranded motorist on a highway, we are less likely to offer help than on a country road. To explore bystander inaction in clear emergencies, Darley and Latané (1968) simulated the Genovese drama. They placed people in separate rooms from which the subjects would hear a victim crying for help. To create this situation, Darley and Latané asked some New York University students to discuss over a laboratory intercom their problems with university life. They told the students that to guarantee their anonymity, no one would be visible, nor would the experimenter eavesdrop. During the ensuing discussion, the participants heard one person, when the experimenter turned his microphone on, lapse into an epileptic seizure. With increasing intensity and speech difficulty, he pleaded for someone to help.

Of those led to believe they were the only listener, 85 percent left their room to seek help. Of those who believed four others also overheard the victim, only 31 percent went for help. Were those who didn't respond apathetic and indifferent? When the experimenter came in to end the experiment, she did not find this response. Most immediately expressed concern. Many had trembling hands and sweating palms. They believed an emergency had occurred but were undecided whether to act.

After the smoke-filled room, the woman-in-distress, and the seizure experiments, Latané and Darley asked the participants whether the others' presence had influenced them. We know the other bystanders had a dramatic effect. Yet the participants almost invariably denied the influence. The typical reply? "I was aware of the others, but I would have reacted just the same if they weren't there." This response reinforces a familiar point: We often do not know why we do what we do. That is why experiments such as these are revealing. A survey of uninvolved bystanders following a real emergency would have left the bystander effect hidden.

Further experiments revealed situations in which others' presence sometimes does *not* inhibit people from offering help. Irving Piliavin and his colleagues (1969) staged an emergency in a laboratory on wheels, the unwitting subjects being 4450 riders of New York's subway. On each of 103 occasions, a confederate entered a subway car and stood in the center next to a pole. After the train pulled out of the station, he staggered, then collapsed. When the victim carried a cane, one or more bystanders almost always promptly offered help. Even when the victim carried a bottle and smelled of liquor, he was often promptly offered aid—aid that was especially prompt when several male bystanders were close by. Why? Did the presence of other passengers provide a sense of security to those who helped? Was it because the situation was unambiguous? (The passengers couldn't help noticing and realizing what was happening.)

To test this latter possibility, Linda Solomon, Henry Solomon, and Ronald Stone (1978) conducted experiments in which New Yorkers either saw and

Compassion fatigue helps explain why those seeking help receive fewer responses from city people than from country people.

heard someone's distress, as in the subway experiment, or only heard it, as in the woman-in-distress experiment (leaving the situation more open to interpretation). When the emergencies were very clear, those in groups were only slightly less likely to help than were those alone. However, when the emergencies were somewhat ambiguous, the subjects in groups were far less likely to help than were solitary bystanders.

New Yorkers, like other urbanites, are seldom alone in public places, which helps account for why city people often are less helpful than country people. "Compassion fatigue" and "sensory overload" from encountering so many people in need further restrain helping in large cities. This explains what happened when Robert LeVine and colleagues (1994) approached several thousand people in 36 cities, dropping an unnoticed pen, asking for change, simulating a blind person needing help at a corner, and so forth. The bigger and more densely populated the city, the less likely people were to help.

In the subway experiment, the passengers sat face-to-face, allowing them to see the alarm on one another's faces. To explore the effect of facial communication, Darley, Allan Teger, and Lawrence Lewis (1973) had people working either face-to-face or back-to-back when they heard a crash in the adjacent room as several metal screens fell on a workman. Unlike those working alone, who almost always offered help, pairs working back-to-back seldom offered help. A person working face-to-face with a partner could notice the other's facial expression and know that the person had also observed the event. Apparently, this led both people to interpret the situation as an emergency and to feel some responsibility to act, for these pairs were virtually as likely to give aid as were those working alone.

Finally, all the experiments we have considered involved groups of strangers. Imagine yourself facing any of these emergencies with a group of friends. Would your acquaintance with the other bystanders make a difference? Experiments conducted in two Israeli cities and at the University of Illinois at Chicago reveal that the answer is yes (Rutkowski & others, 1983; Yinon & others, 1982). Cohesive groups are *less* inhibited about helping than are solitary individuals. To summarize: The presence of other bystanders inhibits helping *if* the emergency is *ambiguous* and the other bystanders are *strangers* who *cannot easily read one another's reactions*.

These experiments raise again the issue of research ethics. Is it right to force hundreds of subway riders to witness someone's apparent collapse? Were the researchers in the seizure experiment ethical when they forced people to decide whether to abort the discussion to report the problem? Would you object to being in such a study? Note that it would have been impossible to get your "informed consent"; doing so would have destroyed the cover for the experiment.

In defense of the researchers, they were always careful to debrief the participants. After explaining the seizure experiment, probably the most stressful, the experimenter gave the participants a questionnaire. One hundred percent said the deception was justified and that they would be willing to take part in similar experiments in the future. None of the participants reported feeling angry at the experimenter. Other researchers similarly report that the overwhelming majority of subjects in such experiments say afterward that their participation was both instructive and ethically justified (Schwartz & Gottlieb, 1981). In field experiments, such as the one in the subway car, an accomplice assisted the victim if no one else did, thus reassuring bystanders that the problem was being dealt with.

Remember that the social psychologist has a twofold ethical obligation: to protect the participants and to enhance human welfare by discovering influences upon human behavior. Such discoveries can alert us to unwanted influences and show us how we might exert positive influences. The ethical principle thus seems to be: After protecting participants' welfare, social psychologists fulfill their responsibility to society by doing such research.

SITUATIONAL INFLUENCES: HELPING WHEN SOMEONE ELSE DOES

If aggressive models can heighten aggression (Chapter 12) and if unresponsive models can heighten nonresponding, then will helpful models promote helping? Imagine hearing a crash followed by sobs and moans. If another bystander said: "Uh oh. This is an emergency! We've got to do something," would this stimulate others to help?

The evidence is clear: Prosocial models do promote altruism. Some examples:

■ James Bryan and Mary Ann Test (1967) found that Los Angeles drivers were more likely to offer help to a female driver with a flat tire if a quarter mile earlier they witnessed someone helping another woman change a tire.

■ In another experiment, Bryan and Test observed that New Jersey Christmas shoppers were more likely to drop money in a Salvation Army kettle if they had just seen someone else do the same.

■ Philippe Rushton and Anne Campbell (1977) found British adults usually unwilling to donate blood, unless they were approached after observing a confederate consent to donating.

Sometimes models contradict in practice what they preach. Parents may tell their children, "Do as I say, not as I do." Experiments show that children learn moral judgments both from what they hear preached and what they see practiced (Rice & Grusec, 1975; Rushton, 1975). When exposed to hypocrites, they imitate: They do what the model does and say what the model says.

"We are, in truth, more than half what we are by imitation. The great point is, to choose good models and to study them with care."
Lord Chesterfield, *Letters*, January 18, 1750

SITUATIONAL INFLUENCES: TIME PRESSURES

Darley and Batson (1973) discerned another determinant of helping in the Good Samaritan parable. The priest and the Levite were both busy, important people, probably hurrying to their duties. The lowly Samaritan surely was less pressed for time. To see whether people in a hurry would behave as the priest and Levite did, Darley and Batson cleverly staged the situation described in the parable.

After collecting their thoughts prior to recording a brief extemporaneous talk (which, for half the participants, was on the Good Samaritan parable), Princeton Theological Seminary students were directed to a recording studio in an adjacent building. En route, they passed a man sitting slumped in a doorway, head down, coughing and groaning. Some of the students had been sent off nonchalantly: "It will be a few minutes before they're ready for you, but you might as well head on over." Of these, almost two-thirds stopped to offer help. Others were told, "Oh, you're late. They were expecting you a few minutes ago . . . so you'd better hurry." Of these, only 10 percent offered help.

Reflecting on these findings, Darley and Batson remarked:

A person not in a hurry may stop and offer help to a person in distress. A person in a hurry is likely to keep going. Ironically, he is likely to keep going even if he is hurrying to speak on the parable of the Good Samaritan, thus inadvertently confirming the point of the parable. (Indeed, on several occasions, a seminary student going to give his talk on the parable of the Good Samaritan literally stepped over the victim as he hurried on his way!)

This is one of the most ironically humorous scenes ever noted in a social psychology experiment: a contemporary "priest" passing by a slumped, groaning victim while pondering the parable of the Good Samaritan.

Are we being unfair to the seminary students, who were, after all, hurrying to *help* the experimenter? Perhaps they keenly felt the social-responsibility norm but found it pulling them two ways—toward the experimenter and toward the victim. In another enactment of the Good Samaritan situation, Batson and his associates (1978) directed 40 University of Kansas students to an experiment in another building. Half were told they were late; half knew they had plenty of time. Half thought their participation was vitally important to the experimenter; half thought it was not essential. The results: Those who, like the White Rabbit in *Alice's Adventures in Wonderland*, were late for a very important date seldom stopped to help. Those on their way to an unimportant appointment usually stopped to help.

Can we conclude that those who were rushed were callous? Did the seminarians notice the victim's distress and then consciously choose to ignore it?

No. In their hurry, they never fully grasped the situation. Harried, preoccupied, rushing to meet a deadline, they simply did not take time to tune in to the person in need.

PERSONAL INFLUENCES: FEELINGS

We have considered external influences on the decision to help—number of bystanders, modeling, hurrying, and characteristics of the person in need. We also need to consider internal factors, such as the helper's emotional state or personal traits.

Guilt

Throughout recorded history, guilt has been a painful emotion, so painful that cultures have institutionalized ways to relieve it: animal and human sacrifices, offerings of grain and money, penitent behavior, confession, denial. In ancient Israel, the sins of the people were periodically laid on a "scapegoat" animal that was then led into the wilderness to carry away the people's guilt (de Vaux, 1965).

To examine the consequences of guilt, social psychologists have induced people to transgress: to lie, to deliver shock, to knock over a table loaded with alphabetized cards, to break a machine, to cheat. Afterward, the guilt-laden participants may be offered a way to relieve their guilt: by confessing, by disparaging the one harmed, or by doing a good deed to offset the bad one. The results are remarkably consistent: People will do whatever can be done to expunge the guilt and restore their self-image.

Picture yourself as a participant in one such experiment conducted with Mississippi State University students by David McMillen and James Austin (1971). You and another student, each seeking to earn credit toward a course requirement, arrive for the experiment. Soon after, a confederate enters, portraying himself as a previous subject looking for a lost book. He strikes up a conversation in which he mentions that the experiment involves taking a multiple-choice test, for which most of the correct answers are "B." After the accomplice departs, the experimenter arrives, explains the experiment and then asks, "Have either of you been in this experiment before or heard anything about it?"

Would you lie? The behavior of those who have gone before you in this experiment—100 percent of whom told the little lie—suggests that you would. After you have taken the test (without receiving any feedback on it), the experimenter says: "You are free to leave. However, if you have some spare time, I could use your help in scoring some questionnaires." Assuming you have told the lie, do you think you would now be more willing to volunteer some time? Judging from the results, the answer again is yes. On average, those who had not been induced to lie volunteered only two minutes of time. Those who had lied were apparently eager to redeem their self-image; on average they offered a whopping 63 minutes. One moral of this experiment was well expressed by a seven-year-old girl, who, in one of our own experiments, wrote: "Don't Lie or youl Live with gilt" (and you will feel a need to relieve it).

Our eagerness to do good after doing bad reflects both our need to reduce *private* guilt and restore our shaken self-image and our desire to reclaim a positive *public* image. We are more likely to redeem ourselves with helpful behavior when other people know about our misdeeds (Carlsmith & Gross, 1969). But even when our guilt is private, we act to reduce it. Dennis Regan and his associates (1972) demonstrated this in a New York shopping center. They led women to think they had broken a camera. A few moments later a confederate, carrying a shopping bag with candy spilling out, crossed paths with each woman. Compared to women not put on the guilt trip—only 15 percent of whom bothered to alert the confederate to the spillage—nearly four times as many of the guilt-laden women did so. The guilt-laden women had no need to redeem themselves in the confederate's eyes. So their helpfulness is best explained as a way of relieving their private guilt feelings. Other ways of relieving guilt—as by confession—reduce guilt-induced helping (Carlsmith & others, 1968).

"Open confession is good for the soul."
Old Scottish proverb

All in all, guilt leads to much good. By motivating people to confess, apologize, help, and avoid repeated harm, it boosts sensitivity and sustains close relationships.

Negative Mood

If guilt increases helping, do other negative feelings do the same? If, while depressed over a bad grade, you saw someone spill papers on the sidewalk, would you be more likely than usual to help? Or less likely?

At first glance, the results are confusing. Putting people in a negative mood (by having them read or think about something sad) sometimes increases altruism, sometimes decreases it. Such an apparent contradiction excites the scientist's detective spirit. If we look closely, we find order amid the confusion. First, the studies in which negative mood decreased helping usually involved children (Isen & others, 1973; Kenrick & others, 1979; Moore & others, 1973); those that found increased helping usually studied adults (Aderman & Berkowitz, 1970; Apsler, 1975; Cialdini & others, 1973; Cialdini & Kenrick, 1976). Why do you suppose a negative mood affects children and adults differently?

Robert Cialdini, Douglas Kenrick, and Donald Baumann (1981; Baumann & others, 1981) surmise that for adults, altruism is self-gratifying. It carries its own inner rewards. Blood donors feel better about themselves for having donated. Students who've helped pick up dropped materials feel better about themselves after helping (Williamson & Clark, 1989). Thus, when an adult is in a guilty, a sad, or an otherwise negative mood, a helpful deed (or any other mood-improving experience) helps neutralize the bad feelings.

This implies (and experiments confirm) that a negative mood won't boost helping if a person first receives some other mood boost (finds money or listens to a humorous tape) (Cialdini & others, 1973; Cunningham & others, 1980; Kidd & Berkowitz, 1976). Likewise, if people believe a drug has temporarily fixed their mood state, then a negative mood does not affect willingness to help (Manucia & others, 1984). To repeat: *If* being helpful is a way to improve mood, a sad adult is helpful.

Why doesn't this work with children? Cialdini, Kenrick, and Baumann argue that altruism is not similarly rewarding for children. When reading stories, young children view unhelpful characters as happier than helpful ones; as children grow older, their views reverse (Perry & others, 1986). Although young children exhibit empathy, they do not take much pleasure in being helpful; such behavior is a product of *socialization*—or so Cialdini and his colleagues supposed.

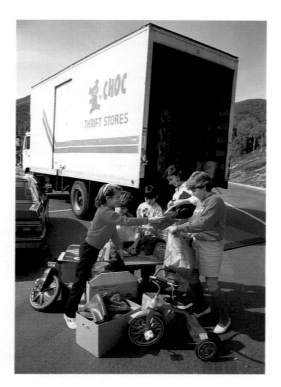

Schoolchildren packing toy donations for the needy. As children mature, they usually come to take pleasure in being helpful to others.

To test their belief, they had children in early elementary school, late elementary school, and high school reminisce about sad or neutral experiences prior to a chance to donate prize coupons privately to other children (Cialdini & Kenrick, 1976). When sad, the youngest children donated slightly less, the middle groups donated slightly more, and the teenage group donated significantly more. Only the teenagers seemed to find generosity a self-gratifying technique for cheering themselves up.

As the researchers note, these results are consistent with the view that we are born selfish. But such results are also consistent with the view that altruism naturally grows with age as children come to see things from another person's point of view (Bar-Tal, 1982; Rushton, 1976; Underwood & Moore, 1982).

Exceptions to the Feel Bad–Do Good Scenario

Among well-socialized adults, should we always expect to find the "feel bad–do good" phenomenon? No. In the previous chapter, we saw that one negative mood, anger, produces anything but compassion. Another exception is depression, which is characterized by brooding self-concern (Carlson & Miller, 1987; Wood & others, 1990). Yet another exception is profound grief. People who suffer the loss of a spouse or a child, whether through death or separation, often undergo a period of intense self-preoccupation, a state that makes it difficult to be giving (Aderman & Berkowitz, 1983; Gibbons & Wicklund, 1982).

In a powerfully involving laboratory simulation of self-focused grief, William Thompson, Claudia Cowan, and David Rosenhan (1980) had Stanford University students privately listen to a taped description of a person (whom they were to imagine was their best friend of the other sex) dying of cancer. The experiment focused some subjects' attention on their own worry and grief:

> He (she) could die and you would lose him, never be able to talk to him again. Or worse, he could die slowly. You would know every minute could be your last time together. For months you would have to be cheerful for him while you were sad. You would have to watch him die in pieces, until the last piece finally went, and you would be alone.

For others, it focused their attention on the friend:

> He spends his time lying in bed, waiting those interminable hours, just waiting and hoping for something to happen. Anything. He tells you that it's not knowing that is the hardest.

The researchers report that regardless of which tape the participants heard, they were profoundly moved and sobered by the experience, yet not the least regretful of participating (although some participants who listened to a boring control condition tape were regretful). Did their mood affect their helpfulness? When immediately thereafter they were given a chance to anonymously help a graduate student with her research, 25 percent of those whose attention had been self-focused helped. Of those whose attention was other-focused, 83 percent helped. The two groups were equally touched. But only the other-focused participants found helping someone especially rewarding. In short, the feel bad–do good effect occurs with people whose attention is on others, people for whom altruism is therefore rewarding (Barnett & others, 1980; McMillen & others, 1977). So unless they are self-preoccupied, sad people are sensitive, helpful people.

Feel Good, Do Good

Are happy people unhelpful? Quite the contrary. There are few more consistent findings in the entire literature of psychology: Happy people are helpful people. This effect occurs with both children and adults, regardless of whether the good mood comes from a success, from thinking happy thoughts, or from any of several other positive experiences (Salovey & others, 1991). One woman recalled her experience after falling in love:

> At the office, I could hardly keep from shouting out how deliriously happy I felt. The work was easy; things that had annoyed me on previous occasions were taken in stride. And I had strong impulses to help others; I wanted to share my joy. When Mary's typewriter broke down, I virtually sprang to my feet to assist. Mary! My former "enemy"! (Tennov, 1979, p. 22)

In experiments the one helped may be someone seeking a donation, an experimenter seeking help with paperwork, a woman who drops papers. Alice Isen, Margaret Clark, and Mark Schwartz (1976) had a confederate, who had supposedly spent her last dime on a wrong number, call people who had received a free sample of stationery 0 to 20 minutes earlier. As Figure 14–4 shows, their willingness to relay the phone message rose during the five minutes afterward. Then, as the good mood wore off, helpfulness dropped.

If sad people are sometimes extra helpful, how can it be that happy people are also helpful? Experiments reveal several factors are at work (Carlson & others, 1988). Helping softens a bad mood and sustains a good mood. A positive mood is, in turn, conducive to positive thoughts and positive self-esteem, which

"It's curious how, when you're in love, you yearn to go about doing acts of kindness to everybody."
P. G. Wodehouse, *The Mating Season*, 1949

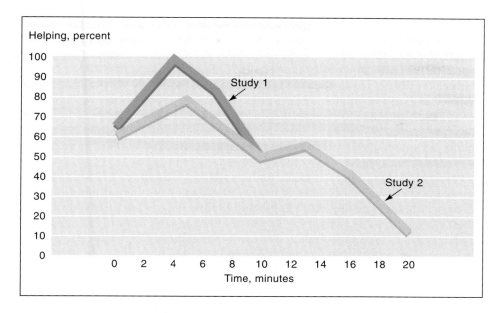

■ **FIGURE 14–4**
Percentage of those willing to relay a phone message 0 to 20 minutes after receiving a free sample. Of control subjects who did not receive a gift, only 10 percent helped.
(Data from Isen & others, 1976.)

predispose us to positive behavior (Berkowitz, 1987; Cunningham & others, 1990; Isen & others, 1978). In a good mood—after being given a gift or while feeling the warm glow of success—people are more likely to have positive thoughts and to have positive associations with being helpful. Positive thinkers are likely to be positive actors.

Recall from Chapter 5 the effect on cognition of depressed versus happy moods.

PERSONAL INFLUENCES: PERSONALITY TRAITS

We have seen that mood and guilt dramatically affect altruism. Are there similar dramatic effects from enduring personality traits? Surely some traits must distinguish the Mother Teresa types.

For many years social psychologists were unable to discover a single personality trait that predicted altruistic behavior with anything close to the predictive power of the situation, guilt, and mood factors. Modest relationships were found between helping and certain personality variables, such as need for social approval. But by and large, the personality tests were unable to identify the helpers. Recent studies of rescuers of Jews in Nazi Europe reveal a similar conclusion: Although the social context clearly influenced willingness to help, there was no definable set of altruistic personality traits (Darley, 1995).

If that has a familiar ring, it could be from a similar conclusion by conformity researchers (Chapter 7): Conformity, too, seemed more influenced by the situation than by measurable personality traits. Perhaps, though, you recall from Chapter 2 that who we are does affect what we do. Attitude and trait measures seldom predict a *specific* act, which is what most experiments on altruism measure, in contrast to the lifelong altruism of a Mother Teresa. But they better predict average behavior across many situations.

Personality researchers have responded to the challenge, first, by demonstrating individual differences in helpfulness and showing that these differences persist over time and are noticed by one's peers (Hampson, 1984; Rush-

"There are . . . reasons why personality should be rather unimportant in determining people's reactions to the emergency. For one thing, the situational forces affecting a person's decision are so strong."
Bibb Latané and John Darley, (1970, p. 115)

ton & others, 1981). Second, researchers are gathering clues to the network of traits that predispose a person to helpfulness. Preliminary indications are that those high in emotionality, empathy, and self-efficacy are most likely to be concerned and helpful (Bierhoff & others, 1991; Eisenberg & others, 1991; Tice & Baumeister, 1985). Third, personality influences how people react to particular situations (Carlo & others, 1991; Romer & others, 1986; Wilson & Petruska, 1984). High self-monitoring people, being attuned to other people's expectations, are especially helpful if they think helpfulness will be socially rewarded (White & Gerstein, 1987). Others' opinions matter less to internally guided, low self-monitoring people.

This interaction of person and situation also appears in the 172 studies that have compared the helpfulness of nearly 50,000 male and female subjects. After analyzing these results, Alice Eagly and Maureen Crowley (1986) report that when faced with potentially dangerous situations in which strangers need help (such as with a flat tire or a fall in a subway), men more often help. (Eagly and Crowley also report that among 6767 individuals who have received the Carnegie medal for heroism in saving human life, 90 percent have been men.) But in safer situations, such as volunteering to help with an experiment or spend time with retarded children, women are slightly more likely to help. Thus, the gender difference interacts with (depends on) the situation. And Eagly and Crowley suspect that if researchers were to study caring behavior in long-term, close relationships, rather than in short-term encounters with strangers, they would discover that women are significantly more helpful.

PERSONAL INFLUENCES: RELIGIOSITY

With Nazi submarines sinking ships faster than the Allied forces could replace them, the troop ship SS *Dorchester* steamed out of New York harbor with 902 men headed for Greenland (Elliott, 1989; Parachin, 1992). Among those leaving anxious families behind were four chaplains, Methodist preacher George Fox, Rabbi Alexander Goode, Catholic priest John Washington, and Reformed Church minister Clark Poling. Some 150 miles from their destination, submarine *U-456* caught the *Dorchester* in its cross hairs. Within moments of the torpedo's impact, stunned men were pouring out from their bunks as the ship began listing. With power cut off, the escort vessels, unaware of the unfolding tragedy, pushed on in the darkness. On board, chaos reigned as panicky men came up from the hold without life jackets and leapt into overcrowded lifeboats.

As the four chaplains arrived on the steeply sloping deck they began guiding the men to their boat stations. They opened a storage locker, distributed life jackets, and coaxed the men over the side. When Petty Officer John Mahoney turned back to retrieve his gloves, Rabbi Goode responded, "Never mind. I have two pairs." Only later did Mahoney realize that the Rabbi was not conveniently carrying an extra pair; he was giving up his own.

In the icy, oil-smeared water, Pvt. William Bednar heard the chaplains preaching courage and found the strength to swim out from under the ship until he reached a life raft. Still on board, Grady Clark watched in awe as the chaplains handed out the last life jacket and then, with ultimate selflessness, gave away their own. As Clark slipped into the waters he looked back at an unforgettable sight: the four chaplains standing—their arms linked—praying, in Latin, He-

The four chaplains' ultimate selflessness inspired this painting, which hangs in Pennsylvania's Chapel of the Four Chaplains near Valley Forge.

brew, and English. Other men, now serene, joined them in a huddle as the *Dorchester* slid beneath the sea. "It was the finest thing I have ever seen or hope to see this side of heaven," said John Ladd, another of the 230 survivors.

Does the chaplains' heroic example rightly suggest that faith somehow promotes courage and caring? Most studies of altruism explore spontaneous helping acts. Confronted with a minor emergency, people are intrinsically slightly more responsive (Trimble, 1993). Now, some researchers have also begun exploring planned helping—the sort of sustained helping provided by AIDS volunteers, Big Brother and Big Sister helpers, and supporters of campus service organizations (Amato, 1990; Clary & Snyder, 1991, 1993; Omoto & others, 1993). It is when making intentional choices about long-term helping that religiosity predicts altruism.

At Earlham College, Peter Benson and his colleagues (1980) found that religiously committed students volunteered more hours as tutors, relief workers, and campaigners for social justice than did religiously uncommitted students. Among the 12 percent of Americans whom George Gallup (1984) classified as "highly spiritually committed," 46 percent said they were presently working among the poor, the infirm, or the elderly—many more than the 22 percent among those "highly uncommitted" (Figure 14–5). In a follow-up Gallup survey (Colasanto, 1989), charitable and social service volunteering was reported by 28 percent of those who rated religion "not very important" in their lives and by 50 percent of those who rated it "very important." In another Gallup survey, 37 percent of those attending church yearly or less, and 76 percent of those attending weekly, reported thinking at least a "fair amount" about "your responsibility to the poor" (Wuthnow, 1994).

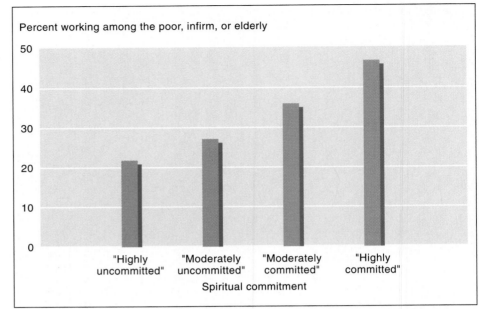

Percent working among the poor, infirm, or elderly

Spiritual commitment

"Highly uncommitted" — "Moderately uncommitted" — "Moderately committed" — "Highly committed"

■ **FIGURE 14–5**
Religion and long-term altruism. Those whom George Gallup (1984) classifies as "highly spiritually committed" are more likely to report working among the needy.

"Religion is the mother of philanthropy."
Emerson Andrew, *Attitudes toward Giving*, 1953

Moreover, Sam Levenson's jest—"When it comes to giving, some people stop at nothing"—is seldom true of church and synagogue members. In a 1987 Gallup survey, Americans who said they never attended church or synagogue reported giving away 1.1 percent of their incomes (Hodgkinson & others, 1990). Weekly attenders were two and a half times as generous. This 24 percent of the population gave 48 percent of all charitable contributions. The other three-quarters of Americans give the remaining half. Follow-up 1990 and 1992 Gallup surveys confirmed this pattern: In 1992, nonattenders reported giving 0.6 percent of their household income (Hodgkinson & Weitzman, 1990, 1992). Those attending religious services once or twice a month gave 1.6 percent. Weekly attenders gave twice again as much, 3.2 percent. The desire for social and personal rewards may help motivate such generosity (Batson & others, 1989). Nevertheless, the religious links with planned helping are significant.

SUMMING UP

Several situational influences work to inhibit or to encourage altruism. As the number of bystanders at an emergency increases, any given bystander is (1) less likely to notice the incident, (2) less likely to interpret it as an emergency, and (3) less likely to assume responsibility.

When are people most likely to help? (1) After observing someone else helping and (2) when not hurried. Personal influences such as moods also matter. After transgressing, people often become more willing to offer help, apparently hoping to relieve guilt or to restore self-image. Sad people also tend to be helpful. However, this feel bad–do good effect is not found in young children, thus suggesting that the inner rewards of helping are a product of later socialization. Finally, there is a striking feel good–do good effect: Happy people are helpful people.

In contrast to altruism's potent situational and mood determinants, personality test scores have served as only modest predictors of helping. However, new evidence indicates that some people are consistently more helpful than others and that the effect of personality or gender may depend on the situation. Religiosity predicts long-term altruism, as reflected in volunteerism and charitable contributions.

■ WHOM DO WE HELP?

*W*hom do we feel most compelled to help? Does gender matter? Does race? Type of need?

When considering the social-responsibility norm, we noted the tendency to help those most in need, those most deserving. In the subway experiment, the "victim" was helped more promptly when carrying a cane than when carrying a liquor bottle. Grocery store shoppers are more willing to give change to a woman who wants to buy milk than to one who wants to buy cookie dough (Bickman & Kamzan, 1973).

GENDER

If, indeed, perception of another's need strongly determines one's willingness to help, will women, if perceived as less competent and more dependent, *receive* more help than men? In the United States, this is indeed the case. Alice Eagly and Maureen Crowley (1986) located 35 studies that compared help received by male or female victims. (Virtually all the studies involved short-term encounters with strangers in need—the very situations in which people expect males to be chivalrous, note Eagly and Crowley.) When the potential helpers were males, female victims were more likely to receive aid. When the potential helpers were females, female and male victims were equally likely to receive aid. Several experiments have found that women with disabled cars (for example, with a flat tire) get many more offers of help than do men (Penner & others, 1973; Pomazal & Clore, 1973; West & others, 1975). Similarly, solo female hitchhikers receive far more offers of help than do solo males or couples (Pomazal & Clore, 1973; M. Snyder & others, 1974). Of course, men's chivalry toward lone women may be motivated by something other than altruism. So it won't come as a great surprise to learn that men more frequently help attractive women (Mims & others, 1975; Stroufe & others, 1977; West & Brown, 1975).

Women not only receive more offers of help in certain situations, they also seek more help. They are twice as likely to seek medical and psychiatric help. They are the majority of callers to radio counseling programs and clients of college counseling centers. They more often welcome help from friends. Arie Nadler (1991), a Tel Aviv University expert on help seeking, attributes this to gender differences in independence versus interdependence (Chapter 6).

SIMILARITY

Because similarity is conducive to liking (Chapter 13) and liking is conducive to helping, we are also biased toward those *similar* to us. The similarity bias applies to both dress and beliefs. Tim Emswiller and his fellow researchers

(1971) had confederates, dressed either conservatively or in counterculture garb, approach "straight" and "hip" Purdue University students seeking a dime for a phone call. Fewer than half the students did the favor for those dressed differently from themselves. Two-thirds did so for those dressed similarly. Similarly, Scottish shoppers were less willing to make change for someone if the person wore a T-shirt with a pro-gay slogan (Gray & others, 1991). On election day, 1972, Stuart Karabenick, Richard Lerner, and Michael Beecher (1973) had Nixon and McGovern workers "accidentally" drop campaign leaflets near voting places. The workers were helped by fewer than half the passers-by who preferred the other candidate but by more than two-thirds of those whose preference was the same.

Does the similarity bias extend to race? During the 1970s, researchers explored this question with confusing results: Some studies found a same-race bias (Benson & others, 1976; Clark, 1974; Franklin, 1974; Gaertner, 1973; Gaertner & Bickman, 1971; Sissons, 1981). Others found no bias (Gaertner, 1975; Lerner & Frank, 1974; Wilson & Donnerstein, 1979; Wispe & Freshley, 1971). And still others—especially those involving face-to-face situations—found a bias toward helping those of a different race (Dutton, 1971, 1973; Dutton & Lake, 1973; Katz & others, 1975). Is there a general rule that resolves these seemingly contradictory findings?

Few people want to appear prejudiced. Thus one possibility is that people favor their own race but keep this bias secret to preserve a positive image. If so, the same-race bias should appear only when failure to help someone of another race can be attributed to factors other than race. This is what happened in experiments by Samuel Gaertner and John Dovidio (1977, 1986). For example, University of Delaware White women were less willing to help a Black than a White "woman in distress" *if* their responsibility could be diffused among the bystanders ("I didn't help the Black woman because there were others who could"). When there were no other bystanders, the women were equally helpful to the Black and the White women. The rule seems to be: When norms for appropriate behavior are well defined, Whites don't discriminate; when norms are ambiguous or conflicting, racial similarity may bias responses.

For me, the laboratory came to life recently as I walked from a dinner meeting in Washington, D.C., to my hotel. On a deserted sidewalk, a well-dressed, distraught-seeming man about my age approached me and pled for a dollar. He explained that he had just come over from London and after visiting the Holocaust Museum had accidentally left his wallet in a taxi. So here he was stranded, now needing a $24 taxi fare to a friend's home in suburban D.C.

"So how's one dollar going to get you there?," I asked.

"I asked people for more, but no one would help me!," he nearly sobbed, "so I thought maybe if I asked for less I could collect taxi fare."

"But why not take the Metro?" I challenged.

"It stops about five miles from Greenbriar, where I need to go," he explained. "Oh my, how am I ever going to get there? If you could help me out, I will mail you back the money on Monday."

Here I was, as if a subject in an on-the-street altruism experiment. Having grown up in a city, and as a frequent visitor to New York and Chicago, I am accustomed to panhandling and have never rewarded it. But I also consider myself a caring person. Moreover, this fellow was unlike any panhandler I had ever met. He was sharply dressed. He was intelligent. He had a convincing story. And he looked like me! If he's lying, he's a slimeball, I said to myself, and giving him money would be stupid, naive, and rewarding slimeballism. If he's a truth-teller and I turn my back on him, I'm a slimeball.

He had asked for $1. I gave him $30, along with my name and address, which he gratefully took, and quickly disappeared into the night.

As I walked on, I began to realize—correctly as it turned out—that I had been a patsy. Having lived in Britain, why had I not tested his knowledge of England? Why had I not taken him to a phone booth to call his friend? Why had I at least not offered to pay a taxi driver and send him on his way, rather than give him the money? And why after a lifetime of resisting scams, had I succumbed to this one?

Sheepishly, because I like to think myself not influenced by ethnic stereotypes, I had to admit that it was not only his socially skilled, personal approach but also the mere fact of his similarity to me.

I n crisis or short-term needs situations, women receive more offers of help than men, especially from men. Women also seek more help. We are most likely to help those judged to both need and deserve it and those similar to us.

S U M M I N G   U P

■ HOW CAN WE INCREASE HELPING?

To increase helping, we can reverse the factors that inhibit helping. Or we can teach altruistic norms and socialize people to see themselves as helpful.

As social scientists, our goal is to understand human behavior, thus also suggesting ways to improve it. We therefore wonder how we might apply insights from research to increase altruism.

UNDOING THE RESTRAINTS ON HELPING

One way to promote altruism is to reverse those factors that inhibit it. Given that hurried, preoccupied people are less likely to help, can we think of ways to encourage them to slow down and turn their attention outward? If the presence of others diminishes each bystander's sense of responsibility, how can we enhance responsibility?

Reduce Ambiguity, Increase Responsibility

If Latané and Darley's decision tree (Figure 14–2) describes the dilemmas bystanders face, then assisting people to interpret an incident correctly and to assume responsibility should increase their involvement. Leonard Bickman and his colleagues (1975, 1977, 1979) tested this presumption in a series of experiments on crime reporting. In each, supermarket or bookstore shoppers witnessed a shoplifting. Some witnesses had seen signs that attempted to sensitize them to shoplifting and to inform them how to report it. But the signs had

Help-giving increases among people who expect to see one another again. Here leaflets offering crisis counseling are distributed to commuters on the 5:33 after the Long Island Railroad massacre in December 1993, when a gunman on a rampage killed 5 commuters on that train and injured 19.

little effect. Other witnesses heard a bystander interpret the incident: "Say, look at her. She's shoplifting. She put that into her purse." (The bystander then left to look for a lost child.) Still others heard this person add, "We saw it. We should report it. It's our responsibility." Both face-to-face comments substantially boosted reporting of the crime.

The potency of personal influence is no longer in doubt. Robert Foss (1978) surveyed several hundred blood donors and found that neophyte donors, unlike veterans, were usually there at someone's personal invitation. Leonard Jason and his collaborators (1984) confirmed that personal appeals for blood donation are much more effective than posters and media announcements—*if* the personal appeals come from friends. Nonverbal appeals can also be effective when they are personalized. Mark Snyder and his co-workers (1974) found that hitchhikers doubled the number of ride offers by looking drivers straight in the eye. A personal approach, as my panhandler knew, makes one feel less anonymous, more responsible.

Henry Solomon and Linda Solomon (1978; Solomon & others, 1981) confirmed the benefits of reducing anonymity. They found that bystanders who had identified themselves to one another—by name, age, and so forth—were more likely to offer aid to a sick person than were anonymous bystanders. Similarly, when a female experimenter caught the eye of another shopper and gave her a warm smile prior to stepping on an elevator, that shopper was far more likely than other shoppers to offer help when the experimenter later said, "Damn. I've left my glasses. Can anyone tell me what floor the umbrellas are on?" Even a trivial momentary conversation with someone. ("Excuse me, aren't you Suzie Spear's sister?" "No, I'm not") dramatically increased the person's later helpfulness.

Helpfulness also increases when one expects to meet the victim and other witnesses again. Using a laboratory intercom system, Jody Gottlieb and Charles

Carver (1980) led University of Miami students to believe they were discussing problems of college living with other students. (Actually, the other discussants were tape-recorded.) When one of the supposed fellow discussants had a choking fit and cried out for help, she was helped most quickly by subjects who believed they would soon be meeting the discussants face-to-face. In short, anything that personalizes bystanders—a personal request, eye contact, stating one's name, anticipation of interaction—increases willingness to help.

Personal treatment makes bystanders more self-aware and therefore more attuned to their own altruistic ideals. Recall from earlier chapters that people made self-aware by acting in front of a mirror or TV camera exhibit increased consistency between attitudes and actions. By contrast, "deindividuated" people are less responsible. Thus, circumstances that promote self-awareness—name tags, being watched and evaluated, undistracted quiet—should also increase helping. Shelley Duval, Virginia Duval, and Robert Neely (1979) confirmed this. They showed some University of Southern California women their own image on a TV screen or had them complete a biographical questionnaire just before giving them a chance to contribute time and money to people in need. Those made self-aware contributed more. Similarly, pedestrians who have just had their picture taken by someone became more likely to help another pedestrian pick up dropped envelopes (Hoover & others, 1983). Self-aware people more often put their ideals into practice.

Guilt and Concern for Self-Image

Earlier we noted that people who feel guilty will act to reduce guilt and restore their self-worth. Can heightening people's awareness of their transgressions therefore increase desire to help? A Reed College research team led by Richard Katzev (1978) wondered. So when visitors to the Portland Art Museum disobeyed a "Please do not touch" sign, experimenters reprimanded some of them: "Please don't touch the objects. If everyone touches them, they will deteriorate." Likewise, when visitors to the Portland Zoo fed unauthorized food to the bears, some of them were admonished with, "Hey, don't feed unauthorized food to the animals. Don't you know it could hurt them?" In both cases, 58 percent of the now guilt-laden subjects shortly thereafter offered help to another experimenter who had "accidentally" dropped something. Of those not reprimanded, only one-third helped.

People also care about their public image. When Robert Cialdini and his colleagues (1975) asked some of their Arizona State University students to chaperon delinquent children on a zoo trip, only 32 percent agreed to do so. With other students the questioner first made a very large request—that the students commit two years as volunteer counselors to delinquent children. After getting the **door-in-the-face** in response to this request (all refused), the questioner then counteroffered with the chaperoning request, saying, in effect, "OK, if you won't do that, would you do just this much?" With this technique, nearly twice as many—56 percent—agreed to help.

Cialdini and David Schroeder (1976) offer another practical way to trigger concern for self-image: Ask for a contribution so small that it's hard to say no without feeling like a Scrooge. Cialdini (1995) discovered this when a United Way canvasser came to his door. As she solicited his contribution, he was mentally preparing his refusal—until she said magic words that demolished his fi-

Door-in-the-face technique: A strategy for gaining a concession. After someone first turns down a large request (the door-in-the-face), the same requester counteroffers with a more reasonable request.

nancial excuse: "Even a penny will help." "I had been neatly finessed into compliance," recalled Cialdini. "And there was another interesting feature of our exchange as well. When I stopped coughing (I really had choked on my attempted rejection), I gave her *not* the penny she had mentioned but the amount I usually allot to legitimate charity solicitors. At that, she thanked me, smiled innocently, and moved on."

Was Cialdini's response atypical? To find out, he and Schroeder had a solicitor approach suburbanites. When the solicitor said, "I'm collecting money for the American Cancer Society," 29 percent contributed an average of $1.44 each. When the solicitor added, "Even a penny will help," 50 percent contributed, an average of $1.54 each. When James Weyant (1984) repeated this experiment, he found similar results: The "even a penny will help" boosted the number contributing from 39 to 57 percent. And when 6000 people were solicited by mail for the American Cancer Society, those asked for small amounts were more likely to give—and gave no less on average—than those asked for larger amounts (Weyant & Smith, 1987). When approaching previous donors, bigger requests (within reason) do elicit bigger donations (Doob & McLaughlin, 1989). But with door-to-door solicitation, there is more success with requests for small contributions, which are difficult to turn down and still allow the person to maintain an altruistic self-image.

Labeling people as helpful can also strengthen a helpful self-image. After they had made a charitable contribution, Robert Kraut (1973) told some Connecticut women, "you are a generous person." Two weeks later, these women were more willing than those not so labeled to contribute to a different charity. Likewise, Angelo Strenta and William DeJong (1981) told some students a personality test revealed that "you are a kind, thoughtful person." These students were later more likely than others to be kind and thoughtful toward a confederate who dropped a stack of computer cards.

SOCIALIZING ALTRUISM

If we can learn altruism, then how might we teach it? Here are three ways.

Teaching Moral Inclusion

Rescuers of Jews in Nazi Europe, leaders of the American antislavery movement in the 1840s and 1850s, and medical missionaries share at least one thing in common: They include people who differ from them within the human circle to which their moral values and rules of justice apply. These people are *morally inclusive*, as illustrated by one rescuer who faked a pregnancy on behalf of a pregnant hidden Jew—thus including the soon-to-be-born child within the circle of her own children's identities (Fogelman, 1994).

Moral exclusion—omitting certain people from one's circle of moral concern—has the opposite effect. It justifies all sorts of harm, from discrimination to genocide (Opotow, 1990; Staub, 1990; Tyler & Lind, 1990). Exploitation or cruelty becomes acceptable, even appropriate, toward those we regard as undeserving or as nonpersons. The Nazis excluded Jews from their moral community; so does anyone who participates in enslavement, death squads, or torture. To a lesser extent, moral exclusion describes any of us who concentrate our concerns, favors, and financial inheritance upon "our people" (for example, our children) to the exclusion of others.

A first step toward socializing altruism is therefore to counter the natural ingroup bias favoring kin and tribe by broadening the range of people whose well-being concerns us. Daniel Batson (1983) notes how religious teachings do this. They extend the reach of kin-linked altruism by urging "brotherly and sisterly" love toward all "children of God" in the whole human "family." If everyone is part of our family, then everyone has a moral claim on us. The boundaries between "we" and "they" fade. Nurturing children to have a secure sense of self also helps, by enabling them to accept social diversity without feeling threatened (Deutsch, 1990).

Modeling Altruism

Earlier we learned that when we see unresponsive bystanders, we, too, are unlikely to help. If we see someone helping, we are more likely to offer assistance. A similar modeling effect occurred within the families of European Christians who risked their lives to rescue Jews in the 1930s and 1940s and of the civil rights activists of the late 1950s. In both cases these exceptional altruists had warm and close relationships with at least one parent who was, similarly, a strong "moralist" or committed to humanitarian causes (London, 1970; Oliner & Oliner, 1988; Rosenhan, 1970). Their family—and often their friends and church—had taught them the norm of helping and caring for others. This "prosocial value orientation" led them to include people from other groups in their circle of moral concern and to feel responsible for others' welfare (Staub, 1989, 1991, 1992). People reared by extremely punitive parents, as were many delinquents, chronic criminals, and Nazi mass murderers, show much less of the empathy and principled caring that typify altruistic rescuers.

Modeling also helps increase blood donations, as Irwin Sarason and his colleagues (1991) discovered after soliciting nearly 10,000 students at 66 high schools across America. The researchers compared students who experienced the procedure that blood centers believed most effective in recruiting students with students who viewed a slide show that included 38 photos of high school blood drive scenes. Those exposed to the modeling were 17 percent more likely to donate.

Do television's positive models promote helping, much as its aggressive portrayals promote aggression? Television's prosocial models have actually had even greater effects than its antisocial models. Susan Hearold (1986) statistically combined 108 comparisons of prosocial programs with neutral programs or no program. She found that, on average, "If the viewer watched prosocial

> **Moral exclusion:** The perception of certain individuals or groups as outside the boundary within which one applies moral values and rules of fairness. Moral *inclusion* is regarding others as within one's circle of moral concern.

> *"We consider humankind our family."*
> Parliament of the World Religions, *Towards a Global Ethic,* 1993

Children can learn to be altruistic, friendly and self-controlled by looking at television programs depicting such behavior patterns."
National Institute of Mental Health, *Television and Behavior*, 1982

programs instead of neutral programs, he would [at least temporarily] be elevated from the 50th to the 74th percentile in prosocial behavior—typically altruism."

In one such study, researchers Lynette Friedrich and Aletha Stein (1973; Stein & Friedrich, 1972) showed preschool children "Mister Rogers' Neighborhood" episodes each day for four weeks as part of their nursery school program. ("Mister Rogers" is an educational program designed to enhance young children's social and emotional development.) During this viewing period, children from less educated homes became more cooperative, helpful, and likely to state their feelings. In a follow-up study, kindergartners who viewed four "Mister Rogers" programs were able to state its prosocial content, both on a test and in puppet play (Friedrich & Stein, 1975; also Coates & others, 1976).

Attributing Helpful Behavior to Altruistic Motives

Overjustification effect:
See Chapter 4.

Another clue to socializing altruism comes from research on the overjustification effect: When the justification for an act is more than sufficient, the person may attribute the act to the extrinsic justification rather than to an inner motive. Rewarding people for doing what they would do anyway therefore undermines intrinsic motivation. We can state the principle positively: By providing people with just enough justification to prompt a good deed (weaning them from bribes and threats when possible), we may increase their pleasure in doing such deeds on their own.

Daniel Batson and his associates (1978, 1979) put the overjustification phenomenon to work. In several experiments they found that University of Kansas students felt most altruistic after they agreed to help someone without payment or implied social pressure. When pay had been offered or social pressures were present, people felt less altruistic after helping. In another experiment, the researchers led students to attribute a helpful act to compliance ("I guess we really don't have a choice") or to compassion ("The guy really needs help"). Later, when the students were asked to volunteer their time to a local service agency, 25 percent of those who had been led to perceive their previous helpfulness as mere compliance now volunteered; of those led to see themselves as compassionate, 60 percent volunteered. The moral? Simple: When people wonder, "Why am I helping?" it's best if the circumstances enable them to answer, "Because help was needed, and I am a caring, giving, helpful person."

As you may recall from Chapter 4, rewards undermine intrinsic motivation when they function as controlling bribes. An unanticipated compliment, however, can make people feel competent and worthy. When Joe is coerced with, "If you quit being chicken and give blood, we'll win the fraternity prize for most donations," he isn't likely to attribute his donation to altruism. When Jocelyn is rewarded with, "That's terrific that you'd choose to take an hour out of such a busy week to give blood," she's more likely to walk away with an altruistic self-image—and thus to contribute again (Piliavin & others, 1982; Thomas & Batson, 1981; Thomas & others, 1981).

Learning about Altruism

Researchers have found another way to boost altruism, one that provides a happy conclusion to this chapter. Some social psychologists worry that as people become more aware of social psychology's findings, their behavior may

BEHAVIOR AND ATTITUDES AMONG RESCUERS OF JEWS

Goodness, like evil, often evolves in small steps. The Gentiles who saved Jews often began with a small commitment—to hide someone for a day or two. Having taken that step, they began to see themselves differently, as people who help. Then they became more intensely involved. Given control of a confiscated Jewish-owned factory, Oskar Schindler began by doing small favors for his Jewish workers, who were earning him handsome profits. Gradually, he took greater and greater risks to protect them. He got permission to set up workers' housing next to the factory. He rescued individuals separated from their families and reunited loved ones. Finally, as the Russians advanced, he saved some 1200 Jews by setting up a fake factory in his home town, and taking along his entire group of "skilled workers" to staff it. (Rappoport & Kren, 1993).

Others, like Raoul Wallenberg, began by agreeing to a personal request for help, and ended up repeatedly risking their lives. Wallenberg became Swedish ambassador to Hungary, where he saved tens of thousands of Hungarian Jews from extermination at Auschwitz. One of those given protective identity papers was six-year-old Ervin Staub (1993), now a University of Massachusetts social psychologist whose experience set him on a lifelong mission to understand why some people perpetrate evil, some stand by, and some heroically help.

Munich, 1948: Oskar Schindler with some of the Jews he saved from the Nazis during World War II.

change, thus invalidating the findings (Gergen, 1982). Will learning about the factors that inhibit altruism reduce their influence? Sometimes, such "enlightenment" is not our problem but one of our goals.

Experiments with University of Montana students by Arthur Beaman and his colleagues (1978) reveal that once people understand why the presence of bystanders inhibits helping, they become more likely to help in group situations. The researchers used a lecture to inform some students how bystander inaction can affect the interpretation of an emergency and feelings of responsibility. Other students heard either a different lecture or no lecture at all. Two weeks later, as part of a different experiment in a different location, the participants found themselves walking (with an unresponsive confederate) past someone slumped over or past a person sprawled beneath a bicycle. Of those who had not heard the helping lecture, a fourth paused to offer help; twice as many of those "enlightened" did so. Having read this chapter, you, too, have perhaps changed. As you come to understand what influences people's responses, will your attitudes and your behavior be the same?

Coincidentally, shortly before I wrote the last paragraph, a former student, now living in Washington, D.C., stopped by. She mentioned that she recently found herself part of a stream of pedestrians striding past a man lying unconscious on the sidewalk. "It took my mind back to our social psych class and the accounts of why people fail to help in such situations. Then I thought, well, if I just walk by, too, who's going to help him?" So she made a call to an emergency help number and waited with the victim—and other bystanders who now joined her—until help arrived.

Another student, happening upon a drunk man beating up a street person near midnight in a Vienna subway station, flowed by with the crowd.

> Finally, I was convinced enough of the truth we learned in social psychology to go back and pull the drunk off the street person. Suddenly he was very mad at me and chased me through the subway until police came, arrested him, and got an ambulance for the victim. It was pretty exciting and made me feel good. But the coolest part was how a little insight into social-psychological aspects of our own behavior can help us overcome the power of the situation and change our predicted actions.

S U M M I N G   U P

Research suggests that we can enhance helpfulness in two ways. First, reverse those factors that inhibit helping. We can take steps to reduce the ambiguity of an emergency situation or to increase feelings of responsibility. We can even use reprimands or the door-in-the-face technique to evoke guilt feelings or a concern for self-image.

Second, we can teach altruism. Research into television's portrayals of prosocial models shows the medium's power to teach positive behavior. Children who view helpful behavior tend to act helpfully.

If we want to coax altruistic behavior from people, we should remember the overjustification effect: When we coerce good deeds, with either excessive rewards or threats, intrinsic love of the activity often diminishes. If we provide people with enough justification for them to decide to do good, but not much more, they will attribute their behavior to their own altruistic motivation and henceforth be more willing to help.

■ FOR FURTHER READING

Clark, M. S. (Ed.) (1991). *Prosocial behavior.* Newbury Park, CA: Sage. Prominent researchers discuss their research on the causes and effects of helping.

Fogelman, E. (1994). *Conscience and courage: Rescuers of Jews during the Holocaust.* New York: Doubleday Anchor. In life and death situations, who helps? Under what circumstances? Draws from interviews with 300 rescuers.

Gilkey, L. (1966). *Shantung compound.* New York: Harper & Row. A first-person account of human nature laid bare among 1800 westerners crowded into a Japanese internment camp during World War II. Self-centeredness prevailed but was interspersed by incidents of selfless altruism.

Hunt, M. (1990). *The compassionate beast: What science is discovering about the humane side of humankind.* New York: William Morrow. Drawing on extensive interviews with leading researchers, Hunt offers a personalized and provocative tour through the new altruism research.

Oliner, S. P., & Oliner, P. M. (1988). *The altruistic personality: Rescuers of Jews in Nazi Europe.* New York: The Free Press. From interviews with over 400 European rescuers and nonrescuers, the Oliners explore the moral and social roots of heroic behavior.

Schroeder, D. A., Penner, L. A., Dovidio, J. F., & Piliavin, J. A. (1995). *The social psychology of helping and altruism: Problems and puzzles.* New York: McGraw-Hill. Four leading researchers offer the first textbook on prosocial behavior—when and why people help.

CONFLICT AND PEACEMAKING

There is a speech that has been spoken in many languages by the leaders of many countries. It goes like this: "The intentions of our country are entirely peaceful. Yet, we are also aware that other nations, with their new weapons, threaten us. Thus we must defend ourselves against attack. By so doing, we shall protect our way of life and preserve the peace" (L. F. Richardson, 1969). Almost every nation claims concern only for peace but, mistrusting other nations, arms itself in self-defense. The result: a world in which developing countries have 8 soldiers for every doctor, a world with 51,000 nuclear weapons stockpiled, a world that spends $2 billion per day on arms and armies (Sivard, 1991).

Conflict:
A perceived incompatibility of actions or goals.

The elements of such **conflict** (a perceived incompatibility of actions or goals) are similar at all levels, from nations in an arms race, to Bosnian Serbs warring against Muslims, to baseball players and owners disputing salaries, to a feuding married couple. Whether their perceptions are accurate or inaccurate, people in conflict sense that one side's gain is the other's loss. "I'd like the music off." "I'd like it on." "We want more pay." "We can't give it to you." "We want peace and security." "So do we, but you threaten us."

A relationship or an organization without conflict is probably apathetic. Conflict signifies involvement, commitment, and caring. If understood, if recognized, it can stimulate renewed and improved human relations. Without conflict, people seldom face and resolve their problems.

Peace, in its most positive sense, is more than the suppression of open conflict, more than a tense, fragile, surface calmness. Peace is the outcome of a creatively managed conflict, one in which the parties reconcile their perceived differences and reach genuine accord. "We got our increased pay. You got your increased profit. Now we're helping each other achieve our aspirations."

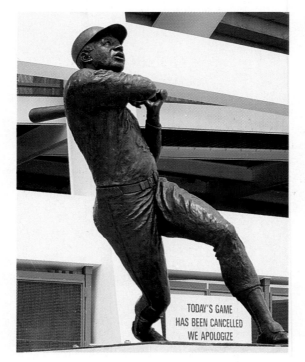

Conflicts, as between baseball players and owners, can be mutually destructive. But when the parties find a way to help each other attain their goals, the result can also be constructive.

■ CONFLICT

*W*hat kindles conflict? Social-psychological studies have identified several in- gredients. What's striking (and what simplifies our task) is that these in- gredients are common to all levels of social conflict, whether interpersonal, inter- group, or international.

SOCIAL DILEMMAS

Several of the problems that most threaten our human future—nuclear arms, the greenhouse effect, pollution, overpopulation, natural resource depletion— arise as various parties pursue their self-interest but do so, ironically, to their collective detriment. Anyone can think: "It would cost me lots to buy expen- sive pollution controls. Besides, by itself my pollution is trivial." Many others reason similarly, and the result is befouled air and water.

In some societies individuals benefit by having many children who, they as- sume, can assist with the family tasks and provide security in the parents' old age. But when most families have many children, the result is the collective devastation of overpopulation. Thus, choices that are individually rewarding become collectively punishing. We therefore have an urgent dilemma: How can we reconcile the individuals' well-being, including their right to pursue their personal interests, with the community's well-being?

To isolate and illustrate this dilemma, social psychologists have used labo- ratory games that expose the heart of many real social conflicts. By showing us how well-meaning people become trapped in mutually destructive behav- ior, they illuminate some fascinating, yet troubling, paradoxes of human exis- tence. Consider two examples: the Prisoner's Dilemma and the Tragedy of the Commons.

The Prisoner's Dilemma

One dilemma derives from an anecdote concerning two suspects questioned separately by the district attorney (Rapoport, 1960). They are jointly guilty; however, the DA has only enough evidence to convict them of a lesser offense. So the DA creates an incentive for each to confess privately: If one confesses and the other doesn't, the DA will grant the confessor immunity (and will use the confession to convict the other of a maximum offense). If both confess, each will receive a moderate sentence. If neither confesses, each will receive a light sentence. The matrix of Figure 15–1 summarizes the choices. Faced with such a dilemma, would you confess?

To minimize their own sentence, many would, despite the fact that mutual confession elicits more severe sentences than mutual nonconfession. Note from the matrix that no matter what the other prisoner decides, each is better off confessing. If the other confesses, one then gets a moderate sentence instead of a severe one. If the other does not confess, one goes free. Of course, each pris- oner reasons the same way. Hence, the social trap.

In some 2000 studies (Dawes, 1991), university students have faced varia- tions of the Prisoner's Dilemma with the outcomes being not prison terms but

name from the centrally located pasture area in old English towns, but the "commons" can be air, water, whales, cookies, or any shared and limited re- source. If all use the resource in moderation, it may replenish itself as rapidly as it's harvested. The grass will grow, the whales will reproduce, and the cookie jar gets restocked. If not, there occurs a tragedy of the commons.

chips, money, or course points. As Figure 15–2 illustrates, on any given decision, a person is better off defecting (because such behavior exploits the other's cooperation or protects against the other's exploitation). However—and here's the rub—by not cooperating, both parties end up far worse off than if they trusted each other and gained a joint profit. This dilemma often traps each

BEHIND THE SCENES

I am brash enough to believe that laboratory studies of conflict can illumine our understanding of the dynamics of war, peace, and social justice. From small groups to nations, the social processes appear similar. Thus social psychologists who study conflict are in much the same position as the astronomers. We cannot conduct true experiments with large-scale social events. But we can identify the conceptual similarities between the large scale and the small, as the astronomers have between the planets and Newton's apple. By experimenting with small-scale social situations, we may thus be able to understand, predict, and influence large-scale social processes. That is why the games people play as subjects in our laboratory may advance our understanding of war, peace, and social justice.

MORTON DEUTSCH, *Columbia University*

Imagine 100 farmers surrounding a commons capable of sustaining 100 cows. When each grazes one cow, the common feeding ground is optimally used. But then someone reasons: "If I put a second cow in the pasture, I'll double my output, minus the mere 1 percent overgrazing." So this farmer adds a second cow. So do each of the other farmers. The inevitable result? The Tragedy of the Commons—a grassless mud field.

Many real predicaments parallel this story. Environmental pollution is the sum of many minor pollutions, each of which benefits the individual polluters much more than they could benefit themselves (and the environment) if they stopped polluting. We litter public places—dorm lounges, parks, zoos—but keep our personal spaces clean. And we deplete our natural resources because the immediate personal benefits of, say, taking a long, hot shower outweigh the seemingly inconsequential costs. Whalers knew others would exploit the whales if they didn't and that taking a few whales would hardly diminish the species. Therein lay the tragedy. Everybody's business (conservation) became nobody's business.

The elements of the commons dilemma have been isolated in laboratory games. Put yourself in the place of Arizona State University students playing Julian Edney's Nuts Game (1979). You and several others sit around a shallow bowl that initially has 10 metal nuts. The experimenter explains that your goal is to accumulate as many nuts as possible. Each of you at any time may take as many as you want, and every 10 seconds the number of nuts remaining in the bowl will be doubled. Would you leave the nuts in the bowl to regenerate, thus producing a greater harvest for all?

Likely not. Unless they were given time to devise and agree upon a conservation strategy, 65 percent of Edney's groups never reached the first 10-second replenishment. Often the people knocked the bowl on the floor grabbing for their share.

Is such individualism uniquely American? Kaori Sato (1987) gave students in a more collective culture, Japan, opportunities to harvest—for actual money—trees from a simulated forest. When the students shared equally the costs of planting the forest, the result was like those in western cultures. More than half the trees were harvested before they had grown to the most profitable size.

Edney's nut bowl and Sato's forest remind me of the cookie jar in our home. What we *should* have done is conserve cookies during the interval between weekly restockings, so that each day we could each munch two or three. Lacking regulation and fearing that other family members would soon deplete the resource, what we actually did was maximize our individual cookie consumption by downing one after the other. The result: Within 24 hours the cookie glut ended, the jar sat empty, and we again awaited its replenishment.

The Prisoner's Dilemma and the Tragedy of the Commons games have several similar features. First, both tempt people to explain their own behavior situationally ("I had to protect myself against exploitation by my opponent") and to explain their partners' behavior dispositionally ("she was greedy," "he was untrustworthy"). Most never realize that their counterparts are viewing them with the same fundamental attribution error.

Second, motives often change. At first, people are eager to make some easy money, then to minimize their losses, and finally to save face and avoid defeat (Brockner & others, 1982; Teger, 1980). These shifting motives are strikingly similar to President Johnson's apparently shifting motives during the buildup of the 1960s Vietnam war. At first, his speeches described America's concern for democracy, freedom, and justice. As the conflict escalated, his expressed concern became protecting America's honor and avoiding the national humiliation of losing a war.

Third, most real-life conflicts, like the Prisoner's Dilemma and Commons Dilemma, are **non-zero-sum games**. The two sides' profits and losses need not add up to zero. Both can win; both can lose. Each game pits the immediate interests of individuals against the well-being of the group. Each is a diabolical

Non-zero-sum games: Games in which outcomes need not sum to zero. With cooperation, both can win; with competition, both can lose. (Also called *mixed-motive situations*.)

When after eight years of war, more than a million casualties, and ruined economies, Iran and Iraq finally laid down their arms, the border over which they had fought was exactly the same as when they started.

social trap that shows how, even when individuals behave "rationally," harm can result. No malicious person planned for Los Angeles to be smothered in smog, nor for the horrendous destruction of the Bosnian conflict, nor for the earth's atmosphere to be warmed by a blanket of carbon dioxide.

Not all self-serving behavior leads to collective doom. In a plentiful commons—as in the world of the eighteenth-century capitalist economist Adam Smith (1776, p. 18)—individuals who seek to maximize their own profit may also give the community what it needs: "It is not from the benevolence of the butcher, the brewer, or the baker, that we expect our dinner," he observed, "but from their regard to their own interest."

Resolving Social Dilemmas

In those situations that are indeed social traps, how can we induce people to cooperate for their mutual betterment? Research with the laboratory dilemmas has revealed several methods for promoting cooperation.

Regulation

Reflecting on the Tragedy of the Commons, Garrett Hardin (1968) wrote: "Ruin is the destination to which all men rush, each pursuing his own best interest in a society that believes in the freedom of the commons. Freedom in a commons brings ruin to all." Consider: If taxes were entirely voluntary, how many would pay their full share? Surely, many would not, which is why modern societies do not depend on voluntary charity to meet their needs for social and military security.

We also develop laws and regulations for our common good. An International Whaling Commission sets an agreed-upon "harvest" that enables whales to regenerate. The United States and the Soviet Union mutually commit themselves to the Atmospheric Test Ban Treaty that reduces radiation in our common air. When enforced, environmental regulations equalize the burden for all; no steel company need fear that other companies will gain a competitive advantage by disregarding their environmental responsibilities.

Similarly, participants in laboratory games often seek ways to regulate their behavior for what they know to be their common good. Players of the Nuts Game may agree to take but 1 or 2 nuts every 10 seconds, leaving the rest to regenerate, or they may elect a leader to decide each person's share (Messick & others, 1983; Samuelson & others, 1984).

But in everyday life, regulation has costs—costs of administering and enforcing the regulations, costs of diminished personal freedom. A volatile political question thus arises: At what point does a regulation's cost exceed its benefits?

Small Is Beautiful

There is another way to resolve social dilemmas: Make the group small. In small commons, each person feels more responsible, effective, and identified with the group's success (Kerr, 1989). Although group identification occurs more readily in small groups, anything that gives people a "we feeling"—even just a few minutes of discussion or just believing that one shares similarities with others in the group—will increase cooperation (Brewer, 1987; Orbell & others, 1988).

In small rather than large groups, individuals are also more likely to take no more than their equal share of available resources (Allison & others, 1992). On the Puget Sound island where I grew up, our small neighborhood shared a communal water supply. On hot summer days when the reservoir ran low, a light came on, signaling our 15 families to conserve. Recognizing our responsibility to one another, and feeling like our conservation really mattered, each of us conserved. Never did the reservoir run dry.

In a much larger commons—say, a city—voluntary conservation is less successful. Because the harm one does diffuses across many others, each individual can rationalize away personal accountability. Some political theorists and social psychologists therefore argue that, where feasible, the commons should be divided into smaller territories (Edney, 1980). In his 1902 *Mutual Aid*, the Russian revolutionary Pyotr Kropotkin set down a vision of small communities making decisions for the benefit of all by consensus, thereby reducing the need for central government (Gould, 1988).

"For that which is common to the greatest number has the least care bestowed upon it."
Aristotle

Communication

To escape a social trap, people must communicate. In the laboratory, group communication sometimes degenerates into threats and name calling (Deutsch & Krauss, 1960). More often, communication enables groups to cooperate more—much more (Bornstein & others, 1988, 1989; Jorgenson & Papciak, 1981). Discussing the dilemma forges a group identity, which enhances concern for the group's welfare. More important, discussion enables people to commit themselves to cooperation (Kerr & Kaufman-Gilliland, 1994).

A clever experiment by Robyn Dawes (1980, 1994) illustrates. Imagine that an experimenter offered you and six strangers each a choice: You could each have $6. Or you could give it to the others, knowing that the experimenter would double your gift and allocate $2 to each of the strangers. No one will

Distrust fuels conflict. Members of the Michigan Militia, distrusting the United States government, prepare to defend themselves against possible government intrusion into their lives and the confiscation of their weapons.

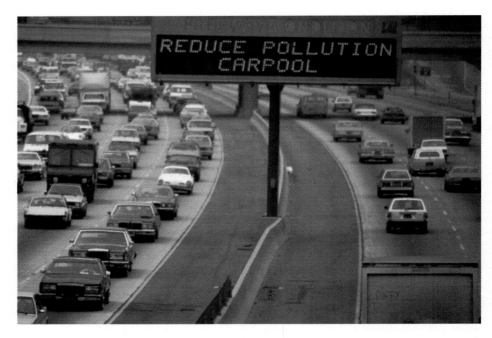

To change behavior, many cities have changed the payoff matrix. Fast carpool-only lanes increase the benefits of carpooling and the costs of driving alone.

"My own belief is that Russian and Chinese behavior is as much influenced by suspicion of our intentions as ours is by suspicion of theirs. This would mean that we have great influence on their behavior—that, by treating them as hostile, we assure their hostility."
U.S. Senator J. William Fulbright
(1971)

be told whether you chose to give or keep. So, if all seven cooperate and give, everyone pockets $12. If you alone keep the $6 and the others give, you pocket $18. If you give and the others keep, you pocket nothing. Clearly, cooperation is mutually advantageous, but it requires sacrifice and risk. Dawes found that, without discussion, about 30 percent of people gave; with discussion, about 80 percent gave.

Open, clear, forthright communication also reduces mistrust. Without communication, those who expect others not to cooperate usually refuse to cooperate themselves (Messé & Sivacek, 1979; Pruitt & Kimmel, 1977). One who mistrusts almost has to be uncooperative (to protect against exploitation). Noncooperation, in turn, feeds further mistrust ("What else could I do? It's a dog-eat-dog world"). In experiments, communication reduces mistrust, enabling people to reach agreements that lead to their common betterment.

Changing the Payoffs

Cooperation rises when experimenters change the payoff matrix to make cooperation more rewarding, exploitation less rewarding (Komorita & Barth, 1985; Pruitt & Rubin, 1986). Changing payoffs also helps resolve actual dilemmas. In some cities, freeways clog and skies smog because people prefer the convenience of driving themselves directly to work. Each knows that one more car does not add noticeably to the congestion and pollution. To alter the personal cost-benefit calculations, many cities now give carpoolers incentives, such as designated freeway lanes or reduced tolls.

Appeals to Altruistic Norms

In Chapter 14, we saw how increasing people's feelings of responsibility for others boosts altruism. Can we therefore assume that appeals to altruistic motives will prompt people to act for the common good?

The evidence is mixed. On the one hand, it seems that just *knowing* the dire consequences of noncooperation has little effect. In laboratory games, people realize that their self-serving choices are mutually destructive, yet they continue to make them (Cass & Edney, 1978; Edney & Harper, 1978). Outside the laboratory, warnings of doom and appeals to conserve have brought little response. Shortly after taking office in 1976, President Carter declared that America's response to the energy crisis should be "the moral equivalent of war" and urged conservation. The following summer, Americans consumed more gasoline than ever before. *Knowing* the good does not necessarily lead to *doing* the good.

Still, most people do adhere to norms of social responsibility, reciprocity, equity, and keeping one's commitments (Kerr, 1992). The problem is how to tap such feelings. When permitted to communicate, participants in laboratory games frequently appeal to the social-responsibility norm: "If you defect on the rest of us, you're going to have to live with it for the rest of your life" (Dawes & others, 1977). Noting this, researcher Robyn Dawes (1980) and his associates gave people a short sermon about group benefits, exploitation, and ethics. Then the people played a dilemma game. The appeal worked: People were convinced to forgo immediate personal gain for the common good. (Recall, too, from Chapter 14, the disproportionate volunteerism and charitable contributions by people who regularly hear sermons in churches and synagogues.)

Could such appeals work in large-scale dilemmas? Jeffery Scott Mio and his colleagues (1993) found that, after reading about the commons dilemma (as you have), theatre patrons littered less than patrons who read about voting. Moreover, when cooperation obviously serves the public good, one can usefully appeal to the social-responsibility norm (Lynn & Oldenquist, 1986). Basketball players will pass up a good shot to offer a teammate a better shot. In the struggle for civil rights, many marchers willingly agreed, for the sake of the larger group, to suffer harassment, beatings, and jail. In wartime, people make great personal sacrifices for the good of their group. As Winston Churchill said of the Battle of Britain, the actions of the Royal Air Force pilots were genuinely altruistic: A great many people owed a great deal to those who flew into battle knowing there was a high probability they would not return.

To summarize, we can minimize destructive entrapment in social dilemmas by establishing rules that regulate self-serving behavior, by keeping groups small, by enabling people to communicate, by changing payoffs to make cooperation more rewarding, and by invoking altruistic norms.

"Never in the field of human conflict was so much owed by so many to so few."
Sir Winston Churchill, House of Commons, August 20, 1940

COMPETITION

Hostilities often arise when groups compete for jobs and housing; when interests clash, conflict erupts. This was powerfully evident in the Shantung compound, a World War II internment camp into which the invading Japanese military herded foreigners residing in China. According to one of those interned, Langdon Gilkey (1966), the need to distribute the barely adequate food and floor space provoked frequent conflicts among the doctors, missionaries, lawyers, professors, businesspeople, junkies, and prostitutes. The effects of competition for space, jobs, and political power have been tragically evident in Northern Ireland, where between 1969 and 1994 hostilities between the ruling Protestant majority and the Catholic minority claimed 3200 lives. (A comparable population proportion would number close to 400,000 in the United States, 40,000 in Canada, and 27,000 in Australia.)

But does competition by itself provoke hostile conflict? To find out, we could experiment. Craig Anderson and Melissa Morrow (1995) did so by having people alternate with someone else playing Nintendo's Super Mario Brothers. Half played as competition (comparing points), half as cooperation (combining points). Given the competitive mindset, people unnecessarily killed (by stomping or fireballing) 61 percent more of the game creatures. Competition primed aggression.

Will competition also trigger destructive behavior under more realistic circumstances? To experiment, we could randomly divide people into two groups, have the groups compete for a scarce resource, and note what happens. This is precisely what Muzafer Sherif (1966) and his colleagues did in a dramatic series of experiments with typical 11- and 12-year-old boys. The inspiration for these experiments dated back to Sherif's witnessing, as a teenager, Greek troops invading his Turkish province in 1919.

> They started killing people right and left. [That] made a great impression on me. There and then I became interested in understanding why these things were happening among human beings. . . . I wanted to learn whatever science or specialization was needed to understand this intergroup savagery. (Quoted by Aron & Aron, 1989, p. 131)

After studying the social roots of savagery, Sherif introduced these apparent essentials into several three-week summer camping experiences. In one such study, he divided 22 unacquainted Oklahoma City boys into two groups, took them to a Boy Scout camp in separate buses, and settled them in bunkhouses about a half-mile apart. For most of the first week, they were unaware of the other group's existence. By cooperating in various activities—preparing meals, camping out, fixing up a swimming hole, building a rope bridge—each group soon became close-knit. They gave themselves names: "Rattlers" and "Eagles." Typifying the good feeling, a sign appeared in one cabin: "Home Sweet Home."

Group identity thus established, the stage was set for the conflict. Toward the end of the first week, the Rattlers "discovered the Eagles on 'our' baseball field." When the camp staff then proposed a tournament of competitive activities between the two groups (baseball games, tugs-of-war, cabin inspections, treasure hunts, and so forth), both groups responded enthusiastically. This was win-lose competition. The spoils (medals, knives) would all go to the tournament victor.

The result? The camp gradually degenerated into open warfare. It was like a scene from William Golding's novel *Lord of the Flies*, which depicts the social disintegration of boys marooned on an island. In Sherif's study, the conflict began with each side calling the other names during the competitive activities. Soon it escalated to dining hall "garbage wars," flag burnings, cabin ransackings, even fistfights. Asked to describe the other group, the boys said "they" were "sneaky," "smart alecks," "stinkers," while referring to their own group as "brave," "tough," "friendly."

The win-lose competition had produced intense conflict, negative images of the outgroup, and strong ingroup cohesiveness and pride. All this occurred without any cultural, physical, or economic differences between the two groups and with boys who were their communities' "cream of the crop." Sherif noted

Competition kindles conflict. Here, in the Sherif experiment, one group of boys raids the bunkhouse of another.

that had we visited the camp at this point, we would have concluded these "were wicked, disturbed, and vicious bunches of youngsters" (1966, p. 85). Actually, their evil behavior was triggered by an evil situation. Fortunately, as we will see, Sherif not only made strangers into enemies; he then made the enemies into friends.

PERCEIVED INJUSTICE

"That's unfair!" "What a ripoff!" "We deserve better!" Such comments typify conflicts bred by perceived injustice. But what is "justice"? According to some social-psychological theorists, people perceive justice as *equity*—the distribution of rewards in proportion to individuals' contributions (Walster & others, 1978). If you and I have a relationship (employer-employee, teacher-student, husband-wife, colleague-colleague), it is equitable if:

$$\frac{\text{My outcomes}}{\text{My inputs}} = \frac{\text{Your outcomes}}{\text{Your inputs}}$$

If you contribute more and benefit less than I do, you will feel exploited and irritated; I may feel exploitative and guilty. Chances are, though, that you more than I will be sensitive to the inequity (Greenberg, 1986; Messick & Sentis, 1979).

We may agree with the equity principle's definition of justice yet disagree on whether our relationship is equitable. If two people are colleagues, what will each consider a relevant input? The one who is older may favor basing pay on seniority, the other on current productivity. Given such a disagreement, whose definition is likely to prevail? More often than not, those with social power convince themselves and others that they deserve what they're getting (Mikula, 1984). This has been called a "golden" rule: Whoever has the gold makes the rules.

As this suggests, the exploiter can relieve guilt by valuing or devaluing inputs to justify the existing outcomes. Men may perceive the lower pay of women as equitable, given women's "less important" inputs. As we noted in Chapter 11, those who inflict harm may blame the victim and thus maintain their belief in a just world.

"Do unto others 20% better than you would expect them to do unto you, to correct for subjective error."
Linus Pauling (1962)

TABLE 15–1 *Gallup Polls Reveal Increased Perceptions of Gender Inequality*
All things considered, who has a better life in this country— men or women?

	1975	1989
Men	32%	49%
Women	28	22
Same	31	21
No opinion	9	8

From De Stefano & Colasanto, 1990.

And how do those who are exploited react? Elaine Hatfield, William Walster, and Ellen Berscheid (1978) detected three possibilities. They can accept and justify their inferior position ("We're poor; it's what we deserve, but we're happy"). They can demand compensation, perhaps by harassing, embarrassing, even cheating their exploiter. If all else fails, they may try to restore equity by retaliating.

An interesting implication of equity theory—an implication that has been confirmed experimentally—is that the more competent and worthy people feel (the more they value their inputs), the more they will feel underbenefitted and thus eager to retaliate (Ross & others, 1971). Intense social protests generally come from those who believe themselves worthy of more than they are receiving. Since 1970, professional opportunities for women have significantly increased. Ironically, though understandably to an equity theorist, so have people's feelings that women's status is *in*equitable (Table 15–1).

So long as women compared their opportunities and earnings with other women, they felt generally satisfied—as they still do with their disproportionate share of family labor (Jackson, 1989; Major, 1989, 1993). Now that women are more likely to see themselves as men's equals, their sense of relative deprivation has grown. If secretarial work and truck driving have "comparable worth" (for the skills required), then they deserve comparable pay; that's equity, say advocates of gender equality (Lowe & Wittig, 1989).

Critics argue that equity is not the only conceivable definition of justice. (Pause a moment: Can you imagine any other?) Edward Sampson (1975) says equity theorists wrongly assume that the economic principles that guide western, capitalist nations are universal. Some noncapitalist cultures define justice not as equity but as equality or even fulfillment of need: "From each according to his abilities, to each according to his needs" (Karl Marx). When rewards are distributed to those within one's group, people socialized under the influence of collectivist cultures, such as China and India, likewise favor need or equality more than do individualistic Americans (Hui & others, 1991; Leung & Bond, 1984; Murphy-Berman & others, 1984). In collectivist, age-respecting Japan, pay is less often based on productivity, more often on seniority (Kitayama & Markus, in press). In individualistic America, 53 percent of people favor basing pay on performance, as do only 32 percent in Britain and 26 percent in

"Awards should be 'according to merit'; for all people agree that what is just in distribution must be according to merit in some sense, though they do not all specify the same sort of merit."
Aristotle

Spain. And should government reduce income differences or guarantee incomes? Yes, say 39 percent of Americans, 48 percent of Canadians, and 65 percent of Britishers (Brown, 1995). Even within individualistic cultures, criteria other than equity sometimes define justice (Deutsch, 1985). In a family or an altruistic institution, the criterion may be need. In a friendship, it may be equality. In a competitive relationship, the winner may take all the reward.

How universal, then, is the tendency to define justice as equity? And on what basis *should* rewards be distributed? Need? Equality? Merit? Some combination of these? Political philosopher John Rawls (1971) invites us to consider a future in which our own place on the economic ladder was unknown. Which standard of justice would we prefer? Gregory Mitchell and his colleagues (1993) report that American University students want enough priority placed on equality to meet their own needs, should they find themselves at the bottom, but also some reward for productivity.

MISPERCEPTION

Recall that conflict is a *perceived* incompatibility of actions or goals. Many conflicts contain but a small core of truly incompatible goals; the bigger problem is the misperceptions of the other's motives and goals. The Eagles and the Rattlers did indeed have some genuinely incompatible aims. But their perceptions subjectively magnified their differences (Figure 15–3).

In earlier chapters we considered the seeds of such misperception. The *self-serving bias* leads individuals and groups to accept credit for their good deeds and shuck responsibility for bad deeds, without according others the same benefit of the doubt. A tendency to *self-justify* further inclines people to deny the wrong of evil acts that cannot be shucked off. Thanks to the *fundamental attri-*

> "Solutions to the distribution problem are nontrivial. Children fight, colleagues complain, group members resign, tempers flare, and nations battle over issues of fairness. As parents, employers, teachers, and presidents know, the most frequent response to an allocation decision is 'not fair.'"
> Arnold Kahn & William Gaeddert (1985)

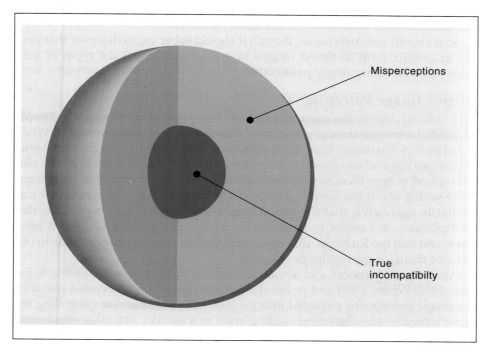

Misperceptions

True incompatibilty

■ **FIGURE 15–3**
Many conflicts contain a core of truly incompatible goals surrounded by a larger exterior of misperceptions.

Self-confirming, mirror-image perceptions are a hallmark of intense conflict, as in the former Yugoslavia. This photo shows soldiers in the uniform of the Yugoslav army rounding up suspected Croatian soldiers (in civilian clothes) after they over-ran the town of Vukovar in November 1991, when the current war among ethnic groups began.

Gorbachev displayed the complex style of thinking that facilitates reaching mutually beneficial agreements. But, as the collapse of the former Soviet Union shows, even complex thinkers can be overwhelmed by intractable economic problems and conflicts of interest.

When, however, the two sides have clashing perceptions, at least one of the two is misperceiving the other. And when such misperceptions exist, noted Bronfenbrenner, "It is a psychological phenomenon without parallel in the gravity of its consequences . . . for *it is characteristic of such images that they are self-confirming.*" If A expects B to be hostile, A may treat B in such a way that B fulfills A's expectations, thus beginning a vicious circle. Morton Deutsch (1986) explains:

> You hear the false rumor that a friend is saying nasty things about you; you snub him; he then badmouths you, confirming your expectation. Similarly, if the policy-makers of East and West believe that war is likely and either attempts to increase its military security vis-à-vis the other, the other's response will justify the initial move.

Mirror-image perceptions: Reciprocal views of one another often held by parties in conflict; for example, each may view itself as moral and peace-loving and the other as evil and aggressive.

Negative **mirror-image perceptions** have been an obstacle to peace in many places:

■ Both sides of the Arab-Israeli conflict insisted that "we" are motivated by our need to protect our security and our territory, while "they" want to obliterate us and gobble up our land (Heradstveit, 1979; R. K. White, 1977). Given such intense mistrust, negotiation is difficult.

■ At Northern Ireland's University of Ulster, J. A. Hunter and his colleagues (1991) showed Catholic and Protestant students videos of a Protestant attack at a Catholic funeral and a Catholic attack at a Protestant funeral. Most students attributed the other side's attack to "bloodthirsty" motives but its own side's attack to retaliation or self-defense.

■ Muslims and Hindus in Bangladesh exhibit the same ingroup-favoring perceptions (Islam & Hewstone, 1993).

Destructive mirror-image perceptions also operate in conflicts between small groups and between individuals. As we saw in the dilemma games, both parties may say, "We want to cooperate. But their refusal to cooperate forces us to react defensively." In a study of executives, Kenneth Thomas and Louis Pondy (1977) uncovered such attributions. Asked to describe a significant recent conflict, only 12 percent felt the other party was cooperative; 74 percent perceived themselves as cooperative. The executives explained that they had "suggested," "informed," and "recommended," while their antagonist had "demanded," "disagreed with everything I said," and "refused."

Group conflicts are often fueled by an illusion that the enemy's top leaders are evil but their people, though controlled and manipulated, are pro-us. This evil leader–good people perception characterized Americans' and Soviets' views of each other during the cold war. The United States entered the Vietnam war believing that in areas dominated by the communist Vietcong "terrorists," many of the people were allies-in-waiting. As suppressed information later revealed, these beliefs were mere wishful thinking.

Another type of mirror-image perception is each side's exaggeration of the other's position. People with opposing views on issues such as abortion and capital punishment often differ less than they suppose. Each side overestimates the extremity of the other's views and presumes that "our" beliefs *follow* from the facts while "their" beliefs *dictate* their interpretation of facts (Robinson & others, 1991).

Shifting Perceptions

If misperceptions accompany conflict, then they should appear and disappear as conflicts wax and wane. And they do, with startling ease. The same processes that create the enemy's image can reverse that image when the enemy becomes an ally. Thus the "bloodthirsty, cruel, treacherous, buck-toothed little Japs" of World War II soon became—in American minds (Gallup, 1972) and in the American media—our "intelligent, hardworking, self-disciplined, resourceful allies." Our World War II allies, the Soviets, then became the "warlike, treacherous" ones.

The Germans, whom Americans after two world wars hated, then admired, and then again hated, were once again admired—apparently no longer plagued by what earlier was presumed to be cruelty in their national character. So long as Iraq was attacking Iran, even while using chemical weapons and massacring its own Kurds, many nations supported it. Our enemy's enemy is our friend. When Iraq ended its war with Iran and invaded oil-rich Kuwait, Iraq's behavior suddenly became "barbaric." Clearly, images of our enemies not only justify our actions but also change with amazing ease.

The extent of misperceptions during conflict provides a chilling reminder that people need not be insane or abnormally evil to form these distorted images of their antagonists. When in conflict with another nation, another group, or simply a roommate or parent, we readily develop misperceptions that allow us to perceive our own motives and actions as wholly good and the other's as totally evil. Our antagonists usually form a mirror-image perception of us. So, trapped in a social dilemma, competing for scarce resources, or perceiving injustice, the conflict continues until something enables both parties to peel away their misperceptions and work at reconciling their actual differences.

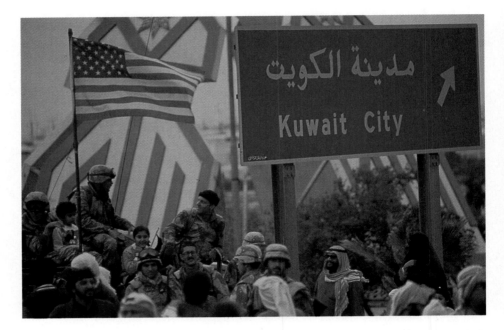

Shifting perceptions. North Americans, once Iraq's friends, became Iraq's enemy and Kuwait's friends during the Persian Gulf War of 1991.

SUMMING UP

Whenever two people, two groups, or two nations interact, their perceived needs and goals may conflict. Many social problems arise as people pursue individual self-interest, to their collective detriment. Two laboratory games, the Prisoner's Dilemma and the Tragedy of the Commons, capture this clash of individual versus communal well-being. In real life, as in laboratory experiments, we can avoid such traps by establishing rules that regulate self-serving behavior; by keeping social groups small so people feel responsibility for one another; by enabling communication, thus reducing mistrust; by changing payoffs to make cooperation more rewarding; and by invoking altruistic norms.

When people compete for scarce resources, human relations often sink into prejudice and hostility. In his famous experiments, Muzafer Sherif found that win-lose competition quickly made strangers into enemies, triggering outright warfare even among normally upstanding boys.

Conflicts also arise when people feel unjustly treated. According to equity theory, people define justice as the distribution of rewards in proportion to one's contributions. Conflicts occur when people disagree on the extent of their contributions and thus on the equity of their outcomes. Other theorists argue that people sometimes define justice not as equity but as equality, or even in terms of people's needs.

Conflicts frequently contain a small core of truly incompatible goals, surrounded by a thick layer of misperceptions of the adversary's motives and goals. Often, conflicting parties have *mirror-image perceptions*. When both sides believe "we are peace-loving—they are hostile," each may treat the other in ways that provoke confirmation of its expectations. International conflicts are also fed by an evil leader–good people illusion.

■ PEACEMAKING

*A*lthough toxic forces can breed destructive conflict, we can harness other forces to bring conflict to a constructive resolution. What are these ingredients of peace and harmony?

We have seen how conflicts are ignited: by social traps, competition, perceived injustices, and misperceptions. Although grim, the picture is not hopeless. Sometimes closed fists become open arms as hostilities evolve into friendship. Social psychologists have focused on four strategies for helping enemies become comrades. We can remember these as the four C's of peacemaking: contact, cooperation, communication, conciliation.

> *"We know more about war than we do about peace—more about killing than we know about living."*
> General Omar Bradley,
> 1893–1981, former U.S. Army
> Chief of Staff

CONTACT

Might putting two conflicting individuals or groups into close contact enable them to know and like each other? We have seen why it might. In Chapter 13, we saw that proximity—and the accompanying interaction, anticipation of interaction, and mere exposure—boosts liking. In Chapter 4, we noted that the recent downturn in blatant racial prejudice in the United States followed closely on the heels of desegregation, showing that "attitudes follow behavior." If this social-psychological principle now seems obvious, remember: That's how things usually seem—once you know them. To the U.S. Supreme Court in 1896 (*Plessy* v. *Ferguson*), the idea that desegregated behavior might influence racial attitudes was anything but obvious. What seemed obvious at the time was, "Legislation is powerless to eradicate racial instincts."

During the last 30 years in the United States, segregation and prejudice have diminished together. But was interracial contact the *cause* of these improved attitudes? Were those who actually experienced desegregation affected by it?

Does Desegregation Improve Racial Attitudes?

School desegregation has produced measurable benefits, such as leading more Blacks to attend and succeed in college (Stephan, 1988). Does desegregation of schools, neighborhoods, and workplaces also produce favorable *social* results? The evidence is mixed.

On the one hand, many studies conducted during and shortly after the desegregation following World War II found Whites' attitudes toward Blacks improving markedly. Whether the people were department store clerks and customers, merchant marines, government workers, police officers, neighbors, or students, racial contact led to diminished prejudice (Amir, 1969; Pettigrew, 1969). For example, near the end of World War II, the Army partially desegregated some of its rifle companies (Stouffer & others, 1949). When asked their opinions of such desegregation, 11 percent of the White soldiers in segregated companies approved. Of those in desegregated companies, 60 percent approved.

When Morton Deutsch and Mary Collins (1951) took advantage of a made-to-order natural experiment, they observed similar results. In accord with state law, New York City desegregated its public housing units; it assigned families to apartments without regard to race. In a similar development across the river in Newark, Blacks and Whites were assigned to separate buildings. When surveyed, White women in the desegregated development were far more likely to favor interracial housing and to say their attitudes toward Blacks had improved. Exaggerated stereotypes had wilted in the face of reality. As one woman put it, "I've really come to like it. I see they're just as human as we are."

Surveys of nearly 4000 Europeans reveal that friendship is a key to successful contact: If you have a minority-group friend, you become much more likely to express sympathy and support for the friend's group, and even somewhat more support for immigration by that group. It's true of West Germans' attitudes toward Turks, French people's attitudes toward Asians and North Africans, Netherlanders' attitudes toward Surinamers and Turks, and Britishers' attitudes toward West Indians and Asians (Pettigrew, 1995). Likewise, antigay feeling is lower among people who know gays personally (Herek, 1993).

Findings such as these influenced the Supreme Court's 1954 decision to desegregate U.S. schools and helped fuel the civil rights movement of the 1960s (Pettigrew, 1986). Yet studies of the effects of school desegregation have been less encouraging. Social psychologist Walter Stephan (1986) reviewed all such studies and concluded that racial attitudes have been little affected by desegregation. For Blacks the more noticeable consequence of desegregated schooling is their increased likelihood of attending integrated (or predominantly White) colleges, living in integrated neighborhoods, and working in integrated settings.

Many student exchange programs have likewise had less-than-hoped-for positive effects on student attitudes toward their host countries. For example, when eager American students study in France, often living with other Americans as they do so, their stereotypes of the French tend not to improve (Stroebe & others, 1988).

So, sometimes desegregation improves racial attitudes; sometimes it doesn't. Such disagreements excite the scientist's detective spirit. What explains the difference? So far, we've been lumping all kinds of desegregation together. Actual desegregation occurs in many ways and under vastly different conditions.

When Does Desegregation Improve Racial Attitudes?

Might the amount of interracial *contact* be a factor? Indeed it seems to be. Researchers have gone into dozens of desegregated schools and observed with whom children of a given race eat, loiter, and talk. Race influences contact. Whites disproportionately associate with Whites, Blacks with Blacks (Schofield, 1982, 1986). Academic tracking programs often amplify resegregation by separating academically advantaged White students into predominantly White classes.

In contrast, the more encouraging older studies of store clerks, soldiers, and housing project neighbors involved considerable interracial contact. Other studies involving prolonged, personal contact—between Black and White prison inmates and between Black and White girls in an interracial summer camp—show similar benefits (Clore & others, 1978; Foley, 1976).

The social psychologists who advocated desegregation never claimed that contact of *any* sort would improve attitudes. They expected poor results when contacts were competitive, unsupported by authorities, and unequal (Pettigrew, 1988; Stephan, 1987). Before 1954, many prejudiced Whites had frequent contacts with Blacks—as shoeshine men and domestic workers. As we saw in

Chapter 11, such unequal contacts breed attitudes that merely justify the continuation of inequality. So it's important that the contact be **equal-status contact**, like that between the store clerks, the soldiers, the neighbors, the prisoners, and the summer campers.

The contact in desegregated schools was often unequal. White students were often more active, more influential, more successful (Cohen, 1980a; Riordan & Ruggiero, 1980). When a seventh-grade Black girl from an academically inferior school is dropped suddenly into a predominantly White middle-class junior high school with White middle-class teachers who expect less of her, she is likely to be perceived, by her classmates and by herself, as having lower academic status.

Equal-status contact:
Contact made on an equal basis. Just as a relationship between people of unequal status breeds attitudes consistent with their relationship, so do relationships between those of equal status. Thus, to reduce prejudice, interracial contact should be between persons equal in status.

COOPERATION

Although equal-status contact can help, it is sometimes not enough. It didn't help when Muzafer Sherif stopped the Eagles versus Rattlers competition and brought the groups together for noncompetitive activities, such as watching movies, shooting off fireworks, and eating. By this time, their hostility was so strong that what contact provided was the opportunity for taunts and attacks. When an Eagle was bumped by a Rattler, his fellow Eagles urged him to "brush off the dirt." Obviously, desegregating the two groups had hardly promoted their social integration.

Given entrenched hostility, what can a peacemaker do? Think back to the successful and unsuccessful desegregation efforts. The Army's racial mixing of rifle companies not only brought Blacks and Whites into equal-status contact but also made them interdependent. Together, they were fighting a common enemy, striving toward a shared goal.

Contrast this interdependence with the competitive situation in the typical classroom, desegregated or not. Is the following scene familiar (Aronson, 1980)? Students compete for good grades, teacher approval, and various honors and privileges. The teacher asks a question. Several students' hands shoot up; other students sit, eyes downcast, trying to look invisible. When the teacher calls on one of the eager faces, the others hope for a wrong answer, giving them a chance to display their knowledge. The losers in this academic sport often resent the "nerds" or "geeks" who succeed. The situation abounds with both competition and painfully obvious status inequalities; we could hardly design it better to create divisions among the children.

Does this suggest a second factor that predicts whether the effect of desegregation will be favorable? Does competitive contact divide and *cooperative* contact unite? Consider what happens to people who together face a common predicament.

Common External Threats

Together with others, have you ever been victimized by the weather; harassed as part of your initiation into a group; punished by a teacher; or persecuted and ridiculed because of your social, racial, or religious identity? If so, you may recall feeling close to those with whom you shared the predicament. Perhaps previous social barriers were dropped as you helped one another dig out of the snow or struggled to cope with a common enemy.

Shared predicaments are a powerful trigger for cooperation: Koreans band together to protect their businesses during the Los Angeles riots; New Yorkers work together to free a snowbound car.

"*I couldn't help but say to [Mr. Gorbachev], just think how easy his task and mine might be in these meetings that we held if suddenly there was a threat to this world from some other species from another planet. [We'd] find out once and for all that we really are all human beings here on this earth together.*"
Ronald Reagan, December 4, 1985, speech

Such friendliness is common among those who experience a shared threat. John Lanzetta (1955) observed this when he put four-man groups of Naval ROTC cadets to work on problem-solving tasks and then began informing them over a loudspeaker that their answers were wrong, their productivity inexcusably low, their thinking stupid. Other groups did not receive this harassment. Lanzetta observed that the group members under duress became friendlier to one another, more cooperative, less argumentative, less competitive. They were in it together. And the result was a cohesive spirit.

Having a common enemy unified the groups of competing boys in Sherif's camping experiments—and in many subsequent experiments (Dion, 1979). Americans' feelings of patriotism and unity were aroused by conflicts with Germany and Japan during World War II, with the Soviet Union during the cold war, with Iran during 1980, and with Iraq during 1991. Soldiers who together face combat often maintain lifelong ties with their comrades (Elder & Clipp, 1988). Few things so unite a people as having a common hatred.

Times of interracial strife may therefore be times of heightened group pride. For Chinese university students in Toronto, facing discrimination heightens a sense of kinship with other Chinese (Pak & others, 1991). Just being reminded of an outgroup (say, a rival school) heightens people's responsiveness to their own group (Wilder & Shapiro, 1984). When keenly conscious of who "they" are, we also know who "we" are.

Leaders may even *create* a threatening external enemy as a technique for building group cohesiveness. George Orwell's novel *Nineteen Eighty-Four* illustrates the tactic: The leader of the protagonist nation uses border conflicts with the other two major powers to lessen internal strife. From time to time the enemy shifts, but there is always an enemy. Indeed, the nation seems to need an enemy. For the world, for a nation, for a group, having a common enemy is powerfully unifying. In 1994, Saddam Hussein's grip on power in Iraq was threatened by a suffocating economy, growing dog-eat-dog criminality, and a restive military. His response: to provoke another conflict with the outside world, by again threatening to invade Kuwait (Socolovsky, 1994).

Superordinate Goals

Superordinate goal:
A shared goal that necessitates cooperative effort; a goal that overrides people's differences from one another.

Closely related to the unifying power of an external threat is the unifying power of **superordinate goals,** goals compelling for all in a group and requiring cooperative effort. To promote harmony among his warring campers, Sherif introduced such goals. He created a problem with the camp water supply, necessitating their cooperation to restore the water. Given an opportunity to rent a movie, one expensive enough to require the joint resources of both groups, they again cooperated. When a truck "broke down" on a camping trip, a staff member casually left the tug-of-war rope nearby, prompting one boy to suggest that they all pull the truck to get it started. When it started, a backslapping celebration ensued over their victorious "tug-of-war against the truck."

After working together to achieve such superordinate goals, the boys began eating together and enjoyed themselves around a campfire. Friendships sprouted across group lines. Hostilities plummeted (Figure 15–5). On the last day, the boys decided to travel home together on one bus. During the trip they no longer sat by groups. As the bus approached Oklahoma City and home, they, as one, spontaneously sang "Oklahoma" and then bade their friends farewell. With isolation and competition, Sherif made strangers into bitter enemies. With superordinate goals, he made enemies into friends.

Are Sherif's experiments mere child's play? Or can pulling together to achieve superordinate goals be similarly beneficial with adults in conflict? Robert Blake and Jane Mouton (1979) wondered. So in a series of two-week experiments involving more than 1000 executives in 150 different groups, they re-created the essential features of the situation experienced by the Rattlers and Eagles. Each group first engaged in activities by itself, then competed with another group, and then cooperated with the other group in working toward jointly chosen superordinate goals. Their results provided "unequivocal evidence that adult reactions parallel those of Sherif's younger subjects."

Extending these findings, Samuel Gaertner, John Dovidio, and their collaborators (1993) report that working cooperatively has especially favorable effects under conditions that lead people to define a new, inclusive group that dissolves their former subgroups. Old feelings of bias against another group

■ FIGURE 15–5
After competition, the Eagles and Rattlers rated each other unfavorably. After they worked cooperatively to achieve superordinate goals, hostility dropped sharply.
(Data from Sherif, 1966, p. 84.)

diminish when members of the two groups sit alternately around a table (rather than on opposite sides), give their new group a single name, and then work together under conditions that foster a good mood. "Us" and "them" become "we." To combat Germany, Italy, and Japan during World War II, the United States and the U.S.S.R., along with other nations, formed one united group named the Allies. So long as the superordinate goal of defeating a common enemy lasted, so did supportive U.S. attitudes toward the Soviets.

The cooperative efforts by Rattlers and Eagles ended in success. Would the same harmony have emerged if the water had remained off, the movie unaffordable, the truck still stalled? Likely not. In experiments with University of Virginia students, Stephen Worchel and his associates (1977, 1978, 1980) confirmed that *successful* cooperation between two groups boosts their attraction for one another. However, if previously conflicting groups *fail* in a cooperative effort *and* if conditions allow them to attribute their failure to each other, the conflict may worsen. Sherif's groups were already feeling hostile to one another. Thus, failure to raise sufficient funds for the movie might have been attributed to the one group's "stinginess" and "selfishness." This would have exacerbated rather than alleviated their conflict.

Cooperative Learning

So far we have noted the apparently meager social benefits of typical school desegregation and the apparently dramatic social benefits of successful, cooperative contacts between members of rival groups. Could putting these two findings together suggest a constructive alternative to traditional desegregation practices? Several independent research teams speculated yes. Each wondered whether, without affecting academic achievement, we could promote interracial friendships by replacing competitive learning situations with cooperative ones. Given the diversity of their methods—all involving students on integrated study teams, sometimes in competition with other teams—the results are striking and very heartening.

Are students who participate in existing cooperative activities, such as interracial athletic teams and class projects, less prejudiced? Robert Slavin and Nancy Madden (1979) analyzed survey data from 2400 students in 71 American high schools and found encouraging results. Those of different races who play and work together are more likely to report having friends of another race and to express positive racial attitudes. Charles Green and his colleagues (1989) confirmed this in a study of 3200 Florida middle school students. Compared to students at traditional, competitive schools, those at schools with interracial learning "teams" had more positive racial attitudes.

From this correlational finding, can we conclude that cooperative interracial activity improves racial attitudes? Again, the way to find out is to experiment. Randomly designate some students, but not others, to work together in racially mixed groups. Slavin (1985) and his colleagues divided classes into interracial teams, each composed of four or five students from all achievement levels. Team members sat together, studied a variety of subjects together, and at the end of each week competed with the other teams in a class tournament. All members contributed to the team score by doing well, sometimes by competing with other students whose recent achievements were similar to their own, sometimes by competing with their own previous scores. Everyone had a chance to succeed. Moreover, team members were motivated to help one an-

Interracial cooperation—on athletic teams, in class projects and extracurricular activities—melts differences and improves racial attitudes.

other prepare for the weekly tournament—by drilling each other on fractions, spelling, or historical events—whatever was the next event. Rather than isolating students from one another, team competition brought them into closer contact and drew out mutual support.

Another research team, led by Elliot Aronson (1978, 1979; Aronson & Gonzalez, 1988), elicited similar group cooperation with a "jigsaw" technique. In experiments in Texas and California elementary schools, they assigned children to racially and academically diverse six-member groups. The subject was then divided into six parts, with each student becoming the expert on his or her part. In a unit on Chile, one student might be the expert on Chile's history, another on its geography, another on its culture. First, the various "historians," "geographers," and so forth got together to master their material. Then each returned to the home group to teach it to their classmates. Each group member held, so to speak, a piece of the jigsaw. The self-confident students therefore had to listen to and learn from the reticent students, who in turn soon realized they had something important to offer their peers. Other research teams—led by David Johnson and Roger Johnson (1987, 1994) at the University of Minnesota, Elizabeth Cohen (1980) at Stanford University, Shlomo Sharan and Yael Sharan (1976) at Tel Aviv University, and Stuart Cook (1985) at the University of Colorado—have devised additional methods for cooperative learning.

From all this research—more than 650 studies—what can we conclude? With cooperative learning, students learn not only the material but other lessons as well. Cooperative learning, said Slavin (1980), is an "effective means of increasing positive race relations and achievement in desegregated schools." Aronson reported that "children in the interdependent, jigsaw classrooms grow to like each other better, develop a greater liking for school, and develop greater self-esteem than children in traditional classrooms" (1980, p. 232).

FOCUS

BRANCH RICKEY, JACKIE ROBINSON, AND THE INTEGRATION OF BASEBALL

On April 10, 1947, 19 words that forever changed the face of baseball would also put social psychological principles to the test. In the sixth inning of a Brooklyn Dodgers exhibition game with their top minor league club, the Montreal Royals, radio announcer Red Barber read a statement from Dodger president, Branch Rickey: "The Brooklyn Dodgers today purchased the contract of Jackie Roosevelt Robinson from the Montreal Royals. He will report immediately." Five days later, Robinson became the first African American since 1887 to play major league baseball. In the fall, Dodger fans realized their dreams of going to the World Series. Robinson, after enduring racial taunts, beanballs, and spikes, was voted *Sporting News* rookie of the year and in a poll finished second to Bing Crosby as the most popular man in America. Baseball's racial barrier was forever broken.

Motivated by both his Methodist morality and a drive for baseball success, Rickey had been planning the move for some time, report social psychologists Anthony Pratkanis and Marlene Turner (1994a,b). Three years earlier, Rickey had been approached by the sociologist-chair of the Mayor's Committee on Unity and asked to desegregate his team. His response was to ask for time, so the hiring would not be attributed to pressure—and for advice on how best to do it. In 1945, Rickey cast the lone vote in a 15 to 1 owners' vote against bringing Blacks into baseball. In 1947 he made his move using principles identified by Pratkanis and Turner, including these:

■ *Create a perception that change is inevitable.* Leave little possibility that protest or resistance can turn back the clock. The announcer Red Barber, a traditional Southerner, recalled that in 1945 Rickey took him to lunch and explained very slowly and strongly that his scouts were searching for "the first black player I can put on the white Dodgers. I don't know who he is or where he is, but he is coming." An angered

Barber at first intended to quit, but in time decided to accept the inevitable and keep the world's "best sports announcing job." Rickey was equally matter of fact with the players in 1947, offering to trade any player who didn't want to play with Robinson.

■ *Establish equal status contact with a superordinate goal.* As one sociologist explained to Rickey, when relationships focus on an overarching goal, such as winning the pennant, "the people involved would adjust appropriately." One of the players initially opposed to Robinson later helped him with his hitting, explaining, "When you're on a team, you got to pull together to win."

■ *Puncture the norm of prejudice.* Rickey led the way, but others helped. Team leader, shortstop Pee Wee Reese, a Southerner, set a pattern of sitting and eating with Robinson. One day in Cincinnati, as the crowd was hurling slurs—"get the nigger off the field"—Reese left his shortstop position, walked over to Robinson at first base, smiled and spoke to him, and then—with a hushed crowd watching—put his arm around Robinson's shoulder.

■ *Cut short the spiral of violence by practicing nonviolence.* Rickey, wanting "a ballplayer with guts enough not to fight back," role-played for Robinson the kind of insults and dirty play he would experience, and gained Robinson's commitment not to return violence with violence. When Robinson was taunted and spiked, he left the responses to his teammates. Team cohesion was thereby increased.

■ *Individuate the new group member.* Treat the person as an individual—in this case, as Jackie Robinson and not as "the Negro ballplayer." Rickey engaged his media friends in introducing Robinson as an accomplished individual in sports, academics, and the military.

Robinson and Bob Feller later became the first players in baseball history elected to the Hall of Fame in their first year of eligibility. As he received the award, Robinson asked three persons to stand beside him: his mother, Mallie, his wife, Rachel, and his friend, Branch Rickey.

Cross-racial friendships also begin to blossom. The exam scores of minority students improve (perhaps because academic achievement is now peer-supported). After the experiments are over, many teachers continue using cooperative learning (D. W. Johnson & others, 1981; Slavin, 1990). "It is clear," wrote race-relations expert John McConahay (1981), that cooperative learning "is the most effective practice for improving race relations in desegregated schools that we know of to date."

Should we have "known it all along"? At the time of the 1954 Supreme Court decision, Gordon Allport spoke for many social psychologists in predicting, "Prejudice . . . may be reduced by equal status contact between majority and minority groups in the pursuit of common goals" (1954, p. 281). Cooperative learning experiments have confirmed Allport's insight. Robert Slavin (1985) is therefore optimistic: "Thirty years after Allport laid out the basic principles operationalized in cooperative learning methods, we finally have practical, proven methods for implementing contact theory in the desegregated classroom."

So, cooperative, equal-status contacts exert a positive influence on boy campers, industrial executives, college students, and schoolchildren. Does the principle extend to all levels of human relations? Are families unified by pulling together to farm the land, restore an old house, or sail a sloop? Are communal identities forged by barn raisings, group singing, or cheering on the football team? Is international understanding bred by international collaboration in science and space, by joint efforts to feed the world and conserve resources, by friendly personal contacts between people of different nations? Indications are that the answer to all these questions is yes (Brewer & Miller, 1988; Desforges & others, 1991; Deutsch, 1985, 1994). Thus an important challenge facing our divided world is to identify and agree on our superordinate goals and to structure cooperative efforts to achieve them.

COMMUNICATION

Conflicting parties have other ways to resolve their differences. When husband and wife, or labor and management, or nation X and nation Y disagree, they can **bargain** with one another directly. They can ask a third party to **mediate** by making suggestions and facilitating their negotiations. Or they can **arbitrate** by submitting their disagreement to someone who will study the issues and impose a settlement.

Bargaining

If you or I want to buy or sell a new car, are we better off adopting a tough bargaining stance—opening with an extreme offer so that splitting the difference will yield a favorable result? Or are we better off beginning with a sincere "good-faith" offer?

Experiments suggest no simple answer. On the one hand, those who demand more will often get more. Robert Cialdini, Leonard Bickman, and John Cacioppo (1979) provide a typical result: In a control condition, they approached various Chevrolet dealers and asked the price of a new Monte Carlo sports coupe with designated options. In an experimental condition, they approached other dealers and first struck a tougher bargaining stance, asking for and rejecting a price on a *different* car ("I need a lower price than that. That's a lot"). When they then asked the price of the Monte Carlo, exactly as in the control condition, they received offers that averaged some $200 lower.

Tough bargaining may lower the other party's expectations, making the other side willing to settle for less (Yukl, 1974). But toughness can sometimes backfire. Many a conflict is not over a pie of fixed size but over a pie that shrinks if the conflict continues. When a strike is prolonged, both labor and manage-

"The greenhouse effect, the depletion of the ozone layer and the global ecological crisis [is] the most serious issue facing this country and the world. . . . The cooperation required will be unprecedented. But we know what to do."
Vice President Albert Gore, 1989

Bargaining:
Seeking an agreement through direct negotiation between parties to a conflict.

Mediation:
An attempt by a neutral third party to resolve a conflict by facilitating communication and offering suggestions.

Arbitration:
Resolution of a conflict by a neutral third party who studies both sides and imposes a settlement.

ment lose. Being tough can also diminish the chances of actually reaching an agreement. If the other party responds with an equally extreme stance, both may be locked into positions from which neither can back down without losing face. In the weeks before the Persian Gulf war, President Bush threatened, in the full glare of publicity, to "kick Saddam's ass." Saddam Hussein communicated in kind, threatening to make "infidel" Americans "swim in their own blood." After such belligerent statements, it was difficult for each side to evade war and save face.

Mediation

A third-party mediator may offer suggestions that enable conflicting parties to make concessions and still save face (Pruitt, 1981). If my concession can be attributed to a mediator, who is gaining an equal concession from my antagonist, then neither of us will be viewed as caving in to the other's demands.

Turning Win-Lose into Win-Win

Mediators also help resolve conflicts by facilitating constructive communication. Their first task is to help the parties rethink the conflict and gain information about the other party's interests (Thompson, 1991). Typically, people on both sides have a competitive "win-lose" orientation. Thus, after a negotiation they are successful if their opponent is unhappy with the result, and unsuccessful if their opponent is pleased (Thompson & others, 1995). By prodding them to set aside their conflicting demands and to think instead about each other's underlying needs, interests, and goals, the mediator aims to replace this win-lose orientation with a cooperative "win-win" orientation. In experiments, Leigh Thompson (1990) found that, with experience, negotiators become better able to make mutually beneficial tradeoffs and thus to achieve win-win resolutions.

A classic story of such a resolution concerns the two sisters who quarreled over an orange (Follett, 1940). Finally they compromised and split the orange in half, whereupon one sister squeezed her half for juice while the other used the peel to make a cake. In experiments at the State University of New York at Buffalo, Dean Pruitt and his associates induced bargainers to search for **integrative agreements**. If the sisters had agreed to split the orange, giving one sister all the juice and the other all the peel, they would have hit on such an agreement, one that integrates both parties' interests (Kimmel & others, 1980; Pruitt & Lewis, 1975, 1977). Compared to compromises, in which each party sacrifices something important, integrative agreements are more enduring. Because they are mutually rewarding, they also lead to better ongoing relationships (Pruitt, 1986).

Integrative agreements: Win-win agreements that reconcile both parties' interests to their mutual benefit.

Unraveling Misperceptions with Controlled Communications

Communication often helps reduce self-fulfilling misperceptions. Perhaps you can recall experiences similar to that of this college student:

> Often, after a prolonged period of little communication, I perceive Martha's silence as a sign of her dislike for me. She, in turn, thinks that my quietness is a result of my being mad at her. My silence induces her silence, which makes me even more silent . . . until this snowballing effect is broken by some occurrence that makes it necessary for us to interact. And the communication then unravels all the misinterpretations we had made about one another.

The outcome of such conflicts often depends on *how* people communicate their feelings to one another. Roger Knudson and his colleagues (1980) invited married couples to come to the University of Illinois psychology laboratory and relive, through role playing, one of their past conflicts. Before, during, and after their conversation (which often generated as much emotion as the actual previous conflict), the couples were closely observed and questioned. Couples who evaded the issue—by failing to make their positions clear or failing to acknowledge their spouse's position—left with the illusion that they were more in harmony and agreement than they really were. Often, they came to believe they now agreed more when actually they agreed less. In contrast, those who engaged the issue—by making their positions clear and by taking one another's views into account—achieved more actual agreement and gained more accurate information about one another's perceptions. That helps explain why couples who communicate their concerns directly and openly are usually happily married (Grush & Glidden, 1987).

Such findings have triggered new programs that train couples and children how to manage conflicts constructively (Horowitz and Boardman, 1994). Children, for example, learn that conflict is normal, that people can learn to get along with those who are different, that most disputes can be resolved with two winners, and that nonviolent communication strategies are an alternative to a world of bullies and victims. This "violence prevention curriculum . . . is not about passivity," notes Deborah Prothrow-Stith (1991, p. 183). "It is about using anger not to hurt oneself or one's peers, but to change the world."

Conflict researchers report that a key factor is *trust* (Ross & Ward, 1995). If you believe the other person is well-intentioned, not out to exploit you, you are then more likely to divulge your needs and concerns. Lacking such trust, you probably will be cautious, fearing that being open will give the other party information that might be used against you.

"[There is] a psychological barrier between us, a barrier of suspicion, a barrier of rejection; a barrier of fear, of deception, a barrier of hallucination. . . ."
President Anwar al-Sadat, to the Israeli Knesset, 1977

Communication facilitators work to break down barriers, as in this diversity training exercise for teenagers.

FOCUS

HOW TO FIGHT CONSTRUCTIVELY

With every close relationship comes conflict. If managed constructively, conflict provides opportunities for reconciliation and a more genuine harmony. Psychologists Ian Gotlib and Catherine Colby (1988) offer advice on how to avoid destructive quarrels and to have good quarrels.

DO NOT

1. Apologize prematurely.
2. Evade the argument, give the silent treatment, or walk out on it.
3. Use your intimate knowledge of the other person to hit below the belt and humiliate.
4. Bring in unrelated issues.
5. Feign agreement while harboring resentment.
6. Tell the other party how they are feeling.
7. Attack indirectly by criticizing someone or something the other person values.
8. Undermine the other by intensifying their insecurity or threatening disaster.

DO

1. Fight privately, away from children.
2. Clearly define the issue and repeat the other's arguments in your own words.
3. Divulge your positive and negative feelings.
4. Welcome feedback about your behavior.
5. Clarify where you agree and disagree and what matters most to each of you.
6. Ask questions that help the other find words to express the concern.
7. Wait for spontaneous explosions to subside, without retaliating.
8. Offer positive suggestions for mutual improvement.

When the two parties mistrust each other and communicate unproductively, a third-party mediator—a marriage counselor, a labor mediator, a diplomat—sometimes helps. After coaxing the conflicting parties to rethink their perceived win-lose conflict, the mediator often has each party identify and rank its goals. When goals are compatible, the ranking procedure makes it easier for each to concede on less important goals so that both achieve their chief goals (Erickson & others, 1974; Schulz & Pruitt, 1978). Once labor and management both believe that management's goal of higher productivity and profit is compatible with labor's goal of better wages and working conditions, they can begin to work for an integrative win-win solution. If workers will forgo benefits that are moderately beneficial to them but very costly to management (perhaps company-provided dental care), and if management will forgo moderately valuable arrangements that workers very much resent (perhaps inflexibility of working hours), then both sides may gain (Ross & Ward, 1995). Rather than seeing itself as making a concession, each side can see the negotiation as an effort to exchange bargaining chips for things more valued.

When the parties then convene to communicate directly, they are usually *not* set loose in the hope that, eyeball to eyeball, the conflict will resolve itself. In the midst of a threatening, stressful conflict, emotions often disrupt the ability to understand the other party's point of view. Communication may become most difficult just when it is most needed (Tetlock, 1985). The mediator will therefore often structure the encounter to help each party understand and feel understood by the other. The mediator may ask the conflicting parties to re- strict their arguments to statements of fact, including statements of how they feel and how they respond when the other acts in a given way: "I enjoy hav- ing music on. When you play it loud, I find it hard to concentrate. That makes me crabby." Also, the mediator may ask people to reverse roles and argue the other's position, or to restate one another's positions before replying with their own: "My turning up the stereo bugs you."

Neutral third parties may also suggest mutually agreeable proposals that would be dismissed—"reactively devalued"—if offered by either side. Con- stance Stillinger and her colleagues (1991) found that a nuclear disarmament proposal that Americans dismissed when attributed to the Soviet Union seemed more acceptable when attributed to a neutral third party. Likewise, people will often reactively devalue a concession offered by an adversary ("they must not value it"); the same concession may seem less like a token gesture when sug- gested by a third party.

These peacemaking principles, based partly on laboratory experiments, partly on practical experience, have helped mediate both international and in- dustrial conflicts (Blake & Mouton, 1962, 1979; Fisher, 1994; Wehr, 1979). One small team of Arab and Jewish Americans, led by social psychologists Herbert Kelman and colleagues (Kelman & Cohen, 1979, 1986; Rouhana & Kelman, 1994), have conducted workshops bringing together influential Arabs and Is- raelis, and Pakistanis and Indians. Using methods such as those we've con- sidered, Kelman and colleagues counter misperceptions and have participants creatively seek solutions for their common good. Isolated, the participants are free to speak directly to their adversaries without fear of their constituents' sec- ond-guessing what they are saying. The result? Those from both sides typically come to understand the other's perspective and how the other side responds to their own group's actions.

When direct communication is impossible, a third party can meet with one party, then the other. Henry Kissinger's "shuttle diplomacy" in the two years after the Arab-Israeli war of 1973 produced three disengagement agreements between Israel and its Arab neighbors. Kissinger's strategy gave him control over the communications and enabled both sides to concede to him without appearing to capitulate to one another (Pruitt, 1981).

Negotiation sometimes receives a boost from smaller mediating efforts. In 1976, Kelman drove an Egyptian social scientist, Boutros Boutros-Ghali (who in 1991 became the UN secretary general), to the Boston airport. En route, they formulated plans for an Egyptian conference on misperceptions in Arab-Israeli relations. The conference later took place, and Kelman conveyed its promising results to influential Israelis. A year later, Boutros-Ghali became Egypt's act- ing foreign minister, and Egyptian President Anwar Sadat made his historic trip to Israel, opening a road to peace. Afterward, Boutros-Ghali said happily to Kelman, "You see the process that we started at the Boston airport last year" (Armstrong, 1981).

A year later, mediator Jimmy Carter secluded Sadat and Israeli Prime Min- ister Menachem Begin at Camp David. Rather than begin by having each side state its demands, Carter had them identify their underlying interests and goals—security for Israel, authority over its historic territory for Egypt. Thir- teen days later, the trio emerged with "A Framework for Peace in the Middle East," granting each what they desired—security in exchange for territory (Ru-

Former President Jimmy Carter, an international mediator with an impressive track record, announces a temporary negotiated ceasefire between Bosnian Serbs and Muslims in December 1994.

bin, 1989). Six months later, after further mediation by President Carter during visits to both countries, Begin and Sadat signed a treaty ending a state of war that had existed since 1948.

Arbitration

Some conflicts are so intractable, the underlying interests so divergent, that a mutually satisfactory resolution is unattainable. Bosnian Serbs and Muslims could not both have jurisdiction over the same homelands. In a divorce dispute over custody of a child, both parents cannot enjoy full custody. In these and many other cases (disputes over tenants' repair bills, athletes' wages, and national territories), a third-party mediator may—or may not—help resolve the conflict.

If not, the parties may turn to *arbitration* by having the mediator or another third party *impose* a settlement. Disputants usually prefer to settle their differences without arbitration, so they retain control over the outcome. Neil McGillicuddy and others (1987) observed this preference in an experiment involving disputants coming to the Dispute Settlement Center in Buffalo, New York. When people knew they would face an arbitrated settlement if mediation failed, they tried harder to resolve the problem, exhibited less hostility, and thus were more likely to reach agreement.

However, in cases where differences seem large and irreconcilable, the prospect of arbitration may have an opposite effect (Pruitt, 1986). The disputants may freeze their positions, hoping to gain an advantage when the arbitrator chooses a compromise. To combat this tendency, some disputes, such

"In the research on the effects of mediation one finding stands out: The worse the state of the parties' relationship is with one another, the dimmer the prospects that mediation will be successful."
Kenneth Kressel & Dean Pruitt (1985)

as those involving salaries of individual baseball players, are settled with "final-offer arbitration" in which the third party chooses one of the two final offers. Final-offer arbitration motivates each party to make a reasonable proposal.

Typically, however, the final offer is not so reasonable as it would be if each party, free of self-serving bias, saw its own proposal through others' eyes. Negotiation researchers report that most disputants are made stubborn by "optimistic overconfidence" (Kahneman & Tversky, 1995). Successful mediation is hindered when, as often happens, both parties believe they have a two-thirds chance of winning a final-offer arbitration (Bazerman, 1986, 1990).

CONCILIATION

Sometimes tension and suspicion run so high that communication, much less resolution, becomes all but impossible. Each party may threaten, coerce, or retaliate against the other. Unfortunately, such acts tend to be reciprocated, thus escalating the conflict. So, would a strategy of appeasing the other party by being unconditionally cooperative produce a satisfying result? Often not. In laboratory games, those who are 100 percent cooperative often get exploited. Politically, a one-sided pacifism is out of the question anyway.

GRIT

Is there a third alternative—one that is conciliatory, rather than retaliatory, yet strong enough to discourage exploitation? Social psychologist Charles Osgood (1962, 1980) advocated one such alternative. Osgood called it "graduated and

GRIT:
Acronym for "graduated and reciprocated initiatives in tension reduction"—a strategy designed to deescalate international tensions.

"Don't worry, dear—it's just a *peace* offensive."

People perceive that they respond more favorably to conciliation, but that others might be responsive to coercion.

reciprocated initiatives in tension reduction," nicknamed **GRIT,** a label that suggests the determination it requires. GRIT aims to reverse the conflict spiral by triggering reciprocal deescalation. To do so, it draws upon social-psychological concepts, such as the norm of reciprocity and the attribution of motives.

GRIT requires one side to initiate a few small deescalatory actions, undertaken after *announcing a conciliatory intent*. The initiator states its desire to reduce tension, declares each conciliatory act prior to making it, and invites the adversary to reciprocate. Such announcements create a framework that helps the adversary correctly interpret what otherwise might be seen as weak or tricky actions. They also bring public pressure on the adversary to follow the reciprocity norm.

Next, the initiator establishes credibility and genuineness by carrying out, exactly as announced, several verifiable *conciliatory acts*. This intensifies the pressure to reciprocate. Making conciliatory acts diverse—perhaps offering medical information, closing a military base, and lifting a trade ban—keeps the initiator from making a significant sacrifice in any one area and leaves the adversary freer to choose its own means of reciprocation. If the adversary reciprocates voluntarily, its own conciliatory behavior may soften its attitudes.

GRIT *is* conciliatory. But it is not "surrender on the installment plan." The remaining aspects of the plan protect each side's self-interest by *maintaining retaliatory capability*. The initial conciliatory steps entail some small risk but do not jeopardize either one's security; rather, they are calculated to begin edging both sides down the tension ladder. If one side takes an aggressive action, the other side reciprocates in kind, making it clear it will not tolerate exploitation. Yet, the reciprocal act is not an overresponse that would reescalate the conflict. If the adversary offers its own conciliatory acts, these, too, are matched or even slightly exceeded. Conflict expert Morton Deutsch (1993) captures the spirit of GRIT in advising negotiators to be "'firm, fair, and friendly': *firm* in resisting intimidation, exploitation, and dirty tricks; *fair* in holding to one's moral principles and not reciprocating the other's immoral behavior despite his or her provocations; and *friendly* in the sense that one is willing to initiate and reciprocate cooperation."

Does GRIT really work? In laboratory dilemma games the most successful strategy has proved to be simple "tit-for-tat," which begins with a cooperative opening play and thereafter matches the other party's last response (Axelrod & Dion, 1988; Komorita & others, 1992; Smith, 1987). Tit-for-tat tries to cooperate and is forgiving, yet does not tolerate exploitation. In a lengthy series of experiments at Ohio University, Svenn Lindskold and his associates (1976 to 1988) have tested other aspects of the GRIT strategy. Lindskold (1978) reports that his own and others' studies provide "strong support for the various steps in the GRIT proposal." In laboratory games, announcing cooperative intent *does* boost cooperation. Repeated conciliatory acts *do* breed greater trust (although self-serving biases often make one's own acts seem more conciliatory and less hostile than those of the adversary). Maintaining an equality of power *does* protect against exploitation.

Lindskold is not contending that the world of the laboratory experiment mirrors the more complex world of everyday life. Rather, experiments enable us to formulate and verify powerful theoretical principles, such as the reciprocity norm and the self-serving bias. Notes Lindskold (1981): "It is the theories, not the individual experiments, that are used to interpret the world."

"Perhaps the best policy in the nuclear age is to speak softly and carry a small- to medium-sized stick."
Richard Ned Lebow and Janice Stein (1987)

Applications in the Real World

GRIT-like strategies have occasionally been tried outside the laboratory, with promising results. During the Berlin crisis of the early 1960s, U.S. and Soviet tanks faced one another barrel to barrel. The crisis was defused when the Americans pulled back their tanks step by step. At each step, the Soviets reciprocated. More recently, small concessions by Israel and Egypt (for example, Israel allowing Egypt to open up the Suez Canal, Egypt allowing ships bound for Israel to pass through) helped reduce tension to a point where the negotiations became possible (Rubin, 1981).

To many, the most significant attempt at GRIT was the so-called Kennedy experiment (Etzioni, 1967). On June 10, 1963, President Kennedy gave a major speech, "A Strategy for Peace." In it he noted, "Our problems are man-made . . . and can be solved by man," and then announced his first conciliatory act: The United States was stopping all atmospheric nuclear tests and would not resume them unless another country did. In the Soviet Union, Kennedy's speech was published in full. Five days later Premier Khrushchev reciprocated, announcing he had halted production of strategic bombers. There soon followed further reciprocal gestures: The United States agreed to sell wheat to Russia, the Soviets agreed to a "hot line" between the two countries, and the two countries soon achieved a test-ban treaty. For a time, these conciliatory initiatives warmed relations between the two countries.

As they warmed again, within all our memories, President Bush in 1991 ordered the elimination of all land-based U.S. tactical nuclear warheads and took strategic bombers off high alert, putting their bombs in storage. Although leaving intact his least vulnerable and most extensive nuclear arsenal—submarine-based missiles—he invited Mikhail Gorbachev to reciprocate. Eight days later Gorbachev did, taking his bombers off alert, storing their bombs, and announcing the removal of nuclear weapons from short-range rockets, ships, and submarines.

Might conciliatory efforts also help reduce tension between individuals? There is every reason to expect so. When a relationship is strained and communication nonexistent, it sometimes takes only a conciliatory gesture—a soft answer, a warm smile, a gentle touch—for both parties to begin easing down the tension ladder, to a rung where contact, cooperation, and communication again become possible.

"I am not suggesting that principles of individual behavior can be applied to the behavior of nations in any direct, simple-minded fashion. What I am trying to suggest is that such principles may provide us with hunches about international behavior that can be tested against experience in the larger arena."
Charles E. Osgood (1966)

SUMMING UP

Although conflicts are readily kindled and fueled by social dilemmas, competition, and misperceptions, some equally powerful forces, such as contact, cooperation, communication, and conciliation, can transform hostility into harmony.

Might putting people into close contact reduce their hostilities? Despite some encouraging early studies, other studies show that in schools mere desegregation has little effect upon racial attitudes. But when interracial contact is prolonged and intimate, and when it is structured to convey *equal status*, hostilities often lessen.

Contacts are especially beneficial when people work together to overcome a common threat or to achieve a superordinate goal. Taking their cue from experiments on cooperative contact, several research teams have replaced competitive classroom learning situations with opportunities for cooperative learning, with heartening results.

Conflicting parties can also seek to resolve their differences by bargaining either directly or through a third-party mediator. Third-party mediators can help by prodding the antagonists to replace their competitive win-lose view of their conflict with a more cooperative win-win orientation. Mediators can also structure communications that will peel away misperceptions and increase mutual understanding and trust. When a negotiated settlement is not reached, the conflicting parties may defer the outcome to an arbitrator, who either dictates a settlement or selects one of the two final offers.

Sometimes tensions run so high that genuine communication is impossible. In such cases, small conciliatory gestures by one party may elicit reciprocal conciliatory acts by the other party. One such conciliatory strategy, GRIT (graduated and reciprocated initiatives in tension reduction), aims to alleviate tense international situations.

Those who mediate tense labor-management and international conflicts sometimes use another peacemaking strategy. They instruct the participants, as this chapter instructed you, in the dynamics of conflict and peacemaking in the hope that understanding can help us establish and enjoy peaceful, rewarding relationships.

■ FOR FURTHER READING

Fisher, R., Ury, W. L., & Patton, B. M. (1991). *Getting to yes: Negotiating agreement without giving in* (2d ed.). Boston: Penguin Books. A resoundingly successful (more than 2 million copies sold) summary of practical negotiation principles. Advocates replacing a win-lose with a "mutual gains approach."

Johnson, D. W., & Johnson, R. T. (1987). *Learning together and alone: Cooperative, competitive and individualistic learning* (2d ed.). Englewood Cliffs, NJ: Prentice-Hall. Offers teachers strategies for implementing various goals, including steps for creating interdependent learning activities.

Pruitt, D. G., & Rubin, J. Z. (1986). *Social conflict: Escalation, stalemate, and settlement.* New York: Random House. Two prominent social psychologists draw on both research and anecdote to explain how conflicts arise, escalate, and are resolved.

Rubin, J. Z., & Rubin, C. (1989). *When families fight: How to manage conflict with those you love.* New York: Arbor House/William Morrow. Identifies the reasons families fight and how they can manage conflict more constructively.

Worchel, S., & Simpson, J. A. (Eds.) (1992). *Conflict between people and groups: Causes, processes, and resolutions.* Chicago: Nelson-Hall. Expert social psychologists offer state-of-the-art reviews of the roots and fruits of interpersonal, intergroup, and international conflicts.

GLOSSARY

Acceptance: Conformity that involves both acting and believing in accord with social pressure.

Adaptation-level phenomenon: The tendency to adapt to a given level of stimulation and thus to notice and react to changes from that level.

Aggression: Physical or verbal behavior intended to hurt someone. In laboratory experiments, this might mean delivering electric shocks or saying something likely to hurt another's feelings. By this social psychological definition, one can be socially assertive without being aggressive.

Altruism: A motive to increase another's welfare without conscious regard for one's self-interests.

Arbitration: Resolution of a conflict by a neutral third party who studies both sides and imposes a settlement.

Attitude: A favorable or unfavorable evaluative reaction toward something or someone, exhibited in one's beliefs, feelings, or intended behavior.

Attitude inoculation: Exposing people to weak attacks upon their attitudes so that when stronger attacks come, they will have refutations available.

Attractiveness: Having qualities that appeal to an audience. An appealing communicator (often someone similar to the audience) is most persuasive on matters of subjective preference.

Attribution theory: The theory of how people explain others' behavior—for example, by attributing it either to internal *dispositions* (enduring traits, motives, and attitudes) or to external *situations*.

Autokinetic phenomenon: Self (*auto*) motion (*kinetic*). The apparent movement of a stationary point of light in the dark. Perhaps you have experienced this when thinking you have spotted a moving satellite in the sky, only to realize later that it was merely an isolated star.

Availability heuristic: An efficient but fallible rule-of-thumb that judges the likelihood of things in terms of their availability in memory. If instances of something come readily to mind, we presume it to be commonplace.

Bargaining: Seeking an agreement through direct negotiation between parties to a conflict.

Base-rate fallacy: The tendency to ignore or underuse base-rate information (in-formation that describes most people) and instead to be influenced by distinctive features of the case being judged.

Behavioral confirmation: A type of self-fulfilling prophecy whereby people's social expectations lead them to act in ways that cause others to confirm their expectations.

Behavioral medicine: An interdisciplinary field that integrates and applies behavioral and medical knowledge about health and disease.

Belief perseverance: Persistence of one's initial conceptions, as when the basis for one's belief is discredited but an explanation of why the belief might be true survives.

Bogus pipeline: A false procedure that fools people into disclosing their attitudes. Participants are first convinced that a new machine can use their psychological responses to measure their private attitudes. Then they are asked to predict the machine's reading, thus revealing their attitudes.

Bystander effect: The finding that a person is less likely to provide help when there are other bystanders.

Catharsis: Emotional release. The catharsis view of aggression is that aggressive drive is reduced when one "releases" aggressive energy, either by acting aggressively or by fantasizing aggression.

Central route persuasion: Persuasion that occurs when interested people focus on the arguments and respond with favorable thoughts.

Channel of communication: The way the message is delivered—whether face to face, in writing, on film, or in some other way.

Clinical psychology: The study, assessment, and treatment of people with psychological difficulties.

Coactors: A group of people working simultaneously and individually on a noncompetitive task.

Cognitive dissonance: Tension that arises when one is simultaneously aware of two inconsistent cognitions. For example, dissonance may occur when we realize that we have, with little justification, acted contrary to our attitudes or made a decision favoring one alternative despite reasons favoring another.

Cohesiveness: A "we feeling"—the extent to which members of a group are bound together, such as by attraction for one another.

Collectivism: The concept of giving priority to the goals of one's groups (often one's extended family or work group) and defining one's identity accordingly.

Communitarianism: An effort to synthesize aspects of both individualism (respecting basic individual rights) and collectivism (caring for the well-being of families and communities).

Companionate love: The affection we feel for those with whom our lives are deeply intertwined.

Complementarity: The supposed tendency, in a relationship between two people, for each to complete what is missing in the other. The questionable complementarity hypothesis proposes that people attract those whose needs are different, in ways that complement their own.

Compliance: Conformity that involves publicly acting in accord with social pressure while privately disagreeing.

Confederate: An accomplice of the experimenter.

Confirmation bias: A tendency to search for information that confirms one's preconceptions.

Conflict: A perceived incompatibility of actions or goals.

Conformity: A change in behavior or belief as a result of real or imagined group pressure.

Correlational research: The study of the naturally occurring relationships among variables.

Counterfactual thinking: Imagining alternative scenarios and outcomes that might have happened, but didn't.

Credibility: Believability. A credible communicator is perceived as both expert and trustworthy.

Crowding: A subjective feeling of not enough space per person.

Cult: A group typically characterized by (1) the distinctive ritual of its devotion to a god or a person, (2) isolation from the surrounding "evil" culture, and (3) a charismatic leader. (A *sect*, by contrast, is a spinoff from a major religion.)

Culture: The enduring behaviors, ideas, attitudes, and traditions shared by a large group of people and transmitted from one generation to the next.

Deindividuation: Loss of self-awareness and evaluation apprehension; occurs in group situations that foster anonymity and draw attention away from the individual.

Demand characteristics: Cues in an experiment that tell the participant what behavior is expected.

Dependent variable: The variable being measured, so-called because it may *depend* on manipulations of the independent variable.

Depressive realism: The tendency of mildly depressed people to make accurate rather than self-serving judgments, attributions, and predictions.

Disclosure reciprocity: The tendency for one person's intimacy of self-disclosure to match that of a conversational partner.

Discrimination: Unjustifiable negative behavior toward a group or its members.

Displacement: The redirection of aggression to a target other than the source of the frustration. Generally, the new target is a safer or more socially acceptable target.

Door-in-the-face technique: A strategy for gaining a concession. After someone first turns down a large request (the door-in-the-face), the same requester counteroffers with a more reasonable request.

Egoism: A motive (supposedly underlying all behavior) to increase one's own welfare. The opposite of *altruism,* which aims to increase another's welfare.

Empathy: The vicarious experience of another's feelings; putting oneself in another's shoes.

Equal-status contact: Contact made on an equal basis. Just as a relationship between people of unequal status breeds attitudes consistent with their relationship, so do relationships between those of equal status. Thus, to reduce prejudice, interracial contact should be between persons equal in status.

Equity: A condition in which the outcomes people receive from a relationship are proportional to what they contribute to it. Note: Equitable outcomes needn't always be equal outcomes.

Ethnocentrism: A belief in the superiority of one's own ethnic and cultural group, and a corresponding disdain for all other groups.

Evaluation apprehension: Concern for how others are evaluating us.

Evolutionary psychology: The study of the evolution of behavior using the principles of natural selection; assumes that natural selection favors information processing and behaviors that, in particular environments, contribute to the preservation and spread of one's genes.

Experimental realism: Degree to which an experiment absorbs and involves its participants.

Experimental research: Studies that seek clues to cause-effect relationships by manipulating one or more factors (independent variables) while controlling others (holding them constant).

Explanatory style: One's habitual way of explaining life events. A negative pessimistic, depressive explanatory style attributes failures to stable, global, and internal causes.

False consensus effect: The tendency to overestimate the commonality of one's opinions and one's undesirable or unsuccessful behaviors.

False uniqueness effect: The tendency to underestimate the commonality of one's abilities and one's desirable or successful behaviors.

Field research: Research done in natural, real-life settings outside the laboratory.

Foot-in-the-door phenomenon: The tendency for people who have first agreed to a small request to comply later with a larger request.

Free riders: People who benefit from the group but give little in return.

Frustration: The blocking of goal-directed behavior.

Fundamental attribution error: The tendency for observers to underestimate situational influences and overestimate dispositional influences upon others' behavior. (Also called *correspondence bias,* because we so often see behavior as corresponding to a disposition.)

Gender: In psychology, the characteristics, whether biologically or socially influenced, by which people define male and female. Because "sex" is a biological category, social psychologists often refer to biologically based gender differences as "sex differences."

Gender role: A set of behavior expectations (norms) for males or females.

GRIT: Acronym for "graduated and reciprocated initiatives in tension reduc-

tion"—a strategy designed to deescalate international tensions.

Group: Two or more people who, for longer than a few moments, interact with and influence one another and perceive one another as "us."

Group polarization: Group-produced enhancement of members' preexisting tendencies; a strengthening of the members' *average* tendency, not a split within the group.

Group-serving bias: Explaining away outgroup members' positive behaviors; also attributing negative behaviors to their dispositions (while excusing such behavior by one's own group).

Groupthink: "The mode of thinking that persons engage in when concurrence-seeking becomes so dominant in a cohesive in-group that it tends to override realistic appraisal of alternative courses of action." Irving Janis (1971)

Health psychology: A subfield of psychology that provides psychology's contribution to behavioral medicine.

Hindsight bias: The tendency to exaggerate, *after* learning an outcome, one's ability to have foreseen how something turned out. Also known as the *I-knew-it-all-along phenomenon.*

Hostile aggression: Aggression driven by anger and performed as an end in itself.

Hypothesis: A testable proposition that describes a relationship that may exist between events.

Illusion of control: Perception of uncontrollable events as subject to one's control or as more controllable than they are.

Illusory correlation: Perception of a relationship where none exists, or perception of a stronger relationship than actually exists.

Independent variable: The experimental factor that a researcher manipulates.

Individualism: The concept of giving priority to one's own goals over group goals and defining one's identity in terms of personal attributes rather than group identifications.

Informational influence: Conformity that results from accepting evidence about reality provided by other people.

Informed consent: An ethical principle requiring that research participants be told enough to enable them to choose whether they wish to participate.

Ingratiation: The use of strategies, such as flattery, by which people seek to gain another's favor.

Ingroup: "Us"—a group of people who share a sense of belonging, a feeling of common identity.

Ingroup bias: The tendency to favor one's own group.

Instinctive behavior: An innate, unlearned behavior pattern exhibited by all members of a species.

Instrumental aggression: Aggression that is a means to some other end.

Insufficient justification effect: Reduction of dissonance by internally justifying one's behavior when external justification is "insufficient."

Integrative agreements: Win-win agreements that reconcile both parties' interests to their mutual benefit.

Interaction: The effect of one factor (such as biology) depends on another factor (such as environment).

Just-world phenomenon: The tendency of people to believe that the world is just and that people therefore get what they deserve and deserve what they get.

Kin selection: The idea that evolution has selected altruism toward one's close relatives to enhance the survival of mutually shared genes.

Leadership: The process by which certain group members motivate and guide the group.

Learned helplessness: The hopelessness and resignation learned when a human or animal perceives no control over repeated bad events.

Locus of control: The extent to which people perceive their lives as internally controllable by their own efforts and actions or as externally controlled by chance or outside forces.

Low-ball technique: A tactic for getting people to agree to something. People who agree to an initial request will often still comply when the requester ups the ante. People who receive only the costly request are less likely to comply with it.

Matching phenomenon: The tendency for men and women to choose as partners those who are a "good match" in attractiveness and other traits.

Mediation: An attempt by a neutral third party to resolve a conflict by facilitating communication and offering suggestions.

Mere-exposure effect: The tendency for novel stimuli to be liked more or rated more positively after the rater has been repeatedly exposed to them.

Mirror-image perceptions: Reciprocal views of one another often held by parties in conflict; for example, each may view itself as moral and peace-loving and the other as evil and aggressive.

Misinformation effect: Witnessing an event, receiving misleading information about it, and then incorporating the "misinformation" into one's memory of the event.

Moral exclusion: The perception of certain individuals or groups as outside the boundary within which one applies moral values and rules of fairness. Moral *inclusion* is regarding others as within one's circle of moral concern.

Mundane realism: Degree to which an experiment is superficially similar to everyday situations.

Naturalistic fallacy: The error of defining what is good in terms of what is observable. For example: What's typical is normal; what's normal is good.

Need to belong: A motivation to bond with others in relationships that provide ongoing, positive interactions.

Non-zero-sum games: Games in which outcomes need not sum to zero. With cooperation, both can win; with competition, both can lose. (Also called *mixed-motive situations.*)

Normative influence: Conformity based on a person's desire to fulfill others' expectations, often to gain acceptance.

Norms: Rules for accepted and expected behavior. Norms *prescribe* "proper" behavior. (In a different sense of the word, norms also *describe* what most others do—what is *normal.*)

Outgroup: "Them"—a group that people perceive as distinctively different from or apart from their ingroup.

Outgroup homogeneity effect: Perception of outgroup members as more similar to one another than are ingroup members. Thus "they are alike; we are diverse."

Overconfidence phenomenon: The tendency to be more confident than correct—to overestimate the accuracy of one's beliefs.

Overjustification effect: The result of bribing people to do what they already like doing; they may then see their action as externally controlled rather than intrinsically appealing.

Passionate love: A state of intense longing for union with another. Passionate lovers are absorbed in one another,

feel ecstatic at attaining their partner's love, and are disconsolate on losing it.

Peripheral route persuasion: Persuasion that occurs when people are influenced by incidental cues, such as a speaker's attractiveness.

Personal space: The buffer zone we like to maintain around our bodies. Its size depends on our familiarity with whomever is near us.

Physical-attractiveness stereotype: The presumption that physically attractive people possess other socially desirable traits as well: What is beautiful is good.

Pluralistic ignorance: A false impression of how other people are thinking, feeling, or responding.

Possible selves: Images of what we dream of or dread becoming in the future.

Prejudice: An unjustifiable negative attitude toward a group and its individual members.

Primacy effect: Other things being equal, information presented first usually has the most influence.

Priming: Activating particular associations in memory.

Prosocial behavior: Positive, constructive, helpful social behavior; the opposite of antisocial behavior.

Proximity: Geographical nearness. Proximity (more precisely, "functional distance") powerfully predicts liking.

Racism: (1) Individual's prejudicial attitudes and discriminatory behavior toward people of a given race, or (2) institutional practices (even if not motivated by prejudice) that subordinate people of a given race.

Random assignment: The process of assigning participants to the conditions of an experiment such that all persons have the same chance of being in a given condition. (Note the distinction between random *assignment* in experiments and random *sampling* in surveys. Random assignment helps us infer cause and effect. Random sampling helps us generalize to a population.)

Random sample: Survey procedure in which every person in the population being studied has an equal chance of inclusion.

Reactance: A motive to protect or restore one's sense of freedom. Reactance arises when someone threatens our freedom of action.

Realistic group conflict theory: The theory that prejudice arises from competition between groups for scarce resources.

Recency effect: Information presented last sometimes has the most influence. Recency effects are less common than primacy effects.

Reciprocity norm: An expectation that people will help, not hurt, those who have helped them.

Regression toward the average: The statistical tendency for extreme scores or extreme behavior to return toward one's average.

Relative deprivation: The perception that one is less well off than others to whom one compares oneself.

Representativeness heuristic: The strategy of judging the likelihood of things by how well they represent, or match, particular prototypes; may lead one to ignore other relevant information.

Reward theory of attraction: The theory that we like those whose behavior is rewarding to us or whom we associate with rewarding events.

Role: A set of norms that define how people in a given social position ought to behave.

Self-awareness: A self-conscious state in which attention focuses on oneself. It makes people more sensitive to their own attitudes and dispositions.

Self-disclosure: Revealing intimate aspects of oneself to others.

Self-efficacy: A sense that one is competent and effective. Distinguished from self-esteem, a sense of one's self-worth. A bombardier might feel high self-efficacy and low self-esteem.

Self-esteem: A person's overall self-evaluation or sense of self-worth.

Self-handicapping: Protecting one's self-image by creating a handy excuse for failure.

Self-monitoring: Being attuned to the way one presents oneself in social situ-

ations and adjusting one's performance to create the desired impression.

Self-perception theory: The theory that when unsure of our attitudes, we infer them much as would someone observing us—by looking at our behavior and the circumstances under which it occurs.

Self-presentation: The act of expressing oneself and behaving in ways designed to create a favorable impression or an impression that corresponds to one's ideals.

Self-reference effect: The tendency to process efficiently and remember well information related to oneself.

Self-schema: Beliefs about self that organize and guide the processing of self-relevant information.

Self-serving bias: The tendency to perceive oneself favorably.

Sexism: (1) Individual's prejudicial attitudes and discriminatory behavior toward people of a given sex, or (2) institutional practices (even if not motivated by prejudice) that subordinate people of a given sex.

Sleeper effect: A delayed impact of a message; occurs when we remember the message but forget a reason for discounting it.

Social comparison: Evaluating one's opinions and abilities by comparing oneself to others.

Social-exchange theory: The theory that human interactions are transactions that aim to maximize one's rewards and minimize one's costs.

Social facilitation: (1) Original meaning—the tendency of people to perform simple or well-learned tasks better when others are present. (2) Current meaning—the strengthening of dominant (prevalent, likely) responses owing to the presence of others.

Social identity: The "we" aspect of our self-concept. The part of our answer to "Who am I?" that comes from our group memberships. Examples: "I am Australian." "I am Catholic."

Social learning theory: The theory that we learn social behavior by observing and imitating and by being rewarded and punished.

Social loafing: The tendency for people to exert less effort when they pool their efforts toward a common goal than when they are individually accountable.

Social psychology: The scientific study of how people think about, influence, and relate to one another.

Social representations: Socially shared beliefs. Widely held ideas and values, including our assumptions and cultural ideologies. Our social representations help us make sense of our world.

Social-responsibility norm: An expectation that people will help those dependent upon them.

Stereotype: A belief about the personal attributes of a group of people. Stereotypes can be overgeneralized, inaccurate, and resistant to new information.

Stereotype vulnerability: A disruptive apprehension that one will verify a negative stereotype.

Superordinate goal: A shared goal that necessitates cooperative effort; a goal that overrides people's differences from one another.

Theory: An integrated set of principles that explain and predict observed events.

Two-factor theory of emotion: Arousal $\times$ label = emotion.

Two-step flow of communication: The process by which media influence often occurs through opinion leaders, who in turn influence others.

REFERENCES

Abbey, A. (1987). Misperceptions of friendly behavior as sexual interest: A survey of naturally occurring incidents. *Psychology of Women Quarterly,* **11**, 173–194. (p. 75)

Abbey, A. (1991). Misperception as an antecedent of acquaintance rape: A consequence of ambiguity in communication between women and men. In A. Parrot (Ed.), *Acquaintance rape.* New York: John Wiley. (p. 75)

Abbey, A., & Andrews, F. M. (1985). Modeling the psychological determinants of life quality. *Social Indicators Research,* **16**, 1–34. (p. 480)

Abbey, A., Ross, L. T., & McDuffie, D. (1993). Alcohol's role in sexual assault. In R. R. Watson (Ed.), *Drug and alcohol abuse reviews, vol 5: Addictive behaviors in women.* Totowa, NJ: Humana Press. (p. 441)

Abelson, R. (1972). Are attitudes necessary? In B. T. King & E. McGinnies (Eds.), *Attitudes, conflict and social change.* New York: Academic Press. (p. 125)

Abelson, R. P., Kinder, D. R., Peters, M. D., & Fiske, S. T. (1982). Affective and semantic components in political person perception. *Journal of Personality and Social Psychology,* **42**, 619–630. (p. 281)

Abrams, D. (1991). AIDS: What young people believe and what they do. Paper presented at the British Association for the Advancement of Science conference. (p. 56)

Abrams, D. (1994). Social self-regulation. *Personality and Social Psychology Bulletin,* **20**, 473–483. (p. 407)

Abrams, D., Wetherell, M., Cochrane, S., Hogg, M. A., & Turner, J. C. (1990). Knowing what to think by knowing who you are: Self-categorization and the nature of norm formation, conformity and group polarization. *British Journal of Social Psychology,* **29**, 97–119. (p. 337)

Abramson, L. Y. (Ed.). (1988). *Social cognition and clinical psychology: A synthesis.* New York: Guilford. (p. 188)

Abramson, L. Y., Metalsky, G. I., & Alloy, L. B. (1989). Hopelessness depression: A theory-based subtype. *Psychological Review,* **96**, 358–372. (p. 174)

Acitelli, L. K., & Antonucci, T. C. (1994). Gender differences in the link between marital support and satisfaction in older couples. *Journal of Personality and Social Psychology,* **67**, 688–698. (p. 197)

Ackermann, R., & DeRubeis, R. J. (1991). Is depressive realism real? *Clinical Psychology Review,* **11**, 565–584. (p. 173)

Adair, J. G., Dushenko, T. W., & Lindsay, R. C. L. (1985). Ethical regulations and their impact on research practice. *American Psychologist,* **40**, 59–72. (p. 25)

Adams, D. (Ed.) (1991). *The Seville statement on violence: Preparing the ground for the constructing of peace.* UNESCO. (p. 441)

Aderman, D., & Berkowitz, L. (1970). Observational set, empathy, and helping. *Journal of Personality and Social Psychology,* **14**, 141–148. (p. 548)

Aderman, D., & Berkowitz, L. (1983). Self-concern and the unwillingness to be helpful. *Social Psychology Quarterly,* **46**, 293–301. (p. 549)

Adler, R. P., Lesser, G. S., Meringoff, L. K., Robertson, T. S., & Ward, S. (1980). *The effects of television advertising on children.* Lexington, Mass.: Lexington Books. (p. 307)

Adler, S. J. (1994). *The jury.* New York: Times Books. (p. 376)

Adorno, T., Frenkel-Brunswik, E., Levinson, D., & Sanford, R. N. (1950). *The authoritarian personality,* New York: Harper. (p. 415)

Agnew, C. R., Currey, D. P., & Thompson, V. D. (1994). Will racism theories with significant empirical support please stand up? Paper presented at the American Psychological Association convention. (p. 409)

Agostinelli, G., Sherman, S. J., Presson, C. C., & Chassin, L. (1992). Self-protection and self-enhancement biases in estimates of population prevalence. *Personality and Social Psychology Bulletin,* **18**, 631–642. (p. 60)

Agres, S. J. (1987). Rational, emotional and mixed appeals in advertising: Impact on recall and persuasion. Paper presented at the American Psychological Association convention. (Available from Lowe Marschalk, Inc., 1345 Avenue of the Americas, New York, N.Y., 10105.) (p. 281)

Aiello, J. R., Thompson, D. E., & Brodzinsky, D. M. (1983). How funny is crowding anyway? Effects of room size, group size, and the introduction of humor. *Basic and Applied Social Psychology,* **4**, 193–207. (p. 319)

Ainsworth, M. D. S. (1973). The development of infant-mother attachment. In B. Caldwell & H. Ricciuti (Eds.), *Review of child development research* (Vol. 3). Chicago: University of Chicago Press. (p. 509)

Ainsworth, M. D. S. (1979). Infant-mother attachment. *American Psychologist,* **34**, 932–937. (p. 509)

Ainsworth, M. D. S. (1989). Attachments beyond infancy. *American Psychologist,* **44**, 709–716. (p. 509)

Ajzen, I. (1982). On behaving in accordance with one's attitudes. In M. P. Zanna, E. T. Higgins, & C. P. Herman (Eds.). *Consistency in social behavior: The Ontario Symposium,* vol. 2. Hillside, N.J.: Erlbaum. (p. 128)

Ajzen, I., & Fishbein, M. (1977). Attitude-behavior relations: A theoretical analysis and review of empirical research. *Psychological Bulletin,* **84**, 888–918. (p. 128)

Ajzen, I., & Timko, C. (1986). Correspondence between health attitudes and behavior. *Basic and Applied Social Psychology,* **7**, 259–276. (p. 129)

Albee, G. (1979, June 19). Politics, power, prevention, and social change. Keynote address to Vermont Conference on Primary Prevention of Psychopathology. (p. 228)

Aldag, R. J., & Fuller, S. R. (1993). Beyond fiasco: A reappraisal of the groupthink phenomenon and a new model of group decision processes. *Psychological Bulletin,* **113**, 533–552. (p. 345)

Alicke, M. D., & Davis, T. L. (1989). The role of *a posteriori* victim information in judgments of blame and sanction. *Journal of Experimental Social Psychology,* **25**, 362–377. (p. 374)

Alicke, M. D., Klotz, M. L., Breitenbecher, D. L., Yurak, T. J., & Vredenburg, D. S. (1995). Personal contact, individuation and the better than average effect. *Journal of Personality and Social Psychology,* **68**, 804–825. (p. 54)

Allee, W. C., & Masure, R. M. (1936). A comparison of maze behavior in paired and isolated shell-parakeets (*Melopsittacus undulatus Shaw*) in a two-alley problem box. *Journal of Comparative Psychology,* **22**, 131–155. (p. 315)

609

Allen, V. L., & Levine, J. M. (1969). Consensus and conformity. *Journal of Experimental Social Psychology*, **5**, 389–399. (p. 254)

Allen, V. L., & Wilder, D. A. (1980). Impact of group consensus and social support on stimulus meaning: Mediation of conformity by cognitive restructuring. *Journal of Personality and Social Psychology*, **39**, 1116–1124. (p. 260)

Allgeier, A. R., Byrne, D., Brooks, B., & Revnes, D. (1979). The waffle phenomenon: Negative evaluations of those who shift attitudinally. *Journal of Applied Social Psychology*, **9**, 170–182. (p. 257)

Allison, S. T., Beggan, J. K., McDonald, R. A., & Rettew, M. L. (1995). The belief in majority determination of group decision outcomes. *Basic and Applied Social Psychology*, **16**, 367–382. (p. 418)

Allison, S. T., Jordan, M. R., & Yeatts, C. E. (1992). A cluster-analytic approach toward identifying the structure and content of human decision making. *Human Relations*, **45**, 49–72. (p. 575)

Allison, S. T., Mackie, D. M., Muller, M. M., & Worth, L. T. (1993). Sequential correspondence biases and perceptions of change: The Castro studies revisited. *Personality and Social Psychology Bulletin*, **19**, 151–157. (p. 80)

Allison, S. T., McQueen, L. R., & Schaerfl, L. M. (1992). Social decision making processes and the equal partitionment of shared resources. *Journal of Experimental Social Psychology*, **28**, 23–42. (p. 106)

Allison, S. T., & Messick, D. M. (1985). The group attribution error. *Journal of Experimental Social Psychology*, **21**, 563–579. (p. 418)

Allison, S. T., & Messick, D. M. (1987). From individual inputs to group outputs, and back again: Group processes and inferences about members. In C. Hendrick (Ed.), *Group processes: Review of personality and social psychology*, Vol. 8. Newbury Park, Ca.: Sage. (p. 418)

Allison, S. T., Messick, D. M., & Goethals, G. R. (1989). On being better but not smarter than others: The Muhammad Ali effect. *Social Cognition*, **7**, 275–296. (p. 55)

Allison, S. T., Worth, L. T., & King, M. W. C. (1990). Group decisions as social inference heuristics. *Journal of Personality and Social Psychology*, **58**, 801–811. (p. 418)

Alloy, L. B., & Abramson, L. Y. (1979). Judgment of contingency in depressed and nondepressed students: Sadder but wiser? *Journal of Experimental Psychology: General*, **108**, 441–485. (p. 173)

Alloy, L. B., Albright, J. S., Abramson, L. Y., & Dykman, B. M. (1990). Depressive realism and nondepressive optimistic illusions: The role of the self. In R. E. Ingram (Ed.), *Contemporary psychological approaches to depression: Theory, research and treatment*. New York: Plenum. (p. 173)

Alloy, L. B., & Clements, C. M. (1992). Illusion of control: Invulnerability to negative affect and depressive symptoms after laboratory and natural stressors. *Journal of Abnormal Psychology*, **101**, 234–245. (p. 176)

Allport, F. H. (1920). The influence of the group upon association and thought. *Journal of Experimental Psychology*, **3**, 159–182. (p. 315)

Allport, G. (1954). *The nature of prejudice*. Cambridge, Mass.: Addison-Wesley. (p. 595)

Allport, G. W. (1958). *The nature of prejudice* (abridged). Garden City, NY: Anchor Books. (pp. 402, 404, 405, 413)

Allport, G. W. (1978). *Waiting for the Lord: 33 Meditations on God and Man* (Edited by P. A. Bertocci). New York: Macmillan. (p. 56)

Allport, G. W., & Postman, L. (1958). *The psychology of rumor*. New York: Henry Holt and Co., 1975. (Originally published, 1947). Also in E. E. Maccoby, T. M. Newcomb, & E. L. Hartley (Eds.), *Readings in social psychology*. New York: Holt, Rinehart and Winston. (p. 413)

Allport, G. W., & Ross, J. M. (1967). Personal religious orientation and prejudice. *Journal of Personality and Social Psychology*, **5**, 432–443. (p. 404)

Altemeyer, B. (1988). *Enemies of freedom: Understanding right-wing authoritarianism*. San Francisco: Jossey-Bass. (p. 416)

Altemeyer, B. (1992). Six studies of right-wing authoritarianism among American state legislators. Unpublished manuscript, University of Manitoba. (p. 416)

Altermeyer, B., & Hunsberger, B. (1992). Authoritarianism, religious fundamentalism, quest, and prejudice. *International Journal for the Psychology of Religion*, **2**, 113–133. (p. 403)

Altman, I., & Vinsel, A. M. (1978). Personal space: An analysis of E. T. Hall's proxemics framework. In I. Altman & J. Wohlwill (Eds.), *Human behavior and the environment*. New York: Plenum Press. (p. 212)

Alwin, D. F. (1990). Historical changes in parental orientations to children. In N. Mandell (Ed.), *Sociological studies of child development*, Vol. 3. Greenwich, Ct.: JAI Press. (p. 217)

Alwin, D. F., Cohen, R. L., & Newcomb, T. M. (1991). *Political attitudes over the life span: The Bennington women after fifty years*. Madison, WI: University of Wisconsin Press. (p. 293)

Amabile, T. M., & Glazebrook, A. H. (1982). A negativity bias in interpersonal evaluation. *Journal of Experimental Social Psychology*, **18**, 1–22. (p. 414)

Amato, P. R. (1979). Juror-defendant similarity and the assessment of guilt in politically motivated crimes. *Australian Journal of Psychology*, **31**, 79–88. (p. 370)

Amato, P. R. (1986). Emotional arousal and helping behavior in a real-life emergency. *Journal of Applied Social Psychology*, **16**, 633–641. (p. 531)

Amato, P. R. (1990). Personality and social network involvement as predictors of helping behavior in everyday life. *Social Psychology Quarterly*, **53**, 31–43. (p. 553)

Ambady, N., & Rosenthal, R. (1992). Thin slices of expressive behavior as predictors of interpersonal consequences: A meta-analysis. *Psychological Bulletin*, **111**, 256–274. (p. 115)

Ambady, N., & Rosenthal, R. (1993). Half a minute: Predicting teacher evaluations from thin slices of nonverbal behavior and physical attractiveness. *Journal of Personality and Social Psychology*, **64**, 431–441. (p. 115)

American Enterprise (1991, March/April). Women and the use of force. Pp. 85–86. (p. 197)

American Enterprise (1992, January/February). Women, men, marriages & ministers. P. 106. (p. 216)

American Psychological Association (1981). Ethical principles of psychologists. *American Psychologist*, **36**, 633–638. (p. 29)

American Psychological Association (1992). Ethical principles of psychologists and code of conduct. Washington, D.C.: American Psychological Association, **47**, 1597–1611. (p. 29)

American Psychological Association (1993). *Violence and youth: Psychol-*

ogy's response. *Vol I: Summary report of the American Psychological Assocation Commission on Violence and Youth.* Washington DC: Public Interest Directorate, American Psychological Association. (pp. 440, 441, 468)

Amir, Y. (1969). Contact hypothesis in ethnic relations. *Psychological Bulletin,* 71, 319–342. (p. 587)

Anderson, C. A. (1982). Inoculation and counter-explanation: Debiasing techniques in the perseverance of social theories. *Social Cognition, 1,* 126–139. (p. 96)

Anderson, C. A. (1989). Temperature and aggression: Ubiquitous effects of heat on occurrence of human violence. *Psychological Bulletin,* 106, 74–96. (p. 454)

Anderson, C. A., Deuser, W. E., & DeNeve, K. M. (1995). Hot temperatures, hostile affect, hostile cognition, and arousal: Tests of a general model of affective aggression. *Personality and Social Psychology Bulletin,* 21, 434–448. (p. 456)

Anderson, C. A., & Harvey, R. J. (1988). Discriminating between problems in living: An examination of measures of depression, loneliness, shyness, and social anxiety. *Journal of Social and Clinical Psychology,* 6, 482–491. (p. 179)

Anderson, C. A., Horowitz, L. M., & French, R. D. (1983). Attributional style of lonely and depressed people. *Journal of Personality and Social Psychology,* 45, 127–136. (p. 62)

Anderson, C. A., Lepper, M. R., & Ross, L. (1980). Perseverance of social theories: The role of explanation in the persistence of discredited information. *Journal of Personality and Social Psychology,* 39, 1037–1049. (p. 95)

Anderson, C. A., Miller, R. S., Riger, A. L., Dill, J. C., & Sedikides, C. (1994). Behavioral and characterological attributional styles as predictors of depression and loneliness: Review, refinement, and test. *Journal of Personality and Social Psychology,* 66, 549–558. (p. 178)

Anderson, C. A., & Morrow, M. (1995). Competitive aggression without interaction: Effects of competitive versus cooperative instructions on aggressive behavior in video games. *Personality and Social Psychology Bulletin,* in press. (p. 578)

Anderson, C. A., & Sechler, E. S. (1986). Effects of explanation and counterexplanation on the development and use

of social theories. *Journal of Personality and Social Psychology,* 50, 24–34. (p. 96)

Anderson, N. H. (1968). A simple model of information integration. In R. B. Abelson, E. Aronson, W. J. McGuire, T. M. Newcomb, M. J. Rosenberg, & P. H. Tannenbaum (Eds.), *Theories of cognitive consistency: A sourcebook.* Chicago: Rand McNally. (p. 78)

Anderson, N. H. (1974). Cognitive algebra: Integration theory applied to social attribution. In L. Berkowitz (Ed.), *Advances in experimental social psychology,* Vol. 7. New York: Academic Press. (p. 78)

Anthony, T., Copper, C., & Mullen, B. (1992). Cross-racial facial identification: A social cognitive integration. *Personality and Social Psychology Bulletin,* 18, 296–301. (p. 420)

Antill, J. K. (1983). Sex role complementarity versus similarity in married couples. *Journal of Personality and Social Psychology,* 45, 145–155. (p. 198)

Apsler, R. (1975). Effects of embarrassment on behavior toward others. *Journal of Personality and Social Psychology,* 32, 145–153. (p. 548)

Archer, D., & Gartner, R. (1976). Violent acts and violent times: A comparative approach to postwar homicide rates. *American Sociological Review,* 41, 937–963. (p. 473)

Archer, D., & Gartner, R. (1984). Violence and crime in cross-national perspective. New Haven, CT: Yale University Press. (p. 438)

Archer, D., Iritani, B., Kimes, D. B., & Barrios, M. (1983). Face-ism: Five studies of sex differences in facial prominence. *Journal of Personality and Social Psychology,* 45, 725–735. (p. 411)

Archer, J. (1991). The influence of testosterone on human aggression. *British Journal of Psychology,* 82, 1–28. (p. 441)

Archer, R. L., & Cook, C. E. (1986). Personalistic self-disclosure and attraction: Basis for relationship or scarce resource. *Social Psychology Quarterly,* 49, 268–272. (p. 516)

Arendt, H. (1963). *Eichmann in Jerusalem: A report on the banality of evil.* New York: Viking Press. (p. 252)

Argyle, M., & Henderson M. (1985). *The anatomy of relationships.* London: Heinemann. (p. 203)

Argyle, M., Shimoda, K., & Little, B. (1978). Variance due to persons and situations in England and Japan. *British Journal of Social and Clinical Psychology,* 17, 335–337. (p. 227)

Arkes, H. R. (1990). Some practical judgment/decision making research. Paper presented at the American Psychological Association convention. (p. 289)

Arkin, R. M., Appleman, A., & Burger, J. M. (1980). Social anxiety, self-presentation, and the self-serving bias in causal attribution. *Journal of Personality and Social Psychology,* 38, 23–35. (pp. 54, 68)

Arkin, R. M., & Baumgardner, A. H. (1985). Self-handicapping. In J. H. Harvey & C. Weary (Eds.), *Attribution: Basic issues and applications.* New York: Academic Press. (p. 68)

Arkin, R. M., & Burger, J. M. (1980). Effects of unit relation tendencies on interpersonal attraction. *Social Psychology Quarterly,* 43, 380–391. (p. 482)

Arkin, R. M., Cooper, H., & Kolditz, T. (1980). A statistical review of the literature concerning the self-serving attribution bias in interpersonal influence situations. *Journal of Personality,* 48, 435–448. (p. 54)

Arkin, R. M., Lake, E. A., & Baumgardner, A. H. (1986). Shyness and self-presentation. In W. H. Jones, J. M. Cheek, & S. R. Briggs (Eds.), *Shyness: Perspectives on research and treatment.* New York: Plenum. (p. 66)

Arkin, R. M., & Maruyama, G. M. (1979). Attribution, affect, and college exam performance. *Journal of Educational Psychology,* 71, 85–93. (p. 54)

Arms, R. L., Russell, G. W., & Sandilands, M. L. (1979). Effects on the hostility of spectators of viewing aggressive sports. *Social Psychology Quarterly,* 42, 275–279. (p. 473)

Armstrong, B. (1981). An interview with Herbert Kelman. *APA Monitor,* January, pp. 4–5, 55. (p. 599)

Aron, A., & Aron, A. N. (1994). Love. In A. L. Weber & J. H. Harvey (eds.), *Perspective on close relationships.* Boston: Allyn & Bacon. (p. 517)

Aron, A., & Aron, E. (1989). *The heart of social psychology,* 2nd ed. Lexington, MA: Lexington Books. (pp. 237, 578)

Aron, A., Dutton, D. G., Aron, E. N., & Iverson, A. (1989). Experiences of falling in love. *Journal of Social and Personal Relationships,* 6, 243–257. (p. 497)

Aronson, E. (1980). *The social animal.* New York: Freeman. (p. 589)

Aronson, E. (1988). *The social animal.* New York: Freeman. (pp. 499, 589)

Aronson, E., Blaney, N., Stephan, C., Sikes, J., & Snapp, M. (1978). *The jigsaw classroom.* Beverly Hills, Calif.: Sage Publications. (p. 593)

Aronson, E., Brewer, M., & Carlsmith, J. M. (1985). Experimentation in social psychology. In G. Lindzey & E. Aronson (Eds.), *Handbook of social psychology,* vol. 1. Hillsdale, N.J.: Erlbaum. (p. 28)

Aronson, E., & Bridgeman, D. (1979). Jigsaw groups and the desegregated classroom: In pursuit of common goals. *Personality and Social Psychology Bulletin, 5,* 438–446. (p. 593)

Aronson, E., & Gonzalez, A. (1988). Desegregation, jigsaw, and the Mexican-American experience. In P. A. Katz & D. Taylor (Eds.), *Towards the elimination of racism: Profiles in controversy.* New York: Plenum. (p. 593)

Aronson, E., & Linder, D. (1965). Gain and loss of esteem as determinants of interpersonal attractiveness. *Journal of Experimental Social Psychology, 1,* 156–171. (p. 499)

Aronson, E., & Mettee, D. R. (1974). Affective reactions to appraisal from others. *Foundations of interpersonal attraction.* New York: Academic Press. (p. 499)

Aronson, E., & Mills, J. (1959). The effect of severity of initiation on liking for a group. *Journal of Abnormal and Social Psychology, 59,* 177–181. (p. 299)

Aronson, E., Turner, J. A., & Carlsmith, J. M. (1963). Communicator credibility and communicator discrepancy as determinants of opinion change. *Journal of Abnormal and Social Psychology, 67,* 31–36. (pp. 284, 285)

Asch, S. E. (1946). Forming impressions of personality. *Journal of Abnormal and Social Psychology, 41,* 258–290. (pp. 78, 286)

Asch, S. E. (1955, November). Opinions and social pressure. *Scientific American,* pp. 31–35. (pp. 238, 254, 255)

Asendorpf, J. B. (1987). Videotape reconstruction of emotions and cognitions related to shyness. *Journal of Personality and Social Psychology, 53,* 541–549. (p. 179)

Asher, J. (1987, April). Born to be shy? *Psychology Today,* pp. 56–64. (p. 440)

Ashmore, R. D. (1990). Sex, gender, and the individual. In L. A. Pervin (Ed.), *Handbook of personality: Theory and research.* New York: Guilford Press. (p. 196)

Associated Press (1988, July 10). Rain in Iowa. *Grand Rapids Press,* p. A6. (p. 108)

Astin, A., Korn, W. S., & Riggs, E. R. (1993). *The American freshman: National norms for Fall 1993.* Los Angeles: Higher Education Research Institute, Graduate School of Education, UCLA. (pp. 197, 224, 272, 399, 445)

Astin, A. W. (1972). *Four critical years.* San Francisco: Jossey-Bass. (p. 290)

Astin, A. W., Green, K. C., & Korn, W. S. (1987). *The American freshman: Twenty year trends.* Los Angeles: Higher Education Research Institute, UCLA. *(a)* (pp. 224, 272)

Astin, A. W., Green, K. C., Korn, W. S., & Schalit, M. (1987). *The American freshman: National norms for Fall 1987.* Los Angeles: Higher Education Research Institute, UCLA. *(b)* (pp. 224, 272, 399)

Astin, A. W., Korn, W. S., Sax, L. J., & Mahoney, K. M. (1994). *The American freshman: National norms for fall 1994.* Higher Education Research Institute, Graduate School of Education & Information Studies, UCLA. (p. 272)

Atwell, R. H. (1986, July 28). Drugs on campus: A perspective. *Higher Education & National Affairs,* p. 5. (p. 266)

Augoustinos, M., & Innes, J. M. (1990). Towards an integration of social representations and social schema theory. *British Journal of Social Psychology, 29,* 213–231. (p. 9)

Averill, J. R. (1983). Studies on anger and aggression: Implications for theories of emotion. *American Psychologist, 38,* 1145–1160. (p. 443)

Axelrod, R., & Dion, D. (1988). The further evolution of cooperation. *Science, 242,* 1385–1390. (p. 602)

Axom, D. (1989). Cognitive dissonance and behavior change in psychotherapy. *Journal of Experimental Social Psychology, 25,* 234–252. (p. 186)

Axom, D., & Cooper, J. (1985). Cognitive dissonance and psychotherapy: The role of effort justification in inducing weight loss. *Journal of Experimental Social Psychology, 21,* 149–160. (p. 186)

Axsom, D., Yates, S., & Chaiken, S. (1987). Audience response as a heuristic cue in persuasion. *Journal of Personality and Social Psychology, 53,* 30–40. (p. 294)

Ayres, I. (1991). Fair driving: Gender and race discrimination in retail car negotiations. *Harvard Law Review, 104,* 817–872. (p. 400)

Azrin, N. H. (1967, May). Pain and aggression. *Psychology Today,* pp. 27–33. (p. 452)

Babad, E., Bernieri, F., & Rosenthal, R. (1991). Students as judges of teachers' verbal and nonverbal behavior. *American Educational Research Journal, 28,* 211–234. (p. 115)

Babad, E., Hills, M., & O'Driscoll, M. (1992). Factors influencing wishful thinking and predictions of election outcomes. *Basic and Applied Social Psychology, 13,* 461–476. (p. 57)

Bachman, J. G., Johnston, L. D., O'Malley, P. M., & Humphrey, R. N. (1988). Explaining the recent decline in marijuana use: Differentiating the effects of perceived risks, disapproval, and general lifestyle factors. *Journal of Health and Social Behavior, 29,* 92–112. (p. 278)

Bachman, J. G., & O'Malley, P. M. (1977). Self-esteem in young men: A longitudinal analysis of the impact of educational and occupational attainment. *Journal of Personality and Social Psychology, 35,* 365–380. (p. 21)

Baer, R., Hinkle, S., Smith, K., & Fenton, M. (1980). Reactance as a function of actual versus projected autonomy. *Journal of Personality and Social Psychology, 38,* 416–422. (p. 265)

Bailey, J. M., Gaulin, S., Agyei, Y., & Gladue, B. A. (1994). Effects of gender and sexual orientation on evolutionary relevant aspects of human mating psychology. *Journal of Personality and Social Psychology, 66,* 1081–1093. (p. 201)

Bairagi, R. (1987). Food crises and female children in rural Bangladesh. *Social Science, 72,* 48–51. (p. 390)

Bandura, A. (1979). The social learning perspective: Mechanisms of aggression. In H. Toch (Ed.), *Psychology of crime and criminal justice.* New York: Holt, Rinehart & Winston. (pp. 450, 451)

Bandura, A. (1982). Self-efficacy: Mechanism in human agency. *American Psychologist, 37,* 122–147. (p. 50)

Bandura, A. (1986). *Social foundations of thought and action: A social cognitive theory.* Englewood Cliffs, N.J.: Prentice-Hall. (p. 47)

Bandura, A., Ross, D., & Ross, S. A. (1961). Transmission of aggression through imitation of aggressive models. *Journal of Abnormal and Social Psychology, 63,* 575–582. (p. 449)

Bandura, A., & Walters, R. H. (1959).

Adolescent aggression. New York: Ronald Press. (p. 450)

Bandura, A., & Walters, R. H. (1963). *Social learning and personality development.* New York: Holt, Rinehart and Winston. (p. 467)

Bar-Tal, D. (1982). Sequential development of helping behavior: A cognitive-learning approach. *Development Review*, **2**(2), 101–124. (p. 549)

Barash, D. (1979). *The whisperings within.* New York: Harper & Row. (pp. 438, 536, 537)

Baratz, D. (1983). How justified is the "obvious" reaction. *Dissertation Abstracts International 44/02B*, 644B (Univ. Microfilms No. DA 8314435). Reported by N. L. Gage (1991, January–February). The obviousness of social and educational research results. *Educational Researcher*, pp. 10–16. (p. 14)

Bargh, J. A. (1989). Conditional automaticity: Varieties of automatic influence in social perception and cognition. In J. S. Uleman & J. A. Bargh (Eds.), *Unintended thought: Causes and consequences for judgment, emotion, and behavior.* New York: Guilford. (p. 100)

Bargh, J. A. (1994). The four horsemen of automaticity: Awareness, intention, efficiency, and control in social cognition. In R. S. Wyer & T. K. Srull (Eds.), *Handbook of social cognition*, 2nd ed. (Vol. 1). Hillsdale, NJ: Erlbaum. (pp. 89, 100)

Barnes, R. D., Ickes, W., & Kidd, R. F. (1979). Effects of the perceived intentionality and stability of another's dependency on helping behavior. *Personality and Social Psychology Bulletin*, **5**, 367–372. (p. 535)

Barnett, M. A., King, L. M., Howard, J. A., & Melton, E. M. (1980). Experiencing negative affect about self or other: Effects on helping behavior in children and adults. Paper presented at the Midwestern Psychological Association convention. (p. 550)

Barnett, P. A., & Gotlib, I. H. (1988). Psychosocial functioning and depression: Distinguishing among antecedents, concomitants, and consequences. *Psychological Bulletin*, **104**, 97–126. (p. 175)

Baron J., & Hershey, J. C. (1988). Outcome bias in decision evaluation. *Journal of Personality and Social Psychology*, **54**, 569–579. (p. 426)

Baron, L., & Straus, M. A. (1984). Sexual stratification, pornography, and rape in the United States. In N. M. Malamuth & E. Donnerstein (Eds.), *Pornography and sexual aggression.* New York: Academic Press. (p. 459)

Baron, R. A. (1977). *Human aggression.* New York: Plenum Press. (p. 474)

Baron, R. M., Mandel, D. R., Adams, C. A., & Griffen, L. M. (1976). Effects of social density in university residential environments. *Journal of Personality and Social Psychology*, **34**, 434–446. (p. 455)

Baron, R. S. (1986). Distraction-conflict theory: Progress and problems. In L. Berkowitz (Ed.), *Advances in experimental social psychology*, Orlando, Fla.: Academic Press. (p. 320)

Baron, R. S., Kerr, N. L., & Miller, N. (1992). *Group process, group decision, group action.* Pacific Grove, CA: Brooks/Cole. (p. 447)

Barry, D. (1995, January). Bored Stiff. *Funny Times*, p. 5. (p. 201)

Barzun, J. (1975). *Simple and direct.* New York: Harper & Row, pp. 173–174. (p. 142)

Bass, E., & Davis, L. (1988). *The courage to heal.* New York: Harper & Row. (p. 168)

Batson, C. D. (1983). Sociobiology and the role of religion in promoting prosocial behavior: An alternative view. *Journal of Personality and Social Psychology*, **45**, 1380–1385. (p. 561)

Batson, C. D. (1991). *The altruism question: Toward a social-psychological answer.* Hillsdale, NJ: Erlbaum. (pp. 530, 533)

Batson, C. D. (1995). Prosocial motivation: Why do we help others? In A. Tesser (ed.), *Advanced social psychology.* New York: McGraw-Hill. (p. 530)

Batson, C. D., Bolen, M. H., Cross, J. A., & Neuringer-Benefiel, H. E. (1986). Where is the altruism in the altruistic personality? *Journal of Personality and Social Psychology*, **50**, 212–220. (p. 530)

Batson, C. D., Cochran, P. J., Biederman, M. F., Blosser, J. L., Ryan, M. J., & Vogt, B. (1978). Failure to help when in a hurry: Callousness or conflict? *Personality and Social Psychology Bulletin*, **4**, 97–101. (p. 562)

Batson, C. D., Coke, J. S., Jasnoski, M. L., & Hanson, M. (1978). Buying kindness: Effect of an extrinsic incentive for helping on perceived altruism. *Personality and Social Psychology Bulletin*, **4**, 86–91. (pp. 546, 562)

Batson, C. D., Duncan, B. D., Ackerman, P., Buckley, T., & Birch, K. (1981). Is empathic emotion a source of altruistic motivation? *Journal of Personality and Social Psychology*, **40**, 290–302. (p. 531)

Batson, C. D., Flink, C. H., Schoenrade, P. A., Fultz, J., & Pych, V. (1986). Religious orientation and overt versus covert racial prejudice. *Journal of Personality and Social Psychology*, **50**, 175–181. (p. 404)

Batson, C. D., Fultz, J., & Schoenrade, P. A. (1987). Distress and empathy: Two qualitatively distinct vicarious emotions with different motivational consequences. *Journal of Personality*, **55**, 19–40. (p. 531)

Batson, C. D., Harris, A. C., McCaul, K. D., Davis, M., & Schmidt, T. (1979). Compassion or compliance: Alternative dispositional attributions for one's helping behavior. *Social Psychology Quarterly*, **42**, 405–409. (p. 562)

Batson, C. D., Oleson, K. C., Weeks, J. L., Healy, S. P., Reeves, P. J., Jennings, P., & Brown, T. (1989). Religious prosocial motivation: Is it altruistic or egoistic? *Journal of Personality and Social Psychology*, **57**, 873–884. (p. 554)

Batson, C. D., Schoenrade, P., & Ventis, W. L. (1993). *Religion and the individual: A social-psychological perspective.* New York: Oxford University Press. (p. 403)

Batson, C. D., & Ventis, W. L. (1982). *The religious experience: A social psychological perspective.* New York: Oxford University Press. (p. 403)

Baumann, D. J., Cialdini, R. B., & Kenrick, D. T. (1981). Altruism as hedonism: Helping and self-gratification as equivalent responses. *Journal of Personality and Social Psychology*, **40**, 1039–1046. (p. 548)

Baumeister, R. F. (1982). A self-presentational view of social phenomena. *Psychological Bulletin*, **91**, 3–26. (p. 145)

Baumeister, R. F. (1985). Four selves and two motives: Outline of self-presentation theory. Paper presented to the Midwestern Psychological Association convention. (p. 145)

Baumeister, R. F. (1991). *Meanings of life.* New York: Guilford. (pp. 201, 519)

Baumeister, R. F., Chesner, S. P., Senders, P. S., & Tice, D. M. (1988). Who's in charge here? Group leaders do lend help in emergencies. *Personality and Social Psychology Bulletin*, **14**, 17–22. (p. 81)

Baumeister, R. F., & Ilko, S. A. (1995).

Shallow gratitude: Public and private acknowledgement of external help in accounts of success. *Basic and Applied Social Psychology*, **16**, 191–209. (p. 66)

Baumeister, R. F., & Leary, M. R. (1995). The need to belong: Desire for interpersonal attachment as a fundamental human motivation. *Psychological Bulletin*, **117**, 497–529. (p. 478)

Baumeister, R. F., & Scher, S. J. (1988). Self-defeating behavior patterns among normal individuals: Review and analysis of common self-destructive tendencies. *Psychological Bulletin*, **104**, 3–22. (p. 67)

Baumeister, R. F., Smart, L., & Boden, J. (1996). The dark side of high self-esteem. *Psychological Review*. (p. 62)

Baumeister, R. F., & Wotman, S. R. (1992). *Breaking hearts: The two sides of unrequited love*. New York: Guilford. (p. 519)

Baumgardner, A. H. (1991). Claiming depressive symptoms as a self-handicap: A protective self-presentation strategy. *Basic and Applied Social Psychology*, **12**, 97–113. (p. 67)

Baumgardner, A. H., & Brownlee, E. A. (1987). Strategic failure in social interaction: Evidence for expectancy disconfirmation process. *Journal of Personality and Social Psychology*, **52**, 525–535. (p. 67)

Baumgardner, A. H., Kaufman, C. M., & Levy, P. E. (1989). Regulating affect interpersonally: When low esteem leads to greater enhancement. *Journal of Personality and Social Psychology*, **56**, 907–921. (p. 61)

Baumhart, R. (1968). *An honest profit*. New York: Holt, Rinehart & Winston. (p. 54)

Baxter, T. L., & Goldberg, L. R. (1987). Perceived behavioral consistency underlying trait attributions to oneself and another: An extension of the actor-observer effect. *Personality and Social Psychology Bulletin*, **13**, 437–447. (p. 85)

Bayer, E. (1929). Beitrage zur zeikomponenten theorie des hungers. *Zeitschrift fur Psychologie*, **112**, 1–54. (p. 315)

Bazerman, M. H. (1986, June). Why negotiations go wrong. *Psychology Today*, pp. 54–58. (p. 601)

Bazerman, M. H. (1990). *Judgment in managerial decision making*, 2nd ed. New York: Wiley. (p. 601)

Beaman, A. L., Barnes, P. J., Klentz, B., & McQuirk, B. (1978). Increasing helping rates through information dissem-ination: Teaching pays. *Personality and Social Psychology Bulletin*, **4**, 406–411. (p. 563)

Beaman, A. L., & Klentz, B. (1983). The supposed physical attractiveness bias against supporters of the women's movement: A meta-analysis. *Personality and Social Psychology Bulletin*, **9**, 544–550. (p. 492)

Beaman, A. L., Klentz, B., Diener, E., & Svanum, S. (1979). Self-awareness and transgression in children: Two field studies. *Journal of Personality and Social Psychology*, **37**, 1835–1846. (p. 331)

Beauvois, J. L., & Dubois, N. (1988). The norm of internality in the explanation of psychological events. *European Journal of Social Psychology*, **18**, 299–316. (p. 88)

Beck, A. J., Kline, S. A., & Greenfeld, L. A. (1988). Survey of youth in custody, 1987. U.S. Department of Justice, Bureau of Justice Statistics Special Report. (p. 450)

Beck, A. T., & Young, J. E. (1978, September). College blues. *Psychology Today*, pp. 80–92. (p. 177)

Beck, S. B., Ward-Hull, C. I., & McLear, P. M. (1976). Variables related to women's somatic preferences of the male and female body. *Journal of Personality and Social Psychology*, **34**, 1200–1210. (p. 490)

Becker, B. J. (1986). Influence again: Another look at studies of gender differences in social influence. In J. S. Hyde & M. Linn (Eds.), *The psychology of gender: Advances through meta-analysis*. Baltimore: Johns Hopkins University Press. (p. 260)

Bell, B. E., & Loftus, E. F. (1988). Degree of detail of eyewitness testimony and mock juror judgments. *Journal of Applied Social Psychology*, **18**, 1171–1192. (p. 358)

Bell, B. E., & Loftus, E. F. (1989). Trivial persuasion in the courtroom: The power of (a few) minor details. *Journal of Personality and Social Psychology*, **56**, 669–679. (p. 358)

Bell, P. A. (1980). Effects of heat, noise, and provocation on retaliatory evaluative behavior. *Journal of Social Psychology*, **110**, 97–100. (p. 454)

Belson, W. A. (1978). *Television violence and the adolescent boy*. Westmead, England: Saxon House, Teakfield Ltd. (p. 465)

Bem, D. J. (1972). Self-perception theory. In L. Berkowitz (Ed.), *Advances in experimental social psychology*. Vol. 6. New York: Academic Press. (pp. 150, 157)

Bem, D. J., & McConnell, H. K. (1970). Testing the self-perception explanation of dissonance phenomena: On the salience of premanipulation attitudes. *Journal of Personality and Social Psychology*, **14**, 23–31. (p. 97)

Bennett, R. (1991, February). Pornography and extrafamilial child sexual abuse: Examining the relationship. Unpublished manuscript, Los Angeles Police Department Sexually Exploited Child Unit. (p. 460)

Bennis, W. (1984). Transformative power and leadership. In T. J. Sergiovani & J. E. Corbally (Eds.), *Leadership and organizational culture*. Urbana: University of Illinois Press. (p. 351)

Benson, P. L., Dehority, J., Garman, L., Hanson, E., Hochschwender, M., Lebold, C., Rohr, R., & Sullivan, J. (1980). Intrapersonal correlates of nonspontaneous helping behavior. *Journal of Social Psychology*, **110**, 87–95. (p. 553)

Benson, P. L., Karabenick, S. A., & Lerner, R. M. (1976). Pretty pleases: The effects of physical attractiveness, race, and sex on receiving help. *Journal of Experimental Social Psychology*, **12**, 409–415. (p. 556)

Benvenisti, M. (1988, October 16). Growing up in Jerusalem. *New York Times Magazine*, pp. 34–37. (p. 407)

Berenbaum, S. A., & Hines, M. (1992). Early androgens are related to childhood sex-typed toy preferences. *Psychological Science*, **3**, 203–206. (p. 207)

Berg, J. H. (1984). Development of friendship between roommates. *Journal of Personality and Social Psychology*, **46**, 346–356. (pp. 500, 514)

Berg, J. H. (1987). Responsiveness and self-disclosure. In V. J. Derlega & J. H. Berg (Eds.), *Self-disclosure: Theory, research, and therapy*. New York: Plenum. (p. 516)

Berg, J. H., & McQuinn, R. D. (1986). Attraction and exchange in continuing and noncontinuing dating relationships. *Journal of Personality and Social Psychology*, **50**, 942–952. (p. 500)

Berg, J. H., & McQuinn, R. D. (1988). Loneliness and aspects of social support networks. Unpublished manuscript, University of Mississippi. (pp. 178, 516)

Berg, J. H., & Peplau, L. A. (1982). Loneliness: The relationship of self-disclosure and androgyny. *Personality and Social Psychology Bulletin*, **8**, 624–630. (p. 515)

Berger, P. (1963). *Invitation to sociology: A humanistic perspective.* Garden City, N.Y.: Doubleday Anchor Books. (p. 267)

Berglas, S., & Jones, E. E. (1978). Drug choice as a self-handicapping strategy in response to noncontingent success. *Journal of Personality and Social Psychology*, **36**, 405–417. (p. 67)

Berkowitz, L. (1954). Group standards, cohesiveness, and productivity. *Human Relations*, **7**, 509–519. (p. 255)

Berkowitz, L. (1968, September). Impulse, aggression and the gun. *Psychology Today*, pp. 18–22. (p. 443)

Berkowitz, L. (1972). Frustrations, comparisons, and other sources of emotional arousal as contributors to social unrest. *Journal of Social Issues*, **28**, 77–91. (a) (p. 444)

Berkowitz, L. (1972). Social norms, feelings, and other factors affecting helping and altruism. In L. Berkowitz (Ed.), *Advances in experimental social psychology* (Vol. 6). New York: Academic Press. (b) (pp. 444, 535)

Berkowitz, L. (1978). Whatever happened to the frustration-aggression hypothesis? *American Behavioral Scientists*, **21**, 691–708. (p. 443)

Berkowitz, L. (1981, June). How guns control us. *Psychology Today*, pp. 11–12. (p. 443)

Berkowitz, L. (1983). Aversively stimulated aggression: Some parallels and differences in research with animals and humans. *American Psychologist*, **38**, 1135–1144. (p. 453)

Berkowitz, L. (1984). Some effects of thoughts on anti- and prosocial influences of media events: A cognitive-neoassociation analysis, *Psychological Bulletin*, **95**, 410–427. (p. 468)

Berkowitz, L. (1987). Mood, self-awareness, and willingness to help. *Journal of Personality and Social Psychology*, **52**, 721–729. (p. 551)

Berkowitz, L. (1989). Frustration-aggression hypothesis: Examination and reformulation. *Psychological Bulletin*, **106**, 59–73. (pp. 443, 453)

Berkowitz, L. (1995). A career on aggression. In G. G. Brannigan & M. R. Merrens (eds.), *The social psychologists: Research adventures.* New York: McGraw-Hill. (p. 443)

Berkowitz, L., & Geen, R. G. (1966).

Film violence and the cue properties of available targets. *Journal of Personality and Social Psychology*, **3**, 525–530. (p. 467)

Berkowitz, L., & LePage, A. (1967). Weapons as aggression-eliciting stimuli. *Journal of Personality and Social Psychology*, **7**, 202–207. (p. 443)

Bernard, J. (1976). *Sex differences: An overview.* New York: MSS Modular Publications. (p. 196)

Bernieri, F. J., Davis J. M., Rosenthal, R., & Knee, C. R. (1994). Interactional synchrony and rapport: Measuring synchrony in displays devoid of sound and facial affect. *Personality and Social Psychology Bulletin*, **20**, 303–311. (p. 154)

Bernieri, F. J., & Rosenthal, R. (1991). Interpersonal coordination: Behavior matching and interactional synchrony. In R. Feldman & R. Rime (Eds.), *Fundamentals of nonverbal behavior.* New York: Cambridge University Press. (p. 154)

Berry, D. S., & Zebrowitz-McArthur, L. (1988). What's in a face: Facial maturity and the attribution of legal responsibility. *Personality and Social Psychology Bulletin*, **14**, 23–33. (p. 368)

Berscheid, E. (1981). An overview of the psychological effects of physical attractiveness and some comments upon the psychological effects of knowledge of the effects of physical attractiveness. In W. Lucker, K. Ribbens, & J. A. McNamera (Eds.), *Logical aspects of facial form (craniofacial growth series).* Ann Arbor: University of Michigan Press. (pp. 488, 489)

Berscheid, E. (1985). Interpersonal attraction. In G. Lindzey & E. Aronson (Eds.), *The handbook of social psychology.* New York: Random House. (p. 481)

Berscheid, E., Boye, D., & Walster (Hatfield), E. (1968). Retaliation as a means of restoring equity. *Journal of Personality and Social Psychology*, **10**, 370–376. (p. 139)

Berscheid, E., Dion, K., Walster (Hatfield), E., & Walster, G. W. (1971). Physical attractiveness and dating choice: A test of the matching hypothesis. *Journal of Experimental Social Psychology*, **7**, 173–189. (pp. 486, 487)

Berscheid, E., Graziano, W., Monson, T., & Dermer, M. (1976). Outcome dependency: Attention, attribution, and attraction. *Journal of Personality and Social Psychology*, **34**, 978–989. (p. 483)

Berscheid, E., & Peplau, L. A. (1983). The

emerging science of relationships. In Kelley, H. H., Berscheid, E., Christensen, A., Harvey, J. H., Huston, T. L., Levinger, G., McClintock, E., Peplau, L. A. & Peterson, D. R. (Eds.), *Close relationships.* New York: Freeman. (p. 481)

Berscheid, E., Snyder, M., & Omoto, A. M. (1989). Issues in studying close relationships: Conceptualizing and measuring closeness. In C. Hendrick (Ed.), *Review of personality and social psychology*, Vol. 10. Newbury Park, Ca.: Sage. (p. 505)

Berscheid, E., & Walster (Hatfield), E. (1978). *Interpersonal attraction.* Reading, Mass.: Addison-Wesley. (pp. 496, 497)

Bersoff, D. N. (1987). Social science data and the Supreme Court: Lockhart as a case in point. *American Psychologist*, **42**, 52–58. (p. 379)

Beyer, L. (1990, Fall issue on women). Life behind the veil. *Time*, p. 37. (p. 401)

Bianchi, S. M. (in press). The changing economic roles of women and men. In R. Farley (Ed.), *Changes and challenges: America in the 1990s.* New York: Russell Sage. (p. 225)

Bickman, L. (1975). Bystander intervention in a crime: The effect of a mass-media campaign. *Journal of Applied Social Psychology*, **5**, 296–302. (p. 557)

Bickman, L. (1979). Interpersonal influence and the reporting of a crime. *Personality and Social Psychology Bulletin*, **5**, 32–35. (p. 557)

Bickman, L., & Green, S. K. (1977). Situational cues and crime reporting: Do signs make a difference? *Journal of Applied Social Psychology*, **7**, 1–18. (p. 557)

Bickman, L., & Kamzan, M. (1973). The effect of race and need on helping behavior. *Journal of Social Psychology*, **89**, 73–77. (p. 555)

Bierbrauer, G. (1979). Why did he do it? Attribution of obedience and the phenomenon of dispositional bias. *European Journal of Social Psychology* **9**, 67–84. (p. 251)

Bierhoff, H. W., Klein, R., & Kramp, P. (1991). Evidence for the altruistic personality from data on accident research. *Journal of Personality*, **59**, 263–280. (p. 552)

Bierly, M. M. (1985). Prejudice toward contemporary outgroups as a generalized attitude. *Journal of Applied Social Psychology*, **15**, 189–199. (p. 416)

Biernat, M. (1991). Gender stereotypes and the relationship between masculinity and femininity: A developmental analysis. *Journal of Personality and Social Psychology, 61,* 351–365. (p. 417)

Biernat, M., & Wortman, C. B. (1991). Sharing of home responsibilities between professionally employed women and their husbands. *Journal of Personality and Social Psychology, 60,* 844–860. (p. 222)

Bigam, R. G. (1977, March). Voir dire: The attorney's job. *Trial 13,* p. 3. Cited by G. Bermant & J. Shepard in "The voir dire examination, juror challenges, and adversary advocacy." In B. D. Sales (Ed.), *Perspectives in law and psychology (Vol. II): The trial process.* New York: Plenum Press, 1981. (p. 378)

Billig, M., & Tajfel, H. (1973). Social categorization and similarity in intergroup behaviour. *European Journal of Social Psychology, 3,* 27–52. (p. 407)

Biner, P. M. (1991). Effects of lighting-induced arousal on the magnitude of goal valence. *Personality and Social Psychology Bulletin, 17,* 219–226. (p. 457)

Binham, R. (1980, March-April). Trivers in Jamaica. *Science 80,* pp. 57–67. (p. 537)

Bishop, G. D. (1991). Understanding the understanding of illness: Lay disease representations. In J. A. Skelton & R. T. Croyle (Eds.), *Mental representation in health and illness.* New York: Springer-Verlag. (p. 181)

Björkqvist, K. (1994). Sex differences in physical, verbal, and indirect aggression: A review of recent research. *Sex Roles, 30,* 177–188. (p. 200)

Blackburn, R. T., Pellino, G. R., Boberg, A., & O'Connell, C. (1980). Are instructional improvement programs off target? *Current Issues in Higher Education, 1,* 31–48. (p. 63)

Blair, S. L., & Lichter, D. T. (1991). Measuring the division of household labor: Gender segregation of housework among American couples. *Journal of Family Issues, 12,* 91–113. (p. 224)

Blake, R. R., & Mouton, J. S. (1962). The intergroup dynamics of win-lose conflict and problem-solving collaboration in union-management relations. In M. Sherif (Ed.), *Intergroup relations and leadership.* New York: Wiley. (p. 599)

Blake, R. R., & Mouton, J. S. (1979). Intergroup problem solving in organizations: From theory to practice. In W. G. Austin and S. Worchel (Eds.), *The social psychology of intergroup relations.*

Monterey, Calif.: Brooks/Cole. (pp. 591, 599)

Blanchard, F. A., & Cook, S. W. (1976). Effects of helping a less competent member of a cooperating interracial group on the development of interpersonal attraction. *Journal of Personality and Social Psychology, 34,* 1245–1255. (p. 141)

Blanck, P. D., Rosenthal, R., & Cordell, L. H. (1985). The appearance of justice: Judges' verbal and nonverbal behavior in criminal jury trials. *Stanford Law Review, 38,* 89–164. (p. 373)

Blass, T. (1990). Psychological approaches to the Holocaust: Review and evaluation. Paper presented to the American Psychological Association convention. (p. 263)

Blass, T. (1991). Understanding behavior in the Milgram obedience experiment: The role of personality, situations, and their interactions. *Journal of Personality and Social Psychology, 60,* 398–413. (p. 263)

Block J., & Funder, D. C. (1986). Social roles and social perception: Individual differences in attribution and error. *Journal of Personality and Social Psychology, 51,* 1200–1207. (p. 83)

Blucher, J. (1994, October 27). Tuning in to violence: Are "Power Rangers" and other TV shows making children more aggressive? *Anchorage Daily News,* pp. E1–E2. (p. 467)

Blundell, W. E. (1986). *Storyteller step by step: A guide to better feature writing.* New York: Dow Jones. Cited by S. H. Stocking & P. H. Gross (1989), *How do journalists think? A proposal for the study of cognitive bias in newsmaking.* Bloomington, IN: ERIC Clearinghouse on Reading and Communication Skills, Smith Research Center, Indiana University. (p. 120)

Bochner, S. (1994). Cross-cultural differences in the self-concept: A test of hofstede's individualism/collectivism distinction. *Journal of Cross-Cultural Psychology, 25,* 273–283. (p. 44)

Bodenhausen, G. V. (1990). Stereotypes as judgmental heuristics: Evidence of circadian variations in discrimination. *Psychological Science, 1,* 319–322. (p. 417)

Bodenhausen, G. V. (1993). Emotions, arousal, and stereotypic judgments: A heuristic model of affect and stereotyping. In D. M. Mackie & D. L. Hamilton (eds.), *Affect, cognition, and stereotyping: Interactive processes in group*

perception. San Diego, CA: Academic Press. (p. 281)

Bodenhausen, G. V., Kramer, G. P., & Susser, K. (1994). Happiness and stereotypic thinking in social judgment. *Journal of Personality and Social Psychology, 66,* 621–632. (p. 418)

Bodenhausen, G. V., Sheppard, L. A., & Kramer, G. F. (1994). Negative affect and social judgment: The differential impact of anger and sadness. *European Journal of Social Psychology, 24,* 45–62. (p. 112)

Boggiano, A. K., Barrett, M., Weiher, A. W., McClelland, G. H., & Lusk, C. M. (1987). Use of the maximal-operant principle to motivate children's intrinsic interest. *Journal of Personality and Social Psychology, 53,* 866–879. (p. 155)

Boggiano, A. K., Harackiewicz, J. M., Bessette, J. M., & Main, D. S. (1985). Increasing children's interest through performance-contingent reward. *Social Cognition, 3,* 400–411. (p. 155)

Boggiano, A. K., & Ruble, D. N. (1985). Children's responses to evaluative feedback. In R. Schwarzer (Ed.), *Self-related cognitions in anxiety and motivation.* Hillsdale, N.J.: Erlbaum. (p. 156)

Bohner, G., Bless, H., Schwarz, N., & Strack, F. (1988). What triggers causal attributions? The impact of valence and subjective probability. *European Journal of Social Psychology, 18,* 335–345. (p. 74)

Bolt, M., & Brink, J. (1991, November 1). Personal correspondence. (p. 15)

Bond, C. F., Jr., & Anderson, E. L. (1987). The reluctance to transmit bad news: Private discomfort or public display? *Journal of Experimental Social Psychology, 23,* 176–187. (p. 145)

Bond, C. F., Jr., DiCandia, C. G., & MacKinnon, J. R. (1988). Responses to violence in a psychiatric setting: The role of patient's race. *Personality and Social Psychology Bulletin, 14,* 448–458. (p. 430)

Bond, C. F., Jr., & Titus, L. J. (1983). Social facilitation: A meta-analysis of 241 studies. *Psychological Bulletin, 94,* 265–292. (p. 317)

Bond, M. H. (1988). Finding universal dimensions of individual variation in multi-cultural studies of values: The Rokeach and Chinese Value Surveys. *Journal of Personality and Social Psychology, 55,* 1009–1015. (pp. 12, 264)

Bond, R., & Smith, P. B. (in press). Culture and conformity: A meta-analysis of studies using Asch's line judgment task. *Psychological Bulletin.* (p. 264)

Boninger, D. S., Gleicher, F., & Strathman, A. (1994). Counterfactual thinking: From what might have been to what may be. *Journal of Personality and Social Psychology,* **67,** 297–307. (p. 106)

Borchard, E. M. (1932). *Convicting the innocent: Errors of criminal justice.* New Haven: Yale University Press. Cited by E. R. Hilgard & E. F. Loftus (1979) "Effective interrogation of the eyewitness." *International Journal of Clinical and Experimental Hypnosis,* **17,** 342–359. (p. 361)

Borgida, E. (1981). Legal reform of rape laws. In L. Bickman (Ed.), *Applied social psychology annual.* Vol. 2. Beverly Hills, Calif.: Sage Publications, pp. 211–241. (p. 371)

Borgida, E., & Brekke, N. (1985). Psycholegal research on rape trials. In A. W. Burgess (Ed.), *Rape and sexual assault: A research handbook.* New York: Garland. (p. 425)

Borgida, E., Locksley, A., & Brekke, N. (1981). Social stereotypes and social judgment. In N. Cantor & J. Kihlstrom (Eds.), *Cognition, social interaction, and personality.* Hillsdale, N.J.: Lawrence Erlbaum. (p. 429)

Borgida, E., & White, P. (1980). Judgmental bias and legal reform. Unpublished manuscript, University of Minnesota. (p. 373)

Bornstein, G., & Rapoport, A. (1988). Intergroup competition for the provision of step-level public goods: Effects of preplay communication. *European Journal of Social Psychology,* **18,** 125–142. (p. 575)

Bornstein, G., Rapoport, A., Kerpel, L., & Katz, T. (1989). Within- and between-group communication in intergroup competition for public goods. *Journal of Experimental Social Psychology,* **25,** 422–436. (p. 575)

Bornstein, R. F. (1989). Exposure and affect: Overview and meta-analysis of research, 1968–1987. *Psychological Bulletin,* **106,** 265–289. (p. 483)

Bornstein, R. F., & D'Agostino, P. R. (1992). Stimulus recognition and the mere exposure effect. *Journal of Personality and Social Psychology,* **63,** 545–552. (p. 484)

Bossard, J. H. S. (1932). Residential propinquity as a factor in marriage selection. *American Journal of Sociology,* **38,** 219–224. (p. 482)

Bothwell, R. K., Brigham, J. C., & Malpass, R. S. (1989). Cross-racial identification. *Personality and Social Psychology Bulletin,* **15,** 19–25. (pp. 419–420)

Bothwell, R. K., Deffenbacher, K. A., & Brigham, J. C. (1987). Correlation of eyewitness accuracy and confidence: Optimality hypothesis revised. *Journal of Applied Psychology,* **72,** 691–695. (p. 360)

Bourgeois, M. J., Horowitz, I. A., & Lee, L. F. (1993). Effects of technicality and access to trial transcripts on verdicts and information processing in a civil trial. *Personality and Social Psychology Bulletin,* **19,** 219–226. (p. 377)

Bowen, E. (1988, April 4). What ever became of Honest Abe? *Time.* (p. 3)

Bower, G. H. (1986). Prime time in cognitive psychology. In P. Eelen (Ed.), *Cognitive research and behavior therapy: Beyond the conditioning paradigm.* Amsterdam: North Holland Publishers. (p. 100)

Bower, G. H. (1987). Commentary on mood and memory. *Behavioral Research and Therapy,* **25,** 443–455. (pp. 111, 174)

Bower, G. H., & Masling, M. (1979). Causal explanations as mediators for remembering correlations. Unpublished manuscript, Stanford University. (p. 143)

Bowlby, J. (1980). *Loss, sadness and depression. Vol. III of Attachment and loss.* London: Basic Books. (p. 509)

Boyatzis, C. J., Matillo, G. M., & Nesbitt, K. M. (in press). Effects of "The Mighty Morphin Power Rangers" on children's aggression with peers. *Child Study Journal.* (p. 467)

Bradley, W., & Mannell, R. C. (1984). Sensitivity of intrinsic motivation to reward procedure instructions. *Personality and Social Psychology Bulletin,* **10,** 426–431. (p. 155)

Brandon, R., & Davies, C. (1973). *Wrongful imprisonment: Mistaken convictions and their consequences.* Hamden, Conn.: Archon Books. (p. 359)

Brauer, M., Judd, C. M., & Gliner, M. D. (1995). The effects of repeated expressions on attitude polarization during group discussions. *Journal of Personality and Social Psychology,* **68,** 1014–1029. (p. 337)

Bray, R. M., & Kerr, N. L. (1982). Methodological considerations in the study of the psychology of the courtroom. In N. L. Kerr & R. M. Bray (Eds.), *The psychology of the courtroom.* Orlando, Fla.: Academic Press. (p. 383)

Bray, R. M., & Noble, A. M. (1978). Authoritarianism and decisions of mock juries: Evidence of jury bias and group polarization. *Journal of Personality and Social Psychology,* **36,** 1424–1430. (p. 380)

Breckler, S. J., & Wiggins, E. C. (1989). Affect versus evaluation in the structure of attitudes. *Journal of Experimental Social Psychology,* **25,** 253–271. (p. 125)

Bregman, N. J., & McAllister, H. A. (1982). Eyewitness testimony: The role of commitment in increasing reliability. *Social Psychology Quarterly,* **45,** 181–184. (p. 364)

Brehm, J. W. (1956). Post-decision changes in desirability of alternatives. *Journal of Abnormal Social Psychology,* **52,** 384–389. (p. 149)

Brehm, S., & Brehm, J. W. (1981). *Psychological reactance: A theory of freedom and control.* New York: Academic Press. (p. 265)

Brehm, S. S., & Smith, T. W. (1986). Social psychological approaches to psychotherapy and behavior change. In S. L. Garfield & A. E. Bergin (Eds.), *Handbook of psychotherapy and behavior change,* 3rd ed. New York: Wiley. (pp. 188, 266)

Brenner, S. N., & Molander, E. A. (1977). Is the ethics of business changing? *Harvard Business Review,* January-February, pp. 57–71. (p. 54)

Bretl, D. J., & Cantor, J. (1988). The portrayal of men and women in U.S. television commercials: A recent content analysis and trends over 15 years. *Sex Roles,* **18,** 595–609. (p. 411)

Brewer, M. B. (1979). In-group bias in the minimal intergroup situation: A cognitive-motivational analysis. *Psychological Bulletin,* **86,** 307–324. (p. 408)

Brewer, M. B. (1987). Collective decisions. *Social Science,* **72,** 140–143. (p. 574)

Brewer, M. B. (1988). A dual process model of impression formation. In T. Srull & R. Wyer (Eds.), *Advances in social cognition,* Vol. 1. Hillsdale, N.J.: Erlbaum. (p. 428)

Brewer, M. B., & Lui, L. (1984). Categorization of the elderly by the elderly: Effects of perceiver's category membership. *Personality and Social Psychology Bulletin,* **10,** 585–595. (p. 429)

Brewer, M. B., & Miller, N. (1988). Contact and cooperation: When do they work? In P. A. Katz & D. Taylor (Eds.), *Towards the elimination of racism: Profiles in controversy.* New York: Plenum. (p. 595)

Brewer, M. B., & Silver, M. (1978). Ingroup bias as a function of task characteristics. *European Journal of Social Psychology,* **8**, 393–400. (p. 407)

Brickman, P. (1978). Is it real? In J. Harvey, W. Ickes, & R. Kidd (Eds.), *New directions in attribution research.* Vol. 2. Hillsdale, N.J.: Erlbaum. (p. 219)

Brickman, P., & Campbell, D. T. (1971). Hedonic relativism and planning the good society. In M. H. Appley (Ed.), *Adaptation-level theory.* New York: Academic Press. (p. 446)

Brickman, P., Coates, D., & Janoff-Bulman, R. J. (1978). Lottery winners and accident victims: Is happiness relative? *Journal of Personality and Social Psychology,* **36**, 917–927. (pp. 446, 448)

Brigham, J. C. (1990). Target person distinctiveness and attractiveness as moderator variables in the confidence-accuracy relationship in eyewitness identifications. *Basic and Applied Social Psychology,* **11**, 101–115. (p. 360)

Brigham, J. C., & Cairns, D. L. (1988). The effect of mugshot inspections on eyewitness identification accuracy. *Journal of Applied Social Psychology,* **18**, 1394–1410. (p. 365)

Brigham, J. C., & Malpass, R. S. (1985). The role of experience and contact in the recognition of faces of own- and other-race persons. *Journal of Social Issues,* **41**, 139–155. (p. 420)

Brigham, J. C., Ready, D. J., & Spier, S. A. (1990). Standards for evaluating the fairness of photograph lineups. *Basic and Applied Social Psychology,* **11**, 149–163. (p. 365)

Brigham, J. C., & Williamson, N. L. (1979). Cross-racial recognition and age: When you're over 60, do they still all look alike? *Personality and Social Psychology Bulletin,* **5**, 218–222. (p. 419)

British Psychological Society (1991). *Code of conduct ethical principles & guidelines.* Leicester. (p. 29)

Brock, T. C. (1965). Communicator-recipient similarity and decision change. *Journal of Personality and Social Psychology,* **1**, 650–654. (p. 280)

Brock, T. C., & Brannon, L. A. (1991, April 4). Tobacco ad warning should be shocking (letter). *Wall Street Journal.* (p. 283)

Brockner, J., & Hulton, A. J. B. (1978).

How to reverse the vicious cycle of low self-esteem: The importance of attentional focus. *Journal of Experimental Social Psychology,* **14**, 564–578. (p. 47)

Brockner, J., Rubin, J. Z., Fine, J., Hamilton, T. P., Thomas, B., & Turetsky, B. (1982). Factors affecting entrapment in escalating conflicts: The importance of timing. *Journal of Research in Personality,* **16**, 247–266. (p. 573)

Brodt, S. E., & Zimbardo, P. G. (1981). Modifying shyness-related social behavior through symptom misattribution. *Journal of Personality and Social Psychology,* **41**, 437–449. (p. 180)

Bronfenbrenner, U. (1961). The mirror image in Soviet-American relations. *Journal of Social Issues,* **17**(3), 45–56. (p. 582)

Brook, P. (1969). Filming a masterpiece. *Observer Weekend Review,* July 26, 1964. Cited by L. Tiger in *Men in groups.* New York: Random House, p. 163. (p. 133)

Broome, A., & Wegner, D. M. (1994). Some positive effects of releasing socially anxious people from the need to please. Paper presented to the American Psychological Society convention. (p. 179)

Brown, H. J., Jr. (1990). *P.S. I love you.* Nashville, TN: Rutledge Hill. (p. 56)

Brown, J. D. (1986). Evaluations of self and others: Self-enhancement biases in social judgments. *Social Cognition,* **4**, 353–376. (p. 62)

Brown, J. D. (1990). Evaluating one's abilities: Shortcuts and stumbling blocks on the road to self-knowledge. *Journal of Experimental Social Psychology,* **26**, 149–167. (p. 60)

Brown, J. D. (1991). Accuracy and bias in self-knowledge: Can knowing the truth be hazardous to your health? In C. R. Snyder & D. F. Forsyth (Eds.), *Handbook of social and clinical psychology: The health perspective.* New York: Pergamon Press. (p. 47)

Brown, J. D., Collins, R. L., & Schmidt, G. W. (1988). Self-esteem and direct versus indirect forms of self-enhancement. *Journal of Personality and Social Psychology,* **55**, 445–453. (p. 62)

Brown, J. D., & Dutton, K. A. (1994). From the top down: Self-esteem and self-evaluation. Unpublished manuscript, University of Washington. (p. 39)

Brown, J. D., & Gallagher, F. M. (1992). Coming to terms with failure: Private self-enhancement and public self-ef-

facement. *Journal of Experimental Social Psychology,* **28**, 3–22. (p. 60)

Brown, J. D., Novick, N. J., Lord, K. A., & Richards, J. M. (1992). When Gulliver travels: Social context, psychological closeness, and self-appraisals. *Journal of Personality and Social Psychology,* **62**, 717–727. (p. 492)

Brown, J. D., & Rogers, R. J. (1991). Self-serving attributions: The role of physiological arousal. *Personality and Social Psychology Bulletin,* **17**, 501–506. (p. 60)

Brown, J. D., & Siegel, J. M. (1988). Attributions for negative life events and depression: The role of perceived control. *Journal of Personality and Social Psychology,* **54**, 316–322. (p. 176)

Brown, J. D., & Taylor, S. E. (1986). Affect and the processing of personal information: Evidence for mood-activated self-schemata. *Journal of Experimental Social Psychology,* **22**, 436–452. (pp. 111, 175)

Brown, L. R., Hane, H., & Ayres, E. (Eds.) (1993). *Vital signs 1993: The trends that are shaping our future.* New York: Norton. (p. 273)

Brown, P. A. (1995, April 9). Survey shows Americans are different (reporting on Roper Center for Public Opinion Research study). Scripps Howard News Service, *Grand Rapids Press,* p. A10. (p. 580)

Brown, R. (1965). *Social psychology.* New York: Free Press. (p. 203)

Brown, R. (1987). Theory of politeness: An exemplary case. Paper presented to the Society of Experimental Social Psychology meeting. Cited by R. O. Kroker & L. A. Wood, 1992, Are the rules of address universal? IV: Comparison of Chinese, Korean, Greek, and German usage. *Journal of Cross-Cultural Psychology,* **23**, 148–162. (p. 203)

Brown, R., & Smith, A. (1989). Perceptions of and by minority groups: The case of women in academia. *European Journal of Social Psychology,* **19**, 61–75. (p. 422)

Brown, R., & Wootton-Millward, L. (1993). Perceptions of group homogeneity during group formation and change. *Social Cognition,* **11**, 126–149. (p. 419)

Brownell, K., & Rodin, J. (1994). The dieting maelstrom: Is it possible and advisable to lose weight? *American Psychologist,* **49**, 781–789. (p. 182)

Browning, C. (1992). *Ordinary men: Reserve police battalion 101 and the final so-*

lution in Poland. New York: Harper-Collins. (p. 252)

Bruck, C. (1976, April). Zimbardo: Solving the maze. *Human Behavior*, pp. 25–31. (p. 262)

Bryan, J. H., & Test, M. A. (1967). Models and helping: Naturalistic studies in aiding behavior. *Journal of Personality and Social Psychology*, **6**, 400–407. (p. 545)

Buckhout, R. (1974, December). Eyewitness testimony. *Scientific American*, pp. 23–31. (p. 360)

Buehler, R., & Griffin, D. (1994). Change of meaning effects in conformity and dissent: Observing construal processes over time. *Journal of Personality and Social Psychology*, **67**, 984–996. (p. 260)

Buehler, R., Griffin, D., & Ross, M. (1994). Exploring the "planning fallacy": When people underestimate their task completion times. *Journal of Personality and Social Psychology*, **67**, 366–381. (p. 101)

Bundy, T. (1989, January 25). Interview with James Dobson. *Detroit Free Press*, pp. 1A, 5A. (p. 459)

Burchill, S. A. L., & Stiles, W. B. (1988). Interactions of depressed college students with their roommates: Not necessarily negative. *Journal of Personality and Social Psychology*, **55**, 410–419. (p. 175)

Burger, J. M. (1987). Increased performance with increased personal control: A self-presentation interpretation. *Journal of Experimental Social Psychology*, **23**, 350–360. (p. 350)

Burger, J. M. (1991). Changes in attributions over time: The ephemeral fundamental attribution error. *Social Cognition*, **9**, 182–193. (p. 84)

Burger, J. M., & Burns, L. (1988). The illusion of unique invulnerability and the use of effective contraception. *Personality and Social Psychology Bulletin*, **14**, 264–270. (p. 57)

Burger, J. M., & Palmer, M. L. (1991). Changes in and generalization of unrealistic optimism following experiences with stressful events: Reactions to the 1989 California earthquake. *Personality and Social Psychology Bulletin*, **18**, 39–43. (p. 56)

Burger, J. M., & Pavelich, J. L. (1994). Attributions for presidential elections: The situational shift over time. *Basic and Applied Social Psychology*, **15**, 359–371. (p. 84)

Burgess, R. L., & Huston, T. L. (Eds.)

(1979). *Social exchange in developing relationships*. New York: Academic Press. (p. 512)

Burn, S. M. (1992). Locus of control, attributions, and helplessness in the homeless. *Journal of Applied Social psychology*, **22**, 1161–1174. (p. 50)

Burns, D. D. (1980). *Feeling good: The new mood therapy*. New York: Signet. (p. 173)

Burnstein, E., Crandall, R., & Kitayama, S. (1994). Some neo-Darwinian decision rules for altruism: Weighing cues for inclusive fitness as a function of the biological importance of the decision. *Journal of Personality and Social Psychology*, **67**, 773–789. (p. 537)

Burnstein, E., & Kitayama, S. (1989). Persuasion in groups. In T. C. Brock & S. Shavitt (Eds.), *The psychology of persuasion*. San Francisco: Freeman. (p. 348)

Burnstein, E., & Vinokur, A. (1977). Persuasive argumentation and social comparison as determinants of attitude polarization. *Journal of Experimental Social Psychology*, **13**, 315–332. (p. 337)

Burnstein, E., & Worchel, P. (1962). Arbitrariness of frustration and its consequences for aggression in a social situation. *Journal of Personality*, **30**, 528–540. (p. 443)

Burr, W. R. (1973). *Theory construction and the sociology of the family*. New York: Wiley. (p. 482)

Burros, M. (1988, February 24). Women: Out of the house but not out of the kitchen. *New York Times*. (p. 53)

Burt, R. S. (1986). Strangers, friends and happiness. *GSS Technical Report No. 72*. Chicago: National Opinion Research Center, University of Chicago. (p. 480)

Bushman, B. J. (1993). Human aggression while under the influence of alcohol and other drugs: An integrative research review. *Current Directions in Psychological Science*, **2**, 148–152. (p. 441)

Bushman, B. J., & Cooper, H. M. (1990). Effects of alcohol on human aggression: An integrative research review. *Psychological Bulletin*, **107**, 341–354. (p. 441)

Bushman, B. J., & Geen, R. G. (1990). Role of cognitive-emotional mediators and individual differences in the effects of media violence on aggression. *Journal of Personality and Social Psychology*, **58**, 156–163. (p. 468)

Buss, D. M. (1984). Toward a psychology of person-environment (PE) corre-

lation: The role of spouse selection. *Journal of Personality and Social Psychology*, **47**, 361–377. (p. 496)

Buss, D. M. (1985). Human mate selection. *American Scientist*, **73**, 47–51. (pp. 495, 496)

Buss, D. M. (1989). Sex differences in human mate preferences: Evolutionary hypotheses tested in 37 cultures. *Behavioral and Brain Sciences*, **12**, 1–49. (p. 490)

Buss, D. M. (1991). Evolutionary personality psychology. *Annual Review of Psychology*. Palo Alto: CA: Annual Reviews, Inc. (p. 202)

Buss, D. M. (1994a). *The evolution of desire: Strategies of human mating*. New York: Basic Books. (p. 206)

Buss, D. M. (1994b). The strategies of human mating. *American Scientist*, **82**, 238–249. (p. 206)

Buss, D. M. (1995a). Evolutionary psychology: A new paradigm for psychological science. *Psychological Inquiry*, **6**, 1–30. (pp. 206, 210)

Buss, D. M. (1995b). Psychological sex differences: Origins through sexual selection. *American Psychologist*, **50**, 164–168. (p. 205)

Butcher, S. H. (1951). *Aristotle's theory of poetry and fine art*. New York: Dover Publications. (p. 472)

Butler, A. C., Hokanson, J. E., & Flynn, H. A. (1994). A comparison of self-esteem lability and low trait self-esteem as vulnerability factors for depression. *Journal of Personality and Social Psychology*, **66**, 166–177. (p. 176)

Buunk, B. P., & Van Yperen, N. W. (1991). Referential comparisons, relational comparisons, and exchange orientation: Their relation to marital satisfaction. *Personality and Social Psychology Bulletin*, **17**, 709–717. (p. 514)

Bylsma, W. H., & Major, B. (1994). Social comparisons and contentment. *Psychology of Women Quarterly*, **18**, 241–249. (p. 446)

Byrne, D. (1971). *The attraction paradigm*. New York: Academic Press. (pp. 492, 493)

Byrne, D., & Clore, G. L. (1970). A reinforcement model of evaluative responses. *Personality: An International Journal*, **1**, 103–128. (p. 512)

Byrne, D., & Wong, T. J. (1962). Racial prejudice, interpersonal attraction, and assumed dissimilarity of attitudes. *Journal of Abnormal and Social Psychology*, **65**, 246–253. (p. 418)

Bytwerk, R. L. (1976). Julius Streicher and the impact of *Der Stürmer*. *Wiener Library Bulletin*, **29**, 41–46. (p. 272)

Bytwerk, R. L., & Brooks, R. D. (1980). Julius Streicher and the rhetorical foundations of the holocaust. Paper presented to the Central States Speech Association convention. (p. 284)

Cacioppo, J. T., Claiborn, C. D., Petty, R. E., & Heesacker, M. (1991). General framework for the study of attitude change in psychotherapy. In C. R. Snyder & D. R. Forsyth (Eds.), *Handbook of social and clinical psychology*. New York: Pergamon. (p. 304)

Cacioppo, J. T., & Petty, R. E. (1986). Social processes. In M. G. H. Coles, E. Donchin, & S. W. Porges (Eds.), *Psychophysiology*. New York: Guilford Press. (p. 158)

Cacioppo, J. T., Petty, R. E., Feinstein, J., & Jarvis, B. (in press). Dispositional differences in cognitive motivation: The life and times of individuals varying in need for cognition. *Psychological Bulletin*. (p. 295)

Cacioppo, J. T., Petty, R. E., & Morris, K. J. (1983). Effects of need for cognition on message evaluation, recall, and persuasion. *Journal of Personality and Social Psychology*, **45**, 805–818. (p. 281)

Cacioppo, J. T., Priester, J. R., & Bernston, G. G. (1993). Rudimentary determinants of attitudes. II: Arm flexion and extension have differential effects on attitudes. *Journal of Personality and Social Psychology*, **65**, 5–17. (p. 153)

Cacioppo, J. T., Uchino, B. N., Crites, S. L., Snydersmith, M. A., Smith, G., Berntson, G. G., & Lang, P. J. (1991). Relationship between facial expressiveness and sympathetic activation in emotion: A critical review, with emphasis on modeling underlying mechanisms and individual differences. *Journal of Personality and Social Psychology*, **62**, 110–128. (p. 153)

Calhoun, J. B. (1962, February). Population density and social pathology. *Scientific American*, pp. 139–148. (p. 455)

Campbell, D. T. (1975). On the conflicts between biological and social evolution and between psychology and oral tradition. *American Psychologist*, **30**, 1103–1126. *(b)* (pp. 8, 536, 537)

Campbell, D. T. (1975). The conflict between social and biological evolution and the concept of original sin. *Zygon*, **10**, 234–249. *(a)* (pp. 8, 536, 537)

Campbell, E. Q., & Pettigrew, T. F. (1959). Racial and moral crisis: The role of Little Rock ministers. *American Journal of Sociology*, **64**, 509–516. (p. 409)

Cann, A., Calhoun, L. G., & Selby, J. W. (1979). Attributing responsibility to the victim of rape: Influence of information regarding past sexual experience. *Human Relations*, **32**, 57–67. (p. 371)

Cantril, H., & Bumstead, C. H. (1960). *Reflections on the human venture.* New York: New York University Press. (p. 347)

Caplan, N. (1970). The new ghetto man: A review of recent empirical studies. *Journal of Social Issues*, **26**, 59–73. (p. 50)

Carducci, B. J., Cosby, P. C., & Ward, D. D. (1978). Sexual arousal and interpersonal evaluations. *Journal of Experimental Social Psychology*, **14**, 449–457. (p. 502)

Carli, L. L. (1991). Gender, status, and influence. In E. J. Lawler & B. Markovsky (Ed.), *Advances in group processes: Theory and research*, vol. 8. Greenwich, CT: JAI Press. (p. 199)

Carli, L. L., Columbo, J., Dowling, S., Kulis, M., & Minalga, C. (1990). Victim derogation as a function of hindsight and cognitive bolstering. Paper presented at the American Psychological Association convention. (p. 425)

Carli, L. L., & Leonard, J. B. (1989). The effect of hindsight on victim derogation. *Journal of Social and Clinical Psychology*, **8**, 331–343. (p. 425)

Carlo, G., Eisenberg, N., Troyer, D., Switzer, G., & Speer, A. L. (1991). The altruistic personality: In what contexts is it apparent? *Journal of Personality and Social Psychology*, **61**, 450–458. (p. 552)

Carlsmith, J. M., & Anderson, C. A. (1979). Ambient temperature and the occurrence of collective violence: A new analysis. *Journal of Personality and Social Psychology*, **37**, 337–344. (p. 454)

Carlsmith, J. M., Ellsworth, P., & Whiteside, J. (1968). Guilt, confession and compliance. Unpublished manuscript, Stanford University. Cited by J. L. Freeman, D. O. Sears, & J. M. Carlsmith in *Social psychology*. Englewood Cliffs, N.J.: Prentice-Hall, 1970, pp. 275–276. (p. 548)

Carlsmith, J. M., & Gross, A. E. (1969). Some effects of guilt on compliance. *Journal of Personality and Social Psychology*, **11**, 232–239. (p. 547)

Carlson, J., & Hatfield, E. (1992). *The psychology of emotion.* Fort Worth, TX: Holt, Rinehart & Winston. (p. 506)

Carlson, J., & Miller, N. (1987). Explanation of the relation between negative mood and helping. *Psychological Bulletin*, **102**, 91–108. (p. 549)

Carlson, M., Charlin, V., & Miller, N. (1988). Positive mood and helping behavior: A test of six hypotheses. *Journal of Personality and Social Psychology*, **55**, 211–229. (p. 550)

Carlson, M., Marcus-Newhall, A., & Miller, N. (1990). Effects of situational aggression cues: A quantitative review. *Journal of Personality and Social Psychology*, **58**, 622–633. (p. 443)

Carlston, D. E., & Shovar, N. (1983). Effects of performance attributions on others' perceptions of the attributor. *Journal of Personality and Social Psychology*, **44**, 515–525. (p. 68)

Carroll, D., Davey Smith, G., & Bennett, P. (1994, March). Health and socioeconomic status. *The Psychologist*, pp. 122–125. (p. 19)

Cartwright, D. S. (1975). The nature of gangs. In D. S. Cartwright, B. Tomson, & H. Schwartz (Eds.), *Gang delinquency.* Monterey, Calif.: Brooks/Cole. (pp. 335, 450)

Carver, C. S., Kus, L. A., & Scheier, M. F. (1994). Effect of good versus bad mood and optimistic versus pessimistic outlook on social acceptance versus rejection. *Journal of Social and Clinical Psychology*, **13**, 138–151. (p. 175)

Carver, C. S., & Scheier M. F. (1978). Self-focusing effects of dispositional self-consciousness, mirror presence, and audience presence. *Journal of Personality and Social Psychology*, **36**, 324–332. (p. 85)

Carver, C. S., & Scheier, M. F. (1981). *Attention and self-regulation.* New York: Springer-Verlag. (p. 180)

Carver, C. S., & Scheier, M. F. (1986). Analyzing shyness: A specific application of broader self-regulatory principles. In W. H. Jones, J. M. Cheek, & S. R. Briggs (Eds.), *Shyness: Perspectives on research and treatment.* New York: Plenum. (p. 129)

Cash, T. F., & Janda, L. H. (1984, December). The eye of the beholder. *Psychology Today*, pp. 46–52. (p. 489)

Caspi, A., & Herbener, E. S. (1990). Continuity and change: Assortative marriage and the consistency of personality in adulthood. *Journal of Personality and Social Psychology*, **58**, 250–258. (p. 492)

Cass, R. C., & Edney, J. J. (1978). The commons dilemma: A simulation testing the effects of resource visibility and territorial division. *Human Ecology, 6,* 371–386. (p. 577)

Castro, J. (1990, Fall issue on women). Get set: Here they come. *Time.* Pp. 50–52. (p. 222)

Ceci, S. J. (1993). Cognitive and social factors in children's testimony. Master Lecture, American Psychological Association convention. (p. 363)

Ceci, S. J., & Bruck, M. (1993). Child witnesses: Translating research into policy. *Social Policy Report* (Society for Research in Child Development), 7(3), 1–30. (p. 363)

Ceci, S. J., & Bruck, M. (1993). Suggestibility of the child witness: A historical review and synthesis. *Psychological Bulletin, 113,* 403–439. (p. 363)

Ceci, S. J., & Peters, D. (1984). Letters of reference: A naturalistic study of the effects of confidentiality. *American Psychologist, 39,* 29–31. (p. 134)

Census Bureau (1993, May 4). Voting survey, reported by Associated Press. (p. 98)

Centerwall, B. S. (1989). Exposure to television as a risk factor for violence. *American Journal of Epidemiology, 129,* 643–652. (p. 466)

Chagnon, N. A. (1988). Life histories, blood revenge, and warfare in a tribal population. *Science, 239,* 985–991. (p. 439)

Chaiken, S. (1979). Communicator physical attractiveness and persuasion. *Journal of Personality and Social Psychology, 37,* 1387–1397. (p. 280)

Chaiken, S. (1980). Heuristic versus systematic information processing and the use of source versus message cues in persuasion. *Journal of Personality and Social Psychology, 39,* 752–766. (p. 281)

Chaiken, S., & Eagly, A. H. (1978). Communication modality as a determinant of message persuasiveness and message comprehensibility. *Journal of Personality and Social Psychology, 34,* 605–614. (p. 291)

Chaiken, S., & Eagly, A. H. (1983). Communication modality as a determinant of persuasion: The role of communicator salience. *Journal of Personality and Social Psychology, 45,* 241–256. (p. 291)

Chaiken, S., & Maheswaran, D. (1994). Neuristic processing can bias systematic processing: Effects of source credibility, argument ambiguity, and task

importance on attitude judgment. *Journal of Personality and Social Psychology, 66,* 460–473. (p. 275)

Chance, J. E. (1985). Faces, folklore, and research hypotheses. Presidential address to the Midwestern Psychological Association convention. (p. 420)

Chance, J. E., & Goldstein, A. G. (1981). Depth of processing in response to own- and other-race faces. *Personality and Social Psychology Bulletin, 7,* 475–480. (p. 419)

Chapman, L. J., & Chapman, J. P. (1969). Genesis of popular but erroneous psychodiagnostic observations. *Journal of Abnormal Psychology, 74,* 272–280. (p. 165)

Chapman, L. J., & Chapman, J. P. (1971, November). Test results are what you think they are. *Psychology Today,* pp. 18–22, 106–107. (p. 165)

Check, J., & Malamuth, N. (1984). Can there be positive effects of participation in pornography experiments? *Journal of Sex Research, 20,* 14–31. (p. 460)

Cheek, J. M., & Melchior, L. A. (1990). Shyness, self-esteem, and self-consciousness. In H. Leitenberg (Ed.), *Handbook of social and evaluation anxiety.* New York: Plenum. (p. 178)

Chen, H. C., Reardon, R., & Rea, C. (1992). Forewarning of content and involvement: Consequences for persuasion and resistance to persuasion. *Journal of Experimental Social Psychology, 28,* 523–541. (p. 294)

Chen, S. C. (1937). Social modification of the activity of ants in nest-building. *Physiological Zoology, 10,* 420–436. (p. 315)

Chickering, A. W., & McCormick, J. (1973). Personality development and the college experience. *Research in Higher Education,* No. 1, 62–64. (p. 335)

Chodorow, N. J. (1978). *The reproduction of mother: Psychoanalysis and the sociology of gender.* Berkeley, CA: University of California Press. (p. 197)

Chodorow, N. J. (1989). *Feminism and psychoanalytic theory.* New Haven, CT: Yale University Press. (p. 197)

Christensen, L. (1988). Deception in psychological research: When is its use justified? *Personality and Social Psychology Bulletin, 14,* 664–675. (p. 29)

Christian, J. J., Flyger, V., & Davis, D. E. (1960). Factors in the mass mortality of a herd of sika deer, *Cervus Nippon. Chesapeake Science, 1,* 79–95. (p. 455)

Church, G. J. (1986, January 6). China. *Time,* pp. 6–19. (p. 325)

Chwalisz, K., Diener, E., & Gallagher, D. (1988). Autonomic arousal feedback and emotional experience: Evidence from the spinal cord injured. *Journal of Personality and Social Psychology, 54,* 820–828. (p. 448)

Cialdini, R. B. (1984). *Influence: How and why people agree to things.* New York: William Morrow. (p. 150)

Cialdini, R. B. (1988). *Influence: Science and practice.* Glenview, Il.: Scott, Foresman/Little, Brown. (pp. 138, 142)

Cialdini, R. B. (1991). Altruism or egoism? That is (still) the question. *Psychological Inquiry, 2,* 124–126. (p. 533)

Cialdini, R. B. (1995). A full-cycle approach to social psychology. In G. G. Brannigan & M. R. Merrens (eds.), *The social psychologists: Research adventures.* New York: McGraw-Hill. (p. 559)

Cialdini, R. B., Bickman, L., & Caoppo, J. T. (1979). An example of consumeristic social psychology: Bargaining tough in the new car showroom. *Journal of Applied Social Psychology, 9,* 115–126. (p. 595)

Cialdini, R. B., Borden, R. J., Thorne, A., Walker, M. R., Freeman, S., & Sloan, L. R. (1976). Basking in reflected glory: Three (football) field studies. *Journal of Personality and Social Psychology, 39,* 406–415. (p. 407)

Cialdini, R. B., Cacioppo, J. T., Bassett, R., & Miller, J. A. (1978). Lowball procedure for producing compliance: Commitment then cost. *Journal of Personality and Social Psychology, 36,* 463–476. (p. 137)

Cialdini, R. B., Darby, B. L., & Vincent, J. E. (1973). Transgression and altruism: A case for hedonism. *Journal of Experimental Social Psychology, 9,* 502–516. (p. 548)

Cialdini, R. B., Green, B. L., & Rusch, A. J. (1992). When tactical pronouncements of change become real change: The case of reciprocal persuasion. *Journal of Personality and Social Psychology, 63,* 30–40. (p. 156)

Cialdini, R. B., & Kenrick, D. T. (1976). Altruism as hedonism: A social development perspective on the relationship of negative mood state and helping. *Journal of Personality and Social Psychology, 34,* 907–914. (pp. 548, 549)

Cialdini, R. B., Kenrick, D. T., & Baumann, D. J. (1981). Effects of mood on prosocial behavior in children and adults. In N. Eisenberg-Berg (Ed.), *The development of prosocial behavior*. New York: Academic Press. (p. 548)

Cialdini, R. B., & Richardson, K. D. (1980). Two indirect tactics of image management: Basking and blasting. *Journal of Personality and Social Psychology*, **39**, 406–415. (p. 414)

Cialdini, R. B., & Schroeder, D. A. (1976). Increasing compliance by legitimizing paltry contributions: When even a penny helps. *Journal of Personality and Social Psychology*, **34**, 599–604. (p. 559)

Cialdini, R. B., Vincent, J. E., Lewis, S. K., Catalan, J., Wheeler, D., & Danby, B. L. (1975). Reciprocal concessions procedure for inducing compliance: The door-in-the-face technique. *Journal of Personality and Social Psychology*, **31**, 206–215. (p. 559)

Clancy, S. M., & Dollinger, S. J. (1993). Photographic depictions of the self: Gender and age differences in social connectedness. *Sex Roles*, **29**, 477–495. (p. 197)

Clark, K., & Clark, M. (1947). Racial identification and preference in Negro children. In T. M. Newcomb & E. L. Hartley (Eds.), *Readings in social psychology*. New York: Holt. (p. 392)

Clark, M. S. (1984). Record keeping in two types of relationships. *Journal of Personality and Social Psychology*, **47**, 549–557. (p. 514)

Clark, M. S. (1986). Evidence for the effectiveness of manipulations of desire for communal versus exchange relationships. *Personality and Social Psychology Bulletin*, **12**, 414–425. (p. 514)

Clark, M. S., & Bennett, M. E. (1992). Research on relationships: Implications for mental health. In D. Ruble, P. Costanzo (ed.), *The social psychology of mental health*. New York: Guilford. (p. 60)

Clark, M. S., & Mills, J. (1979). Interpersonal attraction in exchange and communal relationships. *Journal of Personality and Social Psychology*, **37**, 12–24. (p. 514)

Clark, M. S., & Mills, J. (1993). The difference between communal and exchange relationships: What it is and is not. *Personality and Social Psychology Bulletin*, **19**, 684–691. (p. 514)

Clark, M. S., Mills, J., & Corcoran, D. (1989). Keeping track of needs and inputs of friends and strangers. *Personality and Social Psychology Bulletin*, **15**, 533–542. (p. 514)

Clark, M. S., Mills, J., & Powell, M. C. (1986). Keeping track of needs in communal and exchange relationships. *Journal of Personality and Social Psychology*, **51**, 333–338. (p. 514)

Clark, R. D., III (1974). Effects of sex and race on helping behavior in a nonreactive setting. *Representative Research in Social Psychology*, **5**, 1–6. (p. 556)

Clark, R. D., III (1995). A few parallels between group polarization and minority influence. In S. Moscovici, H. Mucchi-Faina, & A. Maass (eds.), *Minority influence*. Chicago: Nelson-Hall. (p. 349)

Clark, R. D., III, & Maass, A. (1990). The effects of majority size on minority influence. *European Journal of Social Psychology*, **20**, 99–117. (p. 348)

Clark, R. D., III, & Maass, S. A. (1988). The role of social categorization and perceived source credibility in minority influence. *European Journal of Social Psychology*, **18**, 381–394. (p. 255)

Clarke, A. C. (1952). An examination of the operation of residual propinquity as a factor in mate selection. *American Sociological Review*, **27**, 17–22. (p. 482)

Clary, E. G., & Snyder, M. (1991). A functional analysis of altruism and prosocial behavior: The case of volunteerism. In M. Clark (Ed.), *Prosocial behavior*. Newbury Park, CA: Sage. (p. 553)

Clary, E. G., & Snyder, M. (1993). Persuasive communications strategies for recruiting volunteers. In D. R. Young, R. M. Hollister, & V. A. Hodgkinson (eds.), *Governing, leading, and managing nonprofit orgnaizations*. San Francisco: Jossey-Bass. (pp. 529, 553)

Cleghorn, R. (1980, October 31). ABC News, meet the Literary Digest. *Detroit Free Press*. (p. 23)

Clifford, M. M., & Walster, E. H. (1973). The effect of physical attractiveness on teacher expectation. *Sociology of Education*, **46**, 248–258. (p. 488)

Cline, V. B., Croft, R. G., & Courrier, S. (1973). Desensitization of children to television violence. *Journal of Personality and Social Psychology*, **27**, 360–365. (p. 469)

Clore, G. L., Bray, R. M., Itkin, S. M., & Murphy, P. (1978). Interracial attitudes and behavior at a summer camp. *Journal of Personality and Social Psychology*, **36**, 107–116. (p. 588)

Clore, G. L., Wiggins, N. H., & Itkin, G. (1975). Gain and loss in attraction: Attributions from nonverbal behavior. *Journal of Personality and Social Psychology*, **31**, 706–712. (p. 499)

Coates, B., Pusser, H. E., & Goodman, I. (1976). The influence of "Sesame Street" and "Mister Rogers' Neighborhood" on children's social behavior in the preschool. *Child Development*, **47**, 138–144. (p. 562)

Codol, J.-P. (1976). On the so-called superior conformity of the self behavior: Twenty experimental investigations. *European Journal of Social Psychology*, **5**, 457–501. (pp. 63, 69)

Cohen, B., Waugh, G., & Place, K. (1989). At the movies: An unobtrusive study of arousal and attraction. *Journal of Social Psychology*, **129**, 691–693. (p. 503)

Cohen, E. G. (1980). A multi-ability approach to the integrated classroom. Paper presented at the American Psychological Association convention. *(b)* (p. 593)

Cohen, E. G. (1980). Design and redesign of the desegregated school: Problems of status, power and conflict. In W. G. Stephan & J. R. Feagin (Eds.), *School desegregation: Past, present, and future*. New York: Plenum Press. *(a)* (p. 589)

Cohen, M., & Davis, N. (1981). *Medication errors: Causes and prevention*. Philadelphia: G. F. Stickley Co. Cited by R. B. Cialdini (1989). Agents of influence: Bunglers, smugglers, and sleuths. Paper presented at the American Psychological Association convention. (p. 246)

Cohen, S. (1980). Training to understand TV advertising: Effects and some policy implications. Paper presented at the American Psychological Association convention. (p. 308)

Cohen, S. (1988). Psychosocial models of the role of social support in the etiology of physical disease. *Health Psychology*, **7**, 269–297. (p. 479)

Cohen, S., Tyrrell, D. A. J., & Smith, A. P. (1993). Negative life events, perceived stress, negative affect, and susceptibility to the common cold. *Journal of Personality and Social Psychology*, **64**, 131–140. (p. 181)

Cohen, S., & Williamson, G. M. (1991). Stress and infectious disease in humans. *Psychological Bulletin*, **109**, 5–24. (p. 181)

Colasanto, D. (1989, November). Americans show commitment to helping those in need. *Gallup Report*, No. 290, pp. 17–24. (p. 553)

Colasanto, D., & Shriver, J. (1989, May). Mirror of America: Middle-aged face marital crisis. *Gallup Report* No. 284, pp. 34–38. (p. 518)

Cole, D. L. (1982). Psychology as a liberating art. *Teaching of Psychology*, **9**, 23–26. (p. 165)

Coleman, L. M., Jussim, L., & Abraham, J. (1987). Students' reactions to teachers' evaluations: The unique impact of negative feedback. *Journal of Applied Social Psychology*, **17**, 1051–1070. (p. 498)

Collins, N. L., & Miller, L. C. (1994). Self-disclosure and liking: A meta-analytic review. *Psychological Bulletin*, **116**, 457–475. (p. 516)

Colman, A. M. (1991). Crowd psychology in South African murder trials. *American Psychologist*, 46, 1071–1079. See also, A. M. Colman (1991), Psychological evidence in South African murder trials. *The Psychologist*, **14**, 482–486. (p. 335)

Colombo, J. R. (Ed.) (1994). *The 1994 Canadian global almanac*. Toronto: Macmillan Canada. (p. 200)

Colvin, C. R., Block, J., & Funder, D. C. (1995). Overly-positive self evaluations and personality: Negative implications for mental health. *Journal of Personality and Social Psychology*, **68**, 1152–1162. (p. 62)

Converse, P. E., & Traugott, M. W. (1986). Assessing the accuracy of polls and surveys. *Science*, **234**, 1094–1098. (p. 23)

Conway, F., & Siegelman, J. (1979). *Snapping: America's epidemic of sudden personality change.* New York: Delta Books. (pp. 300, 301)

Conway, M., & Ross, M. (1985). Remembering one's own past: The construction of personal histories. In R. Sorrentino & E. T. Higgins (Eds.), *Handbook of motivation and cognition.* New York: Guilford. (p. 99)

Cook, S. W. (1985). Experimenting on social issues: The case of school desegregation. *American Psychologist*, **40**, 452–460. (p. 593)

Cook, T. D., & Curtin, T. R. (1987). The mainstream and the underclass: Why are the differences so salient and the similarities so unobtrusive? In J. C. Masters & W. P. Smith (Eds.), *Social comparison, social justice, and relative deprivation: Theoretical, empirical, and policy perspectives.* Hillsdale, N.J.: Erlbaum. (p. 422)

Cook, T. D., & Flay, B. R. (1978). The persistence of experimentally induced attitude change. In L. Berkowitz (Ed.), *Advances in experimental social psychology.* Vol. 11. New York: Academic Press. (p. 277)

Coombs, R. H. (1991, January). Marital status and personal well-being: A literature review. *Family Relations*, **40**, 97–102. (p. 511)

Coontz, S. (1992). *The way we never were: American families and the nostalgia trap.* New York: Basic Books. (p. 391)

Cooper, H. (1983). Teacher expectation effects. In L. Bickman (Ed.), *Applied social psychology annual*, Vol. 4. Beverly Hills, Ca.: Sage. (p. 115)

Cooper, J., & Fazio, R. H. (1984). A new look at dissonance theory. In L. Berkowitz (Ed.), *Advances in experimental social psychology*, Vol. 17. New York: Academic Press. (p. 158)

Copeland, J., & Snyder, M. (in press). When counselors confirm: A functional analysis. *Personality and Social Psychology Bulletin.* (pp. 68, 167)

Cota, A. A., & Dion, K. L. (1986). Salience of gender and sex composition of ad hoc groups: An experimental test of distinctiveness theory. *Journal of Personality and Social Psychology*, **50**, 770–776. (p. 267)

Cotton, J. L. (1981). Ambient temperature and violent crime. Paper presented at the Midwestern Psychological Association convention. (p. 454)

Cotton, J. L. (1986). Ambient temperature and violent crime. *Journal of Applied Social Psychology*, **16**, 786–801. (p. 454)

Cottrell, N. B., Wack, D. L., Sekerak, G. J., & Rittle, R. M. (1968). Social facilitation of dominant responses by the presence of an audience and the mere presence of others. *Journal of Personality and Social Psychology*, **9**, 245–250. (p. 320)

Courneya, K. S., & Carron, A. V. (1992). The home advantage in sport competitions: A literature review. *Journal of Sport and Exercise Psychology*, **14**, 13–27. (p. 318)

Court, J. H. (1985). Sex and violence: A ripple effect. In N. M. Malamuth & E. Donnerstein (Eds.), *Pornography and sexual aggression.* New York: Academic Press. (p. 459)

Courtney, J. G., Longnecker, M. P., Theorell, T., & de Verdier, M. G. (1993). Stressful life events and the risk of colorectal cancer. *Epidemiology*, **4**, 407–414. (p. 183)

Cousins, N. (1978, September 16). The taxpayers revolt: Act two. *Saturday Review*, p. 56. (p. 121)

Cousins, N. (1989). *Head first: The biology of hope.* New York: Dutton. (p. 184)

Coyne, J. C., Burchill, S. A. L., & Stiles, W. B. (1991). In C. R. Snyder & D. O. Forsyth (Eds.), *Handbook of social and clinical psychology: The health perspective.* New York: Pergamon. (p. 175)

Crabb, P. B., & Bielawski, D. (1994). The social representation of material culture and gender in children's books. *Sex Roles*, **30**, 6979. (p. 222)

Craig, M. E. (1990). Coercive sexuality in dating relationships: A situational model. *Clinical Psychology Review*, **10**, 395–423. (p. 461)

Crandall, C. S. (1988). Social contagion of binge eating. *Journal of Personality and Social Psychology*, **55**, 588–598. (p. 255)

Crandall, C. S. (1994). Prejudice against fat people: Ideology and self-interest. *Journal of Personality and Social Psychology*, **66**, 882–894. (p. 416)

Crano, W. D., & Mellon, P. M. (1978). Causal influence of teachers' expectations on children's academic performance: A cross-legged panel analysis. *Journal of Educational Psychology*, **70**, 39–49. (p. 115)

Crawford, T. J. (1974). Sermons on racial tolerance and the parish neighborhood context. *Journal of Applied Social Psychology*, **4**, 1–23. (p. 288)

Crocker, J. (1981). Judgment of covariation by social perceivers. *Psychological Bulletin*, **90**, 272–292. (p. 107)

Crocker, J. (1994, October 14). Who cares what they think? Reflected and deflected appraisal. Presentation to the Society of Experimental Social Psychology meeting. (p. 45)

Crocker, J., & Gallo, L. (1985). The self-enhancing effect of downward comparison. Paper presented at the American Psychological Association convention. (p. 448)

Crocker, J., Hannah, D. B., & Weber, R. (1983). Personal memory and causal attributions. *Journal of Personality and Social Psychology*, **44**, 55–56. (p. 427)

Crocker, J., & Luhtanen, R. (1990). Collective self-esteem and ingroup bias. *Journal of Personality and Social Psychology*, **58**, 60–67. (p. 407)

Crocker, J., Luhtanen, R., Blaine, B., & Broadnax, S. (1994). Collective self-esteem and psychological well-being among White, Black, and Asian college students. *Personality and Social Psychology Bulletin, 20,* 503–513. (p. 45)

Crocker, J., & McGraw, K. M. (1984). What's good for the goose is not good for the gander: Solo status as an obstacle to occupational achievement for males and females. *American Behavioral Scientist, 27,* 357–370. (p. 421)

Crocker, J., Thompson, L. L., McGraw, K. M., & Ingerman, C. (1987). Downward comparison, prejudice, and evaluations of others: Effects of self-esteem and threat. *Journal of Personality and Social Psychology, 52,* 907–916. (p. 414)

Crosby, F., Bromley, S., & Saxe, L. (1980). Recent unobtrusive studies of black and white discrimination and prejudice: A literature review. *Psychological Bulletin, 87,* 546–563. (p. 394)

Crosby, F., Pufall, A., Snyder, R. C., O'Connell, M., & Whalen, P. (1989). The denial of personal disadvantage among you, me, and all the other ostriches. In M. Crawford & M. Gentry (Eds.), *Gender and thought.* New York: Springer-Verlag. (p. 400)

Crosby, F. J. (Ed.) (1987). *Spouse, parent, worker: On gender and multiple roles.* New Haven, CT: Yale University Press. (p. 511)

Cross, P. (1977). Not *can* but *will* college teaching be improved? *New Directions for Higher Education,* Spring, No. 17, pp. 1–15. (p. 63)

Cross, S. E., Liao, M-H., & Josephs, R. (1992). A cross-cultural test of the self-evaluation maintenance model. Paper presented at the American Psychological Association convention. (p. 44)

Cross-National Collaborative Group (1992). The changing rate of major depression. *Journal of the American Medical Association, 268,* 3098–3105. (pp. 77, 445)

Crossen, C. (1993). *Tainted truth: The manipulation of face in America.* New York: Simon & Schuster. (p. 25)

Croxton, J. S., Eddy, T., & Morrow, N. (1984). Memory biases in the reconstruction of interpersonal encounters. *Journal of Social and Clinical Psychology, 2,* 348–354. (p. 99)

Croxton, J. S., & Miller, A. G. (1987). Behavioral disconfirmation and the observer bias. *Journal of Social Behavior and Personality, 2,* 145–152. (p. 87)

Croxton, J. S., & Morrow, N. (1984). What does it take to reduce observer bias? *Psychological Reports, 55,* 135–138. (p. 87)

Croyle, R. T., & Cooper, J. (1983). Dissonance arousal: Physiological evidence. *Journal of Personality and Social Psychology, 45,* 782–791. (p. 158)

Crutchfield, R. A. (1955). Conformity and character. *American Psychologist, 10,* 191–198. (p. 238)

Cunningham, J. D. (1981). Self-disclosure intimacy: Sex, sex-of-target, cross-national, and generational differences. *Personality and Social Psychology Bulletin, 7,* 314–319. (p. 517)

Cunningham, M. R. (1986). Measuring the physical in physical attractiveness: Quasi-experiments on the sociobiology of female facial beauty. *Journal of Personality and Social Psychology, 50,* 925–935. (p. 490)

Cunningham, M. R., Roberts, A. R., Barbee, A. P., Druen, P. B., & Wu, C-H. (1995). "Their ideas of beauty are, on the whole, the same as ours": Consistency and variability in the cross-cultural perception of female physical attractivness. *Journal of Personality and Social Psychology, 68,* 261–279. (p. 490)

Cunningham, M. R., Shaffer, D. R., Barbee, A. P., Wolff, P. L., & Kelley, D. J. (1990). Separate processes in the relation of elation and depression to helping: Social versus personal concerns. *Journal of Experimental Social Psychology, 26,* 13–33. (p. 551)

Cunningham, M. R., Steinberg, J., & Grev, R. (1980). Wanting to and having to help: Separate motivations for positive mood and guilt-induced helping. *Journal of Personality and Social Psychology, 38,* 181–192. (p. 548)

Cutler, B. L., Moran, G., & Narvy, D. J. (1992). Jury selection in insanity defense cases. *Journal of Research in Personality, 26,* 165–182. (p. 378)

Cutler, B. L., & Penrod, S. D. (1988). Context reinstatement and eyewitness identification. In G. M. Davies & D. M. Thomson (Eds.), *Context reinstatement and eyewitness identification.* New York: Wiley. *(a)* (pp. 364, 366)

Cutler, B. L., & Penrod, S. D. (1988). Improving the reliability of eyewitness identification: Lineup construction and presentation. *Journal of Applied Psychology, 73,* 281–290. *(b)* (p. 364)

Cutler, B. L., Penrod, S. D., & Dexter, H. R. (1989). The eyewitness, the expert psychologist and the jury. *Law and Human Behavior, 13,* 311–332. (pp. 367, 373)

Cutler, B. L., Penrod, S. D., & Stuve, T. E. (1988). Juror decision making in eyewitness identification cases. *Law and Human Behavior, 12,* 41–55. (p. 366)

Cutrona, C. E. (1986). Behavioral manifestations of social support: A microanalytic investigation. *Journal of Personality and Social Psychology, 51,* 201–208. (p. 479)

Dabbs, J. M., & Janis, I. L. (1965). Why does eating while reading facilitate opinion change? An experimental inquiry. *Journal of Experimental Social Psychology, 1,* 133–144. (p. 281)

Dabbs, J. M., Jr. (1992). Testosterone measurements in social and clinical psychology. *Journal of Social and Clinical Psychology, 11,* 302–321. (p. 441)

Dabbs, J. M., Jr., Carr, T. S., Frady, R. L., & Riad, J. K. (1995). Testosterone, crime, and misbehavior among 692 male prison inmates. *Personality and Individual Differences, 18,* 627–633. (p. 441)

Dabbs, J. M., Jr., de La Rue, D., & Williams, P. M. (1990). Testosterone and occupational choice: Actors, ministers, and other men. *Journal of Personality and Social Psychology, 59,* 1261–1265. (p. 208)

Dabbs, J. M., Jr., Hargrove, M. F., & Heusel, C. (1993). Testosterone differences among college fraternities: Well-behaved vs. rambunctious. Unpublished manuscript, Georgia State University. (p. 208)

Dabbs, J. M., Jr., & Morris, R. (1990). Testosterone, social class, and antisocial behavior in a sample of 4,462 men. *Psychological Science, 1,* 209–211. (pp. 208, 441)

D'Agostino, P., & Fincher-Kiefer, R. (1992). Need for cognition and the correspondence bias. *Social Cognition, 10,* 151–163. (p. 87)

Dallas, M. E. W., & Baron, R. S. (1985). Do psychotherapists use a confirmatory strategy during interviewing? *Journal of Social and Clinical Psychology, 3,* 106–122. (p. 167)

Daly, M., & Wilson, M. (1989). Killing the competition: Female/female and male/male homicide. *Human Nature, 1,* 81–107. (p. 200)

Daniels, R. (1975). *The decision to relocate the Japanese Americans.* New York: Lippincott. (p. 428)

Darley, J. (in press). How organizations socialize individuals into evil-doing. In D. Messick and Ann Tenbrunsel (eds.), *Behavioral research and business ethics.* New York: Russell Sage. (p. 250)

Darley, J. M. (1995). Book review essay. *Political Psychology,* in press. (p. 551)

Darley, J. M., & Batson, C. D. (1973). From Jerusalem to Jericho: A study of situational and dispositional variables in helping behavior. *Journal of Personality and Social Psychology, 27,* 100–108. (p. 546)

Darley, J. M., & Berscheid, E. (1967). Increased liking as a result of the anticipation of personal contact. *Human Relations, 20,* 29–40. (p. 483)

Darley, J. M., & Gross, P. H. (1983). A hypothesis-confirming bias in labelling effects. *Journal of Personality and Social Psychology, 44,* 20–33. (p. 430)

Darley, J. M., & Latané, B. (1968). Bystander intervention in emergencies: Diffusion of responsibility. *Journal of Personality and Social Psychology, 8,* 377–383. (pp. 526, 540, 543)

Darley, J. M., Teger, A. I., & Lewis, L. D. (1973). Do groups always inhibit individuals' response to potential emergencies? *Journal of Personality and Social Psychology, 26,* 395–399. (p. 544)

Darley, S., & Cooper, J. (1972). Cognitive consequences of forced noncompliance. *Journal of Personality and Social Psychology, 24,* 321–326. (p. 309)

Darrow, C. (1933), cited by E. H. Sutherland & D. R. Cressy, *Principles of criminology.* Philadelphia: Lippincott, 1966, p. 442. (pp. 367, 369)

Dashiell, J. F. (1930). An experimental analysis of some group effects. *Journal of Abnormal and Social Psychology, 25,* 190–199. (p. 315)

Davis, B. M., & Gilbert, L. A. (1989). Effect of dispositional and situational influences on women's dominance expression in mixed-sex dyads. *Journal of Personality and Social Psychology, 57,* 294–300. (p. 199)

Davis, C. G., Lehman, D. R., Wortman, C. B., Silver, R. C., & Thompson, S. C. (1995). The undoing of traumatic life events. *Personality and Social Psychology Bulletin, 21,* 109–124. (p. 106)

Davis, J. H., Kameda, T., Parks, C., Stasson, M., & Zimmerman, S. (1989). Some social mechanics of group decision making: The distribution of opinion, polling sequence, and implications for consensus. *Journal of Personality and Social Psychology, 57,* 1000–1012. (p. 380)

Davis, J. H., Kerr, N. L., Atkin, R. S., Holt, R., & Meek, D. (1975). The decision processes of 6- and 12-person mock juries assigned unanimous and two-thirds majority rules. *Journal of Personality and Social Psychology, 32,* 1–14. (pp. 380, 382, 383)

Davis, J. H., Kerr, N. L., Strasser, G., Meek, D., & Holt, R. (1977). Victim consequences, sentence severity, and decision process in mock juries. *Organizational Behavior and Human Performance, 18,* 346–365. (p. 380)

Davis, J. H., Stasson, M. F., Parks, C. D., Hulbert, L., Kameda, T., Zimmerman, S. K., & Ono, K. (1993). Quantitative decisions by groups and individuals: Voting procedures and monetary awards by mock civil juries. *Journal of Experimental Social Psychology, 29,* 326–346. (p. 305)

Davis, K. E. (1985, February). Near and dear: Friendship and love compared. *Psychology Today,* pp. 22–30. (p. 509)

Davis, K. E., & Jones, E. E. (1960). Changes in interpersonal perception as a means of reducing cognitive dissonance. *Journal of Abnormal and Social Psychology, 61,* 402–410. (p. 139)

Davis, L., & Greenlees, C. (1992). Social loafing revisited: Factors that mitigate—and reverse—performance loss. Paper presented at the Southwestern Psychological Association convention. (p. 326)

Davis, M. H. (1979). The case for attributional egotism. Paper presented at the American Psychological Association convention. (p. 54)

Davis, M. H., & Franzoi, S. L. (1986). Adolescent loneliness, self-disclosure, and private self-consciousness: A longitudinal investigation. *Journal of Personality and Social Psychology, 51,* 595–608. (p. 177)

Davis, M. H., & Stephan, W. G. (1980). Attributions for exam performance. *Journal of Applied Social Psychology, 10,* 235–248. (p. 54)

Dawes, R. M. (1976). Shallow psychology. In J. S. Carroll & J. W. Payne (Eds.), *Cognition and social behavior.* Hillsdale, N.J.: Lawrence Erlbaum. (p. 170)

Dawes, R. M. (1980). Social dilemmas. *Annual Review of Psychology, 31,* 169–193. (p. 577)

Dawes, R. M. (1980). You can't systematize human judgment: Dyslexia. In R. A. Shweder (Ed.), *New directions for methodology of social and behavioral science: Fallible judgment in behavioral research.* San Francisco: Jossey-Bass. (pp. 119, 575)

Dawes, R. M. (1989, January). Resignation letter to the American Psychological Association. *APS Observer,* pp. 14–15. (p. 170)

Dawes, R. M. (1990). The potential nonfalsity of the false consensus effect. In R. M. Hogarth (Ed.), *Insights in decision making: A tribute to Hillel J. Einhorn.* Chicago: University of Chicago Press. (p. 58)

Dawes, R. M. (1991). Social dilemmas, economic self-interest, and evolutionary theory. In D. R. Brown & J. E. Keith Smith (Eds.), *Frontiers of mathematical psychology: Essays in honor of Clyde Coombs.* New York: Springer-Verlag. (p. 569)

Dawes, R. M. (1994). *House of cards: Psychology and psychotherapy built on myth.* New York: Free Press. (pp. 169, 575)

Dawes, R. M., Faust, D., & Meehl, P. E. (1989). Clinical versus actuarial judgment. *Science, 243,* 1668–1674. (p. 168)

Dawes, R. M., McTavish, J., & Shaklee, H. (1977). Behavior, communication, and assumptions about other people's behavior in a commons dilemma situation. *Journal of Personality and Social Psychology, 35,* 1–11. (p. 577)

Dawkins, R. (1976). *The selfish gene.* New York: Oxford University Press. (pp. 536, 537)

Dawson, N. V., Arkes, H. R., Siciliano, C., Blinkhorn, R., Lakshmanan, M., & Petrelli, M. (1988). Hindsight bias: An impediment to accurate probability estimation in clinicopathologic conferences. *Medical Decision Making, 8,* 259–264. (p. 18)

Deci, E. L., & Ryan, R. M. (1985). *Intrinsic motivation and self-determination in human behavior.* New York: Plenum. (p. 156)

Deci, E. L., & Ryan, R. M. (1987). The support of autonomy and the control of behavior. *Journal of Personality and Social Psychology, 53,* 1024–1037. (p. 49)

Deci, E. L., & Ryan, R. M. (1991). A motivational approach to self: Integration in personality. In R. Dienstbier (Ed.) Vol. 38. Perspectives on motivation (pp. 237–288), Lincoln, NE: University of Nebraska Press. *Nebraska Symposium on Motivation.* (pp. 154, 156)

Deford, F. (1983, November 7). Sometimes the good die young. *Sports Illustrated,* pp. 44–50. (p. 526)

de Jong-Gierveld, J. (1987). Developing and testing a model of loneliness. *Journal of Personality and Social Psychology, 53,* 119–128. (p. 177)

Delgado, J. (1973). In M. Pines, *The brain changers.* New York: Harcourt Brace Jovanovich. (p. 132)

Dembroski, T. M., Lasater, T. M., & Ramirez, A. (1978). Communicator similarity, fear arousing communications, and compliance with health care recommendations. *Journal of Applied Social Psychology, 8,* 254–269. (p. 280)

Dengerink, H. A., & Myers, J. D. (1977). Three effects of failure and depression on subsequent aggression. *Journal of Personality and Social Psychology, 35,* 88–96. (p. 455)

DePaulo, B. M., Kenny, D. A., Hoover, C. W., Webb, W., & Oliver, P. V. (1987). Accuracy of person perception: Do people know what kinds of impressions they convey? *Journal of Personality and Social Psychology, 52,* 303–315. (p. 62)

Derlega, V., Metts, S., Petronio, S., & Margulis, S. T. (1993). *Self-disclosure.* Newbury Park, CA: Sage. (p. 515)

Dermer, M., Cohen, S. J., Jacobsen, E., & Anderson, E. A. (1979). Evaluative judgments of aspects of life as a function of vicarious exposure to hedonic extremes. *Journal of Personality and Social Psychology, 37,* 247–260. (p. 448)

Dermer, M., & Pyszczynski, T. A. (1978). Effects of erotica upon men's loving and liking responses for women they love. *Journal of Personality and Social Psychology, 36,* 1302–1309. (p. 502)

Desforges, D. M., Lord, C. G., Ramsey, S. L., Mason, J. A., Van Leeuwen, M. D., West, S. C., & Lepper, M. R. (1991). Effects of structured cooperative contact on changing negative attitudes toward stigmatized social groups. *Journal of Personality and Social Psychology, 60,* 531–544. (p. 595)

DeStefano, L., & Colasanto, D. (1990, February). Unlike 1975, today most Americans think men have it better. *Gallup Poll Monthly,* No. 293, 25–36. (pp. 197, 580)

Deutsch, M. (1985). *Distributive justice: A social psychological perspective.* New Haven: Yale University Press. (pp. 581, 595)

Deutsch, M. (1986). Folie à deux: A psychological perspective on Soviet-American relations. In M. P. Kearns (Ed.), *Persistent patterns and emergent structures in a waving century.* New York: Praeger. (p. 584)

Deutsch, M. (1990). Psychological roots of moral exclusion. *Journal of Social Issues, 46,* 21–25. (p. 561)

Deutsch, M. (1993). Educating for a peaceful world. *American Psychologist, 48,* 510–517. (p. 602)

Deutsch, M. (1994). Constructive conflict resolution: Principles, training, and research. *Journal of Social Issues, 50,* 13–32. (p. 595)

Deutsch, M., & Collins, M. E. (1951). *Interracial housing: A psychological evaluation of a social experiment.* Minneapolis: University of Minnesota Press. (p. 587)

Deutsch, M., & Gerard, H. B. (1955). A study of normative and informational social influence upon individual judgment. *Journal of Abnormal and Social Psychology, 51,* 629–636. (p. 257)

Deutsch, M., & Krauss, R. M. (1960). The effect of threat upon interpersonal bargaining. *Journal of Abnormal and Social Psychology, 61,* 181–189. (p. 575)

deVaux, R. (1965). *Ancient Israel (Vol. 2): Religious institutions.* New York: McGraw-Hill. (p. 547)

Devine, P. G. (1989). Stereotypes and prejudice: Their automatic and controlled components. *Journal of Personality and Social Psychology, 56,* 5–18. (p. 395)

Devine, P. G. (1995). Prejudice and outgroup perception. In A. Tesser (ed.), *Advanced social psychology.* New York: McGraw-Hill. (p. 395)

Devine, P. G., Evett, S. R., & Vasquez-Suson, K. A. (in press). Exploring the interpersonal dynamics of intergroup contact. In R. Sorrentino & E. T. Higgins (eds.), *Handbook of motivation and cognition: The interpersonal content,* vol. 3. New York: Guilford. (pp. 395, 421)

Devine, P. G., Hirt, E. R., & Gehrke, E. M. (1990). Diagnostic and confirmation strategies in trait hypothesis testing. *Journal of Personality and Social Psychology, 58,* 952–963. (p. 167)

Devine, P. G., & Malpass, R. S. (1985). Orienting strategies in differential face recognition. *Personality and Social Psychology Bulletin, 11,* 33–40. (p. 419)

de Vries, N. K., & Van Knippenberg, A. (1987). Biased and unbiased self-evaluations of ability: The effects of further testing. *British Journal of Social Psychology, 26,* 9–15. (p. 69)

Dexter, H. R., Cutler, B. L., & Moran, G. (1992). A test of voir dire as a remedy for the prejudicial effects of pretrial publicity. *Journal of Applied Social Psychology, 22,* 819–832. (p. 372)

Diamond, S. S. (1993). Instructing on death: Psychologists, juries, and judges. *American Psychologist, 48,* 423–434. (p. 377)

Diener, E. (1976). Effects of prior destructive behavior, anonymity, and group presence on deindividuation and aggression. *Journal of Personality and Social Psychology, 33,* 497–507. (pp. 328, 330)

Diener, E. (1979). Deindividuation, self-awareness, and disinhibition. *Journal of Personality and Social Psychology, 37,* 1160–1171. (p. 330)

Diener, E. (1980). Deindividuation: The absence of self-awareness and self-regulation in group members. In P. Paulus (Ed.), *The psychology of group influence.* Hillsdale, N.J.: Erlbaum. (p. 331)

Diener, E., & Crandall, R. (1979). An evaluation of the Jamaican anticrime program. *Journal of Applied Social Psychology, 9,* 135–146. (p. 475)

Diener, E., Fraser, S. C., Beaman, A. L., & Kelem, R. T. (1976). Effects of deindividuation variables on stealing among Halloween trick-or-treaters. *Journal of Personality and Social Psychology, 33,* 178–183. (p. 329)

Diener, E., & Wallbom, M. (1976). Effects of self-awareness on antinormative behavior. *Journal of Research in Personality, 10,* 107–111. (p. 331)

DiFonzo, N. (1994). The fundamental attribution error in persistence studies. Poster presented at the American Psychological Society convention. (p. 95)

Dillehay, R. C., & Nietzel, M. T. (1980). Constructing a science of jury behavior. In L. Wheeler (Ed.), *Review of personality and social psychology* (Vol. 1). Beverly Hills, Calif.: Sage Publications. (p. 383)

Dindia, K., & Allen, M. (1992). Sex differences in self-disclosure: A meta-analysis. *Psychological Bulletin, 112,* 106–124. (p. 197)

Dion, K. K. (1972). Physical attractiveness and evaluations of children's transgressions. *Journal of Personality and Social Psychology, 24,* 207–213. (p. 488)

Dion, K. K. (1973). Young children's stereotyping of facial attractiveness. *Developmental Psychology, 9,* 183–188. (p. 488)

Dion, K. K. (1979). Physical attractiveness and interpersonal attraction. In M. Cook & G. Wilson (Eds.), *Love and attraction.* New York: Pergamon Press. (p. 488)

Dion, K. K., & Berscheid, E. (1974).

Physical attractiveness and peer perception among children. *Sociometry*, **37**, 1–12. (p. 488)

Dion, K. K., & Dion, K. L. (1978). Defensiveness, intimacy, and heterosexual attraction. *Journal of Research in Personality*, **12**, 479–487. (p. 516)

Dion, K. K., & Dion, K. L. (1985). Personality, gender, and the phenomenology of romantic love. In P. R. Shaver (Ed.), *Review of personality and social psychology*, vol. 6. Beverly Hills, Ca.: Sage. (p. 505)

Dion, K. K., & Dion, K. L. (1991). Psychological individualism and romantic love. *Journal of Social Behavior and Personality*, **6**, 17–33. (p. 507)

Dion, K. K., & Dion, K. L. (1993). Individualistic and collectivistic perspectives on gender and the cultural context of love and intimacy. *Journal of Social Issues*, **49**, 53–69. (p. 216)

Dion, K. K., Pak, A. W-P., & Dion, K. L. (1990). Stereotyping physical attractiveness: A sociocultural perspective. *Journal of Cross-Cultural Psychology*, **21**, 378–398. (p. 215)

Dion, K. K., & Stein, S. (1978). Physical attractiveness and interpersonal influence. *Journal of Experimental Social Psychology*, **14**, 97–109. (p. 280)

Dion, K. L. (1979). Intergroup conflict and intragroup cohesiveness. In W. G. Austin, & S. Worchel (Eds.), *The social psychology of intergroup relations*. Monterey, Calif.: Brooks/Cole. (p. 590)

Dion, K. L. (1985). Responses to perceived discrimination and relative deprivation. In J. M. Olson, C. P. Herman, & M. P. Zanna (Eds.), *Relative deprivation and social comparison: The Ontario symposium*, vol. 4. Hillsdale, N.J.: Erlbaum. (p. 446)

Dion, K. L. (1987). What's in a title? The Ms. stereotype and images of women's titles of address. *Psychology of Women Quarterly*, **11**, 21–36. (p. 391)

Dion, K. L., & Cota, A. A. (1991). The Ms. stereotype: Its domain and the role of explicitness in title preference. *Psychology of Women Quarterly*, **15**, 403–410. (p. 391)

Dion, K. L., & Dion, K. K. (1988). Romantic love: Individual and cultural perspectives. In R. J. Sternberg & M. L. Barnes (Eds.), *The psychology of love*. New Haven, Conn.: Yale University Press. (p. 507)

Dion, K. L., Dion, K. K., & Keelan, J. P. (1990). Appearance anxiety as a dimension of social-evaluative anxiety: Exploring the ugly duckling syndrome. *Contemporary Social Psychology*, **14**(4), 220–224. (p. 487)

Dion, K. L., & Schuller, R. A. (1991). The Ms. stereotype: Its generality and its relation to managerial and marital status stereotypes. *Canadian Journal of Behavioural Science*, **23**, 25–40. (p. 391)

Ditto, P. H. (1994). Walking the line between passion and reason: Motivated judgment in an adaptive context. Paper presented to the American Psychological Society convention. (p. 59)

Ditto, P. H., & Lopez, D. F. (1992). Motivated skepticism: Use of differential decision criteria for preferred and nonpreferred conclusions. *Journal of Personality and Social Psychology*, **63**, 568–584. (p. 93)

Dixon, B. (1986, April). Dangerous thoughts: How we think and feel can make us sick. *Science 86*, pp. 63–66. (p. 183)

Dohrenwend, B., Pearlin, L., Clayton, P., Hamburg, B., Dohrenwend, B. P., Riley, M., & Rose, R. (1982). Report on stress and life events. In G. R. Elliott & C. Eisdorfer (Eds.), *Stress and human health: Analysis and implications of research* (A study by the Institute of Medicine/National Academy of Sciences). New York: Springer. (p. 479)

Doise, W. (1986). *Levels of explanation in social psychology*. Cambridge: Cambridge University Press. (p. 12)

Dollard, J., Doob, L., Miller, N., Mowrer, O. H., & Sears, R. R. (1939). *Frustration and aggression*. New Haven, Conn.: Yale University Press. (p. 442)

Donnerstein, E. (1980). Aggressive erotica and violence against women. *Journal of Personality and Social Psychology*, **39**, 269–277. (p. 460)

Donnerstein, E., & Berkowitz, L. (1981). Victim reactions in aggressive erotic films as a factor in violence against women. *Journal of Personality and Social Psychology*, **41**, 710–724. (p. 460)

Donnerstein, E., Linz, D., & Penrod, S. (1987). *The question of pornography*. London: Free Press. (pp. 458, 463)

Doob, A. N., & Kirshenbaum, H. M. (1973). Bias in police lineups—partial remembering. *Journal of Police Science and Administration*, **1**, 287–293. (p. 365)

Doob, A. N., & McLaughlin, D. S. (1989). Ask and you shall be given: Request size and donations to a good cause. *Journal of Applied Social Psychology*, **19**, 1049–1056. (p. 560)

Doob, A. N., & Roberts, J. (1988). Public attitudes toward sentencing in Canada. In N. Walker & M. Hough (Eds.), *Sentencing and the public*. London: Gower. (p. 105)

Doty, R. M., Peterson, B. E., & Winter, D. G. (1991). Threat and authoritarianism in the United States, 1978–1987. *Journal of Personality and Social Psychology*, **61**, 629–640. (p. 416)

Douglass, F. (1845/1960). *Narrative of the life of Frederick Douglass, an American slave: Written by himself*. (B. Quarles, Ed.). Cambridge, Mass.: Harvard University Press. (p. 134)

Dovidio, J. F. (1991). The empathy-altruism hypothesis: Paradigm and promise. *Psychological Inquiry*, **2**, 126–128. (p. 533)

Dovidio, J. F., Allen, J. L., & Schroeder, D. A. (1990). Specificity of empathy-induced helping: Evidence for altruistic motivation. *Journal of Personality and Social Psychology*, **59**, 249–260. (p. 532)

Dovidio, J. F., Gaertner, S. L., Anastasio, P. A., & Sanitioso, R. (1992). Cognitive and motivational bases of bias: Implications of aversive racism for attitudes toward Hispanics. In S. Knouse, P. Rosenfeld, & A. Culbertson (Eds.), *Hispanics in the workplace*. Newbury Park, CA: Sage. (p. 395)

Dovidio, J. R., Brigham, J. C., Johnson, B. T., & Gaertner, S. L. (in press). Stereotyping, prejudice, and discrimination: Another look. In N. Macrae, M. Hewstone, & C. Stangor (eds.), *Foundation of stereotypes and stereotyping*. New York: Guilford. (pp. 391, 417)

Downs, A. C., & Lyons, P. M. (1991). Natural observations of the links between attractiveness and initial legal judgments. *Personality and Social Psychology Bulletin*, **17**, 541–547. (p. 369)

Drabman, R. S., & Thomas, M. H. (1974). Does media violence increase children's toleration of real-life aggression? *Developmental Psychology*, **10**, 418–421. (p. 469)

Drabman, R. S., & Thomas, M. H. (1975). Does TV violence breed indifference? *Journal of Communications*, **25**(4), 86–89. (p. 469)

Drabman, R. S., & Thomas, M. H. (1976). Does watching violence on television cause apathy? *Pediatrics*, **57**, 329–331. (p. 469)

Draguns, J. G. (1990). Normal and abnormal behavior in cross-cultural perspective: Specifying the nature of their relationship. *Nebraska Symposium on Motivation 1989, 37,* 235–277. (p. 177)

Driskell, J. E., & Mullen, B. (1990). Status, expectations, and behavior: A meta-analytic review and test of the theory. *Personality and Social Psychology Bulletin,* **16,** 541–553. (p. 256)

Duclos, S. E., Laird, J. D., Schneider, E., Sexter, M., Stern, L., & Van Lighten, O. (1989). Emotion-specific effects of facial expressions and postures on emotional experience. *Journal of Personality and Social Psychology, 57,* 100–108. (p. 151)

Duncan, B. L. (1976). Differential social perception and attribution of intergroup violence: Testing the lower limits of stereotyping of blacks. *Journal of Personality and Social Psychology,* **34,** 590–598. (p. 394)

Dunning, D., Griffin, D. W., Milojkovic, J. D., & Ross, L. (1990). The overconfidence effect in social prediction. *Journal of Personality and Social Psychology,* **58,** 568–581. (p. 100)

Dunning, D., Meyerowitz, J. A., & Holzberg, A. D. (1989). Ambiguity and self-evaluation. *Journal of Personality and Social Psychology, 57,* 1082–1090. (p. 55)

Dunning, D., Perie, M., & Story, A. L. (1991). Self-serving prototypes of social categories. *Journal of Personality and Social Psychology,* **61,** 957–968. (p. 55)

Dunning, D., & Ross, L. (1988). Overconfidence in individual and group prediction: Is the collective any wiser? Unpublished manuscript, Cornell University. (p. 346)

Dunning, D., & Stern, L. B. (1994). Distinguishing accurate from inaccurate eyewitness identifications via inquiries about decision processes. *Journal of Personality and Social Psychology, 67,* 818–835. (p. 365)

Dutton, D. G. (1971). Reactions of restauranteurs to blacks and whites violating restaurant dress regulations. *Canadian Journal of Behavioural Science,* **3,** 298–302. (p. 556)

Dutton, D. G. (1973). Reverse discrimination: The relationship of amount of perceived discrimination toward a minority group and the behavior of majority group members. *Canadian Journal of Behavioural Science, 5,* 34–45. (p. 556)

Dutton, D. G., & Aron, A. (1989). Romantic attraction and generalized liking for others who are sources of conflict-based arousal. *Canadian Journal of Behavioural Science, 21,* 246–257. (p. 502)

Dutton, D. G., & Aron, A. P. (1974). Some evidence for heightened sexual attraction under conditions of high anxiety. *Journal of Personality and Social Psychology, 30,* 510–517. (p. 502)

Dutton, D. G., & Lake, R. A. (1973). Threat of own prejudice and reverse discrimination in interracial situations. *Journal of Personality and Social Psychology, 28,* 94–100. (p. 556)

Duval, S., Duval, V. H., & Neely, R. (1979). Self-focus, felt responsibility, and helping behavior. *Journal of Personality and Social Psychology,* **37,** 1769–1778. (p. 559)

Duval, S., & Wicklund, R. A. (1972). *A theory of objective self-awareness.* New York: Academic Press. (p. 84)

Eagly, A. (1994). Are people prejudiced against women? Donald Campbell Award invited address, American Psychological Association convention. (pp. 196, 399, 400)

Eagly, A., & Mladinic, A. (1994). Are people prejudiced against women? Some answers from research on attitudes, gender stereotypes, and judgments of competence. In W. Stroebe & M. Hewstone (eds.), *European review of social psychology,* vol. 5. Chichester, England: Wiley. (pp. 261, 399)

Eagly, A. H. (1986). Some meta-analytic approaches to examining the validity of gender-difference research. In J. S. Hyde & M. C. Linn (Eds.), *The psychology of gender: Advances through meta-analysis.* Baltimore: Johns Hopkins University Press. (p. 196)

Eagly, A. H. (1987). Sex differences in social behavior: A social-role interpretation. Hillsdale, N.J.: Erlbaum. (pp. 197, 226)

Eagly, A. H. (1995). The science and politics of comparing women and men. *American Psychologist, 50,* 145–158. (p. 196)

Eagly, A. H., Ashmore, R. D., Makhijani, M. G., & Longo, L. C. (1991). What is beautiful is good, but . . . : A meta-analytic review of research on the physical attractiveness stereotype. *Psychological Bulletin,* **110,** 109–128. (p. 488)

Eagly, A. H., & Carli, L. L. (1981). Sex of researcher and sex-typed communications as determinants of sex differences in influenceability: A meta-analysis of social influence studies. *Psychological Bulletin,* **90,** 1–20. (p. 260)

Eagly, A. H., & Chaiken, S. (1992). *The psychology of attitudes.* San Diego: Harcourt Brace Jovanovich. (p. 274)

Eagly, A. H., & Crowley, M. (1986). Gender and helping behavior: A meta-analytic review of the social psychological literature. *Psychological Bulletin,* **100,** 283–308. (pp. 197, 552, 555)

Eagly, A. H., & Johnson, B. T. (1990). Gender and leadership style: A meta-analysis. *Psychological Bulletin, 108,* 233–256. (pp. 199, 350)

Eagly, A. H., & Karau, S. J. (1991). Gender and the emergence of leaders: A meta-analysis. *Journal of Personality and Social Psychology, 60,* 685–710. (p. 199)

Eagly, A. H., Karau, S. J., & Makhijani, M. G. (1995). Gender and the effectiveness of leaders: A meta-analysis. *Psychological Bulletin, 117,* 125–145. (p. 199)

Eagly, A. H., Makhijani, M. G., & Klonsky, B. G. (1992). Gender and the evaluation of leaders: A meta-analysis. *Psychological Bulletin, 111,* 3–22. (p. 199)

Eagly, A. H., Mladinic, A., & Otto, S. (1991). Are women evaluated more favorably than men? *Psychology of Women Quarterly, 15,* 203–216. (pp. 261, 399)

Eagly, A. H., & Steffen, V. J. (1986). Gender and aggressive behavior: A meta-analytic review of the social psychological literature. *Psychological Bulletin, 100,* 309–330. (p. 200)

Eagly, A. H., & Wood, W. (1985). Gender and influenceability: Stereotype versus behavior. In V. E. O'Leary, R. K. Unger, & B. S. Wallston (Eds.), *Women, gender, and social psychology.* Hillsdale, N.J.: Erlbaum. (p. 261)

Eagly, A. H., & Wood, W. (1991). Explaining sex differences in social behavior: A meta-analytic perspective. *Personality and Social Psychology Bulletin, 17,* 306–315. (p. 226)

Eagly, A. H., Wood, W., & Chaiken, S. (1978). Casual inferences about communicators and their effect on opinion change. *Journal of Personality and Social Psychology, 36,* 424–435. (p. 278)

Easterlin, R. A. (in press). Will raising the incomes of all increase the happiness of all? *Journal of Economic Behavior and Organization.* (p. 445)

Ebbesen, E. B., Duncan, B., & Konecni, V. J. (1975). Effects of content of verbal aggression on future verbal aggression: A field experiment. *Journal of Experimental Social Psychology, 11,* 192–204. (p. 473)

Edney, J. J. (1979). The nuts game: A concise commons dilemma analog. *Environmental Psychology and Nonverbal Behavior, 3,* 252–254. (p. 572)

Edney, J. J. (1980). The commons problem: Alternative perspectives. *American Psychologist, 35,* 131–150. (p. 575)

Edney, J. J., & Harper, C. S. (1978). The commons dilemma: A review of contributions from psychology. *Environmental Management, 2,* 491–507. (p. 577)

Edwards, C. P. (1991). Behavioral sex differences in children of diverse cultures: The case of nurturance to infants. In M. Pereira & L. Fairbanks (Eds.), *Juveniles: Comparative socioecology.* Oxford: Oxford University Press. (p. 222)

Efran, M. G. (1974). The effect of physical appearance on the judgment of guilt, interpersonal attraction, and severity of recommended punishment in a simulated jury task. *Journal of Research in Personality, 8,* 45–54. (p. 368)

Einon, D. (1994). Are men more promiscuous than women? *Ethology and Sociobiology, 15,* 131–143. (p. 209)

Eisenberg, N., Fabes, R. A., Schaller, M., Miller, P., Carlo, G., Poulin, R., Shea, C., & Shell, R. (1991). Personality and socialization correlates of vicarious emotional responding. *Journal of Personality and Social Psychology, 61,* 459–470. (p. 552)

Eisenberg, N., & Lennon, R. (1983). Sex differences in empathy and related capacities. *Psychological Bulletin, 94,* 100–131. (p. 198)

Elashoff, J. R., & Snow, R. E. (1971). *Pygmalion reconsidered.* Worthington, Ohio: Charles A. Jones. (p. 115)

Elder, G. H., Jr. (1969). Appearance and education in marriage mobility. *American Sociological Review, 34,* 519–533. (p. 487)

Elder, G. H., Jr., & Clipp, E. C. (1988). Wartime losses and social bonding: Influences across 40 years in men's lives. *Psychiatry, 51,* 177–197. (p. 590)

Eldersveld, S. J., & Dodge, R. W. (1954). Personal contact or mail propaganda? An experiment in voting turnout and attitude change. In D. Katz, D. Cartwright, S. Eldersveld, & A. M. Lee (Eds.), *Public opinion and propaganda.* New York: Dryden Press. (p. 289)

Elkin, I. (1986). Outcome findings and therapist performance. Paper presented at the American Psychological Association convention. (p. 170)

Ellickson, P. L., & Bell, R. M. (1990). Drug prevention in junior high: A multi-site longitudinal test. *Science, 247,* 1299–1305. (p. 306)

Elliot, A. J., & Devine, P. G. (1994). On the motivational nature of cognitive dissonance: Dissonance as psychological discomfort. *Journal of Personality and Social Psychology, 67,* 382–394. (p. 158)

Elliott, G. C. (1986). Self-esteem and self-consistency: A theoretical and empirical link between two primary motivations. *Social Psychological Quarterly, 49,* 207–218. (p. 133)

Elliott, L. (1989, June). Legend of the four chaplains. *Reader's Digest,* pp. 66–70. (p. 552)

Ellis, B. J., & Symons, D. (1990). Sex difference in sexual fantasy: An evolutionary psychological approach. *Journal of Sex Research, 27,* 490–521. (p. 201)

Ellis, H. D. (1981). Theoretical aspects of face recognition. In G. H. Davies, H. D. Ellis, & J. Shepherd (Eds.), *Perceiving and remembering faces.* London: Academic Press. (p. 419)

Ellsworth, P. (1985, July). Juries on trial. *Psychology Today,* pp. 44–46. (p. 379)

Ellsworth, P. (1989, March 6). Supreme Court ignores social science research on capital punishment. Quoted by *Behavior Today,* pp. 7–8. (p. 379)

Ellyson, S. L., Dovidio, J. F., & Brown, C. E. (1991). The look of power: Gender differences and similarities in visual dominance behavior. In C. Ridgeway (Ed.), *Gender and interaction: The role of microstructures in inequality.* New York: Springer-Verlag. (p. 199)

Elwork, A., Sales, B. D., & Alfini, J. J. (1982). *Making jury instructions understandable.* Charlottesville, Va.: The Michie Co. (p. 376)

Emmons, R. A., Larsen, R. J., Levine, S. & Diener, E. (1983). Factors predicting satisfaction judgments: A comparative examination. Paper presented at the Midwestern Psychological Association. (p. 480)

Emswiller, T., Deaux, K., & Willits, J. E. (1971). Similarity, sex, and requests for small favors. *Journal of Applied Social Psychology, 1,* 284–291. (p. 555)

Engs, R., & Hanson, D. J. (1989). Reactance theory: A test with collegiate drinking. *Psychological Reports, 64,* 1083–1086. (p. 266)

Ennis, B. J., & Verrilli, D. B., Jr. (1989). Motion for leave to file brief amicus cu-

riae and brief of Society for the Scientific Study of Religion, American Sociological Association, and others. U.S. Supreme Court Case No. 88–1600, Holy Spirit Association for the Unification of World Christianity, *et al.,* v. David Molko and Tracy Leal. On petition for write of certiorari to the Supreme Court of California. Washington, DC: Jenner & Block, 21 Dupont Circle NW. (p. 302)

Ennis, R., & Zanna, M. P. (1991). Hockey assault: Constitutive versus normative violations. Paper presented at the Canadian Psychological Association convention. (p. 448)

Enzle, M. E., & Hawkins, W. L. (1992). A priori actor negligence mediates a posteriori outcome. *Journal of Experimental Social Psychology, 28*(2), 169–185. (p. 374)

Epstein, S. (1980). The stability of behavior: II. Implications for psychological research. *American Psychologist, 35,* 790–806. (p. 262)

Epstein, S., & Feist, G. J. (1988). Relation between self- and other-acceptance and its moderation by identification. *Journal of Personality and Social Psychology, 54,* 309–315. (p. 61)

Erev, I., Bornstein, G., & Gallili, R. (1993). Constructive intergroup competition as a solution to the free rider problem: A field experiment. *Journal of Experimental Social Psychology, 29,* 463–478. (p. 326)

Erickson, B., Holmes, J. G., Frey, R., Walker, L., & Thibaut, J. (1974). Functions of a third party in the resolution of conflict: The role of a judge in pretrial conferences. *Journal of Personality and Social Psychology, 30,* 296–306. (p. 598)

Erickson, B., Lind, E. A., Johnson, B. C., & O'Barr, W. M. (1978). Speech style and impression formation in a court setting: The effects of powerful and powerless speech. *Journal of Experimental Social Psychology, 14,* 266–279. (p. 278)

Erikson, E. H. (1963). *Childhood and society.* New York: Norton. (p. 509)

Ernst, J. M., & Heesacker, M. (1993). Application of the elaboration likelihood model of attitude change to assertion training. *Journal of Counseling Psychology, 40,* 37–45. (p. 304)

Eron, L. D. (1985). The social responsibility of the researchers. In J. H. Goldstein (Ed.), *Reporting science: The case of aggression.* Hillsdale, N.J.: Erlbaum. (p. 466)

Eron, L. D. (1987). The development of aggressive behavior from the perspective of a developing behaviorism. *American Psychologist, 42,* 425–442. (p. 465)

Eron, L. D., & Huesmann, L. R. (1980). Adolescent aggression and television. *Annals of the New York Academy of Sciences, 347,* 319–331. (p. 466)

Eron, L. D., & Huesmann, L. R. (1984). The control of aggressive behavior by changes in attitudes, values, and the conditions of learning. In R. J. Blanchard & C. Blanchard (Eds.), *Advances in the study of aggression,* vol. 1. Orlando, Fla.: Academic Press. (pp. 466, 467, 474)

Eron, L. D., & Huesmann, L. R. (1985). The role of television in the development of prosocial and antisocial behavior. In D. Olweus, M. Radke-Yarrow, and J. Block (Eds.), *Development of antisocial and prosocial behavior.* Orlando, Fla.: Academic Press. (p. 466)

Esser, J. K., & Lindoerfer, J. S. (1989). Groupthink and the space shuttle Challenger accident: Toward a quantitative case analysis. *Journal of Behavioral Decision Making, 2,* 167–177. (p. 343)

Esses, V. M., Haddock, G., & Zanna, M. P. (1993a). Values, stereotypes, and emotions as determinants of intergroup attitudes. In D. Mackie & D. Hamilton (Eds.), *Affect, cognition and stereotyping: Interactive processes in intergroup perception.* San Diego, CA: Academic Press. (p. 395)

Esses, V. M., Haddock, G., & Zanna, M. P. (1993b). The role of mood in the expression of intergroup stereotypes. In M. P. Zanna & J. M. Olson (eds.), *The psychology of prejudice: The Ontario symposium,* vol. 7. Hillsdale, NJ: Erlbaum. (p. 417)

Esses, V. M., & Webster, C. D. (1988). Physical attractiveness, dangerousness, and the Canadian criminal code. *Journal of Applied Social Psychology, 18,* 1017–1031. (p. 369)

Etzioni, A. (1967). The Kennedy experiment. *The Western Political Quarterly, 20,* 361–380. (p. 603)

Etzioni, A. (1991, May–June). The community in an age of individualism (interview). *The Futurist,* pp. 35–39. (p. 217)

Evans, G. W. (1979). Behavioral and physiological consequences of crowding in humans. *Journal of Applied Social Psychology, 9,* 27–46. (p. 319)

Evans, R., & Berent, I. (1993). *Getting your words' worth.* New York: Warner Books. (p. 17)

Evans, R. I., Smith, C. K., & Raines, B. E. (1984). Deterring cigarette smoking in adolescents: A psycho-social-behavioral analysis of an intervention strategy. In A. Baum, J. Singer, & S. Taylor (Eds.), *Handbook of psychology and health: Social psychological aspects of health,* vol. 4, Hillsdale, N.J.: Erlbaum. (p. 306)

Farquhar, J. W., Maccoby, N., Wood, P. D., Alexander, J. K., Breitrose, H., Brown, B. W., Jr., Haskell, W. L., McAlister, A. L., Meyer, A. J., Nash, J. D., & Stern, M. P. (1977, June 4). Community education for cardiovascular health. *Lancet,* 1192–1195. (p. 290)

Faust, D., & Ziskin, J. (1988). The expert witness in psychology and psychiatry. *Science, 241,* 31–35. (p. 168)

Fazio, R. (1987). Self-perception theory: A. current perspective. In M. P. Zanna, J. M. Olson, & C. P. Herman (Eds.), *Social influence: The Ontario symposium,* vol. 5. Hillsdale, N.J.: Erlbaum. (p. 160)

Fazio, R. H. (1990). Multiple processes by which attitudes guide behavior: The mode model as an integrative framework. *Advances in Experimental Social Psychology, 23,* 75–109. (p. 130)

Fazio, R. H. (1995). Attitudes as object-evaluation associations: Determinants, consequences, and correlates of attitude accessibility. In R. E. Petty and J. A. Krosnick (Eds.), *Attitude strength: Antecedents and consequences.* Hillsdale, NJ: Erlbaum. (p. 130)

Fazio, R. H., & Zanna, M. P. (1981). Direct experience and attitude-behavior consistency. In L. Berkowitz (Ed.), *Advances in experimental social psychology,* Vol. 14. New York: Academic Press. (p. 130)

Fazio, R. H., Zanna, M. P., & Cooper, J. (1977). Dissonance versus self-perception: An integrative view of each theory's proper domain of application. *Journal of Experimental Social Psychology, 13,* 464–479. (p. 160)

Fazio, R. H., Zanna, M. P., & Cooper, J. (1979). On the relationship of data to theory: A reply to Ronis and Greenwald. *Journal of Experimental Social Psychology, 15,* 70–76. (p. 160)

FBI (1994). *Uniform crime report of the United States 1993.* Washington, DC: Superintendent of Documents. (pp. 200, 444)

Feather, N. T. (1983). Causal attributions and beliefs about work and unemployment among adolescents in state and independent secondary schools. *Australian Journal of Psychology, 35,* 211–232. *(a)* (pp. 69, 88)

Feather, N. T. (1983). Causal attributions for good and bad outcomes in achievement and affiliation situations. *Australian Journal of Psychology, 35,* 37–48. *(b)* (pp. 69, 88)

Feeney, J. A., & Noller, P. (1990). Attachment style as a predictor of adult romantic relationships. *Journal of Personality and Social Psychology, 58,* 281–291. (p. 509)

Feeney, J., Peterson, C., & Noller, P. (1994). Equity and marital satisfaction over the family life cycle. *Personality Relationships, 1,* 83–99. (p. 515)

Feierabend, I., & Feierabend, R. (1968, May). Conflict, crisis, and collision: A study of international stability. *Psychology Today,* pp. 26–32, 69–70. (p. 444)

Feierabend, I., & Feierabend, R. (1972). Systemic conditions of political aggression: An application of frustration-aggression theory. In I. K. Feierabend, R. L. Feierabend, & T. R. Gurr (Eds.), *Anger, violence, and politics: Theories and research.* Englewood Cliffs, N.J.: Prentice Hall. (p. 444)

Fein, S., & Hilton, J. L. (1992). Attitudes toward groups and behavioral intentions toward individual group members: The impact of nondiagnostic information. *Journal of Experimental Social Psychology, 28,* 101–124. (p. 429)

Fein, S., Hilton, J. L., & Miller, D. T. (1990). Suspicion of ulterior motivation and the correspondence bias. *Journal of Personality and Social Psychology, 58,* 753–764. (p. 81)

Feingold, A. (1988). Matching for attractiveness in romantic partners and same-sex friends: A meta-analysis and theoretical critique. *Psychological Bulletin, 104,* 226–235. (p. 487)

Feingold, A. (1990). Gender differences in effects of physical attractiveness on romantic attraction: A comparison across five research paradigms. *Journal of Personality and Social Psychology, 59,* 981–993. (p. 486)

Feingold, A. (1991). Sex differences in the effects of similarity and physical attractiveness on opposite-sex attraction. *Basic and Applied Social Psychology,* **12**, 357–367. (p. 486)

Feingold, A. (1992). Gender differences in mate selection preferences: A test of the parental investment model. *Psychological Bulletin,* **112**, 125–139. (p. 206)

Feingold, A. (1992). Good-looking people are not what we think. *Psychological Bulletin,* **111**, 304–341. (pp. 488, 489)

Feinsilber, M. (1994, July 5). Women still have far to go in corridors of power. Associated Press writer report in *Holland Sentinel,* p. A4. (p. 199)

Feldman, K. A., & Newcomb, T. M. (1969). *The impact of college on students.* San Francisco: Jossey-Bass. (p. 335)

Feldman, R. S., & Prohaska, T. (1979). The student as Pygmalion: Effect of student expectation on the teacher. *Journal of Educational Psychology,* **71**, 485–493. (p. 115)

Feldman, R. S., & Theiss, A. J. (1982). The teacher and student as Pygmalions: Joint effects of teacher and student expectations. *Journal of Educational Psychology,* **74**, 217–223. (p. 115)

Felson, R. B. (1984). The effect of self-appraisals of ability on academic performance. *Journal of Personality and Social Psychology,* **47**, 944–952. (p. 51)

Fenigstein, A. (1984). Self-consciousness and the overperception of self as a target. *Journal of Personality and Social Psychology,* **47**, 860–870. (pp. 39, 180)

Fenigstein, A., & Carver, C. S. (1978). Self-focusing effects of heartbeat feedback. *Journal of Personality and Social Psychology,* **36**, 1241–1250. (p. 84)

Fenigstein, A., & Vanable, P. A. (1992). Paranoia and self-consciousness. *Journal of Personality and Social Psychology,* **62**, 129–138. (p. 180)

Fergusson, D. M., Horwood, L. J., & Shannon, F. T. (1984). A proportional hazards model of family breakdown. *Journal of Marriage and the Family,* **46**, 539–549. (p. 519)

Fernandez-Collado, C., & Greenberg, B. S., with Korzenny, F., & Atkin, C. K. (1978). Sexual intimacy and drug use in TV series. *Journal of Communication,* **28**(3), 30–37. (p. 469)

Feshbach, N. D. (1980). The child as "psychologist" and "economist": Two curricula. Paper presented at the American Psychological Association convention. (p. 308)

Feshbach, S. (1980). Television advertising and children: Policy issues and al-

ternatives. Paper presented at the American Psychological Association convention. (p. 307)

Festinger, L. (1954). A theory of social comparison processes. *Human Relations,* **7**, 117–140. (p. 337)

Festinger, L. (1957). *A theory of cognitive dissonance.* Stanford: Stanford University Press. (p. 145)

Festinger, L., & Carlsmith, J. M. (1959). Cognitive consequences of forced compliance. *Journal of Abnormal and Social Psychology,* **58**, 203–210. (p. 146)

Festinger, L., & Maccoby, N. (1964). On resistance to persuasive communications. *Journal of Abnormal and Social Psychology,* **68**, 359–366. (p. 294)

Festinger, L., Pepitone, A., & Newcomb, T. (1952). Some consequences of deindividuation in a group. *Journal of Abnormal and Social Psychology,* **47**, 382–389. (p. 327)

Feynman, R. (1967). *The character of physical law.* Cambridge, Mass.: MIT Press. (p. 157)

Fichter, J. (1968). *America's forgotten priests: What are they saying?* New York: Harper. (p. 404)

Fiebert, M. S. (1990). Men, women and housework: The Roshomon effect. *Men's Studies Review,* **8**, 6. (p. 54)

Fiedler, F. E. (1987, September). When to lead, when to stand back. *Psychology Today,* pp. 26–27. (p. 350)

Fiedler, K., Semin, G. R., & Koppetsch, C. (1991). Language use and attributional biases in close personal relationships. *Personality and Social Psychology Bulletin,* **17**, 147–155. (p. 81)

Fields, J. M., & Schuman, H. (1976). Public beliefs about the beliefs of the public. *Public Opinion Quarterly,* **40**, 427–448. (p. 54)

Finch, J. F., & Cialdini, R. B. (1989). Another indirect tactic of (self-) image management: Boosting. *Personality and Social Psychology Bulletin,* **15**, 222–232. (p. 60)

Fincham, F. D., & Bradbury, T. N. (1993). Marital satisfaction, depression, and attributions: A longitudinal analysis. *Journal of Personality and Social Psychology,* **64**, 442–452. (p. 75)

Fincham, F. D., & Jaspars, J. M. (1980). Attribution of responsibility: From man the scientist to man as lawyer. In L. Berkowitz (Ed.), *Advances in experimental social psychology* (Vol. 13). New York: Academic Press. (p. 83)

Findley, M. J., & Cooper, H. M. (1983).

Locus of control and academic achievement: A literature review. *Journal of Personality and Social Psychology,* **44**, 419–427. (p. 47)

Fineberg, H. V. (1988). Education to prevent AIDS: Prospects and obstacles. *Science,* **239**, 592–596. (p. 283)

Fischhoff, B. (1982). Debiasing. In D. Kahneman, P. Slovic, & A. Tversky (Eds.), *Judgment under uncertainty: Heuristics and biases.* New York: Cambridge University Press. (p. 103)

Fischhoff, B., & Bar-Hillel, M. (1984). Diagnosticity and the base rate effect. *Memory and Cognition,* **12**, 402–410. (p. 103)

Fishbein, D., & Thelen, M. H. (1981). Husband-wife similarity and marital satisfaction: A different approach. Paper presented at the Midwestern Psychological Association convention. *(a)* (p. 496)

Fishbein, D., & Thelen, M. H. (1981). Psychological factors in mate selection and marital satisfaction: A review (Ms. 2374). *Catalog of Selected Documents in Psychology,* **11**, 84. *(b)* (p. 496)

Fishbein, M., & Ajzen, I. (1974). Attitudes toward objects as predictive of single and multiple behavioral criteria. *Psychological Review,* **81**, 59–74. (p. 128)

Fisher, G. H. (1968). Ambiguity of form: Old and new. *Perception and Psychophysics,* **4**, 189–192. (p. 361)

Fisher, H. (1994, April). The nature of romantic love. *Journal of NIH Research,* pp. 59–64. (p. 505)

Fisher, R. J. (1994). Generic principles for resolving intergroup conflict. *Journal of Social Issues,* **50**, 47–66. (p. 599)

Fisher, R. P., Geiselman, R. E., & Amador, M. (1989). Field test of the cognitive interview: Enhancing the recollection of actual victims and witnesses of crime. *Journal of Applied Psychology,* **74**, 722–727. (p. 365)

Fisher, R. P., Geiselman, R. E., & Raymond, D. S. (1987). Critical analysis of police interview techniques. *Journal of Police Science and Administration,* **15**, 177–185. (p. 364)

Fisher, R. P., McCauley, M. R., & Geiselman, R. E. (1994). Improving eyewitness testimony with the Cognitive Interview. In D. F. Ross, J. D. Read, & M. P. Toglia (eds.), *Adult eyewitness testimony: Current trends and developments.* Cambridge, England: Cambridge University Press. (p. 365)

Fiske, S. T. (1992). Thinking is for doing:

Portraits of social cognition from Daguerrotype to Laserphoto. *Journal of Personality and Social Psychology, 63,* 877–889. (pp. 195, 119)

Fiske, S. T. (1993). Controlling other people: The impact of power on stereotyping. *American Psychologist, 48,* 621–628. (p. 419)

Fiske, S. T., & Ruscher, J. B. (1993). Negative interdependence and prejudice: Whence the affect? In D. Mackie & D. Hamilton (Eds.), *Affect, cognition and stereotyping: Interactive processes in intergroup perception.* San Diego, CA: Academic Press. (p. 399)

Fitzpatrick, A. R., & Eagly, A. H. (1981). Anticipatory belief polarization as a function of the expertise of a discussion partner. *Personality and Social Psychology Bulletin, 1,* 636–642. (p. 337)

Flay, B. R., Ryan, K. B., Best, J. A., Brown, K. S., Kersell, M. W., d'Avernas, J. R., & Zanna, M. P. (1985). Are social-psychological smoking prevention programs effective? The Waterloo study. *Journal of Behavioral Medicine, 8,* 37–59. (p. 306)

Fleming, I., Baum, A., & Weiss, L. (1987). Social density and perceived control as mediators of crowding stress in high-density residential neighborhoods. *Journal of Personality and Social Psychology, 52,* 899–906. (p. 455)

Fletcher, G. J. O., Danilovics, P., Fernandez, G., Peterson, D., & Reeder, G. D. (1986). Attributional complexity: An individual differences measure. *Journal of Personality and Social Psychology, 51,* 875–884. (p. 80)

Fletcher, G. J. O., Fincham, F. D., Cramer, L., & Heron, N. (1987). The role of attributions in the development of dating relationships. *Journal of Personality and Social Psychology, 53,* 481–489. (p. 514)

Fletcher, G. J. O., Reeder, G. D., & Bull, V. (1990). Bias and accuracy in attitude attribution: The role of attributional complexity. *Journal of Experimental Social Psychology, 26,* 275–288. (p. 75)

Fletcher, G. J. O., & Ward, C. (1989). Attribution theory and processes: A cross-cultural perspective. In M. H. Bond (Ed.), *The cross-cultural challenge to social psychology.* Newbury Park, Ca.: Sage. (p. 424)

Foa, U. G., & Foa, E. B. (1975). *Resource theory of social exchange.* Morristown, N.J.: General Learning Press. (p. 527)

Fogarty, G. J., & White, C. (1994). Differences between values of Australian Aboriginal and non-Aboriginal students. *Journal of Cross-Cultural Psychology, 25,* 394–408. (p. 214)

Fogelman, E. (1994). *Conscience and courage: Rescuers of Jews during the Holocaust.* New York: Doubleday Anchor. (p. 561)

Foley, L. A. (1976). Personality and situational influences on changes in prejudice: A replication of Cook's railroad game in a prison setting. *Journal of Personality and Social Psychology, 34,* 846–856. (p. 588)

Follett, M. P. (1940). Constructive conflict. In H. C. Metcalf & L. Urwick (Eds.), *Dynamic administration: The collected papers of Mary Parker Follett.* New York: Harper. (p. 596)

Forgas, J. P. (1994). The role of emotion in social judgments: An introductory review and an Affect Infusion Model (AIM). *European Journal of Social Psychology, 24,* 1–24. (p. 112)

Forgas, J. P. (1995). Mood and judgment: The affect infusion model (AIM). *Pschological Bulletin, 117,* 39–66. (p. 112)

Forgas, J. P., Bower, G. H., & Krantz, S. E. (1984). The influence of mood on perceptions of social interactions. *Journal of Experimental Social Psychology, 20,* 497–513. (p. 112)

Forgas, J. P., & Moylan, S. (1987). After the movies: Transient mood and social judgments. *Personality and Social Psychology Bulletin, 13,* 467–477. (p. 111)

Form, W. H., & Nosow, S. (1958). *Community in disaster.* New York: Harper. (p. 537)

Försterling, F. (1986). Attributional conceptions in clinical psychology. *American Psychologist, 41,* 275–285. (p. 188)

Forsyth, D. R., Berger, R. E., & Mitchell, T. (1981). The effects of self-serving vs. other-serving claims of responsibility on attraction and attribution in groups. *Social Psychology Quarterly, 44,* 59–64. (p. 68)

Forward, J. R., & Williams, J. R. (1970). Internal-external control and black militancy. *Journal of Social Issues, 26*(1), 75–92. (p. 50)

Foss, R. D. (1978). The role of social influence in blood donation. Paper presented at the American Psychological Association convention. (p. 558)

Foss, R. D. (1981). Structural effects in simulated jury decision making. *Journal of Personality and Social Psychology, 40,* 1053–1062. (p. 383)

Foulke, E., & Sticht, T. G. (1969). Review of research on the intelligibility and comprehension of accelerated speech. *Psychological Bulletin, 72,* 50–62. (p. 279)

Frable, D. E. S., Johnson, A., & Kellman, H. (1994). Seeing masculine men, sexy women and gender differences: Exposure to pornography and cognitive constructions of gender. Paper presented at the American Psychological Association convention. (p. 458)

Frank, J. (1974). *Persuasion and healing: A comparative study of psychotherapy.* New York: Schocken. (p. 303)

Frank, J. D. (1982). Therapeutic components shared by all psychotherapies. In J. H. Harvey & M. M. Parks (Eds.), *The master lecture series: Vol. 1. Psychotherapy research and behavior change.* Washington, DC: American Psychological Association. (p. 303)

Frank, M. G., & Gilovich, T. (1988). The dark side of self and social perception: Black uniforms and aggression in professional sports. *Journal of Personality and Social Psychology, 54,* 74–85. (p. 330)

Frank, M. G., & Gilovich, T. (1989). Effect of memory perspective on retrospective causal attributions. *Journal of Personality and Social Psychology, 57,* 399–403. (p. 84)

Frankel, A., & Snyder, M. L. (1987). Egotism among the depressed: When self-protection becomes self-handicapping. Paper presented at the American Psychological Association convention. (p. 67)

Franklin, B. J. (1974). Victim characteristics and helping behavior in a rural southern setting. *Journal of Social Psychology, 93,* 93–100. (p. 556)

Freedman, J. L. (1988). Television violence and aggression: What the evidence shows. In S. Oskamp (Ed.), *Television as a social issue. Applied social psychology annual,* Vol. 8. Newbury Park, Ca.: Sage. (p. 468)

Freedman, J. L., Birsky, J., & Cavoukian, A. (1980). Environmental determinants of behavioral contagion: Density and number. *Basic and Applied Social Psychology, 1,* 155–161. (p. 319)

Freedman, J. L., & Fraser, S. C. (1966). Compliance without pressure: The foot-in-the-door technique. *Journal of Personality and Social Psychology, 4,* 195–202. (p. 136)

Freedman, J. L., & Perlick, D. (1979). Crowding, contagion, and laughter.

Journal of Experimental Social Psychology, **15**, 295–303. (p. 319)

Freedman, J. L., & Sears, D. O. (1965). Warning, distraction, and resistance to influence. *Journal of Personality and Social Psychology*, **1**, 262–266. (p. 293)

Freedman, J. S. (1965). Long-term behavioral effects of cognitive dissonance. *Journal of Experimental Social Psychology*, **1**, 145–155. (p. 140)

French, J. R. P. (1968). The conceptualization and the measurement of mental health in terms of self-identity theory. In S. B. Sells (Ed.), The definition and measurement of mental health. Washington, D.C.: Department of Health, Education, and Welfare. (Cited by M. Rosenberg, 1979, *Conceiving the self.* New York: Basic Books.) (p. 54)

Frey, K. P., & Eagly, A. H. (1993). Vividness can undermine the persuasiveness of messages. *Journal of Personality and Social Psychology*, **65**, 32–44. (p. 283)

Friedland, N., Keinan, G., & Regev, Y. (1992). Controlling the uncontrollable: Effects of stress on illusory perceptions of controllability. *Journal of Personality and Social Psychology*, **63**, 923–931. (p. 109)

Friedman, H. S., Riggio, R. E., & Casella, D. F. (1988). Nonverbal skill, personal charisma, and initial attraction. *Personality and Social Psychology Bulletin*, **14**, 203–211. (p. 495)

Friedrich, J. (in press). On seeing oneself as less self-serving than others: The ultimate self-serving bias? *Teaching of Psychology.* (p. 64)

Friedrich, L. K., & Stein, A. H. (1973). Aggressive and prosocial television programs and the natural behavior of preschool children. *Monographs of the Society of Research in Child Development*, **38** (4, Serial No. 151). (pp. 562)

Frieze, I. H., Olson, J. E., & Russell, J. (1991). Attractiveness and income for men and women in management. *Journal of Applied Social Psychology*, **21**, 1039–1057. (p. 489)

Froming, W. J., Walker, G. R., & Lopyan, K. J. (1982). Public and private self-awareness: When personal attitudes conflict with societal expectations. *Journal of Experimental Social Psychology*, **18**, 476–487. (p. 129)

Fulbright, J. W. (1972). United Press International, April 5, 1971. Cited by A. C. Elms, *Social psychology and social reliance.* Boston: Little, Brown. (p. 576)

Fultz, J., Batson, C. D., Fortenbach, V. A.,

McCarthy, P. M., & Varney, L. L. (1986). Social evaluation and the empathy-altruism hypothesis. *Journal of Personality and Social Psychology*, **50**, 761–769. (p. 532)

Funder, D. C. (1987). Errors and mistakes: Evaluating the accuracy of social judgment. *Psychological Bulletin*, **101**, 75–90. (p. 119)

Funder, D. C., & Colvin, C. R. (1991). Explorations in behavioral consistency: Properties of persons, situations, and behaviors. *Journal of Personality and Social Psychology*, **60**, 773–794. (p. 263)

Furnham, A. (1982). Explanations for unemployment in Britain. *European Journal of Social Psychology*, **12**, 335–352. (p. 88)

Furnham, A., & Gunter, B. (1984). Just world beliefs and attitudes towards the poor. *British Journal of Social Psychology*, **23**, 265–269. (p. 425)

Gabrenya, W. K., Jr., Wang, Y.-E., & Latané, B. (1985). Social loafing on an optimizing task: Cross-cultural differences among Chinese and Americans. *Journal of Cross-Cultural Psychology*, **16**, 223–242. (p. 326)

Gaebelein, J. W., & Mander, A. (1978). Consequences for targets of aggression as a function of aggressor and instigator roles: Three experiments. *Personality and Social Psychology Bulletin*, **4**, 465–468. (p. 471)

Gaertner, S. L. (1973). Helping behavior and racial discrimination among liberals and conservatives. *Journal of Personality and Social Psychology*, **25**, 335–341. (p. 556)

Gaertner, S. L. (1975). The role of racial attitudes in helping behavior. *Journal of Social Psychology*, **97**, 95–101. (p. 556)

Gaertner, S. L., & Bickman, L. (1971). Effects of race on the elicitation of helping behavior. *Journal of Personality and Social Psychology*, **20**, 218–222. (p. 556)

Gaertner, S. L., & Dovidio, J. F. (1977). The subtlety of white racism, arousal, and helping behavior. *Journal of Personality and Social Psychology*, **35**, 691–707. (p. 556)

Gaertner, S. L., & Dovidio, J. F. (1986). The aversive form of racism. In J. F. Dovidio & S. L. Gaertner (Eds.), *Prejudice, discrimination, and racism.* Orlando, Fl.: Academic Press. (p. 556)

Gaertner, S. L., Dovidio, J. F., Anastasio, P. A., Bachman, B. A., & Rust, M. C.

(1993). The Common Ingroup Identity Model: Recategorization and the reduction of intergroup bias. In W. Stroebe & M. Hewstone (eds.), *European Review of Social Psychology*, vol. 4. London: Wiley. (p. 591)

Galanter, M. (1989). *Cults: Faith, healing, and coercion.* New York: Oxford University Press. (p. 303)

Galanter, M. (1990). Cults and zealous self-help movements: A psychiatric perspective. *American Journal of Psychiatry*, **147**, 543–551. (p. 303)

Galizio, M., & Hendrick, C. (1972). Effect of musical accompaniment on attitude: The guitar as a prop for persuasion. *Journal of Applied Social Psychology*, **2**, 350–359. (p. 281)

Gallup, G., Jr. (1984, March). Religion in America. *The Gallup Report*, Report No. 222. (pp. 553, 554)

Gallup, G., Jr., & Hugick, L. (1990, June). Racial tolerance grows, progress on racial equality less evident. *Gallup Poll Monthly*, pp. 23–32. (p. 393)

Gallup, G. H. (1972). *The Gallup poll: Public opinion 1935–1971.* (Vol. 3). New York: Random House, pp. 551, 1716. (pp. 464, 585)

Gallup, G. H., Jr., & Jones, T. (1992). *The saints among us.* Harrisburg, PA: Morehouse. (p. 404)

Gallup Organization (1990). April 19–22 survey reported in *American Enterprise*, September/October, 1990, p. 92. (pp. 204, 224)

Gallup Poll Monthly (1994, July). Smoke cigarettes—trend. P. 53. (p. 463)

Gamson, W. A., Fireman, B., & Rytina, S. (1982). *Encounters with unjust authority.* Homewood, Ill.: Dorsey Press. (p. 266)

Garb, H. N. (1994). Judgment research: Implications for clinical practice and testimony in court. *Applied and Preventive Psychology*, **3**, 173–183. (p. 170)

Gastorf, J. W., Suls, J., & Sanders, G. S. (1980). Type A coronary-prone behavior pattern and social facilitation. *Journal of Personality and Social Psychology*, **8**, 773–780. (p. 320)

Gates, D. (1993, March 29). White male paranoia. *Newsweek*, pp. 48–53. (p. 422)

Gates, M. F., & Allee, W. C. (1933). Conditioned behavior of isolated and grouped cockroaches on a simple maze. *Journal of Comparative Psychology*, **15**, 331–358. (p. 315)

Gavanski, I., & Hoffman, C. (1987). Awareness of influences on one's own

Green, C. W., Adams, A. M., & Turner, C. W. (1988). Development and validation of the school interracial climate scale. *American Journal of Community Psychology, 16*, 241–259. (p. 592)

Greenberg, J. (1986). Differential intolerance for inequity from organizational and individual agents. *Journal of Applied Social Psychology, 16*, 191–196. (p. 579)

Greenberg, J., Pyszczynski, T., Burling, J., & Tibbs, K. (1992). Depression, self-focused attention, and the self-serving attributional bias. *Personality and Individual Differences, 13*, 959–965. (p. 188)

Greenberg, J., Pyszczynski, T., Solomon, S., Rosenblatt, A., Veeder, M., Kirkland, S., & Lyon, D. (1990). Evidence for terror management theory II: The effects of mortality salience on reactions to those who threaten or bolster the cultural worldview. *Journal of Personality and Social Psychology, 58*, 308–318. (p. 414)

Greenberg, J., Pyszczynski, T., Solomon, S., Simon, L., & Breus, M. (1994). Role of consciousness and accessibility of death-related thoughts in mortality salience effects. *Journal of Personality and Social Psychology, 67*, 627–637. (p. 414)

Greenwald, A. G. (1968). Cognitive learning, cognitive response to persuasion, and attitude change. In A. G. Greenwald, T. C. Brock, & T. M. Ostrom (Eds.), *Psychological foundations of attitudes.* New York: Academic Press. (p. 143)

Greenwald, A. G. (1975). On the inconclusiveness of crucial cognitive tests of dissonance versus self-perception theories. *Journal of Experimental Social Psychology, 11*, 490–499. (p. 157)

Greenwald, A. G. (1980). The totalitarian ego: Fabrication and revision of personal history. *American Psychologist, 35*, 603–618. (p. 99)

Greenwald, A. G., & Banaji, M. R. (1995). Implicit social cognition: Attitudes, self-esteem, and stereotypes. *Psychological Review, 102*, 4–27. (p. 396)

Greenwald, A. G., Carnot, C. G., Beach, R., & Young, B. (1987). Increasing voting behavior by asking people if they expect to vote. *Journal of Applied Psychology, 72*, 315–318. (p. 137)

Greenwald, A. G., & Schuh, E. S. (1994). An ethnic bias in scientific citations. *European Journal of Social Psychology, 24*, 623–639. (p. 396)

Greenwald, A. G., Spangenberg, E. R., Pratkanis, A. R., & Eskenazi, J. (1991). Double-blind tests of subliminal self-help audiotapes. *Psychological Science, 2*, 119–122. (p. 90)

Griffin, B. Q., Combs, A. L., Land, M. L., & Combs, N. N. (1983). Attribution of success and failure in college performance. *Journal of Psychology, 114*, 259–266. (p. 54)

Griffitt, W. (1970). Environmental effects on interpersonal affective behavior. Ambient effective temperature and attraction. *Journal of Personality and Social Psychology, 15*, 240–244. (pp. 454, 512)

Griffitt, W. (1987). Females, males, and sexual responses. In K. Kelley (Ed.), *Females, males, and sexuality: Theories and research.* Albany: State University of New York Press. (p. 200)

Griffitt, W., & Veitch, R. (1974). Preacquaintance attitude similarity and attraction revisited: Ten days in a fallout shelter. *Sociometry, 37*, 163–173. (pp. 454, 493)

Grofman, B. (1980). The slippery slope: Jury size and jury verdict requirements—legal and social science approaches. In B. H. Raven (Ed.), *Policy studies review annual* (Vol. 4). Beverly Hills, Calif.: Sage Publications. (p. 383)

Gross, A. E., & Crofton, C. (1977). What is good is beautiful. *Sociometry, 40*, 85–90. (p. 492)

Grossman, M., & Wood, W. (1993). Sex differences in intensity of emotional experience: A social role interpretation. *Journal of Personality and Social Psychology, 65*, 1010–1022. (p. 198)

Grove, J. R., Hanrahan, S. J., & McInman, A. (1991). Success/failure bias in attributions across involvement categories in sport. *Personality and Social Psychology Bulletin, 17*, 93–97. (p. 53)

Grube, J. W., Kleinhesselink, R. R., & Kearney, K. A. (1982). Male self-acceptance and attraction toward women. *Personality and Social Psychology Bulletin, 8*, 107–112. (p. 414)

Gruder, C. L. (1977). Choice of comparison persons in evaluating oneself. In J. M. Suls & R. L. Miller (Eds.), *Social comparison processes.* Washington: Hemisphere Publishing. (p. 446)

Gruder, C. L., Cook, T. D., Hennigan, K. M., Flay, B., Alessis, C., & Kalamaj, J. (1978). Empirical tests of the absolute sleeper effect predicted from the discounting cue hypothesis. *Journal of Per-*

sonality and Social Psychology, 36, 1061–1074. (p. 277)

Gruman, J. C., & Sloan, R. P. (1983). Disease as justice: Perceptions of the victims of physical illness. *Basic and Applied Social Psychology, 4*, 39–46. (p. 426)

Grunberger, R. (1971). *The 12-year-Reich: A social history of Nazi Germany 1933–1945.* New York: Holt, Rinehart & Winston. (p. 141)

Grush, J. E. (1980). Impact of candidate expenditures, regionality, and prior outcomes on the 1976 Democratic presidential primaries. *Journal of Personality and Social Psychology, 38*, 337–347. (p. 288)

Grush, J. E., & Glidden, M. V. (1987). Power and satisfaction among distressed and nondistressed couples. Paper presented at the Midwestern Psychological Association convention. (p. 597)

Gudykunst, W. B. (1989). Culture and intergroup processes. In M. H. Bond (Ed.), *The cross-cultural challenge to social psychology.* Newbury Park, Ca.: Sage. (p. 406)

Guerin, B. (1993). *Social facilitation.* Paris: Cambridge University Press. (p. 317)

Guerin, B. (1994). What do people think about the risks of driving? Implications for traffic safety interventions. *Journal of Applied Social Psychology, 24*, 994–1021. (p. 54)

Guerin, B., & Innes, J. M. (1982). Social facilitation and social monitoring: A new look at Zajonc's mere presence hypothesis. *British Journal of Social Psychology, 21*, 7–18. (p. 320)

Guiness, O. (1993). *The American hour: A time of reckoning and the once and future role of faith.* New York: Free Press. (p. 518)

Gupta, U., & Singh, P. (1982). Exploratory study of love and liking and type of marriages. *Indian Journal of Applied Psychology, 19*, 92–97. (pp. 506, 507)

Gutmann, D. (1977). The cross-cultural perspective: Notes toward a comparative psychology of aging. In J. E. Birren & K. Warner Schaie (Eds.), *Handbook of the psychology of aging.* New York: Van Nostrand Reinhold. (p. 208)

Hacker, H. M. (1951). Women as a minority group. *Social Forces, 30*, 60–69. (p. 403)

Hackman, J. R. (1986). The design of work teams. In J. Lorsch (Ed.), *Hand-*

book of organizational behavior. Englewood Cliffs, N.J.: Prentice-Hall. (p. 326)

Hadden, J. K. (1969). *The gathering storm in the churches.* Garden City, N.Y.: Doubleday. (p. 404)

Haddock, G., & Zanna, M. P. (1994). Preferring "housewives" to "feminists." *Psychology of Women Quarterly,* **18,** 25–52. (pp. 196, 399)

Haemmerlie, F. M., & Montgomery, R. L. (1982). Self-perception theory and unobtrusively biased interactions: A treatment for heterosocial anxiety. *Journal of Counseling Psychology,* **29,** 362–370. (p. 187)

Haemmerlie, F. M., & Montgomery, R. L. (1984). Purposefully biased interventions: Reducing heterosocial anxiety through self-perception theory. *Journal of Personality and Social Psychology,* **47,** 900–908. (p. 187)

Haemmerlie, F. M., & Montgomery, R. L. (1986). Self-perception theory and the treatment of shyness. In W. H. Jones, J. M. Cheek, & S. R. Briggs (Eds.), *A sourcebook on shyness: Research and treatment.* New York: Plenum. (p. 187)

Hafner, H., & Schmidtke, A. (1989). Do televised fictional suicide models produce suicides? In D. R. Pfeffer (Ed.), *Suicide among youth: Perspectives on risk and prevention.* Washington, DC: American Psychiatric Press. (p. 236)

Hagiwara, S. (1983). Role of self-based and sample-based consensus estimates as mediators of responsibility judgments for automobile accidents. *Japanese Psychological Research,* **25,** 16–28. (p. 69)

Hall, J. A. (1984). *Nonverbal sex differences: Communication accuracy and expressive style.* Baltimore: Johns Hopkins University Press. (pp. 198, 200)

Hall, T. (1985, June 25). The unconverted: Smoking of cigarettes seems to be becoming a lower-class habit. *Wall Street Journal,* pp. 1, 25. (p. 98)

Hallmark Cards (1990). Cited in *Time,* Fall special issue on women. (p. 197)

Hamblin, R. L., Buckholdt, D., Bushell, D., Ellis, D., & Feritor, D. (1969). Changing the game from get the teacher to learn. *Transaction,* January, pp. 20–25, 28–31. (p. 474)

Hamilton, D. L. (1981). Illusory correlation as a basis for stereotyping. In D. L. Hamilton (Ed.), *Cognitive processes in stereotyping and intergroup behavior.* Hillsdale, N.J.: Erlbaum. (p. 427)

Hamilton, D. L., & Bishop, G. D. (1976). Attitudinal and behavioral effects of initial integration of white suburban neighborhoods. *Journal of Social Issues,* **32**(2), 47–67. (p. 427)

Hamilton, D. L., & Gifford, R. K. (1976). Illusory correlation in interpersonal perception: A cognitive basis of stereotypic judgments. *Journal of Experimental Social Psychology,* **12,** 392–407. (p. 422)

Hamilton, D. L., & Rose, T. L. (1980). Illusory correlation and the maintenance of stereotypic beliefs. *Journal of Personality and Social Psychology,* **39,** 832–845. (p. 423)

Hamilton, D. L., & Sherman, J. W. (1994). Stereotypes. In R. S. Wyer, Jr., & T. K. Srull (eds.), *Handbook of social cognition,* 2nd ed. Hillsdale, NJ: Erlbaum. (p. 423)

Hamilton, V. L., Hoffman, W. S., Broman, C. L., & Rauma, D. (1993). Unemployment, distress, and coping: A panel study of autoworkers. *Journal of Personality and Social Psychology,* **65,** 234–247. (pp. 175–176)

Hampson, R. B. (1984). Adolescent prosocial behavior: Peer-group and situational factors associated with helping. *Journal of Personality and Social Psychology,* **46,** 153–162. (p. 551)

Han, S-P., & Shavitt, S. (1994). Persuasion and culture: Advertising appeals in individualistic and collectivistic societies. *Journal of Experimental Social Psychology,* **30,** 326–350. (p. 215)

Haney, C. (1991). The fourteenth amendment and symbolic legality: Let them eat due process. *Law and Human Behavior,* **15,** 183–204. (p. 370)

Haney, C. (1993). Psychology and legal change. *Law and Human Behavior,* **17,** 371–398. (p. 379)

Hans, V. P., & Vidmar, N. (1981). Jury selection. In N. L. Kerr & R. M. Bray (Eds.), *The psychology of the courtroom.* New York: Academic Press. (p. 378)

Hansen, C. H., & Hansen, R. D. (1988). Priming stereotypic appraisal of social interactions: How rock music videos can change what's seen when boy meets girl. *Sex Roles,* **19,** 287–316. (p. 458)

Hansen, C. H., & Hansen, R. D. (1990). Rock music videos and antisocial behavior. *Basic and Applied Social Psychology,* **11,** 357–369. (p. 458)

Hardin, G. (1968). The tragedy of the commons. *Science,* **162,** 1243–1248. (pp. 571, 574)

Hardy, C., & Latané, B. (1986). Social loafing on a cheering task. *Social Science,* **71,** 165–172. (p. 323)

Haritos-Fatouros, M. (1988). The official torturer: A learning model for obedience to the authority of violence. *Journal of Applied Social Psychology,* **18,** 1107–1120. (p. 249)

Harkins, S. G. (1981). Effects of task difficulty and task responsibility on social loafing. Presentation to the First International Conference on Social Processes in Small Groups, Kill Devil Hills, North Carolina. (p. 323)

Harkins, S. G., & Jackson, J. M. (1985). The role of evaluation in eliminating social loafing. *Personality and Social Psychology Bulletin,* **11,** 457–465. (p. 324)

Harkins, S. G., Latané, B., & Williams, K. (1980). Social loafing: Allocating effort or taking it easy? *Journal of Experimental Social Psychology,* **16,** 457–465. (p. 322)

Harkins, S. G., & Petty, R. E. (1981). Effects of source magnification of cognitive effort on attitudes: An information-processing view. *Journal of Personality and Social Psychology,* **40,** 401–413. (p. 294)

Harkins, S. G., & Petty, R. E. (1982). Effects of task difficulty and task uniqueness on social loafing. *Journal of Personality and Social Psychology,* **43,** 1214–1229. (p. 326)

Harkins, S. G., & Petty, R. E. (1987). Information utility and the multiple source effect. *Journal of Personality and Social Psychology,* **52,** 260–268. (p. 294)

Harkins, S. G., & Szymanski, K. (1989). Social loafing and group evaluation. *Journal of Personality and Social Psychology,* **56,** 934–941. (p. 326)

Harper's Index (1991, September). *Harper's Magazine,* p. 15. Data from Amateur Athletic Foundation of Los Angeles. (p. 204)

Harries, K. D., & Stadler, S. J. (1988). Heat and violence: New findings from Dallas field data, 1980–1981. *Journal of Applied Social Psychology,* **18,** 129–138. (p. 454)

Harris, M. J. (1994). Self-fulfilling prophecies in the clinical context: Review and implications for clinical practice. *Applied & Preventive Psychology,* **3,** 145–158. (p. 168)

Harris, M. J., & Rosenthal, R. (1986). Four factors in the mediation of teacher expectancy effects. In R. S.

Feldman (Ed.), *The social psychology of education.* New York: Cambridge University Press. (p. 115)

Harrison, A. A. (1977). Mere exposure. In L. Berkowitz (Ed.), *Advances in experimental social psychology* (Vol. 10). New York: Academic Press, pp. 39–83. (p. 484)

Hart, A. J. (1995). Naturally occurring expectation effects. *Journal of Personality and Social Psychology,* **68,** 109–115. (p. 373)

Hartlage, S., Alloy, A. B., Vazquez, C., & Dykman, B. (1993). Automatic and effortful processing in depression. *Psychological Bulletin,* **113,** 247–278. (p. 112)

Harvey, J. H., Town, J. P., & Yarkin, K. L. (1981). How fundamental is the fundamental attribution error? *Journal of Personality and Social Psychology,* **40,** 346–349. (p. 86)

Hassan I. N. (1980). Role and status of women in Pakistan: An empirical research review. *Pakistan Journal of Psychology,* **13,** 36–56. (p. 223)

Hastie, R., Penrod, S. D., & Pennington, N. (1983). *Inside the jury.* Cambridge, Mass.: Harvard University Press. (pp. 380, 381, 383)

Hastorf, A., & Cantril, H. (1954). They saw a game: A case study. *Journal of Abnormal and Social Psychology,* **49,** 129–134. (p. 8)

Hatfield, E. (1988). Passionate and compassionate love. In R. J. Sternberg & M. L. Barnes (Eds.), *The psychology of love.* New Haven, Conn.: Yale University Press. (p. 501)

Hatfield, E., Cacioppo, J. T., & Rapson, R. (1992). The logic of emotion: Emotional contagion. In M. S. Clark (Ed.), *Review of Personality and Social Psychology.* Newbury Park, CA: Sage. (p. 153)

Hatfield, E., & Rapson, R. L. (1987). Passionate love: New directions in research. In W. H. Jones & D. Perlman (Eds.), *Advances in personal relationships,* Vol. 1. Greenwich, Ct.: JAI Press. (p. 503)

Hatfield, E. & Sprecher, S. (1986). *Mirror, mirror: The importance of looks in everyday life.* Albany, N.Y.: SUNY Press. (pp. 489, 507)

Hatfield, E., Traupmann, J., Sprecher, S., Utne, M., & Hay, J. (1985). Equity and intimate relations: Recent research. In W. Ickes (Ed.), *Compatible and incompatible relationships.* New York: Springer-Verlag. (p. 514)

Haugtvedt, C. P., & Wegener, D. T. (1994). Message order effects in persuasion: An attitude strength perspective. *Journal of Consumer Research,* **21,** 205–218. (p. 287)

Hazan, C., & Shaver, P. R. (1994). Attachment as an organizational framework for research on close relationships. *Psychological Inquiry,* **5,** 1–22. (pp. 509, 519)

Headey, B., & Wearing, A. (1987). The sense of relative superiority—central to well-being. *Social Indicators Research,* **20,** 497–516. (p. 54)

Hearold, S. (1986). A synthesis of 1043 effects of television on social behavior. In G. Comstock (Ed.), *Public communication and behavior,* Vol. 1. Orlando, Fl.: Academic Press. (pp. 468, 561)

Heath, L., & Petraitis, J. (1987). Television viewing and fear of crime: Where is the mean world? *Basic and Applied Social Psychology,* **8,** 97–123. (p. 470)

Hecht, M. A., LaFrance, M., & Haertl, J. C. (1993). Gender differences in smiling: A meta-analysis of archival data. Paper presented to the American Psychological Association convention. (p. 198)

Hedge, A., & Yousif, Y. H. (1992). Effects of urban size, urgency, and cost on helpfulness: A cross-cultural comparison between the United Kingdom and the Sudan. *Journal of Cross-Cultural Psychology,* **23,** 107–115. (p. 537)

Heesacker, M. (1989). Counseling and the elaboration likelihood model of attitude change. In J. F. Cruz, R. A. Goncalves, & P. P. Machado (Eds.), *Psychology and education: Investigations and interventions.* (Proceedings of the International Conference on Interventions in Psychology and Education, Porto, Portugal, July, 1987.) Porto, Portugal: Portugese Psychological Association. (p. 304)

Heider, F. (1958). *The psychology of interpersonal relations.* New York: Wiley. (p. 76)

Heilman, M. E. (1976). Oppositional behavior as a function of influence attempt intensity and retaliation threat. *Journal of Personality and Social Psychology,* **33,** 574–578. (p. 266)

Heine, S. J., & Lehman, D. R. (1995). Cultural variation in unrealistic optimism: Does the West feel more invulnerable than the East? *Journal of Personality and Social Psychology,* **68,** 595–607. (p. 69)

Heine, S. J., & Lehman, D. R. (1995). When the twain meet: Self-assessments and exposure to Western culture. Unpublished manuscript, University of British Columbia. (p. 45)

Hellman, P. (1980). *Avenue of the righteous of nations.* New York: Atheneum. (p. 527)

Hemsley, G. D., & Doob, A. N. (1978). The effect of looking behavior on perceptions of a communicator's credibility. *Journal of Applied Social Psychology,* **8,** 136–144. (p. 278)

Hendrick, C. (1988). Roles and gender in relationships. In S. Duck (Ed.), *Handbook of personal relationships.* Chichester, England: Wiley. (p. 201)

Hendrick, C., & Hendrick, S. (1993). *Romantic love.* Newbury Park, CA: Sage. (p. 500)

Hendrick, S. S., Hendrick, C., & Adler, N. L. (1988). Romantic relationships: Love, satisfaction, and staying together. *Journal of Personality and Social Psychology,* **54,** 980–988. (p. 516)

Hendrick, S. S., Hendrick, C., Slapion-Foote, J., & Foote, F. H. (1985). Gender differences in sexual attitudes. *Journal of Personality and Social Psychology,* **48,** 1630–1642. (p. 200)

Henley, N. (1977). *Body politics: Power, sex, and nonverbal communication.* Englewood Cliffs, N.J.: Prentice-Hall. (p. 199)

Hennigan, K. M., Del Rosario, M. L., Health, L., Cook, T. D., Wharton, J. D., & Calder, B. J. (1982). Impact of the introduction of television on crime in the United States: Empirical findings and theoretical implications. *Journal of Personality and Social Psychology,* **42,** 461–477. (p. 447)

Henry, W. A. III (1994, June 27). Pride and prejudice. *Time,* pp. 54–59. (p. 394)

Henslin, M. (1967). Craps and magic. *American Journal of Sociology,* **73,** 316–330. (p. 108)

Hepworth, J. T., & West, S. G. (1988). Lynchings and the economy: A time-series reanalysis of Hovland and Sears (1940). *Journal of Personality and Social Psychology,* **55,** 239–247. (p. 412)

Heradstveit, D. (1980). *The Arab-Israeli conflict: Psychological obstacles to peace* (Vol. 28). Oslo, Norway: Universitetsforlaget, 1979. Distributed by Columbia University Press. Reviewed by R. K. White, *Contemporary Psychology,* **25,** 11–12. (p. 584)

Herek, G. (1993). Interpersonal contact and heterosexuals' attitudes toward gay men: Results from a national survey. *Journal of Sex Research,* **30**, 239–244. (p. 588)

Herek, G. M. (1986). The instrumentality of attitudes: Toward a neofunctional theory. *Journal of Social Issues,* **42**, 99–114. (p. 402)

Herek, G. M. (1987). Can functions be measured? A new perspective on the functional approach to attitudes. *Social Psychology Quarterly,* **50**, 285–303. (p. 402)

Herek, G. M. (1990). The context of anti-gay violence: Notes on cultural and psychological heterosexism. *Journal of Interpersonal Violence,* **5**, 316–333. (p. 393)

Hewstone, M. (1988). Causal attribution: From cognitive processes to collective beliefs. *The Psychologist,* **8**, 323–327. (p. 12)

Hewstone, M. (1990). The 'ultimate attribution error'? A review of the literature on intergroup causal attribution. *European Journal of Social Psychology,* **20**, 311–335. (p. 425)

Hewstone, M. (1994). Revision and change of stereotypic beliefs: In search of the elusive subtyping model. In S. Stroebe & M. Hewstone (eds.), *European review of social psychology,* vol. 5. Chichester, England: Wiley. (p. 428)

Hewstone, M., Hantzi, A., & Johnston, L. (1991). Social categorisation and person memory: The pervasiveness of race as an organizing principle. *European Journal of Social Psychology,* **21**, 517–528. (p. 417)

Hewstone, M., Hopkins, N., & Routh, D. A. (1992). Cognitive models of stereotype change: Generalization and subtyping in young people's views of the police. *European Journal of Social Psychology,* **22**, 219–234. (p. 429)

Hewstone, M., & Ward, C. (1985). Ethnocentrism and causal attribution in southeast Asia. *Journal of Personality and Social Psychology,* **48**, 614–623. (p. 424)

Higbee, K. L., Millard, R. J., & Folkman, J. R. (1982). Social psychology research during the 1970s: Predominance of experimentation and college students. *Personality and Social Psychology Bulletin,* **8**, 180–183. (p. 25)

Higgins, E. T., & Bargh, J. A. (1987). Social cognition and social perception. *Annual Review of Psychology,* **38**, 369–425. (p. 39)

Higgins, E. T., & McCann, C. D. (1984). Social encoding and subsequent attitudes, impressions and memory:

"Context-driven" and motivational aspects of processing. *Journal of Personality and Social Psychology,* **47**, 26–39. (p. 135)

Higgins, E. T., & Rholes, W. S. (1978). Saying is believing: Effects of message modification on memory and liking for the person described. *Journal of Experimental Social Psychology,* **14**, 363–378. (p. 135)

Higgins, E. T., Rholes, W. S., & Jones, C. R. (1977). Category accessibility and impression formation. *Journal of Experimental Social Psychology,* **13**, 141–154. (p. 100)

Hilgard, E. R., & Loftus, E. F. (1979). Effective interrogation of the eyewitness. *International Journal of Clinical and Experimental Hypnosis,* **27**, 342–357. (p. 365)

Hill, T., Smith, N. D., & Lewicki, P. (1989). The development of self-image bias: A real-world demonstration. *Personality and Social Psychology Bulletin,* **15**, 205–211. (p. 56)

Hilton, J. L., & Darley, J. M. (1985). Constructing other persons: A limit on the effect. *Journal of Experimental Social Psychology,* **21**, 1–18. (p. 117)

Hilton, J. L., & von Hippel, W. (1990). The role of consistency in the judgment of stereotype-relevant behaviors. *Personality and Social Psychology Bulletin,* **16**, 430–448. (p. 92)

Hinde, R. A. (1984). Why do the sexes behave differently in close relationships? *Journal of Social and Personal Relationships,* **1**, 471–501. (p. 201)

Hines, M., & Green, R. (1991). Human hormonal and neural correlates of sex-typed behaviors. *Review of Psychiatry,* **10**, 536–555. (p. 207)

Hinkle, S., Brown, R., & Ely, P. G. (1992). Social identity theory processes: Some limitations and limiting conditions. *Revista de Psicologia Social,* 99–111. (p. 407)

Hinsz, V. B. (1990). Cognitive and consensus processes in group recognition memory performance. *Journal of Personality and Social Psychology,* **59**, 705–718. (p. 346)

Hinsz, V. B., & Davis, J. H. (1984). Persuasive arguments theory, group polarization, and choice shifts. *Personality and Social Psychology Bulletin,* **10**, 260–268. (p. 337)

Hirschman, R. S., & Leventhal, H. (1989). Preventing smoking behavior in school children: An initial test of a cognitive-development program. *Jour-*

nal of Applied Social Psychology, **19**, 559–583. (p. 306)

Hirt, E. R. (1990). Do I see only what I expect? Evidence for an expectancy-guided retrieval model. *Journal of Personality and Social Psychology,* **58**, 937–951. (p. 96)

Hirt, E. R., Zillmann, D., Erickson, G. A., & Kennedy, C. (1992). Costs and benefits of allegiance: Changes in fans' self-ascribed competencies after team victory versus defeat. *Journal of Personality and Social Psychology,* **63**, 724–738. (p. 175)

Hobden, K. L., & Olson, J. M. (1994). From jest to antipathy: Disparagement humor as a source of dissonance-motivated attitude change. *Basic and Applied Social Psychology,* **15**, 239–249. (p. 147)

Hodges, B. H. (1974). Effect of valence on relative weighting in impression formation. *Journal of Personality and Social Psychology,* **30**, 378–381. (p. 78)

Hodgins, H. S., & Zuckerman, M. (1993). Beyond selecting information: Biases in spontaneous questions and resultant conclusions. *Journal of Experimental Social Psychology,* **29**, 387–407. (p. 167)

Hodgkinson, V. A., & Weitzman, M. S. (1990). *Giving and volunteering in the United States: Findings from a national survey.* Washington, DC: Independent Sector. (p. 554)

Hodgkinson, V. A., & Weitzman, M. S. (1992). *Giving and volunteering in the United States.* Washington, DC: Independent Sector. (p. 554)

Hodgkinson, V. A., Weitzman, M. S., & Kirsch, A. D. (1990). From commitment to action: How religious involvement affects giving and volunteering. In R. Wuthnow, V. A. Hodgkinson & Associates (Eds.), *Faith and philanthropy in America: Exploring the role of religion in America's voluntary sector.* San Francisco: Jossey-Bass. (p. 554)

Hoffman, C., & Hurst, N. (1990). Gender stereotypes: Perception or rationalization? *Journal of Personality and Social Psychology,* **58**, 197–208. (p. 403)

Hoffman, L. W. (1977). Changes in family roles, socialization, and sex differences. *American Psychologist,* **32**, 644–657. (p. 409)

Hoffman, M. L. (1981). Is altruism part of human nature? *Journal of Personality and Social Psychology,* **40**, 121–137. (p. 531)

Hofling, C. K., Brotzman, E., Dairymple,

S., Graves, N., & Pierce, C. M. (1966). An experimental study in nurse-physician relationships. *Journal of Nervous and Mental Disease,* **143,** 171–180. (p. 245)

Hogan, R., Curphy, G. J., & Hogan, J. (1994). What we know about leadership: Effectiveness and personality. *American Psychologist,* **49,** 493–504. (pp. 349, 351)

Hogg, M. A., & Abrams, D. (1988). *Social identifications: A social psychology of intergroup relations and group processes.* London: Routledge. (p. 407)

Hogg, M. A., Turner, J. C., & Davidson, B. (1990). Polarized norms and social frames of reference: A test of the self-categorization theory of group polarization. *Basic and Applied Social Psychology,* **11,** 77–100. (p. 337)

Hokanson, J. E., & Burgess, M. (1962). The effects of frustration and anxiety on overt aggression. *Journal of Abnormal and Social Psychology,* **65,** 232–237. *(a)* (p. 473)

Hokanson, J. E., & Burgess, M. (1962). The effects of three types of aggression on vascular processes. *Journal of Abnormal and Social Psychology,* **64,** 446–449. *(b)* (p. 473)

Hokanson, J. E., & Edelman, R. (1966). Effects of three social responses on vascular processes. *Journal of Personality and Social Psychology,* **3,** 442–447. (p. 473)

Hokanson, J. E., & Shetler, S. (1961). The effect of overt aggression on physiological arousal. *Journal of Abnormal and Social Psychology,* **63,** 446–448. (p. 473)

Hollander, E. P. (1958). Conformity, status, and idiosyncrasy credit. *Psychological Review,* **65,** 117–127. (p. 259)

Holmberg, D., & Holmes, J. G. (1994). Reconstruction of relationship memories: A mental models approach. In N. Schwarz & S. Sudman (Eds.), *Autobiographical memory and the validity of retrospective reports.* New York: Springer-Verlag. (p. 98)

Holmes, J. G., & Rempel, J. K. (1989). Trust in close relationships. In C. Hendrick (Ed.), *Review of personality and social psychology,* Vol. 10. Newbury Park, Ca.: Sage. (p. 515)

Holtgraves, T., & Srull, T. K. (1989). The effects of positive self-descriptions on impressions: General principles and individual differences. *Personality and Social Psychology Bulletin,* **15,** 452–462. (p. 68)

Holtzworth, A., & Jacobson, N. S. (1988). An attributional approach to marital dysfunction and therapy. In J. E. Maddux, C. D. Stoltenberg, & R. Rosenwein (Eds.), *Social processes in clinical and counseling psychology.* New York: Springer-Verlag. (p. 74)

Holtzworth-Munroe, A., & Jacobson, N. S. (1985). Causal attributions of married couples: When do they search for causes? What do they conclude when they do? *Journal of Personality and Social Psychology,* **48,** 1398–1412. (p. 74)

Hoorens, V. (1993). Self-enhancement and superiority biases in social comparison. In W. Stroebe & M. Hewstone (Eds.), *European review of social psychology,* vol. 4. Chichester: Wiley. (p. 54)

Hoorens, V. (in press). Self-favoring biases, self-presentation and the self-other asymmetry in social comparison. *Journal of Personality.* (p. 54)

Hoorens, V., & Nuttin, J. M. (1993). Overvaluation of own attributes: Mere ownership or subjective frequency? *Social Cognition,* **11,** 177–200. (p. 483)

Hoorens, V., Nuttin, J. M., Herman, I. E., & Pavakanun, U. (1990). Mastery pleasure versus mere ownership: A quasi-experimental cross-cultural and cross-alphabetical test of the name letter effect. *European Journal of Social Psychology,* **20,** 181–205. (p. 483)

Hoover, C. W., Wood, E. E., & Knowles, E. S. (1983). Forms of social awareness and helping. *Journal of Experimental Social Psychology,* **19,** 577–590. (p. 559)

Hormuth, S. E. (1986). Lack of effort as a result of self-focused attention: An attributional ambiguity analysis. *European Journal of Social Psychology,* **16,** 181–192. (p. 67)

Hornstein, H. (1976). *Cruelty and kindness.* Englewood Cliffs, N.J.: Prentice-Hall. (p. 439)

Horowitz, S. V., & Boardman, S. K. (1994). Managing conflict: Policy and research implications. *Journal of Social Issues,* **50,** 197–211. (p. 597)

House, J. S., Landis, K. R., & Umberson, D. (1988). Social relationships and health. *Science,* **241,** 540–545. (p. 479)

House, R. J., & Singh, J. V. (1987). Organizational behavior: Some new directions for I/O psychology. *Annual Review of Psychology,* **38,** 669–718. (p. 351)

Houston, V., & Bull, R. (1994). Do people avoid sitting next to someone who is facially disfigured? *European Journal of Social Psychology,* **24,** 279–284. (p. 487)

Hovland, C. I., Lumsdaine, A. A., & Sheffield, F. D. (1949). *Experiments on mass communication. Studies in social psychology in World War II* (Vol. III). Princeton, N.J.: Princeton University Press. (pp. 281, 285, 286)

Hovland, C. I., & Sears, R. (1940). Minor studies of aggression: Correlation of lynchings with economic indices. *Journal of Psychology,* **9,** 301–310. (p. 412)

Hoyle, R. H. (1993). Interpersonal attraction in the absence of explicit attitudinal information. *Social Cognition,* **11,** 309–320. (p. 494)

Huddy, L., & Virtanen, S. (1995). Subgroup differentiation and subgroup bias among Latinos as a function of familiarity and positive distinctiveness. *Journal of Personality and Social Psychology,* **68,** 97–108. (p. 418)

Huesmann, L. R., Lagerspetz, K., & Eron, L. D. (1984). Intervening variables in the TV violence-aggression relation: Evidence from two countries. *Developmental Psychology,* **20,** 746–775. (p. 466)

Hugick, L., & McAneny, L. (1992, September). A gloomy America sees a nation in decline, no easy solutions ahead. *Gallup Poll Monthly,* p. 4. (p. 462)

Hui, C. H. (1988). Measurement of individualism-collectivism. *Journal of Research in Personality,* **22,** 17–36. (p. 212)

Hui, C. H. (1990). West meets East: Individualism versus collectivism in North America and Asia. Invited address, Hope College. (p. 215)

Hui, C. H., Triandis, H. C., & Yee, C. (1991). Cultural differences in reward allocation: Is collectivism the explanation? *British Journal of Social Psychology,* **30,** 145–157. (p. 580)

Hull, J. G., & Bond, Jr., C. F. (1986). Social and behavioral consequences of alcohol consumption and expectancy: A meta-analysis. *Psychological Bulletin,* **99,** 347–360. (p. 441)

Hull, J. G., Levenson, R. W., Young, R. D., & Sher, K. J. (1983). Self-awareness-reducing effects of alcohol consumption. *Journal of Personality and Social Psychology,* **44,** 461–473. (p. 331)

Hull, J. G., & Young, R. D. (1983). The self-awareness-reducing effects of alcohol consumption: Evidence and implications. In J. Suls & A. G. Greenwald (Eds.), *Psychological perspectives on the self,* Vol. 2. Hillsdale, N.J.: Erlbaum. (p. 180)

Humphrey, R. (1985). How work roles influence perception: Structural-cognitive processes and organizational behavior. *American Sociological Review,* **50**, 242–252. (p. 220)

Hunt, M. (1990). *The compassionate beast: What science is discovering about the humane side of human kind.* New York: William Morrow. (pp. 198, 533)

Hunt, M. (1993). *The story of psychology.* New York: Doubleday. (p. 47)

Hunt, P. J., & Hillery, J. M. (1973). Social facilitation in a location setting: An examination of the effects over learning trials. *Journal of Experimental Social Psychology,* **9**, 563–571. (p. 317)

Hunter, J. A., Stringer, M., & Watson, R. P. (1991). Intergroup violence and intergroup attributions. *British Journal of Social Psychology,* **30**, 261–266. (p. 584)

Hurtado, S., Dey, E. L., & Trevino, J. G. (1994). Exclusion or self-segregation? Interaction across racial/ethnic groups on college campuses. Paper presented at the American Educational Research Association annual meeting. (p. 393)

Huston, A. C., Donnerstein, E., Fairchild, H., Feshbach, N. D., Katz, P. A., & Murray, J. P. (1992). *Big world, small screen: The role of television in American society.* Lincoln, NE: University of Nebraska Press. (p. 464)

Huston, T. L. (1973). Ambiguity of acceptance, social desirability, and dating choice. *Journal of Experimental Social Psychology,* **9**, 32–42. (p. 487)

Huston, T. L., & Chorost, A. F. (1994). Behavioral buffers on the effect of negativity on marital satisfaction: A longitudinal study. *Personal Relationships,* **1**, 223–239. (p. 505)

Hutton, D. G., & Baumeister, R. F. (1992). Self-awareness and attitude change: Seeing oneself on the central route to persuasion. *Personality and Social Psychology Bulletin,* **18**, 68–75. (p. 331)

Hyde, J. S. (1986). Gender differences in aggression. In J. S. Hyde & M. C. Linn (Eds.), *The psychology of gender: Advances through meta-analysis.* Baltimore: Johns Hopkins University Press. (p. 200)

Hyman, H. H., & Sheatsley, P. B. (1956 & 1964). Attitudes toward desegregation. *Scientific American,* **195**(6), 35–39, and **211**(1), 16–23. (p. 392)

Hyman, R. (1981). Cold reading: How to convince strangers that you know all about them. In K. Frazier (Ed.), *Paranormal borderlands of science.* Buffalo, N.Y.: Prometheus Books. (p. 136)

Ickes, B. (1980). On disconfirming our perceptions of others. Paper presented at the American Psychological Association convention. (p. 85)

Ickes, W. (1993). Traditional gender roles: Do they make, and then break, our relationships? *Journal of Social Issues,* **49**, 7185. (p. 210)

Ickes, W., & Layden, M. A. (1978). Attributional styles. In J. H. Harvey, W. Ickes, & R. F. Kidd (Eds.), *New directions in attribution research* (Vol. 2). Hillsdale, N.J.: Lawrence Erlbaum. (p. 62)

Ickes, W., Layden, M. A., & Barnes, R. D. (1978). Objective self-awareness and individuation: An empirical link. *Journal of Personality,* **46**, 146–161. (p. 331)

Ickes, W., Patterson, M. L., Rajecki, D. W., & Tanford, S. (1982). Behavioral and cognitive consequences of reciprocal versus compensatory responses to preinteraction expectancies. *Social Cognition,* **1**, 160–190. (pp. 263, 427)

Ickes, W., Snyder, M., & Garcia, S. (1990). Personality influences on the choice of situations. In S. Briggs, R. Hogan, & W. Jones (Eds.), *Handbook of Personality Psychology.* New York: Academic Press. (p. 228)

Imai, Y. (1994). Effects of influencing attempts on the perceptions of powerholders and the powerless. *Journal of Social Behavior and Personality,* **9**, 455–468. (p. 54)

Ingham, A. G., Levinger, G., Graves, J., & Peckham, V. (1974). The Ringelmann effect: Studies of group size and group performance. *Journal of Experimental Social Psychology,* **10**, 371–384. (pp. 322, 323)

Inglehart, M. R., Markus, H., & Brown, D. R. (1989). The effects of possible selves on academic achievement—a panel study. In J. P. Forgas & J. M. Innes (Eds.), *Recent advances in social psychology: An international perspective.* North-Holland: Elsevier Science Publishers. (p. 39)

Inglehart, R. (1990). *Culture shift in advanced industrial society.* Princeton, NJ: Princeton University Press. (pp. 510, 511)

Inman, M. L., & Baron, R. S. (1996). The influence of prototypes on perceptions of prejudice. *Journal of Personality and Social Psychology,* in press. (p. 395)

Insko, C. A., Nacoste, R. W., & Moe, J. L. (1983). Belief congruence and racial discrimination: Review of the evidence and critical evaluation. *European Journal of Social Psychology,* **13**, 153–174. (p. 494)

Insko, C. A., Smith, R. H., Alicke, M. D., Wade, J., & Taylor, S. (1985). Conformity and group size: The concern with being right and the concern with being liked. *Journal of Personality and Social Psychology,* **11**, 41–50. (p. 260)

Institute of Medicine (1989). *Behavioral influences on the endocrine and immune systems.* Washington, DC: National Academy Press. (p. 181)

Isen, A. M., Clark, M., & Schwartz, M. F. (1976). Duration of the effect of good mood on helping: Footprints on the sands of time. *Journal of Personality and Social Psychology,* **34**, 385–393. (pp. 550, 551)

Isen, A. M., Horn, N., & Rosenhan, D. L. (1973). Effects of success and failure on children's generosity. *Journal of Personality and Social Psychology,* **27**, 239–247. (p. 548)

Isen, A. M., & Means, B. (1983). The influence of positive affect on decision-making strategy. *Social Cognition,* **2**, 28–31. (p. 111)

Isen, A. M., Shalker, T. E., Clark, M., & Karp, L. (1978). Affect, accessibility of material in memory, and behavior: A cognitive loop. *Journal of Personality and Social Psychology,* **36**, 1–12. (p. 551)

Islam, M. R., & Hewstone, M. (1993). Dimensions of contact as predictors of intergroup anxiety, perceived out-group variability, and out-group attitude: An integrative model. *Personality and Social Psychology Bulletin,* **19**, 700–710. (p. 584)

Isozaki, M. (1984). The effect of discussion on polarization of judgments. *Japanese Psychological Research,* **26**, 187–193. (pp. 333–334)

ISR Newsletter (1975). Institute for Social Research, University of Michigan, **3**(4), 4–7. (p. 140)

Israel, B. A., & Antonucci, T. C. (1987). Social network characteristics and psychological well-being: A replication and extension. *Health Education Quarterly,* **14**, 461–481. (p. 480)

Iwao, S. (1988). Social psychology's models of man: Isn't it time for East to meet West? Invited address to the International Congress of Scientific Psychology, Sydney, Australia. Cited by H. C. Triandis (1989). The self and social behavior in differing cultural contexts. *Psychological Review,* **96**, 506–520. (p. 134)

Jackman, M. R., & Senter, M. S. (1981). Beliefs about race, gender, and social

Self effects in memory for person information. *Social Cognition,* **10**, 30–50. (p. 39)

Kahle, L. R., & Berman, J. (1979). Attitudes cause behaviors: A cross-lagged panel analysis. *Journal of Personality and Social Psychology,* **37**, 315–321. (p. 128)

Kahn, A. S., & Gaeddert, W. P. (1985). From theories of equity to theories of justice. In V. W. O'Leary, R. K. Unger, & B. S. Wallston (Eds.), *Women, gender, and social psychology.* Hillsdale, N.J.: Erlbaum. (p. 581)

Kahn, A. S., Mathie, V. A., & Torgler, C. (1994). Rape scripts and rape acknowledgment. *Psychology of Women Quarterly,* **18**, 53–66. (p. 461)

Kahn, M. W. (1951). The effect of severe defeat at various age levels on the aggressive behavior of mice. *Journal of Genetic Psychology,* **79**, 117–130. (p. 448)

Kahneman, D., & Miller, D. T. (1986). Norm theory: Comparing reality to its alternatives. *Psychological Review,* **93**, 75–88. (p. 106)

Kahneman, D., & Snell, J. (1992). Predicting a changing taste: Do people know what they will like? *Journal of Behavioral Decision Making,* **5**, 187–200. (p. 484)

Kahneman, D., & Tversky, A. (1979). Intuitive prediction: Biases and corrective procedures. *Management Science,* **12**, 313–327. (p. 100)

Kahneman, D., & Tversky, A. (1995). Conflict resolution: A cognitive perspective. In K. Arrow, R. Mnookin, L. Ross, A. Tversky, & R. Wilson (eds.), *Barriers to the negotiated resolution of conflict.* New York: Norton. (p. 601)

Kalick, S. M. (1977). *Plastic surgery, physical appearance, and person perception.* Unpublished doctoral dissertation, Harvard University. Cited by E. Berscheid in, An overview of the psychological effects of physical attractiveness and some comments upon the psychological effects of knowledge of the effects of physical attractiveness. In W. Lucker, K. Ribbens, & J. A. McNamera (Eds.), *Logical aspects of facial form* (craniofacial growth series). Ann Arbor: University of Michigan Press, 1981. (p. 488)

Kalven, H., Jr., & Zeisel, H. (1966). *The American jury.* Chicago: University of Chicago Press. (pp. 367, 379, 381)

Kameda, T., & Sugimori, S. (1993). Psychological entrapment in group decision making: An assigned decision

rule and a groupthink phenomenon. *Journal of Personality and Social Psychology,* **65**, 282–292. (p. 348)

Kamen, L. P., Seligman, M. E. P., Dwyer, J., & Rodin, J. (1988). Pessimism and cell-mediated immunity. Unpublished manuscript, University of Pennsylvania. (p. 184)

Kammer, D. (1982). Differences in trait ascriptions to self and friend: Unconfounding intensity from variability. *Psychological Reports,* **51**, 99–102. (p. 85)

Kandel, D. B. (1978). Similarity in real-life adolescent friendship pairs. *Journal of Personality and Social Psychology,* **36**, 306–312. (p. 495)

Kanekar, S., & Nazareth, A. (1988). Attributed rape victim's fault as a function of her attractiveness, physical hurt, and emotional disturbance. *Social Behaviour,* **3**, 37–40. (p. 75)

Kaplan, M. F. (1989). Task, situational, and personal determinants of influence processes in group decision making. In E. J. Lawler (Ed.), *Advances in group processes* (vol. 6). Greenwich, CT: JAI Press. (p. 339)

Kaplan, M. F., & Schersching, C. (1980). Reducing juror bias: An experimental approach. In P. D. Lipsitt & B. D. Sales (Eds.), *New directions in psycholegal research.* New York: Van Nostrand Reinhold, pp. 149–170. (pp. 371, 382)

Kaprio, J., Koskenvuo, M., & Rita, H. (1987). Mortality after bereavement: A propsective study of 95,647 widowed persons. *American Journal of Public Health,* **77**, 283–287. (p. 479)

Karabenick, S. A., Lerner, R. M., & Beecher, M. D. (1973). Relation of political affiliation to helping behavior on election day, November 7, 1972. *Journal of Social Psychology,* **91**, 223–227. (p. 556)

Karau, S. J., & Williams, K. D. (1993). Social loafing: A meta-analytic review and theoretical integration. *Journal of Personality and Social Psychology,* **65**, 681–706. (pp. 323, 326)

Kassin, S. M., Ellsworth, P. C., & Smith, V. L. (1989). The "general acceptance" of psychological research on eyewitness testimony: A survey of the experts. *American Psychologist,* **44**, 1089–1098. (p. 367)

Kassin, S. M., & Wrightsman, L. S. (1979). On the requirements of proof: The timing of judicial instruction and mock juror verdicts. *Journal of Personality and Social Psychology,* **37**, 1877–1887. (p. 373)

Kato, P. S., & Ruble, D. N. (1992). Toward an understanding of women's experience of menstrual cycle symptoms. In V. Adesso, D. Reddy, & R. Fleming (Eds.), *Psychological perspectives on women's health.* Washington, DC: Hemisphere. (p. 107)

Katz, A. M., & Hill, R. (1958). Residential propinquity and marital selection: A review of theory, method, and fact. *Marriage and Family Living,* **20**, 237–335. (p. 482)

Katz, E. (1957). The two-step flow of communication: An up-to-date report on a hypothesis. *Public Opinion Quarterly,* **21**, 61–78. (p. 291)

Katz, I., Cohen, S., & Glass, D. (1975). Some determinants of cross-racial helping behavior. *Journal of Personality and Social Psychology,* **32**, 964–970. (p. 556)

Katzev, R., Edelsack, L., Steinmetz, G., & Walker, T. (1978). The effect of reprimanding transgressions on subsequent helping behavior: Two field experiments. *Personality and Social Psychology Bulletin,* **4**, 126–129. (p. 559)

Katzev, R., & Wang, T. (1994). Can commitment change behavior? A case study of environmental actions. *Journal of Social Behavior and Personality,* **9**, 13–26. (p. 257)

Kaufman, J., & Zigler, E. (1987). Do abused children become abusive parents? *American Journal of Orthopsychiatry,* **57**, 186–192. (p. 450)

Keating, C. F. (1985). Gender and the physiognomy of dominance and attractiveness. *Social Psychology Quarterly,* **48**, 61–70. (p. 490)

Keating, J. P., & Brock, T. C. (1974). Acceptance of persuasion and the inhibition of counterargumentation under various distraction tasks. *Journal of Experimental Social Psychology,* **10**, 301–309. (p. 294)

Kellerman, J., Lewis, J., & Laird, J. D. (1989). Looking and loving: The effects of mutual gaze on feelings of romantic love. *Journal of Research in Personality,* **23**, 145–161. (p. 500)

Kelley, H. H. (1973). The process of causal attribution. *American Psychologist,* **28**, 107–128. (p. 78)

Kelley, H. H. (1979). *Personal relationships: Their structures and processes.* Hillsdale, N.J.: Lawrence Erlbaum. (p. 512)

Kelley, H. H., & Stahelski, A. J. (1970). The social interaction basis of cooperators' and competitors' beliefs about others. *Journal of Personality and Social Psychology, 16,* 66–91. (p. 116)

Kelley, K., Dawson, L., & Musialowski, D. M. (1989). Three faces of sexual explicitness: The good, the bad, and the useful. In D. Zillmann & J. Bryant (Eds.), *Pornography: Reesearch advances and policy considerations.* Hillsdale, NJ: Erlbaum. (p. 473)

Kelman, H. C., & Cohen, S. P. (1979). Reduction of international conflict: An interactional approach. In W. G. Austin & S. Worchel, *The social psychology of intergroup relations.* Monterey, CA: Brooks/Cole. (p. 599)

Kelman, H. C., & Cohen, S. P. (1986). Resolution of international conflict: An interactional approach. In S. Worchel & W. G. Austin (Eds.), *Psychology of intergroup relations,* 2nd ed. Chicago: Nelson-Hall. (p. 599)

Kendler, K. S., Neale, M., Kessler, R., Heath, A., & Eaves, L. (1993). A twin study of recent life events and difficulties. *Archives of General Psychiatry, 50,* 789–796. (p. 176)

Kennedy, J. F. (1956). *Profiles in courage.* New York: Harper. (p. 259)

Kenny, D. A., & Albright, L. (1987). Accuracy in interpersonal perception: A social relations analysis. *Psychology Bulletin, 102,* 390–402. (p. 62)

Kenny, D. A., & DePaulo, B. M. (1993). Do people know how others view them? An empirical and theoretical account. *Psychological Bulletin, 114,* 145–161. (p. 59)

Kenny, D. A., & Nasby, W. (1980). Splitting the reciprocity correlation. *Journal of Personality and Social Psychology, 38,* 249–256. (p. 497)

Kenrick, D. T. (1987). Gender, genes, and the social environment: A biosocial interactionist perspective. In P. Shaver & C. Hendrick (Eds.), *Sex and gender: Review of personality and social psychology,* vol. 7. Beverly Hills, Ca.: Sage. (pp. 201, 205, 209)

Kenrick, D. T., Baumann, D. J., & Cialdini, R. B. (1979). A step in the socialization of altruism as hedonism: Effects of negative mood on children's generosity under public and private conditions. *Journal of Personality and Social Psychology, 37,* 747–755. (p. 548)

Kenrick, D. T., Gutierres, S. E., & Goldberg, L. L. (1989). Influence of popular erotica on judgments of strangers and mates. *Journal of Experimental Social Psychology, 25,* 159–167. (p. 492)

Kenrick, D. T., & Keefe, R. C. (1992). Age preferences in mates reflect sex differences in reproductive strategies. *Behavioral and Brain Sciences, 15,* 75–133. (p. 207)

Kenrick, D. T., & MacFarlane, S. W. (1986). Ambient temperature and horn-honking: A field study of the heat/aggression relationship. *Environment and Behavior, 18,* 179–191. (p. 454)

Kenrick, D. T., & Trost, M. R. (1987). A biosocial theory of heterosexual relationships. In K. Kelly (Ed.), *Females, males, and sexuality.* Albany: State University of New York Press. (pp. 75, 507)

Kerr, N. L. (1978). Beautiful and blameless: Effects of victim attractiveness and responsibility on mock jurors' verdicts. *Journal of Personality and Social Psychology, 4,* 479–482. *(a)* (p. 374)

Kerr, N. L. (1978). Severity of prescribed penalty and mock jurors' verdicts. *Journal of Personality and Social Psychology, 36,* 1431–1442. *(b)* (p. 374)

Kerr, N. L. (1981). Effects of prior juror experience on juror behavior. *Basic and Applied Social Psychology, 2,* 175–193. (p. 374)

Kerr, N. L. (1983). Motivation losses in small groups: A social dilemma analysis. *Journal of Personality and Social Psychology, 45,* 819–828. (p. 326)

Kerr, N. L. (1989). Illusions of efficacy: The effects of group size on perceived efficacy in social dilemmas. *Journal of Experimental Social Psychology, 25,* 287–313. (p. 574)

Kerr, N. L. (1992). Norms in social dilemmas. In D. Schroeder (Ed.), *Social dilemmas: Psychological perspectives.* New York: Praeger. (p. 577)

Kerr, N. L., Atkin, R. S., Stasser, G., Meek, D., Holt, R. W., & Davis, J. H. (1976). Guilt beyond a reasonable doubt: Effects of concept definition and assigned decision rule on the judgments of mock jurors. *Journal of Personality and Social Psychology, 34,* 282–294. (pp. 326, 380, 383)

Kerr, N. L., & Bruun, S. E. (1981). Ringelmann revisited: Alternative explanations for the social loafing effect. *Personality and Social Psychology Bulletin, 7,* 224–231. (p. 326)

Kerr, N. L., Harmon, D. L., & Graves, J. K. (1982). Independence of multiple verdicts by jurors and juries. *Journal of Applied Social Psychology, 12,* 12–29. (pp. 199, 374)

Kerr, N. L., & Kaufman-Gilliland,

C. M. (1994). Communication, commitment, and cooperation in social dilemmas. *Journal of Personality and Social Psychology, 66,* 513–529. (p. 575)

Kerr, N. L., & MacCoun, R. J. (1985). The effects of jury size and polling method on the process and product of jury deliberation. *Journal of Personality and Social Psychology, 48,* 349–363. (pp. 257, 382)

Kerwin, J., & Shaffer, D. R. (1994). Mock jurors versus mock juries: The role of deliberations in reactions to inadmissible testimony. *Personality and Social Psychology Bulletin, 20,* 153–162. (p. 382)

Kidd, J. B., & Morgan, J. R. (1969). A predictive information system for management. *Operational Research Quarterly, 20,* 149–170. (p. 63)

Kidd, R. F., & Berkowitz, L. (1976). Effect of dissonance arousal on helpfulness. *Journal of Personality and Social Psychology, 33,* 613–622. (p. 548)

Kiecolt-Glaser, J. K., Malarkey, W. B., Chee, M., Newton, T., Cacioppo, J. T., Mao, H-Y., & Glaser, R. (1993). Negative behavior during marital conflict is associated with immunological down-regulation. *Psychosomatic Medicine, 55,* 395–409. (p. 183)

Kiesler, C. A. (1971). *The psychology of commitment: Experiments linking behavior to belief.* New York: Academic Press. (p. 305)

Kiesler, C. A., & Kiesler, S. B. (1969). *Conformity.* Reading, Mass.: Addison-Wesley. (p. 233)

Kihlstrom, J. F. (1994). The social construction of memory. Address to the American Psychological Society convention. (p. 96)

Kihlstrom, J. F., & Cantor, N. (1984). Mental representations of the self. In L. Berkowitz (Ed.), *Advances in experimental social psychology,* vol. 17. New York: Academic Press. (p. 39)

Kim, M-S., & Hunter, J. E. (1993). Attitude-behavior relations: A meta-analysis of attitudinal relevance and topic. *Journal of Communication, 43,* 101–142. (p. 128)

Kimmel, M. J., Pruitt, D. G., Magenau, J. M., Konar-Goldband, E., & Carnevale, P. J. D. (1980). Effects of trust, aspiration, and gender on negotiation tactics. *Journal of Personality and Social Psychology, 38,* 9–22. (p. 596)

Kinder, D. R., & Sears, D. O. (1985). Public opinion and political action. In

G. Lindzey & E. Aronson (Eds.), *The handbook of social psychology*, 3rd ed. New York: Random House. (pp. 93, 289)

Kinnier, R. T., & Metha, A. T. (1989). Regrets and priorities at three stages of life. *Counseling and Values, 33*, 182–193. (p. 107)

Kirmeyer, S. L. (1978). Urban density and pathology: A review of research. *Environment and Behavior, 10*, 257–269. (p. 456)

Kitayama, S., & Markus, H. R. (in press). Construal of the self as cultural frame: Implications for internationalizing psychology. In J. D'Arms, R. G. Hastie, S. E. Hoelscher, & H. K. Jacobson (Eds.), *Becoming more international and global: Challenges for American higher education*. Ann Arbor: University of Michigan Press. (p. 580)

Kitayama, S., Markus, H. R., & Matsumoto, H. (1995). Culture, self, and emotion: A cultural perspective on "self-conscious" emotions. In J. P. Tangney & K. W. Fisher (Eds.), *Self-conscious emotions: The psychology of shame, guilt, embarrassment, and pride: Empirical studies of self-conscious emotions*. New York: Guilford Press, 439–464. (p. 215)

Klaas, E. T. (1978). Psychological effects of immoral actions: The experimental evidence. *Psychological Bulletin, 85*, 756–771. (p. 135)

Klasen, S. (1994). "Missing women" reconsidered. *World Development, 22*, 1061–1071. (p. 401)

Klayman, J., & Ha, Y-W. (1987). Confirmation, disconfirmation, and information in hypothesis testing. *Psychological Review, 94*, 211–228. (p. 101)

Kleck, R. E., & Strenta, A. (1980). Perceptions of the impact of negatively valued physical characteristics on social interaction. *Journal of Personality and Social Psychology, 39*, 861–873. (p. 421)

Klein, J. G. (1991). Negative effects in impression formation: A test in the political arena. *Personality and Social Psychology Bulletin, 17*, 412–418. (p. 497)

Klein, W. M., & Kunda, Z. (1992). Motivated person perception: Constructing justifications for desired beliefs. *Journal of Experimental Social Psychology, 28*, 145–168. (p. 98)

Klein, W. M., & Kunda, Z. (1993). Maintaining self-serving social comparisons: Biased reconstruction of one's past behaviors. *Personality and Social*

Psychology Bulletin, 19, 732–739. (p. 483)

Kleinke, C. L. (1977). Compliance to requests made by gazing and touching experimenters in field settings. *Journal of Experimental Social Psychology, 13*, 218–223. (p. 244)

Klentz, B., Beaman, A. L., Mapelli, S. D., & Ullrich, J. R. (1987). Perceived physical attractiveness of supporters and nonsupporters of the women's movement: An attitude-similarity-mediated error (AS-ME). *Personality and Social Psychology Bulletin, 13*, 513–523. (p. 492)

Klopfer, P. M. (1958). Influence of social interaction on learning rates in birds. *Science, 128*, 903–904. (p. 315)

Knight, G. P., Johnson, L. G., Carlo, G., & Eisenberg, N. (1994). A multiplicative model of the dispositional antecedents of a prosocial behavior: Predicting more of the people more of the time. *Journal of Personality and Social Psychology, 66*, 178–183. (p. 531)

Knight, J. A., & Vallacher, R. R. (1981). Interpersonal engagement in social perception: The consequences of getting into the action. *Journal of Personality and Social Psychology, 40*, 990–999. (p. 483)

Knight, P. A., & Weiss, H. M. (1980). Benefits of suffering: Communicator suffering, benefitting, and influence. Paper presented at the American Psychological Association convention. (p. 279)

Knowles, E. S. (1983). Social physics and the effects of others: Tests of the effects of audience size and distance on social judgment and behavior. *Journal of Personality and Social Psychology, 45*, 1263–1279. (p. 319)

Knox, R. E., & Inkster, J. A. (1968). Postdecision dissonance at post-time. *Journal of Personality and Social Psychology, 8*, 319–323. (p. 149)

Knudson, R. M., Sommers, A. A., & Golding, S. L. (1980). Interpersonal perception and mode of resolution in marital conflict. *Journal of Personality and Social Psychology, 38*, 751–763. (p. 597)

Koehler, D. J. (1991). Explanation, imagination, and confidence in judgment. *Psychological Bulletin, 110*, 499–519. (p. 103)

Koestner, R., & Wheeler, L. (1988). Self-presentation in personal advertisements: The influence of implicit no-

tions of attraction and role expectations. *Journal of Social and Personal Relationships, 5*, 149–160. (p. 487)

Koestner, R. F. (1993). False consensus effects for the 1992 Canadian referendum. Paper presented at the American Psychological Association. (p. 57)

Kolominsky, Y. (1991). Soviet psychology today. Invited address by Vice-President, Soviet Psychological Society, Hope College. (p. 12)

Komorita, S. S., & Barth, J. M. (1985). Components of reward in social dilemmas. *Journal of Personality and Social Psychology, 48*, 364–373. (p. 576)

Komorita, S. S., Parks, C. D., & Hulbert, L. G. (1992). Reciprocity and the induction of cooperation in social dilemmas. *Journal of Personality and Social Psychology, 62*, 607–617. (p. 602)

Koop, C. E. (1987). Report of the Surgeon General's workshop on pornography and public health. *American Psychologist, 42*, 944–945. (pp. 458, 460)

Koriat, A., Lichtenstein, S., & Fischhoff, B. (1980). Reasons for confidence. *Journal of Experimental Social Psychology: Human Learning and Memory, 6*, 107–118. (p. 103)

Korn, J. H., & Nicks, S. D. (1993). The rise and decline of deception in social psychology. Poster presented at the American Psychological Society convention. (p. 29)

Koss, M. P. (1990, August 29). Rape incidence: A review and assessment of the data. Testimony on behalf of the American Psychological Association before the U.S. Senate Judiciary Committee. (p. 461)

Koss, M. P. (1992). The underdetection of rape: Methodological choices influence incidence estimates. *Journal of Social Issues, 48*, 61–75. (p. 462)

Koss, M. P. (1993). Rape: Scope, impact, interventions, and public policy responses. *American Psychologist, 48*, 1062–1069. (p. 461)

Koss, M. P., Dinero, T. E., Seibel, C. A., & Cox, S. L. (1988). Stranger and acquaintance rape. *Psychology of Women, 12*, 1–24. (p. 461)

Koss, M. P., Heise, L., & Russo, N. F. (1994). The global health burden of rape. *Psychology of Women Quarterly, 18*, 509–537. (p. 461)

Kramer, G. P., Kerr, N. L., & Carroll, J. S. (1990). Pretrial publicity, judicial remedies, and jury bias. *Law and Human Behavior, 14*, 409–438. (p. 372)

Kraus, S. J. (1995). Attitudes and the prediction of behavior: A meta-analysis of the empirical literature. *Personality and Social Psychology Bulletin,* **21,** 58–75. (pp. 126, 130)

Kraut, R. E. (1973). Effects of social labeling on giving to charity. *Journal of Experimental Social Psychology,* **9,** 551–562. (p. 560)

Kraut, R. E., & Poe, D. (1980). Behavioral roots of person perception: The deception judgments of customs inspectors and laymen. *Journal of Personality and Social Psychology,* **39,** 784–798. (p. 417)

Kravitz, D. A., & Martin, B. (1986). Ringelmann rediscovered: The original article. *Journal of Personality and Social Psychology,* **50,** 936–941. (p. 322)

Krebs, D. (1970). Altruism—An examination of the concept and a review of the literature. *Psychological Bulletin,* **73,** 258–302. (p. 528)

Krebs, D. (1975). Empathy and altruism. *Journal of Personality and Social Psychology,* **32,** 1134–1146. (p. 528)

Krebs, D., & Adinolfi, A. A. (1975). Physical attractiveness, social relations, and personality style. *Journal of Personality and Social Psychology,* **31,** 245–253. (p. 486)

Kressel, K., & Pruitt, D. G. (1985). Themes in the mediation of social conflict. *Journal of Social Issues,* **41,** 179–198. (p. 600)

Kristof, N. (1993, July 22). China faces huge surplus of males as scans hold key to missing girls. *The Guardian* (England), p. 22. (p. 401)

Kroger, R. O., & Wood, L. A. (1992). Are the rules of address universal? IV: Comparison of Chinese, Korean, Greek, and German usage. *Journal of Cross-Cultural Psychology,* **23,** 148–162. (p. 203)

Krosnick, J. A., & Alwin, D. F. (1989). Aging and susceptibility to attitude change. *Journal of Personality and Social Psychology,* **57,** 416–425. (p. 293)

Krosnick, J. A., Li, F., & Lehman, D. R. (1990). Conversational conventions, order of information acquisition, and the effect of base rates and individuating information on social judgments. *Journal of Personality and Social Psychology,* **59,** 1140–1152. (p. 105)

Krosnick, J. A., & Schuman, H. (1988). Attitude intensity, importance, and certainty and susceptibility to response effects. *Journal of Personality and Social Psychology,* **54,** 940–952. (p. 24)

Krueger, J., & Clement, R. W. (1994). Memory-based judgments about multiple categories: A revision and extension of Tajfel's accentuation theory. *Journal of Personality and Social Psychology,* **67,** 35–47. (p. 57)

Krueger, J., & Clement, R. W. (1994). The truly false consensus effect: An ineradicable and egocentric bias in social perception. *Journal of Personality and Social Psychology,* **67,** 596–610. (p. 57)

Kruglanski, A. W., & Ajzen, I. (1983). Bias and error in human judgment. *European Journal of Social Psychology,* **13,** 1–44. (p. 119)

Kruglanski, A. W., & Webster, D. M. (1991). Group members' reactions to opinion deviates and conformists at varying degrees of proximity to decision deadline and of environmental noise. *Journal of Personality and Social Psychology,* **61,** 212–225. (p. 348)

Kruglanski, A. W., Webster, D. M., & Klem, A. (1993). Motivated resistance and openness to persuasion in the presence or absence of prior information. *Journal of Personality and Social Psychology,* **65,** 861–876. (p. 295)

Kubany, E. S., Bauer, G. B., Pangilinan, M. E., Muroka, M. Y., & Enriquez, V. G. (1995). Impact of labeled anger and blame in intimate relationships. *Journal of Cross-Cultural Psychology,* **26,** 65–83. (p. 473)

Kuiper, N. A., & Higgins, E. T. (1985). Social cognition and depression: A general integrative perspective. *Social Cognition,* **3,** 1–15. (p. 175)

Kuiper, N. A., & Rogers, T. B. (1979). Encoding of personal information: Self-other differences. *Journal of Personality and Social Psychology,* **37,** 499–514. (p. 39)

Kunda, Z. (1990). The case for motivated reasoning. *Psychological Bulletin,* **108,** 480–498. (p. 60)

Kunda, Z., Fong, G. T., Sanitioso, R., & Reber, E. (1993). Directional questions direct self-conceptions. *Journal of Experimental Social Psychology,* **29,** 63–86. (p. 167)

Kunda, Z., & Sherman-Williams, B. (1993). Stereotypes and the construal of individuating information. *Personality and Social Psychology Bulletin,* **19,** 90–99. (p. 427)

Kunst-Wilson, W. R., & Zajonc, R. B. (1980). Affective discrimination of stimuli that cannot be recognized. *Science,* **207,** 557–558. (p. 484)

Lafferty, E. (1994, November 14). Now, a jury of his peers. *TIME,* p. 64. (p. 378)

LaFrance, M. (1985). Does your smile reveal your status? *Social Science News Letter,* **70** (Spring), 15–18. (p. 198)

Lagerspetz, K. (1979). Modification of aggressiveness in mice. In S. Feshbach & A. Fraczek (Eds.), *Aggression and behavior change.* New York: Praeger. (p. 440)

Lagerspetz, K. M. J., Bjorkqvist, K., Berts, M., & King, E. (1982). Group aggression among school children in three schools. *Scandinavian Journal of Psychology,* **23,** 45–52. (p. 471)

Laird, J. D. (1974). Self-attribution of emotion: The effects of expressive behavior on the quality of emotional experience. *Journal of Personality and Social Psychology,* **29,** 475–486. (p. 151)

Laird, J. D. (1984). The real role of facial response in the experience of emotion: A reply to Tourangeau and Ellsworth, and others. *Journal of Personality and Social Psychology,* **47,** 909–917. (p. 151)

Lalancette, M-F., & Standing, L. (1990). Asch fails again. *Social Behavior and Personality,* **18,** 7–12. (p. 264)

Lalonde, R. N. (1992). The dynamics of group differentiation in the face of defeat. *Personality and Social Psychology Bulletin,* **18,** 336–342. (p. 53)

Lamal, P. A. (1979). College student common beliefs about psychology. *Teaching of Psychology,* **6,** 155–158. (p. 96)

Landers, A. (1969, April 8). Syndicated newspaper column. April 8, 1969. Cited by L. Berkowitz in, The case for bottling up rage. *Psychology Today,* September, 1973, pp. 24–31. (p. 472)

Landers, A. (1985, August). Is affection more important than sex? *Reader's Digest,* pp. 44–46. (p. 22)

Landers, S. (1988, July). Sex, drugs 'n' rock: Relation not causal. *APA Monitor,* p. 40. (p. 21)

Langer, E. J. (1977). The psychology of chance. *Journal for the Theory of Social Behavior,* **7,** 185–208. (p. 108)

Langer, E. J., & Benevento, A. (1978). Self-induced dependence. *Journal of Personality and Social Psychology,* **36,** 886–893. (p. 220)

Langer, E. J., & Imber, L. (1980). The role of mindlessness in the perception of deviance. *Journal of Personality and Social Psychology,* **39,** 360–367. (p. 421)

Langer, E. J., Janis, I. L., & Wofer, J. A. (1975). Reduction of psychological stress in surgical patients. *Journal of*

Experimental Social Psychology, **11**, 155–165. (p. 48)

Langer, E. J., & Rodin, J. (1976). The effects of choice and enhanced personal responsibility for the aged: A field experiment in an institutional setting. *Journal of Personality and Social Psychology*, **334**, 191–198. (p. 48)

Langer, E. J., & Roth, J. (1975). Heads I win, tails it's chance: The illusion of control as a function of the sequence of outcomes in a purely chance task. *Journal of Personality and Social Psychology*, **32**, 951–955. (p. 286)

Langlois, J. H., & Roggman, L. A. (1990). Attractive faces are only average. *Psychological Science,* **1**, 115–121. (p. 490)

Langlois, J. H., Roggman, L. A., & Musselman, L. (1994). What is average and what is not average about attractive faces? *Psychological Science,* **5**, 214–220. (p. 490)

Langlois, J. H., & Stephan, C. W. (1981). Beauty and the beast: The role of physical attractiveness in the development of peer relations and social behavior. In S. S. Brehm, S. M. Kassin, & F. X. Gibbons (Eds.), *Developmental social psychology.* New York: Oxford University Press. (p. 488)

Lanzetta, J. T. (1955). Group behavior under stress. *Human Relations,* **8**, 29–53. (p. 590)

Larsen, K. (1974). Conformity in the Asch experiment. *Journal of Social Psychology,* **94**, 303–304. (p. 264)

Larsen, K. S. (1990). The Asch conformity experiment: Replication and transhistorical comparisons. *Journal of Social Behavior and Personality,* **5**(4), 163–168. (p. 264)

Larsen, R. J., & Diener, E. (1987). Affect intensity as an individual difference characteristic: A review. *Journal of Research in Personality,* **21**, 1–39. (p. 440)

Larson, J. R., Jr., Foster-Fishman, P. G., & Keys, C. B. (1994). Discussion of shared and unshared information in decision-making groups. *Journal of Personality and Social Psychology,* **67**, 446–461. (p. 336)

Larsson, K. (1956). *Conditioning and sexual behavior in the male albino rat.* Stockholm: Almqvist & Wiksell. (p. 315)

Larwood, L. (1978). Swine flu: A field study of self-serving biases. *Journal of Applied Social Psychology,* **18**, 283–289. (p. 55)

Larwood, L., & Whittaker, W. (1977). Managerial myopia: Self-serving bi-

ases in organizational planning. *Journal of Applied Psychology,* **62**, 194–198. (p. 63)

Lassiter, G. D., & Dudley, K. A. (1991). The *a priori* value of basic research: The case of videotaped confessions. *Journal of Social Behavior and Personality,* **6**, 7–16. (p. 84)

Lassiter, G. D., & Irvine, A. A. (1986). Videotaped confessions: The impact of camera point of view on judgments of coercion. *Journal of Applied Social Psychology,* **16**, 268–276. (p. 84)

Latané, B. (1981). The psychology of social impact. *American Psychologist,* **36**, 343–356. (p. 253)

Latané, B., & Dabbs, J. M., Jr. (1975). Sex, group size and helping in three cities. *Sociometry,* **38**, 180–194. (p. 540)

Latané, B., & Darley, J. M. (1968). Group inhibition of bystander intervention in emergencies. *Journal of Personality and Social Psychology,* **10**, 215–221. (p. 540)

Latané, B., & Darley, J. M. (1970). *The unresponsive bystander: Why doesn't he help?* New York: Appleton-Century-Crofts. (pp. 539, 551)

Latané, B., & Nida, S. (1981). Ten years of research on group size and helping. *Psychological Bulletin,* **89**, 308–324. (p. 540)

Latané, B., & Rodin, J. (1969). A lady in distress: Inhibiting effects of friends and strangers on bystander intervention. *Journal of Experimental Social Psychology,* **5**, 189–202. (p. 541)

Latané, B., Williams, K., & Harkins. S. (1979). Many hands make light the work: The causes and consequences of social loafing. *Journal of Personality and Social Psychology,* **37**, 822–832. (p. 322)

Laughlin, P. R., & Adamopoulos, J. (1980). Social combination processes and individual learning for six-person cooperative groups on an intellective task. *Journal of Personality and Social Psychology,* **38**, 941–947. (p. 345)

Laughlin, P. R., VanderStoep, S. W., & Hollingshead, A. B. (1991). Collective versus individual induction: Recognition of truth, rejection of error, and collective information processing. *Journal of Personality and Social Psychology,* **61**, 50–67. (p. 345)

Laumann, E. O., Gagnon, J. H., Michael, R. T., & Michaels, S. (1994). *The social organization of sexuality: Sexual practices in the United States.* Chicago: University of Chicago Press. (pp. 73, 200, 461, 469)

Layden, M. A. (1982). Attributional therapy. In C. Antaki & C. Brewin (Eds.), *Attributions and psychological change: Applications of attributional theories to clinical and educational practice.* London: Academic Press. (p. 188)

Lazarsfeld, P. F. (1949). *The American soldier*—an expository review. *Public Opinion Quarterly,* **13**, 377–404. (p. 14)

Leary, M. (1994). *Self-presentation: Impression management and interpersonal behavior.* Pacific Grove, CA: Brooks/Cole. (p. 144)

Leary, M. R. (1982). Hindsight distortion and the 1980 presidential election. *Personality and Social Psychology Bulletin,* **8**, 257–263. (p. 15)

Leary, M. R. (1984). *Understanding social anxiety.* Beverly Hills, Ca.: Sage. (p. 179)

Leary, M. R. (1986). The impact of interactional impediments on social anxiety and self-presentation. *Journal of Experimental Social Psychology,* **22**, 122–135. (p. 179)

Leary, M. R., & Downs, D. L. (1995). Interpersonal functions of the self-esteem motive: The self-esteem system as a sociometer. In M. Kernis (ed.), *Efficacy, agency, and self-esteem.* New York: Plenum. (p. 61)

Leary, M. R., & Maddux, J. E. (1987). Progress toward a viable interface between social and clinical counseling psychology. *American Psychologist,* **42**, 904–911. (pp. 164, 185)

Leary, M. R., Nezlek, J. B., Radford-Davenport, D., Martin, J., & McMullen, A. (1994). Self-presentation in everyday interactions: Effects of target familiarity and gender composition. *Journal of Personality and Social Psychology,* **67**, 664–673. (p. 68)

Leary, M. R., Tambor, E. S., Terdal, S. K., & Downs, D. L. (1995). Self-esteem as an interpersonal monitor: The sociometer hypothesis. *Journal of Personality and Social Psychology,* **68**, 518–530. (p. 61)

Leary, M. R., Tchvidjian, L. R., & Kraxberger, B. E. (1994). Self-presentation can be hazardous to your health: Impression management and health risk. *Health Psychology,* **13**, 461–470. (p. 68)

Lebow, R. N., & Stein, J. G. (1987). Beyond deterrence. *Journal of Social Issues,* **43**(4), 5–71. (p. 570)

Lee, G. R., Seccombe, K., & Shehan, C. L. (1991). Marital status and personal happiness: An analysis of trend data. *Journal of Marriage and the Family,* **53,** 839–844. (p. 510)

Lee, J. A. (1988). Love-styles. In R. J. Sternberg & M. L. Barnes (Eds.), *The psychology of love.* New Haven: Yale University Press. (p. 500)

Lefcourt, H. M. (1982). *Locus of control: Current trends in theory and research.* Hillsdale, N.J.: Erlbaum. (p. 47)

Lefebvre, L. M. (1979). Causal attributions for basketball outcomes by players and coaches. *Psychological Belgica,* **19,** 109–115. (p. 69)

Lehman, D. R., Lempert, R. O., & Nisbett, R. E. (1988). The effects of graduate training on reasoning: Formal discipline and thinking about everyday-life events. *American Psychologist,* **43,** 431–442. (p. 121)

Lehman, D. R., & Nisbett, R. E. (1985). Effects of higher education on inductive reasoning. Unpublished manuscript, University of Michigan. (p. 57)

Leippe, M. R. (1985). The influence of eyewitness nonidentification on mock-jurors. *Journal of Applied Social Psychology,* **15,** 656–672. (p. 358)

Leippe, M. R. (1994). The appraisal of eyewitness testimony. In D. F. Ross, J. D. Read, & M. P. Toglia (Eds.), *Adult eyewitness testimony: Current trends and developments.* New York: Cambridge. (p. 360)

Leippe, M. R., & Eisenstadt, D. (1994). Generalization of dissonance reduction: Decreasing prejudice through induced compliance. *Journal of Personality and Social Psychology,* **67,** 395–413. (p. 148)

Leippe, M. R., & Elkin, R. A. (1987). Dissonance reduction strategies and accountability to self and others: Ruminations and some initial research. Presentation to the Fifth International Conference on Affect, Motivation, and Cognition, Nags Head Conference Center. (pp. 148, 294)

Lemyre, L., & Smith, P. M. (1985). Intergroup discrimination and self-esteem in the minimal group paradigm. *Journal of Personality and Social Psychology,* **49,** 660–670. (p. 414)

Lenihan, K. J. (1965). Perceived climates as a barrier to housing desegregation. Unpublished manuscript, Bureau of Applied Social Research, Columbia University. (p. 54)

Leon, D. (1969). *The Kibbutz: A new way of life.* London: Pergamon Press. Cited

by B. Latané, K. Williams, & S. Harkins (1979), Many hands make light the work: The causes and consequences of social loafing. *Journal of Personality and Social Psychology,* 1979, **37,** 822–832. (p. 326)

Lepper, M. R., & Greene, D. (Eds.) (1979). *The hidden costs of reward.* Hillsdale, N.J.: Erlbaum. (pp. 154–155)

Lepper, M. R., Ross, L., & Lau, R. R. (1986). Persistence of inaccurate beliefs about the self: Perseverance effects in the classroom. *Journal of Personality and Social Psychology,* **50,** 482–491. (p. 96)

Lerner, M. J. (1980). *The belief in a just world: A fundamental delusion.* New York: Plenum. (p. 425)

Lerner, M. J., & Miller, D. T. (1978). Just world research and the attribution process: Looking back and ahead. *Psychological Bulletin,* **85,** 1030–1051. (p. 425)

Lerner, M. J., & Simmons, C. H. (1966). Observer's reaction to the "innocent victim": Compassion or rejection? *Journal of Personality and Social Psychology,* **4,** 203–210. (p. 425)

Lerner, M. J., Somers, D. G., Reid, D., Chiriboga, D., & Tierney, M. (1991). Adult children as caregivers: Egocentric biases in judgments of sibling contributions. *The Gerontologist,* **31,** 746–755. (p. 55)

Lerner, R. M., & Frank, P. (1974). Relation of race and sex to supermarket helping behavior. *Journal of Social Psychology,* **94,** 201–203. (p. 556)

Leung, K., & Bond, M. H. (1984). The impact of cultural collectivism on reward allocation. *Journal of Personality and Social Psychology,* **47,** 793–804. (p. 580)

Leventhal, H. (1970). Findings and theory in the study of fear communications. In L. Berkowitz (Ed.), *Advances in experimental social psychology* (Vol. 5). New York: Academic Press. (p. 282)

Lever, J. (1978). Sex differences in the complexity of children's play and games. *American Sociological Review,* **43,** 471–483. (p. 197)

Levine, A. (1990, May 7). America's youthful bigots. *U.S. News and World Report,* pp. 59–60. (p. 393)

Levine, J. M. (1989). Reaction to opinion deviance in small groups. In P. Paulus (Ed.), *Psychology of group influence: New perspectives.* Hillsdale, N.J.: Erlbaum. (pp. 348, 349)

Levine, J. M., & Moreland, R. L. (1985). Innovation and socialization in small

groups. In S. Moscovici, G. Mugny, & E. Van Avermaet (Eds.), *Perspectives on minority influence.* Cambridge: Cambridge University Press. (p. 349)

Levine, J. M., & Russo, E. M. (1987). Majority and minority influence. In C. Hendrick (Ed.) *Group processes: Review of personality and social psychology,* Vol. 8. Newbury Park, Ca.: Sage. (p. 348)

Levine, R., & Uleman, J. S. (1979). Perceived locus of control, chronic self-esteem, and attributions to success and failure. *Journal of Personality and Social Psychology,* **5,** 69–72. (p. 62)

LeVine, R. V., Martinez, T. S., Brase, G., & Sorenson, K. (1994). Helping in 36 U.S. cities. *Journal of Personality and Social Psychology,* **67,** 69–82. (p. 544)

Levinger, G. (1987). The limits of deterrence: An introduction. *Journal of Social Issues,* **43**(4), 1–4. (p. 570)

Levy, S., Lee, J., Bagley, C., & Lippman, M. (1988). Survival hazards analysis in first recurrent breast cancer patients: Seven-year follow-up. *Psychosomatic Medicine,* **50,** 520–528. (p. 184)

Levy-Leboyer, C. (1988). Success and failure in applying psychology. *American Psychologist,* **43,** 779–785. (p. 282)

Lewicki, P. (1983). Self-image bias in person perception. *Journal of Personality and Social Psychology,* **45,** 384–393. (p. 59)

Lewicki, P. (1985). Nonconscious biasing effects of single instances on subsequent judgments. *Journal of Personality and Social Psychology,* **48,** 563–574. (p. 512)

Lewin, K. (1936). *A dynamic theory of personality.* New York: McGraw-Hill. (pp. 30, 263)

Lewinsohn, P. M., Hoberman, H., Teri, L., & Hautziner, M. (1985). An integrative theory of depression. In S. Reiss & R. Bootzin (Eds.), *Theoretical issues in behavior therapy.* New York: Academic Press. (p. 176)

Lewinsohn, P. M., Mischel, W., Chapline, W., & Barton, R. (1980). Social competence and depression: The role of illusionary self-perceptions. *Journal of Abnormal Psychology,* **89,** 203–212. (p. 62)

Lewinsohn, P. M., & Rosenbaum, M. (1987). Recall of parental behavior by acute depressives, remitted depressives, and nondepressives. *Journal of Personality and Social Psychology,* **52,** 611–619. (p. 111)

Lewis, C. S. (1960). *Mere Christianity.* New York: Macmillan. (pp. 41, 149)

Lewis, C. S. (1974). *The horse and his boy.* New York: Collier Books. (p. 149)

Leyens, J. P., Camino, L., Parke, R. D., & Berkowitz, L. (1975). Effects of movie violence on aggression in a field setting as a function of group dominance and cohesion. *Journal of Personality and Social Psychology, 32,* 346–360. (p. 467)

Liberman, A., & Chaiken, S. (1992). Defensive processing of personally relevant health messages. *Personality and Social Psychology Bulletin, 18,* 669–679. (p. 284)

Lichtenstein, S., & Fischhoff, B. (1980). Training for calibration. *Organizational Behavior and Human Performance, 26,* 149–171. (p. 103)

Liebert, R. M., & Baron, R. A. (1972). Some immediate effects of televised violence on children's behavior. *Developmental Psychology, 6,* 469–475. (p. 26)

Liebrand, W. B. G., Messick, D. M., & Wolters, F. J. M. (1986). Why we are fairer than others: A cross-cultural replication and extension. *Journal of Experimental Social Psychology, 22,* 590–604. (p. 69)

Life (1988, Spring). What we believe. Pp. 69–70. (p. 393)

Lind, E. A., Erickson, B. E., Friedland, N., & Dickenberger, M. (1978). Reactions to procedural models for adjudicative conflict resolution. *Journal of Conflict Resolution, 22,* 318–341. (p. 357)

Lind, E. A., Thibaut, J., & Walker, L. (1976). A cross-cultural comparison of the effect of adversary and inquisitorial processes on bias in legal decision making. *Virginia Law Review, 62,* 271–283. (p. 357)

Lindsay, R. C. L., & Wells, G. L. (1985). Improving eyewitness identifications from lineups: Simultaneous versus sequential lineup presentation. *Journal of Applied Psychology, 70,* 556–564. (p. 366)

Lindsay, R. C. L., Wells, G. L., & Rumpel, C. H. (1981). Can people detect eyewitness-identification accuracy within and across situations? *Journal of Applied Psychology, 66,* 79–89. (p. 358)

Lindskold, S. (1978). Trust development, the GRIT proposal, and the effects of conciliatory acts on conflict and cooperation. *Psychological Bulletin, 85,* 772–793. (p. 602)

Lindskold, S. (1979). Conciliation with simultaneous or sequential interaction: Variations in trustworthiness and vulnerability in the prisoner's dilemma. *Journal of Conflict Resolution, 27,* 704–714. (p. 602)

Lindskold, S. (1979). Managing conflict through announced conciliatory initiatives backed with retaliatory capability. In W. G. Austin and S. Worchel (Eds.), *The social psychology of intergroup relations.* Monterey, Calif.: Brooks/Cole. (p. 602)

Lindskold, S. (1981). The laboratory evaluation of GRIT: Trust, cooperation, aversion to using conciliation. Paper presented at the American Association for the Advancement of Science convention. (p. 602)

Lindskold, S. (1983). Cooperators, competitors, and response to GRIT. *Journal of Conflict Resolution, 27,* 521–532. (p. 602)

Lindskold, S., & Aronoff, J. R. (1980). Conciliatory strategies and relative power. *Journal of Experimental Social Psychology, 16,* 187–198. (p. 602)

Lindskold, S., Bennett, R., & Wayner, M. (1976). Retaliation level as a foundation for subsequent conciliation. *Behavioral Science, 21,* 13–18. (p. 602)

Lindskold, S., Betz, B., & Walters, P. S. (1986). Transforming competitive or cooperative climate. *Journal of Conflict Resolution, 30,* 99–114. (p. 602)

Lindskold, S., & Collins, M. G. (1978). Inducing cooperation by groups and individuals. *Journal of Conflict Resolution, 22,* 679–690. (p. 602)

Lindskold, S., & Finch, M. L. (1981). Styles of announcing conciliation. *Journal of Conflict Resolution, 25,* 145–155. (p. 602)

Lindskold, S., & Han, G. (1988). GRIT as a foundation for integrative bargaining. *Personality and Social Psychology Bulletin, 14,* 335–345. (p. 602)

Lindskold, S., Han, G., & Betz, B. (1986). Repeated persuasion in interpersonal conflict. *Journal of Personality and Social Psychology, 51,* 1183–1188. *(b)* (p. 602)

Lindskold, S., Han, G., & Betz, B. (1986). The essential elements of communication in the GRIT strategy. *Personality and Social Psychology Bulletin, 12,* 179–186. *(a)* (p. 602)

Lindskold, S., Walters, P. S., Koutsourais, H., & Shayo, R. (1981). Cooperators, competitors, and response to GRIT. Unpublished manuscript, Ohio University. (p. 602)

Linssen, H., & Hagendoorn, L. (1994). Social and geographical factors in the explanation of the content of European nationality stereotypes. *British Journal of Social Psychology, 33,* 165–182. (p. 391)

Linville, P. W., Gischer, G. W., & Salovey, P. (1989). Perceived distributions of the characteristics of in-group and out-group members: Empirical evidence and a computer simulation. *Journal of Personality and Social Psychology, 57,* 165–188. (p. 419)

Linz, D. G., Donnerstein, E., & Adams, S. M. (1989). Physiological desensitization and judgments about female victims of violence. *Human Communication Research, 15,* 509–522. (p. 458)

Linz, D. G., Donnerstein, E., & Penrod, S. (1988). Effects of long term exposure to violent and sexually degrading depictions of women. *Journal of Personality and Social Psychology, 55,* 758–768. (p. 458)

Lipsitz, A., Kallmeyer, K., Ferguson, M., & Abas, A. (1989). Counting on blood donors: Increasing the impact of reminder calls. *Journal of Applied Social Psychology, 19,* 1057–1067. (p. 137)

Locke, E. A., & Latham, G. P. (1990). Work motivation and satisfaction: Light at the end of the tunnel. *Psychological Science, 1,* 240–246. (p. 350)

Locke, K. D., & Horowitz, L. M. (1990). Satisfaction in interpersonal interactions as a function of similarity in level of dysphoria. *Journal of Personality and Social Psychology, 58,* 823–831. (p. 496)

Locksley, A., Borgida, E., Brekke, N., & Hepburn, C. (1980). Sex stereotypes and social judgment. *Journal of Personality and Social Psychology, 39,* 821–831. (pp. 407, 429)

Locksley, A., Hepburn, C., & Ortiz, V. (1982). Social stereotypes and judgments of individuals: An instance of the base-rate fallacy. *Journal of Experimental Social Psychology, 18,* 23–42. (p. 429)

Locksley, A., Ortiz, V., & Hepburn, C. (1980). Social categorization and discriminatory behavior: Extinguishing the minimal intergroup discrimination effect. *Journal of Personality and Social Psychology, 39,* 773–783. (p. 407)

Lofland, J., & Stark, R. (1965). Becoming a worldsaver: A theory of conversion to a deviant perspective. *American Sociological Review, 30,* 862–864. (p. 301)

Loftin, C., McDowall, D., Wiersema, B., & Cottey, T. J. (1991). Effects of restrictive licensing of handguns on homicide and suicide in the District of Columbia. *New England Journal of Medicine, 325,* 1615–1620. (p. 443)

Loftus, E. F. (1974, December). Reconstructing memory: The incredible eyewitness. *Psychology Today*, pp. 117–119. (p. 358)

Loftus, E. F. (1979). *Eyewitness testimony*. Cambridge, Mass.: Harvard University Press. *(a)* (pp. 358, 361)

Loftus, E. F. (1979). The malleability of human memory. *American Scientist*, **67**, 312–320. *(b)* (p. 358)

Loftus, E. F. (1980). Impact of expert psychological testimony on the unreliability of eyewitness identification. *Journal of Applied Social Psychology*, **65**, 9–15. (p. 367)

Loftus, E. F. (1993). The reality of repressed memory. *American Psychologist*, **48**, 518–537. (p. 99)

Loftus, E. F., Donders, K., Hoffman, H. G., & Schooler, J. W. (1989). Creating new memories that are quickly accessed and confidently held. *Memory and Cognition*, **17**, 607–616. (p. 99)

Loftus, E. F., & Ketcham, K. (1994). *The myth of repressed memories: False memories and allegations of sexual abuse*. New York: St. Martins. (p. 168)

Loftus, E. F., & Klinger, M. R. (1992). Is the unconscious smart or dumb? *American Psychologist*, **47**, 761–765. (p. 90)

Loftus, E. F., Miller, D. G., & Burns, H. J. (1978). Semantic integration of verbal information into a visual memory. *Journal of Experimental Social Psychology: Human Learning and Memory*, **4**, 19–31. (pp. 361, 362)

Loftus, E. F., & Palmer, J. C. (1974). Reconstruction of automobile destruction: An example of the interaction between language and memory. *Journal of Verbal Learning and Verbal Behavior*, **13**, 585–589. (p. 99)

Loftus, E. F., & Zanni, G. (1975). Eyewitness testimony: The influence of the wording in a question. *Bulletin of the Psychonomic Society*, **5**, 86–88. (p. 365)

Lombardo, J. P., Weiss, R. F., & Buchanan, W. (1972). Reinforcing and attracting functions of yielding. *Journal of Personality and Social Psychology*, **21**, 359–368. (p. 513)

London, P. (1970). The rescuers: Motivational hypotheses about Christians who saved Jews from the Nazis. In J. Macaulay & L. Berkowitz (Eds.), *Altruism and helping behavior*. New York: Academic Press. (p. 561)

Lonner, W. J. (1980). The search for psychological universals. In H. C. Triandis & W. W. Lambert (Eds.), *Handbook of cross-cultural psychology* (vol. 1). Boston: Allyn and Bacon. (p. 202)

Lonner, W. J. (1989). The introductory psychology text and cross-cultural psychology: Beyond Ekman, Whorf, and biased I.Q. tests. In D. Keats, D. R. Munro & L. Mann (Eds.), *Heterogeneity in cross-cultural psychology*. (p. 221)

Lord, C. G., Desforges, D. M., Ramsey, S. L., Trezza, G. R., & Lepper, M. R. (1991). Typicality effects in attitude-behavior consistency: Effects of category discrimination and category knowledge. *Journal of Experimental Social Psychology*, **27**, 550–575. (p. 429)

Lord, C. G., Lepper, M. R., & Preston, E. (1984). Considering the opposite: A corrective strategy for social judgment. *Journal of Personality and Social Psychology*, **47**, 1231–1243. (p. 96)

Lord, C. G., Ross, L., & Lepper, M. (1979). Biased assimilation and attitude polarization: The effects of prior theories on subsequently considered evidence. *Journal of Personality and Social Psychology*, **37**, 2098–2109. (p. 92)

Lord, C. G. & Saenz, D. S. (1985). Memory deficits and memory surfeits: Differential cognitive consequences of tokenism for tokens and observers. *Journal of Personality and Social Psychology*, **49**, 918–926. (p. 421)

Lorenz, K. (1976). *On aggression*. New York: Bantam Books. (p. 437)

Losch, M. E., & Cacioppo, J. T. (1990). Cognitive dissonance may enhance sympathetic tonus, but attitudes are changed to reduce negative affect rather than arousal. *Journal of Experimental Social Psychology*, **26**, 289–304. (p. 158)

Lott, A. J., & Lott, B. E. (1961). Group cohesiveness, communication level, and conformity. *Journal of Abnormal and Social Psychology*, **62**, 408–412. (p. 255)

Lott, A. J., & Lott, B. E. (1974). The role of reward in the formation of positive interpersonal attitudes. In T. Huston (Ed.), *Foundations of interpersonal attraction*. New York: Academic Press. (p. 512)

Louw-Potgieter, J. (1988). The authoritarian personality: An inadequate explanation for intergroup conflict in South Africa. *Journal of Social Psychology*, **128**, 75–87. (p. 416)

Lovdal, L. T. (1989). Sex role messages in television commercials: An update. *Sex Roles*, **21**, 715–724. (p. 411)

Lowe, C. A., & Goldstein, J. W. (1970). Reciprocal liking and attributions of ability: Mediating effects of perceived intent and personal involvement. *Journal of Personality and Social Psychology*, **16**, 291–297. (p. 498)

Lowe, R. H., & Wittig, M. A. (1989). Comparable worth: Individual, interpersonal, and structural considerations. *Journal of Social Issues*, **45**, 223–246. (p. 580)

Lowenthal, M. F., Thurnher, M., Chiriboga, D., Beefon, D., Gigy, L., Lurie, E., Pierce, R., Spence, D., & Weiss, L. (1975). *Four stages of life*. San Francisco: Jossey-Bass. (p. 208)

Loy, J. W., & Andrews, D. S. (1981). They also saw a game: A replication of a case study. *Replications in Social Psychology*, **1**(2), 45–59. (p. 8)

Luginbuhl, J. (1992). Comprehension of judges' instructions in the penalty phase of a capital trial: Focus on mitigating circumstances. *Law and Human Behavior*, **16**, 203–218. (p. 377)

Luginbuhl, J., & Middendorf, K. (1988). Death penalty beliefs and jurors' responses to aggravating and mitigating circumstances in capital trials. *Law and Human Behavior*, **12**, 263–281. (p. 379)

Lumsdaine, A. A., & Janis, I. L. (1953). Resistance to "counter-propaganda" produced by one-sided and two-sided "propaganda" presentations. *Public Opinion Quarterly*, **17**, 311–318. (p. 285)

Lumsden, A., Zanna, M. P., & Darley, J. M. (1980). When a newscaster presents counter-additional information: Education or propaganda? Paper presented to the Canadian Psychological Association annual convention. (p. 273)

Lüüs, C. A. E., & Wells, G. L. (1994). Eyewitness identification confidence. In D. F. Ross, J. D. Read, & M. P. Toglia (eds.), *Adult eyewitness testimony: Current trends and developments*. Cambridge, England: Cambridge University Press. (p. 360)

Lydon, J., & Dunkel-Schetter, C. (1994). Seeing is committing: A longitudinal study of bolstering commitment in amniocenesis patients. *Personality and Social Psychology Bulletin*, **20**, 218–227. (p. 244)

Lykken, D. T., & Tellegen, A. (1993). Is human mating adventitious or the result of lawful choice? A twin study of mate selection. *Journal of Personality and Social Psychology*, **65**, 56–68. (p. 483)

Lynn, M., & Oldenquist, A. (1986). Egoistic and nonegoistic motives in social dilemmas. *American Psychologist, 41,* 529–534. (p. 577)

Maass, A., Brigham, J. C., & West, S. G. (1985). Testifying on eyewitness reliability: Expert advice is not always persuasive. *Journal of Applied Social Psychology, 15,* 207–229. (p. 367)

Maass, A., & Clark, R. D., III (1984). Hidden impact of minorities: Fifteen years of minority influence research. *Psychological Bulletin, 95,* 428–450. (p. 349)

Maass, A., & Clark, R. D., III (1986). Conversion theory and simultaneous majority/minority influence: Can reactance offer an alternative explanation? *European Journal of Social Psychology, 16,* 305–309. (p. 349)

Maass, A., Milesi, A., Zabbini, S., & Stahlberg, D. (1995). Linguistic intergroup bias: Differential expectancies or in-group protection? *Journal of Personality and Social Psychology, 68,* 116–126. (p. 424)

MacArthur, D. (1973). Quoted in J. D. Frank's statement on psychological aspects of international relations before a hearing of the Committee on Foreign Relations, United States Senate, May 25, 1966. Reprinted in D. E. Linder (Ed.), *Psychological dimensions of social interaction: Readings and perspectives.* Reading, Mass.: Addison-Wesley. (p. 582)

Maccoby, N. (1980). Promoting positive health behaviors in adults. In L. A. Bond & J. C. Rosen (Eds.), *Competence and coping during adulthood.* Hanover, N.H.: University Press of New England. (p. 290)

Maccoby, N., & Alexander, J. (1980). Use of media in lifestyle programs. In P. O. Davidson & S. M. Davidson (Eds.). *Behavioral medicine: Changing health lifestyles.* New York: Brunner/ Mazel. (p. 290)

MacCoun, R. J., & Kerr, N. L. (1988). Asymmetric influence in mock jury deliberation: Jurors' bias for leniency. *Journal of Personality and Social Psychology, 54,* 21–33. (p. 381)

Mack, D., & Rainey, D. (1990). Female applicants' grooming and personnel selection. *Journal of Social Behavior and Personality, 5,* 399–407. (p. 489)

MacKay, J. L. (1980). Selfhood: Comment on Brewster Smith. *American Psychologist, 35,* 106–107. (p. 49)

Mackie, D. M. (1987). Systematic and nonsystematic processing of majority and minority persuasive communications. *Journal of Personality and Social Psychology, 53,* 41–52. (p. 348)

MacLachlan, J. (1979, November). What people really think of fast talkers. *Psychology Today,* pp. 113–117. (p. 279)

MacLachlan, J., & Siegel, M. H. (1980). Reducing the costs of TV commercials by use of time compressions. *Journal of Marketing Research, 17,* 52–57. (p. 279)

MacLeod, C., & Campbell, L. (1992). Memory accessibility and probability judgments: An experimental evaluation of the availability heuristic. *Journal of Personality and Social Psychology, 63,* 890–902. (p. 105)

Macrae, C. N., Bodenhausen, G. V., Milne, A. B., & Jetten, J. (1994). Out of mind but back in sight: Stereotypes on the rebound. *Journal of Personality and Social Psychology, 67,* 808–817. (p. 396)

Macrae, C. N., Milne, A. B., & Bodenhausen, G. V. (1994). Stereotypes as energy-saving devices: A peek inside the cognitive toolbox. *Journal of Personality and Social Psychology, 66,* 37–47. (p. 417)

Macrae, C. N., Stangor, C., & Milne, A. B. (1994). Activating social stereotypes: A functional analysis. *Journal of Experimental Social Psychology, 30,* 370–389. (p. 417)

Maddux, J. E. (1991). Personal efficacy. In V. Derlega, B. Winstead, & W. Jones (Eds.), *Personality: Contemporary theory and research.* Chicago: Nelson-Hall. (p. 47)

Maddux, J. E., Norton, L. W., & Leary, M. R. (1988). Cognitive components of social anxiety: An investigation of the integration of self-presentation theory and self-efficacy theory. *Journal of Social and Clinical Psychology, 6,* 180–190. (p. 179)

Maddux, J. E., & Rogers, R. W. (1983). Protection motivation and self-efficacy: A revised theory of fear appeals and attitude change. *Journal of Experimental Social Psychology, 19,* 469–479. (p. 283)

Magnuson, E. (1986, March 10). "A serious deficiency": The Rogers Commission faults NASA's "flawed" decision-making process. *Time,* pp. 40–42, international ed. (p. 343)

Major, B. (1989). Gender differences in comparisons and entitlement: Implications for comparable worth. *Journal of Social Issues, 45,* 99–116. (p. 580)

Major, B. (1993). Gender, entitlement, and the distribution of family labor. *Journal of Social Issues, 49,* 141–159. (p. 580)

Major, B., Schmidlin, A. M., & Williams, L. (1990). Gender patterns in social touch: The impact of setting and age. *Journal of Personality and Social Psychology, 58,* 634–643. (p. 199)

Malamuth, N. M. (1986). Predictors of naturalistic sexual aggression. *Journal of Personality and Social Psychology, 50,* 953–962. (p. 461)

Malamuth, N. M. (1989). The attraction to sexual aggression scale: Part one. *Journal of Sex Research, 26,* 26–49. (p. 461)

Malamuth, N. M., & Brown, L. M. (1994). Sexually aggressive men's perceptions of women's communications: Testing three explanations. *Journal of Personality and Social Psychology, 67,* 699–712. (p. 75)

Malamuth, N. M., & Check, J. V. P. (1981). The effects of media exposure on acceptance of violence against women: A field experiment. *Journal of Research in Personality, 15,* 436–446. (p. 458)

Malamuth, N. M., & Check, J. V. P. (1984). Debriefing effectiveness following exposure to pornographic rape depictions. *Journal of Sex Research, 20,* 1–13. (p. 460)

Malkiel, B. G. (1985). *A random walk down Wall Street,* 4th ed. New York: W. W. Norton. (p. 101)

Malpaas, R. S., & Devine, P. G. (1984). Research on suggestion in lineups and photo-spreads. In G. L. Wells & E. F. Loftus (Eds.), *Eyewitness identification: Psychological perspectives.* New York: Cambridge University Press. (p. 366)

Manis, M. (1977). Cognitive social psychology. *Personality and Social Psychology Bulletin, 3,* 550–566. (p. 118)

Manis, M., Cornell, S. D., & Moore, J. C. (1974). Transmission of attitude-relevant information through a communication chain. *Journal of Personality and Social Psychology, 30,* 81–94. (p. 134)

Manis, M., Nelson, T. E., & Shedler, J. (1988). Stereotypes and social judgment: Extremity, assimilation, and contrast. *Journal of Personality and Social Psychology, 55,* 28–36. (p. 430)

Mann, L. (1981). The baiting crowd in episodes of threatened suicide. *Journal of Personality and Social Psychology, 41,* 703–709. (p. 327)

Manning, F. J., & Fullerton, T. D. (1988). Health and well-being in highly cohesive units of the U.S. Army. *Journal of Applied Social Psychology*, **18**, 503–519. (p. 480)

Mantell, D. M. (1971). The potential for violence in Germany. *Journal of Social Issues*, **27**(4), 101–112. (p. 264)

Manucia, G. K., Baumann, D. J., & Cialdini, R. B. (1984). Mood influences on helping: Direct effects or side effects? *Journal of Personality and Social Psychology*, **46**, 357–364. (p. 548)

Marcus, S. (1974). Review of *Obedience to authority*. New York Times Book Review, January 13, pp. 1–2. (p. 243)

Markman, H. J., Floyd, F. J., Stanley, S. M., & Storaasli, R. D. (1988). Prevention of marital distress: A longitudinal investigation. *Journal of Consulting and Clinical Psychology*, **56**, 210–217. (p. 520)

Marks, G., & Miller, N. (1987). Ten years of research on the false-consensus effect: An empirical and theoretical review. *Psychological Bulletin*, **102**, 72–90. (p. 57)

Marks, G., Miller, N., & Maruyama, G. (1981). Effect of targets' physical attractiveness on assumptions of similarity. *Journal of Personality and Social Psychology*, **41**, 198–206. (p. 60)

Markus, G. B. (1986). Stability and change in political attitudes: Observe, recall, and "explain." *Political Behavior*, **8**, 21–44. (p. 97)

Markus, H., & Kitayama, S. (1991). Culture and the self: Implications for cognition, emotion, and motivation. *Psychological Review*, **98**, 224–253. (pp. 44, 69, 217)

Markus, H., & Nurius, P. (1986). Possible selves. *American Psychologist*, **41**, 954–969. (p. 39)

Markus, H., & Wurf, E. (1987). The dynamic self-concept: A social psychological perspective. *Annual Review of Psychology*, **38**, 299–337. (p. 39)

Markus, H. R., & Kitayama, S. (1994). A collective fear of the collective: Implications for selves and theories of selves. *Personality and Social Psychology Bulletin*, **20**, 568–579. (p. 232)

Marler, P. (1974). Aggression and its control in animal society. Presentation to the American Psychological Association convention. (p. 437)

Marshall, W. L. (1989). Pornography and sex offenders. In D. Zillmann & J. Bryant (Eds.), *Pornography: Research advances and policy considerations*. Hillsdale, NJ: Erlbaum. (p. 459)

Martin, C. L. (1987). A ratio measure of sex stereotyping. *Journal of Personality and Social Psychology*, **52**, 489–499. (p. 398)

Maruyama, G., Rubin, R. A., & Kingbury, G. (1981). Self-esteem and educational achievement: Independent constructs with a common cause? *Journal of Personality and Social Psychology*, **40**, 962–975. (p. 21)

Marvelle, K., & Green, S. (1980). Physical attractiveness and sex bias in hiring decisions for two types of jobs. *Journal of the National Association of Women Deans, Administrators, and Counselors*, **44**(1), 3–6. (p. 489)

Marx, G. (1960). *Groucho and me*. New York: Dell. (p. 52)

Maslow, A. H., & Mintz, N. L. (1956). Effects of esthetic surroundings: I. Initial effects of three esthetic conditions upon perceiving "energy" and "well-being" in faces. *Journal of Psychology*, **41**, 247–254. (p. 513)

Matthews, K. A. (1988). CHD and Type A behaviors: Update on and alternative to the Booth-Kewley and Friedman quantitative review. *Psychological Bulletin*, **104**, 373–380. (p. 181)

Maxwell, G. M. (1985). Behaviour of lovers: Measuring the closeness of relationships. *Journal of Personality and Social Psychology*, **2**, 215–238. (p. 509)

Mayer, J. D., & Salovey, P. (1987). Personality moderates the interaction of mood and cognition. In K. Fiedler & J. Forgas (Eds.), *Affect, cognition, and social behavior*. Toronto: Hogrefe. (pp. 111, 175)

Mazzella, R., & Feingold, A. (1994). The effects of physical attractiveness, race, socioeconomic status, and gender of defendants and victims on judgments of mock jurors: A meta-analysis. *Journal of Applied Social Psychology*, **24**, 1315–1344. (pp. 368, 370)

McAlister, A., Perry, C., Killen, J., Slinkard, L. A., & Maccoby, N. (1980). Pilot study of smoking, alcohol and drug abuse prevention. *American Journal of Public Health*, **70**, 719–721. (pp. 306, 307)

McAndrew, F. T. (1981). Pattern of performance and attributions of ability and gender. *Journal of Personality and Social Psychology*, **7**, 583–587. (p. 286)

McAneny, L. (1994, June). Alcohol in America: Number of drinkers holding steady, but drinking less. *Gallup Poll Monthly*, pp. 14–19. (p. 457)

McCann, C. D., & Hancock, R. D. (1983). Self-monitoring in communicative interactions: Social cognitive consequences of goal-directed message modification. *Journal of Experimental Social Psychology*, **19**, 109–121. (pp. 68, 146)

McCarrey, M., Edwards, H. P., & Rozario, W. (1982). Ego-relevant feedback, affect, and self-serving attributional bias. *Personality and Social Psychology Bulletin*, **8**, 189–194. (p. 62)

McCarthy, J. D., & Hoge, D. R. (1984). The dynamics of self-esteem and delinquency. *American Journal of Sociology*, **90**, 396–410. (p. 21)

McCarthy, J. F., & Kelly, B. R. (1978). Aggression, performance variables, and anger self-report in ice hockey players. *Journal of Psychology*, **99**, 97–101. (b) (p. 448)

McCarthy, J. F., & Kelly, B. R. (1978). Aggressive behavior and its effect on performance over time in ice hockey athletes: An archival study. *International Journal of Sport Psychology*, **9**, 90–96. (a) (p. 448)

McCauley, C. (1989). The nature of social influence in groupthink: Compliance and internalization. *Journal of Personality and Social Psychology*, **57**, 250–260. (p. 343)

McCauley, C. R., & Segal, M. E. (1987). Social psychology of terrorist groups. In C. Hendrick (Ed.), *Group processes and intergroup relations: Review of personality and social psychology*, Vol. 9. Newbury Park, Ca.: Sage. (pp. 303, 335)

McConahay, J. B. (1981). Reducing racial prejudice in desegregated schools. In W. D. Hawley (Ed.), *Effective school desegregation*. Beverly Hills, Calif.: Sage. (p. 595)

McCullough, J. L., & Ostrom, T. M. (1974). Repetition of highly similar messages and attitude change. *Journal of Applied Psychology*, **59**, 395–397. (p. 485)

McDougal, D. (1994, August 13–19). Baywatch! *TV Guide*, pp. 12–17. (p. 464)

McFarland, C., & Ross, M. (1985). The relation between current impressions and memories of self and dating partners. Unpublished manuscript, University of Waterloo. (p. 98)

McFarland, C., Ross, M., & DeCourville, N. (1989). Women's theories of menstruation and biases in recall of menstrual symptoms. *Journal of Personality and Social Psychology, 57,* 522–531. (pp. 107, 108)

McFarland, S. G., Ageyev, V. S., & Abalakina-Paap, M. A. (1992). Authoritarianism in the former Soviet Union. *Journal of Personality and Social Psychology, 63,* 1004–1010. (p. 416)

McGillicuddy, N. B., Welton, G. L., & Pruitt, D. G. (1987). Third-party intervention: A field experiment comparing three different models. *Journal of Personality and Social Psychology, 53,* 104–112. (p. 600)

McGillis, D. (1979). Biases and jury decision making. In I. H. Frieze, D. Bar-Tal, & J. S. Carroll, *New approaches to social problems.* San Francisco: Jossey-Bass. (p. 368)

McGlynn, R. P., Tubbs, D. D., & Holzhausen, K. G. (1995). Hypothesis generation in groups constrained by evidence. *Journal of Experimental Social Psychology, 31,* 64–81. (p. 346)

McGrath, J. E. (1984). *Groups: Interaction and performance.* Englewood Cliffs, N.J.: Prentice-Hall. (p. 314)

McGuire, W. J. (1964). Inducing resistance to persuasion: Some contemporary approaches. In L. Berkowitz (Ed.), *Advances in experimental social psychology* (Vol. 1). New York: Academic Press. (p. 306)

McGuire, W. J. (1978). An information-processing model of advertising effectiveness. In H. L. Davis & A. J. Silk (Eds.), *Behavioral and management sciences in marketing.* New York: Ronald Press. (p. 289)

McGuire, W. J. (1986). The myth of massive media impact: Savagings and salvagings. In G. Comstock (Ed.), *Public communication and behavior,* Vol. 1. Orlando, Fl.: Academic Press. (pp. 289, 468)

McGuire, W. J., & McGuire, C. V. (1986). Differences in conceptualizing self versus conceptualizing other people as manifested in contrasting verb types used in natural speech. *Journal of Personality and Social Psychology, 51,* 1135–1143. (p. 81)

McGuire, W. J., McGuire, C. V., Child, P., & Fujioka, T. (1978). Salience of ethnicity in the spontaneous self-concept as a function of one's ethnic distinctiveness in the social environment. *Journal of Personality and Social Psychology, 36,* 511–520. (p. 268)

McGuire, W. J., McGuire, C. V., & Winton, W. (1979). Effects of household sex composition on the salience of one's gender in the spontaneous self-concept. *Journal of Experimental Social Psychology, 15,* 77–90. (p. 267)

McGuire, W. J., & Padawer-Singer, A. (1978). Trait salience in the spontaneous self-concept. *Journal of Personality and Social Psychology, 33,* 743–754. (p. 267)

McKenzie-Mohr, D., & Dyal, J. A. (1991). Perceptions of threat, tactical efficacy and competing threats as determinants of pro-disarmament behavior. *Journal of Social Behavior and Personality, 6,* 675–696. (p. 50)

McKenzie-Mohr, D., & Zanna, M. P. (1990). Treating women as sexual objects: Look to the (gender schematic) male who has viewed pornography. *Personality and Social Psychology Bulletin, 16,* 296–308. (p. 473)

McMillen, D. L., & Austin, J. B. (1971). Effect of positive feedback on compliance following transgression. *Psychonomic Science, 24,* 59–61. (p. 547)

McNeel, S. P. (1980). Tripling up: Perceptions and effects of dormitory crowding. Paper presented at the American Psychological Association convention. (p. 455)

McNeill, B. W., & Stoltenberg, C. D. (1988). A test of the elaboration likelihood model for therapy. *Cognitive Therapy and Research, 12,* 69–79. (p. 304)

Medalia, N. Z., & Larsen, O. N. (1958). Diffusion and belief in collective delusion: The Seattle windshield pitting epidemic. *American Sociological Review, 23,* 180–186. (p. 236)

Medvec, V. H., Madey, S. F., & Gilovich, T. (1994). When less is more: Counterfactual thinking and satisfaction among Olympic medalists. Unpublished manuscript, Cornell University. (p. 106)

Meech, P., & Kilborn, R. (1992). Media and identity in a stateless nation: The case of Scotland. *Media, Culture and Society, 14,* 245–259. (p. 407)

Meehl, P. E. (1954). *Clinical vs. statistical prediction: A theoretical analysis and a review of evidence.* Minneapolis: University of Minnesota Press. (p. 168)

Meehl, P. E. (1986). Causes and effects of my disturbing little book. *Journal of Personality Assessment, 50,* 370–375. (p. 169)

Meeus, W. H. J., & Raaijmakers, Q. A. W. (1986). Administrative obedience: Carrying out orders to use psychological-administrative violence. *European Journal of Social Psychology, 16,* 311–324. (p. 264)

Meindl, J. R., & Lerner, M. J. (1984). Exacerbation of extreme responses to an out-group. *Journal of Personality and Social Psychology, 47,* 71–84. (p. 414)

Meleshko, K. G. A., & Alden, L. E. (1993). Anxiety and self-disclosure: Toward a motivational model. *Journal of Personality and Social Psychology, 64,* 1000–1009. (p. 179)

Melton, G. B., Monahan, J., & Saks, M. J. (1987). Psychologists as law professors. *American Psychologist, 42,* 502–509. (p. 356)

Memon, A., & Bull, R. (1991). The cognitive interview: Its origins, empirical support, evaluation, and practical implications. *Journal of Community and Applied Social Psychology, 1,* 291–307. (p. 365)

Menand, L. (1991, May 20). Illiberalisms. *New Yorker,* pp. 101–107. (p. 390)

Mendonca, P. J., & Brehm, S. S. (1983). Effects of choice on behavioral treatment of overweight children. *Journal of Social and Clinical Psychology, 1,* 343–358. (p. 186)

Merton, R. K., & Kitt, A. S. (1950). Contributions to the theory of reference group behavior. In R. K. Merton & P. F. Lazarsfeld (Eds.), *Continuities in social research: Studies in the scope and method of the American soldier.* Glencoe, Ill.: Free Press. (p. 447)

Messé, L. A., Kerr, N. L., & Sattler, D. N. (1992). "But some animals are more equal than others": The supervisor as a privileged status in group contexts. In S. Worchel, W. Wood, & J. Simpson (Eds.) *Group process and productivity.* Newbury Park, CA: Sage. (p. 220)

Messé, L. A., & Sivacek, J. M. (1979). Predictions of others' responses in a mixed-motive game: Self-justification or false consensus? *Journal of Personality and Social Psychology, 37,* 602–607. (p. 576)

Messick, D. M., Bloom, S., Boldizar, J. P., & Samuelson, C. D. (1985). Why we are fairer than others. *Journal of Experimental Social Psychology, 21,* 480–500. (p. 54)

Messick, D. M., & Sentis, K. P. (1979). Fairness and preference. *Journal of Experimental Social Psychology, 15,* 418–434. (p. 579)

Messick, D. M., Wilke, H., Brewer, M. B., Kramer, R. M., Zemke, P. E., & Lui, L. (1983). Individual adaptations and structural change as solutions to social dilemmas. *Journal of Personality and Social Psychology*, **44**, 294–309. (p. 574)

Metalsky, G. I., Joiner, T. E., Jr., , Hardin, T. S., & Abramson, L. Y. (1993). Depressive reactions to failure in a naturalistic setting: A test of the hopelessness and self-esteem theories of depression. *Journal of Abnormal Psychology*, **102**, 101–109. (p. 176)

Michaels, J. W., Blommel, J. M., Brocato, R. M., Linkous, R. A., & Rowe, J. S. (1982). Social facilitation and inhibition in a natural setting. *Replications in Social Psychology*, **2**, 21–24. (p. 317)

Michaelson, R. (1993, August). Behavior gets big billing in medical schools today. *The Monitor*, p. 56. (p. 180)

Miell, E., Duck, S., & La Gaipa, J. (1979). Interactive effects of sex and timing in self disclosure. *British Journal of Social and Clinical Psychology*, **18**, 355–362. (p. 516)

Mikula, G. (1984). Justice and fairness in interpersonal relations: Thoughts and suggestions. In H. Taijfel (Ed.), *The social dimension: European developments in social psychology*, Vol. 1, Cambridge: Cambridge University Press. (p. 579)

Milgram, S. (1961, December). Nationality and conformity. *Scientific American*, December, pp. 45–51. (p. 264)

Milgram, S. (1965). Some conditions of obedience and disobedience to authority. *Human Relations*, **18**, 57–76. (p. 240)

Milgram, S. (1974). *Obedience to authority*. New York: Harper and Row. (pp. 240, 241, 247, 252, 256, 261, 262, 269)

Milgram, S. (1977). *The individual in a social world*. Reading, MA: Addison-Wesley. (p. 248)

Milgram, S., Bickman, L., & Berkowitz, L. (1969). Note on the drawing power of crowds of different size. *Journal of Personality and Social Psychology*, **13**, 79–82. (p. 253)

Milgram, S., & Sabini, J. (1983). On maintaining social norms: A field experiment in the subway. In H. H. Blumberg, A. P. Hare, V. Kent, and M. Davies (Eds.), *Small groups and social interaction*, Vol. 1. London: Wiley. (p. 249)

Millar, M. G., & Tesser, A. (1992). The role of beliefs and feelings in guiding behavior: The mismatch model. In L. Martin & A. Tesser (Eds.), *The construction of social judgment*. Hillsdale NJ: Erlbaum. (p. 43)

Miller, A. G. (1986). *The obedience experiments: A case study of controversy in social science*. New York: Praeger. (p. 243)

Miller, A. G., Ashton, W., & Mishal, M. (1990). Beliefs concerning the features of constrained behavior: A basis for the fundamental attribution error. *Journal of Personality and Social Psychology*, **59**, 635–650. (p. 80)

Miller, A. G., Gillen, G., Schenker, C., & Radlove, S. (1973). Perception of obedience to authority. *Proceedings of the 81st annual convention of the American Psychological Association*, **8**, 127–128. (p. 251)

Miller, C. E., & Anderson, P. D. (1979). Group decision rules and the rejection of deviates. *Social Psychology Quarterly*, **42**, 354–363. (p. 259)

Miller, C. T., & Felicio, D. M. (1990). Person-positivity bias: Are individuals liked better than groups? *Journal of Experimental Social Psychology*, **26**, 408–420. (p. 429)

Miller, D. T. (1977). Altruism and threat to a belief in a just world. *Journal of Experimental Social Psychology*, **13**, 113–124. (p. 426)

Miller, D. T., & McFarland, C. (1987). Pluralistic ignorance: When similarity is interpreted as dissimilarity. *Journal of Personality and Social Psychology*, **53**, 298–305. (p. 338)

Miller, D. T., Taylor, B., & Buck, M. L. (1991). Gender gaps: Who needs to be explained? *Journal of Personality and Social Psychology*, **61**, 5–12. (p. 196)

Miller, G. R., & Fontes, N. E. (1979). *Videotape on trial: A view from the jury box*. Beverly Hills, Calif.: Sage Publications. (p. 373)

Miller, J. B. (1986). *Toward a new psychology of women*, 2nd ed. Boston, MA: Beacon Press. (p. 196)

Miller, J. G. (1984). Culture and the development of everyday social explanation. *Journal of Personality and Social Psychology*, **46**, 961–978. (p. 86)

Miller, J. G., Bersoff, D. M., & Harwood, R. L. (1990). Perceptions of social responsibility in India and in the United States: Moral imperatives or personal decisions? *Journal of Personality and Social Psychology*, **58**, 33–47. (p. 535)

Miller, K. I., & Monge, P. R. (1986). Participation, satisfaction, and productivity: A meta-analytic review. *Academy of Management Journal*, **29**, 727–753. (p. 49)

Miller, L. C. (1990). Intimacy and liking: Mutual influence and the role of unique relationships. *Journal of Personality and Social Psychology*, **59**, 50–60. (p. 516)

Miller, L. C., Berg, J. H., & Archer, R. L. (1983). Openers: Individuals who elicit intimate self-disclosure. *Journal of Personality and Social Psychology*, **44**, 1234–1244. (p. 516)

Miller, L. C., Berg, J. H., & Rugs, D. (1989). Selectivity and sharing: Needs and norms in developing friendships. Unpublished manuscript, Scripps College. (p. 514)

Miller, L. E., & Grush, J. E. (1986). Individual differences in attitudinal versus normative determination of behavior. *Journal of Experimental Social Psychology*, **22**, 190–202. (p. 129)

Miller, N., & Campbell, D. T. (1959). Recency and primacy in persuasion as a function of the timing of speeches and measurements. *Journal of Abnormal and Social Psychology*, **59**, 1–9. (p. 287)

Miller, N., & Marks, G. (1982). Assumed similarity between self and other: Effect of expectation of future interaction with that other. *Social Psychology Quarterly*, **45**, 100–105. (p. 483)

Miller, N., Maruyama, G., Beaber, R. J., & Valone, K. (1976). Speed of speech and persuasion. *Journal of Personality and Social Psychology*, **34**, 615–624. (p. 279)

Miller, N. E. (1941). The frustration-aggression hypothesis. *Psychological Review*, **48**, 337–342. (p. 442)

Miller, N. E., & Bugelski, R. (1948). Minor studies of aggression: II. The influence of frustrations imposed by the in-group on attitudes expressed toward out-groups. *Journal of Psychology*, **25**, 437–442. (p. 413)

Miller, P. A., & Eisenberg, N. (1988). The relation of empathy to aggressive and externalizing/antisocial behavior. *Psychological Bulletin*, **103**, 324–344. (p. 530)

Miller, P. C., Lefcourt, H. M., Holmes, J. G., Ware, E. E., & Saley, W. E. (1986). Marital locus of control and marital problem solving. *Journal of Personality and Social Psychology*, **51**, 161–169. (p. 47)

Miller, R. L., Brickman, P., & Bolen, D. (1975). Attribution versus persuasion as a means for modifying behavior. *Journal of Personality and Social Psychology, 31,* 430–441. (p. 116)

Miller, R. S., & Schlenker, B. R. (1985). Egotism in group members: Public and private attributions of responsibility for group performance. *Social Psychology Quarterly, 48,* 85–89. (p. 69)

Miller, R. S., & Simpson, J. A. (1990). Relationship satisfaction and attentiveness to alternatives. Paper presented at the American Psychological Association convention. (p. 492)

Millett, K. (1975). The shame is over. *Ms.,* January, pp. 26–29. (p. 517)

Mims, P. R., Hartnett, J. J., & Nay, W. R. (1975). Interpersonal attraction and help volunteering as a function of physical attractiveness. *Journal of Psychology, 89,* 125–131. (p. 555)

Minard, R. D. (1952). Race relationships in the Pocohontas coal field. *Journal of Social Issues, 8*(1), 29–44. (p. 409)

Mio, J. S., Thompson, S. C., & Givens, G. H. (1993). The commons dilemma as a metaphor: Memory, influence, and implications for environmental conservation. *Metaphor and Symbolic Activity, 8,* 23–42. (p. 577)

Mirels, H. L., & McPeek, R. W. (1977). Self-advocacy and self-esteem. *Journal of Consulting and Clinical Psychology, 45,* 1132–1138. (p. 186)

Mischel, W. (1968). *Personality and assessment.* New York: Wiley. (pp. 126, 261)

Mita, T. H., Dermer, M., & Knight, J. (1977). Reversed facial images and the mere-exposure hypothesis. *Journal of Personality and Social Psychology, 35,* 597–601. (p. 485)

Mitchell, G., Tetlock, P. E., Mellers, B. A., & Ordonez, L. D. (1993). Judgments of social justice: Compromises between equality and efficiency. *Journal of Personality and Social Psychology, 65,* 629–639. (p. 581)

Mitchell, T. R., & Thompson, L. (1994). A theory of temporal adjustments of the evaluation of events: Rosy prospection and rosy retrospection. In C. Stubbart, J. Porac, & J. Meindl (Eds.), *Advances in managerial cognition and organizational information processing.* Greenwich, CT: JAI Press. (p. 98)

Moghaddam, F. M. (1987). Psychology in the three worlds: As reflected by the crisis in social psychology and the move toward indigenous third-world psychology. *American Psychologist, 42,* 912–920. (p. 12)

Moghaddam, F. M. (1990). Modulative and generative orientations in psychology: Implications for psychology in the three worlds. *Journal of Social Issues, 46,* 21–41. (p. 12)

Monson, T. C., Hesley, J. W., & Chernick, L. (1982). Specifying when personality traits can and cannot predict behavior: An alternative to abandoning the attempt to predict single-act criteria. *Journal of Personality and Social Psychology, 43,* 385–399. (p. 263)

Monson, T. C., & Snyder, M. (1977). Actors, observers, and the attribution process: Toward a reconceptualization. *Journal of Experimental Social Psychology, 13,* 89–111. (p. 86)

Monteith, M. J. (1993). Self-regulation of prejudiced responses: Implications for progress in prejudice-reduction efforts. *Journal of Personality and Social Psychology, 65,* 469–485. (p. 396)

Moody, K. (1980). *Growing up on television: The TV effect.* New York: Times Books. (p. 307)

Moore, B. S., Underwood, B., & Rosenhan, D. L. (1973). Affect and altruism. *Developmental Psychology, 8,* 99–104. (p. 548)

Moore, D. L., & Baron, R. S. (1983). Social facilitation: A physiological analysis. In J. T. Cacioppo & R. Petty (Eds.), *Social psychophysiology.* New York: Guilford Press. (p. 319)

Moore, D. W. (1993, July). Americans feel threatened by new immigrants. *Gallup Poll Monthly,* pp. 2–16. (p. 393)

Moran, G., & Comfort, J. C. (1982). Scientific juror selection: Sex as a moderator of demographic and personality predictors of impaneled felony juror behavior. *Journal of Personality and Social Psychology, 43,* 1052–1063. (p. 379)

Moran, G., & Comfort, J. C. (1986). Neither "tentative" nor "fragmentary": Verdict preference of impaneled felony jurors as a function of attitude toward capital punishment. *Journal of Applied Psychology, 71,* 146–155. (p. 379)

Moran, G., & Cutler, B. L. (1991). The prejudicial impact of pretrial publicity. *Journal of Applied Social Psychology, 21,* 345–367. (p. 372)

Moran, G., Cutler, B. L., & De Lisa, A. (1994). Attitudes toward tort reform, scientific jury selection, and juror bias: Verdict inclination in criminal and civil trials. *Law and Psychology Review, 18,* 309–328. (p. 378)

Moran, G., Cutler, B. L., & Loftus, E. F. (1990). Jury selection in major controlled substance trials: The need for extended voir dire. *Forensic Reports, 3,* 331–348. (p. 378)

Moreland, R. L., & Zajonc, R. B. (1977). Is stimulus recognition a necessary condition for the occurrence of exposure effects? *Journal of Personality and Social Psychology, 35,* 191–199. (p. 484)

Morgan, R. (1980). Theory and practice: Pornography and rape. In L. Lederer (Ed.), *Take back the night: Women on pornography.* New York: Morrow. (p. 459)

Morier, D., & Seroy, C. (1994). The effect of interpersonal expectancies on men's self-presentation of gender role attitudes to women. *Sex Roles, 31,* 493–504. (p. 222)

Morris, M. W., & Peng, K. (1994). Culture and cause: American and Chinese attributions for social and physical events. *Journal of Personality and Social Psychology, 67,* 949–971. (p. 215)

Morris, W. N., & Miller, R. S. (1975). The effects of consensus-breaking and consensus-preempting partners on reduction of conformity. *Journal of Experimental Social Psychology, 11,* 215–223. (p. 254)

Morrison, D. M. (1989). Predicting contraceptive efficacy: A discriminant analysis of three groups of adolescent women. *Journal of Applied Social Psychology, 19,* 1431–1452. (p. 129)

Morrow, L. (1983, August 1). All the hazards and threats of success. *Time,* pp. 20–25. (p. 232)

Morse, S. J. & Gruzen, J. (1976). The eye of the beholder: A neglected variable in the study of physical attractiveness. *Journal of Psychology, 44,* 209–225. (p. 490)

Moscovici, S. (1985). Social influence and conformity. In G. Lindzey & E. Aronson (Eds.), *The handbook of social psychology,* 3rd ed. Hillsdale, N.J.: Erlbaum. (p. 348)

Moscovici, S. (1988). Notes towards a description of social representations. *European Journal of Social Psychology, 18,* 211–250. (p. 9)

Moscovici, S., Lage, S., & Naffrechoux, M. (1969). Influence of a consistent minority on the responses of a majority in a color perception task. *Sociometry, 32,* 365–380. (p. 348)

Moscovici, S., & Zavalloni, M. (1969). The group as a polarizer of attitudes. *Journal of Personality and Social Psychology, 12,* 124–135. (p. 333)

Moyer, K. E. (1976). *The psychobiology of aggression*. New York: Harper & Row. (p. 440)

Moynihan, D. P. (1979). Social science and the courts. *Public Interest*, **54**, 12–31. (p. 8)

Mucchi-Faina, A., Maass, A., & Volpato, C. (1991). Social influence: The role of originality. *European Journal of Social Psychology*, **21**, 183–197. (p. 348)

Muehlenhard, C. L. (1988). Misinterpreted dating behaviors and the risk of date rape. *Journal of Social and Clinical Psychology*, **6**, 20–37. (p. 75)

Mueller, C. W., Donnerstein, E., & Hallam, J. (1983). Violent films and prosocial behavior. *Personality and Social Psychology Bulletin*, **9**, 83–89. (p. 468)

Mullen, B. (1986). Atrocity as a function of lynch mob composition: A self-attention perspective. *Personality and Social Psychology Bulletin*, **12**, 187–197. (a) (pp. 319, 328, 471)

Mullen, B. (1986). Stuttering, audience size, and the other-total ratio: A self-attention perspective. *Journal of Applied Social Psychology*, **16**, 139–149. (b) (pp. 319, 328)

Mullen, B., & Baumeister, R. F. (1987). Group effects on self-attention and performance: Social loafing, social facilitation, and social impairment. In C. Hendrick (Ed.), *Group processes and intergroup relations: Review of personality and social psychology*, Vol. 9. Newbury Park, Ca.: Sage. (pp. 320, 324)

Mullen, B., Brown, R., & Smith, C. (1992). Ingroup bias as a function of salience, relevance, and status: An integration. *European Journal of Social Psychology*, **22**, 103–122. (p. 407)

Mullen, B., & Copper, C. (1994). The relation between group cohesiveness and performance: An integration. *Psychological Bulletin*, **115**, 210–227. (p. 341)

Mullen, B., Copper, C., & Driskell, J. E. (1990). Jaywalking as a function of model behavior. *Personality and Social Psychology Bulletin*, **16**, 320–330. (p. 256)

Mullen, B., & Goethals, G. R. (1990). Social projection, actual consensus and valence. *British Journal of Social Psychology*, **29**, 279–282. (p. 57)

Mullen, B., & Hu, L. (1989). Perceptions of ingroup and outgroup variability: A meta-analytic integration. *Basic and Applied Social Psychology*, **10**, 233–252. (p. 419)

Mullen, B., & Riordan, C. A. (1988). Self-serving attributions for performance in naturalistic settings: A meta-analytic review. *Journal of Applied Social Psychology*, **18**, 3–22. (p. 53)

Mullen, B., Salas, E., & Driskell, J. E. (1989). Salience, motivation, and artifact as contributions to the relation between participation rate and leadership. *Journal of Experimental Social Psychology*, **25**, 545–559. (p. 348)

Muller, S., & Johnson, B. T. (1990). Fear and persuasion: A linear relationship? Paper presented to the Eastern Psychological Association convention. (p. 282)

Murphy, C. (1990, June). New findings: Hold on to your hat. *The Atlantic*, pp. 22–23. (pp. 14, 17)

Murphy-Berman, V., Berman, J. J., Singh, P., Pachauri, A., & Kumar, P. (1984). Factors affecting allocation to needy and meritorious recipients: A cross-cultural comparison. *Journal of Personality and Social Psychology*, **46**, 1267–1272. (p. 580)

Murphy-Berman, V., & Sharma, R. (1986). Testing the assumptions of attribution theory in India. *Journal of Social Psychology*, **126**, 607–616. (p. 69)

Murray, J. P., & Kippax, S. (1979). From the early window to the late night show: International trends in the study of television's impact on children and adults. In L. Berkowitz (Ed.), *Advances in experimental social psychology*, vol. 12. New York: Academic Press. (p. 464)

Murray, J. P., & Lonnborg, B. (1989). Using TV sensibly. Cooperative Extension Service, Kansas State University. (p. 468)

Murstein, B. L. (1986). *Paths to marriage*. Newbury Park, Ca.: Sage. (p. 487)

Muson, G. (1978). Teenage violence and the telly. *Psychology Today*, March, pp. 50–54. (p. 465)

Musser, L. M., & Graziano, W. F. (1991). Behavioral confirmation in children's interaction with peers. *Basic and Applied Social Psychology*, **12**, 441–456. (p. 220)

Myers, D. G. (1978). Polarizing effects of social comparison. *Journal of Experimental Social Psychology*, **14**, 554–563. (p. 338)

Myers, D. G. (1993). *The pursuit of happiness*. New York: Avon. (pp. 111, 445)

Myers, D. G. (1995). *Psychology*, 5th ed. New York: Worth Publishers. (p. 99)

Myers, D. G. (1995b). *Society in the balance: America's social recession and renewal*. Unpublished manuscript, Hope College. (p. 519)

Myers, D. G., & Bishop, G. D. (1970). Discussion effects on racial attitudes. *Science*, **169**, 778–789. (p. 334)

Nadler, A. (1991). Help-seeking behavior: Psychological costs and instrumental benefits. In M. S. Clark (Ed.), *Prosocial behavior*. Newbury Park, CA: Sage. (p. 555)

Nadler, A., & Fisher, J. D. (1986). The role of threat to self-esteem and perceived control in recipient reaction to help: Theory development and empirical validation. In L. Berkowitz (Ed.), *Advances in Experimental Social Psychology*, vol. 19. Orlando, FL: Academic Press. (p. 534)

Nadler, A., Goldberg, M., & Jaffe, Y. (1982). Effect of self-differentiation and anonymity in group on deindividuation. *Journal of Personality and Social Psychology*, **42**, 1127–1136. (p. 331)

Nagar, D., & Pandey, J. (1987). Affect and performance on cognitive task as a function of crowding and noise. *Journal of Applied Social Psychology*, **17**, 147–157. (p. 319)

Nail, P. R., & Van Leeuwen, M. D. (1993). An analysis and restructuring of the diamond model of social response. *Personality and Social Psychology Bulletin*, **19**, 106–116. (p. 265)

Napolitan, D. A., & Goethals, G. R. (1979). The attribution of friendliness. *Journal of Experimental Social Psychology*, **15**, 105–113. (p. 81)

National Council for Research on Women (1994). Women and philanthropy fact sheet. *Issues Quarterly*, **1**(2), 9. (p. 197)

National Safety Council (1991). *Accident facts*. Chicago: Author. (p. 106)

Naylor, T. H. (1990). Redefining corporate motivation, Swedish style. *Christian Century*, **107**, 566–570. (p. 350)

NBC News Poll (1977, November 29–30). Cited by *Public Opinion*, January-February, 1979, p. 36. (p. 399)

NCTV (1988). TV and film alcohol research. *NCTV News*, **9**(3–4), 4. (p. 469)

Needles, D. J., & Abramson, L. Y. (1990). Positive life events, attributional style, and hopefulness: Testing a model of recovery from depression. *Journal of Abnormal Psychology*, **99**, 156–165. (p. 176)

Neimeyer, G. J., MacNair, R., Metzler, A. E., & Courchaine, K. (1991). Changing personal beliefs: Effects of forewarning, argument quality, prior bias, and personal exploration. *Journal of Social and Clinical Psychology, 10,* 1–20. (p. 304)

Nelson, T. E., Acker, M., & Manis, M. (1994). Irrepressible stereotypes. Unpublished manuscript, Ohio State University. (p. 430)

Nelson, T. E., Biernat, M. R., & Manis, M. (1990). Everyday base rates (sex stereotypes): Potent and resilient. *Journal of Personality and Social Psychology, 59,* 664–675. (p. 430)

Nemeth, C. (1977). Interactions between jurors as a function of majority vs. unanimity decision rules. *Journal of Applied Social Psychology, 7,* 38–56. (p. 382)

Nemeth, C. (1979). The role of an active minority in intergroup relations. In W. G. Austin and S. Worchel (Eds.), *The social psychology of intergroup relations.* Monterey, Calif.: Brooks/Cole. (p. 348)

Nemeth, C. (1986). Intergroup relations between majority and minority. In S. Worchel and W. G. Austin (Eds.), *Psychology of intergroup relations.* Chicago: Nelson-Hall. (p. 349)

Nemeth, C., & Chiles, C. (1988). Modelling courage: The role of dissent in fostering independence. *European Journal of Social Psychology, 18,* 275–280. (p. 255)

Nemeth, C., & Wachtler, J. (1974). Creating the perceptions of consistency and confidence: A necessary condition for minority influence. *Sociometry, 37,* 529–540. (p. 348)

Nemeth, C. J., & Staw, B. M. (1989). The tradeoffs of social control and innovation in groups and organizations. *Advances in Experimental Social Psychology, 22,* 175–210. (p. 346)

Newcomb, T. M. (1961). *The acquaintance process.* New York: Holt, Rinehart and Winston. (pp. 482, 493)

Newman, H. M., & Langer, E. J. (1981). Post-divorce adaptation and the attribution of responsibility. *Sex Roles, 7,* 223–231. (p. 62)

Newman, L. S. (1993). How individualists interpret behavior: Idiocentrism and spontaneous trait inference. *Social Cognition, 11,* 243–269. (p. 86)

Newport, F. (1993, October). Americans now more likely to say: Women have it harder than men. *Gallup Poll Monthly,* pp. 1118. (p. 224)

Ng, W-J., & Lindsay, R. C. L. (1994). Cross-race facial recognition: Failure of the contact hypothesis. *Journal of*

Cross-Cultural Psychology, 25, 217–232. (p. 420)

Nias, D. K. B. (1979). Marital choice: Matching or complementation? In M. Cook and G. Wilson (Eds.), *Love and attraction.* Oxford: Pergamon. (p. 496)

Nicholson, N., Cole, S. G., & Rocklin, T. (1985). Conformity in the Asch situation: A comparison between contemporary British and U. S. university students. *British Journal of Social Psychology, 24,* 59–63. (p. 264)

Nielsen Media Research (1990). *Report on television.* Summarized in *American Enterprise,* July/August, 1990, p. 98. (p. 464)

Niemi, R. G., Mueller, J., & Smith, T. W. (1989). *Trends in public opinion: A compendium of survey data.* New York: Greenwood Press. (pp. 393, 399, 445, 473)

Nigro, G. N., Hill, D. E., Gelbein, M. E., & Clark, C. L. (1988). Changes in the facial prominence of women and men over the last decade. *Psychology of Women Quarterly, 12,* 225–235. (p. 411)

Nisbett, R. (1988, Fall). The Vincennes incident: Congress hears psychologists. *Science Agenda* (American Psychological Association), p. 4. (p. 91)

Nisbett, R. E. (1993). Violence and U.S. regional culture. *American Psychologist, 48,* 441–449. (p. 451)

Nisbett, R. E., Borgida, E., Crandall, R., & Reed, H. (1976). Popular induction: Information is not necessarily informative. In J. S. Carroll and J. W. Payne (Eds.), *Cognition and social behavior.* Hillsdale, N.J.: Erlbaum. (p. 104)

Nisbett, R. E., Fong, G. T., Lehman, D. R., & Cheng, P. W. (1987). Teaching reasoning. *Science, 238,* 625–631. (p. 120)

Nisbett, R. E., & Ross, L. (1980). *Human inference: Strategies and shortcomings of social judgment.* Englewood Cliffs, N.J.: Prentice-Hall. (pp. 118, 119)

Nisbett, R. E., & Ross, L. (1991). *The person and the situation.* New York: McGraw-Hill. (p. 350)

Nisbett, R. E., & Schachter, S. (1966). Cognitive manipulation of pain. *Journal of Experimental Social Psychology, 2,* 227–236. (p. 41)

Nisbett, R. E., & Wilson, T. D. (1977). Telling more than we can know: Verbal reports on mental processes. *Psychological Review, 84,* 231–259. (p. 41)

Noel, J. G., Forsyth, D. R., & Kelley, K. N. (1987). Improving the perfor-

mance of failing students by overcoming their self-serving attributional biases. *Basic and Applied Social Psychology, 8,* 151–162. (p. 48)

Nolen-Hoeksema, S., Girgus, J. S., & Seligman, M. E. P. (1986). Learned helplessness in children: A longitudinal study of depression, achievement, and explanatory style. *Journal of Personality and Social Psychology, 51,* 435–442. (p. 176)

Noller, P., & Fitzpatrick, M. A. (1990). Marital communication in the eighties. *Journal of Marriage and the Family, 52,* 832–843. (p. 520)

Noon, E., & Hollin, C. R. (1987). Lay knowledge of eyewitness behaviour: A British survey. *Applied Cognitive Psychology, 1,* 143–153. (p. 366)

Norem, J. K., & Cantor, N. (1986). Defensive pessimism: Harnessing anxiety as motivation. *Journal of Personality and Social Psychology, 51,* 1208–1217. (p. 57)

Notarius, C., & Markman, H. J. (1993). *We can work it out.* New York: Putnam. (p. 520)

O'Dea, T. F. (1968). Sects and cults. In D. L. Sills (Ed.), *International encyclopedia of the social sciences* (Vol. 14). New York: Macmillan. (p. 301)

O'Gorman, H. J., & Garry, S. L. (1976). Pluralistic ignorance—a replication and extension. *Public Opinion Quarterly, 40,* 449–458. (p. 54)

Ohbuchi, K., & Kambara, T. (1985). Attacker's intent and awareness of outcome, impression management, and retaliation. *Journal of Experimental Social Psychology, 21,* 321–330. (p. 455)

O'Leary, K. D., Christian, J. L., & Mendell, N. R. (1994). A closer look at the link between marital discord and depressive symptomatology. *Journal of Social and Clinical Psychology, 13,* 33–41. (p. 520)

Oliner, S. P., & Oliner, P. M. (1988). *The altruistic personality: Rescuers of Jews in Nazi Europe.* New York: The Free Press. (p. 561)

Oliver, M. B., & Hyde, J. S. (1993). Gender differences in sexuality: A meta-analysis. *Psychological Bulletin, 114,* 29–51. (p. 200)

Olson, J. M., & Cal, A. V. (1984). Source credibility, attitudes, and the recall of past behaviours. *European Journal of Social Psychology, 14,* 203–210. (p. 278)

Olson, J. M., Roese, N. J., & Zanna, M. P. (1996). Expectancies. In E. T. Higgins & A. W. Kruglanski (eds.), *Social psy-*

chology: Handbook of basic principles. New York: Guilford Press, in press. (p. 116)

Olson, J. M., & Zanna, M. P. (1981). Promoting physical activity: A social psychological perspective. Report prepared for the Ministry of Culture and Recreation, Sports and Fitness Branch, 77 Bloor St. West, 8th Floor, Toronto, Ontario M7A 2R9, November. (p. 129)

Olson, J. M., & Zanna, M. P. (1993). Attitudes and attitude change. *Annual Review of Psychology, 44*, 117–154. (p. 125)

Olweus, D. (1979). Stability of aggressive reaction patterns in males: A review. *Psychological Bulletin, 86*, 852–875. (p. 440)

Olweus, D., Mattsson, A., Schalling, D., & Low, H. (1988). Circulating testosterone levels and aggression in adolescent males: A causal analysis. *Psychosomatic Medicine, 50*, 261–272. (p. 441)

Omoto, A. M., Snyder, M., & Berghuis, J. P. (1993). The psychology of volunteerism: A conceptual analysis and a program of action research. In J. B. Pryor & G. D. Reeder (eds.), *The social psychology of HIV infection*. Hillsdale, NJ: Erlbaum. (p. 553)

Opotow, S. (1990). Moral exclusion and injustice: An introduction. *Journal of Social Issues, 46*, 1–20. (p. 561)

Orbell, J. M., van de Kragt, A. J. C., & Dawes, R. M. (1988). Explaining discussion-induced cooperation. *Journal of Personality and Social Psychology, 54*, 811–819. (p. 574)

Orive, R. (1984). Group similarity, public self-awareness, and opinion extremity: A social projection explanation of deindividuation effects. *Journal of Personality and Social Psychology, 47*, 727–737. (p. 330)

Ornstein, R. (1991). *The evolution of consciousness: Of Darwin, Freud, and cranial fire: The origins of the way we think.* New York: Prentice-Hall. (pp. 136, 246, 299)

Osberg, T. M., & Shrauger, J. S. (1986). Self-prediction: Exploring the parameters of accuracy. *Journal of Personality and Social Psychology, 51*, 1044–1057. (p. 42)

Osberg, T. M., & Shrauger, J. S. (1990). The role of self-prediction in psychological assessment. In J. N. Butcher & C. D. Spielberger (Eds.), *Advances in Personality Assessment*, vol. 8. Hillsdale, NJ: Erlbaum. (p. 42)

Osgood, C. E. (1962). *An alternative to war or surrender.* Urbana, Ill.: University of Illinois Press. (p. 601)

Osgood, C. E. (1980). GRIT: A strategy for survival in mankind's nuclear age? Paper presented at the Pugwash Conference on New Directions in Disarmament, Racine, Wis. (p. 601)

Oskamp, S. (1971). Effects of programmed strategies on cooperation in the prisoner's dilemma and other mixed-motive games. *Journal of Conflict Resolution, 15*, 225–229. (p. 571)

Oskamp, S. (1991). Curbside recycling: Knowledge, attitudes, and behavior. Paper presented at the Society for Experimental Social Psychology meeting, Columbus, Ohio. (p. 129)

Osterhouse, R. A., & Brock, T. C. (1970). Distraction increases yielding to propaganda by inhibiting counterarguing. *Journal of Personality and Social Psychology, 15*, 344–358. (p. 294)

Ostrom, T. M., & Sedikides, C. (1992). Out-group homogeneity effects in natural and minimal groups. *Psychological Bulletin, 112*, 536–552. (p. 418)

Ozer, E. M., & Bandura, A. (1990). Mechanisms governing empowerment effects: A self-efficacy analysis. *Journal of Personality and Social Psychology, 58*, 472–486. (p. 51)

Padgett, V. R. (1989). Predicting organizational violence: An application of 11 powerful principles of obedience. Paper presented at the American Psychological Association Convention. (p. 243)

Pak, A. W., Dion, K. L., & Dion, K. K. (1991). Social-psychological correlates of experienced discrimination: Test of the double jeopardy hypothesis. *International Journal of Intercultural Relations, 15*, 243–254. (p. 590)

Pallak, M. S., Mueller, M., Dollar, K., & Pallak, J. (1972). Effect of commitment on responsiveness to an extreme consonant communication. *Journal of Personality and Social Psychology, 23*, 429–436. (p. 284)

Pallak, S. R., Murroni, E., & Koch, J. (1983). Communicator attractiveness and expertise, emotional versus rational appeals, and persuasion: A heuristic versus systematic processing interpretation. *Social Cognition, 2*, 122–141. (p. 280)

Palmer, E. L., & Dorr, A. (Eds.) (1980). *Children and the faces of television: Teaching, violence, selling.* New York: Academic Press. (p. 307)

Paloutzian, R. (1979). Pro-ecology behavior: Three field experiments on litter pickup. Paper presented at the Western Psychological Association convention. (p. 288)

Pandey, J., Sinha, Y., Prakash, A., & Tripathi, R. C. (1982). Right-left political ideologies and attribution of the causes of poverty. *European Journal of Social Psychology, 12*, 327–331. (p. 88)

Papastamou, S., & Mugny, G. (1990). Synchronic consistency and psychologization in minority influence. *European Journal of Social Psychology, 20*, 85–98. (p. 348)

Parachin, V. M. (1992, December). Four brave chaplains. *Retired Officer Magazine*, pp. 24–26. (p. 552)

Park, B., & Rothbart, M. (1982). Perception of out-group homogeneity and levels of social categorization: Memory for the subordinate attributes of ingroup and out-group members. *Journal of Personality and Social Psychology, 42*, 1051–1068. (p. 419)

Parke, R. D., Berkowitz, L., Leyens, J. P., West, S. G., & Sebastian, J. (1977). Some effects of violent and nonviolent movies on the behavior of juvenile delinquents. In L. Berkowitz (Ed.), *Advances in experimental social psychology* (Vol. 10). New York: Academic Press. (p. 467)

Pascarella, E. T., & Terenzini, P. T. (1991). *How collects affects students: Findings and insights from twenty years of research.* San Francisco: Jossey-Bass. (p. 335)

Patterson, G. R., Chamberlain, P., & Reid, J. B. (1982). A comparative evaluation of parent training procedures. *Behavior Therapy, 13*, 638–650. (p. 450)

Patterson, G. R., Littman, R. A., & Bricker, W. (1967). Assertive behavior in children: A step toward a theory of aggression. *Monographs of the Society of Research in Child Development* (Serial No. 113), *32*, 5. (p. 448)

Patterson, T. E. (1980). The role of the mass media in presidential campaigns: The lessons of the 1976 election. *Items, 34*, 25–30. Social Science Research Council, 605 Third Avenue, New York, N.Y. 10016. (p. 485)

Paulhus, D. (1982). Individual differences, self-presentation, and cognitive dissonance: Their concurrent operation in forced compliance. *Journal of Personality and Social Psychology, 43*, 838–852. (p. 145)

Paulhus, D. L., & Lim, D. T. K. (1994). Arousal and evaluative extremity in social judgments: A dynamic complexity model. *European Journal of Social Psychology, 24,* 89–99. (p. 112)

Pauling, L. (1962). Quoted by Etzioni, A. *The hard way to peace: A new strategy.* New York: Collier. (p. 579)

Paulus, P. B., Brown, V., & Ortega, A. H. (in press). Group creativity. In R. E. Purser & A. Montuori (Eds.), *Social creativity,* vol. 2. Cresskill, NJ: Hampton Press. (p. 346)

Paulus, P. B., Dzindolet, M. T., Poletes, G., & Camacho, L. M. (1993). Perception of performance in group brainstorming: The illusion of group productivity. *Personality and Social Psychology Bulletin, 19,* 78–89. (p. 346)

Pegalis, L. J., Shaffer, D. R., Bazzini, D. G., & Greenier, K. (1994). On the ability to elicit self-disclosure: Are there gender-based and contextual limitations on the opener effect? *Personality and Social Psychology Bulletin, 20,* 412–420. (p. 516)

Peng, Y., Zebrowitz, L. A., & Lee, H. K. (1993). The impact of cultural background and cross-cultural experience on impressions of American and Korean male speakers. *Journal of Cross-Cultural Psychology, 24,* 203–220. (p. 279)

Pennebaker, J. (1990). *Opening up: The healing power of confiding in others.* New York: William Morrow. (p. 479)

Pennebaker, J. W., & O'Heeron, R. C. (1984). Confiding in others and illness rate among spouses of suicide and accidental death victims. *Journal of Abnormal Psychology, 93,* 473–476. (p. 479)

Pennebaker, J. W., Rimé, B., & Sproul, G. (in press). Stereotypes of emotional expressiveness of northerners and southerners: A cross-cultural test of Montesquieu's hypotheses. *Journal of Personality and Social Psychology.* (p. 391)

Penner, L. A., Dertke, M. C., & Achenbach, C. J. (1973). The "flash" system: A field study of altruism. *Journal of Applied Social Psychology, 3,* 362–370. (p. 555)

Pennington, N., & Hastie, R. (1992). A theory of explanation-based decision making. In G. Klein & J. Orasanu (Eds.), *Decision making in complex worlds.* (p. 375)

Pennington, N., & Hastie, R. (1993). The story model for juror decision making. In R. Hastie (ed.), *Inside the juror: The psychology of juror decision making.* New York: Cambridge University Press. (p. 375)

Penrod, S., & Cutler, B. L. (1987). Assessing the competence of juries. In I. B. Weiner & A. K. Hess (Eds.), *Handbook of forensic psychology.* New York: Wiley. (p. 378)

Peplau, L. A., & Gordon, S. L. (1985). Women and men in love: Gender differences in close heterosexual relationships. In V. E. O'Leary, R. K. Unger, & B. S. Wallston (Eds.), *Women, gender, and social psychology.* Hillsdale, N.J.: Erlbaum. (p. 505)

Perdue, C. W., Dovidio, J. F., Gurtman, M. B., & Tyler, R. B. (1990). Us and them: Social categorization and the process of intergroup bias. *Journal of Personality and Social Psychology, 59,* 475–486. (p. 407)

Perkins, H. W. (1991). Religious commitment, Yuppie values, and well-being in post-collegiate life. *Review of Religious Research, 32,* 244–251. (p. 480)

Perlman, D., & Rook, K. S. (1987). Social support, social deficits, and the family: Toward the enhancement of well-being. In S. Oskamp (Ed.), *Family processes and problems: Social psychological aspects.* Newbury Park, CA: Sage. (p. 480)

Perloff, L. S. (1987). Social comparison and illusions of invulnerability. In C. R. Snyder & C. R. Ford (Eds.), *Coping with negative life events: Clinical and social psychological perspectives.* New York: Plenum. (p. 56)

Perls, F. S. (1972). Gestalt therapy [interview]. In A. Bry (Ed.), *Inside psychotherapy.* New York: Basic Books. (pp. 214, 472)

Perls, F. S. (1973). *Ego, hunger and aggression: The beginning of Gestalt therapy.* Random House, 1969. Cited by Berkowitz in The case for bottling up rage. *Psychology Today,* July, pp. 24–30. (pp. 214, 472)

Perrin, S., & Spencer, C. (1981). Independence or conformity in the Asch experiment as a reflection of cultural or situational factors. *British Journal of Social Psychology, 20,* 205–209. (p. 264)

Perry, L. C., Perry, D. G., & Weiss, R. J. (1986). Age differences in children's beliefs about whether altruism makes the actor feel good. *Social Cognition, 4,* 263–269. (p. 548)

Pessin, J. (1933). The comparative effects of social and mechanical stimulation on memorizing. *American Journal of Psychology, 45,* 263–270. (p. 315)

Pessin, J., & Husband, R. W. (1933). Effects of social stimulation on human maze learning. *Journal of Abnormal and Social Psychology, 28,* 148–154. (p. 315)

Peterson, B. E., Doty, R. M., & Winter, D. G. (1993). Authoritarianism and attitudes toward contemporary social issues. *Personality and Social Psychology Bulletin, 19,* 174–184. (p. 417)

Peterson, C., & Barrett, L. C. (1987). Explanatory style and academic performance among university freshmen. *Journal of Personality and Social Psychology, 53,* 603–607. (p. 48)

Peterson, C., Schwartz, S. M., & Seligman, M. E. P. (1981). Self-blame and depression symptoms. *Journal of Personality and Social Psychology, 41,* 253–259. (p. 62)

Peterson, C., & Seligman, M. E. P. (1987). Explanatory style and illness. *Journal of Personality, 55,* 237–265. (p. 183)

Peterson, C., Seligman, M. E. P., & Vaillant, G. E. (1988). Pessimistic explanatory style is a risk factor for physical illness: A thirty-five-year longitudinal study. *Journal of Personality and Social Psychology, 55,* 23–27. (p. 184)

Peterson, J. L., & Zill, N. (1981). Television viewing in the United States and children's intellectual, social, and emotional development. *Television and Children, 2*(2), 21–28. (p. 470)

Peterson, R. S., & Nemeth, C. J. (in press). Focus versus flexibility: Majority and minority influence can both improve performance. *Personality and Social Psychology Bulletin.* (p. 348)

Peto, R., Lopez, A. D., Boreham, J., Thun, M., & Heath, C., Jr. (1992). Mortality from tobacco in developed countries: Indirect estimation from national vital statistics. *Lancet, 339,* 1268–1278. (p. 124)

Pettigrew, T. F. (1958). Personality and socio-cultural factors in intergroup attitudes: A cross-national comparison. *Journal of Conflict Resolution, 2,* 29–42. (p. 409)

Pettigrew, T. F. (1969). Racially separate or together? *Journal of Social Issues, 2,* 43–69. (p. 587)

Pettigrew, T. F. (1978). Three issues in ethnicity: Boundaries, deprivations, and perceptions. In J. M. Yinger & S. J. Cutler (Eds.), *Major social issues: A mul-*

tidisciplinary view. New York: Free Press. (p. 413)

Pettigrew, T. F. (1979). The ultimate attribution error: Extending Allport's cognitive analysis of prejudice. *Personality and Social Psychology Bulletin,* **55,** 461–476. (p. 424)

Pettigrew, T. F. (1980). Prejudice. In S. Thernstrom et al. (Eds.), *Harvard encyclopedia of American ethnic groups.* Cambridge, Mass.: Harvard University Press. (p. 424)

Pettigrew, T. F. (1986). The intergroup contact hypothesis reconsidered. In M. Hewstone & R. Brown (Eds.), *Contact and conflict in intergroup encounters.* Oxford: Basil Blackwell. (p. 588)

Pettigrew, T. F. (1987, May 12). "Useful" modes of thought contribute to prejudice. *The New York Times,* pp. 17–20. (p. 396)

Pettigrew, T. F. (1988). Advancing racial justice: Past lessons for future use. Paper for the University of Alabama Conference: "Opening Doors: An Appraisal of Race Relations in America." (p. 588)

Pettigrew, T. F. (1995). The deprovincialization hypothesis: Generalized intergroup contact effects on prejudice. Unpublished manuscript, University of California, Santa Cruz. (p. 588)

Pettigrew, T. F., & Meertens, R. W. (1995). Subtle and blatant prejudice in western Europe. *European Journal of Social Psychology,* **25,** 57–76. (pp. 395, 413)

Pettingale, K. W., Morris, T., Greer, S., & Haybittle, J. L. (1985, March 30). Mental attitudes to cancer: An additional prognostic factor. *Lancet,* p. 750. (p. 184)

Petty, R. E. (1994). Two routes to persuasion: State of the art. In G. d'Ydewalle, P. Eelen, & P. Berteleson (Eds.), *International pspectives on psychological science,* vol. 2. Hillsdale, NJ: Erlbaum. (p. 274)

Petty, R. E., & Cacioppo, J. T. (1977). Forewarning cognitive responding, and resistance to persuasion. *Journal of Personality and Social Psychology,* **35,** 645–655. (p. 294)

Petty, R. E., & Cacioppo, J. T. (1979). Effects of forewarning of persuasive intent and involvement on cognitive response and persuasion. *Personality and Social Psychology Bulletin,* **5,** 173–176. *(a)* (pp. 284, 294)

Petty, R. E., & Cacioppo, J. T. (1979). Issue involvement can increase or decrease persuasion by enhancing message-relevant cognitive responses. *Journal of Personality and Social Psychology,* **37,** 1915–1926. *(b)* (p. 284)

Petty, R. E., & Cacioppo, J. T. (1986). *Communication and persuasion: Central and peripheral routes to attitude change.* New York: Springer-Verlag. (p. 274)

Petty, R. E., & Cacioppo, J. T. (1986). The elaboration likelihood model of persuasion. In L. Berkowitz (Ed.), *Advances in experimental social psychology,* Vol. 19. New York: Academic Press. (p. 274)

Petty, R. E., Cacioppo, J. T., & Goldman, R. (1981). Personal involvement as a determinant of argument-based persuasion. *Journal of Personality and Social Psychology,* **41,** 847–855. (pp. 143, 281, 295)

Petty, R. E., Gleicher, F., & Baker, S. M. (1991). Multiple roles for affect in persuasion. In J. Forgas (Ed.), *Emotion and social judgments.* London: Pergamon. (p. 281)

Petty, R. E., Haugtvedt, C. P., & Smith, S. M. (1995). Elaboration as a determinant of attitude strength: Creating attitudes that are persistent, resistant, and predictive of behavior. In R. E. Petty & J. A. Krosnick (Eds.), *Attitude strength: Antecedents and consequences.* Hillsdale, NJ: Erlbaum. (p. 275)

Petty, R. E. & Krosnick, J. A. (Eds.). (1995). *Attitude strength: Antecedents and consequences.* Hillsdale, NJ: Erlbaum. (p. 274)

Petty, R. E., Ostrom, T. M., & Brock, T. C. (Eds.). (1981). *Cognitive responses in persuasion.* Hillsdale, N.J.: Erlbaum. (p. 143)

Petty, R. E., Schumann, D. W., Richman, S. A., & Strathman, A. J. (1993). Positive mood and persuasion: Different roles for affect under high and low elaboration conditions. *Journal of Personality and Social Psychology,* **64,** 5–20. (p. 281)

Phillips, D. P. (1982). The impact of fictional television stories on U.S. adult fatalities: New evidence on the effect of the mass media on violence. *American Journal of Sociology,* **87,** 1340–1359. (p. 236)

Phillips, D. P. (1985). Natural experiments on the effects of mass media violence on fatal aggression: Strengths and weaknesses of a new approach. In L. Berkowitz (Ed.), *Advances in experimental social psychology,* Vol. 19. Orlando, Fla.: Academic Press. (p. 236)

Phillips, D. P., Carstensen, L. L., & Paight, D. J. (1989). Effects of mass media news stories on suicide, with new evidence on the role of story content. In D. R. Pfeffer (Ed.), *Suicide among youth: Perspectives on risk and prevention.* Washington, DC: American Psychiatric Press. (p. 236)

Piliavin, I. M., Rodin, J., & Piliavin, J. A. (1969). Good Samaritanism: An underground phenomenon. *Journal of Personality and Social Psychology,* **13,** 289–299. (p. 543)

Piliavin, J. A., Evans, D. E., & Callero, P. (1982). Learning to "Give to unnamed strangers": The process of commitment to regular blood donation. In E. Staub, D. Bar-Tal, J. Karylowski, & J. Reykawski (Eds.), *The development and maintenance of prosocial behavior: International perspectives.* New York: Plenum. (pp. 528, 562)

Piliavin, J. A., & Piliavin, I. M. (1973). The Good Samaritan: Why *does* he help? Unpublished manuscript, University of Wisconsin. (p. 528)

Platz, S. J., & Hosch, H. M. (1988). Cross-racial/ethnic eyewitness identification: A field study. *Journal of Applied Social Psychology,* **18,** 972–984. (p. 420)

Pleck, J. H., Sonenstein, F. L., & Ku, L. C. (1993). Masculinity ideology: Its impact on adolescent males' heterosexual relationships. *Journal of Social Issues,* **49,** 11–29. (p. 201)

Pliner, P., Hart, H., Kohl, J., & Saari, D. (1974). Compliance without pressure: Some further data on the foot-in-the-door technique. *Journal of Experimental Social Psychology,* **10,** 17–22. (p. 137)

Plous, S. (1985). Perceptual illusions and military realities: A social-psychological analysis of the nuclear arms race. *Journal of Conflict Resolution,* **29,** 363–389. (p. 583)

Plous, S. (1993). The nuclear arms race: Prisoner's dilemma or perceptual dilemma? *Journal of Peace Research,* **30,** 163–179. (p. 583)

Pomazal, R. J., & Clore, G. L. (1973). Helping on the highway: The effects of dependency and sex. *Journal of Applied Social Psychology,* **3,** 150–164. (p. 555)

Pomerleau, O. F., & Rodin, J. (1986). Behavioral medicine and health psychology. In S. L. Garfield & A. E. Bergin (Eds.), *Handbook of psychotherapy and behavior change,* 3rd ed. New York: Wiley. (p. 48)

Poole, D. A., Lindsay, D. S., Memon, A., & Bull, R. (1995). Psychotherapy and the recovery of memories of childhood sexual abuse: U.S. and British practitioners' opinions, practices, and experiences. *Journal of Consulting and Clinical Psychology, 63,* 426–437. (p. 168)

Popenoe, D. (1993). The evolution of marriage and the problem of stepfamilies: A biosocial perspective. Paper presented at the National Symposium on Stepfamilies, Pennsylvania State University. (p. 216)

Porter, N., Geis, F. L., & Jennings (Walstedt), J. (1983). Are women invisible as leaders? *Sex Roles, 9,* 1035–1049. (p. 397)

Powell, J. (1989). *Happiness is an inside job.* Valencia, CA: Tabor. (p. 52)

Pozo, C., Carver, C. S., Wellens, A. R., & Scheier, M. F. (1991). Social anxiety and social perception: Construing others' reactions to the self. *Personality and Social Psychology Bulletin, 17,* 355–362. (p. 180)

Prager, I. G., & Cutler, B. L. (1990). Attributing traits to oneself and to others: The role of acquaintance level. *Personality and Social Psychology Bulletin, 16,* 309–319. (p. 85)

Pratkanis, A. R., Greenwald, A. G., Leippe, M. R., & Baumgardner, M. H. (1988). In search of reliable persuasion effects: III. The sleeper effect is dead. Long live the sleeper effect. *Journal of Personality and Social Psychology, 54,* 203–218. (p. 277)

Pratkanis, A. R., & Turner, M. E. (1994a). The year cool Papa Bell lost the batting title: Mr. Branch Rickey and Mr. Jackie Robinson's plea for affirmative action. *Nine: A Journal of Baseball History and Social Policy Perspectives, 2,* 260–276. (p. 594)

Pratkanis, A. R., & Turner, M. E. (1994b). Nine principles of successful affirmative action: Mr. Branch Rickey, Mr. Jackie Robinson, and the integration of baseball. *Nine: A Journal of Baseball History and Social Policy Perspectives, 3,* 36–65. (p. 594)

Pratt, M. W., Pancer, M., Hunsberger, B., & Manchester, J. (1990). Reasoning about the self and relationships in maturity: An integrative complexity analysis of individual differences. *Journal of Personality and Social Psychology, 59,* 575–581. (p. 208)

Pratto, F., Sidanius, J., Stallworth, L. M., & Malle, B. F. (1994). Social dominance orientation: A personality variable predicting social and political attitudes. *Journal of Personality and Social Psychology, 67,* 741–763. (p. 416)

Prentice-Dunn, S., & Rogers, R. W. (1980). Effects of deindividuating situational cues and aggressive models on subjective deindividuation and aggression. *Journal of Personality and Social Psychology, 39,* 104–113. (p. 331)

Prentice-Dunn, S., & Rogers, R. W. (1989). Deindividuation and the self-regulation of behavior. In P. B. Paulus (Ed.), *Psychology of group influence,* 2nd ed. Hillsdale, N.J.: Erlbaum. (p. 331)

Price, G. H., Dabbs, J. M., Jr., Clower, B. J., & Resin, R. P. (1979). At first glance—Or, is physical attractiveness more than skin deep? Paper presented at the Eastern Psychological Association convention, 1974. Cited by K. L. Dion & K. K. Dion. Personality and behavioral correlates of romantic love. In M. Cook & G. Wilson (Eds.), *Love and attraction.* Oxford: Pergamon. (p. 492)

Prohaska, V. (1994). "I know I'll get an A": Confident overestimation of final course grades. *Teaching of Psychology, 21,* 141–143. (p. 57)

Prothrow-Stith, D. (with M. Wiessman) (1991). *Deadly consequences.* New York: HarperCollins. (p. 597)

Pruitt, D. G. (1981). Kissinger as a traditional mediator with power. In J. Z. Rubin (Ed.), *Dynamics of third party intervention: Kissinger in the Middle East.* New York: Praeger. *(a)* (pp. 596, 599)

Pruitt, D. G. (1981). *Negotiation behavior.* New York: Academic Press. *(b)* (p. 596)

Pruitt, D. G. (1986, July). Trends in the scientific study of negotiation. *Negotiation Journal,* pp. 237–244. (pp. 596, 600)

Pruitt, D. G. (1986). Achieving integrative agreements in negotiation. In R. K. White (Ed.), *Psychology and the prevention of nuclear war.* New York: New York University Press. (pp. 596, 600)

Pruitt, D. G., & Kimmel, M. J. (1977). Twenty years of experimental gaming: Critique, synthesis, and suggestions for the future. *Annual Review of Psychology, 28,* 363–392. (p. 576)

Pruitt, D. G., & Lewis, S. A. (1975). Development of integrative solutions in bilateral negotiation. *Journal of Personality and Social Psychology, 31,* 621–633. (p. 596)

Pruitt, D. G., & Lewis, S. A. (1977). The psychology of integrative bargaining. In D. Druckman (Ed.), *Negotiations: A social-psychological analysis.* New York: Halsted. (p. 596)

Pruitt, D. G., & Rubin, J. Z. (1986). *Social conflict.* San Francisco: Random House. (p. 576)

Pryor, J. B. (1987). Sexual harassment proclivities in men. *Sex Roles, 17,* 269–290. (p. 461)

Public Opinion (1984, August/September). Vanity fare, p. 22. (pp. 54, 55)

Purvis, J. A., Dabbs, Jr., J. M., & Hopper, C. H. (1984). The "opener": Skilled user of facial expression and speech pattern. *Personality and Social Psychology Bulletin, 10,* 61–66. (p. 516)

Pyszczynski, T., & Greenberg, J. (1987). Self-regulatory perseveration and the depressive self-focusing style: A self-awareness theory of reactive depression. *Psychological Bulletin, 102,* 122–138. (p. 67)

Pyszczynski, T., Greenberg, J., & Holt, K. (1985). Maintaining consistency between self-serving beliefs and available data: A bias in information evaluation. *Personality and Social Psychology Bulletin, 11,* 179–190. (p. 59)

Pyszczynski, T., Hamilton, J. C., Greenberg, J., & Becker, S. E. (1991). Self-awareness and psychological dysfunction. In C. R. Snyder & D. O. Forsyth (Eds.), *Handbook of social and clinical psychology: The health perspective.* New York: Pergamon. (pp. 176–177)

Quattrone, G. A. (1982). Behavioral consequences of attributional bias. *Social Cognition, 1,* 358–378. (p. 86)

Quattrone, G. A., & Jones, E. E. (1980). The perception of variability within in-groups and out-groups: Implications for the law of small numbers. *Journal of Personality and Social Psychology, 38,* 141–152. (p. 422)

Rachlinski, J. (1990). Prospect theory and civil negotiation. Working paper No. 17. Stanford Center on Conflict and Negotiation, Stanford University. (p. 357)

Radecki, T. (1989, February–March). On picking good television and film entertainment. *NCTV NEWS, 10*(1–2), pp. 5–6. (p. 468)

Rajecki, D. W., Bledsoe, S. B., & Rasmussen, J. L. (1991). Successful personal ads: Gender differences and similarities in offers, stipulations, and outcomes. *Basic and Applied Social Psychology, 12,* 457–469. (p. 487)

Ramirez, A. (1988). Racism toward Hispanics: The culturally monolithic society. In P. A. Katz & D. A. Taylor (Eds.) *Eliminating racism: Profiles in controversy.* New York: Plenum. (p. 396)

Rank, S. G., & Jacobson, C. K. (1977). Hospital nurses' compliance with medication overdose orders: A failure to replicate. *Journal of Health and Social Behavior,* **18,** 188–193. (p. 245)

Rapoport, A. (1960). *Fights, games, and debates.* Ann Arbor: University of Michigan Press. (p. 569)

Rappoport, L., & Kren, G. (1993). Amoral rescuers: The ambiguities of altruism. *Creativity Research Journal,* **6,** 129–136. (p. 563)

Rawls, J. (1971). *A theory of justice.* Cambridge, MA: Belknap Press of Harvard University Press. (p. 581)

RCAgenda (1979). November-December, p. 11. 475 Riverside Drive, New York, N.Y. 10027. (p. 390)

Reed, D. (1989, November 25). Video collection documents Christian resistance to Hitler. Associated Press release in *Grand Rapids Press,* pp. B4, B5. (p. 404)

Reeder, G. D., Fletcher, G. J., & Furman, K. (1989). The role of observers' expectations in attitude attribution. *Journal of Experimental Social Psychology,* **25,** 168–188. (p. 87)

Reeder, G. D., McCormick, C. B., & Esselman, E. D. (1987). Self-reference processing and recall of prose. *Journal of Educational Psychology,* **79,** 243–248. (p. 39)

Regan, D. T., & Cheng, J. B. (1973). Distraction and attitude change: A resolution. *Journal of Experimental Social Psychology,* **9,** 138–147. (p. 294)

Regan, D. T., & Fazio, R. (1977). On the consistency between attitudes and behavior: Look to the method of attitude formation. *Journal of Experimental Social Psychology,* **13,** 28–45. (p. 130)

Regan, D. T., Williams, M., & Sparling, S. (1972). Voluntary expiation of guilt: A field experiment. *Journal of Personality and Social Psychology,* **24,** 42–45. (p. 548)

Reifman, A. S., Larrick, R. P., & Fein, S. (1991). Temper and temperature on the diamond: The heat-aggression relationship in major league baseball. *Personality and Social Psychology Bulletin,* **17,** 580–585. (p. 454)

Reis, H. T., Nezlek, J., & Wheeler, L. (1980). Physical attractiveness in social interaction. *Journal of Personality and Social Psychology,* **38,** 604–617. (p. 486)

Reis, H. T., & Shaver, P. (1988). Intimacy as an interpersonal process. In S. Duck (Ed.), *Handbook of personal relationships: Theory, relationships and interventions.* Chichester, England: Wiley. (p. 516)

Reis, H. T., Wheeler, L., Spiegel, N., Kernis, M. H., Nezlek, J., & Perri, M. (1982). Physical attractiveness in social interaction: II. Why does appearance affect social experience? *Journal of Personality and Social Psychology,* **43,** 979–996. (p. 486)

Reis, T. J., Gerrard, M., & Gibbons, F. X. (1993). Social comparison and the pill: Reactions to upward and downward comparison of contraceptive behavior. *Personality and Social Psychology Bulletin,* **19,** 13–20. (p. 448)

Reisenzein, R. (1983). The Schachter theory of emotion: Two decades later. *Psychological Bulletin,* **94,** 239–264. (p. 457)

Reiss, A. J., Jr., & Roth, J. A. (Eds.) (1993). *Understanding and preventing violence.* Washington, D.C.: National Academy Press. (p. 441)

Reitzes, D. C. (1953). The role of organizational structures: Union versus neighborhood in a tension situation. *Journal of Social Issues,* **9**(1), 37–44. (p. 409)

Remley, A. (1988, October). From obedience to independence. *Psychology Today,* pp. 56–59. (p. 217)

Renaud, H., & Estess, F. (1961). Life history interviews with one hundred normal American males: "Pathogenecity" of childhood. *American Journal of Orthopsychiatry,* **31,** 786–802. (p. 168)

Ressler, R. K., Burgess, A. W., & Douglas, J. E. (1988). *Sexual homicide patterns.* Boston: Lexington Books. (p. 460)

Reychler, L. (1979). The effectiveness of a pacifist strategy in conflict resolution. *Journal of Conflict Resolution,* **23,** 228–260. (p. 571)

Rhine, R. J., & Severance, L. J. (1970). Ego-involvement, discrepancy, source credibility, and attitude change. *Journal of Personality and Social Psychology,* **16,** 175–190. (p. 284)

Rhodes, N., & Wood, W. (1992). Self-esteem and intelligence affect influenceability: The mediating role of message reception. *Psychological Bulletin,* **111,** 156–171. (p. 292)

Rhodewalt, F. (1987). Is self-handicapping an effective self-protective attributional strategy? Paper presented at the American Psychological Association convention. (p. 67)

Rhodewalt, F., & Agustsdottir, S. (1986). Effects of self-presentation on the phenomenal self. *Journal of Personality and Social Psychology,* **50,** 47–55. (p. 186)

Rhodewalt, F., Saltzman, A. T., & Wittmer J. (1984). Self-handicapping among competitive athletes: The role of practice in self-esteem protection. *Basic and Applied Social Psychology,* **5,** 197–209. (p. 67)

Rholes, W. S., Newman, L. S., & Ruble, D. N. (1990). Understanding self and other: Developmental and motivational aspects of perceiving persons in terms of invariant dispositions. In E. T. Higgins & R. M. Sorrentino (Eds.), *Handbook of motivation and cognition: Foundations of social behavior,* Vol. 2. New York: Guilford. (p. 85)

Rice, B. (1985, September). Performance review: The job nobody likes. *Psychology Today,* pp. 30–36. (p. 54)

Rice, M. E., & Grusec, J. E. (1975). Saying and doing: Effects on observer performance. *Journal of Personality and Social Psychology,* **32,** 584–593. (p. 546)

Richardson, L. F. (1960). Generalized foreign policy. *British Journal of Psychology Monographs Supplements,* 1969, **23.** Cited by A. Rapoport in *Fights, games, and debates.* Ann Arbor: University of Michigan Press. p. 15. (p. 568)

Riess, M., Rosenfeld, P., Melburg, V., & Tedeschi, J. T. (1981). Self-serving attributions: Biased private perceptions and distorted public descriptions. *Journal of Personality and Social Psychology,* **41,** 224–231. (p. 68)

Riggs, J. M. (1992). Self-handicapping and achievement. In A. K. Boggiano & T. S. Pittman (Eds.), *Achievement and motivation: A social-developmental perspective.* New York: Cambridge University Press. (p. 67)

Riordan, C. A. (1980). Effects of admission of influence on attributions and attraction. Paper presented at the American Psychological Association convention. (p. 513)

Riordan, C. A., & Ruggiero, J. (1980). Producing equal status interracial interaction: A replication. *Social Psychology Quarterly,* **43,** 131–136. (p. 589)

Robberson, M. R., & Rogers, R. W. (1988). Beyond fear appeals: Negative and positive persuasive appeals to health and self-esteem. *Journal of Applied Social Psychology,* **18,** 277–287. (p. 282)

Robertson, I. (1987). *Sociology*. New York: Worth Publishers. (p. 194)

Robinson, J. P. (1988, December). Who's doing the housework? *American Demographics*, pp. 24–28, 63. (p. 224)

Robinson, R. J., Keltner, D., & Ross, L. (1991). Misconstruing the views of the "other side": Real and perceived differences in three ideological conflicts. Working Paper No. 18, Stanford Center on Conflict and Negotiation, Stanford University. (p. 585)

Rochat, F. (1993). How did they resist authority? Protecting refugees in Le Chambon during World War II. Paper presented at the American Psychological Association convention. (p. 249)

Rodgers, K. (1994, Autumn). Wife assault in Canada (report of a survey by Statistics Canada). *Canadian Social Trends*, pp. 2–8. (p. 436)

Rodin, J. (1992). *Body traps*. New York: William Morrow. (p. 182)

Roese, N. J. (1994). The functional basis of counterfactual thinking. *Journal of Personality and Social Psychology*, **66**, 805–818. (p. 106)

Roese, N. J., & Olson, J. M. (1995). Counterfactual thinking: A critical overview. In N. J. Roese & J. M. Olson (eds.), *What might have been: The social psychology of counterfactual thinking*. Hillsdale, NJ: Erlbaum. (p. 106)

Rogers, C. R. (1958). Reinhold Niebuhr's *The self and the dramas of history*: A criticism. *Pastoral Psychology*, **9**, 15–17. (p. 52)

Rogers, C. R. (1980). *A way of being*. Boston: Houghton Mifflin. (p. 516)

Rogers, R. W., & Mewborn, C. R. (1976). Fear appeals and attitude change: Effects of a threat's noxiousness, probability of occurrence, and the efficacy of coping responses. *Journal of Personality and Social Psychology*, **34**, 54–61. (p. 282)

Rogers, R. W., & Prentice-Dunn, S. (1981). Deindividuation and anger-mediated interracial aggression: Unmasking regressive racism. *Journal of Personality and Social Psychology*, **41**, 63–73. (pp. 394, 395)

Rohrer, J. H., Baron, S. H., Hoffman, E. L., & Swander, D. V. (1954). The stability of autokinetic judgments. *Journal of Abnormal and Social Psychology*, **49**, 595–597. (p. 236)

Rokeach, M. (1968). *Beliefs, attitudes, and values*. San Francisco: Jossey-Bass. (p. 494)

Rokeach, M., & Mezei, L. (1966). Race

and shared beliefs as factors in social choice. *Science*, **151**, 167–172. (p. 418)

Romer, D., Gruder, D. L., & Lizzadro, T. (1986). A person-situation approach to altruistic behavior. *Journal of Personality and Social Psychology*, **51**, 1001–1012. (p. 552)

Rook, K. S. (1984). Promoting social bonding: Strategies for helping the lonely and socially isolated. *American Psychologist*, **39**, 1389–1407. (p. 178)

Rook, K. S. (1987). Social support versus companionship: Effects on life stress, loneliness, and evaluations by others. *Journal of Personality and Social Psychology*, **52**, 1132–1147. (p. 479)

Rosenbaum, M. E. (1986). The repulsion hypothesis: On the nondevelopment of relationships. *Journal of Personality and Social Psychology*, **51**, 1156–1166. (p. 494)

Rosenbaum, M. E., & Holtz, R. (1985). The minimal intergroup discrimination effect: Out-group derogation, not in-group favorability. Paper presented at the American Psychological Association convention. (p. 408)

Rosenberg, L. A. (1961). Group size, prior experience and conformity. *Journal of Abnormal and Social Psychology*, **63**, 436–437. (p. 253)

Rosenblatt, A., & Greenberg, J. (1988). Depression and interpersonal attraction: The role of perceived similarity. *Journal of Personality and Social Psychology*, **55**, 112–119. (p. 496)

Rosenblatt, R. (1993, December 21). The 11th commandment. *Family Circle*, pp. 30–32, 45. (p. 58)

Rosenblatt, R. (1994, April 24). The buck stops somewhere else. *Detroit Free Press Magazine*, pp. 6–13. (p. 124)

Rosenfeld, D. (1979). The relationship between self-esteem and egotism in males and females. Unpublished manuscript, Southern Methodist University. (p. 62)

Rosenfeld, D., Folger, R., & Adelman, H. F. (1980). When rewards reflect competence: A qualification of the over-justification effect. *Journal of Personality and Social Psychology*, **39**, 368–376. (p. 155)

Rosenhan, D. L. (1970). The natural socialization of altruistic autonomy. In J. Macaulay & L. Berkowitz (Eds.) *Altruism and helping behavior*. New York: Academic Press. (p. 561)

Rosenhan, D. L. (1973). On being sane in insane places. *Science*, **179**, 250–258. (p. 166)

Rosenthal, R. (1985). From unconscious experimenter bias to teacher expectancy effects. In J. B. Dusek, V. C. Hall, & W. J. Meyer (Eds.), *Teacher expectancies*. Hillsdale, N.J.: Erlbaum. (p. 114)

Rosenthal, R. (1991). Teacher expectancy effects: A brief update 25 years after the Pygmalion experiment. *Journal of Research in Education*, **1**, 3–12. (p. 115)

Rosenthal, R., & Jacobson, L. (1968). *Pygmalion in the classroom: Teacher expectation and pupils' intellectual development*. New York: Holt, Rinehart & Winston. (p. 115)

Rosenzweig, M. R. (1972). Cognitive dissonance. *American Psychologist*, **27**, 769. (p. 141)

Ross, C. (1979, February 12). Rejected. *New West*, pp. 39–43. (p. 101)

Ross, L. (1977). The intuitive psychologist and his shortcomings: Distortions in the attribution process. In L. Berkowitz (Ed.), *Advances in experimental social psychology* (Vol. 10). New York: Academic Press. (p. 80)

Ross, L. (1981). The "intuitive scientist" formulation and its developmental implications. In J. H. Havell & L. Ross (Eds.), *Social cognitive development: Frontiers and possible futures*. Cambridge, England: Cambridge University Press. (pp. 38, 85)

Ross, L. (1988). Situationist perspectives on the obedience experiments. Review of A. G. Miller's *The obedience experiments*. *Contemporary Psychology*, **33**, 101–104. (p. 240)

Ross, L. Amabile, T. M., & Steinmetz, J. L. (1977). Social roles, social control, and biases in social-perception processes. *Journal of Personality and Social Psychology*, **35**, 485–494. (p. 82)

Ross, L. & Anderson, C. A. (1982). Shortcomings in the attribution process: On the origins and maintenance of erroneous social assessments. In D. Kahneman, P. Slovic, & A. Tversky (Eds.), *Judgment under uncertainty: Heuristics and biases*. New York: Cambridge University Press. (p. 94)

Ross, L. & Lepper, M. R. (1980). The perseverance of beliefs: Empirical and normative considerations. In R. A. Shweder (Ed.), *New directions for methodology of behavioral science: Fallible judgment in behavioral research*. San Francisco: Jossey-Bass. (p. 95)

Ross, L., & Ward, A. (1995). Psychological barriers to dispute resolution. In M. P. Zanna (ed.), *Advances in experimental social psychology*, vol. 27. San Diego: Academic Press. (pp. 597, 598)

Ross, M., & Buehler, R. (1994). Creative remembering. In U. Neisser & R. Fivush (eds.), *The remembering self.* New York: Cambridge University Press. (p. 96)

Ross, M., & Fletcher, G. J. O. (1985). Attribution and social perception. In G. Lindzey & E. Aronson (Eds.), *The Handbook of Social Psychology*, 3rd ed. New York: Random House. (p. 112)

Ross, M., McFarland, C., & Fletcher, G. J. O. (1981). The effect of attitude on the recall of personal histories. *Journal of Personality and Social Psychology*, **40**, 627–634. (p. 98)

Ross, M., & Sicoly, F. (1979). Egocentric biases in availability and attribution. *Journal of Personality and Social Psychology*, **37**, 322–336. (pp. 53, 60)

Ross, M., Thibaut, J., & Evenbeck, S. (1971). Some determinants of the intensity of social protest. *Journal of Experimental Social Psychology*, **7**, 401–418. (p. 580)

Rossi, A. S., & Rossi, P. H. (1993). *Of human bonding: Parent-child relations across the life course.* Hawthorne, NY: Aldine de Gruyter. (p. 197)

Roszell, P., Kennedy, D., & Grabb, E. (1990). Physical attractiveness and income attainment among Canadians. *Journal of Psychology*, **123**, 547–559. (p. 489)

Rothbart, M., & Birrell, P. (1977). Attitude and perception of faces. *Journal of Research Personality*, **11**, 209–215. (p. 93)

Rothbart, M., Fulero, S., Jensen, C., Howard, J., & Birrell, P. (1978). From individual to group impressions: Availability heuristics in stereotype formation. *Journal of Experimental Social Psychology*, **14**, 237–255. (p. 422)

Rothbart, M., & John, O. P. (1985). Social categorization and behavioral episodes: A cognitive analysis of the effects of intergroup contact. *Journal of Social Issues*, **41**(3), 81–104. (p. 428)

Rothbart, M., & Lewis, S. (1988). Inferring category attributes from exemplar attributes: Geometric shapes and social categories. *Journal of Personality and Social Psychology*, **55**, 861–872. (p. 428)

Rothbart, M., & Park, B. (1986). On the confirmability and disconfirmability of trait concepts. *Journal of Personality and Social Psychology*, **50**, 131–142. (p. 428)

Rothbart, M., & Taylor, M. (1992). Social categories and social reality. In G. R. Semin & K. Fielder (eds.), *Language, interaction and social cognition.* London: Sage. (p. 268)

Rotter, J. (1973). Internal-external locus of control scale. In J. P. Robinson & R. P. Shaver (Eds.), *Measures of social psychological attitudes.* Ann Arbor: Institute for Social Research. (p. 47)

Rotton, J., & Frey, J. (1985). Air pollution, weather, and violent crimes: Concomitant time-series analysis of archival data. *Journal of Personality and Social Psychology*, **49**, 1207–1220. (pp. 453, 454)

Rouhana, N. N., & Kelman, H. C. (1994). Promoting joint thinking in international conflicts: An Israeli-Palestinian continuing workshop. *Journal of Social Issues*, **50**, 157–178. (p. 599)

Rowe, D. C., Vazsonyi, A. T., & Flannery, D. J. (1994). No more than skin deep: Ethnic and racial similarity in developmental process. *Psychological Review*, **101**, 396–413. (p. 32)

Ruback, R. B., Carr, T. S., & Hoper, C. H. (1986). Perceived control in prison: Its relation to reported crowding, stress, and symptoms. *Journal of Applied Social Psychology*, **16**, 375–386. (p. 49)

Rubin, J. Z. (1986). Can we negotiate with terrorists: Some answers from psychology. Paper presented at the American Psychological Association convention. (p. 449)

Rubin, J. Z. (1989). Some wise and mistaken assumptions about conflict and negotiation. *Journal of Social Issues*, **45**, 195–209. (pp. 599–600)

Rubin, J. Z. (Ed.) (1981). *Third party intervention in conflict: Kissinger in the Middle East.* New York: Praeger. (p. 603)

Rubin, L. B. (1985). *Just friends: The role of friendship in our lives.* New York: Harper & Row. (p. 198)

Rubin, R. B. (1981). Ideal traits and terms of address for male and female college professors. *Journal of Personality and Social Psychology*, **41**, 966–974. (p. 203)

Rubin, Z. (1970). Measurement of romantic love. *Journal of Personality and Social Psychology*, **16**, 265–273. (p. 500)

Rubin, Z. (1973). *Liking and loving: An invitation to social psychology.* New York: Holt, Rinehart and Winston. (pp. 500, 520)

Ruehlman, L. S., & Wolchik, S. A. (1988). Personal goals and interpersonal support and hindrance as factors in psychological distress and well-being. *Journal of Personality and Social Psychology*, **55**, 293–301. (p. 480)

Rule, B. G., Taylor, B. R., & Dobbs, A. R. (1987). Priming ffects of heat on aggressive thoughts. *Social Cognition*, **5**, 131–143. (p. 454)

Rusbult, C. E. (1980). Commitment and satisfaction in romantic associations: A test of the investment model. *Journal of Experimental Social Psychology*, **16**, 172–186. (p. 512)

Rusbult, C. E., Johnson, D. J., & Morrow, G. D. (1986). Impact of couple patterns of problem solving on distress and nondistress in dating relationships. *Journal of Personality and Social Psychology*, **50**, 744–753. (p. 520)

Rusbult, C. E., Morrow, G. D., & Johnson, D. J. (1987). Self-esteem and problem-solving behaviour in close relationships. *British Journal of Social Psychology*, **26**, 293–303. (p. 520)

Rushton, J. P. (1975). Generosity in children: Immediate and long-term effects of modeling, preaching, and moral judgment. *Journal of Personality and Social Psychology*, **31**, 459–466. (p. 546)

Rushton, J. P. (1976). Socialization and the altruistic behavior of children. *Psychological Bulletin*, **83**, 898–913. (pp. 440, 549)

Rushton, J. P. (1991). Is altruism innate? *Psychological Inquiry*, **2**, 141–143. (p. 537)

Rushton, J. P., Brainerd, C. J., & Pressley, M. (1983). Behavioral development and construct validity: The principle of aggregation. *Psychological Bulletin*, **94**, 18–38. (p. 262)

Rushton, J. P., & Campbell, A. C. (1977). Modeling, vicarious reinforcement and extraversion on blood donating in adults: Immediate and long-term effects. *European Journal of Social Psychology*, **7**, 297–306. (p. 546)

Rushton, J. P., Chrisjohn, R. D., & Fekken, G. C. (1981). The altruistic personality and the self-report altruism scale. *Personality and Individual Differences*, **2**, 293–302. (p. 552)

Rushton, J. P., Russell, R. J. H., & Wells, P. A. (1984). Genetic similarity theory: Beyond kin selection. *Behavior Genetics*, **14**, 179–193. (p. 536)

Russell, B. (1930/1980). *The conquest of happiness.* London: Unwin Paperbacks. (p. 486)

Russell, G. W. (1983). Psychological issues in sports aggression. In J. H. Goldstein (Ed.), *Sports violence.* New York: Springer-Verlag. (p. 473)

Ruvolo, A., & Markus, H. (1992). Possible selves and performance: The power of self-relevant imagery. *Social Cognition, 9,* 95–124. (p. 46)

Ruzzene, M., & Noller, P. (1986). Feedback motivation and reactions to personality interpretations that differ in favorability and accuracy. *Journal of Personality and Social Psychology, 51,* 1293–1299. (p. 69)

Ryckman, R. M., Robbins, M. A., Kaczor, L. M., & Gold J. A. (1989). Male and female raters' stereotyping of male and female physiques. *Personality and Social Psychology Bulletin, 15,* 244–251. (p. 25)

Saad, L., & McAneny, L. (1994, April). Most Americans think religion losing clout in the 1990's. *Gallup Poll Monthly,* pp. 2–4. (p. 469)

Saal, F. E., Johnson, C. B., & Weber, N. (1989). Friendly or sexy? It may depend on whom you ask. *Psychology of Women Quarterly, 13,* 263–276. (p. 75)

Sabini, J., & Silver, M. (1982). *Moralities of everyday life.* New York: Oxford University Press. (p. 250)

Sacco, W. P., & Dunn, V. K. (1990). Effect of actor depression on observer attributions: Existence and impact of negative attributions toward the depressed. *Journal of Personality and Social Psychology, 59,* 517–524. (p. 175)

Sacks, C. H., & Bugental, D. P. (1987). Attributions as moderators of affective and behavioral responses to social failure. *Journal of Personality and Social Psychology, 53,* 939–947. (p. 176)

Sadalla, E. K., Kenrick, D. T., & Vershure, B. (1987). Dominance and heterosexual attraction. *Journal of Personality and Social Psychology, 52,* 730–738. (p. 490)

Saks, M. J. (1974). Ignorance of science is no excuse. *Trial, 10*(6), 18–20. (p. 382)

Saks, M. J. (1977). *Jury verdicts.* Lexington, Mass.: Heath. (p. 382)

Saks, M. J., & Hastie, R. (1978). *Social psychology in court.* New York: Van Nostrand Reinhold. (pp. 357, 367, 378)

Sakurai, M. M. (1975). Small group cohesiveness and detrimental conformity. *Sociometry, 38,* 340–357. (p. 255)

Sales, S. M. (1972). Economic threat as a determinant of conversion rates in authoritarian and nonauthoritarian churches. *Journal of Personality and Social Psychology, 23,* 420–428. (p. 301)

Sales, S. M. (1973). Threat as a factor in authoritarianism: An analysis of archival data. *Journal of Personality and Social Psychology, 28,* 44–57. (p. 416)

Salovey, P., Mayer, J. D., & Rosenhan, D. L. (1991). Mood and healing: Mood as a motivator of helping and helping as a regulator of mood. In M. S. Clark (Ed.), *Prosocial behavior.* Newbury Park, CA: Sage. (p. 550)

Saltzman, A. (1991, June 17). Trouble at the top. *U.S. News & World Report,* pp. 40–48. (p. 222)

Saltzstein, H. D., & Sandberg, L. (1979). Indirect social influence: Change in judgmental processor anticipatory conformity. *Journal of Experimental Social Psychology, 15,* 209–216. (p. 257)

Sampson, E. E. (1975). On justice as equality. *Journal of Social Issues, 31*(3), 45–64. (p. 580)

Samuelson, C. D., Messick, D. M., Rutte, C. G., & Wilke, H. (1984). Individual and structural solutions to resource dilemmas in two cultures. *Journal of Personality and Social Psychology, 47,* 94–104. (p. 574)

Sanbonmatsu, D. M., Akimoto, S. A., & Biggs, E. (1993). Overestimating causality: Attributional effects of confirmatory processing. *Journal of Personality and Social Psychology, 65,* 892–903. (p. 101)

Sanbonmatsu, D. M., Akimoto, S. A., & Gibson, B. D. (1994). Stereotype-based blocking in social explanation. *Personality and Social Psychology Bulletin, 20,* 71–81. (p. 427)

Sanbonmatsu, D. M., & Fazio, R. H. (1990). The role of attitudes in memory-based decision making. *Journal of Personality and Social Psychology, 59,* 614–622. (p. 125)

Sandberg, G. G., Jackson, T. L., & Petretic-Jackson, P. (1985). Sexual aggression and courtship violence in dating relationships. Paper presented at the Midwestern Psychological Association convention. (p. 461)

Sande, G. N., Goethals, G. R., & Radloff, C. E. (1988). Perceiving one's own traits and others': The multifaceted self. *Journal of Personality and Social Psychology, 54,* 13–20. (p. 85)

Sanders, G. S. (1981). Driven by distraction: An integrative review of social facilitation and theory and research. *Journal of Experimental Social Psychology, 17,* 227–251. *(a)* (p. 320)

Sanders, G. S. (1981). Toward a comprehensive account of social facilitation: Distraction/conflict does not mean theoretical conflict. *Journal of Experimental Social Psychology, 17,* 262–265. *(b)* (p. 320)

Sanders, G. S., & Baron, R. S. (1977). Is social comparison irrelevant for producing choice shifts? *Journal of Experimental Social Psychology, 13,* 303–314. (p. 339)

Sanders, G. S., Baron, R. S., & Moore, D. L. (1978). Distraction and social comparison as mediators of social facilitation effects. *Journal of Experimental Social Psychology, 14,* 291–303. (p. 320)

Sanislow, C. A., III, Perkins, D. V., & Balogh, D. W. (1989). Mood induction, interpersonal perceptions, and rejection in the roommates of depressed, nondepressed-disturbed, and normal college students. *Journal of Social and Clinical Psychology, 8,* 345–358. (p. 175)

Sanitioso, R., Kunda, Z., & Fong, G. T. (1990). Motivated recruitment of autobiographical memories. *Journal of Personality and Social Psychology, 59,* 229–241. (p. 60)

Sansone, C. (1986). A question of competence: The effects of competence and task feedback on intrinsic interest. *Journal of Personality and Social Psychology, 51,* 918–931. (p. 155)

Sapadin, L. A. (1988). Friendship and gender: Perspectives of professional men and women. *Journal of Social and Personal Relationships, 5,* 387–403. (p. 198)

Sarason, I. G., Sarason, B. R., Pierce, G. R., Shearin, E. N., & Sayers, M. H. (1991). A social learning approach to increasing blood donations. *Journal of Applied Social Psychology, 21,* 896–918. (p. 561)

Sarnoff, I., & Sarnoff, S. (1989). *Love-centered marriage in a self-centered world.* New York: Hemisphere. (p. 521)

Sato, K. (1987). Distribution of the cost of maintaining common resources. *Journal of Experimental Social Psychology, 23,* 19–31. (p. 572)

Schachter, S. (1951). Deviation, rejection and communication. *Journal of Abnormal and Social Psychology, 46,* 190–207. (pp. 259, 348)

Schachter, S., & Singer, J. E. (1962). Cognitive, social and physiological determinants of emotional state. *Psychological Review, 69,* 379–399. (p. 456)

Schafer, R. B., & Keith, P. M. (1980). Equity and depression among married couples. *Social Psychology Quarterly*, **43**, 430–435. (p. 515)

Schaffner, P. E. (1985). Specious learning about reward and punishment. *Journal of Personality and Social Psychology*, **48**, 1377–1386. (p. 110)

Schaffner, P. E., Wandersman, A., & Stang, D. (1981). Candidate name exposure and voting: Two field studies. *Basic and Applied Social Psychology*, **2**, 195–203. (p. 485)

Schaller, M., & Cialdini, R. B. (1988). The economics of empathic helping: Support for a mood management motive. *Journal of Experimental Social Psychology*, **24**, 163–181. (p. 532)

Schaller, M., & O'Brien, M. (1992). "Intuitive analysis of covariance" and group stereotype formation. *Personality and Social Psychology Bulletin*, **18**, 776–785. (p. 391)

Scheier, M. F., & Carver, C. S. (1992). Effects of optimism on psychological and physical well-being: Theoretical overview and empirical update. *Cognitive Therapy and Research*, **16**, 201–228. (pp. 47, 184)

Schein, E. H. (1956). The Chinese indoctrination program for prisoners of war: A study of attempted brainwashing. *Psychiatry*, **19**, 149–172. (p. 142)

Scher, S. J., & Cooper, J. (1989). Motivational basis of dissonance: The singular role of behavioral consequences. *Journal of Personality and Social Psychology*, **56**, 899–906. (p. 158)

Schiffenbauer, A., & Schiavo, R. S. (1976). Physical distance and attraction: An intensification effect. *Journal of Experimental Social Psychology*, **12**, 274–282. (p. 319)

Schlenker, B. R. (1976). Egocentric perceptions in cooperative groups: A conceptualization and research review. Final Report, Office of Naval Research Grant NR 170–797. (p. 62)

Schlenker, B. R. (1986). Self-identification: Toward an integration of the private and public self. In R. Baumeister (Ed.), *Public self and private self*. New York: Springer-Verlag. (p. 145)

Schlenker, B. R. (1987). Threats to identity: Self-identification and social stress. In C. R. Snyder & C. E. Ford (Eds.), *Coping with negative life events: Clinical and social psychological perspectives*. New York: Plenum Press. (p. 145)

Schlenker, B. R., Britt, T. W., & Pennington, J. (in press). Impression regulation and management: Highlights of a theory of self-identification. In R. M. Sorrentino & E. T. Higgins (Ed.), *Handbook of motivation and cognition: The interpersonal context*, vol. 3. New York: Guilford. (p. 68)

Schlenker, B. R., Dlugolecki, D. W., & Doherty, K. (1994). The impact of self-presentations on self-appraisals and behavior: The power of public commitment. *Personality and Social Psychology Bulletin*, **20**, 20–33. (p. 152)

Schlenker, B. R., & Leary, M. R. (1982). Audiences' reactions to self-enhancing, self-denigrating, and accurate self-presentations. *Journal of Experimental Social Psychology*, **18**, 89–104. *(a)* (p. 69)

Schlenker, B. R., & Leary, M. R. (1982). Social anxiety and self-presentation: A conceptualization and model. *Psychological Bulletin*, **92**, 641–669. *(b)* (pp. 69, 179)

Schlenker, B. R., & Leary, M. R. (1985). Social anxiety and communication about the self. *Journal of Language and Social Psychology*, **4**, 171–192. (p. 179)

Schlenker, B. R., & Miller, R. S. (1977). Egocentrism in groups: Self-serving biases or logical information processing? *Journal of Personality and Social Psychology*, **35**, 755–764. *(b)* (p. 62)

Schlenker, B. R., & Miller, R. S. (1977). Group cohesiveness as a determinant of egocentric perceptions in cooperative groups. *Human Relations*, **30**, 1039–1055. *(a)* (p. 62)

Schlenker, B. R., Phillips, S. T., Boniecki, K. A., & Schlenker, D. R. (1995). Championship pressures: Choking or triumphing in one's own territory? *Journal of Personality and Social Psychology*, **68**, 632–643. (p. 318)

Schlenker, B. R., & Weigold, M. F. (1992). Interpersonal processes involving impression regulation and management. *Annual Review of Psychology*, **43**, 133–168. (p. 68)

Schlenker, B. R., Weigold, M. F., & Hallam, J. R. (1990). Self-serving attributions in social context: Effects of self-esteem and social pressure. *Journal of Personality and Social Psychology*, **58**, 855–863. (p. 62)

Schlesinger, A., Jr. (1949). The statistical soldier. *Partisan Review*, **16**, 852–856. (p. 14)

Schlesinger, A., Jr. (1991, July 8). The cult of ethnicity, good and bad. *Time*, p. 21. (pp. 194, 217)

Schoeneman, T. J. (1994). Individual-ism. In V. S. Ramachandran (Ed.), *Encyclopedia of Human Behavior*. San Diego: Academic Press. (p. 44)

Schofield, J. (1982). *Black and white in school: Trust, tension, or tolerance?* New York: Praeger. (p. 588)

Schofield, J. W. (1986). Causes and consequences of the colorblind perspective. In J. F. Dovidio & S. L. Gaertner (Eds.), *Prejudice, discrimination, and racism*. Orlando, Fl.: Academic Press. (p. 588)

Schooler, J. W., Gerhard, D., & Loftus, E. F. (1986). Qualities of the unreal. *Journal of Experimental Psychology: Learning, Memory, and Cognition*, **12**, 171–181. (p. 99)

Schopler, J., Insko, C. A., Graetz, K. A., Drigotas, S. M., & Smith, V. A. (1991). The generality of the individual-group discontinuity effect: Variations in positivity-negativity of outcomes, players' relative power, and magnitude of outcomes. *Personality and Social Psychology Bulletin*, **17**, 612–624. (p. 334)

Schulz, J. W., & Pruitt, D. G. (1978). The effects of mutual concern on joint welfare. *Journal of Experimental Social Psychology*, **14**, 480–492. (p. 598)

Schulz, R., & Decker, S. (1985). Long-term adjustment to physical disability: The role of social support, perceived control, and self-blame. *Journal of Personality and Social Psychology*, **48**, 1162–1172. (p. 448)

Schuman, H., & Kalton, G. (1985). Survey methods. In G. Lindzey & E. Aronson (Eds.), *Handbook of Social Psychology*, Vol. 1. Hillsdale, N.J.: Erlbaum. (p. 24)

Schuman, H., & Ludwig, J. (1983). The norm of even-handedness in surveys as in life. *American Sociological Review*, **48**, 112–120. (p. 23)

Schuman, H., & Scott, J. (1987). Problems in the use of survey questions to measure public opinion. *Science*, **236**, 957–959. (p. 24)

Schuman, H., & Scott, J. (1989). Generations and collective memories. *American Sociological Review*, **54**, 359–381. (p. 293)

Schwartz, S. H. (1975). The justice of need and the activation of humanitarian norms. *Journal of Social Issues*, **31**(3), 111–136. (p. 535)

Schwartz, S. H., & Gottlieb, A. (1981). Participants' post-experimental reactions and the ethics of bystander research. *Journal of Experimental Social Psychology*, **17**, 396–407. (p. 545)

Schwarz, N. (1994). Judgment in a social context: Biases, shortcomings, and the logic of conversation. In M. Zanna (ed.), *Advances in experimental social psychology*, vol 26. San Diego, CA: Academic Press. (p. 105)

Schwarz, N., Bless, H., & Bohner, G. (1991). Mood and persuasion: Affective states influence the processing of persuasive communications. In M. Zanna (Ed.), *Advances in experimental social psychology*, vol. 24. New York: Academic Press. (p. 281)

Schwarz, N., & Kurz, E. (1989). What's in a picture? The impact of face-ism on trait attribution. *European Journal of Social Psychology, 19*, 311–316. (p. 411)

Schwarz, N., Strack, F., Kommer, D., & Wagner, D. (1987). Soccer, rooms, and the quality of your life: Mood effects on judgments of satisfaction with life in general and with specific domains. *Journal of Applied Social Psychology, 17*, 69–79. (p. 111)

Schwarzwald, J., Bizman, A., & Raz, M. (1983). The foot-in-the-door paradigm: Effects of second request size on donation probability and donor generosity. *Personality and Social Psychology Bulletin, 9*, 443–450. (p. 137)

Schweitzer, K., Zillmann, D., Weaver, J. B., & Luttrell, E. S. (1992, Spring). Perception of threatening events in the emotional aftermath of a televised college football game. *Journal of Broadcasting and Electronic Media*, pp. 75–82. (p. 111)

Scott, J. P., & Marston, M. V. (1953). Nonadaptive behavior resulting from a series of defeats in fighting mice. *Journal of Abnormal and Social Psychology, 48*, 417–428. (p. 448)

Sears, D. O. (1979). Life stage effects upon attitude change, especially among the elderly. Manuscript prepared for Workshop on the Elderly of the Future, Committee on Aging, National Research Council, Annapolis, Md., May 3–5. (p. 292)

Sears, D. O. (1986). College sophomores in the laboratory: Influences of a narrow data base on social psychology's view of human nature. *Journal of Personality and Social Psychology, 51*, 515–530. (p. 292)

Sedikides, C. (1993). Assessment, enhancement, and verification determinants of the self-evaluation process. *Journal of Personality and Social Psychology, 65*, 317–338. (p. 60)

Sedikides, C., & Anderson, C. A. (1992). Causal explanations of defection: A knowledge structure approach. *Personality and Social Psychology Bulletin, 18*, 420–429. (p. 76)

Segal, H. A. (1954). Initial psychiatric findings of recently repatriated prisoners of war. *American Journal of Psychiatry, 61*, 358–363. (p. 141)

Segal, N. L. (1984). Cooperation, competition, and altruism within twin sets: A reappraisal. *Ethology and Sociobiology, 5*, 163–177. (p. 536)

Segall, M. H., Dasen, P. R., Berry, J. W., & Poortinga, Y. H. (1990). *Human behavior in global perspective: An introduction to cross-cultural psychology*. New York: Pergamon. (pp. 200, 224)

Segerstrom, S. C., McCarthy, W. J., Caskey, N. H., Gross, T. M., & Jarvik, M. E. (1993). Optimistic bias among cigarette smokers. *Journal of Applied Social Psychology, 23*, 1606–1618. (p. 184)

Selby, J. W., Calhoun, L. G., & Brock, T. A. (1977). Sex differences in the social perception of rape victims. *Personality and Social Psychology Bulletin, 3*, 412–415. (p. 370)

Seligman, C., Fazio, R. H., & Zanna, M. P. (1980). Effects of salience of extrinsic rewards on liking and loving. *Journal of Personality and Social Psychology, 38*, 453–460. (p. 498)

Seligman, M. E. P. (1975). *Helplessness: On depression, development and death*. San Francisco: W. H. Freeman. (p. 48)

Seligman, M. E. P. (1988). Why is there so much depression today? The waxing of the individual and the waning of the commons. The G. Stanely Hall Lecture, American Psychological Association convention. (p. 216)

Seligman, M. E. P. (1991). *Learned optimism*. New York: Knopf. (pp. 48, 176, 177)

Seligman, M. E. P. (1992). Power and powerlessness: Comments on "Cognates of personal control." *Applied & Preventive Psychology, 1*, 119–120. (p. 176)

Seligman, M. E. P., Nolen-Hoeksema, S., Thornton, N., & Thornton, K. M. (1990). Explanatory style as a mechanism of disappointing athletic performance. *Psychological Science, 1*, 143–146. (p. 48)

Seligman, M. E. P., & Schulman, P. (1986). Explanatory style as a predictor of productivity and quitting among life insurance sales agents. *Journal of Personality and Social Psychology, 50*, 832–838. (p. 48)

Seltzer, L. F. (1983). Influencing the "shape" of resistance: An experimental exploration of paradoxical directives and psychological reactance. *Basic and Applied Social Psychology, 4*, 47–71. (p. 266)

Seta, C. E., & Seta, J. J. (1992). Increments and decrements in mean arterial pressure levels as a function of audience composition: An averaging and summation analysis. *Personality and Social Psychology Bulletin, 18*, 173–181. (p. 320)

Seta, J. J. (1982). The impact of comparison processes on coactors' task performance. *Journal of Personality and Social Psychology, 42*, 281–291. (p. 320)

Shaheen, J. G. (1990, August 19). Our cultural demon—the "ugly Arab." *Washington Post*, Outlook Section. (p. 411)

Sharan, S., & Sharan, Y. (1976). *Small group teaching*. Englewood Cliffs, N.J.: Educational Technology. (p. 593)

Sharma, N. (1981). Some aspect of attitude and behaviour of mothers. *Indian Psychological Review, 20*, 35–42. (p. 394)

Sharpe, D., Adair, J. G., & Roese N. J. (1992). Twenty years of deception research: A decline in subjects' trust? *Personality and Social Psychology Bulletin, 18*, 585–590. (p. 29)

Shaver, P., Hazan, C., & Bradshaw, D. (1988). Love as attachment: The integration of three behavioral systems. In R. J. Sternberg & M. L. Barnes (Eds.), *The psychology of love*. New Haven: Yale University Press. (p. 509)

Shaver, P. R., & Hazan, C. (1993). Adult romantic attachment: Theory and evidence. In D. Perlman & W. Jones (Eds.), *Advances in personal relationships*, vol. 4. Greenwich, CT: JAI. (p. 509)

Shaver, P. R., & Hazan, C. (1994). Attachment. In A. L. Weber & J. H. Harvey (eds.), *Perspectives on close relationships*. Boston: Allyn & Bacon. (p. 509)

Shaw, L. L., Batson, C. D., & Todd, R. M. (1994). Empathy avoidance: Forestalling feeling for another in order to escape the motivational consequences. *Journal of Personality and Social Psychology, 67*, 879–887. (p. 532)

Shaw, M. E. (1981). *Group dynamics: The psychology of small group behavior*. New York: McGraw-Hill. (p. 314)

Sheppard, B. H., & Vidmar, N. (1980). Adversary pretrial procedures and testimonial evidence: Effects of lawyer's role and machiavelianism. *Journal of Personality and Social Psychology*, **39**, 320–322. (p. 364)

Shepperd, J. A. (1993). Student derogation of the Scholastic Aptitude Test: Biases in perceptions and presentations of College Board Scores. *Basic and Applied Social Psychology*, **14**, 455–473. (p. 59)

Shepperd, J. A., & Arkin, R. M. (1991). Behavioral other-enhancement: Strategically obscuring the link between performance and evaluation. *Journal of Personality and Social Psychology*, **60**, 79–88. (p. 67)

Shepperd, J. A., & Wright, R. A. (1989). Individual contributions to a collective effort: An incentive analysis. *Personality and Social Psychology Bulletin*, **15**, 141–149. (p. 326)

Sherif, M. (1937). An experimental approach to the study of attitudes. *Sociometry*, **1**, 90–98. (p. 235)

Sherif, M. (1966). *In common predicament: Social psychology of intergroup conflict and cooperation*. Boston: Houghton Mifflin. (pp. 578, 591)

Sherif, M., & Sherif, C. W. (1969). *Social psychology*. New York: Harper & Row. (p. 235)

Sherman, S. J. (1980). On the self-erasing nature of errors of prediction. *Journal of Personality and Social Psychology*, **39**, 211–221. (p. 117)

Sherman, S. J., Cialdini, R. B., Schwartzman, D. F., & Reynolds, K. D. (1985). Imagining can heighten or lower the perceived likelihood of contracting a disease: The mediating effect of ease of imagery. *Personality and Social Psychology Bulletin*, **11**, 118–127. (pp. 105, 283)

Sherman, S. J., Presson, C. C., Chassin, L., Bensenberg, M., Corty, E., & Olshavsky, R. (1983). Smoking intentions in adolescents: Direct experience and predictability. *Personality and Social Psychology Bulletin*, **8**, 376–383. (p. 130)

Short, J. F., Jr. (Ed.) (1969). *Gang delinquency and delinquent subcultures*. New York: Harper & Row. (p. 450)

Shostak, M. (1981). *Nisa: The life and words of a !Kung woman*. Cambridge, MA: Harvard University Press. (p. 505)

Shotland, R. L. (1989). A model of the causes of date rape in developing and close relationships. In C. Hendrick (Ed.), *Review of Personality and Social Psychology*, Vol. 10. Beverly Hills: Sage. (p. 75)

Shotland, R. L., & Stebbins, C. A. (1983). Emergency and cost as determinants of helping behavior and the slow accumulation of social psychological knowledge. *Social Psychology Quarterly*, **46**, 36–46. (p. 535)

Shotland, R. L., & Straw, M. K. (1976). Bystander response to an assault: When a man attacks a woman. *Journal of Personality and Social Psychology*, **34**, 990–999. (p. 542)

Showers, C., & Ruben, C. (1987). Distinguishing pessimism from depression: Negative expectations and positive coping mechanisms. Paper presented at the American Psychological Association convention. (p. 57)

Shrauger, J. S. (1975). Responses to evaluation as a function of initial self-perceptions. *Psychological Bulletin*, **82**, 581–596. (pp. 61, 498)

Shrauger, J. S. (1983). The accuracy of self-prediction: How good are we and why? Paper presented at the Midwestern Psychological Association convention. (p. 42)

Shure, G. H., Meeker, R. J., & Hansford, E. A. (1965). The effectiveness of pacifist strategies in bargaining games. *Journal of Conflict Resolution*, **9**(1), 106–117. (p. 571)

Sidanius, J., Pratto, F., & Bobo, L. (1994). Social dominance orientation and the political psychology of gender: A case of invariance? *Journal of Personality and Social Psychology*, **67**, 998–1011. (p. 199)

Sigall, H. (1970). Effects of competence and consensual validation on a communicator's liking for the audience. *Journal of Personality and Social Psychology*, **16**, 252–258. (p. 513)

Sigall, H., & Page, R. (1971). Current stereotypes: A little fading, a little faking. *Journal of Personality and Social Psychology*, **18**, 247–255. (p. 127)

Silver, M., & Geller, D. (1978). On the irrelevance of evil: The organization and individual action. *Journal of Social Issues*, **34**, 125–136. (p. 250)

Simon, H. A. (1957). *Models of man: Social and rational*. New York: Wiley. (p. 119)

Simonton, D. K. (1994). *Greatness: Who makes history and why*. New York: Guilford. (p. 351)

Simpson, J. A. (1987). The dissolution of romantic relationships: Factors involved in relationship stability and emotional distress. *Journal of Personality and Social Psychology*, **53**, 683–692. (p. 519)

Simpson, J. A., Campbell, B., & Berscheid, E. (1986). The association between romantic love and marriage: Kephart (1967) twice revisited. *Personality and Social Psychology Bulletin*, **12**, 363–372. (pp. 503, 507)

Simpson, J. A., Gangestad, S. W., & Lerma, M. (1990). Perception of physical attractiveness: Mechanisms involved in the maintenance of romantic relationships. *Journal of Personality and Social Psychology*, **59**, 1192–1201. (p. 492)

Simpson, J. A., Rholes, W. S., & Nelligan, J. S. (1992). Support seeking and support giving within couples in an anxiety-provoking situation: The role of attachment styles. *Journal of Personality and Social Psychology*, **62**, 434–446. (p. 509)

Singer, J. L., & Singer, D. G. (1988). Some hazards of growing up in a television environment: Children's aggression and restlessness. In S. Oskamp (Ed.), *Television as a social issue: Applied Social Psychology Annual*, Vol. 8. Newbury Park, Ca.: Sage. (p. 469)

Singer, M. (1979, July-August). Interviewed by M. Freeman. Of cults and communication: A conversation with Margaret Singer. *APA Monitor*, pp. 6–7. *(b)* (p. 301)

Singer, M. (1979). Cults and cult members. Address to the American Psychological Association convention. *(a)* (p. 301)

Singh, D. (1993). Adaptive significance of female physical attractiveness: Role of waist-to-hip ratio. *Journal of Personality and Social Psychology*, **65**, 293–307. (p. 490)

Sissons, M. (1981). Race, sex, and helping behavior. *British Journal of Social Psychology*, **20**, 285–292. (p. 556)

Sittser, G. L. (1994, April). Long night's journey into light. *Second Opinion*, pp. 10–15. (p. 107)

Sivard, R. L. (1991). *World military and social expenditures*. Washington, DC: World Priorities. (pp. 438, 568, 570)

Six, B., & Krahe, B. (1984). Implicit psychologists' estimates of attitude-behavior consistencies. *European Journal of Social Psychology*, **14**, 79–86. (p. 130)

Skaalvik, E. M., & Hagtvet, K. A. (1990). Academic achievement and self-concept: An analysis of causal predominance in a developmental perpsective. *Journal of Personality and Social Psychology*, **58**, 292–307. (p. 21)

Skill, T., Robinson, J. D., Lyons, J. S., & Larson, D. (1994). The portrayal of religion and spirituality on fictional network television. *Review of Religious Research, 35,* 251–267. (p. 469)

Skinner, B. F. (1971). *Beyond freedom and dignity.* New York: Knopf. (p. 529)

Skitka, L. J., & Tetlock, P. E. (1993). Providing public assistance: Cognitive and motivational processes underlying liberal and conservative policy preferences. *Journal of Personality and Social Psychology, 65,* 1205–1223. (p. 535)

Skov, R. B., & Sherman, S. J. (1986). Information-gathering processes: Diagnosticity, hypothesis-confirmatory strategies, and perceived hypothesis confirmation. *Journal of Experimental Social Psychology, 22,* 93–121. (p. 101)

Slavin, R. E. (1980). Cooperative learning and desegregation. Paper presented at the American Psychological Association convention. (p. 593)

Slavin, R. E. (1985). Cooperative learning: Applying contact theory in desegregated schools. *Journal of Social Issues, 41*(3), 45–62. (p. 592)

Slavin, R. E. (1990, December/January). Research on cooperative learning: Consensus and controversy. *Educational Leadership,* pp. 52–54. (p. 594)

Slavin, R. E., & Madden, N. A. (1979). School practices that improve race relations. *Journal of Social Issues, 16,* 169–180. (p. 592)

Sloan, J. H., Kellerman, A. L., Reay, D. T., Ferris, J. A., Koepsell, T., Rivara, F. P., Rice, C., Gray, L., & LoGerfo, J. (1988). Handgun regulations, crime, assaults, and homicide: A tale of two cities. *New England Journal of Medicine, 319,* 1256–1261. (p. 443)

Slovic, P. (1972). From Shakespeare to Simon: Speculations—and some evidence—about man's ability to process information. *Oregon Research Institute Research Bulletin, 12*(2). (p. 118)

Slovic, P. (1985, January 30). Only new laws will spur seat-belt use. *Wall Street Journal.* (p. 272)

Slovic, P., & Fischhoff, B. (1977). On the psychology of experimental surprises. *Journal of Experimental Psychology: Human Perception and Performance, 3,* 455–551. (p. 14)

Smart, R. G., Adlaf, E. M., & Walsh, G. W. (1991). The Ontario student drug use survey: Trends between 1977 and 1991. Toronto: Addiction Research Foundation. (p. 272)

Smedley, J. W., & Bayton, J. A. (1978). Evaluative race-class stereotypes by race and perceived class of subjects. *Journal of Personality and Social Psychology, 3,* 530–535. (p. 392)

Smith, A. (1976). *The wealth of nations.* Book 1. Chicago: University of Chicago Press. (Originally published, 1776.) (p. 574)

Smith, D. E., Gier, J. A., & Willis, F. N. (1982). Interpersonal touch and compliance with a marketing request. *Basic and Applied Social Psychology, 3,* 35–38. (p. 244)

Smith, H. (1976) *The Russians.* New York: Balantine Books. Cited by B. Latané, K. Williams, and S. Harkins in, Many hands make light the work. *Journal of Personality and Social Psychology,* 1979, *37,* 822–832. (p. 325)

Smith, H. W. (1981). Territorial spacing on a beach revisited: A cross-national exploration. *Social Psychology Quarterly, 44,* 132–137. (p. 211)

Smith, M. B. (1978). Psychology and values. *Journal of Social Issues, 34,* 181–199. (p. 10)

Smith, M. L., Glass, G. V., & Miller, R. L. (1980). *The benefits of psychotherapy.* Baltimore: Johns Hopkins Press. (p. 170)

Smith, P. B., & Tayeb, M. (1989). Organizational structure and processes. In M. Bond (Ed.), *The cross-cultural challenge to social psychology.* Newbury Park, Ca.: Sage. (p. 351)

Smith, S. M., & Petty, R. E. (1995). Personality moderators of mood congruency effects on cognition: The role of self-esteem and negative mood regulation. *Journal of Personality and Social Psychology, 68,* 1092–1107. (p. 40)

Smith, S. M., & Shaffer, D. R. (1991). Celerity and cajolery: Rapid speech may promote or inhibit persuasion through its impact on message elaboration. *Personality and Social Psychology Bulletin, 17,* 663–669. (p. 279)

Smith, T. (1994). Personal correspondence. National Opinion Research Center, University of Chicago. (pp. 393, 445)

Smith, T. W. (1990, December). Personal communication. Chicago: National Opinion Research Center. (p. 399)

Smith, V. L. (1991). Impact of pretrial instruction on jurors' information processing and decision making. *Journal of Applied Psychology, 76,* 220–228. (p. 373)

Smith, V. L. (1991). Prototypes in the courtroom: Lay representations of legal concepts. *Journal of Personality and Social Psychology, 61,* 857–872. (p. 377)

Smith, V. L., & Ellsworth, P. C. (1987). The social psychology of eyewitness accuracy: Misleading questions and communicator expertise. *Journal of Applied Psychology, 72,* 294–300. (p. 363)

Smith, W. P. (1987). Conflict and negotiation: Trends and emerging issues. *Journal of Applied Social Psychology, 17,* 641–677. (p. 602)

Smolowe, J. (1994, August 1). Race and the O. J. case. *Time,* pp. 24–25. (p. 371)

Snodgrass, M. A. (1987). The relationships of differential loneliness, intimacy, and characterological attributional style to duration of loneliness. *Journal of Social Behavior and Personality, 2,* 173–186. (p. 178)

Snodgrass, S. E. (1992). Further effects of role versus gender on interpersonal sensitivity. *Journal of Personality and Social Psychology, 62,* 154–158. (p. 226)

Snodgrass, S. E., Higgins, J. G., & Todisco, L. (1986). The effects of walking behavior on mood. Paper presented at the American Psychological Association convention. (p. 153)

Snyder, C. R. (1978). The "illusion" of uniqueness. *Journal of Humanistic Psychology, 18,* 33–41. (p. 55)

Snyder, C. R. (1980). The uniqueness mystique. *Psychology Today,* March, pp. 86–90. (p. 267)

Snyder, C. R., & Fromkin, H. L. (1980). *Uniqueness; The human pursuit of difference.* New York: Plenum. (p. 267)

Snyder, C. R., & Higgins, R. L. (1988). Excuses: Their effective role in the negotiation of reality. *Psychological Bulletin, 104,* 23–35. (p. 62)

Snyder, C. R., & Smith, T. W. (1986). On being "shy like a fox": A self-handicapping analysis. In W. H. Jones et al. (Eds.), *Shyness: Perspectives on research and treatment.* New York: Plenum. (p. 180)

Snyder, M. (1981). Seek, and ye shall find: Testing hypotheses about other people. In E. T. Higgins, C. P. Herman, & M. P. Zanna (Eds.), *Social cognition: The Ontario symposium on personality and social psychology.* Hillsdale, N.J.: Erlbaum. *(a)* (p. 168)

Snyder, M. (1983). The influence of individuals on situations: Implications for understanding the links between personality and social behavior. *Journal of Personality, 51,* 497–516. (p. 227)

Snyder, M. (1984). When belief creates reality. In L. Berkowitz (Ed.), *Advances in Experimental Social Psychology*, Vol. 18. New York: Academic Press. (pp. 116, 167)

Snyder, M. (1987). *Public appearances/private realities: The psychology of self-monitoring.* New York: Freeman. (pp. 145, 68)

Snyder, M. (1988). Experiencing prejudice first hand: The "discrimination day" experiments. *Contemporary Psychology*, **33**, 664–665. (p. 105)

Snyder, M. (1989). Selling images versus selling products: Motivational foundations of behavioral confirmation. *Advances in Experimental Social Psychology*, **26**, 206–311. (p. 167)]]]

Snyder, M., Berscheid, E., & Glick, P. (1985). Focusing on the exterior and the interior: Two investigations of the initiation of personal relationships. *Journal of Personality and Social Psychology*, **48**, 1427–1439. (p. 504)

Snyder, M., Berscheid, E., & Matwychuk, A. (1988). Orientations toward personnel selection: Differential reliance on appearance and personality. *Journal of Personality and Social Psychology*, **54**, 972–979. (p. 504)

Snyder, M., Campbell, B., & Preston, E. (1982). Testing hypotheses about human nature: Assessing the accuracy of social stereotypes. *Social Cognition*, **1**, 256–272. (p. 168)

Snyder, M., & Copeland, J. (1989). Self-monitoring processes in organizational settings. In R. A. Giacalone & P. Rosenfeld (Eds.), *Impression management in the organization.* Hillsdale, N.J.: Erlbaum. (pp. 68, 145)

Snyder, M., & DeBono, K. G. (1987). A functional approach to attitudes and persuasion. In M. P. Zanna, J. M. Olson, & C. P. Herman (Eds.), *Social influence: The Ontario symposium*, Vol. 5. Hillsdale, N.J.: Erlbaum. (pp. 68. 145)

Snyder, M., & DeBono, K. G. (1989). Understanding the functions of attitudes: Lessons from personality and social behavior. In A. R. Pratkanis, S. J., Breckler, & A. G. Greenwald (Eds.), *Attitude structure and function.* Hillsdale, N.J.: Erlbaum. (p. 295)

Snyder, M., Grether, J., & Keller, K. (1974). Staring and compliance: A field experiment on hitch-hiking. *Journal of Applied Social Psychology*, **4**, 165–170. (pp. 555, 558)

Snyder, M., & Haugen, J. A. (1994). Why does behavioral confirmation occur? A functional perspective on the role of the perceiver. *Journal of Experimental Social Psychology*, **30**, 218–246. (p. 26)

Snyder, M., & Ickes, W. (1985). Personality and social behavior. In G. Lindzey & E. Aronson (Eds.), *Handbook of social psychology* (3rd ed.). New York: Random House. (pp. 227, 261, 416)

Snyder, M., & Simpson, J. (1985). Orientations toward romantic relationships. In S. Duckk & D. Perlman (Eds.), *Understanding personal relationships.* Beverly Hills, Ca.: Sage. (p. 504)

Snyder, M., & Swann, W. B., Jr. (1976). When actions reflect attitudes: The politics of impression management. *Journal of Personality and Social Psychology*, **34**, 1034–1042. (p. 129)

Snyder, M., Tanke, E. D., & Berscheid, E. (1977). Social perception and interpersonal behavior: On the self-fulfilling nature of social stereotypes. *Journal of Personality and Social Psychology*, **35**, 656–666. *(b)* (p. 116)

Snyder, M., & Thomsen, C. J. (1988). Interactions between therapists and clients: Hypothesis testing and behavioral confirmation. In D. C. Turk & P. Salovey (Eds.), *Reasoning, inference, and judgment in clinical psychology.* New York: Free Press. (p. 167)

Socolovsky, J. (1994, October 9). Troubles at home force Saddam to look outward. Associated Press release in the *Holland Sentinel*, p. A5. (p. 590)

Sokoll, G. R., & Mynatt, C. R. (1984). Arousal and free throw shooting. Paper presented at the Midwestern Psychological Association convention, Chicago. (p. 319)

Solano, C. H. Batten, P. G., & Parish, E. A. (1982). Loneliness and patterns of self-disclosure. *Journal of Personality and Social Psychology*, **43**, 524–531. (p. 515)

Solomon, H., & Solomon, L. Z. (1978). Effects of anonymity on helping in emergency situations. Paper presented at the Eastern Psychological Association convention. (p. 558)

Solomon, H., Solomon, L. Z., Arnone, M. M., Maur, B. J., Reda, R. M., & Rother, E. O. (1981). Anonymity and helping. *Journal Social Psychology*, **113**, 37–43. (p. 558)

Sommer, R. (1969). *Personal space.* Englewood Cliffs, N.J.: Prentice-Hall. (p. 211)

Sommers-Flanagan, R., Sommers-Flanagan, J., & Davis, B. (1993). What's happening on music television? A gender role content analysis. *Sex Roles*, **28**, 745–753. (p. 411)

Sonne, J., & Janoff, D. (1979). The effect of treatment attributions on the maintenance of weight reduction: A replication and extension. *Cognitive Therapy and Research*, **3**, 389–397. (p. 189)

Sorenson, S. B., Stein, J. A., Siegel, J. M., Golding, J. M., & Burnam, M. A. (1987). Prevalence of adult sexual assault: The Los Angeles Epidemiologic Catchment Area Study. *American Journal of Epidemiology*, **126**, 1154–1164. (p. 462)

Sparacino, J., & Hansell, S. (1979). Physical attractiveness and academic performance: Beauty is not always talent. *Journal of Personality*, **47**, 449–469. (p. 489)

Sparrell, J. A., & Shrauger, J. S. (1984). Self-confidence and optimism in self-prediction. Paper presented at the American Psychological Association convention. (p. 57)

Spector, P. E. (1986). Perceived control by employees: A meta-analysis of studies concerning autonomy and participation at work. *Human Relations*, **39**, 1005–1016. (p. 350)

Speer, A. (1971). *Inside the Third Reich: Memoirs.* (P. Winston & C. Winston. trans.). New York: Avon Books. (p. 341)

Spencer, S. J., & Steele, C. M. (1995). Under suspicion of inability: Stereotype vulnerability and women's math performance. Unpublished manuscript, Hope College. (p. 405)

Sperling, E. (1994). Japanese-American internment during World War II: The impact of geography on racism. Unpublished, award-winning manuscript in national student history competition, Bainbridge Island, Washington. (p. 411)

Spiegel, D., Bloom, J. R., Kraemer, H. C., & Gottheil, E. (1989, October 14). Effect of psychosocial treatment on survival of patients with metastatic breast cancer. *The Lancet*, 888–891. (p. 184)

Spiegel, H. W. (1971). *The growth of economic thought.* Durham, N.C.: Duke University Press. (p. 63)

Spitzberg, B. H., & Hurt, H. T. (1987). The relationship of interpersonal competence and skills to reported loneliness across time. *Journal of Social Be-*

havior and Personality, **2**, 157–172. (p. 178)

Spivak, J. (1979, June 6). *Wall Street Journal*. (p. 325)

Spivey, C. B., & Prentice-Dunn, S. (1990). Assessing the directionality of deindividuated behavior: Effects of deindividuation, modeling, and private self-consciousness on aggressive and prosocial responses. *Basic and Applied Social Psychology*, **11**, 387–403. (p. 330)

Sprecher, S. (1987). The effects of self-disclosure given and received on affection for an intimate partner and stability of the relationship. *Journal of Personality and Social Psychology*, **4**, 115–127. (p. 516)

Sprecher, S., Aron, A., Hatfield, E., Cortese, A., Potapova, E., & Levitskaya, A. (1994). Love: American style, Russian style, and Japanese style. *Personal Relationships*, **1**, 349–369. (p. 507)

Sprecher, S., & Duck, S. (1994). Sweet talk: The importance of perceived communication for romantic and friendship attraction experienced during a get-acquainted date. *Personality and Social Psychology Bulletin*, **20**, 391–400. (p. 493)

Sprecher, S., & Sedikides, C. (1993). Gender differences in perceptions of emotionality: The case of close heterosexual relationships. *Sex Roles*, **28**, 511–530. (p. 198)

Sprecher, S., Sullivan, Q., & Hatfield, E. (1994). Mate selection preferences: Gender differences examined in a national sample. *Journal of Personality and Social Psychology*, **66**, 1074–1080. (pp. 486–487)

Stangor, C., Lynch, L., Duan, C., & Glass, B. (1992). Categorization of individuals on the basis of multiple social features. *Journal of Personality and Social Psychology*, **62**, 207–218. (p. 196)

Stangor, C., & McMillan, D. (1992). Memory for expectancy-congruent and expectancy-incongruent information: A review of the social and social developmental literatures. *Psychological Bulletin*, **111**, 42–61. (p. 427)

Stangor, C., Sullivan, L. A., & Ford, T. E. (1991). Affective and cognitive determinants of prejudice. *Social Cognition*, **9**, 359–380. (p. 391)

Stark, R., & Bainbridge, W. S. (1980). Networks of faith: Interpersonal bonds and recruitment of cults and sects. *American Journal of Sociology*, **85**, 1376–1395. (pp. 301, 302)

Stasser, G. (1991). Pooling of unshared information during group discussion. In S. Worchel, W. Wood, & J. Simpson (Eds.), *Group process and productivity*. Beverly Hills, CA: Sage. (p. 336)

Stasser, G., Kerr, N. L., & Bray, R. M. (1981). The social psychology of jury deliberations: Structure, process, and product. In N. L. Kerr & R. M. Bray (Eds.), *The psychology of the courtroom*. New York: Academic Press. (p. 381)

Staub, E. (1978). *Positive social behavior and morality: Social and personal influences*, vol. 1. Hillsdale, NJ: Erlbaum. (p. 529)

Staub, E. (1989). *The roots of evil: The origins of genocide and other group violence*. Cambridge: Cambridge University Press. (pp. 247, 249, 561)

Staub, E. (1990). Moral exclusion: Personal goal theory, and extreme destructiveness. *Journal of Social Issues*, **46**, 47–64. (p. 561)

Staub, E. (1991). Altruistic and moral motivations for helping and their translation into action. *Psychological Inquiry*, **2**, 150–153. (p. 533)

Staub, E. (1991). Psychological and cultural origins of extreme destructiveness and extreme altruism. In W. Kurtines & J. Gewirtz (Eds.), *The handbook of moral behavior and development*. Hillsdale, NJ: Erlbaum. (p. 561)

Staub, E. (1992). The origins of caring, helping and nonaggression: Parental socialization, the family system, schools, and cultural influence. In S. Oliner & P. Oliner (Eds.), *Embracing the other: Philosophical, psychological, and theological perspectives on altruism*. New York: New York University Press. (p. 561)

Staub, E. (1993). The psychology of bystanders, perpetrators, and heroic helpers. *International Journal of Intercultural Relations*, **17**, 315–341. (pp. 450, 563)

Staub, E. (1996). Altruism and aggression in children and youth: Origins and cures. In R. Feldman (ed.), *The psychology of adversity*. Amherst, MA: University of Massachusetts Press. (p. 471)

Steblay, N. M. (1987). Helping behavior in rural and urban environments: A meta-analysis. *Psychological Bulletin*, **102**, 346–356. (p. 537)

Steele, C. M. (1988). The psychology of self-affirmation: Sustaining the integrity of the self. In L. Berkowitz (Ed.), *Advances in experimental social psychology*, Vol. 21. Orlando, Fl.: Academic Press. (p. 158)

Steele, C. M., & Aronson, J. (in press). Contending with a stereotype: African-American intellectual test performance and stereotype vulnerability. *Journal of Personality and Social Psychology*. (p. 406)

Steele, C. M., & Southwick, L. (1985). Alcohol and social behavior I: The psychology of drunken excess. *Journal of Personality and Social Psychology*, **48**, 18–34. (p. 441)

Steele, C. M., Southwick, L. L., & Critchlow, B. (1981). Dissonance and alcohol: Drinking your troubles away. *Journal of Personality and Social Psychology*, **41**, 831–846. (p. 159)

Steele, C. M., Spencer, S. J., & Lynch, M. (1993). Self-image resilience and dissonance: The role of affirmational resources. *Journal of Personality and Social Psychology*, **64**, 885–896. (p. 158)

Stein, A. H., & Friedrich, L. K. (1972). Television content and young children's behavior. In J. P. Murray, E. A. Rubinstein, & G. A. Comstock (Eds.), *Television and social learning*. Washington, D.C.: Government Printing Office. (p. 562)

Stein, D. D., Hardyck, J. A., & Smith, M. B. (1965). Race and belief: An open and shut case. *Journal of Personality and Social Psychology*, **1**, 281–289. (p. 418)

Steinem, G. (1988). Six great ideas that television is missing. In S. Oskamp. (Ed.), *Television as a social issue: Applied Social Psychology Annual*, Vol. 8. Newbury Park, Ca.: Sage. (p. 463)

Steiner, I. D. (1982). Heuristic models of groupthink. In M. Brandstatter, J. H. Davis, & G. Stocker-Kreichgauer (Eds.), *Group decision making*. New York: Academic Press, pp. 503–524. (p. 346)

Stephan, C. W., & Stephan, W. G. (1986). Habla Ingles? The effects of language translation on simulated juror decisions. *Journal of Applied Social Psychology*, **16**, 577–589. (p. 370)

Stephan, W. G. (1986). The effects of school desegregation: An evaluation 30 years after *Brown*. In R. Kidd, L. Saxe, & M. Saks (Eds.), *Advances in applied social psychology*. New York: Erlbaum. (p. 588)

Stephan, W. G. (1987). The contact hypothesis in intergroup relations. In C. Hendrick (Ed.), *Group processes and intergroup relations*. Newbury Park, Ca.: Sage. (p. 588)

Stephan, W. G. (1988). School desegregation: Short-term and long-term effects. Paper presented at the national conference "Opening doors: An appraisal of race relations in America," University of Alabama. (p. 587)

Stephan, W. G., Berscheid, E., & Walster, E. (1971). Sexual arousal and heterosexual perception. *Journal of Personality and Social Psychology, 20*, 93–101. (p. 502)

Sternberg, R. J. (1988). Triangulating love. In R. J. Sternberg & M. L. Barnes (Eds.), *The psychology of love.* New Haven: Yale University Press. (pp. 500, 501, 520)

Sternberg, R. J., & Grajek, S. (1984). The nature of love. *Journal of Personality and Social Psychology, 47*, 312–329. (p. 509)

Stiles, W. B., Shuster, P. L., & Harrigan, J. A. (1992). Disclosure and anxiety: A test of the fever model. *Journal of Personality and Social Psychology, 63*, 980–988. (p. 516)

Stille, R. G., Malamuth, N., & Schallow, J. R. (1987). Prediction of rape proclivity by rape myth attitudes and hostility toward women. Paper presented at the American Psychological Association convention. (p. 461)

Stillinger, C., Epelbaum, M., Keltner, D., & Ross, L. (1991). The "reactive devaluation" barrier to conflict resolution. Unpublished manuscript, Stanford University. (p. 599)

Stockdale, J. E. (1978). Crowding: Determinants and effects. In L. Berkowitz (Ed.), *Advances in experimental social psychology* (Vol. 11). New York: Academic Press. (p. 211)

Stokes, J., & Levin, I. (1986). Gender differences in predicting loneliness from social network characteristics. *Journal of Personality and Social Psychology, 51*, 1069–1074. (p. 178)

Stone, A. A., Hedges, S. M., Neale, J. M., & Satin, M. S. (1985). Prospective and cross-sectional mood reports offer no evidence of a "blue Monday" phenomenon. *Journal of Personality and Social Psychology, 49*, 129–134. (p. 41)

Stone, A. L., & Glass, C. R. (1986). Cognitive distortion of social feedback in depression. *Journal of Social and Clinical Psychology, 4*, 179–188. (p. 111)

Stone, L. (1977). *The family, sex and marriage in England, 1500–1800.* New York: Harper & Row. (p. 519)

Stoner, J. A. F. (1962). A comparison of individual and group decisions involving risk. Unpublished master's thesis, Massachusetts Institute of Technology, 1961. Cited by D. G. Marquis in, Individual responsibility and group decisions involving risk. *Industrial Management Review, 3*, 8–23. (p. 332)

Stoppard, J. M., & Gruchy, C. D. G. (1993). Gender, context, and expression of positive emotion. *Personality and Social Psychology Bulletin, 19*, 143–150. (p. 198)

Storms, M. D. (1973). Videotape and the attribution process: Reversing actors' and observers' points of view. *Journal of Personality and Social Psychology, 27*, 165–175. (p. 83)

Storms, M. D., & Thomas, G. C. (1977). Reactions to physical closeness. *Journal of Personality and Social Psychology, 35*, 412–418. (p. 319)

Stouffer, S. A., Suchman, E. A., DeVinney, L. C., Star, S. A., & Williams, R. M., Jr. (1949). *The American soldier: Adjustment during army life* (Vol. 1.). Princeton, N.J.: Princeton University Press. (pp. 447, 587)

Strack, S., & Coyne, J. C. (1983). Social confirmation of dysphoria: Shared and private reactions to depression. *Journal of Personality and Social Psychology, 44*, 798–806. (p. 175)

Straus, M. A., & Gelles, R. J. (1980). *Behind closed doors: Violence in the American family.* New York: Anchor/Doubleday. (p. 450)

Strenta, A., & DeJong, W. (1981). The effect of a prosocial label on helping behavior. *Social Psychology Quarterly, 44*, 142–147. (p. 560)

Stroebe, W., & Diehl, M. (1994). Productivity loss in idea-generating groups. In W. Stroebe & M. Hewstone (Eds.), *European review of social psychology*, vol. 5. Chichester: Wiley. (p. 346)

Stroebe, W., Insko, C. A., Thompson, V. D., & Layton, B. D. (1971). Effects of physical attractiveness, attitude similarity, and sex on various aspects of interpersonal attraction. *Journal of Personality and Social Psychology, 18*, 79–91. (p. 487)

Stroebe, W., Lenkert, A., & Jonas, K. (1988). Familiarity may breed contempt: The impact of student exchange on national stereotypes and attitudes. In W. Stroebe & A. W. Kruglanski (Eds.), *The social psychology of intergroup conflict.* New York: Springer-Verlag. (p. 588)

Stroessner, S. J., Hamilton, D. L., &

Lepore, L. (1990). Intergroup categorization and intragroup differentiation: Ingroup-outgroup differences. Paper presented at the American Psychological Association convention. (p. 417)

Stroessner, S. J., & Mackie, D. M. (1993). Affect and perceived group variability: Implications for stereotyping and prejudice. In D. M. Mackie & D. L. Hamilton (eds.), *Affect, cognition, and stereotyping: Interactive processes in group perception.* San Diego, CA: Academic Press. (p. 417)

Strong, S. R. (1968). Counseling: An interpersonal influence process. *Journal of Counseling Psychology, 17*, 81–87. (p. 304)

Strong, S. R. (1978). Social psychological approach to psychotherapy research. In S. L. Garfield & A. E. Bergin (Eds.), *Handbook of psychotherapy and behavior change*, 2nd ed. New York: Wiley. (p. 303)

Strong, S. R. (1991). Social influence and change in therapeutic relationships. In C. R. Snyder & D. R. Forsyth (Eds.), *Handbook of social and clinical psychology.* New York: Pergamon Press. (p. 303)

Strong, S. R., Welsh, J. A., Corcoran, J. L., & Hoyt, W. T. (1992). Social psychology and counseling psychology: The history, products, and promise of an interface. *Journal of Personality and Social Psychology, 39*, 139–157. (p. 185)

Stroufe, B., Chaikin, A., Cook, R., & Freeman, V. (1977). The effects of physical attractiveness on honesty: A socially desirable response. *Personality and Social Psychology, 3*, 59–62. (p. 555)

Sue, S., Smith, R. E., & Caldwell, C. (1973). Effects of inadmissible evidence on the decisions of simulated jurors: A moral dilemma. *Journal of Applied Social Psychology, 3*, 345–353. (p. 371)

Suls, J., & Tesch, F. (1978). Students' preferences for information about their test performance: A social comparison study, *Journal of Applied Social Psychology, 8*, 189–197. (p. 446)

Suls, J., Wan, C. K., & Sanders, G. S. (1988). False consensus and false uniqueness in estimating the prevalence of health-protective behaviors. *Journal of Applied Social Psychology, 18*, 66–79. (p. 58)

Summers, G., & Feldman, N. S. (1984). Blaming the victim versus blaming the perpetrator: An attributional analysis of spouse abuse. *Journal of Social and Clinical Psychology*, **2**, 339–347. (p. 425)

Sundstrom, E., De Meuse, K. P., & Futrell, D. (1990). Work teams: Applications and effectiveness. *American Psychologist*, **45**, 120–133. (p. 350)

Svenson, O. (1981). Are we all less risky and more skillful than our fellow drivers? *Acta Psychologica*, **47**, 143–148. (p. 54)

Swann, W. B., Jr. (1984). Quest for accuracy in person perception: A matter of pragmatics. *Psychological Review*, **91**, 457–475. (p. 119)

Swann, W. B., Jr. (1987). Identity negotiation: Where two roads meet. *Journal of Personality and Social Psychology*, **53**, 1038–1051. (p. 117)

Swann, W. B., Jr. (1990). To be adored or to be known? The interplay of self-enhancement and self-verification. In R. M. Sorrentino & E. T. Higgins (Eds.), *Foundations of social behavior*, vol. 2. New York: Guilford. (p. 60)

Swann, W. B., Jr., & Ely, R. J. (1984). A battle of wills: Self-verification versus behavioral confirmation. *Journal of Personality and Social Psychology*, **46**, 1287–1302. (p. 117)

Swann, W. B., Jr., & Giuliano, T. (1987). Confirmatory search strategies in social interaction: How, when, why, and with what consequences. *Journal of Social and Clinical Psychology*, **5**, 511–524. (p. 167)

Swann, W. B., Jr., Giuliano, T., & Wegner, D. M. (1982). Where leading questions can lead: The power of conjecture in social interaction. *Journal of Personality and Social Psychology*, **42**, 1025–1035. (p. 294)

Swann, W. B., Jr., Hixon, J. G., & De La Ronde, C. (1992). Embracing the bitter "truth": Negative self-concepts and marital commitment. *Psychological Science*, **3**, 118–121. (p. 102)

Swann, W. B., Jr., & Predmore, S. C. (1985). Intimates as agents of social support: Sources of consolation or despair? *Journal of Personality and Social Psychology*, **49**, 1609–1617. (p. 516)

Swann, W. B., Jr. & Read, S. J. (1981). Acquiring self-knowledge: The search for feedback that fits. *Journal of Personality and Social Psychology*, **41**, 1119–1128. (a) (p. 102)

Swann, W. B., Jr., & Schroeder, D. G. (1994). The search for beauty and truth: A framework for understanding reactions to evaluations. *Personality*

and Social Psychology Bulletin*, in press. (p. 102)

Swann, W. B., Jr., Stein-Seroussi, A., & Giesler, R. B. (1992). Why people self-verify. *Journal of Personality and Social Psychology*, **62**, 392–401. (p. 102)

Swann, W. B., Jr., Stein-Seroussi, A., & McNulty, S. E. (1992). Outcasts in a white lie society. The enigmatic worlds of people with negative self-conceptions. *Journal of Personality and Social Psychology*, **62**, 618–624. (p. 102)

Swann, W. B., Jr., Wenzlaff, R. M., Krull, D. S., & Pelham, B. W. (1991). Seeking truth, reaping despair: Depression, self-verification and selection of relationship partners. *Journal of Abnormal Psychology*, **101**, 293–306. (pp. 175, 499)

Swap, W. C. (1977). Interpersonal attraction and repeated exposure to rewarders and punishers. *Personality and Social Psychology Bulletin*, **3**, 248–251. (p. 485)

Swedish Information Service (1980). *Social change in Sweden*, September, No. 19, p. 5. (Published by the Swedish Consulate General, 825 Third Avenue, New York, N.Y. 10022.) (p. 475)

Sweeney, J. (1973). An experimental investigation of the free rider problem. *Social Science Research*, **2**, 277–292. (p. 323)

Sweeney, L. T., & Haney, C. (1992). The influence of race on sentencing: A meta-analytic review of experimental studies. *Behavioral Sciences and the Law*, **10**, 179–195. (p. 370)

Sweeney, P. D., Anderson, K., & Bailey, S. (1986). Attributional style in depression: A meta-analytic review. *Journal of Personality and Social Psychology*, **50**, 947–991. (p. 174)

Swim, J., Borgida, E., Maruyama, G., & Myers, D. G. (1989). Joan McKay vs. John McKay: Do gender stereotypes bias evaluations? *Psychological Bulletin*, **105**, 409–429. (p. 400)

Swim, J. K. (1994). Perceived versus meta-analytic effect sizes: An assessment of the accuracy of gender stereotypes. *Journal of Personality and Social Psychology*, **66**, 21–36. (pp. 196, 398)

Swim, J. K., Aikin, K. J., Hall, W. S., & Hunter, B. A. (1995). Sexism and racism: Old-fashioned and modern prejudices. *Journal of Personality and Social Psychology*, **68**, 199–214. (p. 400)

Symons, D. (interviewed by S. Keen). (1981, February). Eros and alley cop. *Psychology Today*, p. 54. (p. 490)

Tajfel, H. (1970, November). Experiments in intergroup discrimination. *Scientific American*, pp. 96–102. (p. 406)

Tajfel, H. (1981). *Human groups and social categories: Studies in social psychology*. London: Cambridge University Press. (p. 406)

Tajfel, H. (1982). Social psychology of intergroup relations. *Annual Review of Psychology*, **33**, 1–39. (p. 406)

Tajfel, H., & Billig, M. (1974). Familiarity and categorization in intergroup behavior. *Journal of Experimental Social Psychology*, **10**, 159–170. (p. 406)

Takooshian, H., & Bodinger, H. (1982). Bystander indifference to street crime. In L. Savitz & N. Johnston (Eds.), *Contemporary criminology*. New York: Wiley. (p. 542)

Tang, S-H., & Hall, V. C. (1994). The overjustification effect: A meta-analysis. *Applied Cognitive Psychology*, in press. (p. 155)

Tanke, E. D., & Tanke, T. J. (1979). Getting off a slippery slope: Social science in the judicial processes. *American Psychologist*, **34**, 1130–1138. (pp. 382, 383)

Tannen, D. (1990). *You just don't understand: Women and men in conversation*. New York: Morrow. (p. 197)

Tapp, J. L. (1980). Psychological and policy perspectives on the law: Reflections on a decade. *Journal of Social Issues*, **36**(2), 165–192. (p. 383)

Taylor, D. A., Gould, R. J., & Brounstein, P. J. (1981). Effects of personalistic self-disclosure. *Personality and Social Psychology Bulletin*, **7**, 487–492. (p. 516)

Taylor, D. G., Sheatsley, P. B., & Greeley, A. M. (1978). Attitudes toward racial integration. *Scientific American*, **238**(6), 42–49. (p. 140)

Taylor, D. M., & Doria, J. R. (1981). Self-serving and group-serving bias in attribution. *Journal of Social Psychology*, **113**, 201–211. (p. 63)

Taylor, D. M., Wright, S. C., Moghaddam, F. M., & Lalonde, R. N. (1990). The personal/group discrimination discrepancy: Perceiving my group, but not myself, to be a target for discrimination. *Personality and Social Psychology Bulletin*, **16**, 254–262. (p. 400)

Taylor, S. E. (1979). Remarks at symposium on social psychology and medicine, American Psychological Association convention. (p. 48)

Taylor, S. E. (1981). A categorization approach to stereotyping. In D. L. Hamilton (Ed.), *Cognitive processes in stereo-*

typing and intergroup behavior. Hillsdale, N.J.: Erlbaum. (pp. 418, 429)

Taylor, S. E. (1989). *Positive illusions: Creative self-deception and the healthy mind*. New York: Basic Books. (pp. 56, 173, 448)

Taylor, S. E., & Brown, J. D. (1988). Illusion and well-being: A social psychological perspective on mental health. *Psychological Bulletin*, **103**, 193–210. (p. 174)

Taylor, S. E., Crocker, J., Fiske, S. T., Sprinzen, M., & Winkler, J. D. (1979). The generalizability of salience effects. *Journal of Personality and Social Psychology*, **37**, 357–368. (p. 421)

Taylor, S. E., Fiske, S. T., Etcoff, N. L., & Ruderman, A. J. (1978). Categorical and contextual bases of person memory and stereotyping. *Journal of Personality and Social Psychology*, **36**, 778–793. (p. 417)

Taylor, S. P., & Chermack, S. T. (1993). Alcohol, drugs and human physical aggression. *Journal of Studies on Alcohol*, Supplement No. **11**, 78–88. (p. 441)

Taylor, S. P., & Leonard, K. E. (1983). Alcohol and human physical aggression. *Aggression*, **2**, 77–101. (p. 441)

Taylor, S. P., & Pisano, R. (1971). Physical aggression as a function of frustration and physical attack. *Journal of Social Psychology*, **84**, 261–267. (p. 455)

Tedeschi, J. T., Nesler, M., & Taylor, E. (1987). Misattribution and the bogus pipeline: A test of dissonance and impression management theories. Paper presented at the American Psychological Association convention. (p. 145)

Teger, A. I. (1980). *Too much invested to quit*. New York: Pergamon Press. (p. 573)

Teigen, K. H. (1986). Old truths or fresh insights? A study of students' evaluations of proverbs. *British Journal of Social Psychology*, **25**, 43–50. (p. 16)

Telch, M. J., Killen, J. D., McAlister, A. L., Perry, C. L., & Maccoby, N. (1981). Long-term follow-up of a pilot project on smoking prevention with adolescents. Paper presented at the American Psychological Association convention. (p. 307)

Tennen, H., & Affleck, G. (1987). The costs and benefits of optimistic explanations and dispositional optimism. *Journal of Personality*, **55**, 377–393. (p. 184)

Tennov, D. (1979). *Love and limerence: The experience of being in love*. New York: Stein and Day, p. 22. (p. 550)

Tesser, A. (1988). Toward a self-evaluation maintenance model of social behavior. In L. Berkowitz (Ed.), *Advances in experimental social psychology*, Vol. 21. San Diego, Ca.: Academic Press. (p. 60)

Tesser, A., Martin, L., & Mendolia, M. (1995). The impact of thought on attitude extremity and attitude-behavior consistency. In R. E. Petty and J. A Krosnick (Eds.), *Attitude strength: Antecedents and consequences*. Hillsdale, NJ: Erlbaum. (p. 337)

Tesser, A., Millar, M., & Moore, J. (1988). Some affective consequences of social comparison and reflection processes: The pain and pleasure of being close. *Journal of Personality and Social Psychology*, **54**, 49–61. (p. 407)

Tesser, A., Rosen, S., & Conlee, M. C. (1972). News valence and available recipient as determinants of news transmission. *Sociometry*, **35**, 619–628. (p. 134)

Tetlock, P. E. (1981). Pre- to post-election shifts in presidential rhetoric: Impression management or cognitive adjustment. *Journal of Personality and Social Psychology*, **41**, 207–212. (p. 134)

Tetlock, P. E. (1983). Accountability and complexity of thought. *Journal of Personality and Social Psychology*, **45**, 74–83. (p. 134)

Tetlock, P. E. (1985). Integrative complexity of American and Soviet foreign policy rhetoric: A time-series analysis. *Journal of Personality and Social Psychology*, **49**, 1565–1585. (p. 598)

Tetlock, P. E. (1988). Monitoring the integrative complexity of American and Soviet policy rhetoric: What can be learned? *Journal of Social Issues*, **44**, 101–131. (p. 583)

Tetlock, P. E., Peterson, R. S., McGuire, C., Chang, S., & Feld, P. (1992). Assessing political group dynamics: A test of the groupthink model. *Journal of Personality and Social Psychology*, **63**, 403–425. (p. 345)

Thibodeau, R. (1989). From racism to tokenism: The changing face of blacks in *New Yorker* cartoons. *Public Opinion Quarterly*, **53**, 482–494. (p. 411)

Thomas, G. C., & Batson, C. D. (1981). Effect of helping under normative pressure on self-perceived altruism. *Social Psychology Quarterly*, **44**, 127–131. (p. 562)

Thomas, G. C., Batson, C. D., & Coke, J. S. (1981). Do Good Samaritans discourage helpfulness? Self-perceived altruism after exposure to highly helpful others. *Journal of Personality and Social Psychology*, **40**, 194–200. (p. 562)

Thomas, K. W., & Pondy, L. R. (1977). Toward an "intent" model of conflict management among principal parties. *Human Relations*, **30**, 1089–1102. (p. 585)

Thomas, L. (1978). Hubris in science? *Science*, **200**, 1459–1462. (p. 171)

Thomas, L. (1981). Quoted by J. L. Powell. Testimony before the Senate Subcommittee on Science, Technology and Space, April 22. (p. 437)

Thompson, L. (1990a). An examination of naive and experienced negotiators. *Journal of Personality and Social Psychology*, **59**, 82–90. (p. 596)

Thompson, L. (1990b). The influence of experience on negotiation performance. *Journal of Experimental Social Psychology*, **26**, 528–544. (p. 596)

Thompson, L. (1991). Information exchange in negotiation. *Journal of Experimental Social Psychology*, **27**, 161–179. (p. 596)

Thompson, L. L., & Crocker, J. (1985). Prejudice following threat to the self-concept. Effects of performance expectations and attributions. Unpublished manuscript, Northwestern University. (p. 414)

Thompson, L., Valley, K. L., & Kramer, R. M. (in press). The bittersweet feeling of success: An examination of social perception in negotiation. *Journal of Experimental Social Psychology*. (p. 596)

Thompson, W. C., Cowan, C. L., & Rosenhan, D. L. (1980). Focus of attention mediates the impact of negative affect on altruism. *Journal of Personality and Social Psychology*, **38**, 291–300. (p. 549)

Thompson, W. C., Fong, G. T., & Rosenhan, D. L. (1981). Inadmissible evidence and juror verdicts. *Journal of Personality and Social Psychology*, **40**, 453–463. (p. 383)

Thompson, W. C., & Schumann, E. L. (1987). Interpretation of statistical evidence in criminal trials. *Law and Human Behavior*, **11**, 167–187. (p. 377)

Thorndike, R. L. (1968). Review of *Pygmalion in the classroom*. *American Educational Research Journal*, **5**, 707–711. (p. 115)

Thornton, B., & Moore, S. (1993). Physical attractiveness contrast effect: Implications for self-esteem and evaluations of the social self. *Personality and*

Social Psychology Bulletin, 19, 474–480. (p. 492)

Tice, D. M. (1992). Self-concept change and self-presentation: The looking glass self is also a magnifying glass. *Journal of Personality and Social Psychology, 63*, 435–451. (p. 152)

Tice, D. M., & Baumeister, R. F. (1985). Masculinity inhibits helping in emergencies: Personality does predict the bystander effect. *Journal of Personality and Social Psychology, 49*, 420–428. (p. 552)

Time (1992, March 30). The not so merry wife of Windsor. Pp. 38–39. (p. 519)

Time (1994, June 27). Vox pop Yankelovich survey for TIME/CNN. P. 26. (p. 24)

Time (1994, November 7). Vox pop (poll by Yankelovich Partners Inc.). P. 21. (p. 24)

Time-Life Books (1994). *Tapping hidden power: Journey through the mind and body.* Alexandria, VA: Time-Life Books. (p. 527)

Timko, C., & Moos, R. H. (1989). Choice, control, and adaptation among elderly residents of sheltered care settings. *Journal of Applied Social Psychology, 19*, 636–655. (p. 50)

Tindale, R. S., Davis, J. H., Vollrath, D. A., Nagao, D. H., & Hinsz, V. B. (1990). Asymmetrical social infuence in freely interacting groups: A test of three models. *Journal of Personality and Social Psychology, 58*, 438–449. (p. 381)

Tobin, R. J., & Eagles, M. (1992). U.S. and Canadian attitudes toward international interactions: A cross-national test of the double-standard hypothesis. *Basic and Applied Social Psychology, 13*, 447–459. (p. 582)

Toronto News (1977, July 26). (p. 53)

Tourangeau, R., Rasinski, K. A., Bradburn, N., & D'Andrade, R. (1989). Belief accessibility and context effects in attitude measurement. *Journal of Experimental and Social Psychology, 25*, 401–421. (p. 23)

Towson, S. M. J., & Zanna, M. P. (1983). Retaliation against sexual assault: Self-defense or public duty? *Psychology of Women Quarterly, 8*, 89–99. (p. 370)

Travis, L. E. (1925). The effect of a small audience upon eye-hand coordination. *Journal of Abnormal and Social Psychology, 20*, 142–146. (p. 315)

Triandis, H. C. (1981). Some dimensions of intercultural variation and their implications for interpersonal behavior.

Paper presented at the American Psychological Association convention. (p. 211)

Triandis, H. C. (1982). Incongruence between intentions and behavior: A review. Paper presented at the American Psychological Association convention. (p. 126)

Triandis, H. C. (1994). *Culture and social behavior.* New York: McGraw-Hill. (pp. 224, 105, 450, 519)

Triandis, H. C., Bontempo, R., Villareal, M. J., Asai, M., & Lucca, N. (1988). Individualism and collectivism: Cross-cultural perspectives on self-ingroup relationships. *Journal of Personality and Social Psychology, 54*, 323–338. (pp. 216, 264, 507)

Triandis, H. C., Brislin, R., & Hui, C. H. (1988). Cross-cultural training across the individualism-collectivism divide. *International Journal of Intercultural Relations, 12*, 269–289. (p. 214, 216)

Triandis, H. C., McCusker, C., Betancourt, H., Iwao, S., Leung, K., Salazar, J. M., Setiadi, B., Sinha, J. B. P., Touzard, H., & Zaleski, Z. (1993). An etic-emic analysis of individualism and collectivism. *Journal of Cross-Cultural Psychology, 24*, 366–383. (pp. 213, 214)

Trimble, D. E. (1993). Meta-analysis of altruism and intrinsic and extrinsic religiousness. Paper presented at the Eastern Psychological Association convention. (p. 553)

Trimble, J. E. (1988). Stereotypical images, American Indians, and prejudice. In P. A. Katz & D. A. Taylor (Eds.), *Eliminating racism: Profiles in controversy.* New York: Plenum. (pp. 396, 411)

Triplett, N. (1898). The dynamogenic factors in pacemaking and competition. *American Journal of Psychology, 9*, 507–533. (p. 315)

Trolier, T. K., & Hamilton, D. L. (1986). Variables influencing judgments of correlational relations. *Journal of Personality and Social Psychology, 50*, 879–888. (p. 107)

Trost, M. R., Maass, A., & Kenrick, D. T. (1992). Minority influence: Personal relevance biases cognitive processes and reverses private acceptance. *Journal of Experimental Social Psychology, 28*, 234–254. (p. 348)

Tumin, M. M. (1958). Readiness and resistance to desegregation: A social portrait of the hard core. *Social Forces, 36*, 256–273. (p. 413)

Turner, C. W., Hesse, B. W., & Peterson-Lewis, S. (1986). Naturalistic studies of the long-term effects of television violence. *Journal of Social Issues, 42*(3), 51–74. (p. 465)

Turner, E. A., & Pratkanis, A. R. (1994). An experimental investigation of gender discrimination in childcare employment. Western Psychological Association convention. (p. 390)

Turner, J. C. (1987). *Rediscovering the social group: A self-categorization theory.* New York: Basil Blackwell. (p. 314)

Turner, M. E., & Pratkanis, A. R. (1993). Effects of preferential and meritorious selection on performance: An examination of intuitive and self-handicapping perspectives. *Personality and Social Psychology Bulletin, 19*, 47–58. (p. 67)

Turner, M. E., & Pratkanis, A. R. (1994). Social identity maintenance prescriptions for preventing groupthink: Reducing identity protection and enhancing intellectual conflict. *International Journal of Conflict Management, 5*, 254–270. (p. 340)

Turner, M. E., Pratkanis, A. R., Probasco, P., & Leve, C. (1992). Threat cohesion, and group effectiveness: Testing a social identity maintenance perspective on groupthink. *Journal of Personality and Social Psychology, 63*, 781–796. (p. 340)

TV Guide (1977, January 26), pp. 5–10. (p. 465)

Tversky, A. (1985, June). Quoted by Kevin McKean, Decisions, decisions. *Discover*, pp. 22–31. (p. 118)

Tverksy, A., & Kahneman, D. (1974). Judgment under uncertainty: Heuristics and biases. *Science, 185*, 1123–1131. (pp. 106, 109)

Tversky, A., & Kahneman, D. (1983). Extensional versus intuitive reasoning: The conjunction fallacy in probability judgment. *Psychological Review, 90*, 293–315. (p. 104)

Tyler, T. R. (1988). What is procedural justice? Criteria used by citizens to assess the fairness of legal procedures. *Law and Society Review, 22*, 103–135. (p. 356)

Tyler, T. R. (1989). The psychology of procedural justice: A test of the group-value model. *Journal of Personality and Social Psychology, 57*, 830–838. (p. 356)

Tyler, T. R., & Cook, F. L. (1984). The mass media and judgments of risk: Distinguishing impact on personal and societal level judgments. *Journal of Personality and Social Psychology*, **47**, 693–708. (p. 470)

Tyler, T. R., & Lind, E. A. (1990). Intrinsic versus community-based justice models: When does group membership matter? *Journal of Social Issues*, **46**, 83–94. (p. 561)

Tzeng, M. (1992). The effects of socioeconomic heterogamy and changes on marital dissolution for first marriages. *Journal of Marriage and the Family*, **54**, 609–619. (p. 519)

U.S. Supreme Court, Plessy v. Ferguson. (1986). Quoted by L. J. Severy, J. C. Brigham, & B. R. Schlenker, *A contemporary introduction to social psychology*. New York: McGraw-Hill, p. 126. (p. 383)

Ugwuegbu, C. E. (1979). Racial and evidential factors in juror attribution of legal responsibility. *Journal of Experimental Social Psychology*, **15**, 133–146. (p. 370)

Uleman, J. S. (1989). A framework for thinking intentionally about unintended thoughts. In J. S. Uleman & J. A. Bargh (Eds.), *Unintended thought: The limits of awareness, intention, and control*. New York: Guilford. (p. 77)

Umberson, D., & Hughes, M. (1987). The impact of physical attractiveness on achievement and psychological well-being. *Social Psychology Quarterly*, **50**, 227–236. (p. 489)

Underwood, B., & Moore, B. (1982). Perspective-taking and altruism. *Psychological Bulletin*, **91**, 143–173. (p. 549)

Unger, R. K. (1979). Whom does helping help? Paper presented at the Eastern Psychological Association convention, April. (p. 528)

Unger, R. K. (1985). Epistomological consistency and its scientific implications. *American Psychologist*, **40**, 1413–1414. (p. 9)

United Nations (1991). *The world's women 1970–1990: Trends and statistics*. New York: United Nations. (pp. 199, 222, 401)

Vaillant, G. E. (1977). *Adaptation to life*. Boston: Little, Brown. (p. 97)

Vallone, R. P., Griffin, D. W., Lin, S., & Ross, L. (1990). Overconfident prediction of future actions and outcomes by self and others. *Journal of Personality and Social Psychology*, **58**, 582–592. (p. 101)

Vallone, R. P., Ross, L., & Lepper, M. R. (1985). The hostile media phenomenon: Biased perception and perceptions of media bias in coverage of the "Beirut Massacre." *Journal of Personality and Social Psychology*, **49**, 577–585. (p. 92)

Vancouver, J. B., Rubin, B., & Kerr, N. L. (1991). Sex composition of groups and member motivation III: Motivational losses at a feminine task. *Basic and Applied Social Psychology*, **12**, 133–144. (p. 326)

Van der Plight, J., Eiser, J. R., & Spears, R. (1987). Comparative judgments and preferences: The influence of the number of response alternatives. *British Journal of Social Psychology*, **26**, 269–280. (p. 23)

Vanderslice, V. J., Rice, R. W., & Julian, J. W. (1987). The effects of participation in decision-making on worker satisfaction and productivity: An organizational simulation. *Journal of Applied Social Psychology*, **17**, 158–170. (p. 350)

Van Knippenberg, D., & Wilke, H. (1992). Prototypicality of arguments and conformity to ingroup norms. *European Journal of Social Psychology*, **22**, 141–155. (p. 280)

Van Lange, P. A. M. (1991). Being better but not smarter than others: The Muhammad Ali effect at work in interpersonal situations. *Personality and Social Psychology Bulletin*, **17**, 689–693. (p. 55)

Van Leeuwen, M. S. (1978). A cross-cultural examination of psychological differentiation in males and females. *International Journal of Psychology*, **13**, 87–122. (p. 224)

Van Staden, F. J. (1987). White South Africans' attitudes toward the desegregation of public amenities. *Journal of Social Psychology*, **127**, 163–173. (p. 416)

Van Yperen, N. W., & Buunk, B. P. (1990). A longitudinal study of equity and satisfaction in intimate relationships. *European Journal of Social Psychology*, **20**, 287–309. (p. 514)

Vaughan, K. B., & Lanzetta, J. T. (1981). The effect of modification of expressive displays on vicarious emotional arousal. *Journal of Experimental Social Psychology*, **17**, 16–30. (p. 153)

Vaux, A. (1988). Social and personal factors in loneliness. *Journal of Social and Clinical Psychology*, **6**, 462–471. (p. 178)

Vidmar, N. (1979). The other issues in jury simulation research. *Law and Human Behavior*, **3**, 95–106. (p. 383)

Vidmar, N., & Laird, N. M. (1983). Adversary social roles: Their effects on witnesses' communication of evidence and the assessments of adjudicators. *Journal of Personality and Social Psychology*, **44**, 888–898. (p. 364)

Visher, C. A. (1987). Juror decision making: The importance of evidence. *Law and Human Behavior*, **11**, 1–17. (pp. 358, 367)

Visintainer, M. A., & Seligman, M. E. (1983, July/August). The hope factor. *American Health*, pp. 59–61. (p. 183)

Visintainer, M. A., & Seligman, M. E. P. (1985). Tumor rejection and early experience of uncontrollable shock in the rat. Unpublished manuscript, University of Pennsylvania. See also, M. A. Visintainer et al. (1982). Tumor rejection in rats after inescapable versus escapable shock. *Science*, **216**, 437–439. (p. 183)

Vitelli, R. (1988). The crisis issue assessed: An empirical analysis. *Basic and Applied Social Psychology*, **9**, 301–309. (p. 29)

Vivian, J. E., & Berkowitz, N. H. (1993). Anticipated outgroup evaluations and intergroup bias. *European Journal of Social Psychology*, **23**, 513–524. (p. 408)

Vollrath, D. A., Sheppard, B. H., Hinsz, V. B., & Davis, J. H. (1989). Memory performance by decision-making groups and individuals. *Organizational Behavior and Human Decision Processes*, **43**, 289–300. (p. 382)

Vonk, R. (1993). The negativity effect in trait ratings and in open-ended descriptions of persons. *Personality and Social Psychology Bulletin*, **19**, 269–278. (p. 78)

Wachtler, J., & Counselman, E. (1981). When increasing liking for a communicator decreases opinion change: An attribution analysis of attractiveness. *Journal of Experimental Social Psychology*, **17**, 386–395. (p. 279)

Wagstaff, G. (1982). Attitudes to rape: The "just world" strikes again? *Bulletin of the British Psychological Society*, **35**, 277–279. (p. 427)

Wagstaff, G. F. (1983). Attitudes to poverty, the Protestant ethic, and political affiliation: A preliminary investigation. *Social Behavior and Personality*, **11**, 45–47. (p. 88)

Walker, M., Harriman, S., & Costello, S. (1980). The influence of appearance on compliance with a request. *Journal of Social Psychology*, **112**, 159–160. (p. 256)

Wallace, M. *New York Times*, November 25, 1969. (p. 247)

Wallach, M. A., & Wallach, L. (1983). *Psychology's sanction for selfishness: The error of egoism in theory and therapy*. San Francisco: Freeman. (p. 533)

Wallbott, H. G. (1988). In and out of context: Influences of facial expression and context information on emotion attributions. *British Journal of Social Psychology, 27*, 357–369. (p. 94)

Walster (Hatfield), E. (1965). The effect of self-esteem on romantic liking. *Journal of Experimental Social Psychology, 1*, 184–197. (p. 498)

Walster (Hatfield), E., Aronson, V., Abrahams, D., & Rottman, L. (1966). Importance of physical attractiveness in dating behavior. *Journal of Personality and Social Psychology, 4*, 508–516. (pp. 486, 487)

Walster (Hatfield), E., & Festinger, L. (1962). The effectiveness of "overheard" persuasive communications. *Journal of Abnormal and Social Psychology, 65*, 395–402. (p. 278)

Walster (Hatfield), E., & Walster, G. W. (1978). *A new look at love*. Reading, MA: Addison-Wesley. (p. 513)

Walster (Hatfield), E., Walster, G. W., & Berscheid, E. (1978). *Equity: Theory and research*. Boston: Allyn and Bacon. (pp. 514, 578, 580)

Ward, W. C., & Jenkins, H. M. (1965). The display of information and the judgment of contingency. *Canadian Journal of Psychology, 19*, 231–241. (p. 107)

Warnick, D. H., & Sanders, G. S. (1980). The effects of group discussion on eyewitness accuracy. *Journal of Applied Social Psychology, 10*, 249–259. (pp. 345–346)

Warr, P., & Payne, R. (1982). Experiences of strain and pleasure among British adults. *Social Science and Medicine, 16*, 1691–1697. (p. 479)

Wason, P. C. (1960). On the failure to eliminate hypotheses in a conceptual task. *Quarterly Journal of Experimental Psychology, 12*, 129–140. (pp. 101–102)

Watson, D. (1982). The actor and the observer: How are their perceptions of causality divergent? *Psychological Bulletin, 92*, 682–700. (p. 85)

Watts, W. A. (1967). Relative persistence of opinion change induced by active compared to passive participation. *Journal of Personality and Social Psychology, 5*, 4–15. (p. 130)

Weary, G., & Edwards, J. A. (1994). Social cognition and clinical psychology: Anxiety, depression, and the processing of social information. In R. Wyer & T. Srull (eds.), *Handbook of social cognition*, vol. 2. Hillsdale, NJ: Erlbaum. (p. 111)

Weary, G., Harvey, J. H., Schwieger, P., Olson, C. T., Perloff, R., & Pritchard, S. (1982). Self-presentation and the moderation of self-serving biases. *Social Cognition, 1*, 140–159. (p. 68)

Webster, D. M. (1993). Motivated augmentation and reduction of the overattribution bias. *Journal of Personality and Social Psychology, 65*, 261–271. (p. 87)

Wegner, D. M., & Erber, R. (1992). The hyperaccessibility of suppressed thoughts. *Journal of Personality and Social Psychology, 63*, 903–912. (p. 396)

Wehr, P. (1979). *Conflict regulation*. Boulder, Colo.: Westview Press. (p. 599)

Weiner, B. (1980). A cognitive (attribution)-emotion-action model of motivated behavior: An analysis of judgments of help-giving. *Journal of Personality and Social Psychology, 39*, 186–200. (p. 535)

Weiner, B. (1981). The emotional consequences of causal ascriptions. Unpublished manuscript, UCLA. (p. 443)

Weiner, B. (1985). "Spontaneous" causal thinking. *Psychological Bulletin, 97*, 74–84. (p. 74)

Weinstein, N. D. (1980). Unrealistic optimism about future life events. *Journal of Personality and Social Psychology, 39*, 806–820. (p. 56)

Weinstein, N. D. (1982). Unrealistic optimism about susceptibility to health problems. *Journal of Behavioral Medicine, 5*, 441–460. (p. 56)

Weiss, J., & Brown, P. (1976). Self-insight error in the explanation of mood. Unpublished manuscript, Harvard University. (p. 41)

Wells, G. L. (1984). The psychology of lineup identifications. *Journal of Applied Social Psychology, 14*, 89–103. (p. 366)

Wells, G. L. (1986). Expert psychological testimony. *Law and Human Behavior, 10*, 83–95. (p. 367)

Wells, G. L. (1992). Naked statistical evidence of liability: Is subjective probability enough? *Journal of Personality and Social Psychology, 62*, 739–752. (p. 377)

Wells, G. L. (1993). What do we know about eyewitness identification? *American Psychologist, 48*, 553–571. (p. 366)

Wells, G. L., Ferguson, T. J., & Lindsay, R. C. L. (1981). The tractability of eyewitness confidence and its implications for triers of fact. *Journal of Applied Psychology, 66*, 688–696. (p. 364)

Wells, G. L., & Leippe, M. R. (1981). How do triers of fact enter the accuracy of eyewitness identification? Memory for peripheral detail can be misleading. *Journal of Applied Psychology, 66*, 682–687. (p. 358)

Wells, G. L., Lindsay, R. C. L., & Ferguson, T. (1979). Accuracy, confidence, and juror perceptions in eyewitness identification. *Journal of Applied Psychology, 64*, 440–448. (p. 358)

Wells, G. L., Lindsay, R. C. L., & Tousignant, J. P. (1980). Effects of expert psychological advice on human performance in judging the validity of eyewitness testimony. *Law and Human Behavior, 4*, 275–285. (pp. 358, 367)

Wells, G. L., & Luus, C. A. E. (1990). Police lineups as experiments: Social methodology as a framework for properly conducted lineups. *Personality and Social Psychology Bulletin, 16*, 106–117. (p. 366)

Wells, G. L., & Murray, D. M. (1983). What can psychology say about the *Neil v. Biggers* criteria for judging eyewitness accuracy? *Journal of Applied Psychology, 68*, 347–362. (p. 360)

Wells, G. L., & Turtle, J. W. (1986). Eyewitness identification: The importance of lineup models. *Psychological Bulletin, 99*, 320–329. (p. 366)

Wells, G. L., Wrightsman, L. S., & Miene, P. K. (1985). The timing of the defense opening statement: Don't wait until the evidence is in. *Journal of Applied Social Psychology, 15*, 758–772. (p. 287)

Wener, R., Frazier, W., & Farbstein, J. (1987, June). Building better jails. *Psychology Today*, pp. 40–49. (p. 49)

Wenzlaff, R. M., & Prohaska, M. L. (1989). When misery prefers company: Depression, attributions, and responses to others' moods. *Journal of Experimental Social Psychology, 25*, 220–233. (p. 496)

Werner, C. M., & Kagehiro, D. K., & Strube, M. J. (1982). Conviction proneness and the authoritarian juror: Inability to disregard information or attitudinal bias? *Journal of Applied Psychology, 67*, 629–636. (p. 379)

West, S. G., & Brown, T. J. (1975). Physical attractiveness, the severity of the emergency and helping: A field experiment and interpersonal simulation. *Journal of Experimental Social Psychology*, **11**, 531–538. (p. 555)

West, S. G., Whitney, G., & Schnedler, R. (1975). Helping a motorist in distress: The effects of sex, race, and neighborhood. *Journal of Personality and Social Psychology*, **31**, 691–698. (p. 555)

Weyant, J. M. (1984). Applying social psychology to induce charitable donations. *Journal of Applied Social Psychology*, **14**, 441–447. (p. 560)

Weyant, J. M., & Smith, S. L. (1987). Getting more by asking for less: The effects of request size on donations of charity. *Journal of Applied Social Psychology*, **17**, 392–400. (p. 560)

Wheeler, L., Koestner, R., & Driver, R. E. (1982). Related attributes in the choice of comparison others: It's there, but it isn't all there is. *Journal of Experimental Social Psychology*, **18**, 489–500. (p. 446)

Wheeler, L., Reis, H. T., & Bond, M. H. (1989). Collectivism-individualism in everyday social life: The middle kingdom and the melting pot. *Journal of Personality and Social Psychology*, **57**, 79–86. (p. 215)

White, G. L. (1980). Physical attractiveness and courtship progress. *Journal of Personality and Social Psychology*, **39**, 660–668. (p. 487)

White, G. L., & Kight, T. D. (1984). Misattribution of arousal and attraction: Effects of salience of explanations for arousal. *Journal of Experimental Social Psychology*, **20**, 55–64. (p. 503)

White, H. R., Brick, J., & Hansell, S. (1993). A longitudinal investigation of alcohol use and aggression in adolescence. *Journal of Studies on Alcohol*, Supplement No. 11, 62–77. (p. 441)

White, J. A., & Plous, S. (1994). Self-enhancement and social responsibility: On caring more, but doing less, than others. Unpublished manuscript, Weslyan University. (p. 55)

White, J. W., & Kowalski, R. M. (1994). Deconstructing the myth of the nonaggressive woman. *Psychology of Women Quarterly*, **18**, 487–508. (p. 200)

White, M. J., & Gerstein, L. H. (1987). Helping: The influence of anticipated social sanctions and self-monitoring. *Journal of Personality*, **55**, 41–54. (p. 552)

White, P. A. (1991). Ambiguity in the internal/external distinction in causal attribution. *Journal of Experimental Social Psychology*, **27**, 259–270. (p. 76)

White, P. A., & Younger, D. P. (1988). Differences in the ascription of transient internal states to self and other. *Journal of Experimental Social Psychology*, **24**, 292–309. (p. 81)

White, R. (1984). *Fearful warriors: A psychological profile of U.S.-Soviet relations.* New York: Free Press. (p. 582)

White, R. K. (1971, November). Selective inattention. *Psychology Today*, pp. 47–50, 78–84. (p. 139)

White, R. K. (1977). Misperception in the Arab-Israeli conflict. *Journal of Social Issues*, **33**(1), 190–221. (p. 584)

Whitley, B. E., Jr., & Frieze, I. H. (1985). Children's causal attributions for success and failure in achievement settings: A meta-analysis. *Journal of Educational Psychology*, **77**, 608–616. (p. 53)

Whitman, R. M., Kramer, M., & Baldridge, B. (1963). Which dream does the patient tell? *Archives of General Psychology*, **8**, 277–282. (p. 168)

Whittaker, J. O., & Meade, R. D. (1967). Social pressure in the modification and distortion of judgment: A cross-cultural study. *International Journal of Psychology*, **2**, 109–113. (p. 264)

Whyte, G. (1993). Escalating commitment in individual and group decision making: A prospect theory approach. *Organizational Behavior and Human Decision Processes*, **54**, 430–455. (p. 334)

Wicker, A. W. (1969). Attitudes versus actions: The relationship of verbal and overt behavioral responses to attitude objects. *Journal of Social Issues*, **25**, 41–78. (pp. 125, 126)

Wicklund, R. A. (1979). The influence of self-awareness on human behavior. *American Scientist*, **67**, 187–193. (p. 84)

Wicklund, R. A. (1982). Self-focused attention and the validity of self-reports. In M. P. Zanna, E. T. Higgins, & C. P. Herman (Eds.), *Consistency in social behavior: The Ontario symposium*, Vol. 2. Hillsdale, N.J.: Erlbaum. (p. 84)

Widom, C. S. (1989). Does violence beget violence? A critical examination of the literature. *Psychological Bulletin*, **106**, 3–28. (p. 450)

Wiegman, O. (1985). Two politicians in a realistic experiment: Attraction, discrepancy, intensity of delivery, and attitude change. *Journal of Applied Social Psychology*, **15**, 673–686. (p. 277)

Wiesel, E. (1985, April 6). The brave Christians who saved Jews from the Nazis. *TV Guide*, pp. 4–6. (p. 527)

Wilder, D. A. (1977). Perception of groups, size of opposition, and social influence. *Journal of Experimental Social Psychology*, **13**, 253–268. (p. 254)

Wilder, D. A. (1978). Perceiving persons as a group: Effect on attributions of causality and beliefs. *Social Psychology*, **41**, 13–23. (p. 418)

Wilder, D. A. (1981). Perceiving persons as a group: Categorization and intergroup relations. In D. L. Hamilton (Ed.). *Cognitive processes in stereotyping and intergroup behavior*. Hillsdale, N.J.: Lawrence Erlbaum. (p. 406)

Wilder, D. A. (1990). Some determinants of the persuasive power of in-groups and out-groups: Organization of information and attribution of independence. *Journal of Personality and Social Psychology*, **59**, 1202–1213. (p. 280)

Wilder, D. A., & Shapiro, P. (1991). Facilitation of outgroup stereotypes by enhanced ingroup identity. *Journal of Experimental Social Psychology*, **27**, 431–452. (p. 408)

Wilder, D. A., & Shapiro, P. N. (1984). Role of out-group cues in determining social identity. *Journal of Personality and Social Psychology*, **47**, 342–348. (p. 590)

Wilder, D. A., & Shapiro, P. N. (1989). Role of competition-induced anxiety in limiting the beneficial impact of positive behavior by out-group members. *Journal of Personality and Social Psychology*, **56**, 60–69. (p. 427)

Wilkes, J. (1987, June). Murder in mind. *Psychology Today*, pp. 27–32. (p. 437)

Wilkinson, G. S. (1990, February). Food sharing in vampire bats. *Scientific American*, **262**, 76–82. (p. 537)

Williams, C. L. (1989). *Gender differences at work: Women and men in nontraditional occupations*. Berkeley: University of California Press. (p. 222)

Williams, D. K., Bourgeois, M. J., & Croyle, R. T. (1993). The effects of stealing thunder in criminal and civil trials. *Law and Human Behavior*, **17**, 597–609. (p. 285)

Williams, J. E. (1993). Young adults' views of aging: A nineteen nation study. In M. I. Winkler (ed.), *Documentos: Conferencia del XXIV Congreso Interamericano de Psicología*. (pp. 101–123) Santiago, Chile: Sociedad Interamericana de Psicología. (p. 202)

Williams, J. E., & Best, D. L. (1990a). *Measuring sex stereotypes: A multination study.* Newbury Park, CA: Sage. (pp. 198–199)

Williams, J. E., & Best, D. L. (1990b). *Sex and psyche: Gender and self viewed cross-culturally.* Newbury Park, CA: Sage. (pp. 223, 403)

Williams, K. D., Harkins, S., & Latané, B. (1981). Identifiability as a deterrent to social loafing: Two cheering experiments. *Journal of Personality and Social Psychology,* 40, 303–311. (pp. 324, 325)

Williams, K. D., Jackson, J. M., & Karau, S. J. (1992). Collective hedonism: A social loafing analysis of social dilemmas. In D. A. Schroeder (Ed.), *Social dilemmas: Social psychological perspectives.* New York: Praeger. (p. 324)

Williams, K. D., & Karau, S. J. (1991). Social loafing and social compensation: The effects of expectations of coworker performance. *Journal of Personality and Social Psychology,* 61, 570–581. (p. 326)

Williams, K. D., Nida, S. A., Baca, L. D., & Latané, B. (1989). Social loafing and swimming: Effects of identifiability on individual and relay performance of intercollegiate swimmers. *Basic and Applied Social Psychology,* 10, 73–81. (p. 324)

Williams, R. (1993). *Anger kills.* New York: Times Books. (pp. 181, 391)

Williams, R. M., Jr. (1975). Relative deprivation. In L. Coser (Ed.), *The idea of social structure: Papers in honor of Robert K. Merton.* New York: Harcourt Brace Jovanovich. (p. 446)

Williams, T. M. (Ed.) (1986). *The impact of television: A natural experiment in three communities.* Orlando, Fl.: Academic Press. (p. 466)

Williamson, G. M., & Clark, M. S. (1989). Providing help and desired relationship type as determinants of changes in moods and self-evaluations. *Journal of Personality and Social Psychology,* 56, 722–734. (p. 548)

Willis, F. N., & Hamm, H. K. (1980). The use of interpersonal touch in securing compliance. *Journal of Nonverbal Behavior,* 5, 49–55. (p. 244)

Wills, T. A. (1981). Downward comparison principles in social psychology. *Psychological Bulletin,* 90, 245–271. (p. 62)

Wilson, D. K., Kaplan, R. M., & Schneiderman, L. J. (1987). Framing of decisions and selections of alternatives in health care. *Social Behaviour,* 2, 51–59. (pp. 182, 282)

Wilson, D. K., Purdon, S. E., & Wallston, K. A. (1988). Compliance to health recommendations: A theoretical overview of message framing. *Health Education Research,* 3, 161–171. (p. 282)

Wilson, D. S., & Sober, E. (1994). Re-introducing group selection to the human behavioral sciences. *Behavioral and Brain Sciences,* 17, 585–654. (p. 537)

Wilson, E. O. (1978). *On human nature.* Cambridge, Mass.: Harvard University Press. (pp. 536, 556)

Wilson, G. (1994, March 25). Equal, but different. *The Times Higher Education Supplement, Times of London.* (p. 207)

Wilson, J. P., & Petruska, R. (1984). Motivation, model attributes, and prosocial behavior. *Journal of Personality and Social Psychology,* 46, 458–468. (p. 552)

Wilson, R. C., Gaft, J. G., Dienst, E. R., Wood, L., & Bavry, J. L. (1975). *College professors and their impact on students.* New York: Wiley. (pp. 290, 335)

Wilson, R. S., & Matheny, Jr., A. P. (1986). Behavior-genetics research in infant temperament: The Louisville twin study. In R. Plomin & J. Dunn (Eds.), *The study of temperament: Changes, continuities, and challenges.* Hillsdale, N.J.: Erlbaum. (p. 440)

Wilson, T. D. (1985). Strangers to ourselves: The origins and accuracy of beliefs about one's own mental states. In J. H. Harvey & G. Weary (Eds.), *Attribution in contemporary psychology.* New York: Academic Press. (p. 43)

Wilson, T. D., Dunn, D. S., Kraft, D., & Lisle, D. J. (1989). Introspection, attitude change, and attitude-behavior consistency: The disruptive effects of explaining why we feel the way we do. In L. Berkowitz (Eds.), *Advances in experimental social psychology,* Vol. 22. San Diego, Ca.: Academic Press. (p. 43)

Wilson, T. D., Laser, P. S., & Stone, J. I. (1982). Judging the predictors of one's mood: Accuracy and the use of shared theories. *Journal of Experimental Social Psychology,* 18, 537–556. (p. 41)

Wilson, T. D., Lisle, D. J., Schooler, J. W., Hodges, S. D., Klaaren, K. J., & LaFleur, S. J. (1993). Introspecting about reasons can reduce post-choice satisfaction. *Personality and Social Psychology Bulletin,* 19, 331–339. (p. 43)

Wilson, W. R. (1979). Feeling more than we can know: Exposure effects without learning. *Journal of Personality and Social Psychology,* 37, 811–821. (p. 484)

Winch, R. F. (1958). *Mate selection: A study of complementary needs.* New York: Harper & Row. (p. 495)

Wing, R. R., & Jeffery, R. W. (1979). Outpatient treatments of obesity: A comparison of methodology and clinical results. *International Journal of Obesity,* 3, 261–279. (p. 188)

Winter, F. W. (1973). A laboratory experiment of individual attitude response to advertising exposure. *Journal of Marketing Research,* 10, 130–140. (p. 485)

Wispe, L. G., & Freshley, H. B. (1971). Race, sex, and sympathetic helping behavior: The broken bag caper. *Journal of Personality and Social Psychology,* 17, 59–65. (p. 556)

Wittenberg, M. T., & Reis, H. T. (1986). Loneliness, social skills, and social perception. *Personality and Social Psychology Bulletin,* 12, 121–130. (p. 178)

Wixon, D. R., & Laird, J. D. (1976). Awareness and attitude change in the forced-compliance paradigm: The importance of when. *Journal of Personality and Social Psychology,* 34, 376–384. (p. 97)

Wolf, S. (1987). Majority and minority influence: A social impact analysis. In M. P. Zanna, J. M. Olson, & C. P. Herman (Eds.), *Social influence: The Ontario symposium on personality and social psychology,* Vol. 5. Hillsdale, N.J.: Erlbaum. (p. 349)

Wolf, S., & Latané, B. (1985). Conformity, innovation and the psycho-social law. In S. Moscovici, G. Mugny, & E. Van Avermaet (Eds.), *Perspectives on minority influence.* Cambridge: Cambridge University Press. (p. 349)

Wolf, S., & Montgomery, D. A. (1977). Effects of inadmissible evidence and level of judicial admonishment to disregard on the judgments of mock jurors. *Journal of Applied Social Psychology,* 7, 205–219. (p. 372)

Women on Words and Images (1972). *Dick and Jane as victims: Sex stereotyping in children's readers.* Princeton: Women on Words and Images. Cited by C. Tavris & C. Offir (1977) in *The longest war: Sex differences in perspective.* New York: Harcourt Brace Jovanovich, p. 177. (p. 410)

Wood, J. V. (1989). Theory and research concerning social comparisons of personal attributes. *Psychological Bulletin,* 106, 231–248. (p. 446)

Wood, J. V., Saltzberg, J. A., & Goldsamt, L. A. (1990). Does affect induce self-focused attention? *Journal of Personality and Social Psychology,* 58, 899–908. (pp. 176, 549)

Wood, J. V., Saltzberg, J. A., Neale, J. M., Stone, A. A., & Rachmiel, T. B. (1990). Self-focused attention, coping responses, and distressed mood in everyday life. *Journal of Personality and Social Psychology*, **58**, 1027–1036. (pp. 176, 177)

Wood, W., & Eagly, A. H. (1981). Stages in the analysis of persuasive messages: The role of causal attributions and message comprehension. *Journal of Personality and Social Psychology*, **40**, 246–259. (p. 279)

Wood, W., Lundgren, S., Ouellete, J. A., Busceme, S., & Blackstone, T. (1994). Minority influence: A meta-analytic review of social influence processes. *Psychological Bulletin*, **115**, 323–345. (p. 348)

Wood, W., & Rhodes, N. (1991). Sex differences in interaction style in task groups. In C. Ridgeway (Ed.), *Gender and interaction: The role of microstructures in inequality*. New York: Springer-Verlag. (p. 199)

Wood, W., Rhodes, N., & Whelan, M. (1989). Sex differences in positive well-being: A consideration of emotional style and marital status. *Psychological Bulletin*, **106**, 249–264. (p. 511)

Wood, W., Wong, F. Y., & Chachere, J. G. (1991). Effects of media violence on viewers' aggression in unconstrained social interaction. *Psychological Bulletin*, **109**, 371–383. (p. 468)

Worchel, S., Andreoli, V. A., & Folger, R. (1977). Intergroup cooperation and intergroup attraction: The effect of previous interaction and outcome of combined effort. *Journal of Experimental Social Psychology*, **13**, 131–140. (p. 592)

Worchel, S., Axsom, D., Ferris, F., Samah, G., & Schweitzer, S. (1978). Deterrents of the effect of intergroup cooperation on intergroup attraction. *Journal of Conflict Resolution*, **22**, 429–439. (p. 592)

Worchel, S., & Brown, E. H. (1984). The role of plausibility in influencing environmental attributions. *Journal of Experimental Social Psychology*, **20**, 86–96. (p. 319)

Worchel, S., & Norvell, N. (1980). Effect of perceived environmental conditions during cooperation on intergroup attraction. *Journal of Personality and Social Psychology*, **38**, 764–772. (p. 592)

Word, C. O., Zanna, M. P., & Cooper, J. (1974). The nonverbal mediation of self-fulfilling prophecies in interracial interaction. *Journal of Experimental Social Psychology*, **10**, 109–120. (p. 404)

Workman, E. A., & Williams, R. L. (1980). Effects of extrinsic rewards on intrinsic motivation in the classroom. *Journal of School Psychology*, **18**, 141–147. (p. 156)

Worringham, C. J., & Messick, D. M. (1983). Social facilitation of running: An unobtrusive study. *Journal of Social Psychology*, **121**, 23–29. (p. 320)

Wright, E. F., Lüüs, C. A., & Christie, S. D. (1990). Does group discussion facilitate the use of consensus information in making causal attributions? *Journal of Personality and Social Psychology*, **59**, 261–269. (p. 346)

Wright, P., & Rip, P. D. (1981). Retrospective reports on the causes of decisions. *Journal of Personality and Social Psychology*, **40**, 601–614. (p. 42)

Wrightsman, L. (1978). The American trial jury on trial: Empirical evidence and procedural modifications. *Journal of Social Issues*, **34**, 137–164. (p. 378)

Wu, C., & Shaffer, D. R. (1987). Susceptibility to persuasive appeals as a function of source credibility and prior experience with the attitude object. *Journal of Personality and Social Psychology*, **52**, 677–688. (p. 130)

Wu, D. Y. H., & Tseng, W. S. (1985). Introduction: The characteristics of Chinese culture. In D. Y. H. Wu and W. S. Tseng (Eds.), *Chinese culture and mental health*. San Diego, Ca.: Academic Press. (p. 69)

Wuthnow, R. (1994). *God and mammon in America*. New York: Free Press. (p. 553)

Wylie, R. C. (1979). *The self-concept (Vol. 2): Theory and research on selected topics*. Lincoln, Neb.: University of Nebraska Press. (p. 54)

Wyse, L. (1991, April). The way we are. *Good Housekeeping*, p. 254. (p. 481)

Yinon, Y., Sharon, I., Gonen, Y., & Adam, R. (1982). Escape from responsibility and help in emergencies among persons alone or within groups. *European Journal of Social Psychology*, **12**, 301–305. (p. 545)

Young, W. R. (1977, February). There's a girl on the tracks! *Reader's Digest*, pp. 91–95. (p. 526)

Younger, J. C., Walker, L., & Arrowood, J. A. (1977). Postdecision dissonance at the fair. *Personality and Social Psychology Bulletin*, **3**, 284–287. (p. 149)

Yovetich, N. A., & Rusbult, C. E. (1994). Accommodative behavior in close relationships: Exploring transformation of motivation. *Journal of Experimental Social Psychology*, **30**, 138–164. (p. 520)

Yuchtman (Yaar), E. (1976). Effects of social-psychological factors on subjective economic welfare. In B. Strumpel (Ed.), *Economic means for human needs*. Ann Arbor: Institute for Social Research, University of Michigan. (p. 446)

Yuille, J. C., & Cutshall, J. L. (1986). A case study of eyewitness memory of a crime. *Journal of Applied Psychology*, **71**, 291–301. (p. 358)

Yukl, G. (1974). Effects of the opponent's initial offer, concession magnitude, and concession frequency on bargaining behavior. *Journal of Personality and Social Psychology*, **30**, 323–335. (p. 595)

Yzerbyt, V. Y., & Leyens, J-P. (1991). Requesting information to form an impression: The influence of valence and confirmatory status. *Journal of Experimental Social Psychology*, **27**, 337–356. (p. 497)

Zabelka, G. (1980, August). I was told it was necessary. *Sojourners*, pp. 12–15. (Interview by C. C. McCarthy.) (p. 403)

Zajonc, R. B. (1965). Social facilitation. *Science*, **149**, 269–274. (p. 316)

Zajonc, R. B. (1968). Attitudinal effects of mere exposure. *Journal of Personality and Social Psychology*, **9**, Monograph Suppl. No. 2, part 2. (pp. 483, 484)

Zajonc, R. B. (1970, February). Brainwash: Familiarity breeds comfort. *Psychology Today*, pp. 32–35, 60–62. (p. 483)

Zajonc, R. B. (1980). Feeling and thinking: Preferences need no inferences. *American Psychologist*, **35**, 151–175. (p. 485)

Zajonc, R. B., & Sales, S. M. (1966). Social facilitation of dominant and subordinate responses. *Journal of Experimental Social Psychology*, **2**, 160–168. (p. 317)

Zander, A. (1969). Students' criteria of satisfaction in a classroom committee project. *Human Relations*, **22**, 195–207. (p. 63)

Zanna, M. P. (1993). Message receptivity: A new look at the old problem of open- vs. closed-mindedness. In A. Mitchell (Ed.), *Advertising: Exposure, memory and choice*. Hillsdale, NJ: Erlbaum. (p. 284)

Zanna, M. P., Crosby, F., & Loewenstein, G. (1987). Male reference groups and discontent among female professionals. In B. A. Gutek & L. Larwood (Eds.), *Women's career development*. Newbury Park, Ca.: Sage. (p. 446)

Cartoon, p. 300: *The Far Side* © 1987 Far-works, Inc. Distributed by Universal Press Syndicate. Reprinted with permission. All rights reserved.

CHAPTER 9

Figure 9-4: From K. D. Williams, J. M. Jackson, and S. J. Karau, "Collective hedonism: A social loafing analysis of social dilemmas," *Social Dilemmas: Social Psychological Perspectives,* edited by D. A. Schroeder. Reprinted with permission of Greenwood Publishing Group, Inc., Westport, CT. Copyright © 1992.

Focus box, p. 345: Adapted from I. L. Janis "Counteracting the adverse effects of concurrence-seeking in policy-planning groups: theory and research perspectives," in *Group Decision Making* edited by H. Brandstatter et al., 1982. pp. 477–501. Copyright © 1982. Reprinted by permission of Harcourt Brace & Company Limited.

Cartoon, p. 342: Drawing by Martin; © 1979 The New Yorker Magazine, Inc.

CHAPTER 10

Figure 10-1: From Robert Buckhout, "Eyewitness Testimony," *Scientific American,* December 1974. Copyright © 1974 by Scientific American, Inc. All rights reserved.

Figure 10-2: From G. H. Fisher, "Ambiguity of Form: Old and New, *Perception and Psychophysics,* 4, 1968, pp. 189–192. Reprinted by permission of Psychonomic Society, Inc.

Table 10-1: From S. M. Kassin, P. C. Ellsworth, and V. L. Smith, "The `general acceptance' of psychological research on eyewitness testimony: A survey of the experts," *American Psychologist,* 44, 1989, pp. 1089–1098. Copyright © 1989 by the American Psychological Association. Reprinted with permission.

Cartoon, p. 359: Drawing by Mirachi; © 1984 The New Yorker Magazine, Inc.

Cartoon, p. 363: *The Far Side* © 1994 Far-works, Inc. Distributed by Universal Press Syndicate. Reprinted with permission. All rights reserved.

Cartoon, p. 365: *The Far Side* © 1985 Far-works, Inc. Distributed by Universal Press Syndicate. Reprinted with permission. All rights reserved.

Cartoon, p. 368: The Far Side cartoon by Gary Larson is reprinted by permission of Chronicle Features, San Francisco, CA. All rights reserved.

Cartoon, p. 370: Drawing by Barsotti; © 1988 The New Yorker Magazine, Inc.

Cartoon, p. 373: Drawing by Lorenz; © 1977 The New Yorker Magazine, Inc.

CHAPTER 11

Figure 11-6: From P. G. Devine and R. S. Malpass, "Orienting strategies in differential face recognition," *Personality and Social Psychology Bulletin,* 11, 1985, pp. 33–40, copyright © 1985 by Sage Publications, Inc. Reprinted by permission of Sage Publications, Inc.

Cartoon, p. 401: Drawing by Vietor; © 1981 The New Yorker Magazine, Inc.

Cartoon, p. 408: Drawing by Fisher; © 1987 The New Yorker Magazine, Inc.

Cartoon, p. 412: Drawing by Maslin; © The New Yorker Magazine, Inc.

Cartoon, p. 415: Cartoon by Don Wright reprinted by permission: Tribune Media Services.

Cartoon, p. 416: *Doonesbury* © 1994 G. B. Trudeau. Reprinted with permission of Universal Press Syndicate. All rights reserved.

Cartoon, p. 426: Drawing by Mankoff; © 1981 The New Yorker Magazine, Inc.

CHAPTER 12

Figure 12-7: From C. A. Anderson, W. E. Deuser, and K. M. DeNeve, "Hot temperatures, hostile affect, hostile cognition, and arousal; Tests of a general model of affective aggression," *Personality and Social Psychology Bulletin,* in press. Copyright © 1995 by Sage Publications, Inc. Reprinted by permission of Sage Publications, Inc.

Cartoon, p. 439: Cartoon by John Ruge, *The Saturday Review.*

Cartoon, p. 447: *Peanuts* reprinted by permission of United Feature Syndicate.

Cartoon, p. 465: Cartoon by Mayers, *Funny Times,* February 1994. Reprinted by permission.

Cartoon, p. 470: © 1990 Tom Tomorrow. Reprinted by permission.

CHAPTER 13

Figure 13-1: From R. B. Zajonc, "Attitudinal effects of mere exposure," *Journal of Personality and Social Psychology,* 9, Monograph Suppl. No. 2, part 2, 1968. Copyright © 1968 by the American Psychological Association. Reprinted with permission.

Figure 13-2: From R. J. Sternberg, "Triangulating love," in *The Psychology of Love,* edited by R. J. Sternberg and

M. L. Barnes. © 1988. Reprinted by permission of Yale University Press.

Figure 13-6: From a. Aron and A. N. Aron, "Love," in *Perspective on Close Relationships,* edited by A. L. Weber and J. H. Harvey, Allyn & Bacon, 1994.

Cartoon, p. 491: Cartoon by Sidney Harris, © 1991. Reprinted by permission.

Cartoon, p. 493 (left): Drawing by Maslin; © 1992 The New Yorker Magazine, Inc.

Cartoon, p. 493 (right): Drawing by Koren; © 1992 The New Yorker Magazine, Inc.

Cartoon, p. 494: Drawing by Miller; © 1992 The New Yorker Magazine, Inc.

Cartoon, p. 497: Drawing by Mankoff; © 1994 The New Yorker Magazine, Inc.

Cartoon, p. 503 (top): Cartoon by Peter Kohlsat copyright, 1988, Los Angeles Times Syndicate. Reprinted with permission.

Cartoon, p. 503 (bottom): © 1996 Mell Lazarus. By permission of Mell Lazarus and Creators Syndicate, Inc.

Cartoon, p. 513: Drawing by Weber; © 1989 The New Yorker Magazine, Inc.

Cartoon, p. 518: Drawing by Stevens; © 1993 The New Yorker Magazine, Inc.

CHAPTER 14

Figure 14-1: From C. D. Batson, J. Fultz, and P. A. Schoenrade, "Distress and empathy: Two qualitatively distinct vicarious emotions with different motivational consequences," *Journal of Personality,* 55:1 (Spring 1987), fig. 14:1, p. 14. Copyright Duke University Press, 1987. Reprinted with permission.

Figure 14-2: From J. M. Darley and B. Latane, "Bystander intervention in emergencies: Diffusion of responsibility," *Journal of Personality and Social Psychology,* 8, 1968, pp. 377–383. Copyright © 1968 by the American Psychological Association. Reprinted with permission.

Chapter 14, Cartoon, p. 530: Drawing by Tobey; © 1972 The New Yorker Magazine, Inc.

Cartoon, p. 560: *Hi & Lois* cartoon reprinted with special permission of King Features Syndicate.

CHAPTER 15

Figure 15-4: From P. E. Tetlock, "Monitoring the integrative complexity of American and Soviet policy rhetoric: What can be learned?" *Journal of Social Issues,* Vol. 44, No. 2, 1988, pp. 101–131. Reprinted by permission of The Society for the Psychological Study of Social Issues.

Table 15-1: From L. DeStefano and D. Colasanto, "Unlike 1975, today most Americans think men have it better," *Gallup Poll Monthly*, No. 293, February 1990, pp. 25–36.

Table 15-2: Reprinted from S. Plous, "The nuclear arms race: Prisoner's dilemma or perceptual dilemma?" *Journal of Peace Research*, 30, 1993, pp. 163–179, copyright 1993, by permission of Sage Publications Ltd.

Cartoon, p. 573: Cartoon by Steve Benson reprinted by permission: Tribune Media Services.

Cartoon, p. 601: Cartoon by Baloo from *The Wall Street Journal*. Permission, Cartoon Features Syndicate.

PHOTO CREDITS

CHAPTER 1

Page 1 Mark Richards/PhotoEdit; page 2 Documents Claudio Edinger & Mikki Ansin/Gamma; Liaison; page 9 Ronald C. James; page 11 David Young-Wolff/PhotoEdit; page 13 Courtesy Fathali M. Moghaddam, Georgetown University; page 19 Douglas Carroll; page 22 Courtesy University of Michigan Institute for Social Research Survey Research Center, Ann Arbor. Photo by Kalmbach.; page 26 Benali/Gamma Liaison; page 31 Photo News/Gamma Liaison

CHAPTER 2

Page 36 Nathan Benn/Woodfin Camp; page 40 Photofest; page 42 Rick Blumberg/Stock, Boston; page 43 Michael Grecco/Stock, Boston; page 46 Courtesy Shinobu Kitayam, Kyoto University; page 49 Marc Deville/Gamma Liaison; page 50 Evelyn Scolney/Monkmeyer; page 57 George Goodwin/Monkmeyer; page 61 Barbara Rios/Photo Researchers; page 63 Courtesy Barry Schlenker, University of Florida; page 64 David H. Wells/Image Works; page 69 Chitose Suzuki/Picture Cube

CHAPTER 3

Page 72 Fox/Gamma Liaison; page 75 Conklin/Monkmeyer; page 76 Grant LeDuc/Monkmeyer; page 79 Michael Newman/PhotoEdit; page 86 Courtesy Daniel M. Wegner; page 87 James Schnepf/Gamma Liasion; Page 93 Steve Lehman/SABA; Page 94 Myron Rothbart; page 95 Tom Cheek/Stock, Boston; page 97 D. Hill/Image Works; page 102 UPI/Bettmann; page 106 Robert Nichols/Black Star; page 109 Courtesy of Ellen Langer, Harvard University; page 110 Frank Pedrick/Image Works; page 113 Courtesy Joseph Forgas, University of New South Wales, Sydney, Australia; page 114 D&I MacDonald/Picture Cube

CHAPTER 4

Page 122 Byron/Monkmeyer; page 124 John Coletti/Picture Cube; page 128 Prettyman/PhotoEdit; page 133 Bob Daemmrich/Image Works; page 137 Wyman/Monkmeyer; page 138 Courtesy Robert B. Cialdini, Arizona State University; page 139 Versele-PhotoNews/Gamma Liaison; page 142 Denis Drever/Canada in Stock, Inc.; page 146 Courtesy Leon Festinger; page 148 Photo Works/Monkmeyer; page 150 Amy C. Etra/PhotoEdit; page 151 Courtesy of Fritz Strack; page 154 Bemieri, F. Davis, J., Rosenthal, R. & Knee, C. (1991). Interactional synchrony and the social affordance of rapport: A validation study. Unpublished manuscript, Oregon State University, Corvallis; page 156 J.O. Barcelone/Gamma Liaison; page 160 Courtesy Claude Steele, Stanford University

CHAPTER 5

Page 162 PBJ Pictures/Gamma Liaison; page 166 AP/Wide World; page 169 Bob Daemmrich/Stock, Boston; page 171 Siteman/Monkmeyer; page 173 LeDuc/Monkmeyer; page 175 *Top,* courtesy Lauren Alloy, Temple University; *bottom,* courtesy Lyn Abramson, University of Wisconsin; page 178 Larry Lawfer/Black Star; page 179 Frank Siteman/Picture Cube; page 182 Daniel Needham/Envision; page 184 Jacques Chenet/Gamma Liaison; page 187 Ellis Herwig/Stock, Boston

CHAPTER 6

Page 192 Kal Muller/Woodfin Camp & Associates; page 197 *Left,* Gottlieb/Monkmeyer; *right,* B. Daemmrich/Image Works; page 203 Charles Gupton/Stock, Boston; page 207 Steve Allen/Gamma Liaison; page 208 Courtesy David Buss; page 209 David Barrit/Gamma Liaison;

CHAPTER 7

Page 214 Mitsuhiko Sata/AP/Wide World; page 216 Courtesy C. Harry Hul, University of Hong Kong; page 219 *Left,* Tony Korody/Sygma; *right,* Memo Zack/Sygma; page 222 Courtesy Mark Zanna, University of Waterloo; page 223 *Left,* Willie Hill, Jr./Image Works; *right,* Bob Daemmrich/Image Works; page 227 Evelyn Scolney/Monkmeyer Press

CHAPTER 7

Page 230 George Rose/Gamma Liaison; page 238 Both, William Vendivert; page 240 Stanley Milgram, 1965, from the film Obedience, distributed by the Pennsylvania State University, PCR.; page 245 James Pickerell/Black Star; page 248 Courtesy Stanley Milgram, City University of New York; page 250 Jason Grow/San Jose Mercury News; page 251 University Photographic Services, University of Massachusetts at Amherst; page 254 Photofest; page 257 AP/Wide World; page 259 Ken Lambert/The Washington Times Photo Agency; page 261 Courtesy Alice Eagly, Purdue University; page 263 Michael Grecco/Stock, Boston; page 266 Mark Peterson/SABA; page 268 Joe Sohm/Image Works

CHAPTER 8

Page 270 David Young-Wolff/Photo Edit; page 272 Courtesy of The Children's Defense Fund; page 273 Bob Daemmrich/Image Works; page 274 Courtesy Swan Technologies; page 276 Courtesy Playtex Products, Inc.; page 283 Sidney/Monkmeyer; page 292 Courtesy Shelly Chicken, New York University; page 296 *Top,* courtesy Richard Petty, Ohio State University; *bottom,* courtesy John Cacioppo, Ohio State University; page 298 LeMatin de Lausanne/Gamma Liaison; page 302 Cindy Karp/Black Star; page 308 McLaughlin/Image Works; page 309 Courtesy William McGuire, Yale University

CHAPTER 9

Page 312 Joe Sohm/Image Works; page 316 Rob Crandall/Stock, Boston; page 318 Chromosohm/Sohm/Stock, Boston; page 321 James Terkfurst/Herman Miller, Inc.; page 323 Alan G. Ingham; page 325 James Lemass/Picture Cube; page 327 Rob Crandall/CNN/Stock, Boston; page 328 Courtesy of Philip Zimbardo; page 336 Doug Burrows/Gamma Liaison; page 344 NASA; page 347 Courtesy Irving Janis; page 350 Courtesy Charlan Jeanne Nemeth, University of California, Berkeley; page 351 Liane Enkelis/Stock, Boston

CHAPTER 10

Page 354 AP/Wide World; page 357 Detroit Free Press; page 359 Courtesy Gary L. Wells, Iowa State University; page 361 Dale A. Dunaway/Cincinnati post; page 362 Both, courtesy of Elizabeth Loftus; page 372 AP/Wide World; page 374 Courtesy Norbert Kerr, Michigan State University; page 376 John Giordano/SABA; page 384 A. Jason/Gamma Liaison

CHAPTER 11

Page 386 J. Y. Rabeuf/Image Works; page 394 Renato Rotolo/Gamma Liaison; page 396 Courtesy Patricia Devine; page 397 Frank White/Gamma Liaison; page 398 Porter & Geis, 1981; page 402 Library of Congress; page 406 Scott Peterson/Gamma Liaison; page 409 Courtesy Thomas Pettigrew, University of California, Santa Cruz; page 410 Jon Levy/Gamma Liaison; page 420 Eastcott/Momatiuk/Image Works; page 424 Courtesy Miles Hewstone, University of Bristol; page 428 Bob Daemmrich/Stock, Boston; page 431 Chip Hires/Gamma Liaison; page 432 Courtesy Susan T. Fiske, University of Masscahussets

CHAPTER 12

Page 434 Christine Grunnet/Gamma Liaison; page 438 The Granger Collection; page 440 Jeff Share/Black Star; page 442 Carol Halebian/Gamma Liaison; page 449 Photo Works; page 453 Both, Dr. Nathan Azrin; page 455 John Barr/Gamma Liaison; page 457 Bob Daemmrich/Image Works; page 459 UPI/Bettmann; page 466 Photofest

CHAPTER 13

Page 476 Kindra Clineff/Picture Cube; page 478 Frank Siteman/Picture Cube; page 482 Frank Siteman/Picture Cube; page 486 Dagmar Fabricius/Stock, Boston; page 490 Courtesy Ellen Berscheid, University of Minnesota; page 491 *Far left*, Rick Smolan/Stock, Boston; *center left*, Paul Lau/Gamma Liaison; *center right*, Catherine Karnow/Woodfin Camp & Associates; *far right*, David R. Frazier/Folio, Inc.; page 495 Susan May Tell/SABA; page 496 *Top*, courtesy James Jones, University of Delaware; *bottom*, Photofest; page 502 B. Daemmrich/Image Works; page 504 Courtesy Elaine Hatfield, University of Hawaii; page 506 Rob Nelson/Black Star; page 508 AP/Wide World; page 512 All, Dr. Pawel Lewicki, University of Tulsa, Oklahoma page 515 Kagan/Monkmeyer

CHAPTER 14

Page 524 Kindra Clineff/Picture Cube; page 528 Harold Glaser/Gamma Liaison; page 532 Hermine Dreyfuss/Monkmeyer; page 533 Courtesy Dennis Krebs, Simon Fraser University; page 534 Courtesy C. Daniel Batson, University of Kansas; page 535 Scott Shaw, The Odessa (Texas) American; page 539 Courtesy John M. Darley, Princeton University; page 542 Mark Zemnick; page 544 Stephen Ferry/Gamma Liaison; page 549 Ellis Herwig/Stock, Boston page 553 {cr} Lynn Burkholder/First Impressions; page 558 AP/Wide World page 563 Page Collection/Gamma Liaison

CHAPTER 15

Page 566 Clark/Monkmeyer; page 568 AP/Wide World; page 572 Courtesy Morton Deutsch, Columbia University; page 575 Mark Peterson/SABA; page 576 Mark Richards/PhotoEdit; page 579 Muzafer Sherif; page 584 Chris Morris/Black Star; page 586 G. Bassignac/G. Suassier/L. van der Stockt/Gamma Liaison; page 590 *Left*, Michael Newman/PhotoEdit; *right*, Lee Snider/Image Works; page 593 Frank Siteman/Picture Cube; page 597 M. Antman/Image Works; page 600 AP/Wide World

INDEXES

■ NAME INDEX

■ SUBJECT INDEX